THE ECONOMICS OF
REGULATION

Theory and Practice in the
Transportation and Public Utility Industries

THE IRWIN SERIES IN ECONOMICS

Consulting Editor
LLOYD G. REYNOLDS
Yale University

THE ECONOMICS OF REGULATION

Theory and Practice in the Transportation and Public Utility Industries

CHARLES F. PHILLIPS, Jr.

Professor of Economics
Washington and Lee University

Revised Edition

1969

RICHARD D. IRWIN, INC., Homewood, Illinois

IRWIN-DORSEY LIMITED, Georgetown, Ontario

Revised Edition

First Printing, August, 1969

Library of Congress Catalog Card No. 69–17160

Printed in the United States of America

To
Marjorie Hancock Phillips

PREFACE

Since publication of the original text, there have been encouraging signs of a revival of interest in public utility and transportation economics. This new interest is largely due to the fact that technological change has rapidly eroded the traditional monopoly position of these industries, making them increasingly subject to competiton and resulting in many intriguing and important economic problems.

It has long been recognized that the public utility and transportation industries are vital to the economic growth of the United States, and that they contribute a significant percentage of our national income. But what has not always been appreciated is the fact that regulation has potential positive effects upon the performance of these industries. As originally conceived, regulation sought to insure consumers of adequate utility services at reasonable rates by restricting prices and profits. As presently conceived, regulation must be more than a protector—it must provide positive incentives to induce superior performance. To accomplish this task, broader questions must be raised and new concepts must be developed. As Francis X. Welch has succinctly put it: "Modern regulation is increasingly in need of more headlights and less taillights."[1]

In revising the text, the author has attempted to bring all factual material up to date. More importantly, greater emphasis has been placed on the transportation industry, the pricing of utility services, and the economic effects of regulatory policy. The aim has been to concentrate on the development of regulation and on the challenges which face both the regulatory commissions and the regulated industries. It is still true that more questions are raised than are answered, but the fact is that there are no definitive answers to many of the complex problems surrounding government regulation. For this reason, the author has quoted extensively from those doing research in the regulated sector of the economy and has provided comprehensive footnotes for those who wish to pursue a particular topic further.

Moreover, while we know far too little about the effects of public regulation on the industries involved, or on the economy, it is idle to theorize what the status of these industries would be if regulation were not the accepted public policy. Put another way, regulatory statutes may be amended, the commissions consolidated or bisected, and regulatory concepts changed, but it seems certain that public regulation will continue to be a permanent feature of the American economy. But the more difficult the problem, the more urgent is

---

[1] Francis X. Welch, "Changing Values in the Regulatory Mix," 80 *Public Utilities Fortnightly* 61, 69 (November 9, 1967).

the need of observation, analysis, understanding, evaluation, and interpretation. The author will be fully rewarded if, by pointing up some of the principal areas in which research is needed, others will be led to bring their special abilities and techniques to bear on problems having great significance for the industries and the economy as a whole.

Many people have offered suggestions and comments on this and the original text. My debt to the following is particularly great: Lewis W. Adams, John F. DeVogt, Thomas E. Ennis, Jr., John M. Gunn, Jr., and Frederick J. Nowak, all colleagues at Washington and Lee University; George R. Hall, The Rand Corporation; William R. Hughes, Boston College; David Dale Martin, Indiana University; Lloyd G. Reynolds, Yale University; and Irwin M. Stelzer and Miss Florence Weiss, National Economic Research Associates, Inc. Especially, however, has the revision benefited from the careful analysis and detailed suggestions of James C. Nelson, Washington State University, who reviewed the entire original text. His assistance is acknowledged with deep gratitude. Detailed information and, in many cases, comments on various sections of the two editions, were supplied by representatives of several companies and associations, including the American Gas Association, American Telephone and Telegraph Company, Arthur Andersen & Co., Association of American Railroads, Edison Electric Institute, United Air Lines, United States Independent Telephone Association, and The Western Union Telegraph Company. Finally, all of the state and federal regulatory commissions also supplied requested information. Without this help, these volumes would not have been possible. Of course, the author alone is responsible for the conclusions reached and for all errors.

Mrs. Jill Huntley and Miss Louise P. Moore provided helpful and patient assistance in the research undertaken at the Washington and Lee University School of Law. Likewise, the author is indebted to Mrs. Shirley Martin for secretarial assistance and to his students for their many constructive suggestions as they used the original volume as a text. And last, but certainly not least, the author wishes to express gratitude to his wife, not only for her assistance in the proofreading, but also for her continual encouragement.

To those who read this book, it is again hoped that the problems discussed will be as stimulating and as challenging as they are to the author. Any comments and suggestions on the material included, or excluded, will be appreciated.

Lexington, Virginia   Charles F. Phillips, Jr.
May, 1969

TABLE OF CONTENTS

Natural Gas: *The Allocation of Costs: The Seaboard Formula. Rate Structures. Wholesale Natural Gas Rates.* Conservation: *State Conservation Measures. The FPC and Conservation. The Future.* Controversy and Experimentation.

The Communications Act of 1934. The Telegraph Industry: *The Western Union Telegraph Company. Technological Developments. The Domestic Telegraph Investigation. The Diversification of Western Union.* The Telephone Industry: *The Domestic Telephone Industry. The Development of Telephone Communications. The Telephone Investigation of the 1930's. The Current Telephone Investigation. Western Electric Company.* Competition in the Communications Industry: *The "Above 890 Decision": The Impact of Microwave. Communications and Computers: The Impact of Technology. The Common Carriers' Responses. Some Regulatory and Policy Issues. Task Force on Communications Policy.* Cables and Satellites: A Digression: *Submarine Cables. Space Communications.* Technology, Competition, and the Future.

PART IV.   AN APPRAISAL—AND A CHALLENGE

The Regulatory Process: *Independence from Political Control. The Problem of Industry-Mindedness. Lack of Meaningful Policy Standards. Regulatory Delay.* Regulation as a Substitute for Competition: *The Inherent Difficulties. The Role of Competition. Management: Divided Responsibility. An Obsolete Concept?* A Continuing Challenge: *The Need for Dynamic Standards. The Need for Performance Evaluation. The Future.*

INDEXES

INTRODUCTION

Chapter 1

THE REGULATED INDUSTRIES IN THE AMERICAN ECONOMY

There is something quite special about government regulation of the public utility type: this is the way we behave when we are really keyed up about economizing, when we stop acquiescing and "going along," when we feel quite certain that, for reasons we can identify, the processes of the free market cannot be made satisfactorily to perform the economizing job we want done and, hence, that we must perform the economizing functions by specifically designed laws, agencies, and measures.

—Ben W. Lewis*

The economy of the United States is often described as a competitive, private enterprise system. In such a system, the economy is organized on the decentralized lines of private property and private enterprise. Since competition is relied upon to promote the public welfare, the market is the central institution regulating economic activity. But it has long been accepted that some industries, in which competition is not fully effective, must be regulated by the government to protect the public interest. "Here the visible hand of public regulation was to replace the invisible hand of Adam Smith in order to protect consumers against extortionate charges, restrictions of output, deterioration of service, and unfair discrimination."[1] Those industries which have been subjected to public regulation are collectively known as the regulated industries.

THE REGULATED INDUSTRIES

What are the regulated industries? A classification is somewhat elusive, for in a broad sense all industries are regulated.[2] Governmental laws which affect

---

*Ben W. Lewis, "Ambivalence in Public Policy toward Regulated Industries," 53 *American Economic Review* 38, 40 (1963).
[1] Walter Adams, "The Role of Competition in the Regulated Industries," 48 *American Economic Review* 527 (1958).
[2] "If anyone can find such a thing now as an 'unregulated industry' he can sell it at a profit to the Smithsonian." George Champion, quoted in 79 *Public Utilities Fortnightly* 10 (March 2, 1967).

business include antitrust policy, fair-trade laws, labor legislation, monetary and fiscal policy, and tariff policy. As commonly used, however, the phrase *the regulated industries* refers to a diverse group of businesses which has been subjected to detailed local, state, and federal regulation as to rates and services. The regulated industries can be divided into two major classes: "(1) those enterprises which supply, directly or indirectly, continuous or repeated services through more or less permanent physical connections between the plant of the supplier and the premises of the consumer; and (2) the public transportation agencies."[3] In the first class are enterprises supplying energy (electricity and natural gas), communications services (telephone and telegraph), and water.[4] In the second class are firms providing local and interregional transportation (airlines, bus companies, motor freight carriers, gas and oil pipelines, railroads, and water carriers).

These industries, often referred to as public utilities,[5] differ in several respects from other industries in the economy. These differences will be discussed at length in the following three chapters. To summarize, the regulated industries (with the notable exception of motor and domestic water carriers) tend toward monopoly, or, more accurately, the firms in these industries seem to operate more efficiently as monopolies. Yet, if economic power is not to be controlled by the market, it must be controlled by public authority, for a firm's contribution to the general welfare, rather than being the result of voluntary choice, must be compelled.[6] Some regulation, moreover, may be undertaken for social or political reasons, such as promoting regional development or for national defense purposes. There is a high degree of public interest attached to the services rendered by the regulated industries—a fact that is the primary legal

[3] James C. Bonbright, *Principles of Public Utility Rates* (New York: Columbia University Press, 1961), p. 4. "Despite the distinction . . . between the transportation and the nontransport utilities, even most of the latter utilities do a transportation business if we use 'transportation' in a broad sense to include what are more frequently called 'transmission' and (in gas and electricity parlance) 'distribution.' True, a local utility company may have a production or manufacturing department, as does an electric company which generates its own power or a gas company which manufactures its own gas. But the transmission-distribution phase of the business is a vital part of most public utility systems and may constitute the major component of the total cost of service. Moreover, even though the entire utility system is usually subject to regulation, it is likely to have derived its recognized utility status from the department of the operations concerned with the transfer of the gas, or the electricity, or the telephone messages from one location to another." *Ibid.,* p. 5.

[4] Seventy-one percent of all water supply systems are municipally owned; 29 percent are investor owned. While the private systems are subject to commission control, water utilities are outside the scope of this book.

[5] The public utility concept usually encompasses several fields of economic activity not included in the above classification, such as ice plants, sanitation, elevators, stockyards, and warehouses. For an exhaustive classification of public utilities, see Martin G. Glaeser, *Public Utilities in American Capitalism* (New York: Macmillan Co., 1957), pp. 9–10, n. 2.

[6] "It is the fact that the competitive market *compels* the results of its processes which is the ultimate defense against the demand that economic decisions be made or supervised by politically responsible authorities. Without such market compulsion, that demand appears ultimately irresistible in a society committed to representative government." Carl Kaysen and Donald F. Turner, *Antitrust Policy: An Economic and Legal Analysis* (Cambridge: Harvard University Press, 1959), pp. 48–49.

basis of regulation. Finally, regulation is undertaken by administrative commissions that have been established with jurisdiction over the rates and services of these industries.[7]

There are two common characteristics of the industries under consideration that deserve further discussion. The first is the fact that private ownership is predominant. The second is the existence in varying degrees of public regulation.

Private Ownership

The position of the regulated industries in the American economy is unique. In contrast to most other industrialized countries which have nationalized these industries, we have relied on private ownership, controlled by state and federal agencies, to provide services which are more or less essential to the economy and which are public in their nature.[8] Argued Justice Harlan in *Smyth v. Ames:* "A railroad is a public highway, and none the less so because constructed and maintained through the agency of a corporation deriving its existence and powers from the State. . . . It performs a function of the State."[9] And Justice Brandeis, in the Southwestern Bell Telephone case, remarked that "the company is the substitute for the State in the performance of the public service, thus becoming a public servant."[10]

The combination of private ownership and public control means that some conflicts are inevitable. In the first place, while regulation is essentially a legislative and legal concept, it is also an economic one. Accordingly, the regulated industries are economically motivated as are other private enterprises, but they render a public service and, hence, are subject to detailed governmental regulation, supervised by the judicial system.[11] Two important results are divided responsibility and ambiguous statutes. Explains Shapiro:

> . . . Regulatory statutes with one hand impose responsibility for a certain sector of the economy on a given agency, while with the other leaving ownership, initiative, and nearly all the actual decision-making power in private hands. The agency is apparently intended to get the private decision makers to act in the public interest not by telling them what to do but only by sporadically intervening to tell them what not to do. Furthermore, the statute maker typically invokes the public interest or public convenience and necessity without saying what he means. Just as typically he mixes a number of specific limitations on jurisdiction and a number of concrete policy standards

---

[7] Several industries and activities not discussed in this book are also subject in varying degrees to commission regulation, such as banking, broadcasting, and corporate securities at the federal level, and insurance and milk distribution at the state level.

[8] There are certain exceptions to private ownership, such as some electric power generation, transmission, and distribution, and a limited number of transportation facilities.

[9] 169 U.S. 466, 544 (1898).

[10] *Missouri* ex rel. *Southwestern Bell Tel. Co.* v. *Missouri Public Service Comm.,* 262 U.S. 276, 291 (1923).

[11] C. Woody Thompson and Wendell R. Smith, *Public Utility Economics* (New York: McGraw-Hill Book Co., 1941), p. 12.

with these rather open directives to the agency to use its discretion and take its own initiatives to meet new circumstances. In short, regulatory statutes represent an uneasy compromise between laissez faire and government-control visions of the economy. As such they are likely to embody the ambiguity and internal contradictions of contemporary economic philosophy. . . .[12]

In the second place, there often seems to be a conflict between private and public interests. The basic objective of private corporations is profit maximization, while the public interest demands adequate service at the lowest possible price. However, this conflict is more apparent than real, for a regulated company cannot maximize profit in the long run without providing adequate service at prices acceptable to the public, while the public in the long run cannot receive adequate service at reasonable prices except from a company which is financially healthy.

In the third place, there is a difficult division of authority between the federal government and the fifty state governments. In theory, interstate activities are subject to federal regulation and intrastate activities to state jurisdiction. In actual practice, however, the line is a hard one to draw, since most of the regulated enterprises provide both inter- and intrastate services. While many jurisdictional problems have been solved by past commission and court decisions, several areas of conflict remain. At a minimum, effective regulation under such circumstances requires continuous cooperation between the federal and state commissions.

In the fourth place, as private corporations, the regulated industries are entitled to due process of law in administrative proceedings and to judicial protection of private property. At the commission level, due process of law frequently results in lengthy regulatory proceedings, thereby precluding rapid adjustment to changing economic conditions. In recent years, informal procedures have been established in an attempt to overcome the problems created by lengthy, formal proceedings, but these newer procedures have not gained complete acceptance. The firms within the regulated sector, moreover, may contest commission decisions and orders in the courts. Such appeals, while often necessary, further delay an already complex regulatory situation. But it is important to keep in mind that these legal requirements and protections are a vital part of the regulatory process.

Examples of these conflicts will appear throughout this book. A further set of questions also should be raised. Has the combination of private ownership and public control been wise and successful? Would public ownership be a better alternative? What characteristics, for instance, permit the United States to have the only privately owned railroad system in the world? Even if the present system is considered to be the best, how can it be improved? These questions will be considered in the following chapters.

[12] Martin Shapiro, *The Supreme Court and Administrative Agencies* (New York: The Free Press, 1968), pp. 260–61.

Public Regulation

Given the facts that public policy has sought (*a*) to restrict competitive forces and (*b*) to maintain private ownership, public regulation of these industries becomes necessary. As previously noted, uncontrolled economic power is economically, politically, and socially unacceptable in a democratic society. In the United States, regulation is carried on by local, state, and federal governments. Prior to 1934, regulation of the nontransportation utilities was an almost exclusive function of local and state agencies. As these industries developed, however, they expanded beyond local and state boundaries, serving multiple states or the entire nation. In the telephone and telegraph industries as well as airlines, international operations are common. Federal regulation has thus tended to become more important than state control and will receive primary emphasis in this study.

It must be clearly stated and recognized at the outset that regulation has not developed in a smooth or always logical manner. On the contrary, regulation has experienced "a slow and fitful growth."[13] Every change in policy is certain to meet strong opposition. Take, for example, the current railroad situation. The industry is undergoing a potentially large and economically significant merger movement. Opposition to the approval of railroad mergers appears from the railway unions (who fear the loss of jobs), local and state governments (who fear the loss of service and tax revenues), competing forms of transportation (who fear the possibility of stronger competition), other railroads (who fear they might be left out and thus be unable to compete against the stronger lines), and from the Department of Justice (which fears a lessening of competition). Such strong opposition adds a further reason to the list of factors causing delays in the regulatory process. Compromise is frequently the ultimate outcome.

The fact that regulation is necessary does not imply how much or what kind of regulation is desirable. It is to be expected that the regulated industries favor minimum regulation, while the public may demand the maximum. But economic conditions are changing constantly, and if regulation is to be up-to-date, public policy must change too. Further, since "antitrust and public regulation have, broadly speaking, been the characteristic response of American politics, government, and law to the problems posed by the modern corporation,"[14] a study of public regulation is vital to an evaluation of the desirability of its extension to nonregulated industries or its curtailment (or withdrawal) from existing regulated industries. Would the long-run economic performance of the steel industry, which exhibits many of the characteristics of the regulated industries, be improved by the extension of public regulation to that industry? Would the long-run economic performance of the transportation industry, which dis-

[13] Emery Troxel, *Economics of Public Utilities* (New York: Holt, Rinehart & Winston, Inc., 1947), p. 786.

[14] Abram Chayes, "The Modern Corporation and the Rule of Law," in Edward S. Mason (ed.), *The Corporation in Modern Society* (Cambridge: Harvard University Press, 1959), p. 37.

plays economic and market characteristics close to those of nonregulated industries in general, be enhanced by permitting more freedom to competitive forces? These issues will also be considered in subsequent chapters.

THE SIGNIFICANCE OF THE REGULATED INDUSTRIES

In legal phraseology, the regulated industries are "affected with a public interest." The contribution of these industries to the economy is important and substantial. As Table 1-1 indicates, 7.8 percent of national income (1967) origi-

TABLE 1-1
Percentage of National Income Originating in the Regulated Industries, 1967

Industry	Percentage of National Income	
Transportation		4.0
Motor freight transportation and warehousing	1.4	
Railroad transportation	1.1	
Air transportation	0.6	
Water transportation	0.4	
Local, suburban, and highway passenger	0.3	
Pipeline transportation	0.1	
Transportation services	0.1	
Utilities: electric, gas, and sanitary services		2.0
Communications: telephone and telegraph		1.8
Total Regulated Industries		7.8

Source: U.S. Department of Commerce, *Survey of Current Business* (July, 1968), p. 23.

nates in the regulated industries. The significance of these industries can also be seen in the tremendous sums spent by the public on their services and in the form of aid and subsidies.

Services to Consumers

One measure of the importance of the regulated industries is in the services they provide to consumers. In 1967, nearly 5 percent of total personal consumption expenditures, or approximately $23.9 billion, was made for these services.

Since 1920, the use of electric energy has doubled every 10 years, reaching 1.106 trillion kilowatt-hours in 1967. Electricity is now available to practically every American home, with more than 98 percent of all occupied homes, both urban and rural, connected for electric service. Residential customers used an average of 5,565 kilowatt-hours of electric power during 1967, at an average price of 2.16 cents per kilowatt-hour. Electric motors provide 90 percent of all mechanical power used in industry. The electric industry currently supplies over 68 million customers a year.[15] The United States, with only 6 percent of the

15 See *The Electric Utility Industry,* an annual publication of the Edison Electric Institute (New York).

world's population, produces 36 percent of all the electricity generated in the world.[16]

The gas industry also has experienced a rapid rate of growth. In 1920, gas utilities supplied but 4 percent of the energy used in the country; by 1967, the figure had risen to about one-third. The industry, presently serving 39 million customers annually, has an 826,300 mile network of pipelines and mains that transport gas from wells to the consumer. Net production of natural gas, which continues to have the largest share of the total gas market, reached 17.5 trillion cubic feet in 1967. Proved recoverable reserves of natural gas totaled 289.3 trillion cubic feet—an all-time high.[17] Further, as a result of more intense competition between electricity and gas (as well as oil), both residential and commercial consumers are being offered choices not previously available.

The importance of transportation to American consumers needs little emphasis. The volume of domestic intercity freight and passenger traffic for 1967 is shown in Table 1–2. The industry's significance, however, is far more

TABLE 1–2
Volume of Domestic Intercity Freight and Passenger Traffic, 1967*

Form of Transportation	Freight		Passengers	
	Billions of Ton-Miles	Per-centage	Billions of Passenger-Miles	Per-centage
Railroads[a]	731.2	41.61	15.3	1.50
Motor vehicles:				
Of property	388.5	22.11	. . .	. . .
Of passengers	. . .	. . .	24.9[e]	2.44
Private automobiles	. . .	. . .	889.8	87.18
Inland waterways[b]	274.0	15.59	3.4	0.33
Oil pipelines[c]	361.0	20.54	. . .	. . .
Airlines[d]	2.6	0.15	87.2	8.55
Total	1,757.3	100.00	1,020.6	100.00

* Preliminary.
[a] Includes electric railways, express, and mail.
[b] Includes Great Lakes.
[c] Includes refined products and crude oil, with an allowance for gathering lines.
[d] Includes express, mail, and excess baggage, as well as private flying.
[e] Excludes school bus data.
Source: Interstate Commerce Commission, Bureau of Economics, *Transport Economics* (July, 1968), pp. 3, 4.

than simply the volume of traffic it handles. Improved transportation leads to increases in the productivity of the economy, to the reduction in costs to producers, and to gains in utility to consumers. Improved transportation also affects

[16] Federal Power Commission, *World Power Data, 1965* (Washington, D.C.: U.S. Government Printing Office, 1968).

[17] See *Gas Facts,* an annual publication of the American Gas Association (New York).

the location of industry, the movement of commodities, and the development of regions and cities. Finally, the transportation system plays a vital role in the country's national defense.

Turning to the communications industries, over 85 percent of American families have basic telephone service. The nearly 105 million telephones in use represent almost one-half of the world's telephones. In 1967, the telephone industry carried approximately 140 billion calls, equal to an average daily volume of 387 million local calls and 19.5 million toll calls or an average yearly volume of about 630 conversations per capita. In addition, the American Telephone and Telegraph Company, which handles over 84 percent of the domestic telephone business, has one of the most efficient research laboratories in the world—Bell Telephone Laboratories—and is an important supplier of communication systems for national defense and outer space exploration. While public message telegraph volume has experienced a 60 percent decline since World War II, consumers are served by nearly 12,000 company offices throughout the country. The Western Union Telegraph Company, sole domestic supplier of public message service, has become a significant supplier of other communication services, some of which compete directly with services offered by A.T.&T.

Contribution to the Economy

A second measure of the importance of the regulated industries is their annual contribution to the economy, summarized in Table 1–3.[18] (1) Annual revenues of the regulated industries are nearly $60 billion. The transportation industries account for 48 percent of this total; electric and gas utilities for 32 percent; and communications for 20 percent. (2) The regulated industries have a net investment of approximately $131.8 billion in plant and equipment. (3) These industries employ 3.7 million full-time workers, representing 7.3 percent of the employment of all private industries. (4) The regulated industries have an annual gross payroll (wages and salaries) of $26.7 billion, amounting to 9.2 percent of all private industry. (5) Expenditures for new plant and equipment were over $16 billion in 1965, representing 31.6 percent of all such expenditures by private industry. Such sums have been required by the rapid postwar growth of these industries. Between 1945 and 1966, for example, the communications industry experienced a 500 percent increase in total assets, electric and gas utilities a 330 percent increase, and the transportation industry a 75 percent increase, compared with an increase of 320 percent for all manufacturing industries.[19]

Another indicator of the role played by the regulated industries, not shown in the table, is annual taxes. Over $8 billion is paid yearly by these industries in local, state, and federal taxes. An additional $1.6 billion is collected

---

[18] Table 1–3 must be used with caution. As indicated in the footnotes, some of the data concerning operating revenues and net investment are not for the entire industry. Further, the net investment data for the transportation industries exclude public investment in transport facilities (airways and airports, highways, and water channels).

[19] 81 *Public Utilities Fortnightly* 40 (January 4, 1968).

TABLE 1–3
Selected Statistics of the Regulated Industries, 1965

Industry	Operating Revenues (Millions)	Net Investment (Millions)	Number of Full-Time Employees (Thousands)	Wages and Salaries (Millions)	Expenditure on New Plant and Equipment (Billions)
Transportation	$28,685.8	$ 39,168.5	2,297	$ 17,191	$ 4.54
Railroads	10,207.9	22,917.8[a]	735	5,450	
Motor vehicles:	...	...	...	...	
Property	7,097.2[b]	1,275.2[b]	774	6,216	
Passengers	635.0[c]	313.8[c]	256	1,393	
Air Transportation	4,957.9[d]	3,404.0[d]	229	1,860	
Pipeline transportation ...	...	...	18	153	
Natural gas	4,601.4[e]	8,782.0[e]	...	...	
Oil	903.8[f]	2,232.8[f]	...	...	
Water transportation	282.6[g]	242.9[g]	204	1,585	
Transportation services ..	...	...	81	534	
Utility	$18,984.6	$ 62,357.0	626[k]	$ 4,565[k]	$ 6.94
Electric	13,400.1[h]	51,267.1[h]	...	...	
Natural gas	5,584.5[i]	11,089.9[i]	...	...	
Communications	$12,067.4[j]	$ 30,307.3[j]	775	$ 4,937	$ 4.94
Telephone	11,761.8	29,861.5	...	...	
Telegraph	305.6	445.8	...	...	
Total Regulated Industries	$59,737.8	$131,832.8	3,698	$ 26,693	$16.42
All Private Industries ..	...	...	50,766	$289,788	$51.96
Regulated Industries as Percentage of All Private Industries ...	...	...	7.3%	9.2%	31.6%

[a] Class I line-haul railroads.

[b] Class I motor carriers of property engaged in intercity service.

[c] Class I motor carriers of passengers engaged in intercity service.

[d] Operating revenues exclude subsidy for certificated route air carriers; investment figure is flight equipment and ground property and equipment.

[e] Thirty-two major Class A and Class B pipelines.

[f] Carriers subject to the jurisdiction of the ICC.

[g] Classes A and B carriers.

[h] Classes A and B privately owned electric utilities.

[i] Includes companies subject to the jurisdiction of the FPC.

[j] Telephone data for carriers which operate telephone exchanges and have annual operating revenues exceeding $1 billion and those which operate point-to-point toll service only and have annual operating revenues exceeding $50,000; telegraph data for Western Union only.

[k] Includes sanitary services.

Source: Air Transport Association of America, *1967 Air Transport Facts & Figures;* Federal Communications Commission, *Thirty-Second Annual Report* (1966); Federal Power Commission, *Forty-Sixth Annual Report* (1966); Interstate Commerce Commission, *Eightieth Annual Report* (1966); and U.S. Department of Commerce, *Survey of Current Business* (July, 1967).

in federal excise taxes levied on airline passengers, telephone users, and telegraph customers.

By several economic measures, therefore, the regulated industries make a substantial annual contribution to the American economy and are also important from a national defense point of view. But their full economic significance to the economy's productivity is even greater than these figures indicate, for the services of the regulated industries are just as essential to efficient production and distribution as money and credit are to exchange. Further, data for the regulated segment of those industries under consideration that are comprised of both regulated and nonregulated firms do not reveal the significance of the entire industry. The transportation industry, which includes both for-hire and non-for-hire carriers, is larger than the regulated transportation industry. To some extent, such is also true of the electric, gas, and telephone industries.

Public Aid and Subsidy to Transportation

Over the years, public aid and subsidy to the transportation industries have been tremendous.[20] Beginning with land grants to the railroads in the second half of the nineteenth century, all domestic transportation agencies, except for the pipelines, have received public aid and/or subsidy at some time during their development. Aggregate federal, state, and local spending for domestic air, highway, and water facilities and services, including airline cash subsidies, has been estimated at $298.2 billion through fiscal 1968 (Table 1-4). The largest item of federal expenditures, $56.9 billion or approximately 72 percent, has been for highway development; the second largest amount, $12.5 billion, for airways, airports, and cash subsidies to domestic carriers; the third largest amount, $8.0 billion, for the development of waterways (excluding $321 million for the development of the Tennessee River and $132 million for the St. Lawrence Seaway project); and the fourth largest amount, $1.4 billion,[21] for railroad development (Table 1-5). The major portion of expenditures by local and state governments, $209 billion out of an estimated total of $221 billion or nearly 95 percent, has been for highway development.

The two terms *public aid* and *subsidy* are not synonymous. Both mean that money has been granted for the provision of facilities and services by the various units of government. Some of the money spent as public aid is in the

---

[20] Public aid and subsidy have been extended to the electric industry to assist in the development of atomic power and, under the Rural Electrification Act, low-cost federal loans have been granted to rural electric and telephone companies. Atomic energy and the REA are discussed in Chapter 15.

[21] This figure does not include current government expenditures for research and demonstration projects in local mass transportation and high-speed intercity ground transportation. In 1965, Congress authorized an expenditure of $90 million (Public Law 89-220) for research and development in the field of high-speed intercity ground transportation. Part of this amount is being spent for rail demonstration projects in the northeast (Boston-Washington) corridor. The figure also does not include state and federal aid granted late in 1967 to the New Haven Railroad. *The Wall Street Journal,* December 18, 1967, p. 34.

TABLE 1–4
Summary of Government Expenditures for Domestic Transportation: Airways,
Airports, Airline Cash Subsidies, Highways, and Waterways*

Years	Federal	State and Local [a]	Total [a]
Prior to 1947	$13,732,604,489	$ 48,742,721,615	$ 62,475,326,104
1947	534,102,370	2,994,000,000	3,528,102,370
1948	678,790,053	3,497,000,000	4,175,790,053
1949	861,384,324	3,873,000,000	4,734,384,324
1950	896,368,978	4,208,000,000	5,104,368,978
1951	896,308,768	4,644,000,000	5,540,308,768
1952	963,935,839	5,046,000,000	6,009,935,839
1953	1,080,333,685	5,591,000,000	6,671,333,685
1954	942,875,734	6,593,000,000	7,535,875,734
1955	1,055,817,154	6,839,000,000	7,894,817,154
1956	1,221,572,828	7,821,000,000	9,042,572,828
1957	1,944,045,184	8,332,000,000	10,276,045,184
1958	3,109,201,771	8,355,000,000	11,464,201,771
1959	4,014,005,304	8,197,000,000	12,211,005,304
1960	3,653,058,876	8,588,000,000	12,241,058,876
1961	3,952,608,676	9,266,000,000	13,218,608,676
1962	4,192,740,321	9,782,000,000	13,974,740,321
1963	4,875,781,543	9,967,000,000	14,842,781,543
1964	5,446,064,981	10,109,000,000	15,555,064,981
1965	5,320,193,993	10,865,000,000	16,185,193,993
1966	5,822,145,000	11,670,000,000	17,492,145,000
1967	5,814,816,000	12,439,000,000	18,253,816,000
1968 (est.)	6,380,689,000	13,428,000,000	19,808,689,000
Total	$77,389,444,871	$220,846,721,615	$298,236,166,486

*This table summarizes expenditures for all types of facilities. Data are for fiscal years, except highway expenditures which are on a calendar year basis. Not included are Merchant Marine ($21,451,000,000) and Coast Guard ($8,031,000,000) expenditures.

[a] Does not include state and local expenditures for waterways prior to 1947, as they are not available.

Source: Association of American Railroads, "Government Expenditures for Highway, Waterway, and Air Facilities and Private Expenditures for Railroad Facilities" (Washington, D.C., May, 1968) (mimeographed), table 1. Also see *National Transportation Policy* (Preliminary Draft of a Report Prepared for the Committee on Interstate and Foreign Commerce by the Special Study Group on Transportation Policies in the United States, Senate, 87th Cong., 1st sess.) (Washington, D.C.: U.S. Government Printing Office, 1961), pp. 166–84.

form of repayable grants or is later returned to the government by user fees levied on the carriers. These two situations represent public aid but not subsidy. It is only when public expenditures are not recovered by user fees, or when they take the form of direct cash payments for the purpose of increasing an industry's revenues, that subsidy is involved. At the present time, all modes of transport

TABLE 1-5
Government Expenditures for Domestic Transportation,
by Type of Carrier, through Fiscal 1968*

Industry	Federal	Expenditures (Billions of Dollars) State and Local	Total
Highway	$56.9*a*	$209.0*b*	$265.9
Air............................	12.5	6.9*c*	19.4*c*
Waterways*d*	8.0	4.9*c*	12.9*c*
Railroads*e*	1.4	0.2*f*	1.6
Total	$78.8	$221.0	$299.8

*Data for fiscal 1968 are estimated.

*a*Of this total, $39.4 billion was covered by receipts of the Federal Highway Trust Fund from user charges in the period 1956-68.

*b*Of this total, $123.4 billion was covered by state and local highway user imposts and toll receipts in the period 1921-68.

c Partially estimated.

*d*Includes inland waterways, intracoastal waterways, Great Lakes and coastal harbors. Excludes expenditures for navigation on the Tennessee River ($321 million through fiscal 1967), the United States portion of construction costs for the St. Lawrence Seaway ($132 million through fiscal 1968), the Merchant Marine ($21.5 billion through fiscal 1968), and the Coast Guard ($8.0 billion through fiscal 1968).

e Excludes government programs for research and development in local mass transportation and high-speed intercity ground transportation.

f State only. No estimate is available of the amount expended by local governments. The amount of county and municipal bonds outstanding in 1870 has been estimated at $185 million.

Source: Association of American Railroads, "Government Expenditures for Highway, Waterway, and Air Facilities and Private Expenditures for Railroad Facilities" (Washington, D.C., May, 1968) (mimeographed), tables 2-9; James C. Nelson, *Railroad Transportation and Public Policy* (Washington, D.C.: Brookings Institution, 1959), pp. 67-71; and D. Philip Locklin, *Economics of Transportation* (6th ed.; Homewood, Ill.: Richard D. Irwin, Inc., 1966), chap. vi.

except pipelines receive public aid. Air and water carriers, some railroad passenger service, and perhaps a few types of motor vehicles receive subsidies.[22]

The national purposes for giving financial assistance to transportation development have been well summarized by James C. Nelson:

Clearly, grants to the railroads had the somewhat unique national objective of initially stimulating settlement and use of the undeveloped lands in the West by means of rapid introduction of a new transport technique capable of substantially reducing the cost of long-distance transport and of improving the speed of service. On the other hand, most merchant-marine expenditures have been for the purpose of increasing the supply of ships for military needs

[22] The problems arising from public aid and subsidy are discussed at length in Chapters 13 and 14.

during World Wars I and II and of maintaining, during peace periods, sufficient merchant ships, shipbuilding and repair facilities, and trained personnel for any military eventualities that might arise. Aids to air transport sought to improve postal communication and to hasten the introduction of a new means of transport capable of unique speeds of service, as well as to assure adequate equipment, aircraft-manufacturing facilities, and skilled personnel for national defense. Federal aid to highways had as its principal purposes the improvement of rural postal services and the promotion of interstate commerce through stimulating competitive transport; in addition, there has always been an underlying national defense interest in a highly developed system of interstate highways based on the needs of commerce and, therefore, generally adequate for the needs of the military in time of war. State and local investment in modern highways has largely been in response to the way-service demands of a rapidly multiplying ownership of motor vehicles, as the willingness of user groups to pay user fees and a growing proportion of total highway costs attests. The principal objectives for federal channelization of the inland waterways, including the no-toll policy, have been to give some landlocked areas (principally the Mississippi Valley) lower freight rates than the railroads would otherwise have quoted (even under ICC regulation) and to furnish additional competition against the pre-1930 monopoly power of the railroads; and as in the case of the other agencies, there was also some military interest in having these supplementary facilities in time of war.[23]

Public aid and subsidy are given in many forms to most domestic industries. In the case of the transportation industries, it is the magnitude and the consequences of public assistance that are of significance.

PLAN OF STUDY

The topics covered in this introductory chapter suggest the outline of the book. Admittedly, more questions are raised than are answered, but there are no definitive answers to many of the problems under consideration. It is only with more understanding and discussion that regulation in the United States can continue to be successful. Moreover, controversy is the essence of public policy. The book has been divided into four major sections.

The Economic, Legal, and Administrative Concepts

Public policy in the United States in general has been directed toward maintaining competition. The belief has been that a competitive, free enterprise economic system is the best means of achieving our basic goals, including an efficient allocation of resources, a higher standard of living, and the preservation of personal freedom. In many industries, however, competition is imperfect. Especially is this true of a group of industries which have been singled out and

---

[23] James C. Nelson, "Policy Issues and Economic Effects of Public Aids to Domestic Transport," 24 *Law and Contemporary Problems* 531, 535–36 (Autumn, 1959).

subjected to a vast amount of government regulation. From an economic point of view, such industries (with certain exceptions) tend to be monopolistic; from a legal standpoint, they are "affected with a public interest." To carry out regulatory functions, various administrative agencies have been established by state and federal legislatures. All decisions of these agencies are subject to judicial review. The economic, legal, and administrative concepts of regulation are discussed in Part I.

The Theory of Regulation

Regulation is primarily concerned with rate and service control. Rate regulation occupies much of the time of the administrative agencies. Under this topic fall the questions of supervision of operating expenses, valuation of physical property, rate of return, and the rate structure. Closely connected are problems dealing with service and safety standards. The regulated industries are expected to provide adequate and safe service at reasonable rates. The theory of regulation forms the subject matter of Part II.

The Regulated Industries

In practice, the theory of regulation often must be adapted to specific conditions. For example, while competition among the various modes of transportation has tended to become increasingly intensive, more restrictive regulation has been the general trend. At the same time, the railroads and, to a lesser extent, the airlines have faced financial difficulties. And the United States has so far failed to develop a national transportation policy. The private electric utility industry competes with other fuels and, to an extent, with public and cooperative projects. Government regulation of independent natural gas producers is of recent origin, as is the Federal Power Commission's method of regulating this sector of the natural gas industry. Competition in the communications industry, too, has been growing in recent years. The practice of regulation, including current public policy problems, is considered in Part III.

Problems and Future of Regulation

Regulation has resulted in many complex problems and policy issues. These issues can be divided into two broad categories. The first category includes the procedures of regulation, such as delay, quality of the administrative agencies, and the desirability of independent regulatory commissions. The second category includes the kind of regulation presently found in the United States. As a means of improving economic performance, regulation has many limitations compared with competition. Some have argued in recent years that the real problem is too much regulation as well as regulation of the wrong kind. But regulation is an intensively political process, and policy changes evolve slowly. The problems and future of regulation are discussed in Part IV.

PART I

*The Economic, Legal,
and Administrative
Concepts of Regulation*

Chapter 2

THE ECONOMIC CONCEPTS
OF REGULATION

*Free competition is a basic postulate of our free enterprise
system, but it is not always—in all conditions—in the public
interest; sometimes regulated monopoly, or a measure of controlled monopoly, is in the public interest.*

—Judge Prettyman*

Regulation is an economic, legislative, and legal concept. The
legislature usually decides what industries should be regulated. Such decisions
may be based upon the economic characteristics of certain industries, prevailing
social philosophies, or political considerations. The policies adopted, however,
must conform to existing legal concepts and procedures. Compromise is thus a
basic ingredient of economic policy.

In this chapter, emphasis is placed on the economic characteristics of the
regulated industries. The legal concepts are discussed in the following chapter. It
will become readily apparent that there is often a gap between the economic
criteria justifying regulation on the one hand and legislative and legal concepts
on the other. It is hoped that the subsequent discussion will help to bridge this
gap. Likewise, it will become quickly apparent that while a differentiation can
be made between regulated and nonregulated industries on the basis of their
economic characteristics, the distinction is frequently "a matter of degree."

EXCEPTIONS TO COMPETITIVE POLICY

Kaysen and Turner have suggested that regulation or exemption from
competitive policy may be either necessary or desirable when one or more of
three situations are found within an industry:

1. Situations in which competition, as a practical matter, cannot exist or
   survive for long, and in which, therefore, an unregulated market will not
   produce competitive results.
2. Situations in which active competition exists, but where, because of imperfections in the market, competition does not produce one or more competitive results.

*Judge Prettyman, California v. Federal Power Comm., 296 F. 2d 348, 353 (1961).

3. Situations in which competition exists, or could exist, and has produced or may be expected to produce competitive results, but where in light of other policy considerations competitive results are unsatisfactory in one or more respects.[1]

The first situation refers to the inherently noncompetitive market. From an economic point of view, such a market structure is due to the technology of an industry, so that one ("natural monopoly") or a small number ("natural oligopoly") of optimum-size firms have adequate productive capacity to supply the demand in a market. In the case of the regulated industries, there are also other bases for limiting competition, such as technical limitations and the unique position of the buyer. The second situation refers to interference with the market process to prevent ruinous competition or to promote conservation.[2] The third situation refers to the alteration of market results to serve other public policy goals, including national defense, economic stabilization, regional development, and social equity. Political considerations, in other words, largely determine what activities fall within this third category. For this reason, primary attention is focused on the first two situations.

Each of these situations suggests different kinds of regulatory approaches to meet the various problems they pose. Moreover, more than one situation might well be found in the same industry, although such is not inevitable. At the same time, the justification for regulation implies neither the degree of regulatory activity that is desirable nor the goals that public policy should seek. Safety regulation does not necessarily require control of entry or rates; regulatory policy may seek maximum economic efficiency, the promotion of an industry, or countless other goals. Finally,

. . . regulation can easily expand beyond the scope appropriate to the conditions that first produced it, and often for reasons quite unrelated to those originally deemed pertinent. The new reasons may be sufficient to justify the extended reach, but intelligent policy-making requires that they be treated on their own merits. "Logical" extensions of regulation are not always logical. Similarly, the conditions that first produced regulation may well change to the point that regulation should be reduced or drastically revised.[3]

DETERMINANTS OF MARKET STRUCTURE

The market structure, market conduct, and market performance of the regulated industries will be discussed at length in Part III.[4] What economic

---

[1] Carl Kaysen and Donald F. Turner, *Antitrust Policy: An Economic and Legal Analysis* (Cambridge: Harvard University Press, 1959), pp. 189–90. For a slightly different approach, see Francis M. Bator, "The Anatomy of Market Failure," 72 *Quarterly Journal of Economics* 351 (1958).

[2] Conservation is discussed in connection with the natural gas industry. See Chapter 16, pp. 628–36.

[3] Kaysen and Turner, *op. cit.,* p. 190.

[4] "Market structure is important because the structure determines the behavior of firms in the industry, and that behavior in turn determines the quality of the industry's

characteristics possessed by such industries distinguish them from other domestic industries? Specifically, why provide detailed regulation of electric companies, communications services, and railroad enterprises and leave the large steel companies, drug manufacturers, and automobile producers free from comparable regulation? Clearly, all these industries are "affected with a public interest" and "render an essential service."

Market Structure: Cost Considerations

The classic economic case for extensive regulation of price, investment, service, and other managerial decisions of an industry is the inherently noncompetitive situation. The regulated industries are frequently referred to as "natural" monopolies. The term is misleading.[5] Economies of scale may allow one firm to serve a market at a lower average cost than can several competing firms. But in some of the regulated industries, primarily transportation, competition is limited by legislative policy rather than by technological conditions. In such cases, there is nothing natural or inherent about the resulting market structure. Similarly, interindustry or intermodal competition may be present. While this type of competition may lead to different results than does intraindustry or intramodal competition, it can still serve to limit discretionary control over price. Many regulated industries, therefore, exhibit both monopolistic and competitive elements. It should also be emphasized that economic conditions are constantly changing. Market growth may make entry of a new firm economically feasible; technological advances may lead to either larger or smaller optimum-size plants; substitute products or services may be developed. What is natural at one period of time, then, may become quite unnatural at another. "Perhaps, as others have observed, the notion of a natural monopoly was invented to justify exclusive markets for utility companies after their ineffectual and sometimes wasteful rivalry proved unsatisfactory to both the investor and the consumer interests."[6]

Economies of Scale. In some fields, regulation is predicated on the idea

---

performance." Richard Caves, *American Industry: Structure, Conduct, Performance* (2d ed.; Englewood Cliffs: Prentice-Hall, Inc., 1967), p. 17. Also see Joe S. Bain, *Industrial Organization* (2d ed.; New York: John Wiley & Sons, Inc., 1968).

[5] "One of the most unfortunate phrases ever introduced into law or economics was the phrase 'natural monopoly.' Every monopoly is a product of public policy. No present monopoly, public or private, can be traced back through history in a pure form. . . . '[N]atural monopolies' in fact originated in response to a belief that some goal, or goals, of public policy would be advanced by encouraging or permitting a monopoly to be formed, and discouraging or forbidding future competition with this monopoly." James R. Nelson, "The Role of Competition in the Regulated Industries," 11 *The Antitrust Bulletin* 1, 3 (Jan.–Apr., 1966). For a critical analysis of the natural monopoly concept as a justification for regulation, see Harold Demsetz, "Why Regulate Utilities?" 11 *Journal of Law and Economics* 55 (1968).

[6] Emery Troxel, *Economics of Public Utilities* (New York: Holt, Rinehart & Winston, Inc., 1947), p. 27. Also see Horace Gray, "The Passing of the Public Utility Concept," 16 *Journal of Land & Public Utility Economics* 8 (1940).

that an enterprise can achieve lower costs if placed in the position of a monopolist in a market. As Stelzer has pointed out, there are three aspects of decreasing
cost:

> ... The first is short-run decreasing cost. This reflects the fact that once an
> investment in facilities is made, output can be increased with unit costs
> declining until the physical capacity of the facilities is reached.
>
> The second aspect of decreasing cost relates to the long run. This phenom-
> enon arises from the fact that, at any point in time, the unit cost of adding
> capacity declines as the size of the additional facility increases. Note that
> whereas the short-run decreasing cost situation relates to fuller utilization of
> existing capacity, the long-run decreasing cost situation applies to the econo-
> mies associated with larger rather than smaller additions to capacity.
>
> The third aspect of decreasing cost reflects the fact of technological prog-
> ress. Note that the second aspect is basically a static concept; at any point in
> time, with given technology, larger capacity increments tend to be associated
> with lower unit costs. But this third aspect of decreasing cost is dynamic: as
> technology changes, the real unit costs of adding capacity decline.[7]

As short-run decreasing cost is a characteristic of many industries, this
phenomenon does not provide an economic rationale for detailed regulation.
The long-run decreasing cost situation, however, does provide an economic justification for regulation, as illustrated in Figure 2–1. Assume a given state of

FIGURE 2–1
The Natural Monopoly Situation

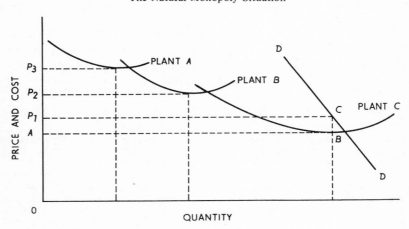

technology. If four firms of equal size were competing in a market, the long-run
price could not be less than P_3 (plant A). If two firms of equal size were serving

---

[7] Irwin M. Stelzer, "Incremental Costs and Utility Rate-Making in the Competitive
Era" (American Bar Association Annual Report, Section of *Public Utility Law, 1967*),
pp. 30–31.

the market, minimum average costs would fall to P_2 (plant B). But the situation would still be unstable, for if economies of scale permitted one of the firms to double its plant, it would be able to supply the entire market (plant C), charging price P_1 and earning a monopoly profit equal to P_1CBA. [8]

The inherently noncompetitive market situation, therefore, is determined by economies of scale. Competition may exist for a time, but only until bankruptcy or merger leaves the field to one firm. Competition is self-destructive and results in a waste of scarce resources. Conceivably, the two or three firms could make an agreement to share the market. Neither the firms nor the public would benefit should this occur. The firms would be high-cost producers, and the consumers would be denied the benefits derived from economies of scale. Moreover, nonprice rivalry between inefficient plants does not lead to an efficient allocation of resources. When economies of scale permit only one optimum-size producer in a market, it is highly desirable for public policy to allow a monopolistic supplier to operate. But the mere fact that a monopolist is allowed to exist does not assure the public of obtaining the benefits of whatever lower costs are achieved. In fact, the monopolist might absorb not only the benefits resulting from the lower cost but also might raise prices. Consequently, the presence of a monopolist calls for some degree of public regulation.

With respect to the regulated industries, significant economies of scale indicating large-scale, monopolistic operations are found in the generation, transmission, and distribution of electric power; the transportation by pipeline of natural gas and petroleum; the distribution of natural gas; the provision of long-distance telephone and telegraph services; and, over local or short-haul routes, in the supplying of railroad transportation. The pipeline industry is illustrative. Unit costs of crude oil pipeline transport decline rapidly with increases in the designated capacity (throughput) per day and the diameter of the pipeline. Thus, a throughput of 25,000 barrels per day in a 10¾-inch line costs 0.237 cents per ton-mile as compared with a cost of 0.0513 cents per ton-mile for a daily throughput of 400,000 barrels in a 32-inch line. [9] The second cost is approximately 22 percent of the first.

In some markets two or more competitors are found, all of which may be relatively efficient producers. Particularly is this true with respect to air, highway, and water transportation and the production of natural gas. In these cases, regulation is based on considerations other than the existence of significant economies of scale. Moreover, all of the regulated industries are subject to varying degrees of interindustry or intermodal competition.

---

[8] The theoretical treatment of long-run decreasing cost resulting from technological advances is the same as depicted in Figure 2–1: over time, only one firm of optimum size will survive in a market. Historically, technological advances have been of major importance in explaining decreasing costs in American industries.

[9] Leslie Cookenboo, Jr., "Costs of Operating Crude Oil Pipe Lines," *Rice Institute Bulletin* (April, 1954). For data on the electric power industry, see Suilin Ling, *Economies of Scale in the Steam-Electric Power Generating Industry* (Amsterdam: North-Holland Publishing Co., 1964).

Fixed and Nonliquid Investment. Economies of scale often require large-scale plants. Such plants, in turn, require large fixed investments. Indeed, an important economic characteristic of the regulated industries (bus, highway freight, and water carriers are exceptions) is their heavy investment in durable equipment. The nation's railroads, for instance, have invested more than $36 billion in road and equipment—an amount equivalent to over $170,000 per mile of road. The investment is largely fixed capital and represents a high percentage of total costs. One result is a low annual rate of capital turnover (the ratio of annual revenues to total investment). For electric utilities, the turnover is once every four years; for the railroads, it is once every three years. In contrast, for most manufacturing industries, annual revenues are frequently greater than total investment.[10]

For some of the regulated industries, their large investment has been irrevocably sunk in the original site; it is highly specialized and nonliquid. If the market for a regulated firm's service began to disappear, its investment could not be moved to some other location where the prospects of success appear greater. Should a company desire to retire from the railroad field, by way of illustration, a significant percentage of its total investment would be lost. A large part of the investment is in grading and excavation, and these have no value except as a roadbed for a railroad. In a similar manner, although perhaps to a somewhat lesser degree, little could be realized on such investments as hydroelectric plants, telephone cables and lines, and natural gas and petroleum pipelines.

The Problem of Unused Capacity. Closely connected with the limitation on intraindustry competition in the regulated industries arising from economies of scale is the problem of unused capacity.[11] This situation results from two factors: first, the diversity of consumer demand; second, engineering considerations, resulting from the general policy requirement that the regulated industries must have the necessary capacity to meet foreseeable increases in demand.

Consider the first factor—the peak demand problem. Most of the regulated industries provide a product or service which is nonstorable (electricity) or which can be stored for only a limited time (natural gas). Yet, consumers expect, indeed demand, instantaneous service. But consumers also have different demands throughout a day, a season, or a year. Since storage is limited, at best, the companies must have adequate capacity to satisfy the peak demand, even though this maximum demand on a system may come only for a few minutes or a few

[10] Stated another way, electric utilities require an investment in plant and equipment of about $4 to produce one dollar in revenue, whereas most manufacturing firms require an investment of approximately 50 cents in plant and equipment to produce one dollar in annual revenue. Thus, electric utilities require about eight times the capital investment of typical manufacturing firms doing equivalent volumes of business.

[11] Unused capacity is not necessarily synonymous with excess capacity. Both are usually thought of in the investment sense—that is, a commitment to an industry of factors of production in excess of current demand. As used in this book, however, unused capacity refers to short-term overinvestment due to seasonal or cyclical fluctuations in demand, or to engineering considerations, while excess capacity refers to large and persistent maladjustments between capacity and long-run demand.

hours at periodic intervals of time. There are many examples: the demand for electricity may be greater in the summer than in the winter, while the demand for natural gas may be just the opposite; urban transport experiences its maximum demand for commutation services in the morning and evening; telephone plant may be used more continuously during the day than during the night hours; airline traffic may be heavier over the weekend than during the week. Except for peak demand periods, therefore, the regulated industries commonly have unused capacity.

When a firm is large, it is able to draw customers with different demand characteristics, or it can transfer equipment from one place to another in order to economize its total investment costs. Multiplant firms may be required. A large electric company can attract commercial, industrial, and residential customers who demand electricity in different amounts at different hours during a given period of time. A large transportation company can move its equipment from one route to another in response to different consumer demands over the two routes. In such ways, a company can minimize its unused capacity.

Consider next the second factor—short-term overinvestment due to engineering considerations. If there are significant economies of scale and if consumer demand is expected to increase in the foreseeable future, cost savings can be achieved by building an optimum-size plant, even though total capacity is greater than required to meet the existing demand. The same conclusion applies to the expansion of a plant. Frequently, such economies of scale result from the indivisibility of some factors of production. Pegrum has pointed this out with respect to the railroad industry as follows:

> A railroad has to make large initial outlays to build a single-track line and acquire the necessary terminal facilities and rolling stock to operate it. When the plant is utilized to capacity, double-tracking will require a large additional investment which cannot profitably be made unless there is a prospect of a large proportionate increase in traffic. Expansion of this type entails difficult problems of market anticipation because the facilities have to be built well in advance of market opportunities. Meanwhile the traffic which is available will have to bear the burden of keeping the railroad in operation until the new traffic has been built up. If, instead of double-tracking, a new railroad were to be built, a complete duplication of the facilities of the existing road would be necessary, and the immediately available traffic would be inadequate to give either road a profit. The building of the second road would cost more than double-tracking the first, although doing this would give the two railroads only the same capacity as the double-tracked one, or perhaps even less.[12]

For one or both of these reasons, therefore, unused capacity is another common characteristic of the regulated industries. But the utilization problem provides only limited support for detailed economic regulation. Unused capacity due to the diversity of consumer demand is a persistent situation. In order to

[12] Dudley F. Pegrum, *Transportation: Economics and Public Policy* (rev. ed.; Homewood, Ill.: Richard D. Irwin, Inc., 1968), p. 139.

attract off-peak users, firms will tend to cut their prices. Such price cuts (off-peak rates) are often economically defensible, but sometimes they result in discrimination among customers, products, or sections of the country, or in severe price wars to the detriment of both the companies and their customers. This problem will be considered at greater length in the following section. Unused capacity due to engineering considerations or economies of scale is only temporary, until markets grow. Thus, while the decreasing cost phenomenon provides a permanent reason for monopoly, the existence of unused capacity only provides a reason for controlling discrimination and, perhaps, a temporary reason for limiting competition.[13]

The Limits to Size. It should not be assumed either that the present size of firms in the economy can be justified solely by economies of scale or that economies of scale are limitless. On the contrary, it appears that there are definite (if imprecise) limits to large-scale enterprises,[14] and the regulated industries are not exceptions. In a careful study of the effects of size (scale) in 37 railroad systems, Healy concluded that "an increase in scale above 10,000 employees is associated with an increase in wages and transportation expenses and with lower rates of return, and above 19,000 with an increase in unit capital requirements."[15] Diseconomies of scale, then, may occur in the railroad industry as a system is expanded beyond the optimum size. In contrast, there are apparently few, if any, significant economies of scale in the air, highway, and water transport industries[16] or in the production of natural gas. And local telephone

[13] Nor does excess capacity provide a strong case for economic regulation. "The kind of intervention usually demanded is that which is likely not to cure the situation but rather to insure that it will persist much longer than it otherwise would. What is usually sought is price support, by public authority or by authorized private agreement, and production quotas are often necessary to make the price support effective. It may be that not even these steps will improve the affected industry's lot—if demand for the product concerned is highly elastic, a raising of price may well make the industry's losses more acute than before. This is likely to be the case where the decline in demand has been caused by the rise of competitive substitutes, as has happened to railroads, coal, and a host of less significant industries. But to the extent that price-fixing restores the profits or cuts the losses of the industry's producers, cure of the basic problem—excess capacity—is simply postponed, and meanwhile resources are being uneconomically used from an over-all standpoint." Kaysen and Turner, *op. cit.,* p. 196.

[14] See Joe S. Bain, *Barriers to New Competition* (Cambridge: Harvard University Press, 1956), esp. chap. iii.

[15] Kent T. Healy, *The Effects of Scale in the Railroad Industry* (New Haven: Committee on Transportation, Yale University, 1961), p. 3. Also see, by the same author, "The Merger Movement in Transportation," 52 *American Economic Review* 436 (1962); and Merrill J. Roberts, *Discussion,* 52 *ibid.* 445 (1962). For a view that economics of scale are not so limited, see John W. Barriger, "The Effect of Mergers on Competition," 7 *Transportation Journal* 5 (Spring, 1968).

[16] H. D. Koontz, "Domestic Air Line Self-Sufficiency," 42 *American Economic Review* 103 (1952); Merrill J. Roberts, "Some Aspects of Motor Carrier Costs: Firm Size, Efficiency and Financial Health," 32 *Land Economics* 228 (1956); Edward W. Smykay, "An Appraisal of the Economies of Scale in the Motor Carrier Industry," 34 *ibid.* 143 (1958); and J. R. Meyer, M. J. Peck, J. Stenason, and C. Zwick, *The Economics of Competition in the Transportation Industries* (Cambridge: Harvard University Press, 1959), pp. 86–101, 135–36.

(exchange) service is often considered to be subject to increasing costs.[17] In some cases, moreover, there may be other means of achieving economies of scale. Two railroads may jointly own terminal facilities; two or more electric utilities may be interconnected, thereby reducing the necessary reserve capacity. Finally, plant economies of scale, necessitating local monopoly operations, may be of far greater importance than multiplant economies, necessitating regional or national monopoly operations.[18]

Technical Limitations. Rivalry in the regulated industries is normally confined to local or regional market areas. Such competition, in addition to economies of scale, may be limited by the fact that equipment must be located below, upon, or over public property. While the number of conduits or mains that can be buried below the street, the number of tracks that can be laid upon it, and the networks of wires that can be strung above it are limited, competing firms are usually possible. But, as the number of conduits or mains increases, the streets are torn up more frequently, thereby creating a public nuisance, and the available space is used up. The number of desirable sites also may be limited, such as those for hydroelectric power plants. Even the number of air lanes is limited, necessitating some control over the schedules and positions of aircraft throughout any twenty-four-hour period.

Local telephone service illustrates the technical limitations to competition. If such service were supplied by two competing companies—a situation which has existed in a number of cities in former years—subscribers might be forced to have two telephones in order to contact every other telephone subscriber in the city. Of course, the two companies might agree to interchange calls (either free or for a fee), but they might not.[19] Such a situation, moreover, also might require two sets of telephone poles and lines throughout the city. The tremendous cost for duplication of facilities is evident. Even if the firms agreed to an interchange of calls, it would be more difficult to achieve an efficient, integrated system (delay in completing calls might be either avoidable or unavoidable) than would be possible from a single telephone company serving the entire city.

Market Structure: Demand Considerations

In legal terminology, there is a high degree of public interest attached to

[17] Local exchange service may be subject to increasing costs because as the number of subscribers increases, the amount of central office equipment required per telephone increases even more rapidly. But there are economies of scale in circuits and switching equipment to provide any given number of connections. Consequently, the judgment as to whether costs are increasing or decreasing depends primarily upon the unit of measurement of output. If calls are taken as the unit, local exchange service clearly shows economies of scale. If the number of subscribers is the measure, it appears that there may be diseconomies. See Charles W. Meyer, "The Cost Function for Local Telephone Service: Increasing or Decreasing?" (Ph.D. dissertation, Johns Hopkins University, 1961); and David A. Bowers and Wallace F. Lovejoy, "Disequilibrium and Increasing Costs: A Study of Local Telephone Service," 41 *Land Economics* 31 (1965).

[18] Bain, *Barriers to New Competition, op. cit.*

[19] See James M. Herring and Gerald C. Gross, *Telecommunications* (New York: McGraw-Hill Book Co., Inc., 1936), pp. 62–66.

the services rendered by the regulated industries. While the major economic criteria justifying detailed regulation result from cost considerations, this statement implies that there are some demand characteristics of the regulated industries that distinguish their services from those of other industries, for many nonregulated firms produce goods or render services that can be regarded as necessities (food, clothing, and shelter, among others).

The Diversity Problem.   One important demand characteristic of the regulated industries is the diversity problem discussed above. Consumers demand instantaneous and uninterrupted service. They can neither store the service nor defer its purchase. However, since consumers' demands for service differ considerably from one period of time to another, the regulated industries commonly have peak hours or peak seasons when their plant is used to capacity and other times when they have varying amounts of unused capacity. In this respect, the services offered by the regulated industries can be distinguished from those rendered by nonregulated enterprises.

The Elasticity of Demand.   A second demand characteristic of the services performed by the regulated industries concerns the elasticity of demand. Two concepts are involved. Price elasticity of demand refers to the effect of a price increase or decrease on consumer expenditures for a good or service under given demand conditions. If the price for a service increases, demand is elastic if consumers decrease their expenditures for this service, inelastic if they increase their expenditures. Conversely, if the price falls, demand is elastic if consumers increase their expenditures for the service, inelastic if they decrease their expenditures. Income elasticity of demand refers to the effect of a change in consumer income on consumer expenditures for a good or service at a given price. If consumers change their expenditures for a service more than proportionately to a change in their incomes, demand is elastic; when they change their expenditures less than proportionately to a change in their incomes, demand is inelastic.

For many types of consumers and for many uses, demand (measured by both price elasticity and income elasticity) is inelastic for the services of the regulated industries.[20] As a result, the revenues and earnings of these industries, with the significant exception of transport firms, tend to show greater stability throughout the business cycle than do the revenues and earnings of nonregulated industries. Such a situation reflects the fact that many consumers consider these services to be indispensable, preferring during a business recession to cut their expenditures for other goods and services before reducing their outlays for electric, gas, and telephone services.

Figures 2–2 and 2–3 reflect this characteristic by showing the sensitivity of dollar sales to income changes.[21] Figure 2–2 shows that sales of electric, gas,

[20] See Chapters 10 and 11.
[21] The sensitivity of *dollar sales* to income changes must be distinguished from the concept of income elasticity of demand. The second refers to the correlation of *unit sales* with income. Thus, income sensitivity is a broader concept and includes more factors which influence sales than does income elasticity.

FIGURE 2-2
Income Sensitivity for Sales of Various Industries
(1929–60 average, growth trend removed)

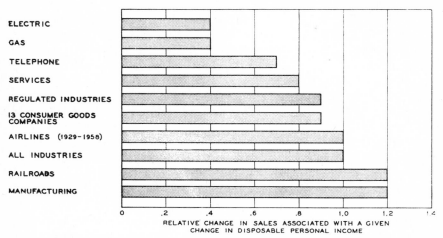

Source: Gerald W. Groepper, "Sensitivity of Corporate Sales to Income Changes," 26 *Journal of Marketing* 47, 51 (1962). Reprinted with permission from the *Journal of Marketing,* national quarterly publication of the American Marketing Association.

FIGURE 2-3
Income Sensitivity for Sales of the Nontransportation Utilities
(1929–60 average, growth trend removed)

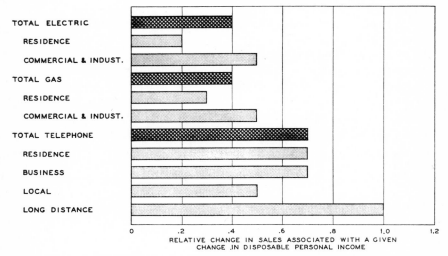

Source: Gerald W. Groepper, "Sensitivity of Corporate Sales to Income Changes," 26 *Journal of Marketing* 47, 51 (1962). Reprinted with permission from the *Journal of Marketing,* national quarterly publication of the American Marketing Association.

and telephone industries are less sensitive to changes in disposable personal income than are transportation services and all manufacturing sales. Figure 2–3, showing the major consumer groups for the nontransportation regulated industries, indicates that their sales to small consumers (residential) as well as local telephone service are less sensitive to changes in disposable income than are sales to large consumers (commercial and industrial) and long-distance telephone service.

The Position of the Consumer. A final demand characteristic concerns the position of the buyer of services offered by the regulated industries. Most regulated firms' markets, as well as their customers' alternatives, are restricted by "the necessarily close connection between the utility plant on the one hand and the consumers' premises on the other."[22] With respect to the average consumer and excepting some transportation services, intraindustry competiton would offer few benefits. As explained by Lewis:

> Even though a utility service is furnished in any community by two or more companies, the position of any consumer is not significantly different from that which he would occupy if he were served by a monopolistic company. He is both free and able to buy his groceries daily from any of many competing stores, but it is not possible for him to buy gas, for example, elsewhere than from the concern with whose distribution system his gas-burning equipment is at the time physically connected. Nothing short of desperation borne of excessive and long-continued abuse would induce him to incur the cost and inconvenience of changing companies, and of course, once the new arrangement had been made he would find himself once more removed from the current of active competition.[23]

There is a closely related factor, namely, interindustry competition. There can be little doubt that coal, electricity, gas, and oil are all in competition for many uses, or that the various modes of transport compete for customers. But, as will be discussed in the following section, such rivalry is imperfect. As a result of the nonstorability of the regulated industries' services, differences in consumer demands, and the inability (or limited ability) of consumers to buy from competing companies, price discrimination is possible and highly attractive to the regulated companies and, under regulation, to their customers.

Market Structure: Noneconomic Factors

These cost and demand characteristics partly explain the present market structures of the regulated industries and the need for detailed economic regulation. At the same time, noneconomic factors also have played a role in shaping public policy decisions. Entry into all regulated industries is rigidly controlled. Evidence indicates that such control has been used for two purposes—to pro-

---

[22] James C. Bonbright, *Principles of Public Utility Rates* (New York: Columbia University Press, 1961), pp. 12–13.

[23] Ben W. Lewis, "Public Utilities," in L. S. Lyon and V. Abramson, *Government and Economic Life* (Washington, D.C.: Brookings Institution, 1940), Vol. II, p. 621.

mote the maximum number of firms economically feasible in a given market and to protect existing firms in a market from new competition. The need to enforce safety requirements and the desire to promote the development of a particular industry have likewise been advanced as justifications for restricting competition. These factors are of particular importance in the transportation industries and will be considered at length in Chapters 13 and 14. The point being stressed is that public policy is determined on both economic and political grounds and that because not all regulated industries possess the same economic and noneconomic characteristics, the basis for their regulation also differs.

COMPETITION, PRICING, AND DISCRIMINATION

The present market structures of the regulated industries vary considerably, ranging from the one firm which provides all public message telegraph service to the thousands of firms which provide highway transport services. Where a single firm serves a market, there is a presumption in favor of regulation to control prices, earnings, and service standards. Where a large number of firms serve a market, there is a presumption in favor of unregulated competition to protect the public interest. In between these two situations, the case for or against economic regulation is more complex and uncertain. A brief review of price theory will provide a background for further analysis.

A Review of Price Theory [24]

In economic theory, four models are usually recognized for purposes of analyzing pricing policies—pure or perfect competition, pure monopoly, oligopoly, and monopolistic competition. These are theoretical models, built upon certain limiting assumptions—assumptions which may not be valid in explaining the price behavior of a particular firm in real life. They are useful, nevertheless, as analytical aids.

Perfect Competition. Perfect competition refers to a market situation in which no seller has any influence over the market price of his product. Five assumptions concerning the structure of the market underlie this model. First, the products being offered are homogeneous, so that there is perfect substitutability among them. Buyers can thus shift quickly from one seller to another in response to a lower price. Second, there is a large number of buyers and sellers, each of them small, so that neither the quantity supplied nor the quantity demanded by any one of them will have an effect on the market price. Third, buyers and sellers possess complete knowledge of market conditions, so that no individual has an advantage over the others. Fourth, there are no restraints on the market or on the independence of any buyer or seller. Economic forces are

[24] For exhaustive studies on pricing, see Joe S. Bain, *Price Theory* (New York: Henry Holt & Co., 1952); and Donald S. Watson, *Price Theory and Its Uses* (2d ed.; Boston: Houghton Mifflin Co., 1968). The welfare concepts of competition are discussed by J. de V. Graaff, *Theoretical Welfare Economics* (Cambridge, England: Oxford University Press, 1957).

free to operate in the market, and individuals are free to act in their own self-interests. Fifth, there are no obstacles preventing the complete mobility of resources, both into and out of an industry.[25]

Given this market structure, the final result is a situation in which no seller or buyer can become better off by altering his own behavior. Equilibrium, in the long run, requires that marginal revenue equals marginal cost (Figure 2–4),[26] for at that point, the firm is maximizing its profit. Producing more units would add

FIGURE 2–4
Long-Run Equilibrium of a Firm in a Perfectly Competitive Industry

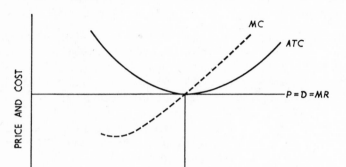

more to total cost than to total revenue; producing fewer units would subtract more from total revenue than from total cost. Further, since price equals minimum average cost, the plant is being used efficiently. The model indicates that the market determines the price of a product and allocates resources. Each seller, by trying to maximize his own profit, works for the best interests of the economy as a whole.

The final market equilibrium also defines in a precise way a socially efficient allocation of resources. In the first place, the firms are of optimum size, so that total production is maximized and all factors of production are fully utilized. Given existing consumer tastes and available technology and resources, no other arrangement of resources would result in an increase in the total value of production. In the second place, consumer satisfaction is maximized. Under conditions of perfect competition, the price represents what consumers are willing to pay for the last unit of a product. The price, in turn, is equal to the cost

25 Pure, as opposed to perfect, competition is a less restrictive concept. It assumes imperfect knowledge, so that instantaneous market adjustments do not result.

26 It is assumed throughout the book that all cost curves include a "normal" profit, defined as the net return required to maintain the equity capital in the business.

of producing the last unit—that is, marginal cost. It follows that the consumer's valuation of the last unit and the cost of producing that unit are equal. Producing more of one good involves giving the consumer additional units which he values less than the cost of production to society; producing less involves foregoing units that the consumer values more than the cost of production. Only when price is equal to marginal cost is consumer satisfaction maximized.[27]

Pure Monopoly. Pure monopoly is at the opposite extreme to conditions of perfect competition. This situation means there is a single seller of a product. The extent of a monopolist's power, however, will depend on the closeness of available substitutes. As used here, pure monopoly implies a situation in which substitutes are lacking.

In the long run, a monopolist has the same objective as a seller operating under conditions of perfect competition—the maximization of profit. Being the only supplier, the demand for the monopolist's product is the entire market demand for the product. In seeking to maximize profit, a seller operating under conditions of perfect competition will adjust his total output so that his marginal cost is equal to his marginal revenue. So, too, with the monopolist. But there is a vital difference, for what distinguishes the monopolist's position is the shape of the demand curve. As this curve slopes downward and to the right (Figure 2–5), marginal revenue and price are no longer the same. Marginal revenue will fall faster than price as output is increased. It is thus apparent that the

FIGURE 2–5
Price Determination under Pure Monopoly

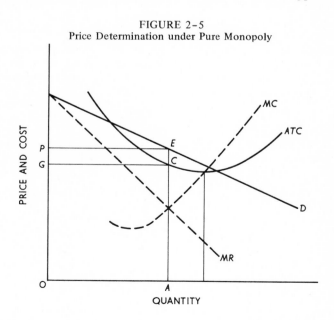

27 The marginal cost pricing principle is further discussed in the appendix to Chapter 11.

monopolist can get a higher price by restricting output and selling less. Assuming that the monopolist charges only one price, his best price in the illustration is P and his output is OA, resulting in a monopoly profit equal to $PECG$.

The results of pure monopoly differ in several important respects from those of perfect competition. The most profitable policy for the monopolist is to produce less, and charge more, than a firm operating under perfect competition. As noted above, the best allocation of resources for society as a whole is to carry production to the point where marginal cost equals price. Here, the value of the last unit of input just equals the value of the last unit of output. The most profitable adjustment for the monopolist, in contrast, is where price is greater than marginal cost. The difference is excess profit to the firm. Consequently, fewer resources are being employed than society would be willing to pay for at going rates. As long as price exceeds marginal cost, use of additional resources would add more to the value of output than in their present use. From the point of view of society, monopoly keeps output from being maximized. And, in addition, the monopolist's plant is not being used efficiently. Society does not get the full potential advantages of economies of scale. In short, price is higher, profits excessive, output smaller, and fewer resources are used under conditions of pure monopoly as compared with perfect competition.

Oligopoly. Both perfect competition and pure monopoly are uncommon market structures. An understanding of these markets does give a means of analyzing two more realistic types of markets found in the modern economy—oligopoly and monopolistic competition. Oligopoly is common in our basic industries, monopolistic competition in consumer goods industries and retailing.

Oligopoly exists when there is a small number of sellers in a market. Each seller, therefore, must take into account the effects of his own price and output decisions on those of his rivals. In other words, each seller recognizes that his actions have a definite effect on the final market outcome. The products produced by oligopolists may be virtually identical—cement, oil, steel—or differentiated but close substitutes—automobiles, cigarettes.

In theory, the condition for profit maximization under oligopoly is the output where marginal cost equals marginal revenue. But because of the existence of close substitutes, a seller must also consider what others are likely to do if he takes a certain course of action. Each seller, moreover, faces the same kind of problem. The result is uncertainty, the inherent characteristic of oligopoly. To illustrate: A price reduction by one seller, assuming that rivals do not follow suit, might lead to a larger sales volume. Yet, can such an assumption be made? Given a small number of sellers, it could reasonably be expected that each will follow a known price reduction made by another. And if all firms reduce their prices, revenues may fall (depending on the elasticity of demand) with little or no change in market shares, but with smaller profits for each seller. The same considerations apply to price increases. No one seller, under normal conditions, will want his price to be far above that of his rivals. If one oligopolist wants to raise his price, he will consider whether or not the others will follow suit. Thus, the initiative taken by one seller to either raise or lower his price may be risky. It is not surprising, then, that price changes in oligopolistic markets may be few and far between. Price leadership is common. Rivalry tends to take the form of quality, advertising, research and development, and innovation. These forms of competition, more difficult for rivals to match, largely determine the market shares held by each producer.

Pricing behavior in oligopoly cannot be precisely formulated, but depends on the assumptions that one makes. Competitive prices, monopoly prices, or prices somewhere between these two extremes are likely outcomes of oligopoly. Some have argued that the most plausible outcome is monopoly pricing[28] or limited joint profit maximization.[29] Others have rejected the assumption of profit maximization altogether, substituting in its place the theory of games,[30] preventative pricing to forestall entry,[31] organizational influences,[32] interfirm organization,[33] and limited sales maximization.[34] Clearly, there is little consensus on oligopoly price theory.

Monopolistic Competition. Monopolistic competition stands between perfect competition and oligopoly. Many industries have numerous suppliers, but each seller has a differentiated product. Products may differ because of quality, color, location, packaging, service, or a particular dealer's reputation. Since many sellers are supplying a similar product, joint action is not feasible. Moreover, there is reason for expecting active price competition. For example, while there is only one gasoline station on a given location, there may be many within a few blocks. Some may give lower prices, others trading stamps, and still others better service. Each automobile dealer normally enjoys an exclusive franchise in a given area, but competition among dealers is keen.

Firms operating under conditions of monopolistic competition will achieve maximum profits at the point where marginal cost equals marginal revenue, as depicted in Figure 2–6. Due to product differentiation, each seller faces a downward sloping demand curve. The seller will produce *OA* units and sell at price *P*, thus giving him the excess profit represented by *GCEP*. Such profits may attract

[28] See G. W. Stocking and M. W. Watkins, *Monopoly and Free Enterprise* (New York: Twentieth Century Fund, Inc., 1951), chap. iv.

[29] William Fellner, *Competition among the Few* (New York: Alfred A. Knopf, 1949).

[30] John von Neumann and Oskar Morgenstern, *Theories of Games and Economic Behavior* (Princeton: Princeton University Press, 1944); and Martin Shubik, *Strategy and Market Structure: Competition, Oligopoly, and the Theory of Games* (New York: John Wiley & Sons, Inc., 1959).

[31] Bain, *Barriers to New Competition, op. cit.;* and Paolo Sylos-Labini, *Oligopoly and Technical Progress*, trans. Elizabeth Henderson (Cambridge: Harvard University Press, 1962).

[32] R. M. Cyert and J. G. March, "Organizational Structure and Pricing Behavior in an Oligopolistic Market," 45 *American Economic Review* 129 (1955), and "Organizational Factors in the Theory of Oligopoly," 70 *Quarterly Journal of Economics* 44 (1956).

[33] Almarin Phillips, *Market Structure, Organization and Performance* (Cambridge: Harvard University Press, 1962).

[34] William J. Baumol, *Business Behavior, Value and Growth* (rev. ed.; New York: Harcourt, Brace & World, 1967). But see B. D. Mabry and D. L. Siders, "An Empirical Test of the Sales Maximization Hypothesis," 33 *Southern Economic Journal* 367 (1967).

FIGURE 2-6
Price Determination under Monopolistic Competition

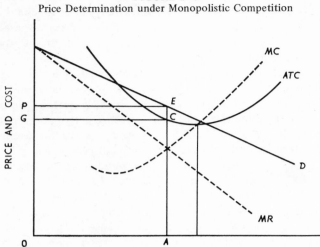

new competition. A new producer, of course, cannot produce exactly the same product, but he can try for a close enough substitute to capture a share of the market. At the same time, existing competitors may pursue more aggressive policies through price reductions or advertising campaigns to attract some of the customers of the original firm. If either event occurs, the demand curve facing the original firm will shift to the left, as in Figure 2-7. In the long run, therefore, the equilibrium point may be where profits are normal (*O'A'* units, *O'P'* price). It should be noted, however, that such an equilibrium is at a point where price equals average total cost, indicating a smaller output and higher cost (due

FIGURE 2-7
Long-Run Equilibrium under Monopolistic Competition

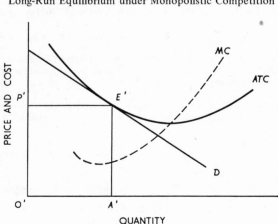

to advertising, research, promotional activities, and so forth) and price than under perfect competition.[35]

What effect does imperfect competition (oligopoly and monopolistic competition) have on economic efficiency? Clearly, imperfect competition does not result in a socially efficient allocation of resources in the same sense as perfect competition. Price is above marginal cost, so that what consumers are willing to pay for the last unit of a good is not equated to the cost to society of the last unit. Stated another way, price is higher and output is smaller under imperfect competition than under perfect competition, and plants are not being operated at their most efficient output levels. Taking a broader view of social efficiency, however, the perfectly competitive definition may not be applicable. If consumers want product differentiation, a situation ignored by the perfectly competitive model, imperfect competition is inevitable. In addition, research and development, technological and product innovation, and advertising are all part of imperfect competition, and again, the model of perfect competition ignores these factors. Perhaps, then, progress and efficiency, in line with consumer wants, will be greater under conditions of oligopoly or monopolistic competition.[36] Whether or not this is true can only be determined from a case-by-case analysis of actual markets in the economy.

Workable Competition

In the economists' theoretical concept of perfect competition, and the added assumption of profit maximization, the market structure of an industry is a necessary and sufficient condition to define one unique market performance that will result. Under conditions of imperfect competition, the market structure of an industry may permit several patterns of market performance, so that there is no single one-to-one correlation between structure and performance. No modern industry conforms exactly to all the conditions necessary for perfect competition. Fortunately, evidences of competitive performance, adequate for public policy purposes, often can be found in markets in which structure is not ideal. In recent years, it has become common to study the workability of competition in various industries.

Workable or effective competition may result from conditions that are less exacting than those demanded for perfection.[37] The major elements of market structure are: (1) the number and size distribution of buyers and sellers; (2) the characteristics of demand; (3) the nature of the price structure; (4) the market-

---

[35] Above-normal profits may still persist in the long run. The original firm might increase its own advertising campaign, thus checking the inroads of its competitors so that price will not fall to $O'P'$. See Edward H. Chamberlin, *The Theory of Monopolistic Competition* (8th ed.; Cambridge: Harvard University Press, 1962).

[36] The outstanding exponent of this view was Joseph Schumpeter. See his *Capitalism, Socialism, and Democracy* (3d ed.; New York: Harper & Bros., 1950), esp. chap. vii.

[37] See Stephen H. Sosnick, "A Critique of Concepts of Workable Competition," 62 *Quarterly Journal of Economics* 380 (1958); and Robert L. Knox, "Workable Competition and Public Policy," 1 *Antitrust Law & Economics Review* 41 (Spring, 1968).

ing or distribution channels utilized; (5) the geographical distribution of supply and demand; (6) the conditions of entry into the industry. Similarly, the leading tests of market performance are: (1) price behavior; (2) capacity-output relationships; (3) progressiveness; (4) the level of profits; and (5) selling expenses.[38] The objective of studying these aspects of an industry's structure and performance has been well summarized by McKie:

> We study such patterns to determine how they work, and how well, and whether they might be improved. It is particularly necessary to determine whether and to what extent the firms in the market have the power to control the outcome. A free-market economy works best when the external pressures of the market hold each firm in check. Market compulsion is the best guarantee of good performance and optimum economic results in the long run. Firms possessing great and unchecked market power may for a time show good performance, especially if performance is judged chiefly by the criterion of progressiveness; but the drawbacks of benevolent despotism are too well known to require elaboration. Public policy does not and should not require perfect competition in most markets, but it should seek to establish or encourage market patterns in which adequate performance is compelled by market structure. To these patterns we give the generic name "workable competition."[39]

The concept of workable competition is admittedly less precise than that of perfect competition. By what standards, for example, should progressiveness, prices, or profits be measured? Further, complete flexibility or optimum resource allocation cannot be insured. The concept does, however, contribute toward these ends. And, since the utopia of perfect competition, with a total absence of market power, is not attainable (many would say undesirable), workable competition is a more useful goal of public policy. It assumes that a situation can be devised whereby the existing market power poses no economic or political threat to consumers.

Competition and Price Discrimination

Past experience suggests that unrestricted competition in the regulated industries (1) may become cutthroat, destructive, or ruinous and (2) often results in severe price discrimination. The latter is of far more importance than is the former, particularly with respect to current conditions and regulatory problems.

Inadequacy of Competition. Historically, it can be argued with a considerable measure of validity that competition within the regulated industries did not seem to afford a sufficient degree of protection for the public.[40] More specifi-

38 Edward S. Mason, "The Current Status of the Monopoly Problem in the United States," 62 *Harvard Law Review* 1265 (1949).

39 James W. McKie, *Tin Cans and Tin Plate* (Cambridge: Harvard University Press, 1959), p. 7.

40 See W. Z. Ripley, "Economic Wastes in Transportation," 21 *Political Science Quarterly* 381 (1906).

cally, whereas competition among automobile producers seemed to result in lower prices and/or a better product, unregulated competition among railroads and public utilities did not produce consistently lower rates for an equally good or improved product. Competition often became cutthroat or ruinous.[41]

Cutthroat competition may occur when investment in plant and equipment is large, fixed, and specialized and when competing firms have unused capacity. Except for motor and water carriers, these factors are all characteristics of the regulated industries. If capital cannot be readily withdrawn from a business, a company will continue operations as long as it can make some return on the capital invested, for a significant portion of the money invested in the business is lost if operations cease. Companies will, therefore, continue operations even at ruinously low rates. Rate wars are likely to occur as the firms try to increase their output or to utilize their plants more fully. Given a small number of competitors, rate reductions are usually met promptly by all rivals. Rates may even fall below marginal costs for a short time. Many examples can be found: a rate of 25 cents per person for carrying passengers from New York to Chicago, established by the railroads during a rate war; a rate of 2.5 cents a kilowatt-hour as a result of a rate war in Chicago. Whereas failure of a corner grocery store to show a profit may result (*a*) in sale of its stock—on which a large percentage of its cost will be realized—and retirement from business, (*b*) conversion, for example, into a drugstore, or (*c*) in its reorganization as a grocery store under different management, in the case of a regulated business, reorganization is usually the only choice.

Any one or a combination of a number of results may follow from such severe competition. One possibility is continuance of the low rates so long that bankruptcy may occur. However, long before this will occur, the service offered by the firms will suffer. Adequate outlays cannot be made for improvements. Maintenance will be neglected. Finally, it is likely, and this is substantiated by past experience, that the competitors will take steps to reduce the severity of rate competition. And in making an agreement, the firms might extract a very high rate from the consumer.

Thus, in the regulated industries, competition may not succeed in a gradual elimination of the weaker firms, with business becoming concentrated in the hands of the more efficient. In fact, a reorganized company may well find itself in a position from which it may even force into bankruptcy a competitor who, up to that time, has been the low-cost producer. Such a possibility follows from the opportunity for a significant write-down of plant and equipment during a reorganization, with an accompanying decrease in capitalization. Accordingly, the company can show profits with a smaller return than was possible preceding the reorganization.

41 On cutthroat or ruinous competition, see A. T. Hadley, *Railroad Transportation* (New York: Putnam, 1885), pp. 63–74; E. Jones, "Is Competition in Industry Ruinous?" 34 *Quarterly Journal of Economics* 473 (1920); J. M. Clark, *Studies in the Economics of Overhead Costs* (Chicago: University of Chicago Press, 1923), esp. chap. xxi; and Kaysen and Turner, *op. cit.,* pp. 195–98.

It has been emphasized repeatedly that the concept of natural monopoly is of limited usefulness in justifying regulation of some industries in the economy. In a similar vein, both the actual existence of rate wars and the threat of rate wars have been overemphasized. There is substantial evidence that cutthroat competition was the exception and not the rule prior to the establishment of regulatory commissions. The spectacular nature of the rate wars which did occur may explain the attention which they have received.[42] But rate wars also exist among nonregulated companies, as gasoline price wars so vividly demonstrate. There are many nonregulated industries, such as steel, which have engaged in severe price wars during periods of general recession or when unused capacity existed.[43] Cutthroat competition, therefore, is not of particular significance in distinguishing between regulated and nonregulated industries.

Price Discrimination. Price discrimination occurs when a seller establishes for the same product or service different rates which are not entirely justified by differences in cost, or the same rate where differences in cost would justify differences in price.[44] Such discrimination arises from the presence of high fixed costs, differences in the elasticity of demand, and the special nature of the regulated industries' services. As noted above, fixed costs may result in competition's driving rates below a point at which all costs are covered (assuming the existence of unused capacity). Moreover, consumers have different demands for these services, and since each consumer must usually deal directly with the company furnishing the service, it would be theoretically possible for a firm to charge each customer a different rate. That is, each customer represents a market for electric, gas, and telephone services and, to an extent, for transportation services.[45] Whereas an individual can buy a car from a dealer and then resell it to a neighbor, a customer cannot do the same with the services rendered by the regulated industries. While price discrimination is not a sole characteristic of the regulated industries, it is a more important one.

As a result of the possibility of adding to profits through price discrimination, this became a common practice in pre-regulation days. Special rates were given to certain buyers, particular commodities, or favored places. Particularly was discrimination found in the railroad industry. With respect to personal discrimination, for example, Locklin has stated:

> The railroad companies sometimes gave a practical monopoly to certain individuals or corporations in supplying wood or coal to particular towns and

42 Troxel, *op. cit.,* p. 40.

43 See Arthur R. Burns, *The Decline of Competition* (New York: McGraw-Hill Book Co., Inc., 1936).

44 A satisfactory definition of price discrimination is elusive. Thus, what costs—marginal or average, short run or long run, out-of-pocket or fully allocated, including or excluding either some or a uniform rate of return—are relevant to a determination of discrimination? Further, what are the same or like services? Is business exchange service, for instance, the same as residential exchange service, or are they different? These problems are considered at greater length in Chapters 10 and 11.

45 The existence of intermodal competition limits the ability of any one mode to charge discriminatory rates.

cities. The monopoly was enforced through preferential rates to the favored dealers and higher rates to the independent dealers. In the same way the buying of grain was monopolized by preferential rates to favored shippers. These monopolies could not have long endured if all shippers had been treated equally by the common carriers.[46]

The gradual realization that discrimination was substantially aiding certain firms to make tremendous profits (the classic example is Standard Oil of New Jersey) and to engage in selling at prices below those possible for companies not receiving special rates or rebates—and thus forcing these unfavored firms out of business—was one of the driving forces behind the movement for regulation. Since nineteenth-century western agricultural regions were especially susceptible to discriminatory practices by the railroads, it is little wonder that the move to regulate the railroad industry was organized by midwestern farmers through the Grange.

It should be noted at this point that discrimination is accepted in the rate structures of the regulated industries, but that such discrimination must be "just and reasonable." Discrimination is both unintentional and purposive. It is unintentional in that some discrimination results from the efforts of the companies and commissions to simplify the rate structures by grouping customers into a limited number of classifications. It is purposive in that discrimination may be the only way in which service can be provided to some customers. Low-density routes may be subsidized by high-density routes, small towns by large cities. Rather than preventing discrimination, regulation merely seeks to control what discrimination takes place.

Interindustry Competition

For most of the regulated industries, interindustry competition is of more significance than is intraindustry competition. Sometimes interindustry rivalry is between regulated firms: competition between the different modes of transportation; electricity with gas; and telephone with telegraph. Sometimes interindustry rivalry is between regulated and nonregulated firms: common carriers compete with contract, exempt, and private modes of transport; electricity and gas with coal and oil; and telephone and telegraph with private microwave. This type of competition raises two important regulatory problems.

In the first place, is interindustry competition an adequate substitute for intraindustry competition? In economic literature, the latter has been stressed, since

> ... intraindustry competition has certain unique characteristics. It is only in competition between firms in the same industry that each competitor has similar cost structures and products, so that each can come near to duplicat-

[46] D. Philip Locklin, *Economics of Transportation* (6th ed.; Homewood, Ill.: Richard D. Irwin, Inc., 1966), p. 199.

ing a rival's prices and service. In contrast, interindustry competition must always be limited, for the differences in cost structures from one industry to another provides sheltered markets in which one industry has an inherent advantage over all rivals. For this reason, competition within an industry is considered necessary in both the literature of economics and the interpretations of the antitrust laws in order to provide the competitive pressures necessary to fully promote efficiency, progress, and lower prices.[47]

Interindustry competition, then, may be imperfect.[48] A residential consumer, for example, will be even slower to switch from one type of fuel to another than from one gas company to another. The fuel change not only involves new equipment but it also involves new appliances, thereby resulting in an even greater cost. Interindustry competition thus tends to be strongest for new customers, such as those deciding which fuel to use for heating when a new home is being constructed.[49] It also tends to be stronger for larger customers than for smaller ones. Due to his low volume, for instance, a residential user does not have the option of an industrial user of installing a private microwave system. Only in the transportation industries, where shippers can substitute between types of carriers more readily, can interindustry competition be expected to yield rates closely related to costs. But even here, the fact that each mode has a different cost structure means that each attracts some noncompetitive traffic. Nevertheless, there are many who feel that technological advances have reduced the volume of noncompetitive traffic to the point where the presence of substantial intramodal competition, fortified by strong intermodal competition, indicates that the transportation industry would be workably competitive in the absence of detailed regulation.

In the second place, interindustry competition presents difficult pricing problems, raising again the issue of "just and reasonable" discrimination. Assume that a regulated firm offers a basic service for which there are no close substitutes and another service for which there is a close substitute supplied by a nonregulated firm. How can the commissions insure that the regulated enterprise does not use the power at its disposal in the "monopoly" area of its business to eliminate (via internal subsidies) competition in the "competitive" area? An answer to this question, in turn, depends on another: should minimum rates be based upon fully allocated costs or incremental costs? These issues will be considered in Chapters 10 and 11. At this point, it should simply be noted that interindustry competition tends to complicate the regulatory task.

47 Meyer and others, *op. cit.,* pp. 240–41 (footnote omitted).

48 For some statistical documentation, see J. B. Vermitten and J. Plantinga, "The Elasticity of Substitution of Gas with Respect to Other Fuels in the United States," 35 *Review of Economics and Statistics* 140 (1953); and John F. Felton, "Competition in the Energy Market between Gas and Electricity," 4 *Nebraska Journal of Economics and Business* 1 (Autumn, 1965).

49 Appliances also wear out, so that rivalry is important in the replacement market. See Alfred M. Casazza, "Competitive Utilities and Happy Investors," 71 *Public Utilities Fortnightly* 19, 21 (March 14, 1963).

ECONOMIC CHARACTERISTICS: A MATTER OF DEGREE

The major economic characteristics of the regulated industries have been set forth. In large measure, they explain why certain enterprises are regulated. To summarize briefly.[50] For electric power generation, transmission, and distribution, and for the transportation and distribution of natural gas, the economic justification for regulation is based on the existence of significant economies of scale (long-run decreasing costs) in a given local or regional market. For telephone and telegraph services, the economic justification for regulation is also based on significant economies of scale, as well as on the expense and inconvenience to consumers of parallel competing systems. Few question the need of regulating these industries.

For the production of natural gas and for the provision of transportation services, economies of scale are of less significance. As a result, the case for regulation is more complex and questionable. Regulation of natural gas producers is based on the proposition that concentration is high enough to raise the probability of monopolistic pricing practices. Such a proposition is highly debatable.[51] Regulation of the railroads was initially based on their oligopolistic market structure over long-haul routes and their monopolistic market structure over short-haul routes. In both cases, discriminatory pricing proved profitable. The development of several competing modes of transport, however, reduced the economic justification for detailed regulation of the railroad industry. But instead of deregulating the railroads, regulation was extended to these competing modes. Bus, highway, and water transport regulation was largely predicated on the need to prevent cutthroat or destructive competition within each of these modes and to prevent undue price discrimination throughout the transportation industry. Airline regulation was primarily based on safety and promotional considerations. The need for detailed regulation of the transportation industry under modern conditions is also highly debatable.[52]

It should be apparent to the reader that the economic characteristics used to justify regulation do not belong solely to the regulated industries; rather, the distinction is one of degree. That is, most of the regulated industries seem to possess these characteristics to a greater degree than do other industries. In many fields, economies of scale may explain the need for large-scale plants, such as typewriters and automobiles.[53] The necessity of enforcing competition in such industries caused Congress to enact the Sherman Antitrust Act in 1890 and to establish the Federal Trade Commission in 1914. Fixed costs and nonliquidity of capital are important in such industries as concrete and steel, so that some degree of cutthroat competition can and does exist. The monopoly element,

---

[50] This summary is partly based on Bain, *Industrial Organization, op. cit.,* pp. 635–37.

[51] See Chapter 16, pp. 617–22.

[52] See Chapters 13 and 14.

[53] See Bain, *Barriers to New Competition, op. cit.,* pp. 53–113.

inherent in the regulated industries, may be found in nonregulated manufacturing and mining industries due to patents or control of raw materials. As mergers may reduce competition in nonregulated industries, an antimerger policy was adopted in 1914 (Clayton Act) and amended in 1950 (Celler-Kefauver Act). Seasonal and cyclical unused capacity is common throughout American industry. And consumers have relatively inelastic demands for goods and services other than those of the regulated industries.

The tendency for many businesses to discriminate in price caused passage of a law limiting such discrimination as early as 1914 (Clayton Act) and strengthening of this law in 1936 (Robinson-Patman Act). Since imperfect competition is common in many industries, price competition is frequently avoided in favor of nonprice competition. As regards the lower cost of monopoly, it must be apparent that a lower immediate cost would be obtained in many fields by the creation of a monopoly. This may easily be illustrated by considering the cost of maintaining competition in the distribution of milk. Certainly, a single company could reduce the cost of distribution in a certain city over what it is at the present time with several competing companies crossing one another's paths with duplicate facilities.

Many industries render essential services—meat-packing plants and grocery stores—and yet escape public regulation. Even in the case of the regulated industries, services are not regarded as being so essential that they should be provided to everyone irrespective of the individual's ability to pay for them.[54] Countless individuals and communities, therefore, are completely without one or more of these services. Safety requirements have been established and enforced, as in the automobile manufacturing industry, without also imposing economic regulation. Finally, some manufacturing industries have avoided detailed regulation, not because they are more competitive but rather because of the difficulties of extending regulation to the manufacture of commodities. "Reliance on a certain degree of competition, fortified by antitrust laws, may therefore be deemed the lesser evil."[55]

What determines, then, which industries are to be regulated? It is the judgment of legislatures and, ultimately, of the Supreme Court. Regulation is applied when it is felt that competition cannot be relied on to provide adequate service at a reasonable price. This decision often has been based on proper economic criteria, but it has sometimes been predicated on political considerations.

54 Lewis, *op. cit.*, p. 622.
55 Bonbright, *op. cit.*, p. 11.

Chapter

3

THE LEGAL CONCEPT OF PUBLIC REGULATION

All business is subject to some kinds of public regulation, but when the public becomes so peculiarly dependent upon a particular business that one engaging therein subjects himself to a more intimate public regulation is only to be determined by the process of exclusion and inclusion and to gradual establishment of a line of distinction.

—Chief Justice Taft*

For many years, the courts attempted to establish a separate category of businesses that were "affected with a public interest" and that required detailed government regulation. A business so designated, known as a public utility, was privately owned and rendered an indispensable service to the community under economic conditions of imperfect competition. In the Supreme Court's words:

Property does become clothed with a public interest when used in a manner to make it of public consequence, and affect the community at large. When, therefore, one devotes his property to a use in which the public has an interest, he, in effect, grants to the public an interest in that use, and must submit to be controlled by the public for the common good. . . .[1]

In 1934, the Court upheld price regulation of the milk industry without classifying that industry as a public utility.[2] As a result, while there is still a distinct public utility concept, some regulation may be applied to any industry when deemed essential to protect the public interest.

By what right does government regulate these activities? How does an activity become classified as a regulated industry? What are the obligations and rights of regulated enterprises? Is government free to go as far as it likes in regulating these activities, or are there certain limitations? These legal concepts will be discussed in this chapter.

*Chief Justice Taft, *Wolff Packing Co.* v. *Court of Industrial Relations*, 262 U.S. 522, 538–39 (1923).
[1]*Munn* v. *Illinois*, 94 U.S. 113, 126 (1877).
[2]*Nebbia* v. *New York*, 291 U.S. 502 (1934).

THE LEGAL BASIS OF GOVERNMENT REGULATION

In the United States, federal regulation of business proceeds under the interstate commerce clause, state regulation under the police power of the state. In both federal and state constitutions there are constitutional safeguards for individual rights. All acts of administrators and legislatures are subject to judicial review.

Constitutional Provisions

Article I, Section 8 of the Constitution enumerates the economic powers delegated to the federal government by the states. From the viewpoint of public regulation of business, the most important clause is the one usually referred to as the interstate commerce clause that gives Congress power "to regulate Commerce . . . among the several States. . . ." In addition, there are the implied powers that have been inferred from the final clause of the same article which authorizes Congress "To make all laws which shall be necessary and proper for carrying into Execution the foregoing Powers, and all other Powers vested by this Constitution in the Government of the United States. . . ." The Supreme Court has interpreted this clause broadly, with the result that the federal government is permitted to do both things expressly stated in the Constitution and things the Court is willing to infer. Said Chief Justice Marshall in one of his most frequently quoted passages:

> Let the end be legitimate, let it be within the scope of the Constitution, and all means which are appropriate, which are plainly adapted to that end, which are not prohibited, but consistent with the letter and spirit of the Constitution, are constitutional.[3]

All governmental powers, except those denied them by the Constitution, are reserved for the several states. State regulation of business proceeds under the police power of the state—that is, power of the state to regulate business to safeguard the health, safety, morals, and general welfare of its citizens. While not mentioned in the Constitution, this power has long been recognized by the courts.[4]

In many areas, this distribution of powers between federal and state governments causes conflicts. In such cases, the former must prevail. According to Article VI: "This Constitution and the Laws of the United States which shall be made in Pursuance thereof . . . shall be the supreme Law of the Land."

The Interstate Commerce Clause. After decades of court decisions, the interstate commerce clause has been broadly interpreted by the courts, and it seems that the clause is unlikely to impose significant limits on federal regula-

---

[3] *McCulloch* v. *Maryland,* 4 Wheaton 316 (1819).
[4] *Brown* v. *Maryland,* 12 Wheaton 419 (1827); *Charles River Bridge* v. *Warren Bridge,* 11 Peters 420 (1837).

tory powers in the future.[5] The first Supreme Court definition of the word "commerce" was in 1824. Commerce, said Chief Justice Marshall, "is traffic, but it is something more: it is intercourse. It describes the commercial intercourse between nations, and parts of nations, in all its branches, and is regulated by prescribing rules for carrying on that intercourse."[6] Thus, Chief Justice Marshall, in refusing to limit the definition of commerce to "buying and selling, or the interchange of commodities,"[7] extended the concept to embrace all processes through which trade is carried on. Further, the phrase "among the several States" also was interpreted broadly.

> The word "among" means intermingled with . . . . Commerce among the States cannot stop at the external boundary line of each State, but may be introduced into the interior.
> Comprehensive as the word "among" is, it may very properly be restricted to that commerce which concerns more States than one . . . . The genius and character of the whole government seem to be, that its action is to be applied to all the external concerns of the nation, and to those internal concerns which affect the States generally; but not to those which are completely within a particular State, which do not affect other States, and with which it is not necessary to interfere, for the purpose of executing some of the general powers of the government. The completely internal commerce of a State, then, may be considered as reserved for the State itself.[8]

Subsequently, this interpretation was applied to railways and communication services.[9]

In 1871, the Court upheld federal regulation of a steamer carrying goods between two ports in Michigan, ruling that the out-of-state origin and destination of these goods made the vessel "an instrument" of interstate commerce.[10] The Court, in 1914, permitted the federal government to fix railway rates between points within the borders of a state because "in all matters having such a close and substantial relation to interstate traffic . . . the control is essential or

---

[5] While the trend of court decisions favors the federal government, it should not be inferred that it has been a smooth and continuous trend. In 1887 and in 1895, the Supreme Court ruled that manufacturing was not commerce, thus excluding the entire sector from federal power (*Kidd* v. *Pearson*, 128 U.S. 1 [1887]; *United States* v. *E. C. Knight Co.*, 156 U.S. 1 [1895]). In 1918, it invalidated a law prohibiting interstate shipment of the products of child labor, ruling that their production was not interstate (*Hammer* v. *Dagenhart*, 247 U.S. 251). And in 1936, the Court invalidated a law providing for wage- and price-fixing in the coal industry, asserting that the effect on interstate commerce was "close and substantial," but not "direct" (*Carter* v. *Carter Coal Co.*, 298 U.S. 238). In later decisions, these rulings have been explicitly reversed. For a review of the cases in this area, see Charles P. Light, Jr., "The Federal Commerce Power," 49 *Virginia Law Review* 717 (1963).

[6] *Gibbons* v. *Ogden,* 9 Wheaton (22 U.S.) 1, 189 (1824).

[7] *Ibid.*

[8] *Ibid.,* pp. 194–95.

[9] *Railway* v. *Van Husen,* 95 U.S. 465 (1872); *Pensacola Telegraph Co.* v. *Western Union,* 96 U.S. 1 (1877).

[10] *Steamer Daniel Bell* v. *United States,* 10 Wallace 557 (1871).

appropriate . . . ."[11] In 1922, the Court approved the regulation of grain eleva-tors, saying that such enterprises, though tied to one location, were situated in the "stream" or "flow" of interstate commerce.[12] Similarly, in the same year, federal regulation of stockyards was approved. While stockyards "are not a place of rest or final destination," stated the Court, they are "a throat through which the current flows, and the transactions which occur therein are only incident to this current from the West to the East, and from one State to another." [13]

More recent cases have served to reinforce and extend these earlier deci-sions.[14] In 1937, the Court upheld the constitutionality of the National Labor Relations Act, saying that Congress cannot be held powerless to regulate "when industries organize themselves on a national scale, making their relation to inter-state commerce the dominant factor in their activities . . . ." The relevant test, the Court added, was whether an interstate activity had a "close and intimate effect" on interstate commerce.[15] In 1938, it ruled that the law applied to a cannery that shipped only a third of its output to other states,[16] and to a power company that sold an insignificant percentage of its current across state lines.[17] In 1941, the Court upheld a law forbidding interstate shipment of goods made by persons paid less than legally determined wages or required to work for more than legally determined hours (Fair Labor Standards Act), holding that "Con-gress . . . may choose the means reasonably adopted to the attainment of the permitted end, even though they involve control of intrastate activities." [18] The following year, when the Court upheld the power of Congress to regulate the quantity of wheat a farmer could sell (under the Agricultural Adjustment Act of 1938), Justice Jackson stated:

> Even if the appellee's activity be local and though it may not be regarded as commerce, it may still, whatever its nature, be reached by Congress if it exerts a substantial economic effect on interstate commerce, and this irre-spective of whether such effect is what might at some earlier time have been defined as "direct" or "indirect." [19]

[11] *Houston, East and West Texas Ry. Co.* v. *United States,* 234 U.S. 342 (1914). Also see *Swift & Co.* v. *United States,* 196 U.S. 375 (1905); and *Southern Ry.* v. *United States,* 222 U.S. 20 (1911).

[12] *Lemke* v. *Farmers Grain Co.,* 258 U.S. 50 (1922).

[13] *Stafford* v. *Wallace,* 258 U.S. 495, 515–16 (1922).

[14] See Robert L. Stern, "The Commerce Clause and the National Economy, 1933–1946," 59 *Harvard Law Review* 645, 883 (1946).

[15] *National Labor Relations Board* v. *Jones & Laughlin Steel Corp.,* 301 U.S. 1, 38, 41 (1937). Also see *National Labor Relations Board* v. *Fruehauf Trailer Co.,* 301 U.S. 49 (1937); and *National Labor Relations Board* v. *Friedman-Harry Marks Clothing Co.,* 301 U.S. 58 (1937).

[16] *Santa Cruz Fruit Packing Co.* v. *National Labor Relations Board,* 303 U.S. 453 (1938).

[17] *Consolidated Edison Co.* v. *National Labor Relations Board,* 305 U.S. 197 (1938).

[18] *United States* v. *Darby Lumber Co.,* 312 U.S. 100, 121 (1941).

[19] *Wickard* v. *Filburn,* 317 U.S. 111, 125 (1942).

In the same year, the Court held that Congress could regulate both building employees who serviced interstate operations[20] and oil drillers.[21] In 1944, it upheld the application of a federal statute to the insurance business;[22] in 1945, to retail trade;[23] in 1946, to a newspaper which sold only 45 copies out of the state.[24]

It would seem that federal authority is almost unlimited. As the Court put it in 1946, federal power to regulate commerce among the several states "is as broad as the economic needs of the nation."[25] Further, federal authority may even be extended to intrastate commerce when necessary to prevent intrastate commerce from imposing a burden on interstate commerce. In 1914, when it upheld an Interstate Commerce Commission order that required a group of railroads to raise intrastate rates so that they would not be discriminatory against interstate commerce, the Court said that "Congress in the exercise of its paramount power may prevent the common instrumentalities of interstate and intrastate commercial intercourse from being used in their intrastate operations to the injury of interstate commerce."[26] Eight years later, in upholding a similar ICC order with respect to an intrastate passenger rate, Chief Justice Taft argued:

> Commerce is a unit and does not regard state lines, and while, under the Constitution, interstate and intrastate commerce are ordinarily subject to regulation by different sovereignties, yet when they are so mingled together that the supreme authority, the nation, cannot exercise complete effective control over interstate commerce without incidental regulation of intrastate commerce, such incidental regulation is not an invasion of state authority. . . .[27]

Federal regulation of intrastate commerce is subject to one limit: it may be used only to remove "undue or unreasonable advantages, preferences, or prejudices" or "unjustly discriminatory" inequalities.[28] But since the mere existence of inequality is not necessarily proof of an undue burden, federal-state jurisdictional conflicts remain.[29]

[20] *Kirschbaum Co.* v. *Walling,* 316 U.S. 517 (1942).
[21] *Warren-Bradshaw Drilling Co.* v. *Hall,* 317 U.S. 88 (1942).
[22] *United States* v. *South-Eastern Underwriters Association,* 322 U.S. 533 (1944).
[23] *United States* v. *Frankfort Distilleries,* 324 U.S. 293 (1945).
[24] *Mabee* v. *White Plains Publishing Co.,* 327 U.S. 178 (1946).
[25] *American Power & Light Co.* v. *Securities & Exchange Comm.,* 329 U.S. 90, 104 (1946).
[26] *Houston, East and West Texas Ry. Co.* v. *United States, op. cit.,* p. 353.
[27] *Wisconsin Railroad Comm.* v. *Chicago, B. & Q. R. Co.,* 257 U.S. 563, 588 (1922). In 1942, the Court said: "The commerce power is not confined in its exercise to the regulation of commerce among the states. It extends to those activities intrastate which so effect interstate commerce, or the exertion of the power of Congress over it, as to make regulation of them appropriate means to the attainment of a legitimate end, the effective execution of the granted power to regulate interstate commerce." *United States* v. *Wrightwood Dairy Co.,* 315 U.S. 110, 119 (1942). Also see *Stafford* v. *Wallace, op. cit.;* and *Chicago Board of Trade* v. *Olsen,* 262 U.S. 1 (1923).
[28] *North Carolina* v. *United States,* 325 U.S. 507 (1945).
[29] See Chapter 4, pp. 115-18.

The Police Powers of the States. The Tenth Amendment provides that those powers not delegated to the federal government and not specifically prohibited to them may be exercised by the states. States have the broad authority to legislate for protection of the health, safety, morals, and general welfare of their citizens. These are collectively known as the "police powers" of the states.

The courts have given the states wide latitude under these police powers to regulate business enterprises. In an early case, Chief Justice Waite recognized that "... this is a power which may be abused; but that is no argument against its existence. For protection against abuses by legislatures the people must resort to the polls, not the courts."[30] And in 1934, the Court said:

> ... a state is free to adopt whatever economic policy may reasonably be deemed to promote the public welfare, and to enforce that policy by legislation adapted to its purpose. The courts are without authority either to declare such policy, or, when it is declared by the legislature, to override it . . . . With the wisdom of the policy adopted, with the adequacy or practicability of the law enacted to forward it, the courts are both incompetent and unauthorized to deal . . . . Price control, like any other form of regulation, is unconstitutional only if arbitrary, discriminatory, or demonstrably irrelevant to the policy the legislature is free to adopt . . . .[31]

There has been a partial retreat from this position in recent years. In 1956, for instance, the Oregon Supreme Court ruled that the right of an owner to sell his property at a price agreeable to him was a valuable property right which the legislature could not take away except in a lawful exercise of its police power to protect the public interest. The Court said, "to be a valid exercise of the police power, the statute and the regulations thereunder must have a well-recognized and direct bearing upon the health, happiness, and well-being of the public as a whole."[32]

Constitutional Safeguards for Corporate Rights. The rights of citizens are protected against invasion by the acts of government in both federal and state constitutions. The limitations on control of business by the federal government are found in the Fifth Amendment: "No person shall ... be deprived of life, liberty, or property without due process of law; nor shall private property be taken for public use, without just compensation." The limitations on state power over business are contained in the contracts clause in Article I, Section 10 of the Constitution: "No State shall ... pass any ... Law impairing the Obligation of Contracts"; and in the Fourteenth Amendment: "No State shall make or enforce any law which shall abridge the privileges or immunities of citizens of the United States; nor shall any State deprive any person of life, liberty, or property, without due process of law; nor deny to any person within its jurisdiction the equal protection of the laws."

[30]*Munn* v. *Illinois, op. cit.,* p. 134.
[31]*Nebbia* v. *New York, op. cit.,* pp. 537, 539.
[32]*General Electric Co.* v. *Wahle,* 207 Ore. 302 (1956).

In both amendments, reference is made to *persons* and *citizens*. Since business enterprises have never been held to qualify as citizens, the clause relating to privileges and immunities has never been applied to limit governmental regulation. The other clauses, however, have been held applicable ever since the Supreme Court declared in 1886 that a corporation is a person.[33]

The significance of these amendments was well summarized by Justice Roberts in a 1934 decision:

> The Fifth Amendment, in the field of federal activity, and the Fourteenth, as respects state action, do not prohibit government regulation for the public welfare. They merely condition the exertion of the admitted power, by securing that the end shall be accomplished by methods consistent with due process. And the guaranty of due process, as has often been held, demands only that the law shall not be unreasonable, arbitrary, or capricious, and that the means selected shall have a real and substantial relation to the object sought to be attained. It results that a regulation valid for one sort of business, or in given circumstances, may be invalid for another sort, or for the same business under other circumstances, because the reasonableness of each regulation depends upon the relevant facts.[34]

Judicial Review.   Under our constitutional system, all acts of legislatures and decisions of administrators are subject to judicial review. The term "judicial review," as Shapiro has noted, has both a particular and a general meaning. "The particular meaning, and the one most often invoked in the United States, is the power to declare statutes and the regulations and acts of government officials and agencies unconstitutional."[35] The courts interpret the Constitution as acts and laws are brought before them. State courts can find a local ordinance or a state law to be in violation of either state or federal constitutions. Federal courts can find state or federal laws to be in violation of the federal Constitution. The final authority is the Supreme Court of the United States.

In the more general sense, judicial review "is the power of a court to review the interpretations made by government agencies and officers (including other courts and judges) in order to determine what interpretation of the statute, regulation or previous ruling, and/or findings of fact supporting them shall be taken as binding upon the parties."[36] It has been well established that orders of a commission

> . . . are final unless (1) beyond the power which it could constitutionally exercise; or (2) beyond its statutory power; or (3) based upon a mistake of

[33] *Santa Clara County* v. *Southern Pacific R.R. Co.,* 118 U.S. 394 (1886).

[34] *Nebbia* v. *New York, op. cit.,* p. 525.

[35] Martin Shapiro, *The Supreme Court and Administrative Agencies* (New York: The Free Press, 1968), p. 2.

[36] *Ibid.,* p. 3. "In this sense judicial review is the power to declare an act or decision of a government official not unconstitutional but simply illegal—not beyond the totality of powers that government may legitimately exercise, but simply beyond the authorization of the statute or other legal rule by which he is supposed to conduct himself." *Ibid.*

law. But questions of fact may be involved in the determination of questions of law, so that an order, regular on its face, may be set aside if it appears that (4) the rate is so low as to be confiscatory and in violation of the constitutional prohibition against taking property without due process of law; or (5) if the Commission acted so arbitrarily and unjustly as to fix rates contrary to evidence, or without evidence to support it; or (6) if the authority therein involved has been exercised in such an unreasonable manner as to cause it to be within the elementary rule that the substance, and not the shadow, determines the validity of the exercise of the power . . . . In determining these mixed questions of law and fact, the court confines itself to the ultimate question as to whether the Commission acted within its power. It will not consider the expediency or wisdom of the order, or whether, on like testimony, it would have made a similar ruling.[37]

ORIGINS OF THE PUBLIC INTEREST CONCEPT

There are four recognizable antecedents of our "public interest" concept. First, there was the "just price" doctrine of medieval times. As Glaeser has explained:

Regulation of private industry has been attempted by government from earliest times. All attempts at such regulation owed much to a very ancient ideal of social justice, which, as applied to economic life by the early Church Fathers, became their very famous doctrine of *justum pretium,* i.e., "just price." They opposed this idea to the contemporaneous doctrine of *verum pretium,* i.e., "natural price," which the Roman law had derived from Stoic philosophy. As contrasted with the doctrine of natural price, which justified any price reached by agreement in effecting exchanges between willing buyers and willing sellers, the "just price" doctrine drew attention to the coercion which may reside in economic circumstances, such as a food famine where a buyer is made willing by his economic necessities. Hence, in order to draw the sting of coercion, the early Church Fathers, following St. Augustine, considered only that trading to be legitimate in which the trader paid a "just price" to the producer, and in selling, added only so much to the price as was customarily sufficient for his economic support. There was to be no unjust enrichment.[38]

The Emperor, during the decline of the Roman Empire, issued price edicts setting maximum prices for some 800 articles based upon their estimated cost of production. His edicts were supported by the Church Fathers under the "just price" doctrine; a doctrine firmly established by the Middle Ages.

Second, during the Middle Ages, guilds operated. These guilds were similar to modern craft unions—members of the same craft belonged to the same guild.

[37]*Interstate Commerce Comm.* v. *Union Pacific R.R. Co.,* 222 U.S. 541, 547 (1912).

[38] Martin G. Glaeser, *Public Utilities in American Capitalism* (New York: Macmillan Co., 1957), p. 196. Reprinted by permission of The Macmillan Company.

The obligation of the crafts was to provide service to anyone who wanted it at reasonable prices. The various crafts were known, therefore, as "common carriers," "common innkeepers," "common tailors," and so forth. As each craft had a monopoly of its trade, they were closely regulated. Third, the idea of an exclusive privilege to monopolize a line of commerce was further developed in France during the sixteenth century. Royal charters were given by the government to plantations and trading companies, granting them monopolies. A charter was the equivalent of the franchise granted to regulated industries today. Here, regulation was strictly applied to these companies to carry out governmental objectives. In Glaeser's words:

> Thus, the grant of monopoly was regarded as a method of accomplishing social results. Since franchises were royal grants, they conferred the special privilege of performing functions which the state itself, for various reasons, did not care to undertake, but which the mercantilist authorities conceived to be governmental in character. These grants of monopoly provided an incentive for the investment of capital and the assumption of risks. That they turned out, in many cases, to be extremely profitable to their grantees, and would in turn need curbing, should not conceal the fact that they were originated by the state as a means of attaining public objects. No distinct line can be drawn between the guilds, the regulated commercial companies of the fourteenth and fifteenth centuries, and the new, joint-stock companies that sprang into being in the sixteenth century with the discoveries and colonizations. In this development, however, is to be found the origin of our modern notion of a public service corporation.[39]

Finally, there was the common law of England from which the legal antecedent of our public interest concept was developed. The common law courts displaced the authorities of the guilds, manors, and towns. Under the common law, certain occupations or callings were singled out and subjected to special rights and duties. These occupations became known as "common callings," and were explained primarily by the conduct of the business. That is, a person who practiced such a calling, as distinguished from a private calling, sought public patronage. Lord Chief Justice Hale (1609–76) of England, in his treatise, *De Portibus Maris*, stated:

> A man, for his own private advantage, may, in a port or town, set up a wharf or crane, and may take what rates he and his customers can agree for cranage, wharfage, housellage, pesage; for he doth no more than is lawful for any man to do, viz., makes the most of his own . . . . If the king or subject have a public wharf, unto which all persons that come to that port must come and unlade or lade their goods as for the purpose, because they are the wharfs only licensed by the queen, . . . or because there is no other wharf in that port, as it may fall out where a port is newly erected; in that case there cannot be taken arbitrary and excessive duties for cranage, wharfage, pesage, and so forth, neither can they be enhanced to an immoderate rate, but the

---

[39] *Ibid.*, p. 201. Reprinted by permission of The Macmillan Company.

duties must be reasonable and moderate, though settled by the king's license or charter. For now the wharf and crane and other conveniences are affected with a public interest and they cease to be *juris privati* only. As if a man set out a street in new building on his land, it is no longer bare private interest, but it is affected with a public interest.[40]

The list of common or public occupations regulated by the English Parliament included those of bakers, brewers, cab drivers, ferrymen, innkeepers, millers, smiths, surgeons, tailors, and wharfingers. A person engaged in a common employment had special obligations that were not attached to private employment, particularly the duty to provide, at reasonable prices, adequate service and facilities to all who wanted them. Closely connected was the "just price" of medieval times. These occupations, then, were to charge a reasonable price that was ethically controlled and not market determined.

Development in America

The same regulations of business which existed in England were tried in the English colonies in North America. In the years prior to the American Revolution, a few colonies attempted to regulate prices for such products as beer, bread, corn, and tobacco, although the most detailed control was exercised over common carriers by land and water. "During the Revolution, generally at the instigation of the Continental Congress, at least eight of the thirteen states passed laws fixing the price of almost every commodity in the market."[41] Some of these laws even provided for the establishment of rates for various kinds of skilled and unskilled labor.

In the course of time, especially after the War of 1812, many, if not all, of these restrictions were either repealed or allowed to become inoperative. America had developed an economic and political liberalism which was adverse to government regulation. Competition was regarded as the best form of control for the general welfare. "Growing up in this environment, public utility regulation was a small cross current in the general economic life of the nation."[42] Only two public interest industries—carriers and waterworks—were subjected to special obligations, and both required franchises to use or cross public streets, highways, and waterways.

Following the war between the states, the doctrine of public interest was revived. Competition did not prove to be so perfect as economic theory had indicated. As agriculture became less important in the total economic activity of the country, and as technological changes resulted in the growth of corporate concentration, competition in business enterprise began to disappear. Financiers, too, used various devices to bring rival companies under common control, cul-

---

[40] Quoted in *Munn* v. *Illinois, op. cit.,* p. 127.

[41] Note, "State Regulation of Prices under the Fourteenth Amendment," 33 *Harvard Law Review* 838, 838–39 (1920) (citations omitted).

[42] Emery Troxel, *Economics of Public Utilities* (New York: Holt, Rinehart & Winston, Inc., 1947), p. 5.

minating in the great merger movement of 1898 to 1902. And management frequently seized the opportunities at hand to increase profits. Gradually, the liberal tradition was modified. Railroad companies were the first to feel this change in economic philosophy. To quote Troxel:

> When the railroad industry was new, the companies were encouraged to expand freely throughout the country. They received land grants from the federal and state governments, the voters gave them tax exemptions and public funds, and their securities were sold to the towns and persons to which they brought transportation service. Yet, even though the legislatures and voters helped the struggling railroad companies, they did not always get low rates. And they did not experience much competition between railroad companies. Railroading never was destined to be a competitive business in the same degree, for instance, that farming was. There never were so many companies serving every hamlet and city that competition controlled the freight rates. Often only one and never more than a few railroads served each town or area. Consequently most of the railroads operated under monopolistic or imperfectly competitive conditions. And the companies took advantage of their pricing situations, exploiting some of the people and towns from which financial aid was obtained. Being built ahead of the demand for railroad service and needing earnings, the railroad systems resorted to discriminatory and noncompetitive pricing, and forgot the promises of their promoters to the populace.[43]

The Grangers (the Patrons of Husbandry) led a nationwide movement for the regulation of railroad companies during the long depression of the 1870's.[44] Regulation began in the Middle West, but soon spread throughout the country. Regulatory commissions, often ineffective, were established.[45] But in subsequent years, commissions were to be strengthened and the list of regulated industries expanded. Today, the legal concept of common callings, with its many duties and obligations, is not static. Stated simply, the public interest with which some businesses are affected is one created by the public policy of the people.

LEADING JUDICIAL OPINIONS

Unless something is unusual about the industry involved, government regulation of private business would violate rights guaranteed by the Fifth and Fourteenth Amendments to the Constitution. When, therefore, is an industry so affected with a public interest that the usual privileges of private property give way to the duties attached to public service? Certainly, meat packing has a direct bearing on the health of the inhabitants of a state, but meat packing has been held by the courts as not sufficiently affected with a public interest to be a

---

[43] *Ibid.,* p. 7.
[44] See Chapter 13, pp. 444–47.
[45] See Chapter 4, pp. 88–89.

public utility.[46] Certainly, the sanitary conditions of drugstores as well as the care with which prescriptions are compounded affect public welfare, yet drugstores are not public utilities. In contrast, such an activity as the operation of a grain elevator has been held by the Supreme Court as sufficiently affected with a public interest to allow a considerable degree of regulation.[47] How do the courts distinguish among these and other activities?

At the outset, it must be recognized that there is no definite way of foretelling the necessary characteristics for distinguishing an industry affected with a public interest from one that is not sufficiently affected to require detailed public regulation. In practice, a business becomes so classified when the courts declare it to be, and they make such declarations only when a business is

> ... so pervasive and varied as to require constant detailed supervision and a very high degree of regulation. Where this is true, it is common to speak of the business as being a "public" one, although it is privately owned. It is to such businesses that the designation "public utility" is commonly applied; or they are spoken of as "affected with a public interest."[48]

This statement is not very helpful. There are, however, three important steps to getting into this classification. First, the public at large or a smaller group must demand regulation. Second, the legislature must deem it necessary to regulate the particular industry in the interest of the people. Third, the courts must recognize the need of regulation. The Supreme Court has long held:

> ... the mere declaration by a legislature that a business is affected with a public interest is not conclusive.... The circumstances of its alleged change from the status of a private business and its freedom from regulation into one in which the public have come to have an interest are always a subject of judicial inquiry.[49]

In the course of passing on regulations imposed on various industries, the courts have laid down certain characteristics of these industries as justifying the regulations allowed. The following illustrative Supreme Court cases will indicate what reasons have been accepted by the courts as grounds for declaring an industry to be affected with a public interest and thus subject to broad regulation.

Munn v. Illinois

Beginning in 1877, in the well-known case of *Munn* v. *Illinois*,[50] and continuing until 1934, the courts attempted to establish a separate category of businesses affected with a public interest, and confined regulation to those that

---

[46] *Wolff Packing Co.* v. *Court of Industrial Relations, op. cit.*

[47] *Munn* v. *Illinois, op. cit.*

[48] Dissenting opinion of Justice Brandeis in *New State Ice Co.* v. *Liebmann*, 285 U.S. 262, 301 (1932).

[49] *Wolff Packing Co.* v. *Court of Industrial Relations, op. cit.*, p. 536. Also see *Tyson & Brother* v. *Banton*, 273 U.S. 418 (1927).

[50] 94 U.S. 113.

they so defined. In general, businesses placed in this category were known as public utilities. The Munn case was the first important statement of the Supreme Court on the public interest concept.

The Illinois constitution of 1870 contained a provision granting to the legislature power to prescribe rates and service for several businesses. In 1871, the state legislature passed a law establishing regulation for grain elevators and warehouses in the city of Chicago. The statute required elevator owners to obtain a license, file a schedule of rates for the storage of grain, and charge no more than the maximum rate specified in the law. The following year, Munn and his partner Scott, who had operated a grain elevator business in Chicago for about eight years, were sued for failure to comply with all the provisions of the statute.[51] Believing that they had a private business, Munn and Scott contested the law on the grounds that it constituted state regulation of interstate commerce and that they were being deprived of property without due process of law.

The important facts of the case are essentially as follows: In 1874, 14 grain storage plants operated in Chicago. These plants were owned by about thirty people and were controlled by nine companies. It was shown that the possible number of sites on which to build such elevators was strictly limited. Moreover, the leaders of these nine firms met periodically to agree on grain storage rates. The situation was described by Chief Justice Waite:

> Thus it was apparent that all the elevating facilities through which these vast [wheat] productions "of seven or eight great States of the West" must pass on the way "to four or five of the States on the sea-shore" may be a "virtual" monopoly. . . . They stand, to use again the language of their counsel, in the very "gateway of commerce," and take toll from all who pass. Their business most certainly "tends to a common charge, and is become a thing of public interest and use." Every bushel of grain for its passage "pays a toll, which is a common charge," and, therefore, according to Lord Hale, every such warehouseman "ought to be under public regulation, viz.: that he . . . take but a reasonable toll." Certainly, if any business can be clothed "with a public interest, and cease to be *juris privati* only," this has been. It may not be made so by the operation of the Constitution of Illinois or this statute, but it is by the facts.[52]

The Court also recognized the growing importance of the Chicago warehouses to midwestern farmers. The Court said the fact that the people of Illinois revised their constitution in 1870 to permit legislative statutes protecting shippers, producers, and consumers,

> . . . indicates very clearly that during the twenty years in which this peculiar business had been assuming its present "immense proportions," something had occurred which led the whole body of the people to suppose that

---

[51] The Criminal Court of Cook County, Illinois, found Munn and Scott guilty and fined them $100.

[52] *Munn* v. *Illinois, op. cit.,* pp. 131–32.

remedies such as are usually employed to prevent abuses by virtual monopolies might not be inappropriate here. For our purposes we must assume that, if a state of facts could exist that would justify such legislation, it actually did exist when the statute now under consideration was passed. For us the question is one of power, not of expediency. If no state of circumstances could exist to justify such a statute, then we may declare this one void, because in excess of the legislative power of the State. But if it could, we must presume it did. Of the propriety of legislative interference within the scope of legislative power, the legislature is the exclusive judge.[53]

The majority opinion was not decided by the precedent rule, as no earlier parallel case involving a utility enterprise existed. The Chief Justice said it was not

... a matter of any moment that no precedent can be found for a statute precisely like this. It is conceded that the business is one of recent origin, that its growth has been rapid, and that it is already of great importance. And it must also be conceded that it is a business in which the whole public has a direct and positive interest. It represents, therefore, a case for the application of a long-known and well-established principle in social science, and this statute simply extends the law so as to meet this new development of commercial progress. There is no attempt to compel these owners to grant the public an interest in their property, but to declare their obligations, if they use it in this particular manner.[54]

The Court recognized, however, that unless the restrictions in question involved special and peculiar circumstances, the statute would violate the Fourteenth Amendment. Chief Justice Waite, quoting extensively from an essay written by Lord Chief Justice Hale two centuries before, said:

This brings us to inquire as to the principles upon which this power of regulation rests, in order that we may determine what is within and what without its operative effect. Looking, then, to the common law, from whence came the right which the Constitution protects, we find that when private property is "affected with a public interest, it ceases to be *juris privati* only." This was said by Lord Chief Justice Hale more than two hundred years ago ... and has been accepted without objection as an essential element in the law of property ever since. Property does become clothed with a public interest when used in a manner to make it of public consequence, and affect the community at large. When, therefore, one devotes his property to a use in which the public has an interest, he, in effect, grants to the public an interest in that use, and must submit to be controlled by the public for the common good, to the extent of the interest he has thus created. He may withdraw his grant by discontinuing the use; but, so long as he maintains the use, he must submit to the control.[55]

[53] *Ibid.*, pp. 132–33.

[54] *Ibid.*, p. 133.

[55] *Ibid.*, pp. 125–26. See Walton H. Hamilton, "Affectation with Public Interest," 39 *Yale Law Journal* 1089 (1930); and Breck P. McAllister, "Lord Hale and the Business Affected with a Public Interest," 43 *Harvard Law Review* 759 (1930).

Finally, the Court argued:

It matters not in this case that these plaintiffs in error had built their warehouses and established their business before the regulations complained of were adopted. What they did was from the beginning subject to the power of the body politic to require them to conform to such regulations as might be established by the proper authorities for the common good. They entered upon their business and provided themselves with the means to carry it on subject to this condition. If they did not wish to submit themselves to such interference, they should not have clothed the public with an interest in their concerns.[56]

Justice Bradley, who concurred with the majority opinion, said later of the Munn case:

The inquiry . . . was as to the extent of the police power in cases where the public interest is affected; and we held that when an employment or business becomes a matter of such public interest and importance as to create a common charge or burden upon the citizens; in other words, when it becomes a practical monopoly, to which the citizen is compelled to resort, and by means of which a tribute can be exacted from the community, it is subject to regulation by the legislative power.[57]

The Court thus held that the state, under the police power, could regulate grain elevator rates in Chicago, since such a large part of all grain passed through the city that a "virtual monopoly" existed. Hence, the principle of monopoly—an economic condition—as a basis for broad regulation was established.[58]

An important dissent in the Munn case was written by Justice Field and concurred in by Justice Stone. Two positions were taken. First, Justice Field thought the state's right to regulate a privately owned business must be based upon some privilege (franchise) conferred on the owner. In his words:

It is only where some right or privilege [franchise] is conferred by the government or municipality upon the owner, which he can use in connection with his property, or by means of which the use of his property is rendered more valuable to him, or he thereby enjoys an advantage over others, that the compensation to be received by him becomes a legitimate matter of regulation. . . . When the privilege ends, the power to regulate ceases.[59]

Second, Justice Field believed the grain elevator business was of no greater public interest than many other businesses. To quote him again:

[56] *Munn* v. *Illinois, op. cit.,* p. 133.
[57] *Sinking Fund Cases,* 99 U.S. 700, 747 (1878).
[58] McAllister (*op. cit.,* p. 769) argues that "Chief Justice Waite's references to monopoly seem to be for the purpose of emphasizing the size and importance of the business and not of delimiting a necessary condition to regulation." This argument is difficult to support, however, in view of the Court's subsequent references to the Munn case and to monopoly conditions. See, for example, *Nebbia* v. *New York, op. cit.,* pp. 531–32.
[59] Dissenting opinion of Justice Field in *Munn* v. *Illinois, op. cit.,* pp. 146–47.

If this be sound law, if there be no protection, either in the principles upon which our republican government is founded, or in the prohibitions of the Constitution against such invasion of private rights, all property and all business in the State are held at the mercy of a majority of its legislature. The public has no greater interest in the use of buildings for the storage of grain than it has in the use of buildings for the residences of families, nor, indeed, anything like so great an interest; and, according to the doctrine announced, the legislature may fix the rent of all tenements used for residences, without reference to the cost of their erection. If the owner does not like the rates prescribed, he may cease renting his houses. He has granted to the public, says the court, an interest in the use of the buildings, and "he may withdraw his grant by discontinuing the use; but, so long as he maintains the use, he must submit to the control." The public is interested in the manufacture of cotton, woolen, and silken fabrics, in the construction of machinery, in the printing and publication of books and periodicals, and in the making of utensils of every variety, useful and ornamental; indeed, there is hardly an enterprise or business engaging the attention and labor of any considerable portion of the community, in which the public has not an interest in the sense in which that term is used by the court in its opinion; and the doctrine which allows the legislature to interfere with and regulate the charges which the owners of property thus employed shall make for its use, that is, the rates at which all these different kinds of business shall be carried on, has never before been asserted, so far as I am aware, by any judicial tribunal in the United States.[60]

Budd *v.* New York

In 1892, the Supreme Court, following the precedent of the Munn decision, declared that the business of elevating, weighing, and discharging grain from ships was rendered under monopoly conditions and was thus "affected with a public interest."[61] The significance of this case, however, lies in the dissenting opinion.

Three justices (Brewer, Brown, and Field) dissented. Their philosophy was one of opposition to the expansion of governmental control over business. Justice Brewer first distinguished between property devoted to a public use and property in whose use the public has an interest.

The vice of the doctrine is, that it places a public interest in the use of property upon the same basis as a public use of property. Property is devoted to a public use when, and only when, the use is one which the public in its organized capacity, to wit, the State, has a right to create and maintain, and, therefore, one which all the public have a right to demand and share in. The use is public, because the public may create it, and the individual creating it is doing thereby and *pro tanto* the work of the State. The creation of all highways is a public duty. Railroads are highways. The State may build them. If an individual does that work, he is *pro tanto* doing the work of the State. He devotes his property to a public use. The State doing the work fixes the

[60]*Ibid.*, pp. 140–41.
[61]*Budd* v. *New York,* 143 U.S. 517 (1892).

price for the use. It does not lose the right to fix the price, because an individual voluntarily undertakes to do the work. But this public use is very different from a public interest in the use. There is scarcely any property in whose use the public has no interest. No man liveth unto himself alone, and no man's property is beyond the touch of another's welfare. Everything, the manner and extent of whose use affects the well-being of others, is property in whose use the public has an interest. . . . I cannot bring myself to believe that when an owner of property has by his industry, skill and money made a certain piece of his property of large value to many, he has thereby deprived himself of the full dominion over it which he had when it was of comparatively little value; nor can I believe that the control of the public over one's property or business is at all dependent upon the extent to which the public is benefited by it.[62]

Justice Brewer recognized three limitations to the proposition that property "honestly acquired" should be controlled by the owner.

. . . First, that he shall not use it to his neighbor's injury, and that does not mean that he must use it for his neighbor's benefit; second, that if he devotes it to a public use, he gives to the public a right to control that use; and, third, that whenever the public needs require, the public may take it upon payment of due compensation.[63]

None of these limitations, he argued, were applicable in the present case. Nor was the majority's concern with monopoly conditions persuasive.

It is suggested that there is a monopoly, and that that justifies legislative interference. There are two kinds of monopoly; one of law, the other of fact. The one exists when exclusive privileges are granted. Such a monopoly, the law which creates alone can break; and being the creation of law justifies legislative control. A monopoly of fact anyone can break, and there is no necessity for legislative interference. It exists where any one by his money and labor furnishes facilities for business which no one else has. A man puts up in a city the only building suitable for offices. He has therefore a monopoly of that business; but it is a monopoly of fact, which any one can break who, with like business courage, puts his means into a similar building. Because of the monopoly feature, subject thus easily to be broken, may the legislature regulate the price at which he will lease his offices? So, here, there are no exclusive privileges given to these elevators. They are not upon public ground. If the business is profitable, any one can build another; the field is open for all the elevators, and all the competition that may be desired. If there be a monopoly, it is one of fact and not of law, and one which any individual can break.[64]

---

[62] Dissenting opinion of Justice Brewer, *ibid.*, pp. 549–50.
[63] *Ibid.*, p. 550.
[64] *Ibid.*, pp. 550–51. As Troxel (*op. cit.*, p. 15) has pointed out, "a monopoly of law was a consequence of private privilege, and was subject to regulation. But the idea of a monopoly of fact involved some strange legal reasoning."

Justice Brewer's dissent contained a prediction, but one which has not come true. He argued:

> I believe the time is not distant when the evils resulting from this assumption of a power on the part of government to determine the compensation a man may receive for the use of his property, or the performance of his personal services, will become so apparent that the courts will hasten to declare that government can prescribe compensation only when it grants a special privilege . . . or when the service which is rendered is a public service, or the property is in fact devoted to a public use.[65]

The majority of the Court, as will be shown below, in fact continued to expand the list of businesses subject to detailed regulation.

Brass *v.* Stoeser

In 1894, the Court gave a further definition of the public interest concept.[66] The North Dakota legislature, in 1891, passed a law fixing the maximum rates for grain storage. Within the state, there were in operation 600 elevators controlled by 125 different owners. While the economic power of these elevator owners was not so great as that enjoyed by the owners of the Chicago elevators, the statute was upheld by the Court.

Unlike the Munn case, in which the noncompetitive practices of the storage companies were an important consideration, the Court did not discuss pricing practices in the Brass case. Rather, the Court recognized the size of the elevators and the volume of business, as well as the judgment of the North Dakota legislature. Stated Justice Shiras: ". . . as we have no right to revise the wisdom or expediency of the law in question, so we would not be justified in imputing an improper exercise of discretion to the legislature of North Dakota."[67] In short, since the legislature obviously sought to protect the state's farmers, the Supreme Court approved the regulatory statute. The Munn case was reaffirmed, and state legislatures were free to exercise their prerogatives in assigning a public utility status to industries.[68]

German Alliance Insurance Co. *v.* Lewis

The next important step in defining the public interest concept was taken in 1914 when the Court upheld regulation of the fire insurance business.[69] The state of Kansas, through its superintendent of insurance, had ordered a 12 percent reduction in fire insurance premiums in 1909. The German Alliance Insurance Company contended that the fire insurance business was private and not dependent on special privileges conferred by the state and, therefore, that there

---

65 *Budd* v. *New York, op. cit.,* p. 552.
66 *Brass* v. *North Dakota* ex rel. *Stoeser,* 153 U.S. 391 (1894).
67 *Ibid.,* p. 403.
68 Troxel, *op. cit.,* p. 16. Justices Brewer, Field, Jackson, and White dissented.
69 *German Alliance Insurance Co.* v. *Lewis,* 233 U.S. 389 (1914).

was no constitutional power for state regulation of rates and charges for services rendered by it. Justice McKenna, speaking for a divided Court, stated:

> We may put aside, therefore, all merely adventitious considerations and come to the bare and essential one, whether a contract of fire insurance is private and as such has constitutional immunity from regulation. Or, to state it differently and to express an antithetical proposition, is the business of insurance so far affected with a public interest as to justify legislative regulation of its rates? And we mean a broad and definite public interest. In some degree the public interest is concerned in every transaction between men, the sum of the transactions constituting the activities of life. But there is something more special than this, something of more definite consequence, which makes the public interest that justifies regulatory legislation. We can best explain by examples. The transportation of property—business of common carriers—is obviously of public concern and its regulation is an accepted governmental power. The transmission of intelligence is of cognate character. There are other utilities which are denominated public, such as the furnishing of water and light, including in the latter gas and electricity. We do not hesitate at their regulation nor at the fixing of the prices which may be charged for their service. The basis of the ready concession of the power of regulation is the public interest. . . .
>
> Against that conservatism of the mind, which puts to question every new act of regulating legislation and regards the legislation invalid or dangerous until it has become familiar, government—state and national—has pressed on in the general welfare; and our reports are full of cases where in instance after instance the exercise of regulation was resisted and yet sustained against attacks asserted to be justified by the Constitution of the United States. The dread of the moment having passed, no one is now heard to say that rights were restrained or their constitutional guaranties impaired.[70]

After reviewing preceding cases in which state regulation of business was upheld, Justice McKenna continued:

> The cases need no explanatory or fortifying comment. They demonstrate that a business, by circumstances and its nature, may rise from private to be of public concern and be subject, in consequence, to governmental regulation. And they demonstrate . . . that the attempts made to place the right of public regulation in the cases in which it has been exerted, and of which we have given examples, upon the ground of special privilege conferred by the public on those affected cannot be supported. "The underlying principle is that business of certain kinds hold such a peculiar relation to the public interest that there is superinteduced upon it the right of public regulation."[71]

Did the insurance business come within the principle? Answered the Court:

> We have shown that the business of insurance has very definite characteris-

[70] *Ibid.*, pp. 406–7, 409.
[71] *Ibid.*, p. 411.

tics, with a reach of influence and consequence beyond and different from that of the ordinary business of the commercial world, to pursue which a greater liberty may be asserted. The transactions of the latter are independent and individual, terminating in their effect with the instances. The contracts of insurance may be said to be interdependent. They cannot be regarded singly, or isolatedly, and the effect of their relation is to create a fund of assurance and credit, the companies becoming the depositories of the money insured, possessing great power thereby and charged with great responsibility. How necessary their solvency is, is manifest. On the other hand to the insured, insurance is an asset, a basis of credit. It is practically a necessity to business activity and enterprise. It is, therefore, essentially different from ordinary commercial transactions, and, as we have seen, according to the sense of the world from the earliest times,—certainly the sense of the modern world,—is of the greatest public concern. It is therefore within the principle we have announced. . . .[72]

The Court thus expanded the public interest doctrine to include more than the mere rendering of service by means of tangible, physical property. The customary legal characteristics of a public utility—monopoly conditions and an indispensable commodity—were not found. Rather, fire insurance was referred to as "practically a necessity," thereby justifying public regulation. As Justice Lamar argued in his dissent (an opinion concurred in by Chief Justice White and Justice Van Devanter): if the state can regulate the premiums of fire insurance contracts, "then the price of everything within the circle of business transactions can be regulated." [73]

Wolff Packing Co. *v.* Court of Industrial Relations

In the Wolff Packing Company case of 1923,[74] the Supreme Court unanimously held that a state of Kansas statute undertaking extensive controls of commodity prices and wage rates was unconstitutional. The Kansas legislature, in 1920, enacted a statute declaring that the manufacture and preparation of food for human consumption, the production of clothing and all fuels, the transportation of these commodities, and the ordinary public utility businesses were affected with a public interest. The Court of Industrial Relations, created to fix wages and other terms for the conduct of such industries, ordered the Wolff Packing Company to increase the wages being paid to its workers by over $400 weekly, despite the fact that the company had lost $100,000 the previous year. The statute was held unconstitutional on the grounds that it was in conflict with the Fourteenth Amendment. The order of the Court of Industrial Relations, accordingly, was canceled.

[72] *Ibid.*, pp. 414–15.
[73] *Ibid.*, p. 420. The dissent also argued that the statute was discriminatory and represented a denial of equal protection of the law, since insurance rates were to be fixed for stock companies but not for either mutual companies or individual persons selling insurance. *Ibid.*, pp. 433–34.
[74] *Wolff Packing Co.* v. *Court of Industrial Relations, op. cit.*

In reaching this decision, Chief Justice Taft said the concept of public interest involved a "peculiarly close relation" between the public and those businesses so classified. He then proceeded to divide those industries affected with a public interest into three classes:

(1) Those which are carried on under the authority of a public grant of privileges which either expressly or impliedly imposes the affirmative duty of rendering a public service demanded by any member of the public. Such are the railroads, other common carriers and public utilities.

(2) Certain occupations, regarded as exceptional, the public interest attaching to which, recognized from earliest times, has survived the period of arbitrary laws by Parliament or Colonial legislatures for regulating all trades and callings. Such are those of the keepers of inns, cabs, and gristmills. . . .

(3) Businesses which, though not public at their inception, may be fairly said to have risen to be such and have become subject in consequence to some government regulation. They have come to hold such a peculiar relation to the public that this is superimposed upon them. In the language of the cases, the owner, by devoting his business to the public use, in effect grants the public an interest in that use, and subjects himself to public regulation to the extent of that interest, although the property continues to belong to its private owner, and to be entitled to protection accordingly. . . .

It is manifest from an examination of the cases cited under the third head that the mere declaration by a legislature that a business is affected with a public interest is not conclusive of the question whether its attempted regulation on that ground is justified. The circumstances of its alleged change from the status of private business and its freedom from regulation into one in which the public have come to have an interest are always a subject of judicial inquiry. . . .

In nearly all the businesses included under the third head above, the thing which gave the public interest was the indispensable nature of the service and the exorbitant charges and arbitrary control to which the public might be subjected without regulation.[75]

Justice Taft's classification of businesses affected with a public interest is as good a general statement as will be found in court decisions, but he did not discuss the characteristics of such enterprises. The first category was based upon the belief that a special privilege, the right of eminent domain or the issuance of a franchise, was the legal basis for detailed regulation. As previously discussed, this was the position taken by those dissenting in the earlier grain elevator cases. It was not until 1934, in the Nebbia case, that this problem was finally clarified.[76] The franchise is not the evidence of public interest; rather, it can be possessed only as a result of that status. The second category was no more than a statement of historical facts. And the third category, one for which Justice Taft gave no illustrations, simply implied the industries that already were subject to

---

[75] *Ibid.*, pp. 535–36, 538.
[76] *Nebbia* v. *New York, op. cit.*

regulation. "The whole classification, in fact, was scarcely more than a tautology."[77]

Moreover, as Justice Taft pointed out:

> In a sense, the public is concerned about all lawful business because it contributes to the prosperity and well-being of the people. The public may suffer from high prices or strikes in many trades, but the expression "clothed with a public interest," as applied to a business, means more than that the public welfare is affected by continuity or by the price at which a commodity is sold or a service rendered. The circumstances which clothe a particular kind of business with a public interest, in the sense of *Munn* v. *Illinois* and the other cases, must be such as to create a peculiarly close relation between the public and those engaged in it, and raise implications of an affirmative obligation on their part to be reasonable in dealing with the public.[78]

The Court thus gave a classification of the businesses considered to be affected with a public interest, but did not attempt to define a public utility. Justice Taft clearly implies that the two concepts are not synonymous, foreshadowing a development made in the later Nebbia case.

Tyson & Brother *v.* Banton

The state of New York, trying to control the pricing practices of ticket scalpers, enacted a law which declared that the price of admission to places of public amusement or entertainment was affected with a public interest and which limited the advance in price of theater tickets sold through brokers to 50 cents per ticket. In 1927, the Supreme Court, in a five to four decision, decided the law was unconstitutional.[79] In the words of the majority:

> The significant requirement is that the property shall be devoted to a use in which the public has an interest, which simply means . . . that it shall be devoted to "a public use." Stated in another form, a business or property, in order to be affected with a public interest, must be such or be so employed as to justify the conclusion that it has been *devoted* to a public use and its use thereby, in effect *granted* to the public. . . .
>
> A theatre is a private enterprise, which, in its relation to the public, differs obviously and widely, both in character and degree, from a grain elevator, standing at the gateway of commerce and exacting toll, amounting to a common charge, for every bushel of grain which passes on its way among the states; or stock yards, standing in like relation to the commerce in live stock; or an insurance company, engaged, as a sort of common agency, in collecting and holding a guaranty fund in which definite and substantial rights are enjoyed by a considerable portion of the public sustaining interdependent relations in respect of their interests in the fund. Sales of theatre tickets bear no relation to the commerce of the country; and they are not interdependent transactions, but stand, both in form and effect, separate and apart from each

---

[77] Troxel, *op. cit.*, p. 17.
[78] *Wolff Packing Co.* v. *Court of Industrial Relations, op. cit.*, p. 536.
[79] *Tyson & Brother* v. *Banton, op. cit.*

other, "terminating in their effect with the instances." And, certainly, a place of entertainment is in no legal sense a public utility; and, quite as certainly, its activities are not such that their enjoyment can be regarded under any conditions from the point of view of an emergency.

The interest of the public in theatres and other places of entertainment may be more nearly, and with better reason, assimilated to the like interest in provision stores and markets and in the rental of houses and apartments for residence purposes; although in importance it falls below such an interest in the proportion that food and shelter are of more moment than amusement or instruction. As we have shown, there is no legislative power to fix the prices of provisions or clothing or the rental charges for houses or apartments, in the absence of some controlling emergency; and we are unable to perceive any dissimilarities of such quality or degree as to justify a different rule in respect of amusements and entertainments.[80]

Justice Sutherland, who wrote the majority opinion, even noted the danger of carrying governmental price-fixing too far. He argued:

If it be within the legitimate authority of government to fix maximum charges for admission to theatres, lectures (where perhaps the lecturer alone is concerned), baseball, football and other games of all degrees of interest, circuses, shows (big and little), and every possible form of amusement, including the lowly merry-go-round with its adjunct, the hurdy-gurdy, . . . it is hard to see where the limit of power in respect of price-fixing is to be drawn.[81]

There were three dissenting opinions in the case. Justice Holmes, in a dissent concurred in by Justice Brandeis, said:

I think the proper course is to recognize that a state legislature can do whatever it sees fit to do unless it is restrained by some express prohibition in the Constitution of the United States or of the State, and that Courts should be careful not to extend such prohibitions beyond their obvious meaning by reading into them conceptions of public policy that the particular Court may happen to entertain. . . . [I] think . . . that the notion that a business is clothed with a public interest and has been devoted to the public use is little more than a fiction intended to beautify what is disagreeable to the sufferers. The truth seems to me to be that, subject to compensation when compensation is due, the legislature may forbid or restrict any business when it has a sufficient force of public opinion behind it. . . .

But if we are to yield to fashionable conventions, it seems to me that theatres are as much devoted to public use as anything well can be. We have not that respect for art that is one of the glories of France. But to many people the superfluous is the necessary, and it seems to me that Government does not go beyond its sphere in attempting to make life livable for them. I am far from saying that I think this particular law a wise and rational provision. That is not my affair. But if the people of the State of New York

[80]*Ibid.*, pp. 433–34, 439–40.
[81]*Ibid.*, p. 442.

speaking by their authorized voice say that they want it, I see nothing in the Constitution of the United States to prevent their having their will. [82]

Justice Stone wrote a second dissent, concurred in by Justices Brandeis and Holmes. He, too, was unable to find anything in the Constitution that would prohibit the state of New York from regulating the price of brokerage charges. Of more significance, however, was his questioning of the usefulness of the phrase "business affected with a public interest." Justice Stone argued that it

> . . . seems to me to be too vague and illusory to carry us very far on the way to a solution. It tends in use to become only a convenient expression for describing those businesses, regulation of which has been permitted in the past. To say that only those businesses affected with a public interest may be regulated is but another way of stating that all those businesses which may be regulated are affected with a public interest. It is difficult to use the phrase free of its connotation of legal consequences, and hence when used as a basis of judicial decision, to avoid begging the question to be decided. The very fact that it has been applied to businesses unknown to Lord Hale, who gave sanction to its use, should caution us against the assumption that the category has now become complete or fixed and that there may not be brought into it new classes of business or transactions not hitherto included, in consequence of newly devised methods of extortionate price exaction. [83]

Thus, price control was appropriate, contended Justice Stone, whenever there existed "a situation or a combination of circumstances materially restricting the regulative force of competition, so that buyers or sellers are placed at such a disadvantage in the bargaining struggle that serious economic consequences result to a very large number of members of the community." [84]

Justice Sanford, in the third dissent, argued that the relevant question was "whether the business of ticket brokers who intervene between the theatre owners and the general public in the sale of theatre tickets is affected with a public interest, and may, under the circumstances disclosed in this case, be regulated by the legislature to the extent of preventing them from selling tickets at more than a reasonable advance upon the theatre prices." [85] He concluded that such regulation was proper:

> . . . ticket brokers, by virtue of arrangements which they make with the theatre owners, ordinarily acquire an absolute control of the most desirable seats in the theatres, by which they deprive the public of access to the theatres themselves for the purpose of buying such tickets at the regular prices, and are enabled to exact an extortionate advance in prices for the sale of such tickets to the public.
>
> In *Munn* v. *Illinois* . . . —although there was no holding that the sale of grain was in itself a business affected with a public interest which could be

82 *Ibid.*, pp. 446–47.
83 *Ibid.*, p. 451.
84 *Ibid.*, pp. 451–52.
85 *Ibid.*, p. 454.

regulated by the legislature—it was held that the separate business of grain elevators, which "stood in the very gateway of commerce" in grain, "taking toll" from all who passed and tending to a common charge, had become by the facts, clothed "with a public interest" and was subject to public regulation limiting the charges to a reasonable toll. So, I think, that here—without reference to the character of the business of the theatres themselves—the business of the ticket brokers, who stand in "the very gateway" between the theatres and the public, depriving the public of access to the theatres for the purchase of desirable seats at the regular prices, and exacting toll from patrons of the theatres desiring to purchase such seats, has become clothed with a public interest and is subject to regulation by the legislature limiting their charges to reasonable exactions and protecting the public from extortion and exorbitant rates.[86]

Ribnik *v.* McBride

The Ribnik decision closely parallels that of the Tyson case. The state of New Jersey became concerned over the abuses of private employment agencies, and passed a law requiring such agencies to secure a license to operate. One of the terms for securing the license was the filing of the agency's proposed charges. Ribnik's application for a license was rejected by the Commissioner of Labor on the ground that his proposed fees were excessive and unreasonable.

In a six to three decision, the Supreme Court ruled that the law was unconstitutional.[87] Again, the Court held that the interest of the public in the matter of employment is not "that *public interest* which the law contemplates as the basis for legislative price control." Argued Justice Sutherland:

> The business of securing employment for those seeking work and employees for those seeking workers is essentially that of a broker, that is, of an intermediary. While we do not undertake to say that there may not be a deeper concern on the part of the public in the business of an employment agency, that business does not differ in substantial character from the business of a real estate broker, ship broker, merchandise broker or ticket broker. In the *Tyson* case . . . we declared unconstitutional an act of the New York legislature which sought to fix the price at which theatre tickets should be sold by a ticket broker, and it is not easy to see how, without disregarding that decision, price-fixing legislation in respect of other brokers of like character can be upheld.[88]

In his dissent, Justice Stone, supported by Justices Brandeis and Holmes, strongly criticized the antisocial practices of employment agencies.

> For thirty years or more the evils found to be connected with the business of employment agencies in the United States have been the subject of repeated investigations, official and unofficial, and of extensive public com-

[86] *Ibid.*, p. 455.
[87] *Ribnik* v. *McBride*, 277 U.S. 350 (1928).
[88] *Ibid.*, pp. 356–57.

ment. They have been the primary reason for the establishment of public employment offices in the various States.

Quite apart from the other evils laid at the door of the private agencies, the data supplied by these investigations and reports afford a substantial basis for the conclusion of the New Jersey legislature that the business is peculiarly subject to abuses relating to fee-charging, and that for the correction of these the restriction to a reasonable maximum charge is the only effective remedy.[89]

Nor could Justice Stone understand the majority's distinction between price control and other forms of regulation. He thought it obvious that,

> ... even in the case of businesses affected with a public interest, other control than price regulation may be appropriate, and price regulation may be so inappropriate as to be arbitrary or unreasonable, and hence unconstitutional. To me it seems equally obvious that the Constitution does not require us to hold that a business, subject to every other form of reasonable regulation, is immune from the requirement of reasonable prices, where that requirement is the only remedy appropriate to the evils encountered. In this respect I can see no difference between a reasonable regulation of price and a reasonable regulation of the use of property, which affects its price or economic return. The privilege of contract and the free use of property are as seriously cut down in the one case as in the other.
>
> To say that there is constitutional power to regulate a business or a particular use of property because of the public interest in the welfare of a class peculiarly affected, and to deny such power to regulate price for the accomplishment of the same end, when that alone appears to be an appropriate and effective remedy, is to make a distinction based on no real economic difference, and for which I can find no warrant in the Constitution itself nor any justification in the opinions of this Court.[90]

Williams *v.* Standard Oil Co.

In 1927, the state of Tennessee adopted a statute enabling the Commissioner of Finance and Taxation to fix the prices at which gasoline could be sold within the state.[91] A "proper" differential between the wholesale and retail price was to be maintained; rebates, price concessions and price discrimination between persons or localities were forbidden. Suit was brought to declare the statute unconstitutional. Justice Sutherland, speaking for the majority,[92] argued:

> It is settled by recent decisions of this Court that a state legislature is without constitutional power to fix prices at which commodities may be sold, services rendered, or property used, unless the business or property involved is "affected with a public interest." ... Nothing is gained by reiterating the statement that the phrase is indefinite. By repeated decisions of this Court,

---

[89]*Ibid.*, pp. 363–65.
[90]*Ibid.*, pp. 373–74.
[91]*Williams* v. *Standard Oil Co.*, 278 U.S. 235 (1929).
[92] Justice Holmes dissented, but did not write an opinion. Justices Brandeis and Stone dissented from the majority's reasoning, but concurred in the result.

beginning with *Munn* v. *Illinois,* . . . that phrase, however it may be characterized, has become the established test by which the legislative power to fix prices of commodities, use of property, or services, must be measured. As applied in particular instances, its meaning may be considered both from an affirmative and a negative point of view. Affirmatively, it means that a business or property, in order to be affected with a public interest, must be such or be so employed as to justify the conclusion that it has been *devoted* to a public use and its use thereby in effect *granted* to the public. . . . Negatively, it does not mean that a business is affected with a public interest merely because it is large or because the public are warranted in having a feeling of concern in respect of its maintenance. . . .

In support of the act under review it is urged that gasoline is of widespread use; that enormous quantities of it are sold in the State of Tennessee; and that it has become necessary and indispensable in carrying on commercial and other activities within the state. But we are here concerned with the character of the business, not with its size or the extent to which the commodity is used. Gasoline is one of the ordinary commodities of trade, differing, so far as the question here is affected, in no essential respect from a great variety of other articles commonly bought and sold by merchants and private dealers in the country. The decisions referred to above make it perfectly clear that the business of dealing in such articles, irrespective of its extent, does not come within the phrase "affected with a public interest." Those decisions control the present case.

There is nothing in the point that the act in question may be justified on the ground that the sale of gasoline in Tennessee is monopolized by appellees, or by either of them, because, objections to the materiality of the contention aside, an inspection of the pleadings and of the affidavits submitted to the lower court discloses an utter failure to show the existence of such monopoly.[93]

The Court ruled, therefore, that the statute was unconstitutional. There was no monopoly in the sale of gasoline. More importantly, since earlier decisions were controlling, the selling of gasoline was not a business "affected with a public interest."

New State Ice Co. v. Liebmann

In 1925, the state of Oklahoma enacted a statute declaring that the manufacture, sale, and distribution of ice was a "public business" and conferring on the Corporation Commission the power of regulation. Among the regulations was the power to license new enterprises on a showing that they were necessary to meet the public need. Liebmann began to construct an ice plant in competition with the New State Ice Company without first obtaining the required license, contending that he was not engaged in a public business but in a common calling, and therefore, no license from the state was necessary.[94]

The majority of the Court found no monopoly conditions or emergency

[93] *Williams* v. *Standard Oil Co., op. cit.,* pp. 239–40.
[94] *New State Ice Co.,* v. *Liebmann, op. cit.*

conditions that justified regulation, believing, instead, that a restriction of the number of ice manufacturing companies might result in monopoly, thereby jeopardizing the interests of consumers. In the words of Justice Sutherland:

> It has been said that the manufacture of ice requires an expensive plant beyond the means of the average citizen, and that since the use of ice is indispensable, patronage of the producer by the consumer is unavoidable. The same might, however, be said in respect of other articles clearly beyond the reach of restriction like that here under review .... We know, since it is common knowledge, that today, to say nothing of other means, wherever electricity or gas is available (and one or the other is available in practically every part of the country), anyone for a comparatively moderate outlay may have set up in his kitchen an appliance by means of which he may manufacture ice for himself. Under such circumstances it hardly will do to say that people generally are at the mercy of the manufacturer, seller, and distributor of ice for ordinary needs. Moreover, the practical tendency of the restriction ... is to shut out new enterprises, and thus create and foster monopoly in the hands of existing establishments, against, rather than in aid of, the interest of the consuming public.[95]

Justice Brandeis, in one of his most famous dissents, concurred in by Justice Stone, showed his willingness to greatly expand public regulation. First, he argued that the Court should not substitute its judgment for that of the legislature with respect to the desirability of regulation. To quote from his dissent:

> Oklahoma declared the business of manufacturing ice for sale and distribution a "public business;" that is, a public utility. So far as appears, it was the first State to do so. Of course, a legislature cannot by mere legislative fiat convert a business into a public utility. ... But the conception of a public utility is not static. The welfare of the community may require that the business of supplying ice be made a public utility, as well as the business of supplying water or any other necessary commodity or service. If the business is, or can be made, a public utility, it must be possible to make the issue of a certificate a prerequisite to engaging in it. ...
>
> The business of supplying ice is not only a necessity, like that of supplying food or clothing or shelter, but the legislature could also consider that it is one which lends itself peculiarly to monopoly. Characteristically the business is conducted in local plants with a market narrowly limited in area, and this for the reason that ice manufactured at a distance cannot effectively compete with a plant on the ground. In small towns and rural communities the duplication of plants, and in larger communities the duplication of delivery service, is wasteful and ultimately burdensome to consumers. At the same time the relative ease and cheapness with which an ice plant may be constructed exposes the industry to destructive and frequently ruinous competition. Competition in the industry tends to be destructive because ice plants have a determinate capacity, and inflexible fixed charges and operating costs, and

95 *Ibid.*, pp. 277–78.

because in a market of limited area the volume of sales is not readily expanded. Thus, the erection of a new plant in a locality already adequately served often causes managers to go to extremes in cutting prices in order to secure business. Trade journals and reports of association meetings of ice manufacturers bear ample witness to the hostility of the industry to such competition, and to its unremitting efforts, through trade associations, informal agreements, combination of delivery systems, and in particular through the consolidation of plants, to protect markets and prices against competition of any character. . . .

The advisability of treating the ice business as a public utility and of applying to it the certificate of convenience and necessity had been under consideration for many years. Similar legislation had been enacted in Oklahoma under similar circumstances with respect to other public services. The measure bore a substantial relation to the evils found to exist. Under these circumstances, to hold the Act void as being unreasonable, would, in my opinion involve the exercise not of the function of judicial review, but the function of a super-legislature. If the Act is to be stricken down, it must be on the ground that the Federal Constitution guarantees to the individual the absolute right to enter the ice business, however detrimental the exercise of that right may be to the public welfare. Such, indeed, appears to be the contention made . . . .

The claim is that manufacturing ice for sale and distribution is a business inherently private, and, in effect, that no state of facts can justify denial of the right to engage in it. To supply one's self with water, electricity, gas, ice, or any other article, is inherently a matter of private concern. So also may be the business of supplying the same articles to others for compensation. But the business of supplying to others, for compensation, any article or service whatsoever may become a matter of public concern. Whether it is, or is not, depends upon the conditions existing in the community affected. If it is a matter of public concern, it may be regulated, whatever the business. The public's concern may be limited to a single feature of the business, so that the needed protection can be secured by a relatively slight degree of regulation. Such is the concern over possible incompetence, which dictates the licensing of dentists . . . or the concern over possible dishonesty, which led to the licensing of auctioneers . . . . On the other hand, the public's concern about a particular business may be so pervasive and varied as to require constant detailed supervision and a very high degree of regulation. Where this is true, it is common to speak of the business as being a "public" one, although it is privately owned. It is to such businesses that the designation "public utility" is commonly applied; or they are spoken of as "affected with a public interest." . . .

A regulation valid for one kind of business may, of course, be invalid for another; since the reasonableness of every regulation is dependent upon the relevant facts. But so far as concerns the power to regulate, there is no difference in essence, between a business called private and one called a public utility or said to be "affected with a public interest." Whatever the nature of the business, whatever the scope or character of the regulation applied, the source of the power invoked is the same. And likewise the constitutional limitation upon that power. The source is the police power. The limitation is that set by the due process clause, which, as construed, requires that the regulation shall not be unreasonable, arbitrary or capricious; and that the means of regulation selected shall have a real or substantial relation to the subject sought to be obtained. The notion of a distinct category of businesses "affected with a public interest," employing property "devoted to a public use," rests upon historical error. The consequences which it is sought to draw from those phrases are belied by the meaning in which they were used centuries ago, and by the decision of this court, in *Munn* v. *Illinois*, . . . which first introduced them into the law of the Constitution. In my opinion, the true principle is that the State's power extends to every regulation of any business reasonably required and appropriate for the public protection. I find in the due process clause no other limitation upon the character or the scope of regulation permissible.[96]

Second, Justice Brandeis rejected the majority's contention that regulation would result in monopoly. Instead he argued:

It is settled that the police power commonly invoked in aid of health, safety and morals, extends equally to the promotion of the public welfare. The cases just cited show that, while, ordinarily, free competition in the common callings has been encouraged, the public welfare may at other times demand that monopolies be created. Upon this principle is based our whole modern practice of public utility regulation. It is no objection to the validity of the statute here assailed that it fosters monopoly. That, indeed, is its design. The certificate of public convenience and invention is a device—a recent social-economic invention—through which the monopoly is kept under effective control by vesting in a commission the power to terminate it whenever that course is required in the public interest. To grant any monopoly to any person as a favor is forbidden even if terminable. But where, as here, there is reasonable ground for the legislative conclusion that in order to secure a necessary service at reasonable rates, it may be necessary to curtail the right to enter the calling, it is, in my opinion, consistent with the due process clause to do so, whatever the nature of the business. The existence of such power in the legislature seems indispensable in our ever-changing society.[97]

Finally, it was suggested that an emergency of sufficient importance to warrant experimental legislative regulation had been created by the depression. Said Justice Brandeis:

To stay experimentation in things social and economic is a grave responsibility. Denial of the right to experiment may be fraught with serious consequences to the Nation. It is one of the happy incidents of the federal system that a single courageous State may, if its citizens choose, serve as a laboratory; and try novel social and economic experiments without risk to the rest of the country. This Court has the power to prevent an experiment. We may

[96] Dissenting opinion of Justice Brandeis, *ibid.*, pp. 283–84, 291–93, 300–303.
[97] *Ibid.*, p. 304.

strike down the statute which embodies it on the ground that, in our opinion, the measure is arbitrary, capricious or unreasonable. We have power to do this, because the due process clause has been held by the Court applicable to matters of substantive law as well as to matters of procedure. But in the exercise of this high power, we must be ever on our guard, lest we erect our prejudices into legal principles. If we would guide by the light of reason, we must let our minds be bold.[98]

Nebbia *v.* New York

The last attempt of the Supreme Court to define the public interest concept is found in the Nebbia case of 1934.[99] In addition, this case marks the Court's abandonment of its attempt to distinguish a peculiar category of industries "affected with a public interest."

In 1933, the New York legislature passed a statute which declared that the milk industry was affected with a public interest. The statute set up a Milk Control Board and provided for control of prices and trade practices of milk producers and distributors. The board proceeded to fix nine cents as the price which a store could charge for a quart of milk. A grocer in Rochester, named Nebbia, had sold two quarts of milk, plus a five-cent loaf of bread, for eighteen cents. Promptly sued for violating the law, Nebbia argued that the milk business was competitive rather than monopolistic, that it had none of the characteristics of a public utility, and that the federal Constitution prohibited a state from regulating the price charged for milk. The Supreme Court, in a five to four decision, rejected this defense. Said Justice Roberts:

> We may as well say at once that the dairy industry is not, in the accepted sense of the phrase, a public utility. We think the appellant is also right in asserting that there is in this case no suggestion of any monopoly or monopolistic practice. It goes without saying that those engaged in the business are in no way dependent upon public grants or franchises for the privilege of conducting their activities. But if, as must be conceded, the industry is subject to regulation in the public interest, what constitutional principle bars the state from correcting existing maladjustments by legislation touching prices? We think there is no such principle. . . .
>
> It is clear that there is no closed class or category of businesses affected with a public interest, and the function of courts in the application of the Fifth and Fourteenth Amendments is to determine in each case whether circumstances vindicate the challenged regulation as a reasonable exertion of governmental authority or condemn it as arbitrary or discriminatory . . . . The phrase "affected with a public interest" can, in the nature of things, mean no more than that an industry, for adequate reason, is subject to control for the public good. In several of the decisions of this court wherein the expressions "affected with a public interest," and "clothed with a public use," have been

[98]*Ibid.*, p. 311. The majority had argued that there were "certain essentials of liberty with which the state is not entitled to dispense in the interest of experiments." *Ibid.*, p. 280.

[99]*Nebbia* v. *New York, op. cit.*

brought forward as the criteria of the validity of price control, it has been admitted that they are not susceptible of definition and form an unsatisfactory test of the constitutionality of legislation directed at business practices or prices. These decisions must rest, finally, upon the basis that the requirements of due process were not met because the laws were found arbitrary in their operation and effect. But there can be no doubt that upon proper occasion and by appropriate measures the state may regulate a business in any of its aspects, including the prices to be charged for the products or commodities it sells.

So far as the requirement of due process is concerned, and in the absence of other constitutional restriction, a state is free to adopt whatever economic policy may reasonably be deemed to promote public welfare, and to enforce that policy by legislation adapted to its purpose. The courts are without authority either to declare such policy, or, when it is declared by the legislature, to override it. If the laws passed are seen to have a reasonable relation to a proper legislative purpose, and are neither arbitrary nor discriminatory, the requirements of due process are satisfied, and judicial determination to that effect renders a court *functus officio.*[100]

Justice Roberts clearly discards monopoly as a prerequisite of the public interest concept, substituting the principle of imperfect competition—a concept covering both monopoly and excessive competition. The Court thus observed:

If the law-making body within its sphere of government concludes that the conditions or practices in an industry make unrestricted competition an inadequate safeguard of the consumer's interests, produce waste harmful to the public, threaten ultimately to cut off the supply of a commodity needed by the public, or portend the destruction of the industry itself, appropriate statutes passed in an honest effort to correct the threatened consequences may not be set aside because the regulation adopted fixes prices reasonably deemed by the legislature to be fair to those engaged in the industry and to the consuming public. And this is especially so where, as here, the economic maladjustment is one of price, which threatens harm to the producer at one end of the series and the consumer at the other. The Constitution does not secure to any one liberty to conduct his business in such fashion as to inflict injury upon the public at large, or upon any substantial group of the people. Price control, like any other form of regulation, is unconstitutional only if arbitrary, discriminatory, or demonstrably irrelevant to the policy the legislature is free to adopt, and hence an unnecessary and unwarranted interference with individual liberty.[101]

Justice McReynolds, in his dissent concurred in by Justices Butler, Sutherland, and Van Devanter, stated:

Is the milk business so affected with public interest that the Legislature may prescribe prices for sales by stores? This Court has approved the contrary view; has emphatically declared that a State lacks power to fix prices in

[100]*Ibid.,* pp. 531–32, 536–37.
[101]*Ibid.,* p. 538.

similar private businesses. . . . Regulation to prevent recognized evils in business has long been upheld as permissible legislative action. But fixation of the price at which "A," engaged in an ordinary business, may sell, in order to enable "B," a producer, to improve his condition, has not been regarded as within legislative power. This is not regulation, but management, control, dictation—it amounts to the deprivation of the fundamental right which one has to conduct his own affairs honestly and along customary lines. The argument advanced here would support general prescription of prices for farm products, groceries, shoes, clothing, all the necessities of modern civilization, as well as labor, when some legislature finds and declares such action advisable and for the public good. This Court has declared that a State may not by legislative fiat convert a private business into a public utility. . . . And if it be now ruled that one dedicates his property to public use whenever he embarks on an enterprise which the Legislature may think is desirable to bring under control, this is but to declare that rights guaranteed by the Constitution exist only so long as supposed public interest does not require their extinction. To adopt such a view, of course, would put an end to liberty under the Constitution.[102]

Some Implications of the Nebbia Case

The Nebbia decision established a new basic doctrine which has become a vital part of our constitutional law. While the exact meaning of the doctrine cannot be precisely determined,[103] two major implications emerge. First, as argued by the dissent in the case, the Court's broadened definition of "affected with a public interest" virtually brings within the regulatory power all modern business enterprises.[104] Second, the "affected with a public interest" concept is no longer synonymous with the traditional "public utility" concept; the latter concept is broader than, and includes, the former.

Extension of Regulation. Since the Nebbia case, the Supreme Court has allowed state and federal governments to extend regulation over many businesses. The Court has upheld state laws fixing maximum warehouse charges for handling and selling leaf tobacco,[105] and curtailing the output of petroleum;[106] and federal laws requiring inspection of tobacco,[107] restricting quantities of

[102] Dissenting opinion of Justice McReynolds, *ibid.,* pp. 552, 554–55.

[103] The implications of the Nebbia case are discussed by Irving B. Goldsmith and Gordon W. Winks, "Price Fixing: From Nebbia to Guffey," 31 *Illinois Law Review* 179 (1936); R. L. Hale, "The Constitution and the Price System: Some Reflections on Nebbia v. New York," 34 *Columbia Law Review* 401 (1934); Irwin S. Rosenbaum, "Ruling on Milk Price Control," 14 *Public Utilities Fortnightly* 795 (1934); and R. W. Harbeson, "The Public Interest Concept in Law and in Economics," 37 *Michigan Law Review* 181 (1938).

[104] "In truth, it would appear that the *Nebbia* case, in attempting to define 'affected with a public interest' in a manner sufficiently broad to sustain price regulation, destroyed that concept." Ronald A. Anderson, *Government and Business* (3d ed.; Cincinnati: South-Western Publishing Co., 1966), p. 315.

[105] *Townsend* v. *Yeomans,* 301 U.S. 441 (1937).

[106] *Railroad Comm.* v. *Rowan & Nichols Oil Co.,* 310 U.S. 573 (1940).

[107] *Currin* v. *Wallace,* 306 U.S. 1 (1939).

tobacco that can be marketed,[108] and providing for establishment of minimum prices for milk.[109] In a 1941 case in which the Supreme Court upheld a state statute fixing maximum compensation that could be collected by a private employment agency, it was argued that "The drift away from *Ribnik* v. *McBride* had been so great that it can no longer be deemed a controlling authority."[110] The Court even referred to the concept of "affected with a public interest" as "discarded" in the Nebbia case.[111] And in 1950, the Court upheld a state law fixing minimum prices for natural gas at the wellhead without invoking the concept at all. The Court simply stated: "Like any other regulation, a price-fixing order is lawful if substantially related to a legitimate end sought to be attained."[112]

Public Utility Status. The most extensive public regulation has been reserved for those activities which have been designated as public utilities (or regulated industries). The public utility status generally has been conferred on an industry that possesses those distinct economic characteristics which indicate that administrative, as opposed to market, regulation can improve the industry's economic performance. Such activities are those closely associated with the processes of transportation and distribution. As summarized by Judge Vinson in a 1943 dissenting opinion:

> The participation by a business in activities *intimately connected with the processes of transportation and distribution* . . . was the characteristic which caused it to be subjected to the impositions implicit in public utility regulation. A somewhat exhaustive enumeration of the businesses which frequently have been designated, operated, and regulated as public utilities illustrates that the gradual growth of the family has involved no departure from the initial concept, but merely reflected scientific progress in the facilities, auxiliaries, and varieties of transportation and distribution.[113]

Judge Vinson then proceeded to state the essential elements of the public utility concept.

> . . . If a business is (1) affected with a public interest, *and* (2) bears an intimate connection with the processes of transportation and distribution, *and* (3) is under an obligation to afford its facilities to the public generally, upon demand, at fair and non-discriminatory rates, *and* (4) enjoys, in a large measure an independence and freedom from business competition brought about either (a) by its acquisition of a monopolistic status, or (b) by the grant of a franchise or certificate from the State placing it in this position, it is . . . a public utility.[114]

[108] *Mulford* v. *Smith,* 307 U.S. 38 (1939).
[109] *United States* v. *Rock Royal Co-operative,* 307 U.S. 533 (1939).
[110] *Olsen* v. *Nebraska,* 313 U.S. 236, 244 (1941).
[111] *Ibid.,* p. 245.
[112] *Cities Service Gas* v. *Peerless Oil & Gas Co.,* 340 U.S. 179, 186 (1950).
[113] *Davies Warehouse Co.* v. *Brown,* 137 F. 2d 201, 212–13 (1943).
[114] *Ibid.,* p. 217. Judge Vinson recognized that the "formula is a limited one," amounting to an affirmative test only. "My formula has no negative or exclusive implications. What I do say is that, at least, *any* business which *does* possess and practice and operate under each and all of these features, is by a preponderance of considered judicial opinion a business in the public utility class." *Ibid.*

The Supreme Court's decisions, however, do not provide consistent criteria from which a more precise definition of the public utility concept may be formulated. Thus, "while monopoly and lack of competition are present in the case of some undoubted public utilities, there are others, carriers by motor vehicle for example, whose business is highly competitive."[115] The Court, in other words, has permitted detailed regulation of some industries with economic characteristics which differ from those possessed by traditional public utilities. At the same time, a legislature cannot confer public utility status on *any* business merely by passing a statute.[116]

OBLIGATIONS AND RIGHTS OF REGULATED INDUSTRIES

The English courts evolved a group of obligations and rights which they attached on common callings or public interest occupations. The obligations were not voluntary but compulsory, and could be avoided only by withdrawal from service. They were later adopted by the American courts. Today, such obligations and rights have been incorporated into, and amplified by, state and federal statutes. As with other matters, however, the courts still retain their prerogative of reviewing the reasonableness of all statutory provisions and their administrative applications. Because these obligations and rights will be discussed at length in succeeding chapters, the following paragraphs merely summarize the major requirements.

Obligations

Regulated industries have four major obligations or responsibilities imposed on them because of their special status. First, they are obligated to serve all who apply for service. Within a market (service) area, and within the limit of its capacity (ability to serve), a regulated company must be prepared to serve any customer who is willing and able to pay for the service. At times, this requirement may mean that a business must provide capital investment in rural areas where it is not profitable to do so, or to maintain an unprofitable type of service. The price of services in these areas cannot be based on cost, but must be subsidized by other services offered by the company. In contrast, nonregulated businesses may legally decline to serve a potential customer for any reason whatsoever.

Second, the regulated industries are obligated to render safe and adequate service. Consequently, there exist regulations of voltage requirements for electricity, heat value and pressure requirements for gas, and published schedules for transportation services. Each service must be supplied by means of the safest equipment available to the industry involved. Moreover, the service rendered must be adequate. For the telephone, telegraph, and power industries, this requirement means service must be provided 24 hours a day; for the transportation

---

[115] *Ibid.,* majority opinion by Judge Maris, p. 207.
[116] Francis X. Welch, *Cases and Text on Public Utility Regulation* (rev. ed.; Washington, D.C.: Public Utilities Reports, Inc., 1968), p. 3.

industries, service must be "in the public interest." All regulated industries must be prepared for foreseeable increases in demand. In short, regulated firms must be ready to give instantaneous service on demand.

Third, regulated industries have the obligation to serve all customers on equal terms. Unjust or undue discrimination among customers is forbidden. Under conditions of near monopoly, discrimination in price and perhaps service may become profitable to a business. As there are few substitute services available, customers would be helpless in such a situation. If reasonable, regulation does permit the classification of customers for the purpose of rate-making. But within each class, the same rate structure must apply. Regulation also permits the use of graduated rate structures; again, they must be reasonable.

Finally, the regulated industries are obligated to charge only a "just and reasonable" price for the services rendered. It is up to the various commissions and the courts to interpret this duty. Nonregulated businesses are under no such restraint, as competition is assumed to regulate prices in the public interest. As will be demonstrated throughout the book, this provision has resulted in considerable controversy between the industries, commissions, and courts.

Rights

All businesses, regulated and nonregulated, have certain rights. The most important general right is the legal protection of private property. In addition, however, regulated industries have four rights that are largely the result of their special status.

First, the regulated industries have the right to collect a reasonable price for their services. Regulatory authorities may not force such a business to operate at a loss.[117] At the same time, a reasonable return is not guaranteed, and under adverse economic conditions it may happen that no rate will cover the cost of service. Barring such a possibility, the courts have insisted on the right to a reasonable price.

Second, the regulated industries have the right to render service subject to reasonable rules and regulations. The public has certain rights and can demand that regulated industries live up to their obligations. For their part, these industries have the right to reasonable office hours, prompt customer payments, service deposits, and contracts, among others. Moreover, these businesses have the right to withdraw service under prescribed conditions and after giving due notice to their customers.

Third, when they furnish adequate service at reasonable rates, the regulated industries have the right of *protection* from competition from an enterprise offering the same service in the same service area.[118] Prior to commencing

[117]Certain services offered by a particular company may be operated at a loss (e.g., passenger railroad service), but a company cannot be forced to operate at an overall loss.

[118]This statement implies that a competing utility providing the same service may be certified. Section 7(g) of the Natural Gas Act is typical of other statutory provisions: "Nothing contained in this section shall be construed as a limitation upon the power of

operations, a regulated firm must receive a certificate of public convenience and necessity from the appropriate regulatory agency and a franchise (generally dealing with the use of city streets and with city utility service) from the relevant local governmental unit. In turn, such certificates and franchises, while not exclusive, offer a regulated firm some freedom from competition in its service area.

Finally, the specific right of eminent domain has been given to most regulated industries. (The exceptions are the airline, motor carrier, and water carrier industries, and coal slurry pipeline companies.) This right enables them to condemn private property and take it for "public use" when necessary to the proper conduct of their business. The regulated industries are required to pay a just compensation for any property so condemned. Land may be taken, for instance, for electric or telephone pole lines or for water mains, to enable a regulated company to provide adequate service for the public.

LIMITATIONS ON GOVERNMENT REGULATION

Once the right to regulate an industry has been established under the police powers of the state or the interstate commerce clause of the federal Constitution, are there any limits on the actions of the regulatory commissions? The answer is very definitely in the affirmative. The Fifth and Fourteenth Amendments to the Constitution guarantee due process of law. As the courts have long held the right to profits as a fundamental characteristic of property, these two Amendments mean that no regulation by a unit of government can reduce profits below a confiscatory level and be upheld as constitutional.

It is to this limitation on the actions of regulatory commissions that many of the difficulties in the effort to achieve effective regulation can be traced. In fact, this limitation is directly responsible for the frequent overruling of a so-called expert body (the regulatory commission) by a legal body that is often untrained in the problems of regulation (the court). As a result, to test the reasonableness of the commissions' orders, the regulated companies have taken to the courts many important decisions made by the commissions. And the companies cannot necessarily be blamed in their actions. These companies are privately owned and privately operated. Regulation, therefore, involves the question of private rights versus public needs, and the line between them often requires judicial interpretation. But from the point of view of effective regulation, this often results in very slow enforcement of the commissions' decisions.[119]

---

the commission to grant certificates of public convenience and necessity for service of an area already being served by another natural gas company." See *Panhandle Eastern Pipe Line Co.* v. *Federal Power Comm.,* 169 F. 2d 881 (1948), *cert. denied,* 335 U.S. 854 (1948).

[119] This paragraph should not be interpreted to mean that judicial review is a bad thing. Quite the contrary. "Court review has been a public benefit. . . . The courts are the

Thus, there is a good deal of uncertainty both as to the fields over which the units of government may practice regulation and as to how far such regulation may be carried. In both instances, the courts have the final word. In both instances, while the courts have laid down some general rules, they continue to take each specific case under review, and the general rules are so vague and flexible that no commission can accurately forecast just what the final court decision will be. Under such conditions, regulation has proceeded by trial and error. Before taking up these matters in greater detail, the following chapter discusses the independent regulatory commissions.

---

constitutional guardians of the powers of the legislatures and of the rights of those affected by legislation." E. R. Johnson, *Government Regulation of Transportation* (New York: D. Appleton-Century Co., 1938), p. 102. In other words, while judicial review has resulted in slow regulation, it is a lesser evil to have judicial review than it would be to abolish it.

| Chapter | THE INDEPENDENT |
| 4 | REGULATORY COMMISSIONS |

The need for a commission arises . . . when the legislative body finds that particular conditions call for continual and very frequent acts of legislation, based on a uniform and consistent policy, which in themselves require intimate and expert knowledge of numerous and complex facts, a knowledge which can only be obtained by processes of patient, impartial, and continued investigation.

—*Joseph B. Eastman**

Regulatory functions may be exercised by administrative agencies or by executive departments. The agency has become the most important form of regulation at both the federal and state levels in the United States. Such was not always the case. Competition was relied on to protect the consumer during the early developmental stages of all now-regulated industries. As a result, charters and franchises to operate in certain specified areas were granted almost indiscriminately by cities and states. Denver, in 1880, granted a general electric utility franchise "to all comers."[1] New York City, in 1887, gave franchises to six electric utility companies at the same time.[2] In fact, the general policy throughout the country was to grant a franchise to any company that applied.[3]

The impossibility of relying on competition as a regulatory force gradually became evident. As outlined in Chapter 2, the economic characteristics of certain industries indicate that they operate more efficiently as monopolies. Detailed government regulation was needed, however, to insure that these potential economic advantages were realized by consumers. Attention in this chapter is focused on early methods of public control and on the development of commission regulation, as well as relations between federal and state commissions, and between commissions and the three branches of government.

*Joseph B. Eastman, "The Place of the Independent Commission," 12 *Constitutional Review* 95, 97 (1928).

[1] Martin G. Glaeser, *Outlines of Public Utility Economics* (New York: The Macmillan Co., 1931), p. 204. The resolution contained one provision: "that said companies do not obstruct the public thoroughfares." *Ibid.*

[2] Burton N. Behling, *Competition and Monopoly in Public Utility Industries* (Urbana: The University of Illinois Press, 1938), p. 19.

[3] *Ibid.*, p. 23.

PRE-COMMISSION METHODS OF REGULATION

Three early methods of government regulation were: (1) by the terms of decisions handed down by courts at common law; (2) by the terms of charters granted by state legislatures; and (3) by the terms of franchises issued by local governments. These methods frequently overlapped, but they are treated separately for discussion purposes.

Judicial Regulation

Present-day regulation is based upon statutes and ordinances enacted by local, state, or federal governments' legislative bodies. As previously noted, however, statutory law was preceded by the common law—the nonlegislative body of principles built up by court decisions. The common law was developed in England during and following the last part of the Middle Ages, and resulted from decisions handed down by the courts in cases brought by private litigants.

There were no preventive features in the common law. Any person who thought himself injured could sue. As conditions changed and new problems arose, many different issues were brought before the courts. Each decision, therefore, either built upon an old precedent or created a new precedent. The common law thus developed from case to case, from one individual lawsuit to another. One major principle of the common law unfolded: monopoly and restraints of trade were held to be contrary to the public interest. Damages might even be awarded in case of injury. The modern parallel is our antitrust laws.

At the same time, the common law recognized certain occupations as "common callings." In these occupations, the general right of refusal to sell was denied. Instead, the common law imposed on such callings the duty of serving all customers, at reasonable prices and without discrimination. The modern parallel here is public regulation of the industries under consideration in this book.

As a method of regulation, the common law had many limitations. Litigation was (and still is) expensive. An individual might not have known that he had been injured, and even when he did, he might have lacked the funds necessary to sue. Not being provided with staffs of trained accountants, economists, engineers, and rate experts, the courts lacked special competence to deal with the issues brought before them, especially those involving intricate industry problems. Expertise was required for effective regulation. Further, even when the courts found a business practice unreasonable, only negative action could be taken. The problem of deciding on new rates and regulation for a future period is a legislative, not a judicial, function. The courts, therefore, could only decide the cases brought before them; they could not take the initiative. And the court system was not able to handle the required volume of cases which arose from regulatory adjudication. Under such limitations, regulation was discontinuous, expensive, and often slow.

Direct Legislative Regulation

Prior to the enactment of general incorporation laws, public utilities were incorporated through the passage of special legislative acts. These charters contained both the usual corporate rights and a number of special privileges, such as the power of eminent domain. Their regulatory provisions varied considerably, but frequently prescribed only maximum rates and/or limited the yield on common stock to stated percentages. In 1886, to illustrate, the New York legislature passed a law to incorporate the New York Mutual Gas Light Company which provided that:

> Whenever the profits which shall be earned by said company, after deducting all expenses and necessary outlays for labor and materials used in carrying on and extending the business of said company shall exceed in any one year the sum of ten per cent upon the whole capital stock of said company, then, and in that event, the excess over the said sum of ten per cent shall be divided, one half of such excess between the consumers of the gas furnished by said company pro rata according to the amount consumed by them respectively, and the other half shall be paid as dividend to such owners and holders of the stock of said company as may be consumers of the gas furnished by said company; provided that no individual owner or holder of said stock shall be entitled to, or shall receive, nor shall there be paid to him, such dividend upon more than fifty shares of said stock.[4]

Toward the end of the nineteenth century, the states started to enact general incorporation laws. The regulatory provisions in these laws were equally ineffective, since they continued to be written in broad, general terms.

Direct legislative regulation of this sort was, above all else, inflexible. Economic conditions were constantly changing as modern technology was developed. Adjustments were required if regulation was to be up-to-date. Each adjustment, however, necessitated an amendment of the law. But legislatures were in session only a small percentage of the time and found their attention being claimed by many other matters. Under such circumstances, continuous regulation was impossible.[5] Little effort was expended to enforce regulatory provi-

---

[4] New York State Public Service Commission, "Utility Regulatory Bodies in New York State, 1855–1953" (Albany, N.Y., 1953), p. 13.

In 1907, West Virginia passed a law that fixed passenger fares on railroads at two cents per mile. The North Dakota legislature passed a law that required daily operation of at least one passenger train and one freight train on every line within the state. See Clair Wilcox, *Public Policies Toward Business* (3d ed.; Homewood, Ill.: Richard D. Irwin, Inc., 1966), p. 20.

[5] As Welch has noted: "It has been stated that the U.S. Supreme Court, when it decided Smyth v Ames (1898) . . . , sounded the death knell of the earlier efforts of the legislature to regulate utilities directly by statute. It did this by setting up such an exacting set of standards . . . for determining the reasonableness of utility rates, that it became apparent that regulation was a full-time job. . . . [A]s a result of Smyth v Ames state regulatory commissions, meaning specifically organized boards, with powers over

sions contained in charters, and in the absence of effective accounting and financial control, rate regulation was inadequate. And just as the courts lacked specialized knowledge of regulatory problems, so did the members of state legislatures. In practice, therefore, noneconomic considerations would often dictate the type of regulation followed. It should also be stressed that the proper function of a legislative body is to enact and formulate policy and not to engage in administrative work. For all of these reasons, direct statutory regulation proved to be a poor method of controlling an industry.

Local Franchise Regulation

Some local (municipal) control was exercised by the enactment of city ordinances, but particularly did local regulation rely on the franchise.[6] In order to enter a field, certain businesses had to acquire a franchise from the relevant city council before they could commence operations. When well drawn, the franchise set exact standards for service to be rendered, rates to be charged or methods of arriving at the rates, accounting methods to be employed, and in the case of term franchises, the method of renewing the franchise or provision for the locality's taking over the company at expiration of the franchise. Such agreements usually were to run for a definite period, although many franchises were granted in perpetuity.

While use of the well-drawn franchise had some merit, in the main the franchise as actually used proved a defective instrument for detailed regulation. When franchises were issued indiscriminately, little regard was paid to the interest of the public. When they were issued in perpetuity, franchises were often exclusive. In either case, they tended to be poorly drafted due to the inexperience of city councilmen.[7] And even when they were well drawn, the company often benefited, since it was common for the utility's lawyers to draft the franchise and then present it to the city council for approval.

Changes in the prescribed rates or in the service standards were made with great difficulty. This difficulty was due to a Supreme Court decision which held that a franchise had the status of a contract which a state could not impair,[8] thus both parties had to approve a change. As expected, the companies resisted

---

specified utility operations, became a virtual necessity." Francis X. Welch, *Cases and Text on Public Utility Regulation* (rev. ed.; Washington, D.C.: Public Utilities Reports, Inc., 1968), p. 577.

[6] For a more complete analysis of franchise regulation, see Delos F. Wilcox, *Municipal Franchises* (Rochester, N.Y.: The Gervaise Press, 1910), Vol. I; Leonora Arent, *Electric Franchises in New York City* (New York: Columbia University Press, 1919); and Herman H. Trachsel, *Public Utility Regulation* (Homewood, Ill.: Richard D. Irwin, Inc., 1950), chaps. iv and v.

[7] "The city of Dayton, Ohio, once contracted with a corporation for the 'disposal of *all* garbage.' In carrying out the provisions of the contract it developed that the city could not require all the people to give their garbage to the collectors, and the company collected many thousands of dollars in damage. Nevertheless, a few years later a new group of officials, unfamiliar with conditions, were willing to incorporate the same provisions in a new contract." Trachsel, *op. cit.*, p. 78.

[8] *Trustees of Dartmouth College* v. *Woodward*, 4 Wheaton 518, 643 (1819).

downward rate changes and the city councilmen upward adjustments. Nor was it easy to change the prescribed service standards, especially when the companies were asked to raise the standards at the same level of rates. In the case of a franchise issued for a definite period of time, another problem arose. Service often became poor as the termination date on the franchise drew near. The company would try to keep its investment as small as possible to avoid loss if the contract were not renewed. The agreements also failed to provide for administrative machinery to keep check on the company to see that it met the terms of its franchise. It was often possible, therefore, for the actual service rendered to fall for long periods of time below the level specified in the franchise.

It was often impossible, consequently, for franchise or charter provisions to be changed, "however ill-considered or antiquated with respect to current needs for regulation they might be."[9] Especially where exclusive franchises were issued, authorities "found themselves in the disagreeable situation of having bargained away their right to allow competition without having retained effective control over rates and service."[10] Thus, as with direct regulation, franchise regulation proved to be inflexible. Detailed requirements were unsatisfactory under changing conditions. New York City granted to a subway corporation a franchise that provided for a five-cent fare, and in Georgia a franchise given a street railway company required it to run cars over its lines as often as once every thirty minutes, day and night. Such detailed requirements obstructed adjustments to changing consumer demands. Moreover, franchises were frequently sought by speculators to be sold to the highest bidder. Some cities, feeling that a franchise carried with it valuable rights, issued one only for a monetary consideration. Chicago, for instance, issued to its utilities franchises that required annual payments of 3 percent of their gross income.[11]

In addition, a more serious drawback to franchise regulation soon became apparent—the significant change in scope of operations. Whereas at first, each company usually serviced but one market area (community), technological developments gradually made it both feasible and advisable to have one company serve two or more towns. As this change took place, it became obvious that state regulation would have to succeed the earlier regulation obtained through the local franchise.

Many cities continue to issue franchises to regulated companies serving their areas. In a few instances, these franchises are a method of regulation. In Texas, incorporated cities control the rates and services of electric, gas, and telephone utilities within their boundaries, with the Railroad Commission exercising appellate jurisdiction over gas rates only. In Minnesota, Nebraska, and South Dakota, municipalities grant permits and set rates for electric and gas utilities. But in most cases, city franchises are limited in function, usually dealing

---

[9] Behling, *op. cit.*, p. 24. Following the Dartmouth College decision, clauses reserving the right to amend franchise or charter provisions were often inserted, but with limited results.

[10] *Ibid.*, p. 25.

[11] Many cities continue to charge annual fees for their franchises.

with the use of city streets. Economic regulation is carried out by the state commissions.

COMMISSION REGULATION

Each of the early methods of regulation proved ineffective. Court control was expensive, slow, and negative in character. Direct legislative control was inflexible, as well as slow. Local franchise control had the same defects. Each of these methods was incapable of adapting to the development of an industrialized and highly complex society—a development requiring expertise, flexible regulation, and continuity of policy.[12] Further, there were no clear lines of authority between state and local governments. "Owing often to the lack of clearness in the general laws, serious questions arose whether a city, in granting the special franchise, was authorized to impose conditions upon applicant companies in addition to those imposed by general statute."[13] Under these conditions, regulation failed to safeguard the interests of consumers, investors, and the companies involved. Gradually the demand for more stringent and continuous control arose, and the states responded by turning to regulatory commissions. These commissions, operating under general legislative statutes, are referred to as "independent" regulatory commissions (agencies).

The initial state commissions, generally those created prior to 1870, were largely fact-finding and advisory bodies, with jurisdiction limited to the railroads. Six states set up such commissions before the Civil War: Rhode Island in 1839, New Hampshire in 1844, Connecticut in 1853, New York and Vermont in 1855, and Maine in 1858. Ohio, in 1867, and Massachusetts, in 1869, followed right after the war. These commissions made recommendations to their state legislatures[14] and to railroad managements, appraised property taken by railroads under the right of eminent domain, and enforced railroad safety standards, but they had no control over rates. Thus, they had to rely heavily on publicity and public opinion to obtain enforcement of their orders.[15]

Shortly after the beginning of the Granger movement in the Midwest, the first commissions with mandatory powers were established. Between 1871 and 1874, Illinois, Iowa, Minnesota, and Wisconsin established commissions with power to set maximum rates, prevent discrimination, and forbid mergers of competing railroad lines. While the Granger laws, except in Illinois, were repealed by the end of the seventies, they established a pattern followed by other states. By 1887, when Congress created the Interstate Commerce Commission

---

[12] Peter Woll, *Administrative Law: The Informal Process* (Berkeley and Los Angeles: University of California Press, 1963), pp. 7–8.

[13] Glaeser, *op. cit.,* p. 204.

[14] As a result of a recommendation of the three commissioners, the New York Railroad Commission was abolished by the legislature in 1857.

[15] See L. D. White, "The Origin of Utility Commissions in Massachusetts," 29 *Journal of Political Economy* 177 (1921).

(partly patterned after the British Railway Commission of 1873) to regulate the nation's railroads, "twenty-five states had established commissions to assist the legislature in this work."[16]

Commission regulation of other industries was slower to develop, reflecting in part their later development. In 1859, an office of Inspector of Gas Meters was established by the New York legislature. In 1885, a Board of Gas Commissioners was created in Massachusetts; two years later, electric light companies were added to its jurisdiction. But most nontransportation industries were not subjected to commission regulation until the beginning of the twentieth century. Many abuses long went unrecognized. Despite evidence of ineffective control long before this time, local authorities were reluctant to give up their regulatory power. In the absence of public agitation, state legislatures were slow to act.

The public clamor for reform, however, became widespread early in the twentieth century as notorious abuses began to appear. In New York, Charles Evans Hughes was elected governor primarily because of his 1905 exposé of insurance scandals. Under his leadership, the legislature enacted the Public Service Commissions Law in May, 1907, creating two district commissions: the First District Commission with jurisdiction over rapid transit, railroad, gas and electric companies in New York City, and the Second District Commission with jurisdiction over the same industries in the remainder of the state.[17] Little more than a month later the Wisconsin legislature, largely on the urging of Governor Robert M. LaFollette, expanded the powers and duties of its existing Railroad Commission to cover such utilities as gas, light, power, and telephone companies. These powerful state commissions became the models, and gradually other states followed suit, either by establishing new commissions or by extending the powers and duties of existing commissions.

By 1920, more than two-thirds of the states had regulatory commissions.[18] Their jurisdictions and powers were often limited, as was clearly shown after the stock market crash of 1929 and the resulting financial scandals. Thereafter, state commissions were strengthened, their jurisdictions extended, and their powers increased. Today all 50 states plus the District of Columbia have commissions (Table 4–1) known as public utility or public service commissions, railroad commissions, corporation commissions, or commerce commissions. Five federal commissions also have been established with jurisdiction over the interstate activities of the industries under consideration.

[16] Glaeser, *op. cit.,* p. 234.

[17] The two district commissions were abolished in 1921 when the New York State Public Service Commission was established.

[18] The development of state regulatory commissions is discussed by: Glaeser, *op. cit.,* pp. 233–63; William E. Mosher and Finla G. Crawford, *Public Utility Regulation* (New York: Harper & Bros., 1933), pp. 14–26; Robert E. Cushman, *The Independent Regulatory Commissions* (New York: Oxford University Press, 1941), pp. 19–41; Irston R. Barnes, *The Economics of Public Utility Regulation* (New York: F. S. Crofts & Co., Inc., 1942), pp. 173–75; and National Association of Regulatory Utility Commissioners, "Report of the Committee on Secretarial Offices" (Washington, D.C., 1963).

TABLE 4-1
Dates of Establishment of State Regulatory Commission Laws

State	Original	Present
Alabama	1881	1915
Alaska (PSC)	1960	1963
Alaska (TC)	1966	1966
Arizona	1911	1912
Arkansas (PSC)	1899	1935
Arkansas (CC)	1957	1957
California	1879	1912
Colorado	1907	1914
Connecticut	1853	1911
Delaware	1949	1949
District of Columbia	1913	1913
Florida	1887	1951
Georgia	1879	1922
Hawaii	1913	1913
Idaho	1913	1951
Illinois	1871	1921
Indiana	1913	1933
Iowa	1878	1963
Kansas	1911	1933
Kentucky (RR)	1880	1934
Kentucky (DMT)	1924	1934
Kentucky (PSC)	1934	1934
Louisiana	1898	1921
Maine	1858	1914
Maryland	1910	1910
Massachusetts	1869	1919
Michigan	1909	1919
Minnesota	1871	1911
Mississippi	1884	1938
Missouri	1875	1913
Montana	1907	1913
Nebraska	1906	1906
Nevada	1907	1919
New Hampshire	1844	1911
New Jersey	1911	1911
New Mexico (CC)	1912	1941
New Mexico (PSC)	1941	1941
New York	1907	1921
North Carolina	1891	1949
North Dakota	1889	1919
Ohio	1911	1913
Oklahoma	1907	1907
Oregon	1907	1931
Pennsylvania	1907	1937
Rhode Island	1912	1939
South Carolina	1896	1922
South Dakota	1889	1897
Tennessee	1883	1919
Texas	1891	1891
Utah	1917	1941
Vermont	1886	1908
Virginia	1816	1902
Washington	1905	1949
West Virginia	1913	1915
Wisconsin	1874	1905
Wyoming	1915	1915

The State Regulatory Commissions [19]

The jurisdiction (sometimes limited) of the state commissions, including the District of Columbia, is shown in Table 4–2 and can be summarized as follows:

Motor buses	51	Contract carrier trucks	45
Telephone	50	Water carriers	30
Common carrier trucks	49	Gas pipelines	29
Railroads	49	Oil pipelines	27
Gas utilities	48	Electric cooperatives	21
Electric utilities	47	Air transport	20
Telegraph	47	Municipal: electric and gas	10

Fifty of the regulatory commissions have jurisdiction over one or more additional businesses, including express and livery companies, sightseeing vehicles, pullman companies, toll bridges and roads, and warehouses. Moreover, in states where one or more of the regulated industries are not subject to commission control, the statutes frequently provide other means of insuring service at a reasonable rate. The most common of these methods, as noted earlier, is local regulation.

State commissions vary somewhat in regulatory powers. A majority have authority to issue licenses, franchises, or permits for the initiation of service, for construction or abandonment of facilities, and related matters. With respect to rates, commissions generally have power to require prior authorization of rate changes, to suspend proposed rate changes, to prescribe interim rates, and to initiate rate investigations. Most commissions have authority to control the quantity and quality of service, to prescribe uniform systems of accounts, and to require annual reports. Over three-fourths of the commissions are authorized to regulate the issuance of securities.

Personnel. The majority of the states have three- or five-member commissions, but three agencies (Kentucky DMT, Oregon, and Rhode Island) are composed of one commissioner, and two states (Massachusetts and South Carolina) have seven-member commissions (Table 4–3). Commissioners are appointed (thirty-eight agencies) or elected either by popular vote (sixteen agencies) or by the legislature (two agencies). The most common legal qualifications are that commissioners must be qualified electors, citizens, and residents without financial interests in the industries regulated. Other more specific requirements vary widely. For example, seventeen states have a minimum age requirement (ranging from twenty-one in Rhode Island to thirty-five in Oklahoma); three states (Alabama, New Hampshire, and Oregon) require "competent persons;" one state

[19] Unless otherwise noted, the data in this section come from three sources: Subcommittee on Intergovernmental Relations, Senate Committee on Government Operations, *State Utility Commissions* (Committee Print, 1967); Federal Power Commission, "Federal and State Commission Jurisdiction and Regulation, Electric, Gas and Telephone Utilities, 1967" (Washington, D.C.: U.S. Government Printing Office, 1968); and a questionnaire by the author to the state commissions.

TABLE 4-2

Jurisdiction of State Regulatory Commissions, 1968

Commission						Industries Regulated[1]											
	E	G	SH	W	M	ECO	A	B	C	GPL	OPL	SR	RR	T	WC	TT	O
Alabama Public Service Commission	E	G	SH	W[2]			A	B	C		OPL	SR	RR	T	WC	TT	O[3]
Alaska Public Service Commission	E	G	SH	W		ECO										TT	O[4]
Alaska Transportation Commission							A	B	C								
Arizona Corporation Commission	E	G	SH	W		ECO	A	B	C				RR	T		TT	O[5]
Arkansas Commerce Commission							A	B	C	GPL	OPL	SR	RR	T	WC		O[6]
Arkansas Public Service Commission	E	G	SH	W		ECO		B		GPL	OPL	SR				TT	
California Public Utilities Commission	E	G	SH	W		ECO	A[7]	B	C	GPL	OPL	SR	RR		WC	TT	O[8]
Colorado Public Utilities Commission	E	G	SH	W	M[9]	ECO	A	B	C	GPL	OPL	SR	RR	T	WC	TT	O[10]
Connecticut Public Utilities Commission	E	G		W				B	C		OPL	SR	RR	T		TT	O[11]
Delaware Public Service Commission	E	G		W		ECO		B				SR	RR	T		TT	O[12]
District of Columbia Public Service Comm.	E	G						B	C			SR		T		TT	O[13]
Florida Public Service Commission	E	G		W[2]				B	C				RR	T	WC	TT	O[14]
Georgia Public Service Commission	E	G		W				B	C			SR	RR			TT	O[15]
Hawaii Public Utilities Commission	E	G		W			A	B	C				RR[16]	T	WC	TT	O[17]
Idaho Public Utilities Commission	E	G		W				B	C	GPL	OPL	SR	RR		WC	TT	O[18]
Illinois Commerce Commission	E	G	SH	W			A	B	C	GPL	OPL	SR	RR		WC	TT	O[19]
Indiana Public Service Commission	E	G	SH	W	M	ECO		B	C			SR	RR			TT	O[20]
Iowa State Commerce Commission	E	G	SH	W				B[9]	C	GPL[2]	OPL		RR			TT	O[17]
Kansas State Corporation Commission	E	G	SH	W		ECO		B	C	GPL	OPL	SR	RR	T		TT	O[21]
Kentucky Dept. of Motor Transportation								B			OPL			T			
Kentucky Public Service Commission	E	G	SH	W		ECO		B		GPL	OPL	SR				TT	
Kentucky Railroad Commission													RR		WC		O[22]
Louisiana Public Service Commission	E	G	SH	W	M	ECO		B	C	GPL	OPL	SR	RR		WC	TT	O[23]
Maine Public Utilities Commission	E	G	SH	W	M	ECO		B	C	GPL		SR	RR	T	WC	TT	O[24]
Maryland Public Service Commission	E	G	SH	W	M		A	B	C[25]			SR	RR	T	WC	TT	O[26]
Massachusetts Dept. of Public Utilities	E	G		W			A[16]	B	C			SR	RR	T	WC	TT	O[27]
Michigan Public Service Commission	E	G	SH	W		ECO	A[16]	B	C[28]		OPL		RR	T	WC	TT[29]	O[30]
Minnesota R.R. and Warehouse Commission	E	G		W				B	C			SR	RR			TT[29]	O[31]

Footnotes on pp. 94–95.

TABLE 4-2—Continued

	Industries Regulated[1]																
Commission	E	G	SH	W	M	ECO	A	B	C	GPL	OPL	SR	RR	T	WC	TT	O
Mississippi Public Service Commission	E	G		W				B	C	GPL			RR			TT	O[32]
Missouri Public Service Commission	E	G	SH	W				B[2]	C	GPL		SR	RR			TT	O[33]
Montana Board of Railroad Commissioners[34]	E	G	SH	W	M			B	C	GPL	OPL	SR	RR	T	WC	TT	O[35]
Nebraska State Railway Commission				W			A	B	C		OPL	SR	RR	T	WC	TT	O[36]
Nevada Public Service Commission[37]	E	G		W		ECO	A	B	C	GPL	OPL	SR	RR	T	WC	TT	O[38]
New Hampshire Public Utilities Commission	E	G	SH	W	M[9]	ECO		B	C		OPL	SR	RR		WC	TT	O[39]
New Jersey Bd. of Public Utilities Commissioners	E	G	SH	W	M[9]	ECO		B		GPL	OPL	SR	RR		WC	TT	O[40]
New Mexico Public Service Commission	E	G	SH	W	M[41]	ECO		B		GPL			RR			TT	O[42]
New Mexico State Corporation Commission							A					SR	RR	T			
New York State Public Service Commission[43]	E	G	SH	W[2]	M			B	C	GPL	OPL	SR	RR		WC[44]	TT	O[45]
North Carolina Utilities Commission	E	G		W				B	C	GPL		SR	RR		WC	TT	O[46]
North Dakota Public Service Commission	E	G	SH	W				B	C	GPL	OPL	SR[9]	RR	T[9]	WC	TT	O[47]
Ohio Public Utilities Commission	E	G	SH	W				B	C	GPL	OPL	SR	RR		WC	TT[29]	O[48]
Oklahoma Corporation Commission	E	G		W				B	C	GPL	OPL	SR	RR	T[2]		TT	O[49]
Oregon Public Utility Commissioner	E	G	SH	W				B	C			SR	RR	T		TT	O[50]
Pennsylvania Public Utility Commission	E	G	SH	W	M[9]		A	B	C	GPL	OPL	SR	RR	T	WC	TT	O[51]
Rhode Island Division of Public Utilities	E	G	SH	W	M		A	B	C		OPL	SR	RR	T	WC	TT	O[52]
South Carolina Public Service Commission	E	G		W				B	C			SR	RR	T		TT	O[17]
South Dakota Public Utilities Commission								B					RR				O[53]
Tennessee Public Service Commission	E	G		W				B	C[28]	GPL	OPL		RR	T		TT	O[54]
Texas Railroad Commission								B	C	GPL	OPL		RR			TT	
Utah Public Service Commission[55]	E	G	SH	W		ECO		B	C			SR	RR	T[9]	WC	TT	O[56]
Vermont Public Service Board	E	G		W				B	C[28]			SR	RR		WC	TT	O[57]
Virginia State Corporation Commission	E	G		W	M	ECO	A	B	C	GPL		SR	RR		WC	TT	O[58]
Washington Util. and Trans. Commission	E	G		W			A	B	C		OPL	SR	RR		WC	TT	O[59]
West Virginia Public Service Commission	E	G		W	M	ECO	A	B	C	GPL	OPL	SR	RR	T	WC	TT	O[60]
Wisconsin Public Service Commission	E	G	SH	W	M	ECO[2]		B	C	GPL		SR	RR	T[9]	WC	TT	O[61]
Wyoming Public Service Commission	E	G	SH	W	M[9]	ECO	A	B	C	GPL	OPL	SR	RR	T[9]	WC	TT	O[22]
Total	47	48	27	46	16	21	20	51	49	29	27	39	49	27	30	50	50

Footnotes on pp. 94–95.

TABLE 4-2—Continued

1 E = Electric. G = Gas. SH = Steam Heating. W = Water. M = Municipal Electric and Gas Plants. ECO = Electric Cooperatives. A = Air Transport. B = Motor Buses. C = Common and Contract Trucks. GPL = Gas Pipelines. OPL = Petroleum Pipelines. SR = Street Railways. RR = Railroads. T = Taxicabs. WC = Water Carriers. TT = Telephone and Telegraph. O = Other.

2 Jurisdiction limited.

3 Express and sleeping car companies; toll bridges, ferries, and roads.

4 Sewage systems.

5 Warehouses for cotton and wool; security laws; certificates of incorporation and licenses to domestic and foreign corporations.

6 Warehouses; tax equalization.

7 Rates only.

8 Warehousemen; wharfingers; private toll bridges; express companies; freight forwarders; car loaning, loading, renting, or other car corporation or person; radio (telephone).

9 No jurisdiction within municipal limits.

10 Mobile radio (telephone).

11 Express and livery companies; CATV systems.

12 Express companies; trolley coaches.

13 Sightseeing vehicles; security dealers and salesmen.

14 Express and sleeping car companies; tolls on public canals; toll bridges; ferries; auto transportation brokerage; sewage systems; radio common carriers.

15 Electric railway; express and terminal companies; docks and wharves.

16 Securities only.

17 Warehouses.

18 Public wharves and warehouses.

19 Warehouses; docks and wharves; sewage systems.

20 Rural private sewage disposal plants.

21 Gas and oil conservation; blue-sky laws; municipal flood control and drainage projects.

22 Express companies.

23 Toll roads and bridges; express and pullman companies; canals (except irrigation canals); sewage systems.

24 Warehouses; docks and wharves; pullman companies.

25 Common carriers and tank carriers of flammable or combustible liquids for compensation.

26 Toll bridges and sewage systems.

27 Blue-sky laws.

28 Common carriers only.

29 Telephone only.

30 Docks, wharves, and bridge companies.

31 Warehouses; grain inspection; weights and measures; livestock weighing and buying.

32 Express and sleeping car companies.

33 Express companies; sewage systems.

34 Ex officio Public Service Commission.

35 Express companies; coal slurry pipelines; VHF booster and translator television systems.

36 Toll roads and bridges; warehouses; irrigation companies; express and pullman companies; sale of liquid fuel.

37 Ex officio tax commissioner.

38 Sewage systems; express companies; coal slurry pipelines; CATV systems.

39 Toll roads and bridges.

40 Sewage systems; express companies; subways; canals.

41 Electric plants only if municipality elects to come under commission jurisdiction.

42 Express and sleeping car companies; insurance rates; cotton gin rates.

43 Also New York State Department of Public Service.

44 Water carriers if they participate in joint rates with railroads in through movements by both rail and water.

45 Express companies, car companies, sleeping car companies, freight companies, baggage and transfer companies, and other common carriers as defined by statute; grade crossing elimination, protection, and reconstruction.

TABLE 4-2 — *Concluded*

46 Grain elevators; express and brokers; private sewage companies.
47 Warehouses and stockyard companies.
48 Toll rates of causeway at Cedarpoint, Ohio; bridge and sewage companies.
49 Cotton gins; gas and oil conservation.
50 Docks; wharves; canals; sewage systems; streetcars; ferries; turnpike tunnels and bridges; mobile radio; grade crossing elimination, protection, and reconstruction.
51 Real estate; insurance; banking; securities; upholstery; liquor control; express companies; tow trucks.
52 Sewage systems; common carrier radio.
53 Private sewage systems; express, car loading, and pullman companies.
54 Gas and oil conservation.

55 Also Business, Securities and Trade Commission.
56 Sewage systems; culinary water companies; warehousemen.
57 Ferries; store reservoirs; express companies.
58 Sewage systems; express, car loading, and pullman companies; banking and insurance; blue-sky laws; certificates of incorporation and licenses to domestic and foreign corporations.
59 Warehouses; docks and wharves; toll bridges; sleeping car companies; express companies; freight brokers; freight forwarders; garbage and refuse collection; port districts.
60 Toll bridges; sewage systems; coal slurry pipelines; ferries; express companies; public dams.
61 Docks and wharves partially; sewage systems partially; toll roads and bridges; water reservoir companies; regulation of navigable waters.

(Arizona) requires "maturity;" and in one state (Massachusetts) the law states that one of the seven members "shall be a woman." Only five states have specific educational and professional requirements.[20]

Most commissioners have had professional training and practice or business background. However, only a few have had previous experience with a regulatory commission prior to their appointment or election. Their understanding of the complex legal, economic, accounting, and engineering problems confronting them as commissioners increases with their tenure of service. The terms fixed by law run from two years to indefinite appointments, with six-year terms being the most frequent. While some commissioners are reappointed or reelected, most of them serve a single term or less. Moreover, commissioners are sometimes appointed because of political considerations rather than because of their qualifications for the job. Removal from office, while rare (only six known removals since 1933), is provided for in many of the legislative statutes. Generally, removal may be made by executive order or by impeachment for "just cause." The most common reasons for such action are neglect of duty, misconduct in office, incompetence, and malfeasance.

State commission staffs, varying in size from three (Kentucky RC) to 795 (California), totaled 5,989 full-time and 65 part-time employees at the end of 1967. About half of the commissions had two or fewer attorneys; three or fewer engineers; three or fewer accountants; and two or fewer rate analysts. Four commissions had no engineers; six had no rate analysts; seven had no accountants; eight had no full-time attorneys; and twenty-six had no security analysts. Only five commissions had economists on their staffs. Except for the larger commissions, therefore, many feel that both the size and composition of the professional staffs are inadequate to undertake an extensive regulatory program.[21] In an effort to maintain highly skilled staffs, the National Association of Regulatory Utility Commissioners (an association of state and federal regulatory personnel) has established for its members an annual regulatory development course which covers regulatory principles and their applications.

Financial Matters. In 1967, fifteen states paid commissioners $20,000 or over, compared with only four states in 1961. The 1967 median salary was nearly $16,000. Staff salaries varied widely, but a majority paid professional personnel under $11,000 a year. These salaries often make it difficult for the commissions, as well as other governmental agencies, to attract and retain

---

[20] In the words of Chairman Lundy of the New York commission: "The task of the utility regulator is one which requires the wisdom of Solomon, the patience of Job, the determination of a bulldog and the hide of a rhinoceros" (National Association of Regulatory Utility Commissioners, *Annual Proceedings, 1966* [Washington, D.C., 1967], p. 14).

[21] In many states the commissions can obtain assistance from the state attorney general and his staff, as well as employ experts in utility regulatory matters when needed or request assistance from federal commissions. But such part-time assistance, compared with a full-time staff, makes it more difficult to develop a comprehensive program.

TABLE 4-3
State Regulatory Commissions and Selected Statistics, 1967

State	Number of Commissioners	Term, Years	Method of Selection[a]	Yearly Salary Chairman	Yearly Salary Commissioners	No. of Staff Members Full-Time	No. of Staff Members Part-Time	Commission Expenditures, 1967[b]
Alabama	3	4	DE	$18,500	$18,000	25	0	$ 350,000*
Alaska PSC	3	6	G-L	(c)	(c)	9	0	87,855*
Alaska TC	2	4,6	G-L	18,000	17,500	10	2	219,300*
Arizona	3	6	DE	13,000	13,000	100	0	774,096*
Arkansas CC	3	2,4,6	G	15,000	15,000	20	0	74,500*
Arkansas PSC	3	6	G-S	15,000	15,000	24	0	227,614
California	5	6	G-S	25,500	25,000	795	0	10,073,629*
Colorado	3	6	G	18,000	18,000	57	0	570,470*
Connecticut	3	6	G-L	24,340	20,240	44	0	435,766*
Delaware	3	6	G-S	4,500d	4,500d	6	2	78,000*
District of Columbia	3	3	P-S	25,900	25,900	29	0	333,814*
Florida	3	4	DE	18,500	18,500	161	0	3,105,548*
Georgia	5	6	DE	22,500	22,500	42	0	512,114*
Hawaii	5	4	G-S	(e)	(e)	27	0	320,301*
Idaho	3	6	G-S	14,500	14,500	17	0	238,631*
Illinois	5	5	G-S	25,000	23,000	250	0	1,982,828*
Indiana	3	4	G	22,000	22,000	48	3	414,570*
Iowa	3	6	G-S	13,000	13,000	97	0	997,750*
Kansas	3	4	G-S	14,000	13,500	143	13	1,386,240*
Kentucky DMT	1	ind.	G	20,000	. . . .	135	0	1,102,819*
Kentucky PSC	3	4	G	10,000d	10,000d	32	4	382,910*
Kentucky RC	3	4	DE	3,600d	3,000d	1	2	28,997*
Louisiana	3	6	DE	12,500	12,500	30	0	335,325*
Maine	3	7	G-C	13,000	12,000	42	0	409,165*
Maryland	3	6	G	9,000d	8,000d	52	0	525,600*
Massachusetts	7	7	G-C	15,000	11,500	118	2	1,028,945*
Michigan	3	6	G-S	19,000	18,000	97	0	1,322,471*
Minnesota	3	6	DE	17,000	17,000	339	0	4,093,375*

Footnotes on p. 99.

TABLE 4-3—Continued

State	Number of Commissioners	Term, Years	Method of Selection[a]	Yearly Salary		No. of Staff Members		Commission Expenditures, 1967[b]
				Chairman	Commissioners	Full-Time	Part-Time	
Mississippi	3	4	DE	$15,000	$15,000	45	0	$ 550,000*
Missouri	5	6	G-S	20,000	20,000	49	0	933,942*
Montana	3	6	DE	10,000	10,000	16	0	210,000*
Nebraska	5	6	DE	10,000	10,000	48	5	528,739*
Nevada	3	4	G	16,000	14,400	23	0	283,000*
New Hampshire	3	6	G-C	12,480[f]	11,960[f]	20	0	194,685*
New Jersey	3	6	G-S	22,000	18,000	113	3	968,354*
New Mexico PSC	3	6	G-S	12,500	12,500	9	1	196,500*
New Mexico SCC	3	6	DE	12,000	12,000	85	0	907,746*
New York	5[g]	10	G-S	32,265	29,160	623	0	6,086,429*[h]
North Carolina	5	8	G	21,000	20,000	56	0	633,991*
North Dakota	3	6	DE	11,000	11,000	28	0	271,338
Ohio	3	6	G	16,000	16,000	124	0	1,434,413*
Oklahoma	3	6	DE	12,000	12,000[i]	204	0	1,344,922*
Oregon	1	4	G	18,640	. . .	188	0	1,967,116*
Pennsylvania	5	10	G	20,000	19,000	351	0	2,870,108*
Rhode Island	1	ind.	G	12,000	. . .	14	0	156,161*
South Carolina	7	4	L	15,500	15,000	54	1	612,041*
South Dakota	3	6	DE	10,800	10,800	19	0	202,218*
Tennessee	3	6	DE	17,500	17,500	15	1	513,706*
Texas	3	6	DE	22,500	22,500	426	18	3,117,497*
Utah	3	6	G-S	11,000	10,000	17	3	221,512*
Vermont	3	6	G-S	16,500	3,500[j]	13	0	223,843*
Virginia	3	6	L	22,000	21,400	300	0	5,188,000*
Washington	3	6	G	20,000	14,500[k]	139	0	1,520,822*
West Virginia	3	6	G	16,000	16,000	100	0	600,000*
Wisconsin	3	6	G-S	18,500	15,000[l]	120	5	1,349,585*
Wyoming	3	6[m]	G-S	13,000	12,500	40	0	242,928
Total 1967 Expenditures								$64,742,229

TABLE 4-3–*Concluded*

[a] DE = Direct Election. G = Governor. G-C = Governor with approval of the Council. G-L = Governor with approval of the Legislature. G-S = Governor with approval of the Senate. L = Legislature. P-S = President with approval of the Senate.

[b] Figures marked with asterisk represent fiscal year (1966–67). All others represent calendar year (1967).

[c] Part-time; $35 per day.

[d] Part-time.

[e] Part-time; $10 per day; maximum $1,000 per annum.

[f] $312 yearly increment; maximum for chairman, $14,040; maximum for other commissioners, $13,208.

[g] May be increased by two additional commissioners on certification to the governor and legislature that they are required by the work load.

[h] Does not include expenditures for capital construction activities (such as highway and railroad crossing safety program).

[i] One commissioner receives $15,000.

[j] Two commissioners are part-time.

[k] One commissioner receives $17,500.

[l] One commissioner receives $16,500.

[m] Two commissioners appointed for six years; one commissioner for four years.

trained people. As a result, the annual turnover in commission staffs is relatively high, as better paying jobs with more promising futures open up.

All regulated companies, and hence their customers, pay their own expenses of regulation. Since 1930, commission funds also have come increasingly from fees and charges imposed on the companies under their jurisdiction. Forty-one commissions receive a portion or all of their general funds in this manner; the remaining fifteen receive all of their general funds from legislative appropriations. The assessments to cover the annual costs of regulation usually take the form of a percentage tax on each company's gross revenues. Special assessments are usually made for specific types of investigations or cases.

Total expenditures of the state regulatory commissions (including the District of Columbia) were nearly $65 million in fiscal 1967. But of this amount, about three-fourths was spent by seventeen agencies, leaving an average of approximately $403,000 for each of the remaining thirty-nine commissions.[22] Limited financial resources, some maintain, inhibit effective state regulation.

Organization. State commissions are organized along functional lines, with separate departments for rates, engineering, accounting, financial and legal work; along industry lines, with separate departments for each type of industry regulated; or some combination of the two. Typical of a larger agency is the New York State Public Service Commission, whose organization is shown in Figure 4-1. In addition, a few commissions have an officer designated as the "public counselor."[23] It is the duty of this officer to appear in all hearings before the commission and the courts on behalf of the customers of the company under investigation.

Duties and Responsibilities. The range and complexity of issues that come before the regulatory commissions are vast. The duties and responsibilities of a commissioner were outlined by a member of the Massachusetts commission as follows:

> . . . to be familiar with the history of regulation; to understand the meaning of objectivity in the light of the dual capacity of a public utility commissioner as a party and as judge, and to cultivate in his own judgments this quality; to become familiar with the fundamental characteristics of the industries over which he exercises control; to exercise a wide discretion over the procedures followed before the commission, having in mind the basic guides of fairness to the parties and uniformity of application; and, FINALLY, to cultivate a public awareness of the limitations of regulatory control over the basic economic conditions which give rise to increasing rates in some industries and diminishing services in others.[24]

---

[22] Table 4-3 overstates the annual expenditures related to the regulated industries, since the figures represent total commission expenditures. Some commissions (see Table 4-2) have jurisdiction over other industries. To illustrate: Expenses related solely to the regulation of the industries under discussion totaled $539,112 for the Minnesota commission and $326,000 for the Texas commission in fiscal 1967.

[23] The state of Maryland has a special counsel for public utility matters that is established outside of the Public Service Commission.

[24] David M. Brackman, quoted in 66 *Public Utilities Fortnightly* 981 (1960).

These duties impose a time-consuming task on regulatory commissions. Further, all the commissions have found their work loads increasing rapidly in the past few years. The New York State Public Service Commission reported that in 1967, 849 new proceedings were instituted, 602 days of hearings were held (involving 38,270 pages of testimony and hundreds of exhibits), 408 formal

FIGURE 4-1
Organization Chart of New York State Public Service Commission

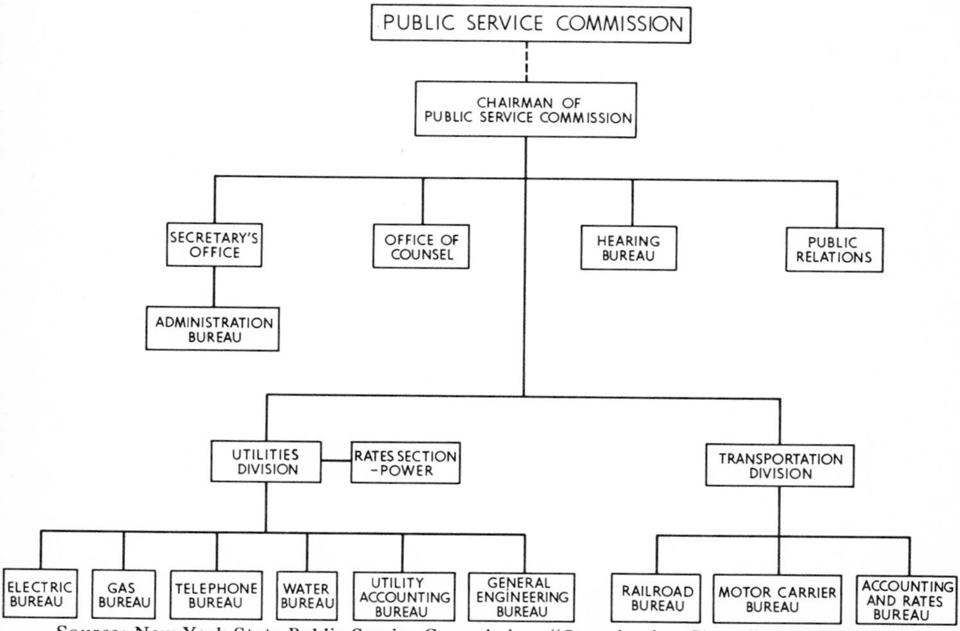

Source: New York State Public Service Commission, "Organization Charts" (1968), Chart I.

cases were determined without the necessity of public hearings, and 2,049 orders were adopted.[25] These covered such diverse subjects as rates, capitalization, grade crossings, certificates of convenience and necessity, construction of electric generating facilities, accounts and records, and maintenance of service. In addition, 11,585 informal complaints were received from individual customers.[26] The variety of New York's work load is not unique, but typical of most other state commissions.

The Federal Regulatory Commissions

There are five federal commissions with jurisdiction over interstate activi-

---

[25] New York State Public Service Commission, *Annual Report, 1967* (Albany, N.Y., 1968), pp. 117–20.
[26] *Ibid.*, pp. 121–22.

ties of the regulated industries. These commissions are organized to handle particular functional groups (Table 4–4).

The *Interstate Commerce Commission,* oldest and largest of the federal agencies, was established in 1887 to regulate the railroads. In addition to the railroads, the ICC's authority has been expanded to oil pipelines (1906), motor carriers (1935), and water carriers (1940). The commission's jurisdiction over interstate telephone and telegraph services, granted in 1910, was transferred in 1934 to the Federal Communications Commission.

The *Federal Power Commission,* first set up in 1920 with three cabinet officers to regulate power projects on navigable rivers, was reorganized in 1930 with five full-time commissioners. Besides its original duties, jurisdiction of the agency has been broadened twice. In 1935, Congress gave it authority to regulate the transmission and sale at wholesale of electric energy in interstate commerce. In 1938, the FPC was given jurisdiction over the transmission and sale for resale of natural gas in interstate commerce under the Natural Gas Act.

The *Securities and Exchange Commission* was organized in 1934 to administer the Securities Act of 1933 and the Securities Exchange Act of 1934. The commission regulates the conditions of sale of new securities, and some of the practices of the stock exchanges. In 1935, the SEC was given power, under the Public Utility Holding Company Act of that year, to regulate the finances and corporate structures of electric and gas utility holding companies.

The *Federal Communications Commission,* established in 1934, succeeded the Federal Radio Commission of 1927, which regulated radio and television broadcasting. From the ICC, the FCC took over regulation of interstate and foreign telephone and telegraph services in 1934.

The *Civil Aeronautics Board,* created in 1938, has economic control of commercial air transportation. The Federal Aviation Agency (formerly the Civil Aeronautics Administration and now the Federal Aviation Administration), created in 1958, was transferred to the Department of Transportation in 1967. The Administration has responsibility for development of the physical facilities for air transportation and for safety regulation.[27]

Duties, Finances, Organization, and Personnel. Federal regulatory agencies are bipartisan by law, and members must be citizens with no financial interest in

---

[27] Six other federal regulatory commissions should be noted. (1) The *Board of Governors of the Federal Reserve System* was established in 1913 to control credit. (2) The *Federal Trade Commission* was created in 1914 to enforce part of the antitrust laws. (3) The *National Labor Relations Board,* established in 1935 to administer the collective bargaining provisions of the Wagner Act, was retained to regulate labor relations under the Taft-Hartley Act of 1947. (4) The *Small Business Administration* was created in 1953 as part of the Department of Commerce, and given independent status in 1958, to promote small business, chiefly through loans. (5) The *Federal Home Loan Bank Board* was established in 1955 (succeeding a board in an executive agency) to control credit for home financing. (6) The *Federal Maritime Commission* was created in 1961 (succeeding the Federal Maritime Board) to control shipping in domestic and foreign offshore commerce. There are other federal commissions, such as the *Atomic Energy Commission* and the *United States Tariff Commission,* but their functions are primarily developmental or advisory.

TABLE 4-4

Selected Statistics for Federal Regulatory Agencies

Agency	Date Established	Number of Members	Term, Years	Number of Staff Members	Budget, Fiscal 1967 (Thousands of Dollars)	Jurisdiction
Interstate Commerce Commission	1887	11	7	1,929	$27,169	Railroads; motor carriers; shipping by coast-wise, intercoastal, and inland waters; oil pipe-lines; express companies; freight forwarders; sleeping-car companies
Federal Power Commission	1920, 1930	5	5	1,131	14,220	Electric power, natural gas and natural gas pipe-lines, water-power sites
Securities and Exchange Commission ...	1934	5	5	1,360	16,721	Securities and financial markets, electric and gas utility holding companies
Federal Communications Commission ..	1934	7	7	1,458	17,852	Radio, television, telephone, telegraph, cables
Civil Aeronautics Board	1938	5	6	770	11,312	Airlines

Source: *The Budget of the United States Government, Fiscal Year 1969, Appendix* (Washington, D.C.: U.S. Government Printing Office, 1968).

the industries they regulate. No other qualifications for commissioners have been established. Appointments are made by the President, with Senate approval, for terms ranging from five to seven years. Almost all commissioners have had a legal background. The salary of a federal commissioner is $38,000; for a chairman, $40,000. These salaries would appear adequate to attract and retain the caliber of men required. The tenure of members varies considerably among the commissions. For the ICC, where reappointment is common, commissioners have averaged nearly two terms (about thirteen years' service). For the FPC, commissioners have averaged just over one term. The turnover has been more rapid in the case of the three remaining federal agencies: commissioners have averaged 69 percent of a term for the FCC, 67 percent of a term for the SEC, and 43 percent of a term for the CAB.[28]

Congressional appropriations for the five federal commissions totaled just over $87 million in fiscal 1967. The ICC enjoys the largest staff—nearly 2,000; the FCC has a staff of over 1,400. In 1949, the Hoover Commission found these staff members to be well qualified and conscientious[29]—a finding that appears equally true today. The annual turnover rate, however, is high.

The organization of the federal commissions is similar to that of the state agencies. The organizational chart of the Interstate Commerce Commission is shown in Figure 4–2. The statutory duties of the federal commissions also are comparable to those of the state commissions. And, finally, the federal commissions are finding their work loads increasing. In fiscal 1966, for example, the ICC received 11,572 formal cases; 36 percent more than the 8,511 cases received in fiscal 1964.[30] Table 4–5 illustrates the diversity of the Civil Aeronautics Board's work load for fiscal 1967. The table (third column) also reflects another regulatory problem of major significance: the commissions have found it increasingly difficult to keep up with their greater work loads. This problem, considered in Chapter 18, contributes to "regulatory lag."

STATUS AND FUNCTIONS OF THE COMMISSIONS

At both the state and federal levels, the regulatory agencies occupy a unique position in the structure of American government. Their independent status and combined functions deserve brief discussion.

Independence of the Commissions

The regulatory agencies are often called "independent" commissions. That is, the commissions are in theory independent of the other branches of government. At the federal level and with certain exceptions at the state level as well,

28 Data, covering the period 1933–65, from David T. Stanley, Dean E. Mann, and Jameson W. Doig, *Men Who Govern: A Biographical Profile of Federal Political Executives* (Washington, D.C.: The Brookings Institution, 1967), chap. iv.
29 Commission on Organization of the Executive Branch of the Government, *Task Force Report on Regulatory Commissions* (Washington, D.C.: U.S. Government Printing Office, 1949), p. 23.
30 Interstate Commerce Commission, *Eightieth Annual Report* (1966), p. 6.

FIGURE 4-2

Organization Chart of the Interstate Commerce Commission

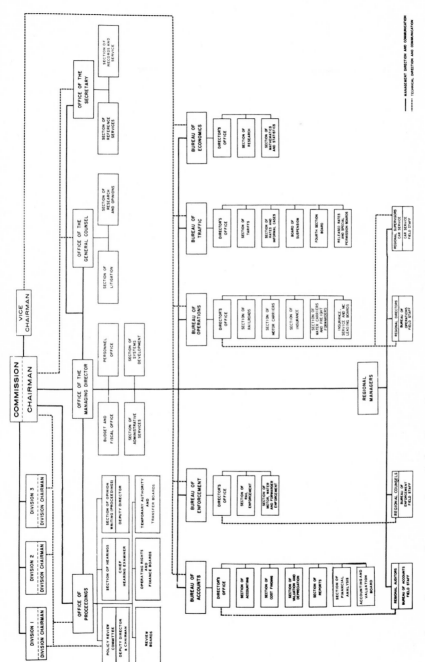

Source: Interstate Commerce Commission, *Eighty-First Annual Report* (1967), facing p. 98.

TABLE 4-5
Work Load Categories, Civil Aeronautics Board, Fiscal 1967*

Item	Received or Initiated	Decided or Otherwise Disposed of	On Hand at End of Fiscal Year
1. Regular route activities:			
a) Formal hearings	83	73	63
b) Informal matters	203	199	45
2. Cargo and charter licensing:			
a) Supplemental carrier matters	347	330	47
b) Airfreight forwarder matters	72	49	130
c) Individual flight authorization applications	908	894	39
3. Antitrust activities:			
a) Acquisitions of control	2,195	2,357	59
b) Agreements	1,048	1,041	178
4. Subsidy rates	45	56	27
5. Guaranteed loans: Aircraft purchase loan-guarantee applications and waivers	18	18	0
6. Commercial rates:			
a) Tariff filings (regular) pages screened	48,035	47,616	1,723
b) Special tariff permission applications	1,575	1,599	10
c) Tariff referrals and complaints for processing on the merits	956	956	41
d) Passenger and property rate investigations	14	19	6
e) Free transportation tariff applications	1,635	1,635	0
f) Service mail rates	14	10	13
g) Intercarrier rate agreements	1,027	861	190
h) Passenger and property rate exemption applications	208	225	13
7. Major international air agreement consultations and negotiations.................................	. . .	15	. . .
8. Passenger and shipper service complaints	3,036	2,561	917
9. Economic enforcement investigations	290	260	67
10. Economic enforcement legal activities	469	449	198
11. Regulation of carrier accounting and reporting systems (regulations, interpretations, waivers, etc.)	986	967	1,358
12. Policing and conformance of air carrier reports	2,136	2,063	341
13. Accounting and financial analysis	144	143	4
14. Field audit of air carriers	77	73	64
15. Statistical and cost-finding activities	563	553	78

*Table includes only the more significant categories.
· Source: Civil Aeronautics Board, *Reports to Congress* (1967), pp. 78-79.

four major factors make for independence. Appointments are for definite but staggered terms. No more than a majority of the commissioners may be from the same political party. "Although a president may not find it difficult to locate persons in the opposition party who share his points of view, this provision does insure a lack of partisan responsibility."[31] Removal of commissioners from office is limited. Statutes generally confine the executive's power of removal to "inefficiency, neglect of duty, or malfeasance in office."[32] Even where there are no statutory limitations on the executive's power of removal, legal barriers exist. Argued Justice Sutherland in the Humphrey's case:

> The authority of Congress, in creating quasi legislative or quasi judicial agencies, to require them to act in discharge of their duties independently of executive control cannot well be doubted; and that authority includes, as an appropriate incident, power to fix the period during which they shall continue, and to forbid their removal except for cause in the meantime. For it is quite evident that one who holds his office only during the pleasure of another cannot be depended upon to maintain an attitude of independence against the latter's will.[33]

Removal may also be difficult because of the "political inadvisability of such a traumatic step."[34] Finally, procedural features of the commissions inhibit executive control. "Where decision must be made on the basis of the record made in hearings, an overhead directive power is necessarily excluded, except to choice and prosecution of cases. Moreover, the tendency of the commissions to operate through case-to-case proceedings obscures the opportunity to develop policy by overhead directives."[35]

Independent status was aimed at keeping political influence over commission work and decisions at a minimum and, hence, making the agencies more efficient. They were to have the advantages of expertise, continuity, flexibility, and impartiality. But this independent status was quickly challenged in the courts. Under our constitutional law, a legislature cannot divest itself of its powers. Consequently, since regulatory agencies operate under general legislative powers, their creation was challenged as an unconstitutional delegation of legislative power. To this contention the Supreme Court declared in 1894:

[31] Emmette S. Redford, *American Government and the Economy* (New York: Macmillan Co., 1965), p. 550.

[32] At the federal level, this is true for the CAB and ICC, but there are no statutory limitations on the President's removal power of members of the FCC, FPC, and SEC. All but six of the states have statutory provisions regarding removal. See Subcommittee on Intergovernmental Relations, Senate Committee on Government Operations, *State Utility Commissions, op. cit.,* Table 1 and pp. 65–67.

[33] *Humphrey's Executor* v. *United States,* 295 U.S. 602, 629 (1935). The principle of security was reaffirmed in *Wiener* v. *United States,* 357 U.S. 349 (1958). See Reginald Parket, "The Removal Power of the President and Independent Administrative Agencies," 36 *Indiana Law Journal* 63 (1960).

[34] William L. Cary, *Politics and the Regulatory Agencies* (New York: McGraw-Hill Book Co., Inc., 1967), p. 10.

[35] Redford, *op. cit.,* p. 550.

. . . there can be no doubt of the general power of a State to regulate the fares and freights which may be charged and received by railroad or other carriers, and that this regulation can be carried on by means of a commission. Such a commission is merely an administrative board created by the State for carrying into effect the will of the State as expressed by its legislation.[36]

It is thus firmly established that an administrative body may be delegated legislative power as long as the legislature lays down general provisions or standards to guide the agency. ". . . Congress can not delegate any part of its legislative power except under the limitation of a prescribed standard . . . ."[37] In practice, however, the legislative standards are frequently broad—such as the general requirement that rates must be "just and reasonable"—and commissions, therefore, have wide discretion. Many regulatory problems arise from these broad, delegated powers because of their interpretation by the commissions or by the courts.

How Independent Are the Commissions?

While in theory the regulatory agencies are independent, they nevertheless have a direct relationship to the executive, legislative, and judicial branches of their respective governments. Sometimes referred to as the "headless fourth branch of government," the regulatory agency is created by, and dependent on, the other three. As a result, the administrative process is inherently a political activity, closely connected with other governmental policies.

Relation to the Executive Branch.[38] The executive branch of government comes into contact with regulatory commissions in several ways. The governor (in many states) and the President have the power to appoint commissioners as terms expire or members resign and with some exceptions to name the chairmen.[39] Appointments to high positions in the commissions also may be cleared

---

[36]*Reagan* v. *Farmers' Loan & Trust Co.,* 154 U.S. 362, 393–94 (1894).

[37]*United States* v. *Chicago, Milwaukee, St. Paul & Pacific R.R. Co.,* 282 U.S. 311, 324 (1931).

"Some courts have taken the view that the legislature cannot delegate its lawmaking function at all, but have concluded that authorizing an administrative agency to 'fill in the details' of legislation is valid as not being an exercise of the legislative power. Other courts have stated that the legislature *can* delegate part of its function to an agency as long as sufficient general standards to be used by the agency are included in the grant of authority. The difference in the two foregoing approaches to delegation is largely a matter of semantics." Robert N. Corley and Robert L. Black, *The Legal Environment of Business* (2d ed.; New York: McGraw-Hill Book Co., Inc., 1968), p. 99. Compare *Yakus* v. *United States,* 321 U.S. 414 (1944) with *Panama Refining Co.* v. *Ryan,* 293 U.S. 388 (1935).

[38]For a more complete discussion, upon which this summary is largely based, see Marver H. Bernstein, *Regulating Business by Independent Commission* (Princeton: Princeton University Press, 1955), pp. 109–13, 126–54; Bernard Schwartz, *The Professor and the Commissions* (New York: Alfred A. Knopf, Inc., 1959), pp. 205–34; Emmette S. Redford, "The President and the Regulatory Commissions," 44 *Texas Law Review* 288 (1965); and David M. Welborn, "Presidents, Regulatory Commissioners and Regulatory Policy," 15 *Journal of Public Law* 1 (1966).

[39]The governors of twenty-six states have the power to appoint the chairmen of the regulatory agencies. The President has the power to name all chairmen except for the head of the ICC.

with the executive branch before being made by the various chairmen. And, while the statutory and legal power of removal is limited, a governor or the President can use, and has used, a variety of means to force the resignation of a commissioner whose conduct or policies the chief executive disapproves.

The commissions' budgets and legislative matters generally are handled by the executive branch. At the federal level, for example, the Bureau of the Budget, which is part of the executive offices of the President, "is the Cerberus at the gate of any program."[40] Proposed testimony before congressional committees must be cleared through the Bureau. All budget requests and legislative recommendations must pass through it for ultimate approval by the White House. Moreover, while Congress does not always adopt appropriations or enact legislation recommended by the President, the fact remains that Presidential backing is usually required to obtain budget requests and legislative proposals. "Thus a hostile or unsympathetic President or Bureau of the Budget can severely cripple the activities of a commission, while a friendly and sympathetic President or budget bureau can contribute much to the commission's effectiveness."[41]

The executive branch frequently consults with the commissioners. It can initiate legislation affecting regulatory policy or appoint special study commissions. It can express preferences about general policy. At times, the executive branch has tried to influence the initiation of specific investigations or the outcome of specific decisions. The commissions are also dependent on the executive branch (through the offices of the state attorneys general or the Department of Justice) to enforce and defend their orders.[42]

Finally, various executive offices have an interest in particular cases before the commissions or are directly involved with the industries controlled by the commissions. Governments are large buyers of regulated industries' services. It is not uncommon, therefore, to find an executive office (such as the General Services Administration) intervening in a rate case. Further, a regulatory commission may not have complete jurisdiction over an industry. Prior to the establishment of the Department of Transportation, for instance, at least 23 federal agencies or parts of federal agencies dealt with transportation matters.[43] Nor were all of these agencies transferred to the new department. In addition, the Department of Justice is concerned with the antitrust aspects of regulation; the

[40] Cary, *op. cit.,* p. 12. Also see testimony of Elmer M. Staats, *Federal Administrative Procedure* (Hearings before the Subcommittee on Administrative Practice and Procedure of the Committee of the Judiciary, Senate, 86th Cong., 2d sess.) (Washington, D.C.: U.S. Government Printing Office, 1960), pp. 22–46; and *Budget Bureau Censorship and Control of Independent Agency Fiscal and Other Matters* (Study by the staff of the Special Subcommittee on Legislative Oversight for the Committee on Interstate and Foreign Commerce, House, 86th Cong., 2d sess.) (Washington, D.C.: U.S. Government Printing Office, 1960).

[41] D. Philip Locklin, *Economics of Transportation* (6th ed.; Homewood, Ill.: Richard D. Irwin, Inc., 1966), p. 283.

[42] See Robert L. Stern, "The Solicitor General's Office and Administrative Agency Litigation," 46 *American Bar Association Journal* 154 (1960).

[43] Hugh S. Norton, *Modern Transportation Economics* (Columbus: Charles E. Merrill Books, Inc., 1963), p. 227.

Atomic Energy Commission with nuclear power development; the Department of Interior with right-of-way applications across public land for transmission lines; and the Rural Electrification Administration with the promotion of rural electric and telephone services.

The involvement of more than one agency raises two problems. First, coordination of policy is more difficult. Second, the executive branch can turn to any one of these agencies for advice and counsel. Assuming that the policy-making role of a regulatory agency is of minimal importance, the chief executive "is likely to give only passing attention to appointments to that body," while the executive agencies, "not being judicial in nature, can take a much freer policy line."[44]

Relation to the Legislative Branch. Being an administrative body, a regulatory commission is created by legislative authority and depends on legislation for its powers. Moreover, a commission may exercise only such powers as the legislature confers on it. Early attempts to prescribe detailed standards by franchise or statute were unsuccessful. It was gradually realized, therefore, that regulatory laws must be written in very general terms, and that the exact meaning and application of these statutes must be left to the commissions subject, of course, to judicial review. A majority of the commissions are thus authorized to prescribe "just and reasonable" rates and to prevent "undue" discrimination, but no criteria are found in the law as to what constitutes a reasonable rate or when a rate is unduly discriminatory. The legislative branch cannot be expected to specify rules to govern every possible situation. Thus, a commission is vested with broad authority to apply general legislative principles to the many specific instances that arise.

A commission is also dependent on the legislature for its annual appropriation[45] and for both the number and salaries of its staff. Budget control, in particular, gives legislative committees the opportunity to direct commissions as the following quote from the 1964 report of the House Appropriations Committee indicates:

> The Federal Power Commission is an important agency, but it has grown almost 40 percent in jobs since 1960. Along with growth in jobs there is much complaint that the Agency is foot-dragging in its disposal of cases. The Committee urges the Commission to cut down its delay in disposing of cases as it is hurting the industries it has to regulate . . . . The Commission is spending too much time in empire building and trying to expand its jurisdiction.[46]

---

[44] *Ibid.*, pp. 229–30.

[45] One important exception: as previously noted, some state commissions receive part or all of their annual appropriations from assessments levied on the industries under their jurisdiction.

[46] House Appropriations Committee, *Report on Independent Offices Appropriation Bill, 1964* (House Report No. 824, 88th Cong., 1st sess.) (Washington, D.C.: U.S. Government Printing Office, 1963), p. 9. It should be noted that the backlog of cases complained about in the report has been cut substantially since 1963.

Because they are created by the legislative branch, regulatory commissions must report directly to this body. The legislature has the right to conduct investigations or hold hearings on all aspects of a commission's policy or performance. Such investigations or hearings, especially at the federal level, may directly interfere in a commission's rule-making authority. Finally, in many states and at the federal level, commissioners must be confirmed by the whole legislature or by the Senate.

The legislative branch thus has a large responsibility for the strength or weakness of commission regulation. If a commission receives a statute that clearly defines its objectives, a grant of sufficient jurisdiction and powers, and adequate appropriations and staff to carry out its responsibilities, the legislative branch has done its part. If, however, goals and objectives are poorly defined, jurisdiction and powers inadequate, and control over the budget used to exert legislative influence, the effectiveness of a regulatory commission will be sharply diminished.

Relation to the Judicial Branch.[47] As the power given to a regulatory commission is of necessity broad, there is always danger that the constitutional rights of parties involved will be endangered by the arbitrary and unreasonable exercise of this power. To avoid this danger, the courts must act as a check on the actions of administrative agencies. The courts also must interpret the rulings of regulatory commissions from the point of view of the Constitution and of existing legislation. Judicial review is well established and the courts have the power to review and set aside, if necessary, commission orders. Yet,

> . . . it is difficult to determine just how far the courts should go in interfering with the acts of administrative bodies; for if the courts insist upon reopening matters supposedly determined by a commission and substitute their judgment for that of the commission, the latter becomes a worthless body which impedes rather than aids in the regulating process.[48]

In the early days of railroad regulation, difficulties were experienced because the courts exercised an unlimited right of review over ICC decisions. The courts insisted on reviewing all evidence, both old and new. As a result, the railroads refused to take seriously the commission's hearings, and the commission's orders, in turn, frequently were reversed by the courts. The situation is well illustrated by the Alabama Midland case decided by the Supreme Court in 1897.[49] In making a decision as to the reasonableness of rates to Troy, Alabama, a knowledge as to the existence or nonexistence of water competition was essential. In the evidence presented before the commission at its hearing, the presence of water competition was shown. Later, when evidence was presented

---

[47] See Frank E. Cooper, *Administrative Agencies and the Courts* (Ann Arbor: University of Michigan Law School, 1951); Louis L. Jaffe, *Judicial Control of Administrative Action* (Boston: Little, Brown & Co., Inc., 1965); and Martin Shapiro, *The Supreme Court and Administrative Agencies* (New York: The Free Press, 1968).

[48] Locklin, *op. cit.,* p. 274.

[49] *Interstate Commerce Comm.* v. *Alabama Midland Ry. Co.,* 168 U.S. 144 (1897).

to the Court, it was shown that the river—the water competition shown in the evidence before the ICC—was dry half of the year, that it was but three feet deep, and that the presence of overhanging trees made the use of boats impossible.[50]

In 1910, the Supreme Court clarified the proper scope of judicial review. Recognizing the advantages of commission regulation, the Court held that review must be confined to questions of power and right, and not to matters which could be left to the administrative discretion of a commission. In the words of the Court:

> Beyond controversy, in determining whether an order of the Commission shall be suspended or set aside, we must consider (*a*) all relevant questions of constitutional power or right; (*b*) all pertinent questions as to whether the administrative order is within the scope of the delegated authority under which it purports to have been made; and (*c*) . . . whether, even although the order be in form within the delegated power, nevertheless it must be treated as not embraced therein, because the exertion of authority which is questioned has been manifested in such an unreasonable manner as to cause it, in truth, to be within the elementary rule that the substance, and not the shadow, determines the validity of the exercise of the power.[51]

As a result of this, and of subsequent decisions, the findings of fact of a regulatory commission are ordinarily conclusive. Except in reparation cases, the courts will not substitute their judgment for that of a commission in determining the facts of a particular case. Yet, until 1942, the Supreme Court did not hesitate to specify the factors that should guide commission decisions. It enumerated specific measures of value to be considered in determining fair value in 1898[52] and listed a number of factors to be considered in determining a fair rate of return in 1923.[53] The Court narrowed the boundaries of judicial review in 1942, stating:

> The Constitution does not bind rate-making bodies to the service of any single formula or combination of formulas. Agencies to whom this legislative power has been delegated are free, within the ambit of their statutory authority, to make the pragmatic adjustments which may be called for by particular circumstances. Once a fair hearing has been given, proper findings made, and other statutory requirements satisfied, the courts cannot intervene in the

---

[50] "The same case is not tried before the court which is tried before the Commission. The trial before the Commission, therefore, with all its attendant expense and consumption of time, goes practically for nothing. . . . A procedure like the present one tends to bring the body into disrepute and is grossly unfair to it and to the complainants who appear before it." Interstate Commerce Commission, *Annual Report, 1897*, pp. 31–32.

[51] *Interstate Commerce Comm. v. Illinois Central R. R. Co.*, 215 U.S. 452, 470 (1910).

[52] *Smyth v. Ames*, 169 U.S. 466, 546–47 (1898).

[53] *Bluefield Water Works & Imp. Co. v. Public Service Comm. of West Virginia*, 262 U.S. 679, 692–93 (1923).

absence of a clear showing that the limits of due process have been overstepped. If the commission's order, as applied to the facts before it and viewed in its entirety, produces no arbitrary result, our inquiry is at an end.[54]

The courts have other functions in the regulatory process. As a commission is not a court, it has only limited power to compel observance of its orders. The courts, therefore, must enforce orders and laws by injunctions or mandamus. The courts also may compel a commission to perform its duties under the law. Often, when a statute is broad and lacking in precise objectives, a commission may not think its authority covers a certain issue or activity, or a commission may simply refuse to act. In such situations, the courts may compel action.[55]

Independence: An Outdated Concept? In creating regulatory commissions, legislatures sought to establish agencies that were free from control of the executive and of the legislature, in order to insure continuity of policy and to keep political pressures to a minimum. But both branches of government have influence over the commissions. As former SEC Chairman Cary has put it: ". . . government regulatory agencies are stepchildren whose custody is contested by both Congress and the Executive, but without very much affection from either one."[56]

In recent years, the *concept of independence* has been challenged, and the argument advanced that administrative and policy-making functions should be transferred to executive departments or agencies. The essence of the argument supporting this view is that commissions performing these functions—functions which are closely related to the broadest objectives of government—should be politically responsible. Further, the commissions would be left to perform their quasi-judicial functions for which they should be independent.[57] Such a transfer of functions, however, has long been opposed by the legislative branch. Argues former Congressman Harris: "These agencies should not in any way be subservient to the White House or anyone else."[58] This important issue will be examined in Chapter 18.

A Combination of Functions

Regulatory commissions have been characterized as quasi-judicial and quasi-legislative. Contrary to the basic pattern of American government, which is

---

[54] *Federal Power Comm.* v. *Natural Gas Pipeline Co.,* 315 U.S. 575, 586 (1942).

[55] See, for example, *Phillips Petroleum Co.* v. *Wisconsin,* 347 U.S. 672 (1954).

[56] Cary, *op. cit.,* p. 4.

[57] See President's Committee on Administrative Management, *Report with Special Studies* (Washington, D.C.: U.S. Government Printing Office, 1937), pp. 39–42; Frederick F. Blachly and Miriam E. Oatman, *Federal Regulatory Action and Control* (Washington, D.C.: Brookings Institution, 1940), chap. ix; James M. Landis, *Report on Regulatory Agencies to the President-Elect* (Washington, D.C.: U.S. Government Printing Office, 1960); and Redford, "The President and the Regulatory Commissions," *op. cit.,* pp. 297–98.

[58] Oren Harris, quoted in 67 *Public Utilities Fortnightly* 222 (1961).

based upon the doctrine of separation of powers, a commission assumes the tasks of administrator, judge, and legislator. When investigating rates or service and safety standards, a commission is performing an administrative function. When holding hearings, examining evidence, and making decisions, a commission is acting as judge of a company's conduct. Moreover, a commission can even determine the rules it wants to administer, and it can decide to prosecute a company and to gather evidence against the firm. It then considers its own evidence as well as the evidence presented by the company, and makes a decision. When prescribing certain rules of conduct for a company, such as fixing rates, a commission is acting in a legislative capacity. As stated by the Supreme Court:

> The function of rate-making is purely legislative in its character, and this is true, whether it is exercised directly by the legislature itself or by some subordinate or administrative body, to whom the power of fixing rates in detail has been delegated. The completed act derives its authority from the legislature and must be regarded as an exercise of the legislative power.[59]

That regulatory commissions combine various functions has been the subject of considerable controversy. Argues a former chairman of the Federal Communications Commission: "I do not believe it is possible to be a good judge on Monday and Tuesday, a good legislator on Wednesday and Thursday, and a good administrator on Friday."[60] The American Bar Association, in particular, has long been critical of the adjudicating function of administrative bodies. The ABA believes that administrative exercise of judicial powers "violates the fundamental doctrine of separation of powers and thus imperils the even more fundamental 'rule of law.' "[61] Thus, the association has recommended the abolition of all independent commissions and the establishment of an administrative court system.[62] In the absence of abolition, the ABA has sought "to judicialize administrative procedure."[63] The aim has been "to establish a meaningful concept of due process of law with reference to administrative proceedings, thereby protecting the citizen under the jurisdiction of administrative agencies."[64] While the commissions have been concerned with due process, they have also been conscious of regulatory lag. Consequently, they have developed informal procedures in addition to formal procedures.[65]

---

[59] *Knoxville* v. *Knoxville Water Co.,* 212 U.S. 1, 8 (1909).

[60] Newton W. Minow, quoted in 72 *Public Utilities Fortnightly* 11 (December 5, 1963).

[61] Roy L. Cole, "Administrative Agencies and Judicial Powers," 44 *American Bar Association Journal* 953, 954 (1958).

[62] See Woll, *op. cit.,* pp. 15–18.

[63] *Ibid.,* p. 19.

[64] *Ibid.,* p. 21.

[65] See Chapter 5, pp. 139–40.

THE FEDERAL-STATE JURISDICTIONAL PROBLEM[66]

For many years, state commissions and even some of the regulated industries were opposed to federal regulation. Opposition was especially strong prior to 1935. Opponents generally argued that federal regulation was unnecessary, that it would raise the cost of regulation, and that it was bureaucratic. "Federal regulation was even likened to Communism and Socialism."[67] One state commissioner put it this way: "There can be no such thing as concurrent jurisdiction or even co-operation between the states and the Federal government on the subject of rate-making."[68] And two leaders of the electrical industry argued:

> The interests of the public are already fully safeguarded. . . . Federal regulation would only lead to confusion and besides it would greatly increase the cost of the service.
>
> [Federal regulation will] raise from the several states the last vestige of utility control and deprive them of rights which distinctly belong to the states. . . . It would substitute for a regulation sensitive to local public opinion the absentee treatment of a Federal Bureau in Washington.[69]

After 1935, opposition to federal regulation sharply declined. In part, this was due to a change in the political climate brought about by the depression and the New Deal. And in part, it was due to the uncovering of notorious abuses, particularly through the use of the holding company devise, and the growing realization that the states were unable to effectively regulate interstate activities.

Federal-State Conflicts

In the preceding chapter, it was pointed out that the courts have long recognized three fields of jurisdiction in the United States: (1) the field in which the federal power is exclusive; (2) the field in which the state power is exclusive; and (3) the field in which the state and federal governments have concurrent powers. Concurrent power means that either may act, but if both legislate on the same subject matter, the federal law supersedes the state law. Only in the absence of federal legislation can the state act in this field.[70] In general, all inter-

---

[66] While major jurisdictional problems have concerned state and federal regulatory spheres, there have been a number of cases involving local and state authority. See, for example, *Re East Ohio Gas Co.*, 41 PUR 3d 75 (Ohio, 1961); *Florida* ex rel. *Utilities Operating Co.* v. *Mason*, 172 So. 2d 225 (1964); *Coast Cities Coaches* v. *Dade County*, 178 So. 2d 703 (1965); and *Re Northwest Natural Gas, Inc.*, 67 PUR 3d 523 (N.J., 1967).

[67] C. Woody Thompson and Wendell R. Smith, *Public Utility Economics* (New York: McGraw-Hill Book Co., Inc., 1941), p. 229.

[68] National Association of Regulatory Utility Commissioners, *Annual Proceedings, 1931* (Washington, D.C., 1932), p. 150.

[69] From addresses by H. Erickson and H. Sands, respectively, delivered at a conference, August 29, 1928, and published by the National Electric Light Association, as cited in Thompson and Smith, *op. cit.*, p. 229.

state activities are under the jurisdiction of federal agencies, and intrastate activities under the control of state commissions. The courts have restricted the jurisdiction of the states, however, if intrastate activities interfere with federal regulation of interstate commerce.[71]

Congress, in order to alleviate jurisdictional disputes, has tried to outline federal authority in its legislation. For example, the Public Utility Act of 1935, which extended the authority of the Federal Power Commission, reads in part:

> The provisions of this Part shall apply to the transmission of electric energy in interstate commerce and to the sale of electric energy at wholesale in interstate commerce, but shall not apply to any other sale of electrical energy or deprive a State or State commission of its lawful authority now exercised over the exportation of hydroelectric energy which is transmitted across a State line. The Commission shall have jurisdiction over all facilities for such transmission or sale of electric energy, but shall not have jurisdiction, except as specifically provided in this Part ... over facilities used for the generation of electric energy or over facilities used in local distribution or only for the transmission of electric energy in intrastate commerce, or over facilities for the transmission of electric energy consumed wholly by the transmitter.[72]

Attempts have also been made to ease jurisdictional conflicts through closer federal-state cooperation. By statute, the federal commissions are authorized to confer with state authorities and to hold joint hearings with them on matters within federal jurisdiction which affect the rate-making authority of the states. The Federal Power Commission has statutory authority to assist the state commissions by making cost studies, supplying information and reports, and loaning its rate or other experts. Some statutes permit federal agencies to refer matters within their jurisdiction to joint state boards composed of members of state commissions from affected states, while the Motor Carrier Act of 1935 requires decisions by joint state boards where no more than three states are involved. The Federal Communications Commission has used on several occasions panels of cooperating state commissioners listening to the evidence and participating in the discussion.[73] And both state and federal commissioners are

---

[70] An 1851 Supreme Court decision suggested that federal inaction should be interpreted as implying that no regulation should be exercised, thus prohibiting state action. *Cooley* v. *The Board of Wardens of the Port of Philadelphia*, 53 U.S. 298 (1851). Later decisions indicate otherwise. See, for example, *Munn* v. *Illinois*, 94 U.S. 113 (1877); and *Peik* v. *Chicago & Northwestern Ry. Co.*, 94 U.S. 164 (1877).

[71] See Chapter 3, pp. 46–49.

[72] Public Utility Act of 1935, Title II, Part II, Sec. 201 (b).

[73] Experience under all these provisions has shown limitations. "Joint hearings and joint boards are infrequently used, except where this is compulsory (in motor-carrier regulation). Even then, there are serious problems. There is much absenteeism on the part of board members, and the work of the boards is done substantially by examiners assigned by the Interstate Commerce Commission, with little contribution being made by the joint boards." Redford, *American Government and the Economy, op. cit.*, p. 153. Also see David M. Welborn, "National-State Cooperation in Regulatory Administration," 33 *State Government* 199 (1960); and James W. Karber, "Challenge: A Way of Life for the Future," 80 *Public Utilities Fortnightly* 19, 24–25 (November 9, 1967).

brought together in the National Association of Regulatory Utility Commissioners and in regional associations.

Some Current Areas of Conflict. While opposition to federal regulation has diminished, the conclusion should not be drawn that harmony between state and federal commissions has been achieved. The state commissions, in particular, fear the continual encroachment of the federal agencies into areas once exclusively the province of the states. Argues former Chairman Karber of the Illinois Commerce Commission:

> It is not at all clear that the best interests of all the users of utility services can best be served by federal control over all the utility operations. Yet there are indications that this is the path which most of the federal agencies seem to be taking. . . . In their desire to expand their powers, however, the federal agencies ignore the constitutional rights of the state legislatures to decide how much regulation is necessary for the public interest. The federal agencies do not have the constitutional power to impose their own ideas of appropriate regulatory standards and procedures upon all the state commissions. [74]

Thus, despite years of experience, jurisdictional boundaries have not been firmly established, as illustrated by the following Supreme Court decisions concerning the jurisdiction of the Federal Power Commission. In 1942, the Court held that an order requiring an intrastate subsidiary of an interstate natural gas pipeline to make an extension was properly to be issued by the FPC and not by the state commission. [75] In 1947, the Court ruled that a company which produced and bought gas in Louisiana and, in turn, sold the gas in the same state to three interstate pipeline companies was subject to federal regulation. [76] In 1950, the Court upheld the right of the FPC, at the request of the City of Cleveland, to determine the cost of transporting gas from the southern border of Ohio through the pipelines of the East Ohio Gas Company, a large distributor, and to determine the value of the company's facilities, even though all were confined within the State. [77] In 1954, despite language to the contrary in the Natural Gas Act,

[74] *Ibid.*, p. 24. Also see "Proper Spheres of State and Federal Regulation," in National Association of Regulatory Utility Commissioners, *Annual Proceedings, 1963* (Washington, D.C., 1964), pp. 320-38; "Report of the Committee on Regulatory Procedure," in National Association of Regulatory Utility Commissioners, *Annual Proceedings, 1965* (Washington, D.C., 1966), pp. 62-70; and James W. Karber, "The Regulatory Jurisdictional Problem: State or Federal?" 82 *Public Utilities Fortnightly* 17 (October 24, 1968).

[75] *Illinois Natural Gas Co.* v. *Central Illinois Public Service Co.*, 314 U.S. 498 (1942). Said the Court: ". . . the proposed extension . . . is so intimately associated with the commerce [of gas transportation], and would so affect its volume moving into the state and distribution among the states, as to be within the Congressional power to regulate those matters which materially affect interstate commerce, as well as the commerce itself." *Ibid.*, p. 509.

[76] *Interstate Natural Gas Co.* v. *Federal Power Comm.*, 331 U.S. 682 (1947). Argued the Court: ". . . it is clear that the sales in question were quite as much in interstate commerce as they would have been had the pipes of the petitioner crossed the state line before reaching the points of sale." *Ibid.*, pp. 687-88.

[77] *Federal Power Comm.* v. *East Ohio Gas Co.*, 338 U.S. 464 (1950). In response, Congress in 1954 enacted the Hinshaw amendment to the Natural Gas Act which exempts any company from the Act if it buys and consumes all gas within one state and its

the Court decided that the FPC had jurisdiction over all natural gas producers.[78] In 1964, the Court ruled that the FPC and not state agencies had jurisdiction over all wholesale rates of electricity for resale within a single state, even if only a small part of a company's power is brought in from another state.[79] Early in 1965, the Court upheld the FPC's claim of jurisdiction over natural gas sales to an interstate pipeline which were subject to "restricted use" agreements providing that the gas either would be used within a state or that it would be transported to another state for use in the pipeline company's own facilities.[80] And later in the same year, the Court held that construction of pumped storage hydroelectric projects which utilize headwaters of navigable rivers to generate energy for interstate power systems required licenses from the FPC, regardless of whether such projects affected commerce on navigable waters.[81]

A RÉSUMÉ

It has been suggested that regulatory commissions were established to meet existing problems and as a result were not based on a carefully developed philosophy of government.[82] Summarize Corley and Black:

> As our industrial society has grown and become more and more complex, the social and economic problems which confront government have multiplied fantastically. Not only have these problems increased in number, but interrelationships and conflicting social goals have complicated their solution. Also, advances in technology have required special training and experience to make an intelligent attempt at the solution of problems in many areas. Having decided that regulation of one sort or another is desirable, governments of necessity have employed the device of the administrative agency to lighten the burdens imposed on the executive branch, legislative bodies, and courts by this growth and development. The multitude of administrative agencies performing governmental functions today has resulted from limitations due to the lack of time to devote to making, enforcing, and interpreting laws and the lack of expert familiarity with all aspects of all these problems to make informed and effectual decisions concerning them.[83]

---

rates, services, and facilities are regulated by a state commission. As of May 3, 1968, 159 companies had been exempted, either fully or partially (1 *FPC News* 14–15 [May 3, 1968]).

[78] *Phillips Petroleum Co.* v. *Wisconsin, op. cit.* See Chapter 16, pp. 602–3.

[79] *Federal Power Comm.* v. *Southern California Edison Co.*, 376 U.S. 205 (1964).

[80] *California* v. *Lo-Vaca Gathering Co.*, 379 U.S. 366 (1965). Argued Justice Douglas: "Were suppliers of gas and pipeline companies free to allocate by contract gas from a particular source to a particular use, havoc would be raised with the federal regulatory scheme. . . ." *Ibid.*, p. 369. Also see *Re United Gas Pipe Line Co.*, 50 PUR 3d 186 (1963). In 1967, the FPC asserted jurisdiction over an electric company that operates entirely within a single state, on the grounds that it connects with another utility which in turn connects with an out-of-state utility. *Re Florida Power & Light Co.*, 68 PUR 3d 249 (1967). The decision has been appealed.

[81] *Federal Power Comm.* v. *Union Electric Co.*, 381 U.S. 90 (1965).

[82] Cushman, *op. cit.*, pp. 28–29.

[83] Corley and Black, *op. cit.*, p. 97.

Irrespective of their origin, Woll has noted that the rise of the administrative branch poses many serious questions "both for constitutional government and for the more newly created democratic norms of our society." He explains:

> Constitutional government requires limitation through counterbalancing the departments and through the requirement that governmental agencies act in accordance with traditional legal rights protected by the Constitution. Democratic government requires participation by the people in the formulation of public policy. There is no provision in the Constitution designed to control administrative agencies, and the very ambiguities of the Constitution permit Congress to create a "headless fourth branch," the independent regulatory commissions. The constitutional limitations, then, which are operative with respect to the three traditional branches of government do not control the activities of administrative agencies. [84]

Should, therefore, administrative commissions be abolished and administrative courts established in their place? Should the present commissions remain, but with their administrative and policy-making functions transferred to the executive branch? To date, negative answers have been given to these and other questions concerning the status of independent regulatory commissions. As Senator Cummings argued many years ago:

> . . . the whole policy of our regulation of commerce is based upon our faith and confidence in administrative tribunals. If we are not willing to entrust the commercial fortunes of the United States to the honor, the learning, and the integrity of administrative tribunals, we had better suspend and cease any attempted regulation of commerce. [85]

And yet, regulatory commissions have been severely criticized in recent years. The caliber of commissioners and adequacy of staffs have been questioned. Regulatory lag has resulted in continuing debate over commission procedures and practices. It has been argued that the commissions have tended to become protectors of the regulated rather than guardians of the public interest—that their performance has been deficient. With the growth of competition, particularly in the transportation industry, the desirability of substantially reducing regulation has been, and is being, explored.

Finally, the broad problem concerning the proper jurisdiction of state and federal agencies remains unresolved. While accepting federal regulation, many believe that federal agencies have gone too far in regulating essentially "fringe interstate matters" and, unless this trend is reversed, that "the entire fabric of state regulation of local matters may well disintegrate." [86] But there is no easy or obvious solution to the jurisdictional problem, and it is likely to remain unresolved as long as an attempt is made to distinguish between intrastate and interstate commerce for regulatory purposes.

---

[84] Woll, *op. cit.,* pp. 1–2.
[85] LI *Congressional Record,* Part II (June 25, 1914), p. 11104.
[86] Albert L. Sklar, former Chairman of the Maryland Public Service Commission, quoted in 72 *Public Utilities Fortnightly* 68 (November 21, 1963).

PART II

The Theory of
Regulation

THE GOALS, TASK, PHASES, AND PROCEDURES OF REGULATION

Chapter 5

> We are asking much of regulation when we ask that it follow
> the guide of competition. As Americans, we have set up a
> system that indicates we have little faith in economic planning
> by the government. Yet, we are asking our regulators to exer-
> cise the judgment of thousands of consumers in the evaluation
> of our efficiency, service, and technical progress so that a fair
> profit can be determined. Fair regulation is now, and always
> will be, a difficult process. But it is not impossible.
>
> —Ralph M. Besse*

Regulation, as it has developed in the United States, is concerned with rates, service, safety and, to a lesser extent, the efficiency of management. In most of the industries under consideration, rate regulation has
occupied much of the commissions' time and has been the subject of continuous
controversy. Rate regulation has two aspects: control of the rate level (earnings)
and control of the rate structure (prices). As to the rate level, the regulated
industries are permitted to earn a "fair rate of return on the fair value of their
property." This return must be neither so high as to exploit consumers nor so
low as to discourage investors. The allowable rate of return, therefore, must fall
within these limits. As to the rate structure, the regulated industries are permitted to practice price discrimination in order to expand the use of their
services. Such discrimination must be "just and reasonable," with no favoritism
toward any buyer or group of buyers.

While rate regulation has been the major concern of the commissions and
the courts, attention also has been paid to the problems of quality and quantity
of service, safety of operation, and efficiency of management. Consumers expect
high standards of service from the regulated industries, for "it does the buyer no
good to pay a lower price if the quality or quantity he gets for his money is
lowered in the same proportion, giving him gas, for instance, of four-fifths the
former heating power for four-fifths the former price."[1] They also expect safe

---

*Ralph M. Besse, speech before the American Bar Association Annual Meeting
(Boston, Mass., August 25, 1953).

[1] J. M. Clark, *Social Control of Business* (2d ed.; New York: McGraw-Hill Book
Co., Inc., 1939), p. 337.

123

service, because the best or fastest service available is useless if gas leaks cause explosions or one out of four commercial airplanes crash. And, "it does the buyer no good to compel the producer to accept half the former net earnings if he gets in exchange a management half as efficient, for the poor management will add more to the costs of operation than the regulating commission can take away in reducing earnings."[2]

The goals of regulation, the task and phases of rate regulation, and commission procedures are discussed in this chapter. In the following six chapters, accounting and financial control, the rate level, the rate of return, and the rate structures of the regulated industries will be examined at length. Finally, service and safety standards will be considered in Chapter 12.

THE GOALS OF REGULATION

The job of a regulated industry is "to provide the public with as much and as good service as the public wants and is willing to pay for. The goal of regulation, within the limits set by its authority and its capacity, is to translate this task into operating terms, and see to it that it is carried out."[3] Five basic objectives have been employed by the regulatory commissions in translating this task into operating terms:

1. Commissions have sought to prevent excessive (monopoly) profits and unreasonable (inequitable) price discrimination among customers, commodities, and places.

2. Commissions have tried to assure adequate earnings so that the regulated industries could continue to develop and expand in accordance with consumer demand. Profits, however, are not guaranteed.

3. Commissions have sought to provide service to the maximum number of consumers. In some instances, competition has been limited to permit internal subsidy (low-density routes may be subsidized by earnings on high-density routes). In other cases, the government has given direct (cash) or indirect (facilities) subsidies.

4. Commissions have often promoted the development of an industry or a region. Again, subsidies have been given to achieve this objective, as in the case of local-service airlines and water carriers, or an industry's rate structure designed to promote the industrial development of a region, as in the case of some differential rates in the transportation industry.

5. Commissions, in some instances, have been concerned with insuring maximum public safety. This has been an important objective in the provision of transport services, particularly in the air and motor carrier industries.

These are not the only possible alternative goals or objectives for regula-

[2] *Ibid.*
[3] Ben W. Lewis, "Emphasis and Misemphasis in Regulatory Policy," in William G. Shepherd and Thomas G. Gies (eds.), *Utility Regulation: New Directions in Theory and Policy* (New York: Random House, 1966), p. 219.

tion. A few have argued that regulation should seek "social," as opposed to "business," objectives. The term is difficult to define, but it generally "refers to any policy of rate control designed to make the supply of utility services responsive to social needs and social costs, and rejecting as even tolerable measures of these needs and these costs the prices that consumers are able and willing to pay for the services and the money costs that the enterprise must incur in their production."[4] A larger number have argued that regulation is too often conceived of as a restrictive or negative force; that it must become more dynamic with greater emphasis on achieving (a) maximum economic performance, by providing explicit incentives to reward efficiency and penalize inefficiency, and (b) proper resource allocation.[5]

The conflicting nature of these goals and objectives is evident. Cramton has referred to transportation regulation as "the arena of 'ambiguous protectionism': that unnatural state in which the salt of competition is joined in uneasy mixture with the pepper of protectionism and the whole porridge seasoned with the paprika of subsidy and promotion."[6] Put another way, subsidy and promotion may favor one industry over another, making it more difficult for the second to compete or to earn adequate profits for growth. Unless government regulation seeks to achieve maximum economic efficiency and minimum cost services, maladjustments cannot be avoided.

The regulated industries are no longer, if they ever were, isolated from the rest of the economy. It is possible that the expanding regulated sector has been taking too large a share of the nation's resources, especially of investment.[7] At a minimum, regulation must be viewed in the context of the entire economy—and evaluated in a similar context. The regulated industries have always operated within the framework of a competitive economy. They must obtain capital, labor, and materials in competition with nonregulated industries. Adequate profits are not guaranteed to them. Regulation, then, should provide incentives to adopt new methods, improve quality, increase efficiency, cut costs, develop new markets, and expand output in line with consumer demand. In short, regulation is a substitute for competition and should attempt to put the regulated industries under the same restraints competition places on nonregulated industries.

The fact that the regulated industries are an integral part of the American

[4] James C. Bonbright, *Principles of Public Utility Rates* (New York: Columbia University Press, 1961), p. 110. On social objectives, see *ibid.*, chap. vii; and Horace Gray, "The Passing of the Public Utility Concept," 16 *Journal of Land & Public Utility Economics* 8 (1940).

[5] See Shepherd and Gies, *op. cit.*; and Harry M. Trebing (ed.), *Performance under Regulation* (East Lansing: Michigan State University Public Utilities Studies, 1968).

[6] Roger C. Cramton, "The Effectiveness of Economic Regulation—A Legal View," in Shepherd and Gies, *op. cit.*, p. 259.

[7] Harvey Averch and Leland L. Johnson, "Behavior of the Firm under Regulatory Constraint," 52 *American Economic Review* 1052 (1962); and Stanislaw H. Wellisz, "Regulation of Natural Gas Pipeline Companies: An Economic Analysis," 71 *Journal of Political Economy* 30 (1963). This thesis is discussed in Chapter 18.

economy is obvious. But the interdependence among these industries is often overlooked. In transportation activities,

> . . . the relative cost data indicate that airlines should probably not carry passengers for trips of under two hundred miles, an activity in which they regularly lose substantial money. Airline operation in these short hauls in turn hurts the railroads, who are efficient carriers of this business where volume is sufficiently large, that is, between large urban centers. Furthermore, keeping the railroads in the short-haul passenger business where volume is not sufficient is definitely detrimental to the buses, which are, generally speaking, the most efficient mode of short-haul passenger transport on low- and medium-density runs.
>
> In sum, there is mounting evidence that regulatory bodies have made the economic goal of cost minimization subservient to the political objective of service maintenance. As time has passed, technological changes have increased the number of services that are economically unremunerative and at the same time made it increasingly difficult to privately finance such services. This situation has been worsened further by the failure of regulatory bodies to take account of the interdependency of different transportation systems so that the maintenance of an uneconomic service by one carrier often converts possibly remunerative traffic of another carrier into an actual loss.[8]

Interdependence is not confined to the transportation system. Coal, electricity, gas, and oil actively compete for many uses. One important competitive area, to illustrate, is boiler fuel for electric generating plants. Coal currently provides 66 percent of this fuel compared with the 26 percent provided by natural gas.

> Since about half of the cost of coal at the generating plant comprises transportation charges, the current round of rate cuts by the railroads has made the cost of coal even more competitive with natural gas. (This action by the railroads has been inspired by the specter of new forms of competition they face: from coal pipelines, extra high-voltage transmission lines, and mine-mouth generating plants.) Also, while rates set by natural gas distributors must be approved by regulatory authorities, the coal companies have no such bother in writing contracts; but they can, and often do, intervene in gas rate hearings to thwart gas sales.[9]

Even in the telephone industry, competition from privately operated microwave communications systems has become significant.[10]

When it is stated that regulation should follow the guide of competiton, much is being asked. In the first place, since perfect competition does not exist

---

8 J. R. Meyer, M. J. Peck, J. Stenason, and C. Zwick, *The Economics of Competition in the Transportation Industries* (Cambridge: Harvard University Press, 1959), p. 14.

9 Alfred M. Casazza, "Competitive Utilities and Happy Investors," 71 *Public Utilities Fortnightly* 19, 23–24 (March 14, 1963).

10 See Bernard P. Herber, "The Impact of Microwave on the Telephone Business," 70 *Public Utilities Fortnightly* 214 (1962).

in the nonregulated sector of the economy, it is extremely difficult to specify with any precision that competitive standard which regulation should seek. Consequently, as Lewis has pointed out,

> It is probably true that regulation can never achieve more than a rough approximation of the results which perfect competition probably would have worked out in these industries—that is, it must be regarded as a "make-shift" for a condition of competition which never has existed and never can exist— and society must be prepared to accept some degree of maladjustment as inevitable.[11]

In the second place, social and political considerations make it difficult to reverse long-standing policies and goals. It might be argued with validity that present-day conditions indicate the desirability of neutral governmental policies toward the regulated industries, meaning that no industry should receive unfair advantage through promotion, user charge, subsidy, taxation, or economic regulation. Even if one were to consider this goal as ideal, however, is it practical? Take the user fee problem with respect to inland waterways. Millions of dollars have been invested in waterways over the past years by public agencies. This investment is fixed in that the resources devoted to such facilities have already been committed and cannot be withdrawn. If user fees were to be imposed on such facilities, they should only cover annual maintenance and operating costs. On new investment, user fees should cover full annual costs, including amortization and interest on the investment and payments in lieu of taxes. But vested interests have been created, since public policy has long provided free waterways, thereby making it difficult to obtain changes. Further, determining the amount of the subsidy is a complex and controversial art.[12]

In the third place, the regulatory process is inherently slower than the competitive process and, more importantly, creates vested interests itself. As described by Bernstein:

> It is impossible to avoid the conclusion that regulation of particular industries by independent commissions tends to destroy rather than promote competition. The historical tradition of commissions is anti-competitive. Their basic methods, especially their reliance upon the case by case approach, place small business firms at a disadvantage. The growing passivity of the commissions' approach and the inconvenience of dealing with large numbers of firms strengthen the commissions' tendency to identify their view of the public interest with the position of the dominant regulated firms. In short, regula-

[11] Ben W. Lewis, "Public Utilities," in L. S. Lyon and V. Abramson, *Government and Economic Life* (Washington, D.C.: Brookings Institution, 1940), Vol. II, p. 625. "Society may, of course, quite appropriately seek other than 'competitive' ends. But it should not depart from a program of harmonizing the processes and policies of public utility regulation with the larger competitive economy, without conscious purpose, and without seeking to ascertain the extent and implications of its departure." *Ibid.*, pp. 625–26.

[12] See Chapter 14, pp. 515–17.

tion of particular businesses stacks the cards against the small competitive firms and weakens the force of competition. [13]

All three of these factors suggest that the development of consistent regulatory goals, and the adoption of policies to achieve these goals, is exceedingly difficult. Adding to the problem have been technological developments which have greatly increased the competitive relationships between the regulated industries and between the regulated and nonregulated sectors of the economy. As will be demonstrated in the following chapters, regulation is now, and always will be, a difficult process. It is only with better understanding and increased knowledge of economic, political, and social factors that regulation can be an efficient substitute for competition.

THE TASK OF RATE REGULATION

Before discussing the theory of regulation in detail, it is desirable to outline the overall task of rate regulation. The method of establishing rates constitutes one of the most fundamental differences between the regulated industries and the remainder of our private enterprise system. In the nonregulated sector, rates are largely determined by the action of competitive forces—market supply and demand. In the regulated sector, because of the absence or the control of these competitive forces, rates are generally determined by a regulatory commission acting under broad powers conferred on it by the legislature, subject, of course, to judicial review.

Each aspect of rate regulation is treated separately in the next few chapters, but in reality they overlap in many instances. Thus, annual depreciation must be included in operating costs and accrued depreciation subtracted from the value of a company's tangible and reproducible property; service and safety standards have an important relation to the rates which a company must charge consumers. For these and other similar reasons, the various problems of regulation are closely interwoven.

There are, moreover, significant differences in rate regulation among the regulated industries; differences that will be outlined in subsequent chapters. For example: the rate base-rate of return approach is used for firms supplying electricity and natural gas, pipeline transport, and communications services. A similar approach is used in regulating air carriers and natural gas producers, although rates are established for each class of carrier and on an area basis, respectively. But the approach has not been employed in recent years in the regulation of rail, motor, and water carrier rate levels, primarily because of the presence of pervasive competition.

[13] Marver H. Bernstein, in *Airlines* (Report of the Antitrust Subcommittee of the Committee on the Judiciary, House, 85th Cong., 1st sess.) (Washington, D.C.: U.S. Government Printing Office, 1957), p. 4.

The Revenue-Requirement Standard

The basic standard of rate regulation is the revenue-requirement standard, often referred to as the rate base-rate of return standard. Simply stated, a regulated firm must be permitted to set rates which will (*a*) cover operating costs and (*b*) result in a reasonable rate of return on the property devoted to the business. This return must enable the firm to maintain its financial credit as well as to attract whatever capital may be required in the future for replacements, expansion, and technological innovation, and it must be comparable to that earned by other businesses with corresponding risks.

There are two aspects of rate regulation: the rate level or determination of a firm's general level of rates and the rate structure or determination of specific rates and the relationships between rates. In the words of the Supreme Court:

> The establishment of a rate for a regulated industry often involves two steps of different character, one of which may appropriately precede the other. The first is the adjustment of a general revenue level to the demands of a fair return. The second is the adjustment of a rate schedule conforming to that level, so as to eliminate discriminations and unfairness from its details.[14]

The Rate Level. The first aspect of rate regulation, the determination of a firm's total revenue requirement, can be expressed as a formula:

$$R = O + (V - D)r$$

where R is the total revenue required,
O is the operating costs,
V is the gross value of the tangible and intangible property,
D is the accrued depreciation of the tangible and reproducible property, and
r is the rate of return.

The formula indicates that determining the total revenue required involves three major steps. First, allowable operating costs must be ascertained. These include all types of operating expenses (wages, salaries, fuel, maintenance, advertising, research, and charitable contributions) plus annual charges for depreciation and operating taxes. Operating costs represent the largest percentage of a firm's total revenue requirement. Many of these costs are determined by normal competitive factors (wages, salaries, fuel, and maintenance) or by various levels of government (taxes). Others are determined by the individual firms (expenditures on advertising, research and development, and charitable contributions). A regulated firm legally may spend any amount it chooses for such purposes, but a commission may not allow all expenditures made for rate-making purposes. When expenditures are disallowed, they, in effect, are charged to a firm's stockholders rather than to its customers.

[14] *Federal Power Comm.* v. *Natural Gas Pipeline Co.,* 315 U.S. 575, 584 (1942).

Second, the net or depreciated value of the tangible and intangible property, or net investment in the property, of the enterprise must be determined. This net value or investment $(V-D)$ is referred to as the *rate base*, sometimes "valuation." Referring again to legal phraseology, a regulated company is entitled to earn a "fair rate of return" on this net value or investment, i.e., on the rate base. The determination of the rate base has been the source of major controversies between the regulated industries and the commissions ever since the early days of regulation.

Tangible property represents the value of, or investment in, plant and equipment "used and useful" in providing a particular firm's services. Methods of arriving at the value of a company's property differ. In recent years with an increasing price level, the companies have argued in favor of reproduction cost valuations or the value of plant and equipment expressed in current dollars, while the commissions generally have favored original cost valuations or the cost of plant and equipment when purchased or built. Regardless of the measure used, accrued depreciation must be subtracted so as to reflect the depreciated cost or value of the property. Land is usually separated from other tangible property. It is commonly valued either at its original cost or at the value of adjacent property, although qualified appraisals are sometimes accepted by the commissions. No depreciation is subtracted since land tends to appreciate in value over time.

In addition to tangible property, the rate base includes an allowance for working capital and depending on the circumstances amounts for overhead construction costs, water rights, and leaseholds. In former years, the regulated companies also argued that several intangibles—especially franchise value, going concern value, and good will—should be considered in rate-making, but current commission practices exclude these items.

The foregoing discussion assumes that the rate base is determined from the left-hand or asset side of the balance sheet, which represents the depreciated original cost of assets "used and useful" in the enterprise as well as an allowance for working capital. The rate base may also be determined from the right-hand side of the balance sheet, which constitutes the capital employed in the business. This second method is known as the invested-capital or prudent-investment rate base, and was long advocated by Justice Brandeis. "The thing devoted by the investor to the public use," he argued in the Southwestern Bell case, "is not specific property, tangible and intangible, but capital embarked in the enterprise."[15] Regulatory statutes permit some commissions to use either method, while limiting other commissions to only one.

Third, a "fair rate of return" must be determined. This rate is usually expressed as a percentage of the depreciated value of a company's property. Thus, a rate base of $100 million combined with a 7 percent fair rate of return will result in an annual allowance of $7 million as the fair-return component of

[15] Concurring opinion in *Missouri* ex rel. *Southwestern Bell Tel. Co.* v. *Missouri Public Service Comm.*, 262 U.S. 276, 290 (1923).

the firm's revenue requirement. (To this figure must be added the allowable operating costs to determine the firm's rate level.)

Whatever rate of return is allowed, it should perform two functions. It should be fair to investors so as to avoid the confiscation of their property. It should also preserve the credit standing of the company to enable it to attract new capital to maintain, improve, and expand its services in response to consumer demand. The regulated companies must compete for investment funds in the capital market with nonregulated businesses. Moreover, they are not guaranteed a fair rate of return; they are entitled to a fair return only if it can be earned. As expressed by the Supreme Court:

> . . . it may be safely generalized that the due process clause never has been held by this Court to require a commission to fix rates on the present reproduction value . . . or on the historical valuation of property whose history and current financial statements showed the value no longer to exist. . . . The due process clause has been applied to prevent governmental destruction of existing economic values. It has not and cannot be applied to insure values that have been lost by the operation of economic forces. [16]

The Rate Structure. The second aspect of rate regulation, the determination of a firm's rate structure, involves the establishment of rates (prices) to be charged consumers. The problem is complex. For some regulated companies, nonallocable (common or joint) costs represent a significant percentage of total costs. All regulated companies have various degrees of monopoly power in the market areas they serve and all have unused capacity some of the time. For these reasons, rate structures are differentiated; both supply (cost of service) and demand (value of service) considerations enter into their development. The nontransportation utilities, for example, sell the same service to different classes of buyers, with the classes largely determined by differences in demand elasticities. They do not charge each class the same rate. Often, differences in rates can be justified by differences in costs. Sometimes, they cannot and discrimination occurs.

In the absence of regulation, price discrimination may be favorable to the supplying companies and to some buyers but unfavorable to the vast majority of consumers. As has already been pointed out, there is a potential for a firm with monopoly power to charge more where demand is relatively inelastic and alternatives are lacking, and less where demand is relatively elastic and alternatives are available. Moreover, special prices or rebates may be given to those in the strongest bargaining position. Yet, because most of the regulated companies operate under conditions of decreasing costs, discrimination may be socially desirable. The seller who discriminates might well enjoy higher sales, lower costs, and larger profits, while the seller who is forbidden to discriminate might have smaller sales, higher costs, and smaller profits or even losses. Consumers, too,

---

[16] *Market Street Ry. Co. v. California Railroad Comm.*, 324 U.S. 548, 567 (1945).

may benefit from discrimination: lower prices usually result in a greater demand for—and, hence, consumption of—the company's services. The commissions and the courts, therefore, must control the utility's rate structure to prevent undue and unjust discrimination and to insure that the benefits of discrimination are realized.

Competition adds another dimension to the rate structure problem. As competition increases in strength, rates are forced toward the cost of service. But cost is a term with a variety of meanings, including marginal cost, incremental cost, out-of-pocket cost, average cost, and fully allocated cost. There is the need, consequently, to define properly the costs relevant to competitive rates, so that regulated firms will neither gain unfair competitive advantages nor be deprived of opportunities to compete for customers.

THE PHASES OF RATE REGULATION

An electric utility executive has pointed out that the history of regulation consists of three major phases—legislative, judicial, and administrative.[17] The legislative phase began with the *Munn* v. *Illinois* decision in 1877,[18] when the Supreme Court upheld the right of the state of Illinois to regulate grain elevators under its police powers. By implication, the constitutionality of other state laws regulating private firms was also established. The Court ruled, however, that the regulation of rates was a legislative function and that recourse against the abuse of that function must be at the polls and not from the courts. In 1890, the Court reversed its position, saying that the reasonableness of rates was subject to judicial review.[19] This decision marked the beginning of the judicial phase that was to last over four decades.

Throughout this period, the judiciary was to dominate regulatory policy. The *Smyth* v. *Ames* decision in 1898[20] listed a number of factors that the commissions should consider in determining the value of a company's property, but it did not assign a weight to each one. So started the valuation controversy concerning original versus reproduction cost, which was to occupy much of the commissions' and companies' time for many years. The Court, especially after the first World War, emphasized reproduction cost, as did the companies, while many commissions favored original cost. Then, in the Bluefield case of 1923,[21] the Supreme Court enumerated a number of factors the commissions should

---

[17]Ralph M. Besse, "Seventy-five Years of Public Utility Regulation in a Competitive Society" (mimeographed, 1953). Also see William H. Anderson, "The Supreme Court and Recent Public Utility Valuation Theory," 21 *Journal of Land & Public Utility Economics* 12 (1945).

[18]94 U.S. 113 (1877).

[19]*Chicago, Milwaukee & St. Paul Ry.* v. *Minnesota,* 134 U.S. 418 (1890).

[20]169 U.S. 466 (1898).

[21]*Bluefield Water Works & Imp. Co.* v. *Public Service Comm. of West Virginia,* 262 U.S. 679 (1923).

consider in determining the rate of return. Again, however, no weights were assigned to the various factors. In general, the Court found that a utility was entitled to a return "equal to that generally being made at the same time and in the same general part of the country on investments and in other business undertakings which are attended by corresponding risks and uncertainties."[22] The comparability-of-earnings standard, which had been developed in earlier cases, was reaffirmed.

These two judicial decisions, in particular,

> ... put the regulatory commissions on the spot. The rule of *Smyth* v. *Ames* required that full consideration be given to the many economic factors pertinent to valuation. It limited regulation to those factors arising as a result of elimination of competition, since valuation of property would be changed only as a result of changing economic conditions. The Bluefield case said that the fair rate of return for a utility should be gauged by that received in competitive industry of similar risk. Regulators were faced with the choice of either searching out the facts and reaching a decision in line with those facts, or having their decisions overruled by the courts. [23]

The Hope Natural Gas case of 1944[24] marks the beginning of the administrative phase, although the reasoning of this decision was foreshadowed in a number of earlier cases.[25] The Supreme Court held that the procedure and method of determining both the rate base and the rate of return should be left to the commissions.[26] Thus began the doctrine of the "end result." Only in cases of obvious injustice would the Court interfere with the rulings of the regulatory agencies.

According to Kahn, "The most important thing the Hope Natural Gas decision did was to invite regulatory commissions to break out of the mold into which they had been confined for forty-five years by *Smyth* v. *Ames* and start thinking about the economic requirements of effective public utility regulation."[27] In accepting this invitation, the commissions have been faced with the task of determining the criteria to be used in rate regulation. In establishing a reasonable or fair return, for instance, they have found reasonableness and fairness difficult terms to define. "The Supreme Court's concept of a reasonable return is really a notion of a zone of reasonableness. Confiscation of the property of a private company is the lower limit of the zone; exploitation of buyers,

[22]*Ibid.*, p. 692.

[23]Besse, *op. cit.*, p. 8.

[24]*Federal Power Comm.* v. *Hope Natural Gas Co.*, 320 U.S. 591 (1944).

[25]*McCardle* v. *Indianapolis Water Co.*, 272 U.S. 400 (1926); *Los Angeles Gas & Electric Corp.* v. *Railroad Comm. of Calif.*, 289 U.S. 287 (1933); *Federal Power Comm.* v. *Natural Gas Pipeline Co.*, 315 U.S. 575 (1942).

[26]The Hope Natural Gas decision applies only to the federal commissions and to appeals from state courts. State regulatory commissions are still bound by their own constitutional or statutory requirements.

[27]Alfred E. Kahn, "Inducements to Superior Performance: Price," in Trebing, *op. cit.*, p. 88 (citations omitted).

which is revealed by pricing practices and monopoly profits, is the upper limit. If the return is reasonable, it must fall between these limits."[28] Clearly, then, the required earnings of a company cannot be represented by a specific sum, nor determined by a precise formula. Rather, they will vary with the economic conditions of both the company and the economy. And what appears to be reasonable to one person or at one time may seem unreasonable to or at another.

Historically, far fewer cases involving questions of rate structure have been appealed to the courts. Most of these questions have been settled at the commission level. In many cases, commissions have been satisfied with the structures suggested by the companies and have adopted them without significant change. In other cases, particularly at the federal level, rate structures different from those proposed by the companies have been prescribed by the commissions. But as intra- and interindustry competition has increased in intensity, the commissions have become more involved in rate structure problems and in the development of proper pricing criteria and objectives.

The administrative phase of regulation, therefore, is relatively new. Freed from court domination, the federal and state commissions, acting within broad legislative provisions, have the responsibility for establishing their own criteria to determine both the rate level and the rate structure. And as long as the "end result" is just and reasonable, the courts (at least the Supreme Court) will not interfere. As will become readily apparent in the following chapters, there are few established or consistent criteria, so that regulatory practices vary considerably from commission to commission. Some, for example, use original cost valuations; others, reproduction cost valuations; still others, a combination of the two (known as fair value). For each problem raised, there are as many potential solutions as there are commissions and companies. Whether any uniform criteria can or should be established and accepted by all interested parties is doubtful, for the present diversity, despite its complexity, permits experimentation. Such experimentation, in turn, helps to prevent rigidity in the entire regulatory process.

COMMISSION PROCEDURES[29]

Commissions, as previously discussed, have considerable authority to regulate the earnings and rates of many important industries in the economy. To an increasing extent, they are taking the initiative in investigating companies under their jurisdiction. Even so, however, much of their work originates in requests

---

[28] Emery Troxel, *Economics of Public Utilities* (New York: Holt, Rinehart & Winston, Inc., 1947), p. 224.

[29] For a more complete analysis of this topic, see Frank E. Cooper, *State Administrative Law* (Indianapolis: The Bobbs-Merrill Co., Inc., 1965), Vols. I and II; Eugene D. Anderson, *ICC Practice and Procedure* (Indianapolis: The Bobbs-Merrill Co., Inc., 1966); and Francis X. Welch, *Cases and Text on Public Utility Regulation* (rev. ed.; Washington, D.C.: Public Utilities Reports, Inc., 1968), chap. xiii.

filed by the regulated companies and in complaints made by customers or competitors.

There are two types of proceedings: those initiated for the purpose of rule-making (such as the establishment of rules of practice and procedure for practicing lawyers, uniform systems of accounts, and safety standards) and those initiated for the purpose of settling a contested issue (such as proposed rate changes or merger applications). In turn, two general types of procedures are used by the commissions: formal and informal. Customer complaints are almost always dealt with by informal methods; rule-making proceedings by both formal and informal methods; and contested issues by formal methods. In recent years, there has been a trend toward the use of informal procedures in much of the commissions' activities—a trend due to the growing complexity of the regulatory process, as well as the need for more rapid commission decisions.

Formal Procedures

The requests filed by the regulated companies in the post-World War II period have largely dealt with the general level of rates and, in the case of railroads, with abandonment of service and with mergers. Such requests may be handled in formal proceedings. These proceedings vary considerably among the commissions, so that it is impossible to give an accurate description that will apply to every situation. In general, however, formal proceedings follow the provisions of the Federal Administrative Procedure Act, which provides:

Sec. 4. Except to the extent that there is involved (1) any military, naval, or foreign affairs function of the United States or (2) any matter relating to agency management or personnel or to public property, loans, grants, benefits, or contracts—

(a) *Notice.*—General notice of proposed rule making shall be published in the Federal Register (unless all persons subject thereto are named and either personally served or otherwise have actual notice thereof in accordance with law) and shall include (1) a statement of the time, place, and nature of public rule making proceedings; (2) reference to the authority under which the rule is proposed; and (3) either the terms or substance of the proposed rule or a description of the subjects and issues involved. Except where notice or hearing is required by statute, this subsection shall not apply to interpretative rules, general statements of policy, rules of agency organization, procedure, or practice, or in any situation in which the agency for good cause finds (and incorporates the findings and a brief statement of the reasons thereof in the rules issued) that notice and public procedure thereon are impracticable, unnecessary, or contrary to the public interest.

(b) *Procedures.*—After notice required by this section, the agency shall afford interested persons an opportunity to participate in the rule making through submission of written data, views, or arguments with or without opportunity to present the same orally in any manner; and, after consideration of all relevant matter presented, the agency shall incorporate in any rules adopted a concise general statement of their basis and purpose. Where rules are required by statute to be made on the record after opportunity for an agency hearing, the requirements of sections 7 and 8 shall apply in place of the provisions of this subsection.

(c) *Effective Dates.*—The required publication or service of any substantive rule (other than one granting or recognizing exemption or relieving restriction or interpretative rules and statements of policy) shall be made not less than thirty days prior to the effective date thereof except as otherwise provided by the agency upon good cause found and published with the rule.

(d) *Petitions.*—Every agency shall accord any interested person the right to petition for the issuance, amendment, or repeal of a rule.

Formal hearings, which normally follow these procedures, take time, work, and money. Assume, for example, that Company X files for a rate increase.[30] The company, with the concurrence of the commission or its staff, will generally select a "test period," frequently the latest 12-month period for which complete data are available. The purposes of such a test period are as follows. In the first place, the commission must examine company expenses. Only reasonable expenses are allowed for rate-making purposes. In the second place, the commission must have a basis for estimating future revenue requirements. This estimate is, perhaps, the most difficult problem in a rate case. A commission is setting rates for the future, but it has only past experience (expenses, cost, and demand conditions) to use as a guide. Frequently, future estimates of expenses will be made, thereby resulting in either an increase or decrease of the test period expenses. But the commissions have been hesitant to make future forecasts of consumer demand, often preferring instead to assume that the test period demand conditions will hold in the immediate future. For this reason, the actual rate of return earned by a regulated company may turn out to be quite different from the rate allowed by the commission in a particular rate case.

The case will be set down on the commission's docket for public hearings, and due notice will be given. When the case is called, testimony—sometimes oral and sometimes written ("canned")—will be presented by the company, the commission's staff, and interveners (interested parties).[31] Such testimony is usually

---

[30] Most regulatory commissions have the authority to suspend proposed rate increases for a period of time. Thus, the Interstate Commerce Commission may suspend a proposed change for seven months. At the end of this statutory period, the applicant may put the change into effect unless the commission has ruled otherwise. Proposed rate changes must usually be filed 30 days before they can become effective. See "Variations in Rate Tariff Suspension Periods," 74 *Public Utilities Fortnightly* 83 (October 22, 1964); and "Suspension of New and Existing Rate Tariff," 74 *Public Utilities Fortnightly* 58 (December 17, 1964).

[31] The FCC's requirements for intervention are typical. Petitions for leave to intervene in a formal proceeding must be filed within thirty days from the date of publication of the hearing issues in the *Federal Register*. Each petition "must set forth the interest of petitioner in the proceedings, must show how such petitioner's participation will assist the commission in the determination of the issues in question, and must be accompanied by the affidavit of a person with knowledge as to the facts set forth in the petition. The presiding officer, in his discretion, may grant or deny such petition or may permit intervention by such persons limited to particular issues or to a particular stage of the

presented by outside experts, as well as by both company and staff personnel.[32] All witnesses are sworn, the evidence is recorded, and witnesses may be questioned by the examiner[33] or commission and cross-examined by counsel for opposing parties. In some instances, hearings will be held in the community or communities affected. At the federal level, the examiner will then issue his decision (the "initial decision") on the case. The decision must be written and accompanied by formal findings of fact and conclusions of law. It is then subject to review by the full commission, and the commission's decision, in turn, may be appealed to the courts.

It is not uncommon for important cases to require several sets of hearings and to take from one to five years before a final commission order is issued. When a decision is appealed to the courts, another two to four years may be added. As a result, formal proceedings often involve delay to the disadvantage of all the parties involved.

Shortened Procedure.[34] In an attempt to save both time and expense, shortened procedures have been developed. One of the most important and widely used is the prehearing conference. The Rules of Practice of the Civil Aeronautics Board are typical:

Prior to any hearing there will ordinarily be a prehearing conference before an Examiner. . . . Written notice of the prehearing conference shall be sent by the Chief Examiner to all parties to a proceeding and to other persons who appear to have an interest in such proceeding. The purpose of such a conference is to define and simplify the issues and the scope of the proceeding, to secure statements of the positions of the parties, . . . to schedule the exchange of exhibits before the date set for hearing, and to arrive at such agreements as will aid in the conduct and disposition of the proceeding. For example, consideration will be given to: (1) Matters which the Board can consider without the necessity of proof; (2) admissions of fact and the genuineness of documents; (3) admissibility of evidence; (4) limitation of the number of witnesses; (5) reducing of oral testimony to exhibit form; (6) procedure at the hearings, etc. If necessary, the Examiner may require further

---

proceeding." For a more complete discussion, see Charles F. Phillips, Jr., "Interveners in the Telephone Investigation," 78 *Public Utilities Fortnightly* 26 (December 22, 1966).

[32] The potential dual role of a commission's staff in an adversary proceeding has been the subject of considerable debate. It is common for the staff to participate in formal hearings before the commission by presenting evidence and cross-examining witnesses. The staff, upon completion of the hearings, may then review and summarize the record, prepare recommendations for commission action, participate in the commission's deliberations and, finally, draft the initial decision. The issue is discussed at length in Chapter 18.

[33] A trial or hearing examiner is an official in the federal and in some of the state administrative agencies who performs the function of a judge—hearing evidence, listening to lawyers' arguments, and rendering an opinion. All such opinions may be appealed to the full commission. In many of the states, one of the commissioners may be assigned to hear a particular case; his decision may then be appealed to the full commission.

[34] For a more complete discussion of this topic, see Peter Woll, *Administrative Law: The Informal Process* (Berkeley and Los Angeles: University of California Press, 1963).

conference, or responsive pleadings, or both. The Examiner may also on his own motion or on motion of any party direct any party to a proceeding (air carrier or non-air carrier) to prepare and submit exhibits setting forth studies . . . relevant to the issues in the proceeding.[35]

Following the prehearing conference, "The Examiner shall issue a report of the prehearing conference, defining the issues, giving an account of the results of the conference, specifying a schedule for the exchange of exhibits and rebuttal exhibits, the date of hearings, and specifying a time for the filing of objections to such report."[36] The report is sent to all parties in the proceeding and, based upon their objections, may be revised by the examiner. The final report "shall constitute the official account of the conference and shall control the subsequent course of the proceeding, but it may be reconsidered and modified at any time to protect the public interest or to prevent injustice."[37] Finally, CAB examiners have the right to "hold conferences, before or during the hearings, for the settlement or simplification of issues."[38]

The regulatory agencies have adopted other informal methods as well to shorten formal proceedings. The Interstate Commerce Commission, for instance, uses a "modified procedure." As explained by Woll:

> The Rules of Practice of the ICC provide that if modified procedure is to be used, either by order of the Commission or by desire of the parties, statements of fact with regard to a particular case, together with exhibits, are to be filed in writing by the defendant, followed by the rebuttal of the complainant. Further, "if cross examination of any witness is desired the name of the witness and the subject matter of the desired cross examination shall, together with any other request for oral hearings, including the basis thereof, be stated. . . ." And, "the order setting the proceeding for oral hearing, if hearing is deemed necessary, will specify the matters upon which the parties are not in agreement and respecting which oral evidence is to be introduced." In this manner, under modified procedure, the ICC has adopted a selective formal procedure with regard to witnesses and evidence.[39]

The purposes of prehearing conferences and other informal methods are to simplify and clarify the issues in the case at hand and to dispose of minor issues prior to the initiation of formal proceedings. "The facts with respect to a particular case can be developed either independently by the agency or through the introduction of various forms of exhibits and stipulations of fact."[40] In both theory and practice, shortened procedures result in speedier regulatory decisions.

[35] Civil Aeronautics Board, Procedural Regulations, Part 302–"Rules of Practice in Economic Proceedings" (Washington, D.C.: U.S. Government Printing Office, 1961), p. 7.

[36] *Ibid.*

[37] *Ibid.*

[38] *Ibid.*

[39] Woll, *op. cit.,* pp. 39-40 (footnotes omitted).

[40] *Ibid.,* p. 57.

Informal Procedures

Informal procedures are frequently used to deal with customer complaints. Any customer may present a complaint directly to a regulatory commission. After an investigation, if the complaint has merit, a solution satisfactory to all concerned is arrived at without undue delay. Customer complaints commonly concern such matters as service interruptions, inaccurate metering, disputes over bills, poor voltage, and other similar grievances. Moreover, some commissions adopt informal procedures even when such issues as rates and rate of return are under consideration. Company and commission representatives meet periodically to discuss mutual regulatory problems and to reach agreements. Written statements or testimony from the parties involved may become part of the official transcript of the proceeding. Interested parties, however, are usually not permitted to intervene as in formal proceedings.

The advantages of informal procedures are threefold. First, time and money are saved. Decisions which might take several months to reach in formal hearings can often be made in several days of concentrated conferences.[41] Second, the commissioners, as opposed to their staffs, become better acquainted with the problems confronting the industries under their jurisdiction because they take an active part in informal conferences. Third, an informal atmosphere is usually more conducive to mutual understanding and respect than is a formal, courtroom-type proceeding.[42]

The FCC and Constant Surveillance.[43] The development and use of informal procedures are best illustrated with reference to the Federal Communications Commission and its regulation of the telephone industry. The need for constant or continuing surveillance was explained in 1938 as follows:

> Many of the problems of interstate telephone rate regulation are continuing in nature, calling at all times for frank, informal discussion between company and commission representatives. The atmosphere of the council table seems ordinarily much more conducive to the development of positive results in such matters than does the adversary air which tends to surround

[41] "Informal settlement of rate level cases is especially desirable since it eliminates the need for expensive litigation and very often makes it possible for customers to begin paying lower rates much sooner than would be possible if full litigation were necessary." Chairman White, Federal Power Commission, quoted in National Association of Regulatory Utility Commissioners, *Annual Proceedings, 1966* (Washington, D.C., 1967), p. 403.

"This industry [airline] is too dynamic and moves too fast for procedures and proceedings the determination of which is measured in terms of years to be the best way to keep its fares in line with changing conditions and requirements." Chairman Murphy, Civil Aeronautics Board, quoted in *ibid.*

[42] "Many tasks call for round-tables and unbuttoned vests, not for witness chairs and courtroom trappings." K. C. Davis, *Administrative Law Treatise* (St. Paul: West Publishing Co., 1958), p. 284.

[43] See Francis X. Welch, "Constant Surveillance: A Modern Regulatory Tool," 8 *Villanova Law Review* 340 (1963). For a discussion on the use of informal procedures by the state commissions, see National Association of Regulatory Utility Commissioners, *Annual Proceedings, 1965* (Washington, D.C., 1966), pp. 65–67.

most formal proceedings. The aspect of a game or contest which inevitably envelopes the respective advocates (be they lawyers, accountants, engineers, or what not) in formal rate cases makes for bickering and bitterness, as well as for delay and expense.

If the essential factors can be soundly defined and weighted, and if their factual background can be fully and frankly developed, the positive and direct methods of informal negotiation should prove effective, and desired ends should be attainable with a minimum expenditure of time, money and effort. Only through some such concept of regulatory functions can an end apparently be brought to the sorry spectacle of "ten year rate cases." *In rate making, time is always of the essence*, and certain of the state commissions are today making notable progress in the development of informal regulatory machinery. [44]

To implement this policy, [45] the FCC and the Bell Telephone System have developed routines for submitting regular reports (about 300 yearly) on a monthly, quarterly, and semiannual basis. Special reports are submitted when needed. At all times, therefore, the Commission has at its disposal "a veritable fluoroscope of Bell telephone system operating performance." [46] Informal proceedings are usually initiated by the FCC's Common Carrier Bureau. "The agenda for those conferences is decided and prepared, and in the final stages the full commission may sit to hear the informal and uninhibited discussion by company spokesmen and experts called in to explain the company's position under various topics on the agenda." [47] The Commission also maintains field offices which inspect and audit Bell System operations throughout the country.

Between the investigation ordered by Congress in 1935 and the full-scale investigation initiated late in 1965, the FCC did not hold a formal hearing on the entire interstate telephone rate structure. (The Commission did hold many formal hearings on specific issues and rates.) But the FCC has not been lax in regulating such rates. Some fifty negotiated interstate telephone rate changes during this period resulted in a net savings to the public of over $1.5 billion annually, based on 1967 volumes of business. Interstate rates decreased by 24 percent between 1940 and 1967. There were similar reductions in intrastate revenue requirements, totaling more than $350 million annually, based on 1967 volumes of business, due to changes in separations procedures. [48]

[44] Federal Communications Commission, "Final Report of the Telephone Rate and Research Department" (Washington, D.C., 1938), p. 68 (footnote omitted; emphasis in original). Some regulatory statutes require formal hearings, while others leave the type of proceeding to the commission.

[45] The FCC's use of constant surveillance has been tested and upheld in the courts. See *Public Utilities Comm. of State of California* v. *United States*, 356 F. 2d 236 (9th Cir. 1966), *cert. denied*, 385 U.S. 816 (1966).

[46] Welch, "Constant Surveillance . . . ," *op. cit.*, p. 352.

[47] *Ibid.*

[48] Significantly, the FCC has indicated that it intends to return to constant surveillance upon completion of the general investigation initiated in 1965. "We have not repudiated continuing surveillance. We agree with Bell that it is often an effective and highly efficient method of regulation and we appreciate the cooperation which has con-

SUMMARY

As the American economy has developed, the regulatory process has become extremely complex. "Technological and economic change have revolutionized traditional relationships, and eroded conventional conceptions of market structure, conduct, and performance. And the future promises more of the same."[49] Modern technology has tended to blur the common distinction between regulated and nonregulated industries. One result is a growing tendency to treat the regulated industries "as only one part of the economy, rather than as isolated entities."[50] Significant competition, both among regulated industries and between regulated and nonregulated industries, has developed. "Behavior which might be reasonable given a market structure approximating a natural monopoly may be fraught with disaster once that structure is exposed to potential erosion by competitive product or process innovations."[51] To these factors must be added the multiplicity of regulatory goals. Economic, political, and social goals all are interwoven into the regulatory process.

To cope with these complexities, new procedures have been, and are being, developed. Increasingly is emphasis being placed on informal procedures as opposed to formal procedures. This trend has been attacked and defended at length.[52] But the fact remains that informal procedures have been adopted in an attempt to reduce regulatory lag and to cope with rapid technological change. At the same time, far too little attention has been devoted to analyzing the economic effects of regulation. The same forces which call for new procedures also call for new and continuing economic analysis. What, for example, is the proper role of competition in the regulatory process? If competitive forces continue to grow stronger, can regulation be relaxed? Does the present regulatory system offer adequate incentives to efficiency? Admittedly, such questions are difficult to answer, but they should be kept in mind as attention is directed to the detailed principles of regulation in the following chapters.

One final point. In considering the problems of regulation, it should be emphasized that they are policy problems. As explained by Lewis:

> . . . They are not problems of right and wrong, for which there is only one right solution as distinct from all other solutions—which are, perforce, wrong. The "principles" of public-utility regulation are not "scientific principles" or

---

tributed to its past success. Under appropriate circumstances, we intend to use the method again. Indeed, we believe that the standards and criteria developed on the record here will enable us to employ continuing surveillance even more effectively in the future." Federal Communications Commission, "Memorandum Opinion and Order," Docket No. 16258 (FCC 65-1144, December 22, 1965), p. 6.

[49] Walter Adams and Joel B. Dirlam, "Market Structure, Regulation, and Dynamic Change," in Trebing, *op. cit.,* p. 131.

[50] William G. Shepherd, "Conclusion," in Shepherd and Gies, *op. cit.,* p. 270.

[51] Adams and Dirlam, *op. cit.,* p. 138.

[52] The pros and cons of informal versus formal procedures are considered at length in Chapter 18.

"natural laws." Essentially, regulation has an identifiable job to do, and its organization and operation should be established and determined functionally in the light of that job; it is a matter of defining a goal and proceeding economically to achieve it. Regulation involves the human adjustment of resources to accomplish humanly established ends. Regulation is limited and guided both by what we want and by what we are willing to give in order to get what we want. To say that there are no immutable laws of regulation is not to say that regulation is, by nature, amorphous, loose, aimless, adrift. It can be just as purposeful and tight and firm as we care to make it. The point is that regulation and regulatory policies must be *made;* they are not revealed to us, nor do we discover them.[53]

[53] Lewis, "Emphasis and Misemphasis in Regulatory Policy," *op. cit.*, pp. 214-15.

Chapter

6

ACCOUNTING

AND

FINANCING

It seems that accounting as an art, adjustable and flexible, even under strict regulatory control, produces many variations as a result of managerial discretion.

—John F. Kavanaugh*

Two aspects of regulation, while of vital significance in overall regulatory activity, are largely historical. At the turn of the century and continuing into the early 1930's, methods of both accounting and financing were abused by American industry. This situation was partly due to the infancy of the accounting profession and of business. However, it was also a result of the opportunities for enormous profits which often accrued to the unscrupulous.

From the point of view of the regulated industries, the development of uniform systems of accounts and of control over financing by the commissions has decreased the *opportunity* for abuses in this area. Of equal importance, the *desire* has decreased as the business system has matured. Despite these changes, it is essential that the need for and development of accounting and financing regulation be examined. Moreover, several issues, such as cost allocation methods and supervision of capital structures, deserve attention. These are the topics of the present chapter.

REGULATION OF ACCOUNTING

In the early days of regulation, little attention was paid to the methods of accounting used by the regulated industries. Notorious abuses appeared. Operating expenses were overstated, the investment in plant and equipment was impossible to ascertain, utility and nonutility businesses were not separated, and over-capitalization—often at the expense of the investor—was common due to the lack of reliable figures.[1] Under these conditions, the goals of regulation were

---

*John F. Kavanaugh, "Accounting for Overhead Costs," in *Proceedings, National Conference of Electric and Gas Utility Accountants* (New York: Edison Electric Institute, 1952), p. 331.

[1] Earl H. Barbee, "As Represented: Adventures in Public Utility Accounting," 11 *Journal of Land & Public Utility Economics* 25 (1935).

frustrated; effective regulation requires commission control of accounting procedures.

The Objectives of Accounting Regulation

Several basic objectives of accounting regulation can be realized under uniform systems of accounts. In the first place, rate regulation requires accurate records of revenues, operating costs, depreciation expenses, and investment in plant and equipment, among others. Here, uniformity is often essential, since rate regulation may be undertaken on an industry or group basis. In the transportation industries, for example, the commissions must compare the net investment of two or more companies within the same industry. Uniformity is also desirable so that the regulated companies are not subject to different accounting regulations in each of the states in which they operate—a situation that would require keeping several different sets of records.[2]

In the second place, accounting regulation is needed so as to distinguish between expenditures that should be charged to capital and those that should be charged to income. (This control is exercised for all business by the Securities and Exchange Commission and independent auditors.) Expenditures that represent investment in capital assets (plant and equipment) should be charged to fixed asset accounts rather than to operating expense accounts. Similarly, expenditures that represent costs of doing business should be charged to operating expense accounts rather than to capital. If these distinctions are not made, earnings can be inflated by charging operating expenses to capital, or concealed by charging capital to operating expenses. Again, uniformity is essential, for without it, the accounting practices of the various companies would differ. One firm might charge all replacements to operating expenses, even if the expenditures were for improved equipment. Another firm might distinguish between an expenditure that represented a replacement in kind and one that represented an improvement, charging the first to operating expenses and the second to capital. Such varied practices would make impossible industry-wide regulation, which requires comparisons among the firms in the particular industry.

In the third place, as regulated companies are entitled to a fair rate of return on the fair value of their property, an accurate statement of a company's property account is one of the most important objectives of accounting regulation and uniform systems of accounts. Prior to the mid-1930's, some of the worst abuses occurred with respect to property valuations: values were often increased arbitrarily, and property was exchanged between affiliated companies at inflated prices. As explained by Troxel:

> These write-ups and "inside" property exchanges were parts of holding-company finance, parts of the reckless expansion and questionable business

---

[2] Interstate companies, however, must separate their total operating costs, expenses, investment, and so forth, between their interstate and intrastate operations. Intrastate costs, moreover, must be allocated to each state in which such companies do business. See pp. 153–62.

conduct of public utility promoters. Sometimes a plant was exchanged several times, or was included in several successive consolidations. And as each exchange or consolidation was effected, the plant was recorded at higher and higher book values. Some affiliated companies exchanged properties, indeed, because they wanted to write up their property values. When holding companies or their management companies added fees to the acquisition prices of properties, further write-ups occurred. Some write-ups were imaginary "overhead" expenses of construction work. And another kind of book value revision was common too: managers made an "inside" revaluation of property and credited the increment to the capital surplus account. Other companies wrote up book values to the reproduction costs of their properties; or they wrote up property accounts to whatever figures suited their financial purposes.[3]

Regulatory commissions, therefore, must have control over a company's property account. But at this point, an important distinction must be made. All commissions require that property accounts show the original cost of property items. The rate of return, moreover, is based on the value of, or investment in, property used and useful in providing a particular service. However, the value of a company's property in an accounting sense is not necessarily the same as the value of a company's property for rate-making purposes. In rate-making cases, valuation may be based upon original cost, reproduction cost, or some figure between these two measures.[4]

In the fourth place, carrier and utility business must be separated from noncarrier and nonutility business. The regulated companies are permitted to earn a fair rate of return on the property devoted to carrier or utility purposes. A great majority of such companies, however, have other investments, expenses, and sources of revenue. They may have investments or make loans to other companies; they may own other businesses; they may sell electric or gas appliances. With few exceptions (such as telephone directory revenues), these outside expenses and revenues are not subject to regulation. The commissions can permit a company to earn neither more than a fair return to make up for other unprofitable undertakings nor less when a company has additional sources of income that are profitable.

In the fifth place, accounting regulation is of aid to the commissions and companies in evaluating the reasonableness of rates. The regulated companies provide many different types of service. Unit cost information is essential in controlling price discrimination and in determining the profitability of competitive rates. It must be emphasized, however, that the cost of providing a particular service cannot be determined from accounting data alone. Directly allocated costs can be charged to different service accounts; common or joint costs cannot. This problem will be discussed below.

[3] Emery Troxel, *Economics of Public Utilities* (New York: Holt, Rinehart & Winston, Inc., 1947), pp. 123-24.
[4] The problem is discussed at length in Chapter 8.

Finally, accounting regulation is beneficial to investors. Before effective accounting regulation was undertaken, accounts were frequently misrepresented and earnings raised or lowered to suit a company's immediate purpose. Investors lacked reliable information on which to make intelligent investment decisions. Commissions, too, lacked reliable data and found it impossible to regulate the issuance of new securities. Overcapitalization, stock watering, and excessive indebtedness became common. During the depression of the thirties, millions were lost by investors when reorganizations (railroads) were necessary and holding company (electric and gas) abuses were uncovered.

The Development of Uniform Systems

The courts have long upheld the commissions' right to prescribe accounting practices. In 1912, for example, the Supreme Court said:

> If the Commission is to successfully perform its duties in respect to reasonable rates, undue discriminations, and favoritism, it must be informed as to the business of the carriers by a system of accounting which will not permit the possible concealment of forbidden practices. . . . Further, the requiring of information concerning a business is not regulation of that business. [5]

In a later case, the Court went even further, implying its approval of almost any method of accounting regulation adopted by the commissions. The Court argued:

> Whether the Commission should make special classifications to fit exceptional cases lies within the discretion conferred, and courts ought not to be called upon to interfere with or correct alleged errors with respect to accounting practice. If we were in disagreement with the Commission as to the wisdom and propriety of the order, we are without power to usurp its discretion and substitute our own. [6]

Uniform systems of accounts, however, developed slowly. [7] Early legislative statutes either made no provision for commission control of accounting methods, or, when provision was made, the commissions often did not act. Massachusetts was the first state to direct its commission to prescribe uniform accounting systems: for railroads in 1876, gas companies in 1885, and electric utilities in 1887. The regulatory agencies of New York and Wisconsin were given jurisdiction over the accounting practices of public utilities in 1905 and 1907,

[5] *Interstate Commerce Comm.* v. *Goodrich Transit Co.*, 224 U.S. 194, 211 (1912). Also see *Kansas City Southern Ry. Co.* v. *United States*, 231 U.S. 423 (1913).

[6] *Norfolk & Western Ry. Co.* v. *United States*, 287 U.S. 134, 141 (1932). Four years later, the Court stated: "Error or unwisdom is not equivalent to abuse. What has been ordered must appear to be 'so entirely at odds with fundamental principles of correct accounting' . . . as to be the expression of a whim rather than an exercise of judgment." *American Tel. & Tel. Co.* v. *United States*, 299 U.S. 232, 236–37 (1936).

[7] See Jay H. Price, Jr., Richard Walker, and Leonard Spacek, "Accounting Uniformity in the Regulated Industries," 30 *Law and Contemporary Problems* 824, 830–35 (1965).

respectively, and they prescribed uniform systems for electric and gas utilities in 1909.

In other instances, the regulated companies developed their own uniform accounting systems. The National Electric Light Association, an organization of private electric utilities, devised the first important standard classification of electric accounts. In 1907, the Association of American Railway Accountants in cooperation with the Interstate Commerce Commission developed a similar system of accounting for the nation's railroads. In 1913, the ICC established a uniform system for telephone companies (over which it then had jurisdiction), and in 1922, the National Association of Regulatory Utility Commissioners (NARUC) prescribed uniform systems of accounts for electric and gas companies. These systems served as models, and by 1925, 40 states had adopted or approved such uniform classifications.[8] These early systems, though better than no systems at all,

> . . . had significant defects. They gave too much accounting authority to the utility companies. When the first draft of the uniform electric system was drawn up in 1920, representatives of private electric companies did much of the work. And the accounting ideas of private electric systems were evident in the final draft of the uniform system. Managers of utility companies could fix, in part, the book valuation standard for property, and could choose the method of depreciation accounting.[9]

Major revisions in accounting control of electric, gas, and telephone companies were made during the depression of the thirties. The Federal Communications Commission adopted in 1935, with only minor modifications, the uniform system for telephone companies which had been promulgated by the ICC in 1913, and in 1937, the NARUC approved a similar system for intrastate telephone companies. In 1936, systems of accounts were developed for electric companies by the Federal Power Commission and the NARUC, and by the NARUC for gas companies. Shortly after Congress passed the Natural Gas Act in 1938, the FPC prescribed a uniform system of accounts for all interstate natural gas companies. And in the Motor Carrier Act of 1935, the Civil Aeronautics Act of 1938, and the Transportation Act of 1940, provisions were made for the Interstate Commerce Commission and Civil Aeronautics Board to prescribe uniform systems of accounts for motor carriers, airlines, and water carriers. These systems were subsequently developed. Since this time, the uniform systems have been modified on numerous occasions, but they remain substantially as developed during the thirties.

The systems prescribed by the federal commissions went into effect immediately, but the state commissions had to adopt the systems before they became effective. Today, most of the state commissions have adopted either the federal or the NARUC accounting systems, although they are often modified in detail to

---

[8] *Re Montana Power Co.,* 42 PUR 3d 241, 252 (Mont., 1962).
[9] Troxel, *op. cit.,* p. 121.

fit local situations or problems. Thus, forty-one of the state commissions regulating private electric utilities prescribe the FPC or NARUC systems of accounts, four have their own systems, and two are without uniform systems, while forty of the state commissions regulating telephone companies prescribe the FCC uniform system of accounts, six have their own systems, and four have not prescribed systems of accounts.[10]

Comparability and Rate Regulation

As is true with almost all regulatory procedures, uniform systems of accounts represent a tool. There are many important differences of opinion with respect to the scope, content, and application of the various provisions of any uniform system. Because of alternative accounting principles, uniform accounting standards have not been adopted by the regulatory commissions.[11] Consequently, while there is widespread comparability of financial reports filed by companies within each jurisdiction, there is little interjurisdictional comparability.[12]

There is a related issue: Do the regulatory commissions have authority over financial reporting to the public? The Federal Power Commission has assumed jurisdiction by requiring that reports to stockholders conform to the accounting requirements set forth in its uniform systems of accounts. Its authority was upheld in 1964.[13] No other commission has claimed jurisdiction over public financial statements, although the Interstate Commerce Commission requires that "any variance" from its prescribed accounting rules in financial statements be "clearly disclosed in footnotes to the statements."[14]

Further, it is important to keep in mind that a commission

... is not bound in its rate proceedings by any system of accounts it may have prescribed or by what is revealed in a review of the systems of accounts. Utility regulation, the making of business decisions, and the determination of

10 Federal Power Commission, "Federal and State Commission Jurisdiction and Regulation, Electric, Gas, and Telephone Utilities, 1967" (Washington, D.C.: U.S. Government Printing Office, 1968), p. 18.

11 See Price, Walker, and Spacek, *op. cit.*, pp. 839–47; and two articles by Gordon R. Corey, "Some Controversial Aspects of Accounting," 79 *Public Utilities Fortnightly* 46 (January 5, 1967) and "Problems in Uniform Accounting," 79 *ibid*. 23 (January 19, 1967).

12 See Alfred L. Burke, "The Investor Looks at Accounting Problems in the Utility Industry," 21 *Financial Analysts Journal* 27 (Sept.–Oct., 1965); and Homer E. Sayad, "Consistency in Utility Financial Statements," 80 *Public Utilities Fortnightly* 17 (September 14, 1967).

13 *Appalachian Power Co.* v. *Federal Power Comm.*, 328 F. 2d 237 (4th Cir. 1964), *cert. denied*, 379 U.S. 829 (1964). Late in 1967, the FPC revised its regulations to require electric utilities and natural gas pipeline companies to add to their annual reports a statement from independent certified, or licensed, public accountants attesting to the conformity of certain schedules in the reports with the commission's accounting requirements. FPC, News Release No. 15288 (December 29, 1967).

14 ICC Order No. 33581 (1964).

values cannot be reduced to an automatic process by which the correct decision can be made by reference to books of accounts.[15]

In rate proceedings, therefore, a commission may (and occasionally does) disallow certain expenditures for rate-making purposes or may place a value on a regulated company's property (in determining the rate base) that exceeds the original cost of that property as shown in the uniform system of accounts. These problems are considered in succeeding chapters.

Uniform Systems of Accounts

The uniform systems of accounts used by the federal commissions are similar to those adopted by the National Association of Regulatory Utility Commissioners. They can be illustrated with reference to the uniform system prescribed by the Federal Power Commission for Class A and Class B interstate electric utilities.[16]

Balance Sheet Accounts. A condensed balance sheet form is shown in Figure 6-1. On the asset side, the most important account is "Utility Plant." The FPC, along with the other federal commissions, requires that property accounts show the original cost of all items entered. It is important to realize, however, that the term "original cost" has a special meaning—that is, it represents "the cost of such property to the person first devoting it to public service."[17] This definition is not the conventional accounting meaning, for accountants generally value property at its cost to the existing company (the investment cost). Thus, when a utility builds its own plant, the total cost of construction is entered under the appropriate utility plant account. When property is acquired as a gift, it is entered on the basis of the estimated value at the time of donation. But when property is purchased from another company, it is recorded in the plant account on the basis of its original cost, even though the acquiring firm may have paid more or less than this figure for the property.[18] The costs of additions and improvements are added when incurred, whether paid for from accrued depreciation, retained earnings, or the proceeds of security issues; any excess cost of replacing property in kind over the original cost of the property

---

[15] *Re Montana Power Co.*, 42 PUR 3d 241, 253 (Mont., 1962). Also see *Federal Power Comm. v. Hope Natural Gas Co.*, 320 U.S. 591, 643-44 (1944).

[16] Federal Power Commission, *Uniform System of Accounts Prescribed for Public Utilities and Licensees*, effective January 1, 1961 (Washington, D.C.: U.S. Government Printing Office, 1960). The accounts shown in Figures 6-1 and 6-2 are from this publication.

[17] *Ibid.*, p. 2.

[18] The difference between the original cost and a higher purchase price (the usual situation) is either added to operating expenses or amortized over a period of years. If, however, the commission feels that the difference is not "legitimate" (such as representing an excessive price for property transferred between affiliated companies), it is charged to earned or capital surplus, and thus charged to the company's stockholders. Many state commissions, it should be noted, use the accountants' concept of original cost, thereby charging the entire purchase price to the plant account.

FIGURE 6-1
Condensed Balance Sheet Accounts

Assets and Other Debits	*Liabilities and Other Credits*
Utility plant [a]	Proprietary capital [e]
Other property and investments [b]	Long-term debt [f]
Current and accrued assets [c]	Current and accrued liabilities [g]
Deferred debits [d]	Deferred credits [h]
	Operating reserves [i]
	Contributions in aid of construction [j]
	Accumulated deferred income taxes [k]

[a] Electric plant less accumulated provision for depreciation and amortization.

[b] Nonutility property less accumulated provision for depreciation and amortization, investments in associated companies, other investments, special funds.

[c] Cash, special deposits, working funds, temporary cash investments, notes and accounts receivable, receivables from associated companies, materials and supplies, other current and accrued assets.

[d] Unamortized debt discount and expense, extraordinary property losses, other deferred debits.

[e] Common capital stock, preferred capital stock, other paid-in capital, earned surplus.

[f] Bonds, advances from associated companies, other long-term debt.

[g] Notes payable, accounts payable, payables to associated companies, customer deposits, taxes accrued, interest accrued, other current and accrued liabilities.

[h] Unamortized premium on debt, customer advances for construction, other deferred credits.

[i] Property insurance reserve, injuries and damages reserve, provisions and benefits reserve, amortization reserve—federal, miscellaneous operating reserves.

[j] "This account shall include donations or contributions in cash, services, or property from states, municipalities or other governmental agencies, individuals, and others for construction purposes."

[k] Accumulated deferred income taxes—accelerated amortization, liberalized depreciation, and other.

retired is added to the account. Abandoned property is written off. Finally, the cost of construction work in progress is also added.

As previously discussed, the regulatory commissions must make a distinction between charges made to capital and charges made to income. The commissions have prescribed lists of retirement units to handle this problem. A retirement unit list contains those property items whose costs are recorded in the plant account when they are acquired, whose costs are charged to depreciation expense during their useful lives, and which are withdrawn from the plant account when they are retired. While the commissions prescribe these lists, specifying the grouping of similar items of plant, the regulated companies may subdivide each of the commission-prescribed categories for their own analysis.

All federal commissions and most of the state commissions also require the maintenance of continuing property records or inventories. Property items found in the list of retirement units are arranged according to their technical characteristics, location (usually by plants, taxing districts, or the operating systems of each company), date of installation, and original cost. When a property item is retired, it is withdrawn from the continuing property record. In addition to showing the original cost of property, such records provide useful information for measuring the service life of property and for aiding in the computation of depreciation rates. And when reproduction cost valuations are desired, they can be obtained by multiplying each property item by its current price, including the current cost of installation.[19] Such a procedure is quicker and cheaper than taking a complete inventory every time a new valuation is required.

Finally, the uniform balance sheet requires the separation of utility and nonutility businesses, and provides special accounts to record transactions among affiliated companies. The first is necessary for rate regulation; the second to prevent abuses or excessive charges among affiliated enterprises.

Income Accounts. Whereas the balance sheet shows the financial position of a company at a specific moment of time, the income statement reflects the results of operations over a specified period of time. If commissions are to supervise operating expenses, they must have accurate and reliable uniform data. This information is contained in the prescribed income accounts. All expenditures charged to operating expense accounts must be "just and reasonable"; if they are not, they are charged to stockholders rather than to consumers.

The income accounts illustrated in Figure 6–2 are largely self-explanatory. Detailed instructions for each type of expense are given to indicate in which account they should be entered. It should be noted that nonutility income is reported separately from utility income. For regulatory purposes, the most important account is "Total Operating Income," which represents the company's income from utility business. It should also be noted that donations to charitable, social, or welfare programs are charged to stockholders,[20] as are the rare penalties and fines levied by the commissions for violating regulatory statutes.

All uniform systems of accounts require depreciation accounting. Over the past half century, the depreciation practices of the regulated industries have changed significantly. Prior to the thirties, most of the companies, with the notable exception of the Bell Telephone System, practiced retirement accounting, whereby either the whole investment cost of property is charged to depreciation expense only when retired from service, or part of the investment cost is charged to a partial reserve and accumulated during the useful life of the property. As a result, the companies were able to control their annual reported earnings: when actual earnings were high, they could make large charges to depreciation expense, thereby lowering reported earnings and avoiding regulatory rate and earnings reductions; when actual earnings were low, they could

---

[19] In the Bell System, for example, despite the fact that Western Electric's prices are currently lower than in 1950, the reproduction cost new of the telephone companies' plant is higher than in 1950 because the increased cost of installing the equipment has more than offset the decreased price of the equipment.

[20] The practice of charging donations to stockholders is not universal among the commissions. See Chapter 7, pp. 186–87.

FIGURE 6-2
Condensed Income Accounts

Operating revenues
Operating expenses[a]
    Operating income[b]
Income from electric plant leased to others
Other utility operating income[c]
    Total operating income[d]
Other income[e]
    Total income[f]
Miscellaneous income deductions[g]
    Income before interest charges[h]
Interest charges[i]
    Net income[j]
Earned surplus[k]

[a] Includes operating expense, maintenance expense, depreciation expense, amortization of electric plant, taxes, provisions for deferred income taxes, income taxes deferred in prior years—credit.

[b] Operating revenues minus operating expenses.

[c] Income from operations of other utility plant (gas, railway, etc.).

[d] Income from utility plant operations plus income from plant leased to others.

[e] Income from nonutility business, such as merchandising, jobbing, and contract work, nonoperating rental income, and interest and dividend income.

[f] Total operating income plus nonutility income.

[g] Includes miscellaneous amortization, donations for charitable, social, or community welfare purposes, and penalties or fines for violation of statutes pertaining to regulation.

[h] Total income minus miscellaneous income deductions.

[i] Includes interest on long-term debt, amortization of debt discount and expense, interest charged to construction—credit.

[j] Income before interest charges minus interest charges.

[k] Beginning balance of earned surplus plus net income minus dividends on preferred and common stock equals earned surplus at end of period.

make few, if any, charges to depreciation expense, thereby making it possible to pay some common stock dividends by overstating reported earnings. Nor were the rates of depreciation uniform. In its 1926 investigation of depreciation accounting, for instance, the Interstate Commerce Commission found that wooden freight cars had been given service lives ranging from 3 to 60 years by different carriers; steam locomotives, from 4 to 55 years; steel passenger cars, from 5 to 50 years; and wooden passenger cars, from 5 to 66 years.[21]

During the thirties and early forties, the commissions gradually required the regulated companies to accrue depreciation, making annual charges to depreciation expense so as to distribute the original cost over the service life of the property. This practice is known as depreciation accounting, as distinguished from retirement accounting. In addition, the commissions have prescribed the various plant accounts for which depreciation charges are to be set up, and have

[21] *Depreciation Charges of Steam Railroad Companies*, 118 ICC 295, 336–37 (1926).

established rates of depreciation for the most important types of property. Depreciation charges generally are computed on the basis of the original cost of the property.[22] Depreciation accounting will be considered in greater detail in Chapter 7.

Cost Allocation Methods

The property of many regulated companies is used in common to (*a*) furnish service to different customer classes, (*b*) provide different services, or (*c*) supply both intrastate and interstate services. In these circumstances, cost allocation methods are required. The methods used to allocate common or joint costs[23] for rate-making purposes are discussed in later chapters. Two cases, however, deserve separate treatment: the separation of expenses between railroad freight and passenger services, and the separation of costs between intrastate and interstate telephone services. In both instances, detailed cost allocation methods —known as separations procedures—have been adopted by the Interstate Commerce Commission and, until 1965, accepted on an interim basis by the Federal Communications Commission, respectively.[24]

Accounting regulation offers little guidance in developing cost allocation methods, since common or joint costs cannot generally be identified with any customer class, specific service, or jurisdiction. As Justice Douglas has put it:

> A separation of properties is merely a step in the determination of costs properly allocable to the various classes of services rendered by a utility. But where as here several classes of services have a common use of the same property difficulties of separation are obvious. Allocation of costs is not a matter for the slide-rule. It involves judgment on a myriad of facts. It has no claim to an exact science.[25]

Stated another way, each cost allocation method contains elements of arbitrari-

[22] When the regulated companies switched from retirement accounting to depreciation accounting, it was often impossible to set up a depreciation account showing the depreciation already accrued on their property. Such a requirement would have seriously impaired the financial condition of many companies by decreasing or eliminating entirely their surplus accounts. Consequently, for those companies that formerly used retirement accounting, present depreciation reserves usually show only the accrued depreciation since the transition to the depreciation accounting system.

[23] Common and joint costs are similar in that they arise when the production of one product results in the output of another. But there is a theoretical distinction between the two: joint costs require that the joint products be produced in fixed proportions (i.e., beef and hides), while the proportions can vary when common costs are involved. Moreover, common and joint costs can be both variable and fixed with respect to changes in output. That is, while fixed costs generally belong to the business as a whole, they may be partially traceable to particular services and, conversely, while variable costs generally are traceable to particular services, they may be partially common or joint to two or more services.

[24] Railroad separations procedures were discussed in the *Minnesota Rate Cases*, 230 U.S. 352 (1913); telephone separations in *Smith* v. *Illinois Bell Tel. Co.*, 282 U.S. 133 (1930).

[25] *Colorado Interstate Gas Co.* v. *Federal Power Comm.*, 324 U.S. 581, 589 (1945).

ness. The results obtained by the application of a particular method are affected by the method employed.

Railroad Industry. Under the current ICC methods of separating railroad freight and passenger accounts,[26] all railroad expenses, taxes, and net equipment and joint facility rents are divided into: (1) those solely related to freight service, (2) those solely related to passenger and allied services, (3) those common to both freight service and passenger and allied services, and (4) those related to neither freight nor passenger service—that is, the costs of nontransport activities. It is the third category that raises substantial difficulties.

The general rule for separating expenses states: "The test of whether an item of expense is direct or common should be based upon whether the service performed or the use of the facility is related solely to the freight service or to the passenger service, on the one hand or on the other hand, is common to both freight and passenger services."[27] The common costs are normally allocated to freight and passenger services according to the proportion of common physical units of each service. Thus, maintenance of way and structures on common running tracks is divided between the two services in proportion to the gross ton-miles over the tracks by each service, yard switching according to the total switching locomotive-hours of each service, miscellaneous general expenses in proportion to the total costs incurred by each service.[28] Taxes and net equipment and joint facility rents are separated in a similar manner.[29] On the basis of these separations procedures, and with the exception of four years during World War II, passenger and allied services have been operated at a deficit since 1936 (Table 6-1).

These procedures, however, have been the subject of considerable criticism. First, the procedure fails to provide a uniform treatment of costs, because the railroads treat accounts differently. Some roads, for example, treat the enginehouse expense account as common, while others treat it as solely related.[30] Second, the allocation of common costs according to the proportion of common physical units of each service assumes that freight and passenger service units are identical. "Yet some railroad men maintain that a gross ton-mile of passenger service adds twice as much to maintenance costs as a gross ton-mile of freight service, whereas other railroad men maintain that at current levels of freight traffic a gross ton-mile of passenger service requires no significant additional maintenance expenditures."[31]

[26] This discussion is based upon Interstate Commerce Commission, *Rules Governing the Separation of Operating Expenses, Railway Taxes, Equipment Rents, and Joint Facility Rents between Freight Service and Passenger Service on Class I Line-Haul Railroads* (mimeographed, 1953).

[27] *Ibid.,* Sec. 121.02.

[28] *Ibid.,* Secs. 121.2, 121.42, and 121.66.

[29] *Ibid.,* Secs. 121.67–121.77.

[30] Dwight Ladd, *Cost Data for the Management of Railroad Passenger Service* (Boston: Harvard Graduate School of Business Administration, 1957), pp. 63–73.

[31] John R. Meyer, Merton J. Peck, John Stenason, Gerald Kraft, and Robert Brown, *Avoidable Costs of Passenger Train Service* (A report prepared by a research

TABLE 6-1
Financial Data on Passenger Train Service, Class I Railroads, 1936–67
(in millions of dollars)

Year	Rail Operating Revenues Assignable to Passenger and Allied Services	Expenses, Taxes, and Rents		Net Railway Operating Income, Passenger and Allied Services
		Related Solely to Passenger and Allied Services	Related and Apportioned to Passenger and Allied Services	
1936	$ 628	$ 577	$ 861	$233 def.
1937	665	. . .	907	242 def.
1938	611	. . .	866	255 def.
1939	632	. . .	883	251 def.
1940	635	. . .	897	262 def.
1941	751	677	977	226 def.
1942	1,348	849	1,259	89
1943	2,080	1,058	1,800	280
1944	2,248	1,212	2,014	234
1945	2,173	1,231	1,943	230
1946	1,644	1,239	1,784	140 def.
1947	1,400	1,273	1,827	427 def.
1948	1,435	1,401	1,995	560 def.
1949	1,296	1,340	1,946	650 def.
1950	1,394	1,321	1,903	509 def.
1951	1,449	1,499	2,130	681 def.
1952	1,497	1,499	2,139	642 def.
1953	1,416	1,454	2,121	705 def.
1954	1,312	1,388	1,982	670 def.
1955	1,267	1,352	1,904	637 def.
1956	1,282	1,403	1,979	697 def.
1957	1,238	1,390	1,962	724 def.
1958	1,202	1,284	1,812	610 def.
1959	1,203	1,241	1,747	544 def.
1960	1,176	1,187	1,661	485 def.
1961	1,153	1,136	1,561	408 def.
1962	1,149	1,137	1,543	394 def.
1963	1,107	1,116	1,506	399 def.
1964	1,085	1,103	1,495	410 def.
1965	1,042	1,086	1,463	421 def.
1966	1,018	1,028	1,418	400 def.
1967	878	1,015	1,363	485 def.

Source: James C. Nelson, *Railroad Transportation and Public Policy* (Washington, D.C.: Brookings Institution, 1959), pp. 474–75; Association of American Railroads, "Statistics of Railroad Passenger Service" (Washington, D.C., 1966); and Interstate Commerce Commission, Bureau of Economics, *Transport Economics* (August, 1968), p. 1.

Third, the ICC's procedure of assigning to passenger service the expenses incurred solely for that service, plus a share of common expenses, results in a misleading passenger "deficit" figure. A significant percentage of the fully apportioned costs would still be incurred even if the railroads were to abandon all passenger service. The ICC has estimated that about 75 percent of the passenger operating expenses are solely related to this service and would probably be saved if the service were abandoned; the remaining 25 percent represents the apportionment of passenger costs incurred in common for both freight and passenger service.[32] Professor Berge has argued that this distinction is essential, as fully allocated costs have no value for either regulatory or managerial decisions. Implying that the principal function of railroads is freight service and that passenger service is a by-product, he proposes as the proper measure of the costs of passenger service "the use of avoidable costs." In his words: "The profitability of passenger service to any railroad whose principal business is carrying freight is best measured by the extent to which the revenues added by passenger service exceed the expenses which could be avoided by its elimination."[33]

Finally, and closely connected with the above, is the fact that the ICC has never required a cost separation of passenger service (parlor and sleeping car, coach, commutation, dining car services) and allied services (baggage, express, mail, milk). In 1953, the commission estimated that about 72 percent of that year's passenger deficit could be attributed to passenger service and 28 percent to allied services.[34]   f 3

To remedy these problems, the ICC made a lengthy study of proposed changes suggested by its Bureau of Accounts.[35] In 1958, however, the commis-

---

committee of the Aeronautical Research Foundation) (Cambridge, Mass., 1957), p. 8. Using refined statistical costing techniques, the report concluded that present ICC accounting methods understate the true passenger deficit. The authors found that the 1955 passenger deficit was $708 million as opposed to the ICC's reported $476 million deficit. One important difference between the study's methods and those of the ICC was that the study estimated larger depreciation expenses. The estimated deficit drops to $604 million if the ICC's depreciation expense estimate is used. *Ibid.*, p. 35.

32 *Railroad Passenger Train Deficit*, 306 ICC 417 (1959). Until 1949, the revenues assignable to passenger and allied services covered the expenses, taxes, and net rents solely related to that service and part of the apportioned costs (Table 6-1). Since that time (except for 1950), revenues from passenger and allied services have failed to cover even the solely related expenses, taxes, and net rents. For a more complete discussion, see James C. Nelson, *Railroad Transportation and Public Policy* (Washington, D.C.: Brookings Institution, 1959), pp. 293-96. It should be emphasized that these figures relate to the railroads as a whole; some roads have profitable passenger service.

33 Stanley Berge, *The Railroad Passenger Service—Costs and Financial Results* (Evanston, 1956), quoted in Meyer and others, *Avoidable Costs of Passenger Train Service, op. cit.*, p. 17.

34 Interstate Commerce Commission, *Sixty-Seventh Annual Report* (1953), p. 39. This problem is discussed further in Chapter 10.

35 Interstate Commerce Commission, Bureau of Accounts, Cost Finding and Valuation, *Proposed Formula for Determining Cost of Providing Rail Passenger Service by Classes of Traffic and Comparing the Costs with the Service* (mimeographed, 1956). Proposals were made also by Berge, *op. cit.;* Meyer and others, *op. cit.*

sion concluded that the present separations procedures were adequate for the purpose intended and that no satisfactory alternative proposal had been made. In the commission's words:

> No proposal for revision of the present rules was offered which has not been examined and found by the Commission to be inadequate. Out-of-pocket costs are not uniformly defined by accountants or statisticians, and the development and annual reporting of such costs, although useful in special cases involving individual trains or services, does not appear to be warranted on this record. . . . Moreover, determinations in many proceedings, such as many involving adjustment of freight rates, require the assignment or apportionment of all railroad costs. The conclusion is warranted that the present separation rules are sound and result in useful information. The possible need for future modifications, however, will receive continuing consideration and study. [36]

Telephone Industry. The Bell Telephone System furnishes both interstate and intrastate communications services. [37] Interstate services, which include interstate-message toll telephone, private line telephone, telegraph, data, and program transmission (video and audio), teletypewriter exchange (TWX) services, and wide area telephone services, are subject to the jurisdiction of the FCC. Intrastate services, which represent local exchange and intrastate toll services (similar to the interstate services listed above), are subject to the jurisdiction of the state commissions. The Long Lines Department of A.T.&T. is engaged solely in interstate and overseas activities. Much of the property of the twenty-four operating companies, however, is used in common for both interstate and intrastate services. The costs incurred in rendering such services cannot be directly assigned to those services. The state and federal regulatory agencies

---

[36] *Separation of Operating Expenses, Freight and Passenger,* 302 ICC 735, 737 (1958).

In an analysis released in August, 1968, the ICC's Bureau of Economics concluded that in the period 1954–1967, the railroads "realized total incremental revenues of $35 million" on their passenger operations. The bureau's "net incremental operating revenue" figures were computed by subtracting operating expenses related solely to passenger and allied services (thereby excluding taxes and rents) from total passenger service revenues. Interstate Commerce Commission, Bureau of Economics, *Transport Economics* (August, 1968), pp. 2–3. In October, 1968, the ICC announced the initiation of a new investigation to determine the "actual net costs" of intercity railroad passenger service and the "methods of reducing or meeting such costs." *The Wall Street Journal,* October 17, 1968, p. 8.

[37] The discussion in this section relates primarily to the operations of The American Telephone and Telegraph Company and its affiliated operating companies. It is based on National Association of Regulatory Utility Commissioners, *Separations Manual—Standard Procedures for Separating Telephone Property Costs, Revenues, Expenses, Taxes and Reserves* (Washington, D.C., 1963, and 1964 and 1965 Addenda), and on information supplied by Bell System representatives. The *Separations Manual* also applies to independent telephone companies and has been used in rate case presentations by some independent companies before state commissions and for developing independent company costs underlying intercompany settlements between independents and the Bell System and between two independent companies.

have thus cooperated in developing uniform methods of allocating common costs between the various jurisdictions.

The present separations procedures have evolved from many years of study by all interested parties. Moreover, they have been changed and modified on numerous occasions.[38] These separations methods are built around the "actual use" principle, namely, that (1) all costs of plant used solely for one service are assigned directly to that service, and (2) all costs of plant used jointly for two or more services are allocated among the services on an actual use basis which considers both relative occupancy and relative time in use measurements.[39] Measurements of time in use are determined on a unit basis (e.g., traffic units per call) in studies of traffic handled or work performed during a representative test period, and apply to a full 24-hour period rather than busy hour volumes.[40] Thus, telephone circuit plant is separated on the basis of minutes of use (i.e., minutes of holding time or conversation time), manual switching plant on the basis of operator work time, and dial switching plant on the basis of minutes of use; while reserves, expenses, and taxes generally are separated on the same basis as the current costs or the book costs of the related plant.[41] For settlements within the Bell System, all revenues collected from interstate operations are pooled each month, and expenses and taxes allocated to interstate operations by each company are repaid to them out of these revenues.[42] The remaining net

---

[38] See Richard Gabel, *Development of Separations Principles in the Telephone Industry* (East Lansing: Michigan State University Public Utilities Studies, 1967); and testimony of H. L. Baker, "Background Information and History of Separations for the Telephone Communications Industry," FCC Docket No. 16258 (FCC Staff Exhibit No. 25, dated November 14, 1966).

The latest changes in separations procedures were made by an FCC order early in 1969. Federal Communications Commission, "Report and Order," Docket No. 17975 (FCC 69-65, January 29, 1969). This order suggests that the FCC will take a more active and influential role in determining separations procedures in the future than it has in the past.

[39] Telephone plant is divided into two broad classifications: interexchange plant, which is plant used primarily to furnish long distance services; and exchange plant, which is plant used primarily to furnish local services.

[40] While the *Separations Manual* is designed for interstate-intrastate separations only, some of its procedures either may be used without modifications or may be adapted for use in intrastate toll-exchange services separations. One state commission—California—requires such separations in intrastate rate cases and has approved separations procedures for this purpose. The remaining state commissions determine a fair rate of return on the combined investment devoted to local exchange and intrastate toll services.

[41] *Separations Manual, op. cit.*, pp. 16–17.

[42] In addition to expenses and taxes, from total interstate revenues are deducted the amounts of settlements between Bell System companies and independent companies for the independent's share of the revenues for interstate services furnished jointly by the independent companies and the Bell System. The amounts of these settlements are based upon separations studies of independent company costs incurred in providing the joint services. The settlement received by each independent company is made in accordance with an agreement between the independent and a Bell System associated company. Most independent companies are covered by a settlement agreement employing uniform settlement schedules based on nationwide cost studies negotiated for the independents by the United States Independent Telephone Association. The remaining companies have agree-

revenue, which represents the amount for return, is distributed to the Long Lines Department and the operating companies on the basis of the net investment each contributes to the total net investment of interstate services. If the Long Lines Department, for example, provides 35 percent of the total net investment, it will receive 35 percent of the remaining net revenue.

As in the case of railroad separations procedures, the telephone methods of allocating common costs have been subject to criticism and review.[43] Between 1945 and 1961, interstate toll rates, particularly for very long distances, decreased significantly, while intrastate toll rates increased moderately. This rate behavior resulted in the so-called "disparity problem," that is, rates for interstate toll calls generally below those for intrastate toll calls of approximately equal distances.[44] Although the relationship between interstate and intrastate rates is constantly changing, on July 1, 1967, when the latest study was made, intrastate long-distance rates averaged 15 to 30 percent higher than interstate rates for comparable distances for station-to-station calls; 30 to 80 percent higher for person-to-person calls (Table 6–2).[45] Some critics have maintained that the separations procedures place too great a burden on intrastate service. However, there appear to be two major reasons that account for the movement of interstate and intrastate rates in opposite directions:

> One reason, and possibly the more important of the two, is that the introduction of technological improvements, particularly in the field of interexchange circuitry where carrier techniques have been extensively developed, has had significantly different impacts on interstate and intrastate services. These improvements have resulted in very substantial reductions in the unit costs per circuit mile for the longer haul circuits used primarily to furnish interstate services. However, these improvements have caused only relatively moderate decreases in the costs per circuit mile for the shorter haul interexchange circuits used largely to provide intrastate toll services. Further, while the application of technological advances in switching and exchange circuitry has been very effective in holding down overall costs, the impact of these improvements has not been sufficient in the exchange service field to offset the impact of inflationary forces, especially those on wages, which have persisted in the post–World War II period, despite decided improvements in

---

ments calling for settlements based on individual company cost studies. While this latter type of agreement involves only a small proportion of the total companies, such agreements cover about one-half of the total settlements.

[43] See Curtis M. Bushnell, "Regulatory Responsibilities in Telephone Cost Allocations," Part I: 72 *Public Utilities Fortnightly* 52 (November 7, 1963), Part II: 72 *ibid.* 32 (November 21, 1963); and Gabel, *op. cit.*, chap. vi.

[44] Delaware and Pennsylvania have based their entire intrastate toll rate structure on the interstate structure, so that the rates for both services are the same for comparable distances.

[45] See National Association of Regulatory Utility Commissioners, *A Study of Message Toll Telephone Rate Disparities* (Washington, D.C., 1967); and Sanford F. Smith, "Disparities in Message Toll Telephone Rates," 79 *Public Utilities Fortnightly* 25 (March 30, 1967).

TABLE 6-2
Summary of Percentages of Disparity for a Six-Minute Message, June 1, 1967

| | *Number of State Schedules* | | | | | | | |
| | *Greater than Interstate* | | | | | *Equal to Inter-state* | *Lower than Interstate* | *Total* |
Miles	*1%-20%*	*21%-50%*	*51%-100%*	*Over 100%*	*Total*			
1. Station messages from 4:30 A.M. to 6:00 P.M. Monday thru Friday —"day" rate:								
25	6	5	1	—	12	30	9	51
50	3	33	5	—	41	9	—	50
100[a]	10	21	4	—	35	11	—	46
200[a]	13	20	2	—	35	4	2	41
300[a]	23	10	—	—	33	4	—	37
400[a]	17	7	—	—	24	2	2	28
2. Station messages from 6:00 P.M. to 8:00 P.M. Monday thru Saturday and from 4:30 A.M. to 6:00 P.M. Saturday—"evening" rate:								
25	6	2	—	—	8	29	14	51
50	6	24	2	—	32	9	9	50
100[b]	5	15	19	—	39	6	1	46
200[a,b]	9	20	4	—	33	4	3	40
300[a,b]	12	16	—	—	28	4	4	36
400[a,b]	7	13	—	—	20	3	4	27
3. Station messages from 8:00 P.M. to 4:30 A.M. every day and from 4:30 A.M. to 8:00 P.M. Sunday—"night" rate:								
25	6	2	—	—	8	27	16	51
50	9	19	—	—	28	8	14	50
100	7	24	3	—	34	7	6	47
200	12	3	—	—	15	2	25	42
300	12	6	1	—	19	2	17	38
400	9	2	1	—	12	3	14	29
4. Person messages from 4:30 A.M. to 6:00 P.M. Monday thru Saturday —"day" rate:								
25	12	22	6	—	40	5	6	51
50	3	16	24	3	46	4	—	50
100	6	11	22	4	43	4	—	47
200[a]	4	12	20	4	40	1	—	41
300[a]	5	12	18	1	36	1	—	37
400[a]	3	13	11	—	27	1	—	28
5. Person messages from 6:00 P.M. to 4:30 A.M. every day and from 4:30 A.M. to 6:00 P.M. Sunday—"night" rate:								
25[c]	11	22	6	—	39	5	6	50
50[c]	5	12	23	3	43	5	1	49
100[c]	3	7	18	16	44	2	—	46
200[c]	2	6	23	9	40	1	—	41
300[c]	4	4	22	6	36	1	—	37
400	3	7	17	2	29	—	—	29

[a] Omits California.
[b] Omits Utah.
[c] Omits Wisconsin.

Source: National Association of Regulatory Utility Commissioners, *A Study of Message Toll Telephone Rate Disparities* (Washington, D.C., 1967).

productivity. Hence, in the longer haul interstate toll service field, the cost improvements due to technological advances have more than kept pace with inflationary forces, while in the shorter haul intrastate toll and exchange service fields, these cost improvements have not been adequate to entirely offset such forces.

The second reason is that there have been a number of service extensions and improvements in the exchange service field which have necessitated increases in monthly and nonrecurring exchange service charges but which, in reality, have provided customers as a whole with more service per dollar than before. These improvements include the establishment of extended and metropolitan area exchange services, which appreciably lowered the customers' short haul interexchange service bills, the upgrading of local service by the elimination of most of the multi-party and four-party subscriber lines, and improvements in exchange circuit transmission.[46]

Application of the actual use principle under conditions of decreasing unit costs for long-haul plant and relatively constant unit costs for short-haul plant and exchange plant accounted for the diverse movement of interstate and intrastate rates. But since 1961, both interstate and intrastate rates have moved in the same direction (both downward). Moreover, as a result of (*a*) a larger percentage increase in interstate toll calls relative to intrastate calls and (*b*) cooperative changes in separations procedures, the disparity between interstate and intrastate toll rates has narrowed considerably in the past few years.

Equally important, while there are basic differences of opinion over methodology, the toll rate disparity is not the result of separations procedures alone. The disparity problem is created by the jurisdictional division of authority between the federal and state governments. Costs differ substantially among the jurisdictions regulating toll telephone rates, reflecting primarily differences in length of haul and to some degree differences in terrain, density of population, volume of calls, plant investment, and other miscellaneous factors. For example:

> States having a predominance of short-haul traffic are necessarily burdened with higher unit costs than states with an average longer haul traffic. In the interstate area there is a very high volume of long-haul traffic over high density routes. This, in turn, reduces the cost per mile of the long lines plant. The effect of such high volume of long-haul traffic over high density routes is reflected in the cost per message minute mile. To put it another way, the average length of haul for intrastate calls is 47 miles, while for interstate calls it is 400 miles.[47]

In other words, one way to eliminate the disparity problem would be to transfer responsibility for interstate and intrastate toll calls to one jurisdiction, thereby permitting the development of a uniform nationwide toll rate structure. "Such

---

[46] Information furnished by the American Telephone and Telegraph Company (July 30, 1968).

[47] E. William Henry, "Communications Problems—1965," in National Association of Regulatory Utility Commissioners, *Annual Proceedings, 1965* (Washington, D.C., 1966), p. 506.

charge would be calculated without regard to whether the particular toll call was intrastate or interstate, and without regard to whether it occurred wholly within a small state like Rhode Island, a very large state like Texas, a heavily populated state like New York or a sparsely populated state like Wyoming."[48] Another way to eliminate the disparity problem would be for all the commissions to act cooperatively, perhaps through the National Association of Regulatory Utility Commissioners, in setting uniform toll rates.

REGULATION OF FINANCING

Prior to the 1930's the financing of utilities, except for railroads, was almost completely unregulated. The general attitude of the times toward overcapitalization was expressed by Senator LaFollette: "The public need not concern itself with all the villanies of overcapitalization."[49] And the chairman of the Wisconsin commission stated the general feeling toward the control of corporate securities: "Regulation of corporate securities is . . . for the benefit of investors and . . . it has no bearing . . . upon the question of rates."[50] After the stock market crash in 1929, however, the public attitudes changed completely as a result of the many abuses uncovered—overcapitalization, stock watering, excessive dividends, and the like. These abuses, it should be noted again, were not limited to the regulated companies, but were widespread throughout American industry. Many of the regulatory commissions were granted jurisdiction over the financing of the utility companies.

The abuses which brought about this type of regulation have long since been removed through the surveillance of the commissions and refinements in the art of accounting and auditing. It is important, nevertheless, to understand why the commissions were granted these powers and the methods by which they corrected the abuses.[51]

Control of Capitalization

For many years, it was widely believed by the commissions that the financial policies of the regulated industries had no effect upon either rates or service. Among the commissions, only those of California, Massachusetts, New York, Texas, and Wisconsin, in addition to the Interstate Commerce Commission, exercised active supervision of financial matters prior to 1930. Most of the commissions apparently accepted the proposition that financial decisions should be the responsibility of management.

48 *Ibid.* As the former FCC Chairman notes, however, "such a course would destroy the authority and discretion vested in the regulatory body of each separate state. It would also be contrary to the basic principle of our federal system, in which the individual states maintain and play a fundamental regulatory role in intrastate matters." *Ibid.*
49 Cited in Troxel, *op. cit.,* p. 141.
50 *Ibid.*
51 Financial abuses by electric and gas holding companies and their subsequent correction under the Public Utility Holding Company Act of 1935 are discussed in Chapter 15.

Relation of Capitalization to Rates and Service. The capitalization of a company refers to the amount of outstanding securities—long-term debt, preferred and common stock. A company is considered to be undercapitalized when the amount of outstanding securities is below the value of its property (assets); overcapitalized when the amount of outstanding securities exceeds the value of its property. For the regulated industries, a distinction must be made between capitalizable and noncapitalizable assets. Simply stated, the first refers to property devoted to carrier and utility business, the second to property devoted to noncarrier and nonutility purposes. This distinction, and the reasons for making it, are the same as those discussed under accounting regulation. It is sufficient to state again, therefore, that rates should be set on the basis of a fair rate of return on the value of the property devoted to carrier and utility business.[52]

It is now generally recognized that abuses of capitalization can prevent effective regulation. In extreme cases, overcapitalization has resulted in higher rates charged by a company or in deteriorating quality and quantity of service offered. This situation arose because utility rates are set by regulation. Under competitive conditions, capitalization cannot affect rates. Even if a company were overcapitalized, it would be unable to raise its rates above those of its competitors. Likewise, under monopoly conditions, capitalization is unrelated to rates. While an overcapitalized company might find it possible to raise its rates to earn a profit on its inflated capitalization, a monopolist has the power to charge excessive rates whether overcapitalized or not.[53] Under regulation, however, capitalization may affect rates.

In theory, a regulated company is entitled to earn a fair rate of return on the fair value of its property. If the theory were strictly adhered to, capitalization would have no affect on rates. But such does not occur in practice. Assume that the value of a company's property, on an original cost basis, is $5 million. If the commission allows a 5 percent rate of return, the company will earn $250,000. Further, assume that the company's capitalization is $10 million, that is, the company is overcapitalized. On $4 million of bonds at 4 percent, it must pay $160,000, leaving $90,000. On $3 million of preferred stock at 5 percent, it must pay $150,000. Obviously, this is impossible. In other words, the company is unable to meet its fixed obligations. To do so, the company would need a rate of return of 6.2 percent, and even then, it would be unable to pay any dividends on its common stock.

In practice, therefore, commissions would be faced with a difficult decision when confronted with such a situation. Unless the company were allowed, through increased rates, a rate of return sufficient to meet its fixed obligations, it would be forced into bankruptcy and reorganization—an alternative which may be less desirable over the long-run than higher rates. Bankruptcy not only inflicts losses upon investors, making it difficult or impossible for the utility to

---

[52] *Securities of Louisville & Nashville R.R.,* 76 ICC 718 (1923).
[53] D. Philip Locklin, *Economics of Transportation* (6th ed.; Homewood, Ill.: Richard D. Irwin, Inc., 1966), p. 532.

attract capital in the future, but service improvements and growth may be deferred. In extreme cases, the provision of any service at all may be imperiled. "As between the two alternatives—high rates or poor service—the public will usually choose the former." [54]

For these reasons, overcapitalization does affect the rates and services of regulated companies. The solution, of course, is for the commissions to exercise supervision over the financing of these companies so as to prevent the problem of overcapitalization from arising.

Commission Control of Capitalization. There are three important problems concerning commission supervision of capitalization. What is the proper measure of a company's capitalization? How can overcapitalization be corrected? How can overcapitalization be prevented?

Measures of Capitalization. It was earlier noted that a regulated company's capitalization should not exceed the value of its capitalizable assets. But what is the proper basis of valuation to use? The value of a company's assets can be measured by original or actual cost, reproduction cost, and market values. While the terms are the same, the considerations which govern the choice of the proper valuation method as a basis of capitalization are not the same as those governing the choice of a standard for determining the rate base. [55] The commissions, for sound reasons, commonly use the original or actual cost as a basis for capitalization. [56]

Reproduction cost fluctuates with the price level. If capitalization were based on this value, a company might be properly capitalized at one time but overcapitalized at another simply because of a change in the price level. Such a situation would be undesirable, for a company cannot easily change its capitalization, especially if the price level and, hence, reproduction cost is falling. A company's capitalization should not fluctuate with the price level. [57] Nor can a regulated company's capitalization be based upon the market value of its assets or its capitalized earnings, because circular reasoning would be involved. The earnings of a regulated company depend on the rates established by a commission. Thus, whereas an unregulated company may have a proper capitalization when its outstanding securities equal its capitalized earnings, even though the

[54] *Ibid.,* p. 533.
[55] See Chapter 8.
[56] Original cost has two common meanings: the cost of assets when first devoted to public service and the cost of assets to the existing company. While a majority of the commissions use the first meaning when valuing assets for capitalization purposes, some state commissions, as well as the Federal Power Commission and the Securities and Exchange Commission, use the second.
[57] "An estimate of what it would cost to reproduce the properties now, . . . or even what a purchaser may have agreed to pay . . . , are too fanciful to warrant serious consideration." *Re California Water Supply Co.,* PUR 1928C 516, 525 (Cal., 1928). Also see *Chicago Junction Case,* 71 ICC 631 (1922); *Grand Trunk Western R.R. Co., Unification & Securities,* 158 ICC 117 (1929); *Re Mondovi Tel. Co.,* PUR 1931C 439 (Wis., 1931); *Re Stoughton Light & Fuel Co.,* 26 PUR (NS) 160 (Wis., 1936); *Re Central Illinois Electric & Gas Co.,* 5 SEC 115 (1939); *Re Waynesboro Gas Co.,* 53 PUR (NS) 247 (Pa., 1944); and *Re Winnebago Nat. Gas Corp.,* 31 PUR 3d 79 (Wis., 1959).

resulting capitalization is higher than the original or actual cost of its assets, this is an improper measure for a regulated company whose earnings are not determined by market forces.[58]

The commissions have long held, therefore, that the proper measure of a regulated company's capitalization is the original or actual cost of the company's capitalizable assets.[59] Except in unusual circumstances, such as reorganization, capitalization will be permitted to increase only as the investment in property rises, and a commission may try to reduce a company's capitalization as investment falls. This statement does not imply that a regulated company should be considered as overcapitalized when its earnings are insufficient to meet its fixed obligations. While in such a situation it might be desirable for a company to reduce its capitalization, as long as its "securities outstanding represent funds actually invested in the property," the company is not overcapitalized.[60] The railroad industry illustrates this point. In recent years, the total amount of bonds and stock outstanding has been about 47 percent of the railroads' total investment in road and equipment. Thus, the railroads as a whole cannot be considered as overcapitalized on the basis of investment, even though some individual railroads cannot justify their present capitalizations on the basis of current earnings.

Methods of Correcting Overcapitalization. Particularly in the electric, gas, and railroad industries was overcapitalization a serious problem following the stock market crash of 1929. Use of the holding company device was primarily responsible for the financial difficulties of the electric and gas utilities. In the case of the railroads, construction costs were inflated because of widespread use of the construction company,[61] property purchased at excessive prices, securities sold at a discount when investors were unwilling to pay par for them, and excessive amounts of securities issued in reorganization cases when companies offered to replace defaulted bonds with securities whose par values were even higher.

[58] "[W]e do not consider the capitalized value of earning capacity as an appropriate basis for the issue of securities under the provisions of section 20a." *Grand Trunk Western R.R. Co., Unification & Securities, op. cit.,* pp. 134–35.

[59] For many years, the Massachusetts commission restricted a regulated company's capitalization to the amount of cash contributed by investors, not to the company's actual investment. The effect was to exclude investment from retained earnings, on the ground that such funds were contributed by consumers rather than investors. This practice was overturned by the Massachusetts Supreme Court in 1951. *New England Teleph. & Teleg. Co. v. Dept. of Public Utilities,* 327 Mass. 81, 97 NE 2d 509 (1951).

[60] Locklin, *op. cit.,* p. 539.

[61] In the 1860's and 1870's, a railroad's directors would frequently organize a construction company for the purpose of voting profitable contracts to themselves—as the construction company—for construction of the railroad. As payment for construction, the company would receive the land grants and state and local bonds offered to the railroad as a subsidy, or bonds and stock of the railroad. To illustrate: "The Logan, Crawfordsville & South Western Railroad voted all its municipal subsidy bonds, capital stock, and bonds to the director-contractors. The road actually cost about a million dollars, while $4,000,000 in securities were issued." *Ibid.,* p. 113.

The commissions used several methods to correct the excessive capitalizations which occurred before they were given jurisdiction over the financial affairs of the regulated industries. The most common method was reorganization and will be discussed below. Capitalization readjustments were made in at least four other ways. First, the current book value of common stock was scaled down by writing off excessive values of property. Second, earned surplus was accumulated by restricting or entirely withholding dividend payments. Third, stockholders contributed cash or securities to a company. Fourth, authority to issue new securities was denied when the proceeds were to be used to reimburse the company's treasury for construction expenditures already made. While all these methods were used,[62] they had disadvantages. Reorganization remained as the most effective and most frequently used way of eliminating excessive overcapitalization.

Methods of Preventing Overcapitalization. It is far easier to prevent than to correct overcapitalization. A majority of the state commissions have the power to regulate or control purchases, mergers, and consolidations (45 states); issuance of securities (42 states); property and security transactions with affiliated companies (37 states); and purchase of securities of other utilities (30 states). In addition, a few state commissions (18) have the authority to regulate dividends.[63] The federal commissions, except for natural gas and telephone companies, have similar powers. The commissions have frequently exercised these powers to prevent overcapitalization.[64] Most of the commissions have made certain exceptions so that the companies have some necessary flexibility. The Interstate Commerce Commission, for instance, permits a railroad to issue notes maturing in two years or less as long as the total of all such notes outstanding does not exceed more than 5 percent of the par value of all outstanding securities of the company.

In regulating security issues, a few commissions control the selling prices of the securities. The most active commission in this respect is the Massachusetts commission, which fixes the issuing prices of the common stocks of electric and

---

[62] See, for example, *Re Michigan Gas & Electric Co.* (SEC), Holding Co. Act Release No. 4780 (Dec., 1943); *Re Niagara Falls Power Co.* (SEC), Holding Co. Act Release No. 4911 (Feb., 1944); *Re Commonwealth Tel. Co.*, PUR 1932D 299 (Wis.); *Re Laclede Gas Light Co.*, 11 SEC 40 (1942); *Securities of St. Louis–San Francisco Ry.*, 79 ICC 92 (1923).

[63] Federal Power Commission, "Federal and State Commission Jurisdiction and Regulation, Electric, Gas, and Telephone Utilities, 1967" (Washington, D.C.: U.S. Government Printing Office, 1968), pp. 22–24. Also see "Regulatory Restrictions on Dividends," 79 *Public Utilities Fortnightly* 71 (March 30, 1967); and Robert H. Plattner, "State Regulatory Control of Dividend Policy," 81 *ibid.* 29 (February 15, 1968).

[64] See, for example, *Securities Application of Detroit & Toledo Shore Line R.R.*, 70 ICC 322 (1921); *Re White Mt. Power Co.*, 18 PUR (NS) 321 (N.H., 1937); *Re Northern Pennsylvania Power Co.*, 15 PUR (NS) 390 (Pa., 1936); *Re Federal Water & Gas Corp.* (SEC), Holding Co. Act Release No. 6052 (Sept., 1945); *Rochester Gas & Electric Corp.* v. *Maltbie*, 76 N.Y.S. 2d 671 (1948); *Re Old Dominion Electric Cooperative*, 86 PUR (NS) 129 (Va., 1950).

gas utilities.[65] More common is regulation of the selling costs of new security issues by requiring competitive bidding. These costs, known as "flotation costs," represent the difference between the amount paid by investors and the amount received by the issuing company.

It was the long-standing practice of the regulated companies to float issues of new securities through one or more of the large investment banking houses. Which investment bank a company would use often depended on tradition or which bank was represented on the company's board of directors. Prior to 1940, however, investment banking houses frequently made excessive charges for their services by agreeing not to compete against each other.[66] The commissions, in an effort to reduce flotation charges, began to require competitive bidding as opposed to direct placement. A 1919 Massachusetts statute required competitive bidding on electric and gas bonds; the Interstate Commerce Commission started competitive bidding on railroad equipment-trust obligations in 1926; and other commissions followed suit during the thirties and early forties.[67] Exceptions will be made for small issues (the Securities and Exchange Commission exempts all issues under one million dollars), when a company can show that direct placement of securities will result in a better price, or when the market conditions are unfavorable for competitive bidding. Otherwise, mortgage bonds and debentures are subject to competitive bidding in ten states and underwriting of new common stock in eight states.[68] A majority of the federal commissions also require competitive bidding on new security issues.

Control of the Capital Structure

Regulatory commissions are not only concerned with a company's total capitalization, but also with the capital structure. The term capital structure refers to the composition of a company's capitalization—that is, to the proportion between debt and equity that make up the capitalization. Historically, the regulated industries have issued about 50 percent of their securities in the form

[65] Troxel, *op. cit.*, p. 151. Also see *Re Long Island Light Co.*, 5 PUR (NS) 456 (N.Y., 1934); *Re Pennsylvania Electric Co.*, 6 PUR (NS) 22 (Pa., 1934); *Re California–Oregon Tel. Co.*, 32 PUR (NS) 317 (Cal., 1940).

[66] See Irston R. Barnes, *The Economics of Public Utility Regulation* (New York: F. S. Crofts & Co., 1942), pp. 729–39.

[67] See, for example, *Western Maryland Equipment Trust*, 111 ICC 434 (1926); *Re New Hampshire Gas & Electric Co.*, 40 PUR (NS) 285 (N.H., 1941); Securities and Exchange Commission, *Seventh Annual Report, 1941*, pp. 98–102; *In re Competitive Bidding in Sale of Securities*, 257 ICC 129 (1944); *Re Competitive Bidding Rule for Public Utility Securities*, 63 PUR (NS) 140 (Cal., 1946); *Re Rochester Tel. Corp.*, 64 PUR (NS) 30 (N.Y., 1946).

[68] Federal Power Commission, "Federal and State Commission Jurisdiction and Regulation, Electric, Gas, and Telephone Utilities, 1967," *op. cit.*, p. 26. Thirty-one state commissions have authority to require competitive bidding on mortgage bonds and debentures; twenty-eight on underwriting of new common stock. *Ibid.* Also see "Exemption from Competitive Bidding Requirements," 61 *Public Utilities Fortnightly* 417 (March 13, 1958) and 75 *ibid.* 71 (January 21, 1965).

of bonds, 25 percent in preferred stock, and 25 percent in common stock. These proportions, however, vary widely among individual companies. Manufactured gas companies and railroads, which have often used even larger amounts of debt financing, have undergone many bankruptcy proceedings. Other companies, which have maintained lower debt to equity ratios, have been criticized as being too conservative.

Importance of Capital Structure. A company's capital structure is important for three major reasons. First, if the proportion of debt to equity is high, fixed charges will also be high, thereby creating difficulties for a company in times of low earnings and increasing the chances of bankruptcy. A company must meet its fixed charges or go through the process of reorganization. During the depression of the thirties, the dangers of large debt ratios were evident. To illustrate: in 1932, 122 out of 162 Class I railroads, operating nearly 74 percent of the total mileage of Class I roads, failed to earn their fixed charges.[69]

Second, it is widely held that the cost of capital is related to a company's capital structure.[70] As the proportion of debt increases, "the added *financial risks* for both the debt and equity holders result in higher and higher costs for both debt and equity capital."[71] The commissions, in determining a fair rate of return, commonly consider the cost of capital as the minimum necessary return needed to maintain a company's credit standing.[72] Therefore, the higher the cost of capital, the higher a company's total earnings (and, hence, rates) must be to preserve its credit rating.

Third, the capital structure determines control of a company. Before the commissions exercised supervision over their capital structures, the regulated companies often issued large amounts of bonds and preferred stock, incurring heavy interest and fixed dividend obligations, in addition to nonvoting common stock, to avoid losing control by issuing voting common stock. Particularly was this true of the electric and gas holding companies. While this situation may have benefited those in control, it was detrimental to the debt holders, stockholders, and the economy, for bankruptcy often resulted from these burdensome capital structures. For all these reasons, effective regulation requires commission supervision of capital structures.

---

[69] Locklin, *op. cit.,* p. 547.

[70] The assumption that the average cost of capital is a function of a company's capital structure is questioned by Franco Modigliani and Merton H. Miller, "The Cost of Capital, Corporation Finance and the Theory of Investment," 48 *American Economic Review* 261 (1958). The traditional view is defended in two replies by Joseph R. Rose and David Durand, 49 *American Economic Review* 638, 639 (1959); Alexander Barges, *The Effect of Capital Structure on the Cost of Capital* (Englewood Cliffs: Prentice-Hall, Inc., 1963); and J. Fred Weston, "A Test of Cost of Capital Propositions," 30 *Southern Economic Journal* 105 (1963). Also see William J. Baumol and Burton G. Malkiel, "The Firm's Optimal Debt-Equity Combination and the Cost of Capital," 81 *Quarterly Journal of Economics* 547 (1967).

[71] J. J. Scanlon, *Financial Expansion and the Problems of Corporate Capital Structure* (Urbana: University of Illinois Bulletin, 1968) (Weinstein Lecture series, Department of Finance), p. 5.

[72] See Chapter 9.

What Is a Proper Capital Structure? At the outset, it must be recognized that there is no one proper or ideal capital structure. Rather, a company's capital structure is a function of its business risks and, thus, is largely a matter of business judgment. For manufacturing firms, whose earnings are subject to sharp fluctuations, a debt ratio of 4.5 to 35 percent is common. The railroads' debt ratio stood at nearly 34 percent at the end of 1966, compared with a 61 percent ratio (bonds and preferred stock) for private electric utility companies.[73] Further, it should be noted that

> ... a capital structure evolves. It is rooted in the history of the firm, and is the present reflection of financial decisions made at various times in the past and in the light of considerations then obtaining. Ordinarily, a firm's capital structure cannot be changed radically overnight—short of Draconian measures which would probably entail a cost greater than the benefits sought to be obtained by such a radical change.[74]

The American Telephone and Telegraph Company has maintained a debt to total capital ratio of about one-third for many years. This financial policy of the company has been debated widely. These debates serve to illustrate the differences of opinion concerning a proper capital structure.

The facts: At the end of 1967, the company's total capitalization was about $34 billion; the ratio of debt to total capital stood at 35 percent. Of this capitalization, approximately $30 billion was added in the period 1946 to 1967, with nearly $23 billion of this amount coming from new securities issued to private investors (bonds and equity).

The critics: Critics of A.T.&T.'s postwar financing argue that the company has been too conservative. A higher debt ratio, they state, would have reduced the cost of capital and increased the market price of the company's common stock. Financing by debt costs less than by equity—5 to 6 percent interest on debt compared to 10 to 11 percent earnings on equity. Moreover, interest charges on debt are deductible from income subject to taxes. As a result (assuming a 48 percent corporate income tax rate), the company must earn $1.92 to pay a dollar in dividends, compared with only $1.00 to pay a dollar in interest. It has been estimated that if the debt ratio had increased from 35 to 40 percent in 1959, A.T.&T. could have saved nearly $100 million in taxes and lower capital costs, and could have saved nearly double that amount if the debt ratio had risen to 45 percent.[75]

---

[73] These figures are averages. The debt to equity ratio of a particular company within a group may differ significantly. There are railroads, for example, with little or no funded debt; other roads have practically all their capitalizations in the form of funded debt.

[74] Scanlon, *op. cit.*, p. 8.

[75] Gilbert Burck, "Is A.T.&T. Playing It Too Safe?," *Fortune*, September, 1960, p. 276. One authority has estimated that for electric utilities, "a change of 10 per cent of capitalization from equity to debt saves 1.10 percentage points in the cost of capital, or a saving of about 11 per cent." Donald C. Cook, "Special Problems of Electric Regulation," Part II, 74 *Public Utilities Fortnightly* 30, 31 (November 19, 1964).

Such calculations assume that equity and debt holders would have taken the same return on their investment, even though the debt ratio had risen. The critics maintain that they would have done so, first, because other utilities have maintained a higher debt ratio and their securities are rated as high as those of A.T.&T.; second, since with a higher debt ratio there is greater leverage for any given level of return on total capital, the earnings on each share are higher. Higher earnings, in turn, would make it possible to increase dividends, which would tend to result in a rise of the stock's market price. Finally, the critics conclude, even if the company were forced to pay somewhat higher interest rates as its debt ratio increased, this would be offset by the tax savings.

The defense: A.T.&T. takes issue with all of these contentions. In the immediate postwar years, the company points out, its debt ratio reached 54 percent, but its bond rating dropped and it had trouble placing its bonds. Summarizes a former company official:

> . . . [O]nce the System's debt ratio rises appreciably, there is an immediate reaction in the market and it becomes more expensive to finance by debt. In other words, higher debt adds to investment risks—both debt and equity, and even the bond buyers, whose investments in effect are underwritten by the share owners, demand a greater return for the greater risk taken. The share owners, in turn, also demand (and are entitled to) a greater return for their greater risks. When all of these factors are added up, the claimed cost of capital advantages realized from financing by debt are actually non-existent. Over the long-run, it is the over-all risks of the business that determine the over-all capital costs, regardless of how these risks are divided among the classes of investors. No one has been able to prove successfully to the contrary.[76]

The company also maintains that it must keep "a reserve of borrowing capacity." Explains treasurer Scanlon:

> A business like ours, faced with the necessity for frequent and heavy new borrowings, must maintain a high grade credit rating on its debt. Such a credit rating cannot be achieved with a debt burden which the financial markets consider to be high for that business. In our case this need is underscored by the fact that shortly we shall have to commence the refunding of our large volume of existing debt. This refunding will be over-laid on the heavy requirements for additional new debt financing to finance current growth.[77]

For these reasons, A.T.&T.'s management believes "that its policy of maintaining its debt ratio in the 30-40 per cent range is proper, considering the kind of business it is, its riskiness and its future prospects and problems."[78] However, the company has recently announced its intention of moving its debt ratio up to

---

[76] L. Chester May, "Bell System Financing," *Bell Telephone Magazine*, Autumn, 1960, p. 28.
[77] Scanlon, *op. cit.*, p. 15. The Bell System must refinance over $11 billion of debt securities now outstanding between 1970 and 2005.
[78] May, *op. cit.*, p. 29.

40 percent by 1970 or 1971, "at which time we can consider what range of debt ratio would then appear appropriate in the light of conditions obtaining at that time."[79]

These, then, are the major arguments between the critics of A.T.&T. and the company itself. The debate continues. Which side is correct? There is no one answer to this question, although the widespread acceptance of A.T.&T.'s securities suggests public approval of its financial policies. But the debate is of importance, for it indicates that business judgment, rather than a mathematical formula, is the major determining factor of a company's capital structure.

Commission Control of Capital Structures. The most important problem faced by the commissions is excessive indebtedness. Two questions are raised. How do commissions control indebtedness? How can indebtedness be reduced?

Control of Indebtedness. Past experience showed the commissions that large amounts of debt securities often are undesirable, but no satisfactory method of limiting indebtedness has been developed. A few state commissions have fixed the ratio of bonds to stock that a regulated company may not exceed. Others have refused to approve increases in indebtedness when companies already have large amounts of debt securities, have restricted bond issues, or have ruled that stock instead of bonds should be issued.[80] These methods, however, have limitations. For example, since the financial conditions of individual companies vary, no one ratio of debt to equity is correct. The refusal to approve a bond issue may lead to no issue at all, for if a company's earnings are insufficient to maintain its stock at par, it is in no position to issue more stock; bonds are the only way new capital can be raised. As a result of these problems, few commissions are willing to substitute their judgments for those of management, except in reorganization cases.[81]

Rather than adopt an arbitrary debt limit, some commissions have established requirements for additional bond issues, particularly for mortgage bonds.[82] "Today the SEC and several state commissions regularly examine the values of mortgaged properties, control the issuance of additional bonds under each mortgage, require sinking funds for most bond issues, specify provisions for depreciation and maintenance costs, and limit the payments of common-stock

[79] Scanlon, *op. cit.*

[80] See, for example, *Bonds of Chesapeake & Ohio Ry.*, 105 ICC 748 (1926); *Securities of Yankton, Norfolk & Southern R.R. Co.*, 154 ICC 669 (1929); *Re Nelson Tel. Co.*, 28 PUR (NS) 116 (Wis., 1939); *Re El Paso Electric Co.*, 8 SEC 366 (1941).

[81] For rate-making purposes, however, a few commissions will use a hypothetical capital structure when they feel the company's debt ratio is too low. See Chapter 9.

[82] Three types of bonds are commonly issued by the regulated companies: (1) mortgage bonds, which are secured by the entire property of the issuing company (equipment-trust obligations, which are common in the railroad industry, are secured by specific property, such as railroad cars); (2) debenture bonds, which are secured by the general credit of the issuing company, but which are subject to the prior claim of the mortgage bond; (3) revenue or income bonds, which are secured by the earnings of the issuing company after interest on any outstanding mortgage or debenture bonds has been paid.

dividends."[83] Restriction on dividend payments is also used when a company is in financial difficulty. Some commissions will prescribe minimum amounts of earned surplus that must be available before dividends can be paid, or will prohibit dividend payments altogether.[84]

Methods of Reducing Indebtedness. Short of reorganization, indebtedness can be reduced in four principal ways. First, the debt to equity ratio can be lowered by confining new security issues to common stock.[85] Second, bonds can be retired by issuing common stock or out of earnings.[86] Unless bonds have a "call provision," only maturing issues can be retired in this manner. Some commissions now require such a provision so that bonds can be repaid and retired before their maturity at the company's option.[87] When earnings and stock market conditions are favorable, redemption may be a desirable way to reduce indebtedness. Retirement also may be accomplished out of earnings. In a few cases, as noted above, commissions have prohibited or restricted dividend payments until indebtedness has been reduced. Oftentimes, however, retirement from earnings is impossible; unless a company has adequate earnings, it will have to use all its available resources for improvements and additions.

Third, the refunding of bond and note issues offers another method of reducing indebtedness. When these issues mature, they must be paid. Commonly, new issues are sold in order to obtain the money for the maturing bonds and notes. Commissions sometimes will require that stock issues be used to refund debt, thereby reducing a company's debt.[88] Callable bonds can be refunded when interest rates are low. Here, new bonds are sold at the lower interest rates and the proceeds used to retire the higher interest bonds. While the capital structure remains unchanged, the burden of debt is reduced, as the company's annual interest charges are lower.

Indebtedness can be reduced, finally, through voluntary agreements with bondholders. Income bonds and common stock have been substituted for fixed interest securities, the maturity date of bonds extended, and the rate of interest reduced.[89] While not a popular method, bondholders are often willing to accept such adjustments when a company faces bankruptcy.

83 Troxel, *op. cit.,* p. 160.

84 See, for example, *Re Interstate Light & Power Co.,* PUR 1933A 319 (Wis.); *Re Luzerne County Gas & Electric Corp.,* 9 SEC 359 (1941); *Re Missouri Edison Co.,* 11 SEC 1125 (1942); *Re Laclede Gas Light Co.,* 11 SEC 40 (1942); *Re Stockbridge & Sherwood Tel. Co.,* 37 PUR 3d 313 (Wis., 1960).

85 *Re Consolidated Edison Co. of N.Y.,* Case 22092 (N.Y., 1962).

86 Frequently, the redemption of sinking fund and serial bonds is scheduled so as to match depreciation accruals. In this way, the cash generated through depreciation is used to retire outstanding bonds; when the asset is fully depreciated, the bonds used to finance it originally are also retired.

87 A "call premium" or "call penalty" is often added before a callable bond issue will be accepted by investors. See "Limitations on the Redemption of Senior Securities," 60 *Public Utilities Fortnightly* 417 (1957).

88 *Re Mid-Georgia Natural Gas Co.,* 35 PUR 3d 477 (Ga., 1960).

89 These procedures have been used on numerous occasions in the railroad industry. See Locklin, *op. cit.,* p. 555; and *Annual Reports* of the Interstate Commerce Commission.

Reorganization

Financial reorganization offers the most effective, but also the most drastic, way of revising a company's capitalization and capital structure.[90] When a company is unable to meet its debts, bankruptcy results. The company or its creditors may file a petition in court, requesting a financial reorganization. If approved, the court will appoint one or more trustees to operate the company until a reorganization plan has been drawn up, submitted, and approved. The procedure for railroad reorganization cases, under Section 77 of the Bankruptcy Act, has been summarized by Locklin:

Within six months after approval of the petition the debtor corporation is required to file a plan of reorganization with the court and with the Interstate Commerce Commission. Reorganization plans may also be filed by the trustees, creditors, stockholders, or other interested parties. After public hearings on the reorganization plans the Commission is to render a report approving a plan of reorganization. This plan may be different from that presented by any party. Before approving a plan, however, the Commission must find that it conforms to certain requirements. Among these are the following: (1) The plan must be "compatible with the public interest"; (2) the fixed charges must be within the earning capacity of the carrier; and (3) the plan must be fair and equitable, affording due recognition to the rights of each class of creditors and stockholders, and conforming to the requirements of the law of the land regarding the participation of the various classes of creditors and stockholders. The plan of reorganization approved by the Commission is then submitted to the court for its approval. The court is not empowered to approve a plan that has not been approved by the Commission. If the court will not accept the plan approved by the Commission, the matter is referred back to the Commission for reconsideration. After a plan has been approved by the court, it is submitted for approval to such classes of creditors and stockholders as under the circumstances may be necessary. After approval by creditors or stockholders representing two thirds of the amount of such claims or stock, the judge must confirm the plan. Upon confirmation of the plan it is binding upon all parties.[91]

Railroad Reorganization.[92] Except for electric and gas utilities under the Public Utility Holding Company Act of 1935, the most significant reorganization cases have concerned the nation's railroads. Since 1872 (Table 6–3), the railroads have been undergoing continuous financial reorganizations. As of April 30, 1948, the Interstate Commerce Commission had approved reorganization plans resulting in the elimination of $2,543,202,369 of debt, and a reduction of $111,083,511 in fixed charges.[93]

[90] Merger represents an alternative to financial reorganization. Particularly is this alternative of significance in the railroad industry. See Chapter 14.

[91] Locklin, *op. cit.,* pp. 550–51.

[92] See William H. Moore, "Railroad Fixed Charges in Bankruptcy Proceedings," 47 *Journal of Political Economy* 100 (1939); Robert T. Swaine, "A Decade of Railroad Reorganization under Section 77 of the Federal Bankruptcy Act," 56 *Harvard Law Review* 1037, 1193 (1943); and De F. Billyou, "Railroad Reorganization since Enactment of Section 77," 96 *Univ. of Pennsylvania Law Review* 793 (1948).

[93] Locklin, *op. cit.,* pp. 549, 552.

Prior to 1933, the ICC played a small role in reorganization cases. Reorganization plans were drawn up by representatives of the various classes of security holders, and after receiving court approval, applications were made to the com-

TABLE 6-3
Railroad Receiverships and Trusteeships,
Selected Years, 1872–1963

Year [a]	Mileage in Receivership	Percentage of Total Railroad Mileage in Receivership
1872	1,160	. . .
1875	11,125	. . .
1880	8,522	. . .
1885	14,733	. . .
1890	8,553	. . .
1895	37,856	21.30
1900	4,178	2.17
1905	796	.37
1910	5,257	2.18
1915	30,223	11.73
1920	16,290	6.27
1925	18,687	7.23
1930	9,486	3.64
1935	68,345	27.02
1940	75,270	30.63
1945	39,714	16.59
1950	12,223	5.16
1955	1,938	.83
1960	1,259	.55
1963	1,748	.77

[a] As of June 30, 1872 to 1915, inclusive. As of December 31, 1920 to 1963, inclusive.
Source: Figures from 1872 to 1895 are from D. Philip Locklin, *Economics of Transportation* (5th ed.; Homewood, Ill.: Richard D. Irwin, Inc., 1960), p. 547. The remainder of the figures are from Interstate Commerce Commission, *Seventy-Eighth Annual Report* (1964), p. 135.

mission for permission to issue the securities necessary to carry out the plans. Even though it favored more thorough reorganizations, the commission was reluctant to disapprove of any plans, because receivership would be prolonged.

In March, 1933, Congress enacted Section 77 of the Bankruptcy Act, giving the commission more control over reorganization plans.[94] Two years later, the provisions of Section 77 were completely rewritten for railroad reorgani-

[94] Ch. 204, Sec. 77, 47 Stat. 1474 (1933). See Max Lowenthal, "The Railroad Reorganization Act," 47 *Harvard Law Review* 18 (1933).

zations.[95] With respect to security issues, the statute states that the reorganization plan

> ... shall provide for fixed charges (including fixed interest on funded debt, interest on unfunded debt, amortization of discount on funded debt, and rent for leased railroads) in such an amount that, after due consideration of the probable prospective earnings of the property in light of its earnings experience and all other relevant facts, there shall be adequate coverage of such fixed charges by the probable earnings available for the payment thereof.[96]

In general, the commission's policy is to limit a company's total capitalization to an amount based upon a conservative estimate of future earnings, rather than upon property valuations. As explained by the commission in an early case: "If this reorganization is to be successful, the capital structure of the reorganized company must be realistically related to its actual earning power, and consideration given to the investment in its property only to the extent that such investment is justified by the probable earnings reasonably foreseeable in the future."[97] And, in 1943, this position was upheld by the Supreme Court:

> A basic requirement of any reorganization is the determination of a capitalization which makes it possible ... to give the new company a reasonable prospect for survival. ... Only "meticulous regard for earning capacity" ... can give the new company some safeguards against the scourge of overcapitalization. Disregard of that method of valuation can only bring ... "a harvest of barren regrets."[98]

Similar views have been expressed by the Securities and Exchange Commission and some state commissions in public utility reorganization cases.[99]

The commission's policy of basing capitalization upon future earnings has been severely criticized.[100] The most serious criticism is that by underestimating the future earnings of a company, stock has been declared worthless needlessly —that is, future earnings have been higher than estimated at the time of reorganization. Suppose, for example, that a railroad with a funded debt of $300 million is undergoing financial reorganization. If the commission estimates the

---

[95] 49 Stat. 911 (1935), 11 U.S.C. Sec. 205 (1958). See Leslie Craven and Warner Fuller, "The 1935 Amendments of the Railroad Bankruptcy Law," 49 *Harvard Law Review* 1254 (1936).

[96] 49 Stat. 911 (1935), 11 U.S.C. Sec. 205 (b) (4) (1958).

[97] *Western Pacific R.R. Co. Reorganization,* 230 ICC 61, 87 (1939).

[98] *Group of Investors* v. *Chicago, Milwaukee, St. Paul & Pacific R.R. Co.,* 318 U.S. 523, 540–41 (1943).

[99] See, for example, *Re United Tel. & Electric Co.,* 3 SEC 679 (1938); *Re Louer,* 35 PUR (NS) 351 (N.Y., 1940); and *Re George,* 41 PUR (NS) 193 (Pa., 1941).

[100] William Polatsek, "The Wreck of the Old 77," 34 *Cornell Law Quarterly* 532 (1949); and *Railroad Reorganizations* (Senate, Committee on Interstate and Foreign Commerce, 82 Cong., 2nd sess.; Committee Print) (Washington, D.C.: U.S. Government Printing Office, 1952). For a more general discussion of debt ratios, see Melvin G. Dakin, "Public Utility Debt Ratios and the Public Interest—Reasonable Fixed Charges and Just and Reasonable Rates," 15 *Vanderbilt Law Review* 195 (1961).

future annual net earnings of the road to be $15 million and sets 6 percent as the proper rate for capitalizing the earnings, a total capitalization of $250 million could be supported. Since the indebtedness of the company exceeded $250 million, the stock of the bankrupt road would be declared worthless. Now suppose that the annual net earnings of the company turned out to be $21 million. These earnings would have justified a total capitalization of $350 million and would have permitted the old stockholders to retain an interest in the reorganized company.

In 1948, Congress passed an amendment to the Bankruptcy Act partially to remedy this situation.

> This amendment requires the Commission, upon petition of any party in a reorganization proceeding which has been approved by the Commission but which is still before the courts, to notify the court of any changes, facts, or developments which make it necessary or expedient to re-examine the plan of reorganization previously approved. In response to such notification the court must return the plan to the Commission for further consideration. [101]

A CONCLUDING COMMENT OF CAUTION

At the outset of this chapter, it was stated that the material covered in the chapter was largely of historical importance. This point needs reemphasis. With respect to accounting procedures, the establishment of uniform systems of accounts has solved the earlier abuses which resulted from irregular accounting practices. Moreover, there is no disagreement concerning the need for such systems. They are used as the starting point in evaluating a regulated company's rates and in developing cost allocation methods. But since uniform systems only specify an accounting form, there remain differences of opinion over the scope, content, and application of the various provisions. [102] The regulated industries take the general position that accounting principles should be the same for both regulated and nonregulated business. Therefore, they argue, the principal objective of the regulatory commissions in this area should be the uniform application of these principles. [103] Current accounting and depreciation problems center about the proper statement of income, inflation, and competition, and will be considered at length in subsequent chapters.

Similarly, with respect to financial matters, the excesses brought to light in the early 1930's have largely been corrected. There is no evidence, for example,

---

[101] Locklin, *op. cit.,* pp. 554–55. See *Missouri Pacific R.R. Co. Reorganization*, 282 ICC 629 (1952).

[102] "A prescribed system of accounts is a prerequisite to effective control of utilities by a regulatory body. However, by no stretch of the imagination can the system of accounts be viewed as furnishing an interpretation of the accounting results." *Re Montana Power Co.*, 42 PUR 3d 241, 253 (Mont., 1962).

[103] For a discussion of one relevant question—who will develop accounting principles?—see Robert N. Anthony, "Showdown on Accounting Principles," 41 *Harvard Business Review* 99 (May–June, 1963). Also see William J. Powell, "The Case for the Regulatory Accountant," 75 *Public Utilities Fortnightly* 36 (January 7, 1965).

that regulated companies (in general) are overcapitalized at the present time, or that their capital structures are unjustified. Disagreements as to the proper capital structure for a particular company are to be expected, but overcapitalization, stock watering, excessive dividends, and so forth are primarily problems of the past.

Chapter 7

OPERATING EXPENSES, DEPRECIATION, AND TAXES

Expenses (using that term in its broad sense to include not only operating expenses but depreciation and taxes) are facts. They are to be ascertained, not created, by the regulatory authorities. If properly incurred, they must be allowed as part of the composition of the rates. Otherwise, the so-called allowance of a return upon investment, being an amount over and above expenses, would be a farce.

—*Judge Prettyman**

Previously, it was seen that the problem of rate regulation can be expressed by the formula $R = O + (V - D)r$, where R is the total revenue to be obtained, O is the operating costs, V is the value of the tangible and intangible property, D is the accrued depreciation of the tangible and reproducible property, and r is the rate of return. Establishment of the total revenue requirement thus involves three steps: (1) determination of the costs of operation, (2) determination of the value of the property minus accrued depreciation, known as the rate base, and (3) determination of the rate of return.

Operating costs make up the largest sum that must be covered in fixing rates. Commonly, they range from three-fourths to four-fifths of total revenues for public utilities and from two-thirds to four-fifths in the case of airlines and railroads. These costs include all types of operating expenses (materials and supplies, fuel, wages and salaries, maintenance, among others), as well as annual depreciation charges and taxes. For a typical electric and telephone company, operating expenses average about 44 percent of revenues, depreciation about 12 percent, and taxes about 22 percent; for the railroads, the comparable figures are 73 percent for operating expenses, 6 percent for depreciation, and 10 percent for taxes.

Some operating costs are determined by normal competitive forces and by tax authorities; others basically are determined by individual companies. Yet, commission supervision as to their reasonableness is essential for effective regulation.

*Judge Prettyman, *Mississippi River Fuel Corp.* v. *Federal Power Comm.*, 163 F. 2d 433, 437 (1947).

THE NECESSITY FOR SUPERVISION

The need for commission supervision of operating expenses might seem questionable given the development of uniform systems of accounts and the self-interest of the regulated companies.[1] As earlier noted, however, uniform systems only specify the form and content of the statement of expense; they do not solve controversies over permissible expenditures or their computation. Nor is self-interest always sufficient. Commissions seldom challenge expenditures controlled by competitive forces, such as those for plant maintenance, raw materials, and labor. Conflicts do arise over whether certain expenditures should be charged to operating expenses to be paid for by customers, or deducted from allowable operating expenses to be paid for by owners out of earnings.

Management might vote itself high salaries and pensions. Payments to affiliated companies for goods and services might be excessive. Expenses for advertising, rate investigations, litigation, and public relations should be closely scrutinized by the commissions to determine if they are extravagant or if they represent an abuse of discretion. In all cases, moreover, the commissions should require proof as to the reasonableness of a firm's charges to operating expenses.

Depreciation and taxes, too, receive special attention by the regulatory commissions. The accounting for depreciation affects rate regulation in two ways: (1) as a current operating cost and (2) as a deduction from the value of the tangible and reproducible property in determining a firm's rate base. For many years, some regulated companies made large depreciation charges to operating costs in years of good earnings and low charges in years of poor earnings, while deducting little for accrued depreciation in determining the rate base. Such practices benefited investors, but not consumers. Taxes present important regulatory problems. The regulated industries often are referred to as "tax collectors *par excellence*." As taxes are included in operating costs (with a few exceptions), they can usually be passed on to the consumer in the form of higher rates. There is a conflict, therefore, between the commissions and consumers who seek minimum rates and tax authorities who seek maximum revenues. Discriminatory tax policies, especially in the case of the railroads, also add to an already complex regulatory situation.

THE LEGAL VIEW AND MANAGERIAL JUDGMENT

The right of the commissions to exercise supervision over all three component parts of operating costs—operating expenses, depreciation, and taxes—has been approved by the courts.

---

[1] The growth of intense and widespread competition in the transportation industry, for example, has provided a constant spur to keep operating expenses at a minimum. For this industry, therefore, the basic modern problem has been to establish rates that would permit adequate cost coverage plus provide a reasonable return to capital.

Operating Expenses

As early as 1892, the Supreme Court recognized that the power to determine reasonable rates required supervision of operating expenses. As expressed by Justice Brewer:

> ... It is agreed that the defendant's operating expenses for 1888 were $2,404,516.54. Of what do these operating expenses consist? Are they made up partially of extravagant salaries; fifty to one hundred thousand dollars to the president, and in like proportion to subordinate officers? Surely, before the courts are called upon to adjudge an act of the legislature fixing the maximum passenger rates for railroad companies to be unconstitutional ... , they should be fully advised as to what is done with the receipts and earnings of the company; for if so advised, it might clearly appear that a prudent and honest management would, within the rates prescribed, secure to the bondholders their interest, and to the stockholders reasonable dividends. While the protection of vested rights of property is a supreme duty of the courts, it has not come to this, that the legislative power rests subservient to the discretion of any railroad corporation which may, by exorbitant and unreasonable salaries, or in some other improper way, transfer its earnings into what it is pleased to call "operating expenses."[2]

In upholding the commissions' right of supervision over operating expenses, however, the courts have distinguished between expenditures resulting from "arm's length bargaining" and have recognized the functions of management. With respect to the first, when expenditures are controlled by competitive forces, they are seldom challenged. For example, the regulated companies engage in collective bargaining with their employees as do nonregulated enterprises. Except in rare circumstances, the resulting contracts are not questioned by the commissions. But in the absence of "arm's length bargaining," particularly when transactions occur between affiliated companies, commission supervision is required.

With respect to the second, how far can and should a commission be allowed to go in exercising supervision over a company's operating expenses? Two cases provide a partial answer to this question. In 1923, the Missouri commission refused to include in Southwestern Bell's operating expenses the 4.5 percent of its gross revenue that the company was paying to the American Telephone and Telegraph Company as rent for telephone instruments and for managerial services. The Supreme Court overruled the commission, saying:

> The Commission is not the financial manager of the corporation and it is not empowered to substitute its judgment for that of the directors of the corporation; nor can it ignore items charged by the utility as operating expenses unless there is an abuse of discretion in that regard by the corporate officers.[3]

2 *Chicago & Grand Trunk Ry. Co.* v. *Wellman,* 143 U.S. 339, 345–46 (1892).
3 *Missouri* ex rel. *Southwestern Bell Tel. Co.* v. *Missouri Public Service Comm.,* 262 U.S. 276, 289 (1923), quoting from *Illinois Public Service Comm.* ex rel. *Springfield* v. *Springfield Gas & Elec. Co.,* 291 Ill. 209, 234 (1920).

Thirteen years later, in a case involving regulation of stockyard charges by the Secretary of Agriculture, the Supreme Court approved rejection of certain marketing costs on the ground that they were unwise. Said Justice Roberts:

> The contention is that the amount to be expended for these purposes is purely a question of managerial judgment. But this overlooks the consideration that the charge is for a public service, and regulation cannot be frustrated by a requirement that the rate be made to compensate extravagant or unnecessary costs for these or any purposes.[4]

To disallow an expenditure, then, a commission must prove "an abuse of discretion" on the part of management. Such an abuse, in turn, results from "a showing of inefficiency or improvidence"[5] or from "extravagant or unnecessary costs."[6] Regulated companies, in other words, cannot spend freely and expect all expenditures to be included as allowable operating expenses. In effect, this means the commissions are permitted to question both the judgment and integrity of management. And if rates must be high enough to yield sufficient revenue to cover all operating expenses, the consumer has the right to expect that such expenditures will be necessary and reasonable.

At the same time, managerial good faith is presumed.[7] The regulated companies must be given the opportunity to prove the necessity and reasonableness of any expenditure challenged by a commission. To justify an expenditure, a company must show that the expense was actually incurred (or will be incurred in the near future), that the expense was necessary in the proper conduct of its business, and that the amount of the expenditure was reasonable.[8] Moreover, it must be emphasized again that a regulated company may still spend its money in any way it chooses. Management's function is to set the level of expenses; the commission's duty is to determine what expense burden the ratepayer must bear.[9]

Depreciation and Depletion

The right of a regulated company to a depreciation cost allowance was stated by the Supreme Court in 1909. In the Knoxville Water Company decision, the Court recognized that a plant "begins to depreciate in value from the moment of its use," and added:

[4] *Acker* v. *United States*, 298 U.S. 426, 430–31 (1936). Also see *Smith* v. *Illinois Bell Tel. Co.*, 282 U.S. 133 (1930); and *Western Distributing Co.* v. *Public Service Comm. of Kansas*, 285 U.S. 119 (1932).

[5] *West Ohio Gas Co.* v. *Public Utilities Comm. of Ohio*, 294 U.S. 63, 72 (1935).

[6] *Acker* v. *United States, op. cit.,* p. 31.

[7] *West Ohio Gas Co.* v. *Public Utilities Comm. of Ohio, op. cit.*

[8] *Re Ripon United Teleph. Co.*, PUR 1924A, 171 (Wis., 1923); and *Commerce Comm.* v. *Public Service Co. of No. Illinois*, 4 PUR (NS) 1 (Ill., 1934).

[9] *Re Honolulu Gas Co.*, 36 PUR 3d 309 (Hawaii, 1960). As one expert has put it: "Utility managements may not be arbitrary and capricious. And neither may regulators." A. J. G. Priest, "Utility Advertising and Other Operating Expenses," 75 *Public Utilities Fortnightly* 23, 27 (April 29, 1965).

Before coming to the question of profit at all the company is entitled to earn a sufficient sum annually to provide not only for current repairs but for making good the depreciation and replacing the parts of the property when they come to the end of their life. The company is not bound to see its property gradually waste, without making provision out of earnings for its replacement.[10]

In later cases, the Court also approved depreciation provisions for the effects of obsolescence and inadequacy.[11]

Regulated companies are expected to account fully for the depreciation of their plants. In the Court's words:

It is not only the right of the company to make such a provision, but it is its duty to its bond and stockholders, and, in the case of a public service corporation at least, its plain duty to the public. . . . If, however, a company fails to perform this plain duty and to exact sufficient returns to keep the investment unimpaired, . . . the fault is its own.[12]

If, therefore, regulated companies fail to make adequate charges to cover depreciation costs and do not accumulate the necessary depreciation reserves, they cannot increase their charges at a later time in order to recover the deficiencies from consumers. The key phrase is "adequate charges" and has been the subject of considerable dispute between the companies and the commissions.[13]

In 1934, the Supreme Court held that an allowance for the depletion of irreplaceable natural resources was required.

To withhold from a public utility the privilege of including a depletion allowance among its operating expenses, while confining it to a return of 6½% upon the value of its wasting assets, is to take its property away from it without due process of law, at least where the waste is inevitable and rapid. . . . Plainly the state must either surrender the power to limit the return or else concede to the business a compensating privilege to preserve its capital intact.[14]

Taxes

The Supreme Court decided in the Galveston case of 1922 that taxes, including the federal income tax, were operating costs rather than reductions of investors' returns. Said Justice Brandeis:

[10] *Knoxville* v. *Knoxville Water Co.,* 212 U.S. 1, 13 (1909).
[11] *Denver* v. *Denver Union Water Co.,* 246 U.S. 178 (1918); *Kansas City Southern Ry. Co.* v. *United States,* 231 U.S. 423 (1913); *Lindheimer* v. *Illinois Bell Tel. Co.,* 292 U.S. 151 (1934).
[12] *Knoxville* v. *Knoxville Water Co., op. cit.,* p. 14.
[13] See pp. 197–207.
[14] *Columbus Gas & Fuel Co.* v. *Public Service Comm. of Ohio,* 292 U.S. 398, 404–5 (1934).

In calculating whether the five-cent fare will yield a proper return, it is necessary to deduct from gross revenue the expenses and charges; and all taxes which would be payable if a fair return were earned are appropriate deductions. There is no difference in this respect between state and federal taxes or between income taxes and others. [15]

In practice, all kinds of taxes—property, income, sales, franchise, social security, and miscellaneous taxes—are classified as reasonable costs of service. The significant exceptions to this rule are state taxes on capital stock and excess profits taxes levied during World War II and the Korean conflict.

COMMISSION SUPERVISION OF EXPENSES

Commissions have the legal right to supervise a company's operating expenses. Thus, for rate-making purposes, they can control the cost of service. Moreover, since commissions have authority over accounting procedures, they can prescribe general rules for expenditures. In practice, however, commissions have not been vigorous in prescribing such rules. Operating expenses are normally subject to careful scrutiny in rate proceedings, and a commission's decisions provide guides during interim periods.

Methods of Supervision

Operating expenses may be controlled in two broad ways: (1) by disallowing improper charges already incurred in rate proceedings and (2) by prohibiting extravagant or unnecessary charges before they are incurred.

In a rate proceeding, a commission has the opportunity to separate the reasonable and unreasonable costs of service. This method of supervision consists of refusing to permit a company to charge a particular expense to operating expenses. In so doing, the expense is charged to investors. As a method of control, however, the disallowance technique has one important limitation. If a commission disallows a significant percentage of a company's operating expenses (expenses which have already been incurred), the revenue of the company will be inadequate to attract sufficient capital.

For this reason, authority to question expenditures before they are incurred is more satisfactory. At least nineteen state commissions have authority to require that annual budgets be submitted in advance of their effective dates. [16] A majority of the state statutes also require that all intracompany contracts be

---

[15] *Galveston Elec. Co.* v. *Galveston*, 258 U.S. 388, 399 (1922). Also see *Georgia Ry. & Power Co.* v. *Railroad Comm. of Georgia*, 262 U.S. 625, 632–33 (1923).

[16] Subcommittee on Intergovernmental Relations, Senate Committee on Government Operations, *State Utility Commissions* (Committee Print, 1967), Table V facing p. 34. Thirty-four state commissions have authority to require advance submission of budgets on capital expenditures. Federal Power Commission, "Federal and State Commission Jurisdiction and Regulation, Electric, Gas, and Telephone Utilities, 1967" (Washington, D.C.: U.S. Government Printing Office, 1968), p. 24.

filed with the commissions. In both cases, the commissions have the opportunity to consider a company's expenditures before they are incurred.

Supervision of Specific Expenses

An examination of several important costs usually scrutinized by the commissions will illustrate the problems and principles involved in this area.

Costs of Regulation. Should costs of regulation incurred by both the regulated companies and by the commissions be passed on to consumers? In a majority of the states, regulatory expenses of the commissions are assessed to the regulated industries in the form of special taxes. Such assessments are allowable expenses. Allowed, too, is the amount spent in preparing the various reports required by the commissions. But in the rare case of a company's being fined for failing to comply with a statutory requirement, commission order, or rate tariff, the expense is not allowable. [17]

A more complex problem arises with respect to a company's rate case expenses, for consumers should not be forced to pay for "elaborate defenses of private interest." [18] Companies must spend money preparing testimony and exhibits, and hiring lawyers and experts. These expenditures, if reasonable and necessary, are allowed and generally amortized over a five-year period, although periods from two to ten years have been approved. [19] However, advertising expenses incurred by a company to present its case in the newspapers for a rate increase are not always included in operating expenses. [20] When a regulated company exercises its right to appeal a commission decision to the courts, the motives of the company are crucial. The expenses of appeal will be allowed if the rates established by the commission, for instance, are found to be confiscatory. The expenses of appeal will not be allowed when a company merely wants to delay enforcement of a commission decision or, under certain circumstances, when the appeal is unsuccessful. Thus, the Pennsylvania Supreme Court has held that a company is not entitled to recover the full expense of litigation arising from an attempt to increase rates unnecessarily, and the

[17] See "Fines and Penalties against Utilities," 79 *Public Utilities Fortnightly* 62 (April 13, 1967).

[18] Emery Troxel, *Economics of Public Utilities* (New York: Holt, Rinehart & Winston, Inc., 1947), p. 240.

[19] See *Driscoll* v. *Edison Light & Power Co.*, 307 U.S. 104, 120–21 (1939); *Re Public Service Elec. & Gas Co.*, Docket No. 584–10646 (N.J., 1960); *Re Pacific Power & Light Co.*, 34 PUR 3d 36 (Or., 1960); *Re General Teleph. Co. of Wisconsin*, 34 PUR 3d 497 (Wis., 1960); *Re Continental Oil Co.*, 42 PUR 3d 1 (FPC, 1962); *Re United Illum. Co.*, 42 PUR 3d 187 (Conn., 1962); and *Re Area Rate Proceeding for Permian Basin*, 59 PUR 3d 417 (FPC, 1965). Also see "Proper Period for Amortization of Rate Case Expense," 67 *Public Utilities Fortnightly* 59 (January 5, 1961); and "Rate Case Expense must be Reasonable and Necessary," 77 *Public Utilities Fortnightly* 65 (March 3, 1966).

[20] See *Public Utilities Comm.* v. *New England Teleph. & Teleg. Co.*, 80 PUR (NS) 397 (Me., 1949); *Re New England Teleph. & Teleg. Co.*, 83 PUR (NS) 414 (Vt., 1950); *City of Fort Smith* v. *Southwestern Bell Teleph. Co.*, 247 SW 2d 474 (1952); and *Southern Bell Teleph. & Teleg. Co.* v. *Louisiana Public Service Comm.*, 118 So. 2d 372 (1960).

Wisconsin commission once declined to include the costs of a company which refused to reduce rates voluntarily and spent $2,700 fighting the reduction in a formal proceeding.[21]

Salary and Pension Costs. Commissions do not attempt to control wage rates, as they are subject to usual labor-management collective bargaining agreements.[22] Salary and pension costs, however, have been occasionally challenged. If excessive, they would constitute a source of concealed profit: excessive earnings could be turned into high salaries or pensions rather than into rate reductions.

In questioning a company's salaries, a commission normally considers gross revenues, total operating costs, and the quality and duties of management. The New Mexico commission, holding that a salary of $25,000 for a nonresident proprietor of a gas utility was excessive in relation to the company's total operating revenues of less than $700,000, reduced the allowable figure to $12,000.[23] The Connecticut commission held a general officer salary expense of nearly $13,000 excessive for a bus company having total operating expenses of $66,000.[24] The New York commission, after comparing a company with other New York companies and finding no evidence of a notable difference in managerial efficiency, reduced the cost allowance for executive salaries.[25] And the California commission disallowed $2,150,000 of supervisory salaries actually paid by a telephone company when the record disclosed no reason for a substantial increase in the number of management personnel at division level and higher.[26]

Despite these decisions, it should not be thought that the salaries of the regulated companies as a whole are excessive in comparison to those of other industries.[27] Even though they are regulated, they must still compete with the nonregulated sector of the economy for top executives. The general commission practice, therefore, is to leave the determination of officers' salaries to each company. As the Michigan commission held several years ago, the directors are

---

[21] Eli W. Clemens, *Economics and Public Utilities* (New York: Appleton-Century-Crofts, Inc., 1950), p. 130. Also see *Ohio Edison Co. v. Public Utility Comm.*, 45 PUR 3d 1 (Ohio, 1962); and *Pennsylvania Public Utility Comm. v. York Teleph. & Teleg. Co.*, 53 PUR 3d 146 (Pa., 1963).

[22] See "Rate Making as Affected by Negotiations for Wage Increases," 71 *Public Utilities Fortnightly* 69 (March 14, 1963).

[23] *Re Vernah S. Moyston, d/b/a Hobbs Gas Co.*, 48 PUR 3d 459, 462 (N.M., 1963). Also see *Re Cascade Town Co.*, 41 PUR 3d 256 (Colo., 1961).

[24] *Re Airfield Service Co.*, 46 PUR 3d 246 (Conn., 1962). Also see *Re Pleasant Green Water Co.*, 55 PUR (NS) 99 (Utah, 1944); *Re Wilkinson County Teleph. Co.*, 31 PUR 3d 318 (Ga., 1959); *Re Bozrah Light & Power Co.*, 34 PUR 3d 398 (Conn., 1960); *Re Henderson Teleph. Co., Inc.*, 36 PUR 3d 458 (Nev., 1960); and *Re Cherokee Teleph. Co.*, 45 PUR 3d 91 (Ga., 1962).

[25] *Re Orange & Rockland Elec. Co.*, 49 PUR (NS) 257, 301-4 (N.Y., 1943).

[26] *Re Pacific Teleph. & Teleg. Co.*, 53 PUR 3d 513, 568-70 (Cal.. 1964), *aff'd* 401 P. 2d 353 (1965).

[27] See a summary of a 1967 study by National Economic Research Associates concerning gas and electric utilities compensation in 80 *Public Utilities Fortnightly* 45 (July 20, 1967).

the "best judges of the value of executive officers . . . , both to the utility and to the public."[28] It is only in holding company structures, in cases where company officers are also important stockholders, or where smaller companies are involved, that serious problems arise regarding executive salaries.

Pension plans are regarded as legitimate costs of a regulated company, since they are considered as part of an employee's total compensation and necessary to attract and retain good personnel. The cost of such plans must be reasonable, and the plans must be in existence at the time of the rate case.[29] A problem often arises over unfunded pension liability when a plan covers both existing and retired employees, as well as new employees. "The unfunded liability problems exist because the retirement fund is deficient, at the time it is established, in the amount of the accruals due on past services performed by all but new employees."[30] A majority of the commissions have held that the unfunded liability should be amortized over a twenty- to thirty-year period and included in operating expenses, but a few commissions have disallowed such expenses on the ground that they involve costs related to past services.[31]

Public Relations Expenses. American industry spends huge sums annually on various public relations activities, including institutional advertising, political contributions, and lobbying activities at the state and federal levels. All of these expenses raise questions concerning the propriety of including them in operating expenses.

National advertising campaigns (both by trade associations and by individual companies) are directed especially toward the idea that private ownership is superior to public ownership (electric utilities), that regulatory treatment is unjust (railroads), and that the imposition of user fees would be detrimental (water carriers). Expenditures are also made to make the companies better known to customers and potential investors. Commission and court decisions indicate that these expenditures, if they promote good will, are allowable for rate-making purposes.[32] Expenditures of a political nature, however, have generally been regarded as investor costs.[33]

Contributions, Donations, and Dues. American industry also spends significant amounts annually in the form of contributions, donations, and dues.

[28] *Re Detroit Edison Co.,* 16 PUR (NS) 9, 25 (Mich., 1936).

[29] See "Pension Expense," 78 *Public Utilities Fortnightly* 66 (September 15, 1966).

[30] Paul J. Garfield and Wallace F. Lovejoy, *Public Utility Economics* (Englewood Cliffs: Prentice-Hall, Inc., 1964), p. 51.

[31] Amortization was allowed in *Re Utilities & Industries Corp.,* 52 PUR 3d 37, 52 (N.Y., 1963) and *Re Alaska Electric Light & Power Co.,* 70 PUR 3d 481, 489–90 (Alaska, 1967); disallowed in *Re Chesapeake & Potomac Teleph. Co.,* 57 PUR 3d 1, 24–25 (D.C., 1964).

[32] See *Re Consolidated Edison Co. of New York,* 41 PUR 3d 305 (N.Y., 1961); *General Teleph. Co. of Wisconsin* v. *Wisconsin Public Service Comm.,* 46 PUR 3d 1 (1962); and "Public Relations Expense," 77 *Public Utilities Fortnightly* 67 (January 20, 1966).

[33] See "Accounting and Rate Case Treatment of Political Advertising Expenses," 66 *Public Utilities Fortnightly* 417 (1960).

Contributions to charity and educational institutions are not easily classified. Twenty-nine state commissions have held that if such contributions are reasonable, they can be included in operating expenses, since they benefit a company by building good will and strengthening the economic well-being of the community.[34] Refusal to include contributions is based on the belief that they might be a means of influencing public opinion and on the fact that their inclusion would place consumers in the position of becoming involuntary contributors to charity.[35]

When donations to industrial and economic development funds or dues to trade and professional associations (including local and state chambers of commerce) are at issue, they have usually been included in operating expenses.[36] Such donations and dues make a direct contribution to the well-being of the company involved. But dues in civic and service clubs are sometimes excluded on the basis that they do not directly benefit a company in providing service to its customers.[37]

Advertising and Promotional Expenses. The regulated companies constantly seek new customers and larger sales in order to attain the full utilization of their facilities and to realize economies of scale. Advertising costs, expended to increase the demand for service or to retain existing customers, are classified as operating expenses. As the Supreme Court has stated: "A business never stands still. It either grows or decays. Within the limits of reason, advertising or development expenses to foster normal growth are legitimate charges upon income for rate purposes. . . ."[38] It is of interest to note that in a few instances,

---

[34] "Public utilities must be good citizens and the public expects contributions such as these. It would be a rather strained construction to say that such items, in reasonable amounts, are not a permissible part of the operating costs of a public utility." *Re General Teleph. Co. of Florida*, 44 PUR 3d 247, 254 (Fla., 1962). Also see *Re New England Teleph. & Teleg. Co.*, 35 PUR 3d 100 (Vt., 1960); *United Gas Corp.* v. *Mississippi Public Service Comm.*, 38 PUR 3d 252 (1961); and *Re United Gas Pipe Line Co.*, 54 PUR 3d 285 (FPC, 1964).

[35] "Dues, donations, and contributions, if included as an expense for rate-making purposes, become an involuntary levy on ratepayers, who, because of the monopolistic nature of utility service, are unable to obtain service from another source and thereby avoid such a levy. Ratepayers should be encouraged to contribute directly to worthy causes and not involuntarily through an allowance in utility rates." *Re Pacific Teleph. & Teleg. Co.*, 53 PUR 3d 513, 586 (Cal., 1964). Also see *Re Michigan Bell Teleph. Co.*, 32 PUR 3d 395 (Mich., 1960); *Re Henderson Teleph. Co.*, 41 PUR 3d 248 (Nev., 1961); and *Re Chesapeake & Potomac Teleph. Co.*, 57 PUR 3d 1 (D.C., 1964).

[36] See *Re Southwestern Bell Teleph. Co.*, 34 PUR 3d 257 (Kan., 1960); *Re Michigan Consol. Gas Co.*, 36 PUR 3d 289 (Mich., 1960); and *Re Consumers Power Co.*, 38 PUR 3d 355 (Mich., 1961).

[37] See *Re Southern California Gas Co.*, 35 PUR 3d 300 (Cal., 1960); *Re Public Service Co. of North Carolina*, 33 PUR 3d 398 (N.C., 1960); *Re Henderson Teleph. Co.*, 41 PUR 3d 248 (Nev., 1961); and *Re Accounting Treatment for Donations, Dues, and Lobbying Expenditures*, 71 PUR 3d 440 (N.Y., 1967).

[38] *West Ohio Gas Co.* v. *Public Utilities Comm. of Ohio, op. cit.*, p. 72. Also see *Southern Bell Teleph. & Teleg. Co.* v. *Georgia Public Service Comm.*, 49 SE 2d 38 (1948); *Central Maine Power Co.* v. *Maine Public Utilities Comm.*, 136 A. 2d 726 (1957); and *City of El Dorado* v. *Arkansas Public Service Comm.*, 362 SW 2d 680 (1962).

commissions have ordered companies to expand their sales promotion activities beyond the amounts they estimated were necessary and have granted funds for this purpose.[39]

With the growing intensity of interfuel competition, promotional activities of electric and gas utilities have expanded rapidly in both importance and scope, and have received scrutiny by the commissions, the courts, and Congress. These activities fall into seven categories:

I. Advertising cost sharing programs.
II. Construction cost allowances.
III. Sales bonuses.
IV. Maximum cost guarantees.
V. Financing assistance.
VI. Equipment and appliance rental programs, and
VII. Varied sales promotion activities such as Open House Parties, Prize Contests, and the lending of company personnel for showing houses and apartments.[40]

Several of these allowances and practices have been challenged by competing suppliers, but their use has generally been upheld as long as they are granted on a uniform basis, and are reasonable and nondiscriminatory.[41] However, allowances for conversion to gas or electric heat must be uniform regardless of from what type of fuel the conversion is made; utilities may not guarantee maximum annual costs; and electric companies may not provide free underground line extensions to all-electric customers.[42]

Utility Merchandising Expenses. Electric and gas utilities often sell appli-

[39]See *Re San Jose City Lines*, 7 PUR 3d 80 (Cal., 1954); and *Re Pacific Greyhound Lines*, 53 C PUR 634 (Cal., 1954).

[40]Wallace R. Burke, "Promotional Activities," in National Association of Regulatory Utility Commissioners, *Annual Proceedings, 1966* (Washington, D.C., 1967), p. 39.

[41]See *Re Savannah Electric & Power Co.*, 45 PUR 3d 88 (Ga., 1962); *Re Delaware Power & Light Co.*, 56 PUR 3d 1 (Del., 1964); *Watkins v. Atlantic City Electric Co.*, 60 PUR 3d 213 (N.J., 1965); *Gifford v. Central Maine Power Co.*, 63 PUR 3d 205 (Me., 1965), *aff'd* 217 A. 2d 200 (1966); *Rossi v. Garton*, 211 A. 2d 806 (1965); *Virginia State Corp. Comm. v. Appalachian Power Co.*, 65 PUR 3d 283 (Va., 1966); *Re Promotional Practices of Electric and Gas Utilities*, 65 PUR 3d 405 (Conn., 1966); *Re Promotional Activities by Gas and Electric Corporations*, 68 PUR 3d 162 (N.Y., 1967); and *Re Promotional Practices of Electric and Gas Utilities*, 69 PUR 3d 317 (Ill., 1967). Also see Peter B. Spivak, "The Regulator's Views of Utility Competition," 79 *Public Utilities Fortnightly* 28 (February 2, 1967); Grant S. Lewis, "Promotional Activities of Public Utilities," 80 *ibid.* 44 (October 26, 1967); "Regulatory Policy and Promotional Practices," 80 *ibid.* 72; T. Justin Moore, Jr., "Competitive Activities of Regulated Utilities" (American Bar Association Annual Report, Section of *Public Utility Law, 1967*), pp. 15–25; Burke, *op. cit.*, pp. 38–51; "Promotional Rates and Allowances for Electric Service," 81 *Public Utilities Fortnightly* 99 (June 6, 1968); and *Promotional Practices by Public Utilities and Their Impact upon Small Business* (Hearings before the Subcommittee on Activities of Regulatory Agencies of the Select Committee on Small Business, House, 90th Cong., 2d sess.) (Washington, D.C.: U.S. Government Printing Office, 1968) and, under the same title, House Report No. 1984, 90th Cong., 2d sess. (1968).

[42]See cases cited in preceding footnote and "Underground Wiring Conjoined with Promotional Allowances," 80 *Public Utilities Fortnightly* 58 (July 20, 1967).

ances as a promotional activity. These appliances are sold to customers either directly or indirectly by means of sales to architects and builders. In many cases, appliance sales do not show a profit; the utility gains through an increased use of its service.

The merchandising of appliances by utilities has been the subject of constant controversy. Local merchants often claim that such sales represent a form of "unfair" competition, because utilities can write off their appliance sales losses to general business expenses, have larger financial resources, and can obtain quantity discounts from manufacturers.[43] Others argue that appliance merchandising, like general sales promotion, is simply another method of obtaining new business. This position has been summarized by Troxel:

> Before domestic consumers can buy more electricity or gas, they often must buy more stoves, refrigerators, and other equipment. . . . Perhaps they do not buy more water heaters or other appliances because the appliance prices are too high. If this is true, a reduction of appliance prices can increase the sales of electricity or gas. The losses are new business expenses. And the losses, like general advertising expenditures, can be covered by the additional earnings that the company obtains from the demand increases. Appliance sales can be sensibly classed as a part of public utility operations.[44]

The commissions require for accounting purposes that expense and revenue accounts for the appliance business of an electric or gas utility be separated from other accounts. Salaries and commissions of salesmen, the cost of appliance advertising, and any losses on appliance sales, generally are excluded from operating expenses for purposes of rate making.[45] Similarly, any profits on appliance sales are not included in a company's annual utility earnings. The merchandising of appliances, therefore, is treated as a nonutility business.

Transactions among Affiliated Companies. The widespread existence of holding companies results in two important problems in the control of expenditures. Operating companies normally pay either the holding company or a subsidiary service company an annual fee for accounting, legal, and financial services. Operating companies also commonly purchase all or some of their equipment, materials, and supplies from affiliated manufacturing firms. These transactions, because of the absence of arm's length bargaining, require careful scrutiny by the commissions, but they "should not be given any consideration in the absence of evidence of unfair dealing."[46]

With respect to annual service fees, a majority of the state commissions have authority over the management contracts that are signed by operating

43 Richard A. Harvill, "The Opposition to Public Utility Appliance Merchandising," 8 *Journal of Land & Public Utility Economics* 290 (1932).

44 Troxel, *op. cit.*, p. 244.

45 See *Re Nevada Power Co.*, 43 PUR 3d 511 (Nev., 1962); *Re Columbia Gas of New York*, 61 PUR 3d 491 (N.Y., 1965); and *Re Northern Gas Co.*, 70 PUR 3d 260 (Wyo., 1967).

46 *Southwestern Bell Tel. Co.* v. *Kansas State Corp. Comm.*, 386 P. 2d 515, 552 (1963).

companies, and copies of such contracts must be filed with the commissions. In some cases, the contracts must be submitted for approval before they become effective. In other cases, the contracts are subject to approval or disapproval after they have become effective. But in either situation, a commission always has the opportunity in a rate case to question a payment made to an affiliated company.

In general, service fees will not be approved unless the company can show some specific services rendered by the management firm. This requirement follows the principle expressed by the SEC in a 1943 case:

> Each service company should confine itself to functions which the operating subsidiaries cannot perform as efficiently and economically themselves. These services should be limited to services of an "operating nature" as distinguished from managerial, executive, or policy-forming functions. [47]

At the federal level, the service contracts of electric and gas holding companies are closely controlled by the SEC. In the Public Utility Holding Company Act of 1935, the commission was authorized to approve service companies if it finds that services will be performed efficiently and economically "at a cost fairly and equitably allocated among" operating subsidiaries and "at a reasonable saving over the cost of comparable services or construction performed or goods sold by independent persons." [48] The commission prescribes a standard system of accounts for service companies. Charges are limited to the costs of the services performed; all proposed modifications in service contracts must be approved by the commission. [49]

The Federal Communications Commission has no similar control over the service charges made by communications firms, but it has control in rate proceedings. The Bell System operating subsidiaries, for example, currently pay the American Telephone and Telegraph Company 1 percent of exchange and toll revenues annually. [50] This annual fee is for a variety of services, including accounting, legal, and financial services; research and development; and advice and assistance in engineering, plant, traffic, commercial, and other operating fields. In 1945, A.T.&T.'s license contract was investigated by a committee of state commission and FCC representatives. [51] Various recommendations were

[47] *Re Columbia Engineering Corp.* (SEC), Holding Co. Act Release No. 4166 (March, 1943).

[48] Securities and Exchange Commission, "General Rules and Regulations under the Public Utility Holding Company Act of 1935" (Washington, D.C.: U.S. Government Printing Office, 1958), Rule 88, pp. 26–27.

[49] See, for example, *Re Columbia Gas System Service Corporation* (SEC), Holding Co. Act Release No. 14699 (September, 1962).

[50] One state commission, California, requires that service charges be determined by the cost of service. See *Re Pacific Teleph. & Teleg. Co.*, 53 PUR 3d 513, 582–86 (Cal., 1964), *aff'd* 401 P. 2d 353 (1965). Also see Joseph R. Rose, "The Bell Telephone System Rate Cases," 37 *Virginia Law Review* 699, 722–23 (1951).

[51] National Association of Regulatory Utility Commissioners, *Report on Service Charges by the American Telephone & Telegraph Company to the Associated Bell Telephone Companies and Long Lines Department* (New York, 1945).

made, but the annual fee (which at that time was 1½ percent) was found reasonable. Further, no state commission has ever found it necessary to revise the service charges under the license contract.[52]

With respect to prices for equipment charged operating companies by affiliated manufacturing firms, the commissions generally consider two criteria of reasonableness, both based on Supreme Court decisions: (1) whether the prices charged operating companies are lower than those charged by other manufacturers for comparable equipment and supplies[53] and (2) whether the profits earned on sales to operating companies are lower than those of comparable large manufacturing companies.[54] Using these criteria, there are few cases in which commissions have made disallowances, either in operating expenses or in the rate base. For example, in some 330 rate cases involving the Bell System since 1930, the California commission is the only one to make significant disallowances, not because Western Electric's prices were too high, but because of its long-held belief that an affiliated manufacturer should earn no more than a regulated utility.[55] A typical commission finding on the subject is illustrated by the following quote from a 1953 Wyoming commission decision:

> In connection with the matter of the rate base, some mention should also be made of the cost of plant materials included therein. The applicant, as is well known, is a part of the Bell System and has intercorporate relations with the Western Electric Company, Inc. It is the practice of applicant to purchase practically all of its telephone apparatus and equipment and outside plant material from Western Electric. By reason of applicant's relation with

[52] See A. J. G. Priest, "Operating Expenses in the Spotlight," 77 *Public Utilities Fortnightly* 15, 19–24 (February 3, 1966).

[53] *Houston v. Southwestern Bell Tel. Co.*, 259 U.S. 318, 323 (1922).

[54] *Smith v. Illinois Bell Tel. Co., op. cit.*, pp. 152–53. Also see *Illinois Bell Tel. Co. v. Gilbert*, 3 F. Supp. 595 (1933).

[55] *Re Pacific Teleph. & Teleg. Co.*, 23 PUR 3d 209 (Cal., 1958); and *Re Pacific Teleph. & Teleg. Co.*, 53 PUR 3d 513 (Cal., 1964), *aff'd* 401 P. 2d 353 (1965). This reasoning was rejected by the District of Columbia commission in *Re Chesapeake & Potomac Teleph. Co.*, 57 PUR 3d 1, 19–20 (D.C., 1964).

    In a 1952 case, the Missouri commission made a disallowance in Southwestern Bell's rate base because of Western Electric's 1948 earnings, which were above 12 percent on Bell System business, but refused to make any disallowance for subsequent years. *Re Southwestern Bell Teleph. Co.*, 92 PUR (NS) 481 (Mo., 1952). In a 1957 case, the Michigan commission made a small adjustment in Michigan Bell's operating expenses. *Re Michigan Bell Teleph. Co.*, 20 PUR 3d 397 (Mich., 1957), rehearing denied, 24 PUR 3d 109 (Mich., 1958). Other commissions consider Western Electric's profits in arriving at the rate of return to be allowed an operating company. See *Re Wisconsin Teleph. Co.*, 93 PUR (NS) 490 (Wis., 1952); and *Re Southwestern Bell Teleph. Co.*, 93 PUR (NS) 161 (Kan., 1952).

    A few cases in which disallowances have been made involved independent telephone companies. See, for example, *Re United Teleph. Co.*, 27 PUR 3d 128 (Kan., 1958); *Re General Teleph. Co. of Wisconsin*, 34 PUR 3d 497 (Wis., 1960), *aff'd sub nom. General Teleph. Co. of Wisconsin v. Wisconsin Public Service Comm.*, 46 PUR 3d 1 (1962); *Pennsylvania Public Utility Comm. v. York Teleph. & Teleg. Co.*, 53 PUR 3d 146 (Pa., 1963); and *Re General Teleph. Co. of Upstate New York*, Case 22522 (N.Y., 1963), *aff'd sub nom. General Teleph. Co. of Upstate New York v. Lundy*, 17 NY 2d 373 (1966).

Western, it is necessary to consider whether or not the prices paid by applicant are reasonable, having regard for the earnings of Western Electric. As a part of its case, applicant introduced evidence to show that the amounts paid by it to Western for such materials were generally lower than amounts it would be required to pay elsewhere and also that the average earnings of Western Electric (7.9 percent on its net investment) have not reached unreasonable proportions for a manufacturing company when compared with earnings of nonrelated manufacturing companies.

It would seem that applicant, with respect to this matter, has sustained its burden of showing that the material prices are reasonable and, for purposes here, those prices have been accepted.

In reaching this conclusion we are supported by reports from the Special Committee of NARUC co-operating with the FCC, which has made, and is continuing to make, studies of this operation.[56]

Evaluation of Commission Control

The above items do not represent a complete list of the costs of service incurred by the regulated industries, nor are they the only expenses scrutinized in rate cases. Rather, they are representative, and illustrate the problems and nature of commission control of operating expenses. One conclusion stands out: few of the commissions have formulated rules or established standards to govern expenditures, but supervision of expenses has been vigorous in rate-making proceedings. Generally, the commissions and the courts have taken the view that expenditures represent a managerial decision, and they have been hesitant to substitute their judgments.

But the line they have sought to draw between regulation and management is unreal. The substantive problems with which the two must deal are the same. If regulation is to fulfill the function of competition as a disciplinarian, it must invade the sphere of management. Where it refuses to do so, there is no safeguard for the public interest. This is the inescapable dilemma of regulatory control.[57]

Clemens has argued that more effective commission control of operating expenses would require the use of expense ratios.[58] By comparing the expense

---

[56]*Re Mountain States Teleph. & Teleg. Co.*, 97 PUR (NS) 114, 118–19 (Wyo., 1953). Also see *Re Mountain States Teleph. & Teleg. Co.*, 1 PUR 3d 129 (Colo., 1953); *Re New England Teleph. & Teleg. Co.*, 2 PUR 3d 464 (Mass., 1953); *Re Mountain States Teleph. & Teleg. Co.*, 7 PUR 3d 115 (Ariz., 1954); *Re Ohio Bell Teleph. Co.*, 8 PUR 3d 136 (Ohio, 1954); *Re Northwestern Bell Teleph. Co.*, 23 PUR 3d 267 (Minn., 1958); and *Re Southern Bell Teleph. & Teleg. Co.*, 66 PUR 3d 1 (Fla., 1966).

[57]Clair Wilcox, *Public Policies Toward Business* (3d ed.; Homewood, Ill.: Richard D. Irwin, Inc., 1966), p. 307.

"Regulators have frequently disallowed some expenditures, and curtailed others as being excessive or unwarranted. But the policing job is endless, aimless, and dubious, mainly because of the sheer impossibility of small staffs tracking myriads of payments. Comparability studies can only isolate some gross distortions, between firms or over time." Sidney Weintraub, "Rate Making and an Incentive Rate of Return," 81 *Public Utilities Fortnightly* 23, 25 (April 25, 1968).

[58]Clemens, *op. cit.*, pp. 131–38.

ratios of different companies—expenses as a percentage of revenues, expenses per unit of consumption, and expenses per customer—the commissions would have a basis for analyzing company expenditures. Suppose, for instance, that a commission discovered a rise in a company's production cost of electricity from 7 to 7.5 mills per kilowatt-hour. Does this rise indicate an increase in coal cost or an inefficient boiler room operation in which heat is being wasted? Admittedly, care must be exercised in using expense ratios:

> They are comparable only to a degree. A utility with a large industrial load will not operate under the same cost conditions as one with a large residential load. The costs of one utility may be high because the demand tends to be concentrated at one hour of the day or at a certain day of the year. Expense ratios are merely points of departure for further questioning and analysis.[59]

Expense ratios, however, may uncover valuable information that would otherwise go undetected. While many of the regulated companies use ratio analysis, only a few of the commissions have done so.[60]

More elaborate measures of efficiency have been or are being developed by Iulo,[61] and by Dodge and Trebing[62] with respect to the electric utility industry. The Iulo study attempted to measure relative performance using levels of unit costs as the measure, while the Dodge-Trebing research employs the rate of change in total factor productivity as a measure. Shepherd has noted that attempts to measure, explain, and predict the performance of electric utility firms are difficult because of "the multiplicity of elements in performance and the problem of weighting them, data scarcities, difficulty in disentangling cause and effect, and so on" and has questioned the applicability of the approach of these studies to other utility industries.[63] Yet, as Trebing has summarized:

> Any speculation on the relative merits of Professor Iulo's approach on the one hand, or the direct measurement of the firm's real productivity, on the other, seems premature at this stage of development. The former emphasizes the short run, and the latter emphasizes the long run and assumes far fewer constraints on management's ability to influence results. But which approach is more applicable to the general process of regulation or to a given commission problem can only be judged after greater research and investigation.[64]

---

[59]*Ibid.,* p. 132.

[60]The California commission, for example, often compares the sales promotion expense per customer of different companies in determining a reasonable allowance. See *Re Southern California Gas Co.,* 35 PUR 3d 300 (Cal., 1960).

[61]William Iulo, *Electric Utilities—Costs and Performance* (Pullman: Bureau of Economic and Business Research, Washington State University, 1961). Also see, by the same author, "Problems in the Definition and Measurement of Superior Performance" in Harry M. Trebing (ed.), *Performance under Regulation* (East Lansing: Michigan State Public Utilities Studies, 1968), pp. 3–19.

[62]William H. Dodge, "Productivity Measures and Performance Evaluation" in Trebing, *Performance under Regulation, op. cit.,* pp. 20–32.

[63]William G. Shepherd, "Comment," in Trebing, *Performance under Regulation, op. cit.,* pp. 33, 35.

[64]Harry M. Trebing, "Toward an Incentive System of Regulation," 72 *Public Utilities Fortnightly* 22, 33 (July 18, 1963).

DEPRECIATION AS A COST

The concern in this section is with depreciation as an annual charge to operating costs, thereby shown in the income statement. Accrued depreciation, recorded in the depreciation reserve (a balance sheet account) as a deduction from the value of a company's tangible and reproducible property for rate base purposes, will be discussed in the following chapter.

The Meaning of Depreciation

The National Association of Regulatory Utility Commissioners has defined depreciation as follows:

(a) Depreciation is the expiration or consumption, in whole or in part, of the service life, capacity, or utility of property resulting from the action of one or more of the forces operating to bring about the retirement of such property from service;

(b) The forces so operating include wear and tear, decay, action of the elements, inadequacy, obsolescence, and public requirements;

(c) Depreciation results in a cost of service.[65]

Depreciation thus involves the gradual deterioration and eventual destruction of the value of physical facilities used in the process of providing service. The several causes of depreciation are commonly divided into two broad categories. (1) Physical depreciation is caused by usage, rust, rot, and decay—all through the passage of time. Trucks and tires wear out; telephone and electric poles slowly rot; gas and water mains gradually corrode. Physical depreciation also results from unforeseeable and uninsurable contingencies such as accidents and disasters. (2) Functional depreciation occurs when facilities are rendered obsolete by new technology, are made inadequate by growth in demand, or are made useless by changes in public requirements. One authority has estimated that about 20 percent of all past retirements have resulted from physical causes; the remaining 80 percent from functional causes.[66] As will be discussed below, functional depreciation represents a special regulatory problem.

The basic purpose of depreciation accounting is to recover from revenues the costs invested in the physical plant contributing to the production of those revenues. By matching capital recovery with capital consumption, a more accurate measure of current costs of operation is possible. Stated another way, depreciation accounting is necessary to reimburse the owners for their original contribution of capital to the business and should properly be charged to

---

[65] National Association of Regulatory Utility Commissioners, *Report of the Committee on Depreciation, 1943* (Washington, D.C., 1943), p. xiv. On utility depreciation practices, see National Association of Regulatory Utility Commissioners, *Public Utility Depreciation Practices* (Washington, D.C., 1968).

[66] L. R. Nash, "A New Depreciation Fallacy," 30 *Public Utilities Fortnightly* 761, 766 (1942).

consumers as a cost of the service they receive. "It is the exhaustion of service life, not the particular cause of retirement, that is important." [67]

It should be noted that the basic purpose of depreciation accounting is *not* to finance replacements. Even if facilities are not to be replaced, depreciation must be charged to operating expenses in order to record the cost of property consumed in providing service, thereby maintaining the integrity of the investment. Nor does depreciation result in a fund. "The depreciation reserve is an account *contra* to the plant account." [68] Further, a distinction must be made between provisions for depreciation and for maintenance. While both are costs, maintenance keeps facilities in good condition while they are in use but does not reimburse the owners for their capital. Only depreciation charges perform the reimbursement function. This important distinction was stated by Chief Justice Hughes as follows:

> Broadly speaking, depreciation is the loss, not restored by current maintenance, which is due to all the factors causing the ultimate retirement of the property. These factors embrace wear and tear, decay, inadequacy, and obsolescence. Annual depreciation is the loss which takes place in a year. In determining reasonable rates for supplying public service, it is proper to include in the operating expenses, that is, in the cost of producing the service, an allowance for consumption of capital in order to maintain the integrity of the investment in the service rendered. [69]

Depreciation Accounting

The regulatory commissions require depreciation accounting. [70] Under this accounting system, balances are established in the depreciation reserve account. Credits to this account result from annual charges during the useful life of the property. [71] The annual charge depends on three factors: (1) the value of the property less its estimated salvage value, (2) the estimated useful life of the

[67] National Association of Regulatory Utility Commissioners, *Report of the Committee on Depreciation, op. cit.*, p. xv.

[68] *Ibid.*

[69] *Lindheimer* v. *Illinois Bell Tel. Co., op. cit.*, p. 167.

[70] For many years, some of the regulated companies favored retirement accounting, whereby replacements are not charged to operating costs until they are actually made. See H. E. Riggs, "The Two Radically Different Concepts of Depreciation," 9 *Public Utilities Fortnightly* 559 (1932).

[71] "The annual depreciation estimate for a company within a particular industry is a tailor-made proposition. No two companies are ever alike. There is a whole host of reasons why this is so. The more obvious are natural causes. Companies that operate in tropical areas are much more familiar with the ravages caused by hurricanes, high humidity, tropical rot, fungus, and other familiar phenomena in such areas. Companies that operate in northern climates are familiar with the ravages of wind and snow and ice, of alternate freezing and thawing. Companies that operate near the seashore where there are prevailing winds from the sea know the damage done by salt air." Edward C. Edgar and G. R. Faust, "System Growth and Obsolescence—Their Effect on Depreciation," 81 *Public Utilities Fortnightly* 15, 17 (February 15, 1968).

property over which this sum is written off, and (3) the method used in distributing the sum over this life.

As will be discussed in the following section, property may be valued at its original cost, at its replacement cost, or at some intermediate point between these two. In 1930, the Supreme Court ruled that the annual depreciation accrual of public utilities should be based on the "present value" of the depreciable property [72]—a ruling consistent with its earlier decisions emphasizing fair value in determining the rate base. If followed, the annual depreciation charge would fluctuate with price changes, rising as the price level increased and falling as prices declined. The Court subsequently overruled the United Railways case on this point (as well as on fair value), thus recognizing that the recovery of past investments is the main purpose of depreciation accounting. [73] As a result, original cost accounting is now the general rule for valuating depreciable property. Salvage values are then estimated and deducted from the original cost in order to determine the amount to be recovered through depreciation charges.

The useful life of the various property items, which determines the length of the depreciation period, is established in three basic ways. First, and the most frequently used method, is engineering estimates. Second, when estimates made by the company and by the commission differ or when it is desirable to adopt a uniform depreciation rate, the commissions may set the length of the depreciation period. Third, as commissions are reluctant to allow depreciation rates in excess of those permitted for tax purposes, taxes may determine the depreciation period. Particularly is the third method important when accelerated depreciation (discussed below) is permitted for tax purposes. Welch has stated that the process of estimating the useful life of property items

> . . . is something very similar to the actuarial experience used by insurance companies for fires, accidents, and other hazards covered by insurance, even human life. Given a broad enough experience, such actuarial tables can be surprisingly accurate. Thus, a single pole for a pole line might be assigned a life expectancy of twenty years and be knocked down by an automobile the day after it is put into service. Or it may be destroyed by lightning ten years after that. And it may be standing and giving good service thirty years later. But given enough experience with enough poles, and making due adjustments for local hazards (such as sleet in the North, and termites in the South), the average life table assignment will generally be found to work out very close to actual experience. [74]

In practice, a separate rate is not computed for each item of property. Rather, property items are grouped, and an average rate is applied to all items within each group.

Finally, the depreciation charge can be distributed over the expected

---

[72] *United Railways* v. *West,* 280 U.S. 234 (1930).
[73] *Federal Power Comm.* v. *Hope Natural Gas Co.,* 320 U.S. 591 (1944).
[74] Francis X. Welch, *Cases and Text on Public Utility Regulation* (rev. ed.; Washington, D.C.: Public Utilities Reports, Inc., 1968), p. 415.

useful life of the property in two frequently used ways. The straight line method, by which rates remain the same each year, is the simplest and most commonly used. Thus, a piece of property costing $10,000 with no salvage value and an estimated life of ten years would be depreciated at the rate of $1,000 per year. In a growing and expanding company, the accruals are usually reinvested in the business, but they are not credited with interest. The annual depreciation charges are intended to add up to the original cost of the property when retired. The sinking fund method is more complicated. A reserve is set up on the company's books and equal charges assigned to it each year. It is assumed, moreover, that the charges are invested and interest earned. Therefore, the fixed portion of the annual depreciation charge need not be so large as under the straight line method, but only large enough so that the yearly charges plus the accumulated compound interest will be equal to the cost of the property at the time of retirement. Using the same illustration as above, an annual charge of $758.68 and the addition of compound interest at 6 percent would bring the reserve up to $10,000 at the end of ten years. The two methods are compared in Table 7-1. As indicated, the straight line method is preferred by most of the regulated companies and regulatory commissions because of its simplicity.

Current Depreciation Problems

While the use of depreciation accounting is firmly established, four problems frequently arise in rate cases. First, how should the commissions deal with functional depreciation? Second, in view of a constant inflationary trend in prices since the end of World War II, should depreciation allowances be based upon reproduction cost? Third, how should accelerated depreciation be treated?

TABLE 7-1
Comparison of Straight Line and Sinking Fund Methods*

	Straight Line		Sinking Fund		
Year	Annual Depreciation Expense	Depreciation Reserve Accumulation	Annual Depreciation Expense	Annual Interest Accumulation	Depreciation Reserve Accumulation
1	$ 1,000	$ 1,000	$ 758.68	...	$ 758.68
2	1,000	2,000	758.68	$ 45.52	1,562.88
3	1,000	3,000	758.68	93.77	2,415.33
4	1,000	4,000	758.68	144.92	3,318.93
5	1,000	5,000	758.68	199.14	4,276.75
6	1,000	6,000	758.68	256.61	5,292.04
7	1,000	7,000	758.68	317.52	6,368.24
8	1,000	8,000	758.68	382.08	7,509.01
9	1,000	9,000	758.68	450.54	8,718.23
10	1,000	10,000	758.68	523.09	10,000.00
Totals	$10,000		$7,586.80	$2,413.20	

*The following assumptions underlie the computations: original investment, $10,000; no salvage value; estimated useful life, 10 years; annual interest, 6 percent.

Fourth, how should the investment tax credit be treated? Each of these problems will be discussed in turn.

The Problem of Obsolescence. Functional depreciation, as previously noted, may be of more importance than physical depreciation. Functional depreciation is due to changes in technology, demand, or public requirements.[75] Dial telephone systems have been substituted for manual switchboards, leading to the retirement of much equipment. To meet expanding consumer demand, electric companies have installed more economical boilers, stokers, turbines, and generators, resulting in the retirement of many small plants and their equipment. The private automobile has displaced some of our urban transportation systems, resulting in unused capacity. And governmental bodies have condemned property for highways, urban renewal, and slum improvement or have required that underground cables be used in place of overhead lines in the interest of beautification. In these and many other cases, plant and equipment have been outdated and retired. Functional depreciation, however, raises a serious regulatory problem: engineers can estimate with some accuracy physical depreciation, but the rate of obsolescence is determined by changing technology. As a result, no separate allowance is made for obsolescence in depreciation accounting, but it is a major consideration in setting overall depreciation rates.[76]

The Investment Decision. A business firm, in deciding whether it should replace existing equipment with more efficient equipment, will consider the expected return on the new investment. To be profitable, an innovation must result in an increase in earnings due to higher total revenues, lower total operating costs, or a combination of the two.[77] Significantly, in estimating future costs and revenues, depreciation on the replaced equipment is not a relevant cost. It is assumed, however, that a nonregulated company will be permitted to write off the unrecovered investment in old equipment. But for regulated companies, the unrecovered investment in old equipment may be a relevant factor in making an investment decision, as is a commission's policy regarding the expected increase in earnings.

The regulatory commissions control both depreciation charges and annual earnings for rate-making purposes. Assume that a new innovation is profitable— that is, it is expected to result in higher earnings. If a commission refuses to permit the company to write off the unrecovered investment and if the higher earnings resulting from the new investment are used to reduce rates, management may decide to withhold the new investment. Even if a commission permits the company to write off the old investment but uses the increase in earnings to reduce rates, the additional investment may not be made. In short, commission

---

75 For a more complete discussion, see Edgar and Faust, *op. cit.,* pp. 15–28.

76 For example, a basic purpose in the revised depreciation guidelines announced in 1962 was to give greater weight to obsolescence. See U.S. Treasury Department, Internal Revenue Service, "Depreciation Guidelines and Rules" (Washington, D.C.: U.S. Government Printing Office, 1962).

77 See Howard L. Timms, *The Production Function in Business* (rev. ed.; Homewood, Ill.: Richard D. Irwin, Inc., 1966).

policy regarding depreciation charges and annual earnings is critical in the investment decisions of regulated companies.

Innovation, moreover, can benefit consumers even though a company's earnings increase. Rate reductions may be possible immediately. The rise in earnings, for instance, may be greater than required. Similarly, service improvements may result from innovation. In either situation, the consumer benefits from innovation, as does the company and the economy.

Regulatory Policy. Two methods of dealing with the depreciation problem due to obsolescence have been suggested.[78] First, commissions can define obsolete equipment as stand-by capacity, leaving it in the rate base. Depreciation of the old equipment is stopped, but the company receives a return on its value. Unless the stand-by capacity is actually necessary, this solution to the problem is unsatisfactory, for it compels consumers to pay a permanent return on investments that are useless. Second, commissions can permit the rapid amortization of obsolete equipment, while the equipment that replaced it is being depreciated at the normal rate. This solution results in current consumers paying the costs of obsolescence. Furthermore, by amortizing the costs over a five-year period, for example, the costs would be recovered gradually, and some of the benefits of the new technology could be passed on to consumers immediately. The amortization policy is clearly superior to allowing a permanent return on obsolete equipment values.

Most commissions have permitted companies to make adequate annual charges for depreciation in anticipation of future obsolescence. Some have followed the practice of defining obsolete equipment as stand-by capacity, either in whole or in part. Others have approved amortization. Regulatory policy, therefore, is far from consistent.

The Reproduction Cost Controversy.[79] The basic purpose of depreciation accounting is the recovery of past investment in plant and equipment, and is properly a cost of providing service. In recent years, moreover, because of inflationary price trends, many have argued that annual depreciation charges should be based upon current cost rather than upon original cost.[80] Only in this way, it is argued, will a company be able to maintain unimpaired the capital invested in the enterprise.

Consider an inflationary situation (Table 7–2). If a company purchases a machine for $2,000, with an estimated life of five years and no salvage value, straight line depreciation would result in an annual charge of $400 based upon original cost. Now assume that the price level rises throughout the five-year

[78] These suggestions are made and fully analyzed by Troxel, *op. cit.*, pp. 362–68. The rate of return problem is considered in Chapter 9.

[79] The discussion in this section is limited to the controversy over the use of reproduction cost in determining annual depreciation allowances. The property valuation—rate base—controversy is considered in the following chapter.

[80] The terms current cost, reproduction cost, and price level depreciation are used synonymously. On the reproduction cost controversy, see Francis J. Walsh, Jr., *Inflation and Corporate Accounting* (New York: The National Industrial Conference Board, 1962).

period. In terms of the purchasing power of the dollar, the company has recovered only $1,691 of its original investment. As a result, the current-cost advocates argue, depreciation based upon original cost has failed to measure the real consumption of capital. Further, when taxes are levied on taxable income which reflects original cost depreciation allowances, a portion of the tax

TABLE 7-2
Original Cost versus Reproduction Cost Depreciation Allowance*

Year	Depreciation Accruals Based on Original Cost	Consumer Price Index	Depreciation Accruals Based on Price Index	Capital Recovered in Terms of Year 1 Dollars	
				With Original Cost Depreciation	With Reproduction Cost Depreciation
1	$ 400	100	$ 400	$ 400	$ 400
2	400	110	440	364	400
3	400	120	480	333	400
4	400	130	520	308	400
5	400	140	560	286	400
Totals	$2,000		$2,400	$1,691	$2,000

*The following assumptions underlie the computations: original investment, $2,000; no salvage value; estimated life, five years; straight line depreciation.

represents a tax on capital as well as on real income. The capital invested in the enterprise, therefore, is eroded. This situation can be corrected by expressing depreciation allowances in current dollars, as illustrated. The result is to return to the company its original $2,000 investment in terms of constant purchasing power.[81] In times of deflation, the opposite adjustments would be made, and depreciation allowances would be decreased.

Representatives of the regulated industries are not the only ones advocating reproduction cost depreciation. Any industry with a large investment in plant and equipment in relation to annual revenues will be severely hit by changes in the price level. Assume two industries: one with an investment in plant and equipment equal to four times annual revenues, the other with investment equal to one-half annual revenues. If the price level rises 50 percent, it takes either an 8 percent increase in revenues or a 22 percent decrease in operating expenses to offset the tax burden for the first, as compared to a 1 percent increase in revenues or a 1 percent decrease in operating expenses for the second.[82]

[81] Current cost depreciation allowances differ from replacement depreciation. To use the same example depicted in Table 7-2, the $2,400 resulting from current cost depreciation may be greater than or less than the amount needed to replace the machine.
[82] F. Warren Brooks, "Needed Reform for Utility Tax Depreciation," 52 *Public Utilities Fortnightly* 407, 412 (1953). Brooks states that "for the average large electric utility in 1952, 83 per cent of the income taxes paid were levied on real income and 17 per cent were levied on capital." *Ibid.*, p. 411.

The economics of original cost and reproduction cost will be considered at length in the next chapter. At this point, however, three comments are pertinent. First, if the reproduction cost concept is accepted, it should apply to all American industry, not just the regulated industries. Second, acceptance of the reproduction cost concept would involve a change in tax policy. There is no logical reason why depreciation methods for accounting purposes should not be the same as for tax purposes. And from a practical standpoint, commissions are reluctant to allow depreciation rates in excess of those permitted for tax purposes. Under 1968 federal tax laws (i.e., a 48 percent income tax rate), a company must collect $1.92 from its customers for each $1.00 it retains for the extra depreciation allowance. Only a few commissions, therefore, have permitted depreciation allowances in excess of those allowed by current tax laws.[83]

Third, when depreciation charges are based upon original cost, the cost of capital assets consumed and charged to consumers does not vary with changes in the price level. When depreciation charges are based upon replacement costs, however, the annual charges fluctuate. In times of rising prices, the customers of regulated companies would contribute an increased number of dollars equivalent to the decline in the dollar's purchasing power, while in times of falling prices complete recovery of purchasing power by the companies would constitute less than the number of dollars in their capital accounts. This problem will be considered in the following chapter, but it must be remembered that consistency is important. If the reproduction cost concept is accepted, it should apply in periods of rising prices and in periods of falling prices.[84]

Accelerated Depreciation. A third problem involves the accounting and rate-making effects of the Revenue Act of 1954. Under the act, business firms are permitted to adopt accelerated depreciation in calculating taxable income, thereby charging higher depreciation expenses in the early years of the service life of assets than would be allowed under straight line depreciation and lower rates in later years. The effect is to produce lower tax payments with respect to the early years which are offset by increased tax payments in the remaining years. This act poses a problem for the regulatory commissions: should they include, as operating costs, the higher income taxes to which companies would be subject were they to report taxable income on a straight line basis ("normalization" method), or should they include only the taxes actually paid ("flow through" method) by the companies? If the normalization method is adopted, the companies, in effect, are granted during the early years of the property's life an interest-free loan of the difference between taxes paid and

[83] In Iowa, depreciation based upon reproduction cost is an allowable deduction in determining net income for rate-making purposes. A few commissions have granted additional depreciation allowances over those allowed for tax purposes and have granted higher rates to cover partly the additional income taxes of the companies. See *Re The Peoples Gas Light & Coke Co.,* 97 PUR (NS) 33 (Ill., 1953). Also see Louis E. Mullen, "Tax Depreciation Adjusted for Price Level Changes," 82 *Public Utilities Fortnightly* 29 (August 29, 1968).

[84] An alternative to the reproduction cost concept, considered in Chapter 9, is to raise or lower the allowed rate of return as investment conditions warrant.

taxes due under the straight line method.[85] The implication is that the act results in a tax deferral rather than a permanent tax saving. The difference could be used for modernization and expansion or for other financial needs. If the flow through principle is adopted, the tax deferrals are denied to the companies and can be used to raise reported earnings or to reduce consumer rates.

The normalization and flow through methods are compared in Table 7–3. Assume that a company invests $10,000 in new equipment, that its estimated useful service life is ten years, and that the estimated salvage value is $1,075. Using the straight line method, $892.50 would be charged to depreciation expense annually. Using accelerated depreciation (assuming the double declining balance method), the annual depreciation charge would start at $2,000 and decline to $268 over the ten-year period. In either case, the company would receive a tax saving during the first four years. But the effect on net income would not be identical: normalization accounting would have no effect on net income, while under flow through accounting, net income would be increased in the first four years and decreased in the last six years of the equipment's service life.

The Controversy. Accelerated depreciation has been the subject of considerable controversy. First, assuming a constant tax rate, the tax deductions from accelerated depreciation will be greater than the tax deductions available from straight line depreciation as long as a firm continues to grow. For this reason, some have argued that accelerated depreciation actually results in a permanent deferral (tax savings).[86] Second, the commissions have been debating the intent of Congress in passing the act in an attempt to decide whether they should adopt the normalization or flow through method. The Florida commission, on the one hand, has held that the intent of Congress was to provide an incentive for expansion and modernization, adding:

> . . . it appears that the use of accelerated depreciation will not result in a reduction of income taxes, will not create additional income, will not materially change total new financing requirements of the utilities, but will result only in shifting some part of such taxes and new financing from the early years to the later years of the useful life of the new permanent additions and replacements. This undoubtedly will be of benefit to the utilities, and by normalizing taxes and depreciation in their books of account will not be detrimental to present or future ratepayers but, in fact, should be beneficial to the public generally in that the same will tend to assure the necessary expansion and growth to meet all needs.[87]

The Pennsylvania Superior Court, on the other hand, in upholding a decision of the state commission, ruled otherwise:

[85] For accounting purposes, the tax effect of the depreciation difference is placed in a reserve for deferred income taxes.

[86] *Re Alabama-Tennessee Natural Gas Co.,* 52 PUR 3d 118 (FPC, 1964), *aff'd,* 359 F. 2d 318 (1966), *cert. denied,* 385 U.S. 847 (1966).

[87] *Re Gulf Power Co.,* 10 PUR 3d 273 (Fla., 1956).

TABLE 7–3
Illustration of Effect of Accelerated Depreciation, for Tax Purposes, on Net Income*

A. NORMALIZATION ACCOUNTING

Year	Straight Line Depreciation (a)	Accelerated Depreciation (b)	Effect on Taxable Income (c = b − a)	Effect on Taxes Payable (d = c × .48)	Credit (or Charge) to Deferred Taxes (e = −d)	Effect on Net Income (f = d + e)
1	$ 892.50	$ 2,000.00	$−1,107.50	$−531.60	$+531.60	0
2	892.50	1,600.00	− 707.50	−339.60	+339.60	0
3	892.50	1,280.00	− 387.50	−186.00	+186.00	0
4	892.50	1,024.00	− 131.50	− 63.12	+ 63.12	0
5	892.50	819.00	+ 73.50	+ 35.28	− 35.28	0
6	892.50	655.00	+ 237.50	+114.00	−114.00	0
7	892.50	524.00	+ 368.50	+176.88	−176.88	0
8	892.50	419.00	+ 473.50	+227.28	−227.28	0
9	892.50	336.00	+ 556.50	+267.12	−267.12	0
10	892.50	268.00	+ 624.50	+299.76	−299.76	0
	$ 8,925.00	$ 8,925.00	0	0	0	0
Salvage value . . .	1,075.00	1,075.00				
Total	$10,000.00	$10,000.00				

B. FLOW THROUGH ACCOUNTING

Year	Straight Line Depreciation (a)	Accelerated Depreciation (b)	Effect on Taxable Income (c = b − a)	Effect on Taxes Payable (d = c × .48)	Effect on Net Income (e = −d)
1	$ 892.50	$ 2,000.00	$−1,107.50	$−531.60	$+531.60
2	892.50	1,600.00	− 707.50	−339.60	+339.60
3	892.50	1,280.00	− 387.50	−186.00	+186.00
4	892.50	1,024.00	− 131.50	− 63.12	+ 63.12
5	892.50	819.00	+ 73.50	+ 35.28	− 35.28
6	892.50	655.00	+ 237.50	+114.00	−114.00
7	892.50	524.00	+ 368.50	+176.88	−176.88
8	892.50	419.00	+ 473.50	+227.28	−227.28
9	892.50	336.00	+ 556.50	+267.12	−267.12
10	892.50	268.00	+ 624.50	+299.76	−299.76
	$ 8,925.00	$ 8,925.00	0	0	0
Salvage value	1,075.00	1,075.00			
Total	$10,000.00	$10,000.00			

*The following assumptions underlie the computations: original investment, $10,000; salvage value, $1,075.00; estimated useful life, ten years; accelerated depreciation, 20 percent declining balance method; 48 percent federal income tax rate.

Congress merely says that by making more money available to growing business they will probably be induced to spend it on expansion which in turn should increase production and hence better the standard of living. Counsel asserts that, since utilities are an important segment of the national economy, they must likewise benefit. The weakness in this assertion is in failing to recognize the distinct nature of a utility as a regulated quasi-monopoly. As such it may obtain funds for modernization and expansion at the current reasonable cost, and it is allowed to pass this cost on to its customers in an annual depreciation allowance and its annual allowable net return as well. In fixing the rate of return the commission takes cognizance of the cost of capital to the utility. It appears therefore that this general desire of Congress to provide working capital and funds for modernization and expansion is, and has been for many years, adequately met for public utilities through rate proceedings. Utilities are not confronted with the same problem in raising funds for necessary expansion as other business. Every public utility shall furnish adequate and reasonable service to the public, and it is allowed to charge such just and reasonable rates as will enable it to properly function.[88]

Third, the regulated companies have been debating the wisdom of adopting accelerated depreciation even when permitted by the commissions. They generally favor its use if the normalization method is permitted. As explained by one utility executive in making four conclusions concerning the adoption of accelerated depreciation:

Conclusion No. 1: The taking of accelerated depreciation under accounting treatment prescribing normalization of the tax expense produces lower costs of utility service, and as such should be fostered.

Conclusion No. 2: Appropriate regulatory treatment lies in consideration of the applicable rate of return rather than in adjustment of the rate base. Otherwise the prospective regulatory treatment would tend to preclude the taking advantage of the opportunity made available by Congress, and there would be no benefits to divide among anybody.

Conclusion No. 3: The appropriate rate of return to be applied, when significant amounts of property and plant have been built from accumulated provisions growing out of accelerated depreciation, is something less than that which would otherwise be applicable by an amount sufficient to reflect the absence, with respect to such funds, of the pure interest component among the various factors making up the over-all rate of return.

Conclusion No. 4: The accumulation growing out of the taking of accelerated depreciation for tax purposes should preferably be credited to a restricted surplus account, although crediting such accumulations to a Reserve for Future Federal Income Taxes is an acceptable though somewhat less desirable alternate.[89]

[88] *City of Pittsburgh* v. *Pennsylvania Public Utility Comm.,* 17 PUR 3d 249 (Pa., 1957).

[89] F. Warren Brooks, "Accelerated Depreciation" (speech before the Midwest Association of Regulatory Utility Commissioners) (mimeographed, 1957). But see Donald

Some regulated companies, including the Bell System,[90] have not taken advantage of accelerated depreciation. Their decision to use straight line depreciation for both accounting and tax purposes is largely based on three considerations. (1) Congress might suspend, modify, or repeal the accelerated tax depreciation provisions at some future date, thereby resulting in a sudden decline in per share earnings and a possible drop in the market price of a company's stock. (2) A multistate company, subject to several jurisdictions, might find some commissions permitting normalization and others flow through; a situation which would result in confusion on the part of investors and expensive record keeping on the part of a company. (3) Flow through, which is required by many of the commissions, impairs the financial integrity of a company by: (*a*) failing to recognize current costs, since a tax cost is understated during the early life of the property; (*b*) increasing investor risk, since future depreciation deductions might not be available to offset the past costs which were not recognized under this method, while economic conditions or regulatory commissions might not allow future rate increases; and (*c*) endangering the ability of a company to raise funds because of large amounts of unprovided-for costs overhanging the business.[91]

Commission Treatment. The Civil Aeronautics Board follows the normalization method.[92] The Federal Power Commission, which at first permitted normalization,[93] adopted the flow through method early in 1964.[94] The Interstate Commerce Commission, arguing that the accelerated depreciation allowances for tax purposes "are not intended to be a standard for measuring the

---

C. Cook, "The Flow Through of Tax Benefits," 77 *Public Utilities Fortnightly* 170 (June 9, 1966), for an argument that accelerated depreciation should be adopted even if flow through is required by the commissions.

[90] It has been estimated that if the Bell System had elected to use accelerated depreciation in 1954, its income tax liabilities would have been reduced by a total of $1.6 billion by the end of 1965, resulting in cumulative reductions in charges to consumers of about $3 billion. Testimony of A. L. Stott, FCC Docket No. 16258 (Bell Exhibit 38, October 17, 1966), Attachment C; and Testimony of William J. Powell, FCC Docket No. 16258 (FCC Staff Exhibit No. 29), p. 10.

[91] See Gerald J. Glassman, "Objections to Taking Liberalized Depreciation," 77 *Public Utilities Fortnightly* 29 (March 31, 1966); Herman Green, "Proper Regulatory Treatment of Liberalized Depreciation," 78 *ibid.* 31 (July 7, 1966); and C. N. Ostergren, "Accelerated Depreciation and Rate Making Once More," 81 *ibid.* 48 (January 18, 1968).

[92] *General Passenger Fare Investigation,* E-16068 (CAB, 1960).

[93] *Re Panhandle Eastern Pipe Line Co.,* 3 PUR 3d 396 (FPC, 1954), *aff'd sub nom. City of Detroit* v. *Federal Power Comm.,* 230 F. 2d 810 (1955); and *Re El Paso Natural Gas Co.,* 29 PUR 3d 469 (FPC, 1959).

[94] *Re Alabama-Tennessee Natural Gas Co.,* 52 PUR 3d 118 (FPC, 1964), *aff'd,* 359 F. 2d 318 (1966), *cert. denied,* 385 U.S. 847 (1966). The FPC's decision did not affect the funds which had already been accumulated, but it prevented additional accumulations. Further, in 1966, the FPC held that the increased federal income tax payments resulting from the decision of a natural gas pipeline company to discontinue the use of accelerated depreciation are not a reasonable and prudent business expense. *Re Midwestern Gas Transmission Co.,* 64 PUR 3d 433, 444 (FPC, 1966).

rate at which service loss is incurred," requires the flow through method.[95] The Federal Communications Commission has not rendered a decision on this issue. There is a wide divergence among the state commissions. As of July 1, 1967, twenty state commissions permitted various forms of the normalization method for rate-making purposes, twenty-three (including the District of Columbia commission) had either ordered or favored the flow through method, and two permitted either method.[96]

Investment Tax Credit. The final depreciation problem concerns the Revenue Act of 1962 which provides, as an incentive to investment, that a business firm can deduct from its federal income tax a specified percentage of its new investment in most plant and equipment which it puts into service during the taxable year.[97] For nonregulated firms, the percentage is graduated up to 7 percent of such property, depending on the estimated life.[98] For most regulated companies, the percentage is graduated up to 3 percent, but natural gas producers and pipeline operators as well as transportation companies are entitled to the full 7 percent.

How should the regulatory commissions treat the investment tax credit for rate-making purposes? Unlike accelerated depreciation, which only affects the time when such depreciation may be used for tax purposes, the tax credit results in a permanent savings to a company. Two questions are pertinent.[99] First, who should benefit from the tax credit? The benefits could accrue either to the companies or to their customers, or the benefits could be shared by the two groups. Second, regardless of who receives the benefits, should they be taken in the year of the investment or spread out over the useful life of the property acquired?

From an accounting standpoint, the two major methods of treating the tax credit are normalization and flow through.[100] Normalization would result in

---

95 24 *Federal Register* 1401 (1959).

96 Federal Power Commission, "Federal and State Commission Jurisdiction and Regulation, Electric, Gas, and Telephone Utilities, 1967," *op. cit.*, p. 38. Also see Stone & Webster Service Corp., "Accounting and Ratemaking Treatment of Income Tax Effects of Accelerated Amortization, Liberalized Depreciation, Investment Tax Credit, Guideline Depreciation" (New York, 1964, and revision, 1966), summarized in 75 *Public Utilities Fortnightly* 62 (January 21, 1965); and Eugene F. Brigham, "Public Utility Depreciation Practices and Policies," 19 *National Tax Journal* 144 (1966).

97 The investment tax credit provision of the Revenue Act of 1962 was suspended by Congress on October 10, 1966, but reinstated effective March 10, 1967.

98 To qualify for the full credit, the property must have a life of eight years or more. Property having a life of six or seven years qualifies for two-thirds of the basic credit; property having a life of four or five years qualifies for one-third of the basic credit.

99 Francis X. Welch, "Utility Accounting and Investment Tax Credit" (American Bar Association Annual Report, Section of *Public Utility Law, 1963*), p. 55.

100 The Revenue Act of 1962 provided that the tax base of the property was to be lowered by an amount equal to the tax credit. Thus, a third method, known as 48 percent flow through and 52 percent normalization, was proposed, under which 48 percent of the tax credit would be reflected as an increase in net income in the year the credit was received and 52 percent would be spread over the productive life of the

spreading the amount of the credit (i.e., income) over the productive life of the property. Flow through would result in the tax credit being reflected as an increase in net income in the year the credit is received. As of July 1, 1967, twenty-six state commissions had ordered or favored normalization for rate-making purposes, twelve had ordered or favored flow through, and five state commissions (including the District of Columbia commission) plus the FPC and FCC permitted either method.[101]

The federal commissions are prohibited from adopting the flow through method without the consent of the taxpayer, according to the Revenue Act of 1964. That act reiterates that the purpose of the investment tax credit is to provide an incentive for modernization and growth of private industry, including regulated firms. Specifically, the act states that in the case of regulated industries receiving the 3 percent investment tax credit, federal commissions can pass the savings on to customers in the form of lower rates only over the service life of the applicable property, but it prevents federal commissions from passing such savings along at any time in the case of those industries which receive the 7 percent credit.

Depletion Charges

The objective of depreciation accounting is to charge consumers the cost of maintaining intact the capital funds of a company. For the minerals industries, however, other problems arise, of which two are major. First, the fair market value of a mine, quarry, or well cannot be determined accurately for tax purposes; they usually have an unknown content. Second, these industries are subject to increasing costs in the exploration and discovery of new domestic reserves. Increasing costs result because as more easily accessible deposits are depleted, their replacement comes from less accessible deposits. The processes of exploration and discovery, moreover, are expensive, and the risk of loss is large. Finally, there is often a lag of five years or more between exploration and production. The President's Materials Policy Commission explained:

> It is customary under U.S. tax laws to permit a business to recover tax free its investment in physical assets as they wear out or become obsolete. Ordinarily the recovered investment can be applied toward replacing physical assets. But for many minerals there is considerable uncertainty as to whether reserves can be replaced, and considerable risk entailed in attempting to

---

property by being set up as a reserve for future taxes. The theory behind this method was that only 48 percent of the tax credit represented a permanent savings or increase in net income, since the remaining 52 percent would be used to pay the higher future taxes due to lower depreciation allowances for tax purposes. The Revenue Act of 1964, however, provides that the tax credit is not to be used to reduce the tax base, thereby eliminating this method.

[101] Federal Power Commission, "Federal and State Commission Jurisdiction and Regulation, Electric, Gas, and Telephone Utilities, 1967," *op. cit.* Also see Stone & Webster Service Corp., "Accounting and Ratemaking Treatment of Income Tax Effects . . . ," *op. cit.;* and Brigham, *op. cit.*

replace them. Moreover, for some major minerals the real cost of replacement keeps rising because of the progressive depletion of natural resources.[102]

For these reasons, Congress has granted special allowances to the minerals industries. These allowances for the gas and oil industries are as follows. (1) With minor exceptions, drilling, exploration, and development costs can be fully depreciated in the year in which they are incurred. (2) In place of the fair market value of property, 27.5 percent of the gross income from a gas or oil well can be deducted from taxable income, provided that such allowance does not exceed 50 percent of the net income from a well.

The pros and cons of these allowances have been debated for years, and these arguments need not be repeated here.[103] It should be noted, however, that these allowances frequently permit the gas and oil industries total write-offs that exceed total costs. But this incentive may be necessary if domestic exploration and development are to continue at desirable rates.

TAXES AS A COST

Since 1922, taxes, with but minor exceptions, have been included in operating costs. The local, state, and federal tax payments of the regulated industries have increased rapidly and now represent a substantial percentage of their gross revenues. For the private electric utilities, for example, the ratio of taxes to operating revenues was 22 percent in 1967, compared with 18 percent in 1948 and 6.5 percent in 1917.[104] As tax payments are costs of service, conflicts between the regulation and taxation of the regulated industries are inevitable.

Legislatures and tax authorities, seeking revenue for governmental purposes, usually disregard the relation between company taxes on the one hand, and rates, investment, and service improvements on the other. The commissions commonly wish to use any excess earnings either to reduce rates or for service improvements. If regulated companies have excess earnings and taxes are increased, the earnings are diverted to tax revenues rather than to consumers. If the commissions permit only a limited range of reasonable returns, taxes are shifted to the buyers of service. Moreover, the regulated industries are taxed even more heavily than nonregulated businesses, thereby frequently creating a

102 The President's Materials Policy Commission, *Resources for Freedom* (Washington, D.C.: U.S. Government Printing Office, 1952), Vol. I, pp. 34–35.

103 See *Compendium of Papers on Broadening the Tax Base* (House, Committee on Ways and Means) (Washington, D.C.: U.S. Government Printing Office, 1959), Vol. 2, pp. 933–1060.

104 In absolute terms, private electric utilities paid an estimated $1.7 billion in federal and $1.5 billion in local and state taxes in 1967. In comparison, the Bell System paid $2.9 billion in operating taxes in 1967; an amount equal to more than $5 per share of A.T.&T. stock or more than $35 per average telephone in service. In addition, telephone users paid over $955 million in federal excise taxes.

competitive handicap. In recent years, these conflicts have sharpened as the magnitude of taxes imposed on the regulated industries has increased.[105]

The Regulated Industries as Tax Collectors

Why are the regulated industries often called "tax collectors *par excellence*"?[106] In the first place, they are generally large corporate enterprises, which simplifies the administration and collection of taxes. In the second place, their investment in plant and equipment in relation to annual revenue is greater than that of most industries. The regulated industries, consequently, are peculiarly subject to the property tax. In the third place, given relatively inelastic demand curves for some of their services, higher prices are unlikely to lead to significant decreases in consumer demand. When rates are below the value of service, taxes can usually be passed on to buyers.

In the fourth place, many communities derive a significant portion of their annual revenues from taxes levied on the property of regulated companies. As far as the railroads are concerned, it is common knowledge that local taxing districts frequently adjust jurisdictional boundaries to include as much railroad property as possible. Finally, lacking strong political support and often showing good earnings, legislatures appear to consider that further taxation of regulated industries is a safe way to increase tax revenues. Some punitive taxes have also been levied on these industries. In short, the regulated industries are often used as tax collectors, and are a politically acceptable source of local, state, and federal governmental revenues. As explained by one lawmaker:

> . . . a continuation of the excise tax on telephone and telegraph service will not, after all, jeopardize a continued profit in the business of the public utilities affected, because each one of them operates under rates set by public utility regulatory bodies which allow rates sufficiently high to enable the companies to meet their tax situations and at the same time operate at a profit, *even if their business should be slightly reduced.* [107]

Categories of Taxes

The types of taxes imposed on the regulated industries can be grouped into three categories. First, some of the taxes applied to the regulated industries are also applied uniformly to nonregulated industries. These include corporate and state income taxes, social security taxes, state unemployment compensation taxes, and the federal excess profits tax (levied during World War II and the

---

[105] One writer concludes that the history of utility taxation can be divided into three periods: those of (*a*) subsidy, terminating at about the end of the nineteenth century, (*b*) neutral treatment, terminating with the depression of the 1930's, and (*c*) "special burdens," from the 1930's to date. Harold M. Groves, *Financing Government* (5th ed.; New York: Holt, Rinehart & Winston, Inc., 1958), p. 336.

[106] Clemens, *op. cit.*, pp. 526-27.

[107] Senator S. L. Holland, quoted in 66 *Public Utilities Fortnightly* 101 (1960). (Italics added by author.)

Korean conflict).[108] Second, other taxes are applied to all businesses, but unequally. The regulated industries, for example, frequently pay more property taxes per dollar of investment than are paid by other business property owners. Third, some taxes are levied only on the regulated industries, such as franchise taxes, federal excise taxes on airline passenger fares and on telephone and telegraph services, and consumer utility taxes.

The Incidence of Taxes

Treatment of taxes as an operating cost means there is a tendency, in the long run, to shift them to consumers, but it does not follow that such a shift is always successful. Several exceptions should be noted.[109] (1) If there is a lag in the regulatory process, tax increases are borne, in the short run, by the regulated companies. Regulatory procedure is often slow, and a company seldom finds it possible to obtain an immediate offsetting rate increase when a new tax is placed on it or an old tax is increased. The situation may be serious for a company that was just earning a fair return, or less than a fair return, before the tax was added or increased. (2) When a company is already charging rates close to the value of service, so that an increase in rates will result in either a decline in profits or an increase in deficits, taxes are borne by the company. In some cases, the company may be unable to earn a fair return at any reasonable price; a situation faced by many street-railway companies.

(3) Similarly, if a regulated company is earning less than a fair return but competitive conditions will not permit a rate increase, taxes are borne—at least in part—by the company. This situation has relevance in the railroad industry at the present time and is also applicable to electric utilities where they face competition from public power projects. (4) In the transportation industries, a tax levied on one particular carrier is borne by that carrier, because rates are set for groups of carriers on a regional (motor carriers and railroads) or industry-wide (airlines) basis. Within these rate-making groups, each type of carrier generally follows a single-rate policy.

Even when taxes are shifted to consumers, the burden is unequally distributed. The regulated industries are allowed to practice price discrimination by classifying customers into various groups and charging different rates for each group. Take, for instance, the electric industry. As industrial rates are more competitive (demand is relatively elastic) than residential rates (demand is relatively inelastic),[110] a large percentage of the tax burden may fall on the

---

[108] The federal excess profits tax is discussed by Troxel, *op. cit.,* pp. 253–54.

[109] Jesse V. Burkhead, "The Changing Incidence of Public Utility Taxation," 15 *Journal of Land and Public Utility Economics* 383 (1939). Nonregulated firms, too, will tend to shift the tax burden to consumers in the long run. Early in 1969, the New York commission rejected the argument that regulated firms should be permitted to tie consumer rates to changes in tax rates or the base on which taxes are levied. See *The Wall Street Journal,* March 13, 1969, p. 5.

[110] The elasticity of demand does not depend on the type of user of a particular product. Rather, the demand for any product will be relatively elastic in some price ranges and relatively inelastic in other price ranges. The statement in the text implies that at current rates, the demand of industrial users is more elastic than the demand of residential users. The economics of price discrimination is discussed in Chapter 10.

residential. The same situation is found in the transportation industry among different commodities or modes of transport, and in the telephone industry among different sizes of exchange areas.

There is an important tax problem concerning the incidence of local taxes. In most cases, a regulated company serves a large area and is, therefore, subject to several local tax jurisdictions. Where should local taxes rest: on the consumers of the company throughout its market area, or on the consumers of the city which levied the tax? In practice, the commissions tend to follow the first alternative when the tax in question is a franchise tax and the second for gross receipts and other taxes. Franchise taxes are "going concern" taxes, it is argued, and should be included in general operating expenses. But if all taxes were so handled, one city would be permitted, in effect, to tax service users in other cities.[111] Moreover, many commissions require the regulated companies to pass local taxes on to consumers in each of the cities levying such taxes by making a surcharge on each bill. The Idaho commission, in making such a requirement, indicated that unless handled in this manner, consumers would not realize that these "hidden taxes" were being passed on to them, thereby tending to lull the public into a frame of mind which allows government expenditures to be increased without strong opposition.[112]

Taxes and Competition

The taxes levied on the regulated industries impose a proportionately higher tax burden on their services than do the taxes imposed on the commodities and services of nonregulated industries. This treatment tends to lead to an uneconomic allocation of resources by allocating too few resources to these industries. Moreover, a tax on a decreasing-cost industry will raise prices by more than the tax and unduly restrict consumption.[113] But of even more importance is the fact that many taxes imposed on the regulated industries are discriminatory and have an important effect on both the supply of particular types of services and competitive relationships.

The most significant example of this situation is found in the transportation industry,[114] where the heavily taxed railroads (and pipelines to a lesser extent) compete for traffic with other subsidized forms of transportation. The railroads are taxed more heavily than are motor carriers.[115] Moreover, while motor carriers (and airlines) pay user fees, there is a basic difference between

[111] *State* ex rel. *Pacific Teleph. & Teleg. Co.* v. *Dept. of Public Service*, 52 PUR (NS) 6, 54 (Wash., 1943).

[112] *Re Intermountain Gas Co.*, 35 PUR 3d 342 (Idaho, 1960). See also *Re Bell Teleph. Co. of Nevada*, 31 PUR 3d 392 (Nev., 1959); *Re Florida Water Service*, 32 PUR 3d 320 (Fla., 1960); and *Re Missouri Utilities Co.*, 43 PUR 3d 423 (Mo., 1962). In Illinois, even franchise taxes are treated in this manner. See *Village of Maywood* v. *Illinois Commerce Comm.*, 178 NE 2d 345 (1962).

[113] These two propositions are discussed by Clemens, *op. cit.*, pp. 542–44.

[114] It has been estimated that 18 percent of all federal taxes and 35 percent of all state taxes are levied on transportation. Roy J. Sampson and Martin T. Farris, *Domestic Transportation: Practice, Theory and Policy* (Boston: Houghton Mifflin Co., 1966), p. 12.

[115] Haskel Benishay and Gilbert R. Whitaker, Jr., "Tax Burden Ratios in Transportation," 43 *Land Economics* 44 (1967).

property taxes and user fees: ". . . user charges are assessed to pay for the construction, maintenance and administrative costs of *publicly* provided transportaton facilities whereas ad valorem taxes on *private* right-of-way are assessed to pay for the general costs of government."[116] The subsidy question, closely related to the problem of user fees, will be considered in a later chapter, but the property tax situation deserves brief mention. Here, the conflicts between taxation and regulation are glaring.

In the transportation industry, only railroads and pipelines build and maintain their rights-of-way. All tangible property, real and personal, is subject to ad valorem property taxation in the majority of states and to special property taxes in the others. The tax rate of each governmental body is supposed to be uniform on all taxable property within its jurisdiction. State equalization agencies have been established to adjust local assessments to a uniform level. The problem, however, is compounded by the fact that railroad and pipeline operating property usually is centrally assessed for general taxation, but nonoperating property is locally assessed.[117] This divided responsibility for assessing value violates the principle of unit appraising. Further, in many states, the equalization boards have not been active in achieving uniform levels.

One result is that the property of railroads is frequently assessed at a substantially higher percentage of value than is true for other property subject to the same ad valorem tax.[118] Such disparity of assessment was upheld by the Supreme Court in a 1940 decision.[119] Thus, while the railroads have filed countless suits in several states to obtain equal treatment, they have been successful only where state law prohibits a separate classification.[120] The

[116] *National Transportation Policy* (preliminary draft by the Special Study Group on Transportation Policies in the United States, Senate Committee on Interstate and Foreign Commerce) (Washington, D.C.: U.S. Government Printing Office, 1961), p. 450.

[117] For a discussion of the problems and inequities of assessments in Nebraska, see F. O. Woodward, "The Assessment Value of Telephone Properties," *Nebraska Journal of Economics and Business*, Spring, 1962, pp. 49–59.

[118] In 1960, the Association of American Railroads submitted to the Senate Commerce Committee's special study group a study which showed that in 1957, $141,187,829 in excess taxes was extracted from railroads in 31 states solely because railroad property was assessed and valued higher than other property subjected to the same rates. This sum amounted to nearly one-third of the total railroad payments of $441,395,977 to local and state governments in that year. *National Transportation Policy, op. cit.*, pp. 486–87. See *ibid.*, pp. 445–91, for a complete discussion of the tax problem.

[119] ". . . states may classify property for taxation; may set up different modes of assessment, valuation, and collection; may tax some kinds of property at higher rates than others; and in making all these differentiations may treat railroads and other utilities with that separateness which their distinctive characteristics and function in society make appropriate." *Nashville, Chattanooga & St. Louis Ry. Co.* v. *Browning*, 310 U.S. 362, 368 (1940).

[120] See *Chicago, Burlington & Quincy R. Co.* v. *State Board of Equalization and Assessment of the State of Nebraska*, 101 NW 2d 856 (1960); and *Louisville & Nashville R. Co.* v. *Tennessee Public Service Comm.*, 249 F. Supp. 894 (1966). In a 1968 decision, the Supreme Court cautioned states against attempting to levy on interstate corporations property taxes that represent more than a fair share of a company's facilities within the state. *Norfolk & Western Railway Co.* v. *Missouri State Tax Comm.*, 88 S. Ct. 995 (1968).

railroads, therefore, have taken their case against discriminatory taxation to state legislatures and to Congress.[121] While Congress has yet to act on the issue, several states have agreed to reduce future assessment ratios applicable to railroads (and other utilities) gradually over a period of years.[122]

Earning less than a fair rate of return and facing increased competition from other forms of transportation, the tax problem is a serious one for the railroads. The real difficulty, of course, is that the $367 million (Class I railroads, 1967) paid to local and state governments in taxes represents a significant portion of their annual revenues. Particularly is this true at the local level. At the same time, a further complication is added to an already complex regulatory situation.

A Lighter Tax Burden?

The argument that excessive taxation is acceptable because the regulated industries can more easily collect the necessary revenues is untenable. A good case can be made for the proposition that the rate of taxation for regulated industries should be no higher, relative to net earnings, than the tax rates of nonregulated industries. Indeed, Troxel has argued that there is a possible case for lighter taxation:

> Many nonutility companies can obtain more than "normal" returns; they can obtain more earnings than they need to maintain the current output. A few companies often control the markets for nonutility commodities; only a few companies produce most of the nation's steel, rubber tires, autos, sulphur, aluminum, and many other products. Operating in duopoly and oligopoly situations, these companies stabilize prices, take noncompetitive attitudes toward each other, and are not subject to public price controls. These firms often have a better opportunity to get excessive returns than that of even a poorly regulated utility company. Considering these facts, tax authorities can justify higher tax rates on some nonutility earnings than on utility company earnings.[123]

Even the achievement of equalization, however, will be difficult. In the field of taxation, principles and practices are often far apart, and political considerations are strong. Any equitable readjustments of the tax system will always be opposed by the groups benefiting from the existing system. "In taxation, as in regulation, as in public ownership, as in all government, abstract

[121] See *Tax Assessments on Common Carrier Property* (Hearings before the Subcommittee on Transportation and Aeronautics of the Committee on Interstate and Foreign Commerce, House, 88th Cong., 2d sess.) (Washington, D.C.: U.S. Government Printing Office, 1965); and *Discriminatory Taxation of Common Carriers* (Hearings before the Subcommittee on Surface Transportation of the Committee on Commerce, Senate, 90th Cong., 1st sess.) (Washington, D.C.: U.S. Government Printing Office, 1967). Also see Paul J. Hartman and Paul H. Sanders, "The Power of Congress to Prohibit Discrimination in the Assessment of Property of Interstate Carriers for State Ad Valorem Taxes," 33 *I.C.C. Practitioners' Journal* 654 (1966).

[122] These states include Arkansas, Colorado, Illinois, Indiana, Maryland, Michigan, Ohio, and Texas. *The Wall Street Journal,* November 8, 1963, p. 1.

[123] Troxel, *op. cit.,* p. 257.

principles of policy give way to practical considerations of politics. In the best of all second-rate worlds, politics is a factor."[124]

Consolidated Tax Returns

For rate-making purposes, taxes present few problems. One exception concerns consolidated tax returns that an affiliated group of companies is permitted to file under the Internal Revenue Code. Certain benefits accrue to companies that file such returns. The losses of any affiliate can be set off against the taxable income of other affiliates in the group;[125] the parent company is freed from paying federal income taxes on dividends from its subsidiaries. In determining an affiliate's cost of service, the usual practice is to allocate to that company a share of the consolidated taxes.

When a parent company has both utility and nonutility or jurisdictional and nonjurisdictional affiliates, however, a question arises as to the proper allocation procedure. A 1964 FPC decision, involving United Gas Pipe Line Co., a subsidiary of United Gas Corporation, is illustrative.[126] United Gas elected to file consolidated federal income tax returns for the years 1957–61. Because its two oil and gas production and exploration affiliates (Union and Overseas) had net losses over the five-year period, the group's tax liability was thereby reduced. In the rate case, United Gas Pipe Line claimed that its allowance for federal income taxes should be at the full 52 percent rate (the rate then applicable) or about $12 million for the test year. The FPC rejected this claimed allowance and allocated the actual consolidated taxes paid among the companies in the group or approximately $9.9 million for United Gas Pipe Line for the test period.[127]

On appeal, the company claimed that the FPC improperly applied nonjurisdictional losses to jurisdictional income. But the Supreme Court upheld the commission, saying, in part:

> There is no frustration of the tax laws inherent in the Commission's action. The affiliated group may continue to file consolidated returns and through this mechanism set off system losses against system income, including the United's fair return income. The tax law permits this, but it does not seek to control the amount of income which any affiliate will have. Nor does it attempt to set United's rates. This is the function of the Commission, a

---

[124] Clemens, *op. cit.,* p. 547.
[125] A net loss in any year can be carried back to the three preceeding years or carried forward to the succeeding five years.
[126] *Re United Gas Pipe Line Co.,* 54 PUR 3d 285 (FPC, 1964).
[127] The FPC's allocation was based on a formula developed in an earlier decision, whereby (1) the companies are separated into regulated (jurisdictional) and nonregulated (nonjurisdictional) groups, (2) the net aggregate taxable income is determined for each group, and (3) the net total consolidated tax liability is apportioned over a representative period of time between the two groups, and among the companies in the regulated group, on the basis of their respective taxable incomes; "provided that the allowance so computed for the regulated company shall not exceed what its tax liability would be for rate-making purposes, if computed on a separate return basis." *Re Cities Service Gas Co.,* 49 PUR 3d 229, 236 (FPC, 1963).

function performed here by rejecting that part of the claimed tax expense which was no expense at all, by reducing cost of service and therefore rates, and by allowing United only a fair return on its investment.[128]

In short, when a group of affiliated companies elects to file a consolidated tax return, a commission may pass on to customers in the form of lower rates any resulting benefits. But the Court was careful to note that the decision to file such a return belongs to the companies.

CONCLUSIONS

Commission supervision of operating costs raises one broad question and countless specific problems. The specific problems have been outlined in some detail in this chapter. They are a vital part of the broader question: How far should the regulatory commissions go in substituting their judgment for that of management?[129] The answer to this question, in turn, will largely depend on one's personal philosophy.

Some feel that since the regulated companies operate within a free enterprise system, they should be subjected to the same general rules that are applicable to nonregulated firms. If nonregulated firms can make annual contributions to charitable and educational institutions, or if they are permitted to benefit from filing consolidated income tax returns, so, too, should the regulated companies be afforded the same opportunities. Others believe that the very existence of regulation indicates that the regulated companies can and should be treated differently from nonregulated firms. As they are public service enterprises, their basic obligation is to render adequate service at the lowest possible rates. Thus, charitable and educational contributions, they feel, should not be allowed as operating expenses, since they contribute little toward the achievement of this basic obligation, while the benefits from consolidated income tax returns should be passed on to consumers.

The dilemma is clear. A commission has the authority to disallow operating costs if management abuses its discretion. But an abuse of discretion is a matter of judgment. Conflicts, therefore, are inevitable. Particularly is this true with respect to the determination of the rate base and the rate of return.

---

[128] *Federal Power Comm.* v. *United Gas Pipe Line Co.*, 386 U.S. 237, 246–47 (1967). In a dissenting opinion, Justice Harlan (joined by Justices Douglas and Stewart), argued: "... no allocation whatever could be required by the Commission in this case because nonjurisdictional income was more than sufficient to absorb all nonjurisdictional losses and there was no showing that jurisdictional activities would actually benefit from nonjurisdictional losses. To permit the FPC in such circumstances to allocate would in effect extend the Commission's jurisdiction to areas not encompassed within the authority given the Commission by the Natural Gas Act." Dissenting opinion, *ibid.*, pp. 256–57.

[129] See "Managerial and Regulatory Functions Distinguished," 74 *Public Utilities Fortnightly* 67 (July 2, 1964); and "Management–Utility and Commission Powers," 79 *ibid.* 57 (March 2, 1967). Also see "Purchasing Policies of Utilities–A Need for More FPC Oversight?" 83 *ibid.* 41 (April 10, 1969).

Chapter

8

THE RATE BASE

The thing sought is the fair value of the utility property used and useful in the public service, and this cannot be found by applying a fair value to each operating unit and then by addition, obtain the total value thereof, but it requires that a comprehensive view of all the elements of property, both tangible and intangible, to be taken and considered, "not as a separate thing, but, as an inseparable part of one complete harmonious entity, and exercising a reasonable judgment as to the value of that entity," having in mind the cost of reproduction new, the cost of reproduction less depreciation, depreciation, actual or historical cost of all the property in place, the actual or historical cost of all the property used and useful in public service at the date of the inquiry, service capacity, service being rendered, and all other elements of value.
—Idaho Public Utilities Commission*

Determination of the rate base—the value of a company's property used and useful in the public service minus accrued depreciation—is one of the most important and most difficult problems confronting both the commissions and the regulated industries. No other conflict in the history of regulation has received so much attention or been the subject of so much litigation. There has always been agreement that the price for the service of a regulated company should be high enough to cover operating expenses, depreciation, and taxes, and also allow a fair return on the fair value of the capital invested in the business. Consumers expect to pay "just and reasonable" prices for the services they demand; investors expect to receive a "fair" return on the capital they invest. But how should the commissions establish the value of a company's property?

The major controversy has been over the determination of the depreciated value of tangible and reproducible property and is discussed in the first four sections of this chapter. The final section concerns the valuation of land, overhead construction costs, working capital allowances, and intangibles.

*Idaho Public Utilities Commission, *Re Boise Water Co.,* PUR 1926D 321, 357-58.

Elements versus Measures of Value

At the outset, it will be useful to distinguish between the elements of value or the things to be valued and the measures of value or the ways in which they are valued.[1]

The Elements of Value. The elements of value refer to the tangible and intangible assets (property) of a company which together comprise the rate base. The elements are usually listed under four headings. Of these the first element is tangibles, which includes "used and useful" land, buildings, and equipment (plant). The decision as to what property is "used and useful" is normally left to management, although certain items claimed by companies may be questioned and excluded from the rate base by the commissions. As listed by Welch, these items are:

(1) Duplicate and unnecessary property; (2) obsolete and inadequate property; (3) property to be abandoned; (4) abandoned and superseded property; (5) overdeveloped property and facilities for future needs; (6) real estate: buildings, leaseholds, and water rights; (7) incomplete and contemplated construction; (8) property used for nonutility purposes; (9) property of other utility departments (as in the case of a combination gas and electric utility company); (10) property not owned; (11) property donations—voluntary or involuntary; (12) deposits and moneys advanced by customers.[2]

The second, incidentals during construction, includes administration; brokerage, legal and promotional fees; interest; insurance; taxes; and contingencies. These items are commonly referred to as "overhead" construction costs. The third is working capital, a current asset which provides a company money to meet its current obligations. The fourth, intangibles, includes good will, franchise value, water rights, leaseholds, and going concern value.

The Measures of Value. Once the items of property to be included in the rate base have been determined, their value must be established. The measures of value refer to the various methods of computation used in determining the total value of a company's property.

A word of caution: In discussing the rate base valuation problem, it must be recognized that "fair value" is not value in the economic sense. Regulatory commissions are not finding the value of property; they are making it. In the case of nonregulated companies, value is the result of market processes. The value of a company's property is determined by the profitability of the business, and represents the capitalized sum of the earnings above all operating costs at

---

[1] This distinction is drawn by Francis X. Welch, *Cases and Text on Public Utility Regulation* (rev. ed.; Washington, D.C.: Public Utilities Reports, Inc., 1968), pp. 292–93.

[2] *Ibid.*, p. 360. "Not all of the foregoing classes have invariably been excluded from rate bases in rate cases. Some have been partially allowed under particular circumstances. Some have been included on a 'de minimis' basis in case of very small items. Property held for future use, for example, has been included at full value where it was scheduled to go into public service at a very early date and where no claim was made for interest during construction." *Ibid.*

the current rate of interest or rate of return. In the case of regulated companies, this cannot be done, for the earnings depend on the rates established by the commissions. If high rates are set, value will be high; if low rates are set, value will be low. Circular reasoning is thus involved if fair value for rate-making purposes is thought of in the economic sense—rates cannot be based on a value which is dependent on the rates. This distinction, long overlooked, was finally recognized by the Supreme Court in 1944:

> The fixing of prices, like other applications of the police power, may reduce the value of the property which is being regulated. But the fact that the value is reduced does not mean that the regulation is invalid. . . . It does, however, indicate that "fair value" is the end product of the process of rate making, not the starting point as the Circuit Court of Appeals held. The heart of the matter is that rates cannot be made to depend upon "fair value" when the value of the going enterprise depends on earnings under whatever rates may be anticipated.[3]

For purposes of rate making, therefore, value depends on the measures of value used by the companies and commissions.

Throughout commission and court decisions, several measures of tangible and reproducible property value, some subsequently rejected, have been discussed and employed. While these measures will be discussed at length in the following sections, they can be summarized as follows:[4]

I. Measures of Construction Cost Value
   1. *Actual, "First" Original, or Original Cost.* The amount actually paid for installing the original plant and equipment, plus additions, when first devoted to public service.
   2. *Book or Investment Cost.* The amount actually paid for installing the present plant and equipment, plus additions, as shown in the investment accounts on the company's books.
   3. *Historical Cost or Prudent Investment.* The original cost minus any fraudulent, unwise, or extravagant expenditures.
   4.* *Capitalization Cost.* The capital invested in the business as measured by the outstanding bonds, stock, and other securities.

II. Measures of Reproduction Cost Value
   5. *Current or Reproduction Cost; Price Level Accounting.* The cost of plant and equipment, plus additions, estimated at price levels prevailing at the date of valuation.
   6.* *Split Inventory Value.* The original cost (reproduction cost) of plant and equipment installed before a specified date, and the reproduction cost (original cost) of property installed thereafter.
   7.* *Taxation Value.* The value of property as assessed for taxation purposes.
   8.* *Market Value.* The capitalized value of a company (i.e., its probable earnings capacity).

[3] *Federal Power Comm.* v. *Hope Natural Gas Co.,* 320 U.S. 591, 601 (1944).
[4] The measures marked with an asterisk have been generally rejected as proper measures of value.

9.* *Exchange or Purchase Value.* The value of a company as determined by the price another party is willing to pay for the property.

PROPERTY VALUATION: LEGAL CONCEPTS

Prior to the famous case of *Smyth* v. *Ames* in 1898,[5] determining the rate base was a commission and legislative problem. Deciding an 1877 case, the Supreme Court took the position that rate making was a legislative rather than a judicial function. As explained by the Court:

> Rights of property which have been created by the common law cannot be taken away without due process; but the law itself . . . may be changed at the will, or even at the whim, of the legislature, unless prevented by constitutional limitations. . . . To limit the rate of charge for services rendered in a public employment . . . is only changing a regulation which existed before . . . .
>
> We know that this is a power which may be abused; but that is no argument against its existence. For protection against abuses by legislatures the people must resort to the polls, not to the courts.[6]

In 1886, the Court reversed its position, recognizing that "this power to regulate is not a power to destroy, and limitation is not the equivalent of confiscation."[7] Rates fixed under legislative authority, therefore, were subject to judicial review and might be set aside if they were found to deprive investors of their property without due process of law. And a few years later, for the first time, the Court held that a rate-fixing statute of Texas confiscated the property of a railroad company.[8] But the Court established no standards by which to judge the reasonableness of commission valuations until the Smyth decision.

The "Fair Value" Doctrine

The state of Nebraska in 1893 passed a law which established a Board of Transportation. Among other things, the board was given the authority to determine the rates charged for hauling freight. One of its first orders, setting maximum rates, was challenged by the railroads on the basis that the rates were confiscatory. The roads contended that much of their property had been constructed during and after the Civil War when prices were high, and that they were entitled to a return on their original cost. The state, represented by William Jennings Bryan, based its measure of reasonable earnings on the lower reproduction cost. The property valuation problem thus came to the front.

The Supreme Court held that the rates were confiscatory by any measure. This finding was not, however, the importance of the decision, for the Court went on, in a dictum not essential to its decision, to state the measures of value

[5] 169 U.S. 466 (1898).
[6] *Munn* v. *Illinois,* 94 U.S. 113, 134 (1877).
[7] *Stone* v. *Farmers' Loan & Trust Co.,* 116 U.S. 307, 331 (1886).
[8] *Reagan* v. *Farmers' Loan & Trust Co.,* 154 U.S. 362 (1894).

by which confiscation could be judged. This dictum later became the legal basis of the "fair value" doctrine. Said Justice Harlan:

> The corporation may not be required to use its property for the benefit of the public without receiving just compensation for the services rendered by it. How such compensation may be ascertained, and what are the necessary elements in such an inquiry, will always be an embarrassing question. . . .
>
> We hold, however, that the basis of all calculations as to the reasonableness of rates to be charged by a corporation . . . must be the fair value of the property being used by it for the convenience of the public. And in order to ascertain that value, the original cost of construction, the amount expended in permanent improvements, the amount and market value of its bonds and stock, the present as compared with the original cost of construction, the probable earning capacity of the property under particular rates prescribed by statute, and the sum required to meet operating expenses, are all matters for consideration, and are to be given such weight as may be just and right in each case. We do not say that there may not be other matters to be regarded in estimating the value of the property. What the company is entitled to ask is a fair return upon the value of that which it employs for the public convenience. On the other hand, what the public is entitled to demand is that no more be extracted from it . . . than the services rendered by it are reasonably worth.[9]

The Court thus enumerated six specific measures of value to be considered in determining fair value: (1) the original cost of construction and the amount spent on permanent improvements, (2) the amount of bonds and stock, (3) the market value of bonds and stock, (4) the present as compared with the original cost of construction, (5) the probable earning capacity of the property, and (6) operating expenses. Perhaps fearing that something might have been forgotten, the Court added: "We do not say that there may not be other matters to be regarded. . . ." However, the Court did not say which measure is controlling. Each must be considered and be given "such weight as may be just and right . . . ."

Of the measures specifically mentioned, four were subsequently rejected as proper measures of value.[10] Earning capacity and the market value of bonds and stock involve circular reasoning, because they depend on the company's earnings which, in turn, depend on the rates charged.[11] The amount of bonds and stock also has been rejected, for to base a valuation for rate-making purposes on this

---

[9] *Smyth* v. *Ames, op. cit.,* pp. 546–47.

[10] In later cases, two other measures also were rejected: taxation value as being unreliable for rate-making purposes (*Brooklyn Union Gas Co.* v. *Prendergast,* 7 F. 2d 628 [1926]) and exchange value because regulated companies are not commonly bought and sold in the market (concurring opinion of Justice Brandeis in *Missouri* ex rel. *Southwestern Bell Tel. Co.* v. *Missouri Public Service Comm.,* 262 U.S. 276 [1923]).

[11] *Knoxville* v. *Knoxville Water Co.,* 212 U.S. 1 (1909); *Minnesota Rate Cases,* 230 U.S. 352 (1913).

amount would encourage stock watering and overcapitalization.[12] And operating expenses have nothing to do with the determination of the rate base.[13] As a result, two measures remain: (1) original cost, including expenditures on permanent improvements; and (2) present, current, or reproduction cost.

The Court's measures of value have been criticized and defended at length ever since 1898. Some have argued that the decision presented so many broad and vague measures as to make it useless as a guide to the commissions for rate-making purposes. Justice Frankfurter, for example, later referred to the "hodge-podge of the rule in *Smyth v. Ames*,"[14] calling it a "mischievous formula for fixing utility rates" and "useless as a guide to adjudication."[15] Others have argued that the Court was simply trying to place emphasis on the concept of reasonableness without being too doctrinaire about the use of any particular formula to achieve it. Consequently, the commissions were given considerable latitude in determining a proper valuation measure.[16] "But it is important to remember that it did lay down the 'fair return on fair value formula' for determining the reasonableness of utility rates, and it is still followed by the regulatory commissions in a number of states. . . ."[17]

Reproduction Cost versus Prudent Investment: 1898 to 1933

Before World War I, regulated companies generally based their valuation estimates on original cost, while commissions based theirs on reproduction cost. But during the war, construction costs soared, and reproduction cost became higher than original cost. Consequently, the two parties changed sides. The companies now began to demand consideration of reproduction cost; the commissions started to urge original cost. This switch has led one observer to comment: "The position of the various contestants has been largely opportunistic."[18]

Until the early thirties, the Supreme Court was divided. The majority's leading spokesman was Justice Butler, a railroad lawyer appointed to the Court

---

[12]*Knoxville* v. *Knoxville Water Co., op. cit.* In the absence of either stock watering or overcapitalization, a company's total capitalization (i.e., the amount of capital contributed to the enterprise) may be used in rate cases. See discussion below on the prudent investment measure and *General Passenger Fare Investigation*, E–16068 (CAB, 1960).

[13]Chapter 7.

[14]Dissenting opinion in *Federal Power Comm.* v. *Hope Natural Gas Co., op. cit.*, p. 627.

[15]Concurring opinion in *Driscoll* v. *Edison*, 307 U.S. 104, 122 (1939). Also see Robert L. Hale, "Conflicting Judicial Criteria of Utility Rates—the Need for Judicial Restatement," 38 *Columbia Law Review* 959 (1938).

[16]A. J. G. Priest, "Major Public Utility Decisions in Perspective," 46 *Virginia Law Review* 1327 (1960).

[17]Welch, *op. cit.*, p. 280. Also see G. Stanley Joslin and Arthur S. Miller, "Public Utility Rate Regulation: A Re-examination," 43 *Virginia Law Review* 1027 (1957).

[18]D. Philip Locklin, *Economics of Transportation* (6th ed.; Homewood, Ill.: Richard D. Irwin, Inc., 1966), p. 356.

by President Harding, while the minority's leading spokesman was Justice Brandeis, a liberal appointed by President Wilson. Justice Butler emphasized reproduction cost; Justice Brandeis, prudent investment. A brief discussion of the leading decisions will illustrate the valuation controversy, as far as the Court was concerned, during this period.

Emphasis on Reproduction Cost. Around the turn of the century, the majority emphasized reproduction cost largely because the original cost of property was difficult, if not impossible, to determine. As we have seen, accounting practices varied widely among the regulated companies, and costs were often inflated by extravagant and fraudulent expenditures. Referring to original cost in one case, the Court said: "The property may have cost more than it ought to have cost...."[19] A few years later, the same view was expressed when the Court argued that "the only evidence in favor of a higher value in the present case, is the original cost of the work seemingly inflated by improper charges to that account and by injudicious expenditures.... No doubt cost may be considered, and will have more or less importance according to circumstances."[20]

As the price level began to rise, however, the principle that reproduction cost was a better measure of value than original cost became firmly established. In 1909, and again in 1913, the Court argued that the companies were entitled to any increase in property values. Said the Court:

> There must be a fair return upon the reasonable value of the property at the time it is being used for the public.... And we concur with the court below in holding that the value of the property is to be determined as of the time when the inquiry is made regarding the rates. If the property, which legally enters into the consideration of the question of rates, has increased in value since it was acquired, the company is entitled to the benefit of such increase.[21]

> * * *

> It is clear that in ascertaining the present value we are not limited to the consideration of the amount of the actual investment. If that has been reckless or improvident, losses may be sustained which the community does not underwrite. As the company may not be protected in its actual investment, if the value of its property be plainly less, so the making of a just return for the use of the property involves the recognition of its fair value if it be more than its cost. The property is held in private ownership and it is that property, and not the original cost of it, of which the owner may not be deprived without due process of law.[22]

In several postwar cases, the Supreme Court continued to emphasize reproduction cost. The Court overruled the Missouri commission in 1923 on the grounds that the property of the company had been valued at prewar prices. In

[19] *San Diego Land & Town Co.* v. *National City,* 174 U.S. 739, 757 (1899).
[20] *San Diego Land & Town Co.* v. *Jasper,* 189 U.S. 439, 443 (1903).
[21] *Willcox* v. *Consolidated Gas Co.,* 212 U.S. 19, 41, 52 (1909).
[22] *Minnesota Rate Cases, op. cit.,* p. 454.

the Court's words: "It is impossible to ascertain what will amount to a fair return upon properties devoted to public service without giving consideration to the cost of labor, supplies, etc., at the time the investigation is made."[23] In the same year, a decision of the West Virginia commission was overruled. The Court argued:

> The record clearly shows that the commission in arriving at its final figure did not accord proper, if any, weight to the greatly enhanced costs of construction in 1920 over those prevailing about 1915 and before the war, as established by uncontradicted evidence; and the company's detailed estimated cost of reproduction new, less depreciation, at 1920 prices, appears to have been wholly disregarded. This was erroneous.[24]

The greatest judicial emphasis on reproduction cost came in the Indianapolis Water Company case of 1926. The original cost of the company's property was $10 million. Its estimated reproduction cost was $22 million. The Indiana commission valued the property at $15.3 million, while the company insisted on $19 million. The Supreme Court, accepting the company's claim, held that rates based on any valuation below $19 million would be confiscatory. Said Justice Butler:

> ... in determining present value, consideration must be given to prices and wages prevailing at the time of the investigation; and, in the light of all the circumstances, there must be an honest and intelligent forecast as to probable price and wage levels during a reasonable period in the immediate future. In every confiscation case, the future as well as the present must be regarded. It must be determined whether the rates complained of are yielding and will yield, over and above the amounts required to pay taxes and proper operating charges, a sum sufficient to constitute just compensation for the use of the property employed to furnish the service; that is, a reasonable rate of return on the value of the property at the time of the investigation and for a reasonable time in the immediate future. ... It is well established that values of utility properties fluctuate, and that owners must bear the decline and are entitled to the increase.[25]

Three years later, the Court set aside the valuation of railroad properties that had been made over many years by the Interstate Commerce Commission. Although holding that the weight to be accorded to the various measures of value was not at issue and recognizing that "there are some, perhaps many, railroads the ultimate value of which should be placed far below the sum necessary for reproduction," the Court ruled that the commission had failed to give sufficient consideration to reproduction cost.[26]

[23]*Missouri* ex rel. *Southwestern Bell Tel. Co.* v. *Missouri Public Service Comm.,* op. cit., pp. 287–88.
[24]*Bluefield Water Works & Improvement Co.* v. *West Virginia Public Service Comm.,* 262 U.S. 679, 689 (1923).
[25]*McCardle* v. *Indianapolis Water Co.,* 272 U.S. 400, 408–9, 410 (1926).
[26]*St. Louis & O'Fallon Ry. Co.* v. *United States,* 279 U.S. 461, 487 (1929).

Measurement of "Fair Value." There are two pertinent comments concerning the Court's emphasis on reproduction cost. First, the Court consistently
refused to adopt this measure of value as the only controlling one. Instead, it
merely stated that "consideration" must be given to reproduction cost in rate
cases. In upholding the Georgia commission's refusal to base a valuation entirely
on reproduction cost, the Court said:

> Here the Commission gave careful consideration to the cost of reproduc-
> tion; but it refused to adopt reproduction cost as the measure of value. It
> declared that the exercise of a reasonable judgment as to the present "fair
> value" required some consideration of reproduction costs as well as of
> original costs, but that "present fair value" is not synonymous with "present
> replacement cost," particularly under abnormal conditions. . . .
> The refusal of the Commission and of the lower court to hold that, for
> rate-making purposes, the physical properties of a utility must be valued at
> the replacement cost less depreciation was clearly correct.[27]

The same position was taken in the Los Angeles Gas case: "This Court has . . .
declared that, in order to determine present value, the cost of reproducing the
property is a relevant fact which should have appropriate consideration. . . . But
again, the Court has not decided that cost of reproduction furnishes an exclusive
test."[28]

Second, the Court refused, just as consistently, to adopt a precise formula
for measuring fair value. In the Minnesota Rate Cases, the Court said: "The
ascertainment of . . . value is not controlled by artificial rules. It is not a matter
of formulas, but there must be a reasonable judgment having its basis in a proper
consideration of all relevant facts."[29] In several cases, the Court suggested that
the commissions should determine a relatively "normal" level of prices based on
"an honest and intelligent forecast" of future price trends. But in a 1922 case, it
accepted a reproduction cost valuation that was 33 percent above original cost,
even though it was argued that prices had risen 110 percent; while in a 1923
case, it rejected a 25 percent increase in valuation, even though it was shown
that prices had risen 100 percent.[30]

In 1923, the so-called "split inventory" method was introduced, in which
value was based upon prewar reproduction cost for prewar investment and
original cost for investment made during and after the war.[31] And in a 1935
case, the Court rejected the Maryland commission's method of measuring fair
value. As Troxel has explained, the commission

---

[27] *Georgia Ry. & Power Co.* v. *Railroad Comm.,* 262 U.S. 625, 629–30 (1923).
[28] *Los Angeles Gas & Elec. Co.* v. *Railroad Comm. of Calif.,* 289 U.S. 287, 307
(1933).
[29] *Minnesota Rate Cases, op. cit.,* p. 434. See similar opinions expressed in
McCardle v. *Indianapolis Water Co., op. cit.,* p. 410; and *Los Angeles Gas & Elec. Co.* v.
Railroad Comm. of Calif., op. cit., p. 308.
[30] *Galveston Elec. Co.* v. *Galveston,* 258 U.S. 388 (1922); *Missouri* ex rel. *Southwestern Bell Tel. Co.* v. *Missouri Public Service Comm., op. cit.*
[31] *Georgia Ry. & Power Co.* v. *Railroad Comm., op. cit.*

... used sixteen indexes of general prices and construction costs. These indexes ranged from the wholesale price index of the Bureau of Labor Statistics to an index of Western Electric prices. Arbitrary weights were assigned to each index. Then the composite index was used to translate a fair property valuation of 1923 and the cost of subsequent property additions (less property abandonments and accrued depreciation) into a fair value in 1932. The Supreme Court rightly objected to this strange method of reproduction-cost valuation.[32]

In general, the commissions based their estimates of reproduction cost on averages of past prices, frequently using the preceding five-year period. And the Court, despite its suggestion that consideration should be given to "probable future values," usually accepted these estimates.

Prudent Investment and Dissent. During this period, the minority of the Supreme Court repeatedly rejected the emphasis being given to reproduction cost. Justice Brandeis characterized the Smyth rule of determining fair value as "legally and economically unsound," and argued that its application, in practice, had shown it to be "delusive."[33] In a series of separate opinions, he argued that the proper measure of value should be prudent investment—that is, the original cost minus any fraudulent, unwise, or extravagant expenditures that should not be a burden on the public. Perhaps the best statement of his position was in the Southwestern Bell case:

> The thing devoted by the investor to the public use is not specific property, tangible and intangible, but capital embarked in the enterprise. Upon the capital so invested the Federal Constitution guarantees to the utility the opportunity to earn a fair return. Thus, it sets the limit to the power of the state to regulate rates. . . .
>
> The investor agrees, by embarking capital in a utility, that its charges to the public shall be reasonable. His company is the substitute for the State in the performance of the public service; thus becoming a public servant. The compensation which the Constitution guarantees an opportunity to earn is the reasonable cost of conducting the business. . . . The reasonable rate to be prescribed by a commission may allow an efficiently managed utility much more. But a rate is constitutionally compensatory, if it allows to the utility the opportunity to earn the cost of the service as thus defined.
>
> The adoption of the amount prudently invested as the rate base and the amount of the capital charge as the measure of the rate of return would give definiteness to these two factors involved in rate controversies which are now shifting and treacherous, and which render the proceedings particularly burdensome and largely futile. Such measures offer a basis for decision which is certain and stable. The rate base would be ascertained as a fact, not determined as matter of opinion. It would not fluctuate with the market

[32] Emery Troxel, *Economics of Public Utilities* (New York: Holt, Rinehart & Winston, Inc., 1947), p. 296n. See *West v. Chesapeake & Potomac Tel. Co.*, 295 U.S. 662 (1935).

[33] Concurring opinion in *Missouri* ex rel. *Southwestern Bell Tel. Co.* v. *Missouri Public Service Comm., op. cit.*, pp. 290, 291.

price of labor, or materials, or money. It would not change with hard times or shifting populations. It would not be distorted by the fickle and varying judgments of appraisers, commissions, or courts.[34]

The prudent investment standard would shift attention from the left-hand or asset side to the right-hand side of the balance sheet which constitutes the capital embarked in the enterprise. The aim of Justice Brandeis was to achieve a measure of value that would be "certain and stable" and that would "not be determined as matter of opinion." Instead of fluctuating rate base valuations, he was perfectly willing to vary the allowable rate of return as conditions warranted. In part, Justice Brandeis' prudent investment measure has been adopted. The uniform systems of accounts require original cost entries. But with the steady inflationary trend in the economy, his hope that this measure would represent a readily ascertainable value for rate-making purposes proved too optimistic; original cost is not synonymous with fair value.

Justice Brandeis was not alone in attacking the Court's fair value doctrine. Justice Stone argued:

> In assuming the task of determining judicially the present fair replacement value of the vast properties of public utilities, courts have been projected into the most speculative undertaking imposed upon them in the entire history of English jurisprudence. . . . When we arrive at a theoretical value based upon such uncertain and fugitive data we gain at best only an illusory certainty.[35]

Three years later, Justice Black wrote:

> Wherever the question of utility valuation arises today, it is exceedingly difficult to discern the truth through the maze of formulas and the jungle of metaphysical concepts sometimes conceived, and often fostered, by the ingenuity of those who seek inflated valuations to support excessive rates. . . . Completely lost in the confusion of language—too frequently invented for the purpose of confusing—commissions and courts passing upon rates for public utilities are driven to listen to conjectures, speculations, estimates and guesses, all under the name of "reproduction costs."[36]

As far as the Court was concerned, therefore, the valuation controversy was between the merits of prudent investment and reproduction cost. Consistently it refused to resolve the controversy. Even the majority, while placing considerable emphasis on reproduction cost, refused to say how much weight should be given to this measure of value, and declined to determine a uniform procedure for the companies and commissions to follow. The Court simply held that "fair value" demanded consideration of reproduction cost as well as original cost and directed the commissions to exercise their enlightened judgment.

---

[34] *Ibid.*, pp. 290–91, 306–7.

[35] Dissenting opinion (supported by Justices Brandeis and Cardozo) in *West* v. *Chesapeake & Potomac Tel. Co.*, *op. cit.*, p. 689.

[36] Dissenting opinion in *McCart* v. *Indianapolis Water Co.*, 302 U.S. 419, 428–29 (1938).

Outside the Court itself, dissent was equally strong. The Interstate Commerce Commission criticized the fair value doctrine as early as 1927 and defended the use of either original cost or prudent investment in making rate base valuations.[37] The position of most economists was well stated by Lewis when he referred to the "hybrid 'fair value' ('trance') method"[38] as "the unpredictable product of incalculable considerations"[39] which

> . . . consists of an examination by the commission of evidence relating to reproduction cost and prudent investment, together with evidence of intangible values and observed condition of the property, the application of judgment whose processes defy analysis or description, and the selection of a final value figure which bears no derivative relation to any figures in evidence and no ascertainable relation to any functional purpose of rate making. The determination is typically accompanied by explicit denials that a formula was employed or that the result is a compromise, together with a statement that the commission is quite incapable of retracing and setting forth the processes by which the value figure was reached. . . . The peculiar contribution of the "fair value" method to rate regulation is indecision and confusion.[40]

Judicial Shift to the "End Result": 1933 to the Present

With dissatisfaction being expressed both inside and outside of the Supreme Court, it was perhaps inevitable that a shift in emphasis would be forthcoming. That shift began with the Los Angeles Gas case in 1933 and culminated with the Hope Natural Gas case in 1944.

In the Los Angeles Gas case, the California commission made two valuations—one based on "historical cost" and the other on "fair value." It then reduced the company's gas rates. The new rates were estimated to produce a 7.7 percent rate of return on historical cost and 7 percent on fair value. The Court, upholding the order, held that the choice of valuation measures was within the discretion of the commission. Said Chief Justice Hughes:

> The legislative discretion implied in the rate making power necessarily extends to the entire legislative process, embracing the method used in reaching the legislative determination as well as that determination itself. We are not concerned with either, so long as constitutional limitations are not transgressed. When the legislative method is disclosed, it may have a definite bearing upon the validity of the result reached, but the judicial function does not go beyond the decision of the constitutional question. That question is whether the rates as fixed are confiscatory. And upon that question the complainant has the burden of proof and the Court may not interfere with

[37]*Excess Income of St. Louis & O'Fallon Ry. Co.*, 124 ICC 3, 26–39 (1927).
[38]Ben W. Lewis, "Public Utilities," in L. S. Lyon and V. Abramson (eds.), *Government and Economic Life* (Washington, D.C.: Brookings Institution, 1940), Vol. II, p. 692.
[39]*Ibid.*, p. 696.
[40]*Ibid.*, pp. 692–93.

the exercise of the State's authority unless confiscation is clearly established.[41]

In four valuation cases decided in 1934 and 1938, the Court approved measures of value based upon original cost.[42] In a 1935 decision, it rejected a reproduction cost valuation based upon several price indices.[43] And in a 1942 case, the Court upheld an order of the Federal Power Commission reducing pipeline rates. While the issue of original versus reproduction cost did not arise, the Court said: "The Constitution does not bind rate-making bodies to the service of any single formula or combination of formulas. Agencies to whom this legislative power has been delegated are free ... to make the pragmatic adjustments which may be called for by particular circumstances."[44] It was the minority's concurring opinion (Justices Black, Douglas, and Murphy), however, that attracted the attention:

> ... we think this is an appropriate occasion to lay the ghost of *Smyth v. Ames*, ... which has haunted utility regulation since 1898. ...
> As we read the opinion of the Court, the Commission is now freed from the compulsion of admitting evidence on reproduction cost or of giving any weight to that element of "fair value." The Commission may now adopt, if it chooses, prudent investment as a rate base—the base long advocated by Mr. Justice Brandeis.[45]

The Hope Natural Gas Case. Two years later, the Court abandoned the Smyth rule that prescribed the use of a fair value rate base. The Federal Power Commission ordered a company to reduce its wholesale gas rates by more than 60 percent ($3.6 million annually). In making this decision, the commission used the "actual legitimate cost" of $33.7 million as the rate base and allowed a return of 6.5 percent. The company, which estimated that the reproduction cost of its property was $97 million and the trended original cost was $105 million, claimed it should be allowed to earn 8 percent on a $66 million fair value rate base. In a five to three decision, the Court upheld the commission. Speaking for the majority, Justice Douglas said:

> We held in *Federal Power Commission v. Natural Gas Pipeline Co.* that the Commission was not bound to the use of any single formula or combination of formulae in determining rates. Its rate-making function, moreover, involves the making of "pragmatic adjustments." And when the Commission's order is challenged in the courts, the question is whether that order "viewed in its

41 *Los Angeles Gas & Elec. Co.* v. *Railroad Comm. of Calif., op. cit.,* pp. 304–5.
42 *Lindheimer* v. *Illinois Bell Tel. Co.,* 292 U.S. 151 (1934); *Dayton Power & Light Co.* v. *Public Utilities Comm. of Ohio,* 292 U.S. 290 (1934); *Railroad Comm. of Calif.* v. *Pacific Gas & Elec. Co.,* 320 U.S. 388 (1938); *Denver Union Stock Yard Co.* v. *United States,* 304 U.S. 470 (1938).
43 *West* v. *Chesapeake & Potomac Tel. Co., op. cit.*
44 *Federal Power Comm.* v. *Natural Gas Pipeline Co.,* 315 U.S. 575, 586 (1942).
45 Concurring opinion, *ibid.,* pp. 602, 606. See Robert L. Hale, "Does the Ghost of Smyth v. Ames Still Walk?" 55 *Harvard Law Review* 1116 (1942).

entirety" meets the requirements of the Act. Under the statutory standard of "just and reasonable" it is the result reached not the method employed which is controlling. It is not theory but the impact of the rate order which counts. If the total effect of the rate order cannot be said to be unjust and unreasonable, judicial inquiry under the Act is at an end. The fact that the method employed to reach that result may contain infirmities is not then important. Moreover, the Commission's order does not become suspect by reason of the fact that it is challenged. It is the product of expert judgment which carries a presumption of validity. And he who would upset the rate order under the Act carries the heavy burden of making a convincing showing that it is invalid because it is unjust and unreasonable in its consequences.

. . . Rates which enable the company to operate successfully, to maintain its financial integrity, to attract capital, and to compensate its investors for the risks assumed certainly cannot be condemned as invalid, even though they might produce only a meager return on the so-called "fair value" rate base.[46]

All three of the dissenting opinions argued that there is a connection between the method of determining the "end result" and the end result itself. "My disagreement with the Court," stated Justice Reed, "arises primarily from its view that it makes no difference how the Commission reached the rate fixed so long as the result is fair and reasonable. For me the statutory command to the Commission is more explicit."[47] Justice Frankfurter expressed a similar view when he argued:

It will not do to say that it must all be left to the skill of experts. Expertise is a rational process and a rational process implies expressed reasons for judgment. It will little advance the public interest to substitute for the hodge-podge of the rule in *Smyth v. Ames* . . . , an encouragement of conscious obscurity or confusion in reaching a result, on the assumption that so long as the result appears harmless its basis is irrelevant.[48]

And Justice Jackson, approving the prudent investment theory in utility rate cases, thought natural gas belonged in a separate category from other public utility industries. In his opinion:

The heart of this problem is the elusive, exhaustible, and irreplaceable nature of natural gas itself. Given sufficient money, we can produce any desired amount of railroad, bus, or steamship transportation, or communications facilities, or capacity for generation of electric energy, or for the manufacture of gas of a kind. In the service of such utilities one customer has little concern with the amount taken by another, one's waste will not deprive another, a volume of service can be created equal to demand, and today's demands will not exhaust or lessen capacity to serve tomorrow. But the wealth of Midas and the wit of man cannot produce or reproduce a natural

[46] *Federal Power Comm.* v. *Hope Natural Gas Co., op. cit.,* pp. 602, 605 (citations omitted).
[47] Dissenting opinion, *ibid.,* p. 623.
[48] Dissenting opinion, *ibid.,* p. 627.

gas field. We cannot even reproduce the gas, for our manufactured product has only about half the heating value per unit of nature's own.[49]

Implications of the Hope Decision. There are two important, but conflicting, implications of the Hope decision. On the one hand, it removed an obstacle to effective regulation that had been created by the courts. Comments Welch:

> ... the departure from the old fair return–fair value doctrine, in effect, frees the regulatory commissions from the federal court domination and close supervision which prevailed in former years. This does not mean that the regulatory problem of fixing reasonable rates is all settled. To the contrary, reasonable rates will probably be a troublesome question as long as there is regulation. This does, however, place a greater responsibility on commissions, since reasonable rates now become more a matter of expert commission judgment and less a matter of rules or formulas.[50]

Moreover, attention was shifted from the rate base to the rate of return—a shift that many believed was long overdue. And as long as the "end result" is reasonable, "judicial inquiry . . . is at an end."[51]

On the other hand, the Court still has the right of review. But it presented no criteria by which the end result was to be judged. Troxel argues:

> If many commission decisions are reviewed in a thorough and factual manner, the Court cannot escape measurements of fair returns; it cannot fail to recognize that the choice of methods affects the ends. If the decisions are not reviewed for their reasonableness, the Court really turns back to the Munn decision without admitting the reversion.[52]

Consequently, the Court at some future date may be forced to reconsider its position in the property valuation controversy.

Most of the regulatory commissions continue to use the rate base/rate of return concept in rate regulation.[53] But there have been attempts to experiment

---

[49] Dissenting opinion, *ibid.*, p. 629. This problem is discussed in Chapter 16.

[50] Welch, *op. cit.* (1961 ed.), p. 311. It should be emphasized again that the Court did not forbid the use of the fair value doctrine; instead, it merely removed the *Smyth* v. *Ames* requirement that prescribed the use of a fair value rate base.

[51] In determining the "end result," however, the courts require the use of fair and proper procedures. Thus, a year after the Hope decision, the Supreme Court set aside an FPC order on the ground that the commission had failed to furnish sufficient evidence to support its findings. "We have repeatedly emphasized," said Justice Douglas, "the need for clarity and completeness in the basic or essential findings on which administrative orders rest. . . . Their absence can only clog the administrative function and add to the delays in rate-making." *Colorado-Wyoming Gas Co.* v. *Federal Power Comm.*, 324 U.S. 626, 634 (1945).

[52] Troxel, *op. cit.*, p. 278.

[53] The two most significant exceptions to the rate base method are found in the regulation of motor carriers and railroads. In the regulation of the former industry, the operating ratio method is widely employed. (See Chapter 9, pp. 271-75.) In the regulation of the latter industry, the ICC for many years has largely based its measure of the required level of revenues on increased operating expenses.

with alternative approaches. In a 1947 decision, the Wisconsin commission attempted to fix telephone rates without determining either a rate base or a rate of return.[54] The decision was reversed by the Wisconsin circuit court. Argued Judge Reis:

> The Commission . . . disavowed its own accepted precept of rate making. *It outlawed rate base.* It denied the *need* of finding fair value—or of making any finding whatever, other than the elicitation of the end result that old rates were unreasonable and new rates are reasonable . . . .
>
> Our conclusion is that by failing to find, and by decrying its duty to find, *a base upon which to fix the fair profit*—the Commission has gone beyond the four quarters of the statute which vitalizes it; and perchance has impinged upon the due process clause of the Constitution itself.[55]

In a 1956 decision, the Florida commission used the "cost of capital" as a substitute for the rate base. While it based rates on the company's revenue requirements, it also determined the value of the company's physical rate base and then translated the amount of revenue required into a percentage of such rate base.[56] And, finally, in the regulation of airlines, motor carriers, natural gas producers, and railroads, rates are commonly set on a group or area basis, rather than upon an individual company cost of service basis.

PROPERTY VALUATION: ECONOMIC CONCEPTS

Over the past several decades, many arguments, sometimes conflicting, have been presented in favor of, as well as against, each of the various measures of value. In this section, the major economic arguments will be analyzed. Although a distinction is frequently made between "reproduction cost" (or "current cost") and "replacement cost" on the one hand, and among "original cost," "book cost," and "prudent investment" on the other, these terms will be used synonymously and referred to as reproduction cost and original cost, respectively.

The Economics of Reproduction Cost

The economic case for reproduction cost is based upon its effectiveness in obtaining a proper allocation of the nation's resources.[57] During inflation, according to the argument, if the rates of regulated industries are based upon

[54] *City of Two Rivers* v. *Commonwealth Teleph. Co.*, 70 PUR (NS) 5 (Wis., 1947).

[55] *Commonwealth Teleph. Co.* v. *Wisconsin Public Service Comm.*, 71 PUR (NS) 65, 69, 71 (1947), *aff'd*, 32 NW 2d 247 (1948). Also see *New England Teleph. & Teleg. Co.* v. *State*, 64 A. 2d 9 (1949); and *Milwaukee & Suburban Transp. Corp.* v. *Wisconsin Public Service Comm.*, 108 NW 2d 729 (1961).

[56] *Re Peninsula Teleph. Co.*, 17 PUR 3d 109 (Fla., 1956). This approach is defended in two articles by Harold M. Somers: " 'Cost of Money' as the Determinant of Public Utility Rates," 4 *Buffalo Law Review* 289 (1955) and "The 'End Result' Approach to Public Utility Regulation," 16 *ibid*. 689 (1967).

[57] James C. Bonbright, *Principles of Public Utility Rates* (New York: Columbia University Press, 1961), p. 225. This discussion draws heavily from this study.

original cost valuations, they will be lower than the rates of nonregulated industries, which tend to reflect reproduction costs. The rates of regulated industries, in other words, will not be covering current costs of production. Such a situation will result in an excessive increase in demand for the services of the regulated industries relative to demand for other commodities and, in turn, will require an expansion in the capacity of the regulated industries' plants in order to satisfy the new demand.

On two grounds, economic resources will be improperly allocated. First, because consumers will not be paying current production costs, the regulated industries will be supplying services for wasteful consumption. Second, the new investment required will result in a disproportionate amount of resources being allocated to these industries. Likewise, when prices fall and the rates of regulated industries are maintained above those of nonregulated industries, consumption and investment in the regulated industries are unduly restricted, again resulting in a poor allocation of resources.[58]

The argument of the regulated industries in favor of reproduction cost valuations is similar, although often stated in a different manner. Their position can be summarized as follows. The earnings of nonregulated industries rise during inflation. For the regulated industries to (1) obtain necessary replacement funds, (2) maintain the real income of investors and prevent confiscation of their property, and (3) preserve their credit standing, their earnings also should rise. Increased earnings can be obtained by making adjustments in property valuations (and annual depreciation charges) in line with changes in the price level.[59]

While there is merit in these arguments, four basic problems arise from the concept and use of reproduction cost that make questionable its use as a proper measure of value.

The Resource Allocation Argument. The proposition that reproduction cost valuations will lead to a better allocation of resources is subject to four limitations. First, rates based on reproduction cost valuations will not result in "optimum" prices. The reproduction cost measure

> ... identifies reasonable rates with rates sufficient, in the aggregate, to cover total costs of service replacement including a capital-attracting rate of return on the hypothetical investment in a new plant. With a public utility or railroad system still operating at a scale at which further enhancements in rates of output can take place with less than a proportionate increase in operating and capital costs (conditions of decreasing unit costs), such rates will exceed the incremental or marginal costs of service. Yet, under the economists' theory of optimum pricing, the important relationship between

---

[58] The classic economic defense of reproduction cost is made by Harry G. Brown in two articles: "Railroad Valuation and Rate Regulation," 23 *Journal of Political Economy* 505 (1925) and "Economic Basis and Limits of Public Utility Regulation," 53 *American Bar Association Reports* 717 (1928).

[59] William A. Paton and Howard C. Greer, "Utility Rates Must Recognize Dollar Depreciation," 51 *Public Utilities Fortnightly* 333 (1953); and H. A. Coxe, "The Modern Case for Fair Value," 76 *ibid.* 15 (December 3, 1965).

prices and costs is an equality, under equilibrium conditions, between prices and *marginal* costs. Hence, if optimum resource allocation were to be accepted as the primary objective of rate-making policy, as the replacement-cost advocates insist, what would be required is not a mere transfer from an actual-cost standard to a replacement-cost standard, but rather a transfer from *any* standard of total cost to a standard of incremental cost.[60]

Second, the resource allocation argument fails to take into account the tax factor. In the preceding chapter, it was pointed out that the regulated industries are subject to heavy local, state and federal taxes, and that these taxes represent a significant percentage of the companies' annual revenues. Bonbright argues:

> Viewed from the standpoint of the consumers and of the companies that render utility service, the payment of these taxes is a part of the necessary costs of service. Viewed, however, from the standpoint of the nation or of the community, this payment cannot be relied upon to reflect, even in a rough and ready way, the *social* costs of service rendition—the burdens that the community as a whole could save by refraining from supplying the service. Yet the resource-allocation defense of replacement-cost rate control involves the assumption that the expenses incurred by the private producer of the service reflect social costs.[61]

Third, there is some evidence to support the contention that an original cost valuation is not any further removed from a reproduction cost valuation for the property of the regulated industries than it is for the property of the nonregulated industries. Both types of industries have plant and equipment that are the result of separate investments made over many years. At any given time, therefore, the depreciated original cost of each property item will differ. Moreover, as replacement takes place at a more or less uniform rate, in addition to new construction, the total depreciated original cost is kept close to replacement cost. For example, on the assumption that a company's property is retired at a uniform rate, that straight line depreciation is used, and that net investment is 5 percent annually, Bernstein estimates that,

> ... if the average length of useful life of the property were ten years, 20.9 per cent of the property in a prudent investment valuation would be valued at

---

[60] Bonbright, *op. cit.,* pp. 229–30. It is important to emphasize that this same argument applies to any rates which are based upon costs, no matter how the costs are measured. "Reliance upon costs does serve, however, to keep utility prices somewhere within the range of . . . standards relied upon almost universally in our private enterprise economy, and, as well, within an acceptable area of 'fairness' to utility owners and users." Lewis, *op. cit.,* p. 686. The marginal cost pricing proposal is discussed in the appendix to Chapter 11.

[61] Bonbright, *op. cit.,* p. 231. The tax factor creates an interesting paradox. During inflationary periods, it is argued, the rates of regulated industries will be too low if based upon original cost valuations, thereby encouraging wasteful consumption. "But if this danger were really believed to exist despite the heavy prevailing levels of utility taxation, the remedy would not need to be sought for by the adoption of a replacement-cost principle of rate making. Instead, it could be secured far more easily and expeditiously by an increase in utility taxes!" *Ibid.,* p. 232.

the prices of the current year, and 77 per cent of the property would be valued at the prices of the five most recent years. If the average length of useful life of the property were twenty years, 12.6 per cent of the property would be valued at the prices of the current year, and 52 per cent of the property would be valued at the prices of the five most recent years.[62]

Whether these assumptions are fully valid is not at issue. The important point is that unless the ratio of reproduction cost to original cost for the regulated industries differs significantly from the comparable ratio for the nonregulated industries, the resource allocation argument is invalid.[63]

The final limitation is past experience. The regulated industries usually have been able to expand their output significantly without necessitating new investment in plant and equipment. These industries frequently have either unused or stand-by capacity which they can use to meet increases in demand. "They can 'stretch' existing plant capacity a long way, as the experience during the Second World War shows, before they must build more plant or ration service."[64] Even during the depression of the thirties when the prices of regulated industries were more inflexible than those of nonregulated industries, significant shifts from the services of the regulated to the commodities of the nonregulated industries were not evidenced. This suggests that the demand for regulated industries' services is relatively inelastic. Furthermore, it implies that only in the unlikely event of a long period of hyperinflation or deflation is it probable that original cost valuations will lead to distortions in the allocation of resources between regulated and nonregulated industries.[65]

---

[62] E. M. Bernstein, *Public Utility Rate Making and the Price Level* (Chapel Hill: University of North Carolina Press, 1937), p. 124. Also see *Chesapeake & Potomac Tel. Co. v. Public Service Comm.*, 187 A. 2d 475 (1963).

[63] A McGraw-Hill study (*Business Week*, November 26, 1966, p. 101) resulted in the following data:

	Percent of Industrial Capacity Installed			
	Prior to Dec., 1950	Dec., 1950 to Dec., 1956	Jan., 1959 to Dec., 1961	Jan., 1962 to Dec., 1966
All business	24%	18%	22%	36%
Manufacturing industries	24	19	21	36
Airlines	*	6	26	68
Railroads	49	20	13	18
Other transportation and communications	19	16	23	42
Electric utilities	24	21	26	29

*Less than .5%.

[64] Troxel, *op. cit.,* p. 303.

[65] "It should be borne in mind that any really cataclysmic changes in the general price level could not be handled effectively, in the case of public utility rates, by employing either reproduction cost valuations or variable rates of return on prudent

An Imaginary Measure. Reproduction cost is an imaginary cost. The inherent uncertainties of the concept have been summarized by Wilcox:

(1) What is it that is being reproduced: a modern replacement for an old plant, the old plant in its original condition, or the old plant as it stands today? The assumption made in the McCardle case was that the company, starting fresh, would build its old plant in its depreciated condition, a purely imaginary procedure in which sane managements are unlikely to engage.

(2) Under what conditions is reproduction cost to occur: those originally existing or those existing at the present time? If the former, are allowances to be made to cover the possible cost, today, of cutting paths through forest long since razed, and hauling supplies by horse and wagon rather than train or truck? If the latter, are sums to be allowed for tearing down the buildings that might conceivably be standing where a railroad has its lines, or for ripping up and then relaying pavements that did not exist when a water company first laid its mains? Company lawyers have lively imaginations. And though the more absurd of their inventions have been rejected by the courts, a certain residue remains.

(3) What methods of reproduction are to be assumed: simultaneous rebuilding of the whole plant involving large-scale operations and employing modern techniques, or piecemeal reconstruction on a small scale with techniques no longer in use? The latter assumption is the usual rule. And here, again, a procedure is imagined that no sane management would countenance.

(4) What prices are to be taken as representing reproduction cost: the spot prices of a particular day, the average prices of a recent period, or figures based on forecasts of the future? If spot prices, they change from day to day; the chosen day may not be representative. If average prices, they may be raised or lowered by changing the selected period. If either, the costs computed are those of the past and not the future. But if future prices are to be employed, valuation becomes a matter of guesswork, with the companies, presumably, guessing high and the commissions guessing low. Yet it was said by Justice Butler, speaking for the Court in the McCardle case, that forecasts of future prices should be made.[66]

As a result of these inherent uncertainties, three conclusions follow. First, even expert and enlightened judgment will lead to vastly different fair value estimates of the same property. In the New York Telephone case, six estimates were made: the majority of the commission, $367 million; a federal court, $397 million; the minority of the commission, $405.5 million; the court-appointed "master," $518 million; and two independent appraisals—one of $529 million,

---

investment. If general price increases, for instance, should occur suddenly and on a tremendous scale the situation probably would call for the bold application of an emergency percentage increase directly to the rates themselves, without resort to any time-consuming intermediate procedure." Lewis, *op. cit.*, p. 690.

[66] Clair Wilcox, *Public Policies Toward Business* (3d ed.; Homewood, Ill.: Richard D. Irwin, Inc., 1966), p. 317.

the other of $615 million.[67] Under these conditions, the determination of property valuations becomes a matter of bargaining between the companies and the commissions. The final valuation chosen cannot be explained or defended on any economic grounds.

Second, the use of reproduction cost adds to regulatory delay. A typical rate case takes many months before the commission issues its final decision. The company then may appeal the decision to the courts, hoping for a more favorable valuation. And litigation is not only expensive but also results in delay.

Finally, reproduction cost valuations are expensive. There are two frequently used methods of taking a company's inventory for valuation purposes. (1) Prior to the establishment of continuing property records, company and commission engineers had to spend months obtaining an inventory of the entire plant and equipment and estimating its current value. "In theory, it means counting and valuing every nut and bolt and other items of property. . . . Even for a small utility company, this could be a burdensome, costly, and time-consuming job."[68] (2) When continuing property records are required, the inventory procedure is simplified. There still remains the problem, however, of valuing the property items, in addition to the problem of estimating accrued depreciation. The most widely used and inexpensive method of valuing property items is by "trending" original cost, which will be discussed in the following section; the accrued depreciation problem will be considered later in the chapter.

Maintenance of Investors' Real Income. The argument that the real income of investors should be maintained also has shortcomings. The argument assumes that the cost of reproducing a regulated company's property is a good measure of changes in the cost of living index. However, the index of construction costs, which should be used in reproduction cost valuations, and the index of living costs, which measures investors' purchasing power, are not the same. While they usually move in the same direction, the construction cost index has been considerably above the cost of living index for many years. In order to maintain investors' real income, reproduction cost valuations must be based upon the cost of living index. But if this index is below the index of construction costs, the companies would receive less than the necessary "reproduction cost"; if it is above, they would receive more.

More importantly, the use of either index overcompensates a company's common stockholders when prices rise, and undercompensates them when prices fall. As interest on bonds and dividends on preferred stock are fixed or subject

---

[67] Cited in Felix Frankfurter, *The Public and Its Government* (New Haven: Yale University Press, 1930), p. 105.

[68] Welch, *op. cit.,* p. 317. The New York Telephone Company paid $6 million for property inventories and reproduction cost valuations during the twenties, and the New York Edison Company nearly $5 million for a single valuation, while the Interstate Commerce Commission paid $45 million and the railroads nearly $138 million to determine property valuations on the basis of 1914 prices. Leland Olds, "The Public Utility Issues," 24 *Yale Review* 704 (1935); and John Bauer and Nathaniel Gold, *Public Utility Valuation for Purposes of Rate Control* (New York: The Macmillan Co., 1934), p. 120.

to a limited return, they do not change with the price level. Earnings on common stock, therefore, will change by more than the price level. Assume that a company has an $8 million capitalization, an original cost property valuation of $8 million, and an allowable rate of return of 6 percent. Its annual earnings will be $480,000. On $3 million of bonds at 4 percent, it pays $120,000. On $2 million of preferred stock at 5 percent, it pays $100,000. The amount remaining is $260,000. On $3 million of common stock, it can pay 8.7 percent. Now assume that the cost of living index doubles, and the company is revalued at $16 million. With its return still at 6 percent, it earns $960,000. It still pays $220,000 on its bonds and preferred stock. But it now has $740,000 left, resulting in a yield of 24.7 percent on its common stock.

To maintain the real income of all investors, the returns on each type of security would necessarily have to be flexible. To maintain the real income of common stockholders, only their investment ($3 million in the above example) needs to be revalued as the price level rises. Conversely, if the cost of living index declines, the dividends on common stock will fall even more sharply. "Just as regulation is not likely to permit the latter exigency to develop as a mere incident of a falling price level, so public policy need not support the magnifying of profits produced by a fortuitous rise in prices."[69]

Spokesmen for the regulated industries argue that a full inflation adjustment applied to total capitalization is fair, for

> ... the equivalent of the stockholders' claim for the full inflation adjustment occurs as a normal incident in non-regulated industry in the form of "trading on the equity." The return on which the stockholder should be able to count consists of the earnings on his own dollars plus the difference between the earnings on the dollars furnished by bondholders and the fixed return which the company has agreed to pay to these investors for the use of their dollars. It is this total return which belongs to the common stock, and it is this total return, not alone the earnings on the common stock capital, which should be protected from erosion due to inflation.[70]

Statistics fail to show, however, that nonregulated industries are able to fully compensate for inflation by increasing their earnings in line with changes in the cost of living index.[71] Nor is it obvious that these results are desirable for either the regulated or nonregulated industries. And since regulation removes some of the risks to which a nonregulated industry is susceptible, the assumption that since a certain result occurs in nonregulated industry it should also occur in regulated industry is questionable.

The reproduction cost argument implies a second assumption—namely,

[69] Lewis, *op. cit.,* pp. 687–88.

[70] Arthur L. Lanigan, "Fair Value Regulation" (speech before the Symposium on Economics of Public Utilities, sponsored by The Chesapeake & Potomac Telephone Companies, Sept. 8–10, 1960) (mimeographed), p. 20.

[71] See Ralph C. Jones, *Effects of Price Level Changes on Business Income, Capital, and Taxes* (New York: American Accounting Association, 1956).

that the allowable fair rate of return is firmly fixed. In fact, the rate of return is flexible, and if an inflation adjustment is necessary (a subject considered in the next chapter), the commission can increase it as the cost of capital changes. The regulated industries contend that this solution is socially and politically unacceptable, as the rate of return would be much higher than that customarily looked on as the reasonable earning power of money. Furthermore, they argue, the adjustment would be in the wrong place, since it is the value of the property which is affected by inflation. But, as Wilcox has observed, the public "does not complain when the same effect is achieved through revaluation. For here, it does not realize what is going on. The companies center their attention on the rate base rather than the rate of return because valuation is a mystery and earnings can thus be boosted with greater ease."[72] In theory, by stabilizing property valuations, regulatory attention can be shifted to the rate of return—that is, to the earnings a company needs to maintain its credit standing. Earnings regulation is thereby tied in with a company's investment and service requirements. In practice, as will be discussed in the next chapter, there is some truth to the companies' contention.

Preservation of Companies' Credit Standing. Closely connected with maintenance of investors' real income is the argument that the regulated companies must preserve their credit standing in order to attract additional capital for improvements and expansion. There is no one who would deny the validity of this argument. The question arises, therefore, as to whether the use of reproduction cost valuations will accomplish this goal better than will the use of original cost valuations. For two reasons, the reproduction cost measure of value may impair rather than preserve a company's credit standing.

In the first place, reproduction cost valuations result in a constantly fluctuating rate base. The Interstate Commerce Commission, for example, pointed out in the St. Louis & O'Fallon case that if the nation's railroads were valued on the basis of 1914 prices, their value would have been nearly $18 billion; in 1920, their value would have become $41 billion; and in 1923, their value would have dropped to $31 billion.[73] And, as pointed out above, only the common stockholders receive the gains and losses from reproduction cost valuations. "Obviously any method of valuation which concentrates upon the stockholders the gains and losses arising from changes in rates tends to increase risks and introduce a speculative element in the provision for capital that is not conducive to obtaining capital at the lowest cost."[74]

In the second place, in some of the regulated industries, companies cannot earn a fair rate of return on even an original cost rate base, and they certainly could not earn a fair rate of return on the higher reproduction cost.[75] The

[72] Wilcox, *op. cit.,* pp. 316–17.

[73] *Excess Income of St. Louis & O'Fallon Ry. Co., op. cit.,* pp. 31–32.

[74] Locklin, *op. cit.,* p. 360.

[75] Bonbright (*op. cit.,* p. 232) states the argument this way: "Whenever economic conditions disqualify an actual-cost basis, they will probably also disqualify a replacement-cost basis," and he feels that it applies to the regulation of railroad rates, local-transit fares, and natural gas rates.

railroads afford an obvious example. Faced with increased competition from subsidized competitors, they have failed to earn a fair rate of return on any measure of property value for many years. But railroad rates still must be established. In recent years, the fair rate of return standard has been subordinated to considerations of competitive rates and the prevention of undue discrimination.[76]

The Economics of Original Cost

On *economic* grounds, reproduction cost valuations are exceedingly difficult to defend. Original cost valuations have two major advantages, but the measure is not devoid of controversy.

Administrative Advantages. Original cost is easily understood, results in inexpensive valuations, and can be efficiently administered. The accounting practices of the regulated industries are controlled and are based upon original costs. Therefore, because the commissions can easily obtain original cost valuations that are not subject to estimates and speculation, they are able to dispose of rate cases in the shortest possible period of time and with a minimum expense to all concerned. It must not be implied that rate making should become a mechanical or routine process based solely on accounting data and formulas. On the contrary, while this danger is always present, by simplifying the process of establishing the rate base, attention can be shifted to the rate of return; a determination that will always be the subject of controversy.[77] Rather, the advantages of original cost valuations lie in that they (1) reduce the number of controversial issues per rate case and (2) force the companies and commissions to consider the relation of rate regulation to investment needs. This consideration represents the basic purpose of rate regulation and is of much more significance than property valuations. As Troxel has put it:

> Trying to achieve these ends [successful operation, financial integrity, and attraction of capital], commissions must look to the future; even if they rely on past experiences and allow enough earnings to cover the present interest and dividend obligations, they still must keep their eyes on the future demands for service, future operating expenses, and other future investment conditions. The future is more significant than the past; earnings and costs in years to come are more important than historical facts about property costs. past earnings, and recorded expenses.[78]

[76] Competition in the transportation industry also has resulted in significant excess capacity. Since much of this capacity would never be rebuilt were the carriers to start over today, reproduction cost valuations are meaningless for purposes of rate controls. See Chapter 10, below.

[77] In fact, there is always the possibility that rate regulation will become routine under any valuation procedure. As will be discussed in the following chapter, during the long period that reproduction cost was emphasized by the judiciary, the rate of return was usually based upon a conventional, traditional, or customary return. Only in the past few years has any attempt been made to establish a rationale for or basic principles of setting the allowable rate of return.

[78] Troxel, *op. cit.,* pp. 305–6.

It should be emphasized again that there may be some controversy, under an original cost basis, among the three frequently used measures—original cost, book or investment cost, and prudent investment. But compared with that inevitably arising over reproduction cost and fair value, this controversy is relatively minor.

Credit Standing and Capital Attraction. The use of an original cost rate base enables the regulated companies to maintain their credit standing and to attract new capital. Investors receive a rate of return on the money which they have invested in a company. At the time an investment decision is made, investors consider the expected future rate of return. The expected or anticipated rate, of course, will vary with the financial position of the company and the general economic situation of the country. For this reason, the allowable rate of return cannot be inflexible. The important point, however, is that an original cost rate base serves this purpose better than one based upon reproduction cost. As Bonbright has explained: "Whatever scheme of rate regulation will put investors in a position to draw this balance between present outlay and anticipated future return with the most confidence is the scheme most likely to permit a well-managed company to maintain sound financial health at a minimum 'cost of capital' to the consumers."[79]

Many executives of the regulated companies will agree with the validity of these advantages of original cost valuations, at least in theory. Yet, somewhat ironically, they frequently use the same arguments when advocating reproduction cost valuations. Their argument for reproduction cost is predicated on two beliefs: the inevitability of continuing inflation in the economy, so that reproduction cost valuations will remain above, or at least equal to, those based on original cost; and, the previously mentioned factor that commissions are unlikely to make the necessary adjustments for inflation in the allowable rate of return. The truth of the first belief can be proven quickly: if the price level should fall sharply, many present supporters of reproduction cost valuations and price level depreciation would become advocates of original cost measures. The second belief will be discussed in the following chapter.

PROPERTY VALUATION: CURRENT COMMISSION PRACTICES

The Supreme Court has indicated its willingness to leave the choice of proper measures of value to the commissions. What measures do the commissions employ? When reproduction cost or fair value measures are used, how are values determined? What problems have been encountered? Answers to these questions are considered in this section.

Current Measures of Value

Four federal commissions are concerned with the valuation problem. All four—Civil Aeronautics Board, Federal Communications Commission, Federal

[79] Bonbright, *op. cit.,* p. 187.

Power Commission, and Interstate Commerce Commission—base property valuations on original cost.[80] But there are certain exceptions. Thus, land and rights generally are included in the rate base on the basis of their "present value"; the ICC gives considerable weight to reproduction cost in the regulation of oil pipelines.[81]

Among the state commissions, practices vary considerably. In a study of the impact of the Hope decision on utility valuations, Rose found that twenty-seven state commissions changed from fair value to an original cost basis.[82] More recently, largely due to continuation of an inflationary trend, there has been a noticeable change back to fair value. In regulating electric, gas, or telephone utilities, twenty-six states use "original cost"; two, "prudent investment"; nineteen, "fair value," "reasonable value," or "all elements considered"; one, "average net investment"; one, "reproduction cost"; and one has not determined a method.[83]

Measures of Reproduction Cost

Where reproduction cost or fair value measures are employed, two important problems arise.[84] First, how should reproduction cost be determined? Second, what weight should the commissions attach to this measure in arriving at a fair value rate base? Only generalized answers can be given to these questions, for each rate case is unique in that the evidence presented and accepted varies according to the case, industry, state, and year.

With respect to the first question, reproduction cost estimates usually are obtained in three ways. (1) General price indices are used. These indices include

[80] *General Passenger Fare Investigation*, E-16068, pp. 33–38 (CAB, 1960); F. F. Blachly and M. E. Oatman, "Actual Legitimate Cost as a Basis for Utility Regulation—The Experience of the Federal Power Commission," 36 *Georgetown Law Journal* 487 (1948); *Increased Freight Rates, Eastern, Western & Southern Territories, 1956*, 300 ICC 633, 656 (1957).

[81] See *Report on Consent Decree Program of the Department of Justice* (Antitrust Subcommittee of the Committee on the Judiciary, House, 86th Cong., 1st sess.) (Washington, D.C.: U.S. Government Printing Office, 1959), pp. 262–64.

[82] Joseph R. Rose, "The Hope Case and Public Utility Valuation in the States," 54 *Columbia Law Review* 188 (1954).

[83] Federal Power Commission, "Federal and State Commission Jurisdiction and Regulation, Electric, Gas, and Telephone Utilities, 1967" (Washington, D.C.: U.S. Government Printing Office, 1968), pp. 11–12. The District of Columbia commission uses original cost; the Texas commission, which regulates gas but not electric or telephone utilities, uses fair value. Indiana, Kentucky, Mississippi, North Carolina, and Pennsylvania prescribe fair value by statute; Delaware authorizes fair value by statute; Florida and North Dakota require prudent investment by statute; the Ohio commission uses reproduction cost because of an interpretation of its statute by the state supreme court (*Illinois Bell Tel. Co.* v. *Illinois Commerce Comm.*, 414 Ill. 275, 289 [1953]); Maine by statute prohibits consideration of "current value"; and a New York statute prescribes an original cost standard for electric and gas utilities, and a fair value standard for telephone and transportation companies.

For a complete discussion of the various concepts of "value" found in state statutes, see Joseph R. Rose, "Confusion in Valuation for Public Utility Rate-Making," 47 *Minnesota Law Review* 1 (1962).

[84] A third problem, concerning accrued depreciation, is considered in the next section.

the Bureau of Labor Statistics' "Consumers' Price Index" and "Index of Wholesale Prices of All Commodities," or a Gross National Product deflator. The resulting estimate, frequently referred to as "reproduction cost new," represents the original cost of the property expressed in dollars of current purchasing power. (2) Construction cost indices are used. The most widely employed construction cost index is the "Handy–Whitman Index," based upon utility construction costs. The resulting valuation is known as "trended" original cost.[85] As with general price indices, the purpose of the index is to translate original costs into values expressed in current dollars. (3) Unit cost pricing is employed. This method involves pricing like units of property directly by means of price indices representing the price movement of the specific property under consideration.[86]

The advantages and disadvantages of each of these methods have been enumerated in journal articles, as well as in commission and court decisions for many years. If reproduction cost valuations are to be made, unit cost pricing would seem to be the most desirable. General price indices measure purchasing power changes and are entirely unrelated to the cost of reproducing the property of any particular company. Such a valuation represents an imaginary figure. Construction cost indices, while more closely related to the actual cost of constructing buildings and equipment, have the same general drawbacks. However, when like units of property cannot be easily identified or separated, either general price indices or construction cost indices must be used in obtaining a reproduction cost valuation.

With respect to the second question concerning the weighting problem, the commissions generally do not allow the full valuation estimate based upon reproduction cost or trended original cost.[87] As a result, the final valuation figure chosen represents a compromise. Rose concluded in his study of state commission valuation procedures:

> The Illinois Commission has assigned one-quarter weight to reproduction cost and three-quarters to original cost; Alabama has assigned one-third to reproduction cost and two-thirds to original cost; Minnesota, Delaware, Pennsylvania and Arizona have given approximately equal weight to each element. North Carolina and Indiana have also attributed equal weight to

---

[85] The process of trending original cost is explained by Ezra B. Whitman and Ernest C. North, "Trending Public Utility Construction Cost Indices," 52 *Public Utilities Fortnightly* 285 (1953); Ernest C. North, "Trending Utility Plant Costs," 66 *ibid*. 88 (1960); and Edward C. Edgar, "The Rate Base—Its Nature, Composition and Role in Regulation" in *The Economics of Regulation of Public Utilities* (papers presented at a Conference at Northwestern University, 1966), pp. 107–50.

[86] The process of unit cost pricing is explained by Henry E. Crampton, "A Practical Approach to the Development of the Current Cost of Utility Plant" (speech at the Public Utility Valuation and Rate Making Conference, Iowa State University) (mimeographed, 1963).

[87] See "Trended Original Cost as Substitute for Reproduction Cost," 59 *Public Utilities Fortnightly* 273 (1957); and "Use of Trended Original Cost in Fixing a Rate Base," 66 *ibid*. 665 (1960).

each in some proceedings, but in others have given greater weight to original cost. New Mexico, Maryland, and New Jersey have used original cost as the principal factor and added an increment to compensate for reproduction cost, while Missouri has given "greater weight" to original cost than to reproduction cost. And in Kentucky, Nebraska, and Montana, where the statutes also require fair value, no generalization at all can be made concerning the findings of the regulatory authorities.[88]

Attrition

A problem frequently arising in rate cases, but usually when an original cost rate base is used, concerns an allowance for several related factors commonly referred to as "attrition," regulatory lag, erosion, and inflation. As described by the Massachusetts commission:

> This terminology has been used to describe the tendency of the rate of return to diminish in a period of comparatively high construction costs, since new plant is being added which, . . . is relatively expensive. . . . As the high cost plant comes into service, it tends to increase the applicable rate base at a more rapid pace than the resultant earnings, and the rate of return decreases accordingly.[89]

The need for a special allowance, therefore, is based upon one or more of the following situations: (1) increasing construction costs, (2) a rate of return calculated in a year prior to that for which the return is intended, and (3) the loss of proper earnings between the time a company files for a rate increase and the date on which the increase, if any, is granted. These factors can be illustrated by the following example. Suppose a commission sets a company's rate base at $10 million and allows a 6 percent rate of return, resulting in annual earnings of $600,000. If, however, the company completes construction of a $1 million new plant and puts it into operation during the next year, and if total earnings increase to $627,000, the rate of return will be 5.70 percent. And because rate regulation is not continuous (in most cases), this situation may exist for a year or more before the commission can complete a new rate case. Especially is this an important problem for companies that are expanding rapidly.

The commissions use four methods to deal with the problem of attrition. First, they may use a "year end" rate base, which includes property under construction at the end of the test period, rather than a rate base on the

---

[88] Rose, "Confusion in Valuation . . . ," *op. cit.,* pp. 23–24 (citations omitted). To illustrate: In a 1959 case, the Illinois commission found the depreciated original cost of the company's plant to be $162 million; two company witnesses estimated the trended original cost at $482 and $485 million; and one witness presented two estimates of reproduction cost, $451 and $439 million. After considering "all relevant factors," the commission arrived at a "fair value" rate base of $230 million. *Re The Peoples Gas Light & Coke Co.,* 27 PUR 3d 209 (Ill., 1959).

[89] *New England Teleph. & Teleg. Co.* v. *Mass. Department of Public Utilities,* 6 PUR 3d 65, 78 (Mass., 1954).

beginning or average of the whole test period.[90] Second, a separate allowance for attrition may be added to the rate base valuation. The New Jersey commission added $25.5 million to cover the effects of attrition on one company's earnings and the Maryland commission added an attrition allowance of $146,000 (about 3 percent) to the net investment rate base of a gas company.[91] Third, an allowance may be made in the allowable rate of return. The Virginia Supreme Court increased one company's rate of return by .23 percent to account for attrition; the Colorado commission added .20 percent in one case; and the New York commission increased the allowable return by .5 percent for one company.[92] Fourth, where no separate attrition adjustment is made, especially in fair value states, the commissions have frequently stated that they take this factor—along with others—into account in determining a fair rate of return.[93]

ACCRUED DEPRECIATION

Whatever measure of value is used to determine the rate base, depreciation must be deducted. In accounting terms, this deduction from a company's property valuation is known as "accrued depreciation." And, as with other regulatory problems, both the role and measurement of accrued depreciation have been the subject of controversy. A former president of the National Association of Regulatory Utility Commissioners has stated:

> More confusion has arisen with respect to, or has been injected into, regulatory thinking with regard to depreciation in rate making than seems possible.
>
> In rate making, the deduction has run the gamut from:
> (1) no deduction at all, to
> (2) deduction of an engineering determination,
> (3) deduction of the accumulated accounting reserve for depreciation, and
> (4) to the deduction of a computed amount which it is alleged the accountants *should* have accumulated if they had known what they were doing.
>
> The pendulum has indeed swung far, and the process hasn't been free from political influences.[94]

90 "Use of a Year-end Rate Base to Offset Effects of Inflation," 64 *Public Utilities Fortnightly* 241 (July 30, 1959); and "The Year-end Rate Base," 78 *ibid.* 69 (December 22, 1966).

91 *Re New Jersey Bell Teleph. Co.,* 31 PUR 3d 453 (N.J., 1959); and *Re Columbia Gas of Maryland,* 57 PUR 3d 460 (Md., 1965). Also see "Rate Base Allowance for Attrition," 80 *Public Utilities Fortnightly* 59 (December 7, 1967).

92 "Offsets to Attrition and Regulatory Lag," 66 *Public Utilities Fortnightly* 585, 587 (1960). Also see *Re Consolidated Edison Co. of New York,* 41 PUR 3d 305 (N.Y., 1961).

93 "Offsets to Attrition and Regulatory Lag," *op. cit.,* pp. 585–86; and *Re Montana Power Co.,* 42 PUR 3d 241 (Mont., 1962).

94 Cited by Ralph M. Besse, "Deductibility of Depreciation Reserves for Rate Base Purposes" (speech before the National Conference of Electric and Gas Utility Accountants) (mimeographed, 1950), p. 1.

The Need for Accrued Depreciation

The meaning of, and need for, depreciation accounting have already been discussed.[95] The need for accrued depreciation was succinctly stated by the Interstate Commerce Commission in a 1931 case:

> An article when new contains a certain number of units of service and as those units are exhausted the article depreciates. In order to make any figure, whether of original cost or cost of reproduction, representative of the condition of the property at the time of the inquiry it would seem on principle to be necessary to make due allowance for the expired units of service life.[96]

Consequently, if the straight line method of depreciation is used, a unit of property that has a life of 30 years and that has been employed for 15 years in providing service would be depreciated 50 percent.[97]

Consistency with Depreciation Accounting

Closely connected with the above is the need for consistency; depreciation in the accounting sense and in the valuation sense are the same. Property that is used up in service is a charge to operating costs. As it is consumed, the investment in the property is decreased by an equal deduction from its value. In the words of the Federal Power Commission:

> The determination of the annual allowances (annual expenses) for depletion, depreciation, and amortization (sometimes referred to jointly as depreciation) and the accrued depreciation in the properties must be consistent. This is a simple statement of what should be regarded as a universal truth in the regulation of rates. It is so regarded by the overwhelming majority of regulatory authorities of the country, and by students and writers on the subject. It is so regarded by sound business management outside of the utility rate case field.[98]

The need for consistency, however, has not always been recognized. Following the Knoxville Water Company case of 1909, "observed depreciation" was usually accepted as a measure of accrued depreciation.[99] According to this concept, depreciation is "a subnormal or rundown condition of a physical plant—one which is below the proper maximum condition in which the plant can be and should be permanently maintained in order to render adequate

[95] See Chapter 7, pp. 195–97.
[96] *Excess Income of Richmond, Fredericksburg & Potomac R.R. Co.*, 170 ICC 451, 468 (1931).
[97] When the sinking-fund method is used, the depreciation reserve is not deducted from the rate base. The reason is that the company is required to pay interest on the amount in the reserve. The annual charges to depreciation would be insufficient unless interest is earned on the entire fund already accumulated.
[98] *Re Canadian River Gas Co.*, 43 PUR (NS) 205, 218 (1942).
[99] *Knoxville v. Knoxville Water Co., op. cit.*

service."[100] The physical deterioration of a plant, as estimated by expert engineers, was commonly measured as the "percent condition" of old equipment relative to new. Thus, a percent condition of 90 would mean that small amounts of deferred maintenance and accrued depreciation should be deducted from the property valuation. In approving observed depreciation in one 1926 case, the Court held: "The testimony of competent valuation engineers who examined the property and made estimates in respect of its condition is to be preferred to mere calculations based on averages and assumed probabilities."[101] Yet, the Court's inconsistency can be seen from another 1926 decision in which it rejected a commission's effort to deduct accrued depreciation, saying: "Consumers pay for service, not for the property used to render it. Their payments are not contributions to depreciation . . . or to capital of the company."[102]

When depreciation accounting is used in computing operating costs and either observed depreciation or no depreciation in determining the rate base, the company gains at the expense of consumers, and the whole concept of accrued depreciation becomes void of meaning. The first would increase revenues by increasing allowable operating costs. The second would also increase revenues by decreasing the deduction from the property value and, in addition, would force consumers to pay a rate of return on an investment already charged to operating costs. The two positions are inconsistent, as recognized by the New York commission in 1932:

> It is obvious that it is to the advantage of a company in a rate case to make the accrued depreciation as low as possible (and thereby make the value as high as possible) and the annual charge for depreciation as high as possible, as each works to justify high rates. On the other hand, it is equally obvious that the consumer would be benefited, at least momentarily, by the establishment of a high accrued depreciation and a low annual charge, because each would work to produce low rates.
>
> Neither is correct; each is fallacious. The former produces an excessive value for the property, because it does not recognize all of the factors affecting value nor all of the factors which are made so prominent in determining the annual allowance for depreciation to be included in operating expenses. It is grossly unfair and most inconsistent to claim or maintain, for example, that an item of property will have a life of one hundred years when determining its value and then to increase operating expenses by including 2 or 3 per cent, which rates would in fifty or thirty-three years, respectively, amortize, without accumulated interest, the entire cost of the property. If a thing is to have a life in service of one hundred years, operating expenses

---

[100] H. E. Riggs, "The Two Radically Different Concepts of Utility Depreciation," 9 *Public Utilities Fortnightly* 559, 560 (1932). Observed depreciation, also known as deferred maintenance, is closely related to retirement accounting.

[101] *McCardle* v. *Indianapolis Water Co., op. cit.,* p. 416.

[102] *Board of Public Utility Commrs.* v. *New York Tel. Co.,* 271 U.S. 23, 31–32 (1926).

should be charged on the basis of one hundred years' life, and value likewise would be determined on this basis. . . .[103]

The Supreme Court has never explicitly accepted the depreciation reserve as the proper measure of accrued depreciation. In the Hope case, however, the Federal Power Commission rejected a percent condition deduction for accrued depreciation.

> The fallacy of the "per cent condition" theory of accrued depreciation is plain here. To illustrate, under the hypothesis of the company's witness, . . . the property would be found to have depreciated only 25 per cent throughout its life . . . , and then suffer a precipitous loss in the brief final stage of service. Such a theory is opposed by reason and facts.[104]

The Court did not comment on this position, but as it declared itself to be concerned only with the end result, it would seem that the commissions are now free to adopt their own methods of determining the depreciation deduction.

Accrued Depreciation and Original Cost Valuations

The majority of commissions deduct the depreciation reserve as shown on the company's books when an original cost rate base valuation is used.[105] As noted at length above, this position is economically sound. But under certain conditions, commissions deduct what is called the "reserve requirement." The reserve requirement is simply a commission's estimate of what a company's depreciation reserve should be. Compared with this hypothetical reserve, a company may have either an excessive or, more commonly, a deficient depreciation reserve. Excessive reserves occur when a company makes conservative estimates of service life and obsolescence by fixing high annual rates of depreciation or when a commission prescribes conservative rates.[106] Deficient reserves result from low annual depreciation rates, the use of retirement accounting prior to effective commission control, the inability to recover from

---

[103] *Re Yankers R.R. Co.,* PUR 1933D 61 (N.Y., 1932). Moreover, "engineers took some very substantial liberties with what we would now consider to be the realities. Many were the instances of 50 to 75-year old office buildings considered in 98 percent condition. Over-all condition of total utility property was seldom conceded to be less than 90 percent." Besse, *op. cit.,* p. 2. In one case, for example, a company's depreciation reserve totaled approximately $48 million, but it claimed only $15.8 million as observed depreciation. *Lindheimer v. Illinois Bell Tel. Co., op. cit.*

[104] *Cities of Cleveland and Akron v. Hope Natural Gas Co.,* 44 PUR (NS) 1, 17 (1942).

[105] Federal Power Commission, "Federal and State Commission Jurisdiction and Regulation, Electric, Gas, and Telephone Utilities, 1967," *op. cit.,* pp. 11–12.

[106] In the Hope case, to illustrate, the commission found the company had an excessive reserve and deducted a reserve requirement of approximately $22 million, nearly $18 million less than the actual reserve of $40 million. *Cities of Cleveland & Akron v. Hope Natural Gas Co., op. cit.*

earnings the depreciation which has already occurred, and unexpected technological obsolescence.

When a commission uses the reserve requirement for rate-making purposes, care must be exercised. If, for example, a company has a deficient depreciation reserve and a higher reserve requirement is deducted from the property valuation, the financial condition of the company can be seriously affected. Especially is this true when original cost valuations are used in determining property values. For this reason, many commissions refuse to adjust the depreciation reserve unless a company ignores depreciation expenses so that dividends can be higher. But commission procedure is far from uniform.[107] In large part, this is because some commissions do not have legislative power to approve or disapprove rates of depreciation for accounting purposes, while others possessing the power have not exercised it.

There are exceptions to the general rule that the depreciation reserve should be deducted from the property value. Thus, when a company fails to earn a fair rate of return, its customers are not providing all the depreciation accruals. Only the reserves provided by customers should be deducted.[108] Moreover, commissions must consider a firm's earnings. As Troxel has put it:

> If the depreciation reserve increases more than the investments in plant additions and plant replacements and if the rate of return does not change, the return on a fixed property valuation obviously decreases. Additions to the recovered depreciation exceed additional investments in the plan. A firm can use the extra funds to retire bonds and notes, or to make investments in government and private securities. But the liquidation of outstanding debts is not always easy to arrange. And when a company invests in government or corporate bonds, it obtains a 2 to 4 per cent rather than a 5 to 7 per cent return in public utility operations. Considering the earnings effects of depreciation-reserve deductions, a commission must not reduce the reasonable return just because the net property value of a firm decreases. If the company needs the recovered depreciation funds for future reinvestments, the regulators should not reduce the earnings that are available for dividend payments. The important fact is a reasonable return and the need for reinvestment funds, not the accounting procedure of property valuation. Unless the commissions remember the paramount importance of reasonable

---

[107] See Troxel, *op. cit.,* pp. 348–51; and "Accrued Depreciation Not Measured by Accounting Computations," 66 *Public Utilities Fortnightly* 60 (1960).

[108] Bonbright (*op. cit.,* pp. 211–12), however, argues that the full reserve should be deducted even if it is not earned. "This conclusion is in harmony with the general principle, applied alike under a fair-value rule and under an actual-cost rule, that past deficiencies in corporate revenues do not give rise to valid claims for offsetting recoveries in later years. In refusing to grant such recoveries, rate regulation should and does recognize the resulting necessity of giving to companies the somewhat risky opportunity to enjoy higher rates of return than might otherwise be required in order to attract capital. But any resulting higher 'costs of capital' are well worth paying for as a means of avoiding the evils of capitalized deficits." *Ibid.,* p. 212.

earnings as they deduct depreciation reserves, they can drive investors away from public utility enterprises.[109]

Accrued Depreciation and Fair Value

In fair value jurisdictions, the proper measure of accrued depreciation is subject to wide differences of opinion. Frequently, the deduction for depreciation is based on the "field method" or "office method." The field method involves a physical inspection of representative samples of the various types of the company's property "in order to ascertain outward manifestation of depreciation."[110] The office method involves "an age-life study of the property existing in the various plant accounts, i.e., a study of the relationship of the age of the property as determined from book records to the expected life of such property."[111] The two methods may be used together, with each given a specific weight so as to determine a composite percentage of depreciation. As the Ohio commission explained in a 1962 case:

> The commission's engineering staff, on the basis of their own studies, estimated that the depreciation to be deducted from the reproduction cost new as of the date certain was 8.4 per cent. Their estimate was based upon both a field study and an actuarial or office study. The field study consisted of an actual inspection of all of the company's larger installations, as well as an actual inspection of samples of those types of property that are commonly designated as the "mass accounts." The latter include poles, pole lines, aerial wire, etc. The results of the field inspections were converted into percentages by accounts and an average percentage of depreciation was determined for each property account.
>
> The staff's office study consisted of age-life analyses by property accounts. The average service life and the average expired life was estimated for the property in each account. The ratios of expired life to average service life were then applied to depreciation curves. Each of these curves is derived from property mortality data and represents the loci of points each of which shows the percentage of depreciation associated with a given percentage of expired life. Thus, once the type of curve appropriate to the particular account is selected and the ratio of expired life to average service life is determined for the property in the account, the percentage of depreciation is simply the point on the vertical axis corresponding to the point on the curve given by the ratio of expired life to average service life. In this way a percentage of depreciation was estimated for each property account. The results of the office study and the field study were then averaged by accounts to arrive at the staff's final estimate of depreciation.[112]

[109] Troxel, *op. cit.,* pp. 346–47.
[110] *Ohio Edison Co.* v. *City of Mansfield,* 41 PUR 3d 452, 456 (Ohio, 1961).
[111] *Ibid.,* p. 457. See "Accrued Depreciation Not Measured by Accounting Computations," *op. cit.*
[112] *Re Citizens Teleph. Co.,* 43 PUR 3d 471, 474 (Ohio, 1962).

Bonbright has argued that it is difficult to reconcile commission treatment of depreciation "with any basic 'theory' of reasonable public utility rates."[113] When fair value is used, he suggests:

> If this value [fair value] were to be derived from a record of actual construction cost, the allowance for "depreciation" should reflect any fall in value, not otherwise recognized, that may have taken place since the date of the construction. If, as is more plausible for older properties, the value were to be deducted from an estimate of current replacement cost—and the relevant replacement cost, despite some judicial opinions to the contrary, is the cost of a modern substitute plant—the deduction for "depreciation" should summarize the value inferiority of the existing property, including the inferiority due to liability to earlier retirement. This deduction, moreover, should be subject to a partial offset for any superior quality of the present plant over the hypothetical modern substitute—a superiority often claimed in the early railroad valuations, in the form of allowances for roadbed solidification.[114]

But it is difficult to explain the logic of deducting observed depreciation, however measured, from a reproduction cost or fair value rate base determined by general price indices. Such a property valuation, as noted earlier, represents a purely imaginary figure.

OTHER ELEMENTS OF VALUE

While the determination of the depreciated value of the tangible and reproducible property has occupied most of the courts', commissions', and companies' time, several other elements of value also have received attention— land and rights, "overhead" construction costs, working capital allowances, and intangibles. Each will be briefly discussed below.

Valuation of Land

Except for natural gas and railroad companies, the valuation of land is of little importance in rate-making cases. Unlike most other items in the rate base, land represents a small portion of total property, it has no cost of production, and it tends to appreciate in value. Generally, commissions value land on an original cost basis, although an estimate of its current value is used when fair value property valuations are made.[115]

---

113 Bonbright, *op. cit.,* p. 193, n. 2.
114 *Ibid.,* p. 195.
115 Welch has argued that all land should be valued at its present value regardless of the measure used for other property items. "Assume that a utility enterprise, whether by foresight or good luck, is located on land which is rapidly increasing in real estate market value. Keeping that increased value out of the rate base penalizes or handicaps the utility in comparison with other enterprises. It tends to undermine incentive for advance progressive planning. The utility's earnings are to that extent kept below the earnings of the others." Welch, *op. cit.*, p. 359.

In the case of the railroads, much of the land was acquired as a gift or at low prices. Nevertheless, for many years, the railroads based their estimates of land values on multiples of adjacent land values. The use of multipliers was defended on the theory that if they were required to purchase this land at the time of the rate case, they would probably have to pay more than the market value. In a 1913 case, however, the Supreme Court condemned these practices, arguing that "it is impossible to assume, in making a judicial finding of what it would cost to acquire the property, that the company would be compelled to pay more than its fair market value."[116] The Court held that the present fair value of land should be determined on the basis of the market value of adjacent land. The Interstate Commerce Commission has approved of this method ever since. Consequently, railroads receive "the benefit of the unearned increment resulting from increasing land values, a not inconsiderable item when the lands in large city terminals and the rights of way into the city are valued on this basis."[117]

The Supreme Court approved the Federal Power Commission's procedure of valuing natural gas land on an original cost basis in 1934.[118] Troxel has argued that this is the proper measure:

> The market price of gas land is not altogether independent of utility service prices: utility consumers buy most of the gas of Appalachian fields, and they buy much of the natural gas output in other areas. If circular reasoning is avoided, a property value cannot be based on the prices that are subject to public control. Another consideration goes against a return on the market price of natural gas land. Gas companies obtain revenue from consumers that is used to cover the gas exploration costs. Since buyers pay some or all the costs of gas discoveries, they should not pay a return, too, on increases in land prices.[119]

But beginning in 1954, the commission has permitted, in effect, the present value standard, thereby also allowing investors an annual return on an unearned increment.[120]

"Overhead" Construction Costs

Certain expenses, commonly called "overhead" construction costs, incurred by a company cannot be easily identified with the value of any specific property items. These expenses include costs of incorporation; legal, engineering, and administrative services; and interest, insurance, and taxes during construction. Unless they have been charged to operating costs, an allowance for overhead construction costs has usually been included in the rate base. Prior to

---

[116] *Minnesota Rate Cases, op. cit.,* p. 451.
[117] Locklin, *op. cit.,* p. 372.
[118] *Dayton Power & Light Co.* v. *Public Utilities Comm. of Ohio, op. cit.*
[119] Troxel, *op. cit.,* p. 281.
[120] See Chapter 16, pp. 607–15.

the development of uniform systems of accounts, 15 percent of the total value of the property was the frequent allowance, although several commissions have never accepted any percentages without supporting figures showing actual cost. With the development of uniform systems, however, the companies are expected to enter all costs incurred during construction.[121]

One overhead item—interest—requires brief explanation. A few commissions permit regulated companies to include plant under construction in the rate base and, thereby, to earn a full rate of return on funds used for construction purposes.[122] The majority, however, follow the practice of withholding from the rate base plant under construction until the plant is put into operation—that is, until it has become "used and useful" property.[123] When this procedure is employed, an expanding company is not earning a return on its capital during the construction period. To provide an incentive for expansion and an adequate compensation for a company's advance commitment of capital, regulated companies generally capitalize interest during construction. As explained by Rydell:

> Capitalization of interest is merely an accounting process whereby the construction work in progress account is charged with actual or imputed interest for the use of funds. Actual interest is the interest paid or accrued on the use of borrowed funds, and imputed interest is an amount calculated by applying an arbitrary interest rate to equity funds used for construction purposes.[124]

---

[121] Typical is the following 15 percent claimed allowance (*Re Alton Water Co.,* 35 PUR 3d 284 [Ill., 1960]):

1. Organization expense	1.00%
2. Engineering and supervision during design and construction	5.00%
3. Administrative and legal costs	2.00%
4. Omissions and contingencies	2.00%
5. Interest lost on nonproductive investment during construction	4.95%
Total claimed	14.95%

[122] See *Re American Teleph. & Teleg. Co.,* 71 PUR 3d 273, 288 (FCC, 1967). In the airline industry, the CAB permits equipment purchase deposits to be included in the airlines net investment rate base. See *General Passenger Fare Investigation*, E-16068, pp. 38–41 (CAB, 1960).

[123] There are certain exceptions, such as the inclusion of plant that is about to be put into service.

[124] Ferd Rydell, "Interest during Construction," Part I, 79 *Public Utilities Fortnightly* 39 (May 11, 1967). (For Part II, see 79 *ibid.* 22 [May 25, 1967].) Most utilities capitalize interest during construction at a composite rate of 6 percent; a rate "which gives effect to the cost of borrowed funds and the cost of equity funds devoted to construction." Arthur Andersen & Co., *Principles Underlying the Capitalization of Interest during Construction* (New York, 1953), p. 16.

The capitalized interest is added to the investment in plant under construction, and this total included in the book cost of such plant when it goes into service.[125]

An alternative to these two procedures, and one used by some commissions, is to allow a higher rate of return to cover interest during construction. The difficulty of such a method is that it imposes

> . . . upon those persons who must calculate the proper percentage rate the obligation of attempting to do indirectly, and without benefit of adequate accounting data, what the overt allowances for interest during construction do directly and systematically. Anyone who has faced the difficult problem of establishing a fair rate of return or of estimating "cost of capital" can hardly welcome a change in the rules of rate-base determination that would needlessly add to his difficulties.[126]

Working Capital Allowances

The question of working capital must be considered in every rate case, and several important problems are raised in determining a suitable allowance. Working capital—the funds representing necessary investment in materials and supplies, and the cash required to meet current obligations and to maintain minimum bank balances—is included in the rate base so that investors are compensated for capital they have supplied to a company. The amount required largely depends on a company's purchasing and billing methods, as well as its construction program. When purchases are made on credit, when deposits or payments are required in advance, when accruals are made for the payment of taxes in advance of payment dates, or when customers pay for the service at the time it is used, working capital requirements may be small. When materials and supplies must be purchased long before use, when customers are billed monthly, quarterly, semiannually, or even annually, or when the business is seasonal, such requirements may be large.

The most frequently used method of determining the necessary working capital allowance is to (*a*) estimate the operating expenses requiring cash outlays during the period between production and customer payments and (*b*) subtract customers' deposits and tax accruals.[127] To illustrate the procedure: The Indiana commission determined that the annual operating expenses, exclusive of taxes

---

[125] See, for example, *Re Nevada Power Co.,* 43 PUR 3d 511 (Nev., 1962); *Re General Teleph. Co. of Missouri*, 43 PUR 3d 366 (Mo., 1962); *Re Chesapeake & Potomac Teleph. Co.*, 57 PUR 3d 1 (D.C., 1964); and *Re Southern Bell Teleph. & Teleg. Co.*, 66 PUR 3d 364 (Fla., 1966).

[126] Bonbright, *op. cit.*, p. 180, n. 8.

[127] See "Tax Offsets against Working Capital," 79 *Public Utilities Fortnightly* 59 (March 16, 1967). In some cases working capital allowances have been ascertained by subtracting current liabilities from current assets. This measure is discussed and rejected in *Re Peoples Gas Light & Coke Co.*, *op. cit.*

and depreciation, of the General Indiana Gas Company were $10,297,575 and estimated an average time lag of forty-five days before receipt of revenue from service supplied to customers. The allowable working capital was then computed as follows:

Expenses for 45 days	$1,441,632.00
Less deferred federal income tax	192,021.00
	$1,249,611.00
Less customers' deposits	741,099.00
Working capital allowance	$ 508,512.00[128]

Valuation of Intangibles

It will be recalled that the Supreme Court, in the Smyth case, listed six specific measures of value and then added: "We do not say that there may not be other matters to be regarded in estimating the value of the property."[129] Almost immediately, the regulated companies claimed allowances for several intangibles, the most important being good will, franchise value, water rights, leaseholds, and going concern value. These items should properly be included in the rate base, they argued, because the value of a company is more than just the value of its physical property. While the commissions and courts have often supported this contention and have made allowances for these items in the past, few are currently included in rate bases.

Good Will. Good will has been defined by the Supreme Court as "that element of value which inheres in the fixed and favorable consideration of customers, arising from an established and well-known and well-conducted business."[130] It is, in short, the value of customer loyalty and is recognized as an element in the market value of competitive firms.

When consumers have no alternative sources of supply, however, as is the case with many of the regulated industries, no special value can be attached to the company-customer relationship. As early as 1909, in the Consolidated Gas case, the Court recognized this point: "The complainant has a monopoly in fact, and a consumer must take gas from it or go without. He will resort to the 'old stand' because he cannot get gas anywhere else." [131] To include good will in the rate base would involve circular reasoning: its value depends on a company's earnings which, in turn, depend on the rates established by the commission. Its

---

[128] *Re Central Indiana Gas Co.,* 37 PUR 3d 138 (Ind., 1960). Also see *Re Southern New England Teleph. Co.,* 42 PUR 3d 310 (Conn., 1962); *Re Rochester Gas & E. Corp.,* 43 PUR 3d 210 (N.Y., 1962); and *Re Ayersville Teleph. Co.,* 66 PUR 3d 475 (Ohio, 1966). Because of the procedure of using customers' deposits and tax accruals to offset cash requirements, it is possible to have a *negative* working capital allowance. In such cases, some commissions have deducted this amount from the rate base. See *Re Pacific Teleph. & Teleg. Co.,* 53 PUR 3d 513 (Cal., 1964); and *Re Southern Bell Teleph. & Teleg. Co.,* 66 PUR 3d 1 (Fla., 1966). Also see *Re American Teleph. & Teleg. Co.,* 70 PUR 3d 129 (FCC, 1967).

[129] *Smyth* v. *Ames, op. cit.,* p. 547.

[130] *Des Moines Gas Co.* v. *Des Moines,* 238 U.S. 153, 165 (1915).

[131] *Willcox* v. *Consolidated Gas Co., op. cit.,* p. 52.

inclusion, therefore, would permit the capitalization of expected future earnings. Good will has not been accepted for purposes of rate making.[132]

Franchise Value. A regulated company must receive a franchise (or a certificate of convenience and necessity) before it may serve a market area. As only one company usually is authorized to serve a given market (exceptions are found in the transportation industry), it represents a monopoly grant. If the company is then permitted to earn an excessive return, the franchise will become valuable. "To measure a separate franchise value, the company estimates the future earnings above a reasonable return on the tangible property value, and discounts these excess earnings at the probable fair rate of return. A franchise valuation is a capitalization of the earnings that regulators should take away from a utility firm."[133]

Inclusion of a franchise value in the rate base, therefore, would require consumers to pay a permanent return on a monopoly privilege which they granted. Moreover, it would prevent justifiable rate reductions to consumers. Only in the few cases when a city has made a charge for a franchise does the sum so invested belong in the rate base. The Court has supported this position since 1912.[134]

Water Rights. Electric, irrigation, and water companies possess water rights to use and dispose of flowing water. Some of these rights are acquired when a company purchases a piece of land—streams and rivers flowing through the land and subsurface water recovered by sinking wells. Other rights are given by local, state, and federal governments. Especially important are the rights granted by the Federal Power Commission which controls the power sites on navigable streams and federal government land. Like franchises, however, these rights have no special value for regulatory purposes; the value of the rights is determined by the expected future earnings of a company.

Only a few cases involving water rights have come before the Supreme Court. In 1914 and again in 1923, water rights valuations were granted.[135] Three years later, in the McCardle case, the Court said that "the evidence sustains an amount in excess of ten per cent to cover water rights and going value. . . ."[136] But in the Indianapolis Water Company case when the company claimed its water rights had a value of at least $1 million, Justice Black, in his dissenting opinion, could not believe

[132] *Omaha v. Omaha Water Co.*, 218 U.S. 180 (1910); *Des Moines Gas Co. v. Des Moines, op. cit.; Los Angeles Gas & Elec. Co. v. Railroad Comm. of Calif., op. cit.*

[133] Troxel, *op. cit.*, p. 310.

[134] *Cedar Rapids Gas Light Co. v. Cedar Rapids,* 223 U.S. 655 (1912); *Galveston Elec. Co. v. Galveston, op. cit.; Georgia Ry. & Power Co. v. Railroad Comm., op. cit.* A franchise value was permitted in an earlier case because the state of New York had approved a franchise valuation in 1884 and had permitted the company to issue securities on the basis of this valuation. *Willcox v. Consolidated Gas Co., op. cit.*

[135] *San Joaquin & Kings River Co. v. County of Stanislaus,* 233 U.S. 454 (1914); *Bluefield Water Works & Improvement Co. v. Public Service Comm. of West Virginia, op. cit.*

[136] *McCardle v. Indianapolis Water Co., op. cit.*, p. 421.

... that, even if the people of Indianapolis and the surrounding community have permitted the Water Company to use this stream for a public service, there has been a grant of a prescriptive property right which can be capitalized by the Company, in order to exact higher water rates from the very people who granted the privilege.[137]

No Supreme Court decision since that time has dealt with the issue of water rights. However, the cost of acquiring water rights, as well as waterpower sites, is usually included in the rate base.[138]

Leaseholds. A common practice of gas companies is to lease, rather than purchase, the land from which they hope to obtain natural gas. The leases are usually bought and paid for, and their cost included in the rate base. If gas is discovered, the market value of a leasehold will tend to rise. Should the increased value also be included in the rate base?

For many years, a few commissions thought so, allowing some or all the increases in the market value of leases. While affording an incentive to exploration, this practice also granted the companies an unearned increment on which to base an annual return. Moreover, as pointed out above, consumers pay for the costs of developing natural gas land. The present practice, and one followed by the Federal Power Commission in determining pipeline rates, is to value leaseholds at their original cost. While the Supreme Court has not always agreed, it approved the commission's measure of value in 1945.[139]

Going Concern Value. Going concern value can be defined as "the difference in value existing between a plant in successful operation and a similar plant assembled but not yet functioning."[140] But no cost measure of this value has ever been devised, making it "purely hypothetical" and the "most intangible of all the intangibles."[141]

Going value has sometimes been thought of in terms of development costs: establishing an organization, recruiting and training personnel, developing administrative procedures, acquiring a market, and soliciting business. It has also been thought of as compensating a firm for the accumulated deficits it may have sustained in the earlier years of its development. Both concepts have been rejected by the Supreme Court.[142] Development costs have already been charged to operating costs; the losses of previous years cannot be compensated unless excess profits can also be recovered, and in any event, past deficits should not be capitalized. There seems to be no cost basis for going concern value.[143]

137 Dissenting opinion in *McCart* v. *Indianapolis Water Co., op. cit.,* p. 433.

138 See *Central Maine Power Co.* v. *Maine Public Utilities Comm.,* 36 PUR 3d 19 (1960).

139 *Colorado-Interstate Gas Co.* v. *Federal Power Comm.,* 324 U.S. 581 (1945); *Panhandle Eastern Pipe Line Co.* v. *Federal Power Comm.,* 324 U.S. 635 (1945).

140 M. C. Waltersdorf, "Going Value in Utility Valuation," 17 *American Economic Review* 26 (1927).

141 Wilcox, *op. cit.,* p. 324.

142 *Galveston Elec. Co.* v. *Galveston, op. cit.*

143 Several other cost measures of going value have been presented in rate cases,

Until 1933, however, going concern value was recognized by the commissions and courts, and a separate allowance was usually included in the rate base. In the Knoxville Water Company case in 1909, the Supreme Court said there was an "added value of the plant as a whole over the sum of the values of its component parts, which is attached to it because it is in active and successful operation and earning a return."[144] In the Des Moines case in 1915, the Court thought the "element of value in an assembled and established plant, doing business and earning money, over one not thus advanced" was "self-evident."[145] Eleven years later, in the McCardle decision, Justice Butler said the "evidence is more than sufficient to sustain 9.5 per cent for going value."[146] As the Court neither required a separate going concern allowance nor said how such values were to be measured, most commissions simply added a flat 10 percent to the value of tangible property in determining the rate base.

The Court reversed its position in 1933. In the Los Angeles Gas case, decided in that year, the Court upheld the California commission's rejection of an allowance of $9 million claimed by the company as going value, observing that "an examination of the evidence offered by the Company . . . shows it to be of a highly speculative and uncertain character."[147] A year later it rejected a similar claim: "Going value is not something to be read into every balance sheet as a perfunctory addition. . . . We cannot in fairness say that after valuing the assets upon the basis of a plant in successful operation, there was left an element of going value to be added to the total."[148] And in the Natural Gas Pipeline case, the Court could not find a basis for a separate going concern value.[149]

Although they may still be influenced by the concept when they determine the value of tangible property, few commissions now add a separate allowance for value as a going concern in rate-making cases.[150] As Troxel has observed, this is as it should be: "The going-concern value depends on a franchise or certificate; it is, in fact, another name for a franchise or certificate value. It is a social value, and belongs to the public instead of the public utility company."[151]

---

including a dollar value for each customer or meter, a percentage of the company's gross revenue for a year or more, and the estimated reproduction cost of developing the business. See two articles by Ben W. Lewis, "Going Value and Rate Regulation," 26 *Michigan Law Review* 720 (1928) and "Going Value," 6 *Public Utilities Fortnightly* 77 (1930).

[144] *Knoxville* v. *Knoxville Water Co., op. cit.,* p. 9. No separate allowance was permitted in *Cedar Rapids Gas Light Co.* v. *Cedar Rapids, op. cit.*

[145] *Des Moines Gas Co.* v. *Des Moines, op. cit.,* p. 165.

[146] *McCardle* v. *Indianapolis Water Co., op. cit.,* p. 415.

[147] *Los Angeles Gas & Elec. Co.* v. *Railroad Comm. of Calif., op. cit.,* p. 317.

[148] *Dayton Power & Light Co.* v. *Public Utilities Comm. of Ohio, op. cit.,* p. 309.

[149] *Federal Power Comm.* v. *Natural Gas Pipeline Co., op. cit.*

[150] But see *Re Kansas City Power & Light Co.,* 43 PUR 3d 433 (Mo., 1962). When valuation is being undertaken for the purpose of a sale, going concern value generally is included.

[151] Troxel, *op. cit.,* p. 327.

THE RATE BASE: CONFUSION AND OPERATIONALISM

In 1898, the Supreme Court declared that rates must be calculated to yield a fair return on the "fair value" of utility property,[152] and thereby started a continuing debate over the meaning and measurement of value. Even the Court's 1944 Hope Natural Gas decision, which "removed fair value, and indeed valuation, as a constitutional requirement,"[153] failed to terminate the long-standing controversy. On economic grounds, it is difficult, if not impossible, to defend any measure of value except original cost. Yet, the controversy continues to plague regulation.

Part of the confusion can be traced to statutory provisions—provisions which "do not include the essentials of an operational concept."[154] In a careful analysis of state statutory enactments, Rose found wide diversity in the definition of "value" and in the association of value with rates. He concluded:

> It is obvious that the instruction that is the essence of "fair value"—to give the matters for consideration (principally original cost and reproduction cost) such weight as may be just and right—is not operational. It offers no criterion or rule to determine what is "just and right" and, therefore, does not provide a method to ascertain a uniquely determinate value of the weight to be assigned to each of the "matters for consideration" in a finding of fair value. In practice, the weights attributed to original cost and reproduction cost in the application of the fair value concept are the results of a purely subjective and arbitrary process, which is characterized euphemistically as the "judgment" of the regulatory authorities. The weights vary from jurisdiction to jurisdiction and from case to case within the same jurisdiction. The fact is that fair value is an indeterminate magnitude lying anywhere between original cost and reproduction cost.[155]

Part of the confusion can also be traced to the conflicting nature of the objections to an original cost rate base. As Bonbright has explained:

> A close reading of the literature written in recent years in support of the fair value rule revealed two greatly different asserted objections to an actual cost rate base. According to one objection, which is in line with the older legal tradition of property rights, investors are entitled to a reasonable return on the value of their property and not on its cost, not even on its replacement cost except to the extent to which this latter cost may happen to serve as a measure or clue to the real value of the property. But according to the other

---

[152] *Smyth* v. *Ames, op. cit.*

[153] Rose, "Confusion in Valuation . . . ," *op. cit.*, p. 2. Declared the Court: "Rates which enable the company to operate successfully, to maintain its financial integrity to attract capital, and to compensate its investors for the risks assumed certainly cannot be condemned as invalid, even though they might produce only a meager return on the so-called 'fair value' rate base." *Federal Power Comm.* v. *Hope Natural Gas Co., op. cit.*, p. 605.

[154] Rose, "Confusion in Valuation . . . ," *op. cit.*, p. 23.

[155] *Ibid.*

objection, which now is receiving much greater emphasis in this post-war period of price inflation, what makes the original cost standard of rate making so deficient in the opinion of those who object to it is not any failure to reflect value rather than cost, but rather its failure to reflect original cost itself when restated in terms of current dollars.

Now, both of these objections to an orthodox original cost or actual cost standard of rate making have some plausibility on the grounds of fairness or of economic analysis; and it would therefore be very nice if both of them could be avoided at one and the same time by the adoption of a fair value rule of rate making. But, unhappily, they cannot both be avoided in this manner—for that matter, in any other manner. By this I mean that a rate base if designed to protect stockholders against the impairment of their capital investment or their real income in terms of purchasing power could be very different from a rate base designed to reflect the actual current values of the current assets as determined by a skillful, hard-boiled appraiser who takes full account of the ravages of obsolescence.[156]

To these two factors must be added a third: uncertainty over the meaning and measurement of a "fair rate of return." Historically, as will be discussed in the next chapter, the commissions have given far more attention to the determination of the rate base than they have to establishing the rate of return. Indeed, the rate of return has often been based upon a "traditional" or "conventional" percentage figure. Given this situation, in addition to the steady postwar inflationary trend in the economy, the regulated companies have been forced to emphasize fair value in rate cases to obtain what they consider to be adequate earnings. Nor can they be criticized for this emphasis, for even though they are subject to a regulatory constraint, regulated companies—like nonregulated firms—seek maximum profits. Thus, when statutory enactments provide for a "fair value" rate base, the regulated companies would be remiss if they failed to present such data. Regulation involves more than economic concepts. Nevertheless, the fact remains that the determination of the rate base is a source of uncertainty and results in confusion. The gap between theory and practice is often wide.

[156] James C. Bonbright, "The Ill-Defined Meaning of a Fair Value Rate Base" (speech before the Iowa State Conference on Public Utility Valuation and the Rate Making Process, May 7–8, 1962) (mimeographed), pp. 49–50.

Chapter 9

THE RATE OF RETURN

From the investor or company point of view it is important that there be enough revenue not only for operating expenses but also for the capital costs of the business. These include service on the debt and dividend on the stock . . . . By that standard the return to the equity owner should be commensurate with returns on investments in other enterprises having corresponding risks. That return, moreover, should be sufficient to assure confidence in the financial integrity of the enterprise, so as to maintain its credit and attract capital.
— *Justice Douglas**

While the property valuation problem has received too much emphasis, determination of the rate of return has received too little. In recent years, however, the combined effects of the Hope decision and of inflation have been to shift regulatory attention from the rate base to the rate of return. At a minimum, a regulated company must be afforded the opportunity not only of assuring its financial integrity so that it can maintain its credit standing and attract additional capital as needed, but also for earnings comparable to those of other companies having corresponding risks. The rate of return also has an incentive function, indicating that an efficient company may be permitted to earn more than the minimum. But in determining a rate, a commission may not set it so high as to exploit consumers. The concept of a fair rate of return, therefore, represents a range or a zone of reasonableness. And its quantitative importance is evident: given the rate base, earnings are one-third higher under an 8 percent return than under a 6 percent rate.

For regulatory purposes, the rate of return is the amount of money earned by a regulated company, over and above operating costs, expressed as a percentage of the rate base. In other words, the rate of return includes interest on long-term debt, dividends on preferred stock, and earnings on common stock and surplus. As Garfield and Lovejoy have put it, "the return is that money earned from operations which is available for distribution among the various classes of contributors of money capital. In the case of common stockholders,

*Justice Douglas, *Federal Power Comm.* v. *Hope Natural Gas Co.,* 320 U.S. 591, 603 (1944).

part of their share may be retained as surplus."[1] The important point to note is that the rate of return includes both profit (in the traditional sense) and interest on debt capital.

The problems associated with determination of the rate of return are considered in this chapter. The leading judicial concepts and commission decisions are discussed in the first two sections. The remainder of the chapter is devoted to an examination of the cost of capital and comparable earnings standards as methods of establishing a fair rate of return.[2]

JUDICIAL CONCEPTS

The judicial concepts of a fair rate of return are few and far between. In some cases, the Supreme Court has enumerated a number of factors that should be considered. In general, however, the Court has limited its discussions on this matter to the question of confiscation. At the same time, the Court has made it clear that a fair rate of return may be higher than a rate which avoids confiscation, that no single rate of return is always fair, and that regulated companies are not guaranteed a fair return.

The Court's Standards of "Fair"

The valuation problem was considered at length in the case of *Smyth* v. *Ames* in 1898, but no attempt was made to define a fair return until 1909. Then, in the Consolidated Gas case of that year, the Supreme Court said:

> There is no particular rate of compensation which must in all cases and in all parts of the country be regarded as sufficient for capital invested in business enterprise. Such compensation must depend greatly upon circumstances and locality; among other things, the amount of risk in the business is a most important factor, as well as the locality where the business is conducted and the rate expected and usually realized there upon investments of a somewhat similar nature with regard to the risk attending them. There may be other matters which in some cases might also be properly taken into account in determining the rate which an investor might properly expect or hope to receive and which he would be entitled to without legislative interference. The less risk, the less right to any unusual returns upon the investments. One who invests his money in a business of a somewhat hazardous character is very properly held to have the right to a larger return without legislative interference, than can be obtained from an investment in Government bonds or other perfectly safe security. . . .[3]

[1] Paul J. Garfield and Wallace F. Lovejoy, *Public Utility Economics* (Englewood Cliffs: Prentice-Hall, Inc., 1964), p. 116.

[2] For an exhaustive analysis of these problems, see Ellsworth Nichols, *Ruling Principles of Utility Regulation: Rate of Return* (Washington, D.C.: Public Utilities Reports, Inc., 1955); and Ellsworth Nichols and Francis X. Welch, *Ruling Principles of Utility Regulation: Rate of Return—Supplement A* (Washington, D.C.: Public Utilities Reports, Inc., 1964).

[3] *Willcox* v. *Consolidated Gas Co.*, 212 U.S. 19, 48–49 (1909).

According to the Court, therefore, a fair rate of return involved two elements—a return on invested capital and a return for risk. In this case, a 6 percent rate of return was held to be nonconfiscatory.

In the Bluefield case of 1923, the Court extended and elaborated on these principles, and in so doing, presented a lengthy list of factors for determining a fair rate of return. The Court argued:

> What annual rate will constitute just compensation depends upon many circumstances and must be determined by the exercise of a fair and enlightened judgment, having regard to all relevant facts. A public utility is entitled to such rates as will permit it to earn a return on the value of the property which it employs for the convenience of the public equal to that generally being made at the same time and in the same general part of the country on investments in other business undertakings which are attended by corresponding risks and uncertainties; but it has no constitutional right to profits such as are realized or anticipated in highly profitable enterprises or speculative ventures. The return should be reasonably sufficient to assure confidence in the financial soundness of the utility and should be adequate, under efficient and economical management, to maintain and support its credit and enable it to raise the money necessary for the proper discharge of its public duties. A rate of return may be reasonable at one time, and become too high or too low by changes affecting opportunities for investment, the money market and business conditions generally.[4]

As in *Smyth* v. *Ames,* the Court lists a number of factors for consideration, including (1) comparisons with other companies having corresponding risks, (2) the attraction of capital, (3) current financial and economic conditions, (4) the cost of capital, (5) the risks of the enterprise, (6) the financial policy and capital structure of the firm, (7) the competence of management, and (8) the company's financial history. The Court did not define these factors, nor did it indicate the relative weight that should be assigned to each. Rather, the commissions are to consider "all relevant facts" and to exercise an "enlightened judgment."

Since the Bluefield case, little has been added by Court decisions. In the McCardle case of 1926, the Court found: "The evidence is more than sufficient to sustain the rate of seven per cent found by the Commission. And recent decisions support a higher rate of return."[5] In the United Railways case of 1930, the Court decided that a 7.5 to 8 percent return was necessary under the attraction of capital standard. Said the Court:

> What is a fair return . . . cannot be settled by invoking decisions of this Court made years ago based upon conditions radically different from those

[4] *Bluefield Water Works & Imp. Co.* v. *Public Service Comm. of West Virginia,* 262 U.S. 679, 692–93 (1923). Also see *Missouri* ex rel. *Southwestern Bell Tel. Co.* v. *Public Service Comm.,* 262 U.S. 274 (1923); and *Lincoln Gas & Elec. Light* v. *City of Lincoln,* 250 U.S. 256 (1919).

[5] *McCardle* v. *Indianapolis Water Co.,* 272 U.S. 400, 419 (1926).

which prevail today. The problem is one to be tested primarily by present day conditions. Annual returns upon capital and enterprise, like wages of employees, cost of maintenance and related expenses, have materially increased the country over. . . . What will constitute a fair return in a given case is not capable of exact mathematical demonstration. . . . There is much evidence in the record to the effect that in order to induce the investment of capital in the enterprise or to enable the company to compete successfully in the market for money to finance its operations, a net return upon the valuation fixed by the commission should not be far from 8 per cent.[6]

During the depression years of the thirties, the Court recognized the decline in interest rates and in business earnings throughout the country, and was willing to accept lower rates of return. In the Dayton Power and Light case of 1934, it approved a 6.5 percent return rather than the 8 percent sought by the company.[7] A year later, the Court made no mention of a 6 percent rate of return allowed by the commission in the Chesapeake and Potomac Telephone case.[8] A 6 percent return was also upheld in the Driscoll case of 1939, in which the Court said:

> When bonds and preferred stocks of well seasoned companies can be floated at low rates, the allowance of an over all rate of return of a modest percentage will bring handsome yields to the common stock. Certainly the yields of the equity issues must be larger than that for the underlying securities. In this instance, the utility operates in a stable community, accustomed to the use of electricity and close to the capital markets, with funds readily available for secure investment. Long operation and adequate records make forecasts of net operating revenues fairly certain. Under such circumstances a six per cent return after all allowable charges cannot be confiscatory.[9]

In both natural gas cases decided in the early forties, the Court approved 6.5 percent rates of return (on original cost rate bases), pointing out that the rate of return to the equity owner should be commensurate with returns on investments in other companies having corresponding risks, as well as being

---

[6] *United Railways & Elec. Co. v. West,* 280 U.S. 234, 249, 251 (1930). Justice Sutherland also argued: "Sound business management requires that after paying all expenses of operation, setting aside the necessary sums for depreciation, payment of interest and reasonable dividends, there should still remain something to be passed to the surplus account. . . ." *Ibid.,* pp. 251–52. Justice Brandeis dissented: "A net return of 6.26 per cent upon the present value of the property of a street railway enjoying a monopoly in one of the oldest, largest and richest cities on the Atlantic Seaboard would seem to be compensatory." *Ibid.,* p. 255.

[7] *Dayton Power & Light Co. v. Public Utilities Comm. of Ohio,* 292 U.S. 290, 311 (1934).

[8] *West v. Chesapeake & Potomac Tel. Co.,* 295 U.S. 662 (1935). Justice Stone, dissenting from the decision, even suggested that a 4.5 percent rate of return would not be confiscatory, noting (among other things) that both railroads and other corporations listed on the Stock Exchange were averaging less than 4 percent on their invested capital. *Ibid.,* pp. 682–83.

[9] *Driscoll v. Edison Light & Power Co.,* 307 U.S. 104, 120 (1939).

sufficient to maintain the credit of the company and to attract capital. In the 1942 case, Chief Justice Stone argued:

> The evidence shows that profits earned by individual industrial corporations declined from 11.3% on invested capital in 1929 to 5.1% in 1938. The profits of utility corporations declined during the same period from 7.2% to 5.1%. For railroad corporations the decline was from 6.4% to 2.3%. Interest rates were at a low level on all forms of investment, and among the lowest that have ever existed. The securities of natural gas companies were sold at rates of return of from 3% to 6%, with yields on most of their bond issues between 3% and 4%. The interest on large loans ranged from 2% to 3.25%. . . . The regulated business here seems exceptionally free from hazards which might otherwise call for special consideration in determining the fair rate of return.[10]

And in the 1944 case, Justice Douglas stated:

> The rate-making process under the Act, i.e., the fixing of "just and reasonable" rates, involves a balancing of the investor and the consumer interests. . . . From the investor or company point of view it is important that there be enough revenue not only for operating expenses but also for the capital costs of the business. These include service on the debt and dividends on the stock. . . . By that standard the return to the equity owner should be commensurate with returns on investments in other enterprises having corresponding risks. That return, moreover, should be sufficient to assure confidence in the financial integrity of the enterprise, so as to maintain its credit and to attract capital. . . . The conditions under which more or less might be allowed are not important here. Nor is it important to this case to determine the various permissible ways in which any rate base on which the return is computed might be arrived at. For we are of the view that the end result in this case cannot be condemned under the Act as unjust and unreasonable from the investor or company viewpoint.[11]

The Hope decision thus represented a restatement of the rate of return principles listed by the Court in its earlier Bluefield decision.[12] These principles, moreover, remain as the judicial "guidelines" for determining a fair rate of return. "Just as jurists try to make reasonable decisions, so the members of the Supreme Court expect reasonable-return judgments from commissions."[13]

[10] *Federal Power Comm.* v. *Natural Gas Pipeline Co.*, 315 U.S. 575, 596–97 (1942).

[11] *Federal Power Comm.* v. *Hope Natural Gas Co., op. cit.,* p. 603. A year later, the Court stated: "We are unable to say . . . that the return [of 6.5 percent] is not commensurate with the risks, that confidence in petitioner's financial integrity has been impaired, or that petitioner's ability to attract capital, to maintain its credit, and to operate successfully and efficiently has been impeded." *Panhandle Eastern Pipe Line Co.* v. *Federal Power Comm.,* 324 U.S. 635, 650 (1945).

[12] However, the Bluefield statement that the allowable rate of return must be applied to the "value" of the company's property was omitted by the Court. See Chapter 8, pp. 228–31.

[13] Emery Troxel, *Economics of Public Utilities* (New York: Holt, Rinehart & Winston, Inc., 1947), p. 378.

Reasonable versus Nonconfiscatory Rates

The earnings of a regulated company cannot be unduly restricted, or such earnings would be confiscatory and would violate the constitutional guarantees of "due process" and "equal protection of the law." Held the Court in an early railroad case:

> The question of the reasonableness of a rate of charge for transportation by a railroad company, involving as it does the element of reasonableness both as regards the company and as regards the public, is eminently a question for judicial investigation, requiring due process of law for its determination. If the company is deprived of the power of charging reasonable rates for the use of its property, and such deprivation takes place in the absence of an investigation by judicial machinery, it is deprived of the lawful use of its property, and thus, in substance and effect, of the property itself, without due process of law and in violation of the Constitution of the United States; and in so far as it is thus deprived, while other persons are permitted to receive reasonable profits upon their invested capital, the company is deprived of the equal protection of the laws.[14]

Is a reasonable or fair rate of return, then, the same as a nonconfiscatory rate? Or, conversely, is an unreasonable or unfair rate one that is confiscatory? The Supreme Court has held that a fair rate of return may be higher than one necessary to avoid confiscation. To quote from a 1925 decision:

> A commission or other legislative body, in its discretion, may determine to be reasonable and just a rate that is substantially higher than one merely sufficient to justify a judicial finding in a confiscation case that it is high enough to yield a just and reasonable return on the value of the property used to perform the service covered by the rate. The mere fact that a rate is non-confiscatory does not indicate that it must be deemed to be just and reasonable.[15]

Several state commissions and state supreme courts also have made this distinction, holding that a "just and reasonable" rate may be higher than a confiscatory rate.[16]

No Single Rate Always Fair

The Supreme Court has clearly indicated that no single rate of return is always fair. Rather, a fair return varies with investment opportunities, the location of a company, the nature of the business, and general economic

---

[14]*Chicago, M. & St. P. Ry. Co.* v. *Minnesota* ex rel. *Railroad & Warehouse Comm.*, 134 U.S. 418, 458 (1890).

[15]*Banton* v. *Belt Line Ry. Corp.*, 268 U.S. 413, 422–23 (1925). See Nathaniel T. Guernsey, "The Test of Reasonable Rates," 14 *Virginia Law Review* 1 (1927).

[16]*Peoples Gas Light & Coke Co.* v. *Slattery*, 373 Ill. 31 (1939); *Re Pacific Teleph. & Teleg. Co.*, 89 PUR (NS) 414 (Cal., 1950); *Re Southwestern Bell Teleph. Co.*, 87 PUR (NS) 97 (Ark., 1951); *Iowa-Illinois Gas & Elec. Co.* v. *Perrine*, 351 Ill. App. 195 (1953).

conditions. In the Consolidated Gas case, the Court said a fair rate of return depends on "circumstances and locality."[17] Following World War I, the Court recognized that prices were rising: ". . . that annual returns upon capital and enterprise the world over have materially increased, so that what would have been a proper rate of return for capital invested in gas plants and similar public utilities a few years ago furnishes no safe criterion for the present or for the future."[18]

A few years later in the Bluefield case, the Court argued: "A rate of return may be reasonable at one time and become too high or too low by changes affecting opportunities for investment, the money market and business conditions generally."[19] Furthermore, because of differences in risk, a fair rate of return will also vary by industry or company. For example, a higher rate may be necessary for a street railway than for an electric or gas company.[20]

No Guarantee of a Fair Return

The Supreme Court also has stated that the regulated companies are not guaranteed a fair rate of return. In a 1933 case, the Court argued:

> The due process clause of the Fourteenth Amendment safeguards against the taking of private property, or the compelling of its use, for the service of the public without just compensation. . . . But it does not assure to public utilities the right under all circumstances to have a return upon the value of the property so used. The use of, or the failure to obtain, patronage, due to competition, does not justify the imposition of charges that are exorbitant and unjust to the public. The clause of the Constitution here invoked does not protect public utilities against such business hazards.[21]

In the Market Street Railway case, the Court stated: "The due process clause has been applied to prevent governmental destruction of existing economic values. It has not and cannot be applied to insure values or to restore values that have been lost by the operation of economic forces."[22] Regulated industries, in other words, are protected against arbitrary action of commissions, but not from normal "business hazards" or from the operation of "economic forces."

Summary of Judicial Decisions

Throughout all of its decisions, the Supreme Court has formulated no specific rules for determining a fair rate of return, but it has enumerated a

---

[17] *Willcox* v. *Consolidated Gas Co., op. cit.*, p. 48. Also see *Driscoll* v. *Edison Light & Power Co., op. cit.*

[18] *Lincoln Gas & Elec. Light* v. *City of Lincoln, op. cit.*, p. 268.

[19] *Bluefield Water Works & Imp. Co.* v. *Public Service Comm. of West Virginia, op. cit.*, p. 693.

[20] *Wabash Elec. Co.* v. *Young*, 287 U.S. 234, 252 (1930).

[21] *Public Service Comm. of Montana* v. *Great Northern Utilities Co.*, 289 U.S. 130, 135 (1935).

[22] *Market Street Ry. Co.* v. *Railroad Comm. of Calif.*, 324 U.S. 548, 567 (1945).

number of guidelines. The Court has made it clear that confiscation of property must be avoided, that no one rate can be considered fair at all times, and that regulation does not guarantee a fair return. The Court also has consistently stated that a necessary prerequisite for profitable operations is efficient and economical management. Beyond this is a list of several factors the commissions are supposed to consider in making their decisions, but no weights have been assigned.

The stated factors can be grouped into two broad standards. First, the "cost of capital" standard, under which the rate of return should enable a company to attract capital on terms that will (*a*) maintain its credit standing, (*b*) protect its financial soundness, and (*c*) maintain the integrity of its existing investment. Second, the "comparability of earnings" standard, under which the rate of return to equity owners "should be commensurate with returns on investments in other enterprises having corresponding risks."

In reality, the concept of a fair rate of return represents a "zone of reasonableness."[23] As explained by the Pennsylvania commission:

> There is a range of reasonableness within which earnings may properly fluctuate and still be deemed just and reasonable and not excessive or extortionate. It is bounded at one level by investor interest against confiscation and the need for averting any threat to the security for the capital embarked upon the enterprise. At the other level it is bounded by consumer interest against excessive and unreasonable charges for service.[24]

As long as the allowed return falls within this zone, therefore, it is just and reasonable. "As the fair value of the property is a judgment figure so is the denominated fair rate of return a judgment determination."[25] It is the task of the commissions to translate these generalizations into quantitative terms.

COMMISSION DECISIONS

Bonbright has warned that those "familiar with the actual practice of American rate regulation need no reminder about the uncertain relationship between the supposed 'principles' of rate-of-return determination . . . and the considerations that actually lead commissions to allow whatever rates of return they do allow in specific rate cases."[26] He continues:

> In the opinions that accompany their rate orders, commissions seldom attempt to disclose the reasons why they find, say, 5.85 per cent fair in one case and 6.2 per cent fair in another. Especially in fair-value jurisdictions, some of the decisions lead one to suspect that the commissions have first

[23] *Federal Power Comm.* v. *Natural Gas Pipeline Co., op. cit.*

[24] *Pennsylvania Public Utility Comm.* v. *Bell Teleph. Co. of Pennsylvania*, 43 PUR 3d 241, 246 (Pa., 1962).

[25] *Re Eastern Rowan Teleph. Co.*, 44 PUR 3d 379, 382 (N.C., 1962).

[26] James C. Bonbright, *Principles of Public Utility Rates* (New York: Columbia University Press, 1961), p. 281.

reached a conclusion as to reasonable revenue requirements in terms of dollars per annum and then have proceeded to translate these requirements into whatever combination of a rate base and a percentage rate of return will be likely to pass muster with the appellate courts or with public sentiment.[27]

To illustrate: The New York commission, in a 1915 decision, reduced the rates of the Edison Company to yield "6 per cent on nearly $100,000,000, which it seems ... must certainly cover the value of the 'capital actually expended in the enterprise'."[28] In a 1933 Texas decision, all mention of the rate of return was confined to a single sentence: "We find that an annual rate of return equal to 7 per cent of the present fair value of the properties as herein found is adequate."[29] The North Carolina commission, in a 1949 decision, explained that the allowed rate of return was determined after consideration of several factors:

> In arriving at a rate of return ... the Commission has given consideration to the financial history of the company; to its earnings in the past as compared with the present; to the cost of rendering service under existing high prices; to the ratio of its debt capital to its equity capital; to the general market trends in the cost of labor, materials, and capital; to the opportunity of investors to invest in other business undertakings of comparable stability and soundness; to the opportunity for growth and expansion and to public demand therefor; to the protection afforded against destructive competition; to the value of the service to telephone users and to the probability of diminishing returns from rates and charges that approach burdensome proportions.[30]

And in a 1963 decision, the Arkansas commission concluded: "In order to be conservative, the commission has decided that a rate of return from 6.25 per cent to 6.50 per cent would be reasonable in this case."[31]

Allowed Rates of Return

Before turning to the standards underlying commission decisions, it is desirable to summarize the rates of return which have been allowed in the past. There are also a number of specific problems, particularly with respect to the transportation industry, that deserve consideration. In discussing the rate of return, it must be emphasized that any rate by itself is meaningless unless considered in connection with the type of rate base employed in a particular case. Obviously, a 6.5 percent rate of return, say, on an original cost rate base of $1 million is far different from the same rate on a $2 million reproduction cost or fair value rate base.

[27] *Ibid.*
[28] *Stadtlander v. The New York Edison Co.,* PUR 1915B, 685 (N.Y., 1915).
[29] *Texas Border Gas Co. v. Laredo,* 2 PUR (NS) 503, 516 (1933).
[30] *Re Southern Bell Teleph. & Teleg. Co.,* 79 PUR (NS) 109, 112 (N.C., 1949).
[31] *Re Fort Smith Gas Corp.,* 50 PUR 3d 105, 111 (Ark., 1963).

The relationship between the allowable rate of return and the type of rate base employed by the commissions has been analyzed in two studies of postwar rate cases—one by Eiteman, involving the Bell Telephone System, the other by Stuart, involving the electric industry.[32] Both studies conclude that when commissions adopt either reproduction cost or fair value rate bases they partially offset the effect of the larger bases by granting lower percentage rates of return, but that the combined effect of the larger rate base and the lower rate of return is to permit higher levels of earnings in reproduction cost and fair value jurisdictions.[33] Eiteman, for example, found that the average rate of return for telephone companies in original cost cases was 5.93 percent, compared with *an equivalent return* of 7.98 percent on original cost in reproduction cost jurisdictions, and 6.62 percent on original cost in fair value cases. The average returns, therefore, were approximately 35 percent higher for reproduction cost companies and 12 percent higher for fair value companies than they were for original cost companies.

The conclusion of these studies supports the argument often advanced by representatives of the regulated industries to the effect that since commissions are reluctant to allow high rates of return, adequate earnings are more easily achieved when a reproduction cost or fair value rate base is employed. Further, the conclusion also is consistent with Bonbright's contention that some commissions appear to determine a firm's total revenue requirement before either the rate base or the rate of return is established.

One other factor should be kept in mind. There is commonly a difference between the rate of return prescribed by a commission and the rate of return earned by a utility. Since a commission, in determining a fair rate of return, is estimating future revenues and expenses, this divergence is not surprising. As long as the rate earned is within the zone of reasonableness, no regulatory action is required; but when it either falls below or exceeds this range, adjustments may be made.

Electric, Gas, and Telephone Industries. The prescribed or allowed rate of return for electric, gas, and telephone companies has varied considerably, depending on the industry and the company, as well as the period of time. During the height of the rate base measurement controversy, many commissions

---

[32] David K. Eiteman, "Independence of Utility Rate-Base Type, Permitted Rate of Return, and Utility Earnings," 17 *Journal of Finance* 38 (1962); and Fredric Stuart, "Rate Base versus Rate of Return," 70 *Public Utilities Fortnightly* 395 (1962). In a later study these findings for electric utilities were confirmed, although it was noted "that the spread between the earnings obtained under the different valuation approaches has narrowed...." John Pike, "Residential Electric Rates and Regulation," 7 *Quarterly Review of Economics & Business* 45, 49 (1967).

[33] The permitted average rates of return:

	Telephone Companies	Electric Companies
Original cost cases	5.93%	5.88%
Fair value cases	5.83	5.78
Reproduction cost cases	5.74	5.65

maintained a "standard" rate of return for long periods of time—8 percent in New York and 7 percent in Pennsylvania, for instance, during the twenties.[34] A company's total earnings, therefore, were closely related to the type of rate base used by a commission. Then, as interest rates declined, the standard rate also fell. During the thirties, the standard rate of return became 6 percent in New York; a rate defended by the commission in the following words:

> It exceeds the actual cost of raising funds for a public utility in this state which is soundly financed and properly conducted. Any utility corporation which cannot earn for its stockholders an adequate return upon the basis of a 6 per cent return has neglected to conduct its affairs upon the basis of sound finance and engineering.[35]

In recent years, more attention has been given to the determination of the allowable fair rate of return. Yet, there are wide variations in the rates of return actually earned, as Table 9–1 illustrates with respect to 189 private electric utilities. In general, rates have been higher in fast-growing areas than for companies in slow-growing areas, and higher for utilities under the jurisdiction of more liberal commissions than for companies under more strict commissions.[36]

TABLE 9–1
Rates of Return for Privately Owned Electric Utilities, 1963–67 *

Rate of Return	1963		1964		1965		1966		1967	
	Number	Percent	Number	Percent	Number	Percent	Number	Percent	Number	Percent
Less than 5.00 . . .	7	3.7	7	3.7	4	2.2	6	3.2	8	4.2
5.00 to 5.99	17	9.1	18	9.6	20	10.7	13	7.0	14	7.4
6.00 to 6.99	53	28.3	45	24.1	43	23.1	42	22.4	43	22.8
7.00 to 7.99	57	30.5	65	34.8	63	33.9	63	33.7	66	34.9
8.00 to 8.99	33	17.7	35	18.7	34	18.3	37	19.8	33	17.5
9.00 to 9.99	17	9.1	11	5.9	17	9.1	19	10.2	17	9.0
10.00 and above . .	3	1.6	6	3.2	5	2.7	7	3.7	8	4.2
Total	187	100.0	187	100.0	186	100.0	187	100.0	189	100.0

* The companies included are those having annual electric operating revenue of $2,500,000 or more for at least three consecutive years in the 1963–67 period.
Source: Federal Power Commission, *Statistics of Privately Owned Electric Utilities in the United States, 1967* (Washington, D.C.: U.S. Government Printing Office, 1968), p. 651.

34 See Joseph R. Rose, "The Rate of Utility Return," 23 *Public Utilities Fortnightly* 113 (1939); and W. R. Buckwalter, "The Rate of Return on Pennsylvania Utilities," 91 *University of Pennsylvania Law Review* 626 (1943).

35 Temporary National Economic Committee, *Economic Standards of Government Price Control*, Monograph No. 32 (Washington, D.C.: U.S. Government Printing Office, 1941), p. 38.

36 Bonbright, *op. cit.*, p. 282. Also see *Electric World*, May 5, 1958, pp. 97–100; Fred P. Morrissey, "Relation of Growth and Rate of Return for Utilities," 60 *Public Utilities Fortnightly* 361 (1957); and *Re Peoples Water & Gas Co.*, 99 PUR (NS) 516 (Fla., 1953).

Table 9-2 summarizes the rates of return prescribed or allowed by federal and state commissions in their most recent decisions. The rates generally have ranged around 6 percent on the type of rate base employed, with a trend in the sixties to rates in excess of 6 percent. This trend has been the result of several factors, notably continued inflation in the economy and the relatively high cost of money.

In the case of natural gas producers, the FPC has approved a return of 12 percent on average production investment.[37] The commission has stated that in establishing this return, it considered the returns permitted to interstate pipelines and, in addition, the greater financial risks of exploration and production.

Transportation Industries. Determination of the rate of return for the transportation industries is largely in the hands of the federal commissions. As compared with electric, gas, and telephone utilities, however, several different concepts and problems arise. In general, determination of the rate of return has been subordinated to establishment of competitive rates. Competition, in other words, has significantly limited the earnings of the major modes of transportation, especially in the post-World War II period.

Railroads. In 1920, Congress prescribed 5.5 percent as the fair rate of return for the nation's railroads, but gave the Interstate Commerce Commission the power to add .5 percent at its discretion to provide funds for capital improvements. In that year, the commission considered the value of the railroads to be $18.9 billion and 6 percent as a fair rate of return. And in 1922, a 5.75 percent return was held to be fair. Since then, the ICC has not found it necessary to specify a fair rate of return for the roads. Economic conditions and the growing strength of competing modes of transport have effectively limited railroad earnings. (The railroads' rate of return on book investment has ranged from 2.0 to 4.4 percent in the period 1945–68.) In the past few years, commission decisions have generally been concerned with the need for increased revenues to meet rising operating costs and with rate differentiation problems, rather than with calculations of the return railroads should be allowed.

Motor Carriers. The fair rate of return concept has not been used by the ICC in regulating the motor carrier industry for many years. Instead, the commission judges the adequacy of revenues by reference to the operating ratio.[38] The operating ratio is the percentage relationship of operating costs to gross operating revenues. Thus, a ratio of 90 would mean that the costs of the carrier absorbed 90 percent of its gross revenues, leaving 10 cents net revenue out of each $1.00 of gross revenue. The use of the operating ratio arises from the

---

[37] *Re Area Rate Proceeding for Permian Basin*, 59 PUR 3d 417, 473 (FPC, 1965).

[38] See Alan Wright, "Operating Ratio—A Regulatory Tool," 51 *Public Utilities Fortnightly* 24 (1953); Laurence S. Knappen, "Transit Operating Ratio—Another View," 51 *ibid.* 485 (1953); Charles W. Knapp, "Economics of Transit Operating Ratio," 56 *ibid.* 467 (1955); and William J. McKenna, "The Operating Ratio: Its Use in Pennsylvania," 82 *ibid.* 21 (July 4, 1968).

TABLE 9-2

Rates of Return, Electric, Gas, and Telephone Utilities

| | Rates of Return Prescribed or Found Reasonable | | | | | | Valuation Standard Generally Applied with Allowances or Adjustments for Related Factors Such as Contributions and Working Capital |
| | Electric | | Gas | | Telephone | | |
Jurisdiction	Percent Prescribed	Date	Percent Prescribed	Date	Percent Prescribed	Date	
FPC	6.00	1964–66	6.50	1967[1]	7.00–7.50	...	Original cost.
FCC	...	...	...	...	7.00–7.50	1967	Do.
Alabama	(2)		6.00	1958	6.20	1963	Fair value.
Alaska	8.50	1967	(2)		(2)		Do.[3]
Arizona	5.78	1961	6.98	1961	(2)		Do.
Arkansas	6.00–6.25	1956	6.34	1965	6.00–6.25	1959	Original cost.
California	6.04–6.76	1964	6.20	1962	6.30	1966[4]	Do.
Colorado	6.15	1960[5]	6.50	1965	6.69	1952	Do.
Connecticut	6.01	1962	5.85	1962	5.98	1962	Do.
Delaware	6.00–7.00	(6)	6.00–7.00	(6)	6.19	1959	Fair value.
District of Columbia	6.30	1966	6.30–6.45	1958	6.25–6.40	1964	Original cost.
Florida	6.95	1966	6.98	1966	6.80	1966	Do.[7]
Georgia	6.00	1952	6.50	1954	6.00	1951	Do.
Hawaii	6.02–6.50	1958–61	6.60	1960	6.70	1960	Do.
Idaho	6.10	1964	(2)		6.50	1963	Do.
Illinois	5.85	1961	5.94	1966	6.39[22]	1967	Fair value.
Indiana	5.63	1957	6.00	1960	5.80	1965	Do.
Iowa	(8)		(8)		(8)		No experience.
Kansas	(9) (10)	1965[11]	3.19–6.62[9]	1964–65	3.75–6.54[10]	1964–65	Original cost.
Kentucky	6.25	1947	6.75	1965[11]	6.10	1961[11]	Fair value.
Louisiana	6.00	1959	6.00	1966	6.00	1960	Original cost.
Maine	5.75		6.49	1964	6.25	1965	Reasonable value.[12]

TABLE 9-2—Continued

State							
Maryland	6.30	1966	6.25	1958	6.35	1964	Fair value.
Massachusetts	6.25	1962[13]	5.90	1960[13]	6.45	1958[13]	Original cost.
Michigan	6.60	1964	6.60	1964	6.80	1961	Do.
Minnesota	[14]		[14]		6.00 + or −	1964-66	All elements considered.
Mississippi	6.00+	1964	6.00+	1959	5.00+	1960	Fair value.
Missouri	[21]	[21]	[21]	[21]	[21]	[21]	Do.
Montana	5.33	1964[15]	5.89	1964[15]	5.79	1964[15]	Do.
Nebraska	[14]		[14]		6.19	1965	Original cost.
Nevada	6.86	1966	5.90	1963	6.38	1966	Do.
New Hampshire	[16]		[16]		[16]	[16]	All elements considered.
New Jersey	[2]		[2]		[2]	[2]	Fair value.[17]
New Mexico	[2]		6.40	1963	5.91	1954	All elements considered.[18]
New York	6.20-6.30	1964	6.40-6.50	1964	6.50	1964	Original cost.
North Carolina	4.08	1963	6.11	1960	5.60	1965	All elements considered.
North Dakota	6.10	1963	6.15	1965	5.90	1960	Prudent investment.
Ohio	5.50-6.00	1963-65	5.75-6.25	1963-65	5.70-6.00	1963-65	Reproduction cost.
Oklahoma	6.00-6.12	1956	6.00-6.37	1966	6.00-6.37	1964	Original cost.
Oregon	6.10-6.20	1960	6.00	1960	6.35	1959[19]	Do.
Pennsylvania	5.90	1960	5.75-6.00	1964-65	6.00-6.40	1959-63	Fair value.
Rhode Island	5.84	1957	[2]		6.25	1957	Original cost.
South Carolina	[21]	[21]	[21]	[21]	[21]	[21]	Do.
South Dakota	[14]		[14]		6.25	1960	Average net investment.
Tennessee	[2]		[2]		6.59	1965	Original cost.
Texas	[14]		6.50	[20]	[14]		Fair value.
Utah	6.15	1962	6.30	1960	6.25	1958	Original cost.

TABLE 9-2—Concluded

Jurisdiction	Electric		Gas		Telephone		Valuation Standard Generally Applied with Allowances or Adjustments for Related Factors Such as Contributions and Working Capital
	Percent Prescribed	Date	Percent Prescribed	Date	Percent Prescribed	Date	
Vermont	6.11	1964	(2)	(20)	6.00	1960	Do.
Virginia	5.75–7.50	(20)	5.75–7.50	1960	5.75–7.50	(20)	Do.
Washington	6.10	1963	5.99	1960	6.50	1959	Do.
West Virginia	(2)		6.30	1965	6.40	1964	Do.
Wisconsin.........	(10)	1967	(10)	1966	(10)	1967	Prudent investment.
Wyoming	5.30	1967	6.75	1967	6.75	1959	Original cost.

1 In settlements the Commission has approved a 6.50 percent rate of return for pipelines.

2 No recent cases.

3 Book value is prima facie until fair value is proved.

4 3.82 percent for Ponderosa Telephone Co. (R.E.A.–1965).

5 Plus 0.2 percent attrition.

6 No formal determination; 6 to 7 percent on fair value is not considered excessive. In actual experience, rates are in range of 5 to 6 percent.

7 For gas and electric, prudent investment is prescribed by statute. For telephone, no method prescribed by statute.

8 Commission acquired rate jurisdiction in 1963. No decisions to date.

9 In progress.

10 Commission varies the return considerably in light of the cost of capital and other relevant factors.

11 On net investment rate base.

12 All elements considered excluding current value.

13 Some rate changes downward in past few years as a result of conference without formal cases.

14 Not regulated by State commission.

15 On fair value rate base.

16 2 mills above the cost of money.

17 Recent cases have found original cost to be the best evidence of fair value.

18 For telephone, book value less historical depreciation.

19 Also 3.6 percent in 1961 (REA 2-percent money).

20 Dates not available.

21 Variable.

22 In this case the evidence presented by the utility was based on net original cost, less investment tax credits, plus materials and supplies; no reproduction cost or fair value figures were entered in the case by Petitioner.

Source: Federal Power Commission, "Federal and State Commission Jurisdiction and Regulation, Electric, Gas, and Telephone Utilities, 1967" (Washington, D.C.: U.S. Government Printing Office, 1968), p. 15.

characteristics of the motor carrier industry. The amount of investment is relatively small in relation to total costs. As explained by the commission:

> In industries where the amount of investment is large in relation to total costs, the rate of return on investment generally has been accepted as appropriate for determining revenue needs. In such industries the risk is related more to the amount of the investment and less to costs. On the other hand, where the amount of the investment is relatively small in relation to total costs, investment is not the primary factor in determining revenue needs. . . . The owners of motor carriers can hardly be expected to look to the return on the amount of their investment as an incentive where the principal risk is attached to the substantially greater amount of expense.[39]

The essential point is that when investment is so small in relation to total costs, "the margin of revenues over expenses required to pay a normal rate of return on capital invested would be so small that a slight miscalculation of probable revenues or expenses could leave the carrier with revenues insufficient to pay operating expenses."[40] For many years, the ICC has found that an operating ratio of approximately 93 percent is reasonable for the motor carriers under its jurisdiction,[41] while state commissions frequently have used higher ratios, ranging between 95 and 98 percent, for motor carriers under their jurisdiction.[42]

[39] *Middle West General Increases,* 48 MCC 541, 552–53 (ICC, 1948). "The motor carriers' risk lies in the substantial expenses he incurs for wages, gasoline, tires, insurance, licenses, and other operating expenses. It is not infrequent for a motor carrier's expenses to be three or four times the investment in property." McKenna, *op. cit.,* p. 21. In contrast, the railroads would probably require an operating ratio of 70 or below in order to earn a fair rate of return. The Civil Aeronautics Board has refused to determine an allowable rate of return for the airline industry based upon the operating ratio standard. See *General Passenger Fare Investigation,* E–16068 (CAB, 1960).

[40] D. Philip Locklin, *Economics of Transportation* (6th ed.; Homewood, Ill.: Richard D. Irwin, Inc., 1966), p. 702.

The operating ratio method has been severely criticized as representing no standard at all, since the necessary rate of return is not related to a rate base. (See, for example, Knappen, *op. cit.,* p. 488.) Locklin argues, however, that the operating ratio deemed reasonable "is not chosen for the purpose of providing an adequate return on capital invested, but for the purpose of providing a margin of revenues over expenses that is not in danger of disappearing entirely if changes in revenues or expenses occur." (Locklin, *op. cit.*) The ICC has recognized that because of the prevalence of intracorporate transactions in the motor carrier industry, expenses must be fully scrutinized. (See *General Increases–Transcontinental,* 319 ICC 792, 803 [1963].) Further, the ICC now publishes rates of return for regulated motor carriers.

[41] *Increased Common Carrier Rates in the East,* 42 MCC 633 (1943); *Increased Common Carrier Rates in New England,* 43 MCC 13 (1949); *Increases, Transcontinental-Intermountain Coast,* 304 ICC 15 (1958); and *General Increases–Middle Atlantic,* 319 ICC 168 (1964).

[42] *Re Salt Lake City Lines,* 43 PUR 3d 193 (Utah, 1962); *Re Gray Lines, Inc.,* Decision No. 63998 (Cal., 1962); *Re New England Motor Rate Bureau,* Docket No. 10200 (Conn., 1963); *Re Dalton-Hinsdale Bus Lines,* DPU 14530 (Mass., 1964); and *Re Nevada Motor Transport Tariff Service,* I&S Docket 353 (Nev., 1966). Several state commissions use both the operating ratio and the rate base methods, although the former is considered the primary test. See *Re Gray Line,* Decision No. 48570 (Cal., 1953); and *Re Louisville Transit Co.,* 53 PUR 3d 41 (Ky., 1963).

Pipelines. For oil pipeline companies, the ICC has approved an 8-percent return on an original cost rate base.[43] In defending this rate, the commission has argued: "The hazards and uncertain future of the common-carrier business of the pipelines suggest the fairness of a somewhat larger rate of return than it would be reasonable to expect would be applied in industries of a more stable character, where the volume of traffic is more accurately predicted."[44] In the case of pipelines used for the transportation of gasoline and other liquid products of petroleum—the "products lines"—a 10 percent return has been considered fair.[45]

For natural gas pipeline companies, the Federal Power Commission in recent years has found that rates of 6.125 to 6.5 percent are fair,[46] although slightly higher rates (6.625 and 6.875 percent) were prescribed in two 1968 cases.[47] Such returns have generally been on original cost rate bases.[48]

Airlines. The Civil Aeronautics Board has a two-fold task in determining the fair rate of return for airlines: (*a*) payments for transporting freight and passengers and (*b*) payments for transporting airmail. Few decisions have been made by the board concerning a fair rate of return on freight and passenger service. In a 1953 report, the CAB recognized that the earnings of the airlines would fluctuate unavoidably with general business conditions, and held that it was undesirable "to regulate this industry by attempting to relate fares to returns in the short run." Rather, earnings should be adjusted "to provide a fair return over a reasonably extended period which includes the good years as well as the bad."[49] In 1956, the board instituted an investigation of the general level of passenger fares. The final report, issued in 1960, while upholding the earlier decision regarding the need to provide an adequate rate of return over time, adopted a rate of 10.25 percent for the Big Four and 11.125 percent for the other domestic trunkline carriers (on a net investment rate base) as a fair rate of return.[50]

---

[43]*Reduced Pipe Line Rates & Gathering Charges,* 243 ICC 115, 142 (1940); *Minnelusa Oil Corp.* v. *Continental Pipe Line Co.,* 258 ICC 41, 54 (1944).

[44]*Reduced Pipe Line Rates & Gathering Charges, op. cit.,* p. 142.

[45]*Minnelusa Oil Corp.* v. *Continental Pipe Line Co., op. cit.,* p. 53.

[46]See *Re Southern Nat. Gas Co.,* 35 PUR 3d 179 (FPC, 1960); *Re Kansas-Nebraska Nat. Gas Co., Inc.,* 38 PUR 3d 136 (FPC, 1961); *Re Panhandle Eastern Pipe Line Co.,* 38 PUR 3d 307 (FPC, 1961); and *Re Alabama-Tennessee Nat. Gas Co.,* 44 PUR 3d 19 (FPC, 1962).

[47]*Panhandle Eastern Pipe Line Co.,* Docket No. RP68-15 (Phase I) (FPC, 1968); and *Natural Gas Pipeline Co. of America,* Docket Nos. RP67-21 and RP68-17 (Phase I) (FPC, 1968).

[48]Until early 1964, the FPC permitted companies under its jurisdiction to include in their rates amounts for deferred taxes arising from liberalized depreciation, and allowed them to earn a 1.5 percent rate of return on these funds. See *Re Northern Nat. Gas Co.,* 38 PUR 3d 149 (1961). In a 1964 decision, the commission changed its policy, thereby precluding companies from earning any return on accumulated funds. See *Re Alabama-Tennessee Nat. Gas Co.,* 52 PUR 3d 118 (FPC, 1964), *aff'd,* 359 F. 2d 318 (1966), *cert. denied,* 385 U.S. 847 (1966).

[49]*General Passenger Fare Investigation,* 17 CAB 230, 234–35 (1953).

[50]*General Passenger Fare Investigation,* E–16068 (CAB, 1960).

The CAB has spent considerable time in determining a fair rate of return for transporting airmail. Here, the board distinguishes between the past and the future. When fixing mail rates for the future, an 8 percent return after taxes has traditionally been allowed;[51] when adjusting mail rates for a past period, 7 percent.[52] The board justifies the lower past rates by the fact that the element of risk is reduced since "uncertainties in estimating future operating results are no longer present."[53]

In 1960, the board decided that a fair rate of return on investment for local service carriers was in the range of a 9 percent minimum and a 12.75 percent maximum for future rate periods. In cases where investment is less than 25-cents per plane-mile, a minimum of 3-cents per plane-mile is to be used. And the traditional 7 percent return for past rate periods was upheld.[54]

Company versus Industry Rates. There are inequalities in the earning power of different companies within each of the regulated industries. For the airlines, motor carriers, and railroads, in particular, this fact leads to an important problem in determining a fair rate of return.

A large part of the domestic route structure is served by two or more of each type of carrier in competition. In such situations, intramodal rates must be the same. Even when a carrier possesses a monopoly of the region it serves, differences in fares may be impossible, since rates higher in one region than in another tend to discourage industry and trade, while lower rates have the opposite effect. As a result, intramodal rates must be uniform despite the fact that one carrier's revenues may be less than another's. In other words, in establishing a fair rate of return for these industries, the needs of an individual carrier must be subordinated to the needs of each type of carrier as a whole or in groups. And when a rate is prescribed in this manner, some carriers will earn more than the allowed rate, while others will earn less.

The problem can be illustrated with reference to the airline industry.[55] Prior to the United-Capital merger, the CAB divided the domestic trunk line carriers into two groups—the Big Four and the Medium Eight. It then established a fair rate of return for each group and determined an overall weighted industry rate. It is readily apparent from Table 9–3 that earnings will vary between the carriers. Assuming an average industry return of 10.6 percent on investment, the return that individual carriers would have earned in 1958 ranged from 13.95 percent to −3.30 percent.

---

[51] *Colonial Airlines, Mail Rates*, 4 CAB 71, 86 (1942); *Northeast Airlines, Mail Rates*, 4 CAB 181, 189 (1943); *All American Aviation, Mail Rates*, 4 CAB 354, 368 (1943).

[52] *Delta Air Lines, Mail Rates*, 9 CAB 645, 656–57 (1948); *Chicago & Southern Air Lines, Mail Rates*, 9 CAB 786, 804 (1948); *Northwest Airlines, Inc., System Mail Rate*, E–25894 (CAB, 1967).

[53] *Delta Air Lines, Mail Rates, op. cit.*, p. 656.

[54] *Rate of Return, Local Service Carriers Investigation*, 31 CAB 685 (1960).

[55] See Locklin, *op. cit.*, pp. 341–42, 703–4, for a similar discussion with reference to the railroad and motor carrier industries, respectively.

The impossibility of setting a rate for each carrier is evident. To base the rate on the needs of the poorest situated carrier would result in the vast majority of the carriers' customers paying fares greatly in excess of the cost of furnishing the service and would give exorbitant returns to these carriers. To base the rate on the needs of the most favorably situated carrier would have a disastrous

TABLE 9-3
Hypothetical Airline Rates of Return on Investment Resulting
from 10.6% Industry Rate of Return, 1958

Carrier	Rate of Return
American	13.95%
United	12.78
Delta	12.63
Capital	12.00
Braniff	10.20
Western	9.83
TWA	9.39
Northwest	9.11
National	8.13
Eastern	7.64
Continental	6.09
Northeast	−3.30
Industry Weighted Average	10.60%

Source: *General Passenger Fare Investigation,* E-16068 (CAB, 1960), p. 25.

impact on many of the other carriers and on the development of air transportation. The rate of return, therefore, must be determined at some point between the needs of the most profitable and the least profitable carriers. It is to meet this problem that the board adjusts carrier rates to provide a fair return over an extended period of time.

THE COST OF CAPITAL STANDARD

Since the end of World War II, there has been a significant shift in regulatory emphasis, and the rate of return has become a more important part of rate cases. This emphasis has been accompanied by the development of a cost of capital standard, sometimes referred to as the "differentiated rate of return," which has resulted in substantial controversy between the commissions and the regulated industries.[56] Since many commissions consider that the determination of the cost of capital is at least a first step in arriving at a fair rate of return, this section is devoted to an analysis of its meaning, application, and interpretation

[56] See *Public Utilities Reports* for court and commission decisions. Cases are summarized also in *Public Utilities Fortnightly.*

by the commissions. The following section will consider the comparability of earnings standard.

Definition of Cost of Capital

Justice Brandeis expounded the cost of capital concept in his 1923 concurring opinion in the Southwestern Bell case:

> In essence, there is no difference between the capital charge and operating expenses, depreciation, and taxes. Each is a part of the current cost of supplying the service; and each should be met from current income. When the capital charges are for interest on the floating debt paid at the current rate, this is readily seen. But it is no less true of a legal obligation to pay interest on long-term bonds, entered into years before the rate hearing and to continue for years thereafter; and it is true also of the economic obligation to pay dividends on stock, preferred or common.[57]

As used by Justice Brandeis and by several commissions in recent years, the term "cost of capital" may be defined as the annual percent which a company must receive to maintain its credit, to pay a return to the owners of the enterprise, and to insure the attraction of capital in amounts adequate to meet future needs. Mathematically, the cost of capital is a composite of the cost of the several classes of capital used by a company—debt, preferred stock, and common stock (par value plus earned and capital surplus)—weighted on the basis of an appropriate capital structure.[58] Assume a capital structure composed of 50 percent long-term debt, 15 percent preferred stock, and 35 percent common stock and surplus (Table 9-4). Suppose this company's debt has a net annual cost of 4.5 percent, the preferred stock 5.5 percent, and the common stock equity return is 11 percent. The overall cost of capital would then be 6.925 percent.

In applying this deceptively simple standard, commissions face numerous and difficult problems "which almost defy solution."[59] Four major problems will be discussed below: (1) the appropriate capital structure for determining the cost of capital, (2) determination of the allowable cost of debt and equity capital, (3) the incentive to efficiency, and (4) the problem of inflation.

[57]Concurring opinion in *Missouri* ex rel. *Southwestern Bell Tel. Co.* v. *Public Service Comm., op. cit.,* p. 306.

[58]"Unless a utility company has heavy investments in nonutility assets, this invested capital should approximate an actual-cost or net-investment rate base except for investment in plant under construction, for which adjustments are usually made by the temporary exclusion of the investment from the rate base combined with the later introduction into the rate base of an allowance for 'interest during construction' after the plant has gone into service." Bonbright, *op. cit.,* p. 242, n. 4. See Chapter 8, pp. 251-53.

[59]Joseph R. Rose, " 'Cost of Capital' in Public Utility Rate Regulation," 43 *Virginia Law Review* 1079, 1082 (1957). Also see Fred P. Morrissey, "A Reconsideration of Cost of Capital and a Reasonable Rate of Return," 31 *Land Economics* 229 (1955); and two articles by Harold M. Somers: " 'Cost of Money' as the Determinant of Public Utility Rates," 4 *Buffalo Law Review* 289 (1955) and "The 'End Result' Approach to Public Utility Regulation," 16 *ibid.* 689 (1967).

TABLE 9-4
Estimated Cost of Capital

	Percentage of Capital Structure	Annual Cost	Weighted Cost
Bonds	50%	4.5%	2.250%
Preferred stock	15%	5.5%	.825%
Common stock and surplus	35%	11.0%	3.850%
Overall Cost of Capital	100%	...	6.925%

The Capital Structure

The traditional theory of business finance holds that the average cost of capital to a firm varies with the capital structure upon which it is based.[60] The interest rate on debt is normally lower than the cost of equity capital. Consequently, within limits determined by such factors as the risk of a business, the overall cost may be somewhat lower when the debt-equity ratio is high than when the debt-equity ratio is low.

Given this theory, some argue that the regulatory commissions should base their cost of capital estimates on what they consider a "typical" or "ideal" capital structure without regard to the actual capitalization of the particular company being considered. Others argue that cost estimates should be based upon either the actual capital structure or the structure that is expected in the near future.

Commission Decisions. The commissions have yet to develop a consistent position on these two opposing views. Some state commissions seek an approximation of an ideal capital structure through the use of a hypothetical capitalization. As explained by the Alabama Supreme Court:

> The ideal capital structure would allow a debt-equity ratio in amounts that the company would get its full benefit in the amount of debt capital, and

[60] As previously noted, Franco Modigliani and Merton H. Miller have questioned the assumption that the average cost of capital is a function of a company's capital structure. "The Cost of Capital, Corporate Finance and the Theory of Investment," 48 *American Economic Review* 261 (1958). These two authors concluded that the cost of capital is primarily a function of basic business risk and not of how that risk may be apportioned between debt and equity holders. (They subsequently modified their position to acknowledge the effect of savings in federal income tax charges resulting from the deductibility of bond interest payments. "Corporate Income Taxes and the Cost of Capital: A Correction," 53 *ibid*. 433 [1963].) But see two replies by Joseph R. Rose and David Durand, 49 *ibid*. 638, 639 (1959); Alexander Barges, *The Effect of Capital Structure on the Cost of Capital* (Englewood Cliffs, N.J.: Prentice-Hall, Inc., 1963); and J. Fred Weston, "A Test of Cost of Capital Propositions," 30 *Southern Economic Journal* 105 (1963). For empirical studies of the electric utility industry, see Merton H. Miller and Franco Modigliani, "Some Estimates of the Cost of Capital to the Electric Utility Industry, 1954-57," 66 *American Economic Review* 333 (1966); and Eugene F. Brigham and Myron J. Gordon, "Leverage, Dividend Policy, and the Cost of Capital," 23 *Journal of Finance* 85 (1968).

yet not have the debt component so high as to discourage prudent investors. This ideal capital structure is not static. However, many commissions and courts for rate-making purposes have concluded that a debt-equity ratio of 45 per cent debt 55 per cent equity most nearly approximates a proper debt-equity ratio.[61]

The Massachusetts commission thus rejected both the actual capitalization (62 percent debt) and one proposed by the company (35 percent debt), adopting a hypothetical capital structure of 45 to 50 percent debt. The commission pointed out that the company's actual capital structure had a debt ratio that was too high, while the proposed ratio represented an inefficient capital structure because it did not include an amount of debt which could be reasonably assumed by the company.[62] The Mississippi commission, in a 1956 decision, held:

> (4) Southern Bell's capital structure during the test period, with an average debt ratio of 21.7 per cent, is imprudent and uneconomical, and imposes an unjust and unwarranted financial burden on the telephone subscribers. For the purpose of assessing the propriety of the company's intrastate rates which prevail during the test period, we have reformed the capital structure on the basis of a debt ratio in the range of 45 per cent to 50 per cent, which we find is prudent, fair, and equitable.[63]

And the District of Columbia commission rejected a telephone company's actual capital structure of 15 percent debt and 85 percent equity as being unrealistic, adopting for rate-making purposes a hypothetical capital structure of 40 percent debt and 60 percent equity. "In our judgment," said the commission, "this capital structure, when applied to the cost of debt and equity, will amply afford sufficient earnings to pay a reasonable dividend and allow an increment for surplus."[64]

Other state commissions have adopted the actual capitalization. The New York commission has declared that to disregard the "actual historic structure" created with the commission's approval "would unsettle investors" and remove from management control over the capital structure. It added that "having approved a company's capital structure . . . the company and the public have the right to rely upon our using the capital structure which we have approved as the basis for determining its rate of return."[65] The commission has indicated,

---

[61] *Alabama* v. *Southern Bell Teleph. & Teleg. Co.,* 47 PUR 3d 65, 67 (1962).

[62] *New England Teleph. & Teleg. Co.* v. *Dept. of Public Utilities,* 327 Mass. 81, 97 N.E. 2d 509 (1951).

[63] *Re Southern Bell Teleph. & Teleg. Co.,* 16 PUR 3d 415, 461 (Miss., 1956).

[64] *Re The Chesapeake & Potomac Teleph. Co.,* 57 PUR 3d 1, 39 (D.C., 1964). Also see *Re Mountain States Teleph. & Teleg. Co.,* 2 PUR 3d 75 (Utah, 1953); *Re Southern Bell Teleph. & Teleg. Co.,* 4 PUR 3d 195 (Ala., 1954); *Re Illinois Bell Teleph. Co.,* 7 PUR 3d 493 (Ill., 1955); *Re Northwestern Bell Teleph. Co.,* 20 PUR 3d 385 (S.D., 1957); *Re New England Teleph. & Teleg. Co.,* 42 PUR 3d 57 (N.H., 1961); *Re Southern New England Teleph. Co.,* 42 PUR 3d 310 (Conn., 1962).

[65] *Re New York Teleph. Co.,* 84 PUR (NS) 267, 290 (N.Y., 1950).

however, that it will disregard the actual capital structure when it is "wasteful."[66] The Colorado commission has said that it "could adopt a hypothetical structure for rate making in the event that applicants' actual financial structure is not in the long run public interest . . . keeping in mind that responsibility for financial decisions rests with management."[67] The Arizona commission has rejected the use of hypothetical capital structures on the grounds that they involve "pure speculation," while actual capitalizations are "more realistic."[68] The Florida commission has long held that capital structures "fall within the prerogatives of management" and that "invasion of the field of management in such a sensitive area is justified only when the public interest requires the exercise of extreme measures for its protection and benefit."[69]

Finally, the Civil Aeronautics Board has based recent rate decisions on the capital structure expected "in the near future." In an examiner's words:

> It cannot be found that a hypothetical capital structure should be used. . . . The suggestion of a return based on a lower debt ratio than that planned for the future period under consideration is, in effect, a suggestion to allow an expense which would be consistent with sound management if it were to be incurred but which is not expected to be incurred under the plans of the carriers.
>
> If actual debt/equity ratios are used, the cost-of-capital approach will bring to investors the return on their investment which is found to be the cost of acquiring the type of capital (debt or equity) which they own. On the other hand, use of a hypothetical capital structure and the optimum debt/equity ratio will bring to equity investors during the period when the carriers have higher than optimum debt ratios a much higher rate of return than the cost of acquiring that type of capital.[70]

Actual or Hypothetical Capital Structure?   Locklin has argued that most commissions "disregard actual capital structures and set up an ideal or normal structure for the purpose. To do otherwise would burden the public with the higher costs of obtaining capital that result from a capital structure that is something less than ideal, and may, in fact, be quite unsound."[71] And Rose argues: "When a commission in determining cost of capital disregards the actual capital structure or a capital structure proposed by management it is no more

---

[66] *Re New York Teleph. Co.*, 11 PUR 3d 320, 332 (N.Y., 1955).

[67] *Re Mountain States Teleph. & Teleg. Co.*, 1 PUR 3d 129, 140 (Colo., 1954).

[68] *Re Mountain States Teleph. & Teleg. Co.*, 7 PUR 3d 115, 122 (Ariz., 1954).

[69] *Re Florida Power & Light Co.*, 67 PUR 3d 113, 162 (Fla., 1966).

[70] *General Passenger Fare Investigation,* Initial Decision, E-16068 (CAB, 1960), Appendix A, pp. 34–36.

The Federal Communications Commission rejected the adoption of a hypothetical capital structure for the Bell System, but noted that in fixing the allowable rate of return it would take into account the "extraordinary amount of risk insurance respondents have given its stockholders by its low debt ratio policy." *Re American Teleph. & Teleg. Co.*, 70 PUR 3d 129, 193 (FCC, 1967).

[71] Locklin, *op. cit.*, p. 382 (footnotes omitted).

invading the domain of management than when it disregards unreasonable expenses for labor, fuel, or other productive factors in prescribing rates."[72]

The author, however, is inclined to the view that in normal circumstances the actual or planned capital structure should be used in computing the cost of capital.[73] Undoubtedly there are instances of unsound capital structures, and commissions should modify the rule in such situations.[74] But as was discussed in Chapter 6,[75] there is no ideal capital structure, and even expert opinion can differ. The existing capitalization may well have resulted from sound and economical decisions when made, although a different structure might attract capital at a lower cost at the time of a rate case.[76] While hindsight is often superior to foresight, financial decisions must be made on the basis of a judgment of present and future conditions. "It seems, then, that it is economically sound to leave with management the decision as to proper debt ratio, at least within that area where the directors are not usurping or defaulting on their duties as directors."[77]

Moreover, as Bonbright has argued, "the use of a hypothetical or 'typical' capitalization substitutes an estimate of what the capital cost *would be* under nonexisting conditions for what it *actually is or will soon be* under prevailing conditions."[78] Unless the rate of return to equity capital is adjusted upward, and it seldom is, the company is forced to adopt the hypothetical debt ratio to earn its allowed rate. But if the hypothetical debt ratio is significantly higher than the actual debt ratio, it may take several years of financing exclusively by means of debt to attain the higher ratio. During this period, the company is unable to realize the rate on equity found to be required. Further, issuance of securities is under control of the vast majority of the regulatory commissions, so that there is a check on unsound financing. The fact that some commissions have not exercised this control in the past is no excuse to substitute their opinions in the present. For these reasons, it seems economically sound to leave the decision as to the proper capital structure with management.

[72] Rose, " 'Cost of Capital' in Public Utility Rate Regulation," *op. cit.*, pp. 1088–89.

[73] One exception, for instance, is where a company is a wholly owned subsidiary which obtains its capital through its parent corporation. In such circumstances, commissions commonly use the capital structure of the consolidated system. See *Re Tennessee Gas Transmission Co.*, 35 PUR 3d 270 (FPC, 1960); and *Re Gulf Power Co.*, Docket No. 7763–EU, Order No. 4086 (Fla., 1967).

[74] As the Supreme Court argued in the Market Street Railway case, the due process clause "has not and cannot be applied to insure values or to restore values that have been lost by the operation of economic forces." *Market Street Ry. Co.* v. *Railroad Comm. of Calif., op. cit.*, p. 567.

[75] See Chapter 6, pp. 169–71.

[76] A company's financing decision at any point of time depends upon such factors as the condition of the market, the availability of funds, and the financial condition of the company. These factors are constantly changing.

[77] G. Stanley Joslin and Arthur S. Miller, "Public Utility Rate Regulation: A Re-Examination," 43 *Virginia Law Review* 1027, 1060 (1957).

[78] Bonbright, *op. cit.*, pp. 243–44.

The Annual Cost of Capital

The second step in determining the overall cost of capital involves establishment of the cost of senior capital and of equity capital. These costs are then applied to the capitalization of a company to find the weighted cost of capital.

The Cost of Senior Capital. Few problems arise in computing the cost of senior capital. Three methods are commonly used by the commissions in determining the cost of debt capital: (1) the actual fixed charges on the bonds, known as imbedded cost; (2) the imbedded cost for existing debt and current cost, based on market prices, for additional indebtedness contemplated in the immediate future; (3) a combination of imbedded and current costs (with no specific weightings) for existing and contemplated debt. A 1961 survey on the practices of state regulatory commissions indicated that 16 fall in the first group, 14 in the second, and 15 in the third.[79] The cost of preferred stock is determined by its annual dividend requirements. In addition, allowances are usually made for the costs of financing, such as discounts and premiums on sale, call premiums paid when bonds are retired before maturity, underwriting fees, and other flotation costs.

Except for the purpose of new financing or of refunding, basing the cost of existing senior capital upon the hypothetical cost of doing senior financing under current conditions of the bond and stock market is questionable. As in the case of reproduction cost property valuations, such a procedure offers an alternative not available to a company.[80]

The Cost of Equity. The most difficult problem in determining the overall cost of capital arises in estimating the cost of equity capital. The relevant question is: "How much must a company earn to induce investors to hold and to continue to buy common stock?" In answering this question, it is important to realize that circular reasoning is involved. In the absence of a fixed, expressed, or implied commitment as to the dividend rate, the actual cost of floating a stock issue is indeterminate. Investors' decisions are largely based on a company's expected earnings and upon their stability, as well as upon alternative uses of investment funds. But, since the allowable amount of earnings is the object of a rate case, a commission's decision will, in turn, affect investors' decisions.

In attempting to establish the cost of equity, two ratios are commonly computed and analyzed—the earnings-price ratio and the dividend-price ratio.

Earnings-Price Ratio. If a company's reported annual earnings are $11.25 per share and the average market price of its stock for that same year is $150, the earnings-price ratio is 7.5 percent. (The ratio must be increased to allow

[79] Robert G. Towers, "Cost of Debt for Rate of Return," 68 *Public Utilities Fortnightly* 20, 20–22 (1961). Five state commissions (Alaska, Connecticut, Iowa, Minnesota, and Nebraska) were not included in the tabulation. Also see "Determination of Debt Cost in the Rate of Return," 81 *Public Utilities Fortnightly* 53 (May 23, 1968).

[80] But see Eugene M. Lerner, "The FCC's 7.5 Per Cent Ruling," 80 *Public Utilities Fortnightly* 40, 41–43 (October 12, 1967).

for flotation and underpricing costs involved in the issuance of additional stock. An allowance of 10 percent is common and would result in an adjusted ratio of 8.3 percent—7.5 percent divided by 0.90.) This ratio implies that if the earnings-price ratio of a company has been running fairly consistently at 7.5 percent, then the stock will continue to sell at approximately its book value if future earnings per share amount to 8.3 percent of this book value.

Dividend-Price Ratio. If a stock has an average market value of $150 and the annual dividend is $9.00, the dividend-price ratio is 6 percent. This ratio thus represents the yield received by the investor at the average market price. Whereas the earnings-price ratio implies that investors are guided on the basis of earnings, the dividend-price ratio implies that investors are guided by dividend yields.[81]

For many years, it was thought that investors bought utility stocks largely on the basis of dividends.[82] More recently, however, studies indicate that the market is valuing utility stocks with reference to total per share earnings, so that the earnings-price ratio has assumed increased emphasis in rate cases.[83] Both ratios must be used with a great deal of caution because they may fail to indicate an adequate rate of return to attract capital. As stated by the California commission in a 1954 decision:

> Earnings-price ratios and dividend-price ratios merely reflect the prospective investors' appraisal of the market value of stock and as such are influenced by prevailing market and economic conditions and the individual requirements of the purchaser. While useful for comparative purposes and of value in presenting background information, they are not conclusive in themselves in the determination of the allowable fair return on investment in operative properties. It is one thing to say that these ratios indicate the terms under which a new investor might devote his money to the business; it is another thing to say that these terms represent or limit the return the applicant is entitled to receive on the capital committed to the service. It seems to us that reliance on ratios of this nature results in a restricted view of the subject of rate-of-return. Obviously, the price at which a security is bought on the market reflects anticipated earnings rather than past results of operations and it by no means follows that the rates at which present market sales prices are related to the past earnings represents the returns the purchasers at those prices are willing to accept in the future.

[81] Both earnings-price and dividend-price ratios "should cover representative periods of operation. Ratios used on a 'spot' basis, for a period of a month, or even a year, might produce very unsatisfactory results. Prices of utility stocks of the most stable type are influenced by short-run considerations—threats of war, tax legislation, changing governmental regulations, strikes, elections—all affect stock prices in one way or another. For dividend yields or earnings-price ratios to be really significant they must be considered over a sufficiently long period of time for the abnormal and unusual pressures to average out." Lionel W. Thatcher, "Cost-of-Capital Techniques Employed in Determining the Rate of Return for Public Utilities," 30 *Land Economics* 85, 92 (1954).

[82] See Eli W. Clemens, "Some Aspects of the Rate-of-Return Problem," 30 *Land Economics* 32, 34–35 (1954).

[83] See Fred P. Morrissey, "Current Aspects of the Cost of Capital to Utilities," 62 *Public Utilities Fortnightly* 217 (1958).

With the wide range in the claims now before us and with the opposing opinions of the witnesses to be considered, it is apparent that our final determination of rate of return must represent the exercise of judgment on our part, having in mind the lawful interests of the ratepayer and the utility.[84]

In the postwar period, earnings, dividends, and market prices per share have been increasing for most of the regulated companies. Market prices have advanced faster, however, than either earnings or dividends per share, so that earnings-price and dividend-price ratios have declined. The increase in market prices relative to their book values clearly indicates that investors are buying stock in anticipation of *future* advances in per share earnings. As a result, a growth factor must be added in computing the cost of equity capital.[85]

Closely connected with the prospects for future growth of both earnings and dividends per share is the pay-out ratio:

Pay-Out Ratio. If a company has annual reported earnings of $11.25 per share and a dividend rate of $9.00, the pay-out ratio is 80 percent. This ratio depends on the relationship between earnings and dividends. The difference between per share earnings and the dividend rate represents the amount available to the company for reinvestment (i.e., earned surplus).[86]

The importance of the pay-out ratio can be quickly demonstrated. A company can increase its per share earnings in two ways—by increasing the rate of return on its book equity and/or by increasing its per share book value. The pay-out ratio influences the second.[87] Assume that a company earns a 6 percent return for several years on its total capital structure and a 10 percent return on its common stock. If its pay-out ratio is 80 percent and if the remaining 20 percent is reinvested in plant and equipment, earnings and dividends per share will increase at the rate of 2.0 percent (20 percent of 10) per year. It would

---

[84]*Re Pacific Teleph. & Teleg. Co.,* 5 PUR 3d 396, 405 (Cal., 1954). Also see Ralph E. Badger, "Important Concepts as to Fair Return and Cost of Money," 66 *Public Utilities Fortnightly* 93, 96–98 (1960); Walter A. Morton, "Creative Regulation," 39 *Land Economics* 367, 370–74 (1963); Stephen H. Fletcher, "Current Problems in the Determination of the Cost of Equity Capital for Rate of Return Purposes" (American Bar Association Annual Report, Section of *Public Utility Law, 1963*), pp. 46–50; *Re Southern Bell Teleph. & Teleg. Co.,* 66 PUR 3d 1, 98–101 (Fla., 1966); and "Earnings–Price Ratios Test Equity Capital Cost," 81 *Public Utilities Fortnightly* 59 (January 18, 1968).

[85]See Ezra Solomon, *The Theory of Financial Management* (New York: Columbia University Press, 1963), pp. 55–68.

[86]In addition to reinvestment, a surplus account serves two other basic functions. First, certain charges and credits are made directly to surplus rather than taken through the income statement. Thus, when original cost accounting was instituted by regulatory commissions, some companies had to write down the book value of their property. These and other direct surplus charges are called an "erosion" of surplus. Second, retained earnings permit a company to maintain a more stable dividend record throughout the business cycle, thereby aiding in securing a favorable market for its stock.

[87]A second method of increasing per share book value is by selling new equity, provided that the net proceeds are in excess of the book value of presently outstanding stock.

appear, therefore, that a low pay-out ratio would lead to maximum growth in per share earnings with a minimum of new stock issues.[88]

A decision concerning the proper earnings-price, dividend-price, and pay-out ratios is further complicated by the fact that all are interrelated. These ratios, in turn, depend on the price premium for the growth factor which influences investor expectations. Tatham illustrates the point when, in discussing the appropriate relationship between book value and market price, he states:

> It has been widely recognized that some fairly substantial price premium is justified. It is also true that the market price premium varies largely in accordance with the earnings growth rate. But, since the earnings growth rate, in turn, is to a considerable degree controlled by the regulatory permissible *level* of earnings (rate of return), we are dealing with a series of interrelated factors that have some of the aspects of the Gordian knot. What is needed is some index, independent of the influence of earnings, that will reasonably indicate what an appropriate market price premium over book value should be.[89]

It is little wonder, therefore, that estimates of the cost of equity capital differ significantly.[90] In a 1961 case, for instance, five witnesses presented the estimates shown in Table 9-5. The New Hampshire commission concluded that a 7.75 percent return on equity would provide for a $1.72 per share dividend rate (assuming a pay-out ratio of 87.7 percent) and annual retained earnings per share of $0.24.[91] Further, the overall return of 6.11 percent would cover interest 3.3 times.[92]

[88] Willard F. Stanley, "Impact of Dividend Pay-Out on Price-Earnings Ratios," 67 *Public Utilities Fortnightly* 145 (1961); and "Dividend Payments as a Consideration in Determining a Reasonable Return," 69 *Public Utilities Fortnightly* 273 (1962).

[89] Charles Tatham, "Commentary on 'Common Stock Earnings Allowance for Utilities as Adjusted for Growth'," 39 *Land Economics* 53, 54 (1963). Kosh has argued that the increase in market prices relative to book values means that the cost of equity capital has declined and that current earnings are in excess of the cost of equity capital as required by the market. David A. Kosh, "Recent Trends in Cost of Capital," 72 *Public Utilities Fortnightly* 19, 21-26 (September 26, 1963). Bonbright, however, has argued that "market prices are beyond the control, though not beyond the influence, of rate regulation. Moreover, even if a commission did possess the power of control, any attempt to exercise it [so as to prevent the market prices of utility equities from rising to substantial premiums above book values] . . . would result in harmful, uneconomic shifts in public utility rate levels. . . . Regulation is simply powerless to assure the purchasers of public utility equities that future corporate earnings will suffice to maintain market prices on par with book values or with any other dollar figure." Bonbright, *op. cit.*, pp. 255, 256.

[90] The mechanics of determining the annual cost of equity, once these matters have been considered, is as follows. Assume that the current relationship between book value and market price is accepted. Assume, further, a dividend yield of 5.3 percent on market price and an underpricing factor of 10 percent. The result is a rate of 5.9 percent (5.3 percent divided by .90). Finally, assume a 70 percent pay-out ratio. The resulting annual cost of equity capital would be 8.4 percent (5.9 percent divided by .70). This cost would then be weighted with the cost of senior capital and applied to either the actual or hypothetical capital structure to find the overall rate of return.

[91] *Re New England Teleph. & Teleg. Co.*, 42 PUR 3d 57, 61 (N.H., 1961).

[92] *Ibid.* The commission then added 0.2 percent as a "margin," resulting in a 6.3 percent rate of return. *Ibid.*, p. 62.

TABLE 9-5
Estimates of the Cost of Equity Capital

	Debt Ratio	Cost of Equity	Cost of Capital
McIninch	...	9.5–10%	...
Conrad	35%	10–11%	8.0%
Barker	35%	10%	7.75–8.5%
Lowell	35–40%	10–11%	8.0%
Kosh	45–50%	6.95–8%	5.5–6.05%
Commission	45%	7.75%	6.11%

Source: *Re New England Teleph. & Teleg. Co.*, 42 PUR 3d
57, 60–61 (N.H., 1961).

Conclusions on Cost of Capital. It is clear that "the cost of common stock capital is not reduceable to any standard mathematical formula or procedure because the responsible treatment of the same evidence of the cost of common stock capital, such as earnings–price ratios and dividend yields, necessarily vary with economic circumstances of the time and place and most particularly with the shifts from pessimism to optimism." Further, "the evaluation of the elements of fair rate of return is a function in which good judgment as well as arithmetic should be applied to bring about an equitable economic result."[93]

With no precise mathematical formula for computing the cost of equity capital, a large element of judgment inevitably enters. Bonbright feels that the only cost of equity "that can be determined with confidence is a *minimum* or *partial cost.*" He continues:

That is to say, the analyst, by a study of earnings–price ratios and of other market data, may be able to reach a credible conclusion that the cost of common-stock capital comes to *at least* some specified per cent; but the extent of the probable deficiency is necessarily a matter of surmise. Hence, if the minimum estimated cost is to be used in the determination of a computed "overall cost of capital," the resulting computation should be subject to a material, "judgment-reached" enhancement in order to give reasonable assurance of full-cost coverage.[94]

Here, as is true with many other aspects of regulation, the quality of the commissions is crucial.

[93] Testimony of Herbert Dorau in *Alabama* v. *Southern Bell Teleph. & Teleg. Co.,* *op. cit.*, pp. 72–73.
[94] Bonbright, *op. cit.*, p. 254. In an effort to overcome the problems inherent in determining the cost of equity capital, it has been proposed that common stock be placed on a contractual basis. See Arthur P. Becker, "Fixed Dividends for All Public Utility Stock," 21 *Journal of Land & Public Utility Economics* 243 (1945); and John Bauer, *Transforming Public Utility Regulation* (New York: Harper & Bros., 1950), chaps. x and xi. There is little support, however, for such a proposal.

The Incentive to Efficiency

The cost of capital standard, as discussed above, has one serious limitation: it makes no specific allowance for efficiency. Justice Brandeis argued that an efficient utility might properly be allowed more than a rate of return barely above the level of confiscation.[95] And the Florida commission has stated:

> Inefficient operations sometimes penalize the guilty utility and this matter of efficiency compared with inefficiency in the operations of a public utility has given rise to considerable controversy in regulatory circles as to the impact efficiency, or the lack of it, should have in fixing the allowable return. It does not appear to be reasonable to penalize a public utility's customers or subscribers for the inefficiencies of the utility. It would seem to be more reasonable that a utility should be allowed something more in the rate of return if it has demonstrated its ability to operate efficiently. While it is difficult to accurately evaluate this factor because of its imponderable nature, it would appear reasonable to conclude that a public utility is operating efficiently if it has a minimum of service complaints, is constantly improving its service, but is still able to produce higher earnings on lower rates than comparable or similar utilities in the same general area.[96]

Competition is supposed to compel management efficiency as firms seek ways of reducing costs in order to maximize profits and increase sales. Under regulation, however, if rates are fixed so as to enable all companies—those that are well managed and those that are not—to cover their costs plus receive a fair rate of return, there is no stimulus for efficiency comparable to the stimulus of competition.

American experience with regulated private ownership hardly justifies the unqualified indictment that some writers have made against it on this score. But a plausible case, at least, could be made for the thesis that what has saved regulation from being a critical influence in the direction of mediocrity and tardy technological progress has been its very "deficiencies" in the form of regulatory lags and in the form of acquiescence by commissions in fairly prolonged periods of theoretically "excessive" earnings on the part of companies whose public repute and whose comparative rates of charge for service have not made them vulnerable to popular attack.[97]

To be sure, present regulatory methods provide some incentives, most of which are unintended. The most significant incentive, and a highly efficient one, involves the allowable rate of return. Since a fair return represents a range, there is an incentive for operating efficiency to bring earnings into the upper portion of the allowable range. Further, if a company obtains a return in the upper range

[95] Concurring opinion in *Missouri* ex rel. *Southwestern Bell Tel. Co.* v. *Public Service Comm.*, *op. cit.*, p. 290.
[96] *Re General Teleph. Co. of Florida*, 44 PUR 3d 247, 255 (Fla., 1962). Also see *New England Teleph. & Teleg. Co.* v. *New Hampshire*, 44 PUR 3d 498, 506 (1962); and *Re Florida Power Corp.*, Docket No. 9426–EU, Order No. 4341 (Fla., 1968).
[97] Bonbright, *op. cit.*, p. 262.

of the zone of reasonableness, most commissions will approve the higher level. There is also an incentive for small utilities to be efficient, since their earnings as a group are often lower than the rate authorized by the regulatory commissions.[98] And a few commissions have made a specific allowance for efficiency in setting a fair rate of return.[99] But there is no intended, consistent policy among the commissions.

Various proposals to deal with this problem have been made, but none has ever been adopted. The most frequently stated suggestion is for commissions to make adjustments in the rate of return so as to reward efficiency or penalize inefficiency.[100] A commission, for example, might allow a 6 percent rate of return under "standard" management, while permitting a 7 percent rate under "exceptional" management and a 5 percent rate under "substandard" management. Any such program would be difficult to administer. Efficiency is a relative concept.[101] Cost reductions may be due to causes other than improvements in management efficiency, such as to increases in demand (assuming decreasing cost industries). To identify the gains resulting from management efficiency, commissions would find it necessary to devise objective standards of performance and methods of measurement.[102] So far, little attention has been devoted to the development of such techniques. Their development, nevertheless, should be encouraged.

The problem of inefficiency, however, raises a new dilemma. Should a commission find it necessary to impose a penalty for inefficiency, a serious obstacle might be placed on the ability of a company to attract and to hold capital. A reduction in earnings would almost certainly make it more difficult for a company to confront investors, thereby causing efficiency to decline even further.[103] Methods of rewarding efficiency might be developed, but penalties for inefficiency may be impractical.[104]

Finally, the absence of specific incentives does not mean that commissions

---

[98] Richard B. Blatz, "Efficiency Incentives for Telephone Companies," 72 *Public Utilities Fortnightly* 19 (September 12, 1963).

[99] Thus, the New Hampshire commission allowed 0.20 percent in excess of the cost of capital as an efficiency allowance. *New England Teleph. & Teleg. Co.* v. *New Hampshire, op. cit.,* p. 506. Other commissions take efficiency into consideration in determining the overall rate of return. *Re General Teleph. Co. of Upstate New York,* 41 PUR 3d 1, 24 (N.Y., 1961).

[100] See Irvin Bussing, *Public Utility Regulation and the So-Called Sliding Scale* (New York: Columbia University Press, 1936); and Sidney Weintraub, "Rate Making and an Incentive Rate of Return," 81 *Public Utilities Fortnightly* 23 (April 25, 1968).

[101] Clair Wilcox, *Public Policies Toward Business* (3d ed.; Homewood, Ill.: Richard D. Irwin, Inc., 1966), p. 332.

[102] For one such attempt, see William Iulo, *Electric Utilities—Costs and Performance* (Pullman: Washington State University Press, 1961).

[103] *Re Rochester Teleph. Corp.,* 24 PUR 3d 262 (N.Y., 1958).

[104] "But one might hope that the restriction of a company, by virtue of a commission finding of inferior management, to a minimum rate of return measured, say, by a 'barebones' estimate of cost of capital, would become so intolerable to the corporate stockholders that they would soon enforce a change of management." Bonbright, *op. cit.,* p. 263.

can ignore the problem. At the minimum, regulatory agencies must make sure they avoid policies that penalize efficiency. For example, if a commission requires the deduction from the rate base of the unamortized costs of assets unexpectedly retired because of obsolescence, but permits their retention in the rate base as long as the assets are not replaced by superior, but available, substitutes, efficiency is discouraged.[105] The same is true "if every act that raises profit is offset by a regulatory act that reduces it. . . ."[106] Much more thinking remains to be done in the whole area of incentives to efficiency for the regulated industries.[107]

The Inflation Problem

Since the Hope decision in 1944, the majority of federal and state commissions have adopted the original cost less accrued depreciation method of determining the rate base and have applied a rate of return at least partially estimated by the cost of capital standard. The resulting earnings, it is argued, should be sufficient to meet the contractual obligations of the company, to reward common stockholders, and to attract any necessary new capital. But owing to price inflation in the economy since World War II, this procedure has become a source of controversy before the regulatory commissions. Specifically, should investors be compensated for inflation? Such compensation could be made in two ways: by converting either the original cost rate base or the equity portion of the investment into dollars of the current year, or by making an appropriate adjustment in the rate of return. It was argued in the preceding chapter[108] that the second method is preferable to the first if an adjustment is necessary.

Two arguments are commonly advanced in support of a policy of raising earnings during inflation. The first is economic: unless earnings are kept in line with those in other industries, regulated industries will not be able to attract needed capital on reasonable and equitable terms. The second is ethical: unless commissions allow an adjustment in relation to the current purchasing power of the dollar, there is an unfair expropriation of the real value of the company's property and, hence, of the common stockholders' investment.

To be sure, these claims are not independent of each other, since the question whether existing investors have a fair claim to indemnity for *past* inflation may be held to depend on the question whether uncommitted prospective investors are willing to supply new capital without receiving any

---

[105] *Ibid.,* p. 265.

[106] Morton, "Creative Regulation," *op. cit.,* p. 371.

[107] Thus, late in 1963, Federal Power Commissioner Woodward called for a system of "incentive regulation" to encourage in the natural gas industry "efficiency, drive, better planning of construction and programming of operations." He warned that there is a danger "that under regulation, private initiative will be killed, resources will not be allocated in the most efficient manner, and the over-all cost of service will be increased." Federal Power Commission, Release No. 12914 (September 17, 1963).

[108] See Chapter 8, pp. 236–38.

protection against *future* inflation. Nevertheless, the answer to the one issue does not necessarily carry with it the answer to the other.[109]

The two arguments will be considered in turn.

The Attraction of Capital. All the evidence available suggests that the regulated industries have been able to attract capital on terms comparable with nonregulated industries in the postwar inflationary period.[110] The true test of the ability to attract capital is to be found in the capital market. Since 1946, the regulated industries have raised large amounts of new capital for plant expansion and improvements, indicating sufficient confidence in their securities on the part of investors. For the public utilities, most of this capital has been obtained by the issuance of nonconvertible bonds, debentures, and nonconvertible preferred stock—all securities with fixed returns and all securities which offer the investor no protection against inflation. Public utility bonds have been highly regarded by institutional investors, notably life insurance companies and pension funds, who were attracted to fixed income securities because of their fixed dollar obligations. Yet, during this same period, utilities have also raised large amounts of common stock equity. In fact, Morrissey has calculated that "the utility industry has accounted for approximately 50 per cent of new equity issues in the post-war period—a trend likely to continue."[111]

However, it must be emphasized that most commissions have permitted regulated companies under their jurisdictions to earn incomes in excess of the minimum cost of capital. This fact, combined with an average pay-out ratio of 70 percent and the flotation of new common stock issues at prices in excess of the book values of old stocks, has provided an upward trend in the earnings per share of the regulated companies. Investors have found, therefore, that the market values of their stocks have more than kept pace with changes in the cost of living index.[112] Regulated companies, in other words, have received some sort of inflation allowance either through the rate base (in reproduction cost and fair value jurisdictions) or the rate of return (in original cost jurisdictions). Moreover, large amounts of new capital are not synonymous with sufficient quantities of new capital. Some of the regulated companies, for example, particularly in the

[109] Bonbright, *op. cit.,* p. 267. It should be emphasized again that the arguments supporting an inflation adjustment pertain to original cost jurisdictions; a reproduction cost or fair value rate base makes a full or partial allowance for inflation.

[110] See Fergus J. McDiarmid, "Are Public Utility Stocks an Inflation Hedge?" 80 *Public Utilities Fortnightly* 33 (October 12, 1967).

[111] Morrissey, "Current Aspects of the Cost of Capital to Utilities," *op. cit.,* pp. 217–18. The airline and railroad industries have had trouble in meeting their heavy postwar capital needs, but their earnings are regulated more by demand and competitive factors than by regulatory authorities.

[112] See Fred P. Morrissey, "Inflation and Public Utility Regulation," I *California Management Review* 74 (1959). One study, for example, estimated that "per share earnings of electric utility stocks, over the past ten years [1948–58], have shown a compound annual growth at a rate of 2.9 per cent; natural gas distribution companies, 6 per cent; and natural gas pipeline companies, 8.8 per cent." Badger, *op. cit.,* p. 95. Also see McDiarmid, *op. cit.,* pp. 37–38.

immediate postwar period, faced severe capital restrictions. Bonbright has argued:

> In view of this financial history, the question really at issue is that of a choice between a scheme of rate regulation expressly designed to make the dollar earnings on stock equities rise and fall with changes in general price levels, and the more familiar regulatory practice which makes no direct provision for inflation but which undertakes to compensate stockholders for running the *risks* of inflation by the concession of what might otherwise be needlessly high "fair rates of return."[113]

On this issue he concludes:

> While the experience down to date indicates that equity capital can be secured without such adjustments, it also suggests that this capital can be secured only by the concession of rates of return that offer to stockholders a kind of compensation for the very absence of protection. This being the probable situation, the provision of overt adjustments, whether in the rate base or in the rate of return, may prove the more satisfactory arrangement alike to investors and consumers. The possible advantage of this latter arrangement is that the compensation for inflation would then be paid only if, and to the extent that, inflation actually occurs instead of being paid merely in contemplation of the danger that it *may* occur. But the only way to test this possible advantage is by experiment; and the experiment, in my opinion, is well worth trying out in a number of jurisdictions.[114]

Fairness to Stockholders. The second argument in support of an inflation adjustment has been advanced by Morton. In an article published in 1952, he argued that in computing the cost of capital, the equity portion should be adjusted upward by the use of a general price index, with 1946 as the base year. To deny such an inflationary adjustment to the common stockholders of the regulated industries, he continued, is unfair and constitutionally confiscatory. Interestingly enough, his argument is based on the grounds of fairness and not financial necessity. To quote from the article:

> Instead of giving a utility a reasonable return because it is just, we now ask what rate is necessary to maintain it as a going concern and to attract new capital. Justice is a moral concept. Necessity is a power concept. The demands of fairness are not always those of power. We have already shown that a utility will continue to function as a going concern and attract new capital even if no compensation is made for inflation to capital already irrevocably committed. An inflation adjustment is not necessary to maintain the financial soundness and integrity of the concern. As long as necessity is the sole guide to action, the property of a utility can be taken without compensation by means of inflation, provided the will to do so is accompanied by legal and political power. Under these circumstances, holders of utility property can hardly be expected to submit to expropriation without

[113] Bonbright, *op. cit.*, p. 270.
[114] *Ibid.*, p. 274.

trying to use political power to protect themselves. Within the constitutional framework, political power is, after all, the ultimate arbitor of all rights to liberty and property.

The erroneous notion that the market somewhat automatically compensates for inflation rests on the belief that economic power is capable of protecting itself. In unregulated industry this is true. Any interest having economic power to compel a fair return can exert that power; it does not need to resort to the courts. Appeal to the courts under the 14th Amendment (and 5th) is made when the individual is incapable of defending himself against arbitrary action. A utility cannot protect itself against inflation by its power to control the supply of services because that power is limited and circumscribed by regulation. Potential investors can exert some economic power by withholding capital but past investors are wholly dependent upon constitutional interpretation.[115]

Professor Morton's argument rests on two basic assumptions: first, that inflation results in the impairment of stockholders' "real" capital and, second, that nonregulated industries can protect their stockholders from such capital impairment by exercising their "economic power." The first assumption is valid, but the second is questionable.[116] These comments aside, the most significant drawbacks to an inflationary adjustment made on the basis of fairness are that such an adjustment would be selective and not remedial[117] and that in being fair to the common stockholders of the regulated industries, unfairness to others would result.[118]

In the first place, the holders of bonds and preferred stocks receive no safeguards against inflation. While they receive other safeguards (such as less risk), justice or fairness would seem to indicate that they, too, should share in any inflation allowance, for inflation also results in the impairment of their "real" capital. In the second place, the buyers of common stocks, whether of regulated or nonregulated companies, were never promised a return that would protect their capital against price inflation (in fact, they were never promised any return at all). Provided that investors are fully informed about the facts of their investments, as required by the Federal Securities Act, and that commissions are consistent in their policies,[119] common stockholders have no claim to

115 Walter A. Morton, "Rate of Return and the Value of Money in Public Utilities," 28 *Land Economics* 91, 119 (1952).

116 See Chapter 8, pp. 236–39.

117 Martin G. Glaeser, *Public Utilities in American Capitalism* (New York: Macmillan Co., 1957), p. 399.

118 See *Re New York Teleph. Co.,* 91 PUR (NS) 231 (N.Y., 1951); *Re Michigan Bell Teleph. Co.,* 91 PUR (NS) 129 (Mich., 1951); *Re Wisconsin Elec. Power Co.,* 93 PUR (NS) 97 (Wis., 1952).

119 Consistency in regulatory rate-making policy is closely connected to the fairness issue. Stockholders who purchase the common stocks of companies which are in fair value jurisdictions, for example, have the right to expect that commissions will continue to adhere to a fair value theory. See Bonbright, *op. cit.*, pp. 272–73.

preferential treatment.[120] In the third place, inflationary adjustments would tend to "unsettle regulation." As Thatcher puts it:

> It would strengthen the very inflationary forces against which representatives of the companies warn us. Principles such as those proposed by witnesses urging an inflation adjustment, like those urged by proponents of "fair value" or "reproduction cost," if consistently carried onward into the future, as they should be if they are recognized in rate cases, would in fact endanger the future stability of companies in times of falling prices and hopelessly confuse the regulatory process.[121]

Finally, an inflation adjustment might not achieve its intended goal. Clemens has argued:

> ... it is improbable—at least over the short run—that the plan would produce a return to common stockholders of stabilized purchasing power. It is more likely that it would stabilize the *expected* purchasing power of the market value of the equity investment—something entirely different and of limited desirability. This arises from the fact that the formula consists of two variables, the cost of money and the price or inflation adjustment. The inflation adjustment standing alone would give the investor an income of constant purchasing power, but it would not do so if it were coupled with the cost of money computed from market yields. Investors would simply discount expected inflation or deflation and bid up, or bid down, the value of the stock accordingly. Under conditions of expected inflation, yields would be lower than otherwise; under conditions of expected deflation, yields would be higher. In other words, a stock that normally yielded 5.5% might sell to yield only 5.0% if inflation were expected and the inflationary adjustment were assured; if deflation were expected it would be discounted and the stock would sell to yield say 6.0%. Only if the market anticipated no change in the price level, in future income, or in future institutional arrangements would the equity investors' actual income be adjusted to purchasing power. This process of discounting would in effect constitute an exchange of future and present earnings.
>
> It is likely that in the long-run the return would move upward with prices but, assuming inflation, the inflationary adjustment might be offset to a degree by the lower yield at which inflation-protected securities would probably sell. However, a cyclical pattern would be imposed upon the income flow; income would be higher in times of expected deflation; lower in times of expected inflation.[122]

---

120 In the words of the California commission: ". . . the law contemplates that people who buy securities are charged with the knowledge that certain risks will be attached to their ownership and that one of the risks is the possibility of the decline in purchasing power of the dollar." Quoted in Glaeser, *op. cit.*, p. 398.

121 Thatcher, *op. cit.*, p. 111. Also see *Re Mountain States Teleph. & Teleg. Co.*, 2 PUR 3d 75 (Utah, 1953); *Re New York Teleph. Co.*, 5 PUR 3d 33 (N.Y., 1954); *Re Pacific Teleph. & Teleg. Co.*, 5 PUR 3d 396 (Cal., 1954).

122 Clemens, *op. cit.*, pp. 38–39.

Conclusions on Inflation Adjustment. In the author's opinion, some inflation adjustment is necessary if the regulated companies are to continue to attract capital. However, the adjustment should be made on the basis of capital attraction rather than on the basis of fairness. The regulated industries must compete for investment funds with nonregulated industries in the capital market. "The fact that funds were available to finance construction does not mean that utility earnings were adequate or commensurate with the returns of other industries having corresponding risks and uncertainties, that owners were receiving reasonable returns, or that there should be no compensation for inflation."[123] However, the need for an "overt" or systematic adjustment has yet to be demonstrated.

THE COMPARABLE EARNINGS STANDARD

In the Hope decision, Justice Douglas, in discussing the requirements of a fair rate of return, stated: "By that standard the return to the equity owner should be commensurate with returns on investments in other enterprises having corresponding risks."[124] As indicated at the beginning of the chapter, this was not the first time the "comparable earnings" standard had received judicial attention.[125] Admittedly, the standard raises many important and difficult questions, but it also offers the possibility of resolving both the fairness and inflation issues.

The crucial element in the comparable earnings standard is the measurement of risk. On the one hand, regulation tends to eliminate some of the risks to which nonregulated industries are subject. Competition is controlled in the regulated sector of the economy: ruinous rate cutting by competitors is prohibited and entry is limited. On the other hand, regulation cannot eliminate all risk. Markets may disappear with shifts in industrial location and population, and with changes in consumer tastes. Revenues may decline in business recessions. Technological innovation may result in the new competition of substitute products produced by other industries. While competition is controlled, it is not eliminated: gas competes with coal, electricity, and oil; railroads with motor and water carriers, airlines, and the private automobile. The regulated industries compete with nonregulated firms for investment funds and productive resources. And a fair rate of return is not guaranteed. In short, the combination of technological innovation and oligopolistic market structures

---

[123] John H. Bickley, "How to Compensate for Inflation," 73 *Public Utilities Fortnightly* 27, 34 (May 7, 1964).
[124] *Federal Power Comm.* v. *Hope Natural Gas Co., op. cit.,* p. 603.
[125] See pp. 261–64.

suggests that the regulated industries *as a group* may be as risky as nonregulated industries *as a whole.*[126]

Perhaps the most significant aspect of the comparable earnings standard is that it seeks to measure alternative investment opportunities available to investors. In a 1920 case, Judge Hand argued:

> The recurrent appeal to a just rate and a fair value assumes that the effort is to insure such a profit as would induce the venture originally and that the public will keep its faith so impliedly given. That, I think, involves a tacit comparison of the profit possible under the rate with profits available elsewhere; i.e., under those competitive enterprises which offer an alternative investment. The implication is that the original adventurer would compare future rates, varying as they would with the going profit, and would find them enough, but no more than enough, to induce him to choose this investment. By insuring such a return it is assumed that the supply of capital will be secured necessary to the public service. As the profits in the supposed alternative investment will themselves vary, so it is assumed to be a condition of the investors' bargain that their profit shall measurably follow the general rates. It is, of course, not relevant here to discuss these presuppositions, since they have now the support of authoritative law.[127]

An important question involves the relationship between the cost of capital standard and the comparable earnings test. Bonbright believes the comparable earnings test is a secondary or ancillary standard, thus regarding the cost of capital standard as primary.[128] Welch argues that the comparable earnings test "may be used by both commissions and courts as an upper limit on a reasonable rate of return."[129] Leventhal, however, believes "that the attraction of capital standard and the comparable earning standard are interrelated and will merge into each other in the long run. Unless the utility is permitted to earn a return comparable to that available elsewhere on similar risks, it will not be able in the long run to attract capital."[130]

---

[126] See Burton A. Kolb, "The Rise and Fall of Public Utilities: An Appraisal of Risk," 37 *The Journal of Business of the University of Chicago* 329 (1964). It should be recognized that the comparable earnings standard logically implies an original cost rate base. Nonregulated enterprises report earnings on an original cost basis. Therefore, to argue that a 10 percent return on equity capital, for instance, indicated by the comparable earnings standard, should be applied to a fair value rate base would be inconsistent.

[127] *Consolidated Gas Co. of New York* v. *Newton,* 267 Fed. 231, 237 (S.D.N.Y., 1920).

[128] Bonbright, *op. cit.,* pp. 255–56.

[129] Francis X. Welch, *Cases and Text on Public Utility Regulation* (rev. ed.; Washington, D.C.: Public Utilities Reports, Inc., 1968), p. 488.

[130] Harold Leventhal, testimony before the Federal Communications Commission, September, 1962. (Testimony supplied to the author by the American Telephone and Telegraph Company.) See, by the same author, "Vitality of the Comparative Earnings Standard for Regulation of Utilities in a Growth Economy," 74 *Yale Law Journal* 989 (1965).

Commission Decisions

In postwar rate cases, the regulated companies, with increasing frequency, have presented comparable earnings evidence. As with other regulatory matters, a consistent policy has failed to emerge from these cases. It is clear, however, that the comparable earnings standard has gained some acceptance. Thus, the Civil Aeronautics Board in its 1960 passenger fare investigation found that the earnings–price ratio centered around 13 percent for the Big Four, but added 3 percent "derived from a comparison of industries according to indicia of relative risk."[131] Other commissions, while not making a specific allowance for risk, have considered the comparable earnings test in establishing a cost of equity capital.[132]

In reaching these decisions, commissions have measured risk in several different ways.[133] Sometimes, comparisons have been made with other regulated firms, either within a state[134] or nationally,[135] while in other cases, commissions have considered comparisons with nonregulated enterprises.[136] In almost all these cases, moreover, the commissions have emphasized that the comparable earnings test is not the sole determinant of a fair rate of return.[137] They have also emphasized that care must be exercised to be sure that the other business enterprises are "truly comparable."[138]

Summary

In concluding this discussion on the comparable earnings standard, the following excerpts from the 1961 Report of the Committee on Corporate

[131] *General Passenger Fare Investigation,* E-16068 (CAB, 1960), p. 23. For a complete discussion on this point, see *ibid.* pp. 17-28.

[132] See *Re General Teleph. Co. of Michigan,* 41 PUR 3d 469 (Mich., 1961); *Re Montana Power Co.,* 42 PUR 3d 241 (Mont., 1962); *Re American Louisiana Pipe Line Co.,* 45 PUR 3d 78 (FPC, 1962); *Re Montana-Dakota Utilities Co.,* 47 PUR 3d 54 (N.D., 1962).

[133] The Supreme Court has used broad comparisons of risk. In the Consolidated Gas case the Court held that 6 percent was "sufficiently above the local mortgage market to compensate for the additional and noninsurable hazard." *Willcox* v. *Consolidated Gas Co., op. cit.* In the Lincoln Gas case, the comparison was with "banking, merchandising, and other business in the vicinity." *Lincoln Gas & Elec. Light* v. *City of Lincoln, op. cit.* In the Hope case, broad groups of industrials, utilities, and railroads were the basis for comparison. *Federal Power Comm.* v. *Hope Natural Gas Co., op. cit.*

[134] *Re Southern New England Teleph. Co.,* 42 PUR 3d 310, 334-37 (Conn., 1962).

[135] *Re American Louisiana Pipe Line Co., op. cit.,* pp. 80-84; *General Passenger Fare Investigation, op. cit.; Re Florida Power Corp.,* Docket No. 7767-EU, Order No. 4139 (Fla., 1967).

[136] *Re General Teleph. Co. of Michigan, op. cit.,* pp. 473-75.

[137] *Re Hartford Gas Co.,* 44 PUR 3d 401, 405 (Conn., 1962); *Re El Paso Nat. Gas Co.,* 45 PUR 3d 262 (FPC, 1962).

[138] See *United Gas Pipe Line Co.* v. *Louisiana Public Service Comm.,* 39 PUR 3d 349 (1961); *Southwestern Bell Teleph. Co.* v. *State Corp. Comm.,* 51 PUR 3d 113 (1963).

Finance to the National Association of Regulatory Utility Commissioners are pertinent:

> Events of the year 1960 give emphasis to some comments in your Committee's report of last year. We said:
>
> ". . . if the utilities are to prosper—they will have to offer their investors opportunities commensurate with those available from similar, alternative investments."
>
> "Here Commissions must be aware, however, that competition in the money markets is on a two-fold basis, i.e., with consideration not only of the *level* of earnings, but also in terms of the *quality*, or risk-status of the investment."

As pointed out in an earlier section of this report, during the recent recession the return on net assets for manufacturing companies declined from 11.7% in 1959 to 10.5% in 1960, a drop of 10.3%, and total net income fell 4%. On the other hand, net income of public utilities *increased* by 8%, and return on net assets was unaffected, remaining at a 10% level.

This experience points out quite markedly the difference in volatility in earnings of industrial as compared with utility equities. The greater stability of utility earnings suggest[s] the conclusion that utilities need not offer as high a level of equity earnings as industrials in order to attract capital. It should be recognized however, that there are dangers in one year comparisons and that there is a need for use of a sufficiently long period of time in order to smooth out cyclical fluctuations.

It is also important in making such comparisons to keep in mind the directive of the Supreme Court when it said:

". . . but it (the public utility) has no constitutional right to profits such as are realized or anticipated in highly profitable enterprises or speculative ventures. . . ."

As is well known, the earnings of unregulated industry vary between industries and between companies within industry groups. For example, while manufacturing corporations, overall, earned 10.5 per cent on equity in 1960, the rate earned by subsidiary groups ranged from 6.5 per cent for the sugar industry to 22 per cent for the drug manufacturers. It is clear, therefore, in using this test that care must be taken to meet the court's directive of eliminating the ". . . highly profitable enterprises. . . ."

All of these factors suggest that as a guidepost for setting the level of utility earnings, industrial earnings must be used within caution and handled with judgment and skill.

In determining the earnings of alternate investment opportunities, as evidence for the equity cost rate, the objection to the use of earnings of unregulated industry is often met by the use of earnings of comparable regulated utilities. While these provide a certain standard of measurement, their use involves some loss of objectivity since all utilities are regulated. Furthermore, many different regulatory standards are used throughout the country.

This entire discussion points up the fact that as in the case of determining the cost of total capital, the use of the comparable earnings test to determine the cost of equity capital likewise is not subject to mathematical precision. Rather it is necessary to review all factors carefully and skillfully and to exercise informed judgment in order to arrive at an equitable determination.[139]

THE RATE OF RETURN: "BETWEEN SCYLLA AND CHARYBDIS"

Justice Holmes once commented that rate regulation involved a middle course, determined by judgment and fairness, "between Scylla and Charybdis." As he explained:

> On the one side, if the franchise is taken to mean that the most profitable return that could be got, free from competition, is protected by the Fourteenth Amendment, then the power to regulate is null. On the other hand if the power to regulate withdraws the protection of the Amendment altogether, then the property is nought. This is not a matter of economic theory, but of fair interpretation of a bargain. Neither extreme can have been meant. A midway between them must be hit.[140]

The search for this midway position involves consideration of many complex factors. Clearly, the method of determining a fair rate of return is far from settled. The frequently used cost of capital standard is a beginning and represents a significant improvement over the earlier commission practices of basing the allowable return on a customary or traditional figure. But such a return is a minimum. It "determines a floor, below which rate of return is so low as to become confiscatory. . . . If a utility cannot recover its capital cost, it cannot continue indefinitely to serve the public and, per se, present investors in the enterprise will suffer the loss of all or a part of their investment."[141]

If the cost of capital sets the lower limit, what determines the upper limit? Most of the regulated industries are comprised of growing firms which need to raise large amounts of new capital. In addition, there are the problems raised by the need for incentives for efficiency, the effects of regulatory lag or erosion, inflation, and the fairness issue. This question as to the upper limit will always present one of the most difficult problems those concerned with regulation must face, just as it represents a source of controversy for the nonregulated industries. An adequate rate of return is essential for all industries—a fact which is undebatable in a capitalistic economy. The difficulty arises over the definition of "adequate." And the difficulty is compounded for the regulated industries due to the need to consider economic, legal, and political factors.

In connection with determining the rate of return, a suggestion made by

---

[139] National Association of Regulatory Utility Commissioners, *Annual Proceedings, 1961* (Washington, D.C., 1962), pp. 108–10.

[140] *Cedar Rapids Gas Light Co.* v. *Cedar Rapids,* 223 U.S. 655, 669 (1912).

[141] Badger, *op. cit.,* p. 101.

Troxel deserves careful consideration. He argues that rate regulation could be improved by distinguishing between the average rate of return and the marginal rate of return. The average is a return based upon a company's total investment, the marginal on each additional investment. The marginal return could be measured in two ways. First, the measurement could be made "after the investment is made and after the additional returns start to come in. Dealing with actual facts, the company or commission computes the marginal rate of return as a ratio of the additional return to the additional investment; obtaining $7,500 from an additional investment of $150,000, a company gets a marginal rate of return of 5 per cent."[142] Second, the measurement could be undertaken before the investment is made.

> Under these conditions the marginal rate is an expectation—a ratio of the expected net return to the additional plant investment. Defined in this way, the marginal rate of return means the same thing as the marginal efficiency of capital. And it is controlled primarily by the earnings regulation, demand conditions, taxes, raw material costs, and wages that are anticipated in connection with the additional plant investment.[143]

If regulatory thinking were in terms of the marginal rate of return or the marginal efficiency of capital,

> ... new light is thrown on the cost of capital as a measure of the reasonable rate of return. The marginal rate of return is controlled by managerial expectations—anticipations of regulatory action, demand behavior, and expenditures on additional service production. On the other hand, the market rates of borrowing are prices of capital. Clearly, then, the marginal rate of return is not the same thing as the cost of capital. Yet utility commissions use current costs of capital to determine the fair rate of return. Either the utility companies pay these borrowing costs, the commissioners say, or no borrowing can be done. True; but the utility company does not borrow unless the marginal rate of return is above the market rates of interest. The marginal rate of return is one side and the interest rate the other of a relationship that controls investment decisions. Interest rates are controlled by the conditions of capital markets; marginal rates of return either are fixed by commissions or are anticipated by company managers. Interest rates measure the cost of capital; marginal rates of return measure the prescribed or expected increments in net earnings. They are separate conditions that are related to each other as investments are made. Wishing to examine the opportunities for plant expansions and improvements and trying to attract new investments into utility operations, commissions consider more than the current borrowing costs; they also study the earnings expectations of the companies.[144]

Professor Troxel recognizes that there are difficulties in measuring the

[142] Troxel, *op. cit.*, p. 391.
[143] *Ibid.*, pp. 391–92.
[144] *Ibid.*, p. 392.

marginal rate of return—earnings expectations are uncertain, and the marginal efficiency of capital varies over time and among different companies. "Yet, even if the measurement and control of the marginal rate of return is uncertain, a commission broadens earnings regulation as it studies the current investment conditions and looks forward to new investments. Some experimentation and speculation can improve the matter-of-fact regulation of reasonable returns."[145]

A reading of commission decisions over the past few years shows that far more attention is being directed to current investment conditions and the need for future capital. The use of the comparable earnings standard, in spite of its incomplete development, illustrates this trend. But despite these advances in the theory and measurement of a fair rate of return, much more thinking remains for the future.[146]

[145] *Ibid.*, p. 395.
[146] See Harry M. Trebing and R. Hayden Howard (eds.), *Rate of Return under Regulation: New Directions and Perspectives* (East Lansing: Michigan State University Public Utilities Studies, 1969).

Chapter 10

THE RATE STRUCTURE

Rates should be designed to hold existing business, promote new business, be just and equitable to the customer, promote good public relations and provide a fair return to the utility thereby making it possible to attract new capital to meet the industry's growth. No formula can be designed to attain these ends, but two basic factors must be constantly kept in mind—cost of service and value of service.

—*American Gas Association**

The preceding three chapters concerned determination of the rate level. The end result is the total revenue requirement of a regulated company. The next step is the rate structure—determination of the specific rates that will yield the required revenues.

Like most private firms, many of the regulated industries consider market (demand) factors as well as cost (supply) factors in determining their rate structures. This practice, at times, results in discrimination. Customers are classified into various groups, and the price charged each group is different. And within each group, prices are generally reduced as the quantity purchased increases, with the result that customers may not even pay the same average price per unit. Commissions, therefore, must exercise control of the rate structure to assure equity among customers. The legal standards are broad. First, each specific rate must be "just and reasonable." Second, "undue" or "unjust" discrimination among customers is prohibited. The rate structure thus involves determination of specific rates and determination of rate relationships.

The bases of price differentiation, the theory of price discrimination, and the rate structures of the transportation industries are considered in this chapter.

COST AND DEMAND: PRICE DIFFERENTIATION [1]

There are two bases for price differentiation. The first is differences in costs or the "cost of service." The second is differences in demand or the "value

---

*American Gas Association, *Report of Rate Committee* (New York, 1953), p. 3.
[1] The content and outline of the first two sections closely follow Clair Wilcox, *Public Policies Toward Business* (3d ed.; Homewood, Ill.: Richard D. Irwin, Inc., 1966), pp. 334-40, and are used with the author's permission.

of service." The seller does not discriminate when rates are based upon costs, even though some customers pay more than others. But when rates are based upon demand, discrimination occurs.

Cost of Service

Differences in rates may be due to differences in costs. It is more expensive to serve some customers than others. Special equipment may be required. Refrigerator cars are more expensive than flat cars, individual line telephone service more costly than multi-party lines. Customers who use the service only occasionally are more expensive to serve than those who use it continuously. The costs of billing each type of customer, for example, may be approximately the same, so that average costs are higher for the first group than for the second. In providing transportation services, commodities that are bulky in relation to their weight take up more space than those whose density is high; commodities that are fragile are more expensive to handle than those that are sturdy. For the telephone and transportation industries, terminal costs are as high for short distances as for long distances, so that costs per mile decline with distance.

Costs also vary according to the time of use. Customers who use the service during the peak demand period are more expensive to serve than off-peak users. A basic factor in determining the size of a plant is the peak demand. Therefore, it costs less to serve those customers who use the service without burdening the business as a whole by adding to the peak demand period. Further, if off-peak usage is increased, the company may obtain a better utilization of its plant throughout the day, thereby resulting in a larger total output over which fixed costs may be spread. Special rates, therefore, may be offered to off-peak users.

Value of Service

Differences in the rates of the regulated industries are more frequently due to differences in demand. A customer's demand is based upon his need or desire for the service, his ability to pay for it, and the availability of substitutes. Customers have relatively elastic demands when they have little need for the service, when they have insufficient incomes to pay for the service, or when they can provide it for themselves or purchase it from a competing seller. Customers have relatively inelastic demands when their need and ability to pay for the service are great and when no alternative sources of supply or substitutes are available.

From the seller's point of view, discrimination may offer marked advantages. When he can fully utilize his plant and earn a fair rate of return by charging a single price, he is unlikely to practice price discrimination. But a price low enough to maintain full production may yield insufficient revenues to cover costs, while one set high enough to cover costs may result in unused capacity. In such a situation, he will be able to increase his revenues by charging a higher price where demand is inelastic and a lower price where demand is elastic.

This situation is illustrated in Table 10-1. Assume that an enterprise has a plant with a capacity of 3,800 units. Assume further that total cost includes a

TABLE 10-1
Enterprise Selling at a Single Price

Price	Sales	Total Revenue	Total Cost	Profit or Loss
$11.00	100	$1,100	$ 1,600	−$ 500
10.00	200	2,000	2,150	− 150
9.00	300	2,700	2,650	+ 50
8.00	400	3,200	3,100	+ 100
7.00	500	3,500	3,500	0
6.00	700	4,200	4,250	− 50
5.00	1,000	5,000	5,400	− 400
4.00	1,400	5,600	6,700	− 1,100
3.00	2,000	6,000	8,200	− 2,200
2.00	2,800	5,600	10,000	− 4,400
1.00	3,800	3,800	13,000	− 9,200

fair return on the investment in the plant, so that the final column represents either excess profit or loss. If the firm's output is sold at a single price, the rate will be $8.00 and sales will be 400 units. Profits are maximized. At this price, the plant is not fully utilized. A glance at the table will show that it is impossible for the firm to both cover costs and maintain full production as long as a single price is charged.

If discrimination is practiced, however, the situation is quite different, as shown in Table 10-2. Now, by dividing customers into separate classes and charging each one a different price, total revenue will increase. Prices will range

TABLE 10-2
Enterprise Practicing Price Discrimination

Price	Sales	Sales in Each Class	Revenue from Each Class	Total Revenue	Total Cost	Profit or Loss
$11.00	100	100	$1,100	$ 1,100	$ 1,600	−$ 500
10.00	200	100	1,000	2,100	2,150	− 50
9.00	300	100	900	3,000	2,650	+ 350
8.00	400	100	800	3,800	3,100	+ 700
7.00	500	100	700	4,500	3,500	+ 1,000
6.00	700	200	1,200	5,700	4,250	+ 1,450
5.00	1,000	300	1,500	7,200	5,400	+ 1,800
4.00	1,400	400	1,600	8,800	6,700	+ 2,100
3.00	2,000	600	1,800	10,600	8,200	+ 2,400
2.00	2,800	800	1,600	12,200	10,000	+ 2,200
1.00	3,800	1,000	1,000	13,200	13,000	+ 200

from a high of $11.00 to a low of $3.00, output will expand to 2,000 units, and excess profits will rise to $2,400. But, as will be demonstrated below, such a schedule would be considered as "unduly" discriminatory.

THE ECONOMICS OF DISCRIMINATION

When a firm sells the same or similar services at rates which are not proportional to costs, discrimination results. Stated another way, discrimination occurs when rates are based upon differences in demand, rather than differences in costs. Consequently, some buyers will pay more than the cost of the particular service; others will pay less. It must be noted, however, that discrimination is not unlimited. As sellers cannot force customers to pay more than they believe the service to be worth, the upper ceiling is the value of service. A price set above this limit would result in reduced sales. The lower limit is the seller's marginal (sometimes referred to as out-of-pocket) costs. Any sales made at a price below this limit would result in losses, since these costs can be avoided by not producing the output. Most commissions, therefore, will not allow any rate to be established below marginal cost. When fixed costs are high, as in most of the regulated industries, these limits are wide, thereby leaving considerable latitude for discrimination.

Unavoidable versus Intentional Discrimination

Discrimination is partially unavoidable. The cost of providing a particular service is difficult, if not impossible, to determine accurately. Some variable costs, such as labor and fuel, are easily identified with a unit of output. Other costs, however, are commonly or jointly incurred in rendering different types of service. Rather than varying directly with output, they decline in importance as output increases. These costs include interest, depreciation, investment in plant and equipment, and administrative overhead. When investment is large, as in the airline, electric, telephone, and railroad industries, such costs represent a significant percentage of total costs. When the same plant or equipment is used to provide several types of service, there is no one correct way to allocate these costs among the different units of service.[2] The following example illustrates the cost allocation and pricing dilemma.

Assume that a railroad can move 60 cars a day from points A to B at a total cost of $600. Further, assume that this sum is divided into $360 for fixed costs and $240 for variable costs—that is, if the train did not run, the railroad would save $240 a day, but would still have to expend $360 a day to maintain its track for other trains, to operate its stations, and so on. This

---

[2] In discussing the problem of cost allocation for railroad service, Hadley once remarked that "God Almighty did not know the cost of carrying a hundred pounds of freight from Boston to New York." Quoted by Winthrop M. Daniels, *The Price of Transportation* (New York: Harper & Bros., 1932), p. 48.

means that the average per car cost is $10, of which only $4.00 is a variable cost.

With these cost figures in mind, the railroad is asked to propose a rate at which it will carry 10 additional cars, these cars to carry a product not carried by the road up to that time—for example, wheat. If the 10 cars are added, fixed costs will remain just as they were for 60 cars; a total of $360. Variable costs will be increased by the sum of $4.00 for each added car (assuming that no special cars or services are required), thus making total variable costs $280. This means that the total cost of transporting the 70 cars will be $640 or approximately $9.14 a car. But how much of this total cost should be attributed to the added 10 cars? Certainly, total cost was $600 for the 60 cars, and this figure was increased to $640 when the 10 cars were added. Hence, is not the cost of the added cars but $40 or $4.00 a car? Instead of a charge of $9.14 plus profit a car, should not the company charge $10.00 (plus profit) for the original 60 cars and $4.00 (plus profit) for the 10 cars of wheat? Or will the lower charge for the 10 cars of wheat be an unfair discrimination against the products carried in the other 60 cars? In other words, should the 10 cars of wheat pay part of the fixed costs? If so, how much?

The basic problem, then, is how common or joint costs should be apportioned among different services. As was demonstrated in Chapter 6, when separations procedures were discussed,[3] any method of apportionment is subject to dispute. Even if firms tried to base their rates upon costs, therefore, a substantial element of judgment is involved.

Discrimination is also intentional. As previously shown, when one rate is charged for a service, a company may not be able to utilize its capacity fully. Only by discrimination may idle capacity be eliminated. Furthermore, discrimination is often socially desirable. If it allows a company to expand its sales and utilize its facilities more fully, average costs are reduced as fixed costs are spread over more units of output and the firm's profits are increased. Fuller utilization, in turn, may result in lower prices for *all* customers and in a wider use of the regulated industry's services—a goal of regulation. Some services might be offered that would not be available under uniform rates: transportation services over low density routes often are subsidized by revenues from high density routes. Regional development also may be encouraged: low electric rates have encouraged its use and attracted industry to the TVA area; low transportation rates may allow one part of the country to compete in another section. These advantages, however, are unlikely to be realized unless rates are controlled. It is one of the jobs of the commissions to distinguish between those rate structures that are socially desirable and those that are not. As Sharfman has pointed out, there is an inherent danger in discrimination:

The "value of service" principle, as a basis for rate-making, provides at best a vague and indeterminate formula, rather easily construed as justifying any

[3] See Chapter 6, pp. 153–62.

system of rates found expedient by the carrier. Taking the words in their most obvious sense, no rate can exceed the value of the service and still continue to be paid by the shipper.[4]

The Conditions for Discrimination

Rate discrimination is not possible unless the market can be separated into distinct sectors so that (1) customers who are charged the higher rate cannot buy in the low-rate sector and (2) those buying at the lower rate cannot resell in the high-rate sector.[5] For industries selling transferable products, this is usually not possible.[6] However, for the regulated industries which sell services, such a division of the market is possible. Moreover, they are able to control the use of their services, since they generally deliver them to the customer as they are consumed. If a telephone company charges an industrial customer more than it charges a residential user, the industrial one cannot obtain the lower rate by connecting his telephone with the residential one's lines. Similarly, if a railroad company charges more for hauling automobiles than for hauling vegetables, the automobile manufacturer cannot get the lower rate by having his product loaded onto refrigerator cars. Customers of the regulated industries cannot shift between the established sectors. This condition also implies that the discriminating firm is either free from competition or that competition is controlled. If two firms supplied the same market, their rivalry for business would force rates down.

Two other conditions for discrimination also must exist.[7] The elasticities of demand in the established sectors of the market must be considerably different. That is, if the elasticities are equal or similar, so, too, will be the marginal revenue curves, and discrimination would serve no purpose. Finally, the cost of separating the market into sectors must not be too large. Rate discrimination involves some extra expense. Different bills, for example, usually must be printed for each type of customer, and bookkeeping becomes more complex. For discrimination to be profitable, the increase in revenues must be greater than the additional expenses incurred.

The Case for Discrimination

Discrimination may be advantageous for two reasons. First, it may result in a fuller utilization of a firm's plant and equipment, and a wider consumption of its services. Second, it may lead to lower prices for all customers. The first was illustrated above, where adoption of price discrimination raised output from 400 units to 2,000 units. The second can be seen in Table 10–3. Here, the prices,

[4] I. Leo Sharfman, *The Interstate Commerce Commission* (New York: Commonwealth Fund, 1936), Vol. IIIB, pp. 321–22.

[5] Wilcox, *op. cit.*, pp. 338–39.

[6] This statement does not imply that price discrimination is unimportant in the nonregulated sector of the economy. When competition is imperfect and when sellers lack complete information about each product, discrimination may occur.

[7] George J. Stigler, *The Theory of Price* (3d ed.; New York: The Macmillan Co., 1966), p. 210.

sales, and costs are the same as those in the previous tables. But now it is assumed that a regulatory commission controls the firm's rate structure. It was suggested earlier that the rate structure shown in Table 10-2 involves "undue" discrimination due to the presence of excess profits. If discrimination were not allowed, therefore, the commission would force the seller to produce 500 units, which would sell for $7.00 each, as shown in Table 10-1. At this price, there would be no excess profits.

By allowing discrimination, the commission could establish the rate schedule shown in Table 10-3. A fair return is earned from a scale of prices that begins at $2.00 and rises to $5.00, while the volume of output is raised to 2,800 units. It should be noted that every price is well below the $7.00 that would have to be charged if discrimination were not allowed. This schedule is made possible because by serving the low-rate customers who cannot afford the service at a higher rate, the firm's fixed costs are spread over more units. As a result of the adoption of such a schedule, no customers are harmed. On the contrary, all of them have been helped: the $5.00 customers have saved $2.00 per unit, while the $4.00, $3.00, and $2.00 rates are required to obtain customers that otherwise could not afford the service.

TABLE 10-3
Enterprise Practicing Price Discrimination under Regulation*

Price	Sales	Sales in Each Class	Revenue from Each Class	Total Revenue	Total Cost	Profit or Loss
$5.00	1,000	1,000	$5,000	$ 5,000	$ 5,400	−$ 400
4.00	1,400	400	1,600	6,600	6,700	− 100
3.00	2,000	600	1,800	8,400	8,200	+ 200
2.00	2,800	800	1,600	10,000	10,000	0
1.00	3,800	1,000	1,000	11,000	13,000	− 2,000

*This rate structure is only one of several possible structures that might be established by a company and accepted by a commission.

Such discrimination cannot be justified, however, unless (*a*) there are high fixed costs and chronic unused capacity, so that costs per unit are reduced as the fixed costs are spread over a larger volume of output; (*b*) the lower rates are needed to attract new business; (*c*) all rates cover at least variable costs and make some contribution to fixed (overhead) costs; and (*d*) regulation is undertaken to keep total earnings reasonable and to keep discrimination within bounds.[8] If these conditions exist, discrimination is desirable, since it leads to either an increased use of the facilities or to a lower rate for the customers discriminated against. At the same time, it is important to remember that each rate must be set with the thought that all rates together should return to the company sufficient revenue to cover its total costs of service, including the rate of return allowed by

[8] Wilcox, *op. cit.*, p. 340.

the commission. This statement does not imply that such revenue is guaranteed; rather it simply means that this end should be kept in view.

CRITERIA OF A SOUND RATE STRUCTURE

Bonbright, in his study on public utility rates, lists eight criteria of a sound or desirable rate structure. They are as follows:

1. The related, "practical" attributes of simplicity, understandability, public acceptability, and feasibility of application.
2. Freedom from controversies as to proper interpretation.
3. Effectiveness in yielding total revenue requirements under the fair-return standard.
4. Revenue stability from year to year.
5. Stability of the rates themselves, with a minimum of unexpected changes seriously adverse to existing customers. (Compare "The best tax is an old tax.")
6. Fairness of the specific rates in the apportionment of total costs of service among the different consumers.
7. Avoidance of "undue discrimination" in rate relationships.
8. Efficiency of the rate classes and rate blocks in discouraging wasteful use of service while promoting all justified types and amounts of use:
    (a) in the control of the total amounts of service supplied by the company;
    (b) in the control of the relative uses of alternative types of service (on-peak versus off-peak electricity, Pullman travel versus coach travel, single-party telephone service versus service from a multi-party line, etc.).[9]

Admittedly, these criteria are broad and ambiguous (what, for example, is "undue" discrimination?). They also overlap without offering any rules of priority in case of conflicts. How is the "cost of service" to be measured—marginal cost, average cost, or fully distributed cost? Clearly, the measure largely depends on the purpose that a rate is to fulfill. But the criteria are of value "in reminding the rate maker of considerations that might otherwise escape his attention, and also useful in suggesting one important reason why problems of practical rate design do not readily yield to 'scientific' principles of optimum pricing."[10]

Bonbright further suggests that the three primary criteria are numbers 3, 6, and 8, namely,

    ... (a) the revenue-requirement or financial-need objective, which takes the form of a fair-return standard with respect to private utility companies;
    (b) the fair-cost-apportionment objective, which invokes the principle that

[9] James C. Bonbright, *Principles of Public Utility Rates* (New York: Columbia University Press, 1961), p. 291. Also see Russell E. Caywood, "Electric Utility Rate Making Today," 81 *Public Utilities Fortnightly* 51, 53–54 (June 6, 1968).
[10] Bonbright, *op. cit.*, p. 291.

the burden of meeting total revenue requirements must be distributed *fairly* among the beneficiaries of the service; and (c) the optimum-use or consumer-rationing objective, under which the rates are designed to discourage the wasteful use of public utility services while promoting all use that is economically justified in view of the relationships between costs incurred and benefits received.[11]

With these criteria in mind, we turn to a discussion of the rate structures of the regulated industries.

RATE STRUCTURES IN PRACTICE

An unregulated monopolist would tend to base his rates on the value of service, thereby maximizing profits. Yet, regulatory statutes and commissions have long recognized, and permitted, rates based upon this principle. But there is a major difference: under regulation, price discrimination, as shown in the preceding discussion, may be economically and socially desirable. Over the years, some of the regulated industries have been forced to move toward a cost of service standard. Primarily this has been due to the increased competition to which many of these industries have been subjected. As a result, present rate structures are often a complex and confusing mixture of cost of service and value of service considerations. Where competition is strong, rates tend toward the cost of service standard; where competition is weak, toward the value of service. The remainder of this chapter discusses and analyzes the rate structures of the transportation industries.

Railroad Freight Rates

The transportation industries exhibit the most complex rate structures found among the regulated industries. Their rate structures also reflect the impact of strong competition between the various modes of transport. Particularly is this true of railroad freight rates. Here, rate differentiation is highly developed, and of even more importance, discrimination is a serious problem.

Cost Considerations. A railroad does not charge the same rate on all commodities or a uniform rate per mile for different hauls. In part, these rate differences can be explained by examining costs. First, the cost of carrying one commodity (rates are usually stated in cents per hundred pounds or per ton) may be greater than the cost of another. (1) The cost per unit of weight is greater for bulky commodities than for those whose density is high. Articles that are of odd shapes and sizes use more space than those that can be compactly loaded. In some cases (melons, crates of fresh fruits), full carloads are impossible without causing damage to the commodities. (2) Since a railroad company is liable for loss or damage, fragile articles and perishable products cost more than sturdy ones, as do goods susceptible to pilfering (alcoholic beverages, cigarettes)

[11]*Ibid.*, p. 292. Also see John M. Clark, *Studies in the Economics of Overhead Costs* (Chicago: University of Chicago Press, 1923), p. 322.

and explosives. (3) When commodities are carried in volume, costs may be lower due to more economical loading and handling. (4) Commodities that move in steady volume throughout the year cost less than those that move irregularly. Train schedules can be worked out in advance, resulting in a minimum of expense and empty cars. When commodities move only seasonally, however, the railroads' facilities are taxed at certain times and are idle at others. (5) Commodities that require special equipment or services are more expensive to handle. Caretakers are frequently provided for livestock, refrigerator cars are used for hauling fresh fruits, and special sidings or terminal facilities are provided for loading and unloading certain agricultural products.

Second, the cost of different hauls may vary. The cost of carrying freight can be divided into terminal costs and line-haul costs. Since terminal costs do not vary with the length of shipment, they are as high for short hauls as for long hauls. Line-haul costs, however, are higher for short hauls, since they often involve fewer cars per train, more frequent stops, and poorer loading. Consequently, costs per mile, particularly when the haul is in excess of 150 miles, decline with the distance traveled.[12] Even for equal distances, line-haul costs may be different. A mile costs more where traffic is sparse than where it is plentiful. Costs are higher when mountains must be crossed than on the plains, and more in winter than in summer. It costs more to move goods in the direction of heavy traffic, since the peak load is being increased, than when they move in the direction of empty cars.[13]

The costs of railroad freight, therefore, vary with both the type of commodity being hauled and the distance traveled. From a cost standpoint, railroad rates should theoretically be based upon distance. Rather than a straight-line scale, moreover, rates should be based upon the "tapering principle." That is, the cost per mile increases with distance but at a decreasing rate. There are three justifications for the tapering principle. First, terminal costs (loading and unloading, freight house equipment), which do not vary with the distance traveled, can be spread over a greater distance on a longer haul. Thus, if the terminal cost were 58 cents a ton for handling certain freight and the line-haul cost were 2 cents per ton-mile, the rate per mile for a 10-mile haul would be 7.8 cents and for a 500-mile haul 2.1 cents per mile. Second, as pointed out above, the line-haul cost is considered to be lower for longer hauls. Long hauls, for example, use through freights which make fewer stops and operate more efficiently. Finally, the tapering principle is used to prevent rates from restricting the movement of long-haul traffic. If rates increased in proportion to distance, they would soon become so high that the movement of traffic would be prevented. Long distance rates, therefore, are kept low enough to enable the traffic to move greater distances.

In actual practice, railroad freight rates depart markedly from a distance rate structure. Once again, it must be noted that in large measure this is

---

[12] *Southern Class Rate Investigation,* 100 ICC 513, 643 (1925).
[13] Line-haul costs are analyzed in Emery Troxel, *Economics of Transportation* (New York: Holt, Rinehart & Winston, Inc., 1955), pp. 98–102.

unavoidable. There is simply no method by which a railroad can obtain the precise cost of rendering a specific service.

Demand Considerations. As a result of (*a*) the difficulty of finding the cost of carrying a specific commodity and (*b*) the favorable results obtainable through discrimination, there is little attempt to set specific railroad rates on the basis of cost, if cost is used in the sense of including both fixed and variable costs. Railroad rate differentiation is largely based upon demand characteristics or how much the potential buyer of the service values it.[14]

For high valued commodities, freight rates represent a small percentage of the selling price, and high rates will not affect the movement of these goods. For bulky and heavy commodities, freight rates represent a substantial percentage of their selling price; if rates are too high, these goods will not move by rail. Moreover, competitive conditions influence the demand for railroad transportation. As long as the rate charged covers the variable costs of hauling a particular commodity and adds something toward fixed costs, the railroad's net revenue will increase if the commodity is moved. Faced with competition from other modes of transport, the railroads will tend to cut their rates toward variable costs in order to maintain their traffic. Competition for markets also influences demand. Thus, the California orange industry has been allowed to develop to its present-day importance by a railroad rate on California fruit which permits it to compete with Florida fruit in Eastern markets. To change this situation at the present time would spell disaster for the California orange industry. The same is true of the location of many industrial factories. They have been located where conditions seem the most favorable, specific freight rates being one of the factors taken into consideration.

Freight Classification and Commodity Rates. Currently, over 10,000 groups of commodities are hauled by the railroads. When differences in packing and manner of shipment are taken into account, the number expands to nearly 25,000 separate descriptions. There are in the continental United States more than 35,000 railroad stations to and from which rates must be published. Moreover, commodities can move between these stations over many different routes.[15] If rates were specified commodity by commodity and haul by haul, there would be an almost infinite number of separate rates. Instead, differentiation between commodities is accomplished in three ways: (1) by freight classifications, (2) by exceptions to classifications, and (3) by commodity rates. But in spite of these devices to simplify the structure of railroad rates, there are over 75,000 freight tariffs[16] in use, ranging in size from a few pages to over

---

[14] See Interstate Commerce Commission, Bureau of Transport Economics and Statistics, *Value of Service in Rate-Making,* Statement No. 5912 (1959).

[15] Commodities may also move between two points by a combination of different modes of transport. See Chapter 12, pp. 408–9.

[16] Specific rates are published in "freight tariffs." Class tariffs contain the rates applicable on the various classes shown in the classification. Commodity tariffs contain the commodity rates. Local tariffs are published by individual railroads and show the rates for commodities moving between points on their own lines. Agency tariffs show the rates between points on different lines, that is, joint rates.

1,500 pages, and some 43 trillion rates are on file with the Interstate Commerce Commission.

Freight Classification. The freight classification system is the process of grouping thousands of commodities into a limited number of classes for purposes of rate making. All commodities in the same class (rating) are subject to the same rate. As explained by the ICC:

> The primary purpose of a freight classification is to assign each article, or a group of articles, to a class according to well-known classification principles or elements which recognize distinctions from a transportation standpoint, along fairly broad lines, in order to meet the needs of commerce. None of the principles or elements should be controlling, but all that are relevant should be considered. Among them are: Weight per cubic foot and value per pound as packed for shipment; liability to loss, damage, waste, or theft in transit; likelihood of injury to other freight with which it may come in contact; risks due to hazards of carriage; kind of container or package as bearing upon the matter of liability or risk; expense of, and care in, handling; ratings on analogous articles; fair relation of ratings as between all articles; competition between articles of different descriptions but largely used for similar purposes; commercial conditions and units of sales; trade conditions; value of service; volume of movement for the entire country in either less than carloads or carloads; adaptability to movement in carloads; and carload minimum weights just to carriers and shippers. These transportation characteristics would be substantially similar on most articles irrespective of the territory in which the movement occurs.[17]

By 1889, the railroads had developed three major classification territories: the Official, Southern, and Western Territories (Figure 10-1).[18] There were seven regular classes in the Official Classification, twelve in the Southern, and ten in the Western.[19] Identical commodities were differently classified in each region.[20] On May 30, 1952, regional classifications were replaced by the *Uniform Freight Classification.*[21] There are 31 classes, numbered from 400 to 13. Class 100 is considered to be the base, and the other classes are multiples of Class 100 if they are a higher number or percentages of Class 100 if they are

---

[17]*Class Rate Investigation, 1939,* 262 ICC 447, 508–9 (1945).

[18]On the early history of classification, see *Suspension of Western Classification No. 51,* 25 ICC 442, 453–59 (1912).

[19]D. Philip Locklin, *Economics of Transportation* (6th ed.; Homewood, Ill.: Richard D. Irwin, Inc., 1966), p. 162.

[20]Several methods were used in establishing a rate when a commodity moved from a point in one territory to a point in another territory having a different level of rates. The common method was to apply the lower rate for the entire distance and then to add a "differential" or "arbitrary"—that is, a specific amount which varied with the length of the haul in the higher-rate territory. See Locklin, *op. cit.,* pp. 182–83; and *Southern Class Rate Investigation,* 128 ICC 567, 602 (1927).

[21]The *Uniform Freight Classification* resulted from *Class Rate Investigation, 1939,* 262 ICC 447 (1945), *aff'd sub nom. New York* v. *United States,* 65 F. Supp. 856 (1946), *aff'd,* 331 U.S. 284 (1947). Also see E. A. Nightingale, "Uniform Freight Classification and Uniform Class Rates," 20 *I.C.C. Practitioners' Journal* 171 (1952), for an analysis of this decision.

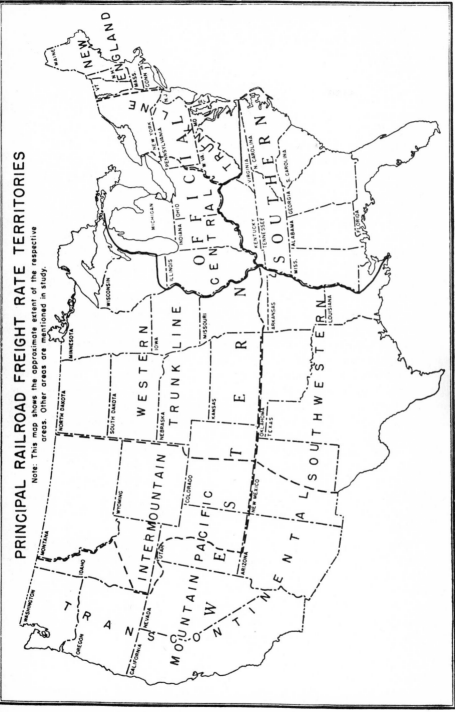

PRINCIPAL RAILROAD FREIGHT RATE TERRITORIES

Note: This map shows the approximate extent of the respective areas. Other areas are mentioned in study.

Source: Interstate Commerce Commission, Bureau of Transport Economics and Statistics, *Value of Service in Rate-Making*, Statement No. 5912 (1959), p. 9.

lower. Thus, Class 13 is a rating equal to 13 percent of Class 100 for a specified haul and for all commodities in Class 13. Class ratings are made for both carload and less-than-carload lots. A sample page from the *Uniform Freight Classification* is shown in Figure 10-2. There is one significant exception to nationwide uniformity: due to higher costs, the level of rates in the Mountain-Pacific Territory is above that found in the rest of the country.[22]

While most less-than-carload freight moves under classification ratings, carload freight typically moves under either exceptions or commodity rates.

Exceptions to the Classification. Individual or groups of railroads have the legal right to depart from the freight classification rating by publishing "exceptions." When an exception rate is published, it supersedes the regular class rating. Prior to 1952, competition often compelled the railroads to publish exceptions, thereby moving traffic at a lower rate than provided for in the freight classification. When the *Uniform Freight Classification* was being established, an attempt was made to incorporate exception ratings into the classification, with the aim of canceling many of the exceptions previously in effect. While not completely successful, the number of exception ratings has declined in recent years. In addition, the Interstate Commerce Commission has taken a stronger stand in recent years by requiring the railroads to fully justify exceptions.

Commodity Rates. Over 80 percent of the railroad's total revenues from carload freight are derived from traffic moving under commodity rates. A commodity rate is a published rate which governs the movement of a specific commodity usually between particular points. It may be expressed as a percentage of Class 100 rates, or more frequently, it is unrelated to the class rates, applying only to a limited number of points or to the movement of a commodity between all points. The commodity rate also supersedes, and is usually below, the class rate. Since the basic purpose of these rates is to encourage a commodity to move in volume, especially in carload lots and over long distances, they are of major significance for bulk commodities. Those commodities which normally move on commodity rates include coal, cement, brick, grain, and livestock. A sample page from a soybean oil tariff is shown in Figure 10-3.

Freight-Rate Structures. There are three general types of freight-rate structures: (1) distance-rate structures, where rates are related to distance; (2) group-rate structures, where points of origin or destination, or both, are grouped together; and (3) equalization and differential systems, where rates are related to a base rate. It is important to recognize, however, that these types of rate structures often overlap and that a particular rate structure may be comprised of two, or even of all three, of these types.

---

[22] In *Class Rates, Mountain-Pacific Territory,* 296 ICC 555, 611 (1955), it was estimated that for hauls of 300 miles, Mountain-Pacific costs were 2 to 10 percent higher than the level for the country as a whole; for hauls of 500 miles, 7 percent higher; for hauls of 1,000 miles, 3 to 4 percent higher.

Item	ARTICLES	Less Carload Ratings	Carload Minimum (Pounds)	Carload Ratings
★2605	**ADVERTISING MATTER:** Displays, advertising, store or window: Cellular, expanded or foamed plastic, or cellular, expanded or foamed plastic combined with other materials, the weight of the cellular, expanded or foamed plastic exceeding 50%, in boxes..	300	10,000R	85
	Cellular, expanded or foamed plastic combined with other materials, the weight of the cellular, expanded or foamed plastic not exceeding 50%; or glass wool or glass wool combined with other materials, in boxes.......................................	200	10,000R	85
6980-A	**ATHLETIC, GYMNASTIC OR SPORTING GOODS:** Balls: Table tennis, in boxes...................	◆300	10,000R	150
7120-A	Bowling alleys or bowling alley parts: Masking units, in boxes or crates.....................	◆150	18,000R	70
7230-A	Decoy birds: ▲Pulpboard or woodpulp, in boxes................	◆150	▲10,000R	◆85
	▲Plastic, in boxes.....................	◆110	▲10,000R	◆85
	▲Wooden, in boxes...................	100	24,000R	55
7860-A	Skis or ski poles, in packages...................	100	◆24,000R	▲55
11500-A	**BOATS, see Note 1, Item 11441, OR PARTS NAMED:** Boat construction kits: ▲Hulls or hull sections, SU: Not nested, in boxes or crates....................	◆300	▲10,000R	◆85
	Nested, see Note 1½, Item 11501, in boxes or crates..........................	◆100 {	◆◆ 24,000R	}◆55
★11501	▲Hulls completely KD, other than in SU sections, ribs in bundles, other parts in boxes or crates, or wrapped with fibreboard testing not less than 275 pounds, steel strapped.......	85	30,000	50
	Note 1½.—Ratings apply only when hulls or hull sections for 3 or more complete boats are nested in one box or crate.			
12600-A	**BOILERS, FURNACES, RADIATORS, STOVES, RELATED ARTICLES OR PARTS NAMED:** Heaters, gas, with or without clay radiants, in mixed carloads with one or more of the following articles, see Note 54, Item 13266: Boards, stove; postal or letter boxes, sheet steel; coal hods (scuttles); collars, stove pipe, sheet steel; chimney caps, sheet steel; elbows, furnace or stove pipe; pipe or ducts, stove, sheet steel or tin plate; pipe, ducts or elbows (air or smoke flues), heating furnace, sheet steel or tin plate; ◆posts, iron or steel; rainproofs, sheet steel; stove pipe drum ovens; stoves or ranges, charcoal, coal or wood, sheet iron; or thimbles, stove pipe.....................................	......	24,000R	45
12790-A	Ovens, ▲portable, for tops of stoves or ranges: SU, in boxes or crates..................................	150	16,000R	60
	KD, in boxes or crates................................	70	24,000R	40
	SU and KD, mixed CL..................................	......	24,000R	40
13120-A	Stoves or ranges, iron or steel: Charcoal, coal or wood, see Notes 36 and 38, Items 13121 and 13122: Sheet, noibn: SU, in boxes, crates or ◆Package 1309, see Note 48, Item 13183.....................	100 {	12,000R 24,000R	70 40
	KD, bodies nested, or tops and bases separated, bases in tops, in boxes or crates.......	85	24,000R	40
★14157	**BOXES OR CRATES, INCLUDING FIBREBOARD, PAPER OR PULPBOARD BOTTLES OR CANS:** Boxes: Lunch, empty, fibreboard: SU, in barrels, boxes or crates....................	400	12,000R	85
	KD, flat or folded flat, in barrels, boxes or crates.....................	85	20,000R	55
14160-A	Lunch, empty, other than ▲fibreboard, iron, steel or tin: SU, in barrels, boxes or crates.....................	◆150	12,000R	85
	KD, flat or folded flat, in barrels, boxes or crates.....................	85	20,000R	55
15210-A	**BRICK, BLOCKS, SLABS, TILE OR RELATED ARTICLES:** Blocks, ◆plates or tubes, segment sewer or ▲sewage treatment, aluminum oxide, ◆cast stone or vitrified clay: Loose......................	70	60,000	17½
	LCL, in barrels, boxes or crates; CL, in packages.............................	50	60,000	17½
17247-A	**BUILDING METAL WORK, INCLUDING ROOF TRIMMINGS OR GUTTERING OR VENTILATORS:** Church steeples, metal or metal and wood combined: SU or in SU sections, not telescoped, loose or in packages....................	250	10,000R	85
	In SU sections, telescoped, ◆or spires SU and belfrys KD flat, loose or in packages..........	150	10,000R	85
17720-A	Moldings, brass, bronze or copper, ◆*** or metal or wood covered with brass, bronze, copper or nickel silver, in boxes or crates....................	85	30,000	55
	***"nickel silver" eliminated. See Item 70690.			

For explanation of abbreviations, numbers and other reference marks, see last page of this supplement and pages 204 and 590 of Classification; for packages, see pages 497 to 589 of Classification, as amended.

FIGURE 10–3
Sample Page from Southern Freight Tariff Bureau—Freight Tariff 830—B—Soybean Oil, CL

		SECTION 1		

Rates in cents per 100 pounds

Rates are applicable only via routes shown below; for explanation of routes, see Section 3.

Soybean oil, in tank cars, min. wt. 60,000 lbs., except that weight computed on 98 percent of the shell gallonage capacity of the tank (exclusive of the dome) will govern if less than 60,000 lbs., CL. Applicable only on soybean oil refined in transit at Savannah, Ga., subject to the rules and charges authorized in Central of Georgia Oils Transit Tariff ICC 3375, supplements thereto or successive issues thereof.

TO FORT McPHERSON, GA.

Item	From	Route to Savannah, Ga.	Route from Savannah, Ga.	Rate
	(F27) ILLINOIS			
625	Alhambra.	IC10.	CG1.	145
630	Bloomington	GM10; IC10; IT15.	CG1.	149
635	Champaign	IC10; IT15.	CG1.	145
640	Chicago	CE10; GM10; IC10; MN10.	CG1.	150
645	Decatur	IC10; IT15.	CG1.	145
650	Gibson City	IC10.	CG1.	147
655	Mascoutah	LN15, 20.	CG1.	143
660	Nashville	LN15, 20; MI5	CG1.	142
665	Pana.	IC10.	CG1.	143
670	Peoria.	CIM20; GM10; IC10; IT15	CG1.	149
675	Springfield	GM10; IC10; IT15.	CG1.	147
680	Taylorville	CIM10	CG1.	145
685	Virden.	GM10; IT10, 15.	CG1.	147
	(F27) INDIANA			
700	Frankfort.	MN10.	CG1.	143
705	Indianapolis.	MN10; IC10.	CG1.	143
710	La Fayette.	MN10.	CG1.	145
715	Oaktown.	CE10.	CG1.	138
	(F27) IOWA			
740	Cedar Rapids.	IC10.	CG1.	158
745	Fort Dodge.	IC10.	CG1.	162
750	Iowa Falls.	IC10.	CG1.	161
755	Plainfield.	IC10.	CG1.	160
760	Quimby.	IC10.	CG1.	164
765	Sheldon	IC10.	CG1.	168
770	Sioux City.	IC10.	CG1.	168
775	Waterloo.	IC10.	CG1.	160
	(F27) MISSOURI			
790	St. Louis	GM10; IC10; LN15, 20; SRS15	CG1.	145

	SECTION 2

ROUTING INSTRUCTIONS--GENERAL

Item	Subject	Application
905	ROUTING--EMERGENCY.	F25 The rates named in this tariff will apply only via the routes and junction points authorized herein, except that when in the case of pronounced traffic congestion (not an embargo), washout, wreck, or other similar emergency, or through carriers' error, carriers forward shipments via other junction points of the same carriers or via the lines of other carriers parties to the tariff, the rate to apply will be that specified in this tariff, but not higher than the rate applicable via the route of movement.

	SECTION 3

EXPLANATION OF ROUTES REFERRED TO IN THIS TARIFF

Route	Via	Route	Via
AC5	ACL, Birmingham, Ala., GM&O.	CIM10	C&IM, Cimic, Ill., IC, Birmingham, Ala., CofGa.
AC10	ACL, Birmingham, Ala., IC.	CIM15	C&IM, Springfield, Ill., IC, Birmingham, Ala.,
CE5	C&EI, Evansville, Ind., thence Route LN10.		ACL or CofGa.
CE10	C&EI, Evansville, Ind., L&N, Atlanta, Ga., Birmingham, Ala., or Chattanooga, Tenn., CofGa.	CIM20 GM5	C&IM, Springfield, Ill., IC, Birmingham, Ala., CofGa. GM&O, Birmingham, Ala.: ACL.
CG1	CofGa direct.		ACL, Cordele, Ga., SAL.
CG5	CofGa., Atlanta, Ga., SAL, Birmingham, Ala., GM&O.		CofGa. SAL, Atlanta, Ga.:
CG10	CofGa., Birmingham, Ala., GM&O. CofGa., Montgomery, Ala., GM&O. CofGa., Atlanta, Ga., SAL, Birmingham, Ala., IC. CofGa., Birmingham, Ala., GM&O or IC.		ACL, Cordele, Ga., SAL. CofGa. CofGa., Macon, Ga., SAL. Sou(SRS).
CG15	CofGa., Birmingham, Ala., GM&O or IC.	GM10	GM&O, Montgomery, Ala., CofGa or SAL. GM&O, Birmingham, Ala., CofGa.
CIM5	C&IM, Cimic, Ill., IC, Birmingham, Ala., ACL or CofGa.		

For explanation of reference marks see concluding page(s) of this tariff.

Distance-Rate Structures. The simplest form of rate structure is one in which rates are based on a distance scale. This structure, as previously discussed, is closely related to costs. The computation of rates for different distances has been simplified: instead of being tapered mile by mile, rates are reduced in mileage blocks. A typical scale, for example, employs 5-mile blocks up to 100 miles, 10-mile blocks from 100 to 240 miles, 20-mile blocks from 240 to 800 miles, and 25-mile blocks from 800 to 3,000 miles.[23] Class rates generally follow the distance-rate structure, as do a few commodity rates.

Competition, however, tends to distort distance rates and to prevent adherence to strict distance scales.[24] A railroad may have to depart from a distance scale when faced with competition from another railroad or from a different mode of transport, when there is competition between rival producing centers to sell goods in a common market, or when there is competition of rival markets for the products of a common producing area. Competiton of routes is illustrated in Figure 10-4. Railroad x will have to charge the same rate as railroad y, even though its route involves a longer haul. Another type of competition is market competition. As shown in Figure 10-5, railroad y may reduce its regular rate from $2.00 to $1.50 in order to meet the rate of railroad x. In this way, both railroads will be able to serve the market at M. Competition of directions is illustrated in Figure 10-6. Here, as markets A and B are competing for the product produced at C, the two railroads may charge the same rate. Otherwise, the railroad charging the lowest rate may get the traffic. This type of competition is common in the movement of grain from country points to rival grain markets.

FIGURE 10-4

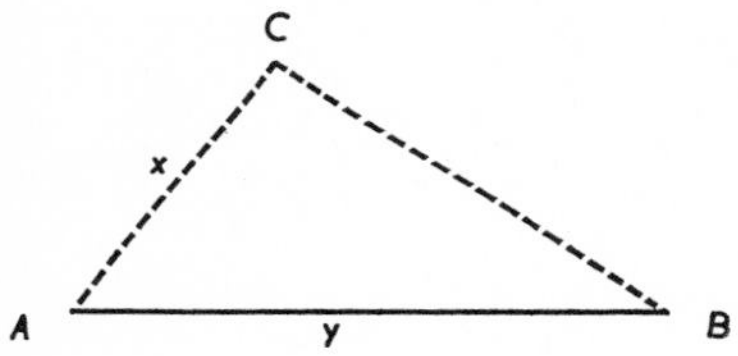

FIGURE 10-5

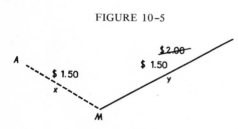

FIGURE 10-6

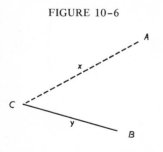

Group-Rate Structures. Frequently, rates from several points of origin or destinations are grouped so that all shippers in the group will pay the same rate regardless of the actual distance traveled. Group-rate structures are established for two principal purposes: to simplify the rate structure and, of more importance, to meet market competition. Distant shippers would often be unable to supply a particular market or markets

---

[23] *Class Rates in the United States,* 294 ICC 662 (1955).
[24] This discussion is based on Locklin, *op. cit.,* pp. 186–89.

in competition with other shippers in the absence of grouping. Thus, group-rate structures have long been of importance in transporting such commodities as coal, milk, lumber, and petroleum. To illustrate: Coal shipped from points in Ohio, Pennsylvania, West Virginia, Virginia, and eastern Kentucky to Toledo, Ohio, are subject to three group rates: the Ohio, Inner Crescent, and Outer Crescent Groups (Figure 10-7). The more distant groups take higher rates. Moreover, rates are usually established on the basis of a fixed differential (discussed below) between the groups.

FIGURE 10-7
Group Coal Rates*

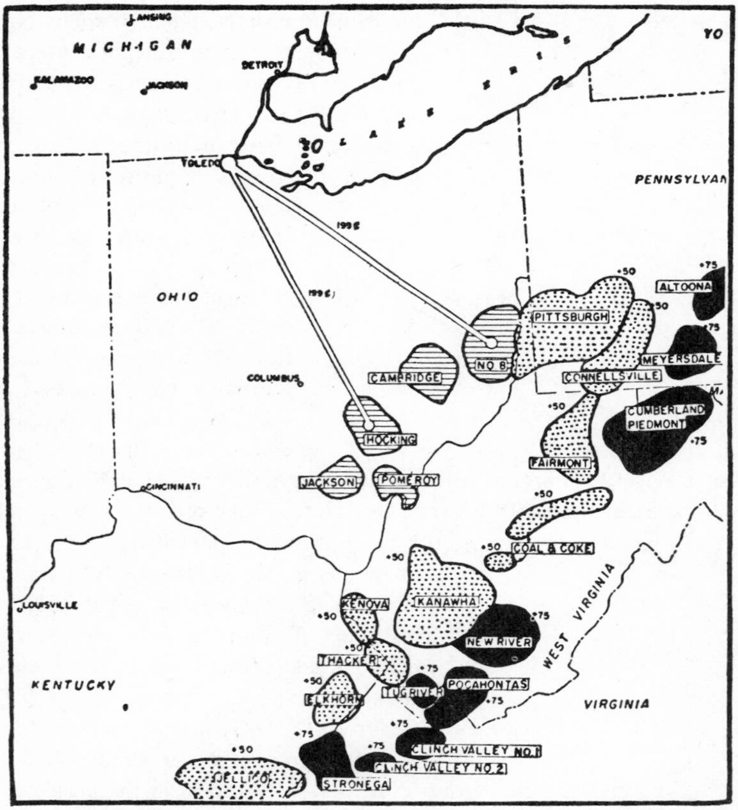

* Ohio (striped), Inner Crescent (dotted), Outer Crescent (black).
Source: D. Philip Locklin, *Economics of Transportation* (6th ed.; Homewood, Ill.: Richard D. Irwin, Inc., 1966), p. 191.

Equalization and Differential Systems. In many cases, rates are equalized between routes or are subject to differentials. The rates between the Missouri

River crossings (Dubuque, Fort Madison, Hannibal, and St. Louis) have generally been the same since 1894, even though distances between them vary from 200 miles between Kansas City and Hannibal to 414 miles between St. Louis and Omaha.[25] Rates between competing terminals and markets are thus equalized. Prior to a 1963 Supreme Court decision,[26] there were differential rates between the North Atlantic ports on import and export traffic. As a result of an agreement by various railroads in 1877, typical freight rates from the Midwest to the Southern ports (Philadelphia, Baltimore, and Hampton Roads) were three to four cents a hundred pounds below those between the Midwest and the Northern ports (New York, Boston, Albany, and Portland). The various differentials were to compensate for ocean rate differentials which gave an advantage to the Northern ports.

Discrimination in Practice. In the early days of the railroad industry, when it enjoyed a monopoly of the nation's transportation, rates tended to be set on the value of service principle. Over the years, as competing modes of transport have developed, many rates on specific commodities have been reduced toward or below the cost of service standard. As a result, present rates reflect a mixture of monopoly and competitive elements, with some based upon demand conditions and others upon cost conditions. The present rate structure clearly discriminates among various commodities and between geographical areas of the country.

Discrimination is partly unavoidable. Given the industry's high fixed costs, and recognizing that most of these costs are joint or common, their allocation among different commodities and hauls must be made on the basis of judgment. And in exercising their judgment, the railroads have tended to allocate fixed costs on the basis of demand considerations. Little attempt has been made to work out an economic allocation.[27]

In larger part, however, discrimination is intentional. Discrimination among commodities occurs in two principal ways. First, commodities move at rates which are multiples or percentages of Class 100. Ideally, the initial rate should be based largely on terminal costs. But if this were true, the initial rates for the other classes of freight would more than cover, or would not cover, such

---

[25] Marvin L. Fair and Ernest W. Williams, Jr., *Economics of Transportation* (rev. ed.; New York: Harper & Bros., 1959), p. 391.

[26] In 1960 and 1961, the ICC issued orders denying the Northern ports permission to equalize the rates. *Equalization of Rates at North Atlantic Ports*, 311 ICC 689 (1960), 314 ICC 185 (1961). The order was reversed by a federal court; a decision affirmed by the Supreme Court. *Boston & Maine Railroad* v. *United States*, 202 F. Supp. 830 (1962), *aff'd per curiam*, 373 U.S. 372 (1963).

[27] In 1956, Dr. James G. Lyne, Editor of *Railway Age*, stated: "The principle of 'charging no more than the traffic will bear' needs to be modified to recognize the fact that a lower ceiling is required than the shipper's ability to pay.... The value of the service is as valid a consideration in ratemaking today as it ever was—the only difference being that a different yardstick has to be used.... Today, the yardstick has to be the cost of any alternative form of transportation." *Transportation Policy* (Hearings before the Subcommittee on Interstate and Foreign Commerce, House, 84th Cong., 2d sess.) (Washington, D.C.: U.S. Government Printing Office, 1956), Part 1, p. 417.

costs. Second, less than 5 percent of the carload freight hauled moves at class rates. Nearly 10 percent moves on exception ratings and approximately 85 percent at commodity rates. These rates are substantially below the corresponding class rates. The rates between commodities are great and cannot be justified by differences in costs: where demand is elastic, rates are low; where inelastic, rates are high. Discrimination was demonstrated vividly in a study made by the Interstate Commerce Commission. The commission compared the carload revenues for certain commodities with both the out-of-pocket costs[28] and the fully distributed costs (including a rate of return on investment) of hauling them. For twenty commodities, the results are shown in Table 10-4, and they

TABLE 10-4
Ratio of Rail Carload Revenues to Out-of-Pocket and Fully
Distributed Costs for Twenty Commodities, 1960

Commodity	Out-of-Pocket Costs	Fully Distributed Costs	Commodity	Out-of-Pocket Costs	Fully Distributed Costs
Sugar beets	54	42	Bituminous coal	110	82
Straw	64	57	Cotton, bales	152	123
Fruits, fresh	66	60	Automobiles, passenger ..	187	171
Petroleum, crude ...	67	54	Iron, pig	187	139
Vegetables, fresh ...	69	63	Rubber, crude	201	160
Dairy products	69	65	Cigarettes	223	185
Pulpwood	75	57	Liquors	246	200
Oranges, grapefruit ..	82	73	Military vehicles	328	256
Gasoline	93	77	Magnesium metal	367	254
Flour wheat	97	77	Explosives	413	324

Source: Interstate Commerce Commission, Bureau of Accounts, Cost Finding Section, *Distribution of the Rail Revenue Contribution by Commodity Groups–1960*, Statement No. 2-62 (Washington, D.C.: U.S. Government Printing Office, 1962).

demonstrate the wide range of discrimination found in the industry. It should also be noted that many commodities are carried at rates which do not even cover out-of-pocket costs. The result is that these rates cannot be justified as socially desirable; the rates may, in fact, reduce the carriers' net revenues and increase the industry's total costs and excess capacity.

Table 10-4 also indicates that high-valued manufacturing commodities make a larger contribution to fixed costs than do the low-valued agricultural, lumber, and mineral commodities. The table, however, does not indicate "the full range of discrimination, because the ICC publishes data only on commodity groups. The details of the discrimination can be inferred from the fact that among the approximately 75,000 tariffs published a distinction has been made between horses for slaughtering and draft horses, sand for glass manufacture

[28] The commission's definition of out-of-pocket costs is roughly similar to the economist's concept of variable cost. See Chapter 11, p. 393.

and sand for cement, and lime for agriculture and lime for industrial use." [29]

Discrimination also occurs between geographical areas. Again, some discrimination is due to the attempt to simplify the rate structure by using mileage blocks and by grouping points of origin or destination. But in most of these cases, rates are established so as to meet the competition of other carriers or to equalize the competitive opportunities between various geographical markets. Figure 10–8 illustrates the point. In other cases, the groupings are extremely

FIGURE 10–8
Railroad Rate Differentiation Due to Competition
from Competing Mode of Transport

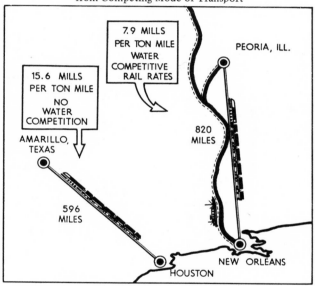

7.9 MILLS PER TON MILE WATER COMPETITIVE RAIL RATES

PEORIA, ILL.

15.6 MILLS PER TON MILE NO WATER COMPETITION

AMARILLO, TEXAS

820 MILES

596 MILES

NEW ORLEANS
HOUSTON

SHIPPING BLACKSTRAP MOLASSES FROM HOUSTON TO AMARILLO, TEXAS AND FROM NEW ORLEANS TO PEORIA, ILL.

Source: *Proposed Amendments to Federal Transportation Laws* (Hearings before the Committee on Commerce, U.S. Senate, 87th Cong., 2d sess.) (Washington, D.C.: U.S. Government Printing Office, 1962), p. 365.

large: transcontinental commodity rates, for instance, have been established whereby shipments from any point in California, Arizona, Nevada, and Idaho to any point in New England, New Jersey, Delaware, Maryland, and most of New York, Pennsylvania, Virginia, and West Virginia take the same rate despite the fact that the distance varies by more than a thousand miles. [30] Clearly, these rates

[29] John R. Meyer, Merton J. Peck, John Stenason, Charles Zwick, *The Economics of Competition in the Transportation Industries* (Cambridge: Harvard University Press, 1959), p. 174.

[30] Locklin, *op. cit.*, p. 189.

bear little relation to differences in costs. Moreover, the rate structure discriminates between short and long hauls. First, short-haul traffic makes a smaller contribution to fixed costs than does long-haul traffic. Such discrimination partly reflects the higher elasticity of demand for short-haul traffic due to truck competition. And, in part, it is historical, for terminal costs once were much lower relative to line-haul costs than they are at the present time.[31] Second, intrastate traffic makes a smaller contribution to fixed costs than does interstate traffic, perhaps reflecting the influence of state regulation of such traffic.[32]

Other Railroad Rates

Class I railroads derive approximately 88 percent of their total operating revenues from freight traffic. The remaining 12 percent is derived from the carriage of passengers and their baggage (5 percent), mail pay (3 percent), express (1 percent), and other revenue (3 percent).[33] The rate structures of these services, which exhibit little discrimination, are briefly discussed in this section.

Passenger Fares. In general, fares for first class or Pullman and coach services are constructed on the basis of a uniform rate per mile, with no recognition of the tapering principle. Fares, as reflected by revenue per passenger-mile, are higher in the Eastern Territory than in the Southern and Western Territories (Table 10-5), but there are many exceptions.[34] There are

TABLE 10-5
Average Revenue per Passenger per Mile, 1967
(cents per passenger mile)

Territory	Commutation	First Class	Coach
Eastern	3.412	5.947	4.095
Southern	3.179	3.510	2.578
Western	3.260	2.852	2.269

Source: Association of American Railroads, Economics and Finance Department.

also exceptions to the practice of making fares proportional to distance. Round-trip fares are approximately 180 percent of the corresponding one-way fares. Commutation fares, frequently lower than coach fares, are often constructed on the tapering principle, and discounts are given when weekly or monthly tickets are purchased. Family fares are in widespread use; special fares are offered for vacation trips, holidays, or special events. And competition has

31 Meyer and others, *op. cit.,* p. 175.
32 *Ibid.*
33 Data supplied by Association of American Railroads, Economics and Finance Department (September, 1968).
34 In the last few years, many changes in passenger fares have been made either by individual railroads or by small groups of railroads and not on a territorial or national basis.

forced certain railroads to group points of origin or destination—equal rates are charged between Chicago and Pacific Coast cities, between California and Kansas City.[35] Moreover, promotional fares are being tried in an attempt to increase passenger business.[36]

Express Rates. Railway Express Agency, Inc., owned since 1929 by 67 of the nation's railroads, was long operated on a cooperative, nonprofit basis. Prior to 1959, the railroads hauled all shipments given to them by the agency at no charge. After deducting its own operating costs, the express agency paid the roads whatever was left at the end of every month. In addition, REA faced rising costs and suffered a tremendous loss of small shipments (less-than-carload traffic), principally to parcel post (which is subsidized by the government) and to trucks.

In 1959, REA and the railroads entered into a new agreement which, among other things, gave the express agency freedom to route traffic as it chooses and changed the basis of pay.[37] A significant improvement program was undertaken, aimed at providing better and faster service at lower rates. And the agency embarked on a diversification program.[38] But it encountered difficulties in financing its capital improvement program, and in 1964, its railroad owners voted to sell a 20 percent ownership in the company to the Greyhound Corporation.[39] The transaction was approved by the ICC, but set aside by the Supreme Court.[40] In mid-1968, REA's owners placed three trustees in voting control of the agency for a ten-year period.[41]

The express agency's rate structure is much simpler than that of the railroad's freight structure. There are three regular classes. First class is for most of the articles carried by express. Second class rates, for beverages and food, are set at 75 percent of first class rates. Printed matter (books, pamphlets, newspapers) are in the third class, and the rate is one cent for each two ounces. Several special commodities are subject to rates that are multiples (1.5 times or double) of first class. These include bulky and easily damaged articles (dressed poultry, gift packages of fresh fruit), articles of exceptional value (coins,

---

[35] Passenger fares are discussed in Troxel, *op. cit.,* pp. 724–35; *Increased Fares, Official Territory, 1956,* 300 ICC 239 (1957); and *Railroad Passenger Train Deficit,* 306 ICC 417 (1959).

[36] These fares are reported annually in Association of American Railroads, Economics and Finance Department, *Railroad Review and Outlook* (Washington, D.C.).

[37] REA now pays for the services as rendered on a basis designed to cover railroad out-of-pocket costs of moving the traffic.

[38] REA's divisions and subsidiaries include Air Express (see p. 338), REA Leasing Corp. (a piggyback trailer pool with REA and 41 railroads as members), Fast Service Shipping Terminals, Inc. (a traffic consolidator), and several international operations.

[39] *Transport Topics,* October 5, 1964, pp. 1, 26.

[40] *Railway Express Agency, Inc., Stock,* Finance Docket No. 23324 (1965), *aff'd sub nom. Denver & Rio Grande Western Railroad Co. v. United States,* 255 F. Supp. 704 (1966), *rev'd,* 387 U.S. 485 (1967). REA and Greyhound subsequently terminated their agreement.

[41] *The Wall Street Journal,* June 12, 1968, p. 4. In fiscal 1967, REA reported a loss of $5.8 million.

currency, securities, orchids), and low-density articles (artificial flowers, furniture, lamp shades). Rates are generally expressed in cents per pound and follow the tapering principle.[42]

Railway Mail Pay. Unlike the compensation paid to the airlines for carrying airmail, which is based on cost and financial need, the railroads are supposed to receive an amount equal only to the cost of carrying surface mail. Since the end of World War II, mail pay rates have more than doubled, but the railroads, in several of these years, have carried mail at rates which did not cover fully distributed costs. The ratio of revenue to cost, excluding a return on investment, was 95 percent for the eastern roads in 1961, 86 percent for the southern roads in 1960, and 87 percent for the western roads in 1958.[43] When it increased rates in 1960—8 percent in the East and 13 percent in the South and West—the Interstate Commerce Commission expressed its belief that the railroads would be able to cover fully distributed costs and earn a 3 percent rate of return before taxes.[44] (The rates of pay are shown in Table 10-6.) But mail revenues can be expected to maintain their downward trend of the last few years as the Post Office Department continues to shift first-class mail to other carriers.

Water Carrier Rates

Three types of waterways are used for domestic water transportation.[45] First, rivers, canals, and other inland waterways which are served by barges and towboats; second, coast and intercoastal waters, serviced by ocean-going vessels among the nation's seaports; third, the Great Lakes, on which freighters provide service. While there are many important cost differences among these diverse modes of transport, there are also significant similarities.[46]

Except for inland waterway vessels, capital investment is large, so that

[42]*Express Rates, Practices, Accounts, and Revenues,* 24 ICC 380, 397, 403 (1912) and 28 ICC 131 (1913); *Express Rates and Ratings between Points in the United States,* 280 ICC 319 (1951) and 286 ICC 467 (1952).

[43]*Railway Mail Pay, 1960,* 311 ICC 579, 592-94 (1960). For earlier mail pay decisions, see 304 ICC 135 (1958); 302 ICC 609 (1957); 292 ICC 101 (1954); 291 ICC 170 (1953); 279 ICC 632 (1950); and 269 ICC 357 (1947).

[44]311 ICC 579, 595 (1960).

[45]Rates for international shipping are determined by "conferences," but such conference agreements are subject to the approval of the Federal Maritime Administration. The "dual-rate" system is also used in international shipping—that is, shippers who agree to ship by conference lines exclusively are given lower rates than other shippers. On shipping conferences, see Daniel Marx, Jr., *International Shipping Cartels: A Study of Industrial Self-Regulation by Shipping Conferences* (Princeton: Princeton University Press, 1953); and John S. McGee, "Ocean Freight Rate Conferences and the American Merchant Marine," 27 *University of Chicago Law Review* 191 (1960). On the dual-rate system, see *Federal Maritime Board* v. *Isbrandtsen,* 356 U.S. 481 (1958); Note, "The American Shipping Industry and the Conference System," 11 *Stanford Law Review* 136 (1958); E. Robert Seaver and Edward Schmeltzer, "The Role of Conferences and the Dual Rate System in Ocean Foreign Trade," 34 *Law and Contemporary Problems* 605 (1959); and James V. Metcalfe, *Principles of Ocean Transportation* (New York: Simmons-Boardman Publishing Corp., 1959), chap. xii.

[46]This summary of cost characteristics is based upon Meyer and others, *op. cit.,* pp. 111–13.

there is a significant difference between fully distributed costs and out-of-pocket costs. A similar characteristic is found in the railroad industry, but it differs markedly from the motor carrier industry. Moreover, water carriers' terminal costs (harbor charges, costs of loading and unloading cargo) are high, while

TABLE 10–6
Rates of Pay, Railway Mail Pay, 1968

Item	East	South and West
a) For each mile of service by		
Railway post office cars and apartments:	*cents*	*cents*
60–foot car	92.15	79.01
30–foot apartment	74.13	67.72
15–foot apartment	47.88	43.73
Storage cars:		
60–foot	101.93	93.11
Lesser units of storage space:		
30–foot	74.13	67.72
27–foot	67.95	62.07
24–foot	61.78	56.43
21–foot	55.60	50.79
18–foot	47.88	43.73
15–foot	41.70	38.09
12–foot	37.07	33.85
9–foot	29.34	26.80
6–foot	20.08	18.34
3–foot	10.81	9.88
b) Terminal charges:		
Per car charges		
Destination storage cars and destination relay storage cars:		
60–foot storage car	$ 88.74	$ 70.26
All other storage cars:		
60–foot storage car	$177.48	$140.52
	cents	*cents*
Per piece charge	21.38	16.93

Source: *Railway Mail Pay, 1960,* 311 ICC 579, 595 (1960). For a complete explanation of each item, see *Railway Mail Pay, 1956,* 304 ICC 135 (1958).

line-haul costs are extremely low. Water carriers, finally, need volume traffic to compensate for the slower service—relative to other modes of transport—that they offer.

Given these cost characteristics, domestic water carriers find that their economic use lies in two types of traffic. These are (1) bulk commodities, for example, grain, petroleum, coal, and sand, for which they are specially designed to be loaded and discharged rapidly and (2) low-to-medium-value goods over long hauls where their low line-haul costs can offset high terminal costs.[47]

[47]*Ibid.,* p. 113.

The rate structures of water carriers, therefore, are similar to those of the railroads. In order to be competitive, the rates of common carriers on inland waterways are commonly based on railroad rates, and the railroad freight classifications are frequently used. The bulk of water traffic, however, moves on commodity rates. Here, rates are often established at a fixed differential below rail rates: common carriers have traditionally maintained port-to-port rates which are 20 percent below the rail rates.[48] But there are many exceptions. Joint rail-barge rates are also extensively in use. Commonly, these rates are computed by deducting from the all-rail rate the 20 percent differential on the water portion of the haul.[49] The rates of contract carriers by water are generally even lower than those of common carriers. These lower rates are due partly to lower costs: contract carriers do not operate on regular routes or according to fixed schedules, and they usually carry commodities in large lots.[50]

In the coastwise and intercoastal trade, steamship lines are organized into "conferences" which attempt to control the rates and competitive practices of their members. In intercoastal trade, some of the conferences have established two classes of steamship lines, known as Class A and Class B lines. Due to their less frequent sailings and slower service, Class B lines have been permitted to set rates on some commodities slightly below those of Class A lines. In addition, port-to-port rates often disregard great differences in distance. For example, in the intercoastal trade, the rates have usually been the same from all Atlantic ports to all Pacific ports.[51]

Water carrier rates, in certain cases, are discriminatory, as was demonstrated in a proceeding relating to the Pacific coastwise rates in 1950. A cost study showed that many steamship rates were insufficient to cover costs plus a fair return to the lines. For some traffic, the excess of cost over revenues was from 7 to 29 cents per 100 pounds. The commission stated, however, that unless the water carriers were to surrender this traffic to the railroads, the rates in effect could not be increased without a similar increase in competing railroad rates.[52]

Motor Carrier Rates

The structure of regulated motor carrier rates is also closely related to that of the railroad industry. Significantly, this similarity is not due to comparable cost considerations. As Locklin has explained:

> This is due in part to the fact that the motor carriers were required by the Motor Carrier Act of 1935 to publish and file rates in a comparatively short

---

[48]*Rail and Barge Joint Rates,* 270 ICC 591, 597 (1948).

[49]In 1948 and 1949, the Interstate Commerce Commission prescribed a different system for computing the joint rail-barge rates on the Mississippi and Warrior Rivers and their tributaries, but the basis on which they were constructed was not explained. *Ibid.* and 272 ICC 229 (1949).

[50]Locklin, *op. cit.,* p. 734.

[51]*Ibid.*

[52]*All Rail Commodity Rates between California, Oregon, & Washington,* 277 ICC 511 (1950).

time, and it was easier to adopt the pattern of railroad rates than to construct an entirely independent structure of rates. They were also in competition with rail carriers and could not charge rates much higher than rail rates. On the other hand, they could charge above-cost rates where the railroad rates permitted.[53]

Despite many changes since this time, Taff estimates that over 80 percent of the entries in the classifications used by the two types of carriers are identical.[54]

Motor Freight Classifications. There are three types of motor freight classifications. First, and the most widely used, is the *National Motor Freight Classification*. As noted above, the ratings follow the railroads' classifications closely. At first, the classification contained different ratings on commodities in the East, South, and West, but when the *Uniform Freight Classification* was adopted by the railroads in 1952, a *National Motor Freight Classification*, with one set of ratings for most commodities, was established. Similar to the railroad industry, motor carriers work through rate bureaus. Currently, there are more than 100 rate and tariff bureaus, and 12 major intraterritorial rate bureaus (Figure 10-9).

Second, in New England a separate classification is used—the *Coordinated Motor Freight Classification*. This classification is important because ratings are based largely on the weight densities of the various commodities carried. These ratings are designed to produce approximately the same revenue per truckload on all commodities carried. Thus, those commodities weighing from 3 to 6 pounds per cubic foot are rated first class; from 6 to 10 pounds, second class; from 10 to 15 pounds, third class; from 15 to 20 pounds, fourth class; and 20 pounds or more, fifth class.[55] Articles which require special treatment (fragile or easily damaged articles) and those which are of high value (liquors) are given a rating one or two classes above their regular weight-density class (the fifth class is the basic class). Lower ratings are applied when necessary to meet railroad competition.

"The development of their own classifications was partly the result of a cost study and also because there was not the degree of rail competition faced by motor carriers in this area as compared with motor carriers located in other areas in the United States."[56] The ICC, which indicated that there was need for experimentation with this method of classifying motor carrier freight, at first questioned its practicability as long as the railroads adhered to their traditional method of classifying freight. But in 1948, the commission concluded that the "trial which the New England motor carriers and shippers [had] given the

[53] Locklin, *op. cit.*, p. 650.
[54] Charles A. Taff, *Commercial Motor Transportation* (3d ed.; Homewood, Ill.: Richard D. Irwin, Inc., 1961), p. 407.
[55] *Motor Carrier Rates, New York City Area–New England,* 62 MCC 427, 432 (1954). Commodities weighing 3 pounds and under are rated either 1½ or 2½ times first class.
[56] Taff, *op. cit.*, p. 419.

FIGURE 10-9

Major Intraterritorial Motor Freight Territories

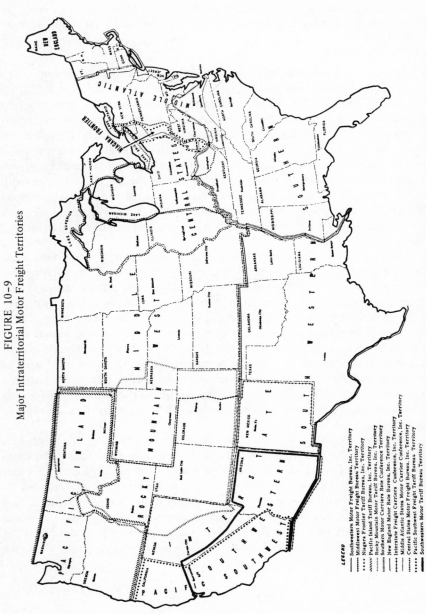

LEGEND

——— Southwestern Motor Freight Bureau, Inc. Territory
——— Middlewest Motor Freight Bureau Territory
• • • • Niagara Frontier Tariff Bureau, Inc. Territory
⟋⟋⟋⟋ Pacific Inland Tariff Bureau, Inc. Territory
⟍⟍⟍⟍ Rocky Mountain Motor Tariff Bureau, Inc. Territory
——— Southern Motor Carriers Rate Conference Territory
——— New England Motor Rate Bureau, Inc. Territory
⊢⊢⊢⊢ Interstate Freight Carriers Conference, Inc. Territory
┴┴┴┴ Middle Atlantic States Motor Carrier Conference, Inc. Territory
——— Central States Motor Freight Bureau, Inc. Territory
• • • • Pacific Southwest Tariff Bureau Territory
▬▬▬ Southwestern Motor Tariff Bureau Territory

Source: Charles A. Taff, *Commercial Motor Transportation* (3d ed.; Homewood, Ill.: Richard D. Irwin, Inc., 1961), p. 461.

density type of classification [had] resulted, in the main, to their mutual advantage."[57]

Finally, because some state regulatory commissions require it for intrastate shipments, a number of motor carriers use the railroads' *Uniform Freight Classification.*

Rate-Making Practices. In general, it appears that motor carriers have a cost advantage over the railroads for short hauls, particularly those of under 100 miles, because terminal costs (pickup and delivery, terminal facilities) tend to be lower. For long hauls, motor carrier line-haul costs (depreciation, taxes, tires, gas) increase more rapidly than those of the railroads. The result is that motor carriers have a cost advantage for short distances and railroads have a cost advantage for long distances.[58] This conclusion leads to four important rate-making practices.

Motor carriers sometimes use railroad distances when their rates are based on a distance scale. From a cost standpoint, highway distances should be used. The practice of employing railroad distances, while it produces rates that are more competitive with railroad rates, may also result in discrimination.[59] Like the railroad industry, motor carriers make a distinction between truckload and less-than-truckload shipments. Truckloads enjoy lower rates. In addition, however, motor carriers have established "volume minimum weights." As explained by the commission:

> A volume minimum is distinguished from a truckload minimum in that the volume rate applies when a shipper tenders the volume minimum weight of a commodity for transportation at one time, even though it may exceed the carrying capacity of the largest vehicle available and must be transported in two or more vehicles, whereas a truckload minimum is generally understood to be the quantity which a carrier can transport in a single vehicle.[60]

The use of volume minimum weights in excess of the capacity of a single truck cannot be justified by cost considerations. Ordinarily, such shipments cannot be transported at a lower cost than a truckload shipment. Their use can only be explained in terms of motor-rail competition. At first, the ICC refused to approve the use of volume minimum weights, but it was later reversed by the Supreme Court.[61] Here, again, discrimination often enters the motor carrier freight rate structure.

Motor carriers have established class and commodity rates and exception ratings. As in the case of the railroads, both exception and commodity rates are generally below the class rate. After adopting the railroads' freight classification

---

[57]*Motor Carrier Rates in New England,* 47 MCC 657, 662-63 (1948). Also see *New England Motor Carrier Rates,* 8 MCC 287, 291–93 (1938).

[58]Meyer and others, *op. cit.,* chap. iv.

[59]*Class Rates between Middle Atlantic & New England Territories,* 67 MCC 741 (1956); *Iron & Steel Articles—Eastern Common Carriers,* 306 MCC 369 (1959).

[60]*Stoves, Alabama & Tennessee to Interstate Points,* 4 MCC 641, n. 643 (1938).

[61]*Eastern-Central Motor Carrier Association* v. *United States,* 321 U.S. 194 (1944).

and class rates, the motor carriers soon found they were unable to carry many commodities profitably. Particularly was this true for low-rated (light and bulky) freight moving long distances. As a solution, the carriers established "minimum rate stops" on certain class rates. This device means that although a commodity may be rated at a lower class in the classification, it will be subject to a higher class rate. On a certain commodity, for example, the fifth class rate might be the lowest rate which a motor carrier would charge, even though the commodity might be rated in the seventh class. In 1945, the commission "reluctantly" approved of minimum rate stops, saying that their use "not only results in undue disadvantage to freight rated in the lower classes but in effect to a certain extent constitutes avoidance of the duty imposed by law upon all motor common carriers to afford reasonable transportation service at reasonable rates in all classes of traffic."[62] The necessity of adopting rate stops demonstrates once more that motor carriers find their major cost advantage in the transport of high-class traffic and that they cannot compete with the railroads and water carriers for low-rated traffic on long hauls.[63] In 1954, it was estimated that nearly 38 per cent of the tonnage moved on class rates, 28 percent on commodity rates, 28 percent on exception ratings, and 6 percent on class-rate stops.[64]

Finally, similar to volume minimum weights are "weight breakdowns"— that is, rates which depend on the size of a shipment regardless of whether the quantity offered is less than a truckload. In New England, for instance, class rates provide different fifth-class rates on six weight groups.[65] The commission has pointed out that this system "is designed to pass on to the shipping public the benefit of a carrier's lower costs, especially for pickup and delivery, in the hauling of larger shipments."[66]

Motor Carrier Rates and Discrimination. Given the cost characteristics of the motor carrier industry, it would seem that their rates would be close to marginal and average costs, and that discrimination would be a relatively rare occurrence. (The significant exception would be in back-haul situations, where true joint costs prevail.) The rates of unregulated motor carriers do appear to be closely related to costs.[67] However, the situation is different with respect to regulated motor carriers, due to restrictive entry control, rate bureaus, and minimum rate and suspension orders. "Thus, they can price under cartel conditions and frequently utilize high rail value-of-service (discriminating) rates as bases for their prices. Sans regulated entry and minimum rates, competitive

---

[62]*Minimum Class Rate Restrictions, Central & Eastern States,* 44 MCC 367 (1945).

[63] Locklin, *op. cit.,* pp. 654–55.

[64] Taff, *op. cit.,* p. 438.

[65] Locklin, *op. cit.,* p. 653.

[66]*Multiple Deliveries–New England,* 69 MCC 77, 78 (1956).

[67] James C. Nelson, "The Effects of Entry Control in Surface Transportation," in *Transportation Economics* (New York: National Bureau of Economic Research, 1965), pp. 398–400, 413–15; and W. Miklius, "Some Characteristics of Nonregulated For-Hire Truck Transportation of Agricultural Commodities," 42 *Land Economics* 226 (1966).

market restraints would insure that the rates of regulated carriers would be closely related to average and marginal costs."[68]

Nor has the regulated motor carrier industry developed a rate structure based upon its own costs. As Taff has put it:

> Although a start has been made in the development and use of cost data in rate making, the regulated for-hire trucking industry has yet to build a motor-carrier price structure starting with the foundation. Rate scales reflecting the distinctive characteristics, the economies, the inherent advantages, as well as cost advantages, have not been devised. The basic rail scales still constitute the foundation of the price structure of motor carriers.[69]

Value of service, therefore, while less evident than in the railroad rate structure, is important in explaining motor carrier rates. So, too, is competition from contract and private trucking and from railroads. From the point of view of the common motor carriers, their failure to develop a rate structure based upon their own costs is serious. In many cases, use of the railroads' rate structure, combined with the emphasis on the value of service standard, results in the common motor carriers' operating under a rate umbrella provided by the railroads, and tends to encourage contract and private trucking competition for high-rated commodities.[70] It is only in the last few years that the commission has made any attempt to investigate the cost of motor carrier operations in a comprehensive manner.[71]

Airline Rates

Less concrete information is available on domestic airline rates than on the other regulated industries.[72] Throughout most of its history, the airline industry has been operating under rapidly changing conditions. Until late in 1948, the industry was primarily concerned with providing first class passenger and mail

[68] James C. Nelson, "Economic Standards for Competitive Freight Rates," 48 *Journal of Farm Economics* 1408, 1412 (1966).

[69] Taff, *op. cit.*, p. 455.

[70] See F. K. Edwards, "Cost Analysis in Transportation," 37 *American Economic Review* 441 (1947); G. W. Wilson, "Effects of Value-of-Service Pricing upon Motor Common Carriers," 63 *Journal of Political Economy* 337 (1955); and Merrill J. Roberts, "Some Aspects of Motor Carrier Costs: Firm Size, Efficiency and Financial Health," 32 *Land Economics* 228 (1956).

[71] Several cost studies are made annually by the Interstate Commerce Commission, Bureau of Accounts, Cost Finding Section. See, for example, *Southern Carrier Cost Study, 1950* (1952); *Cost of Transporting Freight by Class I and Class II Motor Common Carriers of General Commodities, East-South Territory, 1964* (1965); *Cost of Transporting Freight by Class I and Class II Motor Common Carriers of General Commodities, by Regions or Territories, Year 1965* (1967).

[72] The Civil Aeronautics Board has authority to fix rates for domestic air carriers operating between the United States and its territories, but it lacks jurisdiction over the rates of domestic carriers operating in foreign air transport. Such rates are established through the International Air Transport Association. For a discussion of international air transportation policy, see John H. Frederick, *Commercial Air Transportation* (5th ed.; Homewood, Ill.: Richard D. Irwin, Inc., 1961), chap. 10; and Note, "CAB Regulation of International Aviation," 75 *Harvard Law Review* 575 (1962).

services. The demand for passenger service grew rapidly, so that pricing was a relatively simple process. Since that time, however, the rate of growth has slackened. Coach service and promotional rates have been introduced in an effort to attract new customers. The emphasis on freight service has been increased, bringing the airlines into direct competition with other types of carriers. Added to these factors has been the heavy capital needs of the industry to finance new equipment. As a result, rate design has assumed more importance in the past few years. Along with this development have come better cost statistics. The fact remains, however, that there is much disagreement among the domestic carriers over the correct rate structure.

Before discussing the four principal types of airline services offered— passenger, express, freight, and mail—the significant cost and demand characteristics of the industry will be outlined.[73]

Cost Considerations. There are three significant cost considerations. First, airline costs are affected by a number of variables, including: (a) capacity of the plane, (b) length of the flight, (c) ton-miles load factor, (d) number of hours per day planes are utilized, (e) flight frequency, (f) weather, (g) mechanical reliability, (h) adequacy of ground facilities, (i) number of competitors, (j) metropolitan population served, (k) average speed of planes, and (l) net assets of each firm.[74] It can readily be shown, therefore, that one mile may be more expensive than another. Consider, for example, the length of the flight. The larger the number of stations which an airline must maintain over a given route, the higher the costs will tend to be. More stations must be staffed and the average flight between these stations will be shorter. Shorter flights, in turn, result in a higher percentage of ground time in taxiing and warming up, a larger number of take-offs and landings, and a lower average speed per flight. The flight time is increased, and since gasoline consumption per plane mile is greater in reaching flight height than it is at cruising altitude, operating expenses also rise. In addition, if flight equipment utilization is low, the depreciation of such equipment will be high. A report has estimated:

> Costs per available ton mile or available passenger seat mile go down sharply if an airplane can stay aloft for hauls of over 500 miles in length. For example, a 500-mile hop tends to be less than one half as expensive per unit of operation as a 200-mile hop; on the other hand, the economies realizable by lengthening the hop beyond the 500-mile range are significant but not so pronounced. . . .[75]

Second, the common costs of airlines appear to be high, which means there is a complex problem of determining the cost of performing the various

---

[73] The discussion of airline rates largely refers to the eleven domestic trunklines. Some of the information was supplied by United Air Lines.

[74] Jesse W. Proctor and Julius S. Duncan, "A Regression Analysis of Airline Costs," 21 *Journal of Air Law and Commerce* 282 (1954). The authors found that variables (a), (c), and (d) had significant correlation with cost per revenue ton.

[75] Meyer and others, *op. cit.,* p. 136.

types of services.[76] To illustrate: If a particular flight handles passengers, freight, and mail, the costs of the plane's operation, the wages of the pilots and flight engineer, and part of the fuel costs are common to the three services. Other costs can be allocated directly to each type of service, such as the wage(s) of the stewardess(es) to passenger service and the cost of soliciting and handling freight to freight service. As is true in the case of other regulated industries, the allocation of common costs among the various types of services will, in part, be arbitrary.[77]

Third, for the airlines, fixed costs (salaries of management, other administrative overhead) are relatively low. In large part, this is because the airlines do not own their terminals. Rather, they purchase airport services when they are needed.[78] Far more important are variable costs, but here a distinction must be made between constant and direct variable costs.[79] A substantial portion of airline costs do not vary in proportion to changes in the volume of business handled and represent constant variable costs. These costs include many station expenses, as well as supervisory, administrative, and clerical personnel. Moreover, assuming a given number of flights, up to the limit of a plane's capacity the same is true of operating costs (fuel, wages, maintenance). Thus, whether a plane carries five or seventy-five passengers, it may pay out almost the same amount for plane operation and maintenance. The costs will increase, of course, when additional flights are added. The importance of these cost considerations has been well stated by Frederick:

> Thus, with a given number of flights, the only actual *direct* variable costs—those changing more or less in direct proportion to changes in volume of business—are those resulting from the selling of additional tickets, serving of more meals, use of some additional fuel because of the greater weight, etc. And so the *marginal cost*—the addition to total cost from the handling of the additional units of business—is extremely small. As the average load carried per flight rises, the average cost per ton—or passenger-mile drops very sharply, since the total of the constant costs is being spread over more units.[80]

Given these characteristics, the airlines have a strong incentive to gain additional business in order to increase the average load factor on their flights. This situation, not uncommon in the regulated industries, exists because the marginal cost of additional units of business up to the capacity of existing flights is low compared to the average cost per unit of handling the business. In other words, the airlines are subject to decreasing costs. Cutthroat competition might

[76] United Air Lines indicated, in 1948, that 61.4 percent of the company's total costs were common and, therefore, not directly incurred for any particular service. *Air Freight Rate Investigation*, 9 CAB 340.

[77] A similar problem is found in allocating costs within each category of service, such as dividing the wage(s) of the stewardess(es) between first class and coach service, or the cost of handling freight between different commodities.

[78] Meyer and others, *op. cit.,* p. 139.

[79] Frederick, *op. cit.,* p. 133.

[80] *Ibid.,* p. 134.

be expected in the absence of regulation. In general, the CAB has followed the principle of not allowing airline rates to fall below the out-of-pocket costs of any particular service.

Demand Considerations. While the cost of service is one important aspect in establishing airline rates, demand conditions—value of service—must also be considered.[81] In theory, the airlines should follow a price policy which would maximize the profit on each type of service. Stated another way, the rate set for each service should allow the equality of marginal cost and marginal revenue. In practice, as is well known, this is difficult. Moreover, intermodal competition may result in some discriminatory rates. Especially is this likely when there is competition between the airlines, railroads, and motor carriers for certain types of freight. Even in passenger service between sparsely populated areas, rates may not cover fully distributed costs, but continued operation may be regarded as in the public interest. Consequently, the actual contribution to common costs of each type of service largely depends on the value of service.

Passenger Rates. Passenger fares are of two major types—first class and coach service. There are also various promotional rates in effect. Each of these will be discussed in turn.

First Class Service. Prior to 1948, the airlines essentially offered a one-class passenger service. Pricing was relatively simple, as the carriers took the air route distance between two points and multiplied this distance by a standard fare, expressed in cents per mile. Following World War II, the standard fare was 4.5 cents per mile. A few exceptions were found within the rate structure, reflecting competitive routing and regional differences, as well as scattered promotional fares. But while the fare level increased to one of 6.5 cents per mile in late 1948, the relatively simple general structure remained unchanged.

Price consciousness became important in the fall of 1948. This development was primarily due to two causes: failure of anticipated traffic volume to materialize at these rates and, at the same time, increasing costs and competition from the irregular carriers who, by offering low fares and less expensive accommodations, began to take away passengers from the trunkline carriers.[82] Various promotional tariffs were filed with the CAB as experimental and temporary.

Coach Service. One such experiment, which later became permanent, was coach service. The first coach service by a trunkline carrier was established by United Air Lines in 1940 between Los Angeles and San Francisco. It was not until the postwar period, however, that other carriers adopted a similar service on a large scale. Fares were originally at a level of approximately 4 cents per mile; later, they were raised to 4.5 cents per mile. Service was generally provided

---

[81] See Richard W. Klabzuba, "How 'Value of Service' Figures in Fares," 5 *Air Transport World* 27 (January, 1968).

[82] Harold A. Jones and Frederick Davis, "The 'Air Coach' Experiment and National Air Transport Policy," 17 *Journal of Air Law and Commerce* 1, 2-4 (1950).

during off-peak hours, only over high-density routes, and meals were not served in flight.

In 1953, the CAB issued a "Coach Policy Statement" declaring that fares for coach service should not exceed 75 percent of the first class fares.[83] "The Board indicated its belief that a 25 per cent differential is the minimum that will reflect adequately the cost difference between the services, maintain an adequate fare distinction, and provide the incentive to generate additional traffic which is necessary for an economically sound service."[84]

Promotional Fares. With active encouragement from the CAB, the domestic trunklines (as well as many of the local-service lines) have offered in the past few years various promotional fares to increase further the volume of air travel. These fares have frequently been experimental, and several have been revised or discontinued following a test period. Such promotional fares have included night coach fares (with rates as much as 17 percent below regular coach fares); "youth fares" (persons between twelve and twenty-two years of age traveling either at a 50 percent discount on a standby basis, with travel restricted during certain holiday periods, or at a 33-1/3 percent discount on a firm reservation basis, with travel restricted during certain periods of the week); the "Discover America" fare (applicable on a round-trip basis at a 25 percent discount from regular jet coach fares, with certain restrictions as to the time and duration of travel); and "family fares" (under which members of a family can travel at a reduction when traveling with the head of the family).[85]

In addition to the above, there are numerous types of "air shuttle" plans that have been, and are being, tried. On the Boston to New York route, for example, American, Eastern, and Northeast offer such service. Originally, the carriers used older planes, with hourly flights and "no frills" service. American and Eastern guaranteed a seat to everyone showing up for a flight. Early in 1967, however, American began jet shuttle service, with advanced reservations required, light meals served, and liquor for sale to coach passengers. Northeast countered by initiating a comparable service but Eastern, while adding jet flights, decided to retain its no reservation, no frills service.[86]

As a result of these developments, the airlines currently offer a variety of passenger services at various rates. Moreover, a tapering fare was introduced in 1952 when the CAB approved a one-dollar increase in the cost of all tickets. Since that time, there have been five general fare increases: 4 percent plus one dollar a ticket in February, 1958; 4 percent in October, 1958; 2.5 percent plus

---

[83] Civil Aeronautics Board, *Coach Policy for the Certificated Domestic Carriers*, Statement of October 5, 1953.

[84] Frederick, *op. cit.*, p. 260.

[85] See, for example, *Local Discover America Round-trip Fare Revisions Proposed by Northwest Airlines, Inc.*, E–26641 (CAB, 1968); *Night Coach Fares Proposed by Northwest Airlines, Inc.*, E–26652 (CAB, 1968); and *Family Fare Revisions Proposed by the Domestic Trunkline Carriers*, E–26925 (CAB, 1968).

[86] *Business Week*, February 11, 1967, p. 31.

one dollar per one-way ticket in June, 1960; 3 percent in December, 1961; and 3.8 percent in February, 1969.

The carriers, however, are far from unanimous on what the domestic rate structure should be. Some carriers want to reduce the differential between first class and coach fares. Others wish to eliminate shuttle plans entirely. Several favor higher general fares, but there is no agreement on what the percentage increase should be, and a majority argue that the level of first class rates cannot be raised without causing a further decline in that type of service. Thus, United Air Lines recently introduced an experimental one-class jet service, with fares about 10 percent above coach rates, while Continental Air Lines initiated an experimental three-class service, with economy (third class) fares 20 percent below coach rates. It is probable that the carriers will never reach complete agreement, but with better cost and demand studies, the areas of disagreement are bound to narrow.

Express Rates. In 1927, when the American Railway Express Company entered into contracts with a number of airlines, air express service was born. Two years later, this service, as well as the railway express service, was taken over by the Railway Express Agency. A rival organization, General Air Express, was formed by a small group of airlines in 1932, but it was in operation only a few years. All the airlines had joined the REA by 1937.

Air express rates are established jointly by the REA and the airlines, but must be approved by the CAB. Most commodities are subject to the same basic rate, with a general minimum charge of $5.50.[87] Regardless of the actual weight, however, the agency considers 250 cubic inches as a pound. Thus, light and bulky shipments are subject to higher rates without the necessity of designing class rates. There are, however, certain specific commodity rates in effect, for such articles as bonds, securities, gold coins, and other valuables; magazines, newspapers, and periodicals; and live animals and birds.

The distribution of air express revenues is determined by joint agreement as well. Each contract, nevertheless, has the same terms and provisions. The latest contract (1959) provides for deduction of certain specified costs of REA from revenues, with the remainder split 50-50 between the participating airlines and the express company.[88]

Air Freight Rates. An independent air freight service was initiated in 1944

---

[87]*Revised Air Express Rates and Charges Proposed by Railway Express Agency, Inc. and Participating Air Carriers*, E-24491 (CAB, 1966).

[88]On several occasions, the CAB has expressed its concern over some of the contracts between the express company and the airlines. As a result of a 1939 investigation, four provisions in the contracts were found objectionable and later eliminated. *Railway Express Agreements*, 4 CAB 157 (1943). In 1948, the CAB made further criticisms and ordered that new contracts be negotiated. Specifically, the board held that the express company (1) should fix air express rates, rather than the airlines, and (2) should pay the airlines a definite amount for carrying express, based on the costs of performing the service. *Air Freight Forwarder Case*, 9 CAB 473 (1948). The 1959 contracts partially remedied the board's criticisms.

by American Airlines; by 1947, all the trunklines had established a similar service.[89] Air express and air freight are to some extent competitive, but there are important differences in the services offered and the rates charged. Rates for larger shipments are generally lower for air freight; air freight service is slower than air express, since the latter has priority for aircraft space; the airlines commonly make an extra charge for air freight pickup and delivery service; and air freight involves consolidation.[90] Currently, the airlines are developing many interline agreements with truckers under an air-truck program.

The CAB ordered minimum freight rates into effect in 1948 because of a rate war which had developed between the trunklines and the all-cargo carriers.[91] After several modifications, the minimum per-ton rate in effect in 1961 was 20 cents a mile for the first 1,000 miles and 16.25 cents a mile thereafter. In August, 1961, however, the board decided to scrap the rate minimums, arguing that air freight rates were more stable than in 1948.[92]

The airlines have a freight rate structure similar to those of the railroads and motor carriers, but it is not so complex. A one-class system of rates has been adopted by all airlines, although commodity rates for specific articles are published. At first, graduated quantity or volume rates were used, but a consolidated freight tariff established in 1947 abandoned the system of weight breakdowns on shipments weighing less than 16,000 pounds. This move was prompted by the activities of air freight forwarders, who consolidate small shipments into larger ones. They were benefiting from the spread between the rates charged their customers and the lower rates charged by the airlines for the consolidated, larger shipments. Air rates are based upon distance, with the tapering principle employed. The average revenue per ton-mile for all commodities carried by domestic air carriers was 19.89 cents in 1967.

With the approval of the CAB, the airlines have also established "directional rates." That is, rates are lower from the West to the East and from the South to the North than when traffic moves in the opposite directions.[93] Lower directional rates were considered necessary because air freight consists largely of high-valued manufactured articles (electric equipment, wearing apparel, machinery and parts). As these articles are primarily manufactured in the North and East, a high percentage of air freight moves to the South and West, creating a

---

[89] In 1967, the domestic scheduled airline industry handled 98.9 million ton-miles of air express and 2,351.1 million ton-miles of air freight. The trunklines carried just over 50 percent of the total air express and air freight handled. Air Transport Association of America, *Air Transport Facts and Figures, 1968* (Washington, D.C., 1968), pp. 26–27.

[90] *Revised Air Express Rates and Charges Proposed by Railway Express Agency, Inc. and Participating Air Carriers, op. cit.*, p. 2.

[91] *Air Freight Rate Investigation,* 9 CAB 340 (1948).

[92] *Minimum Rates Applicable to Air Freight,* E–17370 (CAB, 1961). The board clearly indicated that if widespread rate cutting below costs should develop in the future, minimum rates would again be imposed. In December, 1965, the board refused to order an investigation of air freight rates, thereby dismissing a petition by Flying Tiger Line (an all-cargo airline). *The Wall Street Journal,* December 10, 1965, p. 2.

[93] *Air Freight Rate Investigation–Directional Rates,* 11 CAB 228 (1950).

serious imbalance of traffic. Moreover, the average length of haul of westbound traffic is greater than that of eastbound traffic, since a large portion of the westbound traffic goes to intermediate points rather than to coastal points.[94] In an effort to stimulate northerly and easterly traffic, the following reductions were adopted: eastbound, no reductions below the 1948 prescribed minimum rates up to 650 miles—beyond this, the directional rates are scaled from 99.88 percent of the minimum to 60 percent at 1,300 miles and over; northbound, the directional rates begin at 551 miles, dropping to 60 percent of the minimum at 1,100 miles. The shorter breaking point for northbound traffic was established in recognition of the shorter distances from south to north. The lower rates do not apply on certain commodities which can move at or above the established minimum rates (art works, cut flowers, gold coins, live animals).

In an attempt to create a reduced-rate service which was faster than surface transportation and which, therefore, would attract additional traffic, but which would be slow enough to prevent substantial diversion from the higher-rated air freight service, American introduced a "deferred air freight" service in 1954. Freight is accepted on a "space-available" basis, and there is a mandatory delay in delivery at destination: it is not released to consignees at destination prior to 7 P.M. the second day after it arrives when the distance traveled is under 2,100 miles, and not before 7 P.M. the third day when over 2,100 miles. At first approved by the CAB for an experimental period,[95] the service was later extended indefinitely.[96] The rates could be no lower than 55 percent of the standard minimum rates.

Mail Rates. The fourth type of service offered by the airlines is the transportation of mail. Under provisions of the Civil Aeronautics Act, the board was directed to take into consideration the "need" of the carrier for compensation in establishing airmail rates which, "together with all other revenue of the air carrier," would enable it "under honest, economical, and efficient management, to maintain and continue the development of air transportation to the extent and of the character and quality required for the commerce of the United States, the Postal Service, and the national defense." Thus, Congress intended that the amount paid to the airlines for carrying mail would give them adequate total revenues.

Prior to 1951, there was no separation of airmail compensation between cost of service and need (subsidy). Since that time, however, the board has annually published such a separation, showing for each carrier the total mail compensation and a breakdown of this figure between what it considers to be a reasonable compensation for the service performed, known as "service mail pay," and the amount it considers to be subsidy, known as "subsidy mail

---

94 Frederick, *op. cit.,* pp. 247-48.
95 *Petition of American Airlines to Modify the Minimum Rate Order*, E–10020 (CAB, 1956).
96 *Deferred Air Freight Rate Renewal Case,* E–13140 (CAB, 1958).

pay." [97] And, since 1953, the airlines have also received payment for carrying nonpriority mail. [98]

"Service" Mail Rates. In 1955, the CAB established a multielement service mail rate formula comprised of a line-haul rate and a terminal charge which varies by class of airport. [99] The objective was to provide a uniform rate of pay for like services. Under the latest methods and rates, [100] the line-haul rate was determined by a cost allocation process. The rate established was based on an overall statistical approach for each type of air carrier, rather than on a detailed cost analysis of the mail service for each individual carrier. Airports were grouped into three classes, based on the revenue tons of all traffic enplaned per year: Class X—25,000 and over, Class Y—5,000 to 24,999, and Class Z—4,999 or less. The larger airports, which handle a larger volume of traffic, were given the lowest terminal charge per pound of mail enplaned. The terminal charge that applies to any shipment is the rate applicable at the originating station. The line-haul rate set by the board was 24 cents per ton-mile. The terminal charges were 2.34 cents per pound enplaned for Class X airports, 4.68 cents for Class Y airports, and 9.36 cents for Class Z airports. The multielement rate was estimated to yield an average of 29.99 cents per nonstop ton-mile for the trunkline carriers and 75.93 cents per nonstop ton-mile for the local-service carriers (based on fiscal 1965 mail volume).

"Subsidy" Mail Rates—Local-Service Carriers. [101] For many years, the subsidy mail rates for local-service lines were typically determined according to the "needs" of each individual carrier. Then, in 1961, the CAB adopted a class subsidy rate, with a uniform formula applicable to all carriers in the group, which reflected industry average cost, revenue, and investment data. [102] The basic aim was to effectuate subsidy reductions by providing stronger incentives for greater operating efficiency.

While the formula has been revised and modified on several occasions, [103] the underlying principle has remained the same: local-service carriers' needs per

---

[97] *Administrative Separation of Subsidy from Total Mail Payments to Domestic Air Carriers* (1951). By Reorganization Plan No. 10 of 1953, the Post Office Department is charged the service mail pay and the CAB the subsidy element. See 20 *Journal of Air Law and Commerce* 210 (1953).

[98] In 1967, the domestic scheduled airline industry carried 567.7 million revenue ton-miles of air mail and 407.8 million revenue ton-miles of nonpriority mail. *Air Transport Facts and Figures, 1968, op. cit.*

[99] *Domestic Trunklines, Service Mail Rates,* 21 CAB 8 (1955); *Service Mail Rates for Allegheny Airlines, et al.,* 21 CAB 894 (1955).

[100] *Domestic Service Mail Rate Investigation,* E–25610 (CAB, 1967).

[101] Since 1956, the only domestic trunkline carrier to receive subsidy has been Northeast Airlines. See *Northeast Airlines, Inc., Subsidy Mail Rates,* E–26191 (CAB, 1967).

[102] *Local Service Class Subsidy Rate Investigation,* 34 CAB 416 (1961).

[103] See *Investigation of the Local Service Class Subsidy Rate,* E–19340 (1963), E–21227 (1964), E–23697 (1966), E–23850 (1966), E–25162 (1967), E–26865 (1968), E–26986 (1968), and 68-7-117 (1968).

available seat-mile vary inversely with density of operations. Under the existing formula, a gross subsidy is computed for each carrier based on various components (such as an amount per weighted departure, an amount per revenue ton-mile, and an amount per available seat-mile) and a "daily need adjustment." The resulting gross subsidy is subject to a ceiling for each carrier. A net subsidy is then computed, representing the gross subsidy adjusted by a "revenue-growth sharing factor." The latter factor reflects experienced improvement in passenger revenues, that is, a carrier's gross subsidy decreases (increases) as passenger growth increases (decreases).

Nonpriority Mail Rates. Late in 1953, the movement of first class and other preferential mail by air was inaugurated on ·an "experimental" basis. Known as nonpriority mail, the purposes of this service were (1) to enable the Post Office Department to achieve greater efficiency and economy in its operations, and thus improve mail service to the public and (2) to enable the air carriers to utilize whatever unused capacity was available, thereby improving their financial position.[104]

The board adopted the same method for compensating the air carriers as it used in 1955 in determining airmail rates.[105] The line-haul rate was set at 15.085 cents per mail ton-mile (revised to 15.115 cents per mail ton-mile in 1966).[106] Four classes of airports were established, based on the revenue tons of all traffic enplaned per year: Class A—7,000 and over, Class B—750 to 6,999, Class C—60 to 749, and Class D—59 or less. The terminal charge per pound enplaned ranged from 1.660 cents for Class A airports to 16.605 cents for Class D airports. These rates were calculated to yield 18.20 cents per mail ton-mile between points within the forty-eight contiguous states and between points within those states and certain offshore points, and 20.6 cents per mail ton-mile between points within the forty-eight contiguous states and Alaska. It was recognized by the board in its 1961 order that the rates established were below fully allocated costs, including taxes and profit. The majority argued that since nonpriority mail is carried only on a voluntary space-available basis and since it can be carried profitably at the rates set, the rates were reasonable. Further, it was pointed out that higher rates would impair the continued use of the service by the Post Office Department.

Airlines Rates and Discrimination. With the introduction of numerous

---

[104] Five railroads affected by this new service filed a complaint for declaratory judgment and injunctive relief. They argued that the establishment of nonpriority mail service was unlawful and beyond the authority granted to the Postmaster General. On December 13, 1954, the injunction was denied. On January 28, 1955, a district court ruled that the Postmaster General had the right to make the experiment, but that he did not have Congressional sanction to make a "prolonged experimental dispatch of first-class mail by air. . . ." *Atchison, Topeka & Santa Fe Railway Co., et al.* v. *Summerfield*, 128 F. Supp. 266, 274 (D.D.C., 1955). No further action has been taken on the matter.

[105] *Nonpriority Mail Rate Case,* 34 CAB 143 (1961).

[106] *Nonpriority Mail Rate Case,* E–24247 (CAB, 1966). One exception: The line-haul rate between Alaskan points and the 48 contiguous states was set at 18.003 cents per mail ton-mile.

promotional and experimental fares in recent years, the airlines' rate structure has become more differentiated. Studies suggest that while many fares are closely related to costs, the present rate structure is often discriminatory. As is true in the case of other carriers, some discrimination is unintentional, resulting from a desire to simplify the rate structure, to experiment with various promotional fares, and from the necessity of choosing an arbitrary method of allocating common costs. In addition, as the airlines' cost structures are not identical, the fact that competing carriers must charge the same rates over competing routes leads to some discrimination. But discrimination also arises from other sources.

In a thorough study of domestic airline passenger fares, Cherington indicated that the airlines' rate structure is discriminatory on short-haul and low traffic density routes, off-peak travel, and in the fare spread between coach and first class service.[107] For short distances, the carriers' unit cost curve is above their unit revenue curve at present rates. The same is true for low traffic density routes. In both cases, the losses have been either subsidized or absorbed by profits on long-haul and high density routes. While the airlines have attempted to build up off-peak service by granting various discounts from regular fares, "There would appear to be a valid argument for imposing some form of premium on peak travel, since it is the heavy fixed costs of handling the peaks which essentially create the problem."[108] Finally, as for the relationship between first class and coach service, Cherington concluded:

> Initially coach service was essentially an off-peak and clearly inferior service, with many fewer amenities, high-density seating, and older equipment. Aside from seat density, these differences . . . have in part disappeared. Originally too, load factors on coach flights were higher, on average, than for first-class flights and coach service was largely confined to long-haul routes. It would seem highly desirable to reexamine the relation or spread between coach and first-class fares. This is particularly true in view of the fact that the Board has essentially tied coach fares to 75% of first-class fares even at short hauls where the impact of ground handling is heaviest and the cost differential between first-class and coach service is probably least.[109]

A recent CAB Staff Report also concluded that "the first class-coach fare relationship is out of proportion to the cost relationship."[110] In addition, the Report concluded that "the current cost analyses indicate that a greater taper is

---

[107] Paul W. Cherington, *Airline Price Policy* (Cambridge: Harvard Graduate School of Business Administration, 1958), pp. 443-49. Also see Richard E. Caves, *Air Transport and Its Regulators* (Cambridge: Harvard University Press, 1962), pp. 155–68; Alan H. Silberman, "Price Discrimination and the Regulation of Air Transportation," 31 *Journal of Air Law and Commerce* 198 (1965); and Civil Aeronautics Board, Rates Division, Bureau of Economics, *A Study of the Domestic Passenger Air Fare Structure* (Washington, D.C., 1968).

[108] Cherington, *op. cit.,* p. 448.

[109] *Ibid.*

[110] *A Study of the Domestic Passenger Air Fare Structure, op. cit.,* p. 71.

warranted than now exists in the fare structure."[111] Particularly did the data indicate that long-haul jet coach fares were high in relation to cost of service,

> . . . even at the relatively low load factors prevailing in the transcontinental markets. The latter suggest that excess capacity is being provided in 'these areas. It is a reasonable inference that the high level of long haul jet coach fares at least tends to support such overscheduling which in turn creates a need for a higher fare level than would otherwise be necessary.[112]

Freight rates also exhibit rate discrimination. While offering what is basically a one-class system, many articles move on exception ratings based upon the value of service. And, in Frederick's words, the deferred freight service is based upon a "simple but dangerous" theory:

> They argue that their aircraft will operate anyhow; that the added expense of taking more traffic will be comparatively little or nonexistent; that if they can obtain some of the traffic now going by ground carriers (chiefly rail express) at some margin over any "added" or "out-of-pocket" expense it will help them just that much. The danger of this theory is twofold. In the first place, the airlines have always had an imperfect knowledge of what this "added" expense might be. In the second place, the theory places the chief burden of sustaining the profits and credit of the air carriers upon the traffic which under no circumstances would want to move on the deferred basis or on the traffic which would be noncompetitive with the ground carriers. Such a burden is likely to increase progressively. Gradually the traffic moving on the low rates ceases to be mere "added" traffic and the "out-of-pocket" expense swells in volume as does the burden on the noncompetitive traffic.[113]

The latter conclusion may apply also to nonpriority mail rates. As previously discussed, these rates were established at a level below the fully allocated costs for the service. While recognizing that nonpriority mail will increase the overall net yield to a carrier per scheduled flight without adding appreciably to the direct costs of that particular flight, as the volume of nonpriority mail grows, so will the out-of-pocket expenses.

Pipeline Rates

The regulation of pipeline rates presents special problems peculiar to these carriers that are closely related to the market structure of the oil and natural gas industries.[114] (1) Most of the oil pipelines are owned and operated by the major refiners. They also carry oil for the independents to the independents' refineries. There is danger, therefore, that the majors may exercise considerable control over the independents by charging high rates or imposing unreasonable restric-.

---

[111] *Ibid.*, p. 68.
[112] *Ibid.*, p. 70.
[113] Frederick, *op. cit.*, pp. 254–55.
[114] In recent years, pipelines have been used to carry coal and other materials. This development will be discussed in Chapter 14.

tions on their services. Both possibilities have occurred in the past. The problem is discussed in Chapter 13. (2) The regulation of natural gas pipeline rates represents a situation in which economics, politics, and regional interests are interwoven in a complex pattern. As a result of the Natural Gas Act of 1938 and a Supreme Court decision in 1954, the Federal Power Commission has a twofold function that involves the regulation of interstate pipeline rates, as well as the wellhead price of gas for both independent and integrated producers. These problems are discussed in Chapter 16.

Chapter 11   THE RATE STRUCTURE (Continued)

> *There are two basic functions of price; to discourage the buyer of a commodity (or service) from using up too much of it, and to induce the supplier to produce enough. But what is the right amount? What is enough and not too much?*
>
> *—Abba P. Lerner**

The first part of this chapter concludes the discussion of rate structures by analyzing those of the electric, gas, telephone, and telegraph industries. The second part reviews the regulation of rate structures by the various commissions. Emphasis is placed on the Interstate Commerce Commission, as it has been the most active commission in this area. In the appendix to the chapter, the role of marginal cost in pricing is examined.

Electric Utility Rates

Over the years, the electric utilities have experimented with numerous types of rate structures. At first, electricity was sold at a uniform rate per kilowatt-hour. Gradually, however, producers began to adopt differentiated rates. Customers were classified according to old and new, with the old paying higher rates than the new. Quantity discounts were set up as a means of encouraging greater consumption. Different classes of customers were established, the most important being for residential use, commercial light and power, industrial power, and street lighting (Table 11–1), with different rates for each class. Within each class, moreover, blocks were set up, measured in kilowatt-hours, and rates were reduced in succeeding blocks. As a result of this past development, modern electric utility rates are highly differentiated.[1] The average price per kilowatt-hour charged varies with both the class of customer and with the monthly quantity purchased.

Cost Considerations. Electric utility rate differentiation is in part based upon cost differences. The variations in the cost of serving different customers

---

*Abba P. Lerner, "Conflicting Principles of Public Utility Price Regulation," 7 *Journal of Law and Economics* 61 (1964).

[1]The development of electric utility rate structures is discussed in Emery Troxel, *Economics of Public Utilities* (New York: Holt, Rinehart & Winston, Inc., 1947), pp. 598–610.

can be illustrated by discussing three important technical concepts—the load factor, the utilization factor, and the diversity factor.

The *load factor* is the average load expressed as a percentage of the peak load. Electric companies are primarily concerned with two types of load

TABLE 11-1
Percentage of Electric Customers, Sales, and
Revenues by Customer Classes, 1967

Classification	Percentage of Customers	Percentage of Sales	Percentage of Revenues
Residential	88.1	29.9	41.7
Commercial	11.1	21.9	28.7
Industrial	.5	43.9	25.3
Other	.3	4.3	4.3
Totals	100.0	100.0	100.0

Source: Edison Electric Institute, *Statistical Year Book* (1968), pp. 31, 37, 43.

curves—annual and customer. Thus, if the average load for a year is 12,000 kilowatts and the peak at any moment of time is 18,000, the annual load factor is 66⅔ percent. Since electricity cannot be stored, and since a utility must provide instantaneous and uninterrupted service, the size of a utility plant is determined by the amount of service taken by its customers at any particular time (peak demand). The peak, it should be noted, may occur only for a short period of time once a year. Utilities attempt to keep their load factor as high as possible, for the higher the average output relative to the peak load, the more units over which to spread the fixed costs. Customers, too, have load factors: the average consumption expressed as a percentage of the maximum consumption. A customer whose average load is high relative to his maximum demand is a more desirable customer than one whose load factor is low.

The *utilization factor* is the peak load expressed as a percentage of the system capacity. Electric utilities must have some reserve capacity to meet emergencies. The necessary reserve will depend on a number of factors, including the size of the area served and the size of the generators and transformers in use. As desirable as a high utilization factor may be, it also serves as a warning to the company that its excess reserve capacity is declining.[2]

The *diversity factor* is the ratio of the sum of noncoincident maximum demands of a system's customers to maximum demand on the whole system. If all customers registered their maximum demands at exactly the same time, the diversity factor would equal one. But because of differences in time use, the sum

[2]The widespread use of interconnections with other electric utilities reduces the necessary reserve capacity. Under these arrangements, utility A can buy power from utility B during emergency situations. See Chapter 15.

of the noncoincident maximum demands is greater than the system's load at any moment of time—that is, the diversity factor is greater than one. A high diversity factor is desirable, since an electric utility seeks to achieve full utilization of its plant and equipment. In addition, as Clemens has pointed out,

> . . . a high diversity factor will compensate for low customer load factors. A customer who used only one kilowatt for one hour a day would be an expensive customer. But twenty-four such customers, each using electricity at a different hour, would give the utility a load factor of 100 per cent. Conversely, a good load factor customer contributes little to the diversity factor. He uses his equipment continuously and increases the peak load as much as he increases the average load. In short a utility can achieve a desirable load factor for itself by having customers with good load factors, or by a high diversity factor, but either is achieved at the expense of the other.[3]

These factors indicate that the cost of supplying electricity to different customers is a function of many variables. For rate-making purposes, an electric utility's total costs are considered to be variable. The allocation of these costs among the different classes of customers, however, represents a difficult task since a major portion of total costs are common or joint. The most frequently used division of total costs is a threefold one: (1) demand, capacity, or load costs; (2) energy, output, or volumetric costs; (3) customer costs.

Demand costs vary with a customer's maximum demand. These costs include investment charges and expenses in connection with generating plants, transmission lines, substations, and part of the distribution system. Suppose two customers have equal monthly consumptions but different demands. Customer A has a load of 10 kilowatts which he operates 200 hours per month, thus consuming 2,000 kilowatt-hours monthly. Customer B has a load of 20 kilowatts which he operates 100 hours per month, resulting in a monthly use of 2,000 kilowatt-hours, the same as for customer A. The cost of serving B, however, is greater than A's cost, because more equipment is needed to supply the larger load.

Output costs vary with the number of kilowatt-hours consumed and are largely composed of fuel and labor expenses. If customer A uses 50 kilowatt-hours per month and customer B uses 500 kilowatt-hours per month, more fuel and labor will be required to produce the electricity demanded by B than by A.

Customer costs vary with the number of customers. These costs include a portion of the distribution system, local connection facilities, metering equipment, meter reading, billing, and accounting. Customer costs, moreover, are independent of consumption. Assume the monthly consumption of three customers to be 10, 50, and 500 kilowatt-hours. Despite the differences in consumption, each customer requires a meter, each meter must be read, and a bill sent to each customer.

It would be practically impossible for an electric utility to charge each

[3] Eli W. Clemens, *Economics and Public Utilities* (New York: Appleton-Century-Crofts, Inc., 1950), p. 284.

customer on the basis of actual cost of service. Rates would simply be too complicated. Customers with similar demand characteristics, therefore, have been classified together, and different rates applied to each class. Industrial users receive lower rates than residential users; large customers are favored over smaller ones.

Types of Electric Rates. The price philosophy of electric utilities has been well summarized by Caywood as follows:

> Electric utility rates should be based on a philosophy which calls for the lowest possible prices consistent with customer requirements, quality service efficiency rendered, fair wages, and a fair return to the utility. Rates should be such that service will be widely available and extensively used; they should be promotional; i.e., they should provide lower prices for larger loads and for longer use of service. Rates should be available for any kind of service a customer desires. In applying rates to individual customers, the spirit on the part of the utility should be one of helpfulness and cooperation, always keeping within the limits set down by the schedules and rules as filed with the regulatory body.[4]

As this statement makes clear, cost considerations alone cannot explain electric utility rates. Demand considerations become apparent when the major types of rate schedules are studied.

Block Meter Rates. The block meter rate or, more precisely, a variation of this type known as the initial charge rate is the most common rate schedule for residential and other small users. An example of this rate:

First 20 kilowatt-hours or less per month, $1.19
Next 30 kilowatt-hours per month, 4¢ per kilowatt-hour
Next 50 kilowatt-hours per month, 3¢ per kilowatt-hour
Next 200 kilowatt-hours per month, 2.3¢ per kilowatt-hour
Over 300 kilowatt-hours per month, 2¢ per kilowatt-hour
Minimum per month or fraction of a month—$1.19

Under this rate schedule, customer costs are partially recovered by making a flat charge for the first kilowatt-hour block or by making a minimum charge even though nothing is consumed. The demand cost element is recognized only indirectly, however, since it is assumed that demand costs are recovered in the higher earlier blocks. Moreover, the use of the block rate permits the rates in each succeeding block to be lower since only output costs need to be covered. And, from the utility's point of view, the major advantage of this rate schedule is its simplicity, making it easily understood by customers.

Wright Demand Rates. The Wright demand rate is commonly used for commercial customers and, at times, for industrial loads. This schedule emphasizes the customer's load factor (demand cost). An example of this rate:

---

[4] Russell E. Caywood, *Electric Utility Rate Economics* (New York: McGraw-Hill Book Co., Inc., 1956), p. 38. Also see Edwin Vennard, *The Electric Power Business* (New York: McGraw-Hill Book Co., Inc., 1962), p. 192.

First 100 kilowatt-hours per kilowatt of demand per month, 6¢ per kilowatt-hour
Over 100 kilowatt-hours per month, 3¢ per kilowatt-hour

Under this rate schedule, all customers with the same load factor would pay the same price per kilowatt-hour regardless of their monthly consumption. As there is no inducement to install additional equipment, the Wright rate is not promotional. Moreover, an examination of the schedule indicates that it contains a hidden demand charge of $3.00 per kilowatt and a uniform energy charge of 3 cents per kilowatt-hour. Yet, there is no assurance that the full demand cost will be collected by the utility: when a buyer's monthly consumption is less than 100 kilowatt-hours, for example, this would be true.

Hopkinson Demand Rate. A two-part Hopkinson demand rate is normally used for medium- and large-sized commercial and industrial customers. This schedule has a block demand and a block energy charge. An example of the Hopkinson rate schedule:

Demand Charge
First 50 kilowatt of demand per month, $2.50 per kilowatt
Next 100 kilowatt of demand per month, $2.00 per kilowatt
Over 150 kilowatt of demand per month, $1.75 per kilowatt

Energy Charge
First 100 kilowatt-hours per month, 5.5¢ per kilowatt-hour
Next 900 kilowatt-hours per month, 3¢ per kilowatt-hour
Next 4,000 kilowatt-hours per month, 2.3¢ per kilowatt-hour
Over 5,000 kilowatt-hours per month, 2¢ per kilowatt-hour

There are two frequently used ways of measuring a customer's demand. One is to measure with a meter the average consumption during the maximum 15- or 30-minute interval during any 3- or 6-month period. The second is to compute the total horsepower rating of a customer's connected equipment.

In actual practice, industrial rate schedules are more complex, as indicated in Table 11–2. Some utility companies add a service charge, making a three-part rate. Off-peak service is sometimes offered at a lower rate than is charged for peak service. Utilities may have a uniform rate for each kilowatt of demand instead of block demand rates. Monthly minimums are common. Discounts may be given for payment of bills within a specified number of days, with an additional charge if bills are not paid within the time limit. Other discounts may be given to industrial buyers who own transformers (voltage discount) or who purchase electricity at the supply-line voltage. When a customer requires additional voltage regulation (power factor), a special charge may be made.[5] A

---

[5] "The power factor is the ratio of the power to the volt-amperes. For direct current, volts multiplied by amperes equals watts. For alternating current, which is most widely used, volt-amperes are the equivalent of watts for lighting uses but not where the

TABLE 11-2
Illustrative Industrial Power Schedule

Availability

Available in the entire territory of the company for any purpose for single-phase and three-phase loads of 50 kilowatts or more.

Monthly Rate

Demand charge:
    First 50 kw @ $2.50 gross per kw of billing demand
    Next 100 kw @ $2.00 gross per kw of billing demand
    Additional @ $1.75 gross per kw of billing demand
Voltage discount:
    20 cents per kilowatt when the service voltage is 22 kilovolts.
Power factor charge:
    25 cents gross per reactive kilovolt-ampere in excess of 50 per cent of the kilowatt demand. The reactive kilovolt-ampere demand shall be determined in the same way as the kilowatt demand.
Energy charge:
    First 25,000 kwh @ 10.0¢ gross per kwh
    Additional @ 0.8¢ gross per kwh
Fuel cost adjustment:
    Increase or decrease of 0.01 cent gross per kilowatt-hour for each change of 0.50 cents per million Btu. above or below 15 cents per million Btu. for the average cost of fuel on hand and delivered at company's generating stations during the second calendar month preceding the billing date.
Prompt payment discount:
    2 per cent for payment within 10 days.

Determination of Billing Demand

The billing demand for any month shall be the highest of the following:
1. The kilowatt demand, which shall be the maximum 15-minute kilowatt demand of the on-peak period plus 50 per cent of the excess of the maximum 15-minute kilowatt demand of the off-peak period over the on-peak demand.
2. 50 per cent of the maximum kilowatt demand of the preceding 11 months.
3. 50 kilowatts.
The off-peak period shall be from 10 P.M. until 6 A.M. daily, and from 12 noon Saturday until 6 A.M. Monday.

Term

Minimum of one year.

Source: Russell E. Caywood, *Electric Utility Rate Economics* (New York: McGraw-Hill Book Co., Inc., 1956), p. 66. Used by permission of McGraw-Hill Book Company.

energy is transformed into mechanical power. Hence at a given wattage a power user may require of alternating generators, conductors and transformers nearly a third greater capacity than the kilowatts he employs and for which he is supposed to pay. The power factor is the coefficient which expresses the significance of this element in the situation. The relation between the kilowatt-hours consumed and the necessary generating capacity and other equipment is in inverse ratio to the power factor of the consumer's apparatus." Emerson P. Schmidt, *Public Utility Economics* (St. Louis: John S. Swift Co., Inc., 1940), p. 134.

fuel cost adjustment is often used to permit a utility to follow the variations in fuel costs either upward or downward.[6] "The special provisions of industrial price schedules (e.g., power-factor adjustments) show distinctly the influence of the engineer in the formulation of pricing practices. Because engineers influence the shape of these schedules, only an engineer, indeed, can interpret and apply their technical provisions."[7]

Discrimination in Practice. That electric utility rate schedules are highly differentiated has been shown. In addition, they are discriminatory. Such discrimination has been introduced into the rate structure in at least three ways. First, there are many different block sizes and block rates which could be chosen. In determining these sizes and rates, both cost and demand considerations are taken into account. If a utility tried to recover its total demand and customer costs in the first block, the initial block rate might be so high that it would not encourage more consumption. These costs are thus spread throughout succeeding blocks, largely according to differences in elasticities of demand. Explains Wilcox:

> Big industrial users have the alternative of generating their own power; their demand, therefore, is highly elastic; their rates are low. Other users lack this alternative; their demand is less elastic; their rates are higher. Householders can use gas rather than electricity for cooking; for this purpose their demand is elastic; the additional kilowatt-hours used in cooking fall in the quantity blocks where rates are low. Householders, on the other hand, are unlikely to substitute gas, kerosene, or candles for electricity in lighting; their demand for this purpose is inelastic; the hours used in lighting fall in the first block where rates are high.[8]

To illustrate a block schedule for residential customers:

First 30 kw.-hrs.—Lighting .... 6 ¢ a kw.-hr.
Next 50 kw.-hrs.—Refrigeration, washer and dryer .... 4 ¢ a kw.-hr.
Next 100 kw.-hrs.—Cooking .... 3 ¢ a kw.-hr.
Next 570 kw.-hrs.—Water heating, air conditioning .... 2 ¢ a kw.-hr.
Over 750 kw.-hrs.—Electric house heating .... 1.5 ¢ a kw.-hr.

Consequently, both block sizes and block rates are established by the utility

---

[6] The fuel clause works as follows: When the price of coal per ton, per million Btu., per kilowatt-hour, or per total tons burned, increases (decreases) a certain amount above (below) a specified price, the energy charge is increased (decreased). To illustrate: "The energy charge will be increased or decreased at the rate of 0.156 mill per kilowatt-hour for each 25 cent increase or decrease in the price of coal above or below the base price of $5 per ton." Caywood, *op. cit.,* p. 54.

[7] Troxel, *op. cit.,* p. 609.

[8] Clair Wilcox, *Public Policies Toward Business* (3d ed.; Homewood, Ill.: Richard D. Irwin, Inc., 1966), p. 344. Also see Ralph K. Davidson, *Price Discrimination in Selling Gas and Electricity* (Baltimore: John Hopkins Press, 1955).

companies on the basis of differences in the value of service for each class of customer.[9]

The second way in which discrimination is evident in the electric utility rate structure is that allocation of demand, output, and customer costs among the different classes of customers is largely arbitrary. Here, socially undesirable discrimination may result. Particularly is this true of demand costs, "the treatment of which has made a nightmare of utility cost analysis. For the problem which it presents is that of imputing joint costs to joint products or by-products and not merely that of distributing those common but nonjoint costs which vary more or less continuously with number of customers or with rates of output."[10]

In his book on electric rates, Caywood discusses three formulas for allocating demand costs among different classes of customers.[11] (1) The "peak responsibility method." Under this formula, the entire demand costs are allocated to those services rendered at the time of the system's peak demand, in proportion to the kilowatt demand at this peak load. Service rendered off-peak would not be apportioned demand costs. (2) The "noncoincident demand method." Here, demand costs are allocated among services in proportion to the maximum demands of the various classes regardless of when each class's maximum demand occurs. (3) The "average and excess demand method." Under this method,

> ... the assumed cost of that portion of the company's plant capacity which would be needed even if all consumers were taking their power at 100 per cent load factor is apportioned among customers in proportion to their average loads. ... But the assumed cost of the excess in actual plant capacity over this lower, hypothetical capacity is apportioned "by applying the noncoincident peak method to the difference between maximum loads and average loads."[12]

The three methods lead to quite different results. Assuming three class loads comprising a system load having a peak of 1,000 kilowatts (Figure 11-1), the results are shown in Table 11-3.

The most frequently used means of allocating demand costs is the second

[9] In recent years, due to the increase in air conditioners and house heating, residential customers' use of electricity has risen faster than any other class of service. A fully electrified home will average 20,000 to 30,000 kilowatt-hours a year. "With these high uses residential service becomes something like commercial service in its characteristics. ... Some type of demand feature is required if the rate is to follow the cost." Vennard, *op. cit.*, pp. 242-43. For examples of how electric utilities have met this problem, see *ibid.*, pp. 243-44.

[10] James C. Bonbright, *Principles of Public Utility Rates* (New York: Columbia University Press, 1961), p. 350.

[11] Caywood, *op. cit.*, pp. 156-67. Bonbright notes that there are at least 29 such formulas in existence. "Most of them have no claim whatever to validity from the standpoint of cost determination, and only a dubious claim to acceptance as compromise measures of reasonable rates." Bonbright, *op. cit.*, p. 351.

[12] Bonbright, *op. cit.*, p. 353.

FIGURE 11-1
Hypothetical Loads

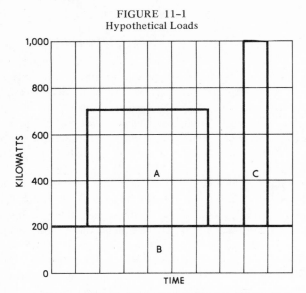

Source: Russell E. Caywood, *Electric Utility Rate
Economics* (New York: McGraw-Hill Book Co., Inc., 1956),
p. 162. Used by permission of McGraw-Hill Book Company.

method—the noncoincident demand method. Three steps are involved. An aggregate maximum demand is obtained by adding together the separate maximum demands of all classes of customers. Then, the percentage of this aggregate that is attributable to each class is determined. Finally, demand costs are allocated to each class in accordance with these percentages. The noncoincident demand method, despite its widespread use, is based upon two fallacies and, in fact, is not really a cost analysis at all. As Wilcox succinctly states:

First, it involves circular reasoning. The differences in demand that are used as a guide in allocating costs are not independent of differences in rates, but are themselves determined by these differences. The companies first fix the rates they want to charge. These rates, in turn, affect the quantities demanded. These quantities are then used to govern the distribution of costs. And the costs are presented, finally, to justify the rates. Q.E.D. Second, the method does not make proper allowance for the factor of diversity. The concept of maximum coincident demand for a utility system as a whole is meaningful. The concept of aggregate noncoincident maximum demands of customer classes is not. A company does have to build a plant big enough to meet the peak of coincident demand. It does not have to build one big enough to meet the aggregate of noncoincident demands. For such demands, by definition, occur at different times. If a customer's maximum comes at the same time as the system's maximum, he may properly be charged with more responsibility for the size of the investment that is required. If it comes at any other time, he should be charged with less. But how much more and how much less is open to debate.[13]

Perhaps no formula of apportionment is perfect. Bonbright has argued, however, that from the standpoint of cost analysis, the "peak responsibility method" would undoubtedly come the closest to receiving support from

TABLE 11-3
Results of Demand Allocation Formulas*

| | | | Allocation | | |
Load	Maximum Demand	Load Factor	PR Method	NCD Method	AED Method
A	500 kw	50%	0 kw	333 kw	371 kw
B	200	100	200	133	200
C	800	10	800	534	429
	1,500 kw		1,000 kw	1,000 kw	1,000 kw

*Assumption: Three classes of loads comprising a system load having a peak demand of 1,000 kilowatts.
Source: Russell E. Caywood, *Electric Utility Rate Economics* (New York: McGraw-Hill Book Co., Inc., 1956), p. 163. Used by permission of McGraw-Hill Book Company.

economists. He points out two major difficulties in using the formula. In the first place, as the periods of peak demand are subject to constant change, apportionment on this basis would necessitate frequent changes in the structure of rates. Such changes may have disruptive effects on consumption. But if the system's annual peak were used and if changes were announced in advance and at stated intervals, gradual adjustments in rates could overcome this difficulty. More important is a second often-voiced objection that the utility plant is required for the service of both on-peak and off-peak users and that both, therefore, should make some contribution toward its capital cost.[14] Once again, the question of how much must be raised.[15]

Closely connected is a third way in which discrimination enters into the rate structure: rates within each class do not vary according to time of use. (There are certain exceptions. Rates do vary by time of use for some large industrial customers; in a few instances, they vary for residential water heating; and, increasingly, they vary for residential space heating.) It was previously pointed out that the size of a utility plant and, hence, the total investment in the business is determined by the quantity of service it must render during periods of peak demand. Just as in the case of apportioning total demand costs among classes, customers within each class who use the service during peak demand

[13] Wilcox, *op. cit.,* p. 346.
[14] "It is obvious that this method is not entirely satisfactory because a class load at the time of the system peak might be zero, while at some other time it might be of considerable size; yet no expense would be allocated to it." Caywood, *op. cit.,* p. 156.
[15] Bonbright, *op. cit.,* pp. 350-68.

periods should contribute a larger percentage toward the class's share of the capital costs than should off-peak users. As there is no attempt to separate these two groups of customers, the rate schedule discriminates against those who use the service in off-peak hours. Here, however, a solution to the problem is more difficult. More elaborate metering equipment would be required to record a buyer's consumption at different periods of time. Customer costs, in turn, might be raised.

But with the industry's drive toward the "fully electrified home," which uses electricity in large amounts for cooling in summer and for heating in winter, more elaborate metering devices will probably be called for. For this purpose the use of "time of day" and "time of season" differential energy rates, which has had more of a vogue in Europe than in America, may be well worth considering.[16]

Gas Distribution Rates

The structure of gas distribution rates differs from that of electric rates.[17] While customers are divided into three major classes—residential, commercial, and industrial (Table 11-4)—most gas distributors have established a "general service rate" schedule that is applicable to all or many classes of firm service. Such general service schedules are of the block meter type (rates are adjusted downward in successive blocks), usually provide for monthly minimum charges, and contain fuel cost adjustment clauses.[18] Space heating falls in the last blocks, thereby making the service more competitive with other fuels. Some gas distributors, however, offer a separate residential rate schedule, including residential heating. Finally, gas distributors also commonly have rate schedules for large volume service (heating and large industrial users) and one or more seasonal, off-peak, and interruptible rate schedules. The latter are designed to help even out the industry's annual load curve, which generally exhibits a winter (heating) peak.

---

[16]*Ibid.,* p. 362. New metering systems being tested and developed might make this feasible in the near future. See report in *Dun's Review and Modern Industry*, November, 1961, pp. 97–102E.

[17]Gas consumers are usually billed on a therm basis. A therm is 100,000 Btu.'s (British thermal units). Consumption, however, continues to be measured in cubic feet. The conversion to therms for billing purposes is done to avoid a loss of revenue. Manufactured gas contains approximately 500 Btu.'s per cubic foot, compared with about 1,000 Btu.'s per cubic foot for natural gas. "If the gas companies do not change their rate schedules when natural gas is substituted for manufactured gas, their revenues decline because the buyers purchase fewer cubic feet of gas. The gas companies can increase the cubic-foot prices, and thereby prevent a decline in the gross revenue and the net revenue." Troxel, *op. cit.*, p. 610.

For a more complete analysis of gas rates, see American Gas Association, *Gas Rate Fundamentals* (rev. ed.; New York, 1969); Davidson, *op. cit.;* and Paul J. Garfield and Wallace F. Lovejoy, *Public Utility Economics* (Englewood Cliffs, N.J.: Prentice-Hall, Inc., 1964), pp. 164–73.

[18]Demand rate schedules, such as the Wright and Hopkinson types, are used infrequently, since demand costs for a gas distributor are far lower in relation to his total costs than those of an electric utility.

Rate differentials are largely based on differences in demand conditions. The gas industry is subject to strong actual and potential competition from electricity, coal, steam, and fuel oil. Rates thus tend to be set according to differences in the elasticities of demand. As a result, lower rates are charged for

TABLE 11-4
Percentage of Gas Customers, Sales and
Revenues by Customer Classes, 1967

Classification	Percentage of Customers	Percentage of Sales	Percentage of Revenues
Residential	91.9	32.4	53.1
Commercial	7.5	11.7	14.8
Industrial	.5	52.0	29.8
Other	.1	3.9	2.3
Totals	100.0	100.0	100.0

Source: American Gas Association, Inc., *1968 Gas Facts* (New York, 1968), p. 3.

industrial than for residential use, for space heating and air conditioning than for cooking and water heating.

Telephone Rates [19]

The domestic structure of telephone rates is highly differentiated and, in large part, discriminatory.[20] The basic pricing objective is to attract as many users as possible, consistent with earning a fair rate of return. The objective is achieved by offering different services to meet the various requirements of different groups at charges within the means of the maximum number of prospective customers. Consequently, while telephone rate structures are based primarily upon the general pattern of cost differences, they strongly reflect the value of service standard.

[19] Some of the information in this section was supplied by the American Telephone and Telegraph Company.

[20] Overseas rates are established on the basis of direct negotiations between A.T.&T. and representatives of the foreign countries involved and are filed with the FCC. In general, the rate structure follows the pattern below:

Rate Mileage Band	Three-Minute Person-to-Person Rate
0–500	$ 4.50
501–1,000	6.00
1,001–2,000	7.50
2,001–3,000	9.00
Over 3,000	12.00

Station-to-station rates are being introduced over various routes and are approximately 25 percent below the person-to-person rate in the corresponding rate mileage band. At the end of 1967, overseas telephone service was available to 190 countries or areas and station-to-station service was available to more than 45 of these countries or areas.

In discussing telephone rates, a distinction must be made between local exchange service and toll service. Special services and equipment are charged for independently of the basic telephone service. A number of bulk communications services also are being offered.

Local Exchange Service. The basic unit for the application of local rates is an exchange—a unit which usually embraces a city, town or village, and its environs. Telephone rates vary widely among states and localities due to many factors.[21] One of the most important reasons for variations among localities is the number of telephones in the exchange that can be called without a toll charge. In Virginia, for example, there are eight rate groups, ranging in size from the smallest village and surrounding rural area to the largest city. The rates in the smallest exchange are slightly more than one-half those in the largest. The justification for this differentiation is considered below. The types of service offered also vary to some extent according to the size of the city.

Flat Rate Service. Except for a few of the largest cities where message rates are common, most local telephone service is sold at flat rates. Subscribers are divided into two broad categories—business and residential. An example of a rate schedule for a medium-size city is the following:

Business:
    One-party service . . . . $16.75 per main telephone per month
    Two-party service . . . .   not offered

Residential:
    One-party service . . . . $ 7.00 per main telephone per month
    Two-party service . . . .   5.75 per main telephone per month
    Four-party service . . . .   not offered

Rates are differentiated on the basis of costs, modified by differences in the elasticities of demand. Business subscribers are charged higher rates than are residential users. Since they have higher calling rates, and since a greater proportion of their calls are concentrated during peak periods, on the average, than residential subscribers, commercial subscribers tend to be more expensive customers. The value of service, moreover, is greater for business users. Differentiation is carried further, however, based upon the number of subscribers for each line. One-party subscribers are charged more, because the cost of serving them is greater and because they are willing to pay for added convenience. Conversely, multiple-party subscribers are charged less, because costs are lower and because low rates are needed to bring about the widest possible use of the service.[22] And the more widely the service is used, the more valuable it is to the subscribers who pay the higher rates.

---

[21] See National Association of Utility Regulatory Commissioners, Telephone Rate Subcommittee, *Local Service Telephone Rates in the United States* (Washington, D.C., 1967).

[22] When subscribers share a line, investment and expenses for outside plant and those items of central office equipment which vary with the number of lines are reduced. At the same time, the usefulness of party line service is limited by its possible effect on

It has been charged that flat rates do not economize the use of telephone plant:

1. Flat rates encourage economic waste. Patrons make unnecessary calls for which equipment and facilities must be provided. This increases the cost of service.

2. The high uniform rate prevents the expansion of service to marginal patrons who would be willing to take limited service on a cost basis.

3. The flat rate is inequitable between customers.

4. The flat rate produces a high peak load that might be avoided in part by measured, off-peak rates.

5. By encouraging calls that are both unduly numerous and unduly long cheap multiple-party line service is made undesirable.[23]

These criticisms of flat rates have some validity, but their widespread use is due to several important advantages. Flat rates encourage customers to use the service more freely, thus enhancing the value of telephone service to all. They help to build up habits of telephone use which further the steady growth of the business and the continuous widening of its field of usefulness. Subscribers generally prefer flat rates because of this freedom of use and the ability to know in advance just what their monthly bills will be. Flat rates are also simpler for the subscriber to understand and for the telephone companies to operate and administer, thereby avoiding possible disputes as to local charges.

Further, it is questionable that a more efficient use of plant could be gained by eliminating flat rates and substituting message rates. Nor would such a change result in large cost savings. While the costs of handling calls would be reduced, the costs of metering would be added and subscribers might well curtail their usage. Since a large portion of the costs of furnishing telephone service is independent of message use, the total savings would be less than proportionate to the reduction of usage. If a telephone company has adequate plant capacity to provide the required service and if earnings are satisfactory with flat rates, there is little incentive for either the commissions or the utility to change the method of charging subscribers.

Message Rate Service. In addition to flat rate service, message rates commonly are offered to business and residential subscribers in the largest cities. A wider spread of telephone charges is sought, since a high proportion of business users have very large and specialized communications requirements, while the residential market covers a wider range of income groups than that found in most small communities. The use of message rates permits the telephone companies to charge lower initial rates than would be possible if unlimited service was provided. As a result, residential subscribers for each type

---

the quality of service. The greater the number of parties per line, the more unsatisfactory the service is likely to be both for the party line customers and for other users who might encounter serious delays in calling party lines. It is for this reason that lines with four or more parties are rapidly disappearing.

[23] Clemens, *op. cit.*, p. 333.

of line service receive an initial bill—a flat charge per month for a limited number of message units.[24] When a subscriber's monthly calls exceed the maximum number of units for which he pays the flat charge, he buys additional units at a uniform price. Examples of message rates are:

Business:
    One-party service . . . . $9.70 per main telephone per month (a)
    Two-party service . . . .   not offered

Residential:
    One-party service . . . . $6.10 per main telephone per month (b)
    Two-party service . . . .   4.70 per main telephone per month (c)

(a) Monthly message charge—1st 95 messages, no message charge; next 2,405, each at 5¢; next 2,500, each at 4.75¢; balance, each at 4.50¢.
(b) Monthly message charge—1st 65 messages, no message charge; balance, each at 5¢.
(c) Monthly message charge—1st 55 messages, no message charge; balance, each at 5¢

The exact limitation of an exchange's local calling area, and the type of rates applied, are both matters of judgment based on local conditions. If the local calling area is too large, local rates may not be low enough to promote maximum development. Conversely, if the area is too small, normal use of the service may be curtailed, and local service will have less value but higher costs. Moreover, a desirable local calling area once fixed is not regarded as static. Especially is this true around the larger cities where conditions tend to change rapidly. Local calling area boundaries, therefore, are extended from time to time, thereby changing traffic over certain routes from toll to local. Frequently, to meet varying customer requirements, optional services with different initial calling areas are offered.

Public Telephone Service. Telephone companies also furnish public telephone service for the use of the public and nonsubscribers. Public facilities are provided at the telephone company's option at locations selected as most suitable and convenient for use by the public. They are usually equipped with coin boxes, although at busy locations (large airports) an attendant may be provided to assist in making connections and to collect the charges for calls. A uniform price, commonly 10 cents per local call, is charged.

Semipublic service is provided and used mainly in locations where there is some transient use (restaurants, gas stations), but not enough to justify public telephone service. Users of the semipublic service pay the same price per call as public users. In some states, the subscriber to the service guarantees a monthly minimum income to the telephone company. The amounts deposited by the public apply toward the guarantee and may substantially reduce the amounts which the subscribers must pay.

[24] A unit is a measure of time, and the number of units per call varies with the distance called within the metropolitan area.

PBX Service. When private-branch exchanges (PBX service) are provided for hotels, large companies, office buildings, and other institutions, telephone companies normally charge for each trunk from the switchboard to the central office. For flat rate PBX trunks, the rate for the first trunk is commonly the same as that for business one-party flat rate service; the charge for each additional trunk is 50 percent more than the first trunk. For message rate PBX trunks, the charge for the first trunk is commonly the same as for business one-party message service; the charge for additional trunks usually is 60 percent of the first trunk, with all messages charged against the first trunk. In addition, there are monthly rental charges for the PBX switchboard and the telephones on the customers' premises connected to the switchboard.

Special Charges. Telephone companies make flat charges for telephone installations and other wiring jobs and for color sets. For supplementary equipment, such as an extension bell, buzzer circuit, and longer desk cord, the subscriber pays both an installation charge and a flat monthly rental for the equipment. The same is true of extension telephones, night lights, and special telephone sets, like the "Princess" and the "Ericofon." In this way, the telephone companies are able to provide basic telephone service at a low rate, while furnishing many extras or luxuries to those who are willing to pay for them. The telephone companies, however, own all equipment which they furnish and do not offer it for sale to the subscriber.

Toll Rates. Toll service or long distance rates vary according to (1) distance, (2) whether completion is requested to a specified person or to anyone who answers, (3) time of day, and (4) length of conversation (holding time).[25] In general, these rates are differentiated due to the costs involved and the value of service, as well as simplicity and ease of understanding. Generally, as the distance of the toll call increases, costs per unit tend to rise because of the greater length of circuits, the additional facilities required to secure satisfactory transmission, the lower volume of traffic over longer routes, and the greater operating labor due to the higher proportion of switched traffic. The costs per mile, however, do not vary directly with increasing distance, since terminal costs become relatively less important in the total cost of any particular call. Consequently, toll charges increase with distance, but at a decreasing rate.[26] Further, long-haul calls tend, on the average, to have greater value to customers, since alternative means of communication involve greater expenditures of time or money, or both.

Toll charges are lower on station-to-station than on person-to-person calls.

[25] For rate-making purposes, a distinction is made between intrastate and interstate toll service. The theory of toll rates, however, is basically the same for both types of service.

[26] Distances within most states are measured point-to-point between toll rate centers for short hauls, and between the centers of specified blocks for the longer hauls and still larger sections for the longest hauls. The distance between rate centers is determined in accordance with the so-called V-H system of mileage measurement. Under this system, the distance is computed from the originating rate center to the center of an area which encloses the terminating rate center. This area becomes progressively larger as the distance increases. Rate distance does not depend upon the actual routing of the call.

This classification recognizes that (a) on certain calls, the calling party desires to speak only with a particular person and may not be sure this person can be readily reached at the called telephone, and (b) generally more operating labor is required, and circuits and equipment are used for a longer time in handling a call when a specified person must be secured. Moreover, the differentials between person-to-person and station-to-station rates decline as the length of the call increases, because the economies of station-to-station operation decline as toll call distance increases. And in many cases, person-to-person overtime charges are now the same as station-to-station overtime charges.

Rates are also lower off-peak than on-peak during business hours.[27] The present rate differentials attempt to offer users an incentive to increase their calls without burdening the business as a whole by building up traffic peaks in the lower rate periods. If successful, a better 24-hour utilization of telephone plant is achieved.

Finally, toll charges vary with the length of conversation. Lower initial period rates are thereby possible, and the service is further developed. Moreover, it is the customer who decides how long a conversation is worth the charge. Conversations are not needlessly prolonged, tying up expensive toll circuits and unnecessarily increasing total costs. Yet, the customer is able to use the service as long as he wishes on those calls when additional conversation time has real value. Lower initial period rates thus are made practicable by both the overtime revenues derived from the longer conversations and the economical use of the circuit.

Local versus Statewide Exchange and Toll Rates. While each exchange is a distinct unit for rate-quoting purposes, the Bell System companies have generally established rates on a statewide basis. Essentially, the statewide basis provides that the total costs of furnishing telephone service and the resulting revenue requirements are considered for the state as a unit. This practice recognizes that

[27]There are (as of August 1, 1968) four rate periods for station-to-station interstate calls: (a) day (Monday-Friday, 7 A.M.-5 P.M.); (b) evening (Monday-Friday, 5 P.M.-7 P.M.); (c) night (Monday-Friday, 7 P.M.-7 A.M., plus all day Saturday and Sunday); and (d) late night—for customer-dialed calls only—midnight to 7 A.M. daily. For interstate person-to-person calls, there are two rate periods: (a) day (Monday-Friday, 7 A.M.-5 P.M.); and (b) night (Monday-Friday, 5 P.M.-7 A.M., plus all day Saturday and Sunday). The following three-minute rates (also as of August 1, 1968) are illustrative:

| | Station-to-Station | | | | Person-to-Person | |
Route	Day	Evening	Night	Late Night	Day	Night
Chicago–Detroit	$ .85	$ .65	$ .60	$ .60	$1.30	$1.10
Boston–Washington	1.15	.85	.65	.60	1.70	1.40
Chicago–New York	1.30	.90	.70	.60	2.20	1.90
Boston–Miami	1.40	1.00	.75	.65	2.40	2.05
San Francisco–Washington ..	1.70	1.25	1.00	.75	3.30	2.85

Intrastate toll rates, although in most states different from interstate rates, follow the same general patterns of differentials between peak and off-peak periods and between station-to-station and person-to-person service.

telephone service, both exchange and toll, furnished by a given company throughout a state is, in reality, an integrated whole, all portions of which are interdependent. The objective is to apply throughout the state a well-balanced and coordinated pattern of rate treatment, providing rates which are uniform under substantially like conditions and producing, in the aggregate, reasonable earnings on the company's total telephone operations within the state.

The statewide basis has five important advantages over separate considera- tion of individual exchanges. First, the statewide basis permits more people to have better service at a reasonable price. Some small areas, if forced to pay their own way, might have no service at all. Needed plant replacements or additions might be postponed if local customers had to cover their full costs, resulting in deterioration of local service within the exchange and of toll service to and from it. Second, on the statewide basis, customers pay like charges for like amounts of service. If each exchange had to stand on its own feet, customers' charges would vary with physical characteristics of the exchange area, age of plant, type of equipment, and other factors affecting costs, but not necessarily affecting the service rendered. The statewide basis averages out such factors.

Third, customers seem better satisfied with statewide rates, because the application of uniform schedules avoids any question of discrimination or unfair advantage to pressure groups in individual exchanges. Fourth, the statewide basis tends to stabilize rate levels by providing a broad rate base. Risks are spread so that a community suffering from flood, storm, or other natural disaster or from some local economic difficulty (e.g., the removal of a major industry) need not pay higher telephone rates such as would be required if telephone operations in that exchange had to meet these conditions single-handed. Finally, the statewide basis is more workable and makes the regulatory process less cumbersome and expensive to both the public and the company involved. It avoids multiplicity of rate cases for each individual exchange. It simplifies handling of questions and complaints by the regulatory commissions and administration by the companies.

At the same time, it should be pointed out that the statewide basis results in some subscribers subsidizing other subscribers. Because exchange telephone service is more valuable to customers in the larger local service areas, they are willing to pay more for their service. Since their average cash income is greater, they are able to pay more. Lower rates in the small towns and rural areas, where average money incomes are relatively low, encourage telephone use and develop- ment in these places. Once again, this is an example of how rate discrimination is used to achieve a socially desirable objective, in this case the widespread development of telephone usage throughout the country.

Bulk Communications Services. In addition to local exchange and toll services, telephone companies offer several services to customers with heavy (bulk) communications needs. Two of these bulk communications services, currently being offered by A.T.&T., are illustrative.[28]

---

[28] Private line services are discussed in Chapter 17. It should be noted that Western Union offers some services that are competitive with many of those offered by telephone companies.

TELPAK Rate Structure. TELPAK makes available packages of channels in various band widths which may be used between specific locations to carry both voice and nonvoice communications. Facilities are furnished on a seven-day per week, twenty-four-hour per day basis only, with a minimum subscription period of one month. The TELPAK rate structure is composed of two elements: a monthly charge per airline mile for designated maximum capacities and a monthly rate per terminal for individual activated channels up to the maximum capacity (Table 11–5).

WATS Rate Schedule. Under the Wide Area Telephone Service offering, known as WATS, subscribers may purchase flat rate service (a customer may call either intrastate or to his choice of six progressively larger interstate zones in the continental United States and Alaska for a flat monthly rate, and may call as often and talk as long as desired within the zone) or measured service (15 hours of conversation per month, with additional use charged by the hour) (Table 11–6).[29] Subscribers also may transmit record messages by utilizing data-phone subsets and teletypewriter machines for which a rental fee is charged.

Telegraph Rates [30]

The Western Union Telegraph Company provides a wide variety of domestic and international services. The present section is concerned with the rate structures of three domestic telegraph services—full-rate telegrams, day letters, and night letters.[31]

For purposes of rate making, the United States is divided into rate squares. The rate squares are 50 miles on a side and are arranged in brick-like fashion. Numbering of the squares is such that the same numerical difference between

[29] In addition to outward WATS, A.T.&T. has introduced inward WATS, a service whereby field employees and customers of a business with inward service can "call collect."

[30] This section is largely based on information supplied by The Western Union Telegraph Company.

[31] In June, 1968, Western Union submitted a new uniform interstate rate proposal (applicable within the continental United States) to the FCC and announced its intention of filing uniform intrastate rate schedules with the state regulatory commissions (*The Wall Street Journal*, July 1, 1968, p. 8). The proposed schedules are as follows:

	Telegram			Overnight Telegram	
	First 15 Words or Less	*Each Additional Word* 16–50 Words	Over 50 Words	First 100 Words or Less	Each Additional Word
Interstate	$2.25	$.09	$.06	$1.70	$.015
Intrastate	1.70	.08	.05	1.30	.01

The interstate tariff became effective on November 1, 1968, but the FCC has instituted an investigation into its lawfulness. The intrastate tariff is in effect in some 40 states.

TABLE 11-5
Interim TELPAK Rate Structure

A. TELPAK CHANNELS AND CHARGES

Classification	Carrier Spectrum Assignment (Kilocycles per Second)	Maximum Equivalent Telephone Grade Channels	Monthly Charge per Airline Mile
TELPAK C.......	240	60	$28
TELPAK D.......	1000 (approximate)	240	60

B. TERMINAL EQUIPMENT CHARGES

	First Station Exchange		Each Additional Station in Exchange	
	A Installation Charge	B Monthly Charge	C Installation Charge	D Monthly Charge
Telephone	$20	$25	$20	$10
Teletypewriter	20	25	20	10
Telephotograph ...	20	100	20	15
Data	20–200	25–625	20–200	20–375

Source: American Telephone and Telegraph Company (August, 1968).

any two rate squares will always represent the same air-line distance and, thus, the same rate. A section of the rate-square map is reproduced in Figure 11–2. To illustrate its use: the numerical difference between New York City (square 2606) and Chicago (square 2777) is 171. This difference represents an air-line distance of 727 miles. Consequently, whenever the difference between two rate squares is

TABLE 11-6
WATS Rate Schedule: Illinois–North

		Measured Time	
	Full Time	First 15 Hours	Each Additional Hour
Intrastate	$ 575	$140	$10.50
Interstate			
Zone 1	700	180	14.00
Zone 2	900	220	16.50
Zone 3	1,200	250	19.50
Zone 4	1,400	270	21.50
Zone 5	1,500	280	22.00
Zone 6	1,950	335	25.50

Source: American Telephone and Telegraph Company (August, 1968).

FIGURE 11-2
Section of the Rate Square Map Used by The Western Union Telegraph Company

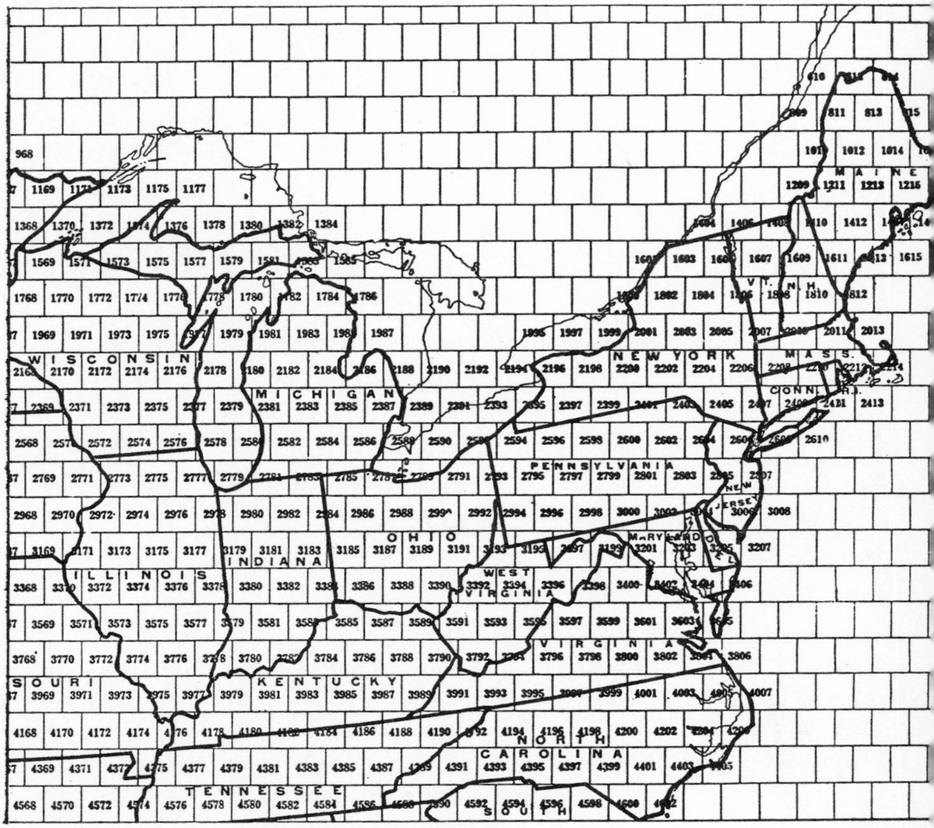

Source: Courtesy of The Western Union Telegraph Company.

171, the air-line distance will be 727 miles and the rate between the two points will be the same.

The rates for telegraph messages are determined by: (1) the air-line distance between the center of the rate square of the point of origin and the center of the rate square of the point of destination, (2) the number of words per message, and (3) the type of service used. The rate for a fifty-word day letter is approximately 45 percent higher than the charge for a fifteen-word full-rate telegram; for a fifty-word night letter the rate is slightly above 85 percent of the charge for a fifteen-word full-rate telegram (Table 11–7). Additional word rates for all three types of service are set at about 84 percent of the basic charge per word.

The differentials between rates for these services are based partly on

TABLE 11-7
Rate Structures for Three Domestic Telegraph Services

Mileage Zones	Full-Rate Telegram		Day Letter		Night Letter	
	15 Words or Less	Each Additional Word	50 Words or Less	Each Additional 5 Words or Less	50 Words or Less	Each Additional 5 Words or Less
0-125	$1.272	$0.0689	$1.855	$0.1484	$1.113	$0.0901
126-225	1.388	0.0742	1.961	0.1537	1.166	0.0901
226-425	1.537	0.0795	2.226	0.1749	1.325	0.1060
426-750	1.696	0.0901	2.438	0.1908	1.484	0.1166
751-1,125 ...	1.855	0.0954	2.650	0.2120	1.590	0.1272
1,126-1,550 ...	2.014	0.1060	2.915	0.2279	1.749	0.1378
1,551-3,000 ...	2.226	0.1166	3.180	0.2491	1.908	0.1484

Source: The Western Union Telegraph Company (July 15, 1968).

differences in costs and partly in consideration of the rates for competing services. The higher rates are charged for the fastest service, the lower rates for less speedy or off-peak services. Some costs, such as those incurred in the acceptance of a telegram from the sender and in the delivery of a telegram to the addressee, do not vary with distance. Other costs, such as station operating costs and line-haul costs, vary with both volume and distance. As telegraph and telephone services are competing substitutes, Western Union must take telephone rates into consideration when establishing its rate structure.[32] Rates need not be equal, however, since there are important differences in the services offered by the two competing media, thereby making them somewhat imperfect substitutes.

Discrimination enters the telegraph rate structure in two primary ways. First, some discrimination is unavoidable. In order to simplify the rate structure, rate squares and block air-line distances are used. The size of the block distances employed are not entirely based upon the cost of providing the service; the value of service is also taken into account. Second, telegraph rates partially disregard differences in station costs. The operating costs of telegraph offices and, hence, the cost per message vary from city to city. They depend on such factors as the amount of industry in a city, the number of telegraph offices required to serve the needs of a community due to its geographical size, and the volume of telegrams handled. These cost factors are averaged for rate-making purposes so that users in cities where the operating costs are low partly subsidize users in high-cost cities. The advantages of a single domestic telegraph rate structure are similar to those for statewide telephone rates.

[32] For example: From New York to points in California, a fifteen-word full-rate telegram costs $2.23; a fifty-word day letter, $3.18; a fifty-word night letter, $1.91. In comparison, the station-to-station three-minute telephone rates are: day, $1.70; evening, $1.25; night, $1.00; late night, $0.75.

COMMISSION REGULATION OF RATE STRUCTURES[33]

The job of controlling the regulated industries' rate structures is left to the commissions, subject, of course, to judicial review. The legal standards are broad: each rate must be "just and reasonable," and the rate structure must avoid "undue" discrimination. Moreover, years of interpretation have failed to witness the development of any clear principles by which a rate structure may be judged as reasonable or unreasonable. A majority of the commissions have been pragmatic, acting only in response to complaints by shippers or customers on a case-by-case approach. Stated another way, far more attention has been paid to the rate level than to the rate structure. The problems associated with commission regulation of rate structures are discussed in this section.

The Rate-Making Power

Contrary to common belief, the commissions do not take the initiative in setting each particular rate that comprises a rate structure. The power to make and change rates rests initially with the regulated industries. The rates of motor carriers, railroads, and some water carriers, for example, either originate through the carriers' freight associations ("bureaus" or "conferences") or represent the action of individual companies.[34] To illustrate: All proposed railroad changes are filed with the Interstate Commerce Commission or with the relevant state commission(s). In the case of the ICC, they take effect in 30 days unless the commission suspends them in response to protests or on its own motion. Individual shippers or groups of shippers may always bring a complaint concerning particular rates. Such a complaint may be brought before the individual railroad(s), the appropriate rate bureau, or the commission: the commission will always review it. But each year, thousands of rates are changed without any formal action by the commission. Thus, in fiscal 1967, the ICC rejected only 1.7 percent of the 215,540 tariffs and schedules filed.[35] When the commission acts in response to a complaint concerning a particular rate, it considers only that rate. When it acts in response to an application for an increase in the general level of rates, however, the commission may substantially modify the entire rate structure.

[33] This discussion draws heavily from D. Philip Locklin, *Economics of Transportation* (6th ed.; Homewood, Ill.: Richard D. Irwin, Inc., 1966), chaps. xix-xxiii, xxxii; Wilcox, *op. cit.*, pp. 348-55; and Dudley F. Pegrum, *Transportation: Economics and Public Policy* (rev. ed.; Homewood, Ill.: Richard D. Irwin, Inc., 1968), pp. 422-36. Also see Truman C. Bigham and Merrill J. Roberts, *Transportation* (2d ed.; New York: McGraw-Hill Book Co., Inc., 1952), chaps. xiii, xv, xvii; Marvin L. Fair and Ernest W. Williams, Jr., *Economics of Transportation* (rev. ed.; New York: Harper & Row, Pubs., 1959), chap. xxvi; Troxel, *op. cit.*, chaps. xxvi, xxviii; and Jordan J. Hillman, *Competition and Railroad Price Discrimination: Legal Precedent and Economic Policy* (Evanston, Ill.: The Transportation Center at Northwestern University, 1968).

[34] Among the transportation industries, only the airlines have not established associations. The Civil Aeronautics Board has long encouraged the airlines to set rates independently.

[35] Interstate Commerce Commission, *Eighty-First Annual Report* (1967), p. 112.

A similar procedure applies to the other regulated industries, although the great majority of all proposed rate changes are by the transportation industries because of their wide variety of rates and the growing importance of intermodal competition.

Statutory Standards

The statutory standards under which the commissions control the rate structures of the regulated industries are necessarily broad. Consider the provisions of the Interstate Commerce Act that apply to the railroad industry. Section 1 of the act requires that all rates, as well as the classification systems used, must be "just and reasonable." Section 2 prohibits personal discrimination, although certain exemptions (free passes to employees) are recognized in later sections of the act. Section 3 covers other forms of discrimination, prohibiting "any undue or unreasonable preference or advantage to any particular person, company, firm, corporation, association, locality, port, port district, gateway, transit point, region, district, territory, or any particular description of traffic" or "any undue or unreasonable prejudice or disadvantage" to the same list. Section 4 applies to a particular type of discrimination between places, forbidding any carrier to charge more, "under substantially similar circumstances and conditions, for a shorter than for a longer distance over the same line, in the same direction, the shorter being included within the longer distance." The commission is authorized to make exceptions "in special cases." Finally, Section 6 requires that rates and fares be published and adhered to. No changes can be made without prior notice, as discussed above.

While there are some important differences (Section 4, for instance, applies only to rail and water carriers), the basic statutory requirements—"just and reasonable" rates and classification systems, and the prevention of "unjust" discrimination—apply to all of the regulated industries. Except for the prohibition against personal discrimination, the legislatures have left the task of interpreting these broad statutory provisions to the commissions and the courts. Since discrimination has been especially serious in railroad rate structures, emphasis is placed on this industry.

Regulation of Railroad Rate Structures

The statutory obligation concerning "just and reasonable" rates refers to specific rates; the statutory obligation to avoid "undue" or "unjust" discrimination among shippers refers to the relationship between two rates.

Particular Rates. When the rate on a particular commodity or a particular haul is being considered, under Section 1 of the Interstate Commerce Act, discrimination is not an issue. Rather, the concern is with reasonableness per se. The commission has no absolute standard by which to judge a "just and reasonable" rate. One approach would be to determine the reasonableness of a rate or a haul by ascertaining the cost of carrying a particular commodity or making a particular haul. An alternative approach, and the one followed by the commission, is to compare the rate that has been questioned with the rate(s) on other commodities in the structure, taking as a standard "analogous" commodities or hauls of equal length. Thousands of rate cases have been decided using this standard. For instance, the commission has held that canned evaporated milk should take the same rate as other canned goods, celery as eggplant, motorcycles as bicycles, chopped alfalfa as baled hay, and lawn mowers as agricultural implements.[36]

Although the analogous commodity standard is commonly used, the ICC will approve a difference in rates when justified on one of three grounds. First, there may be differences in the cost of transporting two commodities. Once again, it should be noted, the deciding factor is not the absolute cost of transporting a particular commodity—a figure that is usually impossible to compute—but the relative costs of handling two. Differences in the cost of service, as previously discussed, may be due to such factors as weight, susceptibility to loss or damage, or volume of traffic. Second, there may be differences in the value of service to shippers. The Interstate Commerce Act specifically requires the commission to consider the effect of rates on the movement of traffic in determining reasonable charges. The commission has long held, therefore, that it is just and reasonable to charge more for hauling finished and valuable goods than for hauling raw materials and cheaper goods. Rates on agricultural products are low because the products would not move at higher charges. And in a case involving wool rates, the commission said: "If the condition of this industry is such that it cannot flourish, that the traffic will not move for the reason that the wool itself will not be produced, that, certainly, is a circumstance which may be considered in comparing this rate with those upon other commodities."[37] Third, in a few isolated instances, the commission has justified rate differences by considering whether the general welfare required a high or low rate on a particular commodity. Thus, low rates were approved on fertilizer because of the "need for continued progress in the use of fertilizer"[38] and on wastepaper because the "utilization of waste materials is of economic value to the country,"[39] while high rates on tobacco were justified on the grounds that it is a luxury rather than a necessity.[40]

When the ICC finds a rate to be unreasonably high, it has the power to prescribe a maximum that may be charged. Prior to 1915, the commission and the Supreme Court held that a maximum need not cover fully allocated costs, provided a carrier could earn a fair return on its entire business. In that year, however, the Court ruled that a maximum rate could not be set below the full

---

[36] 112 ICC 155 (1926); 5 ICC 663 (1893); 109 ICC 465 (1926); 26 ICC 127 (1913); 87 ICC 154 (1923).

[37] *In re Transportation of Wool, Hides & Pelts,* 231 ICC 151, 156 (1912). Also see *Wool & Mohair Rates,* 276 ICC 259, 269 (1949).

[38] *Fertilizers between Southern Points,* 113 ICC 389, 421 (1926).

[39] *Reduced Rates, 1922,* 68 ICC 676, 720 (1922).

[40] *Tobacco Merchants Assn.* v. *Aberdeen & Rockfish R.R. Co.,* 181 ICC 199, 211 (1931).

cost of service, since this would deprive the railroads of property without due process of law and result in burdening other traffic.[41] The Court apparently reversed its stand in 1953, thereby returning to its earlier position by holding that "... so long as rates as a whole afford railroads just compensation for their over-all services to the public the Due Process Clause should not be construed as a bar to the fixing of noncompensatory rates for carrying some commodities when the public interest is thereby served."[42]

A railroad may charge no more than the prescribed maximum, but it may charge less. However, the ICC also has the power to fix the minimum rate. Here, too, it may prescribe a rate that does not cover fully allocated costs. But the commission has consistently refused to approve a rate that does not cover out-of-pocket costs. Consequently, a just and reasonable rate is a matter of judgment. While it may be one that covers or more than covers fully allocated costs, it may not be set below a minimum that covers out-of-pocket costs.

The Rate Structure. Historically, railroads have discriminated in three ways—between persons, between commodities, and between places. The first is now specifically forbidden by law;[43] the second and third are not. In the second and third situations, discrimination is illegal only where it is undue or unreasonable.

Discrimination between Commodities. Two rates may be reasonable per se and yet cause undue discrimination among shippers, for here, the problem is one of the relationship between two rates. Cases involving discrimination among commodities arise when goods that may be substituted for one another compete in the same market or when competition between fabricators is affected by the relation of rates on raw materials to those on finished materials.[44] The commission has generally held that comparable rates are required when (1) commodities are competing substitutes, (2) the rate relationship has been the source of actual injury to the complaining seller in marketing his product, and (3) the cost of transporting the two commodities is similar. It has, therefore, forbidden rates higher on zinc ammonium chloride than on sal ammoniac, on cotton-factory sweepings than on rags, on veneer than on lumber, and on benzol than on gasoline.[45] But comparable rates were not approved for flaxseed and grain (not competitive), for roofing slate and roofing tile (competitive, but no proof of damage), and for metal roofing and hard asbestos roofing (competitive, but the cost of transporting the metal roofing was significantly lower than the asbestos roofing).[46]

[41] *Northern Pacific Railway Co.* v. *North Dakota,* 236 U.S. 585 (1915). Curiously, in its concept of cost the Court did not include a return on investment, so that some commodities could presumably contribute less than others to the railroads' annual profit.

[42] *Baltimore & Ohio Railroad Co.* v. *United States,* 345 U.S. 146, 150 (1953). See R. W. Harbeson, "A New Judicial Test of Reasonable Rates," 21 *I.C.C. Practitioners' Journal* 789 (1955).

[43] For a discussion of personal discrimination, see Locklin, *op. cit.,* chap. xxi.

[44] Wilcox, *op. cit.,* p. 351.

[45] 159 ICC 475 (1929); 147 ICC 740 (1928); 81 ICC 227 (1923); 156 ICC 444 (1929).

[46] 171 ICC 192 (1930); 174 ICC 767 (1931); 167 ICC 693 (1930).

The raw material-finished product relationship is often crucial in determining the location of industry.[47] Freight rates will determine whether the raw material or the finished product is to be transported long distances. They may also discriminate against the producers located near the raw material supply or those located near the market for the finished product. When controversies arise between rival producers, the commission tends to make the differences in rates conform to differences in the cost of service. The goal is to eliminate any artificial advantage or disadvantage, while maintaining the natural advantages of each location. In both situations, however, exceptions will be allowed when the railroads face competition from other modes of transportation.

Discrimination between Places. Cases of place discrimination fall into two categories. Section 4, known as the long-and-short-haul clause, involves a higher charge "for a shorter than for a longer distance over the same line, in the same direction, the shorter being included within the longer distance." This form of place discrimination is forbidden unless expressly permitted by the ICC. All other cases come under Section 3, which prohibits "undue or unreasonable" place discrimination in general. In Section 4 cases, the burden of proof is on the railroad that seeks relief from the provision. In Section 3 cases, however, the burden of proof is on the complaining party, and the procedure is the same as that for cases involving discrimination between commodities. A shipper who complains of a higher rate than one charged at another place must show that (1) the two places are in direct competition and (2) he has suffered actual injury by the difference in rates. A railroad may defend different rates by showing that there are differences in (1) the cost of service, (2) the value of service or (3) the competition faced on the two hauls.

Place discrimination cases arise in two situations—namely, where a railroad faces competition from another carrier and where two producing areas obtain their raw materials from a common source or sell in a common market. By law, the commission is required to grant relief to circuitous lines or routes which are in competition with more direct routes; in other situations, the commission must exercise its judgment. In Figure 11-3, railroad *y* is a circuitous route in competition with railroad *x*. The commission will permit railroad *y* to meet the rate of railroad *x* between *A* and *B*, even though it would be violating the long-and-short-haul clause by charging more between *A* and *C* than between *A* and *B*. In Figure 11-4, a railroad may be permitted to meet the rate set by the water carrier between *A* and *B*, thus charging more for the shorter haul between *A* and *C* than for the longer haul between *A* and *B*. And in Figure 11-5, a railroad may be permitted to charge the same rate for hauling a raw material from *C* to competing producing points *A* and *B*, or for hauling a product to the common market *C*, even though *A* involves a longer haul than does *B*.

Permissible place discrimination is not limitless. Thus, in Figure 11-6, railroads *x* and *y* will not be permitted to charge less for the longer haul from *A*

[47] Locklin, *op. cit.*, pp. 515-17.

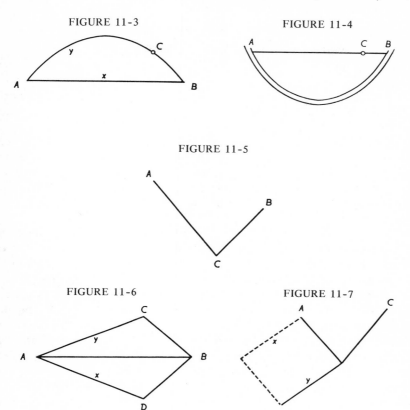

FIGURE 11-3

FIGURE 11-4

FIGURE 11-5

FIGURE 11-6

FIGURE 11-7

to *B* than for the shorter hauls from *A* to *C* and *D* simply because they compete at *B* and not at *C* and *D*. Nor will railroad *y*, in Figure 11–7, be permitted to charge less from *A* to *B*, where it competes with railroad *x*, than it does between the equidistant haul *C* and *B*, where it has no competitors. In cases concerning place discrimination, the railroad seeking relief from the long-and-short-haul clause or the complainant seeking to have a rate equalized with one charged at a competing place is usually required by the commission to show that competitive conditions require relief or equal rates and that the lower rates are "reasonably compensatory"—that they at least cover out-of-pocket costs. In addition, in Section 4 cases the railroad must show that the higher rates at the intermediate points are reasonable per se and that the competition faced is actual and not merely potential.[48]

48 See *ibid.*, chap. xxii.

Regulation of Motor Carrier Rate Structures

In the motor carrier industry, there has been a tendency for competition among the carriers to become ruinous. At first sight, such a situation would seem unlikely because motor carrier costs are mostly variable. However, competition has led to frequent conditions of overcapacity in the industry, and rates have tended to reflect short-run variable costs. In theory, rates should reflect long-run costs. The commission, therefore, has issued minimum rate orders on a number of occasions. "It is not our policy," the commission stated in 1956, "to keep such orders in force any longer than necessary to achieve stabilization of the particular rate structure which is the subject of the order."[49] Minimum rate orders, it was concluded, tend to freeze the rate structure and interfere with "the normal processes of rate-making by negotiations between carriers and shippers."[50]

The same general principles used in similar railroad cases are followed by the commission in determining the reasonableness of motor carrier rates on particular commodities or hauls and in determining justified discrimination.[51] But four important differences should be noted. First, "the Commission has held that because of the limited capacities of motor trucks as compared with railroad freight cars, weight density should be given more consideration in determining classification ratings for motor carriers than it has customarily been given in making rail classifications."[52] Second, in determining minimum rates or in restricting rate reductions proposed by the motor carriers, great emphasis is placed on fully allocated costs. Such a policy is justified, because with high variable costs there is little need for rates which do not cover fully allocated costs. Third, the commission has generally refused to authorize back-haul rates for motor carriers at subnormal levels (that is, below average costs).[53] This policy has been defended as follows:

> ... an unbalanced condition of truck traffic, because of the greater numbers of operators, is apt to be somewhat of an individual matter. That is to say, the traffic of one truck operator may preponderate in one direction, whereas that of a competing operator may preponderate in the other. As between operators, therefore, the application of the "out-of-pocket" cost

---

[49] *New England Motor Rate Increases, 1955,* 67 MCC 75, 77 (1956).

[50] *Ibid.* For a study of California's experience in setting minimum rates, see Howard W. Nicholson, "Motor Carrier Cost and Minimum Rate Regulation," 72 *Quarterly Journal of Economics* 139 (1958).

[51] It should be emphasized that there have been far fewer motor carrier rate discrimination cases because of the absence of true joint cost conditions.

[52] Locklin, *op. cit.,* p. 706. See *Incandescent Electric Lamps or Bulbs,* 47 MCC 601, 603 (1947).

[53] There have been some recent exceptions, such as where the traffic sought would not move at all at higher rates or would move by private carriers (*Aluminum Extrusions from Miami to Chicago,* 325 ICC 188 [1965]) and where the traffic sought would be diverted from the railroads (*Carbon Blacks, Southwest to Indiana, Ohio & Missouri,* 325 ICC 138 [1965]).

method of making rates might well result in a break-down of the rate structure in both directions.[54]

Yet, it should be recognized that this policy results in protective (not economic) regulation by maintaining both excess capacity and high rates.[55] Finally, motor carriers are not subject to the long-and-short-haul clause. The absence of such a provision for motor carriers reflects the smaller fixed costs of these carriers. Nor has long-and-short-haul discrimination ever been an important problem in the industry.

Regulation of Intercarrier Competition

The potential benefits of controlled discrimination have been discussed on numerous occasions in this and the preceding chapter. The ICC, however, has a difficult task in regulating intercarrier competition. "When reduced to its simplest terms the issue is one of evaluating the worth of retaining competition against the cost advantages of concentrating the traffic upon that type of carrier which is shown to be most economical."[56] In short, should the commission promote intercarrier competition regardless of a carrier's cost advantages?

Commission Policy before 1958. It was pointed out in the preceding two sections that the commission will allow, under specified conditions, one type of carrier to meet the lower rates of a competing carrier. Especially have the railroads long been critical of this policy. They have argued that while the commission has frequently allowed them to meet the lower rates of a competing carrier, it has not permitted them to undercut the lower rates even when justified by the cost of service. As a result, the railroads contend, high-cost competing carriers have been protected, and the railroads have been forced to share the traffic with other carriers.

The commission has frequently denied that it was following a policy of protecting competing carriers. In a widely quoted case, the commission said: "... there appears no warrant for believing that rail rates, for example, should be held up to a particular level to preserve a motor-rate structure, or vice versa."[57] But Professor Williams, after analyzing approximately 900 commission decisions, concluded in part:

> With respect to the relationship of rail to motor-carrier rates the Commission seemingly has been moved by a desire to preserve both types of transportation in virtually the whole range of service they had come to occupy at the time its jurisdiction was broadened. Consequently it has given

---

[54] *Refrigerator Material, Memphis, Tenn., to Dayton, Ohio*, 4 MCC 187, 189 (1938).

[55] Hunter Morrison, "Rate Policy of Interstate Commerce Commission for Back-Hauls of Trucks: Pricing and Joint Cost," 19 *Journal of Land & Public Utility Economics* 329 (1943).

[56] Ernest W. Williams, Jr., *The Regulation of Rail-Motor Rate Competition* (New York: Harper & Bros., 1958), pp. 226–27.

[57] *New Automobiles in Interstate Commerce*, 259 ICC 475, 538 (1945).

large emphasis to the preservation of the opportunity to compete and to secure a "fair" share of the traffic. . . . On occasion the railroads have been allowed to go below the motor-carrier rates in compensation of their service deficiencies, but more often they have been compelled to content themselves with rate parity even though their cost structure might have permitted reductions below—sometimes substantially below—a level which would have been judged compensatory for motor carriers.

This result is consistent with a point of view which concerns itself primarily with what must be done "in fairness" to the carriers which have actually been competing for the particular traffic in issue. It is consistent with keeping everyone in the business. It does not, however, contribute to the development of a more economic division of the traffic, to coordination of the services, or to the development of economy in the handling of the available business. And it extends great encouragement to the growth of private and exempt trucking to the detriment of all common carriers, although the growth of such trucking falls with particular severity upon the railroads.[58]

Commission Policy since 1958. Dissatisfaction with commission policy, particularly from the railroads, continued, and in 1958 Congress amended the rate-making rule dealing with intercarrier competition, by adding the following paragraph to Section 15a:

> (3) In a proceeding involving competition between carriers of different modes of transportation subject to this Act, the Commission, in determining whether a rate is lower than a reasonable minimum rate, shall consider the facts and circumstances attending the movement of the traffic by the carrier or carriers to which the rate is applicable. Rates of a carrier shall not be held up to a particular level to protect the traffic of any other mode of transportation, giving due consideration to the objectives of the national transportation policy declared by this Act.

The intent of Congress was to make sure the commission did not follow a policy of protecting high-cost carriers by umbrella rate making.[59]

The effect of the amendment remains uncertain. In a study of the rail investigation and suspension cases involving intermodal competition, published between passage of the amendment and July 24, 1961, Harbeson concluded that all thirty-two decisions (out of fifty-nine) which approved reductions were consistent with the traffic-sharing principle.[60] Then, in 1963, the Supreme Court (in the so-called *Sea-Land* decision) set aside a commission order, arguing:

> If a carrier is prohibited from establishing a reduced rate that is not detrimental to its own revenue requirements merely because the rate will

[58] Williams, *op. cit.,* pp. 210–11, 214–15.

[59] Senate Report No. 1647, 85th Cong., 2d sess. (Washington, D.C.: U.S. Government Printing Office, 1958), p. 3. See comments on the amendment, *Traffic World,* June 25, 1960, p. 12.

[60] Robert W. Harbeson, "The Regulation of Inter-agency Rate Competition under the Transportation Act of 1958," 30 *I.C.C. Practitioners' Journal* 287 (1962).

divert traffic from others, then the carrier is thwarted from asserting its own inherent advantages of cost and service. Nor should the selective character of such a rate reduction, made in response to a particular competitive situation, be permitted, without more, to furnish a basis for rejecting the rate. Section 15a(3), in other words, made it clear that something more than even hard competition must be shown before a particular rate can be deemed unfair or destructive.[61]

The Court, moreover, declined to decide in advance how a carrier's inherent advantages should be measured or protected, but it did suggest that neither out-of-pocket nor fully distributed cost might prove to be the appropriate standard.[62] "The Commission was challenged to formulate, instead, an intelligible economic philosophy of competitive rate regulation consonant with the various statutory imperatives."[63]

In a more recent study, covering all ICC cases involving Section 15a(3) between the Court's 1963 decision and February 23, 1966, Harbeson found that in thirty-two of the thirty-nine cases the proposed reductions were allowed in full or in part. But while this represents a larger proportion of the cases in which the proposed rail rate reductions were approved than was true in the pre-1963 study,

> ... the significance of this comparison is greatly diminished by the fact that, in approximately three-fourths of the cases in the present study in which reductions were approved, the approval rested either on the fact that all or most of the proposed rates were above proponents' fully distributed cost or on the fact that protestants failed to produce evidence of their costs. In only four cases did the Commission go beyond the strict terms of the *Sea-Land* decision by approving rates which were below the fully distributed cost of both proponents and protestants. Furthermore, in each of these latter cases the decision appears to be conditioned, in some degree at least, upon circumstances which limit the permissible scope of rates below the fully distributed cost of both opposing parties.[64]

Finally, in 1968, the Supreme Court (in the *Ingot Molds* case) affirmed an ICC order in which the commission used fully distributed cost as the proper

---

[61] *Interstate Commerce Comm.* v. *New York, New Haven & Hartford R.R. Co.*, 372 U.S. 744, 759 (1963).

[62] *Ibid.*, p. 760. For the ICC's original decision, see *Commodities–Pan-Atlantic Steamship Corp.*, 313 ICC 23 (1960).

[63] Nathaniel L. Nathanson, "Administrative Proposals for Revision of Our National Transportation Policy–Herein of Intermodal Competition and the Minimum Rate Power," 58 *Northwestern Law Review* 583, 599–600 (1963). Also see Ernest W. Williams, Jr., "Transportation Prices: Their Initiation and Regulation," 50 *Virginia Law Review* 377 (1964).

[64] Robert W. Harbeson, "Recent Trends in the Regulation of Intermodal Rate Competition in Transportation," 42 *Land Economics* 315, 326 (1966). But see Harvey A. Levine, "The Railroad Industry's Experience under Section 15a(3) of the Transportation Act of 1958," 35 *I.C.C. Practitioners' Journal* 252 (1968); and Bernard J. McCarney, "ICC Rate Regulation and Rail-Motor Carrier Pricing Behavior: A Reappraisal," 35 *ibid.* 707 (1968).

measure of the low-cost carrier. In upholding the commission, the Court stated that the initial determination of what method of costing should be used to measure the inherent advantage of a carrier is for the ICC.[65] Noting a pending rule-making proceeding before the commission on this issue, the Court added that the agency should be given "reasonable latitude to decide where it will resolve these complex issues, in addition to how it will resolve them."[66]

It can be argued that the preservation of intercarrier competition may be advantageous. In some situations, it may be desirable to offer shippers a choice between different types of transport services; national defense considerations may require maintenance of intercarrier rivalry.[67] In other situations, however, the cost of preserving competition may be too high. The commission, confronted with the task of deciding into which category a particular case falls, has yet to formulate concrete policy standards.

A Case Study: Southern Grain Rates. The issues involved in regulating intercarrier competition can be illustrated by an important case concerning Southern grain rates. Often referred to as the "Big John" case, the proceeding lasted over four years—nearly 32 months before the ICC (the record amounted to 15,815 pages of testimony and 766 exhibits from nearly 150 witnesses in over 139 days of hearings) and another 17 months in the courts (Southern's counsel made 13 appearances in lower federal courts and two before the Supreme Court).

The Case. In the summer of 1961, the Southern Railway Company filed with the ICC schedules, to become effective on August 10, 1961, involving reductions of as much as 64.5 percent under the existing rates on grain moving through the Mississippi and Ohio gateways to thirty-seven specified points in the Southeast. Traditionally, Southern, like the rest of the industry, had based its rates on single-car lots of grain, shipped in loads of 50 tons or less per car. Various transit privileges were offered to shippers, thereby permitting them to interrupt the freight movement for milling, blending, or mixing. At the existing rates, however, the southern railroads had lost the bulk of grain traffic in their

---

[65] *American Commercial Lines, Inc.* v. *Louisville & Nashville R. Co.*, 392 U.S. 571, 592 (1968).

[66] *Ibid.* For the ICC's original decision, see *Ingot Molds from Pennsylvania to Steelton, Ky.*, 323 ICC 758 (1965). For an analysis of the case, see Robert W. Harbeson, "The Supreme Court and Intermodal Rate Competition," 36 *I.C.C. Practitioners' Journal* 1487 (1969).

[67] In at least two cases, the courts have reversed commission decisions which authorized reduced railroad rates that would have adversely affected pipelines and barge lines, respectively, on the ground that insufficient consideration had been given to national defense requirements. *Cantlay & Tanzola* v. *United States*, 115 F. Supp. 72 (1953); *Pacific Inland Tariff Bureau* v. *United States*, 129 F. Supp. 479 (1955); 134 F. Supp. 210 (1955). In a more recent decision, the Supreme Court said the needs of national defense could be controlling. "To justify such a result, we believe it must be demonstrated that the proposed rates in themselves genuinely threaten the continued existence of a transportation service that is uniquely capable of filling a transcendent national defense or other public need." *Interstate Commerce Comm.* v. *New York, New Haven & Hartford R.R. Co.*, op. cit., p. 762.

territory to highway and barge competitors. It was estimated at the time of filing that of the 10.8 million tons of grain shipped annually into the Southeast, 66 percent was carried by unregulated motor carriers, 17 percent by railroads, 11 percent by unregulated barges, and 6 percent by common carrier (regulated) barges.

Southern's proposed rates were based on multiple-car shipments of 450 tons (5 cars), 900 tons (10 cars), and 1,800 tons (20 cars), subject to a minimum of 90 tons per car. To carry the traffic, the line had purchased a fleet of lightweight aluminum hopper cars capable of hauling 100 tons each (the covered hopper car was quickly dubbed "Big John"). Transit privileges were not included. Instead, all rates were for point-to-point transportation; the same service provided by motor carriers and barges. The proposed rates did not cover fully allocated costs, but Southern contended that if it could increase its grain traffic to 3 million tons a year, from the then-existing volume of 600,000 tons, it would net $2 million a year above out-of-pocket cost.

Opposition to the proposed rates came from several sources, including the Waterways Freight Bureau; the Tennessee Valley Authority; large grain merchants on the Tennessee River; the Chicago, Kansas City, St. Louis, Enid (Oklahoma), and Minneapolis boards of trade or grain exchanges; and midwestern millers. Barge operators argued that they were the low-cost carrier and that the proposed railroad rates should cover fully allocated costs. Moreover, they contended that the proposed rates did not even cover out-of-pocket cost, as claimed by Southern, because the cars would be empty on return trips, while boxcars could carry grain one way and different commodities the other. The proposed rates, they argued, would drive barges out of business on the Ohio and Tennessee Rivers. TVA, which supported the bureau, felt that the $200 million of federal money that had been used to build locks and dams on the Tennessee River would have been wasted if the barges were to lose a significant volume of business.[68] The large grain merchants insisted that their extensive facilities on the Tennessee River would become obsolete should the railroads capture a significant share of the grain traffic. These merchants, the regional boards of trade, and midwestern millers all contended that the proposed rates would hurt both the grain farmers and the millers because of the loss of transit privileges. The millers claimed, for example, that they would be put at a competitive disadvantage with southeastern mills, since the proposed rates without transit privileges would be approximately double the rate for shipping an equivalent amount of unprocessed grain.

[68] Grain constituted approximately 46 percent of the waterborne traffic on the Tennessee River. The Department of Agriculture, unlike TVA, supported the proposed rates. Moreover, the department had negotiated with the Southern to ship surplus corn in the new hopper cars at rates considerably lower than those private shippers paid. (Direct negotiations between the federal government and the carriers are permitted by Section 22 of the Interstate Commerce Act.) Others supporting the Southern included the Southern Governors' Conference, the Southeastern Association of Regulatory Utility Commissioners, the American Farm Bureau, the National Grange, and The Farmers' Union.

The Issues.   The leading question in the case was how far the railroads should be allowed to cut freight rates to gain new business. Three issues were involved: (1) What measure of cost should the commission use? The barge operators supported fully allocated cost; the railroads out-of-pocket cost. The 1958 amendment forbids the commission from prohibiting a rate cut merely "to protect the traffic of any other mode of transportation." But the National Transportation Act of 1940 prohibits "destructive" rate cutting. Thus, when do the rate cuts as encouraged by the amendment become destructive as forbidden by the act? (2) In determining the costs of water carriers, should "public costs" (e.g., public funds spent for river improvements) be considered?[69] (3) When there are competing carriers, must all rates or only those of the low-cost carrier be based upon costs (either fully allocated or out-of-pocket costs)? The issue arose because Southern's rail competitors, who were without jumbo cars, filed similar rates for multiple boxcar shipments, subject to a minimum of 50 tons per car.

The Initial Decisions.   In January, 1963, Division 2 of the commission unanimously approved Southern's rates in five-car lots (450 tons).[70] Arguing that the purpose of the proposed rates was "to meet unregulated truck competition," the three-man panel concluded that "Southern's initiative and resoucefulness in coping with substantial unregulated truck competition does not constitute a destructive competitive practice . . . merely because a third mode, claiming it does not suffer from such competition, may be affected by the loss of some traffic."[71] The panel held that "Southern's rates at the proposed minimum weight of 450 tons are compensatory on an over-all basis as returning revenue significantly in excess of out-of-pocket costs."[72] The proposed 450-ton rates of rail carriers other than Southern using conventional equipment and the proposed 900- and 1,800-ton rates of all respondent carriers were not found to be just and reasonable and were ordered canceled.[73]

With respect to the measurement of cost, Division 2 clearly stated its belief that the relevant measure is out-of-pocket cost for intermodal comparisons, where the competition is from unregulated carriers. Further, in determining the costs for water carriers, "public costs" should be included. Said the Division:

> In determining merely the reasonableness of the level of particular rates to be charged shippers by water carriers, the Commission has never considered, as a cost factor, any expenditures of public funds directed and appropriated by the Congress. Nevertheless, it is manifest that in competitive ratemaking

[69] For an analysis of this issue, see Paul H. Banner (ed.), *The Issue of Public Costs in Competitive Transportation Rate Making* (Washington, D.C.: Southern Railway System, 1966).

[70] *Grain in Multiple-Car Shipments—River Crossings to the South*, I&S Docket No. 7656 (January 21, 1963).

[71] *Ibid.*, pp. 72, 73.

[72] *Ibid.*, p. 70. The proposed rates for 450-ton shipments averaged 118 percent of out-of-pocket costs.

[73] *Ibid.*, p. 81. Southern canceled its 900- and 1,800-ton rates on May 6, 1963.

where one mode does assert the inherent advantage of low cost in performing a service, sound economics plainly require that all costs, including "public costs," which go to make up the asserted inherent advantage must, in all justice, be considered. As we understand the term "inherent," it can have no reference other than to permanent, essential, intrinsic characteristics. That an allocation of "public costs" is a factor to be considered in determining whether an inherent advantage exists is clear, and we so find.[74]

Finally, the Division held that Southern's rail competitors could not match the new rates unless new equipment was used, since

> . . . the proposed rates for movements via the other respondents in multiple hoppers and boxcars would not be compensatory. To approve, as compelled by rail competition, the 450-ton rates for the other respondents, would nullify to a large extent the Southern's great expenditures for the more efficient and economical jumbo cars and would sanction the reduction of rates not shown to be just and reasonable.[75]

Accordingly, the proposed rates on 450-ton shipments went into effect on May 11, 1963, about a month after the Supreme Court refused to extend injunctive relief beyond the seven-month suspension period authorized by the Interstate Commerce Act.[76]

Following the filing of numerous petitions for reconsideration, the full commission ordered the proceeding opened on April 12, 1963, and in an order dated July 1, 1963, the commission rejected Southern's rate reductions and required their cancellation not later than August 26, 1963.[77] The commission's majority disagreed with Division 2 that public costs should be considered in determining inherent advantage (arguing that to do so would be administratively impracticable and contrary to history, Congressional intent, and sound accounting principles), but agreed that unregulated trucking was the dominant competitive force and that out-of-pocket cost was the appropriate standard for determining inherent advantage under such circumstances. Yet, despite this latter conclusion, the majority refused to approve Southern's rates on three main grounds: (1) the rates would result in undue prejudice to Tennessee River ports, and undue preference to Ohio and Mississippi river crossings, in violation of

---

[74] *Ibid.,* p. 68. However, the Division's ultimate conclusions turned "on the aspect of the competition to be met, i.e. unregulated truck movements, rather than on the basis of who has the inherent advantage, with or without 'public cost' considered, as between the modes parties to this proceeding." *Ibid.,* p. 70.

[75] *Ibid.,* p. 80.

[76] *Arrow Transportation Co.* v. *Southern Ry. Co.,* 372 U.S. 658 (1963), *affirming* 308 F. 2d 181 (1962). Southern's proposed rates were suspended by the ICC for the seven-month statutory period (through March 9, 1962), and the effective date was further postponed by Southern, voluntarily, through August 7, 1962. The attempts to obtain a temporary restraining order delayed the application of the rates until May 11, 1963.

[77] *Grain in Multiple-Car Shipments—River Crossings to the South,* 321 ICC 582 (1963). The decision included the report of the majority of eight and three dissenting opinions by the members of Division 2.

Section 3(1) of the Interstate Commerce Act;[78] (2) unless other rail carriers having conventional equipment were permitted to adopt Southern's rates, there would be unjust discrimination against shippers not having access to the Southern; and (3) the fact that the barge lines' fully allocated cost was either lower or only slightly above rail out-of-pocket costs on some port-to-port movements indicated that they were also the low-cost carrier on an out-of-pocket cost basis on strictly barge traffic.[79]

On the basis of these considerations, Southern's proposed rates were ordered canceled without prejudice. In fact, it was suggested by the majority that reductions in grain rates of 53.5 percent or an amount approximately 16 percent higher than the level proposed by Southern would be approved upon filing. The increase was needed, it was argued, to "preserve for the barge lines the cost advantages which they enjoy with respect to certain port-to-port movements."[80]

The Court Decisions. The ICC's decision was immediately challenged in the courts by Southern. On August 21, 1963, a federal district court judge issued a temporary restraining order staying the commission's order, pending a court decision on Southern's request for a permanent injunction.[81] The court's decision was handed down on May 20, 1964.[82] In it, Judge Peck upheld Southern's proposed rates, holding that the commission's 1963 order exceeded its statutory authority and was not "supported by substantial evidence in the record."[83] Upon appeal, the Supreme Court, in January, 1965, vacated the district court's order, but remanded the case to the ICC to give the commission the opportunity to justify its original order by adequate findings.[84]

The Final Decision. On August 30, 1965, the commission, upon reconsideration, reversed its previous order and adopted the position originally taken by Division 2; that is, it found the proposed multiple-car rates on 450 tons to be reasonable, but not the rates proposed by other rail carriers based on 50 tons per car.[85] In reaching its decision, the commission held that since Southern's rates

---

78 The barge-rail rate via the Tennessee River ports would be so much higher (due to a minimum charge per ton applicable for a distance up to 346 miles) than the all-rail rate from the Mississippi and Ohio river crossings that a "virtual embargo" would be imposed on grain moving via the former route. *Ibid.*, p. 609.

79 The out-of-pocket cost of barge-rail traffic was found to be substantially above that of all-rail traffic.

80 *Ibid.*, p. 616. Commissioner Freas, in his dissenting opinion, argued that "the majority report represents, albeit in good faith, an attempt to apportion traffic among the several modes. Competition, I submit, cannot and should not be so limited. Nor should regulatory paternalism replace reasonable managerial judgment." *Ibid.*, p. 630.

81 *Cincinnati, New Orleans & Texas Pacific Ry. Co.* v. *United States*, 220 F. Supp. 46 (1963).

82 *Cincinnati, New Orleans & Texas Pacific Ry. Co.* v. *United States*, 229 F. Supp. 572 (1964).

83 *Ibid.*, p. 580.

84 *Arrow Transportation Co.* v. *Cincinnati, New Orleans & Texas Pacific Ry. Co.*, 379 U.S. 642 (1965).

85 *Grain in Multiple-Car Shipments–River Crossings to the South*, 325 ICC 752 (1965).

from the Ohio and Mississippi River crossings were designed to meet pervasive unregulated truck competition and since no similar long-haul truck competition existed from the Tennessee River ports, the rates did not result in undue prejudice to the latter ports. The commission further held that since out-of-pocket costs for all-rail movements under the proposed multiple-car rates were below barge-rail out-of-pocket costs, the rates did not constitute destructive competition against the barge-rail route. And, finally, the commission held that unless the lower rates were approved, a large quantity of grain would continue to move over the barge-truck route, due to the cost advantage of short-haul trucking of grain from the Tennessee ports. The proceeding was ordered discontinued.[86]

Some Implications. The ICC's final decision will tend to lead to more economical transportation of grain to the Southeast and to further economic development of the area.[87] It has been estimated that grain consumers in the South will save nearly $40 million a year in grain transportation charges. Southern's success, moreover, demonstrated to the industry that the new jumbo cars were feasible (thereby forcing its competitors to add this type of equipment to their car fleets) and that traffic could be profitably increased under the multiple-car rates. And Southern predicted that lower grain prices would result in a major expansion of the South's livestock industry that could add some $2 billion a year of new money in the region.[88]

At the same time, while it is undoubtedly true that "the Commission reluctantly reached a conclusion with respect to the 'Big John' rates which economists would presumably regard as sound,"[89] some major questions were

[86] Two subsequent developments should be noted. First, on September 13, 1965, the Southern Railway announced that it would absorb switching charges of other railroads, amounting to as much as $18 per carload for grain handled under the five-car rates. The announced purpose of the action was to "remove any competitive disadvantage which might result to grain shippers or receivers located on other railroads, but who are accessible to Southern through reciprocal switching arrangements, at least until the railroad serving them is able to acquire freight cars and publish rates comparable to the 'Big John' cars and rates." *Railway Age*, September 20, 1965, p. 15.

Second, in its order, the commission ordered the respondents, other than Southern, to cancel all schedules not found to be just and reasonable on or before October 22, 1965. But in October, the commission postponed cancellation of these rates to December 1, 1965, after six southeastern railroads and the Pillsbury Company (a flour and grain merchandising firm) filed petitions requesting an extension. The railroads, lacking adequate jumbo cars, feared diversion of some of their grain traffic to the Southern; the Pillsbury Company argued that the sudden cancellation of the 50-ton rates would cause severe hardship to the affected shippers and receivers of grain. *Traffic World*, October 23, 1965, p. 37.

[87] See John W. Ingram, "The Southern Railway's 'Big John' Grain Rates" (paper given before the Transportation Research Forum, 5th Annual Meeting, Chicago, December 28, 1964); and Edmund A. Nightingale, "Some Effects of Recent Changes in the Railway Grain-Rate Structure on Interregional Competition and Regional Development," in Jack R. Davidson and Howard W. Ottoson (eds.), *Transportation Problems and Policies in the Trans-Missouri West* (Lincoln: University of Nebraska Press, 1967), pp. 105–68.

[88] "ICC Approves 'Big John' Rates," *Ties*, October, 1965, p. 6.

[89] Harbeson, "Recent Trends in the Regulation of Intermodal Rate Competition . . . ," *op. cit.*, p. 324.

left unanswered. If the out-of-pocket cost standard is applicable when the dominant competitors are unregulated carriers, is it not equally applicable in the more common case where competitors are regulated carriers? Does the finding that barge lines could continue to compete successfully because of their rate advantage with respect to some segments of the grain traffic indicate that the commission retains a traffic-sharing philosophy? In not considering public costs in determining which mode had an inherent advantage, except to the extent that user fees are assessed, are nonsubsidized carriers being placed at a competitive disadvantage? How can efficiency be encouraged if it takes over four years of litigation to determine rates for new innovations? Until answers are provided, intermodal rate competition will continue to be subject to uncertain standards and innovation will be retarded.

Regulation of Other Rate Structures

Few other commissions, federal or state, have given as much attention to the regulation of rate structures as has the ICC. Wilcox argues:

> Among the many possible structures that might serve equally well to cover costs and provide investors with a fair return, they have made no effort to discover and adopt the one that would best serve the public interest. Instead, they have left the initiative in fixing particular rates to the companies, accepted the pattern of rates established, subjected it to little scrutiny, and made little effort to have it modified.[90]

This statement does not imply that rate structures have remained constant over time. On the contrary, it implies that adjustments have been made by the industries involved, but often with little investigation by the regulatory agencies. Many changes have been forced on the industries by the growth of competition. Thus, it was the competition of the nonscheduled airlines that made imperative the low-fare coach service of the domestic trunklines. It was the lessons learned from the rate policies of TVA that demonstrated to the private electric utilities the desirability of low promotional rates—rates which have led to a tremendous increase in the consumption of electricity. And it was largely the competition from other modes of transport that forced the railroads to develop more competitive rates. Only in the establishment of natural gas (both the wellhead price and pipeline rates) and telephone rates does it appear that the commissions, particularly the Federal Power Commission and the Federal Communications Commission, have actively participated in the formulation of and changes in rate structures. But even here, competition has played a role. Microwave competition, for instance, undoubtedly accelerated the introduction of new communications services and was a factor in the resulting rate structures.

In general, commissions have acted only in response to complaints or when a company has filed for a rate increase. Few investigations have been started on their own initiative. In part, this situation can be explained by the lack of funds

---

90 Wilcox, *op. cit.,* p. 355.

and of adequate staffs, as well as increasing work loads. Most of the commissions have been compelled to devote their time to the determination of the rate level, leaving little time to spend in investigating the rate structure. But even when the rate level has changed, the commissions have tended to approve across-the-board increases, thereby permitting all rates in the structure to move together and preserving the existing pattern of differentials. And in part, this situation is due to a lack of understanding of the problems involved or, when the problems are understood, to an unwillingness to reform rate structures which have been accepted by customers for many years. In some cases, the commissions do not appear to comprehend the economics of discrimination or the methods used by the regulated companies to justify discrimination. In other cases, they have been unwilling to take a step which would be politically unpopular: those whose rates were lowered would be agreeable to a reform of the rate structure; those whose rates were raised would not.

Even when they have acted, the commissions have developed no clear standards to aid in distinguishing reasonable from unreasonable discrimination. To be sure, detailed separations procedures have been worked out; such procedures represent the first step in the formulation of a rate structure. But when one turns to the second step—specific rates and rate relationships—only two broad principles are found: differences in rates should be related to differences in costs, and rates should not fall below their out-of-pocket costs. Yet, as shown above, there are numerous examples of rates which violate even these general principles.

The end result is that the type or degree of discrimination found in the rate structures of many of the regulated industries is difficult to defend on economic grounds. Caves concludes with respect to airline rates:

> The Board's rulings on issues of discrimination have touched only those forms that have come into its line of vision, and these have appeared usually because they bore some relation to the competitive marketing strategies of the carriers. It has ignored the many possible discriminations in the carriers' fare structure, such as those between coach and first-class passengers, long-haul and short-haul passengers, peak-season and off-season passengers, and so forth. Considering all of the agency's decisions on pricing, the overriding concern has been with "sound economic conditions." Regulation has been sporadic and has operated without any apparent clear-cut standards. Furthermore, the Board generally has been without the cost and demand information necessary for knowing the consequences of various pricing alternatives, and it has been without the accounting control to see that what cost information it did have could be reliably interpreted.[91]

---

[91] Richard E. Caves, *Air Transportation and Its Regulators* (Cambridge: Harvard University Press, 1962), p. 168. Also see Lucile S. Keyes, "Passenger Fare Policies of the Civil Aeronautics Board," 18 *Journal of Air Law and Commerce* 46 (1951). For a discussion of railroad rates, see James C. Nelson, *Railroad Transportation and Public Policy* (Washington, D.C.: Brookings Institution, 1959), chap. x.

And Wilcox states that most commissions

> . . . have accepted, without question, the theory of company accountants that allocates overhead in accordance with the proportionate responsibility of different customers for noncoincident demand. The commissions, moreover, have tended to favor discrimination where it has had the effect of expanding consumption and bringing about a fuller utilization of productive capacity. They have thus approved the creation of low-rate classes, the reduction of rates in successive quantity blocks, and the adoption of objective rate plans. As a result, the wide differentials established between classes, and between large and small users within these classes, have been allowed to stand. In the case of electricity, particularly, the low rates go to big business, where demand is elastic and where protection by government is not required. The high rates go to small business and to households, where demand is inelastic and where such protection is really required. The law thus fails to give to those who need it most the aid it was intended to provide.[92]

THE RATE STRUCTURE: A NEW EMPHASIS?

From the analysis contained in this and the preceding chapter, it is apparent that there is a gap between the theory and the practice of price discrimination. There are indications, however, that the gap is beginning to narrow.

Both management of the regulated industries and those responsible for regulatory policy must share responsibility for the development of the existing situation. Management frequently has failed to exercise its initiative in coming forth with new proposals. Legislatures often have not given the commissions the necessary freedom to adapt their policies to a changing economic, technological, and competitive environment. And commissions too commonly have been preoccupied with promoting "sound economic conditions," thereby hesitating to depart from traditional pricing practices and to allow experimentation. As James C. Nelson, for example, concluded in his 1959 study of railroad transportation:

> Perhaps the most serious deficiency of management has been hesitancy to engage in vigorous competitive pricing and too much dependence upon general rate increases for revenues to offset increases in wages and prices. But the railroads have not been masters of their market fates, as regulatory policy has importantly retarded or discouraged competitive rate reduction.[93]

There are several signs, however, that the situation is changing and that greater emphasis will be placed upon the design of rate structures in the future.

---

92 Wilcox, *op. cit.,* p. 356.

93 Nelson, *op. cit.,* p. 424. Also see Jervis Langdon, Jr., "The Regulation of Competitive Business Forces: The Obstacle Race in Transportation," 41 *Cornell Law Quarterly* 57 (1955); and Gregory S. Prince, "Railroads and Government Policy—A Legally Oriented Study of an Economic Crisis," 48 *Virginia Law Review* 196 (1962).

The regulated industries recently have shown less reluctance to propose cost-oriented, competitive rates; proposals accompanied by detailed economic analyses. Illustrative are the railroads' introduction of unit-train rates for coal and multiple-car rates for grain.[94] The regulatory commissions also have shown a new interest in pricing practices and objectives. Thus, the Interstate Commerce Commission, in 1962, instituted a formal investigation into cost finding principles, theories, and methods;[95] the Federal Communications Commission, in 1965, instituted a formal investigation of the American Telephone and Telegraph Company, one phase of which relates to pricing principles and rate design;[96] and the Civil Aeronautics Board, in 1966, instituted an informal study of the domestic passenger fare structure.[97] Some of the concepts and related policy issues raised by these developments are considered in the appendix to this chapter. But it should be stressed at this point that the significance of the new emphasis on rate design lies in the fact that greater efficiency in all of the regulated industries requires as prerequisites flexibility and adaptability to changing competitive conditions and to new technological opportunities.

APPENDIX: THE ROLE OF MARGINAL COST IN PRICING

The economic literature has long provided the theoretical framework of marginal cost pricing, that is, the pricing of all goods and services at marginal cost.[98] Little attention, however, has been devoted to the problem of translating abstract theory to practical application, particularly with respect to the regulated industries.[99] As previously noted, the marginal cost concept has been used in designing block rates in the electric and gas industries and in establishing a floor below which rates should not fall. But with the exposure of the regulated industries to competitive market forces and to more elastic demand conditions, marginal cost pricing principles have received increased emphasis in regulatory proceedings. It is the purpose of this appendix to discuss, first, the strict, economists' meaning of marginal cost pricing; and second, the more recent use of marginal cost in rate design.

[94] See Paul W. MacAvoy and James Sloss, *Regulation of Transport Innovation: The ICC and Unit Coal Trains to the East Coast* (New York: Random House, 1967).

[95] *Rules to Govern the Assembling and Presenting of Cost Evidence*, ICC Docket No. 34013 (1962).

[96] *In the Matter of American Telephone and Telegraph Company, Charges for Interstate and Foreign Communication Service*, FCC Docket No. 16258 (1965).

[97] Civil Aeronautics Board, *Reports to Congress, Fiscal Year 1966*, p. 13.

[98] See Nancy Ruggles, "The Welfare Basis of the Marginal Cost Pricing Principle," 17 *Review of Economic Studies* 29 (1949–50) and "Recent Developments in the Theory of Marginal Cost Pricing," 17 *ibid.* 107.

[99] The classic article is by Harold Hotelling, "The General Welfare in Relation to Problems of Taxation and of Railway and Utility Rates," 6 *Econometrica* 242 (1938). Also see William S. Vickrey, "Some Implications of Marginal Cost Pricing for Public Utilities," 45 *American Economic Review, Papers and Proceedings* 605 (1955).

Marginal Cost Pricing

The traditional objective of rate regulation is that the rates of a regulated company should cover its total costs of service, including a fair rate of return on the capital employed in the enterprise. This objective, often referred to as the "revenue-requirement" standard, assumes that the resulting rates are fair and equitable to all concerned. Put another way, the establishment of rates is the end of rate making, and both production and consumption are determined incidentally.

There is an alternative objective, known as the "consumer-rationing" standard, that involves the concept of marginal cost pricing. "Under the consumer-rationing test, rates for each kind and amount of service should be based on the cost of this particular service."[100] Rate regulation would thus be adopted as a means to an end. That end would be the achievement of the most efficient volume of production, with the efficiency criterion determined by marginal cost. The objective is to obtain a socially efficient allocation of resources.

The Theory. The importance for a competitive market of selecting the volume of production where marginal cost equals price was explained in Chapter 2. There, it was pointed out that under the equilibrium conditions of pure competition, price, which represents what consumers are willing to pay for the last unit of a good, is equal to the cost of producing that last unit (marginal cost). As a result, the consumers' valuation of the last unit and the cost of producing the last unit are equal. This equilibrium results in a socially optimum volume of output and a minimum cost of producing the volume.

If the regulated companies adopted marginal cost pricing, they would probably be forced to operate at losses.[101] These companies are subject to decreasing costs—that is, as their volume of output increases, their unit costs decrease. When a company is operating in the range of decreasing costs, average

---

[100] James C. Bonbright, "Two Partly Conflicting Standards of Reasonable Public Utility Rates," 47 *American Economic Review, Papers and Proceedings* 386, 388 (1957).

[101] Shepherd disagrees: ". . . marginal-cost pricing will *not necessarily* lead to over-all losses. In most situations, the main substance of marginal-cost pricing of individual units of service may be compatible with adequate profits for the system as a whole. If capacity growth is, generally speaking, coordinated with the growth of demand, then marginal-cost pricing in each submarket will yield adequate total revenues altogether. The main exception to this is the utility, usually with shrinking demand, whose peak-load levels of consumption do not approach capacity under any array of prices which will generate adequate total revenue. In such cases no present user is responsible for the excess capacity, and the utility itself will appropriately bear the financial burden of retiring the excess capacity. The negative profits properly accompany the capital depletion. In the opposite case, if capacity is chronically inadequate, marginal-cost pricing would of course lead to a succession of financial surpluses." William G. Shepherd, "Marginal-Cost Pricing in American Utilities," 33 *Southern Economic Journal* 58, 59-60 (1966).

FIGURE 11-8
Average Cost and Marginal Cost Pricing

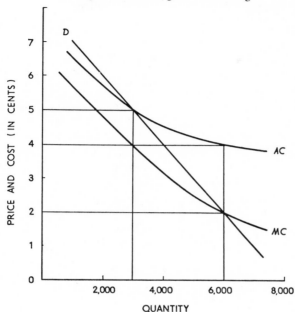

QUANTITY

costs will exceed marginal costs. Prices based on marginal costs, therefore, would mean that the output would be produced at a loss to the firm.[102]

Figure 11-8 illustrates the difference between average cost and marginal cost pricing. For simplicity, it is assumed that the firm produces only one type of service and that normal profits are included in the average cost curve. Under average cost pricing, the firm's volume of output would be 3,000 units and its price 5 cents per unit. Under marginal cost pricing, the volume of output would be expanded to 6,000 units and the price lowered to 2 cents per unit. The firm, however, would be operating at a loss equal to 2 cents per unit or a total of $120. The loss would be subsidized by the government or from other sources of revenue.

Problems of Marginal Cost Pricing.[103] The marginal cost pricing proposal—in the strict, economists' sense of price *equal* to marginal cost—raises

---

[102] It is conceivable that marginal cost pricing might lead to excess profits in a few cases. If a firm's output was expanded beyond the minimum point of its average cost curve, marginal costs would exceed average costs, and excess profits would be earned. Some have suggested that these profits should be taken from the firm through taxes.

[103] For a more complete analysis, upon which this discussion is largely based, see Bonbright, *Principles of Public Utility Rates, op. cit.*, chaps. xvii, xx; Ronald H. Coase,

many unsolved problems concerning its meaning, applicability, and desirability. The following problems are perhaps the most significant, although the list is not all-inclusive.

Short-Run versus Long-Run Marginal Costs. The term short run refers to a period of time in which some productive services are fixed in amount; most typically, the plant capacity (capital) is fixed.[104] Here, a distinction must be made between fixed or constant costs and variable costs. Only variable costs affect the calculation of short-run marginal costs, for they are the only costs which vary with changes in the rate of plant utilization. Thus, if a plant is operating at less than full capacity and fixed costs are high, short-run marginal costs will represent a small fraction of average total costs. In a long-run period of time, the capacity of a plant can be varied. All costs are variable. The long-run marginal costs, therefore, represent the increments in total costs as plants of different sizes (capacities) are put into operation. Figure 11-9 illustrates the differences between short-run and long-run marginal costs.

FIGURE 11-9
Comparison of Short-Run and Long-Run Marginal Costs*

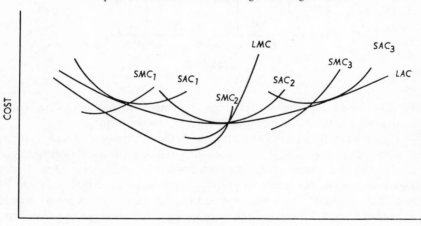

QUANTITY

*In the short run, plant capacity is fixed. For each possible size of plant, there is a corresponding short-run marginal cost curve (*SMC*). In the long run, all costs are considered to be variable. The long-run marginal cost curve (*LMC*) is determined by the long-run average cost curve (*LAC*). It is assumed that a plant could be built to any scale.

"The Marginal Cost Controversy," 13 *Economica* 169 (1946); Robert W. Harbeson, "A Critique of Marginal Cost Pricing," 31 *Land Economics* 54 (1955); Troxel, *op. cit.*, chap. xx; and William S. Vickrey, "Some Objections to Marginal-Cost Pricing," 56 *Journal of Political Economy* 218 (1948).

104 George J. Stigler, *The Theory of Price* (3d ed.; New York: The Macmillan Co., 1966), chaps. v-x.

Short-run marginal costs are extremely volatile. As the volume of output expands, for example, marginal costs change more rapidly than do average costs. This factor seriously limits the usefulness of short-run marginal costs, for rates would have to be changed frequently in accordance with variations in the volume of output. The instability of rates would impose additional burdens on the regulatory commissions, the companies, and consumers.

The Measurement of Long-Run Marginal Costs. In theory, long-run marginal costs seem more desirable for purposes of rate making. Two general problems of measurement arise, however. First, long-run marginal costs are usually indeterminate. "To compute these costs, a company or commission must know the average costs for numerous scales of production; it must have cost information about plants that are not used by the company or that even are not yet used anywhere."[105] Furthermore, total costs may not rise smoothly or continuously with increases in the volume of output. Plant indivisibilities, in other words, may be important in some instances, so that plant expansion takes place in large jumps. Thus, a gas, electric, or telephone company may install at one time adequate distribution capacity to meet estimated growth in service over the next few years in order to minimize costs and the inconveniences caused by tearing up city streets. In this situation, short-run and long-run marginal costs are discontinuous, and rates based on either would tend to be highly unstable.

Second, it is difficult to distinguish between short-run and long-run marginal costs. (1) The regulated industries often have excess or unused capacity. The capacity of a present plant, therefore, may be adequate to supply anticipated increases in demand for several years.

There would be little point, for example, in basing today's railroad passenger rates on the long-run marginal or incremental costs of passenger service if these costs were to be estimated without recognition that an increase in this service may require little or no increase in right of way or in trackage for a long time to come, if ever. For with most American railroads, partial plant redundancy is not just temporary but chronic, perhaps permanent.[106]

(2) The problem is compounded by a closely related factor. The present plant may have adequate capacity to supply anticipated increases in demand with respect to some of its component parts while having just adequate capacity with respect to other parts. A railroad company may have adequate line-haul capacity, but would require additional cars if its freight traffic increased. An electric company might have an adequate distribution network, but would need an enlargement of its generating capacity to supply additional service. (3) Marginal costs are not the same for all customer classifications currently used by the regulated industries. As explained by Troxel:

---

[105] Troxel, *op. cit.,* p. 448.
[106] Bonbright, *Principles of Public Utility Rates, op. cit.,* p. 325.

Electric companies, for example, differentiate between wholesale and retail services; regular buyers are separated from the off-peak customers; and the regular electric consumers commonly are classified into residential, commercial, industrial, street-lighting, and several lesser groups. Even though factual evidence is not available on the cost differences, the marginal costs of wholesale service probably are lower than those of most kinds of retail service because a company incurs less investment costs as the wholesale service increases. The marginal costs of residential service usually seem to be higher than those of industrial service. And off-peak service can be expanded more cheaply than any other kind of service. Realistic price control with marginal costs must be adapted to these service classifications.[107]

Here, rates for off-peak service should be determined by short-run marginal costs, since such service involves no increase in investment or demand costs. But rates for on-peak service may be determined by either short-run or long-run marginal costs.

In summary, measurements of long-run marginal costs are difficult to make, and the distinction between short-run and long-run marginal costs is not always clear.

Marginal Costs for Multiplant Firms. Another complicating problem is that most of the regulated companies have different kinds of productive plant and equipment which are not of equal efficiency. An electric company usually has several generating stations, ranging from modern units to nearly obsolete units (often used as stand-by equipment). A railroad company commonly has several kinds and sizes of freight cars. A natural gas company may be transmitting gas through old, cast-iron pipelines as well as modern, high-pressure steel pipelines. Marginal costs, therefore, will differ for a company according to the kind of equipment used. To avoid this problem, it is common to speak of the "average" marginal costs for each kind or type of service.

The Subsidy and Tax Problem. The use of the marginal cost pricing proposal would, in many cases, require federal subsidies for the regulated industries. While subsidies have frequently been used in the United States to encourage economic development (airlines, water carriers), to raise low incomes (farm programs), and to aid in the national defense program (shipbuilding), they have never been used as a regulatory device to adjust the volume of outputs to ideal levels in accordance with welfare criteria. Their use for such a purpose would require a major change in government economic policy. And there are those who believe the taxes that would be necessary to provide funds for the subsidies would result in other distortions in the economy.

Beckwith has suggested a way of lowering the needed subsidies by changing another customary pricing practice.[108] He would charge consumers directly for many items that they now pay for indirectly, such as telephone

---

107 Troxel, *op. cit.,* p. 450.

108 B. P. Beckwith, *Marginal-Cost, Price-Output Control* (New York: Columbia University Press, 1955).

directories and electric and gas connections. His proposal is to levy flat charges on consumers for these services while charging them the low marginal cost rates for individual units of service.

Required Change in Commission and Court Emphasis. The marginal cost pricing proposal is radical and would require a major shift in the emphasis and thinking of the commissions, courts, and companies. Traditional methods of regulation are difficult to change. To many, marginal cost pricing is based upon peculiar reasoning, and it is not widely understood outside of the economics profession. Even among economists there is no agreement as to the exact meaning of the concept. And the measurement problem remains unresolved. Acceptance of the marginal cost pricing proposal would require a "general upheaval in utility regulation." [109]

The Problem of Optimum Pricing. The desirability of marginal cost pricing for the regulated industries is questionable. It can be shown that unless prices are equal to marginal costs in *all* industries, an optimum allocation of resources (in the Paretian sense) cannot be achieved. [110] Since it is unlikely that marginal cost pricing will be adopted by all industries, its adoption for the regulated industries is difficult to justify. [111]

Marginal Costs as Measures of Minimum Rates

So far the discussion has assumed that all rates are to be established on the basis of marginal costs. This standard poses many perplexing problems. Another use of the marginal cost concept, however, is more familiar in rate making. Frequently, commissions have stated their refusal to allow rates to fall below out-of-pocket costs. If out-of-pocket costs are the same as marginal costs, commissions may be employing marginal costs as measures of minimum rates.

Bonbright has pointed out that the terms out-of-pocket cost and marginal cost may be only approximate synonyms as used by the commissions. In his words:

> "Out-of-pocket cost," itself an ambiguous term, is the popular partial equivalent of "marginal cost," especially in railroad parlance. But it is sometimes used to refer merely to the additional *cash* outlay imposed directly by the production of additional output, whereas "marginal cost" also includes any enhancements in noncash costs (such as depreciation due to wear and tear of equipment) attributable to an increase in rate of output. [112]

[109] Troxel, *op. cit.,* p. 463.

[110] R. G. Lipsey and R. K. Lancaster, "The General Theory of the Second Best," 24 *Review of Economic Studies* 11 (1956-57). But see E. J. Mishan, "Second Thoughts on Second Best," 14 *Oxford Economic Papers* 205 (1962).

[111] One writer, recognizing this problem, states: "To argue in favor of marginal cost pricing for telephone service can be justified on the notion that we 'ought' to move closer to marginal cost pricing in *all* industries, that we have to start somewhere, and that the telephone industry is a good place to start." Leland L. Johnson, *Communications Satellites and Telephone Rates: Problems of Government Regulation* (California: Rand Corp., 1961), p. 110. In the author's view, this is a weak justification.

[112] Bonbright, *Principles of Public Utility Rates, op. cit.,* p. 317, n. 2.

Moreover, whether minimum rates should be based upon short-run or long-run marginal costs represents an important dilemma. The argument in favor of short-run marginal costs as a basis of minimum rates is that rates should be determined by the current costs of providing the service. The aim is to increase consumption in order to make full use of the existing capacity or, when present plant capacity is inadequate to satisfy demand, to raise rates in order to limit consumption. This position,

> . . . that utility rates should approximate short-run marginal costs, at least to the maximum extent permitted by the requirement that rates in the aggregate must cover total costs, is in accord with the view that public utility rate making should accept competitive-price standards of reasonable rates and rate differentials. For, under the theories of pure or perfect competition, prices are supposed to tend to come much more quickly into accord with short-run marginal costs than into accord with long-run marginal costs.[113]

The argument in favor of long-run marginal costs as the correct measures of minimum rates is based on a conviction that a firm's rate level and rate structure should be as stable as possible. If short-run marginal costs were employed, rates would change rapidly as the volume of production increased or decreased. This change, in turn, would pose an increased burden on the regulatory commissions. Further, many argue that consumers often consider long-run, anticipated rates when deciding between substitute services (oil versus gas heating, gas versus electric ranges). Bonbright argues:

> Once these commitments have been made, the demand for utility services consequent thereon will be largely predetermined by the consumers' invest-ment in equipment and will depend only to a minor extent on any temporary changes in rates of charge. In other words, the demand for public utility services is likely to be much less elastic in the short-run than in the long-run.[114]

On balance, should minimum rates be determined by short-run or long-run marginal costs? Despite the greater difficulty of measurement, most economists would probably favor the long run.[115] In using the concept of long-run marginal costs, the added costs of providing a service (e.g., the additional operating expenses and the cost of any additional construction, including a full rate of return thereon) would be taken into account. Only when a firm has significant and continuing excess capacity (such as in off-peak periods) may short-run marginal costs be a better guide to pricing decisions.

Marginal Cost Not a Rate Determinant

Marginal costs thus play a prominent role in pricing in that they set the

---

[113] *Ibid.*, p. 332.

[114] *Ibid.*, p. 333.

[115] See William J. Baumol and Associates, "The Role of Cost in the Minimum Pricing of Railroad Services," 35 *Journal of Business of the University of Chicago* 357, 361–62 (1962).

lower boundary—the floor below which rates should not fall.[116] But they should not determine rates, for the upper boundary is set by demand conditions and regulation.[117] Since this proposition has caused considerable controversy in recent rate cases, its rationale requires brief explanation.

The Role of Fully Allocated Cost. It has been common in rate proceedings to relate the revenues received from each service with the corresponding fully allocated (or fully distributed) cost. To illustrate: In the FCC's domestic telegraph investigation, the Bell System prepared a study (known as the "Seven-Way Cost Study") in which total historic interstate costs and investment were allocated by various methods to each of seven major service categories. The study, which showed that earnings on its various services varied widely (Table 11–8), led the FCC's staff to question the propriety of the Bell System's rate structure.[118] Specifically, have services other than message toll telephone (MTT) been offered at the expense of the MTT user? Stated differently, have MTT customers been forced to subsidize the Bell System's other (competitive) offerings? If so, then the Bell System's competitors, such as Western Union, have been unfairly disadvantaged.[119]

Fully allocated cost studies, however, are of only limited usefulness. They are subject to two basic defects.[120] In the first place, since overhead costs are fixed and are not attributable to any particular traffic or consumer, any

[116] "For maximum economic efficiency, rates should be related to costs, but not to an arbitrary allocation of costs. . . . 'Cost-oriented rates' in the true economic sense are related to the economist's concept of marginal cost—the increase in total expenses as a result of carrying additional ton-miles of traffic. In order to ensure efficiency, marginal, rather than average, cost should be the principal regulatory criterion in applications for rate reductions. . . . [W]here competition and new technology dictate rate reductions, competitive rates could be lowered to the level of marginal cost." *Annual Report of the Council of Economic Advisers* in *Economic Report of the President* (Washington, D.C.: U.S. Government Printing Office, 1966), p. 127.

[117] Baumol and Associates, *op. cit.,* p. 362. Also see John J. Coyle, "Dissimilar Pricing: A Logical Approach to Regulated Rates," 78 *Public Utilities Fortnightly* 32 (September 15, 1966); James C. Nelson, "Economic Standards for Competitive Freight Rates," 48 *Journal of Farm Economics* 1408 (1966); Irwin M. Stelzer, "Incremental Costs and Utility Rate-Making in the Competitive Era" (American Bar Association Annual Report, Section of *Public Utility Law, 1967*), pp. 26–42; and Haskell P. Wald, "The Theory of Marginal Cost Pricing and Utility Rates," 79 *Public Utilities Fortnightly* 15 (June 22, 1967).

[118] "The 7-Way Cost Study . . . tends to confirm the long standing complaint of Western Union that Bell underprices those record services which are competitive with the Western Union services. Accordingly a formal investigation should be instituted promptly by the Commission into the lawfulness of current rate structures and rate levels of the Bell System applicable to its interstate services." *Report of the Common Carrier Bureau of the Federal Communications Commission in the Domestic Telegraph Investigation,* FCC Docket No. 14650 (October 25, 1965), p. 364.

[119] There are many other examples of rates below fully allocated costs. For example, railroads frequently offer freight rates at less than fully allocated costs over competitive routes and electric utilities offer space-heating rates at less than fully allocated costs.

[120] For an analysis of the Seven-Way Cost Study, see testimony of James C. Bonbright in the domestic telegraph investigation (FCC Docket No. 14650), reprinted in *Bell Telephone Magazine* (Winter, 1965–66), pp. 19–23, 45–51.

TABLE 11-8
A.T.&T.'s Earnings on Seven Categories of Interstate Communication Services

Service	Earnings during Busy Hour	Earnings for Total Day
Message toll telephone	9.7%	10.0%
Teletypewriter exchange service	3.4	2.9
Wide area telephone service	13.4	10.2
Telephone grade private line service	4.7	4.7
Telegraph grade private line service	1.4	1.4
TELPAK	.3	.3
All other (including radio and television)	.9	.9
Total	7.5%	7.5%

Source: *Report of the Common Carrier Bureau of the Federal Communications Commission in the Domestic Telegraph Investigation,* FCC Docket No. 14650 (October 25, 1965), Tables 6-3 and 6-4.

allocation of such costs is largely arbitrary. Any formulas for allocating common or joint costs "are insensitive to market factors and to differential cost behavior with changes in the output of different classes of service. They usually express little more than someone's intuitive notions about elementary fairness in cost sharing."[121] In the second place, fully allocated cost studies cannot be used for pricing decisions. By ignoring differences in demand elasticities, such studies do not provide a basis for deciding whether rates should be raised or lowered. As shown in Chapter 2, if a company can supply a service that is priced to cover its associated long-run marginal cost (including a portion of the common plant costs), then the rates on its other services can be lowered, since the common plant costs to be borne by other customers are reduced.[122]

121 Wald, *op. cit.,* p. 20.
122 For similar reasons, fully allocated cost has no validity as a measure of the "low-cost carrier" in Section 15a(3) cases. The low-cost carrier is properly identified by marginal cost. Concludes a recent study:

". . . Imposing a different and higher *cost* standard deprives railroads of traffic which they can transport more economically, artificially stimulates the growth of uneconomic transportation by other means including private transportation, deprives the shipping public of the benefits of low-cost service, and imposes higher commodity prices on the consuming public. However computed, the use of fully distributed costs would be wasteful of economic resources by misdirecting their use and by keeping them idle or underutilized.

"In addition to its inherent defect, this specious 'cost' proposal has another deficiency. To whatever extent carriers which operate on public facilities may not have to meet full economic costs in conducting their business, their 'fully distributed costs' are not consistent with those computed for the railroads. For the railroads a fully distributed cost computation embraces the entire costs. The effect of the use of the 'full cost of the low-cost carrier' doctrine is to obstruct the railroads in pricing their services in competition with other modes to the extent that they may be subsidized. Thus, this proposal constitutes umbrella rate-making to protect any subsidized modes of transportation from legitimate competition by the railroads." Baumol and Associates, *op. cit.,* p. 365.

Major Criticisms of Marginal Costing. Many recognize the need to take both cost and demand factors into account in rate making, but some significant objections have been raised to the use of marginal costs in transport and utility rate design.[123] Five criticisms deserve particular mention.

"Marginal costs are not all-inclusive." It has been argued that marginal costs are not all-inclusive; that the approach fails to take into account all of the costs associated with a new service offering. This charge is correct with respect to the concept of short-run marginal cost,[124] but the long-run concept is open to no such criticism. As defined above, long-run marginal cost (sometimes referred to as "total incremental cost") includes the out-of-pocket expenses of the added service, the portion of the common plant required by that service expansion, the required return thereon, a portion of any increase in overhead expenses which may result from the service expansion, and a portion of the investment required to meet the company's future growth. The concept, then, is all-inclusive.

"Customers make different contributions to overhead costs, resulting in undue discrimination." It has been argued that undue discrimination results when one customer class makes a greater contribution to the overhead costs of the supplier than another.[125] Differentiated rates, however, can benefit all customers, as noted earlier, as long as the new service makes a contribution to the common plant costs.[126] Traffic which is not moved or services which are not offered "cannot possibly help to bear the unallocable costs."[127]

"Marginal costing is inappropriate, absent subsidies." It has been argued that marginal costing is inappropriate, absent subsidies, because of the existence of decreasing costs. This criticism is valid with respect to strict marginal cost pricing, but it is invalid with respect to the long-run marginal cost concept. As long as rates are set with long-run marginal costs as a *floor*, with rates above this floor determined by market forces, no subsidies are required. No service will be

---

123 It should be noted again that there is a distinct difference between costing and pricing. The cost criteria being considered are for use in rate design; appropriate rates, however, cannot be determined from cost data alone.

124 See Roy J. Sampson, "The Case for Full Cost Ratemaking," 33 *I.C.C. Practitioners' Journal* 490, 493-94 (1966).

125 ". . . shippers having an inelastic demand for transport are taxed to subsidize services that fail to cover fully-distributed costs. Such a policy of taxation is arbitrary and inequitable because it is based merely on the carriers' ability to impose the contributions." Joseph R. Rose, "Regulation of Rates and Intermodal Transport Competition," 33 *I.C.C. Practitioners' Journal* 11, 24 (1965).

126 This criticism, however, has led some to advocate prescribing rates based on marginal costs plus a uniform increment "calculated to cover overhead costs, if possible." *Ibid.*, p. 25. Despite the apparent advantages of this approach, "this method of adjusting rates is open to serious objections. It precludes any competition between the different modes of transport. The high-cost carrier is completely excluded from the market unless service advantages give it some of the traffic. . . . Another weakness in this solution of the rate problem is that determination of the 'fixed' amount to be added to direct or out-of-pocket costs is arbitrary, like any apportionment of fixed costs on the basis of averages." Locklin, *op. cit.*, p. 861.

127 Baumol and Associates, *op. cit.*, p. 364.

burdening another, moreover, since no service will be offered at less than the long-run marginal cost associated with it.

"Long-run marginal costs cannot be determined." It has been argued that long-run marginal costs cannot be accurately determined. To be sure, such costs must be estimated, as must demand elasticities. Nevertheless, as Stelzer has pointed out,

> . . . it is surely unreasonable to favor an arbitrary measure of cost over an inexact measure; and it is even more unreasonable to assume (albeit implicitly) that demand has zero elasticity simply because one cannot determine precisely how great the elasticity is. Because we cannot see the future clearly does not mean we should shut our eyes to it. [128]

"Discriminatory pricing tends to promote a misallocation of resources." It has been argued, finally, that price discrimination tends to promote a misallocation of resources. Contends Rose:

> It may allocate excessive resources to inefficient producers (shippers) whose demand for transport happens to be elastic, and inadequate resources to efficient ones, whose demand for transport happens to be inelastic. Similarly, rate discrimination may favor geographical areas having comparative economic disadvantages as against others having comparative economic advantages. Because transport is an essential element in the process of production generally, rate discrimination is bound to have a widespread influence in effecting an inefficient allocation of resources on a large scale. [129]

Certainly there are circumstances under which price discrimination may result in a misallocation of resources and it is one task of regulation to prevent unlimited discrimination. What is being claimed by those favoring the long-run marginal cost concept is that differential pricing "is consistent with the public interest in the economical utilization of resources." [130] But discrimination must not be used indiscriminately.

Conclusions

Marginal cost pricing (e.g., all rates equal to marginal cost) would require the provision of subsidies for most of the regulated industries and has received little regulatory attention in the United States. [131] The idea that no rate should

---

[128] Irwin M. Stelzer, "Pricing in Regulated Industries: A Not-So-Marginal Problem," in Joseph E. Haring (ed.), *The New Economics of Regulated Industries: Rate-Making in a Dynamic Economy* (Los Angeles: Economics Research Center, Occidental College, 1968), p. 133.

[129] Rose, *op. cit.,* pp. 24-25.

[130] Baumol and Associates, *op. cit.,* p. 363. "The value of the marginal cost pricing guide is, first of all, in its usefulness as a point of departure for decisions on rate differentiation by class of service." Wald, *op. cit.,* p. 21.

[131] The marginal cost pricing principle has been more widely employed in France and England. For several years, the Electricité de France, a public electric power system, has used the principle as a basis of setting rates and for investment policy. See Thomas

fall below marginal cost, however, has been widely employed by most commissions for many years. What is relatively recent is the use of the long-run marginal cost concept in establishing promotional rates and rates for new services, as well as in determining permissible rate reductions. And, while several criticisms have been levied against this latter use of the concept, its use seems certain to increase as greater effort is expended on cost and demand analyses.[132]

The marginal cost approach "will not simplify rate making nor will it convert rate making from an art to a mathematical science."[133] But whatever the eventual outcome, the current controversy over the concept serves an important function—namely, to remind all concerned with regulatory problems that there is more than one possible objective or goal of rate making. Current practices must be constantly subjected to careful scrutiny to make sure they are efficient and serving the purpose for which they were intended. Complacency can quickly lead to static and archaic regulation.

Marschak, "Capital Budgeting and Pricing in the French Nationalized Industries," 33 *Journal of Business of the University of Chicago* 133 (1960); James R. Nelson, "Practical Applications of Marginal Cost Pricing in the Public Utility Field," 53 *American Economic Review* 474 (1963); Ronald L. Meek, "An Application of Marginal Cost Pricing: The 'Green Tariff' in Theory and Practice," Part I, "The Theory," 11 *Journal of Industrial Economics* 217 (1963), Part II, "The Practice," 12 *ibid.* 45 (1963); Marcel Boiteux, "The Green Tariff of the Electricité de France," as translated by Eli W. Clemens and Lucienne C. Clemens, 40 *Land Economics* 185 (1964); Eli W. Clemens, "Marginal Cost Pricing: A Comparison of French and American Industrial Power Rates," 40 *Land Economics* 389 (1964); and James R. Nelson (ed.), *Marginal Cost Pricing in Practice* (Englewood Cliffs: Prentice-Hall, Inc., 1964). The French National Railroads have also attempted to base freight rates on marginal costs. See L. Lacoste, "The Role of Cost and Demand in Pricing of Transport Service" (paper before the Transportation Research Forum, Chicago, December 28, 1964). In England, a new Bulk Supply Tariff, based on the marginal cost pricing concept, was put into use starting in 1967. See Wald, *op. cit.*, pp. 23–24.

[132] See, for example, James R. Nelson, "Practical Applications of Marginal Cost Pricing . . . ," *op. cit.;* Stanislaw H. Wellisz, "Regulation of Natural Gas Pipeline Companies: An Economic Analysis," 71 *Journal of Political Economy* 30 (1963); Charles W. Meyer, "Marginal-Cost Pricing for Local Telephone Service," 42 *Land Economics* 378 (1966); James C. Nelson, "Economic Standards for Competitive Freight Rates," *op. cit.;* William G. Shepherd, "Marginal Cost Pricing: First Steps in American Electric and Telephone Rates," 78 *Public Utilities Fortnightly* 15 (July 21, 1966); and L. C. Rosenberg, "Natural-Gas-Pipeline Rate Regulation: Marginal-Cost Pricing and the Zone-Allocation Problem," 75 *Journal of Political Economy* 159 (1967).

[133] Wald, *op. cit.*, p. 24.

Chapter 12 SERVICE AND SAFETY

Whenever the commission, after a hearing after reasonable notice had upon its own motion or upon complaint, finds that the service of any public utility is unreasonable, unsafe, inadequate, insufficient or unreasonably discriminatory, the commission shall determine the reasonable, safe, adequate, sufficient service to be observed, furnished, enforced or employed and shall fix the same by its order, rule or regulation.
                                    —Uniform Public Utilities Act*

The second primary duty of the regulatory commissions involves service and safety regulation. This aspect of regulation is extremely important, because there is no such thing as a reasonable rate for service that is deficient. There is also the possibility, due to limitations on price competition, that service competition might become wasteful or discriminatory. It will be remembered that common callings were required by the common law to render adequate and safe service without undue or unjust discrimination. Most of the common law obligations have been incorporated within state and federal legislation dealing with the regulated industries.

The legislative standards and commission decisions relating to the quality and quantity of service, as well as to safety, will be discussed in this chapter. One word of caution: the importance of this phase of regulation should not be minimized simply because it is covered in a single chapter. Service and safety regulation can be discussed in such a manner because far fewer problems are raised by this aspect of regulation than by rate regulation. With but few exceptions, the regulated industries have maintained high service and safety standards, thereby necessitating little commission attention. The most serious problems have concerned the restriction of entry into the transportation industries, the discontinuance of railroad passenger service, and air and highway safety.

*National Conference of Commissioners on Uniform State Laws, Uniform Public Utilities Act, Sec. 11 (1928).

400

RELATION OF SERVICE AND SAFETY TO RATES

There is a relation—perhaps an obvious one—between the quality and quantity of service, safety, and rates charged consumers. In many cases, an increase in service or safety results in a rise of a company's costs, and higher rates must be charged. Such is the case with the frequency of transportation service or of electric and gas meter tests.[1] A regulated company also may be required to extend service to a small rural area that cannot afford to pay the full cost, thereby resulting in subsidization from service users in larger areas. The type of equipment which a company uses is directly related to the cost of providing the service. And higher safety standards will usually result in higher costs, such as in the airline industry where the cost of equipping every airport with radar would run into millions of dollars.

The regulatory commissions cannot ignore this relation between service, safety, and rates. More importantly, their policies regarding rate regulation will directly affect the quality and quantity of service a company will offer. Take, for instance, the depreciation problem. If a company is permitted to accrue adequate depreciation or to amortize the unrecovered depreciation on its equipment when more modern or higher quality equipment is installed, technological improvements will be encouraged. If, however, a company is not allowed adequate depreciation rates on equipment actually in use, it may not install new equipment until the old is fully depreciated.[2] In short, commission policies have important affects on the quantity and quality of service a regulated company will offer.

Thompson and Smith have pointed out that some types of services bear little relation to rates:

> It should cost but little to train employees to be courteous or to require the meter reader to clean his shoes before crossing the customer's threshold. In general, however, there is some connection between the quality of service and rates. And it goes without dispute that no higher quality or quantity can be demanded of a utility than the users are willing to pay for, assuming the usual economy of management.[3]

Not only is there a relationship between service, safety, and rates, but there exists the possibility that service competition might become undesirable. Assume that two railroads are competing for freight traffic between the same two points. Each must charge the same rate. One line, however, might compete for new business by increasing the services offered: faster delivery, better equipment, more salesmen, transit privileges, additional terminals or warehouses, or more frequent service. If successful, the other line might try or be forced to

---

[1] Cost increases may be partially offset by fuller utilization of plant and equipment or smaller maintenance expenditures.

[2] See Chapter 7, pp. 198–99.

[3] C. Woody Thompson and Wendell R. Smith, *Public Utility Economics* (New York: McGraw-Hill Book Co., Inc., 1941), p. 430.

compete on the same basis. Both would probably find their costs increasing, and unless higher rates were permitted by the commissions, their net revenues would decline. Conceivably, this situation could continue for a long period of time or until one of the lines went bankrupt. Such excessive service competition is parallel to that of destructive price competition. Moreover, the incentives also are similar: under conditions of decreasing costs, an increase in plant utilization will result in lower average total costs. Such an increase can come about as the result of either price reductions or service improvements.[4]

There are numerous examples of competition leading to the provision of duplicating and unprofitable services. Summarizes Locklin:

> . . . pooling agreements have been made by competing railroads in certain instances to reduce wasteful services that had been brought about by competition. Competition in service has often led to wasteful capital expenditures through the construction of duplicating facilities. . . . In 1926 the Baltimore & Ohio and the Reading railroads jointly opened a produce terminal in Philadelphia costing approximately $3,100,000. Not to be outdone, the Pennsylvania Railroad opened a competing terminal, which cost about $6,500,000. Both were used at less than half their capacity, and either alone would have been adequate for the needs of the city. In Buffalo, the Erie and Nickel Plate railroads engaged in a contest with the New York Central to provide terminals. The former spent about $6,700,000 and the New York Central about $2,700,000 in providing rival facilities. Competition between railroads at New York and other ports also resulted in the furnishing of warehousing service by carriers for shippers at nominal charges, which resulted in large losses to the railroads and constituted a drain upon their resources. Competition in service has resulted in the payment by railroads of allowances to industry-owned railroads for switching and spotting services performed by the industry-controlled roads.[5]

Service competition also might become discriminatory. According to Welch:

> Clearly, no utility can refuse service to any customer, otherwise qualified, because of race, color, creed, or political considerations. It can, however, refuse demands for free service or service to persons outside of the service area, or to those who refuse to comply with regulations governing special charges that cover the extra expense of furnishing special or unusual service demands. It can also refuse to serve persons who abuse or forfeit their right to service. . . .[6]

---

[4] Price reductions and service improvements are not perfect substitutes in every situation.

[5] D. Philip Locklin, *Economics of Transportation* (6th ed.; Homewood, Ill.: Richard D. Irwin, Inc., 1966), p. 308 (citations omitted).

[6] Francis X. Welch, *Cases and Text on Public Utility Regulation* (rev. ed.; Washington, D.C.: Public Utilities Reports, Inc., 1968), p. 177. Service may be refused a customer when (1) used for unlawful purposes (bookmaking); (2) the customer refuses to pay for service used; (3) service regulations are violated or service facilities are destroyed; or (4) the company is unable to supply the service "due to circumstances beyond its control." For a complete discussion of these points, see *ibid.*, chap. iv.

Thus, in 1966, the Civil Aeronautics Board's Bureau of Enforcement filed formal complaints against nine domestic airlines, alleging that their special airport lounges ("clubs") constitute "unjust discrimination" because they provide "special and superior services" to selected passengers, while denying such services to other passengers who have paid the same fares.[7]

LEGISLATIVE PROVISIONS

The legislative provisions dealing with service and safety requirements are broad. The Utah public utility law, for example, contains the following provisions:

Whenever the commission shall find after a hearing, that the rules, regulations, practices, equipment, appliances, facilities, or service of any public utility, or the methods of manufacture, distribution, transmission, storage or supply employed by it, are unjust, unreasonable, unsafe, improper, inadequate or insufficient, the commission shall determine the just, reasonable, safe, proper, adequate or sufficient rules, regulations, practices, equipment, appliances, facilities, service or methods to be observed, furnished, constructed, enforced or employed, and shall fix the same by its order, rule, or regulation. The commission, after a hearing, shall prescribe rules and regulations for the performance of any service or the furnishing of any commodity of the character furnished or supplied by any public utility, and on proper demand and tender of rates such public utility shall furnish such commodity or render such service within the time and upon the conditions provided in such rules.[8]

The application of these provisions has been left to the commissions, subject to judicial review. In general, the commissions act only in response to consumer complaints, although a few of the larger commissions have staff members who make systematic inspections and tests to insure adherence to the required standards. Most of the legislative provisions applicable to the transportation industries outline more detailed service and safety standards. These provisions will receive emphasis in the following sections.

QUALITY OF SERVICE

While the regulatory commissions have the power to prescribe and enforce reasonable standards of service, they usually have found it unnecessary to do so. Perhaps, argues Wilcox, this is fortunate:

The danger of prescribing service standards is that technology will be frozen, progress impeded, and managerial initiative impaired. This is a danger that the utility commissions have been able to avoid. In practice, little has

[7] *Time*, July 15, 1966, p. 72. See, for example, *Northwest Airlines, Inc.*, E-24490 (CAB, 1966).
[8] *Public Utility Laws*, state of Utah, issued by Public Service Commission, 1953, p. 56.

been done in the way of developing and enforcing standards of quality. The utilities take the initiative; the commissions intervening only on complaint. On the whole the results appear to be good. With most utilities the quality of service is high.[9]

The quality aspects of service include the following: methods of billing, accuracy of meters, continuity of service, voltage and frequency requirements, deposits and repayments, quality of equipment, treatment of complaints, courtesy to customers, and health standards. With respect to electric and gas utilities, for instance, the New York commission:

(1) ". . . allows use of only those types of meters which have been found to be operating satisfactorily,"
(2) requires the companies "to remove meters from customer premises for inspection and tests at specified intervals,"
(3) requires "gas and electric utilities to provide approved meter testing stations and then makes periodic tests of the meter-proving equipment to make certain that its high standards of accuracy are maintained at all times,"
(4) maintains laboratories "where tests and inspections are made to insure adherence to proper standards," and
(5) maintains a field staff to check on such matters as voltage levels, the heating value of gas, gas pressures, service interruptions, and load growth.[10]

The American Telephone and Telegraph Company has developed an elaborate and detailed system to aid in judging the quality of its telephone service. To illustrate: A performance rating plan has been set up against which to measure monthly each company, department, division, district, and office or unit. The performance measures include: (1) toll and assistance service—speed of answer, wrong number or party, interruptions, time and charges, and courtesy; (2) installation and maintenance service—ability to provide service desired at time desired, keeping appointment dates, and occurrence of troubles; (3) billing service—speed of issuing bills and correctness of charges; (4) business office—speed of attention, correctness and completeness of information given and recorded; and (5) customer opinion—surveys conducted by both the company and outside agencies to determine how the public views the company's performance. The results are tabulated and distributed throughout the organization. Figure 12–1 illustrates the performance rating system.

Service Standards for Railroads

More detailed standards have been prescribed for the transportation

---

[9] Clair Wilcox, *Public Policies Toward Business* (3d ed.; Homewood, Ill.: Richard D. Irwin, Inc., 1966), pp. 296–97.

[10] "The Public Service Commission and . . . You," State of New York, issued by The Public Service Commission, 1967, pp. 8–10. A customer always has the right to request a meter inspection on payment of a fee ranging from 75 cents to $1.50 for a residential user. The fee is returned if a meter is found faulty.

FIGURE 12-1
American Telephone and Telegraph Company: Illustrative Performance Rating System

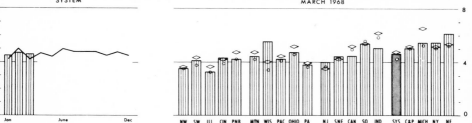

Source: American Telephone and Telegraph Company.

industries, particularly in the case of railroads. The Interstate Commerce Commission has been given authority over such matters as car supply and car service, demurrage, interchange of facilities, establishment of through routes and joint rates, construction of switching connections, transit privileges, and joint use of terminals. Three of these service standards will be discussed in order to illustrate their meaning and importance.[11]

Freight Car Supply. The commission has long held that a railroad must "provide reasonably adequate and suitable equipment for all of the traffic it holds itself out to transport."[12] The railroads need not own the cars they provide. The ICC has the power to require owners of freight cars to permit their use by other carriers, although most railroads have arrangements with each other to supply cars when needed. Frequently, however, the railroads have been unable to furnish shippers with cars when they are wanted. Freight cars may be in short supply during periods of peak traffic (such as movement of the annual grain harvest) or when a shipper requires special types of equipment. When a shortage occurs, shippers may suffer tremendous losses due to their inability to move freight to factories or markets on schedule.[13]

In cases where shortages are caused by shippers' requirements for special types of equipment, the commission has held that railroads must provide the equipment if there is a sufficient amount of traffic to justify the expense involved. For example, carriers must provide refrigerator cars for perishable products and grain doors for cars in which grain is shipped in bulk, but they are

[11] For a more detailed treatment of these topics, see Truman C. Bigham and Merrill J. Roberts, *Transportation* (2d ed.; New York: McGraw-Hill Book Co., Inc., 1952), chap. xviii; and Locklin, *op. cit.,* chap. xxvi.

[12] *Switching at St. Louis and East St. Louis,* 120 ICC 216, 221-22 (1926).

[13] See "Transport Pinch," *The Wall Street Journal,* June 1, 1965, pp. 1, 16; and "Car Supply," *Railway Age,* April 29, 1968, pp. 36-42, 76-78.

not obligated to provide tank cars for oil shipments, cars of uncommon length, or live-poultry cars.[14]

The most serious problem has involved the inadequacy of the freight car supply. In 1962, a Senate subcommittee concluded that the "national ownership of serviceable freight cars has declined to a perilously low level" over the past generation.[15] Statistically, the number of freight cars owned or leased by Class I railroads decreased from 2,427,026 in 1926 to 1,515,139 in 1963.[16] Since 1964, the number of freight cars in service has risen, totaling 1,592,270 in August of 1967.[17] There also have been significant increases in average freight car capacity and improved utilization. Yet, despite these "impressive advances, freight car shortages in calendar 1966 were the worst experienced since World War II."[18]

In view of the existing freight car shortage, it is essential that the current supply of cars is utilized efficiently.[19] Toward this end (*a*) per diem charges are paid for the use of cars not on the owning railroads, (*b*) demurrage charges are levied against shippers detaining cars beyond an established period, and (*c*) car-service orders are issued by the commission to meet specific situations.

Per Diem Charge. The ICC has the authority to determine the "reasonable compensation" (known as the per diem charge) which loaning railroads may receive for their freight cars. First established in 1902 at 20 cents per car, the per diem charge had increased to $2.88 per car by 1959. Some argued, however, that the latter charge was too low to cover the costs of ownership and to provide a reasonable profit, with the result that it was often cheaper for a railroad to rent than to buy cars. On January 1, 1964, the industry introduced a multilevel rate structure, ranging from $2.16 per day for cars worth (depreciated original cost) $1,000 and less to $7.74 for cars worth over $20,000. The scale was modified in 1965, with respect to the more expensive cars, with the upper rate becoming

[14] *Baker* v. *Boston & Maine R.R. Co.,* 65 Atl. 386 (1906); *Chicago Board of Trade* v. *Abilene & Southern Ry. Co.,* 220 ICC 753 (1937); *Chicago, Rock Island & Pacific Ry. Co.* v. *Lawton Refining Co.,* 253 Fed. 705 (1918); *National Supply Co.* v. *Cleveland, Cincinnati, Chicago & St. Louis Ry. Co.,* 140 ICC 66 (1928); *In the Matter of Private Cars,* 50 ICC 652 (1918).

[15] *Freight Car Shortage* (Hearings before the Freight Car Shortage Subcommittee of the Committee on Commerce, Senate, 87th Cong., 1st sess.) (Washington, D.C.: U.S. Government Printing Office, 1962), p. 65.

[16] *National Freight Car Supply* (Senate Report No. 1192, 88th Cong., 2d sess.) (1964), p. 7. In 1964, the ICC estimated that the railroads needed 36,000 more boxcars and 19,000 more gondola cars to meet the existing traffic demands. See *Investigation of Adequacy of Freight Car Ownership,* 323 ICC 48, 52 (1964).

[17] Association of American Railroads, "Facts on Freight Car Supply" (August, 1967), p. 1.

[18] Interstate Commerce Commission, *Eighty-First Annual Report* (1967), p. 84.

[19] In 1959, it was estimated that improved freight car utilization would result in annual savings of almost 112.3 million car-days; a savings equivalent to adding 307,749 cars to the freight car fleet, thereby providing nearly 133,000 additional loadings weekly. James C. Nelson, *Railroad Transportation and Public Policy* (Washington, D.C.: Brookings Institution, 1959), p. 271. Some indication that utilization has improved is the fact that between 1962 and 1966, Class I railroads increased "their revenue ton-miles by 25 percent while carloadings gained just 3.1 percent." Interstate Commerce Commission, *Eighty-First Annual Report, op. cit.,* p. 84.

$12.18.[20] Then, in 1968, the commission (for the first time in its history) ordered the existing rates canceled and established new rates based on both the number of days a car is held and the amount of usage (measured by the number of line-haul miles over which a car moves). Under the new schedule, the per diem charge ranges from 63 cents per day for cars more than thirty years old and costing less than $1,000 to $10.22 per day for cars less than five years old and costing more than $39,000. In addition, mileage charges range from 1.4 cents a mile for the least expensive cars to 4.6 cents a mile for the most expensive.[21]

Several years ago, the commission attempted to impose a penalty per diem charge to encourage deficit railroads to buy a sufficient number of cars for their own loading requirements. A district court, in 1947, ruled that imposition of a penalty charge exceeded the commission's statutory power and that it was "so completely unrelated to the evil sought to be remedied . . . that serious question would arise as to its validity as a regulation."[22] The commission then turned to Congress and, in 1966, was granted authorization to establish incentive per diem rates.[23] But a year later, after an investigation, the commission decided against the imposition of an interim incentive charge, arguing "that there is not available at this time reliable factual data which would enable this Commission to comply with the statutory requirements and make a valid decision. . . ."[24]

Demurrage. The railroads have long granted shippers a period of "free time"—commonly 48 hours except for export traffic at ports where the free time usually is seven days—in which to load and unload freight cars. A demurrage charge is made if a shipper holds a car longer than this free period. In July, 1964, these charges became $5.00 per car per day for the first four days, $10 per car per day for the next four days, and $15 per car for each additional day.[25] The purposes of such charges are to compensate carriers for cars held out of use and to encourage shippers to load and unload promptly. Many believe, however, that demurrage charges are too low to serve their intended purposes, in view of the fact that they are generally below the daily revenues per car that could be earned in carrying traffic.[26]

---

[20] See *Chicago, Burlington & Quincy R. Co.* v. *New York, Susquehanna & Western R. Co.*, 332 ICC 176, 184-85 (1968).

[21] *The Wall Street Journal,* January 31, 1968, p. 4. The new rates became effective August 1, 1969.

[22] *Palmer* v. *United States,* 75 F. Supp. 63, 68 (1947).

[23] Public Law 89-430 (1966), amending Section 1(14)(a) of the Interstate Commerce Act.

[24] *Incentive Per Diem Charges,* 332 ICC 11, 18 (1967).

[25] A few states have enacted "reciprocal demurrage" laws, under which penalties are imposed upon railroads for failure either to furnish cars or to move them promptly when loaded. Such laws "have not proved satisfactory. It seems unfair to penalize a carrier for inability to furnish equipment when a shortage of equipment is brought about by an unusual and unanticipated volume of business or by other circumstances beyond the carrier's control." Locklin, *op. cit.*, p. 566.

[26] "Under earlier monopoly conditions, the effects on carriers were not burdensome so long as freight rates as a whole were adjusted to cover all costs, including car detention cost. But under present highly competitive conditions, rail service as a whole is adversely affected by excessive shipper detention compared with truck service. The resulting car shortages tend to drive traffic to other agencies." Nelson, *op. cit.,* p. 270.

Car-Service Orders. The commission is authorized to issue car-service orders to deal with specific situations. Such orders have frequently been issued to relieve car shortages. To illustrate: In October, 1964, to ease a post-harvest shortage, several eastern railroads were ordered to deliver a specified number of boxcars to western lines;[27] in March, 1966, to ease a daily shortage estimated at 13,000 boxcars, railroads were ordered to return (empty if necessary) all boxcars owned by the Great Northern Railway and Northern Pacific Railway within forty-eight hours of unloading, to reduce free time for unloading at ports to five days, and to increase the per diem charge to $10 per day for the first four days of detention beyond the free time.[28]

Interchange of Facilities and of Traffic. Two closely related powers of the commission provide for the interchange of facilities with other carriers and for the establishment of through routes and joint rates. Section 3 of the Interstate Commerce Act requires the carriers to "afford all reasonable, proper, and equal facilities for the interchange of traffic between their respective lines." In a number of cases, the commission has required a railroad to construct track connections with other lines in order to facilitate the interchange of freight. Some requests have been denied, however, in cases where the volume of traffic to be interchanged did not warrant the expense involved or where the interchange of traffic would divert traffic from one railroad to another.[29] The interchange of facilities lowers the cost of freight transport, since through freight does not need to be unloaded and reloaded at points of interchange.

The meaning of and distinction between through routes and joint rates have been stated as follows:

> As defined by the United States Supreme Court, a through route is "an arrangement, express or implied, between connecting railroads for the continuous carriage of goods from the originating point on the line of one carrier to destination on the line of another." If there is a through route, there is a through rate. This may be a combination rate, that is, the sum of separate rates fixed by the several carriers forming the through route, or it may be a joint rate. A "joint rate" is a single through rate from the point of origin to destination, usually less than the sum of the local rates established by the connecting carriers. Thus there may be through routes with or without joint rates. The power of the Commission extends both to the creation of through routes and to the establishment of joint rates to go with them.[30]

---

[27]*The Wall Street Journal,* October 26, 1964, p. 6.

[28]*Ibid.,* March 16, 1966, p. 5.

[29]*Commercial Club of Faulkton, S. Dak.* v. *Chicago, Milwaukee, St. Paul & Pacific R.R. Co.,* 157 ICC 350 (1929); *Wisconsin Power & Light Co.* v. *Chicago & North Western Ry. Co.,* 220 ICC 475 (1937); *Hilliard Co.* v. *Great Northern Ry. Co.,* 190 ICC 201 (1932); *Chamber of Commerce of Sapulpa, Okla.* v. *St. Louis-San Francisco Ry. Co.,* 181 ICC 457 (1932). The commission's authority does not extend to the construction of sidings and spurs.

[30]Locklin, *op. cit.,* p. 573. The Supreme Court citation is *St. Louis-Southwestern Ry. Co.* v. *United States,* 245 U.S. 136, 139, n. 2 (1917).

Through routes and joint rates may be established between like carriers and between different modes of transport. The commission has authority to *require* their establishment between like common carriers in the rail, water, and motor passenger industries, and between railroads and common water carriers. The commission may only *encourage* the establishment of through routes and joint rates between other common carriers.[31] In general, the ICC has not hesitated to prescribe through routes and joint rates for like common carriers.[32] However, the commission has refused to order through routes and joint rates between railroad and water carriers when the route is unduly circuitous or when "the distance between the points of origin and interchange is about as great as the direct distance by rail between the points of origin and final destination."[33]

From the standpoint of shippers, the public, and some carriers, through routes and joint rates offer important advantages. Thus, a railroad might refuse to handle a shipment originating on another line or might charge an exorbitant rate. Either situation would impose a hardship on both shippers and smaller lines. Since traffic may be moved over shorter routes, wasteful transportation may be reduced. Coordination between different modes of transport is encouraged, although here the commission's power is limited. And through rates may provide shippers with alternative routes over which traffic can be transported, thereby creating or strengthening competition.

Nevertheless, carriers may oppose the establishment of through routes. As Bigham and Roberts have explained:

> From the point of view of an individual line, such arrangements may be disadvantageous. The opening up of an alternative route may deprive the line of a portion of the haul and reduce its revenue. The carrier may possess an especially favorable terminal site for the attraction of traffic, or lines tapping productive territory, and under these circumstances it naturally objects to weakening its competitive position by turning over traffic which it can haul to other lines. In some cases, as in interchanges between railroads and waterways, through routes impose additional expense upon the originating carrier.[34]

---

[31] The Civil Aeronautics Board has authority to establish through routes and joint rates between common air carriers, but neither the CAB nor the ICC may require their establishment between air carriers and other common carriers.

[32] Section 15 of the Interstate Commerce Act provides that "in establishing any such through route the Commission shall not . . . require any carrier by railroad, without its consent, to embrace in such route substantially less than the entire length of its railroad . . . which lies between the termini of such proposed through route" unless needed to provide adequate or more economical service. This limitation, which does not apply when one of the carriers is a water line, is not a serious one.

[33] Bigham and Roberts, *op. cit.,* p. 524.

[34] *Ibid.,* p. 519. The process of dividing joint rates between the various individual carriers is discussed in *Akron, C. & Y. R. Co.* v. *Atchison, T. & S. F. Ry. Co.,* 316 ICC 351 (1962); the establishment of joint rail-water rates in *Interstate Commerce Comm.* v. *Mechling,* 330 U.S. 567 (1947), and *Dixie Carriers* v. *United States,* 351 U.S. 56 (1956).

Joint Use of Terminals. The ICC has the power to require the joint use of terminals. Some railroads have better terminal facilities in large cities than do others, or some have terminals located at more strategic points. Those more favorably located may be in a better position to obtain traffic and may refuse to permit the less favorably situated railroads to use their terminal facilities or to switch traffic on their own lines to the rival systems.

The commission will require joint use of terminal facilities under two conditions. First, it must be shown that joint use is in the public interest. Second, it must also be shown that joint use will not impair the ability of the owning carrier to handle its own business. In other words, there must be a need for joint use, and the carrier owning the terminal must not suffer loss of either traffic or revenue if it is required to permit other lines to use its facilities. The owning carrier is entitled to a reasonable compensation when its facilities are used by another carrier. When these conditions have been met, the commission has favored on numerous occasions the joint use of terminal facilities.[35]

QUANTITY OF SERVICE

The second aspect of service regulation involves the quantitative element. Three problems are predominant—entry restrictions, compulsory extension of existing services, and service abandonment.[36] Each will be examined in turn.

Restriction of Entry

Entry, including both the certification of a new company and the certification of an existing company to serve a new area or a new route, is rigidly controlled by the regulatory commissions.[37] Certificates of public convenience and necessity are required to provide electric, gas, telephone, and telegraph services, and to engage in transportation by air, highway (common carrier), pipeline (natural gas), rail, and water. Each applicant must show that the proposed service is required by public convenience and necessity, and that it is "fit, willing, and able" to perform properly the proposed service and to conform to all relevant regulations. Permits are required for contract motor carriers. The exceptions to entry control are the construction of oil pipelines and municipal power production. The intended purpose of such control is to regulate competition *within* each industry, thereby preventing overinvestment in high fixed-cost industries and encouraging the achievement of economies of scale.

Restriction of entry raises few problems in the electric, gas, telephone, and telegraph industries. The existing companies are usually willing to expand their operations in line with customer demands, and few new suppliers apply for certificates. Such is not the case, however, in the transportation industries.

---

[35] See *Consolidation of Railroads,* 159 ICC 522, 522–23 (1929), 185 ICC 403, 414 (1932).

[36] Consolidations, mergers, and acquisitions are considered in Part III.

[37] Compulsory extension of service is considered in the following section.

Transportation Industries. The most serious problems concerning restriction of entry occur in the transportation industries.[38] Frequently, entry control has been used "in the competitive modes of transport having small fixed costs and slight, if any, economies of scale in terms of size of firm."[39] Entry control has also been used, at times, to control competition *between* the modes of transport. Many of the state statutes as well as federal statutes require "fair and impartial" regulation of all modes. In addition, the Interstate Commerce Act requires the ICC "to recognize and preserve the inherent advantages" of each mode. But in carrying out these provisions, the commissions face many complex problems. Problems concerning intramodal competition are especially significant in the motor carrier and airline industries, as are problems concerning intermodal competition between motor carriers and railroads.

Intramodal Competition. With respect to intramodal competition, the statutory provisions of the Interstate Commerce Act regarding certification of motor carriers are typical. Common carriers are to receive certificates,

> . . . if it is found that the applicant is fit, willing, and able properly to perform the service proposed and to conform to the provisions of this part and the requirements, rules, and regulations of the Commission thereunder, and that the proposed service . . . is or will be required by the present or future public convenience and necessity. . . .[40]

Contract carriers are to be granted permits,

> . . . if it appears . . . that the applicant is fit, willing, and able properly to perform the service of a contract carrier by motor vehicle, and to conform to the provisions of this part and the lawful requirements, rules, and regulations of the Commission thereunder, and that the proposed operation . . . will be consistent with the public interest and the policy declared in section 202(a) of this part. . . .[41]

[38] When the federal regulatory acts with respect to airlines, motor carriers, and water carriers were enacted, a so-called "grandfather clause" was included in each. Under this clause, all carriers were entitled to a certificate or permit as a matter of right if they were in "bona fide operation" on June 1, 1935 (common motor carriers), July 1, 1935 (contract motor carriers), May 14, 1938 (airlines), and January 1, 1940 (common and contract water carriers), and if they had operated continuously since that date, except for interruptions of service caused by conditions over which a carrier had no control. The purpose was to protect carriers who were already in operation at the time each act was enacted. On motor carrier and water carrier grandfather clause cases, see Locklin, *op. cit.*, pp. 689-92, 753-54. Sixteen airlines were granted certificates under the grandfather clause. See John H. Frederick, *Commercial Air Transportation* (5th ed.; Homewood, Ill.: Richard D. Irwin, Inc., 1961), p. 77.

[39] James C. Nelson, "The Effects of Entry Control in Surface Transport," in *Transportation Economics* (New York: National Bureau of Economic Research, 1965), p. 420.

[40] Interstate Commerce Act, Sec. 207(a).

[41] *Ibid.*, Sec. 209(b). "Certificates and permits for motor carriers always designate: (1) the legal characteristics of the service authorized—common or contract; (2) the routes or territories over which such operations may be conducted; (3) the points to or from which a carrier may render the specified service; (4) the commodities or classes of commodities

The word "necessity" has received liberal ICC interpretation, "for there are comparatively few things in life which can be regarded as an absolute 'necessity,' and it was surely not the intent of Congress to use the word in so strict and narrow a sense."[42] It is also easier to obtain a permit than a certificate.[43] To obtain the certificate, an applicant must show that the proposed service is required by public convenience and necessity ("usually an onerous and expensive burden"[44]) and that the existing service is deficient. Thus, the commission has held that "the maintenance of sound economic conditions in the motor-carrier industry would be jeopardized by allowing new operators to enter a field in competition with existing carriers who are furnishing adequate, efficient, and economical service."[45] Competing carriers will be granted certificates or permits only "when the available traffic permits it."[46] The commission has followed a similar, but less restrictive, policy regarding water carriers.[47]

The ICC's certificate and permit restrictions, particularly with respect to motor carriers, have been severely criticized. James C. Nelson, for example, after noting that economies of scale and utilization in the industry appear minimal and that entry limitations "will be economic only if they either lead to utilization of a smaller aggregate of resources in accomplishing the demanded transport, or yield faster, more flexible, and more dependable service at the same resource costs," concludes:

---

which may be transported for compensation; and (5) the extent to which the authorized physical movement of trucks is tied to specific highway routes and gateways. While some restrictions merely confirm voluntary specialization, such detailed specification almost inevitably imposes real handicaps on efficient operations." Nelson, "The Effects of Entry Control . . . ," *op. cit.*, p. 390.

42 *Pan-American Bus Lines Operation,* 1 MCC 190, 202 (1936).

43 See *J-T Transport Co., Inc., Extension—Columbus, Ohio,* 79 MCC 695 (1959), remanded to the commission by the Supreme Court (*Interstate Commerce Comm. v. J-T Transport Co.,* 368 U.S. 81 [1961]); and *Moyer Contract Carrier Application,* 88 MCC 767 (1962).

44 Dudley F. Pegrum, *Transportation: Economics and Public Policy* (rev. ed.; Homewood, Ill.: Richard D. Irwin, Inc., 1968), p. 348. See *I.C.C. Administration of the Motor Carrier Act* (Hearings before Select Committee on Small Business, Senate, 84th Cong., 1st sess.) (Washington, D.C.: U.S. Government Printing Office, 1956), esp. pp. 465–70.

45 *Clark Common Carrier Application,* 1 MCC 445 (1937). Also see *Walter C. Benson Co., Inc., Extension,* 61 MCC 128 (1952); *New York Central R. R. Co., Extension,* 61 MCC 457 (1953); and *Willman Contract Carrier Application,* 77 MCC 535 (1958).

46 *Balch & Martin Motor Express Common Carrier Application,* 47 MCC 75, 78 (1947). In nine states (Arizona, Colorado, Florida, Kentucky, Louisiana, Mississippi, Nebraska, Texas, and Virginia), no certificates may be issued until the existing motor carriers have had an opportunity to establish any needed service. See Locklin, *op. cit.,* pp. 694-95. Also see Marion R. Smyser, "Regulation of Motor Carriers in South Dakota— 'Regulated Monopoly' or 'Regulated Competition,' " 11 *South Dakota Law Review* 27 (1966).

47 See, for example, *McCarthy S.S. Co. Common Carrier Application,* 250 ICC 550 (1942); *Commercial Barge Lines, Inc., Extension—Grain,* 285 ICC 549 (1954); *Luckenbach S.S. Co. v. United States,* 122 F. Supp. 824 (1954); *Pan-Atlantic S.S. Corp. Extension— Intercoastal,* 303 ICC 163 (1957); *Moran Towing & Transp. Co., Inc., Extension—Great Lakes,* 314 ICC 287, 315 ICC 591 (1962).

With its handmaiden, minimum rate control, entry limitation was adopted by the Congress as an alternative to deregulating the railroads in the 1930's and as a measure for protecting these carriers from the forces of depression and the competitive onslaughts of new modes of transport. But whatever the design of the Congress, the ICC's interpretations of the Motor Carrier Act and the Transportation Act of 1940 have been highly restrictive of intramodal competition in the trucking industry and protective of the "grandfather" carriers (particularly those of large size) and the regular-route common carriers of general commodities. Thus, entry regulation has become a means of bringing about soft rather than hard competition between motor carriers, through extreme fragmentation and itemization of markets. Along with minimum rate control, it has fostered administered pricing and service competition.[48]

In the airline industry, a distinction must be made between the certification of a new carrier and the certification of an existing carrier to serve a new route. The CAB's policy toward new carriers was stated in a 1941 case:

... the number of air carriers now operating appears sufficient to insure against monopoly in respect to the average new route case, and we believe that the present domestic air transportation system can by proper supervision be integrated and expanded in a manner that will in general afford the competition necessary for the development of that system in a manner contemplated by the act. In the absence of peculiar circumstances presenting an affirmative reason for a new carrier there appears to be no inherent desirability of increasing the present number of carriers merely for the purpose of numerically enlarging the industry.[49]

Since 1941, the board has issued certificates to new carriers to provide new types of service, but it has never granted a certificate to a new trunkline carrier. Certificates have been issued to local-service carriers, all-cargo carriers, helicopter carriers, and supplemental carriers. In each case, the board felt that "peculiar circumstances" warranted the certification of new carriers. For example, since the traffic potential of local-service routes is limited, the board "was definitely convinced that such services, if they are to be permitted at all, would require specialized planning, specialized equipment, and specialized operators focusing on the development of the local transport market."[50]

---

[48]Nelson, "The Effects of Entry Control . . . ," *op. cit.*, pp. 395, 420–21. Also see Board of Investigation and Research, *Federal Regulatory Restrictions upon Motor & Water Carriers* (Senate Doc. No. 78, 79th Cong., 1st sess.) (1945); *Competition, Regulation, and the Public Interest in the Motor Carrier Industry* (Senate Report No. 1693, 84th Cong., 2d sess.) (1956); and Byron Nupp, "Control of Entry as an Economic and Regulatory Problem," 35 *I.C.C. Practitioners' Journal* 591 (1968).

[49]*Delta Air Corp., Service to Atlanta and Birmingham*, 2 CAB 447, 450 (1941).

[50]Frederick, *op. cit.*, p. 152. Often, these certificates have been on a temporary or experimental basis, i.e., for a three- to five-year period. Many have been extended or made permanent. See Richard E. Caves, *Air Transport and Its Regulators* (Cambridge: Harvard University Press, 1962), pp. 169–76; and Frederick, *op. cit.*, pp. 149–56. In recent years, several local-service carriers have been granted trunkline routes and vice versa.

For the trunkline carriers, entry has occurred only through the authorization of new routes to existing carriers. The board considers the following questions in certification cases:

The primary questions to be considered in the disposition of cases involving applications for new service are, in substance, whether the new service will serve a useful public purpose, responsive to a public need; whether this service can and will be served adequately by existing routes or carriers; whether it can be served by the applicant without impairing the operations of existing carriers contrary to the public interest; and whether any cost of the proposed service to the Government will be outweighed by the benefit which will accrue to the public from the new service.[51]

Due to the tremendous increase in load factors during and after the second World War, the CAB adopted a policy of promoting competition among the domestic trunklines by authorizing competing carriers to enter routes previously served by other lines. TWA and Western were certified to provide service between Los Angeles and San Francisco; National, between New York and Florida; Eastern and Northeast, between Boston and New York.[52] As long as there was a sufficient volume of traffic to support two or more carriers over a route, competition was encouraged. This policy was in keeping with the declaration of policy of the Civil Aeronautics Act, providing that competition should be maintained "to the extent necessary to assure the sound development of an air-transportation system properly adapted to the needs of the foreign and domestic commerce of the United States, of the Postal Service, and of the national defense."

In 1951, the CAB modified its policy regarding competition among the domestic trunklines. In that year, the board said:

Undoubtedly, where it appears on the record of a particular case that an air carrier is failing to attain the high standards of public service contemplated by the Civil Aeronautics Act, and where only provision for an economic competitive service would contribute effectively to the assurance of such standards, a case is made for competition.[53]

One member of the board dissented from this view, arguing that "it changes the policy of the Board from one that favors competition whenever it can be justified to one that opposes it wherever its refusal can be justified."[54]

The board reversed its position again in a series of cases starting in 1955 by issuing a number of certificates to competing carriers. In the *New York-Florida Case*, for instance, the board stated: ". . . the Congress in adopting the

---

[51]*Delta Air Corp., Service to Atlanta and Birmingham, op. cit.*, p. 452.

[52]*Transcontinental & Western Air, North-South California Service*, 4 CAB 254 (1943), 4 CAB 373 (1943); *Colonial Airlines, Atlantic Seaboard Operation*, 4 CAB 552 (1944); *Northeast Airlines, Boston Service*, 4 CAB 686 (1944).

[53]*Southern Service to the West Coast*, 12 CAB 518, 533 (1951).

[54]*Ibid.*, dissenting opinion of Commissioner Lee, p. 586.

Civil Aeronautics Act clearly considered competition to hold the greatest prospect for vigorous development of our national air route system 'with the fullest improvements in service and technological developments.'"[55] One of the major aims of the board was to strengthen smaller lines. Said the board in the *Southwest-Northeast Service Case:* "It is vital, in our opinion, to so develop the national air route structure as to tend to decrease rather than increase the gap between the relative size of the Big Four carriers and the smaller trunks."[56]

By 1961, the board recognized that route extension cases were about over, at least for the immediate future.[57] A combination of the introduction of jet planes and a decrease in the rate of traffic growth had resulted in overcapacity on many routes. In 1963, when it refused to grant Northeast Airlines a permanent certificate to serve the New York to Florida route, the board stated: "We find that the public benefits anticipated when Northeast was certificated have not materialized, that the future prospects for the operation of Northeast's system on a profitable basis are remote, and that there is no present need for a third carrier in the East Coast-Florida markets."[58]

The board's certification policy also has been the subject of considerable debate.[59] From an economic point of view, competing carriers over a given route should be certified if unit costs do not decline substantially with increased volume of traffic. If, however, unit costs do decline substantially as the volume of traffic increases, then one carrier should be certified to carry all the traffic over the route. Since studies suggest that there are no significant economies of

---

[55] 24 CAB 94, 99 (1956). Also see *New York-Chicago Service Case*, 22 CAB 973 (1955); *Denver Service Case*, 22 CAB 1178 (1955); *Southwest-Northeast Service Case*, 22 CAB 52 (1955); *Great Lakes-Southeast Service Case*, 27 CAB 829 (1958); and *New York-San Francisco Nonstop Service Case*, 29 CAB 811 (1959).

[56] 22 CAB 52, 54 (1955).

[57] *Southern Transcontinental Service Case*, 33 CAB 701 (1961).

[58] *New York-Florida Renewal Case,* E-19910, pp. 2–3 (CAB, 1963). The case turned into a lengthy struggle between Northeast and the board. Petitions for reconsideration were denied by Board Order E-20073 (1963). In May, 1964, a circuit court set aside the board's order because of inadequate findings, allowed the carrier to continue service over the route, and remanded the case to the board for further action. *Northeast Airlines, Inc.* v. *Civil Aeronautics Board*, 331 F. 2d 579 (1964). In December, 1964, without holding further proceedings, the board adhered to its original decision. Board Order E-21550 (1964). Petitions for rehearing and reconsideration were denied by Board Order E-21872 (1965). The circuit court again set aside the order on grounds that the board had taken notice of certain new data in reaching its conclusion without affording Northeast an opportunity to rebut and explain such data. *Northeast Airlines, Inc.* v. *Civil Aeronautics Board*, 345 F. 2d 484 (1965). The board then decided to completely reopen the proceeding; a move approved by the court. *Northeast Airlines, Inc.* v. *Civil Aeronautics Board*, 345 F. 2d 488 (1965). In 1967, the board granted Northeast a permanent certificate to fly the route. *Reopened New York-Florida Renewal*, E-24808 (CAB, 1967).

[59] See Caves, *op. cit.,* chap. viii; Lucile S. Keyes, *Federal Control of Entry into Air Transportation* (Cambridge: Harvard University Press, 1951) and "A Reconsideration of Federal Control of Entry into Air Transportation," 22 *Journal of Air Law and Commerce* 192 (1955); H. K. Maclay and W. C. Burt, "Entry of New Carriers into Domestic Trunkline Air Transportation," 22 *ibid.* 131 (1955); and Gilbert L. Bates, "Current Changes in Trunkline Competition," 22 *ibid.* 379 (1955).

scale in the air-transport industry after a moderate size has been attained,[60] it may be concluded

> . . . that the policy of authorizing competitive services over a given route is superior to a policy of granting a carrier a monopoly of the route. The policy should not be carried too far, however, for the establishment of services in excess of what the traffic will support can only lead to dangerously low load factors, impaired earnings, and the jeopardizing of the carriers' ability to provide safe and adequate service. Also, if air carriers are to be subsidized, through air-mail payments or otherwise, it is necessary to prevent more carriers on a given route than the traffic will support.[61]

For the local-service carriers, the board's initial policy was to grant certificates for only a three-year period and to impose restrictions on local-service lines to prevent them from competing with the trunklines.[62] Most of the certificates were later renewed, for periods of three, five, or seven years, but only "covering routes which offer substantial public benefits and hold promise of future economic soundness. . . ."[63] Permanent certificates were granted to the local-service carriers following a Congressional amendment to the Act in 1955.[64] Beginning in 1958, the board undertook a review of local-service operations, announcing a "use it or lose it" policy (under which service is withdrawn from points that do not enplane, over a test period, a minimum of five passengers a day) and adopting a liberalization of earlier restrictions on competition between local-service carriers and trunklines.[65] These reviews gradually evolved into broad proceedings involving the realignment of the entire systems of local-service carriers, with the board issuing amended certificates:

(1) Granting more liberal operating authority through the removal of outdated operating restrictions;

---

[60] See Caves, *op. cit.,* chap. iii. Also see John B. Crane, "The Economics of Air Transportation," 22 *Harvard Business Review* 495 (1944); Harold D. Koontz, "Economic and Managerial Factors Underlying Subsidy Needs of Domestic Trunk Line Air Carriers," 18 *Journal of Air Law and Commerce* 127 (1951) and "Domestic Air Line Self-Sufficiency: A Problem of Route Structures," 42 *American Economic Review* 103 (1952); and John R. Meyer, Merton J. Peck, John Stenason, and Charles Zwick, *Economics of Competition in the Transportation Industries* (Cambridge: Harvard University Press, 1959), esp. pp. 133-44.

[61] Locklin, *op. cit.,* p. 806.

[62] *Service in the Rocky Mountain States Area,* 6 CAB 695 (1946); *Florida Case,* 6 CAB 765 (1946); *West Coast Case,* 6 CAB 961 (1946); *New England Case,* 7 CAB 27 (1946); *Texas-Oklahoma Case,* 7 CAB 481 (1946); *North Central Case,* 7 CAB 639 (1946); *Southeastern States Case,* 7 CAB 863 (1947); *Great Lakes Area Case,* 8 CAB 360 (1947); *Mississippi Valley Case,* 8 CAB 726 (1947); *Arizona-New Mexico Case,* 9 CAB 85 (1948); and *Middle Atlantic Area Case,* 9 CAB 131 (1948).

[63] *Pioneer Certificate Renewal Case,* 12 CAB 1, 4 (1950).

[64] Public Law 38 (1955). See, for example, *West Coast Airlines, Permanent Certificate Case,* 22 CAB 565 (1955).

[65] See *Seven States Area Local Service Case,* 28 CAB 680 (1958); *South Central Area Local Service Case,* 29 CAB 425 (1959); *Pacific Northwest Local Service Case,* 29 CAB 660 (1959); and *Montana Local Service Case,* 29 CAB 1046 (1959). The board's "use it or lose it" policy was upheld in the courts. See *New Castle County Airport Comm.* v. *Civil Aeronautics Board,* 371 F. 2d 733 (1966), *cert. denied,* 387 U.S. 930 (1967).

(2) Giving local-service carriers more access to higher density, short, and medium-haul markets, on a subsidy-ineligible basis, even in instances where such an award may involve competition with trunkline service;

(3) Transferring from trunklines to the local-service carriers certain routes which are marginally profitable for the trunks but which can receive better service from the locals on a more economical and efficient basis;

(4) Consolidating service to two or more points at a single airport where service convenience is improved and economies result;

(5) Improving economies by eliminating service at certain points which have not shown, after a reasonable test period, that they can generate sufficient traffic to justify continued airline service.[66]

The board has made it clear that its aim is to strengthen local-service lines and, thereby, to provide greater public service and to reduce subsidy support.[67]

Intermodal Competition. With respect to intermodal competition, the most serious problems arise in cases involving motor carrier–railroad competition. Assume that a commission receives an application from a motor carrier requesting permission to serve between points A and B; points that are now being served by a railroad. In deciding whether to grant a certificate or permit, the commission cannot disregard the probable effects of a new carrier on the volume of traffic and revenues of the existing one. But what weight should be given to this consideration? Should shippers always have the opportunity of choosing between different modes of transport, regardless of the profitability of the service for either carrier?

In theory, no mode of transportation should be protected from a competing mode unless it is absolutely necessary. Each mode of transport offers certain advantages over others, and shippers should not be denied these benefits. Moreover, even if a commission tries to protect a railroad by refusing to grant a certificate to a motor carrier, it may not be successful. When a shipper believes motor carrier transportation is cheaper than railroad transportation, he has the option of buying and operating his own fleet of trucks when common and contract carriers are not available. Only those shippers who cannot afford to exercise this option are forced to use the available railroad service in the absence of motor carrier service. Therefore, unless it can be shown that the volume of traffic is insufficient to support two modes of transport, so that the certification

---

[66] Civil Aeronautics Board, *Reports to Congress* (1966), p. 4. See, for example, *Lake Central Airlines, Inc., "Use It or Lose It" and Route Realignment Investigation*, E-23589 (CAB, 1966); *Mohawk Route 94 Realignment Investigation*, E-24670 (CAB, 1967); and *Allegheny Airlines, Inc., Segment 8 Renewal and Route Realignment Investigation*, E-25847 (CAB, 1967).

[67] In 1963, the board submitted a plan, in response to a directive from President Kennedy, designed to reduce subsidy payments by about 30 percent over a five-year period. *Report to the President on Airline Subsidy Reduction Program* (1963). See Ronald D. Dockser, "Airline Service Abandonment and Consolidation—A Chapter in the Battle against Subsidization," 32 *Journal of Air Law and Commerce* 496 (1966); and Craig Mathews, "Certificated Air Service at Smaller Communities: The Need for Service as a Determinant of Regulatory Policy," 34 *ibid.* 27 (1968).

For a discussion of the board's certification policy with respect to air-cargo and nonscheduled carriers, see Locklin, *op. cit.*, pp. 811–16.

of a new mode would threaten the solvency of the existing carrier and thereby raise the costs of all carriers involved, there is no economic justification for a policy of protecting one form of transport from the competition of another.

In practice, it is difficult for a commission to follow such a policy of neutrality. Commissions are confronted with many conflicting claims, objections, and pressures in certification cases. As pointed out above, commissions must consider the probable effects of a new carrier on the existing carrier(s). And comparative costs and accurate traffic forecasts are difficult to determine. While it is often impossible to determine the exact grounds on which a commission has refused to grant a certificate to a carrier, Locklin concludes that in only a few cases has the ICC sought to protect the railroads from motor carrier competition.[68] In general, the commission has followed the policy expressed in a 1958 case: "We agree . . . that motor carrier service has certain inherent transportation advantages not found in rail service, and that these advantages warrant a grant of authority even where certain amounts of traffic may be diverted from existing rail carriers."[69]

Less serious, but similar, problems are raised in cases involving bus-railroad passenger service, railroad-water carrier service, airline-railroad freight and passenger service, and airline-bus passenger service. In these situations, however, there has been even less inclination to protect competitors than in the case of motor carrier-railroad competition. The CAB, for instance, has stated: "It is our view that the Board is not required to consider ordinary competitive impact upon the railroads as a public interest factor. . . ."[70]

Compulsory Extension of Service

There are two aspects to the problem of service extension. First, service may be extended within the same general market area that a company presently serves. Second, service may be extended into a new market area. The state and federal legislative provisions are similar to those found in the Interstate Commerce Act, which provide that the commission may, after a hearing, "authorize or require by order any carrier by railroad subject to this Act . . . to provide itself with safe and adequate facilities for performing as a common carrier its car service . . . and to extend its line or lines. . . ."[71] In such cases, the extension must be "reasonably required in the interest of public convenience and necessity" and the expense involved must "not impair the ability of the carrier to perform its duty to the public."

[68] Locklin, *op. cit.,* pp. 854–57. For cases where railroads have received protection, see *Wilson Extension–Dairy Products*, 61 MCC 51 (1952); *California Express, Inc., Extension–Wichita, Kansas*, 77 MCC 118 (1958).

[69] *Carl Subler Trucking, Inc., Common Carrier Application*, 77 MCC 395, 397-98 (1958). Protection has been of more importance in state commission decisions. See Locklin, *op. cit.,* pp. 854–55.

[70] *New York-Florida Case*, 24 CAB 94, 119–20 (1956). Also see *Re Ozark Air Lines, Inc.*, 90 PUR (NS) 161 (1951); *Yazoo Barge Line Common Carrier Application*, 305 ICC 17 (1958); *Coyle Lines, Extension–Chattahoochu & Flint Rivers*, 323 ICC 386 (1964).

[71] Interstate Commerce Act, Sec. 1, par. 21.

Extension within Market Area. A regulated company is required to serve all who ask for, and are willing to pay for, service within the area where it holds itself out to serve.[72] This area is usually specified in the commission's certificate or the city's franchise. As stated by the Supreme Court:

> Corporations which devote their property to a public use may not pick and choose, serving only the portions of the territory covered by their franchises which it is presently profitable for them to serve, and restricting the development of the remaining portions by leaving their inhabitants in discomfort without the service which they alone can render.[73]

As a rule, therefore, a regulated company can be required to extend its service as its specified market area grows. Most companies are willing to do so voluntarily in order to expand or grow with their markets. At times, however, an extension within a market area is not profitable. Here, the commissions will consider the prospective costs and revenues, as well as the social benefits, of such an extension. Some service extensions may be ordered even though costs are greater than revenues.[74] The essential question is the effect of the extension on the total return of the company involved.

The commissions have an alternative to requiring service extension by the existing company: they have the authority to issue a certificate to a new company when the existing company is providing deficient service in its market area.[75] Neither a certificate nor a franchise, in other words, protects a company from the entry of a competitor if a commission finds such entry to be in the public interest.

Extension into New Market. A different problem arises when considering the extension of service beyond a company's present market area, for substantial investment in new plant and equipment is usually required. While many of the commissions have authority to require expansion into a new area, they have used this power sparingly. The CAB, for example, has compelled expansion by local-service carriers, to whom subsidies are paid when service is unprofitable, rather than requiring the domestic trunklines to expand into these areas. Other commissions have limited power over requiring extensions into new markets. Thus, the Federal Power Commission is authorized to order natural gas pipeline extensions to communities that are "immediately adjacent" to a transmission line or "to territory served" by a transmission company, but no farther. And a few commissions lack authority to require extensions into new markets.[76]

---

[72] The obligation to serve, as noted earlier in the chapter, is not absolute.

[73] *New York & Queens Gas Co.* v. *McCall,* 245 U.S. 345, 351 (1917). Also see *Lukrawaka* v. *Spring Valley Water Co.*, 169 Cal. 318 (1915).

[74] *Bierbaum* v. *Union Elec. Co. of Illinois,* 52 PUR (NS) 129, 134 (Ill., 1944).

[75] *City of Sikeston* v. *Missouri Public Service Comm.,* 336 Mo. 985 (Mo., 1935); *Metropolitan Edison Co.* v. *Public Service Comm.,* 19 PUR (NS) 55 (Pa., 1937); *Meyers* v. *Southwestern Bell Teleph. Co.*, 34 PUR 3d 491 (Mo., 1960).

[76] See *New York Public Service Comm.* v. *Bath Elec., Gas & Water Systems,* 42 PUR 3d 353 (N.Y., 1962); *Re Braithwaite,* 44 PUR 3d 205 (Wis., 1962).

As with extensions within a market area, a company is usually willing to expand voluntarily into a new market area. Few cases have resulted and only two have ever reached the Supreme Court. In the first case, the New York commission ordered a gas company to extend its service to several communities adjacent to the city where the firm operated. After giving considerable attention to the prospective costs and revenues, the Court upheld the commission's order for the extension as a reasonable one. The Court warned, however, that: "Under the guise of regulation, the state may not require the company to make large expenditures for the extension of its mains and service into new territory when the necessary result will be to compel the company to use its property for the public convenience without just compensation."[77] The second case involved the only extension of a railroad line ever ordered by the Interstate Commerce Commission.[78] The commission ordered a subsidiary of the Union Pacific to make a 187-mile extension in Oregon that would cost nearly $9 million. The Court refused to uphold the order, believing that the commission's authority did not "embrace the building of what is essentially a new line to reach a new territory."[79] The Court concluded:

> We should expect, if Congress were intending to grant to the Commission a new and drastic power to compel the investment of enormous sums for the . . . service of a region which the carrier had never theretofore entered or intended to serve, the intention would be expressed in more than a clause in a sentence dealing with car service.[80]

When companies, because of the prospective costs and revenues, are unwilling to extend service to new market areas voluntarily, commissions can frequently make such extensions attractive. A company may be permitted to charge higher rates in the new market than are charged in the old market. In this way, the new customers will pay the cost of extending the service. A company may be permitted to raise its rates in the old market, thus charging more for the same service than in the new market.[81] The old customers will thereby subsidize part of the new service. Finally, a company may be permitted to raise rates in both markets, so that the new and old customers will pay the same rates. Both groups will pay the costs of extending the service. Commissions generally prefer either the first or second alternative, and there are many instances where each has been employed. Suburban bus rates commonly are higher than downtown

---

[77] *Woodhaven Gas & Light Co.* v. *Public Service Comm. of New York*, 269 U.S. 244, 248 (1925).

[78] The commission has refused to order extensions on several occasions. See, for example, *Cooke* v. *Chicago, Burlington & Quincy R.R. Co.*, 60 ICC 452 (1922); *Public Service Comm. of Wyoming* v. *Chicago, Burlington & Quincy R.R. Co.*, 185 ICC 741 (1932).

[79] *Interstate Commerce Comm.* v. *Oregon-Washington R.R. & Navigation Co.*, 288 U.S. 14, 40 (1933).

[80] *Ibid.*, p. 35.

[81] Alternatively, if a company has excessive earnings, the commission could require the extension of service rather than order rate reductions. The results are the same.

city rates; city telephone service is usually more expensive, relative to cost, than rural service.

Abandonment of Service

Abandonment of service may be voluntary or involuntary. Voluntary abandonment, either partial or complete, must be approved by the regulatory commissions.[82] Involuntary abandonment involves the commission's revocation or suspension of a company's certificate, permit, or license. It is important to note that abandonment refers to a partial or complete withdrawal of service as opposed to a reduction in a plant's output. Except for railroad services, discontinuance of service has been a relatively minor regulatory problem. By and large commissions have been dealing with expanding industries. Troxel has pointed out, however: "Before the twentieth century ends, many flourishing utility companies probably will stop expanding; some may be decadent. Given time, commissions will face far more petitions for partial or complete abandonments of utility operations than they have encountered in past years."[83]

Complete Abandonment. In practice, the regulatory commissions have little power to prevent complete abandonment of service. When a natural gas field is exhausted, for instance, abandonment is inevitable. Moreover, a regulated company is not obligated to provide service at a loss. Thus, in a 1924 railroad case, the Supreme Court argued that a utility company devotes its property to public service

> ... on condition that the public shall supply sufficient traffic on a reasonable basis to yield a fair return. And if at any time it develops with reasonable certainty that future operations must be at a loss, the company may discontinue operation and get what it can out of the property by dismantling the road. To compel it to go on at a loss, or to give up the salvage value, would be to take its property without just compensation which is a part of due process of law.[84]

Partial Abandonment. When partial abandonment of service is proposed by a regulated company, the commissions have the authority to either approve or disapprove the request. As long as a company earns an adequate total return, it can be required to continue the operation of unprofitable services. If, however, a company's earnings are not reasonable, partial abandonment may be necessary to prevent the impairment of service throughout the whole system. To illustrate: The Missouri commission ruled that a company must be allowed to

---

[82] Two exceptions are noteworthy: motor carriers and water carriers may abandon service without approval of the Interstate Commerce Commission. And while the Commission can revoke the certificate or permit of a motor carrier who voluntarily abandons service, it cannot do so in the case of water carriers.

[83] Emery Troxel, *Economics of Public Utilities* (New York: Holt, Rinehart & Winston, Inc., 1947), p. 480.

[84] *Texas Railroad Comm.* v. *Eastern Texas R.R. Co., 264 U.S. 79,* 85 (1924). See also *Wolff Packing Co.* v. *Court of Industrial Relations, 262 U.S. 522,* 543 (1923).

abandon a rural electric line "unless the customers are willing to pay the proper rates . . . .";[85] the Montana and Wisconsin commissions permitted electric companies to abandon unprofitable steam heating service;[86] the New Hampshire commission allowed a telephone company to discontinue service for summer customers "in view of a continuing financial loss";[87] and the ICC permitted the New York Central to abandon a branch line because losses on the service were affecting the profitability of the whole system.[88]

The Supreme Court's position regarding partial abandonment has not always been clear. In a 1925 case involving a request by a street railway company to abandon less than a mile of its 22-mile route, the Court decided:

> A public utility cannot, because of loss, escape obligations voluntarily assumed . . . . A railway may be compelled to continue the service of a branch or part of a line, although the operation involves a loss . . . . This is true even where the system as a whole fails to earn a fair return upon the value of the property. So far as appears, this company is at liberty to surrender its franchise and discontinue operations throughout the city. It cannot, in the absence of contract, be compelled to continue to operate its system at a loss . . . . But the Constitution does not confer upon the company the right to enjoy the franchise or indeterminate permit and escape from the burdens incident to its use.[89]

A year later, the Court apparently reversed its position. The Court, in placing considerable emphasis on the total earnings of the company, ruled:

> Expenditures in the local interest may be so large as to compel the carrier to raise reasonable interstate rates, or to abstain from making an appropriate reduction of such rates, or to curtail interstate service, or to forego facilities needed in interstate commerce. Likewise, excessive local expenditures may so weaken the financial condition of the carrier as to raise the cost of securing capital . . . , and thus compel an increase in rates.[90]

In the first case, the Court placed emphasis on the public's interest; in the second case on the utility's earnings. While both must receive attention in any case involving partial abandonment, the relative weight assigned to the two factors varies from commission to commission.[91]

Railroad Discontinuance Cases. In recent years, the most significant problems involving service abandonment have concerned the passenger service of

85 *Re Missouri Power & Light Co.*, 17 PUR (NS) 469, 472 (Mo., 1937).

86 *Re Billings Gas Co.*, 26 PUR (NS) 328 (Mont., 1938); *Re Northern States Power Co.*, 35 PUR (NS) 241 (Wis., 1940).

87 *Citizens of Washington* v. *Washington & Cherry Valley Teleph. Co.*, 36 PUR (NS) 190 (N.H., 1940).

88 *New York Central R.R. Co. Abandonment*, 245 ICC 745, 761 (1944).

89 *Fort Smith Light and Traction Co.* v. *Bourland*, 267 U.S. 330, 332–33 (1925). Also see *Broad River Power Co.* v. *South Carolina*, 281 U.S. 537 (1930).

90 *Colorado* v. *United States*, 271 U.S. 153, 163 (1926).

91 *Re Greyhound Corp.*, 37 PUR 3d 113 (N.C., 1961); *Greyhound Corp.* v. *Carter*, 40 PUR 3d 306 (Fla. Sup. Ct., 1961); *Re Deep South Oil Co. of Texas*, 38 PUR 3d 438 (FPC, 1961); *Re Southern P. Co.*, 37 PUR 3d 196 (Calif., 1960); *Re Chicago, B. & Q. R. Co.*, 39 PUR 3d 174 (Neb. Sup. Ct., 1961).

the nation's railroads. Here, the interests of the public and of the companies may diverge sharply. Communities are reluctant to lose rail passenger service, for they may also lose tax revenues and needed commutation service. The railroads, however, continue to sustain losses on passenger service, especially in the eastern part of the country, largely due to unprofitable commutation services. For the railroads as a whole, passenger load factors are less than 25 percent, and the "passenger deficit" has ranged from $394 to $724 million in the last two decades. While this deficit could be covered from earnings on freight service, freight earnings also have been deficient in the post–World War II period. The issue was sharpened in July, 1961, when The New York, New Haven and Hartford Railroad Company filed a petition for reorganization under the Bankruptcy Act. The Interstate Commerce Commission, in a report issued earlier in the year, had concluded that the New Haven's passenger deficit was the primary cause of the line's financial difficulties.[92] The commission, for the first time in its history, recommended a program of direct federal grants to preserve essential passenger services.[93]

Prior to 1958, the ICC had no control over passenger service, either interstate or intrastate. The state commissions had exclusive jurisdiction over the lines within their respective states. Under pressure from the communities which faced the loss of service, state commissions frequently refused to authorize abandonments of unprofitable passenger lines on the ground that there was a public need for the service.[94] The Supreme Court has recognized this position: "It has long been settled . . . that a requirement that a particular service be rendered at a loss does not make such a service confiscatory and thereby an unconstitutional taking of property."[95] Yet, on numerous occasions, the courts were overruling the state commissions, indicating a dissatisfaction with commissions' refusals to permit railroads to abandon unprofitable passenger services, especially in view of the railroads' overall earnings. In upholding a lower court which had refused to sustain the state commission's order, the Kansas Supreme Court said:

> The conclusions of law adopted and applied by the trial court are based solidly on the modern trend of opinion, or philosophy, that passenger trains are operated primarily for the carriage of passengers, and if the public abandons the trains for passenger travel, there is no duty or obligation to

[92] *Passenger Fares, New York, N.H. & H.R. Co.*, 313 ICC 411 (1961).

[93] Interstate Commerce Commission, *Seventy-Fifth Annual Report* (1961), pp. 8–10. Early in 1969, the Association of American Railroads proposed a plan under which "the Federal Government would subsidize passenger trains that the Government decides must be continued despite operating losses. The subsidy would equal the deficit of such operations as decided by the Interstate Commerce Commission. . . ." *The Wall Street Journal*, February 17, 1969, p. 23.

[94] See, for example, *Chicago, Milwaukee, St. Paul & Pacific R. Co.* v. *Board of Railroad Commissioners*, 255 P. 2d 346 (1953); *Delaware & Hudson R. Corp.* v. *Public Service Comm.*, 136 N.Y.S. 2d 510 (1954); *Pennsylvania R.R. Co.* v. *Board of Public Utility Commissioners*, 137 A. 2d 76 (1957).

[95] *Alabama Public Service Comm.* v. *Southern Ry. Co.*, 341 U.S. 341, separate opinion of Justice Frankfurter, p. 352 (1951).

continue their operation at a substantial loss. We do not hesitate to declare that we are in agreement with this position.[96]

The railroads, dissatisfied with state commission decisions in passenger discontinuance cases, were largely responsible for persuading Congress to enact Section 13a of the Interstate Commerce Act in 1958. Under the provisions of this section, passenger service of interstate trains may be discontinued or the service changed on 30 days' notice to the ICC and to the governor of each state involved, regardless of the relevant state laws. The commission was given the power to prevent discontinuance or change of the service for one year if it finds that the service is required by public convenience and necessity and that continued operation will not unduly burden interstate commerce. The ICC also was given more limited authority over intrastate trains. When state laws or state commissions prevent the discontinuance of passenger service or when an application for discontinuance or change of the service is delayed by a state commission for more than 120 days, the railroad may petition the ICC for authority to carry out the proposed discontinuance or change. Such authority may be granted only when the commission finds that discontinuance or change of service is permitted by public convenience and necessity, and where continued operation would result in an undue burden on interstate commerce or on the interstate operations of the carrier.[97]

Under these provisions, the railroads have found it easier to discontinue unprofitable passenger service, and they have made extensive use of the opportunity. The passenger-miles transported by the railroads decreased from nearly 23.3 billion in 1958 to 17.2 billion in 1966; in the same period, railroad mileage operated in passenger service dropped from 106,439 miles to 73,173 miles.[98] State commissions have more readily permitted discontinuances.[99]

[96]*Atchison, Topeka & Santa Fe Ry. Co.* v. *Kansas State Corp. Comm.*, 322 P. 2d 715, 724 (1958). Also see *St. Louis–San Francisco Ry. Co*. v. *State*, 262 P. 2d 168 (1953); *Missouri-Kansas-Texas R. Co.* v. *Oklahoma* 319 P. 2d 590 (1957); *Chicago, Rock Island & Pacific R. Co.* v. *Louisiana*, 100 So. 2d 471 (1958).

[97]Public Law 85-625, enacted August 12, 1958, and known as the Transportation Act of 1958. See Robert L. Bard, "The Challenge of Rail Passenger Service: Free Enterprise, Regulation, and Subsidy," 34 *University of Chicago Law Review* 301 (1967); Hugh S. Norton, "A Modest Proposal to Improve Competition in Passenger Transportation," 18 *Atlanta Economic Review* 17 (1968); and Robert W. Harbeson, "The Rail Passenger Service Problem Revisited," 82 *Public Utilities Fortnightly* 28 (December 19, 1968).

[98]Interstate Commerce Commission, *Eighty-First Annual Report* (1967), Table 24, p. 148. Between 1958 and November 24, 1967, a total of 222 proceedings were instituted by the railroads covering the operation of 1,146 interstate trains, and 49 procedures covering the operation of 466 intrastate trains were filed by the railroads. The ICC permitted discontinuance in a majority of these proceedings. Interstate Commerce Commission, Bureau of Economics, *Transport Economics* (November-December, 1967), pp. 1-2. Also see William E. Thoms and Michael J. Laird, "Derailing the Passenger," 36 *I.C.C. Practitioners' Journal* 1118 (1968).

[99]Five criteria usually are considered by commissions in discontinuance cases: (1) the character and population of the territory involved; (2) the public patronage of the service or lack of it; (3) the facilities remaining; (4) the expense of operation as compared with the revenue from it; and (5) the operations of the carrier as a whole. *North Carolina ex*

Typical is a decision by the Maryland commission in 1959. In granting the request of the Pennsylvania Railroad to discontinue its commuter service between Baltimore and Parkton, Maryland, the commission found that the service involved an annual loss to the railroad of over $100,000 and that there was not even a remote possibility of increasing passenger revenues on the service to overcome the existing loss. To provide adequate public transportation service over the route, a certificate was issued to a bus company. [100]

In 1968, the ICC submitted a report on rail passenger service to Congress, calling for comprehensive changes in federal policy. With respect to intercity rail service, and with the exception of the federal government's demonstration project in the Northeast Corridor,[101] the commission concluded that

... the existing governmental environment does little more than weakly support that level of service which the railroads, themselves, can afford. The quality and quantity of that service are deteriorating. The forces underlying this trend grow stronger. Present programs—public and private—cannot reverse this trend. And we do not believe that any significant action will be taken until a consensus is developed on whether a national intercity rail system is needed. The national ambivalence toward the problem not only fosters inaction and inconsistency in governmental policy, but it encourages railroads to continue the present trends.[102]

---

rel. *Utilities Comm.* v. *Southern Ry. Co.,* 254 N.C. 73 (1961). Also see *Southern Pacific Co.—Discontinuance of Trains Nos. 39 and 40 between Tucumcari, N. Mex., and Los Angeles, Calif.,* 330 ICC 685, 709 (1967).

[100] *Re Pennsylvania R.R. Co.,* 31 PUR 3d 197 (Md., 1959). Also see *Re New York, N.H. & H.R. Co.,* 33 PUR 3d 63 (Conn., 1959); *St. Louis–S. F. R. Co.* v. *City of Fall River,* 35 PUR 3d 486 (Kan. Sup. Ct., 1960); *Maine C. R. Co.* v. *Maine Public Utilities Comm.,* 36 PUR 3d 12 (Me. Sup. Jud. Ct., 1960); *Montana* v. *United States,* 202 F. Supp. 660 (1962).

It should not be implied that every discontinuance request handled by the ICC and state commissions is approved. See, for example, *Re Southern P. Co.,* 37 PUR 3d 196 (Cal., 1960); *North Carolina* ex rel. *Utilities Comm.* v. *Southern Ry. Co., op. cit.*

[101] The project is being undertaken by the Department of Transportation under the High Speed Ground Transportation Act of 1965 (Public Law 89-220). See George Smerk, "Rail Passenger Service in the Northeast Corridor—1947-63," 7 *Quarterly Review of Economics & Business* 5 (1967); and A. S. Lang, "High Speed Transportation," in National Association of Regulatory Utility Commissioners, *Annual Proceedings, 1967* (Washington, D.C., 1968), pp. 530–37.

[102] *Intercity Rail Passenger Service in 1968* (Report and Recommendations of the Interstate Commerce Commission to the Senate Committee on Commerce and the House Interstate and Foreign Commerce Committee) (1968), p. 3. Also see *Railroad Passenger Train Service* (Hearings before the Subcommittee on Transportation and Aeronautics of the Committee on Interstate and Foreign Commerce, House, 90th Cong., 2d sess.) (Washington, D.C.: U.S. Government Printing Office, 1968); and *Study of Essential Railroad Passenger Service* (Hearings before the Subcommittee on Surface Transportation of the Committee on Commerce, Senate, 90th Cong., 2d sess.) (Washington, D.C.: U.S. Government Printing Office, 1968). An ICC hearing examiner, in a 1968 decision, recommended that the commission set "certain minimal standards" for interstate passenger rail service, including some type of meal service on trains traveling more than 250 miles and "adequate" sleeping car accommodations on trains operating between 10 P.M. and 8 A.M. "The time has come," he argued, "when the Commission can no longer act like a county coroner

A great majority of the railroad passenger discontinuance cases have involved intercity trains. But in recent years, several significant cases have involved commutation services in the eastern part of the country, including those of the Boston and Maine and of the New Haven.[103] In an attempt to alleviate the financial burdens and deteriorating quality of such services, programs have been undertaken by all levels of government: the federal government has become engaged in research, experimentation, and capital expenditures related to the development of urban mass transit;[104] state and local governments have granted operating subsidies, made equipment purchases, and granted property tax relief.[105] Yet, while the urban transportation problem is urgent, it is far from solved.[106]

Revocation, Suspension, and Modification of Certificates. A majority of the commissions have the power to revoke, suspend, or modify a certificate, permit, or license they have issued. The West Virginia law with respect to motor carriers provides: "The commission may at any time, for good cause, suspend and, upon not less than fifteen days' notice to the grantee of any certificate and an opportunity to be heard, revoke or amend any certificate."[107] The ICC may revoke a certificate or permit of a motor carrier—but not of a pipeline, railroad, or water carrier—on application of the holder. It may revoke or suspend a certificate or permit on a finding that the holder has willfully failed to comply with the Interstate Commerce Act; with an order, rule, or regulation of the commission; or with the terms of its certificate. No certificate or permit may be revoked on the initiative of the commission, however, until the holder has been given a reasonable period of time to comply with an order, rule, or regulation of the commission.[108] The CAB has similar authority with respect to interstate airlines.[109]

---

and, acting upon death certificates in the form of section 13a(1) notices, inquire by an inquest into the cause of passenger-train demise.... The urgent need is for preventive medicine." *Adequacies—Passenger Service—Southern Pacific Co. between California and Louisiana,* Finance Docket No. 34733 (1968), p. 42. The commission has yet to act on the examiner's recommendations.

103 See *Boston & Maine Corp., Discontinuance,* 324 ICC 705 (1965); *New York, N.H. & H.R.R., Discontinuance,* 327 ICC 151 (1966); and *The Crisis in Passenger Train Service* (Hearings before the Committee on Commerce, Senate, 89th Cong., 1st sess.) (Washington, D.C.: U.S. Government Printing Office, 1965).

104 Housing Act of 1961 (Public Law 87-70); Urban Mass Transportation Act of 1964 (Public Law 88-365).

105 The Massachusetts Bay Transportation Authority, for example, has contracted with both the Boston and Maine and the New Haven to continue much of their commutation services.

106 See *National Transportation Policy* (Preliminary draft of a report prepared for the Committee on Interstate and Foreign Commerce by the Special Study Group on Transportation Policies in the United States, Senate, 87th Cong., 1st sess.) (Washington, D.C.: U.S. Government Printing Office, 1961), Part VII, chap. vii; and Pegrum, *op. cit.,* chap. xxii.

107 *West Virginia Motor Carrier Law, 1961,* issued by the Public Service Commission of West Virginia, p. 9.

108 Interstate Commerce Act, Sec. 212(a).

109 *Pan American World Airways v. Boyd,* 207 F. Supp. 152 (1962).

The commissions have used this authority on occasion, and their right of revocation, suspension, and modification has been upheld by the courts.[110] The CAB has temporarily suspended or modified certificates on numerous occasions, particularly to add or to take away the right of a carrier to provide service between certain points.[111] The ICC has revoked or suspended thousands of motor carrier certificates and permits for failure to comply with the Interstate Commerce Act or an order of the commission, fraud or misrepresentation, failure to file required annual reports, violations of state size and weight regulations, and when carriers have voluntarily abandoned operations.[112]

SAFETY REGULATION

In addition to the quality and quantity of service, regulation is concerned with safety standards. Few safety standards have been established for the electric, gas, telephone, and telegraph utilities.[113] These industries, almost from their inception, have maintained stringent safety standards. Commissions have safety codes, however, to prevent explosions from breaks or leaks in gas transmission and distribution mains, and fires from faulty wiring. Many states require that gas have an odor to aid in early detection of leaks; in the case of natural gas, an artificial odorant is added. In most instances, the customer is responsible for installing facilities within his premises in conformity with local building codes. Safety is a vital part of the Atomic Energy Commission's work: before issuing an operation permit for a nuclear power plant, it must make a positive finding that operation of the facility will provide adequate protection to the health and safety of the public.[114] The Federal Communications Commission is concerned with a different type of safety: the commission must allocate the spectrum space for public safety radio services, such as police, fire, disaster communications, and governmental operations.

The most important safety regulations govern the transportation indus-

[110] *Fuller-Toponce Truck Co.* v. *Public Service Comm.*, 99 U. 28, 96 P. 2d 722 (Utah, 1950); *United Air Lines* v. *CAB*, 198 F. 2d 100 (1952); *Kmeth* v. *Lundy*, 230 N.Y.S. 2d 76 (1962); *Re Hargleroad*, 173 Neb. 151 (1962). The ICC may not revoke a certificate or permit issued to a water carrier. See *United States* v. *Seatrain Lines*, 329 U.S. 424 (1947).

[111] *Caribbean Area Case*, 9 CAB 534 (1948); *Frontier Renewal Case*, 14 CAB 519 (1951); *North Central Route Investigation*, 14 CAB 1027 (1951); *Pacific-Southwest Local Service Case*, E-17950 (CAB, 1962).

[112] See, for example, *Smith Bros. Revocation of Certificate*, 33 MCC 465 (1942); *Public Utility Comm. of Ohio* v. *Riss and Co., Inc., et al.*, 72 MCC 659 (1957).

[113] Occasionally, however, there are differences of opinion with respect to specific facilities or equipment. Thus, in a 1965 decision, the California commission found that the Bell System's handsets were "less safe and healthful" than the "Ericofons" (a non-Bell manufactured instrument) and ordered the Bell System either to allow a hospital to attach the latter equipment to its lines or to provide the hospital with such equipment. *Doctors General Hospital* v. *Pacific Teleph. & Teleg. Co.*, 59 PUR 3d 297 (Cal., 1965), 62 PUR 3d 409 (Cal., 1965). See "Safety of Utility Facilities," 81 *Public Utilities Fortnightly* 55 (January 4, 1968).

[114] See Rob Jones, "Regulatory Decisions Affected by Safety," 79 *Public Utilities Fortnightly* 25 (March 2, 1967).

tries. At the federal level, all responsibility for transport safety was transferred from the commissions (and other federal agencies) to the Department of Transportation, effective April 1, 1967.[115] After illustrating the nature and scope of these regulations, the liability and insurance requirements of the transportation industries will be considered briefly.

National Transportation Safety Board

Section 5 of the Department of Transportation Act of 1966 established within the Department an autonomous National Transportation Safety Board. The section provided that "the Board shall be independent of the Secretary and the other offices and officers of the Department" in the exercise of its functions. The Board was to consist of five members (no more than three from the same political party) appointed by the President with the consent of the Senate, to hold office for five years.

The Board was directed to (1) determine the cause or probable cause of transportation accidents and to report the facts, conditions, and circumstances relating to such accidents; and (2) to review on appeal the suspension, amendment, modification, revocation, or denial of any certificate or license issued by the Secretary or by an Administrator. The Board was further authorized, among other things, to conduct special studies and to make recommendations to the Secretary or Administrators on matters pertaining to the prevention of accidents and the promotion of safety; to initiate on its own motion or conduct rail, highway, or pipeline accident investigations and to make recommendations to the Secretary or Administrators concerning rules, regulations, and procedures for the conduct of accident investigations; and to request from the Secretary or Administrators notification of transportation accidents and reports of such accidents as it deems necessary. In short, the National Transportation Safety Board has broad responsibilities with respect to the investigation of accidents, the determination of their cause, and the steps to be taken to prevent their recurrence.[116]

Airline Safety Regulation

The significance of safety in air transport has been succinctly stated by Frederick:

---

[115] Public Law 89-670 (1966). In 1968, Congress enacted legislation giving the Department of Transportation jurisdiction over safety standards for natural gas transportation facilities (Public Law 90-481). On the need for such standards, see Alan S. Boyd, "DOT—Its Accomplishments and Goals," in National Association of Regulatory Utility Commissioners, *Annual Proceedings, 1967* (Washington, D.C., 1968), pp. 239-41. Also see "Gas Safety—A Fact Not an Argument," 80 *Public Utilities Fortnightly* 44 (July 6, 1967). The Department is expected to promulgate its standards within two years.

[116] Substantial controversy surrounded the combining of investigation and safety regulation, with many arguing that these are separate tasks and best handled if placed in independent hands. The wisdom of the policy adopted can only be determined on the basis of the Board's future record, "although there seem to be good reasons to suppose that it is better equipped to carry out these assignments for rail, water, and motor carriers than the agencies previously charged with them." Pegrum, *op. cit.*, p. 542.

Air transportation is unique among industries in the importance of safety. On the one hand, the safety of air transportation is itself part and parcel of the product the industry sells to the public. On the other hand, because of the new dimension in airspace in which it carries on its business, there is no such thing as an acceptable risk. In most other industries, while safety is a factor affecting costs or even the reputation of the company, the product is usually saleable regardless of the safety record of the industry itself. The economic success of air transportation, on the other hand, rests primarily on public confidence in its safety record.[117]

The Federal Aviation Administration. The responsibilities of the Federal Aviation Administration (of the Department of Transportation), as outlined in the Federal Aviation Act of 1958,[118] are:

(1) The regulation of air commerce in such a manner as to best promote its development and safety and fulfill the requirements of national defense.
(2) The promotion, encouragement, and development of civil aeronautics.
(3) The control of the use of the navigable airspace of the United States and the regulation of both civil and military operations in such airspace in the interest of the safety and efficiency of both.
(4) The consolidation of research and development with respect to air navigation facilities as well as the installation and operation thereof.
(5) The development and operation of a common system of air traffic control and navigation for both military and civil aircraft.[119]

In carrying out these responsibilities, the FAA makes and enforces safety regulations; registers, tests, inspects, and certifies planes; inspects maintenance facilities; examines and rates pilots and mechanics; directs traffic both around airports and in the air; is in charge of federal grants for the development of public airports; and directs aircraft safety research and development. The Administration also operates the Washington National Airport and Dulles International Airport (near Chantilly, Virginia). Dulles was the world's first civil airport designed especially for jet aircraft. Because of its importance, brief mention will be made of the FAA's air traffic control.

Air Traffic Control. One of the Administration's most demanding tasks is the complicated one of air traffic control. The FAA operates and maintains nearly 10,000 facilities of 60 different types for federal air navigation, traffic control, and communications systems. The domestic air traffic control facilities are shown in Figure 12–2. These facilities include 333 flight service stations, 28 air route traffic control centers, 233 airport traffic control towers, 12 international flight service stations, 257 instrument landing systems, and 223 approach light systems. During fiscal 1966, the FAA's air route traffic control

---

[117] Frederick, *op. cit.,* p. 329.
[118] The Federal Aviation Act created the Federal Aviation Agency and transferred to the agency the functions formerly exercised by the Civil Aeronautics Board. These functions have now been transferred to the Department of Transportation.
[119] Robert M. Kane and Allan D. Vose, *Air Transportation* (Dubuque, Iowa: Wm. C. Brown Book Co., 1967), p. 64.

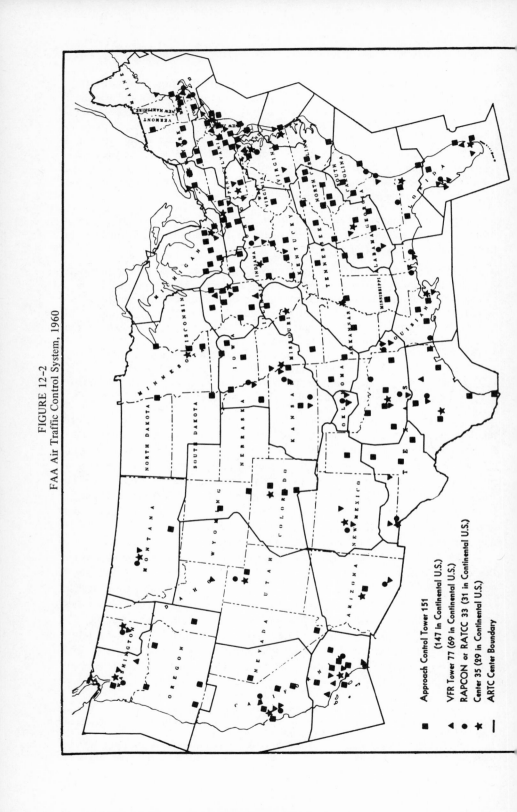

FIGURE 12-2
FAA Air Traffic Control System, 1960

■ Approach Control Tower 151
   (147 in Continental U.S.)

▲ VFR Tower 77 (69 in Continental U.S.)

● RAPCON or RATCC 33 (31 in Continental U.S.)

★ Center 35 (29 in Continental U.S.)

— ARTC Center Boundary

centers handled 13.5 million aircraft operating under instrument flight rules along nearly 133,565 miles of federal airways, airport traffic control towers logged in 41.2 million landings and departures, and the FAA's flight service stations gave 5.4 million pilot briefings.[120]

In insuring efficient and safe utilization of airspace, the FAA must formulate airspace policy and assign airspace use;[121] develop, test, and evaluate air navigation systems, procedures, and facilities; acquire, establish, improve, and operate such facilities; and establish rules and regulations to govern air traffic and the flight of aircraft. Before taking off, each airline pilot must submit his flight plan to the FAA control center, giving his proposed route and altitude. The center makes sure before clearing the flight that no other plane is flying this route at this altitude at the same time. The pilot must obtain also takeoff clearance from the FAA traffic tower. During the flight, the pilot follows the FAA radio range beam, receives FAA weather information, and reports his position to the FAA communications points along the way. At his destination, he gets FAA clearance for the approach and landing. Air traffic control is an extensive operation. To aid in this task, a semiautomatic air traffic control system is being developed.

As part of its air traffic control duties, the FAA is also responsible for seeking a solution to the growing problems of airport congestion, particularly at New York's Kennedy International and LaGuardia, Newark, Chicago's O'Hare, and Washington's National.[122] Many proposals have been made, including the establishment of hourly takeoff and landing quotas (scheduled to go into effect in mid-1969) for these five major airports; scheduling of flights to and from regional airports (such as Westchester Airport near New York City); and new fare schedules designed to reduce peak-hour traveling. In addition, Eastern began a seven-week experiment, late in 1968, with a four-engine STOL—short takeoff and landing—plane that, if successful, promises to help solve the airport congestion problem.[123]

[120] All data from Federal Aviation Agency, *Eighth Annual Report* (1966), pp. 25, 30.

[121] The airspace is divided into two primary categories—controlled and uncontrolled—for air traffic control purposes. The controlled airspace, in turn, is divided into low-altitude airways, intermediate-altitude airways, jet routes, and special-use airspace.

[122] See "The Crowded Skies," *Time*, March 31, 1967, pp. 52-63; and "Air Controllers Battle for More Space in Sky," *Business Week*, July 20, 1968. Also see John Mecklin, "U.S. Airlines: Into the Wild Blue What?," *Fortune*, May, 1966, pp. 146-51, 187-94; S. G. Tipton, *The Airport Situation: Some New Approaches to a Growing National Problem* (Washington, D.C.: Air Transport Association of America, 1967); "Can Airports Cope with the Jet Age?," *Business Week*, July 22, 1967, pp. 54-73; Federal Aviation Administration, *Aviation Demand and Airport Facility Requirement Forecasts for Large Air Transportation Hubs Through 1980* (Washington, D.C., 1967); and *Maintenance of an Adequate Airport System* (Hearings before the Aviation Subcommittee of the Committee on Commerce, Senate, 90th Cong., 1st sess.) (Washington, D.C.: U.S. Government Printing Office, 1968).

[123] "The real crux of the tests is to find whether the STOL's new navigation and guidance system will enable it, in effect, to operate in its own private tunnel in the air, quite outside the patterns laid out for conventional air traffic. Instead of being tracked and guided from the ground, the pilot will follow a precise flight plan, directed by his own equipment.

The NTSB and Accident Investigations. The National Transportation Safety Board is authorized to exercise all functions relating to aircraft accident investigations. The usual steps in such investigations are as follows:

Notification of Accident or Potential Hazard. All accidents involving serious or fatal injury, any air carrier, air collision, fire in flight, structural failure or aircraft or power plant or prop control operations.

Field Investigations. Includes investigation of the accident or review of accident reports to determine adequacy of report.

Laboratory Tests of Failed Parts. Tests of failed parts by appropriate government or commercial laboratories.

Public Hearings. Hearings held when it is in the public interest to bring out the facts.

Technical Analysis and Digest of Evidence. Technical analysis of facts, conditions, and circumstances brought out in hearings, and digest of all the evidence.

Public Report of Findings. Release of public report showing facts, conditions, and circumstances including analysis, probable cause, and recommendations for corrective action.[124]

The goal of an accident investigation is not merely to find the cause of that particular accident, but to correct previous errors so as to prevent re-occurrences. While human errors and limitations continue to be the greatest single cause of aircraft accidents, mechanical and structural failures are also significant. Medical, selecting, and training programs can help to eliminate the human error. So, too, can better weather reporting and traffic control systems. Frequently, however, engineering recommendations have been made following accidents: a modification in the control switch installation of the Viscount, improvement of the power plant fire protection features of C-46 cargo aircraft, installation of an improved bolt in the main gear drag strut of the Fairchild F-27, and removal of the gang bar for compass circuit breakers on Electra aircraft.

As part of its research program, the FAA is developing new devices and procedures to prevent in-flight and airport emergencies. In cooperation with the major users of the nation's airspace, work is progressing on a collision avoidance system that will give a signal indicating the need for or initiating an appropriate avoidance maneuver, and also a pilot warning system that will warn a pilot of a nearby aircraft and assist him to avoid a collision. The Administration is developing all-weather landing systems to improve safety in terminal areas, the scene of approximately 80 percent of all air carrier accidents, and to reduce terminal delays and diversions.

Ground controllers will merely monitor the flight and see that there is no conflict with other aircraft in the area." *Business Week,* September 7, 1968, p. 36. Also see Tom Alexander, "Wheels-Up Time for STOL," *Fortune,* November, 1968, pp. 158-63, 216-20.

[124] Frederick, *op. cit.,* p. 319.

Motor Carrier Safety Regulations

The Federal Highway Administration (of the Department of Transportation) has prescribed detailed rules and regulations regarding safety standards for all types of interstate motor carriers. The FHA's safety standards can be outlined under seven major headings:[125]

Qualifications of drivers. Requirements concerning qualifications of drivers deal with mental and physical condition, driving experience and skill, knowledge of regulations, age, and past record. Every driver must meet certain minimum requirements (e.g., mental, physical, eyesight, and hearing requirements), have at least one year's experience in driving some type of motor vehicle (including experience throughout the four seasons), be twenty-one years of age or older, be "competent by reason of experience or training to operate safely the type of motor vehicle or motor vehicles which he drives," and satisfactorily pass a prescribed physical examination before being employed by a motor carrier. A driver must be re-examined every 36 months. The certificate of physical condition must be kept by the carrier, and each driver must have a copy with him while on duty.

Driving of motor vehicles. Driving of motor vehicles includes many requirements, such as conformity with all speed limits, stopping at all railroad crossings (required of vehicles carrying passengers and inflammable liquids), use of turn signals, emergency signals for disabled, stopped, or parked vehicles, proper distribution and securing of a load, emergency equipment, and duties of drivers in case of accidents.

Parts and accessories. Motor carriers are required to have certain specified parts and accessories. These include the number and placement of lighting devices, reflectors, and electrical equipment; requirements as to the adequacy and performance of brakes; use of safety glass in all windows; specifications concerning fuel systems, coupling devices and towing methods; and miscellaneous parts and accessories, such as tires, sleeper berths, heaters, windshield wipers, and flags on projecting loads.

Recording and reporting of accidents. Every motor carrier that is subject to the Department of Transportation Act is required to report to the Federal Highway Administration every accident in which a motor vehicle operated by it is involved, and from which there results an injury to or death of any person, or property damage to any and all vehicles, cargo, or other property involved to the extent of $250 or more. Specific forms for filing accident reports have been prescribed. At the discretion of the Federal Highway Administration, accident reports are confidential, but they may be offered in evidence by FHA, Department of Transportation, or United States attorneys in federal agency and court proceedings. These reports must be filed as soon as possible and, in every instance, within 15 days after the accident with the regional Federal Highway Administrator. All private carriers are required to

[125] U.S. Department of Transportation, Federal Highway Administration, Bureau of Motor Carrier Safety, *Motor Carrier Safety Regulations* (Washington, D.C.: U.S. Government Printing Office, 1968).

record the same information as regulated carriers and to file the information at their principal place of business.

Hours of drivers' service. No driver is allowed to drive or operate for more than 10 hours following 8 consecutive hours off duty, or to drive for any period after having been on duty 15 hours following 8 consecutive hours off duty. The aggregate hours may be increased to 12 in case of adverse weather conditions in order to complete a run. Drivers of sleeper berth vehicles may cumulate the above mentioned total of at least 8 hours off duty in two periods, of at least 2 hours each, resting in a sleeper berth. The maximum number of on-duty hours is 60 in any 7 consecutive days or, in the case of carriers operating vehicles every day of the week, 70 hours in any period of 8 consecutive days. Each driver must keep a daily log (Figure 12-3) in duplicate; one copy to be retained by the motor carrier and the other by the driver.

Inspection and maintenance. Every motor carrier must be systematically inspected and maintained in safe and proper operating condition. A systematic record (of inspection, repairs, and lubrication, including dates) must be maintained "for each motor vehicle controlled by a motor carrier for the

FIGURE 12-3
Sample Copy of Driver's Daily Log

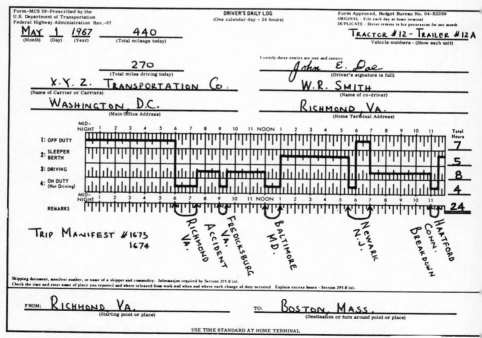

Source: U.S. Department of Transportation, Federal Highway Administration, Bureau of Motor Carrier Safety, *Motor Carrier Safety Regulations* (Washington, D.C.: U.S. Government Printing Office, 1968), p. 68.

period during which such vehicle is subject to the motor carrier's control." *Transportation of explosives and other dangerous articles.* Special regulations have been prescribed for the transportation of explosives and other dangerous articles (e.g., flammable liquids, flammable solids and oxidizing materials, corrosive liquids, compressed gases, and poisons). Vehicles carrying such articles must not be left unattended during the course of transportation, should avoid congested places as far as practicable, should reduce refuelings to a minimum, and drivers must observe certain precautions such as no smoking while driving, avoidance of violent jars, jolts, bumps, and sudden accelerations and decelerations, and care in loading and unloading.

The Transport Safety Record

The comparative transport safety record, for selected years, is shown in Table 12-1. Bus and railroad lines have long had the lowest rate of passenger fatalities per 100 million passenger-miles traveled. Of particular importance, however, is the steady improvement in air transport safety. Further, it is statistically many times safer to ride a mile in a common carrier or fly a mile in a certificated domestic air carrier than to drive one mile in an automobile. But

TABLE 12-1
Comparative Transport Safety Record, Selected Years, 1939-67
(passenger fatality rate per 100,000,000 passenger miles)

Mode of Transport	1939	1949	1955	1960	1965	1967
U.S. Scheduled Airlines:						
Domestic:						
Fatalities	9	93	156	306	205	226
Rate	1.20	1.39	.75	.96	.38	.30
International and Territorial:						
Fatalities	10	4	2	1	21	0
Rate	12.80	.19	.04	.01	.12	.00
Total U.S. Scheduled Airlines:						
Fatalities	19	97	158	307	226	226
Rate	n.a.	n.a.	.62	.75	.31	.22
Motor Buses:						
Fatalities	(1)	120	90	60	100	130[2]
Rate	(1)	.19	.18	.11	.16	.19[2]
Railroads:						
Fatalities	32	29	19	33	12	16
Rate	.14	.08	.07	.16	.07	.09
Autos:						
Fatalities	16,300	15,300	24,700	24,600	32,500	35,200
Rate	3.7	2.0	2.7	2.2	2.4	2.4

n.a. = Not available.
[1] Included in auto statistics.
[2] Preliminary.

Source: Air Transport Association, *Air Transport Facts & Figures, 1959*, p. 30; *1964*, p. 32; and *1968*, p. 40.

while the transport safety record is a good one, the problem is still serious. For example, in addition to actual accidents, there has been a growing number of reported near collisions and other aircraft incidents in the past few years. And the problem of safety is bound to become even more complex as the number of vehicles and aircraft grows.

Carriers' Liability and Insurance

As with other business enterprises, the regulated companies carry insurance for fire, theft, and the like. Common carriers, moreover, generally are held liable for the full value of commodities which they transport, except when loss or damage is caused by acts of God or acts of the public enemy.[126] Common carriers are also liable for injury or death to passengers. The limit of their liability for injury or death has been stated by a court as follows:

> In an airplane accident the limitation of responsibility may be said to consist of a plane in good mechanical condition, handled by a careful pilot, maneuvered in a careful way under conditions that, so far as can be foreseen and overcome by the use of ordinary skill, such as unfavorable weather conditions, so that the ordinary pilot could observe them as such.[127]

In the case of railroads, there are certain exceptions to liability: (1) baggage carried on trains carrying passengers and (2) property, other than ordinary livestock (e.g., racing horses), on which the ICC has specifically authorized "release rates." Release rates are granted on certain articles when the shipper agrees to release the carrier from liability beyond an agreed-on value. Such rates will be authorized by the commission when two conditions exist concurrently—when the commodity is highly susceptible to loss and damage, and when the commodity has a wide range of values.

There are no statutory requirements with respect to insurance for the airlines, railroads, and water carriers. As is to be expected, the airlines carry heavy insurance. As indicated by Frederick:

> No certificated United States airline carries insurance coverage of less than $40,000 per passenger and not less than $150,000 per accident. With respect to airline liability to persons on the ground who are not passengers, none of the certificated airlines carries less insurance coverage than $50,000 per person and $500,000 per accident. With respect to public liability for property damage on the ground for third persons, no certificated airline has insurance coverage of less than $500,000 per accident. These figures represent the least carried by a certificated airline, including the smallest. The average

---

126 See Allen J. O'Brien, "Damage Claims against Air Carriers," 35 *I.C.C. Practitioners' Journal* 652 (1968). Under certain circumstances (e.g., negligent or willful service failures), utilities may also be liable for damages. Compare *Loridans* v. *Southern Bell Teleph. & Teleg. Co.*, 172 So. 2d 323 (1965) with *Coosa Valley Teleph. Co.* v. *Martin*, 133 So. 2d 505 (1961).

127 *Seaman* v. *Curtiss Flying Service, Inc.*, 1929 U.S. Av. R. 48 (1929).

airline carries much higher limits: for example, one middle-sized airline carries insurance of $75,000 for each passenger and $2,000,000 for each accident, and with respect to its liability to persons on the ground it carries insurance coverage of $100,000 per person and $1,000,000 per accident. To cover its potential liabilities for damage to property on the ground, this same airline carries insurance of $1,000,000 per accident.[128]

Minimum insurance requirements have been established for common and contract motor carriers. The need for such requirements stems from the fact that thousands of relatively small motor carriers are often financially weak and sometimes unable to meet claims or judgments against them.[129] Before a motor carrier is issued a certificate or permit, it must provide evidence of security in the form of surety bonds, insurance, or qualifications as a self-insurer in such amounts as the commission may require. At the present time, these requirements are as follows:

1. Cargo liability: Not less than $1,000 on any one motor vehicle for common carriers of property; not less than $2,000 for loss or damage at any one time and place. However, certain low-value commodities, such as coal, lumber, and commercial fertilizer, do not require cargo liability security. Contract carriers of property are not required to file evidence of cargo liability security.
2. Automobile bodily injury or public liability: Not less than $25,000 for injury or death of one person. For all injuries or deaths in any one accident not less than $100,000.
3. Damage to the property of others (excluding cargo): Each accident $10,000.[130]

These requirements, while minimums, are considered by many as too low. The larger carriers carry at least $100,000 per vehicle for cargo liability, $100,000 per person for injury or death, and $300,000 per accident. Such insurance is necessary, since jury grants of $100,000 for a serious injury are not uncommon. Private and exempt carriers are not required to comply with the commission's insurance requirements.

---

[128] Frederick, *op. cit.,* p. 327. The CAB has held that trunkline and local-service carriers' tariff rules must provide that a carrier's limitation of liability for loss of, damage to, or delay in delivery of any personal property, including baggage (whether checked or not) is not less than $500 per passenger. *Baggage Liability Rules Case*, E-24198 (CAB, 1966).

[129] "An average motor carrier in recent years has considered itself fortunate to earn a profit of 5 cents on each dollar in revenue. The average [cargo] claim is about $30.00 and, in order to pay it, a motor carrier realizing 5 cents profit on each dollar must transport $600.00 of revenue freight without profit. To pay a claim of $100.00, the carrier would have to transport $2,000 of revenue freight to come out even, whereas a $1,000 claim would drain away the profit on $20,000 of revenue freight. The claim bill for Class I and II motor common carriers in a recent year exceeded $30 million." Charles A. Taff, *Commercial Motor Transportation* (3d ed.; Homewood, Ill.: Richard D. Irwin, Inc., 1961), pp. 361-62.

[130] *Ibid.,* p. 392.

SERVICE AND SAFETY REGULATION: SUMMARY

Service and safety regulation are vital aspects of the regulatory process. Thousands of service complaints are received annually by the commissions, involving such things as faulty meters, schedule irregularities, reservation difficulties, and inferior service.[131] While these complaints occupy a significant portion of a commission's time, they are normally handled promptly and informally.

Safety regulation, especially for the transportation industries, is of far greater importance. An increase in the number of carriers, as well as in their speed, raises the likelihood of accidents. The National Transportation Safety Board was created to centralize federal accident investigation and prevention. It seems clear that far greater emphasis will be placed on transport safety in the next few years.

[131] The Civil Aeronautics Board, for example, received 1,610 passenger and shipper service complaints in fiscal 1966 and 3,036 such complaints in fiscal 1967. Civil Aeronautics Board, *Reports to Congress* (1967), p. 79.

Chapter	REGULATION OF THE
13	TRANSPORTATION
	INDUSTRIES

A considerable amount of the criticism which has been directed at the transportation regulatory process has been centered around charges of inequality, inconsistency, and delay. Usually, the regulatory agency is the target of these charges. There is ample evidence, however, to support the conclusion that inconsistencies and ambiguities in the law itself, coupled with obsolete provisions carried over from an earlier and different era are, in large part, the real basis for complaint.

—National Transportation Policy *

The transportation industries are subject to the most detailed and complex regulatory activity found in the United States. Government policy toward the various modes of transport has sought two basic objectives—promotion and regulation. It has promoted development of the transportation industries by extending public aid in many forms. It has regulated these industries by controlling entry, rates, combinations, and service. In trying to achieve these two objectives, inconsistencies in policy have resulted. Further, while potential competition among the different modes of transport has developed, regulation has also tightened.

In the present chapter, the development of regulatory laws and the major inconsistencies in public policy are discussed. The following chapter considers the current economic situation of the transportation industries and the leading problem areas.

REGULATION OF THE RAILROAD MONOPOLY: 1850-1933

The development of transportation regulation can be divided into two periods. The first, extending from 1850 to 1933, was the period of promotion and regulation of a railroad monopoly. The second, from 1933 to date, can be

*National Transportation Policy (Preliminary draft of a report prepared for the Committee on Interstate and Foreign Commerce by the Special Study Group on Transportation Policies in the United States, Senate, 87th Cong., 1st sess.) (Washington, D.C.: U.S. Government Printing Office, 1961), p. 12.

441

characterized as a period of growing competition in the transportation industry. Public policy, in turn, has largely been concerned with the need to adjust regulatory laws from a monopolistic situation to a competitive one.

The Rise of Government Intervention

Two forces led to government intervention in the railroad industry: (1) a desire to encourage the early realization of reduced transportation costs to promote economic development and (2) political pressure, particularly from western farmers.

Economic Development. Railroad development in the United States has been dominated from the beginning by private industry. Yet, it is interesting to note that in the early days of railroading, some of the states undertook to carry out construction. Pennsylvania built the Allegheny Portage Railroad and the Philadelphia & Columbia Railroad, while Illinois, Indiana, Michigan, Georgia and other states entered the field in the 1840's and 1850's. Other states acquired railroads when private companies which had been assisted by state subsidies failed. The states soon found that their railroads were involving them in financial difficulties, and most of them gradually sold their railroad assets to private corporations. In a few states, these financial losses so impressed the citizens that provisions were inserted in state constitutions to forbid any further undertakings.

Withdrawal of the states left the field to private enterprise.[1] Even in the 1840's and 1850's, the part played by the states was so small that the whole period from 1827 to about 1870 may be thought of as a period of rapid building by private industry, tremendous financial speculation, and practically no governmental regulation. Railroad development dates from 1827 when the Baltimore and Ohio Railroad was granted a charter by the state of Maryland. In the decade of the 1830's, nearly 3,000 miles of track were laid, largely in the eastern states. The lines were local in nature—that is, they served a small area and, being of various gauge, did not offer a through service for any distance except with a frequent transfer of passengers or merchandise from one line to another. In the 1840's, over 6,000 miles of track were laid. Even as late as this decade, however, the railroad was looked on as a means of transportation which would remain secondary to the canal. Many railroads were built as canal feeders,

---

[1] A few municipalities constructed railroad lines, such as the Schenectady & Troy Railroad which was built by the City of Troy, New York, and opened in 1842. Most of these roads were eventually sold. But see John F. Due, "The City of Princeville Railway—A Case Study in Government Enterprise," 5 *Quarterly Review of Economics & Business* 63 (1965). The federal government constructed the Alaska Railroad in 1916 (now administered by the Department of Transportation). (See Edwin M. Fitch, *The Alaska Railroad* [New York: Frederick A. Praeger, Publishers, 1967].) A few states currently own railroads, including the Long Island Railroad (owned and operated by the Metropolitan Commuter Transportation Authority, an agency of the State of New York), the Western & Atlantic (owned by the State of Georgia and operated by the Louisville & Nashville), and the Atlantic & North Carolina Railroad (majority capital stock owned by the State of North Carolina and leased to and operated by the Atlantic and East Carolina Railway Company).

and some state-granted charters sought to protect canals from the new form of competition. Moreover, by no means were all people convinced of the future significance of the railroads. In 1842, the people of Dorchester, Massachusetts, felt that they should "prevent, if possible, so great a calamity to our town as must be the location of any railroad through it."[2]

The 1850's saw construction of 21,000 miles of railroad track, or over twice as much as had taken place in the two preceding decades. By 1860, the skeleton of the present-day railroad system east of the Mississippi was in existence. No longer were railroads looked on as secondary to canals. The 1850's also saw the beginning of the consolidation movement with the formation in 1853 of the New York Central out of 10 formerly separate lines between New York, Albany, and Buffalo. Gradually, it became possible to travel a considerable distance without continually transferring from one line to another.

Without going into detail, it may be said that railroad mileage continued to expand until 1917. The 1860's saw the laying of about the same amount of rail as the 1850's, with the bulk of the development during this decade coming in the years following the Civil War. In 1869, the first transcontinental railroad was completed. The 1870's saw the addition of over 40,000 miles and represented the high point of any 10-year period of construction. In the 1880's, over 30,000 miles were added, and as late as the decade ending in 1903, railroad mileage increased by about 34,000 miles. By 1916, there were 254,037 miles of railroad line in the United States.

The lack of important railroad regulation prior to 1870 is not difficult to understand. Until quite a system of competing railroads had developed, there was really no railroad problem to regulate. More important (more important because before 1870 there were problems to which regulation might have been applied) was the fact that it took a considerable period of abuse on the part of the railroads to awake the public to the need of regulating them. It was during this early period of railroad development that the people generally looked on the railroad as a great benefactor. They felt that it would be a very important factor in developing the country—as it was—and they actively supported the new method of transportation. Local units of government bought railroad stocks and bonds, made direct loans, and gave station sites and exempted some property from taxation to encourage railroads to locate in their towns. State governments bought bonds, floated large loans, made some land grants, and granted tax-exempt privileges. The federal government, in 1850, began to make land grants. It is estimated that the land grants made by the federal government (not all railroads received land grants) were equal to about 10 percent of the total land area of the continental United States.[3] Without this support, the rapid expansion of the railroad system would have been impossible.

[2] From a 1927 address by B. S. Atkinson, as quoted by D. Philip Locklin, *Economics of Transportation* (6th ed.; Homewood, Ill.: Richard D. Irwin, Inc., 1966), p. 87.

[3] Charles L. Dearing and Wilfred Owen, *National Transportation Policy* (Washington, D.C.: Brookings Institution, 1949), p. 11.

In spite of the fact that no important attempt to regulate the railroads occurred until the 1870's, it is worth noting that many of the earliest state-granted railroad charters upheld the point of view that railroads could be regulated in the public interest. Many charters contained provisions aimed at protecting society. Such provisions are illustrated by schedules of maximum rates, restrictions on discriminatory rates, and the assertion of the state's right to call for lower rates when the earnings on the investment exceeded a specific percentage (10 percent in some cases). Moreover, in the late 1830's and 1840's, a few New England states created railroad commissions. As previously discussed, however, neither the early charter regulation nor commission regulation was of significance other than in its implication that railroads were subject to regulation. The commissions lacked effective power, while charter provisions were inadequate and often not enforced, and when enforced, inflexible. Thus, the late 1870's mark the first real effort to regulate the railroads.

The Granger Laws. It has been said that "The Granger laws marked a reversal of government policy from one of public assistance to one of public control."[4] The Granger laws of the 1870's were laws enacted by a number of midwestern states, beginning in 1871 with Illinois. They were sponsored unofficially by the farmers' organization known as the Grange—hence, the designation "Granger laws."

Fundamentally, the cause of the farmers' drive to get railroad regulation grew out of the depressed conditions in agriculture. The prices received by farmers for their products had suffered a decline; the decline being the result of such things as the diminishing demand in foreign markets for domestic grain as well as an increase in supply owing to the rapid settlement of the West and the adoption of better agricultural methods. It was easy for farmers to place the blame for their depressed conditions on the railroads. While farm prices had declined, railroad rates were still high. Further, the farmers' drive for regulation had considerable merit: the railroads were guilty of engaging in highly discriminatory practices. Railroads, for example, were quoting lower rates from certain competitive points than from noncompetitive points. The farmers felt that these lower rates must be profitable to the railroads or they would not exist. Hence, they reasoned that the higher rates at noncompetitive points must be producing handsome profits.

The Granger movement also drew support from other quarters. The citizens of the country, as well as units of government, who had poured large sums into railroad securities now began to discover that the railroads might not be the public benefactors they originally assumed. Three serious drawbacks to the policy of promoting rapid economic development were gradually recognized:

[4] H. F. Haulik, "The State as Regulator," in H. Taylor (ed.), *Contemporary Economic Problems and Trends* (New York: Harcourt, Brace & World, Inc., 1938), p. 352. The railroads received title to 131,350,534 acres. Robert S. Henry, "The Railroad Land Grant Legend in American History Texts," 32 *Mississippi Valley Historical Review* 171, 172 (1945).

(*a*) there was tremendous overbuilding of railroad lines; (*b*) corruption and ill-advised methods of promotion and finance were assisted; (*c*) public aids were exploited for personal gain. Overexpansion, resulting from speculative building, led to cutthroat competition and, in turn, to instability in rates and to monopolistic agreements and practices. During the 1860's and 1870's, rate wars broke out between New York and Chicago, between Chicago and the Pacific Coast, and in the South. Agreements among the railroads were the outcome. At first, these agreements were informal, merely being understandings with regard to rates. Because they were largely ineffective, formal arrangements—in the form of pools—were undertaken. Pooling agreements were of two major types—traffic pools and money pools. As explained by Locklin:

> In a traffic pool the competitive traffic is divided among the rival carriers. In a money pool the traffic moves over the various lines without interference, but the receipts from the competitive business, or a portion thereof, are divided among the participating carriers. Traffic pools imply an interference with the privilege of shippers to route their traffic, and it was largely for this reason that the money pool was more common. Sometimes, however, a traffic pool was successfully operated by permitting some large shipper to send his shipments over one route or another in amounts that would even up the total flow of traffic according to agreed percentages. Shippers acting in this capacity were called "eveners," and in return for their services to the railroad companies, they received rebates or concessions from the published rates. One of the most famous of these arrangements was the cattle eveners' pool, formed in 1875, in which cattle shipments from Chicago to New York were evened in accordance with agreed proportions by a group of large shippers in return for generous rebates. The Standard Oil Company acted as an evener in connection with shipments of crude petroleum from producing points in Pennsylvania to the seaboard.[5]

Corruption and ill-advised methods of promotion and finance were likewise encouraged and assisted by public aids during this early period. Local and state governments, investors, and consumers were all hurt in the process. The construction company, discussed in Chapter 6, was an important speculative device and frequently served as a medium through which a few people could gain by "milking" an operating company. The speculation inherent in the development of the railroad industry is well illustrated by the history of the Erie

[5] Locklin, *op. cit.,* p. 295. "The pooling movement spread rapidly; in 1879, it was stated there were eight major pools: the Omaha Pool, the Trunk Line Association, the Southern Railway & Steamship Association, the Southwestern Railway Association, the Chicago–Twin Cities Pool, the Chicago Cattle Pool, the Oil Pool, and the Anthracite Pool." George W. Hilton, "The Consistency of the Interstate Commerce Act," 9 *Journal of Law and Economics* 87, 88 (1966). See Henry Hudson, "The Southern Railway and Steamship Association," 5 *Quarterly Journal of Economics* 70 (1890); and Robert E. Riegel, "The Southwestern Pool," 19 *Missouri Historical Review* 12 (1924) and "The Omaha Pool," 22 *Iowa Journal of History and Politics* 569 (1924). Not all pooling agreements were successful, but where they were, competition was eliminated and discrimination practiced.

Railroad, well known in earlier days as the "Scarlet Woman of Wall Street." Chartered in 1832 with its total cost estimated at $3 million, two years later the estimated cost was increased to $6 million, and the state loaned to the company a sum equal to the increased estimate. By 1845, the estimated cost had been increased to $12 million; the state gave up its claim on the original $3 million loan, and the company raised an additional $3 million on a mortgage. In 1851, the road was opened from New York to Lake Erie, but in 1859 it failed to pay interest on its mortgage and went into receivership. A new firm was formed. In 1862, the mortgage was again foreclosed, and a third company formed to run the Erie. In 1868, the construction of the main road was completed. The total cost was $16.5 million as against the original estimated cost of $3 million.

In addition, tales of fraud and financial chicanery committed by men high in railroad circles fanned the growing public concern. This concern was further accentuated by the high-handed manner with which the railroad executives treated the public. People were driven to action when the railroads continued their policy of discriminatory and excessive rates, such rates being, in part, a reflection of the need for obtaining large revenues to make interest payments on greatly inflated capitalizations.

In general, the Granger laws dealt almost entirely with the matter of rates, their main aim being to secure lower rates. While they varied in detail, these laws often set maximum rates or established a commission with authority to set maximum rates, forbade discrimination between places to the extent that rates should not be higher for a shorter haul than for a longer haul, prohibited petty bribery of public officials through the granting of passes, and established a commission to secure enforcement. In their attempt to preserve competition, with the belief that competition among railroads would result in lower rates, some states forbade combinations.

At first, the railroads claimed immunity from regulation. They argued, in the first place, that they were engaged in a private business which could not be subjected to rate regulation, and in the second place, even if they were subject to regulation, they were interstate in character and thus subject only to federal control. The Granger cases grew out of the railroads' efforts to thwart state regulation. In these famous Supreme Court decisions, "the Court cemented the cornerstone of the present system of state regulation of public utilities."[6] The Court held that railroads were affected with a public interest and thus subject to detailed regulation. Moreover, in the absence of federal regulation, the states were held to have the right to regulate, even though the railroads were engaged in interstate commerce.

---

[6] Haulik, *op. cit.,* p. 352. The Granger cases are made up of six Court decisions: *Munn* v. *Illinois,* 94 U.S. 113 (1877), in which the Court set forth the principles for regulating rates charged by grain elevators, subsequently applied in five railroad cases; *Chicago, Burlington and Quincy Railroad Co.* v. *Iowa,* 94 U.S. 155 (1877); *Peik* v. *Chicago and Northwestern Railway Co.,* 94 U.S. 164 (1877); *Chicago, Milwaukee and St. Paul Railroad Co.* v. *Ackley,* 94 U.S. 179 (1877); *Winona and St. Peter Railroad Co.* v. *Blake,* 94 U.S. 180 (1877); and *Stone* v. *Wisconsin,* 94 U.S. 181 (1877).

In spite of the legal success of the Granger laws, their actual success in regulating the railroads was not great.[7] Commissions often proved incompetent, while discrimination among various shipping points, among shippers, and among commodities continued or increased on a large scale. The laws had been passed hurriedly during a wave of emotional outburst against the railroads. As a result, they were crudely drawn and contained many provisions which were too drastic to be enforced. Regulations of various states differed so that railroads doing business in more than one state were subjected to the trouble of not only different rules, but sometimes rules which were conflicting. Even more important, in 1886 came a Supreme Court decision, the Wabash case, which spelled the end of any successful state control. The Court decided, opposite to its decisions in the Granger cases, that the states could not regulate an interstate business *regardless* of the inactivity of the federal government.[8] This decision made it evident that if effective railroad regulation was desired, it had to come from the federal government, since nearly three-fourths of all railroad traffic was interstate in character. In 1887, Congress took action by passing the Act to Regulate Commerce.

The Act to Regulate Commerce, 1887: Its Emasculation

Congress had become interested in the railroad situation prior to the Wabash decision. In 1872, a Senate committee, known as the Windom Committee, was appointed to look into the possibility of achieving lower rates from the Midwest to the East. In its report to the Senate in 1874, the committee charged that the abuses of the railroads were "insufficient facilities, unfair discriminations, and extortionate charges."[9] To correct these abuses, the committee recommended that the federal government construct and operate some railroad lines "which being unable to enter into combinations, will serve as regulators of other lines."[10] Congress took no action. In 1874, 1878, and again in 1884, the House passed bills providing for federal regulation, but it was not until 1885 that the Senate passed such a measure. However, the 1884 House bill (the Reagan bill) and the 1885 Senate bill (the Cullom bill) were quite different, resulting in a deadlock.[11] The Senate then appointed another special committee to investigate the railroad situation. The committee, known as the Cullom Committee,

---

[7]See S. J. Buck, *The Granger Movement* (Cambridge: Harvard University Press, 1913); Charles R. Dietrick, "The Effects of the Granger Acts," 11 *Journal of Political Economy* 237 (1903); A. E. Paine, "The Granger Movement in Illinois," 1 *University of Illinois Studies* 335 (1905); and Charles Fairman, "The So-Called Granger Cases, Lord Hale, and Justice Bradley," 5 *Stanford Law Review* 587 (1953).

[8]*Wabash, St. Louis & Pacific Railway Co. v. Illinois,* 118 U.S. 557 (1886).

[9]*Report of the Select Committee on Transportation—Routes to the Seaboard* (Senate Report No. 307, 43d Cong., 1st sess.), Part 1, p. 71.

[10]*Ibid.,* p. 242. Also see Gerald D. Nash, "Origins of the Interstate Commerce Act of 1887," 24 *Pennsylvania History* 183 (1957).

[11]For comparative texts of the two bills, see 16 *Congressional Record* 1085-86 (1885).

made its report in 1886. After listing 18 charges against the railroads, the committee recommended regulation, not federal-private competition, arguing:

> The evidence upon this point is so conclusive that the committee has no hesitation in declaring that prompt action by Congress upon this important subject is almost unanimously demanded by public sentiment. This demand is occasioned by the existence of acknowledged evils incident to and growing out of the complicated business of transportation as now conducted, evils which the people believe can be checked and mitigated, if not wholly remedied, by appropriate legislation. The committee recognizes the justice of this demand, and believes that action by Congress looking to the regulation of interstate transportation is necessary and expedient. . . .[12]

The Act to Regulate Commerce, usually referred to as the Interstate Commerce Act, was signed by President Cleveland on February 4, 1887.[13] It was largely based upon the Cullom Committee report, was written in general terms, and its interpretation was left to the Interstate Commerce Commission created for the purpose by the act.[14] The primary objectives were to prevent discriminatory rates and to give more reasonable (i.e., lower) rates to shippers.

It was the lack of specific provisions which led to the so-called emasculation of the act by the courts in the years immediately following its passage. While the act gave the commission power to receive complaints concerning violations of the law, to obtain reports from the railroads, to compel testimony, to set up uniform accounting systems, and to make effective the main provisions of the act ("just and reasonable" rates; prohibition of discrimination, rebates, and pooling; and the filing of all rate schedules), it did not specifically state that the commission had power to set rates. No sooner had the commission attempted to make use of the power it thought it had been given by the Act to Regulate Commerce than it found itself shorn of all these powers, except the power of publicity.[15] In 1892, the Supreme Court held that witnesses could refuse to give testimony which might be self-incriminating under the Fifth Amendment to the Constitution.[16] The commission found it impossible, there-

---

[12] *Report of the Senate Select Committee on Interstate Commerce* (Senate Report No. 46, 49th Cong., 1st sess.), Part 1, p. 175.

[13] On the Act of 1887, see C. B. Aitchison, "The Evolution of the Interstate Commerce Act: 1887–1937," 5 *George Washington Law Review* 289 (1937).

The full texts of the surface transportation laws discussed in this chapter are found in *Laws Relating to Interstate Commerce and Transportation*, compiled by Gilman G. Udell (Washington, D.C.: U.S. Government Printing Office, 1961). Also see John Guandolo, *Transportation Law* (Dubuque, Iowa: Wm. C. Brown Co. Publishers, 1965).

[14] The 1887 act provided for a five-member commission. The commission's membership was enlarged to seven (by the Hepburn Act of 1906), to nine (in August, 1917), and to the present eleven members (by the Transportation Act of 1920).

[15] Kolko has argued that "the railroads, not the farmers and shippers, were the most important single advocates of federal regulation from 1877 to 1916." Gabriel Kolko, *Railroads and Regulation, 1877–1916* (Princeton: Princeton University Press, 1965), p. 3. This thesis is questionable. See Robert W. Harbeson, "Railroads and Regulation, 1877–1916: Conspiracy or Public Interest?" 27 *The Journal of Economic History* 230 (1967).

[16] *Counselman v. Hitchcock*, 142 U.S. 547 (1892).

fore, to obtain evidence on rebates and rate discrimination. In 1897, in the Maximum Freight Rate Decision, any power the commission thought it had over the fixing of rates was removed.[17] Previous to this decision, the commission had set aside rates as unreasonable and had prescribed maximum rates. It assumed this power was given it by the act of 1887 which had required that all rates should be just and reasonable. But the Court held the commission was without any rate-setting power: "The power to prescribe rates or fix any tariff is not among the powers granted to the Commission." It pointed out that rate setting was a very important matter and that no such power had been specifically granted to the commission in the act. Certainly, added the Court, if Congress had wanted the commission to have such an important power, it would have said so. As a result of the decision, the commission found itself simply with the power of setting aside one rate after another as unreasonable. And, in another case decided in the same year, the Court reduced the hearings held by the commission to a mere formality by refusing to accept the findings of the agency as final evidence.[18] Instead, the Court insisted on reviewing all evidence, both old and new. The railroads thus refused to take the commission's hearings seriously, preferring instead to take any orders to the courts where the commission was frequently overruled. The Court also weakened the "long-and-short-haul" clause by holding that it did not apply where discrimination resulted from competition between railroads.

The cumulative effect of the Court's decisions on the Interstate Commerce Commission was clearly expressed by Justice Harlan in his dissent in the Alabama Midland case:

Taken in connection with other decisions defining the powers of the Interstate Commerce Commission, the present decision . . . goes far to make that commission a useless body, for all practical purposes, and to defeat many of the important objects designated to be accomplished by the various enactments of Congress relating to interstate commerce. The commission was established to protect the public against the improper practices of transportation companies engaged in commerce among the several states. It has been left, it is true, with power to make reports and to issue protests. But it has been shorn, by judicial interpretation, of authority to do anything of an effective character. It is denied many of the powers which, in my judgment, were intended to be conferred upon it.[19]

Strengthening Federal Regulation

In an effort to strengthen the Interstate Commerce Commission or, rather, in an effort to restore to the commission the powers it had been denied by the

[17] *Interstate Commerce Comm.* v. *Cincinnati, New Orleans and Texas Pacific Railway Co.,* 167 U.S. 479 (1897).

[18] *Interstate Commerce Comm.* v. *Alabama Midland Railway Co.,* 168 U.S. 144 (1897).

[19] Dissenting opinion, *ibid.,* p. 176. See Carl McFarland, *Judicial Control of the Federal Trade Commission and the Interstate Commerce Commission* (Cambridge: Harvard University Press, 1933), esp. pp. 102–14.

Court, Congress passed important railroad legislation in 1903, 1906, and 1910. The Elkins Act of 1903 struck at personal discrimination, that is, rate discrimination between shippers. Prior to this act, the courts held that evidence that a rebate had been received was not enough to prove the existence of discrimination; the commission also had to show that comparable shippers had not received similar rebates. To remove this difficulty, the Elkins Act declared that every departure from a published schedule of rates was to be considered as prima facie evidence of discrimination. Moreover, the recipient of the rebate was made as guilty as the railroad granting it. As the maximum fine for violations was raised to $20,000, large shippers were made less eager to apply pressure on railroads for rebates.

The Hepburn Act of 1906 (many date the real growth of the commission's power from this Act) gave specifically to the commission the right to fix maximum rates.[20] The jurisdiction of the ICC was extended to cover industrial railroads and private car lines. The commission was authorized to control division of rates and charges made for switching and special services rendered by shippers and carriers. To prevent the railroads from refusing to interchange traffic with water carriers, the law gave the commission power to require establishment of joint rates, to fix these rates, and to determine how they should be divided. The act required a 30-day notice of changes in rates. The tendency for hearings before the ICC to become mere formalities was checked by a provision making the commission's orders binding on a railroad with a fine of $5,000 for each day of violation. Recipients of rebates were made liable for triple damages. A provision, known as the commodities clause, forbade the railroads from hauling goods (except for lumber and goods for their own use) they themselves produced. Finally, the Hepburn Act put effective accounting control power into the hands of the commission: the ICC could now examine company books and impose fines for violations.

In 1910, the Mann-Elkins Act, among other things, gave the commission the right to suspend proposed rate changes for a period of six months, during which it was to determine the reasonableness of the rates.[21] Previous to this time, the commission could take no action until the rate was in effect. The act also made effective a "long-and-short-haul" clause. As stated in the 1887 act, the clause might be suspended by the ICC when existing competition at the farther point might hurt the railroad if it charged more for the longer haul than for the shorter one. Since some competition could be shown at nearly any point, the Supreme Court's 1897 Alabama Midland decision virtually set aside the prohibi-

---

[20]The commission's power to fix minimum rates dates from the Transportation Act of 1920.

The Hepburn Act is discussed by F. H. Dixon, "The Interstate Commerce Act as Amended," 21 *Quarterly Journal of Economics* 22 (1906).

[21]On the act, see F. H. Dixon, "The Mann-Elkins Act, Amending the Act to Regulate Commerce," 24 *Quarterly Journal of Economics* 593 (1910).

tion of the original act. Hence, it was necessary for Congress to restate its position on this matter in 1910. Congress did this by forbidding completely, regardless of conditions, the charging of more for a shorter than for a longer haul unless the commission gave its approval.[22]

Philosophy of Pre-World War I Regulation. During the period 1887 to 1917, it clearly was the aim of Congress in regulating general business to enforce competition. A study of the details of railroad regulations passed suggests that Congress was attempting to apply the same policy to the railroads. Although it had established a commission with a considerable degree of control over rates (and, hence, had removed a large part of the need for retaining competition), Congress made no effort to consolidate railroads, to encourage joint operation of terminal facilities, or to remove duplication of mileage. In fact, Congress had gone to the other extreme and forbade pooling of freight, a means by which the railroads might have cooperated in securing shipment by the shortest and cheapest route. Put another way, this early regulatory activity sought to prevent excessive earnings and discrimination, but competition was relied on to create an efficient transportation system.

Yet, in this period can be found the seeds of the current mixture of government regulation and private enterprise. For reasons outlined earlier, competition tends to reduce railroad rates to ruinous levels and to hold them there for long periods of time. During such periods, while society may gain from the lower rates, it loses in that railroad service becomes less adequate. When the railroads lose money, they do not want to spend sufficient sums for maintenance and equipment. This situation was especially significant during the prewar period, since Congress had given the ICC little control over the quality of railroad service. Moreover, Congress had not felt obligated to protect the financial standing of the railroads. It felt that rates should be kept reasonable and that railroad management should look after its own credit position within such a rate structure. It overlooked the fact that without giving to the commission the power to regulate security issues, financial manipulation might take place and weaken the credit position of the railroads, even though the existing rates would be satisfactory under sound financial management. Finally, because the commission was not made to feel a responsibility to protect the financial position of the railroads, it often acted very slowly. In view of the gradual rise of prices following 1896, the hesitancy of the commission in allowing rate increases resulted in a reduction of profit margins of the railroad industry.[23]

---

[22] The act also provided for a Commerce Court to expedite judicial review and enforcement of commission orders. The court was to be composed of five judges from the federal circuit courts, appointed by the President, for five-year terms. The court was impractical and was abandoned in 1913. See S. O. Dunn, "The Commerce Court Question," 3 *American Economic Review* 20 (1913).

[23] See *Advances in Rates, Eastern Case,* 20 ICC 243 (1911); and *Advances in Rates, Western Cases,* 20 ICC 307 (1911).

World War I: Nationalization

The importance of this negative or restrictive policy of railroad legislation became evident with the outbreak of World War I, especially after our entrance as an active participant. The steady fall in the profit margins of the railroads impaired the service-giving ability of the industry. Railroad management's lack of experience in any cooperative endeavor made it difficult for them to attempt to move troops and freight with the greatest dispatch. Although many railroad executives made the greatest effort to cooperate, by the end of 1917 it was evident that a more unified control over railroading was necessary.[24] On December 28, 1917, by proclamation of President Wilson, the federal government took over the nation's railroads. They were operated during the war period by the United States Railroad Administration.

The government operated the railroads from December 28, 1917, to March 1, 1920.[25] In general, effort was concentrated on rapid movement of troops and supplies far more than on running the railroads in order to make them a financial success. As this policy did not result in a balance sheet success of government operation, many have pointed to the period as an illustration of the inefficiencies of government ownership. Obviously, it has little bearing on how the government might operate the railroads in a more normal period. With at least equal truth it could be said that it was the failure of private enterprise which led to the breakdown of the railroad system in 1917 and made government operation a necessity. Both points of view are quite inadequate.

The Transportation Act of 1920

In spite of considerable feeling in certain quarters that the government should continue its operation of the railroads, the Transportation Act of 1920 (the Esch-Cummins Act) made provision for their return to private operation.[26] This act also marked a significant change in public policy toward the railroad industry. The former policy—enforcing competition, plus a commission to regulate rates without necessarily protecting the financial position of the railroads—was replaced with a policy of reducing competition to a certain extent, plus a commission to give reasonable rates but also to protect and develop an efficient railroad system. This change in policy is made

[24] For a comprehensive review of the circumstances leading to the takeover of the railroads by the federal government, see I. L. Sharfman, *The American Railroad Problem* (New York: The Century Co., 1921), chap. iii.

[25] On the administration of the railroads during the war, see Eliot Jones, *Principles of Railway Transportation* (New York: The Macmillan Co., 1924), chap. xxii; Sharfman, *op. cit.*, chaps. iv-v; and Walker D. Hines, *War History of American Railroads* (New Haven: Yale University Press, 1928).

[26] See *Hearings on Extension of Tenure of Government Control of Railroads* (65th Cong., 3d sess.) and *Hearings on Return of the Railroads to Private Ownership* (66th Cong., 1st sess.) (1919).

evident by a brief consideration of the most important aspects of the act.[27]

In place of a policy of enforced competition, the Transportation Act provided that the Interstate Commerce Commission prepare a plan for consolidation of all railroads into a relatively small number of systems of equal strength. While it was expected that competition would continue among the resulting systems, the mere consolidation would result in some limitation on competition. It should be emphasized that the ICC was not given the power to force consolidation on the railroads. It was to prepare a plan and then allow the railroads to consolidate if their proposals were in harmony with the plan. As a matter of fact, combination through holding companies might take place contrary to the plan, since the ICC was given no control over this form of combination. Even combination secured by leasing did not have to follow the plan unless the commission made such a requirement. Thus, only in case combination was secured by the consolidation of physical assets of the railroads did the law really require that the ICC plan be followed.

That Congress had abandoned its policy of enforcing competition was made clear by still other provisions of the act. By one provision, Congress modified its policy toward pooling agreements. In 1887, Congress had adopted a policy of prohibiting all pooling, the assumption being—an assumption founded on fact—that pooling tended to eliminate competition. Now the ICC was authorized to allow pooling it deemed to be "in the interest of better service to the public, or economy of operation." Another provision authorized the commission to require the joint use of terminals, thus reducing competition and making less necessary the duplication of terminal facilities.

The commission's granted power to fix minimum rates, taken in connection with its earlier granted authority to fix maximum rates, permitted the ICC the right to establish the actual rate charged by a railroad. To give the commission an increased degree of control over the financial condition of the railroads, the act provided that all future issues of securities would be at the commission's discretion. It was thought that certain companies had issued excessive amounts of securities, such issues calling for large interest payments that tended to weaken the credit position of the issuers. Under the 1920 act, the commission was to investigate the position of each company wishing to float an issue, and either allow or disallow the issue. The commission was not authorized to take the initiative in proposing the issue or in assuming responsibility for its soundness. Its approval was merely to give notice that it felt the issue should be floated.

Finally, the act stated for the first time a definite policy for the

---

[27]For a discussion of the act, see Forney Johnson, "The Transportation Act, 1920," 6 *Virginia Law Review* 482 (1920); and E. J. Rich, "The Transportation Act of 1920," 10 *American Economic Review* 507 (1920). The act's "recapture" clause is described and held constitutional in *Dayton-Goose Creek Ry. Co.* v. *United States*, 263 U.S. 456 (1924).

determination of the general level of rates. In 1913, Congress had passed the Valuation Act which authorized the ICC to make an appraisal of the value of the railroads' physical assets, such a valuation to serve as a basis for rate making. The Transportaton Act set 5.5 percent (plus .5 percent for improvements) as a fair return to be allowed on this valuation. It should be made clear again that this return was not to be guaranteed. Further, the suggested 5.5 percent return was not to apply to any particular railroad. Rather, it meant the commission was to set rates so that the railroads as a whole would make 5.5 percent on the commission's valuation of their assets. One road might make 15 percent, another 5 percent, and a third might lose money. However, companies making in excess of 6 percent were to have one-half of their excess earnings "recaptured" by the government and used to aid roads with lower earnings.

The results of the Transportation Act of 1920 were disappointing to its ardent supporters. Commission control of security issues and the provisions relating to service were the act's outstanding features. The principle established for fixing the general level of rates was not seriously applied, while "recapture" proved so unsuccessful that it was eventually repealed. As regards combination, nothing tangible was accomplished.[28] Finally, the courts and the commission found themselves in disagreement as to the valuations on which consolidation was to be based.

Railroads' Earnings under Pre-1929 Regulation

An investigation of the financial position of the railroads will reveal that at least since 1910 the railroads were becoming weaker financially. To a significant degree, this can be traced to hesitation of the ICC in granting needed rate increases, but it also resulted from the railroads' failure to pursue aggressively a policy of closer control over operating costs. By 1915, this situation was serious enough to cause Congress to investigate. World War I intervened and served to take attention away from the problem. But in the act of 1920, as noted above, Congress made a firm effort to repair the credit standing of the railroads.

The effort was not wholly successful. In but two of the prosperous years of the 1920's was the suggested rate of return of 5.75 percent realized.[29] In seven of the years of this decade, however, the return was above 5 percent. It was this rise of earnings and their relative stability during the twenties which caused one writer to conclude:

> . . . the pre-depression system of regulation seemed to work reasonably well in many respects, despite the grave difficulties caused by the valuation and consolidation problems, by changing economic conditions, and by the rise of new modes of transport. By following the spirit of the law, the I.C.C.

---

28 See Chapter 14, p. 518.

29 In 1922, Congress raised the suggested fair rate of return from 5.50 to 5.75 percent. The railroads earned the following returns on the commission's valuations during the 1920's: 1921, 3.44; 1922, 4.31; 1923, 5.18; 1924, 5.01; 1925, 5.65; 1926, 5.96; 1927, 5.14; 1928, 5.57; and 1929, 5.80.

was able to help the railroads to recover their financial strength. Yet there were inherent weaknesses in regulation and in the railroad industry. These came into the limelight during the great depression beginning in 1929.[30]

The Railroads and the Great Depression

The Great Depression spelled financial disaster for the railroad industry. Faced with large fixed charges and rapidly falling revenues, 75 Class I railroads were in the hands of the courts by 1932. Whereas in 1929 the railroads were employing 1.66 million men with a total payroll of about $3 billion, by December, 1933, employment had dropped to 952,000 and the payroll to $1.4 billion. Gross operating revenues reached $6.3 billion in 1929 and fell to $3.1 billion in 1933. Car-loadings in March, 1933, were less than 40 percent of the 1923–30 average. In contrast to the 1929 rate of return on net investment of 5.3 percent, in 1930 the return fell to 3.6 percent, in 1931 to 2.2 percent, and in 1932 to 1.4 percent.

Mere operating statistics do not show the full impact of the depression, as they neglect the broader social significance of the railroad industry. Thus, between January, 1928, and July, 1932, the market value of all railroad bonds fell by more than one-half. Railroad stocks, as is to be expected, experienced an even greater decline—from $12.7 billion (August, 1929) to $1.2 billion (July, 1932).

Immediate Steps to Aid the Railroads. In view of the railroads' plight and the vast significance of the industry to the financial structure of the nation, it was obvious early in the depression that something must be done to relieve the railroads. Two direct possibilities existed: a drastic effort might be made to cut the operating expenses of the industry, or an effort might be made to increase railroad revenues. The first was attempted through a cut in railroad wages, a gradual reduction in the number of employees, and a strict economy program in all operating divisions. While the result was a real reduction in operating costs, the presence of heavy fixed charges still left many railroads with revenues less than operating costs. Late in 1931, the Interstate Commerce Commission authorized a 15 percent (approximate) increase in freight rates in an effort to add to the industry's revenues. This step, too, was only partially successful: faced with growing competition from newer modes of transport, higher rates tended to cause traffic which could be transferred to be shifted to some of the railroads' competitors.

Neither the effort to obtain economy nor the attempt to increase revenues was successful in keeping a large number of railroads from going into bankruptcy. It is true that the number of roads taking this step was held down by a government policy of making loans to railroads through the Reconstruction Finance Corporation. But a policy of saving railroads by loans, unless a significant recovery in general business was forthcoming, could be only tempo-

---

[30]Haulik, *op. cit.,* p. 355.

rary. In the Emergency Railroad Transportation Act of 1933, Congress took some steps toward more permanent relief.

The Emergency Railroad Transportation Act of 1933. The Emergency Act of 1933 took what was hoped would be an important step toward reducing the operating costs of the railroads.[31] This step consisted of establishing a temporary office of Federal Coordinator of Transportation and three regional coordinating committees. The coordinator (President Roosevelt appointed ICC Commissioner Joseph B. Eastman) was to make plans for general improvement of the railroad system, aid and encourage railroads to carry out financial reorganizations, and attempt to get the railroads to avoid duplication of facilities. The work of the coordinator was to be carried out without compulsion on the railroads; he was to obtain his aims through voluntary cooperation.

While the immediate results achieved by the coordinator along the lines indicated did not prove to be significant, the several reports he issued as a result of his studies of the railroads' problems were useful in subsequent legislation.[32] In 1936, the office of coordinator was abolished. Primarily, the cause of this failure was twofold: (1) the legislation aroused the railway labor unions, who succeeded in establishing minimum employment and compensation for labor, thus making the proposals for joint use of facilities meaningless, and (2) railroad management found it almost impossible to agree on projects to be undertaken.

The act of 1933 made three other important changes: all combinations were made subject to the commission's jurisdiction, with approval to be denied to any plans not fitting in with the agency's general plan for consolidation; the recapture clause was repealed; and the commission was relieved of attempting to fix the general rate level on the basis of its valuations made under the Valuation Act of 1913. The significance of the third change, a new rule of rate making, will be considered below.

ADJUSTMENT TO COMPETITIVE CONDITIONS: 1933 TO DATE

The transportation legislation enacted prior to 1933 was designed primarily to regulate an industry possessing monopolistic powers. Little attention was paid to other modes of transport which were slowly developing. Beginning in 1933, however, a need for adjustment to new conditions was clearly recognized. Substitute transportation services began to capture a significant percentage of the railroads' former traffic. The nation's railroads, in short, no

---

[31]On the act, see R. W. Harbeson, "The Emergency Railroad Transportation Act of 1933," 42 *Journal of Political Economy* 106 (1934).

[32]See *Regulation of Railroads* (Senate Doc. No. 119, 73d Cong., 2d sess.) (1934); *Regulation of Transportation Agencies* (Senate Doc. No. 152, 73d Cong., 2d sess.) (1934); *Report of the Federal Coordinator of Transportation, 1934* (House Doc. No. 89, 74th Cong., 1st sess.) (1935); *Fourth Report of the Federal Coordinator of Transportation on Transportation Legislation* (House Doc. No. 394, 74th Cong., 2d sess.) (1936). In addition, there were 10 reports, such as *Freight Traffic Report, Report on Freight Car Pooling,* and *Railway Traffic Organization Report.*

longer enjoyed a monopoly position; the transportation revolution was underway.

Competitors of the Railroads

The plight of the railroads during the Great Depression, made evident by
the statistics above, cannot be traced entirely to that event, although the rapid
change from 1929 on was primarily due to the depression. Among other factors
bringing about this condition was the increase in competition from other modes
of transportation. Even by 1929, competition had made important inroads on
the railroads' business. The ICC estimated that by that year, steam railroads
carried but 72.9 percent of the ton-miles of domestic freight. Pipelines were
beginning to divert large amounts of petroleum from the railroads; high-tension
transmission systems for electric power reduced the transportation of fuels;
inland water carriers began to receive government subsidies; airlines were coming
into prominence, carrying mail, passengers, and light merchandise items; the
passenger car was cutting into the railroad passenger business; and the truck was
beginning to draw off a steadily enlarging share of the heavy freight business.

Two facts concerning this increase in competition faced by the railroads
are worth emphasizing. First, each mode of transport has certain cost advantages, so that intermodal competition is imperfect.[33] Second, the type of business
captured by the newer modes of transport is significant in explaining the
railroads' financial problem. The railroads tended to lose their best profit-making
traffic. Motor carriers captured light, valuable merchandise on which rates were
high, leaving the railroads with bulk commodities on which rates were low. Air
carriers gained profitable long-haul passenger traffic, leaving the railroads with
short-haul and commutation traffic which was frequently unprofitable. The
financial position of the railroads became impaired in a relatively short period of
time.

In addition to competition, railroads were adversely affected by still other
factors. With the more careful locating of factories, a reduction in the movement
of either or both raw materials and finished products has taken place. The fall in
exports and imports further reduced the need for railroad facilities. And changes
in production requirements, such as the substitution of other materials for steel,
has affected the volume of traffic handled by the railroads and, at the same time,
has increased the potential traffic that can be hauled economically by competing
modes of transport.

The 1933 Rule of Rate Making

The rule of rate making, contained in the Emergency Act of 1933,
recognized two things: (1) failure of the ICC to set rates so as to provide the
railroads as a whole with a fair rate of return on the fair value of their property

---

[33] See Chapter 2, pp. 41–42.

and (2) growing strength of competing modes of transport. The rule read as follows:

> In the exercise of its power to prescribe just and reasonable rates the Commission shall give due consideration, among other factors, to the effect of rates on the movement of traffic; to the need, in the public interest, of adequate and efficient railway transportation service at the lowest cost consistent with the furnishing of such service; and to the need of revenues sufficient to enable the carriers, under honest, economical, and efficient management, to provide such service.

The ICC was no longer required to establish a fixed return for the railroads.

> The new rule was functional in character, providing for rates that would attract business, assure adequate service and cover its necessary cost, and establish earnings at a level required to insure railway credit, so that new capital could be obtained. In introducing these factors into its consideration, the rule accorded a broad new area of discretion to the ICC.[34]

Yet, the rule required the commission to investigate a large number of factors in a rate case and to substitute its judgment for that of management when necessary. Specifically, the commission was given the power to reject a rate application if it thought the proposed rate would divert railroad traffic to other types of carriers. Subsequent interpretation of this rule resulted in constant disputes between the railroads and the commission. The rule was amended in 1940 and again in 1958.

The Expansion of Regulation to Other Modes of Transport

Prior to 1933, only railroads, pipelines, and those water carriers operated by the railroads were subject to detailed economic regulation. Safety regulations had been prescribed for air and water carriers. A few states had adopted rate and service regulations for motor carriers. Common carriers by water operating on the Great Lakes and in coastwise and intercoastal commerce were subject to the jurisdiction of the United States Shipping Board. Limited supervision of air carriers was exercised by the Postmaster General, and the ICC had authority to fix the rates paid for carrying airmail. But the federal government had no other control over air carriers or water carriers in inland trade, and had no jurisdiction over motor carriers. Such control, however, was soon to develop.

Petroleum Pipeline Regulation. The Hepburn Act of 1906 brought the transportation of petroleum and its products by pipeline under the jurisdiction of the Interstate Commerce Commission. The need for regulation stemmed from the close affiliation between the major oil companies and their pipeline subsidiaries. Until World War II, no firm outside the oil industry had any

---

[34]Clair Wilcox, *Public Policies Toward Business* (3d ed.; Homewood, Ill.: Richard D. Irwin, Inc., 1966), p. 400.

significant investment in petroleum pipelines.[35] The basic problem, then, concerned the relationship between the trunklines and the independent oil producers and refiners. If the major oil companies charged a high rate for transporting the oil of an independent producer to an independent refinery, their profits were increased at the expense of the independents. Further, such a situation often forced the independent to sell his output to one of the major firms at a price advantageous to that firm. The competitive position of the independent was thereby jeopardized.

To avoid these problems, the Hepburn Act declared petroleum pipelines to be common carriers and made their rates subject to regulation by the Interstate Commerce Commission. The commodities clause, however, was explicitly excluded from applying to pipelines. The pipeline companies vigorously protested their new status. At first they refused to carry oil produced by others, insisting instead on buying it from independents in the field. For this reason, they argued that they were not common carriers and, therefore, not covered by the act. In the Pipe Line Cases of 1914, the Supreme Court rejected this contention, thus upholding a similar rejection made by the ICC in a 1912 investigation.[36] Pipelines, argued the Court, are common carriers in fact: "They carry everybody's oil to a market, although they compel outsiders to sell it before taking it into their pipes."[37]

Following this decision, the pipeline companies adopted two other devices in an effort to maintain their advantages over independents. First, they established high minimum tender requirements, refusing to accept shipments that fell below a specified figure. The most common requirement was 100,000 barrels. The independents claimed that this requirement was unreasonable and, in 1922, the commission reduced the minimum tender requirement of the Prairie Pipe Line Company to 10,000 barrels.[38] While the ICC recognized that "pipe lines can not be successfully operated on a driblet basis, and there is a reasonable minimum below which they should not be required to accept oil for transportation," nevertheless, it found that the 100,000 barrel minimum "reserves the pipe lines to a few shippers and essentially deprives the lines of the common-carrier status with which they were impressed by the Interstate Commerce Act."[39] Second, the pipelines charged high rates, or at least this accusation was made by the independents. In 1934, the commission started an investigation of petroleum pipeline rates and, in its report of 1940, found the rates of 21 pipeline companies to be excessive.[40] Since that time, only two other significant cases

35 Locklin, *op. cit.,* p. 602.

36 *The Pipe Line Cases,* 234 U.S. 548 (1914); *In the Matter of Pipe Lines,* 24 ICC 1 (1912).

37 *The Pipe Line Cases, op. cit.,* p. 561.

38 *Brundred Bros.* v. *Prairie Pipe Line Co.,* 68 ICC 458 (1922).

39 *Ibid.,* p. 466. In a 1940 case, the commission again found a minimum tender requirement in excess of 10,000 barrels to be unreasonable. *Reduced Pipe Line Rates and Gathering Charges,* 243 ICC 115 (1940). Texas has prescribed a 500 barrel minimum for that state. Locklin, *op. cit.,* pp. 608–9.

40 *Reduced Pipe Line Rates and Gathering Charges, op. cit.*

involving the reasonableness of pipeline rates have come before the commission.[41]

In addition to rate regulation, the Hepburn Act made petroleum pipeline companies subject to most of the other provisions of the Interstate Commerce Act; the exceptions are outlined in the concluding section to the present chapter. The pipelines also were made subject to the prohibition of rebates under the Elkins Act of 1903.[42] And, in 1941, Congress passed the Cole Act which provided that the President, whenever he found that construction of a pipeline for transporting petroleum was necessary for national defense purposes, could so declare by proclamation, so that the pipeline company could acquire land or rights-of-way by eminent domain. The federal government also was authorized to construct such pipelines if necessary.[43] The provisions of the Cole Act expired on June 30, 1946.

Motor Carriers, 1935. The first regulations relating to the motor carrier industry were enacted by the states. Early regulations were designed primarily for safety purposes and control of the use of public highways. Standards were established governing the lights, brakes, and other equipment of vehicles; the speed at which they might travel; the age of their drivers; and their width, length, height, and weight. By 1932, transportation of passengers by motor vehicle was regulated by all states except Delaware, and transportation of property by 39 states.[44]

---

[41]*Petroleum Rail Shippers' Ass'n.* v. *Alton & Southern Railroad*, 243 ICC 589 (1941); *Minnelusa Oil Corp.* v. *Continental Pipe Line Co.*, 258 ICC 41 (1944).

[42]In 1940, the Department of Justice simultaneously filed suits against three pipeline companies, charging that in paying dividends the companies were giving illegal rebates on published transportation rates to their shipper-owners in violation of the Elkins Act. See Forrest R. Black, "Oil Pipe Line Divorcement by Litigation and Legislation," 25 *Cornell Law Quarterly* 521 (1940). The companies signed a consent decree, limiting their dividends to a maximum of 7 percent on ICC valuation. See Antitrust Subcommittee of the Committee on the Judiciary, *Report on Consent Decree Program of Department of Justice* (House) (Washington, D.C.: U.S. Government Printing Office, 1957, 1958), Part I, Vols. I and II. In 1957, another suit was brought, charging four pipeline companies with violating the 1941 decree on the ground that the allowable 7 percent return was on stockholders' equity rather than on valuation. The Supreme Court rejected this contention. *United States* v. *Atlantic Refining Co. et al.*, 360 U.S. 19 (1959).

For a more complete discussion of pipelines, see George S. Wolbert, Jr., *American Pipe Lines* (Norman: University of Oklahoma Press, 1952); Leslie Cookenboo, Jr., *Crude Oil Pipe Lines and Competition in the Oil Industry* (Cambridge: Harvard University Press, 1955); and Arthur M. Johnson, *The Development of American Petroleum Pipelines: A Study of Private Enterprise and Public Policy, 1862-1906* (Ithaca: Cornell University Press, 1956) and *Petroleum Pipelines and Public Policy, 1906-1959* (Cambridge: Harvard University Press, 1967).

[43]The federal government constructed two crude-oil pipelines during the war: the "Big Inch" (extending from Longview, Texas, to the New York-Philadelphia refining area and sold, in 1947, to the Texas Eastern Transmission Company) and the Southwest Emergency Pipe Line (extending from Corpus Christi to Houston, Texas).

[44]Locklin, *op. cit.*, p. 669. The development of state and federal regulation is outlined by William J. Hudson and James A. Constantin, *Motor Transportation: Principles and Practices* (New York: Ronald Press, 1958), chap. xix; and Charles A. Taff, *Commercial Motor Transportation* (3d ed.; Homewood, Ill.: Richard D. Irwin, Inc., 1961), chap. xx.

Common carriers were first subjected to regulation. The states soon found, however, that these carriers could avoid regulation by operating as contract carriers, and they sought to bring the contract carriers under control. Such carriers resisted this attempt and were upheld by the Supreme Court.[45] But a new scheme for regulating both common and contract carriers was devised by the state of Texas which required certificates of public convenience and necessity for common carriers and permits for contract carriers. The Supreme Court upheld this law in 1932.[46] Other states followed suit.

The problem of intrastate versus interstate operations quickly began to plague the state commissions. In 1925, the Michigan commission refused to issue a permit to an interstate carrier. The Supreme Court overruled the commission, holding that a state could not regulate interstate commerce and, hence, could not deny a permit to an interstate carrier.[47] Pressure for federal regulation arose from the railroads, bus lines, some truckers, and from the state commissions. For the next 10 years, dozens of bills to this end were introduced in Congress. The Interstate Commerce Commission made two lengthy investigations of the need for federal regulation. In 1928, the commission recommended federal regulation of buses; in 1932, it recommended similar regulation of trucks.[48] And in 1934, the federal coordinator issued a report outlining the need for federal regulation of interstate motor carriers and presenting a draft of a proposed bill.[49] In 1935, Congress enacted the Motor Carrier Act which became Part II of the Interstate Commerce Act.

The act established different regulations for the three major types of motor carriers: common, contract, and private.[50] The commission was given the power to establish such safety regulations as it may see fit, and these regulations apply to all interstate carriers. Private carriers were not subject to any economic regulation. Some other carriers were specifically exempt from further regulation, including motor vehicles used by airlines, railroads, water carriers, and freight forwarders for purposes of transferring, collecting, and delivering freight or passengers in their normal operations;[51] local carriers, such as school buses, taxicabs and hotel buses; trucks solely engaged in transporting newspapers; and

---

[45]*Michigan Public Utilities Comm.* v. *Duke,* 266 U.S. 570 (1925); *Frost* v. *Railroad Comm. of Calif.,* 271 U.S. 583 (1926); *Smith* v. *Cahoon,* 283 U.S. 553 (1931).

[46]*Stephenson* v. *Binford,* 287 U.S. 251 (1932).

[47]*Michigan Public Utilities Comm.* v. *Duke, op. cit.*

[48]*Motor Bus & Motor Truck Transportation,* 140 ICC 685 (1928); *Coordination of Motor Transportation,* 182 ICC 263 (1932).

[49]*Regulation of Transportation Agencies, op. cit.* For a discussion of state regulation, see D. V. Harper, *Economic Regulation of the Motor Trucking Industry by the States* (Urbana: University of Illinois Press, 1959).

[50]Transportation brokers also were included in the act. These transport companies own no vehicles, but make arrangements with shippers for the actual performance of transportation services. They must obtain a license to operate from the ICC, and the commission may require accounts and reports, as well as prescribe such rules and regulations as are necessary to protect the public interest.

For a more complete analysis of the 1935 act, see James C. Nelson, "The Motor Carrier Act of 1935," 44 *Journal of Political Economy* 464 (1936); and John J. George, "The Federal Motor Carrier Act of 1935," 21 *Cornell Law Quarterly* 249 (1936).

[51]The airline exemption was added by an amendment to the act in 1938.

carriers transporting livestock, fish, agricultural commodities, and horticultural products, but not manufactured products made from them, if such carriers are used exclusively for hauling these goods.[52] This last exemption is the highly controversial agricultural exemption.

Common carriers were subjected to more detailed economic regulation than were contract carriers. Both must obtain approval to commence interstate operations—certificates for common carriers, permits for contract carriers.[53] Both must obtain liability insurance; common carriers must carry insurance on the goods they haul. The ICC was empowered to prescribe a uniform system of accounts, require reports, control the issuance of securities whenever capitalization exceeds $1 million, and approve or disapprove combinations and mergers for both types of carriers. But here the similarity ends.

Common carriers were required to establish just and reasonable rates which were not unduly discriminatory. They must publish these rates and strictly observe them. The commission must be given a notice of 30 days before a change is made, and the commission has the power to suspend proposed rates for a maximum period of seven months, to fix minimum and maximum rates, and to set the actual rate to be charged by a common carrier. Contract carriers were required to file their minimum rates only, and the commission was given the authority to fix a legal minimum but not a maximum. In 1957, Congress enacted an amendment to the act, requiring contract carriers to publish and adhere to their actual rates. No other regulations were imposed on contract carriers.

Two further provisions of the Motor Carrier Act are of significance. No carrier was to be given both a certificate (for common carrier operations) and a permit (for contract carrier operations) at the same time unless dual operation was shown to be in the public interest. "Dual operation might be abused, affording the carrier an opportunity to discriminate by hauling goods for favored shippers under contract at lower rates. The ability to offer both types of services, moreover, would give the operator an advantage over his competitors in soliciting business."[54] The act also provided for the use of joint boards (federal and state commission representatives) when an application or complaint filed with the ICC involves not more than three states; joint boards may be used at the discretion of the commission when more than three states are involved. The objectives of this provision were twofold: to relieve the commission of some of its work and to decentralize administration of the act.[55]

Air Carriers, 1938. The Civil Aeronautics Act of 1938 established the

---

[52] Horticultural products were included by an amendment to the act in 1952.

[53] A grandfather clause was inserted in the act in order to protect the rights of carriers in operation before the law was passed.

[54] Wilcox, *op. cit.,* p. 411.

[55] Locklin, *op. cit.,* pp. 676–77. See Paul G. Kauper, "Utilization of State Commissioners in the Administration of the Federal Motor Carrier Act," 34 *Michigan Law Review* 37 (1935); and James C. Nelson, "Joint-Board Procedure under the Motor Carrier Act," 13 *Journal of Land and Public Utility Economics* 97 (1937).

present system of federal regulation of air transportation.[56] Prior to the passage of this act, regulation was pragmatic. The Air Commerce Act of 1926 provided for various safety regulations, such as registration of aircraft, examination of pilots, and establishment of minimum safety standards by the Department of Commerce. Under the Air Mail Act of 1934, as amended in 1935, the Post Office Department was given the power to prescribe the number and frequency of flights, intermediate stops, and departure times for planes carrying mail; to prescribe a system of accounts; to award airmail contracts; and to regulate intercorporate relations. The Interstate Commerce Commission was given authority to fix rates for transporting airmail. In addition, the act called for the appointment of a Federal Aviation Commission to study and make recommendations with respect to aviation regulation. The report, made in 1935, formed the basis for the Civil Aeronautics Act of 1938.[57]

The act, as modified by an executive order issued in 1940, transferred the responsibilities formerly exercised by the Department of Commerce to the newly created Civil Aeronautics Board—an independent regulatory commission, but within the Department of Commerce. The board was also empowered to establish the compensation to be paid airlines for carrying the mail, a function formerly exercised by the ICC. In addition, a Civil Aeronautics Administration, also within the Department of Commerce, was set up to perform two primary functions: (1) to promote aviation by establishing and maintaining the airway system as well as planning and administering the airport program and (2) to establish and enforce safety rules, examining airmen, testing aircraft, controlling air traffic, and investigating accidents. The Federal Aviation Act of 1958 created an independent Federal Aviation Agency, outside of the Department of Commerce, and transferred to it all the functions previously assigned to the CAA, as well as responsibility for establishment of safety regulations—a power previously exercised by the CAB. And the Department of Transportation Act of 1966 transferred the safety functions of both the CAB and the FAA to the newly created Department. As a result, the CAB is primarily concerned with economic regulation.

Since air safety regulation was discussed in Chapter 11, emphasis in this section will be on economic regulation. At the outset, it will be well to quote in full the declaration of policy contained in the Civil Aeronautics Act, for it is

[56] The Act of 1938 was replaced by the Federal Aviation Act of 1958. However, the two are essentially the same as far as economic regulation is concerned, differing only in safety regulation.

[57] *Report of the Federal Aviation Commission* (Senate Doc. No. 15, 74th Cong., 1st sess.) (Washington, D.C.: U.S. Government Printing Office, 1935). The Civil Aeronautics Act is discussed in Claude E. Puffer, *Air Transportation* (Philadelphia: Blakiston, 1941), and John H. Frederick, *Commercial Air Transportation* (5th ed.; Homewood, Ill.: Richard D. Irwin, Inc., 1961), chap. iv; the Federal Aviation Act in John W. Gelder, "The Federal Aviation Act of 1958," 57 *Michigan Law Review* 1214 (1959), and Frederick, *ibid.* Also see Howard C. Westwood and Alexander E. Bennett, "A Footnote to the Legislative History of the Civil Aeronautics Act of 1938 and Afterword," 42 *Notre Dame Lawyer* 309 (1967).

evident that Congress sought to promote development of air transportation as well as to regulate this mode in the public interest. The act states:

> In the exercise and performance of its powers and duties under this Act, the Authority shall consider the following, among other things, as being in the public interest, and in accordance with the public convenience and necessity—
>
> (a) The encouragement and development of an air-transportation system properly adapted to the present and future needs of the foreign and domestic commerce of the United States, of the Postal Service, and of the national defense;
>
> (b) The regulation of air transportation in such a manner as to recognize and preserve the inherent advantages of, assure the highest degree of safety in, and foster sound economic conditions in, such transportation, and to improve the relations between, and coordinate transportation by, air carriers;
>
> (c) The promotion of adequate, economical, and efficient service by air carriers at reasonable charges, without unjust discrimination, undue preferences or advantages, or unfair or destructive competitive practices;
>
> (d) Competition to the extent necessary to assure the sound development of an air-transportation system properly adapted to the needs of the foreign and domestic commerce of the United States, of the Postal Service, and of the national defense;
>
> (e) The regulation of air commerce in such manner as to best promote its development and safety; and
>
> (f) The encouragement and development of civil aeronautics. [58]

The provisions of the act concerning economic regulation closely follow those of the Interstate Commerce Act. Only common carriers by air and all carriers of mail are subject to such regulation. Further, the CAB is empowered to exempt any air carrier or class of carriers from economic regulation if it finds that enforcement of these provisions would place an undue burden on the carrier or carriers. Those carriers regulated are required to obtain certificates before starting operations,[59] to provide necessary and adequate facilities, to transport mail whenever required by the Post Office Department, and to obtain approval before abandoning a route previously awarded. Rates must be published and adhered to, and a 30-day notice given to the CAB before a change can be made. The board may suspend proposed rate changes for 180 days. All rates must be just and reasonable, they must not be unduly discriminatory, and the board has the authority to prescribe the minimum, maximum, or lawful rate. In establishing such rates, the board is to take into consideration, among other factors:

> (1) The effect of such rates upon the movement of traffic; (2) the need in the public interest of adequate and efficient transportation of persons and

---

[58] Further evidence of the desire of Congress both to promote and to regulate air transportation is seen in the creation of a new regulatory agency with jurisdiction over the industry. Except for natural gas pipelines, all other modes of transport are under the control of the Interstate Commerce Commission.

[59] A grandfather clause, similar to the one inserted in the Motor Carrier Act of 1935, was included to protect existing air carriers.

property by air carriers at the lowest cost consistent with the furnishing of such service; (3) such standards respecting the character and quality of service to be rendered by air carriers as may be prescribed by or pursuant to law; (4) the inherent advantages of transportation by aircraft; and (5) the need of each air carrier for revenue sufficient to enable such air carrier, under honest, economical, and efficient management, to provide adequate and efficient air carrier service.

A system of accounts may be prescribed for air carriers, and reports may be required. Consolidations, mergers, and acquisitions of control are under the jurisdiction of the board, as are all interlocking relationships between air carriers, or between air carriers and other modes of transport. All pooling agreements must be approved by the CAB. The commission has authority to investigate complaints of "unfair or deceptive practices or unfair methods of competition in air transportation," and to issue cease and desist orders. Finally, in cases involving through service and joint rates between airlines and carriers under the jurisdiction of the Interstate Commerce Commission, a joint board may be established. This board, consisting of an equal number of representatives from the CAB and the ICC, has the same power as the CAB would have if deciding the particular issue itself.

Air safety regulation is entirely in the hands of the federal government, but some economic regulation of intrastate operations is undertaken by the state commissions. Even here, however, state regulation is limited, since the federal government has the power to prevent an aircraft from flying on a federal airway unless it has a federal airworthiness certificate.[60]

Natural Gas Pipelines, 1938. The Natural Gas Act of 1938 extended the jurisdiction of the Federal Power Commission to include the interstate transmission of natural gas and its sale for resale. Prior to enactment of this legislation, such pipeline operations were unregulated. However, unlike petroleum pipeline companies, natural gas pipeline firms are not common carriers. They own all the gas they carry, either producing it themselves or purchasing it from independent producers. The regulatory provisions and problems relating to natural gas pipelines will be discussed in Chapter 16.

The Transportation Act of 1940

The Transportation Act of 1940 was intended to establish a truly national transportation policy.[61] To help achieve this purpose, the jurisdiction of the

---

[60]*Rosenhan* v. *United States,* 131 F. 2d 932 (1942). In a 1943 case, a lower court even upheld the right of the federal government to prevent intrastate flights not on a federal airway unless a federal airworthiness certificate was obtained. *United States* v. *Drumm,* 50 F. Supp. 451 (1943).

On federal-state jurisdiction, see *Western Air Lines* v. *Public Utilities Comm. of Calif.,* 342 U.S. 908 (1954). On state regulation, see Frederick, *op. cit.,* pp. 117-23.

[61]Two reports were primarily responsible for the act: (1) *Immediate Relief for Railroads* (House Doc. No. 583, 75th Cong., 3d sess.) (Washington, D.C.: U.S. Government Printing Office, 1938), and (2) *Report of Committee Appointed September 20, 1938 by the President of the United States to Submit Recommendations upon the General Transportation Situation* (Washington. D.C.: U.S. Government Printing Office.

Interstate Commerce Commission was extended to cover water carriers in domestic commerce. Moreover, the act recognized—for the first time—that the railroad problem was, in reality, a transportation problem.

Water Carrier Regulation. Before 1940, water transportation was subject to several regulatory laws. Under the Act to Regulate Commerce of 1887, the Interstate Commerce Commission was given jurisdiction over common carriers by water which were under the control of railroad companies or which were engaged in joint hauls with railroads. In 1912, the Panama Canal Act made it illegal for any common carrier subject to the Act to Regulate Commerce to own, lease, operate, control, or have any interest in competing common carriers engaged in commerce through the Panama Canal or in the United States, without the express permission of the ICC. The act also empowered the commission to require establishment of joint railroad-water carrier connections; to establish through railroad-water carrier routes and maximum joint rates; and to make sure, and order if necessary, that if one joint arrangement was made, a similar arrangement was made with any other competing water carrier over the same route. The Denison Act of 1928 specifically applied to water carriers on the Mississippi River. It required common water carriers to apply for certificates and, if granted, allowed the ICC to establish through routes and joint rates.

The foregoing regulations were designed to deal with water carriers owned by the railroads or which rendered joint services with the railroads. The Shipping Act of 1916, as amended in 1920, created the United States Shipping Board and gave to this commission jurisdiction over common carriers by water operating on the Great Lakes and in the coastwise trade, as well as control of both common and contract carriers by water operating in the intercoastal trade. Only maximum rates were subject to control.[62] And the Intercoastal Shipping Act of 1933, as amended in 1936 and 1938, increased the rate control powers of the Shipping Board for common carriers engaged in the intercoastal, coastwise, and Great Lakes services. There was no control, before 1940, over water carriers on inland rivers and canals, or on contract carriers except in the intercoastal trade. Further, regulatory authority was divided between the Interstate Commerce Commission and the Shipping Board.

The act of 1940, which became Part III of the Act to Regulate Commerce, gave control over transoceanic shipping to the United States Maritime Commission (now the Federal Maritime Commission) and control over water carriers in domestic interstate commerce to the Interstate Commerce Commission. But the

---

1938). The act is discussed in four articles, each entitled "The Transportation Act of 1940," by T. C. Bigham, 8 *Southern Economic Journal* 1 (1941); R. L. Dewey, 31 *American Economic Review* 15 (1941); J. B. Eastman, 8 *I.C.C. Practitioners' Journal* 331 (1941); and R. W. Harbeson, 17 *Journal of Land and Public Utility Economics* 291 (1941).

[62] In 1933, the Shipping Board was made the Shipping Board Bureau of the Department of Commerce. In 1936, the bureau's jurisdiction was transferred to a newly created United States Maritime Commission; in 1950 to the Federal Maritime Board; and in 1961 to the Federal Maritime Commission.

law relating to domestic commerce allowed so many exemptions that approximately 90 percent of the tonnage hauled by water carriers was not subjected to regulation. Among the exemptions were the following: water carriers used by rail or motor carriers in their normal operations, all private carriers, craft of small size, ferries, contract carriers which have both specialized vessels and cargoes and do not compete with common carriers, carriers which haul liquid cargoes in bulk in tank vessels, and common carriers whose cargoes consist of not more than three bulk commodities (the so-called bulk commodity exemption).

For those water carriers subject to regulation, common carriers must obtain certificates and contract carriers permits to commence operations.[63] As with motor carriers, no water carrier may have both unless approved by the ICC. Interstate rates must be published, observed, and prior notice given of all changes. The ICC can suspend proposed rates in order to conduct an investigation. Minimum, maximum, and actual rates, which are reasonable and not unduly discriminatory, may be fixed by the commission for common carriers. Only minimum rates which neither unduly prejudice common carriers nor are inconsistent with the national transportation policy may be fixed by the commission for contract carriers. For both common and contract carriers, the ICC may prescribe methods of accounting; require reports; and control consolidations, mergers, acquisitions of control, and pooling agreements. A long-and-short-haul clause was included in the act, and through routes and joint rates with railroads may be required.

Other Provisions of the Act of 1940. The Transportation Act of 1940 was enacted at a time when the railroad industry was still in severe financial trouble and when the entire transportation industry was intensely competitive. Congress sought, therefore, to strengthen all modes of transport by restricting, to an extent, competition. Emphasis was placed on a national transportation policy, as the following declaration of policy shows:

> It is hereby declared to be the national transportation policy of Congress to provide for fair and impartial regulation of all modes of transportation subject to the provisions of the Act, so administered as to recognize and preserve the inherent advantages of each; to promote safe, adequate, economical, and efficient service and foster sound economic conditions in transportation and among the several carriers; to encourage the establishment and maintenance of reasonable charges for transportation services, without unjust discrimination, undue preference or advantages, or unfair or destructive competitive practices; to cooperate with the several States and the duly authorized officials thereof; and to encourage fair wages and equitable working conditions;—all to the end of developing, coordinating, and preserving a national transportation system by water, highway, and rail, as well as other means, adequate to meet the needs of the commerce of the United

---

[63] The rights of water carriers in existence when the law was passed were protected by a grandfather clause.

States, of the Postal Service, and of the national defense. All of the provisions of this Act shall be administered and enforced with a view to carrying out the above declaration of policy.

In this declaration of policy, Congress clearly expresses its belief that (1) an adequate national transportation system must include the development of all modes of transport, (2) regulation must be impartial, and (3) the inherent advantages of each type of carrier shall be recognized and preserved. The declaration remains as the overall policy which the Interstate Commerce Commission is expected to observe in its regulatory activities. However, as will be noted in a later section, the policy contains conflicting standards.

Several specific changes in the Interstate Commerce Act were made by the act of 1940. Perhaps the most important, relating to railroad consolidations, will be considered in the following chapter. A significant change was made in the 1933 rule of rate making: in prescribing rates, the original provision that the commission should give due consideration to the "effect of rates on the movement of traffic" was amended by restricting such consideration to the movement of traffic "by the carrier or carriers for which the rates are prescribed." The purpose of the amendment was to prevent the commission from prescribing any rate for a carrier that was designed to protect the traffic of another type of carrier. The act placed the burden of proof on the carrier or carriers in cases involving proposed rate reductions, as well as rate increases. To aid the railroads financially, Congress released those railroads which had received federal land grants (1850–71) from the obligation of transporting mail and nonmilitary government goods and services at reduced rates.[64] The long-and-short-haul clause was clarified, as was the power of the commission to prevent discrimination among regions. Finally, a Board of Investigation and Research was created to study transportation problems and to submit its findings and recommendations to the President and to Congress.[65]

The Transportation Industries in World War II

During the second World War, all modes of transport experienced increases in volume and relatively high earnings. The railroads, however, were relied on to carry the bulk of wartime traffic. As summarized by Wilcox:

> More freight was moved by highway and by air. But expansion of motor traffic was limited by shortages of trucks, parts, and tires. And the volume of air cargoes was relatively insignificant. Coastwise water traffic was sharply curtailed as ships were sunk, and until more pipelines could be built, the

---

[64] An amendment in 1945 eliminated the obligation of these railroads to carry military property and personnel at reduced rates.

[65] The board, in existence four years, made over eighteen reports, including: *Report on Interterritorial Freight Rates* (House Doc. No. 303, 78th Cong., 1st sess.) (1943); *Practices and Procedures of Governmental Control* (House Doc. No. 678, 78th Cong., 2d sess.) (1944); *Federal Regulatory Restrictions upon Motor and Water Carriers* (Senate Doc. No. 78, 79th Cong., 1st sess.) (1944); and *Comparison of Rail, Motor, and Water Carrier Costs* (Senate Doc. No. 84, 79th Cong., 1st sess.) (1944).

railroads had to carry oil from the producing regions to the refineries. The great bulk of the wartime freight was moved by rail. And this was done by the railroads themselves; operation by the government was not required.[66]

The Reed-Bulwinkle Act, 1948

For many years, railroad rate changes, proposed by either a railroad or a shipper, have been submitted to and considered by rate bureaus (trade associations) before being adopted. Rate bureaus are used also by other modes of transport. Legally, each carrier has the right to make a change without the approval of the bureaus; historically, few of them have done so. As a result, rate changes are usually made by all competing railroads at the same time. In a case filed in 1944, the Department of Justice challenged the legality of rate bureaus under the Sherman Antitrust Act. As there was substantial evidence to indicate that the courts would hold such bureaus to violate the law, the railroads sought Congressional exemption. In 1948, over the veto of President Truman, Congress granted their request by enacting the Reed-Bulwinkle Act.

The act exempts from the antitrust laws rate bureaus of carriers subject to the Interstate Commerce Act. The commission was empowered to approve the rules and agreements of the bureaus, and to exercise general surveillance over their activities by requiring reports and inspecting their accounts, records, and files.[67] The new law was attacked as being anticompetitive, leading to monopoly. It was defended by the railroads and some shippers as necessary to prevent rate making from becoming chaotic, since rate bureaus provide a forum where all interested parties can be heard before a rate is changed. Nevertheless, because the act maintained the right of individual action and left shippers free to bring complaints directly to the commission[68] and because both carriers and shippers, particularly in the railroad industry, have exercised their independence and right with growing frequency, rate bureaus are less of a monopolistic device than many originally feared.

The Transportation Act of 1958

In the early 1950's, the financial position of the nation's railroads again began to deteriorate. A number of causes were cited as contributing to the railroads' difficulties: increased competition from other—and often unregulated—modes of transport, losses being sustained on passenger and commutation services, rising costs, labor featherbedding practices, discriminatory local taxation, and unequal treatment under existing regulatory statutes. Several lengthy studies of railroad and general transportation problems were undertaken (see Appendix, Chapter 14) and, in 1958, subcommittees of the House and Senate

---

[66] Wilcox, *op. cit.* (rev. ed., 1960), p. 660.

[67] See George W. Hilton, "Experience under the Reed-Bulwinkle Act," 28 *I.C.C. Practitioners' Journal* 1207 (1961). Also see Stuart Daggett, "Railroad Traffic Associations and Antitrust Legislation," 38 *American Economic Review* 452 (1948).

[68] The act also authorized the Attorney General to take cases before the commission.

committees on interstate and foreign commerce held extensive hearings on "the threat of financial disaster for the railroads."[69] The result was enactment of the Transportation Act of 1958.[70] The act amended the rule of rate making,[71] repealed the federal excise tax on freight, sought to aid the railroad's financial position in three major ways, and made two amendments to the Motor Carrier Act of 1935.

The Excise Tax on Freight. In the early days of the second World War, Congress passed a 3 percent excise tax on freight and a 5 percent (raised to 15 percent in 1944 and reduced to 10 percent in 1954) excise tax on passengers. These taxes were designed primarily to discourage unnecessary shipping and travel. Following the war, however, Congress retained them for revenue purposes. In the fiscal year ending June 30, 1956, the government collected nearly $250 million from the tax on passenger travel and more than $450 million from the tax on freight.

Prior to 1958, all common carriers had repeatedly urged Congressional repeal of the taxes, as had the CAB, ICC, and the Treasury Department, among others. It should be emphasized that the taxes applied only to common carriers.[72] The 3 percent tax was repealed in 1958, but the 10 percent tax was retained.[73]

Aid to the Railroads. The act intended to improve the financial position of the railroads in other specific ways. First, the act provided for a federal government guaranty of fifteen-year commercial loans, up to a total of $500 million outstanding at any time, for capital investment in road and equipment and for maintenance work. The commission, which was to guarantee loans made by public or private institutions, was instructed to make sure a carrier was unable to obtain funds on reasonable terms without the guarantee, and to see that all guaranteed loans carried reasonable interest rates and that the borrowing railroad was in a position to repay the loan. The loan provision was to expire on April 1, 1961, but Congress extended the termination date to June 30, 1963.[74] Second, the ICC was given authority to order abandonment of intrastate passenger trains if it finds after a hearing that the service is not required by public convenience and necessity, or if it imposes a burden on interstate commerce.[75]

---

[69] See, for example, *Problems of the Railroads* (Hearings before the Subcommittee on Surface Transportation of the Committee on Interstate and Foreign Commerce, Senate, 85th Cong., 2d sess.) (Washington, D.C.: U.S. Government Printing Office, 1958), Parts 1-4.

[70] On the act, see R. W. Harbeson, "The Transportation Act of 1958," 35 *Land Economics* 156 (1959).

[71] See Chapter 11, pp. 376-84.

[72] *Problems of the Railroads, op. cit.,* Part 3, pp. 1847-50.

[73] In 1958, a 4.5 percent tax on oil pipelines, enacted in 1932, was allowed to expire. In June, 1962, Congress repealed the 10 percent tax on railroad passenger service, but retained a 5 percent tax on airline passenger travel.

[74] In total, the ICC approved 36 loan guaranty applications, totaling $243,972,360. Interstate Commerce Commission, *Seventy-Ninth Annual Report* (1965), Table 6, p. 106.

[75] See Chapter 12, pp. 422-26.

Third, the commission's power to grant railroads relief from unduly low intrastate rates was clarified. Under the Transportation Act of 1920, the ICC was given authority to prescribe intrastate rates when necessary to prevent discrimination against interstate commerce. In other words, if the commission granted a rate increase in order to give the railroads a fair return, the state commissions were not to be permitted to maintain low intrastate rates resulting in lower revenues than the commission intended to allow. Two 1958 decisions of the Supreme Court increased the difficulties of the railroads in obtaining relief from low intrastate rates.[76] Congress, to remedy these difficulties, declared that the commission could make a finding that intrastate rates placed an undue burden on interstate commerce "without a separation of interstate and intrastate property, revenues, and expenses, and without considering in totality the operations or results thereof of any carrier, or group of carriers wholly within any State."[77] In addition, the commission was given authority to undertake an investigation of any intrastate rates alleged to be unlawful, even though the matter is under consideration by a state commission. This provision was designed to expedite such proceedings.

Amendments to the Motor Carrier Act. The act of 1958 amended the Motor Carrier Act in two important ways. In the first place, Congress froze the list of agricultural commodities, the hauling of which was exempt from economic regulation. Prior to this time, the commission had defined the term "agricultural products" broadly to include "all products raised or produced on farms by tillage and cultivation of the soil (such as vegetables, fruits, and nuts); forest products; live poultry and bees; and commodities produced by ordinary livestock, live poultry, and bees (such as milk, wool, eggs, and honey)," as well as treated or processed commodities.[78] Moreover, several court decisions further increased the commodities subject to the exemption, including some manufactured products.[79] Regulated carriers, particularly the railroads, have always been dissatisfied with the exemption, consistently urging its outright repeal or its

[76] In *Chicago, Milwaukee, St. Paul & Pacific R. Co.* v. *Illinois*, 355 U.S. 300 (1958), the Court held that an undue burden on interstate commerce resulting from low intrastate commutation fares could not be found from a mere showing that the operations in question were performed at an out-of-pocket loss. Rather, it must be shown that such losses were not offset by revenues from other intrastate freight and passenger traffic. In *Public Service Comm. of Utah* v. *United States*, 356 U.S. 421 (1958), the Court held that lower intrastate rates than applied on interstate shipments could not be found to create an undue burden on interstate commerce unless it could be shown that the relative costs of moving intrastate traffic were as great as the costs of interstate traffic.

[77] In the absence of this provision, the railroads would have been forced to develop separations procedures, similar to those used in the telephone industry, to separate interstate and intrastate operations.

[78] *Determination of Exempted Agricultural Commodities*, 52 MCC 511, 519 (1951), as cited in Locklin, *op. cit.,* p. 686.

[79] In a 1956 decision, for example, the Supreme Court held that dressed or frozen poultry were within the exemption. *East Texas Motor Freight Lines, Inc.* v. *Frozen Food Express*, 351 U.S. 49 (1956). Also see *Interstate Commerce Comm.* v. *Yeary Transfer Co.*, 104 F. Supp. 245 (1952), 202 F. 2d 151 (1953); and *Interstate Commerce Comm.* v. *Wagner*, 112 F. Supp. 109 (1953).

extension to themselves. Others, especially agricultural groups, have argued that the exemption has been of direct benefit to the farmer. Thus, neither group was satisfied with freezing of the exempt list in 1958.

The second amendment was designed to prevent contract carriers from evading regulation by pretending to be private carriers. This problem has haunted the ICC ever since its jurisdiction was extended to cover motor carriers in 1935.[80] The amendment provides that no person engaged in any business enterprise other than transportation shall transport property by motor vehicle in interstate or foreign commerce for business purposes unless such transportation is within the scope, and in furtherance, of that person's primary business enterprise (other than transportation).[81] While this amendment clarifies the difference between private and contract carriers, it does not settle its application in any particular case before the ICC.

The Department of Transportation Act, 1966

On March 2, 1966, in a message to Congress, President Johnson recommended establishment of a Cabinet-level Department of Transportation to coordinate the executive functions of the various transport agencies, promote research and development in cooperation with private industry, improve transport safety, and develop investment standards and criteria to assist all levels of government in their transportation investments.[82] Congress held prompt and extensive hearings on bills incorporating most of the President's recommendations and, on October 15, 1966, the legislation was approved, effective April 1, 1967.[83]

The general objectives of the act were set forth in Section 2:

[80] An even more difficult task for the commission is to distinguish between common and contract carriers. By a 1957 amendment, Congress specified that a contract carrier must be transporting "under continuing contracts with one person or a limited number of persons either (a) for the furnishing of transportation services through the assignment of motor vehicles for a continuing period of time to the exclusive use of each person served or (b) for the furnishing of transportation services designed to meet the distinct need of each individual customer."

[81] An amendment enacted the previous year prohibits any for-hire motor carrier operation, unless specifically exempt from economic regulation, without first obtaining commission operating authority.

[82] *Proposed Department of Transportation,* Message from the President of the United States, March 2, 1966 (House Doc. No. 399, 89th Cong., 2d sess.) (Washington, D.C.: U.S. Government Printing Office, 1966).

For a discussion of pre-1966 proposals for reorganization of the executive branch with regard to transportation, see David I. Mackie, "The Necessity for a Federal Department of Transportation," 8 *Journal of Public Law* 1 (1959); and Dudley F. Pegrum, *Transportation: Economics and Public Policy* (rev. ed.; Homewood, Ill.: Richard D. Irwin, Inc., 1968), pp. 532–34.

[83] See *Creating a Department of Transportation* (Hearings before the Subcommittee on Government Operations, House, 89th Cong., 2d sess.) (Washington, D.C.: U.S. Government Printing Office, 1966); and *Establish a Department of Transportation* (Hearings before the Committee on Government Operations, Senate, 89th Cong., 2d sess.) (Washington, D.C.: U.S. Government Printing Office, 1966). Also see *Department of Transportation Act,* House Report No. 1701 (1966) and Senate Report No. 2236 (1966).

The Congress ... finds that the establishment of the Department of Transportation is necessary in the public interest and to assure the coordinated, effective administration of the transportation programs of the Federal Government; to facilitate the development and improvement of coordinated transportation service, to be provided by private enterprise to the maximum extent feasible; to encourage cooperation of Federal, State, and local governments, carriers, labor, and other interested parties toward the achievement of national transportation objectives; to stimulate technological advances in transportation; to provide general leadership to develop and recommend to the President and Congress for approval national transportation policies and programs to accomplish these objectives with full and appropriate consideration of the needs of the public, users, carriers, industry, labor, and the national defense.

The act established an executive department, the Department of Transportation, under a Secretary who was to be appointed by the President with the advice and consent of the Senate. An Undersecretary, four Assistant Secretaries, and the General Counsel were to be similarly appointed. The legislation established within the Department a Federal Aviation Administration, a Federal Railroad Administration, and a Federal Highway Administration, and transferred the Commandant of the Coast Guard, the St. Lawrence Seaway Development Corporation, the Bureau of Public Roads, the Office of the Under Secretary of Commerce for Transportation, the Great Lakes Pilotage Administration, and the Alaska Railroad to the Department (Figure 13-1).[84] The Department was required by the act to consult with other agencies of government to promote a coordinated transportation system, with the proviso that Congress must approve "the adoption, revision, or implementation of (A) any transportation policy, or (B) any investment standards or criteria." An autonomous National Transportation Safety Board, as discussed in Chapter 12, was established within the Department. Finally, the act specified that the enforcement of safety laws was left to the various administrators.

INCONSISTENCIES IN REGULATORY POLICY

There are several significant inconsistencies in public policy toward the transportation industries—inconsistencies in the national transportation policy,

[84] It should be noted that the Federal Maritime Administration, the promotional agency for the merchant marine, was not transferred to the Department. Further, the act specified that the Secretary of Transportation and the Secretary of Housing and Urban Development were to study and report within one year after the effective date of the act (to the President and to Congress) "on the logical and efficient organization and location of urban mass transportation functions in the Executive Branch." (In February, 1968, President Johnson proposed that these functions be transferred to an Urban Mass Transportation Administration to be created within the Department of Transportation. *The Wall Street Journal,* February 27, 1968, p. 34.) See Hugh S. Norton, "The Department of Transportation: A Study of Organizational Futility," 78 *Public Utilities Fortnightly* 19 (December 22, 1966).

FIGURE 13-1
Department of Transportation—Organization and Responsibilities

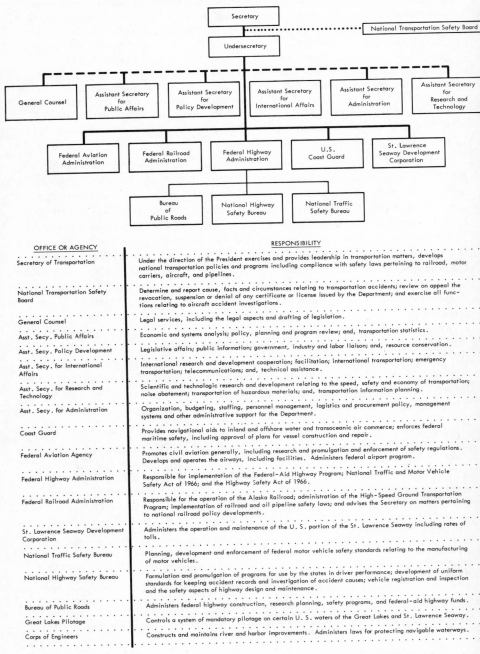

OFFICE OR AGENCY	RESPONSIBILITY
Secretary of Transportation	Under the direction of the President exercises and provides leadership in transportation matters, develops national transportation policies and programs including compliance with safety laws pertaining to railroad, motor carriers, aircraft, and pipelines.
National Transportation Safety Board	Determine and report cause, facts and circumstances relating to transportation accidents; review on appeal the revocation, suspension or denial of any certificate or license issued by the Department; and exercise all functions relating to aircraft accident investigations.
General Counsel	Legal services, including the legal aspects and drafting of legislation.
Asst. Secy. Public Affairs	Economic and systems analysis; policy, planning and program review; and, transportation statistics.
Asst. Secy. Policy Development	Legislative affairs; public information; government, industry and labor liaison; and, resource conservation.
Asst. Secy. for International Affairs	International research and development cooperation; facilitation; international transportation; emergency transportation; telecommunications; and, technical assistance.
Asst. Secy. for Research and Technology	Scientific and technologic research and development relating to the speed, safety and economy of transportation; noise abatement; transportation of hazardous materials; and, transportation information planning.
Asst. Secy. for Administration	Organization, budgeting, staffing, personnel management, logistics and procurement policy, management systems and other administrative support for the Department.
Coast Guard	Provides navigational aids to inland and offshore water and transoceanic air commerce; enforces federal maritime safety, including approval of plans for vessel construction and repair.
Federal Aviation Agency	Promotes civil aviation generally, including research and promulgation and enforcement of safety regulations. Develops and operates the airways, including facilities. Administers federal airport program.
Federal Highway Administration	Responsible for implementation of the Federal-Aid Highway Program; National Traffic and Motor Vehicle Safety Act of 1966; and the Highway Safety Act of 1966.
Federal Railroad Administration	Responsible for the operation of the Alaska Railroad; administration of the High-Speed Ground Transportation Program; implementation of railroad and oil pipeline safety laws; and advises the Secretary on matters pertaining to national railroad policy developments.
St. Lawrence Seaway Development Corporation	Administers the operation and maintenance of the U. S. portion of the St. Lawrence Seaway including rates of tolls.
National Traffic Safety Bureau	Planning, development and enforcement of federal motor vehicle safety standards relating to the manufacturing of motor vehicles.
National Highway Safety Bureau	Formulation and promulgation of programs for use by the states in driver performance; development of uniform standards for keeping accident records and investigation of accident causes; vehicle registration and inspection and the safety aspects of highway design and maintenance.
Bureau of Public Roads	Administers federal highway construction, research planning, safety programs, and federal-aid highway funds.
Great Lakes Pilotage	Controls a system of mandatory pilotage on certain U. S. waters of the Great Lakes and St. Lawrence Seaway.
Corps of Engineers	Constructs and maintains river and harbor improvements. Administers laws for protecting navigable waterways.

Source: Dudley F. Pegrum, *Transportation: Economics and Public Policy* (rev. ed.; Homewood, Ill.: Richard D. Irwin, Inc., 1968), p. 540.

in regulatory (substantive) law, and in promotional activities. Clearly, every provision of transportation law cannot apply equally to all modes of transport. But if the primary objective of government regulatory policy is to achieve a coordinated transportation system, then all modes of transport must receive equal and consistent treatment. Therefore, "each provision of the law should be tested against the questions 'Does it apply to transportation generally; should it; and if not, why not?'"[85]

Inconsistencies in the National Transportation Policy

The most widely quoted Congressional statement of our national transportation policy is found in the Interstate Commerce Act, as amended. But the intent of the declaration, applying to rail, motor, and water carriers, is uncertain, and the factors enumerated are often contradictory. A member of the Interstate Commerce Commission has pointed out some of these problems in the following words:

For example, how can the Commission foster economical transportation and at the same time give controlling weight, as some are contending that the law now requires to "the facts and circumstances attending the movement of the traffic by the carrier or carriers to which the rate is applicable," especially when the reduced rate, proposed for the purpose of meeting the competition of another mode of transportation, is shown by the record to be lower than necessary for that purpose and thus results in unnecessary dissipation of carrier revenues? In permitting such a rate to take effect, would the Commission be giving due weight to the ratemaking factor, which is a part of the ratemaking rule in section 15a, that in passing upon the reasonableness of rates consideration shall be given to the need of revenues sufficient to enable the carriers, under honest, economical, and efficient management, to provide adequate and efficient transportation service? And if in such a case the Commission should find that the rate is not shown to be just and reasonable for that reason, would that action have the effect of holding up the rate of the proponent mode and thus protect the traffic of the competing mode, contrary to a provision in the latest amendment to section 15a?

The Commission is obligated to prevent destructive competition, yet must encourage competition in promoting the general welfare of the national transportation system, and at the same time preserve the inherent advantages of each mode of transport. . . . So, when does competition become destructive and thus undesirable? After an operator has swallowed all opposition in sight, or only after taking over 5, 25, or 50 percent of the existing competition? Or, as some are urging, should the Commission pay no attention

[85] *National Transportation Policy, op. cit.,* p. 119. "To provide guidance in the exercise of regulatory and promotional judgment Congress has established a national transportation policy. To achieve its purpose, the policy should take precedence over any specific provisions of the statutes in the event of conflict between policy provisions and provisions of the statutes. Every broad policy in so complex a field as transportation, however, is likely to require some exceptions thereto. In such cases the fact of the exemption to policy should be specifically stated." *Ibid.,* pp. 119–20.

whatever to the effect of a proposed reduced rate upon the competing mode? If so, how can unfair or destructive competition be prevented and economical transportation promoted?

Once more . . . the policy does declare that the inherent advantages of each mode shall be preserved, and cost, among other things, is an important inherent advantage in many rate situations. It must be assumed that the reason cost as well as other inherent operating advantages are to be preserved is because to do so will give appropriate recognition to that portion of the ratemaking rule which provides that consideration shall be given to the "need, in the public interest, of adequate and efficient railway transportation service at the lowest cost consistent with the furnishing of such service," and to the ultimate objective of the transportation policy, to maintain a national transportation system adequate to meet the needs of the general public and the national defense. Do these objectives warrant the channeling of traffic over the most economical modes of transport? If so, do not those objectives warrant the application of the same principles to the rate relations between carriers of the same mode, so that still greater economics in transportation may be realized for the general public?[86]

Perhaps any general statement of Congressional policy must of necessity be broad. Yet, our present national transportation policy statement contains so many factors which the commission is to consider in its decisions that the intent of Congress can only be assumed or guessed at by the carriers, the commission, and the courts. This problem is largely responsible for the conflicts which have consistently appeared in the application of the law.

Inconsistencies in Regulatory Law

Important inconsistencies also exist in substantive law.

Obviously, there are differences existing in fact which require different laws or regulations for one mode of transportation than for another. To cite an extreme example, it would be ludicrous, in order simply to achieve a paper consistency, to adopt a code of regulations pertaining to airfield runways and to make that code applicable not only to airplanes but likewise to pipelines, railroads, and motor vehicles. . . . However, in most basic respects, where competition exists between modes, all modes of transportation should be responsive to the same tests of public interest.[87]

The major differences of treatment in the law, the significance of which will be discussed in the next chapter, are as follows:

1. Exemptions from Regulation. All air[88] and rail intercity traffic is

---

[86] Rupert L. Murphy, *ibid.,* p. 123.

[87] *Ibid.,* pp. 129–30.

[88] The Civil Aeronautics Board has authority to exempt air carriers from economic regulation. It has done so on several occasions, with exemptions being granted to air taxi operators, irregular air carriers, and airfreight forwarders, among others. Important, too, is the fact that the CAB passes on these exemptions, rather than providing for flat exemptions in the act as is done in the Interstate Commerce Act.

subject to economic regulation, compared with but 10 percent for water carriers, 33⅓ percent for motor carriers (freight), and 78 percent for oil pipelines. For water carriers, the most important exemption applies to the transporting of bulk commodities; for motor carriers, it is the agricultural commodity exemption. Moreover, all private motor and water carriers are exempt from the jurisdiction of the ICC.

2. Rate Regulation. In addition to these commodity exemptions, common and contract carriers are not always subject to the same rate regulations. The ICC may prescribe maximum, minimum, and actual rates for railroads, oil pipelines, and for common motor and water carriers; it may prescribe only legal minimum rates for contract motor and water carriers. The CAB may prescribe maximum, minimum, and actual rates for air carriers, as may the FPC for natural gas pipelines.

3. The Commodities Clause. The Interstate Commerce Act prohibits a railroad from transporting in interstate commerce any article (with the notable exception of lumber) either that it produced or in which it has an interest. No similar restriction applies to any other mode of transport.

4. Long-and-Short-Haul Clause. Water and rail carriers are subject to the long-and-short-haul clause, prohibiting (without express commission approval) the charging of more for a shorter than for a longer haul over the same route in the same direction. Both also are subject to the "aggregate-of-intermediates" clause, prohibiting the charging of more for through service than the sums of the intermediate charges. No such provisions apply to carriers by air, highway, or pipeline.

5. Reparations and Penalties. The Interstate Commerce Act provides for an award of reparations by the ICC when it finds a common water carrier, railroad, or pipeline rate to have been excessive. No such authority is applicable to the rates of air or motor carriers. A similar situation exists with respect to the penalties which are provided for a given offense. The specific penalty is more severe when the offender is a railroad or an employee thereof than when the offense is committed by a carrier or employee of another mode of transport.

6. Security Issues. The Interstate Commerce Commission has control over issuance of securities by railroads and motor carriers. Airlines, water carriers, and pipelines are not regulated in this matter.

7. Extensions and Abandonments. The construction of new oil pipelines or the extension of existing lines is not subject to ICC control. Further, the commission has no control over the abandonment of motor or water carrier operations. All other modes must obtain permission to construct or serve new facilities or areas, to extend existing services, and to abandon any present operation.

8. Interagency Ownership. Without approval from the ICC, railroads are prohibited from owning or controlling a carrier of another mode of transport, and without CAB approval, surface carriers are prohibited from acquiring an interest in air carriers. Motor, water, or air carriers, however, may acquire

ownership of or an interest in railroads; motor and air carriers in water carriers; and water and air carriers in motor carriers.[89] Yet, policy has not been consistent. When the grandfather clauses were inserted in each of the relevant statutory laws, those carriers previously owning or controlling carriers of another mode were permitted to retain such ownership.

9. Miscellaneous Inconsistencies. The above list summarizes the most important differences found in present substantive law. Three additional differences should be noted. (*a*) Only rail and common water carriers are required to establish through routes and joint rates, and provide for interchange of traffic between each other.[90] (*b*) In merger and consolidation cases, railroads must provide employees four years of job protection. There is no similar requirement applicable in connection with approval of unification plans of other carriers. (*c*) A lessor of a barge is a carrier subject to the Interstate Commerce Act; a lessor of a motor vehicle is not.

Disparities among Modes of Transportation

One of the most widely discussed controversies between the railroads and other modes of transport concerns the question of government subsidies. The railroads contend that they must compete against carriers which receive governmental subsidies, giving those carriers unfair competitive advantages. The claimed subsidies take the form of federal right-of-way construction and maintenance, traffic control, and terminal costs (Table 13-1). In 1961, the Transportation Study Group estimated that direct federal aid to highway transportation, navigation, aviation, and the merchant marine totaled no less than $33.6 billion in the period 1917-60.[91]

The railroads, of course, received local, state, and federal financial assistance in their developmental years. Of particular importance were the land grants (approximately 131.4 million acres) received from the federal government.[92] The Federal Coordinator of Transportation estimated that the value of the lands at the time they were granted was nearly $130 million.[93] In return, however, the railroads were obligated to carry government property and personnel at reduced rates (until 1945). The Board of Investigation and Research

---

[89] Carriers may engage in other modes of transport which are "auxiliary to, or supplemental of," their basic service. The leading decisions on interagency ownership are *Kansas City Southern Transport Co., Inc., Common Carrier Application*, 10 MCC 221 (1938), 28 MCC 5 (1941); *American Export Airlines, Inc.*, 3 CAB 619 (1942), 4 CAB 104 (1943); and *United States* v. *Rock Island Motor Transit Co.*, 340 U.S. 419 (1951).

[90] Common motor carriers of passengers are required to establish through routes and joint fares with other passenger common carriers.

[91] *National Transportation Policy, op. cit.*, p. 166. The study group estimated that federal expenses for the same purposes would total $73.9 billion in the period 1961-75. *Ibid.*, p. 172.

[92] Land grants from the states totaled approximately 49 million acres.

[93] Federal Coordinator of Transportation, *Public Aids to Transportation* (House Doc. No. 159, 79th Cong., 1st sess.) (Washington, D.C.: U.S. Government Printing Office, 1945), p. 36.

TABLE 13-1

Disparities among Modes of Domestic Transportation

Item	Railroad	Highway Freight	Highway Passenger[a]	Air	Water
Right-of-way:					
Financed and built by	Railroads	Government	Government	Government	Government
Maintained by	Railroads	Government	Government	Government	Government
Investment cost paid by	Railroads	Government	Government	Government	Government
Property taxes paid by	Railroads	Tax free	Tax free	Tax free	Tax free
Traffic control provided by	Railroads	Government	Government	Government	Government
Terminals:					
Financed and built by	Railroads	Truckers (some by government)	Bus operators (some by government)	Government	Water carriers (some by government)
Maintained by	Railroads	Truckers	Bus operators	Government	Water carriers
Investment cost paid by	Railroads	Truckers	Bus operators	Government	Water carriers
Property taxes paid by	Railroads	Truckers (some tax free)	Bus operators (some tax free)	Tax free	Water carriers (some tax free)
Cash subsidy paid by government	None	None	None	Some airlines (all certificated carriers eligible)	None
Transport diversification restricted:					
Railroads	No	Yes	Yes	Yes	Yes
Truckers	No	No	No	Yes	No
Bus operators	No	No	No	Yes	No
Airlines	No	No	No	Yes	No
Water carriers	No	No	No	Yes	Yes
Rates regulated	Yes	33⅓ percent	Partial	Yes	10 percent
Payment for facilities used	100 percent	Partial	Partial	Only nominal	None

[a] Excluding private automobile.

Source: *Problems of the Railroads* (Hearings before the Subcommittee on Surface Transportation of the Committee on Interstate and Foreign Commerce, Senate, 85th Cong., 2d sess.) (Washington, D.C.: U.S. Government Printing Office, 1958), Part 1, p. 297.

estimated that the railroads (through June 30, 1943) had contributed nearly $580 million through reduced rates.[94] The railroads realized revenues of more than $380 million from the sale of lands received under the federal grants.[95] Even taking into account the present value of the lands still held by the railroads, it appears that the federal government was fully compensated for the land grants. Further, the railroads must pay property taxes on the lands granted, but their competitors pay no such taxes on government-owned rights-of-way.[96]

User Charges. The basic dispute centers around the question of user charges. Are the annual expenditures of local, state, and federal governments recovered by the various types of fees, charges, and taxes imposed on the benefiting carriers? The position of the railroads has been summarized by Prince as follows:

> The exact extent to which these expenditures by state and local governments have been recovered by various types of fees, charges and taxes imposed upon the users is not determinable. However, so far as federal expenditures are concerned, the situation is reasonably clear except for a measure of controversy with respect to the question of adequacy of user charges imposed by the federal government for the recovery of expenditures on the highways. The situation with respect to the use of the waterways is the easiest to analyze because no charge whatsoever is imposed. The federal expenditures for inland navigation are thus out-and-out subsidies in their entirety to the domestic water carriers. Payments of domestic airmail subsidy so designated are on the same footing. Likewise, there are no contributions to offset the expenditures of the federal government for grants-in-aid to the states for airports. A very modest contribution toward reimbursement of the Government for its expenditures on airways may be found in the two cent per gallon aviation gasoline tax which, though its proceeds are now deposited in the highway trust fund, might reasonably be considered a user charge on the airlines. However, the contribution derived from this source is so small as to be fairly described as minimal. The question of how much the airlines should pay as their equitable share of the expenditures on airways is open to some question, but the airline industry does not dispute the soundness of the principle that it should pay its fair share of the cost of the airways, nor does it dispute that it is not doing so at this time.
>
> As to recovery of highway expenditures, the railroads maintain that the heavy trucks and combinations, which are their principal competitors for freight traffic, do not pay a fair share of highway costs by way of a user charge. The representatives of these motor carriers, on the other hand, contend that their payments are at least adequate and probably already too

---

[94] Board of Investigation and Research, *Land Grants to Railroads and Related Rates* (mimeographed, 1944), p. 42. In 1945, a House committee estimated that the railroads had contributed over $900 million through reduced rates. House Report No. 393 (79th Cong., 1st sess.) (Washington, D.C.: U.S. Government Printing Office, 1945), p. 102.

[95] *Land Grants to Railroads and Related Rates, op. cit.,* p. 25.

[96] The exception is pipeline companies which have to cover all their costs, including property taxes.

great. The Bureau of Public Roads, which is not a railroad-dominated agency by any means, agrees with the position of the railroads. Representatives of the trucking industry likewise recognize the soundness of the principle of user charges.[97]

Tax Matters. Two major tax matters affect the railroads.[98] The first, already noted, is the railroads' claim that they are being discriminated against by property taxes levied by local and state governments.[99] The second concerns the industry's contention that it should be allowed to depreciate tunnels for tax purposes.[100] The Internal Revenue Service has ruled that tunnels do not qualify since they do not become "exhausted." But the railroads point out that they do become obsolete when, for example, major alterations are needed to permit passage of bigger cars. With railroad investment in tunnels amounting to over $4 billion, an annual depreciation allowance would approximate $25 million a year.

A CONCLUDING COMMENT

In 1887, Congress enacted the Interstate Commerce Act to regulate the nation's railroads. At that time, the industry had a virtual monopoly of transportation in the country and was guilty of many corrupt and highly discriminatory practices. Over the years, however, other modes of transport have developed and have grown, aided in large part by various government promotional activities. The basic problem has been to promote and regulate each new mode of transport as it has developed without placing the existing modes in an unfair competitive position. The overall objective has been to foster the development of an economically efficient transportation industry.

Congress has been willing to amend the existing statutes, but such adjustments have often been slow and have failed to recognize the changing economic and technological environment of the transportation industry. President Kennedy, in a 1962 message to Congress, argued in part:

> . . . pressing problems are burdening our national transportation system, jeopardizing the progress and security on which we depend. A chaotic

[97] Gregory S. Prince, "Railroads and Government Policy—A Legally Oriented Study of an Economic Crisis," 48 *Virginia Law Review* 196, 227–28 (1962). On the highway user controversy, see *Final Report of the Highway Cost Allocation Study* (House Doc. No. 54, 87th Cong., 1st sess.) (Washington, D.C.: U.S. Government Printing Office, 1961); and Taff, *op. cit.,* chap. iii. The development of the St. Lawrence Seaway is unique in that toll charges are collected to pay for the facilities. Some air carriers also receive cash subsidies. The total subsidy for fiscal 1967 operations was $65.7 million. Of this amount, $56 million went to local-service carriers, $7.2 million for the Alaskan and Hawaiian carriers, and $2.5 million for one trunkline carrier. Civil Aeronautics Board, *Reports to Congress* (1967), p. 45.

[98] There are other tax problems at the local and state levels. Thus, the state of Arkansas recently passed a law stating that railroads abandoning all or most of their operations in the state will be subject to a special "removal" tax on the value of their properties given up in the state.

[99] See Chapter 7, pp. 211–13.

[100] *The Wall Street Journal,* April 27, 1964, p. 2.

patchwork of inconsistent and often obsolete legislation and regulation has evolved from a history of specific actions addressed to specific problems of specific industries at specific times. This patchwork does not fully reflect either the dramatic changes in technology of the past half century or the parallel changes in the structure of competition.

The regulatory commissions are required to make thousands of detailed decisions based on out-of-date standards. The management of the various modes of transportation is subjected to excessive, cumbersome, and time-consuming regulatory supervision that shackles and distorts managerial initiative. Some parts of the transportation industry are restrained unnecessarily; others are promoted or taxed unevenly and inconsistently.

Some carriers are required to provide, at a loss, services for which there is little demand. Some carriers are required to charge rates which are high in relation to cost in order to shelter competing carriers. Some carriers are prevented from making full use of their capacity by restrictions on freedom to solicit business or adjust rates. Restraints on cost-reducing rivalry in ratemaking often cause competition to take the form of cost-increasing rivalry—such as excessive promotion and traffic solicitation, or excessive frequency of service. Some carriers are subject to rate regulation on the transportation of particular commodities while other carriers, competing for the same traffic, are exempt. Some carriers benefit from public facilities provided for their use, while others do not; and of those enjoying the use of public facilities, some bear a large part of the cost, while others bear little or none.

... The resources devoted to provision of transportation service should be used in the most effective and efficient manner possible; and this, in turn, means that users of transport facilities should be provided with incentives to use whatever form of transportation which provides them with the service they desire at the lowest total cost, both public and private. ...

This means a more coordinated Federal policy and a less segmented approach. It means equality of opportunity for all forms of transportation and their users and undue preference to none. It means greater reliance on the forces of competition and less reliance on the restraints of regulation. And it means that, to the extent possible, the users of transportation services should bear the full costs of the services they use, whether those services are provided privately or publicly.[101]

Some of these inconsistencies and obsolete policies may be inevitable; some may not. A more coordinated policy, moreover, is difficult to achieve. These are the problems discussed in the following chapter.

[101] *The Transportation System of Our Nation,* Message from the President of the United States, April 5, 1962 (House Doc. No. 384, 87th Cong., 2d sess.) (Washington, D.C.: U.S. Government Printing Office, 1962), pp. 2, 3.

<table>
<tr><td>Chapter</td><td rowspan="3"></td><td># PUBLIC POLICY AND THE</td></tr>
</table>

Chapter

14

PUBLIC POLICY AND THE

TRANSPORTATION

INDUSTRIES

> *Our present approach to regulation is largely a legacy from an earlier period, when there was a demonstrated need to protect the public interest by a comprehensive and detailed supervision of rates and services. The need for regulation remains; but technological and structural changes today permit greater reliance on competition within and between alternative modes of transportation to make them responsive to the demands for new services and the opportunities for greater efficiency.*
> *—John F. Kennedy**

The basic public policy objectives toward the transportation industries are clear; the methods of obtaining the objectives are not. The United States must have a transportation system that is strong, efficient, and financially stable. Each mode of transport should carry that portion of the traffic it can best serve at the lowest total resource cost. To achieve these objectives, regulatory policies must be neutral among competing carriers. No agency should get unfair advantage through promotion, user charge, subsidy, taxation, or economic regulation. Moreover, regulatory policies should be continuously studied to make sure they are not only neutral, but also of the right type to meet current economic conditions. The basic requirements of a truly national transportation policy, then, are economic efficiency and government neutrality toward competing carriers.

The development of a neutral government policy, however, is easier stated than achieved. In this chapter, attention is focused on the nation's current transportation system and the financial position of the various modes of transport. The concluding section considers the major policy disputes which hinder the development of a consistent national transportation policy.

**John F. Kennedy, *Economic Report of the President* (House Doc. No. 28, 88th Cong., 1st sess.) (1963), p. xxii.*

THE MARKET STRUCTURE OF THE TRANSPORTATION SYSTEM

Regulation of the transportation industries is predicated on the belief that competition cannot be relied on to serve the public interest.[1] On the one hand, there may be too little competition in some markets, resulting in the exploitation of consumers. On the other hand, there may be too much competition in other markets, leading to instability, low profits, and poor customer service. Examples of both situations can be found in the past history of the transportation industries—price discrimination practiced by some pipelines and the railroads, cutthroat competition among the railroads (1870's and 1880's), and excessive competition among motor carriers (1930's).

Yet, is it likely that the conditions which existed in the past are still controlling today? The railroads had a monopoly of the country's transportation when price discrimination was so widely practiced. Further, excessive competition was not confined to the trucking industry during the depression years of the 1930's. In other words, would workable competition be possible in the transportation industries if, as many have suggested, government regulation were relaxed? To provide a basis for analyzing this issue, the market structures of the various modes of transportation must be examined.

The Market Structure of the Railroads

Railroads are classified by the Interstate Commerce Commission in two size classes: Class I railroads are those with annual operating revenues of $5 million or more; Class II railroads are those with annual operating revenues under $5 million. There are 76 Class I and 302 Class II railroads in the country. The Class I lines are by far the most important, owning or leasing approximately 94 percent of the industry's 210,573 miles of line, and accounting for 99 percent of the industry's line-haul traffic and 95 percent of total operating revenues. And within this class, concentration is high: in 1963, eighteen railroads controlled nearly 84 percent of the mileage operated and collected over 60 percent of the freight revenues.[2]

From a competitive standpoint, the relevant concentration figures concern the number of railroads connecting any given pair of cities. The number is limited. To illustrate: Six railroads operate from Chicago to St. Louis; five from New York to Chicago and from Chicago to Kansas City; and four from Chicago to Minneapolis and from Pittsburgh to Chicago. Many important routes, however, are served only by one or two railroads. And minerals, agricultural commodities, and lumber products, which account for nearly 70 percent of rail

---

[1] J. R. Meyer, M. J. Peck, J. Stenason, and C. Zwick, *The Economics of Competition in the Transportation Industries* (Cambridge: Harvard University Press, 1959), p. 203.

[2] The above figures are from Interstate Commerce Commission, *Transport Statistics in the United States, 1963* and *Eighty-First Annual Report* (1967); and Burton N. Behling, *Review of Railroad Operations in 1967* (Washington, D.C.: Association of American Railroads, 1968).

ton-miles, originate from points generally served by only one road.[3] At the same time, potential competition is greater than these figures indicate:

> The average railroad shipment travels 428 miles, of which only half is on the line originating the shipment. A substantial portion of the trip length is on the major routes, such as New York to Chicago, San Francisco to Chicago, and Chicago to St. Louis .... [I]n almost all cases there is more than one line. The shipper has the option by law to route his shipment, so that even though the shipper is served by one railroad line, shipments may eventually enter one of these major routes for which there are alternative railroads, and at that point competition between railroads exists. It makes little difference that shippers at present do not often exercise the prerogative of routing, for rates are generally identical between railroads. If rates should vary between roads, the highly expert traffic departments of industrial shippers can be expected to exercise routing privileges.
>
> Market competition ... further increases the competitiveness between railroads. For example, oranges can move into the Chicago area from Florida over three or four roads, from Los Angeles over three. Each of these roads are competing for a share of the citrus shipments into Chicago, and this share is partly determined by the relative rate charged by each railroad. This kind of competition is particularly significant in setting coal rates.[4]

At best, therefore, the market structure of the railroad industry is one of oligopoly, with two or more roads competing for traffic over the major routes only. As such a structure may lead to cutthroat competition,[5] rate bureaus, through which potentially competitive railroads set rates, have been established and legalized. This method of setting rates not only decreases the function of price-making by individual managements, but also reduces the incentive for individual rate reductions. When a particular management knows a rate decrease will be promptly followed by all competing roads, uncertainty is removed and the possibility of obtaining a competitive advantage by the road initiating the cut is lost. "Furthermore, the whole machinery of rate-making places a high premium on the bureaucratic skills of presenting a case for a rate change (in triplicate), of persuading other traffic men, and of bargaining, accommodation, and compromise, instead of the highly individualistic skills of an aggressive marketing man in a competitive industry. The transformation of traffic departments into self-serving bureaucracies rather than real sales organizations may be the substantial long-run cost of rate bureaus both to the railroad industry and the economy."[6]

---

[3] Meyer and others, *op. cit.*, pp. 205-6. The recent mergers creating the Penn Central and the Chicago and North Western have reduced these numbers.

[4] *Ibid.*, pp. 206-7. Since this book was written, the average railroad shipment has increased to 485 miles, of which about 58 percent is on the line originating the shipment. Data supplied by the Association of American Railroads.

[5] See Chapter 2, pp. 38-40.

[6] Meyer and others, *op. cit.*, p. 211. Railroads have the right, it should be noted again, to set rates independently of a rate bureau, while shippers may take complaints directly to the commission.

The Market Structure of the Trucking Industry

The motor carrier industry is comprised of a large number of firms. In 1967, there were 15,396 motor carriers of property subject to the jurisdiction of the Interstate Commerce Commission: 1,389 Class I carriers (revenues of $1 million or more), 2,769 Class II carriers (revenues of $200,000 to $1 million), and 11,238 Class III carriers (revenues under $200,000).[7] Many of these carriers, however, are relatively large: in 1961, there were 181 Class I common carriers of general commodities having revenues in excess of $5 million; of these carriers, 23 had revenues of more than $20 million and 86 had revenues of $10 million or more.[8] Three areas of the industry, moreover, are specialized and highly concentrated: (*a*) automobile carriers, where the 25 largest firms have 70.3 percent of sales; (*b*) carriers of liquid petroleum products, where the 25 largest concerns have 51.5 percent of the sales; and (*c*) carriers of household goods, where the four largest firms control 49.4 percent of the sales.[9] And, finally, in addition to the intercity carriers, there are thousands of motor carriers engaged in intrastate commerce and in hauling exempt agricultural commodities, as well as private carriers. Thus, in 1960, the ICC estimated the number of exempt trucking firms subject to its safety regulations at 30,666,[10] while in 1964, the California Public Utilities Commission reported that 15,895 motor carriers of property were subject to its authority.[11]

As in the railroad industry, the relevant competitive figure concerns the number of carriers operating between two cities. Here, the number is substantial, generally varying with the volume of traffic on a given route. Summarizes James C. Nelson:

> A considerable number of regulated truckers still operate on dense traffic routes between large, relatively close population centers. For example, David

[7]Interstate Commerce Commission, *Eighty-First Annual Report* (1967), Table 1, p. 128. Also see American Trucking Associations, *American Trucking Trends, 1967* (Washington, D.C., 1968), p. 13. The ICC revised its definitions of Class II and Class III carriers, effective January 1, 1968. Class II carriers are those with annual revenues of $300,000 to $1 million; Class III carriers with annual revenues under $300,000. *Transport Topics*, January 15, 1968, p. 1.

[8]James C. Nelson, "The Effects of Entry Control in Surface Transport," in *Transportation Economics* (New York: National Bureau of Economic Research, 1965), p. 403. In 1954, the 853 largest carriers (4.7 percent of regulated carriers) earned approximately 62.3 percent of the industry's revenue. See Walter Adams, "The Role of Competition in the Regulated Industries," 48 *American Economic Review* 527, 531 (1958).

[9]Walter Adams and James Hendry, *Trucking Mergers, Concentration and Small Business: An Analysis of Interstate Commerce Commission Policy, 1950-1956* (Senate, Select Committee on Small Business) (Washington, D.C.: U.S. Government Printing Office, 1956), pp. 35, 37, 91. The railroads, however, have introduced new types of services which have increased their competitive position with the trucking industry. These services include piggybacking, containerization, and new types of cars to carry bulk commodities and new automobiles. See pp. 524–27.

[10]Interstate Commerce Commission, Bureau of Transport Economics and Statistics, *Gray Area of Transportation Operations* (Washington, D.C., 1960), p. 81.

[11]D. Philip Locklin, *Economics of Transportation* (6th ed.; Homewood, Ill.: Richard D. Irwin, Inc., 1966), p. 643.

Axelrod found that between twenty-five and thirty-nine motor carriers of general commodities operated daily in 1961 between Chicago and such cities as Detroit, St. Louis, Milwaukee, Indianapolis, Cincinnati, and Minneapolis and St. Paul. On the other hand, there are numerous light-density routes that are served by only two or three regulated carriers having like authorizations, or by one carrier in some instances. Even on many routes generating fairly dense traffic flows, the number of general commodity motor carriers authorized to give single-line service varies from two or three up to six or ten common carriers.[12]

More importantly, regulatory policy is primarily responsible for the industry's market structure. Looking only at interstate carriers, the ICC received nearly 9,000 applications in fiscal 1966 and approximately 5,000 applications in fiscal 1967 for permanent common carrier certificates, contract carrier permits, or brokers' licenses.[13] In the absence of commission control over entry, therefore, concentration undoubtedly would be even lower. And, like the railroads, the trucking industry has rate bureaus. But there is a major difference: "Railroads are a concentrated industry with administered prices; regulation and rate bureaus simply centralize the industry further. In contrast, trucking is a substantially less concentrated and a more competitive industry, for which regulation is an awkward fit."[14]

The ease of entry into the trucking industry, due to the absence of significant cost advantages for the large firm, provided the rationale for regulation of the industry—such conditions may lead to excessive competition. The Supreme Court described the circumstances that brought about the Motor Carrier Act by pointing out that the industry "was unstable economically, dominated by ease of competitive entry and a fluid rate picture," so that the industry "became overcrowded with small economic units which proved unable to satisfy the most minimal standards of safety or financial responsibility."[15] There are indications, however, that whatever excess capacity might exist in the industry under regulation, would not exist under competitive (nonregulatory) conditions. Thus, the ICC specifies the commodities to be hauled and the routes to be served in each operating right granted to a motor carrier. In some cases, the commodity restrictions prevent a carrier from obtaining a full load: a carrier authorized to transport canned food is not permitted to carry canned beer. In other cases, the routes authorized are circular, prohibit solicitation of traffic at intermediate points, or prevent soliciting of return traffic. A carrier operating between New York and Montreal is required to operate via Reading, Pennsylvania, a detour of some 200 miles, while a carrier operating between the Pacific Northwest and Salt Lake City may haul commodities eastbound but not westbound.[16] And in granting new operating authority or in extending routes,

[12] Nelson, *op. cit.,* p. 402 (citations omitted).
[13] Interstate Commerce Commission, *Eighty-First Annual Report* (1967), p. 103.
[14] Meyer and others, *op. cit.,* p. 215.
[15] *American Trucking Ass'ns., Inc.* v. *United States,* 344 U.S. 298, 312 (1953).
[16] Adams, *op. cit.,* p. 529.

the commission has not been adverse to protecting existing carriers against competition.[17] Professor Adams concludes:

> In an industry of this sort, entry restrictions tend merely to preserve the capitalized expectations of established carriers—carriers who maintain, on the one hand, that they are efficient and provide superior service and who demand, on the other, government protection from interlopers and competitors. In the final analysis, however, these restrictions do not assure the adjustment of capacity to demand, because the Commission . . . limits the number of firms rather than the number of trucks in operation. Entry control does not prevent established carriers from creating and, in the absence of rate competition, from perpetuating excess capacity. Without competition, moreover, there are no effective pressures to compel either efficient use of existing capacity or elimination of the excess capacity which tends to develop in a cartelized, monopolistically competitive industry. Thus, ironically enough, regulation may breed the very evils it was supposed to eradicate.[18]

The Market Structure of Water Carriers

The domestic water carrier industry can be divided into three geographical systems: (1) Great Lakes, (2) the inland waterways, and (3) the coastal and intercoastal waterways.[19] Carriers in the Great Lakes system are hauling bulk commodities (grain, iron ore, coal, sand, limestone, petroleum, and cement) and, consequently, are largely exempt from economic regulation.[20] There are about eight regulated and thirty-two exempt carriers operating in domestic Great Lakes shipping.[21] Traffic-wise, the inland waterways are the most important, with eight commodities (bituminous coal and lignite; other petroleum and coal products; sand and gravel; crude petroleum; gasoline; unmanufactured marine shells; rafted logs; and grain and grain products) comprising slightly over 78 percent of the total tonnage carried.[22] Again, a significant percentage of this traffic is exempt

[17] Locklin, *op. cit.*, pp. 693-94.

[18] Adams, *op. cit.*, p. 530. Moreover, the exempt trucking markets, under free-entry conditions, exhibit "many-firm and small-scale characteristics." See Nelson, *op. cit.*, pp. 398-400.

[19] "Private carriers by water are frequently called 'proprietary' carriers or 'industrial' carriers. Contract carriers by water are frequently referred to as 'tramps' or 'charterers,' the former term being used generally when referring to vessels operating as contract carriers on the high seas. Some carriers operate both as common and as contract carriers. Industrial carriers sometimes transport for hire, particularly when the proprietary traffic is unbalanced." Locklin, *op. cit.*, pp. 723-24.

[20] Contract and private carriers predominate, because hauling of these commodities is normally handled by subsidiary shipping companies of individual firms (largely steel companies) or by independents under long-term contracts with individual companies. See *Ore Vessel Construction* (Hearings before a Subcommittee of the Committee on Interstate and Foreign Commerce, Senate, 84th Cong., 1st sess.) (Washington, D.C.: U.S. Government Printing Office, 1956), p. 61.

[21] Nelson, *op. cit.*, p. 397.

[22] The American Waterways Operators, Inc., *1966 Inland Waterborne Commerce Statistics* (Washington, D.C., 1968), p. 5.

from economic regulation: of the 1,752 firms operating inland barge and towing vessels, 1,007 are exempt contract carriers and 521 are exempt private carriers.[23] Finally, the common carrier coastwise and intercoastal shipping industry, which has suffered a decline since 1940, is controlled by thirty-seven and thirty-nine vessels, respectively.[24] Private and exempt carriers are of importance, although the exempt carriers are highly concentrated: eleven oil companies and three independent contract operators, for example, control the coastal tanker fleet.[25]

Except for the coastal and intercoastal system, therefore, concentration within the domestic water carrier industry is not very high. Especially is this true when both regulated and unregulated water carriers are considered.[26] This latter consideration is important for, despite the fact that the bulk of water traffic moves on contract or private carriers,[27] potential competition is still significant: regulated water carriers must compete for traffic with each other, with exempt and private water carriers, and with the railroads (in some areas). While it seems unlikely that the removal of entry restrictions on water carriers would change the present market structure, the absence of economic regulation might well result in workable competition in the domestic water carrier industry.

The Market Structure of Pipelines

One of the most highly specialized and highly concentrated modes of transport is the pipeline. The largest percentage of pipelines in operation carry gas or oil. Generally, only one such pipeline serves a given producing and consuming region, although there are some important exceptions. Several pipelines, for example, competitively bring oil to St. Louis and Chicago markets; some from different southwestern fields and some from different regions. In addition, while a few large independents operate in some regions, the majority of these lines are owned by producing companies, commonly on a multiple-ownership basis.[28] Competition among pipeline companies, then, is limited. This degree of concentration can be explained by the costs of pipeline operation—

[23] *Transportation Policy* (Hearings before a Subcommittee of the Committee on Interstate and Foreign Commerce, House, 84th Cong., 2d sess.) (Washington, D.C.: U.S. Government Printing Office, 1956), p. 1513.

[24] *Decline of the Coastwise and Intercoastal Shipping Industry* (Report of the Merchant Marine and Fisheries Subcommittee of the Committee on Interstate and Foreign Commerce, Senate, 86th Cong., 2d sess.) (Washington, D.C.: U.S. Government Printing Office, 1960), p. 3.

[25] Meyer and others, *op. cit.*, p. 238.

[26] For example: "About forty large lines, including fifteen exempt carriers, are described as operating, among other carriers, on the Mississippi system and Gulf coastal waterways; up to five or six major carriers compete for exempt or regulated traffic on each principal waterway." Nelson, *op. cit.*, p. 397.

[27] In 1966, 48.3 percent of total domestic waterborne traffic was handled by private carriers; 42.6 percent by exempt for-hire carriers; and 9.1 percent by regulated carriers. Department of the Army, Corps of Engineers, *Waterborne Commerce of the United States, Calendar Year 1966* (New Orleans, 1968), Part 5, p. 119.

[28] See U.S. Department of Interior, *An Appraisal of the Petroleum Industry of the United States* (1965), p. 37.

unit costs decrease as capacity increases.[29] Competition among pipelines and other modes of transport is also limited. In 1966, pipelines transported 74.15 percent of the crude oil carried in the United States; water carriers transported 17.90 percent; trucks, 7.73 percent; and railroads, .22 percent.[30] Here, again, cost considerations are controlling: it has been estimated that costs of transporting crude oil are about .3 mills per ton-mile by ocean-going tankers; .5 mills by pipeline; and 4 mills by rail.[31] Similar figures apply to natural gas traffic and costs.

Some dozen or more other products also are carried by pipeline, including wood pulp, sulfur, sugar cane, and coal slurry. Of particular interest are coal slurry pipelines, for their potential development indicates the dynamic nature of the present transport system.[32] To be sure, only one such pipeline has been built[33] (with a second line under construction[34]) and little information is available on the relative cost of moving coal by pipeline versus rail transportation.[35] Nevertheless, the potential effect on the traffic of the railroads is clear: In 1956, the year prior to the opening of the Pennsylvania–Ohio pipeline, the railroad serving the route (the New York Central) handled nearly 24,000 carloads of coal. In 1961, the line handled 1,703 carloads, while the electric plant's coal consumption remained relatively constant.[36]

To prevent the loss of coal traffic, railroads made major revisions in coal shipment rates to utilities based on trainload (so-called "unit train" shipments),

[29] Leslie Cookenboo, Jr., *Crude Oil Pipelines and Competition in the Oil Industry* (Cambridge: Harvard University Press, 1955), esp. chap. i.

[30] Association of Oil Pipe Lines, press release of April 26, 1968 (Washington, D.C.), Table 2, p. 3.

[31] Meyer and others, *op. cit.,* p. 149.

[32] See *Coal Slurry Pipeline* (Hearings before the Committee on Commerce, Senate, 87th Cong., 2d sess.) (Washington, D.C.: U.S. Government Printing Office, 1962). The history of coal slurry pipelines is discussed in "Coal Pipeline Background Information" (Washington, D.C.: National Coal Association, 1961).

[33] The only line constructed is an 108-mile line connecting the Hanna Coal Company (a subsidiary of Consolidation Coal) and the Cleveland Electric Illuminating Company's power station at Eastland, Ohio. The line began deliveries in February, 1957, but closed in 1963. Consolidation Coal, in 1963, announced plans to construct a $100 million line from West Virginia to the Atlantic seaboard (*The Wall Street Journal*, May 9, 1963, p. 4), but later scrapped the plans.

[34] Southern Pacific Co., early in 1968, started construction on a 275-mile coal slurry pipeline from the Peabody Coal Co.'s mines in the Black Mesa area of northern Arizona to the Mohave Power Project in Nevada. *Business Week*, February 3, 1968, p. 84.

[35] In 1962, an Interior Department study concluded that it would cost an estimated $2.26 to $3.25 a ton to move coal from West Virginia mines to eastern markets (New York, Philadelphia, and Baltimore) by slurry pipelines, compared with the then-existing average rail rate of $4.59 per ton. *Business Week*, July 21, 1962, p. 38. Since the study, however, railroad rates for hauling coal have been reduced substantially. A more recent study concludes that "Coal pipelines will be most competitive in those areas where there is not existing rail transport and in rugged terrain where a circuitous railroad route is required." T. L. Thompson and E. J. Wasp, "Coal Pipelines—A Reappraisal!" 40 *Pipe Line News* 12, 15 (December, 1968).

[36] *Coal Slurry Pipeline, op. cit.,* pp. 208–9. Interstate coal slurry pipelines are under the jurisdiction of the ICC.

rather than carload, volumes. "Basically, a 'through' freight express, the unit train is loaded with a single shipment at the point of origin and sent to destination without handling at intermediate freight classification yards. The train is then routed back to its point of origin and made ready for another trip."[37] With 100 or more hopper or gondola cars, unit trains are capable of hauling over 8,000 tons. Unit train operations, with their lower volume rates (the average delivered price of rail-borne coal dropped more than $1 a ton between 1957 and 1966), have enabled the railroads to retain coal traffic, thereby keeping coal competitive with nuclear energy as the country's power source for generation of electricity and forestalling the further development of coal slurry pipelines[38] and, perhaps, of mine-mouth generating plants.

The Market Structure of Intercity Passenger Buses

Intercity passenger bus operations are conducted by a large number of relatively small firms and by two large firms. The 176 Class I intercity carriers (annual revenues of $200,000 or more) operate over most of the longer routes, and account for about 80 percent of the passenger miles and nearly 90 percent of total revenues of intercity-bus travel. In addition, there are more than 1,000 Class II (revenues from $50,000 to $200,000) and Class III (under $50,000) intercity carriers.[39] But two carriers—Greyhound Lines (operating 5,422 buses over 102,181 miles of route) and Continental Trailways (operating 2,008 buses over 65,238 miles of route)—dominate the long-haul intercity routes and produce 55 percent of total intercity operating revenues. Greyhound alone accounts for nearly 20 percent of all intercity buses, 46 percent of intercity operating revenues, and 63 percent of the industry's net profits.

Despite some recent improvement, the intercity passenger bus industry has been generally unprofitable in the post-World War II period. In 1955, for example, 56 Class I carriers lost money; in 1959, the comparable number was 22. The industry's rate structure, moreover, "is not the result of any scientific planning. It is the result of the operation of several compelling influences, such as the competition of the private automobile, rail competition, competition

[37]Association of American Railroads, "Facts on Unit Trains" (Washington, D.C., 1967), p. 1. Unit trains are also being used to haul other bulk materials, such as ore, grain, sand, gravel, cement, phosphate rock, lumber, and steel. *Ibid.*, p. 2.

[38]For example, the unit train rate developed for Cleveland Electric Illuminating's coal supply was $1.88 a ton, compared with the then-existing pipeline rate of $2.47 to $2.65 a ton. Association of American Railroads, "The Unit Train: Husky Transport Competitor" (Washington, D.C., 1965), p. 1. Another factor which undoubtedly accounts for the slow development of slurry pipelines is that they do not have the right of eminent domain. On the unit train, see Paul W. MacAvoy and James Sloss, *Regulation of Transport Innovation: The ICC and Unit Coal Trains to the East* (New York: Random House, 1967). Several nonrailroad companies also have purchased fleets of gondola cars for unit train operations, including Consolidation Coal (800 cars) and Wisconsin Electric Power Company (235 cars).

[39]It has been estimated that there are between 700 and 800 intrastate bus companies. See National Association of Motor Bus Owners, *Bus Facts, 1966* (Washington, D.C., 1966), p. 12.

within the industry itself, and the ability of the traffic to bear the charges. The latter element is particularly important in the case of long-haul traffic." [40] For the industry as a whole, revenues are increasingly being derived from the growth of charter and special operations, and from nonpassenger services (package express, mail) and station concessions.[41] Whereas in 1951 almost 92 percent of the operating revenues of Class I carriers was derived from fares paid by passengers using regular-route services, less than 4 percent from charter and special operations, and 4.5 percent from nonpassenger services, in 1966 the proportion of operating revenues derived from regular-route passenger fares had declined to 75.8 percent, while income from charter and special operations accounted for 11.4 percent and nonpassenger services for 12.8 percent.[42]

On short-haul routes, several competing buses operate. Significantly, these routes, particularly in New England and the Central Atlantic states, tend to be the most unprofitable. On long-haul routes, two competing buses are generally found. Intercarrier competition (between bus, rail, and air coach services, as well as competition provided by the private automobile) is keen. In this industry, moreover, entry control permits the largest carriers to subsidize their unprofitable routes from the revenues gained in their most profitable markets. Nevertheless, there seems to be adequate competition among different types of passenger carriers to protect the public interest without restrictions on either entry or rates.[43]

The Market Structure of Air Transport

There are five major classes of domestic air carriers: eleven trunklines, nine local or feeder service carriers, thirteen supplementary carriers or "nonskeds," four helicopter carriers, and five all-cargo lines.[44] The trunklines dominate the industry. They serve the major domestic cities, accounting for 87.4 percent of revenue passenger-miles and 57.7 percent of cargo (comprising freight, express,

---

[40]Charles A. Taff, *Commercial Motor Transportation* (3d ed.; Homewood, Ill.: Richard D. Irwin, Inc., 1961), p. 649. For a discussion of rate making in the industry, see *ibid.*, pp. 652–54.

[41]"Clearly, the efforts of these carriers in promoting their supplemental services have been responsible in large measure for the preservation of essential regular-route passenger services in thousands of communities which otherwise would be without public land transport. Many of these communities simply could not be served were the carriers dependent solely on revenues from passenger fares." Interstate Commerce Commission, *Seventy-Sixth Annual Report* (1962), p. 118.

[42]*Ibid.,* and National Association of Motor Bus Owners, "Supplement to Bus Facts, 1966" (Washington, D.C., 1968), p. 10.

[43]"Bus transportation is available to 96 percent of the 3,377 important communities on the 41,000-mile interstate and defense highway system, rail passenger service is available to 82 percent, and air service within 20 miles to 60 percent. As the size of the community decreases, the availability of rail and air passenger service drops rapidly, whereas bus service does not." Taff, *op. cit.,* p. 613.

[44]Air Transport Association of America, *Air Transport Facts & Figures, 1968* (Washington, D.C., 1968), p. 43. In addition, there are two intra-Hawaiian carriers, five intra-Alaskan carriers, nearly 150 air freight forwarders, and over 2,600 air taxi operators.

and excess baggage) ton-miles. Within this segment, the carriers are of unequal size. The Big Four (American, Eastern, TWA, and United) have 67 percent of revenue passenger-miles, with the remaining 33 percent spread among the other seven trunkline carriers. The local service and helicopter carriers account for 5.5 percent of revenue passenger-miles and 1.4 percent of cargo ton-miles. All of these carriers receive annual government subsidies. The supplemental airlines (performing passenger and cargo charter services) account for 7.1 percent of revenue passenger-miles and 24.3 percent of cargo ton-miles. Over 65 percent of the nonskeds' operating revenues accrue to four of the thirteen carriers of this type. Finally, the five all-cargo carriers (operating scheduled flights carrying freight, express, and mail) account for 16.6 percent of air cargo ton-miles. They serve larger routes only, and except for minimum rates, the CAB has permitted them considerable freedom in developing a rate structure.[45]

Competition in various markets or over particular city-pair routes is limited, although the number of competing carriers has tended to increase in recent years. All but 11 of the 100 largest city-pairs are served by two or more trunkline carriers, while the local-service carriers generally operate over monopoly routes.[46] The disparity in size of the trunklines, as well as size of local-service carriers, is partly inevitable and can be explained by the existing pattern of route distribution. For the airlines, economies of scale are closely related to the density of traffic. It is not surprising, therefore, that the Big Four carriers have 87.5 percent of their passengers originating at stations with 5,000 or more passengers per month and that the local-service carriers, serving primarily low traffic density markets, continue to receive subsidies.[47] Further, fixed costs are relatively high due to such factors as the expense of individual planes and the cost of operating adequate maintenance facilities. These cost characteristics indicate that even in the absence of regulation, the airline industry would be concentrated.

Yet, regulatory policy has had an important effect on the industry's present market structure. In 1938, nineteen trunklines were certified; by 1967, the number had shrunk to eleven. In the early 1940's, the CAB issued twenty temporary certificates to local-service carriers; in 1955, when permanent certificates were authorized by Congress, only thirteen carriers remained and subsequent mergers reduced the number to nine local-service lines. During these periods, no new firms were permitted to enter either segment of the industry. Instead, the CAB followed a policy of extending the routes of existing carriers as the need for new service developed (Table 14–1). A similar situation exists with

[45] All data from Civil Aeronautics Board, *Reports to Congress* (1967), pp. 15, 47, 49–50.

[46] Richard E. Caves, *Air Transport and Its Regulators* (Cambridge: Harvard University Press, 1962), p. 20.

[47] Meyer and others, *op. cit.,* p. 228; and *The Airlines Industry* (Report of the Antitrust Subcommittee of the Committee on the Judiciary, House, 85th Cong., 1st sess.) (Washington, D.C.: U.S. Government Printing Office, 1957).

TABLE 14-1
Growth of Domestic Trunkline Carriers

	Points Served		Route Mileage	
Airlines	Original, 1938	June 30, 1967	Original, 1938	June 30, 1967
American Airlines	59	54	6,826	27,501
Braniff Airways	21	36	2,543	11,184
Continental Air Lines	8	24	624	11,769
Delta Air Lines	13	59	1,091	22,084
Eastern Air Lines	42	85	5,276	34,077
National Airlines	13	36	871	6,279
Northeast Airlines	16	36	648	6,313
Northwest Airlines	21	30	2,507	15,305
Trans World Airlines	27	43	5,749	22,500
United Air Lines	38	89	5,321	30,181
Western Air Lines	12	28	1,237	7,439

Source: Civil Aeronautics Board, *Reports to Congress* (1967), p. 41.

respect to the supplemental carriers where mortality has been high due to the lack of capital and managerial experience and also to "the narrow scope of legal operations defined by the Board."[48]

The CAB has traditionally encouraged air carriers to establish individual rates. Indeed, the carriers are under a legal requirement to secure permission from the board before engaging in industry conferences on such matters as fares. Rate bureaus and traffic conferences, therefore, have played a minor role in the development of the industry's rate structure. Price competition does occur, although Cherington found that such price competition was more frequent in single-carrier markets than in multi-carrier markets.[49] In the latter markets, competition has taken the form of rivalry in the nonprice or service area.

As in the case of the trucking industry, it has been argued that airline regulation is needed to prevent excessive competition, particularly between the trunklines and the supplemental air carriers. And, also like the trucking industry, excess competition is doubtful under present conditions. The authors of a detailed study argue:

[48]Caves, *op. cit.,* p. 14. See *Future of Irregular Airlines in the United States Transportation Industry* (Hearings before a Subcommittee of the Select Committee on Small Business, Senate, 83d Cong., 1st sess.) (Washington, D.C.: U.S. Government Printing Office, 1953).

[49]"One of the considerations ... appears to be that, in a noncompetitive situation, if the fare proves to be unsuccessful, it can be allowed to expire or can be withdrawn at the will of the initiating carrier. Under a competitive situation, the fare may be met by the competitor who then may be unwilling to terminate it." Paul Cherington, *Airline Price Policy: A Study of Domestic Passenger Fares* (Boston: Harvard Graduate School of Business Administration, 1958), p. 160.

In 1938 air transport involved less capital than today and so could attract new firms more on the basis of the glamour of pioneering than on the basis of rational economic calculation. Furthermore, the thirties was a period of excess competition throughout the economy.

In the industry as it exists today, the excessive competition argument for regulation appears dubious. The very small non-sked firms have disappeared, and those that remain operate largely on routes that can support additional carriers, as indicated by recent CAB decisions. Even without the present restrictions, it seems doubtful whether the non-skeds could expand sufficiently to create the general excess capacity that is the consequence of genuinely excessive competition. As the CAB itself states, "Practical economic considerations will prevent the supplemental air carriers from flooding the market, and a supplemental air carrier who is unable to obtain an adequate load will soon seek greener fields elsewhere." Instead of excessive competition, the most likely outcome of the removal of present regulation would be a few more competitors on the eleven most traveled routes and little change in most other airline passenger markets. In short, the inherent self-discipline of a small-numbers market . . . would remain.[50]

There is, however, a complicating factor.[51] The trunklines, as common carriers, have been required to provide service on some routes which were unprofitable. By limiting competition, they were able to subsidize these light-density routes from earnings made on the heavy-density routes. Moreover, the supplemental carriers operated primarily in profitable markets.[52] Given this situation, unrestricted competition would have placed the trunklines at a serious disadvantage. Two solutions to the problem have evolved. First, in 1961 Congress enacted legislation limiting the supplemental carriers to charter operations.[53] Second, the CAB has gradually permitted the trunklines to discontinue service on sparsely traveled routes, with the subsidized local-service carriers being authorized to serve such routes.

Market Structure: Summary

The existing market structures of the various modes of transportation are similar to the market structures of nonregulated industries.

To be sure, the railroad industry and the airlines have highly concentrated market structures, but no more so than automobiles and aluminum. Trucking and inland waterways are composed of numerous small firms, but so is the

[50] Meyer and others, *op. cit.*, p. 232 (footnote omitted).

[51] Samuel B. Richmond, *Regulation and Competition in Air Transportation* (New York: Columbia University Press, 1961), chaps. viii and ix.

[52] The CAB's efforts to deal with nonscheduled or supplemental carriers spans many years. See *Large Irregular Carriers, Exemptions*, 11 CAB 609 (1950); *Large Irregular Air Carrier Investigation*, 22 CAB 838 (1955); *American Airlines v. Civil Aeronautics Board*, 235 F. 2d 845 (1956); *Large Irregular Air Carrier Investigation*, 28 CAB 224 (1959); and *United Air Lines v. Civil Aeronautics Board*, 278 F. 2d 446 (1960).

[53] Public Law 87-528 (1961).

garment industry. Pipeline transportation has the only market structure falling outside the range of market structures in the nonregulated sector of the American economy. Here, the highly concentrated market structure is explained by economies of scale, and so oil pipelines are analogous to regulated natural monopolies, like electric utilities.[54]

Such a conclusion as to the normality of market structures in the transportation industry indicates, but does not prove, that workable competition is possible under substantially reduced regulation.

Competitive Forces or Checks. There are several competitive forces or checks in the transportation industry.[55] First, intramodal competition arises when more than one producer is able and willing to supply a particular product or service. The costs and technological conditions of highway and water operations

. . . are quite conducive to the presence of direct competition, perhaps as conducive as anywhere in the American economy. While such competition is not quite so pronounced in commercial airline operations, especially now that extremely expensive jet airliners have become essential, it is still present. Furthermore, even in railroading there is usually some direct competition, though it is ordinarily limited to two or three alternatives.[56]

Intramodal competition is heightened by rivalry between regulated and unregulated (contract, private, or exempt) modes of transport.[57] Intramodal competition also

. . . is provided by the fact that even if only one or two common-carrier railroads or trucking firms are licensed to operate directly between two points, it is often possible to obtain service by taking only a slightly less direct routing; in such circumstances there will normally be no tariff penalty but only some sacrifice in service, especially of time in transit.[58]

Intermodal competition among different modes of transport provides a second competitive force. The existence and importance of such competition can be seen from Tables 14–2 and 14–3. One fact stands out: the newer forms of transport have captured from the railroads a significant share of both freight and passenger traffic. In 1929, the railroads handled 74.9 percent of intercity ton-miles and 77.1 percent of intercity (for-hire) passenger-miles. In 1967,

[54] Meyer and others, *op. cit.*, p. 239.
[55] John R. Meyer, "Competition, Market Structure and Regulatory Institutions in Transportation," 50 *Virginia Law Review* 212, 214–18 (1964).
[56] *Ibid.*, p. 215.
[57] Competition between regulated and unregulated carriers is largely due to Congressional policy: by preventing common carriers from meeting rates set by unregulated carriers and exempting certain carriers from economic regulation, unregulated competition has been fostered. Significantly, therefore, this source of competition might lessen, but not disappear completely, if Congress should decide to give common carriers more freedom to set rates or should grant all common carriers the same exemptions now given to some regulated and unregulated carriers.
[58] Meyer, *op. cit.*, p. 216.

TABLE 14-2
Percentage Distribution of Intercity Ton-Miles

Agency	1929	1939	1949	1959	1967[p]
Railroads[a]	74.9	62.3	58.4	45.5	41.6
Motor carriers	3.3	9.7	13.8	21.5	22.1
Inland waterways[b]	17.4	17.7	15.2	15.3	15.6
Pipelines (oil)	4.4	10.2	12.6	17.6	20.5
Air carriers[c]	...	...	.03	.05	.15
	100.0	100.0	100.0	100.0	100.0

[p] Preliminary.
[a] Includes electric railways, express, and mail.
[b] Includes Great Lakes.
[c] Includes express, mail, and excess baggage.
Source: Year 1929, Cornelius P. Cotter, *Government and Private Enterprise* (New York: Holt, Rinehart & Winston, Inc., 1960), p. 266; years 1939 and 1949, Interstate Commerce Commission, Statement No. 568 (February, 1956); year 1959, Interstate Commerce Commission, *Seventy-Fifth Annual Report* (1961), p. 15; year 1967, Interstate Commerce Commission, Bureau of Economics, *Transport Economics* (July, 1968), p. 4.

TABLE 14-3
Percentage Distribution of Intercity Passenger-Miles

Agency	1929	1939	1949	1959	1967[p]
Railroads	77.1	67.7	47.4	28.8	11.7
Motor carriers	15.4	26.0	37.8	26.4	19.0
Air carriers	...	2.0	12.9	42.2	66.7
Inland waterways[a]	7.5	4.3	1.9	2.6	2.6
	100.0	100.0	100.0	100.0	100.0

[p] Preliminary.
[a] Includes Great Lakes.
Source: Years 1929 and 1939, Cornelius P. Cotter, *Government and Private Enterprise* (New York: Holt, Rinehart & Winston, Inc., 1960), p. 266; year 1949, Interstate Commerce Commission, Statement No. 280 (January, 1958); year 1959, Interstate Commerce Commission, *Seventy-Fifth Annual Report* (1961), p. 15; year 1967, Interstate Commerce Commission, Bureau of Economics, *Transport Economics* (July, 1968), p. 3.

despite the growth of traffic, these percentages had fallen to 41.6 and 11.7, respectively. And the development of new transportation technology, such as coal slurry pipelines, high-voltage electric transmission lines, and new railroad equipment, suggests that this form of competition will become of even more significance in the future as the inherent cost advantages of each mode of transport are narrowed.[59]

[59] As noted earlier, since each mode of transport has a different cost structure which provides it with certain inherent advantages—as well as sheltered markets—over its rivals, intermodal competition is necessarily imperfect. See Chapter 2, pp. 41-42.

Market competition provides a third competitive force in the transportation industry. In some instances, such as use of oil or gas in place of coal as a boiler fuel in generating electricity, different products can be substituted for one another. In other cases, such as California and Florida citrus fruit, two sources of supply can be found for the same product. Transportation charges, in either situation, are limited by the fact that if the rate on a specific commodity is too high, traffic will be curtailed. Especially is market competition of importance in cases when transportation costs are a significant percentage of the total cost charged to the consumer, such as is true of bulk commodities. A closely related factor is the persistent tendency toward decentralization of industry.

Regional assembly and production centers have become highly attractive in circumstances in which manufacturing or assembly can be conducted on a small scale without too much inefficiency and transportation charges on the finished products are relatively high. The historical fact that transportation rate structures have tended to place much higher mark-ups over actual costs on the shipment of final finished products as against relatively low mark-ups on the movement of raw materials has greatly encouraged this trend.[60]

A final competitive constraint on the transportation industry is the fact that these enterprises operate within a competitive environment. As explained by Meyer:

> This particular competitive check is far more important in terms of its dynamic than its static implications since it primarily places constraints upon the level of managerial inefficiency or lack of adaptation to changed circumstances that will be tolerated. An extremely important fact of life for all private transportation companies in North America and Europe, and to a surprisingly large degree for publicly owned transportation companies as well, is the fact that they must compete for their supplies of capital and other factors of production against unregulated firms. In such circumstances, at least the privately owned transportation companies are subject to the same audits and tests by financial markets and managers as other private industries. The circumstances of being embedded in a generally competitive framework also heightens the effectiveness of all the previously cited constraints upon monopoly powers. Specifically, the mores and conventions of a market economy almost invariably place distinct limitations on how far transportation enterprises and their public regulatory agencies can go in making shippers or consumers absolutely captive. As long as it is impossible to put extremely strict controls on shipper and consumer choices, self-interest will usually lead to exploration of some of the "competitive alternatives" just discussed by those subjected to exorbitant prices or intolerable service levels.[61]

The existence of these various competitive forces adds further support to the proposition that workable competition is possible in the transportation

---

[60]Meyer, *op. cit.*, p. 217.
[61]*Ibid.*, pp. 217–18.

industry under conditions of reduced regulation. It is within this framework that the United States must seek to develop a truly national transportation policy.

THE RELATIVE DECLINE OF COMMON CARRIERS

Since the end of the second World War, the relative position of common carriers in the economy has declined. The emphasis in this section is on the railroads, not because their economic health is of more importance than is the health of other carriers, but because the "decline of the relative importance of railroad transportation is the most significant development in domestic transportation in the last 30 years." [62]

The Financial Plight of the Railroads

For many years, "representatives of the railroad industry have complained that federal transport regulation—and principally rate regulation—has been partially responsible for the railroad adynamy." [63] For example, in a lengthy document entitled "Magna Carta for Transportation," issued in 1961,[64] the Association of American Railroads argued that "our industry is in jeopardy" and warned of "the gathering storm." The railroads blamed this situation on "one of the worst messes Washington has ever blundered into" and declared themselves "tired of being the punching bag for destructive Government policies."

The financial plight of the nation's railroads is shown by the following statistics. (1) The industry's rate of return on net investment (Table 14-4) has not been 6 percent or above since 1920 (except during the war years of 1942 and 1943). (2) The industry's ratio of net income to shareowners' equity has been consistently low throughout this period, never attaining the 6.8 percent of 1929. In contrast with the railroads 1966 ratio of 5.0 percent, the airlines ratio was 23.8 percent and the common motor carriers ratio was 14.1 percent. (3) While the railroads' freight business increased from 602 billion ton-miles in 1946 to 751 billion in 1966, motor carriers' ton-miles increased from 82 billion to 381 billion, and inland water carriers' ton-miles from 28 billion to 281 billion, in the same period. As a result, the railroad's share of total intercity ton-miles declined from 75 percent in 1929 and 67 percent in 1946 to 43 percent in 1966. (4) The industry's share of total operating revenues of all transportation modes has declined from 73.6 percent in 1946 to 52.2 percent in 1966. (5) Freight revenue

[62] *National Transportation Policy* (Preliminary draft of a report prepared for the Committee on Interstate and Foreign Commerce by the Special Study Group on Transportation Policies in the United States, Senate, 87th Cong., 1st sess.) (Washington, D.C.: U.S. Government Printing Office, 1961), p. 4.

[63] Howard W. Davis, "A Review of Federal Rate Regulation and Its Impact upon the Railway Industry," 44 *Land Economics* 1, 2 (1968). "Such representatives have, of course, also been aware of general market conditions contributing to the railroad problem, and they have occasionally even been outspoken about their own management shortcomings in this regard." *Ibid.,* n. 3.

[64] Association of American Railroads, "Magna Carta for Transportation" (Washington, D.C., 1961).

per ton-mile has varied from 1.149 cents for the period 1921–25 to a high of 1.477 in 1958, subsequently declining to 1.271 cents in 1966. (6) Net income (after payment of interest and other fixed charges) of $904 million in 1966 (the highest since 1955) was only .8 percent above the industry's 1929 net income of $897 million. (7) The industry had 630,895 employees in 1966, compared with an average of 1,664,000 in the period 1926–30.[65]

TABLE 14-4
Railroads' Rate of Return on Book Investment, 1890–1968

Year	Return	Year	Return	Year	Return	Year	Return
1890	. . . . .4.0%	1910	. . . . .5.5%	1930	. . . . .3.6%	1950	. . . . .4.3%
1891	. . . . .3.9	1911	. . . . .4.8	1931	. . . . .2.2	1951	. . . . .3.8
1892	. . . . .4.1	1912	. . . . .4.5	1932	. . . . .1.4	1952	. . . . .4.2
1893	. . . . .4.0	1913	. . . . .4.9	1933	. . . . .2.0	1953	. . . . .4.3
1894	. . . . .3.3	1914	. . . . .4.0	1934	. . . . .2.0	1954	. . . . .3.4
1895	. . . . .3.4	1915	. . . . .4.0	1935	. . . . .2.2	1955	. . . . .4.3
1896	. . . . .3.5	1916	. . . . .6.0	1936	. . . . .2.9	1956	. . . . .4.0
1897	. . . . .3.4	1917	. . . . .5.2	1937	. . . . .2.6	1957	. . . . .3.4
1898	. . . . .3.9	1918	. . . . .3.5	1938	. . . . .1.6	1958	. . . . .2.8
1899	. . . . .4.1	1919	. . . . .2.4	1939	. . . . .2.6	1959	. . . . .2.7
1900	. . . . .4.6	1920	1	1940	. . . . .3.0	1960	. . . . .2.1
1901	. . . . .4.9	1921	. . . . .3.0	1941	. . . . .4.4	1961	. . . . .2.0
1902	. . . . .5.2	1922	. . . . .3.9	1942	. . . . .6.6	1962	. . . . .2.7
1903	. . . . .5.3	1923	. . . . .4.7	1943	. . . . .6.0	1963	. . . . .3.1
1904	. . . . .5.0	1924	. . . . .4.6	1944	. . . . .4.9	1964	. . . . .3.2
1905	. . . . .5.2	1925	. . . . .5.2	1945	. . . . .3.9	1965	. . . . .3.7
1906	. . . . .5.7	1926	. . . . .5.5	1946	. . . . .2.8	1966	. . . . .3.9
1907	. . . . .5.8	1927	. . . . .4.7	1947	. . . . .3.5	1967	. . . . .2.5
1908	. . . . .4.7	1928	. . . . .5.1	1948	. . . . .4.4	1968	. . . . .2.6[P]
1909	. . . . .5.1	1929	. . . . .5.3	1949	. . . . .2.9		

[P] Preliminary.
Source: Association of American Railroads.

The Basic Causes

There are several basic causes for the decline of common carriers.[66] In the first place, competition among different modes of transport has advanced rapidly. This growth can be attributed to the rapid advancement of technology, enabling carriers to offer a wider variety of services. The newer types of carriers

[65] All data in this paragraph are from: James C. Nelson, *Railroad Transportation and Public Policy* (Washington, D.C.: Brookings Institution, 1959); Interstate Commerce Commission, *Eighty-First Annual Report* (1967); and Behling, *op. cit.*

[66] See *National Transportation Policy, op. cit.*, pp. 67–71; *Problems of the Railroads* (Hearings before the Subcommittee on Surface Transportation of the Committee on Interstate and Foreign Commerce, Senate, 85th Cong., 2d sess.) (Washington, D.C.: U.S. Government Printing Office, 1958), Parts 1-4; Nelson, *Railroad Transportation and Public Policy, op. cit.*, Part I; and George F. Mott, *Transportation Century* (Baton Rouge: Louisiana State University Press, 1966).

can frequently render more flexible, convenient, and speedier service or can furnish service at a lower cost than can the railroads. "As these modes developed they were in position to offer a service-price combination to various important segments of traffic that the railroads were unable to match. For example, long before the refrigerator truck was a major factor, overnight trucks made great inroads in rail traffic that required the time and expense of refrigerator car service."[67] The loss of high-valued manufactured commodities to the trucks has meant a more than proportionate loss of revenue for the railroads, since rates on these commodities are high in relation to unit costs. While a large percentage of these losses has been over short hauls, the railroads have also been losing high-valued traffic over transcontinental routes.

Second, the railroads have lost traffic as the result of such factors as diversification of industry (fewer long hauls), the decline in the use of coal as a fuel (in the Northeast), and changes in business location (large-volume bulk users have tended to build new plants along navigable waters whenever possible). Business practices also have changed: smaller inventories, for instance, favor airlines and trucks, since these modes can make more frequent deliveries of smaller shipments. Less-than-carload merchandise freight traffic has been captured by motor carriers, while the airlines have captured a large share of the intercity passenger traffic formerly held by the railroads.

Third, government promotional activities have affected the economic position of common carriers. Highways, waterways, airways, and airport facilities have been, and are being, provided at a lower capital cost than is now available to the private railroads. Only the railroads and pipelines must maintain a heavy fixed investment in rights-of-way and pay property taxes on them. Public facilities also have encouraged the development and growth of private carriers. Especially is this true when the rates charged by carriers using public facilities do not reflect adequate payments for their use.

Fourth, government regulatory policy has been a further element in the decline of common carriers. All airlines and railroad operations are subject to state or federal regulation, but only 86 percent of pipeline (oil) traffic, 39.1 percent of truck traffic, and 12.2 percent of water traffic is similarly controlled (Table 14-5). In addition to exempt traffic, private carriers have made significant inroads into traffic once handled by common carriers. Unregulated carriers are neither subject to route limitations nor required to provide unprofitable services (even if considered essential). Regulatory delay in postwar rate cases has cost common carriers millions of dollars annually in revenues. Regulatory policies limiting rate reductions to protect competing modes of transport and traditional markets have resulted in further large revenue losses. And intermodal competition has been affected by the inconsistencies in regulatory policy and disparities among modes of transportation outlined in the preceding chapter.[68]

[67] *National Transportation Policy, op. cit.,* p. 67.
[68] See Chapter 13, pp. 473-81.

TABLE 14-5

Comparison of Total Intercity Traffic by Carrier Type with Intercity Traffic by Federally Regulated Carriers
(billions of ton-miles)

Calendar Year	Airways		Railroads		Water Carriers[a]		Motor Carriers		Oil Pipelines	
	Total Ton-Miles	Percent Regulated	Total Ton-Miles	Percent Regulated	Total Ton-Miles	Percent Regulated	Total Ton-Miles	Percent Regulated	Total Ton-Miles	Percent Regulated
1946	0.1	100.0	602.1	100.0	124.0	6.0	82.0	37.0	92.5	79.0
1947	.2	100.0	664.4	100.0	146.7	6.0	102.1	37.0	104.2	79.0
1948	.2	100.0	647.3	100.0	150.5	6.0	116.1	40.0	119.6	79.0
1949	.2	100.0	534.7	100.0	139.4	6.0	126.6	38.0	114.9	79.0
1950	.3	100.0	596.9	100.0	163.3	6.0	172.9	38.0	129.2	79.0
1951	.4	100.0	655.4	100.0	182.2	6.0	188.0	38.0	152.1	79.0
1952	.4	100.0	623.4	100.0	168.4	6.0	194.6	36.0	157.5	79.0
1953	.4	100.0	614.2	100.0	202.4	6.0	217.2	35.0	169.9	79.0
1954	.4	100.0	556.6	100.0	173.7	6.0	214.6	34.0	179.2	79.0
1955	.5	100.0	631.4	100.0	216.5	6.0	226.2	37.0	203.2	79.0
1956	.6	100.0	655.9	100.0	220.0	6.0	253.8	33.0	230.0	78.0
1957	.6	100.0	626.2	100.0	231.8	6.0	244.9	32.0	222.7	78.0
1958	.6	100.0	558.7	100.0	189.0	6.0	247.0	32.0	211.3	78.0
1959	.8	100.0	582.5	100.0	196.6	6.0	288.5	34.0	227.0	...
1960	.8	100.0	579.1	100.0	220.3	6.0	297.7	35.0	228.6	...
1961	.9	100.0	570.0	100.0	209.7	6.0	313.1	35.0	233.2	...
1962	1.3	100.0	600.0	100.0	475.0	11.1	331.3	33.8	237.7	86.4
1963	1.3	100.0	629.3	100.0	480.6	10.6	331.8	36.3	253.4	85.7
1964	1.5	100.0	666.2	100.0	488.8	11.5	349.8	35.8	268.7	85.4
1965	1.9	100.0	708.7	100.0	489.8	12.2	359.2	39.1	306.4	86.0

[a] Data for inland waterways only from 1946–61; data for coastal, inland waterways, intercoastal, inland, and Great Lakes traffic from 1962–65.

Source: *National Transportation Policy* (Preliminary draft of a Report prepared for the Committee on Interstate and Foreign Commerce by the Special Study Group on Transportation Policies in the United States, Senate, 87th Cong., 1st sess.) (Washington, D.C.: U.S. Government Printing Office, 1961), p. 50; *Transportation Act Amendments—1963* (Hearings before the Surface Transportation Subcommittee of the Committee on Commerce, Senate, 88th Cong., 1st sess.) (Washington, D.C.: U.S. Government Printing Office, 1964), p. 890; Interstate Commerce Commission, Bureau of Economics, *Transport Economics* (February, 1964), p. 5 and (January, 1968), p. 8; and Interstate Commerce Commission, *Seventy-Eighth Annual Report* (1964), p. 61, *Seventy-Ninth Annual Report* (1965), p. 54, and *Eighty-First Annual Report* (1966), p. 54, and *Eightieth Annual Report* (1967), p. 57.

Fifth, all common carriers have experienced rising costs in the postwar period, as have unregulated industries. In particular, union wage rates have increased rapidly. For the railroad industry, which continues to suffer from various featherbedding practices, mounting labor costs have been particularly severe. Finally, management itself is partly responsible for the relative decline of common carriers. An executive of the Association of American Railroads has stated:

> The clearest example of this is the failure of railroad management to anticipate the true economic value of the new and developing modes of transport at a time when there would have been no restrictions upon the right of railroads to employ these new tools of transportation and make of themselves transportation companies rather than merely railroad companies. Also, some of the ills of the railroads may be attributable to a failure of railroad management to appreciate fully the significance of the fact that the railroads are essentially volume carriers, and for most products for other than short distances, the most economic carrier. There have been several consequences of this, but the principal one chargeable to lack of foresight would seem to be in the area of pricing their services so as to retain the volume of business necessary to realize the greatest good from the railroads' inherent advantage as a volume carrier.[69]

To some degree, these comments apply to managements of other carriers as well.

The Basic Economic Results

The relative decline of common carriers raises several important questions:

> What have been and what will be the results of these trends? These are the basic questions. Are we headed for a less than adequate system or lack of system of transportation? Can we accommodate the mass movements of passengers and freight between major centers as our population and economy grow? Will our unlimited growth of private and exempt carriage at the expense of common carriers provide adequate service for the relatively few large shippers and more prosperous persons but entirely inadequate for the many? Finally, would such a structure of transport facilities involve excessive social investment and higher operating expenses so that ton-mile and passenger-mile costs will increase and thereby hinder economic growth?[70]

The deteriorating traffic position of common carriers results in a vicious circle. Falling traffic presents serious revenue and income problems, and leads to overcapacity. To improve earnings, maintenance expenditures are curtailed and services are either discontinued or reduced.[71] Under these conditions, financing

---

[69] Gregory S. Prince, "Railroads and Government Policy—A Legally Oriented Study of an Economic Crisis," 48 *Virginia Law Review* 196, 203 (1962).

[70] *National Transportation Policy, op. cit.,* p. 71.

[71] A financially weak common carrier cannot afford to serve unprofitable routes, even when such service is considered essential from a political or social point of view, for it is unable to subsidize its unprofitable services from revenues on more profitable

costs tend to increase. Since higher financing costs aggravate revenues and income further, the circle is closed. And all these factors tend to raise transportation costs and increase the competitive struggle.

The significance of the railroads' earnings picture has been stated by James C. Nelson:

> Since the railroad industry depends on private capital investment, low and erratic earnings threaten not only the solvency of significant segments of the industry but also the achievement of the gains which high and sustained rates of capital investment could yield. For the principal portion of capital funds for railroad modernization have long come from internal sources; and although conditions in recent years have been more favorable to sale of stock, it seems likely that internal sources will continue to have a key role in railroad capital formation in the future.[72]

Declining traffic leads to overcapacity, a situation faced by common carriers in the postwar period.[73] The railroad industry could handle a substantial increase in both freight and passenger traffic with its present facilities, assuming a balanced distribution. The average passenger load on Class I intercity buses has generally ranged between 18 and 19.6 persons in the years since 1947, compared with a wartime peak of nearly 25. The airline industry's load factor fell from 78.7 percent in 1946 to 56.5 percent in 1967. Consequently, all common carriers have excessive plant and equipment, including standby equipment.

The common carriers have found their financing costs increasing as a consequence of the above trends.

> Just as financing costs tend to decline in a situation of growth and improved competitive position, they will increase if the reverse is true. . . . The carrier in this situation [declining net income] is forced to resort to debt financing rather than equity financing. This in turn saddles the carrier with heavier fixed charges that must be borne during a period of reduced traffic volume. This in turn may lead to receivership for a high investment cost industry like the railroads.[74]

From the mid-1930's to 1952, the railroads reduced their debt ratio to under 50 percent, but since 1953 the ratio has been climbing upward, reaching 54.1 percent in 1960. Even the airline industry, whose earnings have been generally above those of the railroads (Table 14-6), paid nearly 13 percent for equity capital in the late 1950's.[75]

---

operations. Moreover, intermodal competition increases the pressure on common carriers to discontinue such unprofitable services. Thus, as Locklin has noted, if internal subsidization is not possible, "the choice is between direct subsidy—local, state, or federal—or what amounts to the same thing, provision of such services by local, state, or federal governments, with the taxpayers making up the losses." D. Philip Locklin, "Trends in Transport Policy," 22 *Illinois Business Review* 6, 8 (May, 1965).

[72] Nelson, *Railroad Transportation and Public Policy, op. cit.,* p. 229.
[73] See *National Transportation Policy, op. cit.,* pp. 71–74.
[74] *Ibid.,* p. 76.
[75] *Ibid.,* p. 77.

TABLE 14-6
Domestic Trunk Airlines' Rate of Return on Investment, 1939-67*

Year	Return	Year	Return	Year	Return
1939[a]	2.3%	1949	6.1%	1959	7.1%
1940[a]	13.2	1950	11.2	1960	2.8
1941[a]	4.5	1951	14.6	1961	1.5
1942	20.3	1952	14.2	1962	4.1
1943	17.1	1953	11.3	1963	4.3
1944	17.5	1954	10.4	1964	9.6
1945	9.4	1955	11.8	1965	11.2
1946	1.5	1956	9.3	1966	9.7
1947	2.9	1957	4.8	1967	7.7
1948	1.7	1958	6.5		

*Because of the use of two sources of data, the figures since 1957 are not strictly comparable with the earlier figures.

[a] Fiscal year ended June 30.

Source: Years 1939-56; D. Philip Locklin, *Economics of Transportation* (6th ed.; Homewood, Ill.: Richard D. Irwin, Inc., 1966), p. 825; years 1957-67, Air Transport Association of America, *Air Transport Facts & Figures* (Washington, D.C., annually).

No implication is intended that the common carriers have stood idly by, watching their earnings decline and their traffic disappear. Several methods have been employed to reduce expenses. Improved procedures have contributed to a decrease in maintenance expenditures, both as to way and equipment. Advancing technology has resulted in improved utilization of plant and equipment. The railroads, for example, are installing three computer-related systems for better control of freight car distribution and use.[76] Some replacement has been postponed, so that the average age of equipment has been increasing. Some service has been discontinued or reduced. Discontinuance has been of importance in railroad passenger service; reductions have occurred in railroad freight schedules, as well as in airline and bus services in some areas of the country. In addition, common carriers have sought to introduce new equipment and to design incentive rates to gain or retain traffic. To use the railroads again, they have captured about one-half of the transportation of new motor vehicles to distribution centers as a result of introducing multideck rack cars, and they have established unit train operations for moving volume commodities and "rent-a-train" tariffs for handling grain traffic.[77]

The net effect of these developments has been a heightening of intermodal competition. And, in this connection, it is significant that the complaints to the

[76] See Behling, *op. cit.,* p. 15.

[77] The Illinois Central introduced a "Rent-a-Train" grain tariff in 1967. Under the tariff, the shipper makes an annual payment of $1 million with carrier equipment or $700,000 with shipper equipment, plus a charge of 1.175 mills per ton-mile, for hauling an 86-car train. The tariff was permitted to go into effect by the ICC, subject to a formal investigation. Over 70 protests have been filed with the commission.

Interstate Commerce Commission relative to proposed reduced rates have increased from 510 in 1946 to 3,229 in 1967.[78]

TOWARD A NATIONAL TRANSPORTATION POLICY

If the goal of public policy is to develop an economically efficient transportation system, as is here assumed, then several basic and highly controversial changes in current policies are indicated. It is important to emphasize that some causes of the postwar decline of common carriers are economic in nature, while others are due to regulatory policy. Changing traffic patterns resulting from such factors as technological innovation, diversification of industry, and new business practices are expected in a dynamic economy. But when the fortunes of carriers are due to regulatory activities, the desirability of neutral governmental policies becomes clear.

National Transportation Policy Statement

The statement of national transportation policy, contained in the Transportation Act of 1940, contains several inconsistencies and contradictions.[79] Its value as a guide to the Interstate Commerce Commission, therefore, is practically nil. Consider the commission's dilemma: it is told (1) to provide fair and impartial regulation for all modes of transport, (2) to recognize and preserve the inherent advantages of each mode, (3) to provide regulation that fosters sound economic conditions in transportation and among the several carriers, and (4) to prevent unfair or destructive competitive practices.[80] Clearly, the commission cannot abide by each of these principles in the same case. It is little wonder that policy is far from uniform and that decisions seem to lack consistency.

Congress has the minimum responsibility for establishing a clear and concise national transportation policy. Further, such a policy should incorporate both the regulatory and promotional activities of the federal government. The following proposal was made by the Doyle Report in 1961:

National Transportation Policy

It is hereby declared to be the national transportation policy to provide for flexible, coordinated, and impartial promotion and regulation of transportation in interstate commerce to the end that the needs of the commerce of the United States, of the postal service, and of national defense be met.

---

[78] Of the 215,540 tariffs filed with the ICC in fiscal 1967, the Suspension Board considered 4,549. Of the latter, just over 70 percent involved rate decreases. Interstate Commerce Commission, *Eighty-First Annual Report* (1967), pp. 112, 114.

[79] See Martin T. Farris, "Definitional Inconsistencies in the National Transportation Policy," 35 *I.C.C. Practitioners' Journal* 25 (1967).

[80] And the 1958 rule of rate making, to further complicate the issue, provides that "Rates of a carrier shall not be held up to a particular level to protect the traffic of any other mode of transportation, giving due consideration to the objectives of the national transportation policy declared in this chapter. . . ."

To attain this objective, promotional and regulatory programs in transportation shall:

1. Foster a safe, adequate, and coordinated national transportation system composed of all economically suitable modes operating singly and in combination and having as its nucleus privately owned and operated common carriers.

2. Recognize and fully develop the relative service and cost characteristics of each mode as a component part of a coordinated system.

3. Recognize the public interest in safe and economical transportation at just and reasonable charges therefor.

4. Be so administered in promotional programs as to identify national, regional, and local needs for transportation development and to satisfy these needs in the most economical manner through expenditures which consider the relative economic fitness and the characteristics of the several modes, to the end that the transportation resources of the Nation are efficiently allocated.

5. Be so administered in regulatory actions as to recognize cost relationships in the adjustment of rates and charges, without undue discrimination, preference, or advantages as between users of transportation or unfair competitive practices as between carriers.

6. Foster adjustments in the organization and structure of the transportation system and the component modes thereof, through consolidation and otherwise toward maximizing the efficiency of each.

7. Further coordination and cooperation with the several States and the authorized officials thereof toward the development of simplified and effective economic and safety regulation of transportation.

8. Give primary consideration to the national public interest in all cases of conflict with other more limited interests of persons or localities.

All actions of Federal agencies in matters affecting transportation shall be carried out in accordance with the above declaration of policy.[81]

This proposed declaration of policy will not be unanimously accepted by all concerned, but it does illustrate that a clearer and more definite policy statement than the present one is both feasible and desirable.

Control of Entry

Competition in the transportation industry is regulated by the commissions' control of entry. The broad objective of entry control is to assure adequate, safe, and efficient transport services. This objective can be accomplished by entry controls in a number of ways:

First, essential common carrier services can be required of carriers given franchises. Second, the monopoly or limited competition resulting from closed entry and operating-authority restrictions are said to encourage adequate investment and modernization in essential transport by assuring profitable returns and by lessening market risks. Third, standards of service

[81] *National Transportation Policy, op. cit.,* pp. 38–39.

can be improved by encouragement of able and responsible carriers. Fourth, transportation can be more efficient because duplicating fixed investments can be avoided and excess capacity can be reduced. Fifth, economy in transport can be gained through coordination between agencies of transport. Finally, closed entry facilitates the collection of information about the companies performing the service, information very useful both in peace and in war.[82]

Entry control, however, can be a two-edged sword. Instead of promoting efficiency, it may be used to protect inefficiency. Especially is this likely from operating-authority restrictions—that is, specification of the exact route each carrier may serve. Further, entry control is a detailed task which increases the work load of the commissions. On balance, it might be questioned whether the costs of entry control are not greater than the benefits.

Surface Carriers. With respect to surface carriers, there is a strong economic case for removing entry controls, particularly in the motor and water carrier fields.[83] In part, this conclusion is based upon the market structures of these industries outlined earlier in the chapter. Since entry controls were established (1920 for railroads, 1935 for motor carriers, 1940 for water carriers), the structure of the surface transport industry has changed substantially. It is no longer obvious that control of entry is needed to promote efficiency or to prevent destructive competition. It seems probable that competitive forces, if allowed to develop to their fullest extent, would be strong enough to protect the public interest. And, in part, the argument in favor of removing entry controls is based upon past experience. There is little doubt that the combination of entry control and operating-authority restrictions has lessened competition in the trucking industry by creating route monopolies or oligopolies and by reducing the potential flexibility of trucking service.[84] As most water transport is exempt from regulation, entry control has had little effect on the industry's market structure. Only in the pipeline and railroad industries is there a case for entry restrictions, but it is doubtful that free entry would have any effect on the market structure of railroads.[85]

[82] Ernest W. Williams, Jr., and David W. Bluestone, *Rationale of Federal Transportation Policy* (Washington, D.C.: U.S. Government Printing Office, 1960), p. 11.

[83] See James C. Nelson, "New Concepts in Transportation Regulation," in National Resources Planning Board, *Transportation and National Policy* (Washington, D.C.: U.S. Government Printing Office, 1942), esp. pp. 216–37; and Dudley F. Pegrum, "The Economic Basis for Public Policy for Motor Transport," 28 *Land Economics* 244 (1952).

[84] See Adams and Hendry, *op. cit.;* Nelson, "The Effects of Entry Control . . . ," *op. cit.;* Robert A. Nelson, "The Economic Structure of the Highway Carrier Industry in New England," in *Motor Freight Transportation* (Boston: New England Governors' Committee on Public Transportation, 1956); and Byron Nupp, "Control of Entry as an Economic and Regulatory Problem," 35 *I.C.C. Practitioners' Journal* 591 (1968).

For a discussion on the probable structure of the motor carrier industry without entry control, see W. Miklius and D. B. DeLoach, "A Further Case for Unregulated Truck Competition," 47 *Journal of Farm Economics* 933 (1965); and Nelson, "The Effects of Entry Control . . . ," *op. cit.*, pp. 398-400.

[85] Free exit might result in the discontinuance of unprofitable railroad services, particularly passenger service, at a more rapid rate. However, this is probably desirable anyway.

The removal of surface entry controls must, of necessity, be gradual.[86] The first step might be elimination of operating-authority restrictions that prevent competition in the motor and water carrier fields. Ultimately, the present requirements of obtaining certificates and permits should also be eliminated, but this is a long-range program. Until this second step is taken, however, the commissions should consider promotion of efficiency as the most important factor in granting certificates and permits.

Air Carriers. With respect to air carriers, the situation is more complex. While the CAB has never issued a certificate to a new trunkline carrier, it has created competitive conditions by controlling the number of carriers operating over the major domestic routes. At the present time, however, the trunklines have substantial overcapacity due to the introduction of jet and turboprop aircraft. The wisdom of eliminating entry controls at this time, therefore, is questionable. As an alternative, "it would be well to defer new competitive route authorizations where the new aircraft would be a major influence."[87]

The present subsidy given to local service carriers indicates that entry controls also are necessary in this segment of the industry. The basic goal should be to reduce the subsidy paid to these carriers. Duplicating lines, in some cases, can be eliminated.[88] Mergers have eliminated some of the smaller local service carriers, resulting in the strengthening of the larger ones. The method of subsidy payment could be converted from a "need" basis to a "price list" type of payment. "This would in effect pay the local service lines fixed prices for specific types and volumes of service [and] make it possible to operate more effectively in weeding out inefficient practices and unsatisfactory services."[89]

While the retention of entry controls for air transport seems desirable until the overcapacity problem of the trunklines and the subsidy problem of the local service carriers are solved,[90] operating-authority restrictions pose a separate

---

[86] It has been argued, for example, that unlimited entry into the trucking industry might create "utter congestion" on the highways, thereby resulting in high public or social costs and calling "for at least some limitation of the number of firms allowed to operate trucks over the road." Robert A. Nelson and William R. Greiner, "The Relevance of the Common Carrier under Modern Economic Conditions," in *Transportation Economics, op. cit.,* p. 371 and n. 64.

[87] Williams and Bluestone, *op. cit.,* p. 20.

[88] "Where the duplicating carriers are local service lines on subsidy, the Government is paying the cost of duplication. Where one is a trunkline, it can usually be eliminated in the interests of economy, although one of the prices paid is the loss of through trunkline service to the city. However, connections via the local service line would still be available, and the local service lines have generally generated more traffic at smaller points than have the trunklines." *Ibid.,* p. 21.

[89] *Ibid.*

[90] Caves has suggested (*op. cit.,* pp. 447-48) that the move toward relatively free competition in the industry could be accomplished gradually by sorting "the network of air routes into three parts. Class 1 would be the city-pair routes large enough to sustain more than one carrier with entry unrestricted. Class 2 would be those local-service cities or routes that probably could not be served without subsidy. Class 3 would be a residual of cities or city-pair markets that would be profitable for a single carrier. The critical first step would be to open the class of large city-pair markets to all certified carriers not receiving subsidy .... The second step would be to eliminate restrictions on entry of new carriers to city-pair markets in Class 1 .... A final step, once the situation had again

problem. Here, it may be desirable to relax present regulatory policy. Such restrictions have an important bearing on the ability of carriers to compete.[91] To be sure, operating restrictions give the CAB flexibility in controlling competition over domestic routes, but they also may be used to protect carriers.

Exemptions from Regulation

Part II of the Interstate Commerce Act exempts from economic regulation motor vehicles carrying agricultural and horticultural commodities and fish.[92] This section of the act is known as the "agricultural commodity" exemption. As a result of the exemption, plus growth of private and contract carriers, nearly two-thirds of all motor vehicle traffic is exempt from rate regulation. Congress sought, in exempting agricultural commodities, to aid the individual farmer. It was thought that such an exemption would enable the farmer to enjoy adequate and flexible trucking service to move his products from the farm to the initial market.[93] In the original bill, the exemption was for "unprocessed agricultural products," but it was amended on the Senate floor to read "agricultural commodities (not including manufactured products thereof)." The list of exempt commodities, broadened by subsequent Commission and court interpretation, was frozen by Congress in 1958.[94]

Part III of the Interstate Commerce Act exempts water carriers transporting three or fewer bulk commodities in a single vessel or a tow of barges from economic regulation.[95] Here, Congress granted the exemption to water

---

stabilized reasonably, would be to consolidate the first and third classes of markets, leaving only subsidized local-service routes subject to separate regulation." Also see Howard R. Swaine, "A Proposal for Control of Local Service Subsidies," 31 *Journal of Air Law and Commerce* 181 (1965).

[91] See *Southwest-Northeast Case*, E-9758 (CAB, 1955), opinion of member Lee, p. 14.

[92] Motor vehicle operations of agricultural cooperatives are also exempt from regulation; an exemption that "has been used to cloke illegal for-hire operations. So-called agricultural cooperative organizations have been created to engage in transportation operations when they were not real cooperatives. Likewise, some genuine cooperatives have engaged in for-hire transportation of commodities which are unrelated to farm use." Locklin, *Economics of Transportation, op. cit.*, p. 689. See *Agricultural Cooperatives Exemption* (Hearings before the Subcommittee on Transportation and Aeronautics of the Committee on Interstate and Foreign Commerce, House, 90th Cong., 2d sess.) (Washington, D.C.: U.S. Government Printing Office, 1968).

[93] For the history of the agricultural exemption, see Hearings before the Subcommittee on Land and Water Transportation of the Committee on Interstate and Foreign Commerce, Senate, 81st Cong., 2d sess. (Washington, D.C.: U.S. Government Printing Office, 1950), pp. 814–30; *Interstate Commerce Comm. v. Allen E. Kroblin, Inc.*, 113 F. Supp. 599, 602–30 (1953), *aff'd*, 212 F. 2d 555 (1954), *cert. denied*, 348 U.S. 836 (1954); and *Monark Egg Corp. Contract Carrier Application*, 44 MCC 15 (1944).

[94] See *Determination of Exempted Agricultural Commodities*, 52 MCC 511 (1951); *East Texas Motor Freight Lines, Inc. v. Frozen Food Express*, 128 F. Supp. 374 (1955), 351 U.S. 49 (1956); and *Home Transfer & Storage Co. v. United States*, 141 F. Supp. 599 (1956).

[95] The exemption does not apply to transportation which was subject to the Intercoastal Shipping Act of 1933. Moreover, the act specifies that when two or more vessels are navigated as a unit, they shall be considered as a single vessel. And the ICC has

carriers on the grounds that water traffic was not competitive with traffic hauled by other regulated carriers and that such an exemption was needed to reduce opposition to the enactment of federal regulatory legislation.[96] The ICC has consistently argued that the so-called "bulk commodity" exemption places regulated carriers at "a distinct competitive disadvantage and results in discrimination between shippers and localities."[97]

The railroads derive a significant portion of their traffic and revenues from agricultural and bulk commodities. For the year 1961, it is estimated that 15.5 percent of the total rail tons consisted of agricultural commodities, from which was derived 15.0 percent of the railroads' gross freight revenues, and 68.9 percent of such traffic consisted of bulk commodities, from which was derived 41.4 percent of gross freight revenues. Combining these two categories and removing duplications, they represented 76.7 percent of the railroads' freight traffic and 49.8 percent of their gross freight revenues.[98]

From an efficiency point of view, the various modes of transport should be allowed to operate as competitive enterprises whenever possible. The market place, and not a commission, should allocate traffic among the transport agencies. This goal is impossible, however, unless the advantages of low-cost carriers are reflected in their rates and unless active rate competition is permitted. Government neutrality and market allocation of traffic both require that the present exemptions granted to motor and water carriers either be repealed or extended to the railroads. Large private and commercial motor carriers, as well as individual farmers, now benefit from the agricultural exemption. The original argument that water carriers were not competitive with other modes of transport is no longer valid. All three of these modes do compete for both agricultural and bulk commodities, and the exemptions place regulated carriers at a competitive disadvantage. Unless repealed or extended to all carriers, traffic allocation of these commodities will continue to be made on political

---

held that the bulk commodity exemption does not apply when exempt and nonexempt commodities are transported in the same tow of barges. See *Portland Tug & Barge Co. Extension*, 265 ICC 325, 335 (1948); and *Mississippi Valley Barge Co., Exemption*, 311 ICC 105 (1966), *aff'd sub nom. Gulf Canal Lines, Inc.* v. *United States*, 258 F. Supp. 864 (1966), *aff'd per curiam*, 386 U.S. 348 (1967).

The major bulk commodities are grain and grain products; coal and coke; ore, sand, gravel, and stone; petroleum and petroleum products; chemicals; and sulphur.

[96] For the legislative history of the bulk commodity exemption, see H. R. No. 1217 (Report of the Committee on Interstate and Foreign Commerce, House, 76th Cong., 1st sess.) (Washington, D.C.: U.S. Government Printing Office, 1939).

[97] Interstate Commerce Commission, *Seventy-Second Annual Report* (1958), p. 142. ". . . the Commission believes that repeal of the exemption will ultimately be required as the necessary step toward elimination of any inequalities between carriers of different modes." Interstate Commerce Commission, *Eighty-First Annual Report* (1967), p. 95.

[98] *Transportation Act Amendments—1963* (Hearings before the Surface Transportation Subcommittee of the Committee on Commerce, Senate, 88th Cong., 1st sess.) (Washington, D.C.: U.S. Government Printing Office, 1964), Part 2, pp. 779, 788. The figures are for Class I and Class II line-haul railroads.

considerations. Such a result violates the declared policy of Congress: "to provide for fair and impartial regulation of all modes of transportation."[99]

The Civil Aeronautics Board has authority to exempt from economic regulation any air carrier or class of air carrier when it finds that enforcement of any provisions would be "an undue burden on such air carrier or class of air carriers by reason of the limited extent of or unusual circumstances affecting the operations of such air carrier or class of air carriers." Several classes have been exempted, including air taxi operators, Alaskan air and air taxi carriers, irregular carriers, and air freight forwarders. However, there is one important distinction between air carrier exemptions and those discussed in the preceding paragraphs:

> At least, under this system, an expert body which is familiar with the industry passes upon whether the exemption should be granted at all and the extent to which it should go. This is less dangerous to the regulatory scheme than a flat provision for exemptions which has stood for a quarter of a century in the Interstate Commerce Act without much change except in the direction of broadening the exemptions despite the constant recommendations of the expert body (the ICC) that the exemptions be curtailed.[100]

The Minimum Rate Power

Intramodal competition is largely regulated by entry controls, intermodal competition by the minimum rate power. Both the CAB and the ICC have the authority to set minimum rates for carriers under their jurisdictions. As competition in the transportation industry has grown, so, too, has the controversy over the proper measure of minimum rates.[101] It must be emphasized that of all regulatory activities, rate control has the most direct impact on the distribution of traffic among the various modes of transport. And, as with entry controls, rate control can be used either to protect competition or to protect competitors.

[99] President Kennedy, in a message to Congress on April 5, 1962, proposed, among other things, that the agricultural and bulk commodity exemptions be granted to the railroads and that the antitrust laws be applied to prevent predatory and discriminatory practices. See *The Transportation System of Our Nation* (House Doc. No. 384, 87th Cong., 2d sess.). The proposal was reintroduced in 1963 and supported by President Johnson in his Budget Message of January 21, 1964. To date, Congress has not enacted such legislation. It is opposed by motor and water carriers. Some believe the proposal would result in discrimination against shippers and localities, others have argued the exemption would be of little value to the railroads, and the railroads have been hesitant to accept the application of the antitrust laws to rates for exempted commodities. See *ibid.; Transportation Act—1963* (Hearings before the Committee on Interstate and Foreign Commerce, House, 88th Cong., 1st sess.) (Washington, D.C.: U.S. Government Printing Office, 1963), Parts 1 and 2; *Transportation Act Amendments—1963, op. cit.;* Nathaniel L. Nathanson, "Administrative Proposals for Revision of Our National Transportation Policy—Herein of Intermodal Competition and the Minimum Rate Power," 59 *Northwestern Univ. Law Review* 1 (1964); *Transportation Amendments of 1964* (House Report No. 1144, 88th Cong., 2d sess.) (Washington, D.C.: U.S. Government Printing Office, 1964); and John C. Spychalski, "A Railway Agricultural Exemption: One Step Toward Greater Efficiency in Transport?," 35 *I.C.C. Practitioners' Journal* 44 (1967).

[100] *National Transportation Policy, op. cit.,* p. 138.

[101] See Chapter 11, pp. 393–98.

Minimum rate control is of particular importance with respect to the railroads. As earlier outlined, the cost structure of the railroads differs significantly from the cost structures of other modes of transport. Railroads actively compete for freight traffic with motor and water carriers; they also compete with airlines for passenger traffic and, to a lesser extent, for some types of freight traffic. There is little direct competition between pipelines and other types of carriers.[102] The crucial question is how far below fully distributed costs the commission should allow railroad rates to fall in order that railroads can secure traffic also being moved by other modes.

The commission has received broad and inconsistent directives from Congress. Water carriers are to be protected and the inherent advantages of each mode are to be recognized and preserved (Transportation Act of 1940); the rates of a carrier are not to be held up to a particular level to protect the traffic of any other mode of transport (Transportation Act of 1958). The alleged reason for giving special protection to water carriers is the national defense need. But this inconsistency aside, it seems probable that Congress intended to assure that traffic would be moved by the low-cost carrier.

Yet, what is the low-cost carrier? The distinction between costs and rates is essential. "In the determination of cost floors as a guide to the pricing of particular railroad services, or the services of any other transport mode, incremental costs of each particular service are the only relevant costs."[103] Rates for specific services, however, "should be set at such amounts (subject to regulation of maximum rates and to legal rules against unjust discrimination) as will make the greatest total contribution to net income. Clearly, such maximizing rates would never fall below incremental costs."[104] Such a criterion does not lead to predatory pricing. "When a seller is worse off by selling a product or service than he would be if he did not sell it, and knowingly does this to get business from a competitor, then he is engaged in predatory pricing. It is this sort of behavior in transport that the regulation of interagency competition should seek to prevent, and no other."[105]

The incremental or marginal cost criterion of minimum rates assumes that intermodal competition is to be developed to its fullest extent. Competition on such a basis will make it difficult or impossible for some carriers to compete with the low-cost carrier for some types of traffic over some routes. The only alternative is to use the minimum rate power so as to protect competitors, thereby making it possible for each type of carrier to compete over a given

[102] There is some competition between oil pipelines and water carriers, and between pipelines and railroads for liquid products. Also, there is potential competition between coal slurry pipelines and railroads.

[103] William J. Baumol and Associates, "The Role of Cost in the Minimum Pricing of Railroad Services," 35 *Journal of Business of the University of Chicago* 357, 365 (1962).

[104] *Ibid.* It should be noted again that incremental (marginal) costs are not the same as the ICC's "out-of-pocket" costs. See Chapter 11, p. 393.

[105] Dudley F. Pegrum, *Transportation: Economics and Public Policy* (rev. ed.; Homewood, Ill.: Richard D. Irwin, Inc., 1968), p. 432.

route. The price of such a policy is high—increased transportation costs and rates, as well as inefficiency throughout the entire transportation system.[106]

The Commodities Clause

Section 1(8) of the Interstate Commerce Act provides:

> It shall be unlawful for any railroad to transport in interstate or foreign commerce any article or commodity (other than timber and the manufactured products thereof) manufactured, mined or produced by it or under its authority, or which it may own in whole or in part or in which it may have any interest, direct or indirect, except such articles or commodities as may be necessary and intended for its use in the conduct of its business as a common carrier.

The effect of this provision is to limit the railroads in diversifying their operations outside the transportation field. No other mode of transport is subject to the "commodities clause."[107]

In 1906, when the commodities clause was inserted in the Hepburn Act, the railroads held a virtual monopoly of the nation's transportation, and Congress sought to prevent the roads from discriminating against nonrail producers of products they also produced. Congress considered extending the clause in 1939 to all carriers except airlines, but later omitted the provision from the Transportation Act of 1940 because "it was considered far too drastic."[108]

Instead of extending the commodities clause to other carriers, a strong case can be made for its outright repeal. The railroads no longer dominate the transportation system. With traffic and earnings relatively low, diversification into noncarrier fields would seem to be in the public interest. At a minimum, the advantages of railroad diversification are the same as those favoring diversification in unregulated industries; the disadvantages are also the same. If, however, it is deemed desirable to maintain the clause for the railroads, "fair and impartial regulation" would suggest that it should be applied to other regulated carriers.

The railroads have apparently found a device to diversify into nontransportation fields in spite of the commodities clause—the holding company. Several

---

[106] As discussed in the appendix to Chapter 11, the ICC has not accepted the incremental or marginal cost criterion in regulating intermodal competition. The commission's general policy was well summarized in a 1963 decision: "Fully distributed cost is utilized here as the criteria determinative of the low-cost carrier because the primary competition which respondents seek to meet is regulated barge or motor-barge and not private or other carriage not subject to Commission regulation. This is the general rule. As an exception to that rule, an out-of-pocket basis has been approved, for example, where the dominant competitive force was unregulated trucking." *Grain from Idaho, Oregon and Washington to Ports in Oregon and Washington,* 319 ICC 534, 560 (1963). See David Boies, Jr., "Experiment in Mercantilism: Minimum Rate Regulation by the Interstate Commerce Commission," 68 *Columbia Law Review* 599 (1968).

[107] In fact, the ICC has authority to exempt from economic regulation water carriers when engaged solely in transporting goods which they own.

[108] S. R. No. 433 (Report of the Committee on Interstate and Foreign Commerce, Senate, 76th Cong., 1st sess.) (Washington, D.C.: U.S. Government Printing Office, 1939), p. 25.

holding companies have been organized since 1960, including Bangor and Aroostook Corp. by the Bangor and Aroostook Railroad;[109] Kansas City Southern Industries, Inc., by the Kansas City Southern Railway; Illinois Central Industries, Inc., by the Illinois Central Railroad; Katy Industries, Inc., by the Missouri-Kansas-Texas Railway; and Northwest Industries, Inc., by the Chicago & North Western Railway. The ICC has ruled that it lacks jurisdiction over such holding companies since they are not carriers.[110] Hence, the new concerns are freed from commission control over nontransportation diversification.

The new holding companies are of too recent origin to permit any conclusions on their effectiveness. For some railroad companies, particularly the larger ones, the organization of holding companies may be an effective means of skirting the commodities clause. But there are risks as well as advantages, and many smaller railroads will find this method of diversifying closed. The question remains: would it not be more desirable to repeal the commodities clause in order to provide "fair and impartial regulation" and to allow all railroads, if they see fit, to share in the advantages of diversification? It would seem that antitrust policy could be relied on to protect the public interest against undesirable consequences from such diversification.

Governmental Subsidies

The subsidy question is a long-standing one that is still partly unresolved. There is little doubt that air and water transportation are subsidized—that is, part of their costs are borne by taxpayers and not by users. Recent studies suggest that the motor carrier industry as a whole may be paying its share of highway costs, but that heavier vehicles are paying less than their share relative to lighter vehicles. No subsidies are received by either pipeline or railroad companies.[111]

Efficiency and neutrality are impossible unless each mode of transport pays its full cost.

If user charges were imposed, the costs of the carriers which use public facilities would include the cost of such facilities, the effect of "free" facilities would be removed from their rates, the allocation of traffic among the various modes of transport would be more in accord with their economic

---

[109] The Bangor and Aroostook Corp. quickly purchased three firms, and by 1962 one-half of the company's net income came from nonrailroad sources. However, many problems, such as lack of capital, were encountered. (*Business Week*, December 22, 1962, p. 60.) In 1964, the assets of the company were transferred to Punta Alegre Commodities Corp. (now Bangor Punta Operations, Inc.), a wholly owned subsidiary of Punta Alegre Sugar Corp. (now Bangor Punta Corp.).

[110] *The Wall Street Journal*, April 23, 1962, p. 22. United Air Lines, late in 1968, announced plans to form a holding company in a step toward diversifying into nontransportation operations. *Ibid.*, December 19, 1968, p. 2.

[111] Certain railroads are receiving subsidies for commutation services. Certain railroads also are participating in a federal program in the field of high-speed intercity ground transportation, research, development, and demonstration.

characteristics, and the tendency toward overinvestment by carriers which use publicly-provided facilities would be reduced.[112]

Further, the imposition of user charges would result in more careful scrutiny by state and federal legislatures of proposed public transport facilities. Too often have such investment projects been considered "pork barrel" legislation (particularly waterway investment), with little consideration to the effects of public investment on the market allocation of resources.

User charges should cover both explicit and implicit costs. Explicit costs refer to the investment per se, implicit costs to property taxes and interest on the investment. Publicly owned facilities are tax exempt, but privately owned facilities are not. Similarly, there is an imputed cost of capital on public investment equity, just as there is a market determined cost of capital on private investment equity. Unless both explicit and implicit costs are covered by user charges, some modes of transport will be subsidized.

The lack of adequate user charges at the present time indicates that theory and practice are far apart. Two major obstacles have prevented the imposition of full user charges for publicly owned transport facilities. In the first place, there is little agreement on how to calculate the total costs that should be borne by air, motor, and water carriers. The motor carrier problem is typical. The allocation of highway costs involves three steps: (1) calculating the total explicit and implicit costs incurred, (2) allocating these costs between users and nonusers,[113] and (3) allocating the users' share of total costs among the various types of motor vehicles using the roads. As with separations procedures, there is no one correct way of making these calculations.[114]

In the second place, the user charge controversy has become an important political issue. The airlines and motor carriers have long expressed their desire to bear their share of public investment costs; the water carriers have not. Rather, water carriers take the position that the waterways have always been free, that they benefit the entire economy, and that to impose user charges would eliminate some domestic water transportation and would result in higher prices to consumers.[115] Congress has so far accepted these arguments. As a result, the

[112] Williams and Bluestone, *op. cit.*, p. 43.

[113] Nonusers benefit from investment in highways in several important ways. "Highways afford access to land in both urban and rural areas without which the land would be practically useless and worthless. They also perform a 'community service function' that makes community life and activity possible. In addition, they provide one of the principal avenues of intercommunity and long-distance transportation for commercial, recreational, and national defense purposes." Pegrum, *Transportation: Economics and Public Policy, op. cit.*, pp. 490–91.

[114] See *Final Report of the Highway Cost Allocation Study* (House Doc. No. 54, 87th Cong., 1st sess.) (Washington, D.C.: U.S. Government Printing Office, 1961); *Supplementary Report of the Highway Cost Allocation Study* (House Doc. No. 124, 89th Cong., 1st sess.) (Washington, D.C.: U.S. Government Printing Office, 1965); and Robert W. Harbeson, "Some Unsettled Issues in Highway-Cost Allocation," in Paul L. Kleinsorge (ed.), *Public Finance and Welfare* (Eugene: University of Oregon Books, 1966), pp. 187–213.

[115] See William J. Hull and Robert W. Hull, *The Origin and Development of the Waterways Policy of the United States* (Washington, D.C.: National Waterways Confer-

billions of dollars in subsidies that have been spent on transportation facilities and services have not been spent wisely from the viewpoint of the transportation system as a whole.[116]

User charges are essential if the nation is to develop a national transportation policy. Their imposition should be gradual and should be designed primarily to recover future investment in public transport facilities. Past investment is fixed: the resources devoted to such facilities have already been committed and cannot be withdrawn. One likely result of full user charges would be a reduction in air, motor, and water transport, and an increase in railroad transport. But this fact cannot be used as an argument against user charges for, by not levying them, public policy supports overinvestment in the subsidized modes of transport and a misallocation of resources. There is only one alternative and it does not seem attractive: a federal law exempting pipeline and railroad right-of-way property from property taxation and providing for government maintenance of this property. The imposition of universal user charges would seem to be the best method of developing a neutral governmental policy toward the various modes of transport.[117]

Mergers and Consolidations

The railroad industry and, to a lesser extent, the motor carrier industry are undergoing significant changes in structure due to mergers and consolidations. However, since the most pressing issues concern the railroads, emphasis in this section is placed on this industry.[118]

Railroad Mergers. The basic policy issue of railroad mergers is whether intramodal or intermodal competition is to be the goal. The first philosophy has prevailed in the past; the second has gained increased support, especially from

---

ence, Inc., 1967); The National Waterways Conference, Inc., *To Rob Our Youth* and *2¢ and Up!* (Washington, D.C., 1962); Upper Mississippi Waterway Association, *The Waterway Use Tax: A Threat to the Upper Midwest* (Minneapolis, 1967); and *National Transportation Policy, op. cit.*, pp. 197–210.

[116] Charles L. Dearing and Wilfred Owen, *National Transportation Policy* (Washington, D.C.: Brookings Institution, 1949), pp. 353–71.

[117] The Johnson Administration proposed: (1) motor carriers—an increase in diesel fuel taxes from the present 4 cents per gallon to 7 cents and a rise in the annual use tax for trucks weighing more than 26,000 pounds from $3 per pound to $5; (2) water carriers—a 2 cents per gallon fuel tax (increasing to 10 cents per gallon over the next five years) on vessels using the inland waterways system; and (3) airlines—continuation of the 5 percent excise tax on air passenger fares, a new 4 cents per gallon tax on jet fuel used in general aviation, an increase in the tax on general aviation fuel from 2 cents per gallon to 4 cents, a new 2 percent tax on air freight waybills, and repeal of the 2 cents per gallon tax on gasoline used in commercial aviation. *Business Week*, February 6, 1965, p. 72; and *The Budget of the United States, Fiscal Year 1968* (Washington, D.C.: U.S. Government Printing Office, 1967), p. 69. These proposals are similar to those of the Kennedy Administration. See *The Transportation System of Our Nation, op. cit.* In 1968, the Department of Transportation recommended to Congress additional user fees on airline passenger fares, aviation fuel, and air freight waybills to finance a proposed airport expansion and airways safety program. *The Wall Street Journal*, May 22, 1968, p. 34.

[118] See *Transportation Mergers and Acquisitions* (Evanston: Transportation Center at Northwestern University, 1962).

the ICC. As a result of past policy, duplicate facilities, vested labor interests, and overcapacity in the railroad industry have been fostered.

Prior to 1904, railroads were free to consolidate as they saw fit.[119] Between 1884 and 1888 alone, there were some 425 consolidations. Among the most important systems developed were the New York Central, the Pennsylvania Railroad, the Union Pacific Railroad, and the Great Northern-Northern Pacific combine. Then, from 1904 to 1920, antitrust policy was used to prevent railroad mergers: "Competition between railways as well as between other industries is the established policy of the nation."[120] The Northern Securities Company was dissolved, several railroad companies were required to dispose of stock held in other railroad companies, and threatened antitrust prosecution resulted in dissolution of the New Haven monopoly in New England. In several of these cases, the wisdom of trying to maintain intramodal competition was questioned, but the Supreme Court considered this a question for Congress to decide.[121]

Beginning with the Transportation Act of 1920 and ending with the Transportation Act of 1940, Congress directed the ICC to formulate a plan for consolidating the railroads into a limited number of systems.[122] In 1929, the commission published a plan for creating twenty-one independent railroad systems.[123] In 1933, the National Transportation Committee issued a report recommending compulsory consolidation, but Congress rejected the recommendation later in the same year.[124] President Roosevelt appointed two committees to study the railroad problem: both recognized that consolidation would be beneficial, but there was no consensus as to either a plan or a time schedule.[125]

The Transportation Act of 1940 relieved the commission of the obligation to formulate a national plan of consolidation. Instead, Congress stated that the

[119] On the legislative history of railroad consolidations, see J. Stanley Payne, "History of the 'Consolidation' Provisions of the Interstate Commerce Act," 19 *I.C.C. Practitioners' Journal* 453 (1952). On the history of railroad mergers, see *National Transportation Policy, op. cit.*, pp. 229-42.

[120] *Consolidations and Combinations of Carriers,* 12 ICC 277, 305 (1907).

[121] See *United States v. Northern Securities Co.,* 193 U.S. 197, 337-38 (1904); *United States v. Union Pacific R.R.,* 226 U.S. 61 (1912), 226 U.S. 470 (1913); and *United States v. Southern Pacific Co.,* 259 U.S. 214 (1922).

[122] See Wm. N. Leonard, *Railroad Consolidation under the Transportation Act of 1920* (New York: Columbia University Press, 1946); and Charles L. Dearing and Wilfred Owen, *National Transportation Policy* (Washington, D.C.: Brookings Institution, 1949), chap. xv.

[123] *In the Matter of Consolidation of the Railway Properties,* 159 ICC 522 (1929). In 1932, a revised version of the plan was announced. *Consolidation of Railroads,* 185 ICC 403 (1932). These and other plans are outlined in Association of American Railroads, "Consolidations and Mergers in the Transportation Industries" (Washington, D.C., 1960) (mimeographed).

[124] *Report of National Transportation Committee,* February 13, 1933; the recommendation was rejected in the Emergency Railroad Transportation Act of 1933. For a study prepared for the Committee, see H. G. Moulton, *The American Transportation Problem* (Washington, D.C.: Brookings Institution, 1933).

[125] H. R. Doc. No. 583, 75th Cong., 3d sess., pp. 36-39 (1938); "Consolidations and Mergers in the Transportation Industry," *op. cit.*, p. 11, n. 24.

initiative for mergers rested with the railroads and that the commission's function was to pass on the merits of applications under the standards provided in Section 5(2). Four general standards were specified:

(1) the effect of the proposed transaction upon adequate transportation service to the public; (2) the effect upon the public interest of the inclusion, or failure to include, other railroads in the territory involved in the proposed transaction; (3) the total fixed charges resulting from the proposed transactions; and (4) the interest of the carrier employees affected.

The commission has the power to impose, as a condition to approval, the inclusion of another railroad which has requested such inclusion and which is situated in the territory involved. No consolidation may be approved if the total fixed charges are increased, unless a finding is made that such an increase is not contrary to the public interest. Finally, during a period of four years from the date of an order allowing a merger, no employee of any involved railroad shall be placed "in a worse position with respect to . . . employment," unless the carriers and the employees reach another agreement.[126]

Between 1955 (the start of the modern railroad merger movement) and March, 1968, fifty-two unification proposals were filed with the ICC. Of these proposals, thirty-three have been approved, five have been denied, six were either withdrawn or dismissed, and eight are pending.[127] The major unifications approved include three in the East and one in the West: control by the Chesapeake and Ohio of the Baltimore and Ohio; merger of the Norfolk and Western with the Chicago, New York and St. Louis (the Nickel Plate); merger of the Pennsylvania and New York Central railroads; and merger of the Great Northern, Northern Pacific, and Chicago, Burlington and Quincy.[128] Among the applications pending are the proposed merger of the Norfolk and Western and the Chesapeake and Ohio; the proposed control by the Missouri Pacific and

---

[126] The commission has long interpreted this provision as meaning that economy dismissals could be made so long as compensation is provided for displaced workers. The Supreme Court has accepted this position. See *Brotherhood of Maintenance and Way Employees* v. *United States*, 366 U.S. 169 (1961).

[127] Association of American Railroads, "Railroad Merger Scoreboard" (Washington, D.C., 1968) (mimeographed).
     Railroad consolidation proceedings are lengthy legal and political battles. There are dozens of interveners in a typical case, including rail, motor, and water carrier interveners, as well as counties, municipalities, shippers and receivers, civic and labor organizations, and individual states and state regulatory agencies. The Department of Justice also has intervened in many of these proceedings. Thus, the merger of the Pennsylvania and New York Central railroads took nearly six years from the date of application. (The proposal was filed on March 9, 1962; the Supreme Court's approval was handed down on January 15, 1968.) Excluding the court appeals, there were 129 hearing days before two ICC trial examiners, involving 19,750 pages of transcript, 291 prepared statements, 352 exhibits, 463 witnesses, and appearances by 338 attorneys.

[128] *Chesapeake & Ohio Ry. Co.—Control—Baltimore & Ohio R. Co.*, 317 ICC 261 (1962); *Norfolk & Western Ry. Co. & New York, Chicago & St. Louis R. Co. Merger*, 324 ICC 1 (1964); *Pennsylvania R. Co.—Merger—New York Central R. Co.*, 327 ICC 475 (1966); *Great Northern Pacific & Burlington Lines—Merger—Great Northern Ry. Co.*, 331

Mississippi River Corp. of the Atchison, Topeka, and Santa Fe; and the competing proposals filed by the Union Pacific Railroad and the Chicago and North Western Railway to merge with the Chicago, Rock Island and Pacific.[129]

The ICC's decisions clearly indicate that intramodal competition is no longer of primary concern, but that the long-run goal is the strengthening of intermodal competition by developing balanced regional railroad systems. In the Norfolk & Western–Virginian decision, the commission said:

> The monopoly status enjoyed by the railroads in the nineteenth and early twentieth centuries has now disappeared completely with the emergence of strong and growing competitors. . . . While there may be some slight lessening of competition as a result of the proposed merger, we do not regard that fact as of controlling importance. The evidence establishes that, after the merger, strong competition will still be afforded by other forms of transportation. We conclude that the public interest would not be adversely affected by any lessening of competition which may result from the proposed merger.[130]

A similar conclusion was reached in the Seaboard Air Line–Atlantic Coast Line decision:

> While we recognize in general the desirability of preserving intramodal rail competition, it is no longer the all-important factor that it once was in the days when the railroads had a virtual monopoly on all intercity freight traffic. With the development of intense competition in recent years from other modes of transport, the preservation of intramodal rail competition has lost much of its significance in the furtherance of the overall national transportation policy.[131]

While the commission's emphasis on intermodal, as opposed to intramodal, competition has been the subject of considerable debate,[132] regional systems

---

ICC 228 (1967). (The commission's last decision reversed its 1966 denial of the merger. See 328 ICC 460.) On the Pennsylvania-New York Central merger, see Gilbert Burck, "The World's Biggest Merger," *Fortune*, Part I (June, 1965), pp. 176–79, 200–208; Part II (July, 1965), pp. 128–31, 202–15.

129 See Dan Cordtz, "The Fight for the Rock Island," *Fortune*, June, 1966, pp. 140–43, 200–209.

130 *Norfolk & Western Ry. Co.–Merger–Virginian Ry. Co.*, 307 ICC 401, 440 (1959).

131 *Seaboard Air Line R. Co.–Merger–Atlantic Coast Line R. Co.*, 320 ICC 122 (1963). The decision was set aside by a district court on the ground that the commission had not adequately considered the tests of the Clayton Act. But the Supreme Court upheld the commission, arguing that the ICC was not bound by the Clayton Act tests if it concluded that the merger would assist in effectuating the national transportation policy. *Florida East Coast Ry. Co.* v. *United States*, 242 F. Supp. 14 (1965), *rev'd per curiam sub nom. Seaboard Air Line R. Co.* v. *United States*, 382 U.S. 155 (1965). Upon reconsideration, the district court approved the merger; a decision subsequently affirmed by the Supreme Court. *Florida East Coast Ry. Co.* v. *United States*, 259 F. Supp. 993 (1966), *aff'd per curiam*, 386 U.S. 544 (1967).

132 See Michael Conant, "Railroad Consolidations and the Antitrust Laws," 14 *Stanford Law Review* 489 (1962) and *Railroad Mergers and Abandonments* (Berkeley and Los Angeles: University of California Press, 1964); Carl H. Fulda, "Antitrust Aspects of

would seem consistent with economies of scale.[133] Cost reductions can be expected from savings in administrative expenses (simplified car accounting, advertising), operating expenses (elimination of duplicate facilities and services), and financial costs (real estate and tax burdens). In turn, service should improve if these reductions in costs materialize.[134] Any long-range plan, however, must take the smaller and usually weaker lines into consideration, if balanced systems are to be developed.[135] For this reason, it seems clear that the ICC should have a tentative, but flexible, plan outlining the future structure of the industry as a guide in approving merger plans as they are submitted.[136] But past experience suggests that voluntary merger proposals offer the best means of achieving the potential economic benefits from railroad consolidations.

Other Modes. The dilemma between competition and monopoly does not characterize the motor and water carrier fields. Consequently, there seems to be

---

Recent Transportation Mergers," 48 *Minnesota Law Review* 723 (1964); Phil C. Beverly, "Railroad Mergers: The Forces of Intermodal Competition," 50 *American Bar Association Journal* 641 (1964); Robert A. Nelson, "Railroad Mergers and Public Policy," 41 *Land Economics* 183 (1965); and "Advantages and Disadvantages of Carrier Unifications" (panel discussion), 34 *I.C.C. Practitioners' Journal* 956 (1967). The position of the Department of Justice is outlined by Edwin M. Zimmerman, "Carrier Mergers and the Relevance of Antitrust," 34 *ibid.* 958 (1967).

[133] Kent T. Healy, *The Effects of Scale in the Railroad Industry* (New Haven: Committee on Transportation, Yale University, 1961). Also see J. W. Barriger, "Why Consolidation?" (Paper delivered at the Transportation Management Institute, Stanford University, 1959), for a proposal of two nationwide systems.

[134] See J. W. Barriger, "The Effect of Mergers on Competition," 7 *Transportation Journal* 5 (1968).

[135] The ICC has given considerable attention to the effects of railroad mergers on smaller lines. As a condition of approval, for example, the Pennsylvania-New York Central was ordered to indemnify three other roads (Erie-Lackawanna, Delaware & Hudson, and Boston & Maine) against losses they may incur from the merger and to take over the freight and passenger services of the New Haven.

[136] No such plan has yet been formulated. The Bureau of Transport Economics of the Interstate Commerce Commission issued a staff report on *Railroad Consolidations and the Public Interest—A Preliminary Examination* (Statement No. 6201) in 1962. While suggesting a number of possible additions to or changes in present methods, the bureau concluded that the usefulness of additional or modified criteria required further research. Congress, also in 1962, considered legislation aimed at slowing down ICC approval of larger mergers until a long-range plan could be formulated. See *Rail Merger Legislation* (Hearings before the Subcommittee on Antitrust and Monopoly of the Committee on the Judiciary, Senate, 87th Cong., 2d sess.) (Washington, D.C.: U.S. Government Printing Office, 1962), Parts 1 and 2. Also see *The Rail Merger Problem* (Report of the Subcommittee on Antitrust and Monopoly, Senate, 88th Cong., 1st sess.) (Washington, D.C.: U.S. Government Printing Office, 1963). And early in 1963, an interagency committee (representatives from the Departments of Commerce, Justice, and Labor, and from the Council of Economic Advisers) developed general criteria (i.e., "suggested guidelines") applicable to mergers in the airline and railroad industries, but the regulatory agencies were not represented when the criteria were formulated. See Commerce Clearing House, 5 *Trade Regulation Reporter*, Par. 50,177, pp. 55,188–55,189. It may be, as Pegrum has suggested (*Transportation: Economics and Public Policy, op. cit.*, p. 458), that the Department of Transportation "will possibly provide executive leadership for future mergers." See U.S. Department of Transportation, *Western Railroad Mergers* (A Staff Study by the Office of the Assistant Secretary for Policy Development and the Federal Railroad Administration) (Washington, D.C., 1969).

no reason for retaining commission control over mergers in these areas. Rather, mergers can be handled under the antitrust laws. Some hold that ruinous competition would be the result of such a policy,[137] but the idea of "restricting competition in order to preserve it" seems strange indeed.[138] Even pipeline mergers, although they involve natural monopolies, have been subjected to the antitrust laws.[139]

In the air transport field, a distinction must be made between the trunklines and the local service lines. If entry control and route authorizations are to be used so as to develop a competitive trunkline structure, then the antitrust laws can be used to deal with airline mergers. If monopoly is to be the goal, then antitrust policy would seem inappropriate. This choice must be made before a policy can be established with respect to mergers among the trunklines. For the local service lines, it appears that monopoly conditions must continue to prevail until the subsidy problem is resolved.

Interagency Ownership

In the past few years, the nation's railroads have argued that it would be desirable to form transportation companies in the United States, similar to those found in other countries.[140] The railroads argue that "one-package" transportation benefits the shipper by allowing a transportation company to offer complete transport service under one management. In many cases, a shipper may use a combination of different modes to transport a single shipment from the manufacturer to the consumer. If transportation companies were allowed, therefore, the shipper could deal with one company, and that company would be able to use whatever mode or combination of modes that was the best to meet the shipper's requirements. In turn, the economy would benefit from lower transportation costs and a more efficient allocation of resources.

Interagency ownership is not prohibited by statute;[141] rather, it is prohibited by commission interpretation of various statutes.[142] Further, the statutory restrictions only apply to consolidations, mergers, and acquisitions of control. Railroads are prohibited from purchasing a motor carrier firm unless the commission "finds that the transaction proposed will be consistent with the public interest and will enable such carrier to use service by motor vehicle to public advantage in its operations and will not unduly restrain competition."

137 Minority report, *Mergers and Concentration in the Trucking Industry* (Report for the Select Committee on Small Business, Senate, 85th Cong., 1st sess.) (Washington, D.C.: U.S. Government Printing Office, 1958). Also see Adams and Hendry, *op. cit.*

138 Pegrum, *Transportation: Economics and Public Policy, op. cit.*, p. 459, n. 29.

139 See *United States* v. *El Paso Natural Gas Co.*, 376 U.S. 651 (1964).

140 See "Magna Carta for Transportation," *op. cit.*, pp. 40-44.

141 One exception: The ICC is prohibited by statute from permitting railroad control of competing water lines which operate through the Panama Canal. See *Illinois Central R. Co.—Control—John I. Hay Co.*, 317 ICC 39 (1962).

142 See Byron Nupp, "Regulatory Standards in Common Ownership in Transportation," 34 *I.C.C. Practitioners' Journal* 21 (1966).

Railroads may not acquire an interest in water carriers unless the commission finds that such an interest "will not prevent such common carrier by water or vessel from being operated in the interest of the public and with advantage to the convenience and commerce of the people" and that "it will not exclude, prevent, or reduce competition on the route by water under consideration." All surface carriers are prevented from engaging in air transportation unless the CAB finds that the proposed transaction "will promote the public interest by enabling such carrier other than an air carrier to use aircraft to public advantage in its operation and will not restrain competition." There are no statutory restrictions on the ownership of pipelines by other modes of transport. While these statutory provisions apply only to acquisitions, both the CAB and the ICC also have applied them to new certificate cases.[143]

The statutory provisions have been strictly interpreted by the two regulatory commissions. For example, unless covered by grandfather clauses, railroads may acquire motor carriers only under the following conditions:

1. The service to be performed shall be limited to service which is auxiliary to, or supplemental of, rail service.

2. No motor service shall be rendered to or from any point not a station on a rail line of the railroad.

3. No shipments shall be transported by applicant as a common carrier by motor vehicle between any of the following points, or through or to or from more than one of said points: Kansas City, Hume, and Joplin, Mo., Pittsburg, Kans., Shreveport and Lake Charles, La., Beaumont, Tex., Texarkana, Ark.-Tex., and Fort Smith, Ark.

4. All contractual arrangements between the applicant motor carrier and the parent railroad shall be reported to the Commission and shall be subject to revision.

5. The motor carrier service shall be subject to such further specific conditions as the Commission in the future may find it necessary to impose, in order to insure that it will remain auxiliary and supplemental to the rail service.[144]

As a result, motor carrier operations by railroads are approved only when they are "auxiliary and supplemental to" railroad service. The commission has applied similar criteria to railroad-water carrier[145] and motor carrier-water carrier[146] operations, as has the board with respect to surface carrier-airline operations.[147]

---

[143] *Air Freight Forwarder Case*, 9 CAB 473, 509-19 (1948), *aff'd sub nom. National Air Freight Forwarding Corp.* v. *CAB*, 197 F. 2d 384 (D.C. Cir., 1952); *American Trucking Ass'ns, Inc.* v. *United States*, 355 U.S. 141 (1957).

[144] *Kansas City Co. Transp. Co. Common Carrier Application*, 10 MCC 221, 240-41 (1938), 28 MCC 5, 25 (1941). Also see *New York Central Transport Co.— Modification*, 89 MCC 389 (1962).

[145] *Missouri Pacific R.R. Co. and Texas & Pacific Ry. Co., Service by Water*, 245 ICC 143 (1941).

[146] *TTC Corp.—Purchase, Terminal Transport Co., Inc.*, 97 MCC 380 (1965).

[147] *American Export Airlines, Inc.*, 3 CAB 619 (1942), 4 CAB 104 (1943).

The legislative provisions were enacted because of Congressional concern over the possibility of railroad domination of the newer modes of transport. The railroads contend that even if such a possibility existed in the past, it no longer exists today. "The restrictions now serve only to create private preserves for certain favored groups in the economy with the overall effect of preventing effective coordination of the various forms of transport in such a manner as to produce the most efficient and economical transportation for the public." [148]

The economic justification for interagency ownership must rest on the existence of economies of scale. Put another way, in contrast with our present policy of developing each mode independently, what are the benefits of a more permissive regulatory attitude toward interagency ownership? Recent studies indicate that the economic benefits that might be realized from interagency ownership are few. Concludes Pegrum:

> The different agencies would undoubtedly be organized as separate corporations which would afford little opportunity for "spreading the overhead," in addition to the fact that the competitive nature of motor, water, and air transport would make it impossible for them to absorb any significant amount of the railroad burden. Moreover, common ownership by the railroads of competing modes would not assist the railroads as such unless it resulted in reducing the competition among the different agencies of the same company. If this were the outcome, it would be the result of the development of transport monopolies, a possibility that is denied by the proponents, and one that clearly would not be in the public interest.[149]

Evidence suggests, therefore, that interagency ownership may not be economically justified. It might be desirable, however, for the ICC to adopt a more flexible approach to interagency ownership, especially when it can be shown that such ownership will result in increased efficiency. At the same time, it must be emphasized that each mode can be independently developed only if it is permitted an equal competitive opportunity. Such an opportunity can only result from neutral governmental policies toward competing carriers.

Through Routes and Joint Rates: Coordinated Service

Another important policy problem concerns the extent to which the various modes of transport should be encouraged or forced to establish through routes and joint rates.[150] The problem is further compounded by the more

---

148 Prince, *op. cit.*, p. 221.
149 Pegrum, *Transportation: Economics and Public Policy, op. cit.*, p. 463. A similar conclusion was reached by the Transportation Study Group (*National Transportation Policy, op. cit.*, p. 144): "... to permit the railroads (some of which have access to almost vast capital resources) to own or acquire other modes of transportation might very possibly convert our present transportation system into a system of huge and few transportation companies .... [I]t would seem that the far-reaching upheaval in the present competitive situation that might take place if we were to adopt such legislation today would assume the proportions of unscrambling an egg."
150 See Chapter 12, pp. 408–10.

recent widespread development of piggyback, fishyback, birdieback, and containerization services. And the legislative statutes are broad: the ICC may require establishment of through routes and joint rates between rail and water carriers,[151] and between common carriers of passengers, but neither it nor the CAB has authority to require rail-motor, motor-water, or air-surface carrier through routes and joint rates. In these situations, the commissions may, however, authorize such routes and rates.

The coordination of transport services is highly desirable, but if competition is to be allowed to develop in the transportation industry, it is undesirable to make through routes and joint rates mandatory. Joint boards could be authorized to establish such routes and rates when it can be shown that one carrier, or group of carriers, has refused to participate in such arrangements to the detriment of the public interest.[152] Such a policy would mean that the industry itself would be left the job of developing through routes and joint rates. Antitrust policy could deal with unreasonable refusals to coordinate service among the various modes, as well as with the opposite problem of unreasonable exclusive dealings between two different types of carriers.[153]

The difficulties—and dangers—of trying to compel such arrangements are well illustrated by piggyback service, often referred to as "trailer-on-flatcar" (TOFC) service.[154] This term applies to hauling of loaded or empty truck trailers or semitrailers on railroad flatcars.[155] The concept is not new, but it was not until 1954 that piggyback service was tried on a significant scale. In that year, the ICC ruled that the railroads could carry truck trailers without obtaining motor carrier certificates; a decision bitterly opposed by trucking firms.[156] As of 1967, fifty-six Class I railroads were providing piggyback service under five basic plans:

[151] *Rail & Barge Joint Rates,* 270 ICC 591 (1948), *aff'd sub nom. Alabama Great Southern R. Co. v. United States,* 340 U.S. 216 (1957).

[152] Department of Commerce, *Federal Transportation Policy and Program* (Washington, D.C.: U.S. Government Printing Office, 1960), p. 8.

[153] In the late 1930's, when railroads that were members of the Association of American Railroads refused to establish through routes and joint rates with motor carriers, the Department of Justice brought a suit charging that the agreement violated the Sherman Antitrust Act. The suit was settled in 1941 by a consent decree in which the railroads agreed to dissolve the practice. See 68 *Traffic World* 229 (1941). Other cases have been brought: *Interstate Commerce Comm.* v. *Mechling,* 330 U.S. 567 (1947); *Dixie Carriers* v. *United States,* 351 U.S. 56 (1956); and *Arrow Transportation Co.* v. *United States,* 176 F. Supp. 411 (1959), *aff'd per curiam* 361 U.S. 353 (1960).

[154] See Interstate Commerce Commission, Bureau of Economics, *Piggyback Traffic Characteristics,* Statement No. 66-1 (Washington, D.C., 1966); and American Trucking Associations, Inc., Department of Research and Transport Economics, *Who's "In" in Piggyback?* (Washington, D.C., 1967).

[155] The terms fishyback and birdieback refer to the movement of trailers or containers by water and air carriers, respectively. Containerization refers to the practice of having the shipper pack and seal a container himself, then this package, in turn, moves unopened from one mode of transport to another until it reaches the ultimate consignee. On containerization, see Harold B. Meyers, "The Maritime Industry's Expensive New Box," *Fortune,* November, 1967, pp. 150–54, 190–97; and "Rough Road for Capsule Cargo," *The Wall Street Journal,* May 28, 1968, p. 34.

[156] *Movement of Highway Trailers by Rail,* 293 ICC 93, 101 (1954).

Plan I.   The railroad transports motor carriers' trailers. The shipment moves at motor carrier rates. The railroad receives either a division of the rates or a flat charge per trailer. The motor carrier deals with the shipper or his agent, bills the freight, and picks up and delivers the shipment.

Plan II.   The railroad transports its own or leased (from shipper or freight forwarder) trailers. The shipment moves at railroad rates. The railroad picks up and delivers the shipment.

Plan II½.   A variation of Plan II, where the railroad transports its own or leased trailers, but the shipper or his agent picks up and delivers the shipment, and performs the loading and unloading.

Plan III.   The railroad transports trailers owned or leased by the shipper or freight forwarder. The shipper or forwarder provides his own pickup and delivery service. Rates are either based on the commodity and quantity moved or a flat charge per trailer.

Plan IV.   The railroad performs line-haul service only, with both flatcar and trailer furnished (owned or leased) by the shipper or freight forwarder. The railroad makes a charge for movement of the flatcar and trailer, loaded or empty.

Plan V.   Either the railroad or the motor carrier may solicit and accept freight. Part of the haul will involve rail transport, the other part truck transport. The joint motor-rail rates, then, are for door-to-door piggyback service.

The railroads have invested millions of dollars in purchasing specialized flatcars and tie-down equipment, and in developing methods for loading and unloading trailers. All five basic plans, and the variation of Plan II, have received ICC approval, subject to several exceptions.[157] And the growth of the service has been impressive (Table 14-7).[158] At the same time, there is a danger: if either Congress or the ICC interferes, past history strongly suggests that the development of voluntary coordinated service may be impaired. Moreover, an adminis-

---

[157] See *Movement of Highway Trailers by Rail, op. cit.;* and *Iron and Steel Articles between Atlanta, Ga., and St. Louis, Mo.,* 318 ICC 80 (1962). In 1962, the ICC instituted a broad study of piggyback service. Two examiners, in August, 1963, termed piggyback service "one of the most dynamic formulas for transportation of freight this country has ever seen" and recommended that there be no special restraints on the service. They proposed, however, 25 rules intended to encourage more intermodal coordination of service and promote more efficient use of facilities. *Transport Topics,* August 26, 1963, pp. 1, 17 and September 2, 1963, p. 14. The commission's decision generally followed the examiners' recommendations, but it imposed on railroads a new rule to make the service available to motor and water carriers at the same rates as offered to noncarrier shippers. *Substituted Service—Charges and Practices of For-Hire Carriers and Freight Forwarders (Piggyback Service),* 322 ICC 301 (1964). The commission was upheld by the Supreme Court. *American Trucking Ass'ns, Inc.* v. *Atchison, T. & S. F. Ry.,* 387 U.S. 397 (1967). See E. D. Anderson, P. D. Borghesani, and W. H. Towle, "Ex Parte 230: The ICC 'Piggyback' Rulemaking Case," 9 *Boston College Industrial and Commercial Law Review* 23 (1967).

[158] The Teamsters Union, in several 1961 contract negotiations, received from the trucking firms an agreement that they would pay the union a flat $5.00 fee for every trailer they loaded on a railroad flatcar.

TABLE 14-7
Growth of Piggyback Service

Year	Revenue Carloadings	Weekly Average
1955	168,150	3,234
1956	207,783	3,996
1957	249,065	4,790
1958	278,071	5,348
1959	416,508	8,010
1960	554,115	10,656
1961	591,246	11,364
1962	706,441	13,585
1963	797,474	15,336
1964	890,748	17,130
1965	1,034,377	19,892
1966	1,162,731	22,360
1967	1,207,242	23,216
1968	1,337,149	25,714

Source: Economics and Finance Department, Association of American Railroads, *Yearbook of Railroad Facts* (Washington, D.C., 1969), p. 33.

trative burden of considerable magnitude would be imposed on the ICC. It seems desirable, then, to allow the various modes of transport to develop coordinated transport services themselves, subject to the limitations discussed above.[159] Voluntary coordination could be further encouraged by permitting greater freedom of entry for new carriers of all types.

The Problem of Labor

The problem of labor in the transportation field is somewhat unique. Despite the fact that wages account for over 60 percent of air, motor, and rail transport operating expenses, none of the regulatory commissions has authority over labor or labor relations.[160] In the air and railroad fields, labor relations are subject to the Railway Labor Act of 1926; railroad retirements are handled by the Railroad Retirement Board. Labor relations in the remaining modes are subject to the jurisdiction of the National Labor Relations Board.

The special treatment accorded air and railroad labor is due to a number of factors. Transportation plays a strategic role in the economy. The necessity of

[159] There are indications that voluntary coordination will work. See Merrill J. Roberts and Associates, *Intermodal Freight Transportation Coordination: Problems and Potential* (Pittsburgh: Graduate School of Business, University of Pittsburgh, 1966), esp. chap. iii; and Interstate Commerce Commission, Bureau of Economics, *Air-Truck Coordination and Competition*, Statement No. 67-1 (Washington, D.C., 1967).

[160] The Federal Highway Administration is responsible for motor carrier safety and determines the number of hours a driver may work. The Federal Aviation Administration is responsible for airline safety and determines pilot qualification rules, flying time, and retirement age. Railroad labor is protected by statute for four years in merger cases.

maintaining detailed safety regulations means that skilled and trained employees are required. Since a considerable training period is involved, job security has traditionally been a critical issue. Finally, as with other regulated industries, transport services must be provided on a continuous 24-hour, 7-day-a-week basis. Work rules and pay scales, therefore, have developed in a complex manner. The entire situation is further complicated, first, by the existence of craft unions (24 in the railroad industry and 31 in the airline industry) and, second, by technological advances.

Railroads. One observer has labeled labor relations in the railroad industry since 1962 as "little short of chaotic."[161] The basic disputes throughout this period have concerned the wage structure;[162] work rules; road and yard work assignments;[163] and pay for holidays, overtime, expenses away from home, and night shift differentials. Particularly has the issue of work rules been of significance with respect to the employment of firemen; a dispute referred to as the "featherbedding issue."

The struggle over work rules was initiated in 1959 when the carriers demanded negotiations with the unions over basic changes. The railroads made it plain that they wanted to eliminate some 60,000 employees (many being firemen on freight and yard diesel locomotives), a change estimated to save nearly half a billion dollars annually. Since then, the events in the struggle have been the following. In 1960, President Eisenhower appointed a Presidential Railroad Commission which, in February, 1962, issued a 576-page report calling not only for work rule changes that would result in elimination of a substantial number of jobs but also for changes in pay rules. To cushion the impact on employees, income and job security arrangements also were recommended.[164] The carriers accepted the findings, but the unions rejected them.[165] On April 3, 1963, after negotiations with federal mediators failed to resolve the issues, President Kennedy appointed an Emergency Board (Board No. 154) under the

---

161 Pegrum, *Transportation: Economics and Public Policy, op. cit.,* p. 512. For further discussions of the railroad labor problem, see: L. A. Lecht, *Experience under Railway Labor Legislation* (New York: Columbia University Press, 1955); John T. Dunlop, "Manpower in Operating Classifications on the Railroads," in *Transportation Economics, op. cit.,* pp. 423–36; and G. G. Eggert, *Railroad Labor Disputes* (Ann Arbor: University of Michigan Press, 1967). Railroad labor controversies are summarized in the annual publication of the Economics and Finance Department, Association of American Railroads, *Railroad Review and Outlook* (Washington, D.C.).

162 In general, a day's pay is based on hours worked and miles traveled: 100 miles or 5 hours for passenger enginemen, 100 miles or 8 hours for freight enginemen and trainmen, and 150 miles or 7½ hours for passenger trainmen.

163 For example, if a yard crew goes beyond a yard limit to aid a disabled train, every man in the crew gets a whole day's pay at road rates in addition to his regular yard pay.

164 *Report of the Presidential Railroad Commission* (Washington, D.C.: U.S. Government Printing Office, 1962).

165 The unions went to court, but the Supreme Court upheld the right of the railroads to make several work rule changes. *Brotherhood of Locomotive Engineers* v. *Baltimore & Ohio R. Co.,* 372 U.S. 284 (1963).

provisions of the Railway Labor Act. On May 13, 1963, the board also recommended work rule changes. Again, negotiations failed and a nationwide strike seemed imminent. On August 28, 1963, Congress enacted a Joint Resolution banning a strike for six months and requiring compulsory arbitration of two issues—firemen's jobs and the makeup of train crews.[166] The Arbitration Board (Board No. 282) subsequently ruled that 90 percent of the firemen on freight and yard diesels could be eliminated by attrition, as could unneeded train crew jobs (such as brakemen and switchmen). The award of the board was delayed until May 7, 1964, when the unions went to court to test the constitutionality of the compulsory arbitration law.[167] Conflict over the award continued, however, and on March 31, 1966, the firemen struck eight major railroads.[168] A district court ordered them back to work, and when they refused to do so for four days, a contempt citation and a fine were levied against the union.[169] And in January, 1968, the Supreme Court upheld a lower court ruling that termination of the two-year effective period of the award of Arbitration Board 282 did not restore the rates of pay, rules, and working conditions existing prior to the enactment of the Joint Resolution of Congress in 1963.[170]

In September, 1959, a majority of the nation's railroads inaugurated a strike insurance plan, known as "Service Interruption Insurance." Under the plan, a particular railroad may collect fixed costs (interest on debt and the

[166] Public Law 88-108 (1963).

[167] The lower courts upheld the law and the Supreme Court declined review. *Brotherhood of Locomotive Firemen and Enginemen* v. *Certain Carriers Represented by the Eastern, Western, and Southeastern Carriers' Conference Committees*, 225 F. Supp. 11 (1964), 331 F. 2d 1020 (1964), *cert. denied*, 377 U.S. 918 (1964).

One complicating factor is the so-called "full crew" laws currently in effect in five states (Arkansas, Indiana, New York, Ohio and Wisconsin). These laws prohibit railroads from reducing the number of men in a crew below a specific figure, generally five or six. The railroads which operate within these states are seeking repeal of the laws, with only limited success. See "What Is the Crew Size Issue All About?" 59 *Illinois Central Magazine* 2 (April, 1968); *New York Central R. Co.* v. *Lefkowitz*, 282 NYS 2d (1967), *aff'd*, 241 N.E. 2d 730 (1968); *Akron, C. & Y. R. Co.* v. *Public Utilities Comm.*, 224 N.E. 2d 169 (1967); and *Chicago, R.I. & P. R. Co.* v. *Hardin*, 274 F. Supp. 294 (1967), *rev'd*, 89 S. Ct. 323 (1968).

[168] In January, 1966, a National Joint Board established under Arbitration Award No. 282, concluded that there had been virtually no adverse effects from the removal of about 18,000 firemen and more than 3,000 train crewmen.

[169] *Bangor & Aroostook R. Co.* v. *Brotherhood of Locomotive Firemen and Enginemen*, 255 F. Supp. 476 (1966).

[170] *The Wall Street Journal*, January 30, 1968, p. 6. Effective January 1, 1969, four railroad operating unions (the Brotherhood of Railroad Trainmen, the Brotherhood of Locomotive Firemen and Enginemen, the Order of Railway Conductors and Brakemen, and the Switchmen's Union of North America) merged into a single organization—the United Transportation Union.

Other disputes were occurring throughout this period. Presidential intervention was required in a dispute involving the telegraphers in 1962, operating employees in 1964, and shopcraft employees in 1967. The latter dispute resulted in a nationwide strike, Congressional legislation (Public Law 90-54) restraining the strike, and creation of a Special Board to make a final determination (in the absence of agreement) which is binding until January 1, 1969.

expense of supervisory and other forces) if a work stoppage is contrary to the provisions of the Railway Labor Act or if a strike is called to enforce demands contrary to or in excess of the recommendations of an emergency board. The plan was upheld in the courts in 1963.[171]

Airlines. Changing technology also has had an impact on labor relations in the airline industry. The introduction of jet aircraft has created a job security problem concerning both the composition and the size of the cockpit crew. With respect to the composition of the crew, two pilots and a flight engineer occupied each cockpit on piston-engine airplanes. But as the jets were introduced, the jobs changed. The Air Line Pilots Association (ALPA) maintained that safety required three pilots on each jet aircraft. The Flight Engineers International Association (FEIA) maintained that one flight engineer was also needed, despite the fact that many of the functions formerly performed by flight engineers (preflight checkup, minor repairs) were taken over by maintenance crews. And, in a series of strikes beginning in 1958, the unions won their arguments with several lines, resulting in four-man jet crews.

United Air Lines, however, requested the National Mediation Board (which has jurisdiction over labor relations under the Railway Labor Act) to rule on the issue. The board concluded that only three-man crews were required and recommended that United's pilots and engineers vote as to whether one or two unions should represent them. Knowing that they could not win such an election (pilots outnumbered engineers), the FEIA struck the major airlines. The strike ended when the dispute was submitted to a special three-man fact-finding board. The board recommended that crews be cut from four to three and suggested that flight engineers be trained to meet certain pilot qualifications. The issue again resulted in a deadlock in bargaining between the pilots, engineers, and Pan American in 1961, but a strike was avoided when the ALPA and the airline (but not the FEIA) agreed to submit the dispute to a binding special arbitration board. In 1962, the board supported the earlier recommendations of the fact-finding board,[172] and many of the carriers adopted the recommendations in subsequent collective bargaining contracts.

With respect to the size of the cockpit crew, the ALPA's early insistence on the need for three pilots was partly the result of the fact that pilots were being laid off, since one jet could do the work of two or three piston planes. In more recent years, the demand for pilots has increased as the airlines have added more flights. Further, costs have advanced rapidly. Therefore, many airlines took the position that only two-man crews were required on the smaller types of jet passenger planes. Specifically, the dispute centered around the proper size of crew on Boeing 737's; a dispute involving the ALPA and United. After some eighteen months of negotiations, a strike was avoided when the two parties

---

171 *W. P. Kennedy et al.* v. *The Long Island R.R. Co., etc., et al.*, 319 F. 2d 366 (1963), *cert. denied*, 375 U.S. 830 (1963).
172 *The Wall Street Journal*, May 23, 1962, p. 8.

agreed to an intensive six-month operational evaluation (beginning April 28, 1968), after which the dispute will be submitted to binding arbitration.[173]

The trunklines also have instituted a "mutual aid plan" to avoid being "whipsawed" by the airline unions through successive strikes against each line. Under the plan, the carriers agree to share their *increased* revenues which result from a strike called against a competitor, provided the walkout is called before the procedures of the Railway Labor Act are exhausted or that the employees strike to enforce demands in excess of or contrary to the recommendations of an emergency board. The CAB has approved the plan, holding that it does not violate the Railway Labor Act.[174]

Motor Carriers. The only other mode of transport which has had major labor problems in recent years is the trucking industry. Two problems have arisen. First, nearly 90 percent of the over-the-road drivers are members of the International Brotherhood of Teamsters. This union, according to many, is corrupt. Second, in March, 1967, the Teamsters signed the first master (nationwide) contract to replace the five regional contracts formerly in existence.[175] The prospect of a nationwide strike sometime in the future, therefore, must be faced. In view of the importance of trucking in the national transport system, it seems clear that Congress will be forced to take some action.

Urban Transportation

One of the most pressing transport problems concerns urban transportation. In the post–World War II period, "all means of transportation within metropolitan areas are increasingly congested, overburdened and inadequate—suffering greatly from a lack of coordination and long-range planning."[176] The situation is especially serious with respect to commutation services.

[173] *Ibid.,* March 25, 1968, p. 5. Early in 1969, the arbitration panel ruled that United must use three-man crews to operate its 737 passenger jets at least until March, 1970. *Ibid.*, February 26, 1969, p. 14.

[174] *Six-Carrier Mutual Aid Pact,* 29 CAB 168 (1959); *Supplemental Opinion on Reconsideration*, 30 CAB 90 (1959); and *Mutual Aid Investigation*, E-21044 (CAB, 1964). Late in 1967, however, the board ordered a formal investigation into the plan. *Airlines Mutual Aid Agreement*, E-26000 (CAB, 1967). Payments under the plan have been significant: during the strikes of 1960 and 1961, for example, Eastern received nearly $1 million. But complete harmony among the lines has not prevailed. See *The Wall Street Journal*, April 26, 1963, p. 7. To date, no subsidized carrier is a member of the pact. See *Mutual Aid Agreement between American Airlines, Inc., and Mohawk Airlines, Inc.*, E-24213 (CAB, 1966).

[175] See Arthur A. Slone, "James R. Hoffa and His Trucking Triumph," 7 *Business Horizons* 25 (Fall, 1964).

[176] *National Transportation Policy, op. cit.,* p. 552. For a complete discussion of this problem, see *ibid.*, pp. 552–646; Pegrum, *Transportation: Economics and Public Policy, op. cit.*, chaps. xxii–xxiv; J. R. Meyer, J. F. Kain and M. Wohl, *The Urban Transportation Problem* (Cambridge: Harvard University Press, 1965); W. Owen, *The Metropolitan Transportation Problem* (rev. ed.; Washington, D.C.: Brookings Institution, 1966); Lyle C. Fitch and Associates, *Urban Transportation and Public Policy* (San Francisco: Chandler Publishing Co., 1964); and J. Q. Wilson (ed.), *The Metropolitan Enigma* (rev. ed.; Cambridge: Harvard University Press, 1968).

The commutation problem is acute in Boston, New York, Philadelphia, Chicago, and San Francisco, and to a lesser extent in Pittsburgh, Washington, and Baltimore. Public investment in highways has resulted in an increased reliance on the private automobile. At the same time, declining passenger traffic, combined with rising costs, has resulted in an unfavorable price-cost relationship in urban common carrier services. With freight traffic subject to growing intermodal competition, the railroads, in particular, can no longer afford to absorb the annual commutation deficit.

A solution to the urban transportation problem will involve careful and detailed long-range planning by all parties concerned. While such coordination is presently lacking, there are signs that more planning is underway. As noted earlier,[177] local, state, and federal governments have undertaken programs aimed at maintaining commutation services and seeking new ways to move people within cities. In addition to subsidies and loans, cities (such as Boston, Cleveland, and San Francisco) have initiated large-scale investment programs in rapid-transit facilities; Washington, D.C., has conducted an experiment in which ten minibuses circulated within the central business district on a fixed-route with frequent schedules and a low fare; the Department of Transportation has undertaken a program of capital grants and demonstration projects for passenger service on high-speed trains; and the Department of Housing and Urban Development has sponsored several experiments, including the operation of an air-cushion vehicle across San Francisco Bay and an evaluation of the Seattle World's Fair monorail.[178] Moreover, several states have established new agencies to deal with the urban transportation problem, such as the Massachusetts Bay Transportation Authority, the New Jersey Commuter Operating Agency (a unit of the State's Department of Transportation), and the New York Metropolitan Commuter Transportation Authority.[179]

It should be emphasized, however, that a solution to the urban transportation problem will not solve the overall railroad passenger deficit. According to James C. Nelson:

... the trends over several decades indicate that new forms of travel have greatly limited the opportunity of the railways in the passenger business. Although the exact extent of passenger train deficits is uncertain, the rail passenger train business is either distinctly unprofitable or relatively unprofitable in most cases. Either the railways should withdraw from this area or find ways to reduce losses and to increase the profit contributions of the passenger service. A selective approach is needed with the ICC clarifying the deficit and freight burden issues and the state commissions allowing discontinuance of hopelessly unprofitable trains. In addition, management must apply costing

---

[177] See Chapter 12, p. 426.
[178] "Problems of Urban Transportation," *The Morgan Guaranty Survey*, May, 1968, pp. 5–11.
[179] On the Massachusetts Bay Transportation Authority, see *Business Week*, February 20, 1965, pp. 144–48; on the New York Metropolitan Commuter Transportation Authority, see *ibid.*, March 9, 1968, pp. 64–68.

procedures capable of segregating the profitable from the unprofitable trains and service, discontinue the hopelessly unprofitable trains and services, and enhance the profitability of all trains and services having long-term possibilities by either upward or downward fare adjustments, improved service and courtesy, and other measures. In general, the railroads should be freed of their social obligations to operate unprofitable passenger service, but special measures at the local levels of government may be required to solve commuter problems satisfactorily.[180]

HOW MUCH REGULATION?

The divergence between the theory and practice of regulation is best illustrated by the nation's transportation system. Public policies toward the various modes of transport have developed in a piecemeal fashion over three-quarters of a century, with little attention having been given to overall or long-range policy. Economic conditions have changed drastically. Important and serious inconsistencies in policy have developed. Further, each mode continues to be plagued by overcapacity or financial difficulties. There can be little doubt that present policies have tended to promote waste and inefficiency throughout the transportation industries. The basic policy questions, therefore, remain: how much and what type of regulation is needed to promote an efficient transportation system? [181]

Economic efficiency can best be promoted, in the author's opinion, by substantially reducing government regulation of the transportation industries. Competitive forces are as pervasive as in many nonregulated industries, and public policy could strengthen these forces in numerous ways.[182] A heavier reliance on the forces of competition would (1) result in better allocation of traffic and resources than at present and (2) create an environment promoting management incentive and encouraging technological advance. Regulation would still be needed to prevent such abuses as unreasonable rates either on noncompetitive traffic or over noncompetitive routes.

Policy changes, however, will be slow. As Meyer has pointed out: ". . . transportation regulation is a historically established fact, and undoing this history is not easy. At the very least, such undoing would involve some hardship for certain sectors of the transportation industry, certain shippers, and possibly for society as a whole."[183] The burden of reform, moreover, rests partly on management and labor. Many of the suggested changes discussed in this chapter, including the further development of better cost and rate-making techniques, can be undertaken within the existing regulatory framework. Unless manage-

180 Nelson, *Railroad Transportation and Public Policy, op. cit.*, pp. 325–26.

181 For an excellent summary of various answers, see *Proposed Amendments to Federal Transportation Laws, op. cit.*, Part 2.

182 It must be noted, however, that the performance of many unprofitable services complicates reliance on competitive forces.

183 Meyer, *op. cit.*, pp. 229–30.

ment and labor continue to come forward with concrete proposals, there is little hope that sounder public policies will be enacted; political pressures and vested interests are simply too strong to expect commission or legislative initiative. And there is some evidence to support the proposition that private initiative can achieve results: railroad managements' proposals were in large measure responsible for passage of the Transportation Act of 1958 and initiative has been displayed in attempting to recapture freight traffic with new equipment and incentive rates.

At the same time, changes in policy (both regulatory and statutory) also are necessary if a truly national transportation system is to be developed. Here, the Department of Transportation could take the initiative. As Pegrum has written:

> The passage of the Department of Transportation Act marks a clear-cut turning point in the respective roles of regulation and administration in national transportation policy. It seems quite safe to say that regulation will occupy a relatively less, and perhaps absolutely less, important role in transport than it has done in the last 80 years. Policy development is now to be focussed in the executive branch of the government. Whether this will result in severe inroads on regulation remains to be seen, but the Department is bound to have strong influence on regulatory theory. If the Department follows an aggressive approach to the implementation of "pervasive competition" much present regulatory detail will vanish. The pressures of changing technology are working inexorably in that direction. These two factors are bound to modify the scope of activities of the Interstate Commerce Commission and the Civil Aeronautics Board. What will be the role of regulation in transportation as we have known it remains to be seen. The policy of Commissions of protecting regulated carriers from competition among themselves seems destined to suffer severe curtailment, and the Interstate Commerce Commission's "double standard" for competition among regulated carriers and between them and nonregulated ones has probably gone by the boards. A new day has dawned for the development and application of national transport policy but the weather which will accompany it has yet to be ascertained.[184]

In short, if management continues to exhibit the initiative it has shown in recent years and if the Department of Transportation becomes "the focal point for the identification and solution of transportation problems,"[185] the development of a coordinated national transportation policy could become a reality.

APPENDIX: SELECTED BIBLIOGRAPHY OF POSTWAR STUDIES ON NATIONAL TRANSPORTATION POLICY

The bibliographical literature on transportation would fill many volumes. The list below pertains to the major postwar studies on national transportation

---

184 Pegrum, *Transportation: Economics and Public Policy, op. cit.*, p. 543.
185 A. S. Lang, "High Speed Transportation," in National Association of Regulatory Utility Commissioners, *1967 Annual Proceedings* (Washington, D.C., 1968), p. 531.

policy. More general lists of references have been compiled by D. Philip Locklin, *Economics of Transportation* (6th ed.; Homewood, Illinois: Richard D. Irwin, Inc., 1966), at the end of each chapter; and by Dudley F. Pegrum, *Transportation: Economics and Public Policy* (rev. ed.; Homewood, Illinois: Richard D. Irwin, Inc., 1968), pp. 651-62.

Dearing, C. L., and Owen, W., *National Transportation Policy*. Washington, D.C.: Brookings Institution, 1949. This study was made at the request of the Hoover Commission on government reorganization.

Unified and Coordinated Federal Program for Transportation, A report to the President from the Secretary of Commerce (Sawyer Report). Washington, D.C., 1949.

Domestic Land and Water Transportation, Committee on Interstate and Foreign Commerce (Bricker Report), Senate, 82d Cong., 1st sess. Washington, D.C.: U.S. Government Printing Office, 1951.

Revision of Federal Transportation Policy, A report to the President prepared by the Presidential Advisory Committee on Transport Policy and Organization (Weeks Report). Washington, D.C., April, 1955.

Problems of the Railroads, Hearings before the Subcommittee on Surface Transportation of the Committee on Interstate and Foreign Commerce, Senate, 85th Cong., 2d sess., Parts 1-4. Washington, D.C.: U.S. Government Printing Office, 1958; and *Problems of the Railroads*, Subcommittee Report (Smathers Report), 1958.

Meyer, J. R., Peck, M. J., Stenason, J., and Zwick, C., *The Economics of Competition in the Transportation Industries*. Cambridge: Harvard University Press, 1959.

Adequacy of Transportation Systems in Support of the National Defense Effort in the Event of Mobilization, Hearings of Subcommittee on Armed Services (Kilday Report), House, 86th Cong., 1st sess. Washington, D.C.: U.S. Government Printing Office, 1959.

Nelson, J. C., *Railroad Transportation and Public Policy*. Washington, D.C.: Brookings Institution, 1959.

Interstate Commerce Commission, *Railroad Passenger Train Deficit*. Washington, D.C., 1959.

U.S. Department of Commerce, *Federal Transportation Policy and Program* (Mueller Report). Washington, D.C., March, 1960; and Appendix, Williams, Jr., E. W., and Bluestone, D. W., *Rationale of Federal Transportation Policy*. Washington, D.C., April, 1960.

Transportation Diversification, Hearings before a Subcommittee of the Committee on Interstate and Foreign Commerce, House, 86th Cong., 2d sess. Washington, D.C.: U.S. Government Printing Office, 1960.

Decline of the Coastwise and Intercoastal Shipping Industry, Report of the Merchant Marine and Fisheries Subcommittee of the Committee on Interstate and Foreign Commerce, Senate, 86th Cong., 2d sess. Washington, D.C.: U.S. Government Printing Office, 1960.

National Transportation Policy, Preliminary Draft of a Report Prepared for the

Committee on Interstate and Foreign Commerce by the Special Study Group on Transportation Policies in the United States (Doyle Report), Senate, 87th Cong., 1st sess. Washington, D.C.: U.S. Government Printing Office, 1961.

Richmond, S. B., *Regulation and Competition in Air Transportation*. New York: Columbia University Press, 1961.

Fulda, C. H., *Competition in the Regulated Industries: Transportation*. Boston: Little, Brown & Co., 1961.

Rail Merger Legislation, Hearings before a Subcommittee on Antitrust and Monopoly of the Committee on the Judiciary, Senate, 87th Cong., 2d sess., Parts 1 and 2. Washington, D.C.: U.S. Government Printing Office, 1962; and *The Railroad Merger Problem*, Subcommittee Report. Washington, D.C., U.S. Government Printing Office, 1963.

Proposed Amendments to Federal Transportation Laws, Hearings before the Committee on Commerce, Senate, 87th Cong., 2d sess., Parts 1 and 2. Washington, D.C.: U.S. Government Printing Office, 1962.

Caves, R. E., *Air Transport and Its Regulators: An Industry Study*. Cambridge: Harvard University Press, 1962.

Transportation Act—1963, Hearings before the Committee on Interstate and Foreign Commerce, House, 88th Cong., 1st sess., Parts 1 and 2. Washington, D.C.: U.S. Government Printing Office, 1963; and *Transportation Amendments of 1964*, House Report No. 1144. Washington, D.C.: U.S. Government Printing Office, 1964.

Transportation Act Amendments—1963, Hearings before the Surface Transportation Subcommittee of the Committee on Commerce, Senate, 88th Cong., 1st sess., Parts 1 and 2. Washington, D.C.: U.S. Government Printing Office, 1964.

Conant, M., *Railroad Mergers and Abandonments.* Berkeley and Los Angeles: University of California Press, 1964.

Kahn, T. E., *Public Enterprise Economics and Transport Problems.* Berkeley and Los Angeles: University of California Press, 1965.

Transportation Economics. New York: National Bureau of Economic Research, 1965.

Ruppenthal, K. M. (ed.), *Issues in Transportation Economics*. Columbus: Charles E. Merrill Books, Inc., 1965.

The Crisis in Passenger Train Service, Hearings before the Committee on Commerce, Senate, 89th Cong., 1st sess. Washington, D.C.: U.S. Government Printing Office, 1965.

Mott, G. F. (ed.), *Transportation Century.* Baton Rouge: Louisiana State University Press, 1966.

Norton, H. S., *National Transportation Policy: Formation and Implementation.* Berkeley: McCutchan Publishing Co., 1967.

Chapter

15

THE ELECTRIC POWER
INDUSTRY

> *The factors requiring unified planning, construction, and operation of generating and transmission networks have been present from the very beginning of the industry, but the size of the area most efficiently covered by a single network has grown as advances in electric technology have increased the economic transmission distance and enlarged the savings from using larger scale equipment.*
>
> —*Federal Power Commission**

    The combined functions of generating, transmitting, and selling electric energy represent the nation's largest industry. The industry also is one of the country's most important businesses, since nearly every home and commercial enterprise is served by it. With but 6 percent of the world's population, the United States accounts for about 36 percent of the world's production of electric energy. Moreover, it seems certain that the industry will continue to be an expanding one for many years to come. According to the *National Power Survey*, the nation's annual requirements will be 2.8 trillion kilowatt-hours by 1980 (nearly 2¼ times the 1967 total of 1.2 trillion), requiring the addition of approximately 325 million kilowatts to existing installed capacity (of 267 million kilowatts at the end of 1967).[1]

    Effective federal regulation of the electric power industry is of recent origin, dating from 1935. Private electric utilities dominate the industry, but public power projects and cooperatives are of considerable significance. Technological advances in generation (including nuclear power) and transmission have made feasible a rapid growth in interconnections and power pools. The latter, in turn, have resulted in a new wave of consolidations and have raised the issue of reliability. Competition between electric power and the fossil fuels has become even stronger. And in locating and building the new facilities required for the future, the electric utilities have been under increased pressure to consider the conservation of natural resources, the maintenance of scenic or natural beauty, and the preservation of historic sites. The electric power industry well illustrates

---

    *Federal Power Commission, *National Power Survey* (Washington, D.C.: U.S. Government Printing Office, 1964), Vol. I, p. 13.

    [1]*Ibid.*, p. 35.

the problems and challenges of regulating a dynamic industry within which both private and public enterprise operate.

DEVELOPMENT AND STRUCTURE

The electric power industry is one of our youngest industries.[2] As early as 1802, it was demonstrated that an electric current could be used to make a light, but it was not until 1879 that San Francisco could boast of possessing the first central station in the United States, furnishing electric power to its arc lamp system.[3] On October 21, 1879, Thomas A. Edison invented the first commercially practical incandescent lamp, and in December of that year he demonstrated a complete incandescent lighting system; a central plant generated the power which was then transmitted to several houses in which incandescent lamps had been installed. Five years later, on September 4, 1882, the first central station to furnish current for the Edison-type lamp was put into operation at Pearl Street in New York City. The station began by supplying some 400 lamps and had a generating capacity of 560 kilowatts.[4] Later in the year, at Appleton, Wisconsin, the nation's first hydroelectric station was put into operation. And in 1903, the world's first all-turbine station, a 5,000 kilowatt unit, was installed in Chicago.

The current supplied by the earliest stations was direct, and direct current (at the then available voltages) was uneconomical when transmitted over long distances. In 1886, primarily due to the efforts of George Westinghouse, a practical alternating current system was developed. This development made it possible first to "step up" the voltage, through transformers, before the current was transmitted so it could be carried over long distances, then to "step down" the voltage prior to distribution. The present threefold division of the electric power industry was thus established: generation (production of power), transmission (carrying power for long distances), and distribution (dividing power among customers).

Generation

In the twentieth century, the output of electricity has doubled roughly every ten years and has increased at an annual compound rate of about 7 percent. Accompanying this sustained growth have been rapid technological innovations in both generating and transmission equipment.

---

[2] For a more complete history, see John A. Miller, *At the Touch of a Button* (Schenectady, N.Y.: Mohawk Development Service, Inc., 1962); and Edwin Vennard, *The Electric Power Business* (New York: McGraw-Hill Book Co., 1962), chap. i.

[3] In 1875, a dynamo built by Professors William A. Anthony and George S. Moler of Cornell University was used to furnish the electricity lighting the arc lamps of the university's campus.

[4] "By the end of that year, the Edison Electric Illuminating Co. of New York was serving 500 customers using more than 10,000 lamps." *National Power Survey, op. cit.*, p. 10.

Technology. The process of generating electricity has been explained by the Edison Electric Institute as follows:

> An electric current is created when a certain kind of wire is passed through the lines of force emanating from the poles of a magnet, called the magnetic field. This principle is used in the commercial generation of electricity. A generator is a device for passing many wires through a strong magnetic field at a rapid rate. Thus, an appreciable amount of electricity can be generated. The generator is a means of converting mechanical power into electric power.[5]

Electric utility generating plants are of three major types—steam, hydroelectric, and internal combustion. Steam plant production accounted for 81.4 percent of the 1967 output, hydro production for 18.2 percent, and internal combustion production for .4 percent. (Generation by nuclear-fueled steam plants in 1967 was 7.1 billion kilowatt-hours, compared with 2.3 billion in 1962.) Table 15–1 indicates the trends in the production of energy by primary energy sources. In 1920, water power accounted for 40 percent of the nation's production of electricity, coal for 53.09 percent, oil for 5.36 percent, and gas for 1.55 percent. By 1967, water power had declined in importance to 18.17 percent, coal and oil (52.63 percent and 7.4 percent, respectively) had remained constant, and gas had increased to 21.8 percent. In absolute terms, electric utility generating plants consumed 274 million tons of coal in 1967, 2.7 trillion cubic feet of gas, and 161.3 million barrels of oil.

Hydroelectric plants depend on falling water to turn turbines connected to generators. Compared with steam plants, they have several important drawbacks.[6] First, hydroelectric plants must be located at suitable sites on rivers—sites which may be some distance from the points where the power is to be consumed. As a result, a high investment in transmission facilities is required. Steam plants usually can be located nearer to markets. Second, the investment per kilowatt of capacity typically is higher for hydroelectric plants, due to the need of providing expensive dams and considerable land for the reservoirs. Third, there is a wide seasonal variation in water flow. Unlike electricity itself, the water used to drive turbines can be stored. Known as "peaking power," the spillways are closed and the water held back during periods of little use of electricity, then this stored water is used to generate the maximum amount of electric power during peak periods. But storage is limited, and during the summer months, when streams are usually low and demand for electricity high, water is unavailable to generate the required power. A steam plant, therefore, must supplement a hydroelectric plant in most instances, often offsetting the savings of hydro energy. Fourth, when a dam is built to serve multiple purposes, such as flood control, irrigation, and power generation, the functions may work at cross-purposes. Thus, an empty reservoir is needed for flood control, while

[5] Edison Electric Institute, "The Electric Power Industry," in John G. Glover and Rudolph L. Lagai (eds.), *The Development of American Industries* (4th ed.; New York: Simmons-Boardman Publishing Co., 1959), p. 517.

[6] Vennard, *op. cit.,* p. 265.

TABLE 15-1
Total Kilowatt-Hour Production and Source

Energy Source	1920	1930	1940	1950	1960	1967 (pre.)
Total production (billion kilowatt-hours)	39.4	91.1	141.8	329.1	753.4	1,211.8
			Percent of Total			
Hydro	40.00	34.23	33.36	29.15	19.32	18.17
Coal *a*	53.09	55.77	54.57	47.06	53.59	52.63
Oil	5.36	3.07	4.36	10.25	6.12	7.36
Gas	1.55	6.93	7.71	13.54	20.97	21.84
Total	100.00	100.00	100.00	100.00	100.00	100.00

a Includes minor amounts from wood, waste, and nuclear fuels. Nuclear-fueled plants generated .7 percent of total from all sources in 1967.
Source: Federal Power Commission, *Annual Report, 1966*, p. 49; and Edison Electric Institute.

power requires falling water. Finally, greater opportunities for improvement in design are offered by steam plants. Steam turbines have been developed with a capacity of 1 million kilowatts, as compared with the earlier steam engine generators with a 1- to 5-thousand kilowatt capacity. The efficiency of steam generating plants has been improved consistently. Whereas in 1902, power plants averaged 6.7 pounds of coal per kilowatt-hour, for example, the average had dropped to .870 pounds per kilowatt-hour in 1967. Table 15-2 compares the cost of hydro and steam power and shows the change which occurred between 1920 and 1960.

The location of steam plants depends partly on the availability of water and partly on transportation costs. Steam plants require considerable quantities of water for condensing purposes, so that the availability of sufficient water is an important factor. Recent technological advances in extra-high-voltage (EHV) transmission lines have made it more economical to transport energy over wires than to transport coal by rail in certain cases. Consequently, the so-called "mine-mouth power plant" is used in many parts of the country when the available water supply in the coal fields is adequate. To illustrate: Public Service Electric & Gas Company of New Jersey estimated in 1963 that coal at the mine head cost 17 cents per million Btu., while transportation to the company's generators in New Jersey cost an additional 17 cents—a total of 34 cents per million Btu. In contrast, since it cost but 8 cents to ship electricity over EHV lines, mine-mouth power cost a total of only 25 cents per million Btu., representing a difference of 9 cents.[7]

The use of the diesel engine or internal combustion engines has declined over the past three decades. The major advantage of such engines is generation of

[7] Cited in *Business Week*, April 13, 1963, pp. 47-48.

TABLE 15-2
Comparison of Steam and Hydro, 1920 and 1960

	1920	*1960*
a) Hydro: Investment in plant (including 20% for transmission) per kilowatt	$240	$336
Fixed charges: Return on investment	8.0%	6.0%
Depreciation	1.5	1.6
Taxes	1.4	1.8
Total	10.9%	9.4%
b) Steam: Investment in plant per kilowatt	$140	$135
Fixed charges: Return on investment	8.0%	6.0%
Depreciation	2.5	2.7
Taxes	2.0	2.5
Total	12.5%	11.2%
Economy: Btu per kilowatt-hour	30,000	9,300
Coal: Pounds coal (of 14,000 Btu per lb.)	2.14	0.66
Costs per ton	$4.50	$7.00
c) Load characteristics: (55% load factor) kilowatt-hours per kilowatt per year	4,820	4,820

Costs
Mills per kilowatt-hour

	1920	*1960*
a) Hydro		
Fixed charges	5.43	6.55
Fuel	0.00	0.00
Labor and maintenance (including transmission)	0.35	0.89
Total	5.78	7.44
b) Steam		
Fixed charges	3.63	3.14
Fuel	4.82	2.31
Labor and maintenance	1.40	1.01
Total	9.85	6.46

Source: Edwin Vennard, *The Electric Power Business* (New York: McGraw-Hill Book Co., Inc., 1962), p. 267. Used by permission of McGraw-Hill Book Company.

electrical power in small quantities (10,000 kilowatts and under), used for the requirements of municipal, cooperative, and industrial plants, or for reserves to meet peak loads of smaller utility companies.[8] More recently, gas and dual-fuel

[8] Several methods of meeting peak loads have been developed by the industry. One of the most popular is a method known as "pumped storage." During periods of slack demand, power is used to pump water uphill to an upper reservoir. At peak hours, the water is permitted to pass through the turbines to a lower reservoir, thereby providing generation. Reversible units that can both pump and generate are now available, while the development of extra-high-voltage transmission lines has made it economical to transport power to and from the reservoirs.

engines have been developed to utilize the cheaper fuel—gas.[9] Their use, while growing, is still limited.

The total installed generating capacity, by geographic divisions, of the nation's 3,290 electric utility generating plants is shown in Table 15-3. Installed generating capacity (in the contiguous states) increased 36.6 percent over the

TABLE 15-3
Increases in Installed Generating Capacity, 1961–66

Geographic Division	Capacity in Service as of Dec. 31, 1966 (Kilowatts)	Five-Year Increase, 1966 over 1961	
		Kilowatts	Percent
New England	9,029,299	1,592,033	+21.4
Middle Atlantic	34,504,227	6,680,055	+24.0
East North Central	46,733,114	8,267,514	+21.5
West North Central	17,167,923	4,727,237	+38.0
South Atlantic	37,995,992	13,535,733	+55.3
East South Central	25,461,040	7,898,185	+45.0
West South Central	27,661,255	9,544,931	+52.7
Mountain	13,445,105	4,130,625	+44.3
Pacific	34,808,972	9,763,061	+39.0
Contiguous United States	246,806,927	66,139,374	+36.6
Alaska and Hawaii	1,036,198	n.a.	n.a.
Total United States	247,843,125 [a]	n.a.	n.a.

[a] Consists of: (a) 44,977,158 kilowatts hydro; (b) 197,372,782 kilowatts steam-electric, including 1,942,100 kilowatts nuclear and 26,565 kilowatts geothermal; (c) 3,508,856 kilowatts internal combustion; and (d) 1,984,329 kilowatts gas turbine.
n.a. = Not available.
Source: Federal Power Commission, *Annual Report, 1967*, p. 14.

five-year period 1961-66. Of this increase, the largest percentage occurred in the South Atlantic division (Delaware, District of Columbia, Florida, Georgia, Maryland, North and South Carolina, Virginia, and West Virginia), and the lowest in the New England states.

Structure. Electric power in the United States, notes Iulo,

... is supplied by a complex agglomeration of individual electric supply systems of widely differing economic and legal characteristics. These electric supply systems vary in nature from a small rural cooperative distributing power to a hundred or fewer customers to a large corporate utility serving the power needs of two or three million customers in an extensive metropolitan area. An industrial enterprise producing power primarily for its own use and a municipal light and power department provide additional examples of the

[9] Gas turbines are also being developed, but a satisfactory means of utilizing coal as their fuel has yet to be devised.

diversity in electric supply systems' organization. An individual electric supply system may itself generate all the energy demanded by its customers, or it may obtain, by purchase or interchange, all or a portion of its needs from other utilities, governmental agencies, industrial enterprises, or it may utilize any combination of these sources. In many instances, the supplying of electric energy may be the sole activity of the electric supply system; in many other cases, electric service is only one aspect of an enterprise that may provide, in addition, gas, telephone, heating, water, or transportation services. The market served by an electric supply system may include only densely populated and industrialized sections within a relatively limited geographic area; or it may be comprised of sparsely populated rural territory spread over a wide geographic area; or the individual system may serve a region with both rural and metropolitan sections.[10]

Only 472 of the nation's 3,614 electric utility supply systems are privately owned and operated (Table 15-4). Of the remaining 3,142 systems, 986 are owned and operated by cooperatives, and 2,156 are operated by municipalities, state and federal agencies, and special utility districts. In addition, there are 2,234 nonutility plants of 100 kilowatts generating capacity and over that produce primarily for industrial use but sell some of their output to electric utilities. While the number of privately owned and municipal electric systems has declined over the past four decades, the number of rural electric cooperatives and federally owned systems has increased significantly.

The total number of systems, however, is misleading as an indication of capacity and production. With but 13.1 percent of the number of electric utility supply systems, privately owned utilities account for 74.9 percent of installed capacity and 77 percent of total production. The privately owned electric utilities' and industrial systems' shares of capacity and production have declined since reaching their highest points in the 1930's and 1910's, respectively. Conversely, the share of cooperatives and government-owned utilities has shown a continuous growth, particularly in the last two decades. Figure 15–1 shows the sources of electric power supply in 1967.

Transmission

Electricity must be transmitted from the generating plant to consumers. Both the distance traveled and the voltage of the lines used affect total costs. With respect to distance, in 1889 a demonstration of a 13-mile transmission of power took place. By 1900, while more and more power was being transmitted, 25 miles was still looked on as being an exceptional distance. Today, 150 miles is not uncommon, and in several instances, distances of 300 miles are involved. With respect to voltage, 115,000-, 138,000-, and 230,000-volt lines are the most common, although a growing number of extra-high-voltage lines (345,000- and

---

[10]William Iulo, *Electric Utilities–Costs and Performance* (Pullman: Washington State University Press, 1961), pp. 1–2.

TABLE 15-4

Number of Electric Supply Systems, Total Capacity, and Total Production by Type of Ownership, Selected Years, 1902–1965

		Electric Utility Supply Systems							
			Publicly Owned and Cooperatives						
	Privately Owned	Municipal	Federal	Other[a]	Total	Total Utility	Percent Privately Owned to Total	Industrial Supply Systems[b]
1902								
Number of systems	2,805	815	...	...	815	3,620	77.5	n.a.
Total capacity[c]	1	(e)	...	...	(e)	1	100.0	2
Total production[d]	2	(e)	...	...	(e)	3	66.7	3
1912								
Number of systems	3,659	1,562	...	...	1,562	5,221	70.1	n.a.
Total capacity[c]	5	(e)	...	...	(e)	5	100.0	6
Total production[b]	11	1	...	...	1	12	91.7	13
1922								
Number of systems	3,774	2,581	...	...	2,581	6,355	59.4	n.a.
Total capacity[d]	13	1	(e)	(e)	1	14	92.9	6
Total production[d]	42	2	(e)	(e)	2	44	95.5	18
1932								
Number of systems	1,627	1,799	3	...	1,802	3,429	47.4	n.a.
Total capacity[d]	32	2	(e)	(e)	2	34	94.1	8
Total production[d]	74	4	(e)	1	5	79	93.7	20
1940								
Number of systems	n.a.	n.a.	n.a.	n.a.	n.a.	n.a.	n.a.	n.a.
Total capacity[c]	34	3	2	1	6	40	85.0	11
Total production[d]	125	6	9	1	16	142	88.0	38
1950								
Number of systems	821	2,077	55	1,054	3,186	4,007	20.5	3,469
Total capacity[c]	55	5	7	2	14	69	79.7	14
Total production[d]	267	15	40	7	62	329	81.2	60

TABLE 15-4—Continued

| | Privately Owned | Publicly Owned and Cooperatives | | | | Total Utility | Percent Privately Owned to Total | Industrial Supply Systems[b] |
		Municipal	Federal	Other[a]	Total			
1960								
Number of systems	496	2,026	43	1,072	3,141	3,637	13.6	2,234
Total capacity[c]	128	11	22	6	40	168	76.5	18
Total production[d]	579	37	112	26	175	754	76.8	88
1965								
Number of systems	472	2,114	42	986[f]	3,142	3,614	13.1	n.a.
Total capacity[c]	186	17	33	13	63	249	74.9	19
Total production[d]	881	53	153	58	264	1,145	77.0	105

Electric Utility Supply Systems

[a] Includes cooperatives, public utility districts, and state projects.
[b] Primarily produced for industrial use; plants of 100 kilowatts and over.
[c] Millions of kilowatts.
[d] Billions of kilowatt hours.
[e] Less than .5.
[f] Number of cooperatives only; other included in municipal.
n.a. = Not available.
Source: Federal Power Commission.

FIGURE 15-1
Sources of Electric Power Supply, 1967
(millions of kilowatt-hours and percent of total)

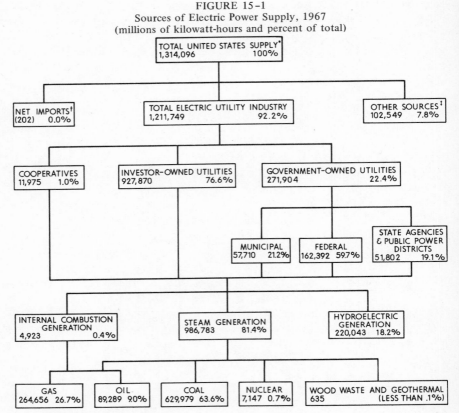

a Includes Alaska and Hawaii.
b Net imports from Canada and Mexico.
c Includes industrial, mine, and railway electric power plants; excludes isolated plants in institutions, hotels, apartment houses, office buildings, amusement parks, etc.
Source: Edison Electric Institute.

500,000-volt) are being built. The industry is even experimenting with transmission lines that can carry 765,000 and 1 million volts of electricity.[11]

From a cost standpoint, these developments are of crucial significance. As the voltage increases, larger quantities of usable energy can be transmitted over longer distances with a smaller loss of energy. A rule of thumb is as follows: the

11 The American Electric Power Corp. has been authorized by the FPC to construct 153 miles of 765,000-volt transmission line. In addition, construction started late in 1966 on the nation's first extra-high-voltage direct-current transmission line, an 825-mile 800,000-volt line from the Dalles Substation of the Bonneville Power Administration in Oregon to the Sylmar Substation of the Los Angeles Department of Water and Power. A second direct-current line is planned, an 863-mile 800,000-volt line from the Dalles Substation to Hoover Dam. Federal Power Commission, *Annual Report, 1967*, p. 15.

power that a transmission line can carry increases by the square of its voltage. If the voltage is tripled, therefore, a line can carry nine times more power and do so more efficiently. Thus, even though a 345,000-volt line costs four or five times as much as a 115,000-volt line, the cost per kilowatt-hour is approximately half as great due to the greater quantity carried. Further, it is estimated that for every 1,000 volts added to a line's capacity, the distance over which electricity can be economically transmitted is increased by one mile, thereby contributing to more effective interconnections and power pools.[12]

Interconnections and Power Pools. In a previous chapter, it was pointed out that the loads of electric utilities vary from hour to hour, day to day, and season to season.[13] Each electric system must have access to enough power to supply the peak load, even though the peak occurs only for a short period of time once a year, as well as to maintain adequate reserves for emergencies and growth. The peak load for the entire country occurs in the summer, although growth in the use of electricity for heating results in a winter peak that is nearly as great. However, since the diversity factor for each utility system depends on the composition of its customers and its geographical location, different systems usually have different peak periods. Interconnections and pooling enable the industry to reduce the peak load of each system by taking advantage of differing diversity factors, thereby decreasing the amount of generating capacity needed. Put another way, when two or more systems are interconnected, their combined simultaneous peak load is less than the sum of the individual systems' peaks because of the diversity factor. Reserve capacity, which costs money but produces no revenue, can be reduced by interconnections.[14]

Virtually all power generated by the electric power industry is produced by plants which are interconnected in five large networks (Figure 15–2). Each network consists of many systems tied together by interconnections. The largest of these networks (consisting of the Interconnected Systems Group, the Pennsylvania-New Jersey-Maryland Interconnection, and the Canada-U.S. Eastern Interconnection) embraces thirty-nine states and two Canadian provinces, covering the entire United States east of Texas and the Rocky Mountains and much of Eastern Canada. Moreover, a nationwide power grid may not be too many years off. The Pacific Northwest-Pacific Southwest intertie is under construction; a system stretching from the Columbia River to Hoover Dam and Los Angeles, and on to Phoenix. And, early in 1967, an experimental East-West tie was successfully accomplished.[15]

---

[12] Transmission costs as a percentage of total electric utility expenditures rose from about 15 percent in the late 1950's to approximately 22 percent in the mid-1960's, largely due to the growth of pooling and interconnections.

[13] See Chapter 11, pp. 346–48.

[14] The various types of contracts made between interconnected companies are discussed by Vennard, *op. cit.,* pp. 252–54. Also see W. Stewart Nelson, *Mid-Continent Area Power Planners: A New Approach to Planning in the Electric Power Industry* (East Lansing: Michigan State University Public Utilities Studies, 1968).

[15] The experiment involved making interconnections between 209 major publicly owned and privately owned electric utilities; interconnections which linked together some

FIGURE 15-2
Major Areas Served by Interconnected Systems

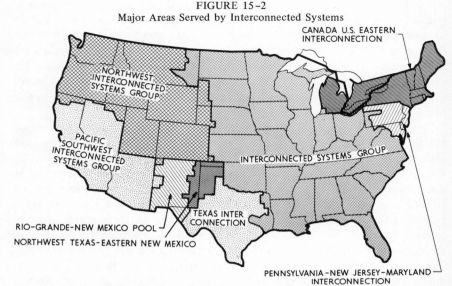

Source: Federal Power Commission, *National Power Survey* (Washington, D.C.: U.S. Government Printing Office, 1964), Vol. I, p. 15.

In addition to interconnections, power pools have been and are being developed throughout the country (Figure 15-3). As explained by Vennard:

Two or more companies may get together and agree to pool their facilities. The combined loads of all the companies in the pool justify building the largest and most efficient generating stations. These pools may take a number of forms.

1. A separate generating company may be formed which is owned by all companies in the pool. The companies then divide up the output of the generating company. The generating company is operated for the maximum benefit to all, and the companies share the savings.

2. Two or more neighboring companies may build a generating station jointly. In this case each company may pay for part of the generating station.

3. A number of companies may agree to pool all of their generating plants and major transmission systems. A committee of engineers plans the requirements of the combined system. In this planning the idea is to build all future plants and transmission lines just as they would be built if one company owned all the facilities. That is to say, they are built for maximum economy regardless of where the plants and lines may be located with respect to the companies' service areas.

265,000 miles of transmission lines in both the United States and Canada and which represented nearly 95 percent of the nation's electrical supply. See Kenneth Holum, "The East-West Electrical Tie Closure," 79 *Public Utilities Fortnightly* 73 (April 27, 1967).

FIGURE 15-3
Major Power Pools

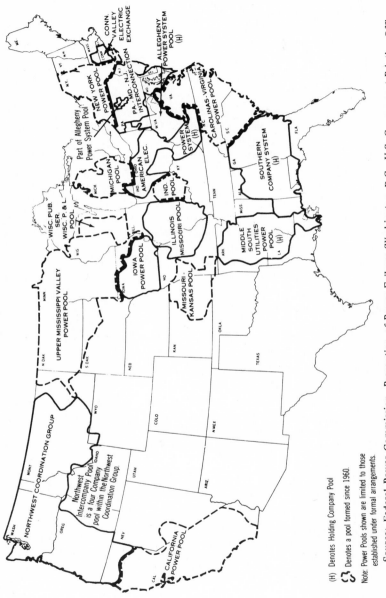

(H) Denotes Holding Company Pool

Denotes a pool formed since 1960.

Note: Power Pools shown are limited to those established under formal arrangements.

Source: Federal Power Commission, *Prevention of Power Failures* (Washington, D.C.: U.S. Government Printing Office, 1967), Vol. I, p. 36.

Each company agrees to pay for construction in its territory, whether it is a power plant or a section of transmission line. Each agrees to operate and maintain the facilities in its territory even though they have been built for the benefit of the whole. A central dispatching office is established, and a central dispatcher operates all power plants in the pool to realize the maximum economy for the whole. A system of payments is worked out so that no company pays more than its share of the costs involved.[16]

With the demand for electricity expected to total more than 2.8 trillion kilowatt-hours by 1980, and 6.7 trillion kilowatt-hours by the end of the century, the advantages of technological developments in the production and transmission of electric power are obvious. But while all major power systems are rapidly becoming capable of operating on an interconnected basis, many believe that the nation's power requirements will be best served by a network of regional pools.

Distribution

Enough has already been said to show that the growth of the electric power industry has given the nation an increasing amount of power, and that Americans have not been slow to use it. Two aspects of distribution, however, deserve examination—electric rates and competition among fuels.

Electric Rates. The trends in electric rates for residential, commercial, and industrial consumers since 1935 are shown in Table 15-5. The relative rate stability is an outstanding characteristic of the electric power industry. While the consumer price index—all items—increased by approximately 150 percent between 1935 and 1967, electric rates (except for industrial service) declined. In large measure, this price behavior simply reflects an expanding industry subject to decreasing costs, but in addition, technological advances have resulted in cost savings greater than the increases in utility costs over the past years.[17]

Retail electric rates vary considerably among states. As of January 1, 1966, the weighted average residential bill for 250 kilowatt-hours of electricity monthly (communities of 2,500 and more population) for each state was $7.34. Average bills ranged from a low of $4.61 (Tennessee) to a high of $10.05

16 Vennard, *op. cit.,* pp. 254–55. "The Pennsylvania-New Jersey-Maryland Interconnection (PJM) is an example of a formal power pool which has gone far toward establishing a mechanism for useful coordination. This pool consists of six full members including one holding company with four operating subsidiaries. In addition, PJM has three associated systems which participate in many of the coordinating functions. The members of PJM coordinate the planning of new generation and transmission facilities. They operate the existing facilities with free flowing ties as though PJM were a single electric system." Federal Power Commission, *Prevention of Power Failures* (Washington, D.C.: U.S. Government Printing Office, 1967), Vol. I, p. 36.

17 See W. Nye Smith, "Economic Evolution of Electric Energy," 71 *Public Utilities Fortnightly* 35 (January 3, 1963); and Federal Power Commission, *Hydroelectric Plant Construction Cost and Annual Production Expenses, 1965* (Washington, D.C.: U.S. Government Printing Office, 1967), and *Steam-Electric Plant Construction Cost and Annual Production Expenses, 1966* (Washington, D.C.: U.S. Government Printing Office, 1967).

TABLE 15-5
Average Bills for Retail Electric Service *

Year	Residential				Commercial 30 Kw., 6,000 Kw.-Hr.	Industrial 1,000 Kw., 200,000 Kw.-Hr.
	250 Kw.-Hr.	500 Kw.-Hr.	750 Kw.-Hr.	1,000 Kw.-Hr.		
1935	$8.91	$13.87	$ ...	$ ...	$182.23	$3,081
1940	7.37	10.55	...	...	170.96	2,828
1945	7.09	10.19	...	...	166.21	2,863
1950	6.98	10.11	...	...	160.75	3,024
1955	7.18	10.30	...	...	159.16	3,168
1960	7.44	10.62	...	...	165.12	3,309
1965	7.38	10.41	14.34	18.59	161.01	3,423
1967	7.37	10.37	14.21	18.32	160.11	3,417
Percent 1967/1935 ...	−17	−25	...	...	−12	+11

*Weighted average bills, based on data for U.S. communities of 2,500 population and more for residential service and 50,000 population and more for commercial and industrial services.
Source: Federal Power Commission, *Annual Report, 1967*, p. 16.

(Alaska).[18] It is clear that the lowest average monthly bills are in those states where public-private power competition is the strongest.

Competition. In 1887, six electric companies were organized in New York City. Five electric companies served Duluth, Minnesota, prior to 1895, while Scranton, Pennsylvania, was being served by four firms in 1906. And in 1907, forty-five electric light firms had the legal right to operate in Chicago.[19] Today, the principle of one utility per market area is well established, although there are exceptions. Both intra- and interindustry competition, however, are of importance, not as regulators of the rate level in the absence of public control but as factors which must be considered in rate making.

The major source of intraindustry competition is public versus private electric power. Private electric utilities (known as investor-owned utilities [20]) are often in direct competition with federal or municipal power projects and cooperatives. The problems arising from this type of competition are discussed later in the chapter. In some instances, where private industrial users have the alternative of supplying electricity for themselves, private utilities have felt compelled to offer lower rates. Indirect competition for industry also is of importance in a few instances. For some industries, such as aluminum, the cost of power is a large item in total production costs.

[18] Federal Power Commission, *Typical Electric Bills, 1966* (Washington, D.C.: U.S. Government Printing Office, 1968), pp. vi, viii.
[19] Burton N. Behling, *Competition and Monopoly in Public Utility Industries* (Urbana: University of Illinois Press, 1938), p. 19.
[20] And, sometimes, referred to as the "I.O.U.s" by their critics. See Lee Metcalf and Vic Reinemer, *Overcharge* (New York: David McKay Co., Inc., 1967).

In recent years, interindustry competition has heightened. Such competition may be between regulated industries (electricity and gas) or between regulated and nonregulated industries (coal and oil). Consider the residential market.[21] Historically, competition between electricity and the fossil fuels in this market has centered on a few household appliances, primarily dryers, ranges, refrigerators, and water heaters. (The electric power industry quickly won the lighting business and, except for gas lighting for decorative purposes, has maintained this business to itself ever since.) The recent competitive struggle has been in three areas. First, there is competition for another appliance: air conditioning. While this area involves competition along traditional lines, it differs from the earlier situations in that gas is invading a market long held by electric power. The gas industry has become a strong competitor for both large installations (e.g., office buildings and shopping centers) and for the household central air conditioning business. And, from the gas industry's point of view, this area offers a major attraction—it represents an ideal load balancer for its winter peak (due to the widespread use of gas for winter space heating). Second, there is competition for the house heating business. Again, this is competition along traditional lines, with electricity invading what was previously an exclusive fuels market. For the electric power industry, this area offers an opportunity to increase consumption to new levels because of the high intensity of use.[22] Third, there is competition for all uses through the "total energy" concept. "Here, for the first time, the electric utilities are facing a type of competition that, when not successfully met, totally eliminates the consumer from the electricity market."[23] Thus, gas turbine generators, by producing on-the-spot electricity, eliminate the need for central-station generated electricity. And there are indications that the competitive battle will continue to intensify in the future. The thermoelectric generator in the furnace is being developed. The fuel cell is being hailed as the "power of the future" and millions of dollars are being expended on its development. If successful, the total energy concept would become a reality for the household market.

Competition in the commercial and industrial markets has also intensified. The alternatives available to the industrial customer have been widened by new technology

> ... beyond the limited one of installing his own generating plant instead of purchasing his power. The possible use of electric resistance heating for glass melting, the electric steel furnace, and the development of solid-state equipment to improve product control and to meet rising specification standards—all have broadened the areas where electric energy and fossil fuels

---

[21] This discussion draws heavily upon Irwin M. Stelzer and Bruce C. Netschert, "Hot War in the Energy Industry," 45 *Harvard Business Review* 14 (November-December, 1967).

[22] "One company reports that average annual consumption for customers using electric heating is 21,959 kwh, compared with 5,842 kwh for customers heating with different fuels." American Electric Power, Inc., *Prospectus*, March 29, 1967, p. 14, as cited in Stelzer and Netschert, *op. cit.*, p. 15.

[23] *Ibid.*, p. 16.

are competitive. The economies of large size and advancing technology have also improved the competitive position of electric energy in satisfying the requirements for heat in a wide range of industrial processes.[24]

Intra- and interindustry competition does not reduce the need for regulation. Competition for industrial users does not protect either residential or commercial consumers. Competition for industry is indirect and confined to those industries for which fuel costs are a large percentage of total production costs. And competition for residential customers is still limited. Nevertheless, limited though it may be, competition is becoming stronger and is a significant factor in rate making, affecting both the development of competitive rates and the use of promotional practices.[25]

Interindustry competition also raises again the long-standing issue of the combination (electric-gas) company. It has been estimated that about one-third of the nation's 26.5 million gas utility customers are served by combination companies.[26] There are many potential cost savings that accrue to combination companies, including fewer administrative jobs and positions; one accounting department; one visit by one meter reader; one bill for both services; and one sales department. A combination company may also be in a better position to provide a balanced service.[27] At the same time, some maintain that these are short-run benefits, and that in the long-run the customer may not gain from combination companies. Such a company may be less aggressive in competitive pricing and promotional activities,[28] and may have "higher costs and higher average selling prices per kilowatt-hour than an enterprise that markets only electricity."[29] Put another way, competition with one's self may not be an adequate substitute for competition between two separate entities.

THE CONSOLIDATION MOVEMENT: THE HOLDING COMPANY

The number of electric systems steadily increased in the United States up to 1917, when a decline set in. The decrease reflects the consolidation

[24] *Ibid.*, p. 20. Also see Alfred M. Casazza, "Competitive Utilities and Happy Investors," 71 *Public Utilities Fortnightly* 19 (March 14, 1963).

[25] Pricing is discussed in Chapter 11; promotional practices in Chapter 7.

[26] Remarks of W. J. Crowley, quoted in 81 *Public Utilities Fortnightly* 47 (March 28, 1968).

[27] ". . . I think honest operators will agree that electricity is better for some [uses] and gas is better for others. This is the story the combination company tells. It offers both, gives honest facts about both on cost and convenience, and is prepared to offer both a price which will be fair and equitable to both the customer and the stockholder. I maintain that this policy will maximize the use of both gas and electricity and will maximize the return on each. In fact, the off-peak sale of either will help the load factor of both." Remarks of F. Eggerstedt, Jr., quoted in *ibid.*, p. 50.

[28] "The 'separate' utility atmosphere is the one where your sales department must learn to sell, rather than make dignified presentations of the merits of both services." Crowley, *op. cit.*, p. 48.

[29] Franklin H. Cook, "Comparative Price Economies of Combination Utilities," 79 *Public Utilities Fortnightly* 31, 38 (January 19, 1967).

movement in this field during the late 1910's and throughout the 1920's. While this movement took place through merger and lease, consolidation by means of the holding company was paramount.[30]

A holding company is an enterprise that owns sufficient stock in another company or in a number of companies so that it may influence the management of the company whose stock it holds (Figure 15-4). Sometimes, the holding company is a stockholding firm entirely and operates no properties directly—a pure holding company. Other holding companies both hold securities and operate some properties in their own names—operating holding companies. By the early 1930's, many electric utility holding companies had assets of $1 billion or more. Further, by 1932, 16 holding companies accounted for 76.4 percent of the energy generated, with three systems (United Corporation, Electric Bond and Share Company, and the Insull interests) accounting for 44.5 percent of the total electricity produced.[31]

Advantages of the Holding Company

The rapid growth of the holding company in the electric utility field was due to a variety of factors. In the main, two sets of forces were dominant. First, the holding company offered certain economies. Second, the holding company offered advantages to its owners which, while often producing harmful effects on the general welfare, encouraged its formation. Some systems (the Electric Bond and Share Company by the General Electric Company) were formed by electrical equipment manufacturers to find markets for their products. Others were organized by investment banking houses (United Corporation by J. P. Morgan and Company) engaged in the flotation of utility securities. Still others were promoted by engineering interests (such as Stone and Webster) which supplied technical services to operating utilities.[32] The basic motive, however, was profit.

Economies. The first advantage of the holding company arises from economies of large scale generation. The introduction of alternating current made it feasible to generate electricity in large central stations and, thereby, to achieve lower costs. In turn, economical service could be rendered over wide areas. Interconnections further increased the service area.[33] In the second place, lower costs of financing were often possible through the holding company. Small companies usually are not well known; buyers for their securities are harder to find. A holding company can sell securities on itself at lower rates of interest and use such funds to buy securities of its operating companies at a lower interest

[30] For a complete discussion of holding companies, see James C. Bonbright and Gardiner C. Means, *The Holding Company* (New York: McGraw-Hill Book Co., Inc., 1932); and Irston R. Barnes, *The Economics of Public Utility Regulation* (New York: F. S. Crofts & Co., 1942), chap. iv.

[31] Barnes, *op. cit.,* p. 85.

[32] *Ibid.,* pp. 66-70.

[33] It should be noted, however, that many holding companies controlled operating companies which were scattered in various parts of the country, making integrated service impossible.

FIGURE 15-4
Electric Bond and Share Company, 1933

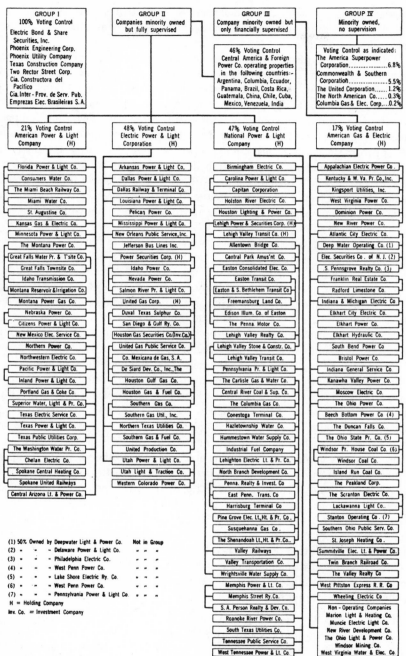

Source: Federal Trade Commission, *Utility Corporations* (Senate Doc. 92, 70th Cong., 1st sess.) (Washington, D.C.: U.S. Government Printing Office, 1935), Part 72-A, Chart II facing p. 88.

rate than if the operating companies tried to find other buyers. As a result, by acting as fiscal agent, holding companies may offer a saving in cost of money to their operating companies.

In the third place, holding companies can perform an engineering and construction service for their operating companies. When the operating companies are small, they cannot afford an engineering staff. Construction jobs come at intervals so that a small operating company cannot be expert in carrying them out. However, a holding company with a large number of operating companies under its control can well afford to set up engineering and construction departments. Hence, if a local company wants to build a new plant, it can turn to its holding company's construction department and be sure that men with continual experience in that line of work will be in charge. Likewise, when an engineering problem arises which the staff of the operating company cannot solve, it can immediately be taken to the holding company's engineering department for solution.

Large scale buying of supplies and equipment has proven to be a fourth source of savings in many fields. A holding company offers an ideal vehicle whereby a number of small companies can pool their purchases. Instead of each company going to a supply house to buy equipment, the orders of all companies are forwarded to the purchasing department of the holding company, which can then afford to go directly to the manufacturers and obtain substantial discounts. Such discounts can be passed on to the operating companies. Finally, many operating companies were originally begun by individuals with little knowledge of the electric utility business. As the field grew, many of these individuals grew with it. They had business ability and a will to keep up with new developments. Their plants were well managed. But a large number of plants were so small that they were unable to offer sufficient financial returns to attract capable managers. A holding company, by combining a number of these poorly managed plants, can group them so that able management may be given to each group. Thus, a holding company, by bringing able managers to the operating companies at a low cost for each such company, may perform a worthwhile service.

Profit Motive. There can be little doubt that the formation of some holding companies was motivated by a desire to achieve economies. But the dominant motive arose from the profits that accrued to users of this system. By facilitating the pyramiding of control, the holding company affords an ideal means for those interested in controlling a large number of companies with a relatively small investment, and in addition, provides a large return on the money invested. Suppose that a holding company is constructed on the following assumptions (Table 15-6):

1. There are 12 operating companies with a total capitalization of $48 million, divided in the following manner: 50 percent in 4 percent bonds, 25 percent in 5 percent preferred stock, and 25 percent in common stock.
2. The operating companies are divided into four groups of three each, with a father holding company over the groups. Each father company owns

TABLE 15-6
Hypothetical Holding Company Pyramid

Company and Capital Structure	Investment	Rate of Return and Its Distribution			
		6 Percent	Per-cent	4 Percent	Per-cent
Operating companies					
50 percent bonds, 4% ...	$24,000,000	$ 960,000	4	$ 960,000	4
25 percent preferred stock, 5%	12,000,000	600,000	5	600,000	5
25 percent common stock	12,000,000	1,320,000	11	360,000	3
Total	$48,000,000	$2,880,000	6	$1,920,000	4
Father holding companies					
50 percent bonds, 4% ...	$ 3,000,000	$ 120,000	4	$ 120,000	4
25 percent preferred stock, 5%	1,500,000	75,000	5	60,000	4
25 percent common stock	1,500,000	465,000	31	...	.
Total	$ 6,000,000	$ 660,000	11	$ 180,000	3
Grandfather holding companies					
50 percent bonds, 4% ...	$ 375,000	$ 15,000	4	...	.
25 percent preferred stock, 5%	187,500	9,375	5	...	.
25 percent common stock	187,500	208,125	111	...	.
Total	$ 750,000	$ 232,500	28	...	.
Great-grandfather holding company					
50 percent bonds, 4% ...	$ 46,875	$ 1,875	4	...	.
25 percent preferred stock, 5%	23,437.50	1,171.88	5	...	.
25 percent common stock	23,437.50	101,015.62	431	...	.
Total	$ 93,750.00	$ 104,062.50	111	...	.

one-half of the common stock of its operating companies, requiring an investment of $1.5 million for each holding company or a total of $6 million for the four. The total capitalization is divided into 50 percent in 4 percent bonds, 25 percent in 5 percent preferred stock, and 25 percent in common stock.

3. The four father companies are now controlled by two grandfather holding companies. Their total capitalization, consisting of one-half of the common stock of the father companies, is $750,000, of which 50 percent is in 4 percent bonds, 25 percent in 5 percent preferred stock, and 25 percent in common stock.

4. A great-grandfather holding company controls the two grandfather companies. Its total capitalization is $93,750, representing one-half of the common stock of the grandfather companies, and is divided into 50 percent of 4 percent bonds, 25 percent of 5 percent preferred stock, and 25 percent in common stock.

If an individual or group owns one-half of the common stock of the great-grandfather company—an investment of $11,718.75—it controls the entire structure. Fanciful? In the case of the Associated Gas and Electric System, erected by H. C. Hopson and Associates, an investment of $300,000 at the top of the structure controlled a utility system having book assets in excess of $1 billion.[34]

The profit potential from the holding company structure also is illustrated in Table 15-6. If the hypothetical pyramid is permitted to earn 6 percent on its investment in the operating properties, then the corresponding return on the common stock of the great-grandfather holding company is 431 percent. Obviously, this is a fantastic rate of return! But large returns were, in fact, earned by several holding companies. According to the Federal Trade Commission, the earnings on the common stocks of five leading holding companies for 1924 and 1925 were as follows: [35]

	1924	1925
American Power & Light Co.	34.8%	40.5%
National Power & Light Co.	16.5	...
North American Co.	28.2	...
Middle West Utilities Co.	19.0	21.5
Standard Gas & Electric Co.	55.2	37.6
Average	30.7	33.2

Even larger profits accrued to the holding companies from their service contracts with operating companies. Again, according to the Federal Trade Commission, the following figures are illustrative: (1) from 1924 to 1929, the Associated Gas and Electric System had net income of $6.5 million for management and construction services alone, representing 193 percent net profit on its service costs; (2) in the same period, Electric Management and Engineering Corporation (owned by National Electric Power Company) received a "minimum" net profit from servicing of $2.9 million or 171 percent net on costs; and (3) from 1924 to 1927, W. S. Barstow and Company, Incorporated, and its subsidiary, W. S. Barstow Management Association, Incorporated, had a combined net income of $4 million or 321 percent on expenses.[36]

[34]Federal Trade Commission, *Utility Corporations* (Senate Doc. 92, 70th Cong., 1st sess.) (Washington, D.C.: U.S. Government Printing Office, 1935), Part 72-A, p. 356.
[35]Federal Trade Commission, *Control of Power Companies* (Senate Doc. 213, 69th Cong., 2d sess.) (Washington, D.C.: U.S. Government Printing Office, 1927), p. 45.
[36]*Utility Corporations, op. cit.,* pp. 662-63.

Holding Company Abuses

While there were advantages to the holding company in the electric utility field, there were also important abuses.[37] Three abuses stand out—pyramiding, write-ups, and excessive service fees.

Pyramiding. Pyramiding itself turned out to be an evil. In the words of the Federal Trade Commission:

> The highly pyramided holding-company group represents the holding-company system at its worst. It is bad in that it allows one or two individuals, or a small coterie of capitalists, to control arbitrarily enormous amounts of investment supplied by many other people. In such a situation few men could be relied on to devote their attention to prudent management of the operating companies, because the speculative element is so overwhelming. It tends, apparently, to make them (1) neglect good management of operating companies, especially by failing to provide for adequate depreciation; (2) exaggerate profits by unsound, deceptive accounting; (3) seek exorbitant profits from service fees from subsidiaries; (4) disburse unearned dividends, because the apparent gains, so obtained, greatly magnify the rate of earnings for the top holding company; and (5) promote extravagant speculation in the prices of such equity stocks on the exchanges. Such concentration of control, even without that speculative pressure, appears objectionable as a matter of sound national welfare . . . . Finally, the exaggerated importance to the top holding company of comparatively small differences in the profit of the operating companies greatly enhances the incentive of the holding company to increase such profits, or to obtain a revenue through the exaction of service and other fees in addition to the ordinary revenue by way of dividends.[38]

The holding company structure is a fair-weather device. Consider again the data shown in Table 15-6. A 6 percent rate of return on the operating companies' investment would yield a 431 percent return on the common stock of the top holding company. But a 4 percent rate of return would not yield even enough revenue to meet the fixed obligations of the father holding company. The entire structure, in other words, would collapse.

Write-ups. Closely connected was a second abuse—excessive write-ups, stock-watering, and inflated capital assets. The Federal Trade Commission estimated that write-ups exceeded $1.4 billion.[39] The Electric Bond and Share Company had total write-ups, for example, of $264 million. Sometimes write-ups occurred when property was purchased, but often they were the result of a revaluation of property already held. Thus, when the Cities Service Power and Light Company was established in 1924 to take over most of the securities held by the Cities Service Company, the former issued $99,999,000 of bonds,

---

[37]The leading source on holding company abuses is *ibid.*
[38]*Ibid.*, p. 860.
[39]*Ibid.*, p. 302.

preferred stock, and common stock against a total investment of $40,057,852, and then recorded the securities on its books at $106,104,403, or at 165 percent more than the amount formerly recorded on the books of Cities Service Company.[40]

These practices alone resulted in higher electric rates to consumers and, due to the stock market crash, financial disaster for millions of investors. From September 1, 1929, to April 15, 1936, 53 holding companies with combined securities of a par value of $1.7 billion went into bankruptcy or receivership. Twenty-three others were forced to default on interest payments or to offer extension plans. As of December 31, 1938, $1.4 billion of a total of $2.5 billion of the preferred stock of holding companies registered with the Securities and Exchange Commission was in arrears in dividends, representing $363 million or 26 percent of the par value of the stock.[41] When the Insull system fell ($238 million investment), holders of debentures received $8.34 per $100 in the final distribution, while other security holders received nothing.[42]

Intracompany Transactions. One of the major abuses of holding companies was charging excessive fees to their operating companies for services rendered. Usually, annual fees were collected in the form of a certain percentage of the operating company's gross revenue, and the resulting fees bore little relationship to the costs of the services furnished. Several examples of excessive fees were given above. Since they were hidden in the costs of the operating companies, excessive fees were covered in setting electric rates and thus paid by the consuming public.

Nor were excessive fees the only source of exploiting operating companies. The operating companies were weakened financially by inadequate depreciation charges, the payment of excessive dividends (sometimes out of capital), and the neglect of annual maintenance. Finally, it should be noted that since the holding company is a corporation separate from the corporation of the operating company whose stock it holds, it is not liable for the debts of the operating company. A holding company thus legally relieves its owners from financial responsibility toward its operating companies.

FEDERAL REGULATION OF ELECTRIC UTILITIES

In Chapter 4, it was pointed out that attempts to regulate private industries by means of the common law, by the terms of franchises and charters, and by ordinances and statutes were unsuccessful. Gradually, therefore, regulation was turned over to state commissions. These commissions, however, were limited in their control of electric utilities in two specific ways: (1) by the development of holding companies and (2) by the interstate transmission of

---

[40]*Ibid.*, pp. 240-41.

[41]Securities and Exchange Commission, *Annual Report, 1943*, p. 25.

[42]Robert H. O'Brien, "Some Current Problems under the Public Utility Holding Company Act," 28 *Public Utilities Fortnightly* 639-47 (1941).

power. State commissions were prohibited for many years from disallowing payments made by operating companies to holding companies in computing expenses unless such payments could be shown as fraudulent. It was not until 1930 that the Supreme Court ruled the commissions could investigate the costs of goods supplied and services rendered to operating companies if the holding companies were intrastate.[43] The largest holding company systems were interstate and not within the jurisdiction of the state commissions. Likewise, state commissions were powerless to regulate interstate transmission of electricity. They could determine the retail rates at which interstate companies sold to local consumers, but not the wholesale rates at which interstate generators sold to local distributors.[44] With the uncovering of holding company abuses, the federal government took steps to remedy these weaknesses in state regulation.

Congress enacted the Public Utility Act (the Wheeler-Rayburn Act) in 1935. Title I of the act increased the jurisdiction of the Securities and Exchange Commission over public utility securities, and gave the commission power to simplify the holding company structures of electric and gas utilities. Title II extended the jurisdiction of the Federal Power Commission over the interstate transmission of electricity.

Holding Companies: Securities and Exchange Commission

Title I, known as the Public Utility Holding Company Act, "was the most stringent corrective measure ever applied to American business."[45] It provided for a broad program of holding company regulation to be carried out under the supervision of the Securities and Exchange Commission.

Legislative Provisions. For purposes of the act, a holding company is defined as any company holding 10 percent or more of the voting stock of another holding company or of a public utility company, or one which has a "controlling influence over the management or policies" of such companies. Congress declared that its policy was to:

1. . . . eliminate the evils . . . connected with public utility holding companies which are engaged in interstate commerce.
2. . . . compel the simplification of public utility holding company systems. . . .
3. . . . provide as soon as practicable for the elimination of public utility holding companies except as otherwise expressly provided in this title.

The act contained many provisions aimed at eliminating holding company evils. The issuing of new securities by interstate holding companies was put under the control of the SEC. The commission was given a large degree of veto power over the purchase and sale of assets by holding companies. With certain

[43]*Smith* v. *Illinois Bell Telephone Co.*, 282 U.S. 133 (1930).
[44]*Rhode Island Public Utilities Comm.* v. *Attleboro Steam and Electric Co.*, 273 U.S. 83 (1927).
[45]Clair Wilcox, *Public Policies Toward Business* (3d ed.; Homewood, Ill.: Richard D. Irwin, Inc., 1966), p. 366.

exceptions, before a holding company may purchase other securities or property in another company it must file with the commission a detailed statement of its proposed purchase. If the proposal tends toward "economical and efficient development of an integrated public utility system" and its terms are such as to protect investors and consumers, it is to be approved by the commission. Otherwise, the SEC may state such changes in the proposed acquisition as it deems "necessary . . . in the public interest." Interstate commerce loans must conform to "such rules and regulations . . . as the commission deems necessary. . . ." Payment of dividends by registered holding companies or any subsidiary company must conform to the commission's requirements. All service contracts were brought under the control of the SEC. And, finally, the commission was given power to prescribe the form and manner of accounting to be used by registered holding companies, affiliates of such companies, service companies, and "every person whose principle business is the performance of . . . contracts for public utility or holding companies."[46]

The Death Sentence Clause. The major corrective provision of the 1935 act is contained in Section 11, which reads, in part:

> It shall be the duty of the Commission, as soon as practicable after January 1, 1938:
>
> (1) To require by order, after notice and opportunity for hearings, that each registered holding company, and each subsidiary company thereof, shall take such action as the Commission shall find necessary to limit the operations of the holding-company system of which such company is a part to a single integrated public-utility system, and to such other businesses as are reasonably incidental, or economically necessary or appropriate to the operations of such integrated public-utility system. . . .
>
> (2) To require by order, after notice and opportunity for hearing, that each registered holding company, and each subsidiary company thereof, shall take steps as the Commission shall find necessary to ensure that the corporate structure or continued existence of any company in the holding-company system does not unduly or unnecessarily complicate the structure, or unfairly or inequitably distribute voting power among security holders, of such holding-company system. In carrying out the provisions of this paragraph the Commission shall require each registered holding company (and any company in the same holding-company system with such holding company) to take such action as the Commission shall find necessary in order that such holding company shall cease to be a holding company with respect to each of its subsidiary companies which itself has a subsidiary company which is a holding company. . . .

Thus, the act provides that all holding companies more than twice removed from their operating subsidiaries are to be abolished. This requirement is the famous "death sentence" clause of the Public Utility Act.

The constitutionality of the act was immediately challenged. The SEC

---

[46] See Securities and Exchange Commission, *General Rules and Regulations under the Public Utility Holding Company Act of 1935* (Washington, D.C.: U.S. Government Printing Office, 1963).

brought suit to compel the Electric Bond and Share Company to register, and the Supreme Court upheld the registration requirements.[47] The North American Company resisted reorganization, contending that the death sentence clause exceeded the powers of Congress under the commerce clause and that it deprived the company of property without due process of law. The Supreme Court rejected these arguments.[48] Finally, the American Power and Light Company contested the simplification of its corporate structure, using the same arguments advanced by the North American Company, as well as the contention that the law involved an unconstitutional delegation of legislative power. Again, the Supreme Court upheld the act.[49]

Developments under the Act. The commission's approach to its task of simplifying holding company structures was one of caution. It invited the companies affected to submit their own reorganization plans. It was not until 1940, therefore, that formal proceedings began. During the period June 15, 1938, to June 30, 1962, 2,419 electric and gas utilities and natural gas pipeline companies came under the jurisdiction of the commission either as registered holding companies or as subsidiaries thereof. Of these companies, 928, with assets aggregating approximately $13 billion, were subject to divestiture.[50]

In compliance with the act, the SEC sought to establish integrated systems which were confined to a single area.[51] Further, the commission basically followed a "one-area rule," limiting a holding company to controlling only one utility system. Two systems could be controlled if three conditions were satisfied: (1) such control was needed to preserve substantial economies; (2) the systems were located in one state, in adjoining states, or in a contiguous foreign country; and (3) the resulting holding company was not so large as to impair the advantages of local management, efficient operation, or effective regulation.[52] The commission opposed the common control of electric and gas utilities unless it could be shown that there were substantial economies of joint operation.[53] It

[47]*Electric Bond & Share Co.* v. *Securities and Exchange Comm.,* 303 U.S. 419 (1938).

[48]*North American Co.* v. *Securities and Exchange Comm.,* 327 U.S. 686 (1946).

[49]*American Power & Light Co.* v. *Securities and Exchange Comm.,* 329 U.S. 90 (1946).

[50]Securities and Exchange Commission, *Twenty-Eighth Annual Report* (1962), pp. 82–84. Of the remaining companies, 793 were released from the commission's jurisdiction as the result of dissolutions, mergers, and consolidations, and 514 by exemption. As of mid-1966, only 26 holding companies were registered under the act. Securities and Exchange Commission, *Thirty-Second Annual Report* (1966), pp. 76–78.

[51]Robert Blum, "SEC Integration of Holding Company Systems," 17 *Journal of Land & Public Utility Economics* 423 (1941).

[52]L. T. Fournier, "Simplification of Holding Companies," 13 *Journal of Land & Public Utility Economics* 138 (1937); *Re The Northern Natural Gas Co.,* Holding Company Act Release No. 5657 (1945); and *Re American Gas & Electric Co.,* Holding Company Act Release No. 6333 (1945).

[53]*Re Columbia Gas & Electric Corp.,* 8 SEC 443 (1941); *Re The United Gas Improvement Co.,* 9 SEC 52 (1941); *Re Philadelphia Co.,* 28 SEC 35 (1948), *aff'd,* 177 F. 2d 720 (1949); and *Re New England Electric System,* Holding Company Act Release No. 15035 (1964), *vacated,* 346 F. 2d 399 (1965), *rev'd and rem'd,* 384 U.S. 176 (1966), *vacated,* 376 F. 2d 107 (1967).

also opposed the ownership by a utility company of a nonutility enterprise unless that enterprise was "reasonably incidental, or economically necessary or appropriate to the operation of" an integrated utility system.[54]

The method by which divestiture was to be achieved was not specified in the act. Some holding companies sold all or part of their security holdings on the open market. Some sold their properties or securities to other holding companies. Independent companies and local governments purchased property in several instances. Securities of some operating companies were distributed to the stockholders of the holding company. Whatever the method, the SEC encouraged voluntary compliance, but under its supervision.

Finally, the SEC was also authorized by the Public Utility Act to reorganize the capital structures of utility companies. Specifically, capital structures were scaled down by eliminating write-ups and by replacing debt and preferred stock with common stock. It has been estimated that long-term debt for 10 large holding company systems decreased from $526 million to $268 million in the period 1934 to 1944.[55] The commission required, and continues to require, competitive bidding for new security issues. And, especially when a company was in arrears of preferred stock dividends, voting rights were redistributed to reduce the control of common stockholders who had small investments in a holding company.[56]

The Public Utility Holding Company Act represents the most stringent law ever passed by Congress. By reorganizing the electric utility holding companies, a major obstacle to effective regulation of rates and service by state and federal commissions was removed. It must not be inferred, however, that the effects of the holding company systems were entirely adverse or that the commission was completely successful in establishing economical integrated systems. It is undoubtedly true that the electric power industry today is far more advanced because of contributions made by the early empire builders.[57] Moreover, as Troxel has pointed out, the commission made mistakes.

Emphasizing physical and geographic conditions, the SEC did not make careful cost studies as integrated operating systems were chosen. The most economical combinations of operating properties were not prescribed. Per-

[54] *Re The North American Co.,* 11 SEC 194 (1942); *Re Peoples Light & Power Co.,* 13 SEC 81 (1943); and *Re Cities Service Co.,* Holding Company Act Release No. 5028 (1944).

[55] R. A. Finlayson, "The Public Utility Holding Company," 19 *Journal of Business,* Part 2, p. 27 (1946). Also see Melvin G. Dakin, "Public Utility Debt Ratios and the Public Interest—Reasonable Fixed Charges and Just and Reasonable Rates," 15 *Vanderbilt Law Review* 195 (1961).

[56] E. M. Dodd, "Fair and Equitable Recapitalization," 55 *Harvard Law Review* 780 (1942), and "Relative Rights of Preferred and Common Stockholders in Recapitalization Plans under the Holding Company Act." 57 *ibid.* 295 (1944); and S. H. Galfand, "Determination of Common Stock Participation in Plans under Section 11 (e) of the Public Utility Holding Company Act," 93 *University of Pennsylvania Law Review* 308 (1945).

[57] See Forrest McDonald, *Insull* (Chicago: University of Chicago Press, 1962).

haps some systems represented the most economical units; others probably were smaller or larger than the economic optimums. The SEC could not be expected to make perfect choices. Careful cost studies took much time, were expensive, and were possible sources of extensive litigation. An optimum choice under current technical conditions could be upset by future technical changes. And a thorough integration necessitated a break-up of operating systems—a reshuffling of generating plants, transmission lines, and distribution systems in the electric industry. The SEC brought integration down to the level of the state commission. If operating properties, too, were carefully integrated, the state commissions were the proper authorities for the job. Neither the state legislatures nor state commissions showed any interest, however, in a reorganization of operating plants and marketing areas.[58]

Regulation of Electricity: Federal Power Commission

The Federal Power Commission has a twofold task with respect to its control of electricity—control of hydroelectric projects on federal waterways and control of interstate transmission of electricity.

Hydroelectric Projects. In 1920, the Federal Power Commission was created under the Federal Water Power Act to regulate construction and operation of hydroelectric projects on navigable domestic waterways.[59] Jurisdiction over such waters results from the government's ownership of vast areas of land and from subsequent Court interpretations of the commerce clause.[60] The commission consisted of the Secretaries of Agriculture, Interior, and War. But since the cabinet members were preoccupied with their own departmental duties and the commission was without its own staff, this structure proved to be unsatisfactory.[61] In 1930, the law was amended, providing for appointment of five full-time commissioners and a full-time staff.

A license must be obtained from the commission before a power plant can be constructed on a federal navigable waterway.[62] There are four types of licenses: the preliminary permit (not to exceed three years, during which time

---

[58] Emery Troxel, *Economics of Public Utilities* (New York: Holt, Rinehart & Winston, Inc., 1947), p. 189.

[59] Prior to 1920, licenses for such projects were granted by special acts of Congress.

[60] See *Gibbons* v. *Ogden,* 22 U.S. 1 (1824); and *United States* v. *River Rouge Co.,* 269 U.S. 411 (1926). The Supreme Court has defined navigable waters broadly to include streams that are not used by commercial traffic (*United States* v. *Utah,* 283 U.S. 64, 83 [1931]), waterways that would be navigable if improvements were undertaken (*United States* v. *Appalachian Electric Power Co.,* 311 U.S. 377, 407 [1940]), and nonnavigable tributaries of navigable streams *(ibid.).*

[61] "With all due respect to them, Congress might just as well have put the King of England, Mussolini, and Albert Einstein on the commission so far as any spontaneous, decisive action originating with the commissioners is concerned." Congressman Celler as quoted in Bernard Schwartz, *The Professor and the Commissions* (New York: Alfred A. Knopf, 1959), p. 33.

[62] When a stream over which Congress has jurisdiction is involved, a declaration of intention must be filed first. The commission undertakes an investigation of the proposed project, and if it finds that interstate or foreign commerce will be affected, a license must be obtained before construction can commence.

the applicant has priority with respect to a proposed project while doing the preliminary work prior to filing an application for a license), the major license (not to exceed fifty years), the minor license (projects having an installed capacity of more than 100 horsepower, but not exceeding 2,000 horsepower), and the minor-part license (a minor part of a complete project or a complete project of less than 100 horsepower of installed capacity). The major licensee agrees to (*a*) keep his plant in good condition; (*b*) follow a prescribed accounting system; (*c*) make annual payments toward the costs of administration and "for the use, occupancy, and enjoyment" of United States land or other property; and (*d*) accept the rate, service, and security regulations of the commission where no state has jurisdiction or where states surrounding the federal waterway being developed find themselves unable to reach agreement on such regulation. At the end of the license period, the license may be renewed with the original company or granted to a new company, or the government can take over the project—except for state and municipal projects—by paying the net investment cost plus reasonable severance damages. During the first twenty years of a license, and if the states have not undertaken regulation, the licensee must make payments to the United States "for the expropriation to the Government of excessive profits." After the first twenty years, the licensee must establish an amortization reserve for the accumulation of excess earnings, that is, earnings which exceed the rate of return on net investment as specified in the license.[63] In granting a major license, the commission is to give priority to applications made by local and state governments, and is to consider how the project will affect the conservation and utilization of the region's water resources for all purposes, such as power, flood control, navigation, and irrigation.

As of June 30, 1967, 599 licenses were in effect: 324 for major projects, 61 for minor projects, 26 for minor-part projects, and 188 for projects involving transmission lines that cross federal lands.[64] The major projects represent 20.2 million kilowatts of generating capacity in service and a potential additional 14 million kilowatts. The total cost of ultimate installations is estimated at over $7 billion. Six preliminary permits also were in effect, involving proposed installations totaling 714,000 kilowatts.

As most states have regulatory commissions, the FPC's authority to regulate the rates, services, and securities of its licensees is limited. The commission has prescribed and enforced a uniform system of accounting. It has enforced the requirement regarding amortization and has made periodic inspections of all projects to insure compliance with license terms. It has ordered 186 net investment cost studies, resulting in disallowance of $71.2 million of a total claimed cost of $2.2 billion as involving write-ups, expenses improperly charged

---

[63] The reserve, in the discretion of the commission, is to be held until the termination of the license or to be applied from time to time in reduction of the net investment. The amortization reserve existing when the license expires serves to reduce the sum payable by the federal government if it decides to take over the project.

[64] All data are from Federal Power Commission, *Annual Report, 1967*, p. 26. Rights-of-way involving transmission lines that cross federal lands are discussed below, on pp. 584–85.

to capital accounts, and so forth. The commission has collected nearly $11.7 million for headwater benefits provided by federally owned improvements. And the FPC is still involved in the task, begun in 1962, of licensing some 500 pre-1935 hydroelectric projects.

Two aspects of the commission's licensing authority deserve brief mention. First, Section 10 (a) of the Federal Power Act requires the commission to take into consideration "recreational purposes" in granting a hydroelectric power project license.[65] For many years this mandate was carried out by including "general terms and conditions in licenses requiring free public access and use of project property for recreational purposes, and facilities for conservation of fish and wildlife resources."[66] Since 1963, however, this aspect of licensing has assumed greater importance. Beginning in that year, the FPC issued a series of orders designed to require license applicants "to develop—in consultation with appropriate Federal, State, and local agencies—a comprehensive program for utilizing project properties for outdoor recreation and for enhancement of fish and wildlife resources."[67] Subsequent court decisions have broadened the phrase "recreational purposes" to encompass the conservation of natural resources, the maintenance of natural beauty, and the preservation of historic sites.[68] Thus, if overhead transmission structures would cause scenic damage, the commission must weigh the aesthetic advantages of underground lines against the cost disadvantages.[69] As the Supreme Court stated in remanding a licensing case to the commission in 1967: in licensing proceedings, the FPC should keep in mind that, "in our affluent society, the cost of a project is only one of several factors to be considered."[70] While under this interpretation of the licensing provisions "it is no longer possible for a utility to commit a long-range harm to society for a short-run profit, assuming that hydroelectric dams will no longer be considered to be economically feasible within a decade or two,"[71] the interpretation adds another complexity to the licensing process.[72]

[65] Section 10 (a) provides: "That the project adopted, including the maps, plans, and specifications, shall be such as in the judgment of the commission will be best adapted to a comprehensive plan for improving or developing a waterway or waterways for the use or benefit of interstate or foreign commerce, for the improvement and utilization of water power development, and for other beneficial public uses, including recreational purposes."

[66] Federal Power Commission, *Annual Report, 1967,* p. 27.

[67] *Ibid.* See *Re License Applications,* 29 FPC 777 (1963); *Re Hydroelectric Licenses—Applications—Recreational Plan Exhibits,* 33 FPC 32 (1965); and *Re Recreational Development at Licensed Projects,* FPC Order No. 313 (1965).

[68] See *Scenic Hudson Preservation Conference* v. *Federal Power Comm.,* 354 F. 2d 608 (1965); and *Udall* v. *Federal Power Comm.,* 358 F. 2d 840 (1966), *rev'd and rem'd,* 387 U.S. 428 (1967).

[69] See Samuel G. Miller, "Electric Transmission Lines—To Bury, Not To Praise," 12 *Villanova Law Review* 497 (1967).

[70] *Udall* v. *Federal Power Comm., op. cit.,* p. 435.

[71] Franklin H. Cook, "Utility Mergers and the Public Interest," 82 *Public Utilities Fortnightly* 35, 40 (August 29, 1968). Also see "Storm King Pumped-storage Project Advances," 82 *ibid.* 42 (August 29, 1968).

[72] There are many other environmental problems confronting the industry. Concern over thermal and air pollution resulted in the enactment of legislation in 1965 (Water Quality Act) and in 1967 (Air Quality Act), while concern over beautification has

Second, licenses for ten projects subject to recapture expired in the period 1966 through 1968; licenses for sixty-nine additional projects expire in the period 1969 through 1974.[73] The Federal Power Act provides for either recapture or relicensing of these major hydroelectric projects. Recapture can only be exercised by Congress. The disposition of expiring licenses for the larger projects could become a highly controversial issue, although the FPC has indicated that if the existing licensee can meet the statutory standards as well as any other applicant, the renewal license should be issued to the original licensee. The criteria used by Congress for recapturing projects and by the FPC for relicensing projects will be crucial. Procedures have been established,[74] and the commission has recommended against recapture of 25 projects.[75] But neither the FPC nor Congress has determined the relevant criteria to be used.

---

resulted in new efforts to redesign overhead transmission facilities and to underground new distribution lines. The industry, moreover, is seeking closer cooperation with "those who are responsible for the development of community and regional plans. More importantly, utilities are pursuing consultations with those who have responsibilities in the fields of conservation, recreation, natural beauty, and air and water quality, all directed more effectively to relate the industry's programs to these disciplines and the national goals to assure a healthy and more beautiful America." Lelan F. Sillin, Jr., " 'Don't Put It Here!'–Natural Resources, Utilities, Pollution, and Beautification," 82 *Public Utilities Fortnightly* 76, 77 (September 12, 1968). Also see Federal Power Commission, Staff Report, *Air Pollution and the Regulated Electric Power and Natural Gas Industries* (Washington, D.C., 1968); *The Electric Utility Industry and the Environment* (A Report to the Citizens Advisory Committee on Recreation and Natural Beauty by the Electric Utility Industry Task Force on Environment) (New York, 1968); and Working Committee on Utilities, *Report to the Vice President and to the President's Council on Recreation and Natural Beauty* (Washington, D.C., 1968).

[73] For a list of these projects, see Federal Power Commission, *Annual Report, 1965*, pp. 66–68, *Annual Report, 1967*, pp. 28–29, and *Annual Report, 1968*, pp. 32–33.

[74] The FPC's procedures with respect to hydroelectric project licenses involve the following steps: (1) the annual publication of a table of expiring licenses subject to recapture within five years; (2) a request to other agencies for their comments five years prior to expiration; (3) the gathering of information from present licensees of their future development plans, including financing, rates, and taxes five years before expiration; and (4) a recommendation to Congress advising it on recapture two years before expiration. *Re Hydroelectric Project Licenses*, 55 PUR 3d 113 (1964). In a 1968 order, the FPC specified that the net investment in a licensed hydroelectric power project shall be the actual legitimate original cost of the project (less retirements, plus additions and betterments) less both accumulated depreciation and all accumulated project excess earnings. *Re Net Investment Hydroelectric Projects*, FPC Order No. 370 (1968). See J. David Mann, Jr., and John C. Mason, "Retroactive Devaluation of Our Hydro Power Projects," 83 *Public Utilities Fortnightly* 13 (January 2, 1969).

In 1968, Congress enacted legislation that (1) prohibits the FPC from relicensing any project it decides should be recaptured; (2) requires the commission to submit its comments and recommendations to Congress; (3) provides that any federal department or agency may recommend recapture and, thereby, cause a stay of the effective date of any relicensing order, up to two years, if the FPC does not recommend recapture; and (4) authorizes the relicensing of obsolete projects for nonpower purposes, subject to regulatory supervision by a state, municipal, or federal agency. Public Law 90-451 (1968).

[75] Twenty-two of the licenses involved small projects (installed capacities of less than 2,000 horsepower). Of the other three, the largest involved the 66,000 kilowatt Bucks Creek project of Pacific Gas & Electric Co. *Re Pacific Gas & Electric Co.*, Project No. 619 (1967).

In addition to its licensing duties, the FPC has made several investigations and reports on the use of water resources in various regions, the waterpower industry, and waterpower sites, and maintains a current inventory of information on developed and undeveloped hydroelectric power resources in the United States. The Chairman of the commission is a member of the Water Resources Council, a council established under the Water Resources Planning Act of 1965 to coordinate the activities of federal agencies engaged in water and land resources planning and development.[76] Finally, the commission, in December, 1964, issued a comprehensive survey of the nation's future power supply (discussed below).

Interstate Transmission. Title II of the Public Utility Act of 1935 gave the Federal Power Commission broad authority over the interstate transmission of electricity. In all those matters in which existing state regulation has proven ineffective or unconstitutional, the commission was authorized to regulate rates and earnings, prescribe an accounting system, control the issuance of securities, mergers, and transfers of facilities, prevent interlocking officers and directors, and "to divide the country into regional districts for the voluntary interconnection and coordination of facilities for the generation, transmission and sale of electric energy." On application of a state commission or of any person engaged in either transmission or sale of electric energy, if such action is in the public interest and does not involve an enlargement of generating facilities, the commission may "direct a public utility to establish physical connection of its transmission facilities with the facilities of one or more other persons . . . to sell energy to or exchange energy with such persons." The commission also has responsibility for approving the rate schedules of public power sold by four marketing agencies—Southeastern Power Administration, Southwestern Power Administration, Bonneville Power Administration, and Bureau of Reclamation (Figure 15–5).

Until recently, few complaints had been filed with the commission, and few investigations had been undertaken on its own initiative. The most important activity of the FPC to date with respect to wholesale electric regulation has been its establishment of a uniform system of accounts—an activity which it has vigorously enforced. It also has cooperated with numerous state commissions in resolving common regulatory problems. But by its own admission, the commission's "function of regulating interstate wholesale electric rates has not received the attention it deserves."[77]

[76] Public Law 89-80 (1965). The council, which replaced the informal Inter-Agency Committee on Water Resources, is composed of six full members (the Secretaries of the Interior; Agriculture; Army; Health, Education, and Welfare; and Transportation; and the Chairman of the Federal Power Commission), two associate members (the Secretaries of Commerce and of Housing and Urban Development), and interested observers (the Bureau of the Budget and the Attorney General). Four regional river basin committees and several coordinating committees have been established, with membership containing both state and federal agencies.

[77] Federal Power Commission, *Annual Report, 1962,* p. 69. Also see Donald C. Cook, "Special Problems of Electric Regulation," Part I, 74 *Public Utilities Fortnightly* 19 (November 5, 1964), Part II, 74 *ibid.* 30 (November 19, 1964).

FIGURE 15–5
Federal Marketing Areas

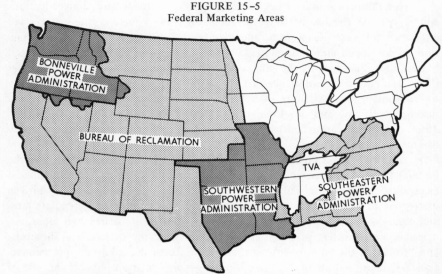

Source: Federal Power Commission, *Prevention of Power Failures* (Washington, D.C.: U.S. Government Printing Office, 1967), Vol. I, p. 33.

In 1962, the FPC reorganized its Bureau of Power with the view of strengthening its regulation of interstate electric activities. The following year, it initiated a program of reviewing all electric rate schedules on file and revised its regulations governing electric rate filings, thereby requiring more detailed cost data. Proposed rate increases filed with the commission were suspended and hearings ordered. Proceedings were initiated by the commission to determine its jurisdiction; subsequent court challenges of its findings were unsuccessful.[78] The net result has been a significant increase in both filings and decisions on interstate rates. In fiscal year 1962, the commission received 477 wholesale electric rate filings, compared with 1,295 in fiscal year 1964 and 2,006 in fiscal year 1967. In the latter year, it approved rate schedules providing for reductions of nearly $4.3 million (of which 30 percent resulted from commission action) and increases of $93,241. At the end of the same year, the commission had forty-two rate studies in progress.[79]

The National Power Survey. Section 202 (a) of the Federal Power Act directs the commission, for "the purpose of assuring an abundant supply of electric energy throughout the United States with the greatest possible economy

[78] See Chapter 4, pp. 117–18.

[79] Federal Power Commission, *Annual Report, 1967,* p. 19. See J. Rhoads Foster, Paul J. Garfield, and Henry Herz, "FPC Regulation of Electric Energy at Wholesale," 51 *Virginia Law Review* 76 (1965); Harry A. Poth, Jr., "Recent Trends in FPC Electric Rate Regulation," 78 *Public Utilities Fortnightly* 25 (August 4, 1966); and Harry W. Keidan, "FPC Cost-of-Service Studies–Electric," 79 *ibid.* 39 (January 5, 1967).

and with regard to the proper utilization and conservation of natural resources," to "divide the country into regional districts for the voluntary interconnection and coordination of facilities for the generation, transmission, and sale of electric energy.... It shall be the duty of the Commission to promote and encourage such interconnection and coordination...." In January, 1962, the commission undertook a nationwide study to aid in carrying out these statutory requirements by developing guidelines for the growth of the electric power industry to 1980. In the FPC's words:

> The goals of the Survey include the development of the need for additional power supply in 1970, 1975, and 1980, and the delineation of means for supplying these additional power needs, taking into consideration general locations and sizes of new plants, relative construction costs, loads, diversities, and other factors. The general outline, including extra-high-voltage transmission facilities, will serve as a nationwide plan providing a framework within which regional and system developments can proceed. The plan will be entirely voluntary. However, the entire power industry in the years to come will benefit from the goals and guides developed by the plan.[80]

The commission established 13 committees with 134 members and advisers representing all segments of the electric power industry, public and private, to study the economic, technological, and legal problems pertinent to the objectives of the Survey. Two dozen advisory committee reports were issued, covering such topics as rate regulation and power pooling agreements, methods of carrying and reducing peak loads, determination of reserve capacity requirements for interconnected systems, forecasts of electric power requirements to 1980, nuclear power developments, and fuels for electric generation. These advisory committee reports were published along with the commission's final report in December, 1964.[81]

The Survey's basic finding is that each of the nation's 3,600 power systems can achieve savings in the costs of generation and transmission of electricity by moving from "isolated or segmented operations, and from existing pools of limited scope, to participation in fully coordinated power networks covering broad areas of the country." The program of coordination outlined by the Survey is designed to meet the nation's estimated annual requirements of 2.8 trillion kilowatt-hours by 1980, more than 2½ times the estimated 1964 total of 1.1 trillion. To produce this energy, the commission notes, the electric power industry will need to add nearly 325 million kilowatts to present installed capacity. The coordinated development proposed, in the absence of further price inflation, could bring about an $11.7 billion savings in plant investment and annual net savings to customers of $11 billion by 1980. Such savings would amount to a reduction of nearly 27 percent in the current cost of electricity,

[80] Federal Power Commission, *Annual Report, 1962*, p. 56.
[81] *National Power Survey, op. cit.* Volume I contains the main report of the commission; Volume II the 24 advisory committee reports and a report on defense implications of the Survey.

resulting in an average unit price of 1.2 cents per kilowatt-hour (as compared with 2.7 cents in 1926 and 1.7 cents in 1962). The target is realistic, argues the commission, because of the economic and technical developments of the electric power industry (as outlined above)—developments that justify a greater degree of coordination than now exists and coordination that will require, in turn, reliance on larger and more efficient generating units connected by means of tie lines (extra-high-voltage transmission lines). In short, the Survey emphasizes that coordinated growth is necessary to meet future power requirements at minimum costs.

The Survey's program, however, raises several important problems which must be resolved before such coordination becomes a reality. To mention but three of these problems: in pooling participation, how are the economic advantages, in terms of taxes and subsidies, to be equalized when publicly-owned or cooperatives' facilities are involved? Can electric companies enter into the formation of power pools or transmission and exchange agreements envisioned in the Survey without violating the antitrust laws? Can the targets set by the Survey best be achieved by regional coordination, as is occurring voluntarily at the present time, or by longer east-west tie lines, as proposed by the commission? The solution to these and other problems may require further legislation.

The Survey, predictably, has met with mixed reactions. Some have argued that the estimated reduction in annual power costs by 1980 is too optimistic;[82] others have expressed fear that the commission will seek new regulatory authority to help shape the future growth and structure of the industry along the lines suggested in the Survey (see below). But while its impact on the electric power industry will not be known for several years, the *National Power Survey* represents a significant undertaking. For one of the few times, all segments of the industry worked together on a common project, thereby leading to better understanding of each other's problems. Regulatory agencies have been criticized frequently for failing to formulate long-range policies and plans. By undertaking the Survey, the FPC is seeking to aid both the industry in meeting its future requirements as efficiently as possible and the commission in carrying out its regulatory functions. Concluded the commission: "It is hoped that this Survey will serve to accelerate interest in more comprehensive industry planning and will direct the attention of all systems in every segment of the industry to the attainable levels of achievement and the relative significance of the various avenues for realizing economic gains for their systems and their customers."[83]

---

[82] But see Joseph C. Swidler, "A Look at National Power Survey Projections," 80 *Public Utilities Fortnightly* 15 (December 7, 1967).

[83] *National Power Survey, op. cit.,* Vol. I, p. 288. See William R. Hughes, "Regulation and Technological Destiny: The National Power Survey," 55 *American Economic Review, Papers and Proceedings* 330 (1966).

The FPC has established six Regional Advisory Committees, composed of representatives from all segments of the electric power industry, to "assist the Commission and the Executive Advisory Committee in its work with and for the Commission and specifically in encouraging the utility systems in each Region to pursue courses of action

Reliability. The Northeast power failure of November 9–10, 1965, and the extensive power interruption in the Pennsylvania-New Jersey-Maryland Interconnection on June 5, 1967, dramatically raised the issue of reliability.[84] Interconnections among electric utility systems offer many economic advantages and interties have progressed rapidly, but the commission's power to require interconnections is limited. To prevent a failure in one part of a system from "cascading" or "snowballing" into other parts, coordinated planning, design, construction, and operation of generating and transmission facilities is required. The issue involves the means of carrying out such coordination.

The Federal Power Commission has recommended to Congress that it be given authority:

(a) to establish regional planning councils, including all segments of the electric utility industry (public, private, cooperative and Federal), to review, test and coordinate plans for bulk power facilities throughout a region, and to disclose electric utility planning to the view of federal and state agencies and the public;

(b) to enable the Commission, with the advice of the regional councils, to establish minimum reliability standards;

(c) to provide for Commission review of extra-high-voltage transmission lines to insure their consistency with high standards of reliability, usefulness, efficient utilization of land and conservation of historic sites and other limited resources; and

(d) to authorize the Commission to require interconnections between bulk power suppliers and to review proposals to abandon bulk power services.[85]

In support of such legislation, the FPC has noted that the structure of the electric power industry includes hundreds of large and small utilities, privately, publicly, cooperatively, and federally owned. The investor-owned utilities have been reluctant to permit participation by small systems (mostly publicly owned) in interconnection contracts and in new generating units, primarily because of the variations in taxes, financing, and earnings requirements of different

---

consistent with the broad goals of the National Power Survey, in reporting the progress being made in attaining these goals, and in up-dating the guidelines of the Survey." FPC Order dated January 10, 1966. See *Electric Power in the Northeast, 1970-1980-1990* (A Report to the Federal Power Commission Prepared by the Northeast Regional Advisory Committee) (Washington, D.C., 1968).

[84] ". . . [T]he term 'reliability' means the ability of a utility system or group of systems to maintain the supply of power. Reliability is gauged by the infrequency of interruption, the size of the area affected, and the quickness with which the bulk power supply is restored if interrupted." *Prevention of Power Failures, op. cit.*, Vol. I, p. xiii. On the two major failures, see Federal Power Commission, *Northeast Power Failure* (Washington, D.C.: U.S. Government Printing Office, 1965) and *Power Interruption, Pennsylvania-New Jersey-Maryland Interconnection* (Washington, D.C., 1968).

[85] Federal Power Commission, *Annual Report, 1967*, p. 5. See *Electric Power Reliability* (Hearings before the Committee on Commerce, Senate, 90th Cong., 1st and 2d sess.) (Washington, D.C.: U.S. Government Printing Office, 1968), Parts 1–3.

systems.[86] The necessary coordination, however, "extends beyond the boundaries of a corporate or other entity, an area or even a region."[87] Further, even though the proposed coordinating mechanisms might require some surrender of management prerogatives, "No management can avoid its share of the responsibility for building adequate interconnected transmission systems."[88]

The industry, particularly the investor-owned utilities, maintains that such massive federal encroachment is unnecessary and undesirable. It is unnecessary because many small systems have been taken into interconnections and pools, while a National Electric Reliability Council (representing twelve regional utility coordinating organizations) has been formed to augment the reliability of bulk power supply in the United States and part of Canada and to maintain liaison with the FPC. It is undesirable because the "administrative procedures through which the FPC acts are not adaptable to the fast and flexible decisions required for proper planning and operation."[89] And, finally, the industry points to its record: "Over the past ten years, on the average, our customers have received uninterrupted electric service 99.98 per cent of the time."[90]

The issue is clear, but the outcome remains uncertain.

PUBLIC POWER AND COOPERATIVES

Government operation of electric utilities is not new in the United States, although its large-scale development dates from the 1930's. Whereas in 1935, public power projects produced but 6 percent of the nation's electric energy, the comparable figure stood at 23.4 percent in 1967. Public power has long generated substantial controversy. Some groups see government operation as socialism, perhaps as the first step toward eventual nationalization of the entire industry, and as a source of unfair competition vis-à-vis private power. Others view government construction in terms of public works projects and see government operation as a device to regulate and control privately operated electric utility companies (the so-called "yardstick" idea) and as a means of promoting regional development.[91]

---

[86] See Donald C. Cook, "Co-ordination and the Small Electric Power System," 80 *Public Utilities Fortnightly* 19 (November 23, 1967); and Abraham Gerber, "Power Pools and Joint Plant Ownership," 82 *ibid.* 23 (September 12, 1968).

[87] *Prevention of Power Failures, op. cit.,* Vol. I, p. 3.

[88] *Ibid.*

[89] Statement of C. A. Erdahl in *Electric Power Reliability, op. cit.,* Part 2, p. 229.

[90] Charles F. Avila, "The Other Side of Electric Service," 81 *Public Utilities Fortnightly* 47, 48 (June 6, 1968).

[91] For an analysis of these views, see Edwin Vennard, *Government in the Power Business* (New York: McGraw-Hill Book Co., 1968). The case for government-private competition is made by Richard Hellman, "Government Competition in the Electric Utility Industry of the United States" (Ph.D. dissertation, Columbia University, 1967).

Municipal Operations [92]

Municipal operations started in the early days of the electric industry, one such system being in operation as early as 1881. By 1921, when the number of municipal systems reached its peak, there were 2,581 such systems. Most of these systems were small: while accounting for nearly 41 percent of all electric systems, they generated but 4.7 percent of the total output of power. Many municipal power systems were built in small towns, and hundreds of them were sold to private companies during the consolidation movement of the 1920's.

During the 1930's, there was a considerable revival of interest in municipal operation. Some municipalities decided that operating their own electric systems might provide them with income which, in turn, might make possible some reduction in local taxation or, at least, check any tax increase. Other municipalities were interested in lower electric rates; the rate practices of the holding companies, in particular, led to demands for reform. Whatever the cause, the liberal loan policy of the federal government made it possible for many communities to realize their desires for their own electric systems. From 1933 to 1938, the federal government paid approximately 45 percent of the total cost of approved municipal projects and provided low-cost loans for the remaining 55 percent as part of its public works program (through the Public Works Administration).

Numerically, municipal systems continue to be of significance, but their percentage of total power production has not increased in the past thirty years. A great majority of all municipal systems are found in federal power regions—the Tennessee Valley, the Pacific Northwest, and the Southwest—and they buy their power from federal systems (Figure 15-6). The remaining municipal systems produce their own electric energy or purchase it from investor-owned companies. No generalizations are possible concerning municipal rate policies: some operate at a profit or at cost, while others operate at a loss.

Cooperatives [93]

In 1935, President Roosevelt, by executive order, established the Rural Electrification Administration.[94] Statutory provision for the REA was made in the Rural Electrification Act of 1936 (the Norris-Rayburn bill). The basic purpose of the REA was to extend electric service to those rural areas of the

[92] The entire state of Nebraska is served by a public electric power system. See Robert E. Firth, *Public Power in Nebraska* (Lincoln: University of Nebraska Press, 1962). In some states, such as Nebraska and Washington, public utility districts—political subdivisions of the state—have been organized.

[93] On the rural electrification program, see Clyde T. Ellis, *A Giant Step* (New York: Vintage Books, 1966).

[94] Executive Order No. 7037 (issued May 11, 1935). The REA is an agency of the Department of Agriculture. The Administrator is named by the President with the consent of the Senate.

FIGURE 15-6
Nonfederal Publicly Owned System
(municipal, state, county, and power districts)

Source: Federal Power Commission, *Prevention of Power Failures* (Washington, D.C.: U.S. Government Printing Office, 1967), Vol. I, p. 33.

country without central station service by providing government loans at low interest rates.[95] Cooperatives were formed by farmers to build power lines; private companies sold power to these co-ops at low wholesale rates. The results have been remarkable. Since 1935, approximately $6.4 billion has been invested by 1,101 borrowers, and 98 percent of all American farms are electrified.[96] Cooperatives presently serve some 5.8 million customers in the forty-six states (all states but Connecticut, Hawaii, Massachusetts, and Rhode Island) in which they operate (Figure 15-7).

The REA's success, ironically, is partly responsible for a growing debate over its future. First, many question the need of continuing two benefits long received by co-ops—their tax-exempt status and the low-cost money they can borrow. The tax benefit is similar to the one received by all users of public

[95] Under the act, the interest rate was to be the average rate paid by the government on its long-term bonds in the preceding fiscal year, and loans could be made for a maximum of twenty-five years. In 1944, the Pace Act set the interest rate at 2 percent and extended the amortization period to thirty-five years.

[96] In 1949, the Rural Electrification Act was amended to authorize the REA to make loans for providing and improving rural telephone service. Slightly over $1 billion has been loaned, and approximately 75 percent of all domestic farms now have telephone service. The 860 rural telephone systems serve 1.8 million subscribers.

FIGURE 15-7
Rural Electric Cooperative Systems

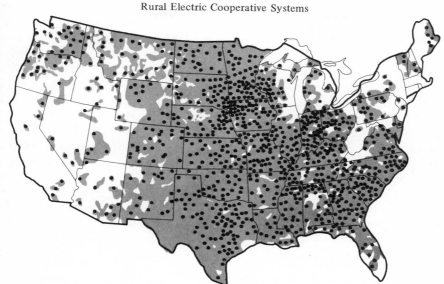

Source: Federal Power Commission, *Prevention of Power Failures* (Washington, D.C.: U.S. Government Printing Office, 1967), Vol. I, p. 33.

power; the loan benefit means that taxpayers are subsidizing the cooperatives. Second, in recent years, many large cooperatives have received loans in order to expand into urban areas or to supply power to industrial users. Five out of every six new co-op customers have been nonfarm in the past few years. As a result, co-ops have come into direct competition with private utilities.[97] Third, the REA has been granting an increasing percentage of its loans to cooperatives for the purpose of constructing power plants.[98] Prior to 1961, the REA followed a policy of granting loans for generating plants and their transmission facilities (known as G&T loans) only when power was not available from private companies or when private companies charged exorbitant wholesale rates. But beginning in May, 1961, several large G&T loans have been made (when "necessary to protect the security and effectiveness of REA-financed sys-

[97]Court challenges of REA loans to finance competing facilities have generally failed. See *Rural Electrification Administration* v. *Central Louisiana Electric Co.*, 354 F. 2d 859 (1966), *cert. denied*, 385 U.S. 815 (1966); and *Northern States Power Co.* v. *Rural Electrification Administration*, 248 F. Supp. 616 (1967), *cert. denied*, 387 U.S. 945 (1967). But see *Western Colorado Power Co.* v. *Colorado Public Utilities Comm.*, 411 P. 2d 785 (1966), *cert. denied*, 385 U.S. 22 (1966).

[98]In addition, in 1968, the REA granted loans totaling just over $1 million to three Vermont cooperatives to enable them to buy shares in a nuclear power plant. *Rural Electric Newsletter*, September 6, 1968, p. 2.

tems"[99]) even though private companies had adequate facilities to supply power at reasonable rates.[100] Fourth, it has been argued that the REA has been financing small, inefficient facilities;[101] a situation due to the fact that the typical rural electric system serves less than 6,000 consumers. Finally, the REA has granted some loans for purposes far removed from supplying power to rural areas.[102] Loans, for example, have been authorized to equip a ski resort in Illinois ($22,000) and to purchase gravel-crushing and gravel-washing machinery for a North Dakota firm ($25,000).

The REA's critics are vocal, the administration's future organization and policies in doubt.[103] Conceivably, the REA will be reorganized into a self-supporting institution. Its G&T loan policy will undoubtedly be reexamined, as will its loans for nonpower purposes. Enactment of the "supplemental financing" legislation proposed by the National Rural Electric Co-operative Association is doubtful.[104] Similarly, it is unlikely that the tax-exempt status of electric co-ops will be repealed. And, in addition to these issues, there remains the question of regulatory control over co-ops which, for the most part, have long been exempt from regulation in a majority of the states and at the federal level.[105]

Federal Operations

The federal government has become an important supplier of electric power. Significantly, its entry into the power field was by the back door. All

---

99 REA Bulletin 20-6 (May 31, 1961).

100 In fiscal 1965, 60 percent of the REA's loans were for G&T facilities. G&T loans are defended by Norman M. Clapp, "REA's Power Supply Program," 81 *Public Utilities Fortnightly* 24 (June 6, 1968). The threat of G&T loans has tended to result in lower wholesale rates to the cooperatives. See Nathaniel E. Shechter, "Low Purchased Energy Costs to the Rural Electric Cooperatives," 42 *Land Economics* 304 (1966). Also see Robert T. Connery, "Generation and Transmission Loan Policy under the Rural Electrification Act," 43 *Denver Law Journal* 269 (1966).

101 See Charles E. Olson, "Inefficiency and Subsidy—A Conflict in Public Policy?," 81 *Public Utilities Fortnightly* 35 (June 6, 1968).

102 Section 5 of the Rural Electrification Act authorizes loans "for the purpose of financing the wiring of the premises of persons in rural areas and the acquisition and installation of electric and plumbing appliances and equipment." Such loans are made to a cooperative which, in turn, makes the loan to a private customer, usually at a 4 percent rate of interest.

103 See Hubert Kay, "There's No Stopping REA—Or Is There?," *Fortune*, February, 1963, pp. 118-21, 170-84. Also see John H. Bickley, "REA—A Brief Study of a Federal Agency," Part I, 83 *Public Utilities Fortnightly* 17 (February 13, 1969); Part II, 83 *ibid.* 27 (February 27, 1969).

104 Under the proposed legislation, Congress would set up two new federally backed banks—electric and telephone banks—to furnish additional low-cost capital for REA-financed systems through "intermediate" and "development" loan programs. A counter proposal was presented by the Edison Electric Institute. See "Modifications Proposed for REA Co-op Financing," 79 *Public Utilities Fortnightly* 54 (April 13, 1967). The need for additional funds is outlined by Norman M. Clapp, "Financing REA Co-op Expansion," 79 *ibid.* 69 (April 27, 1967).

105 In 1967, the FPC held that it lacked jurisdiction over cooperatives financed by the REA. See *Re Dairyland Power Cooperative*, 37 FPC 12 (1967).

seven major federal projects (Table 15-7) were undertaken for other reasons: to prevent floods, to provide navigable waters, to supply water for irrigation, and to store water for urban and industrial consumers. Yet, the dams constructed for these purposes also provided a source of electric power. The controversy which has pointed up federal power projects was thus born.

TABLE 15-7
Major Federal Power Projects—Installed Capacity and
Investment Allocated to Electric Plant, 1966

Project	Capacity (1,000 Kw.)	Investment [a] ($1,000,000)
Tennessee Valley Authority	16,001	2,803
Columbia Basin	6,544	1,866
Missouri Basin	2,434	1,142
Hoover and Parker-Davis	1,690	219
Southeastern Power Administration	1,677	537
Southwestern Power Administration	1,303	398
Central Valley	1,014	290
Total	30,663	7,255

[a] Investment allocated to electric plant; partly estimated.
Source: U.S. Department of Commerce, Bureau of the Census, *Statistical Abstract of the United States, 1968* (Washington, D.C.: U.S. Government Printing Office, 1968), Table 761, p. 517.

Issues in River Valley Development. River valley development, including flood control, navigation, irrigation, and hydroelectric power, raises several issues. As summarized by Watson:

(1) Owing to the fact that they are in the pork barrel or in the one next to it, these projects are subject to strong political influences that tend to distort the application of economic criteria. All government activity is political, obviously; but the water-resource projects are subject to more play from political forces than, say, defense expenditures. The localities and the states where the water projects are constructed form the nuclei of the interest groups that fight for such projects. (2) Within the executive branch of the federal government, bitter rivalry prevails, not eager cooperation. The Bureau of Reclamation in the Department of the Interior operates in seventeen Western states. The Soil Conservation Service of the Department of Agriculture builds flood-control projects on small streams. The Army Corps of Engineers engages in flood control and river and harbor improvements; the electric energy generated by power projects built by the Corps of Engineers is marketed by agencies of the Department of the Interior. Each of the executive agencies has the support of political groups, both in Congress and outside it. Many proposals for administrative reform have been made by bodies such as the Hoover Commission. (3) A continual debate on the engineering features of the water-resource projects goes on: large dams or small ones? Flood control or power? Flood control requires the storage of

water during the flood season, and the emptying of water during dry spells. Power requires an even flow of water the year around. The ideal irrigation cycle is still different. Some of the agencies tend to be flood-control-minded, and others are intent on power. (4) To all this is added the private versus public power struggle. Private power companies want the Federal Power Commission to issue them licenses to build hydro-electric dams on western rivers. The public power groups want large multi-purpose federal projects. (5) There are always more projects than funds available for them. Among the criteria in the selection of projects are benefit-cost ratios—elaborate calculations of estimated future benefits and costs. In general, these ratios are open to serious criticism; benefits tend to be exaggerated. Different agencies make their computations in different ways. (6) On the multi-purpose projects, costs have to be allocated, and charges made to some of the beneficiaries— consumers of electric energy and farmers on irrigated land. Repayment schedules for irrigated land were relatively short early in the century—ten to twenty years. But the tendency has been to lengthen them to forty and to sixty years and even longer.[106]

As river valley development is closely tied to politics, it is not surprising that many projects undertaken cannot be justified by economic criteria.[107] Particularly is the investment criteria open to question. Benefits are frequently overestimated, costs underestimated. For instance, the first situation occurs when excessive estimates are made of the amount of damage that flood control will prevent or the increase in traffic that navigation improvements will attract; the second occurs when the cost of capital is figured on the basis of the rate of interest paid by the government (3.5-4.5 percent). Further, the social value of some multipurpose projects can be questioned. Thus, money has been spent to irrigate new cotton land at the same time the Department of Agriculture is spending money to restrict acreage already under cultivation.[108] And the lack of coordination among interested federal agencies has prevented integrated valley development.

Issues in Public Power Development. In large measure, the controversy over public power is concerned with ideology and efficiency. Some believe that private enterprise is superior to public enterprise and that the private should prevail whenever possible. Others feel that government-operated enterprise tends to be inefficient; bureaucracy and apathetic management are familiar charges of those who oppose public enterprise. These two problems aside, public power development raises several issues worth contemplating.

[106] Donald S. Watson, *Economic Policy: Business and Government* (Boston: Houghton Mifflin Co., 1960), p. 487.

[107] See Otto Eckstein, *Water Resource Development* (Cambridge: Harvard University Press, 1958), pp. 274-77. Also see John V. Krutilla and Otto Eckstein, *Multiple Purpose River Development* (Baltimore: Johns Hopkins Press, 1958); and Stephen C. Smith and Emery M. Castle (eds.), *Economics and Public Policy in Water Resource Development* (Ames, Iowa: Iowa State University Press, 1964).

[108] Leonard W. Weiss, *Case Studies in American Industry* (New York: John Wiley & Sons, Inc., 1967), p. 136.

The first issue concerns the yardstick concept—the idea that public power projects can serve as yardsticks against which the performance of private companies can be measured. In its earliest form, the yardstick concept assumed rate equality: that is, if the government could cover all costs, including a reasonable return, by adopting a particular schedule, then private companies' rates should be cut to these levels. Used in this sense, public power projects are not fair yardsticks. No two power projects are ever exactly the same, so that costs will differ from one project to another. Public and private power costs are not computed in the same way. Private companies must pay higher interest rates. Public power projects do not pay taxes (except as noted below). These two items constitute some 43 percent of the private companies' cost of doing business. And since federal power projects are usually parts of multipurpose projects, there is the question (considered below) of how to allocate the total cost among the various purposes. For these reasons, the cost of supplying public power is lower than the cost of comparable private power, and unless costs are disregarded in establishing rates, the public rates must be lower than the private.

Others, such as Lilienthal, have used the yardstick concept in a different manner.[109] According to this notion, public power rates are properly used in an experimental way, namely, to examine the elasticity of demand for electric power. Used in this way, the yardstick concept makes more sense. Public power projects led the movement toward lower rates in the 1930's. The results are well known: consumption and production increased dramatically as it was shown that the demand for electric energy tends to be elastic. Private companies might have learned this lesson on their own, but it seems possible that the experience of public power projects accelerated the discovery.

A second issue, also of more historic than current interest, revolves around the disposition of water power. The federal government's entry into the generation, transmission, and distribution of power was not made mandatory by construction of dams. The falling water could have been sold to private companies who, in turn, would have built the necessary facilities. Instead, in all the major projects except one,[110] the government has built its own generating facilities and transmission lines. In the distribution of its power, the federal government sells directly to industrial users, municipalities, cooperatives, and federal installations; in only a few instances is power sold to private distributors.[111] The preference clause, as first included in the Reclamation Act of 1906, stated that preference for power generated at federal projects should be given to

[109] David E. Lilienthal, *TVA: Democracy on the March* (New York: Harper & Bros., 1944), pp. 3-4.

[110] On the Colorado, Hoover Dam facilities have been leased to a private company and to a municipality. The lessees generate, transmit, and distribute the power.

[111] Pooling and coordination between federal agencies and private companies, however, are common. Examples are the Northwest power pool involving the Bonneville Power Administration and several private utilities, the seasonal interchange of 1.5 million kilowatts between the Tennessee Valley Authority and 11 private utilities, and the coordination of federal projects in the Southeast by the Southeastern Power Administration with nonfederal systems through the use of privately owned transmission lines.

municipalities for such purposes as street lighting. The current clause specifies that preference should be given to governmental and cooperative distributors. The clause, therefore, has been used to promote municipal and cooperative ownership of distributive systems and has become a partisan issue.

A third issue concerns the cost of public power. As earlier noted, the low rate of interest paid on borrowed funds by the federal government does not reflect the true social cost of capital. Moreover, public power projects do not pay taxes, although some make voluntary payments to local and state governments "in lieu of taxes." [112] There is, in addition, the important problem of the allocation of joint costs. When federal projects are multipurpose, how should the total cost be allocated to each purpose? Several methods are currently in use; each has its limitations. As Wilcox has concluded:

(1) It is suggested that an equal charge be made for each of the purposes for which a dam is used. This would be workable but purely arbitrary. (2) It is suggested that contributions to joint costs be made proportionate to the separable costs of the various uses of common facilities. This, too, would be workable but arbitrary. (3) It is proposed that the contributions be made proportionate to the benefits received by the users of different services. This is justifiable but unworkable. The benefits of some services are difficult to measure. The benefits of others can be measured by the prices which they bring. But since these prices are in question, this method would involve circular reasoning. (4) It is proposed that the alternative cost of building a single-purpose dam for each of the purposes served by a project (where this would be economically justifiable) be computed, and contributions to joint costs be made proportionate to their respective shares in the total of single-purpose costs. The use of alternative possibilities as a basis for allocation has a certain logic. But this procedure necessitates an estimation of the cost of imaginary projects, an exercise in which personal judgment has free play and differences of opinion are certain to result. (5) It is proposed that the share of joint cost charged to each purpose be made proportionate to its use of reservoir capacity. This, too, makes sense. But the cost of different layers in a reservoir is difficult to estimate. The use of reservoir capacity for different purposes is even more so, since it differs from season to season and from day to day. The usefulness of a reservoir in producing power depends, moreover, not only on the volume of water that passes through the turbines but also on the head of water behind the dam. If this procedure were to be used, costs would have to be allocated, in the end, in accordance with an arbitrary rule. [113]

In short, all methods of allocation rest ultimately on judgment, and the final decision is open to dispute.

The allocation of joint costs would be insignificant were it not for a fourth

---

[112] The federal government also makes some payments to state and local governments in the Tennessee Valley area because of property removed from local taxing authority by navigation and flood control projects.

[113] Wilcox, *op. cit.,* pp. 520–21. Also see Eckstein, *op. cit.,* chap. ix; and Joseph S. Ransmeier, *The Tennessee Valley Authority* (Nashville: Vanderbilt University Press, 1942), chaps. vi–xiv.

issue—public power rates.[114] Congress has specified two basic pricing objectives: repayment of the investment allocated to electric power and promotion of the widest possible usage of electricity. The two objectives might conflict. Rates based upon cost calculations might be too high, for instance, to promote widespread consumption in rural areas. In practice, rates have not been based strictly upon cost computations. Emphasis has been placed on low rates to encourage consumption. The policy has been successful. Thus, residential rates in the TVA area averaged .89 cents per kilowatt-hour in 1967, compared with a national average of 2.18 cents. From 1933 to 1967, the number of farms electrified in the region rose from 3 percent to more than 99 percent; the total consumption of power from 1.5 billion kilowatt-hours to 82.1 billion. In some cases, such as TVA, the established rates also have resulted in "excess revenues" so that some of the public money invested in power projects has been returned to the Treasury.[115]

Two closely related matters should be noted. When power is sold by the federal government to distributors, low rates are maintained by regulation. Thus, when TVA enters into contracts with municipal and cooperative distributors, resale prices, finances, accounts, services, and earnings are supervised and specified. Moreover, like private companies, public power rates are discriminatory. Block rates, based on costs and on differences in buyer incomes, are used. Commercial customers pay higher rates than residential buyers; industrial rates are kept low to attract industry. Rates do not take into account differences in transmission costs, thereby being the same for all buyers within a region. Both regulation of distributors and discrimination seek to achieve the objective of expanding the usage of electricity.

A final issue concerns the expansion of public power projects. The entry of the federal government into the production of hydroelectric power was the result of undertaking multipurpose projects. But the government did not stop at that point. The Tennessee Valley Authority, for example, starting with a series of multipurpose dams, obtained both a regional monopoly by buying out private companies and an assured market by promoting public ownership of distribution facilities.[116] In addition to the twenty-nine hydroelectric plants it owns, it has

[114] In theory, rates must at least cover the separate costs of producing power and should be set at a level that would achieve full utilization of capacity. Rates so established might also make some return toward the joint costs.

[115] Through 1958, the TVA paid $185 million of power proceeds and $41.5 million of nonpower proceeds into the Treasury. Under legislation enacted by Congress in 1959, a new repayment schedule was established: beginning with fiscal year 1961, payment of not less than $10 million for each of the first five fiscal years, $15 million for each of the next five years, and $20 million for each year thereafter until the remaining $1 billion of the Authority's debt has been repaid. The same legislation requires an annual payment from power proceeds of a return on the net appropriation investment in power facilities; a return based upon the computed average interest rate payable by the Treasury on its total marketable public obligations as of the beginning of each fiscal year.

[116] Wilcox, *op. cit.,* p. 525. In 1967, the TVA sold 25 percent of its output to other federal agencies (the most important being the Atomic Energy Commission), 23 percent of it to private industries, and 52 percent to distributors. The distributors

continued to expand its power output by building twelve steam plants to "firm up" the supply[117] and to meet increasing demand. In 1967, the Authority had 13.9 million kilowatts of capacity in steam generating plants compared with 4.2 million kilowatts in hydroelectric plants. And in May, 1967, the TVA began construction of its first, and the world's largest, nuclear power plant—a three-unit, 3.5 million kilowatt plant. (Plans for a second nuclear plant—a two-unit, 2.3 million kilowatt plant—also have been announced.) Private interests have consistently tried to limit the growth of public power; regional interests have just as vehemently argued for expansion. To date, regional interests have won out.[118] Expansion has been facilitated by the reinvestment of earnings and by the issuance of revenue bonds. As a result, multipurpose projects—particularly the TVA—have tended to become giant utility enterprises.[119]

Private Lines across Public Lands

A new issue was added to the private-public controversy in 1963. The federal government has vast holdings of public lands. In many cases, especially in the West, electric utilities must build lines across these lands to connect power networks or to carry electricity from a producing to a consuming region. For years, access to public lands was granted by the Federal Power Commission without attachment of strings; duplicate applications for a right-of-way were settled by Congress. In March, 1963, however, the Departments of Agriculture and Interior adopted new rules concerning right-of-way applications for private lines. Under the new regulations:

(1) A right-of-way application across public land for a private transmission line will be denied if the Secretary of the Interior deems it to be "in conflict with the power marketing program of the United States."

(2) If an application is granted, the Interior Department may determine what portion of the proposed line's capacity is "surplus," i.e., built to supply future needs. Such surplus capacity may be used by the federal government—over the entire line, not just the portion on public lands—to transmit federally produced power.

(3) If the Interior Department decides that the surplus capacity is

---

(including 158 municipal and cooperative electric systems, and two small privately-owned systems) served more than 1.9 million customers in parts of seven states.

117 The need to "firm up" the supply, as noted earlier, arises from the conflicting functions of multipurpose projects. The flow of water is regulated to meet the needs of flood control, irrigation, or navigation. Consequently, the flow at any given time may not coincide with the corresponding requirements of electric production. Steam plants, therefore, are built to supplement the irregular output of hydroelectric plants.

118 The TVA is the only federal agency that has full responsibility for supplying all power requirements in the area of its operations. Moreover, Congress so far has refused to establish other valley authorities along the lines of the TVA.

119 On the TVA's policies and achievements, see Lilienthal, *op. cit.;* Gordon R. Clapp, *The TVA: An Approach to the Development of a Region* (Chicago: University of Chicago Press, 1955); Roscoe C. Martin (ed.), *TVA: The First Twenty Years* (University, Alabama: University of Alabama Press, 1956); and John R. Moore (ed.), *The Economic Impact of TVA* (Knoxville: The University of Tennessee Press, 1967).

insufficient it may add, at the government's expense, further transmission line capacity.[120]

The investor-owned utilities' immediate reaction was that the new rules represented a threat to their future growth; public power would be promoted at the expense of private power.[121] No such thing, in fact, has occurred. Instead, as noted earlier, the current trend is toward more coordination and interconnections among public and private systems within the industry.

NUCLEAR POWER

As of mid-1968, fifteen operable nuclear power plants (including one plant in Puerto Rico) had nearly 2.8 million kilowatts of installed capacity, equal to just over 1 percent of total domestic electric power capability (Figure 15-8). Seventy-three nuclear reactors were either being built or planned (Table 15-8) and fourteen additional reactors had been announced but not ordered. These reactors represent 70.1 million kilowatts of installed capacity. In 1966 and 1967, nuclear power accounted for nearly half of all new power-generating capacity ordered by domestic utilities.[122] By 1980, the Atomic Energy Commission estimates that nuclear generating capacity will be in the range of 120 to 170 million kilowatts, or approximately 30 to 35 percent of the nation's total steam electric capacity,[123] and will represent an investment of about $19 billion.[124] It would appear that nuclear power has witnessed a breakthrough into the commercial market.

Nuclear Power and Public Policy [125]

Prior to 1954, the government exercised complete control over the industrial development and production of nuclear power. Under the Atomic Energy Act of 1946 (the McMahon Act), private ownership, production,

[120] *The Wall Street Journal,* June 14, 1963, p. 1; "Memorandum of Understanding," *Federal Register,* April 10, 1964.

[121] See Gerald R. Ford, "Transmission Line Regulation," 71 *Public Utilities Fortnightly* 82 (June 16, 1963).

[122] Some care must be used in interpreting these statistics, since there is a six-to-seven-year lead time in nuclear capacity, compared to a two-to-four-year lead time for fossil fuel capacity.

[123] In a conventional power plant, heat is turned into steam, and steam into electricity. The required heat, in turn, is generated in a coal, gas, or oil burning furnace. Heat may be generated also in a nuclear reactor which uses fissionable material as the fuel. Two types of reactors are currently being developed: converters (reactors that produce less fissionable material than they consume) and breeders (reactors that produce more fissionable material than they consume). Breeders are also of two types: fast breeders and thermal breeders. To date, most of the reactors in operation are of the converter type, although significant research and development is underway on the fast breeder concept. See "The Next Step Is the Breeder Reactor," *Fortune,* March, 1967, pp. 121-23, 198-202; and "GE, Eastern Utilities Plan One-Year Study of Nuclear Breeder Unit," *The Wall Street Journal,* March 16, 1967, p. 6.

[124] James T. Ramey, "Competitive Vigor in Nuclear Power," 46 *Harvard Business Review* 126, 129 (July-August, 1968).

[125] For a more complete discussion, see Philip Mullenbach, *Civilian Nuclear Power* (New York: The Twentieth Century Fund, 1963). On the safety of atomic power plants,

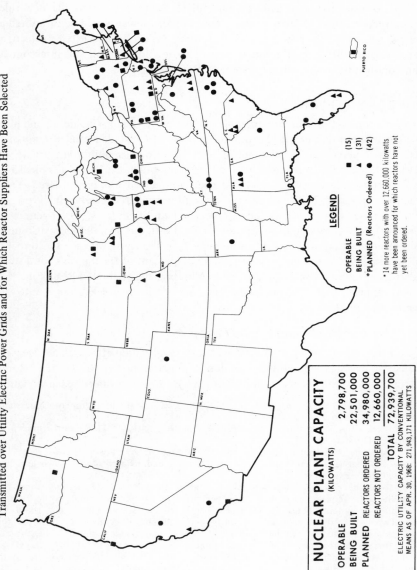

FIGURE 15-8

Nuclear Power Plants in the United States

The Nuclear Power Plants Included in This Map Are Ones Whose Power Is Being Transmitted or Is Scheduled to be Transmitted over Utility Electric Power Grids and for Which Reactor Suppliers Have Been Selected

LEGEND

OPERABLE ■ (15)
BEING BUILT ▲ (31)
*PLANNED (Reactors Ordered) ● (42)

*14 more reactors with over 12,660,000 kilowatts have been announced for which reactors have not yet been ordered.

NUCLEAR PLANT CAPACITY
(KILOWATTS)

OPERABLE   2,798,700
BEING BUILT   22,501,000
PLANNED REACTORS ORDERED   34,980,000
         REACTORS NOT ORDERED   12,660,000
                         TOTAL   72,939,700

ELECTRIC UTILITY CAPACITY BY CONVENTIONAL
MEANS AS OF APR. 30, 1968: 271,943,171 KILOWATTS

Source: Atomic Energy Commission, Division of Technical Information, *Nuclear Reactors Built, Being Built, or Planned in the United States as of June 30, 1968* (Oak Ridge, Tennessee, 1968), p. 29.

TABLE 15-8

Nuclear Power Plants: Operable, Being Built, or Planned (Reactors Ordered), June 30, 1968

Site		Capacity (Kilowatts)	Utility	Start-up
Alabama	Browns Ferry	1,064,500	Tennessee Valley Authority	1970
	Browns Ferry	1,064,500	Tennessee Valley Authority	1971
	Browns Ferry	1,064,500	Tennessee Valley Authority	1972
Arkansas	Dardanelle Lake	850,000	Arkansas Power & Light Co.	1972
California	Humboldt Bay	68,500	Pacific Gas & Electric Co.	1963
	San Clemente	430,000	Southern Calif. Edison and San Diego Gas & Electric Co.	1967
	Corral Canyon	462,000	L.A. Dept. of Water & Power	1973
	Diablo Canyon	1,060,000	Pacific Gas & Electric Co.	1971
	Sacramento County	800,000	Sacramento Municipal District	1973
Colorado	Platteville	330,000	Public Service Co. of Colorado	1971
Connecticut ..	Haddam Neck	462,000	Conn. Yankee Atomic Power Co.	1967
	Waterford No. 1	652,100	Northeast Utilities	1969
	Waterford No. 2	828,000	Northeast Utilities	1974
Florida	Turkey Point No. 3	651,500	Florida Power & Light Co.	1970
	Turkey Point No. 4	651,500	Florida Power & Light Co.	1971
	Red Level	825,000	Florida Power Corp.	1972
	Hutchinson Island	800,000	Florida Power and Light Co.	1973
Georgia	Baxley	786,000	Georgia Power Co.	1973
Illinois	Morris No. 1	200,000	Commonwealth Edison Co.	1959
	Morris No. 2	715,000	Commonwealth Edison Co.	1968
	Morris No. 3	715,000	Commonwealth Edison Co.	1969
	Zion No. 1	1,050,000	Commonwealth Edison Co.	1972
	Zion No. 2	1,050,000	Commonwealth Edison Co.	1973
	Quad Cities No. 1	715,000	Comm. Ed. Co.–Ia.–Ill. Gas & Elec. Co.	1970
	Quad Cities No. 2	715,000	Comm. Ed. Co.–Ia.–Ill. Gas & Elec. Co.	1971
Indiana	Burns Harbor	515,000	Northern Indiana Public Service Co.	1970's
Iowa	Cedar Rapids	537,600	Iowa Electric Light and Power Co.	1973
Maine	Wiscasset	790,000	Maine Yankee Atomic Power Co.	1972
Maryland	Lusby	800,000	Baltimore Gas and Electric Co.	1973
	Lusby	800,000	Baltimore Gas and Electric Co.	1974
Massachusetts .	Rowe	175,000	Yankee Atomic Electric Co.	1960
	Plymouth	625,000	Boston Edison Co.	1971
Michigan	Big Rock Point	70,300	Consumers Power Co.	1962
	South Haven	700,000	Consumers Power Co.	1969
	Lagoona Beach	60,900	Power Reactor Development Co.	1963
	Bridgman	1,060,000	Indiana & Michigan Electric Co.	1972
	Bridgman	1,054,000	Indiana & Michigan Electric Co.	1973
	Midland	650,000	Consumers Power Co.	1974
	Midland	650,000	Consumers Power Co.	1975
Minnesota	Elk River	22,000	Rural Cooperative Power Assoc.	1962
	Monticello	471,700	Northern States Power Co.	1970
	Red Wing No. 1	550,000	Northern States Power Co.	1972
	Red Wing No. 2	550,000	Northern States Power Co.	1974
Nebraska	Fort Calhoun	457,400	Omaha Public Power District	1971
	Brownville	778,000	Consumers Public Power District and Iowa Power and Light Co.	1972
New Jersey ...	Toms River	515,000	Jersey Central Power & Light Co.	1968
	Toms River	810,000	Jersey Central Power & Light Co.	1973

TABLE 15-8–*Continued*

Site		Capacity (Kilowatts)	Utility	Start-up
	Artificial Island	1,050,000	Public Service Gas and Electric Co. of New Jersey	1971
	Artificial Island	1,050,000	Public Service Gas and Electric Co. of New Jersey	1973
New York	Indian Point No. 1	265,000	Consolidated Edison Co.	1962
	Indian Point No. 2	873,000	Consolidated Edison Co.	1969
	Indian Point No. 3	965,300	Consolidated Edison Co.	1971
	Scriba	500,000	Niagara Mohawk Power Co.	1968
	Easton	765,800	Niagara Mohawk Power Co.	1971
	Rochester	420,000	Rochester Gas & Electric Co.	1969
	Shoreham	523,000	Long Island Lighting Co.	1973
	Lansing	829,200	New York State Electric & Gas Co.	1973
	*	1,115,000	Consolidated Edison Co.– Orange and Rockland Utilities, Inc.	1973
North Carolina	*	800,000	Carolina Power and Light Co.	1973
	*	800,000	Carolina Power and Light Co.	1974
	*	800,000	Carolina Power and Light Co.	...
Pennsylvania ..	Peach Bottom No. 1	40,000	Philadelphia Electric Co.	1966
	Peach Bottom No. 2	1,065,000	Philadelphia Electric Co.	1971
	Peach Bottom No. 3	1,065,000	Philadelphia Electric Co.	1973
	*	1,065,000	Philadelphia Electric Co.	1975
	*	1,065,000	Philadelphia Electric Co.	1977
	Shippingport No. 1	90,000	Duquesne Light Co.	1957
	Shippingport No. 2	783,000	Duquesne Light Co.–Ohio Edison Co.	1973
	Three Mile Island	831,000	Metropolitan Edison Co.	1971
	*	1,100,000	Pennsylvania Power and Light	1975
	*	1,100,000	Pennsylvania Power and Light	1977
Puerto Rico ...	Punta Higuera	16,500	Puerto Rico Water Resources Authority	1964
South Carolina	Hartsville	663,000	Carolina Power & Light Co.	1970
	Lake Keowee No. 1	841,100	Duke Power Co.	1971
	Lake Keowee No. 2	841,100	Duke Power Co.	1972
	Lake Keowee No. 3	841,100	Duke Power Co.	1973
South Dakota .	Sioux Falls	58,500	Northern States Power Co.	1964
Vermont	Vernon	513,900	Vermont Yankee Nuclear Power Corp.–Green Mt. Power Corp.	1970
Virginia	Hog Island	783,000	Virginia Electric & Power Co.	1971
	Hog Island	783,000	Virginia Electric & Power Co.	1972
	Louisa County	800,000	Virginia Electric & Power Co.	1974
Washington ...	Richland	790,000	Washington Public Power Supply System	1966
Wisconsin	Genoa	50,000	Dairyland Power Cooperative Edison Co.	1967
	Two Creeks No. 2	454,600	Wisconsin Michigan Power Co.	1971
	Carlton	527,000	Wisconsin Public Service Co.	1972
†	*	1,125,000	Tennessee Valley Authority	1973
†	*	1,125,000	Tennessee Valley Authority	1974

*Site not selected.
†State not selected.
Source: Atomic Energy Commission, Division of Technical Information, *Nuclear Reactors Built, Being Built, or Planned in the United States as of June 30, 1968* (Oak Ridge, Tennessee, 1968), p. 30.

exportation, and importation of fissionable materials were forbidden, as was private ownership of nuclear productive facilities and patents covering productive processes. The Atomic Energy Commission, set up by the law, was authorized to construct its own nuclear facilities and to enter into contracts for research and production. While the AEC undertook a comprehensive program of basic research and experimental development that demonstrated the technical feasibility of nuclear power, the role of private enterprise was limited. In 1951 and 1952, private industry was invited by the commission to investigate the possibility of producing nuclear power. In 1953, Congress authorized funds for the construction of the country's first nuclear plant at Shippingport, Pennsylvania.[126] Yet, it was not until Congress enacted the Atomic Energy Act of 1954 that private enterprise was encouraged to develop a nuclear power industry.

President Eisenhower, early in 1954, proposed that Congress amend the 1946 act to remove, among other things, the severe limitations on private possession of fissionable materials, nuclear productive facilities, and patents. The proposal resulted in substantial controversy. Two issues were critical. The first major debate concerned public versus private power. Proponents of public power sought to authorize the AEC to generate and sell electricity, to give public agencies such as the TVA the same right as private industry to generate nuclear power, and to give municipal and cooperative systems preference in the distribution of public nuclear power. Opponents of public power sought to restrict the development of nuclear power by public agencies, contending that the development of a nuclear power industry would be accelerated under private enterprise. The second major debate concerned patents. Some feared that private ownership of patents would result in a few firms dominating the industry. The AEC had contracted much of its research and development work to a small number of private firms. Most of its reactor development contracts, for instance, were given to only five firms. The head start enjoyed by these firms might result in an unfair advantage over others who might wish to enter the field at a later date.[127]

The 1954 act represented a compromise. While the Atomic Energy Commission retained control,[128] the field was opened up to private enterprise. The AEC was authorized to license the private construction, ownership, and

---

see John F. Hogerton, *Background Information on Atomic Power Safety* (3d ed.; New York: Atomic Industrial Forum, Inc., 1968).

[126] The plant, built at a cost of $120 million, supplies electricity to the Duquesne Light Company of Pittsburgh. Duquesne provided the site, invested $15 million in generating equipment, and contributed $5 million toward the reactor. The government supplied the remaining $100 million.

[127] On the commission's contract system, see Richard A. Tybout, *Government Contracting in Atomic Energy* (Ann Arbor: University of Michigan Press, 1956). On patent issues, see Walter Adams, "Atomic Energy: The Congressional Abandonment of Competition," 55 *Columbia Law Review* 158 (1955); and Bennett Boskey, "Some Patent Aspects of Atomic Power Development," 21 *Law and Contemporary Problems* 113 (1956).

[128] Relations between the AEC and Congress have not always been harmonious. See Robert Dahl and Ralph Brown, Jr., *Domestic Control of Atomic Energy* (New York:

operation of nuclear facilities, and the possession, but not ownership, of fissionable materials. The commission was forbidden from entering into the commercial production of nuclear power, but it could sell power generated in experimental plants. Public agencies were granted an equal right with private utilities to apply for licenses. There were two preference provisions: one gave preference in granting licenses and the other in disposing of energy produced at AEC experimental installations. Private industry was permitted to use government patents and to patent new technology. The patent privilege was not absolute in that compulsory licensing might be required on inventions found by the commission to be "of primary importance."

The Promotion of Nuclear Power

Congress thus rejected the idea of a nuclear power industry built and operated by the federal government. At the same time, private enterprise was unable to undertake the development task alone; the need for nuclear power was nonexistent, while its cost was prohibitive and its success uncertain. The risk involved indicated substantial public assistance for private development, a fact recognized by the act of 1954. Through 1967, the AEC had spent nearly $2.3 billion on the civilian nuclear power program.

The commission's promotional program has included two phases. First, the agency has carried on an extensive research and development program "on a laboratory scale to investigate and understand the basic science and to develop and prove out the general technology."[129] All findings resulting from AEC-sponsored research are now available to private industry without charge. Second, the commission has carried on a "power demonstration" program of utility installations "to verify technology in actual practice, to yield economic information and to provide experience on which to base improvements."[130] This phase of the agency's program has included the provision of reactors and various forms of assistance to utilities that have built their own reactors.

In some cases, the commission builds and operates reactors.[131] The steam produced in these reactors is then sold to the utilities for use in their generators. In cases where private utilities build their own reactors, public assistance is provided in other ways. Nuclear fuel, controlled by the government until 1964, apparently is provided at less than its full cost.[132] Research and development

---

Social Science Research Council, 1951); Morgan Thomas, *Atomic Energy and Congress* (Ann Arbor: University of Michigan Press, 1956); and Harold P. Green and Alan Rosenthal, *Government of the Atom* (New York: Atherton Press, 1963).

[129] Atomic Energy Commission, *Civilian Nuclear Power: A Report to the President—1962* (Washington, D.C.: Atomic Energy Commission, 1962), p. 29.

[130] *Ibid.*

[131] All AEC reactors have been built and operated for publicly owned utility systems except Shippingport. This plant was constructed prior to the 1954 act which permitted private industry to own nuclear plants.

[132] The government's charge for nuclear fuel involves several elements. A lease charge is made for the use of government-owned fuel at 4.75 percent. A further charge is

assistance is provided free of charge, but the commission pays private reactor operators for all economic and technical data they provide. The government also provides $500 million in insurance against accidents at a nominal charge.

The Economic Feasibility of Nuclear Power

The status of nuclear power plant economics as well as future projections about nuclear power are complicated by several conflicting factors. On the one hand, since nuclear technology is relatively young, advances have been rapid. The competitive position of nuclear power improves as size of plant increases, and unit size has been increasing dramatically in recent years—from 500,000 to 800,000 and even to 1.1 million kilowatt plants—as a result of the continued growth in the demand for electricity and the trend toward pooling and interconnections. And while nuclear power plants are more expensive to build per kilowatt of capacity,[133] this disadvantage may be partially offset by savings in the cost of fuel. On the other hand, cost reductions have been achieved by building larger, more efficient conventional power plants. The cost of coal, the principal utility fuel, has declined due to the introduction of unit trains, while technical advances in transmission facilities have made mine-mouth plants economically feasible in some areas. And the future cost of nuclear fuel is uncertain.[134]

For these reasons, estimates of costs are changing constantly. At the present time, the cost of producing power at conventional plants varies between 4 and 9 mills per kilowatt-hour; at nuclear plants in operation, from 7 to 10 mills. At these costs, nuclear power is only competitive in high-cost fuel areas,

---

made for fuel consumed. In some cases, the use charge is waived during the first five years of operation. The commission's charge for disposing of waste is relatively low, while its allowance for plutonium (a by-product) is relatively high. However, unlike private industry would do, the government will not reprocess fuels. See Mullenbach, *op. cit.*, pp. 71–73, 166–75.

[133] A coal-fired steam generating plant can be built at a cost of $105 to $150 per kilowatt of capacity. The first nuclear plants ranged from $246 to $725 per kilowatt. (See William D. Shipman, "Some Economic Implications of Nuclear Power Generation in Large Central Stations," 40 *Land Economics* 1 [1964].) Nuclear plants now being built are expected to cost from $115 to $150 per kilowatt. For a more complete analysis, see Report of Joint Committee on Atomic Energy, *Nuclear Power Economics—1962 through 1967* (Joint Committee Print) (Washington, D.C.: U.S. Government Printing Office, 1968).

[134] In August, 1964, mandatory government ownership of special nuclear material was terminated (Public Law 88-489). Further, no additional quantities of enriched uranium will be leased by the AEC after December 31, 1970, and all leases will terminate by June 30, 1973. The effect of eliminating the government's subsidy is uncertain, but will depend upon two basic cost items: the cost of uranium oxide (which private industry expects to decline under free market conditions) and the cost of nuclear fuel inventory (which will rise). See Ramey, *op. cit.*; Harold B. Meyers, "Another Big Whirl for Uranium," *Fortune*, April, 1968, pp. 128–31; C. D. French and R. C. Woodbury, "Mortgage Financing of Nuclear Fuel," 81 *Public Utilities Fortnightly* 23 (March 28, 1968); and Joseph G. Monks, "Nuclear Fuel Industry Trends," 24 *Financial Analysts Journal* 45 (November–December, 1968).

such as New England, California, and possibly New York. The cost at nuclear plants now being built is expected to be between 5 and 7 mills per kilowatt-hour; those being planned (due to startup in the early 1970's), under 5 mills.[135] But even if these costs do materialize, it will still be several years before nuclear power is as cheap as conventional power throughout the country.[136] At the same time, nuclear power should make long-term inroads because of (a) the greater possibilities of technological improvements in both the fuel cycle and the plant itself and (b) the growing list of problems confronted by utilities operating coal- or oil-fired power stations in urban or highly industrialized areas.[137] The United States has no urgent need for nuclear power. In contrast to the European situation, the domestic cost of generating electricity by conventional methods is relatively low, the supply of fossil fuels abundant. Nevertheless, the AEC estimates that nuclear power may result in cumulative savings in generating costs of approximately $30 billion by the year 2000.

THE NECESSITY OF BALANCE

The growth and development of the electric power industry have been characterized by rapid technological change and bitter controversy. The demand for electricity has doubled every decade; future projections indicate a continuation of this rate. Technological developments, as well as economies of scale, have resulted in both a smaller number of larger systems and lower rates to consumers. Recent technical advances in the areas of generation and transmission, making pooling and interconnections feasible, suggest that the nation's future power requirements may best be served by a network of regional pools.[138]

These achievements, however, have often been overshadowed by the struggle between proponents of private and public ownership. Wildavsky summarizes:

> The public versus private power issue has been one of the most persistent and dramatic controversies in twentieth-century American politics. Perhaps

[135] The TVA, for example, estimates that its first nuclear plant will cost $116 per kilowatt of capacity, with a total cost of 2.39 mills per kilowatt-hour. See Tom O'Hanlon, "An Atomic Bomb in the Land of Coal," *Fortune*, September, 1966, pp. 132–33. Even with pooling, however, there are few utilities capable of installing units as large as those ordered by the TVA (1.1 million kilowatts).

[136] Indeed, it may be until the early 1980's, when the fast breeder reactors are expected to be in widespread use.

[137] These problems include the public's growing concern about air pollution, and the utilities' concern about the high cost of low-sulfur fuels and about obtaining right-of-way for a multiplicity of cross-country transmission lines for mine-mouth plants (even if such plants were economically feasible). See John F. Hogerton, "The Arrival of Nuclear Power," 218 *Scientific American* 21, 29 (February, 1968).

[138] Coordination may ultimately lead to consolidation. One utility executive has stated that within fifty years, there may be no more than 12 to 15 electric power systems in the United States. And he adds: "The electric utility holding company is making a long overdue comeback, and consolidation in the industry will be the trend of the future." Donald C. Cook, quoted in *The Wall Street Journal*, July 15, 1966, p. 1.

the most striking fact is that the power issue has been and is being fought at the city, county, state, and national governmental levels. Any unit of government large enough to be served by its own power plant and with the necessary legal right is a potential arena for the power issue. . . .

The long conflict between public and private power, far from leading to reconciliation, has steadily embittered personal relationships between the antagonists. The animus first developed through clashes on the state and local level has spilled over into the national arena. The harsh truth is that private and public power people have little use for one another. They distrust each other's motives; they question each other's integrity; they doubt each other's devotion to the national good. Each side expects the other to play dirty, and each can produce substantiating evidence from the long history of their dispute.[139]

The private versus public conflict thus permeates every major policy decision, whether it be the future of the Rural Electrification Administration, transmission line rights-of-way across public lands, or the development of nuclear power. Yet, public power is a fact of life: its beneficiaries are vocal and represent a significant political bloc. In some respects, the conflict has been desirable. Public power projects have demonstrated the advantages of promotional rates and have been the leaders in bringing electricity to rural areas. In other respects, the effects have been undesirable. Construction of inefficient plants has been encouraged by government subsidies, and the development of hydroelectric power has been held up in some areas of the country. But regardless of the effects, it is clear that regulation of the electric power industry "involves the endless task of striking fine political, economic, and legal balances in an environment of rapid technological and social change."[140]

Finally, the electric power industry well illustrates the need of adapting regulatory concepts and methods to a changing technological environment. As Shipman has argued:

. . . if the production and transmission of power is essentially a regional matter (which it is rapidly becoming) and if distribution costs vary principally between city and country rather than between this state and that (which is the case), then how can purely interstate variations in rates within a given region be justified in any event? Only where the distribution sector is entirely separate from production and transmission can retail rates be regarded as strictly an intrastate matter and in that case retail rates will reflect wholesale rates which are an interstate matter. Furthermore, if the basic cost information necessary to determine reasonableness of rates is regional in character and is mostly collected by a federal agency as a matter of course, may there not be gross duplication of effort involved in state regulatory commissions continuing to handle rate cases in the traditional manner? There is a strong

---

[139] Aaron Wildavsky, *Dixon-Yates: A Study in Power Politics* (New Haven: Yale University Press, 1962), pp. 5-6.

[140] Merle Fainsod, Lincoln Gordon, and Joseph C. Palamountain, Jr., *Government and the American Economy* (3d ed.; New York: W. W. Norton & Co., Inc., 1959), p. 356.

presumption here . . . that taxpayers, ratepayers, and (with some exceptions) the companies themselves would be better off if the regulatory function as applied to electric power were to lie wholly with regional or national agencies. Of course, it will take much more than nuclear power and EHV transmission to bring about any such reordering of affairs; jurisdictional empires will be defended no matter how small or infirm. But, to paraphrase a famous remark by Bonbright, engineers who insist on pursuing technology across state lines must expect politics, sooner or later, to follow their example.[141]

In sum, innovation in electric power production and transmission may require innovation in regulatory concepts if regulation is to achieve maximum efficiency.

[141] Shipman, *op. cit.*, pp. 10–11 (citation omitted). On the British electric power industry, see William G. Shepherd, *Economic Performance under Public Ownership: British Fuel and Power* (New Haven: Yale University Press, 1965); and R. W. Greenleaf, "Progress and Problems of the British Electrical Supply Industry," 15 *MSU Business Topics* 33 (Autumn, 1967).

Chapter 16

THE NATURAL GAS
INDUSTRY

In no other field of public service regulation is the controlling body confronted with factors so baffling as in the natural gas industry. . . .

—Justice Brandeis*

Prior to the 1920's, natural gas was an unimportant source of domestic energy. It was used basically as a source of pressure to drive petroleum to the surface; then the gas was blown off (vented), burned off (flared), or used in nearby industrial plants. In the late twenties and early thirties, large new oil and gas fields were discovered in the Southwest. At the same time, improvements in pipeline construction, particularly the invention of seamless pipe, increased the distance over which natural gas could be economically transported. These two events radically altered the industry's role in the economy. Today, gas is transported to every part of the country and supplies nearly one-third of the nation's total energy.

The necessity of regulating certain aspects of the natural gas industry, the feasibility of federal versus state control, the most suitable method of regulation, and the development of conservation policy have been the subjects of constant debate. The issues, moreover, are complex. The Supreme Court stated in a 1963 decision: "We recognize the unusual difficulties inherent in regulating the price of a commodity such as natural gas." [1] Both economics and politics have played roles in shaping public policy toward the industry. And the pattern of control is still in the development stage.

THE DEVELOPMENT OF FEDERAL REGULATION

Supplying natural gas [2] to consumers involves three functions: (1) the production and gathering of natural gas in the field, (2) the intra- and interstate

---

*Justice Brandeis, dissenting opinion in *Pennsylvania* v. *West Virginia,* 262 U.S. 553, 621 (1923).

[1] *Wisconsin* v. *Federal Power Comm.,* 373 U.S. 294, 310 (1963).

[2] " 'Natural gas' is a simple hydrocarbon that is gaseous when surfaced from an underground reservoir. This hydrocarbon is composed of 85 to 95 per cent methane, and can be processed to provide 1,000 Btu per cubic foot of energy content, usually at a

transmission of the gas by pipeline from the producing field to consumer markets, and (3) local distribution of the gas to consumers. Similarly, there are three corresponding marketing transactions.[3] The "field price" refers to rates on sales by the producer at the wellhead, or by producers and gatherers at the ends of their gathering lines, or by processors at the tail gate of their processing plants to gatherers, processors, and pipeline companies. The "city gate rate" refers to wholesale rates on sales by pipeline companies to local distribution companies. The "resale rate" refers to the rate charged on retail sales to ultimate customers by the local distributing companies.

The states have long controlled production of natural gas to conserve natural resources.[4] State regulation also has long prevailed over natural gas retail sales under the "affected with a public interest" doctrine. However, the Supreme Court has consistently held that state regulatory authorities lack power to control the rates charged by pipeline companies at the city gates, since interstate commerce is involved.[5] A significant segment of the natural gas industry, therefore, was unregulated. The Natural Gas Act of 1938 sought to remedy this situation by filling the gap.

The Natural Gas Act

The Natural Gas Act of 1938 broadened the jurisdiction of the Federal Power Commission to include the interstate transmission of natural gas and its sale for resale. The act exempted production and gathering of natural gas and its local distribution. It required pipeline companies to file, publish, and adhere to their rate schedules, and to give thirty days' notice of proposed changes. The commission was empowered to suspend proposed changes, except on sales for resale to industrial users, for a period not to exceed five months, and it was directed to establish "just and reasonable" rates as well as to prevent any "undue preference or advantage" to any person or any "unreasonable difference" in rates, service, or facilities among localities and among classes of service. The act

---

pressure of 14.65 pounds pressure per square inch. It is removed from reservoirs or 'traps' that are porous, permeable rock formations in a surrounding seal of impermeable rock and water. The permeable rock may be sand, sandstone, limestone, dolomite, or chalk and may be found from 1,000 to 16,000 feet below surface. The reservoirs may contain not only gas of the requisite quality, but also crude oil ... and 'liquid petroleum gas' .... Typically a number of traps occur close together–side by side or one above the other–so that they form a 'field'." Paul W. MacAvoy, *Price Formation in Natural Gas Fields: A Study of Competition, Monopsony, and Regulation* (New Haven: Yale University Press, 1962), pp. 10–11.

[3] Richard W. Gable, "The Jurisdiction of the Federal Power Commission over the Field Prices of Natural Gas," 32 *Land Economics* 39, 40 (1956).

[4] *Ohio Oil Co.* v. *Indiana*, 177 U.S. 190 (1900); *Champlin Refining Co.* v. *Corporation Comm.*, 286 U.S. 210 (1932); *Thompson* v. *Consolidated Gas Utilities Corp.*, 300 U.S. 55 (1937); *Henderson Co.* v. *Thompson*, 300 U.S. 258 (1937).

[5] *West* v. *Kansas Natural Gas Co.*, 221 U.S. 229 (1911); *Haskel* v. *Kansas Natural Gas Co.*, 224 U.S. 217 (1912); *Public Utilities Comm.* v. *Landon*, 249 U.S. 236 (1918); *Pennsylvania* v. *West Virginia*, 262 U.S. 553 (1923); *Barrett* v. *Kansas Natural Gas Co.*, 265 U.S. 298 (1924).

also authorized the FPC to prescribe and enforce accounting methods and to ascertain the "actual legitimate cost" of pipeline properties.

The commission may order a pipeline company to extend or improve its transportation facilities and to establish physical connections with, and to sell gas to, local distributors unless it finds that the ability of the company to render adequate service would be impaired by such an order. All voluntary extension of facilities and abandonment of service or facilities must be approved by the commission.[6] Under a 1942 amendment, subject to a grandfather clause, certificates must be obtained from the commission for construction, extension, acquisition, or operation of interstate facilities. The commission may determine the service area to which each authorization is limited. Within such an area, a company is permitted to enlarge or extend its facilities without further approval. The commission, however, may issue a certificate to another pipeline company within a service area if it finds that additional service is necessary. The act authorized the FPC to control imports and exports of natural gas. It also instructed the commission to cooperate with state regulatory agencies and provided for establishment of joint boards.

Finally, it should be noted that the FPC was not given control over the security issues of interstate pipelines, nor was it empowered to order interconnections of facilities.

The Certificate Power

The commission's certificate power under the Natural Gas Act is similar to authority invested in other regulatory agencies. The criteria developed by the agency for certification include adequacy of natural gas reserves, physical facilities, financial resources, and market demand.[7] The commission soon found, however, that its exercise of the certificate power raised broad policy questions. In particular, should the certificate provision be employed to promote social goals?

Since the commission allowed interested parties to intervene extensively, certification cases, argues Huitt,

> . . . became the battleground upon which coal, labor, and railroad interests sought to stay the invasion by natural gas of coal-burning market areas. Their case for restricting the growth of the natural-gas industry rested on the basic fact that, while both coal and gas are exhaustible resources, gas reserves are estimated in decades and coal reserves in centuries. From this premise, three arguments were made:
> 1) The coal and railroad industries are large-scale employers of skilled

---

[6] In 1966, the Supreme Court upheld an FPC ruling that the refusal of a natural gas pipeline company to continue receiving gas from a producer, after its contract with the producer had expired and the producer had filed a price increase which was approved by the commission, constituted an abandonment of facilities and of a service. *Re United Gas Pipe Line Co.*, 53 PUR 3d 257 (FPC, 1964), 54 PUR 3d 275 (FPC, 1964), *aff'd*, 350 F. 2d 689 (1965), 385 U.S. 83 (1966).

[7] *Re Kansas Pipe Line and Gas Co.*, 21 FPC 29 (1939).

labor; natural-gas pipe-lines are not. Miners and railroad workers displaced by the substitution of gas for coal cannot be replaced when the gas is gone. Therefore, natural gas should be kept out of markets adequately supplied by coal.

2) Industrialization of the major producing states in the South and Southwest, based on natural gas as a fuel, would help to decentralize industry, foster regional development, and balance the economies of those sections. Therefore, the industrial needs of producing states should be considered in certificate cases.

3) Natural gas is a "luxury" commodity, having great value as a fuel for domestic consumption and as a raw material for the chemical industries, and perhaps for conversion into a liquid fuel. It is economic waste to burn vast quantities at low prices as boiler fuel. Therefore, the certificate power should be used for the selective control of end uses of gas.

These contentions clearly go beyond anything the Congress had in mind when it passed the Natural Gas Act.[8]

The certificate power, therefore, involves far more than simply the establishment of criteria; it involves a determination of the public interest with respect to natural gas. Put another way, natural gas regulation is but a part of the broader program involving utilization of the nation's energy resources. Two questions must be raised. First, should the commission use its certificate power to resolve the divergent economic interests of various groups? Second, should the commission use its certificate power to conserve a scarce resource by controlling the end uses of natural gas? Neither question is unique with the natural gas industry. Both, however, should be answered by Congress and not by the Federal Power Commission. Nevertheless, since Congress has not clarified its position on these questions, they remain as the source of considerable debate and will be considered further in subsequent sections.

THE FIELD PRICE OF NATURAL GAS

Natural gas is produced in five major regions of the country. (1) California, which ships no natural gas out of the state, is an importer of gas. (2) The Appalachian Area, composed of Kentucky, New York, Ohio, Pennsylvania, and West Virginia, is suffering from exhaustion, although some important new finds have been made in recent years. The remaining three regions are located in the Southwest: (3) the Gulf Coast Area, encompassing the state of Louisiana, adjoining regions of Texas, and the area along the Texas Gulf Coast as far south as Mexico; (4) the Mid-Continent region, consisting of the Texas and Oklahoma Panhandles and extending into Kansas; and (5) western Texas and New Mexico, embracing two basins—the Permian Basin and the San Juan Basin. Texas is the

---

[8] Ralph K. Huitt, "Federal Regulation of the Uses of Natural Gas," 46 *American Political Science Review* 455, 455–56 (1952). For a review of the commission's competitive certificate proceedings, see Nelson Lee Smith, "The Federal Power Commission and Pipeline Markets: How Much Competition?" 68 *Columbia Law Review* 664 (1968).

leading producer, accounting for 39 percent of net gas production, closely followed by Louisiana (32 percent). Thirty-three states have natural gas reserves, with the major portion of the nation's proven reserves located in the southwestern states. Texas and Louisiana account for 72 percent of proved natural gas reserves (Table 16–1).

The Natural Gas Act of 1938 appeared to exempt "the production or gathering of natural gas." The apparent exemption soon became a significant economic and political issue.

TABLE 16–1
Net Gas Production and Proved Reserves, 1967

State	Net Gas Production		Proved Gas Reserves[a]	
	Billions of Cubic Feet	Percent of Total	Billions of Cubic Feet	Percent of Total
Texas	7,128.6	38.79%	125,415.1	42.82%
Louisiana	5,917.4	32.19	86,290.0	29.46
Oklahoma	1,517.3	8.25	19,403.8	6.62
New Mexico	954.8	5.19	15,092.5	5.15
Kansas	888.0	4.83	15,283.7	5.22
California	641.4	3.49	7,723.8	2.64
Wyoming	265.8	1.45	3,685.5	1.26
West Virginia	211.5	1.15	2,580.0	0.88
Mississippi	167.1	0.91	1,597.0	0.55
Arkansas	125.7	0.68	2,811.3	0.96
Colorado	119.2	0.65	1,769.3	0.60
Other states[b]	444.0	2.42	11,255.7	3.84
Total	18,380.8	100.00%	292,907.7	100.00%

[a] As of December 31, 1967; figures include offshore reserves.

[b] Includes Alabama, Alaska, Arizona, Florida, Illinois, Indiana, Iowa, Kentucky, Maryland, Michigan, Missouri, Montana, Nebraska, New York, North Dakota, Ohio, Pennsylvania, South Dakota, Tennessee, Utah, Virginia, and Washington.

Source: American Gas Association, Inc., *1968 Gas Facts* (New York, 1968), pp. 8–9.

Jurisdiction over Integrated Producers

Natural gas that enters interstate commerce—some 61 percent of annual net gas production—usually is gathered from various wellheads in a network of field pipes,[9] processed to extract valuable byproducts (liquid hydrocarbons) and to remove impurities (sulphur compounds, nitrogen, and water, among others), and delivered to interstate pipelines. Natural gas transmission companies produce about 8 percent of the gas they carry; the remaining 92 percent represents purchases from independent producers or imports from Canada and Mexico. The

[9] Most of the field and gathering lines that transport gas from individual wells to compressor stations, processing points, or main-line transmission systems are owned and operated by the producer whose gas is transported. A few are owned by long-distance pipeline companies or by independent organizations, and some gathering systems have been developed jointly by long-distance pipeline companies and individual producers.

FPC immediately insisted that it did not have jurisdiction over prices charged by independents to interstate pipeline companies, because (1) such transactions were conducted at arm's length, (2) the commission lacked sufficient staff and funds to undertake the task, and (3) the intent of Congress was to exempt independent producers and gatherers.[10] The commission noted, however, that,

> Further experience with the administration of the Natural Gas Act may reveal that the initial sales of large quantities of natural gas which eventually flow in interstate commerce are by producing or gathering companies which, through affiliation, field agreement, or dominant position in a field, are able to maintain an unreasonable price despite the appearance of competition. Under such circumstances the Commission will decide whether it can assume jurisdiction over arbitrary field prices under the present act or should report the facts to Congress with recommendations for such broadening of the act and provision of additional machinery as may appear necessary to close this gap in effective regulation of the natural gas industry.[11]

The commission faced a different problem when regulating city gate rates charged by integrated pipeline companies. Here, it had to consider the costs incurred or the price paid to obtain gas in the field in determining the reasonableness of the price charged local distributors. The commission did this by using the utility rate base, cost of service method—a company's operating costs (including dry-hole costs on nonproductive lands) plus a return of 6 percent on the original cost of its producing properties less reserves for depreciation.[12] Its authority to follow this procedure was quickly challenged.

The Colorado Interstate Gas Case. The Colorado Interstate Gas case[13] concerned two affiliated companies, Canadian River Gas and Colorado Interstate Gas. Canadian River produced and gathered gas in the Panhandle field in Texas, selling some of the gas within the state and transporting the remainder to a point in New Mexico where it was sold to Colorado Interstate for resale. The commission, in determining the interstate resale rate for Colorado Interstate, included in the rate base both Canadian River's producing and gathering properties and Colorado Interstate's transmission system.

The companies, in contesting the commission's action, contended that Canadian River was a producing and gathering company, and thus exempt from regulation under the act. The FPC argued that Canadian River's sales to Colorado Interstate did not result from arm's length bargaining, and that unless it had control over the price paid by Colorado Interstate, its authority to regulate the rate charged by the pipeline company to local distributors would be severely limited. The Supreme Court upheld the commission. The exemption,

---

[10]*Re Columbian Fuel Corp.*, 2 FPC 200 (1940).

[11]*Ibid.*, p. 208.

[12]*Re Canadian River Gas Co.*, 43 PUR (NS) 205 (1942); *City of Cleveland* v. *Hope Natural Gas Co.*, 44 PUR (NS) 1 (1942); *Re Interstate Natural Gas Co.*, 48 PUR (NS) 267 (1943); *Re Cities Service Gas Co.*, 50 PUR (NS) 65 (1943).

[13]*Re Colorado Interstate Gas Co.*, 3 FPC 32 (1942), *aff'd*, 142 F. 2d 943 (1944), 324 U.S. 581 (1945).

ruled the Court, prevented the agency from controlling such matters as drilling and spacing of wells, but "it [did] not preclude the Commission from reflecting the production and gathering facilities of a natural gas company in the rate base and determining the expenses incident thereto for the purposes of determining the reasonableness of rates subject to its jurisdiction." [14] The commission thus had jurisdiction over the field prices of integrated and affiliated producers.

Jurisdiction over Independent Producers

The commission continued its policy of refusing to regulate independent producers. In September, 1944, it announced a comprehensive investigation into all aspects of the natural gas regulatory problem. In July, 1947, it unanimously endorsed a House bill (the Priest bill) exempting from FPC jurisdiction sales by independent producers to pipeline companies, and in August, 1947, it issued Order 139 declaring the 1938 act denied it this power. In 1948, the natural gas investigation ended in an even split (one vacancy existed on the commission) on the issue: Commissioners Smith and Wimberly favored Congressional exemption of the field sales of independents, [15] and Commissioners Draper and Olds opposed any amendment. [16] The following year, the vacancy was filled by Thomas Buchanan who sided with Commissioners Draper and Olds. Thus, in the short span of three years, the commission had changed its position from unanimous endorsement of the exemption to a 3–2 majority in opposition to amending the statute.

By this time, the issue also was before Congress. The 1947 Priest bill was not enacted. In 1949, Congressman Harris introduced in the House a bill exempting sales by independents to interstate pipelines, which was passed later in the year, 183–131. A companion bill was introduced by Senator Kerr in the Senate where, after strong opposition, it was approved the following year by a vote of 44 to 38. [17] President Truman, on April 18, 1950, vetoed the bill, stating that the

> . . . authority to regulate such sales is necessary in the public interest. . . .
> [T]o withdraw entirely from this field of regulation, however, impelled only
> by imaginary fears, and in the face of a record of accomplishment under the

[14] *Ibid.*, pp. 601–3. Also see *Interstate Natural Gas Co., Inc.* v. *Federal Power Comm.*, 331 U.S. 682 (1947).

[15] Federal Power Commission, *Natural Gas Investigation: Smith-Wimberly Report* (Docket G-580, 1948).

[16] Federal Power Commission, *Natural Gas Investigation: Draper-Olds Report* (Docket G-580, 1948).

[17] During the Senate debates, the confirmation of Commissioner Olds' reappointment to the FPC came before the Senate Committee. "In an endeavor to break the majority opposition of the Commission to such amendatory legislation and deliver a personal rebuff to Olds, gas and oil interests joined forces with the proponents of the legislation in the Senate to defeat Olds' confirmation." Gable, *op. cit.*, pp. 49–50. Also see Joseph P. Harris, "The Senatorial Rejection of Leland Olds: A Case Study," 45 *American Political Science Review* 674 (1951).

present law which is successful from the standpoint of consumer, distributor, carrier and producer alike, would not be in the public interest.[18]

The FPC rescinded Order 139.

The 1954 Phillips Case. The Presidential veto shifted the issue back to the commission, where it did not long remain dormant. On October 28, 1948, the commission initiated an investigation of the Phillips Petroleum Company to determine (*a*) whether the firm was a natural gas company within the meaning of the Natural Gas Act and, if so, (*b*) whether any of its rates were unjust or unreasonable. Phillips, at the time of the investigation, was the nation's largest seller of natural gas to interstate pipelines. It owned 4,380 miles of gathering lines in 5 states (some lines crossed the state border between Oklahoma and Texas) and 35 processing plants. It also purchased and gathered gas from other producers. Its sales were made to five interstate transmission companies. Was Phillips as a producer and gatherer of natural gas exempt from the act?

Hearings were held before an examiner from April 3, 1951, to May 23, 1951. The record made included nearly 5,800 pages of testimony and approximately 4,000 pages of exhibits. Eight states, three cities, a county, and numerous private groups were permitted to intervene in the proceedings. In general, gas-consuming states supported federal regulation, while producers and gas-producing states supported state regulation. The record was certified to the commission which held arguments on July 9 and 10, 1951. Its opinion, issued on August 22, 1951, held that the commission lacked jurisdiction over Phillips on the grounds that all its activities were a part of its producing and gathering business exempt under the act, and that federal regulation of the company's sales made during the course of production and gathering would interfere with effective state conservation efforts.[19] The commission ordered the proceedings terminated.

The commission's decision was appealed by the state of Wisconsin, the cities of Kansas City, Milwaukee, and Detroit, and the county of Wayne, Michigan. On June 7, 1954, the Supreme Court, in a 5 to 3 decision, held that Phillips was subject to the jurisdiction of the FPC and directed the commission to determine whether the firm's prices were just and reasonable.[20] The Court argued, in part:

> ... we believe that the legislative history indicates a congressional intent to give the Commission jurisdiction over the rates of all wholesales of natural gas in interstate commerce, whether by a pipeline company or not and whether occurring before, during, or after transmission by an interstate pipeline company. There can be no dispute that the overriding congressional purpose was to plug the "gap" in regulation of natural gas companies resulting from judicial decisions prohibiting, on federal constitutional grounds, state regulation of many of the interstate commerce aspects of the

---

[18] 96 *Congressional Record* 5304 (1950).
[19] *Re Phillips Petroleum Co.,* 90 PUR (NS) 325 (1951).
[20] *Phillips Petroleum Co. v. Wisconsin,* 347 U.S. 672 (1954).

natural gas business. A significant part of this gap was created by cases holding that "the regulation of wholesale rates of gas and electric energy moving in interstate commerce is beyond the constitutional powers of the States." . . . The committee reports on the bill that became the Natural Gas Act specifically referred to two of these cases and to the necessity of federal regulations to occupy the hiatus created by them. Thus, we are satisfied that Congress sought to regulate wholesales of natural gas occurring at both ends of the interstate transmission systems.

Regulation of the sales in interstate commerce for resale made by a so-called independent natural gas producer is not essentially different from regulation of such sales when made by an affiliate of an interstate pipeline company. In both cases, the rates charged may have a direct and substantial effect on the price paid by the ultimate consumer. Protection of consumers against exploitation at the hands of natural gas companies was the primary aim of the Natural Gas Act. . . . Attempts to weaken this protection by amendatory legislation exempting independent natural gas producers from federal regulation have repeatedly failed, and we refuse to achieve the same result by a strained interpretation of the existing statutory language.[21]

Justice Clark in his dissent stated:

By today's decision, the Court restricts the phrase "production and gathering" to "the physical activities, facilities, and properties" used in production and gathering. Such a gloss strips the words of their substance. If the Congress so intended, then it left for state regulation only a mass of empty pipe, vacant processing plants and thousands of hollow wells with scarecrow derricks, monuments to this new extension of federal power. It was not so understood. . . . There can be no doubt, as the Commission has found, that federal regulation of production and gathering will collide and substantially interfere with and hinder the enforcement of . . . regulatory measures.[22]

The Court thus handed the Federal Power Commission the complex task of determining the wellhead price for thousands of independent natural gas producers—a task which it had not sought.

The Movement for Exemption. The Phillips decision failed to settle the issue. An intensive public relations program was undertaken by producers and trade associations to persuade the public that federal regulation of independent producers was unnecessary. The legislatures of Oklahoma and Kansas enacted laws empowering their state regulatory commissions to establish minimum wellhead prices for natural gas even if they were above the maximum prices set by the FPC. Both statutes were later held unconstitutional on the ground that they were in conflict with the Phillips decision.[23]

The significant battle, however, was waged in Congress. A report in March, 1955, by the President's special Advisory Committee on Energy Supplies and

[21] *Ibid.,* pp. 682–84, 685.
[22] Dissenting opinion, *ibid.,* pp. 695–96.
[23] *Natural Gas Pipeline Co.* v. *Panoma Corp.,* 349 U.S. 44 (1955); *Cities Service Gas Co.* v. *Corporation Comm. of Kansas,* 355 U.S. 391 (1958).

Resources concluded that state rather than federal regulation of gas production was preferable.[24] Identical bills to exempt independent producers from FPC jurisdiction were introduced: one by Representative Harris in the House and the other by Senator Fulbright in the Senate. The House passed the measure in 1955, 209 to 203, and the Senate passed the bill the following year, 53 to 38. But during the course of the Senate debate on the bill, a senator revealed that an oil company lawyer had offered to contribute $2,500 to his campaign fund in an apparent effort to influence his vote. President Eisenhower, while stating that he was "in accord with its basic objectives," nevertheless vetoed the bill, arguing that he could not sign the legislation before the "arrogant" tactics of its supporters had been fully investigated.[25]

In his budget message of January, 1957, President Eisenhower again endorsed exemption of natural gas producers from federal regulation, and some fourteen bills were subsequently introduced in Congress during the year. But in February, 1958, while the matter was pending in the House, it was disclosed that a Texas politician had issued invitations to a $100-a-plate dinner for the House minority leader, noting that his support and influence was needed to insure passage of the measure.[26] Congress took no further action on the proposed legislation. Subsequent proposals also have failed.

Fixing the Field Price

Instead of the 157 natural gas companies subject to its jurisdiction at the end of 1953, the Phillips decision extended the commission's power to 4,365 independent producers who sold to interstate pipelines. In July, 1954, the commission issued an order freezing the wellhead price of natural gas. It directed all producers to apply for certificates, both for present operations and for new service, and to file their rates. By June 30, 1963, 17,809 certificate applications had been filed; of these applications, 5,483 were for services rendered prior to the 1954 decision.[27] But the most difficult task facing the commission was how it should determine the field price of natural gas.

The Wellhead Price: Individual Company Cost of Service. In regulating the field price of gas of interstate pipeline companies, the commission, until a 1954 decision,[28] used the traditional rate base, individual company cost of service approach to rate making. It soon found, however, that this method had serious drawbacks in regulating independent gas producers.[29]

The first problem faced by the commission was one of administrative feasibility. Since the largest 266 producers account for roughly 91 percent of interstate sales, most are small. Their records, in turn, are often incomplete. To

24 Advisory Committee on Energy Supplies and Resources, *Report to the President* (Washington, D.C.: U.S. Government Printing Office, 1955).
25 102 *Congressional Record* 2793 (1956).
26 *Washington Post,* February 11, 1958.
27 Federal Power Commission, *Annual Report, 1963,* p. 140.
28 *Re Panhandle Eastern Pipe Line Co.,* 3 PUR 3d 396 (1954).
29 See *Re Phillips Petroleum Co.,* 35 PUR 3d 199, 208–15 (FPC, 1960).

lessen the impact of regulation, the commission has permitted independent producers to file simplified certificate and rate applications, and has released them from maintaining accounts in accordance with the uniform system and from submitting certain reports. Nevertheless, the cost of service method, requiring a separate rate determination for each producer, would result in an intolerable administrative burden. The commission itself concluded in a 1960 case when it rejected the method: "... if our present staff were immediately tripled, and if all new employees would be as competent as those we now have, we would not reach a current status in our independent producer rate work until 2043 A.D.—eighty-two and one-half years from now."[30]

In the second place, determining the cost of producing natural gas involves an allocation problem. Natural gas is produced to a considerable degree jointly with liquids: with crude oil from oil casinghead reservoirs and with lease liquids (called condensates) from gas condensate reservoirs.[31] The joint production and joint nature of many of the exploration (or finding) and production costs of oil and gas are the source of many of the difficulties in regulating the price of gas sold in interstate commerce, for the "cost" of gas largely depends on the allocation method chosen.

Three allocation methods have been widely employed. (1) Sales Realization. Annual costs, including operating expenses, depreciation, depletion, exploration, and development, are allocated in proportion to the revenues received from the products during the test period. Fixed costs, including net plant and working capital, are allocated in proportion to the value of the reserves remaining in the ground in the test period. (2) Btu. Method. Joint costs are allocated in proportion to the British thermal unit content (i.e., the energy content) of the products. (3) Relative Cost Method. The joint costs of gas and oil are divided in proportion to the costs of the two products in pure gas and pure oil wells. Each of these methods has serious weaknesses.[32] Moreover, since all allocation methods are partly arbitrary, so are the resulting "cost" figures.

Finally, the relationship between investment and service is nebulous in the case of natural gas production. As Justice Jackson observed in the Hope Natural Gas case: "The service one renders to society in the gas business is measured by what he gets out of the ground, not by what he puts into it, and there is little

---

[30] *Ibid.,* p. 210.

[31] In recent years, over 70 percent of domestic gas production has come from gas-only and gas-condensate wells.

[32] See Otto Eckstein, "Natural Gas and Patterns of Regulation," 36 *Harvard Business Review* 126, 129–33 (1958).

The Btu. Method is most often used to allocate exploration costs; the Relative Cost Method to allocate production costs. The two separate allocation methods are used because production costs can be more readily identified with a particular type of production (or lease type), whereas exploration costs (such as geological expenditures) are more general and are therefore said to be incurred "in the indiscriminate search for hydrocarbons." However, in the Area Rate Proceedings (discussed below), the FPC accepted the "directionality" thesis, namely, that producers can direct their exploration efforts towards oil or gas and can assign certain costs respectively.

more relation between the investment and the results than in a game of poker."[33] Stated another way, "A huge investment might yield only a trickle of gas, while a small investment might lead to a bonanza."[34] The rate base, cost of service method would erase any bonanza or windfall profits to successful speculators. Yet, in an industry such as this one, where in the search for gas the elements of risk and chance are so important, the method also tends to penalize the "more astute, fortunate, and efficient" producer.[35] Indeed, as Howard has observed, "the rate-base itself can, conceivably, vanish."[36]

Two consequences of the rate base, individual company cost of service approach also must be considered. First, the rate base method resulted in a structure of field prices described by Justice Jackson as "delirious." In his words:

> To let rate base figures, compiled on any of the conventional theories of rate-making, govern a rate for natural gas seems to me little better than to draw figures out of a hat. These cases confirm and strengthen me in the view I stated in the *Hope* case that the entire rate-base method should be rejected in pricing natural gas, though it might be used to determine transportation costs. . . . These orders in some instances result in three different prices for gas from the same well. The regulated company is a part owner, an unregulated company is a part owner, and the land owner has a royalty share of the production from certain wells. The regulated company buys all of the gas for its interstate business. It is allowed to pay as operating expenses an unregulated contract price for its co-owner's share and a different unregulated contract price for the royalty owner's share, but for its own share it is allowed substantially less than either. Any method of rate-making by which an identical product from a single well, going to the same consumers, has three prices depending on who owns it does not make sense to me.[37]

Second, the cost of service approach discouraged vertical integration since it discriminated against pipeline-produced gas. According to Lindahl:

> The role of the pipelines in providing gas for interstate use has fallen off greatly since the inception of rate control. Eight major interstate pipeline companies produced about 47 percent of the gas which they transported and sold in 1940, whereas these systems produced less than 30 percent of their requirements in 1951. None of the seven large systems which have been created to serve large consuming markets since the Natural Gas Act became effective produces any substantial amount of gas. Taken together these fifteen large major transmission systems produced only 18½ percent of their requirements in 1952.[38]

[33] *Federal Power Comm.* v. *Hope Natural Gas Co.*, 320 U.S. 591, 649 (1944).
[34] *Wisconsin* v. *Federal Power Comm.*, 373 U.S. 294, 299 (1963).
[35] Martin L. Lindahl, "Federal Regulation of Natural Gas Producers and Gathers," 46 *American Economic Review* 532, 538 (1956).
[36] Marshall C. Howard, "Regulation and the Price of Natural Gas," 23 *Southern Economic Journal* 142, 145 (1956).
[37] *Colorado Interstate Gas Co.* v. *Federal Power Comm.*, op. cit., p. 610.
[38] Lindahl, *op. cit.*, p. 536.

Discrimination occurred because with the market price of natural gas rising, independent producers were receiving a higher rate of return than were integrated producers on their gas-producing properties. If vertical integration is desirable—and many feel that it is[39]—a price policy that encourages exploration and development by pipeline companies must be adopted.

The Wellhead Price: Area Rates. In April, 1954, just two months before the Supreme Court's Phillips decision, the commission rejected the rate base, individual company cost of service approach in a case involving the Panhandle Eastern Pipeline Company.[40] In valuing the gas produced by the company, the commission determined a "fair field price" by taking a weighted average of the prices paid by the pipeline company to independent producers in the same area. Prices so determined, argued the commission, resulted from arm's length bargaining and would encourage the exploration for, and development of, gas reserves. A year later, the procedure was held to be improper by a Court of Appeals.[41] The commission might use the average field price method, ruled the Court, but the rate base, cost of service method must be used as a "point of departure." Then, if the resulting rates under the field price method were higher than those based on the cost of service method, the rates would have to be justified by specific evidence showing that they were just and reasonable. The Supreme Court refused to review the case.

This decision forced the commission to return to the rate base, cost of service approach in fixing wellhead prices for integrated producers, and it complicated the FPC's attempt to devise new regulatory methods. In 1956, the commission dismissed a number of rate increase applications of producers on the ground that the evidence presented was insufficient to indicate whether the rates requested were needed to encourage exploration and development.[42]

In the meantime, the commission had before it the remand in the Phillips case, and was investigating the lawfulness of the company's interstate rates. The trial examiner, in April, 1959, fixed the maximum wellhead price that Phillips could charge by computing the cost of production and adding a fair rate of return on the investment.[43] Over a year later, the commission issued its opinion in which it concluded that (*a*) the cost of service approach was "not a sensible, or even a workable, method of fixing the rates of independent producers" since it would "produce fallacious results" and (*b*) the "ultimate solution" to producer regulation lay in the area rate approach—that is, "the determination of fair prices for gas, based on reasonable financial requirements of the industry

[39] See pp. 615–17.

[40] *Re Panhandle Eastern Pipe Line Co., op. cit.*

[41] *City of Detroit* v. *Federal Power Comm.,* 230 F 2d 810 (1955).

[42] *Re Union Oil Co. of California et al.,* Opinion No. 300, Docket Nos. G-4331 et seq. (December 6, 1956).

[43] *Re Phillips Petroleum Co.,* 24 FPC 590 (1959). The examiner and the company were far apart. The examiner allowed a cost of $57 million, compared to Phillips' claim of $92 million. The examiner allocated 30.50 percent of the cost of exploration to gas; the company allocated 62 percent. The examiner allowed a return of 9.25 percent on investment; the company asked for 18 percent.

and not on the particular rate base and expenses of each natural gas company."[44] Concurrently, the commission issued a "Statement of General Policy" to implement its new procedure.[45] The gas fields of the country producing for interstate shipments were divided into twenty-three geographical areas. Two price levels or ceilings were established for each area—initial service rates for new contracts and increased rates ("escalated rates") for existing contracts, in recognition of the fact that "initial prices in new contracts are, and in many cases by virtue of economic factors, must be higher than the prices contained in old contracts." The commission's pricing areas and interim ceilings, as amended through June 30, 1967, are shown in Figure 16-1. These rates were "for the purpose of guidance and initial action by the commission," and it was announced that in the absence of compelling evidence the commission would not certificate initial rates, and would suspend increased rates, that exceeded the set levels.[46] The commission also announced that it would begin a series of hearings, one on each major producing area, to determine final area prices.

The following year, the Court of Appeals affirmed the commission's decision.[47] And in 1963, in a 5 to 4 decision, the Supreme Court did likewise.[48] Justice Harlan argued:

> . . . to declare that a particular method of rate regulation is so sanctified as to make it highly unlikely that any other method could be sustained would be wholly out of keeping with this Court's consistent and clearly articulated approach to the question of the Commission's power to regulate rates. It has repeatedly been stated that no single method must be followed by the Commission in considering the justness and reasonableness of rates . . . and we reaffirm that principle today.
>
> More specifically, the Court has never held that the individual company cost-of-service method is a *sine qua non* of natural gas rate regulation. Indeed

[44]*Re Phillips Petroleum Co.,* 35 PUR 3d 199 (1960). (The commission decided, however, in the case at hand to use cost of service evidence, since the whole case had been tried on that basis.) See Note, "FPC Regulation of Independent Producers of Natural Gas," 75 *Harvard Law Review* 549 (1962); and Edmund W. Kitch, "Regulation of the Field Market for Natural Gas by the Federal Power Commission," 11 *Journal of Law and Economics* 243 (1968).

[45]*Statement of General Policy No. 61-1,* 35 PUR 3d 195 (1960). The policy statement has been revised on several occasions.

[46]Following a 1959 Supreme Court decision (*Atlantic Refining Co.* v. *New York Public Service Comm.,* 360 U.S. 378 [1959]), the FPC evolved a system for determining the maximum initial price (known as the "in-line" price) at which natural gas could move, under sales contracts, during the interval preceding the establishment of just and reasonable rates. After determining the "in-line" prices (based largely on current prices for gas in the area of the proposed sale), the commission conditioned permanent certificates so as to limit the level to which prices might be raised (pursuant to escalation clauses) during a given period or until the relevant area rates had been determined. In granting permanent certificates, the commission also ordered refunds of amounts collected by producers in the past under temporary certificates which contained no refund conditions. The commission's procedures were upheld in *Federal Power Comm.* v. *Sunray DX Oil Co.,* 391 U.S. 9 (1968).

[47]*Wisconsin* v. *Federal Power Comm.,* 303 F. 2d 380 (1961).

[48]373 U.S. 294 (1963).

FIGURE 16-1. Area Price Levels for Independent Producer Natural Gas Sales Per Statement of General Policy No. 61-1 as Amended through June 30, 1967

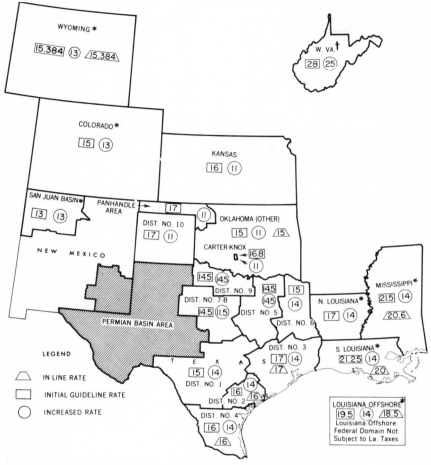

(In cents per thousand cubic feet at 14.65 psia, except as noted)
*At 15.025 psia.   †At 15.325 psia.
Notes: (1) Commission determined Permian Basin area price ceilings—pipeline quality gas:
　　　　　New gas well gas and associated residue gas (contracts since January 1, 1961):   Texas 16.5¢   N.M. 15.5¢
　　　　　All other gas (including gas well gas contracts before January 1, 1961:   Texas 14.5¢   N.M. 13.5¢
　　　　　Minimum price floor, both states: 9¢.
　　　　(2) Increased rate ceilings .6¢ per Mcf (at 14.65 psia) higher than those shown are applicable under rate schedules from which favored-nation and price redetermination provisions have been eliminated, and 1.0¢ per Mcf higher under rate schedules from which all escalation provisions have been eliminated.
　　　　(3) All rates include tax except New Mexico Permian Basin area rates and onshore Louisiana 14.0¢ and 17.0¢ rates.
Source: Federal Power Commission, *Annual Report, 1967,* p. 50.

the prudent investment, original cost, rate base method which we are now told is lawful, established, and effective is the very one the Court was asked to declare impermissible in the *Hope* case, less than twenty years ago.

To whatever extent the matter of costs may be a requisite element in rate regulation, we have no indication that the area method will fall short of statutory or constitutional standards. The Commission has stated in its opinion in this proceeding that the goal is to have rates based on "the reasonable financial requirements of the industry" in each production area . . . and we were advised at oral argument that composite cost-of-service data will be considered in the area rate proceedings. Surely, we cannot say that the rates to be developed in these proceedings will in all likelihood be so high as to deprive consumers, or so low as to deprive producers, of their right to a just and reasonable rate.

We recognize the unusual difficulties inherent in regulating the price of a commodity such as natural gas. We respect the Commission's considered judgment, backed by sound and persuasive reasoning, that the individual company cost-of-service method is not a feasible or suitable one for regulating the rates of independent producers. We share the Commission's hopes that the area approach may prove to be the ultimate solution.[49]

Area Rate Proceedings. On December 23, 1960, the first area rate proceeding, Permian Basin (west Texas and southeastern New Mexico), was initiated; the Southern Louisiana area rate proceeding was instituted on May 10, 1961. These are the only two area proceedings that have been concluded by the commission, although three other proceedings are underway.[50] The ultimate questions to be resolved in the area rate proceedings are how high a reserves–production ratio is needed and what price is required to achieve it.

1. Permian Basin. The Permian Basin is one of the country's major gas-producing areas, accounting for about 11 percent of all gas moving in

---

[49]*Ibid.,* pp. 309–10. Justice Clark, in his dissenting opinion, argued: "The Sisyphean labors of the Commission continue as it marches up the hill of producer regulation only to tumble down again with little undertaken and less done . . . . In this summary fashion [the issuance of the Statement of General Policy] the Commission junked its cost-of-service regulation program, wasted a half dozen years of work thereon, and is now experimenting with a new, untried, untested, inchoate program which, in addition, is of doubtful legality. As a consequence the consumers of gas all over the United States . . . will pay for the Commission's area pricing wild-goose chase. I predict that in the end the consumer will find himself to be the biggest goose of the hunt and the small producer the dead duck." *Ibid.,* pp. 315, 317. Also see Sterling W. Steves, "FPC Gas Tariff—Solution to the Rate Change Dilemma of the Independent Producer?," 15 *Southwestern Law Journal* 46 (1961).

[50]The Hugoton-Anadarko Basin (Texas and Oklahoma Panhandles and Kansas) and the Texas Gulf Coast Area proceedings were instituted on November 27, 1963; the Other Southwest Area (Arkansas, Mississippi, four counties in Alabama, northern Louisiana, Texas Railroad Commission Districts 5, 6, and 9, and most of Oklahoma) proceeding on February 28, 1967. The examiners' decisions have been issued in the first two proceedings. See *Re Hugoton-Anadarko Area Rates,* Docket No. AR64-1 and *Re Texas Gulf Coast Area Rates,* Docket No. AR64-2, as summarized in 1 *FPC News* (September 20, 1968), pp. 1-6.

interstate commerce and supplying markets in twelve states (with 85 percent of the interstate sales destined for California).[51] The commission's decision was issued on August 5, 1965, and was modified in an opinion issued on October 4, 1965.[52] The commission declined to calculate area rates from prevailing field prices. In arriving at costs (prices must be established on the basis of costs), it used the cost of service technique (a composite of all producer costs in the area as reported by them for the test year 1960) for casinghead and residue gas, and a cost computed from industry-wide statistics (using such components as volumes of reserves added versus exploration and development costs, production operating expenses, regulatory expenses, depletion, and royalties) for new nonassociated gas.[53] Each of the cost calculations included a rate base on which a return on investment was allowed. For new gas-well gas, an average rate base approach, based on a twenty-year production life, was adopted. For all other gas, the traditional cost of service approach of total net investment in the test year (1960) was followed. The rate of return allowed, determined by a comparable-earnings standard, was 12 percent on each producer's investment.

A two-price system was adopted (Figure 16-2)—a higher price for new gas-well gas (contracts since January 1, 1961) and a lower price for all other gas.[54] Refunds were ordered for rates that exceeded the ceilings back to the start of the case in 1961 (estimated at more than $68 million), a two and one-half year moratorium (until January 1, 1968) was imposed on filings for prices in excess of the applicable area maximum rate, and restrictions were placed on escalation clauses in existing contracts.[55] A minimum rate of 9 cents per thousand cubic feet was fixed for Permian Basin gas of standard pipeline quality, with provisions for adjustment to reflect deviations from that standard. Finally, the commission instituted a rule-making proceeding for the purpose of relaxing

[51] Federal Power Commission, *Annual Report, 1966*, p. 128.

[52] *Re Permian Basin Area Rates*, 34 FPC 159 (1965), 34 FPC 1068 (1965). The commission's decision generally followed the recommendations of its examiner. (Before the examiner, the proceedings involved 250 days of hearings, 30,365 pages of testimony, 337 exhibits, and 90 witnesses.) The examiner's decision is summarized in 74 *Public Utilities Fortnightly* 86, 86–90 (October 8, 1964). Also see Harold Leventhal, "Reviewing the Permian Basin Area Gas Price Hearings," 73 *ibid.* 19 (March 12, 1964); and A. J. G. Priest, "Factors Leading up to the Permian Basin Decision," 79 *ibid.* 13 (March 2, 1967).

[53] The cost of service technique used by the commission differed from the usual individual company cost of service approach in that (1) the costs of all producer respondents were averaged together and (2) costs were only determined for gas-well gas leases, i.e., costs were not computed for gas produced on casinghead-oil or combination leases. The commission felt that the allocation of costs to gas on these leases was more difficult to compute. It held, however, that the cost of such gas could not be greater than, and is probably less than, the cost of flowing gas-well gas.

[54] The ceiling prices for gas from the Permian Basin produced in New Mexico were lower, reflecting the lower production tax level in that state. In the proceedings before the commission, the producers had sought a one-price ceiling for all Permian Basin gas of about 20 cents per thousand cubic feet; the FPC staff sought a 13.7-cent ceiling for all gas except casinghead, which would be 9 cents.

[55] Escalation clauses are discussed below, pp. 620–21.

FIGURE 16-2
Area Price Levels for Independent Producer Natural Gas Sales in Permian Basin Area
Per Docket No. AR61-1 Proceedings (Opinion No. 468)

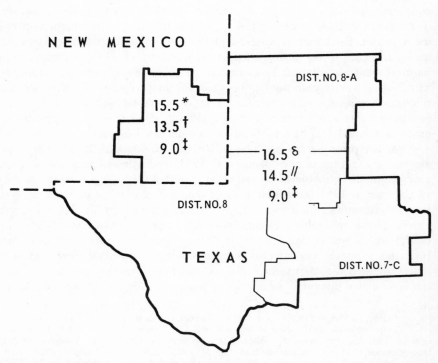

*Base area rate plus production taxes in effect September 1, 1965, for gas well gas and residue gas derived therefrom for gas sales contracts dated on and after January 1, 1961.

†Base area rate plus production taxes in effect September 1, 1965, for gas well gas and residue gas derived therefrom for gas sales contracts dated prior to January 1, 1961, and for all casinghead gas and residue gas derived therefrom.

‡Minimum rate for all gas sales of pipeline quality in Permian Basin.

§Base area rate for gas well gas and residue gas derived therefrom for gas sales contracts dated on and after January 1, 1961.

//Base area rate for gas well gas and residue gas derived therefrom for gas sales contracts dated prior to January 1, 1961, and for all casinghead gas and residue gas derived therefrom.

Note: All rates are subject to adjustment for deviations in gas quality.

Source: Federal Power Commission, *Annual Report, 1966,* p. 132.

the certificate and rate filing requirements for small producers (sales of 10 billion cubic feet per year or under).[56]

The economic rationale of the commission's two-price system requires brief consideration.[57] The separate and higher price for new nonassociated (gas-well) gas was established to encourage the search for new gas reserves, and the lower price for all other gas was aimed at preventing producers from receiving excessive profits. The costs of exploration and development have increased sharply as a result of the postwar inflation. Thus, a one-price system based on costs already incurred (including a fair rate of return) would not provide the necessary incentive for exploration, while a one-price system based on the costs required to replace current production would overcompensate producers on gas already discovered, for which no incentive is needed and for which lower costs were incurred. The two-price system also reflects the fact that the industry can direct its exploration activity to some extent (known as "directionality") toward the search for gas, whereas most gas in the past was discovered as a by-product of the search for oil. Here again, the higher price for new nonassociated gas was to provide an incentive by rewarding the successful directional search for gas, while no incentive is needed for casinghead gas that is forthcoming anyway as a result of the successful search for oil.

Predictably, the Permian Basin decision was appealed to the courts. A lower court, in 1967, sustained the FPC's authority to impose maximum area rates upon producers' jurisdictional sales, but remanded the case to the commission for further proceedings.[58] However, on May 1, 1968, the Supreme Court, in a 7–1 decision, sustained the commission's orders in their entirety.[59] After reviewing the background, the Court said:

> . . . Producers of natural gas cannot usefully be classed as public utilities. They enjoy no franchises or guaranteed areas of service. They are intensely competitive vendors of a wasting commodity they have acquired only by costly and often unrewarded search. Their unit costs may rise and decline with the vagaries of good fortune. The value to the public of the service they perform is measured by the quantity and character of the natural gas they produce, and not by the resources they have expended in its search. . . . The exploration for and the production of natural gas are thus "more erratic and

[56] On the Permian Basin decision, see Comment, "Regulating Independent Gas Producers: The First Area Approach," 115 *University of Pennsylvania Law Review* 84 (1966); James C. Loughlin, "Controversies in the Area Rate Proceedings," 79 *Public Utilities Fortnightly* 36 (February 2, 1967); Stanley Learned, "The Biggest Goose of the Hunt," 20 *New Mexico Business* 4 (April, 1967); and Edmund W. Kitch, "The Permian Basin Area Rate Cases and the Regulatory Determination of Price," 116 *University of Pennsylvania Law Review* 191 (1967).

[57] See Irwin M. Stelzer, "Economic Rationale of the Permian Two-price System," 76 *Public Utilities Fortnightly* 51 (December 9, 1965).

[58] *Skelly Oil Co.* v. *Federal Power Comm.*, 375 F. 2d 6 (1967), 375 F. 2d 35 (1967).

[59] *In re Permian Basin Area Rate Cases,* 390 U.S. 747 (1968). Justice Douglas dissented; Justice Marshall took no part in the decision.

irregular and unpredictable in relation to investment than any phase of any other utility business." ... Moreover, the number both of independent producers and of jurisdictional sales is large, and the administrative burdens placed upon the Commission by an individual company costs-of-service standard were therefore extremely heavy.[60]

The Court then went on to hold that the FPC had authority to adopt a system of area price regulation, to impose a moratorium on the filing of new rates in excess of the maximum area rates, to restrict escalation clauses, and to make special provisions for exempting small producers. The commission's methods also were approved, although with some reservations. For example, with respect to the prescribed rate structure, the Court noted:

> ... We do not suggest that the Commission need not continuously evaluate the revenue and other consequences of its area rate structures. A principal advantage of area regulation is that it centers attention upon the industry's aggregate problems, and we may expect that, as the Commission's experience with area regulation lengthens, it will treat these important questions more precisely and efficaciously. We hold only that, in the circumstances here presented, the Commission's rate structure has not been shown to deny producers revenues consonant with just and reasonable rates.[61]

And the Court concluded: "Although the Commission's position might at several places usefully be clarified, the producers have not satisfied the 'heavy burden' placed upon those who would set aside its decision."[62]

2. Southern Louisiana Area. The Southern Louisiana area (which includes both state and federal offshore domains in the Gulf of Mexico off the Louisiana coast) is also a major gas-producing area, providing about 31 percent of all natural gas moving in interstate commerce and supplying markets in twenty-eight states and the District of Columbia in the eastern and central United States. The commission's opinion, issued on September 25, 1968,[63] generally follows the precedents of the Permian Basin decision.

---

[60] *Ibid.*, pp. 756–57, quoting from *Federal Power Comm.* v. *Hope Natural Gas Co.,* 320 U.S. 591, 649 (1944) (footnotes omitted).

[61] *Ibid.*, p. 822.

[62] *Ibid.*, pp. 812–13. Justice Douglas, in his dissent, said: "The area rate orders challenged here are based on averages. No single producer's actual costs, actual risks, actual returns are known. The 'result reached' as to any producer is not known. The 'impact of the rate order' on any producer is not known. The 'total effect' of the rate order on a single producer is not known.... In absence of knowledge, we cannot possibly perform our function of judicial review, limited though it be.... If the task of regulating producer sales within the framework of the Natural Gas Act is as difficult as the present case illustrates, perhaps the problem should be returned to Congress. But certainly we do little today to advance the cause of responsible administrative action. With all respect, we promote administrative irresponsibility by making an agency's *fiat* an adequate substitute for supported findings." *Ibid.*, pp. 829–30, 831, 841.

[63] *Re Southern Louisiana Area Rates,* 40 FPC 530 (1968). In March, 1969, the FPC affirmed the rate structure and most of the basic conclusions reached in its 1968 opinion, but "at the same time announced a new proceeding aimed at a possible revision

Like the Permian Basin decision, the commission used industry-wide cost data, allowed a 12 percent rate of return on net investment, provided for price adjustments to reflect quality differentials (applicable to future contracts only), ordered refunds, and established simplified procedures for certificate and rate filings for small producers. Unlike the Permian Basin opinion, however, the commission established a three-price structure, providing for ceilings of: 18.5 cents per thousand cubic feet for all casinghead gas and pre-1961 gas-well gas; 19.5 cents for gas-well gas sold under contracts dated January 1, 1961, through September 30, 1968; and 20 cents for gas-well gas sold under contracts dated October 1, 1968, or later.[64] Further, no moratorium was imposed on price increases (although they will remain in effect until "such time as they may be changed by the Commission") and no minimum rate was set for the area.

Integrated and Affiliated Producers. It has long been argued that "the interest of the public definitely lies in the direction of natural gas production by pipeline systems themselves, as distinguished from their complete dependence for gas supply upon purchases from other producers . . . ."[65] The advantages of vertical integration have been succinctly summarized by Falck:

> The very fact that groups of independent producers have been marshaling evidence pointing to declining reserves–production ratios underscores the need to bring the pipelines into the act. The combined efforts of pipelines and producers, assuming both are accorded fair and reasonable price regulation, are needed to assure a dependable long-term future supply of natural gas . . . .

> Quite apart from the supply problem, however, it can be demonstrated that ownership of gas production properties by a pipeline creates real possibilities and opportunities for reducing the overall cost of operation. A pipeline with substantial gas reserves can bargain more effectively in acquiring new gas supplies from independent producers; it is not under pressure to buy specific volumes of gas when it would be disadvantageous to do so, either in terms of time or location; it can avoid some of the more serious economic losses due to the operation of take-or-pay-for clauses in gas purchase contracts; its own achievements in exploration, discovery, and development may serve as a yardstick for measuring the performance of independent producers; it is possible also that pipelines, with their extensive organizations, financial backing and expertise, may make positive contributions to the technology of exploration, development, and production of natural gas; finally, in future years pipelines may use certain of their existing production fields where suitably located as storage reservoirs and thus take care of seasonal variations in demand economically.[66]

of area ceiling prices for gas sales contracts dated after October 1, 1968, from the offshore Southern Louisiana area in the federal domain. . . ." 2 *FPC News* (March 21, 1969), p. 11.

[64] These prices apply to gas subject to the Louisiana production tax. For gas not subject to the tax, the area ceiling rates were set 1.5 cents lower.

[65] *Re Panhandle Eastern Pipe Line Co.*, op. cit., p. 419.

[66] Edward Falck, "Area Gas Pricing for Pipelines?" 73 *Public Utilities Fortnightly* 34, 47 (January 30, 1964).

While recognizing both the advantages of vertical integration and the disadvantages of the cost of service method, the commission continues to use the traditional method for determining the rates of integrated and affiliated producers.[67] However, it has not adopted a consistent policy on whether the rate of return allowed on production properties should be equal to, or greater than, the return on pipeline properties. At first, the commission granted extra compensation for pipeline production. In 1954, for example, it held that gas produced by Panhandle Eastern should go into its cost of service at a fair field price and concluded:

> It is an established fact that this commission cannot compel natural gas companies subject to its jurisdiction to engage in exploration, drilling, and related developmental activities or to acquire and attach gas reserves discovered by others . . . . If there is to be natural gas exploration, development, and production by pipeline systems themselves, therefore—with resultant benefits to the public interest—it follows that this must result from regulatory policies designed to encourage, rather than to penalize, such activities.[68]

In more recent decisions, the commission apparently has reversed its position. In the Southern Natural Gas case of 1963, it argued:

> It has not yet been demonstrated, either generally or with respect to the particular record before us in this case, that exploration and drilling activities conducted by a pipeline company and integrated with marketing activities of the pipeline involve the same degree of risk as exploration and drilling activities of an independent producer. While it may be true that the drilling of any particular well involves the same risk as to its turning out dry, it is the overall financial risk that we are here concerned with. It is well-recognized that a series of dry holes or even a single dry hole may bankrupt an independent producer, and it is equally well-recognized that an independent producer who has the misfortune to discover high-cost gas may very easily find it impossible to dispose of such gas at a price which returns more than a small fraction of his costs of discovery and development. Southern, as a regulated pipeline company, is allowed to recover all of its exploration and development costs in its cost of service, in addition to a return on its investment. Furthermore, Southern has a ready market for its production, and considerable supplies of low-cost gas into which it may blend any

[67]In 1966, the FPC initiated a new proceeding (Docket No. RP66-24) to determine whether natural gas pipeline companies' own gas production should be regulated on an area basis. (This issue previously had been consolidated with the commission's Hugoton-Anadarko Area Rate Proceeding.)

[68]*Re Panhandle Eastern Pipe Line Co., op. cit.*, p. 420. The Court of Appeals reversed the decision, but noted that the commission could consider the need for encouraging exploration and development by a pipeline company in fixing its rates. *Detroit* v. *Federal Power Comm., op. cit.* Also see *Re El Paso Natural Gas Co.*, 13 FPC 421 (1945); *Re Olin Gas Transmission Corp.*, 17 FPC 695 (1957); *Re Colorado Interstate Gas Co.*, 19 FPC 1012 (1958); *Re Panhandle Eastern Pipe Line Co.*, 38 PUR 3d 332 (FPC, 1961); *Panhandle Eastern Pipe Line Co.* v. *Federal Power Comm.*, 305 F. 2d 763 (1962).

high-cost gas it may have discovered and developed. That these factors place Southern in a position considerably more favorable than that occupied by a typical independent producer seems both clear and obvious.[69]

The commission then set forth two guidelines which a pipeline company must meet to warrant a higher rate of return on its production properties:

First, it must demonstrate that the production activity is being carried on for the sole purpose of supplying gas to its pipeline customers. . . . It should not need argument to support the conclusion that if a pipeline is engaging in production operations for the benefit of groups other than its customers, the customers should not be paying a premium return on the production property.

A second essential showing is that the production operation has been so conducted that it is or will be of practical economic advantage to the pipeline's customers. A pipeline whose production properties make no demonstrable contribution to reduction of costs or improvement of service is likewise in no position to demand a premium return on its production investment.[70]

Four commissioners wrote separate opinions, dissenting from that portion of the decision dealing with the rate of return on production properties. Commissioner Woodward found the guidelines to be "vague and indefinite—in effect, they are not guidelines at all."[71] Commissioner Morgan argued that the guidelines did not go far enough: "The plain fact is that utilities which cannot make the required showings stand in no position to demand *any* rate of return—at least on those properties for which they have failed, when challenged, to make such a showing."[72] Commissioner Ross, who wrote the opinion, stated that "before such additional compensation is allowed, there must be a record showing that the pipeline company's production operations are in practical effect a benefit to consumers, and that a special incentive is required to produce these benefits."[73] And Commissioner O'Connor concluded that "a more definite and complete resolution of this problem cannot await a case-by-case determination . . . . Rather, it must be resolved immediately on a general basis."[74]

Is Regulation Necessary?

Regulation of independent producers has been supported by many economists and politicians, as well as by some pipeline and local distribution

---

[69]*Re Southern Natural Gas Co.*, 47 PUR 3d 113, 130–31 (FPC, 1963). Also see *Re El Paso Natural Gas Co.*, 45 PUR 3d 262, 274 (FPC, 1962), where the commission held: "If El Paso's production activities result in lower overall costs and thus lower rates to its consumers, it has every reason to continue such operations in the normal course of the prudent, businesslike operation of its system."

[70]*Re Southern Natural Gas Co.*, op. cit., p. 132.

[71]*Ibid.*, p. 170.

[72]*Ibid.*, p. 161.

[73]*Ibid.*, p. 160.

[74]*Ibid.*, p. 168.

companies. The wellhead price of natural gas has risen rapidly since 1945 (Table 16–2).[75] This price behavior could partly be explained by increasing demand and rising costs. Many also argue that it was due to control over the supply of natural gas by producers. The second argument has so far prevailed; the move to exempt independent producers from federal regulation has failed. The issue is very much alive, however, so that it seems appropriate to ask if regulation is necessary to protect the public interest.

Market Characteristics. On the supply side, there are over 8,000 natural gas producers. Of these, approximately 4,365 sell to interstate pipelines. The degree of concentration is low. The largest firm accounted for 7 percent of new sales to interstate pipelines in 1966, the largest 5 firms for 28 percent, the largest 20 firms for 60 percent. The 266 producers making sales of 2,000,000 Mcf or more either alone or as first named in combination with others supplied 91 percent of the total interstate pipeline purchases and received 92 percent of the total producer revenues.[76] In some gas-producing areas, concentration is higher. Thus, in the Panhandle-Hugoton fields of north Texas, the largest four suppliers accounted for 72 percent of total new sales in 1950–53, while the largest five firms accounted for more than 50 percent of total new sales in the Permian Basin in 1960.[77] These figures suggest that while production of natural gas does not represent a perfect market, "workable competition can prevail in such a market structure in the absence of collusion."[78]

In addition to the number of sellers and the degree of concentration, other factors reinforce the existence of effective competition. First, the various gas-producing fields are in competition for markets. Natural gas pipelines once laid down cannot be readily moved, but extensions and branches can be built to other fields and to other pipelines (interconnections) if a supplier or group of

[75] From a cost standpoint, transportation and distribution costs represent 72 percent of the average value of natural gas at point of consumption, with the wellhead cost of gas representing 28 percent. In 1945, the percentages were 76 and 24, respectively.

[76] Deliveries of natural gas to interstate pipeline companies in 1966 were made by producers in twenty-three states and in Canada and Mexico. (Of the total volume of gas purchased, 96 percent came from domestic producers, 3.6 percent from Canadian sources, and less than 1 percent from Mexican suppliers.) Points of delivery were at wellheads, field gathering points, gasoline and other processing plants and, with respect to the imported gas, at international boundaries. Of the total sales, 69.9 percent were made by producers in two states: Louisiana, 35.8 percent, and Texas, 34.1 percent. In only three other states did sales approximate or exceed 5 percent of the total: Oklahoma, 8.2 percent; New Mexico, 5.8 percent; and Kansas, 5.7 percent. Thus, five states provided nearly 90 percent of the 1966 purchased gas requirements of the nation's interstate natural gas pipeline systems.

In addition to purchases of 11,132,665,729 Mcf of gas from producers, the interstate companies themselves produced 1,004,227,930 Mcf of natural gas.

All data from Federal Power Commission, *Sales by Producers of Natural Gas to Interstate Pipeline Companies, 1966* (U.S. Government Printing Office, 1967).

[77] MacAvoy, *op. cit.,* p. 215; and *In re Permian Basin Area Rate Cases, op. cit.,* p. 793, n. 62.

[78] Lindahl, *op. cit.,* p. 541.

TABLE 16-2
Marketed Production of Natural Gas, Average Wellhead Price,
and Value at Point of Consumption, 1945-67

Year	Marketed Production[a] (Mil. c.f.)	Average Wellhead Price (Cents per Mcf)	Value at Point of Consumption[b] (Cents per Mcf)
1945	3,918,686	4.6	21.4
1950	6,282,060	6.5	26.6
1955	9,405,351	10.4	40.0
1960	12,771,038	14.0	50.1
1965	16,039,753	15.6	52.2
1967[P]	18,390,525	16.0	n.a.

[a] Marketed production is equivalent to natural gas production usefully consumed.

[b] Value is determined by dividing sales volume into revenues received from consumers.

[P] Preliminary.

n.a. = Not available.

Source: American Gas Association, Inc., *1968 Gas Facts* (New York, 1968), p. 30; U.S. Department of Commerce, Bureau of the Census, *Statistical Abstract of the United States, 1968* (Washington, D.C.: U.S. Government Printing Office, 1968), Table 1032, p. 677.

suppliers attempts to control the supply in any field. Consequently, the concentration ratio for a gas-producing field does not indicate a corresponding degree of control over supply.[79] Second, entry into the gas-producing segment of the industry is relatively easy as indicated by the large number of producers. "A monopolist or a monopolizing group which did not control this open end of the supply could not hope to monopolize for long."[80] Third, concentration appears to be decreasing in the important southwestern area, while the total output has increased sharply.[81] For these reasons, McKie has argued:

If any gas producer should attempt to hold out for a higher price than the other producers, he will simply lose his market. If the producer attempts on

[79] James w. McKie, *The Regulation of Natural Gas* (Washington, D.C.: American Enterprise Association, Inc., 1957), p. 28.

[80] *Ibid.*, pp. 32-33. This statement implies that the long-run supply of natural gas is not fixed. Dirlam, however, has argued that "it is extremely doubtful whether any practically conceivable change in the field price of gas could result in any faintly predictable corresponding change in its long-run supply." Joel B. Dirlam, "Natural Gas: Cost, Conservation, and Pricing," 48 *American Economic Review* 491, 494 (1958). The American Petroleum Institute, however, has argued that "the estimates of proved reserves represent only a fraction of the oil and gas that we can depend on, provided that operators are not discouraged from the development of new and existing resources." *Report of the National Fuels and Energy Study Group on an Assessment of Available Information on Energy in the United States* (Senate, 87th Cong., 2d sess.) (Washington, D.C.: U.S. Government Printing Office, 1962), p. 386.

[81] Lindahl, *op. cit.*, p. 541.

his own to restrict supply and force up the price, other producers will quickly fill the gap. Pipelines can turn to other sources, and would not as a rule be crippled by the loss of any one source.[82]

On the buying side, natural gas is purchased in the fields by pipeline companies and local users. The pipeline companies purchase slightly more than 61 percent of annual marketed production. Since there is only a small number of pipeline companies, it might be expected that their bargaining power would be greater than that of their suppliers. MacAvoy found that monopsony pricing did prevail in the three major southwestern producing areas at some time in the past, but that the growth of the pipeline network during the 1950's radically altered the competitive picture.[83] With but few exceptions, such as the isolated central fields of Kansas and Oklahoma which had one pipeline buyer each, gas-producing fields are served by two or three pipeline companies competing for the supply. Further, as noted above, the cost of building an extension or a branch is not prohibitive. "When a new field is discovered, several pipelines in the vicinity may bid for the gas and thus fix its price competitively even though only one of them finally gets it under contract and builds a single line to gather it."[84]

Escalation Clauses. Pipeline companies need, and regulatory policy requires, assurance of an adequate supply of natural gas before a line can be adequately financed and before a certificate to construct a line will be issued by the Federal Power Commission. The commission generally requires not only a 20-year supply be committed to a new pipeline project but also that the field be able to deliver enough gas to support systemwide sales for 12 years.[85] But because market conditions cannot be predicted accurately over such long periods of time, escalation clauses have been inserted into contracts.[86] These clauses, which contain provisions for adjusting the prices at which deliveries are made, are of two major types—"indefinite" and "definite" escalators. Indefinite escalation clauses are of five types. (1) The two-party favored-nation clause provides for an increased price if the buyer pays a higher price to another producer for comparable supplies in the same field. (2) The third-party favored-nation clause provides for upward adjustment of price if a third, unrelated party pays a higher price in the same area. (3) The redetermination clause provides for renegotiation at definite dates on the basis of the then-

---

[82]McKie, *op. cit.,* p. 31.

[83]MacAvoy, *op. cit.,* pp. 243-45.

[84]McKie, *op. cit.,* p. 32.

[85]*Re Midwestern Gas Transmission Co.,* 21 FPC 653, 656 (1959). The commission has made exceptions by permitting some short-term contracts.

[86]In addition to escalation clauses, many contracts have a "take or pay" clause which stipulates the daily quantity to be taken by the pipeline. The buyer must pay for the specified contract quantity whether he takes it or not, while the seller is obligated to provide gas up to some specified maximum daily limit. Under a 1967 FPC order, gas sales contracts by independent natural gas producers must permit a minimum five-year period for pipeline purchasers to take the required volume. *Re New Regulations on Gas Prepayments,* Docket No. R-199, Order No. 334 (FPC, 1967).

existing market price for new supplies in a given area. (4) The spiral escalation clause provides for a price increase if the resale price of the pipeline company rises. (5) The price-index adjustment clause relates changes in the price of gas to changes in a specified price index, such as the index of wholesale prices. Definite escalation clauses are of two types. (1) The step-up clause provides for price increases by specific amounts made at definite dates in the future. (2) The tax reimbursement clause provides that the seller will be reimbursed for increases in production or severance taxes after a specified date. By 1961, about 80 percent of the gas sales contracts on file with the FPC contained either the two-party favored-nation or redetermination clause or both.[87]

Escalation clauses have been severely criticized. Some have objected to all such clauses, arguing that regulatory authorities should maintain prices at the levels specified in the original contracts. Such a policy, however, makes little economic sense. "If demand continues to increase," argues McKie, "the prices for new supply will continue to be bid up. If the prices on 'old' supply are arbitrarily kept down to lower levels, then demand will increase all the more and prices for new supply will go up all the faster, which will pull up the average price."[88] The most intense criticism has been reserved for indefinite escalation clauses. Under spiral clauses, for example, price increases are shared between producers and pipelines, even though such increases may be entirely due to market conditions at only one of the two levels; while under third-party favored-nation clauses, new prices are determined by outside parties. These criticisms resulted in a 1961 commission order outlawing all indefinite price escalation clauses, other than those providing for redetermination once every five years, in contracts executed after April 3, 1961. In the commission's words:

> Increases in producer prices, triggered by indefinite escalation clauses, have resulted in a flood of almost simultaneous filings. These filings bear no apparent relationship to the economic requirements of the producers who file them. The Natural Gas Act contemplates that prices, to be just and reasonable, be related to economic needs. The elimination of indefinite escalation provisions does not, of course, cut off other avenues by which a producer may make provision for filing for increased rates.[89]

---

[87] *Report of the National Fuels and Energy Study Group, op. cit.,* p. 226.

[88] McKie, *op. cit.,* p. 36. In turn, if prices for "old" gas were held at arbitrarily low levels, the conservation problem would be compounded. See pp. 628–36 of this text. Neuner has argued that escalation clauses tend to "result in a level of field prices higher than that which would prevail in a competitive field market." Edward J. Neuner, *The Natural Gas Industry: Monopoly and Competition in Field Markets* (Norman: University of Oklahoma Press, 1960), p. 284.

[89] *Re Automatic Escalation and Favored Nation Clauses,* 25 FPC 379, 609 (1961), 27 FPC 339, 340 (1962). Also see *Pure Oil Co.,* 25 FPC 383 (1961) *aff'd,* 299 F. 2d 370 (1962); and *Federal Power Comm.* v. *Texaco, Inc.,* 377 U.S. 33 (1964). The 1957 Harris Amendment to the Natural Gas Act would have prohibited the use of indefinite clauses in new contracts. See *Amendments to the Natural Gas Act* (Hearings before the Committee on Interstate and Foreign Commerce, Senate, 84th Cong., 1st sess.) (Washington, D.C.: U.S. Government Printing Office, 1955). In 1968, the Supreme Court upheld the

Conclusion. With or without escalation clauses, many believe that workable competition in the production of natural gas would exist in the absence of federal regulation. To cite MacAvoy:

> As has been suggested by this long analysis of price formation in the 1950s, gas markets were diverse in structure and behavior, and were generally competitive or were changing from monopsony toward competition. It would seem possible that this could result in price level changes and in a revolution of pricing patterns in contrast with those associated with monopoly. Markets with such characteristics need not be regulated by the Federal Power Commission to prevent monopoly pricing.[90]

THE CITY GATE PRICE OF NATURAL GAS

Natural gas is transported from the producing fields to local distributors or industrial users by pipeline companies. However, pipeline companies are not common carriers; they own the gas which they transport. Some pipeline companies operate entirely within a state, while others transport gas across state lines, carrying it 2,000 miles or more from where the gas was produced. Currently, there are 225,360 miles of natural gas transmission lines in the country; they extend from the producing fields to every state but Hawaii (Figure 16-3).[91]

Natural gas pipeline companies make two types of sales. Interstate sales for resale, that is, sales to local gas distributors, are referred to as "jurisdictional" (city gate) sales. All others, including interstate sales to industrial customers

---

authority of the FPC to restrict the application of indefinite escalation clauses included in contracts executed before the effective date of April 13, 1961, that is, the area maximum rates may not be exceeded by the implementation of such clauses. *In re Permian Basin Area Rate Cases, op. cit.,* pp. 781-84.

[90]MacAvoy, *op. cit.,* p. 265. Similar conclusions are reached by M. A. Adelman, *The Supply and Price of Natural Gas* (Oxford: B. H. Blackwell Ltd., 1962); L. Cookenboo, Jr., *Competition in the Field Market for Natural Gas* (Houston: Rice Institution, 1958); Lindahl, *op. cit.;* and McKie, *op. cit.* Neuner (*op. cit.,* p. 290) concludes that "if field price regulation is to be avoided, it is essential that contractually imposed barriers to market adjustment be removed." Regulation is supported by Dirlam, *op. cit.;* Paul H. Douglas, "Federal Regulation of Independent Natural Gas Producers Is Essential," 56 *Public Utilities Fortnightly* 622 (1955) and "The Case for the Consumer of Natural Gas," 44 *The Georgetown Law Journal* 566 (1956); and Joseph C. Swidler, "The Public Interest in Effective Natural Gas Regulation," 74 *Public Utilities Fortnightly* 34, 38-40 (October 8, 1964). For a suggestion that the FPC's regulatory authority over gas producers be suspended for a period of years "while the Congress and the public judged the performance of the industry operating without any price regulation," see William R. Connole, "Can Producer Regulation be Temporarily Suspended?" 83 *Public Utilities Fortnightly* 13 (January 30, 1969).

[91]There are also 63,710 miles of field and gathering mains, and 539,200 miles of natural gas distribution lines. American Gas Association, Inc., *1968 Gas Facts,* p. 60. There are indications that Hawaii may receive natural gas supplies from Alaska in the near future. *The Wall Street Journal,* May 27, 1968, p. 8.

FIGURE 16-3

Source: Federal Power Commission, *Annual Report, 1966*, p. 154.

("direct" sales) and intrastate sales, are referred to as "nonjurisdictional" sales.[92] This classification recognizes that the Federal Power Commission's control over pipeline companies is limited to jurisdictional sales.[93] It also indicates that in determining pipeline rates, the commission must allocate joint costs.

The Allocation of Costs: the Seaboard Formula

In setting rates on interstate sales for resale, the commission must first determine a pipeline company's overall system cost of service, and then must allocate this total cost between jurisdictional and nonjurisdictional sales. The allocation process involves five steps.[94]

1. Total costs are grouped by operating functions: production costs, transmission costs, distribution costs and, where applicable, underground storage costs.

2. The items of cost in each of these categories are classified as variable or fixed (constant) costs.

3. Such costs are then classified as commodity or demand costs. Commodity costs include all variable costs (except that portion of purchased gas costs billed as demand costs and manufactured gas costs) and 50 percent of the fixed costs. Demand costs include the remaining 50 percent of fixed costs.

4. Commodity and demand costs are allocated to jurisdictional and nonjurisdictional sales. Demand costs are allocated in proportion to peak period volumes; commodity costs in proportion to annual volumes. In both cases, volumes alone are used to allocate production costs and volumes weighted by mileage to allocate transmission costs.

5. The final step involves the allocation of jurisdictional demand and commodity costs between rate zones or market areas served by the pipeline company on the basis of peak demand volumes and annual volumes, respectively.[95] This step then involves the design of a company's rate structures.

---

[92] Jurisdictional sales are "firm" sales, i.e., they are sales which the pipeline is committed to supply continuously. Most nonjurisdictional sales are "interruptible" sales, i.e., such sales may be interrupted in favor of firm sales at times of insufficiency of gas supply or pipeline capacity to meet all its requirements. As a result, interruptible sales are made at a lower rate than are firm sales, thereby allowing pipeline companies to compete with other fuels in the competitive industrial market.

[93] The FPC, however, does have control over the facilities added to a pipeline to serve industrial customers, as well as control over construction of a pipeline by an industrial customer.

[94] The cost allocation method commonly used is known as the Seaboard formula. See *Re Atlantic Seaboard Corp. et al.*, 43 PUR (NS) 235 (FPC, 1952); and *Re Northern Natural Gas Co.*, 95 PUR (NS) 289 (FPC, 1952), *aff'd mem.*, 346 U.S. 922 (1954). For the commission's earlier allocation decisions, see *Re Colorado Interstate Gas Co., op. cit.;* and *Re Mississippi River Fuel Co.*, 4 FPC 340 (1945).

[95] Southern Natural Gas Company, for example, has three rate zones: Zone 1 includes Mississippi; Zone 2 includes Alabama, plus Columbus and West Point in Georgia; Zone 3 includes the rest of Georgia, plus the Aiken-North Augusta area of South Carolina. *Re Southern Natural Gas Co.*, 47 PUR 3d 113, 119, n. 5 (FPC, 1963).

The Seaboard formula has been the subject of increasing criticism. Wellisz argues that "the formula is not just arbitrary; it is also capricious in its application."[96] Ross contends that the formula is a "pricing formula" as opposed to a "cost formula in any sense."[97] Both conclude that the formula discourages the economic use of a pipeline's facilities and the development of storage facilities, but they disagree as to the proper remedies. For example, the allocation of fixed costs between jurisdictional and nonjurisdictional sales fails to distinguish between peak and off-peak sales. Thus, sales made during the off-peak season (a significant proportion of nonjurisdictional sales) do not add to the peak load problem, and, therefore, "no fixed costs should be arbitrarily ascribed to them."[98] The commission, while recognizing that such criticisms may have merit, has noted in several cases that it has not "slavishly followed Atlantic Seaboard but has made adjustments in individual cases in the area of rate design in order to achieve a reasonable and just result. While this procedure may not satisfy the rate purists, it does serve to treat the pertinent economic factors involved."[99]

Many adjustments in the Seaboard formula (known as "tilts"), therefore, have been permitted. Generally, such adjustments have been made because competition required them; commodity rates have been kept below their theoretical, Seaboard level so that interruptible gas sales are competitive with other fuels (both regulated and unregulated), thereby improving a system's load factor and lowering costs to firm users.[100]

Rate Structures

The goal of the cost allocation formula is to determine the relative levels of commodity and demand charges to be fixed in each zone. In turn, "The objective of rate design is to determine rates that enable the pipeline to sell its gas at charges which recover from the various types of loads their reasonably associated costs of service, keeping in mind the factors pertinent in this regard."[101] What are the factors to be considered? They include:

[96] Stanislaw H. Wellisz, "The Public Interest in Gas Industry Rate Structures," Part II, 70 *Public Utilities Fortnightly* 145, 147 (August 2, 1962). For Part I, see 70 *ibid.* 65 (July 19, 1962).

[97] Homer R. Ross, "How Practical Is the Seaboard Formula?" 71 *Public Utilities Fortnightly* 26, 31 (January 3, 1963).

[98] Wellisz, *op. cit.,* p. 148.

[99] *Re Southern Natural Gas Co., op. cit.,* p. 137.

[100] "We recognize fully the infirmities in the formula and, as indicated by us on a number of recent occasions, we do not consider ourselves bound thereto, as evidenced by our readiness to make substantial adjustments from straight Seaboard rates where warranted. This is particularly so where such adjustments have been necessary to meet competitive circumstances." *Re Midwestern Gas Transmission Co.,* 61 PUR 3d 241, 151–52 (FPC, 1965). Also see *Re Natural Gas Pipe Line Co. of America,* 45 PUR 3d 415 (FPC, 1962); *Re American Louisiana Pipe Line Co.,* 48 PUR 3d 321 (FPC, 1963); *Re United Gas Pipe Line Co.,* 29 FPC 932 (1964), 31 FPC 1342 (1964), 32 FPC 1106 (1964); and *Re United Fuel Gas Co.,* 31 FPC 1342 (1964).

[101] *Re American Louisiana Pipe Line Co., op. cit.,* p. 334.

... the magnitude of the different classes of sales; load factors and load patterns of the pipeline and its customers; the kind of service rendered, i.e., firm or interruptible, peak or off-peak, seasonal or annual, etc.; the comparative prices of competing fuels in the market, and the ability of the company and its customers to make necessary competing sales of gas; and any minimum bill, penalty for unauthorized overruns, or other conditions of service contained in the tariff.[102]

The issues involved in rate design can best be illustrated by an example. Table 16–3 summarizes three sets of rates proposed for the Michigan Wisconsin Pipe Line Company in a 1963 case: the rates filed by the company, the examiner's rates, and rates reflecting costs classified in accordance with the Seaboard formula. The terms of the company's rate schedules are also summarized in a note to the table.[103] At the outset, it should be noted that the rates proposed by both Michigan Wisconsin and the examiner depart from the Seaboard formula: the company's rates would result in the demand charge producing demand revenues some 29 percent, and the examiner's rates some 13 percent, in excess of the costs resulting from the Seaboard formula's classification to demand.[104] Two customers of Michigan Wisconsin supported the company's rate schedule since it would produce a relatively low commodity charge which would facilitate their industrial sales. In contrast, Michigan Gas and Electric Company, a distributing company customer of Michigan Wisconsin, and several "coal interveners" (Fuels Research Council, Inc.; National Coal Association; United Mine Workers of America; Mid-West Coal Producers Institute, Inc.; Upper Lake Docks Coal Bureau, Inc.; and The Chesapeake and Ohio Railway Company) contended that the Seaboard formula rates should be adopted with no deviation, thereby favoring a relatively high commodity charge. Thus, the company's rates would be advantageous to industrial gas users; the rates determined by the Seaboard formula would be competitively advantageous to coal.

The commission upheld the examiner's decision, as illustrated in Table 16-4. The commission argued, in part:

102 *Ibid.*, n. 25.

103 In this case, only one rate zone was involved. When rates for two or more zones are at issue, the level of revenues to be recovered in each zone must be considered in determining the demand and commodity components. See *Re Southern Natural Gas Co., op. cit.*, pp. 147–52.

104 Put another way, the company's rate deviates to demand by some 29 percent and the examiner's rate by some 13 percent. "The percentage of the deviation to demand is computed by determining what is the amount of commodity costs that cannot be recovered by the commodity charge because of competition from other fuels or otherwise (this amount of commodity costs must be recovered by the demand charge and so is transferred to demand costs); and then dividing the amount of such commodity costs by the total of the strictly Seaboard demand costs." *Re American Louisiana Pipe Line Co., op. cit.*, p. 324, n. 6. Of course, assuming that the parties guessed right about the competitive situation, the overall revenues will match the overall costs, but not in the proportions determined by the Seaboard formula.

TABLE 16-3
Proposed Rates: Michigan Wisconsin Pipe Line Company, 1963[a]

Filed Rates of Mich. Wis.	Rates Approved by Examiner	Rates Reflecting Seaboard Classification
ACQ-1 rate		
Demand $3.50	$3.05	$2.65
Commodity . . . . 26 cents	27.85 cents	29.67 cents
Developmental rate . . . . . . 46 cents	45 cents	33 cents
OS-1 . . . . 26 cents	30 cents	
SGS-1 . . . . 46 cents		

[a] Terms: Michigan Wisconsin's contract year is the 12 months beginning each September 1. For service under the ACQ-1 schedule, the company and each customer agree on a maximum daily quantity (MDQ) for each year, which fixes the maximum volume of gas Michigan Wisconsin is obligated to deliver to the customer on any single day. These deliveries are subject to a schedule of monthly contract demands. During the four cold months, November through February, the buyer is entitled to demand 100 percent of his maximum daily quantity, but only 85 percent from March 1-March 15, and 75 percent for the other months of the year. The total volume of gas the customer is entitled to purchase during the contract year, called the annual contract quantity (ACQ), may be stated in terms of the permitted number of days' use of the maximum daily quantity. For example, during the contract year 1961-62, each customer was entitled to a total of 190 days' use of his maximum daily quantity. In 1960-61, each customer's ACQ was 185 days' use of the MDQ. A customer's purchases in excess of his MDQ on a particular day (daily overrun), or in excess of his ACQ in a particular year (annual overrun), if authorized by Michigan Wisconsin, are billed as overrun gas under the OS-1 schedule. If not authorized, a penalty is charged. The SGS-1 rate is a small general service rate.

Source: *Re American Louisiana Pipe Line Co.*, 48 PUR 3d 321, 327, n. 13, n. 14 (FPC, 1963).

TABLE 16-4
Approved Rates: Michigan Wisconsin
Pipe Line Company, 1963

Rate Schedule ACQ-1:
   $3.05 per month per mcf of billing demand
      27.85 cents per mcf of gas delivered
      13.75 cents per mcf of released gas purchased
      10 cents per mcf demand charge adjustment for impaired delivery
      Alternative rate during development period: 45 cents per mcf of gas delivered
Rate Schedule SGS-1:
      For customers whose maximum daily quantity is 6,000 mcf or less
      45 cents per mcf of all gas delivered
      10 cents per mcf demand charge adjustment for impaired delivery
Rate Schedule OS-1:
      30 cents per mcf for all gas delivered

Source: *Re American Louisiana Pipe Line Co.*, 48 PUR 3d 321, 342 (FPC, 1963).

The weight to be accorded a recommended end result depends largely upon the objectivity of the witness. With this fact in mind, the evidence of the staff witnesses, and particularly the judgment of staff witness Hertz respecting his recommended end result is entitled to preponderant weight on this record.

Further, we have tested the examiner's rates against the applicable criteria and find them supportable. . . . We have . . . long recognized that mitigating circumstances may justify rates other than those reflecting a strict Seaboard classification of costs. In rate design particularly, the question is one of overall reasonableness and the Seaboard classification of costs is but one factor in reaching a determination on this question.

Here, the evidence of Michigan Wisconsin and some of the distributing companies supports some deviation to demand, for the resulting lower commodity rate will facilitate industrial sales by the customer companies that would benefit Michigan Wisconsin, the customer companies, and the public. . . . However, in our view, a deviation to demand as large as the 29 per cent deviation proposed under the filed rate, and the resulting shift of a greater share of costs onto the firm gas users (principally domestic consumers), is not supported by evidence of offsetting benefits to the financial status of the distributing companies, the firm gas users, or the pipeline sufficient to justify such a request. Moreover, the Iowa utilities did not convincingly show that the examiner's rate would in fact harm their operations by causing a loss of present industrial sales. On balance, therefore, we conclude that the examiner's ACQ–1 rate with its some 13 per cent deviation to demand represents a reasonable accommodation of the conflicting interests presented by this record.[105]

The foregoing discussion emphasizes once more that the allocation of costs "is not a matter for the slide rule" and "has no claim to an exact science," but "involves judgment on a myriad of facts."[106] The same conclusions are applicable to determining rate structures.

Wholesale Natural Gas Rates

City gate wholesale natural gas rates vary substantially, as illustrated by the data in Table 16–5, which show the wholesale rates for gas to distributors serving the fourteen largest domestic metropolitan areas. The data also indicate that since 1962, city gate wholesale gas rates have decreased, partly reflecting the growing effectiveness of FPC control over both producers and interstate pipeline companies.

CONSERVATION

Natural gas is limited in quantity and is an exhaustible and irreplaceable natural resource. It should, therefore, be conserved. But conservation means

---

[105] *Re American Louisiana Pipe Line Co., op. cit.,* pp. 334–35.
[106] *Colorado Interstate Gas Co.* v. *Federal Power Comm.,* 324 U.S. 581, 589, 591 (1945).

TABLE 16-5
Wholesale Rates for Gas to Distributors Serving the Fourteen
Largest U.S. Metropolitan Areas, 1962 and 1966

| Metropolitan Area | Average Cents per Mcf Charged by Pipeline to Distributor | | Annual Reduction to Distributors Jan. 1, 1962 to Jan. 1, 1966 |
	Jan. 1, 1962	Jan. 1, 1966	
Baltimore	50.07	44.47	$ 2,705,000
Boston	59.39	57.91	316,000
Chicago[a]	35.82	33.13	4,958,000
Cleveland[a]	46.00	43.75	4,922,000
Detroit[a]	39.49	38.24	2,983,000
Los Angeles[a]	34.48	31.85	14,417,000
Minneapolis–St. Paul	40.86	37.09	4,418,000
Newark (New Jersey suburbs of New York)[a]	46.43	44.18	2,837,000
New York (including only New York suburbs)[a]	44.32	42.08	4,937,000
Philadelphia[a]	44.70	43.34	1,521,000
Pittsburgh[a]	40.42	39.10	2,060,000
St. Louis (Missouri portion only)	35.21	33.60	1,411,000
San Francisco-Oakland	34.79	31.17	11,527,000
Washington, D.C.	55.55	49.62	3,563,000
Total	...	...	$62,575,000

[a] Wholesale service furnished by more than one pipeline company. Average rates are computed from the weighted average charges of all suppliers.
Source: Federal Power Commission, *Annual Report, 1966*, p. 139.

different things to different people. The President's Materials Policy Commission in its 1952 report summarized:

Most thoughtful persons agree that conservation is a good idea, but there are wide differences as to how best—and how much—to protect the future claimants against the Nation's treasure of resources. . . . One popular fallacy is to regard our resource base as a fixed inventory which, when used up, will leave society with no means of survival. A related fallacy is that physical waste equals economic waste: the feeling that it is wasteful to use materials in ways that make them disappear. This attitude can lead to devoting a dollar's worth of work to "saving" a few cents worth of waste paper and old string.

These fallacies together lead to a hairshirt concept of conservation which makes it synonymous with hoarding. A sound concept of conservation, in the view of this Commission, is one which equates it with efficient management —efficient use of resources and of manpower and materials: a positive concept compatible with growth and high consumption in place of abstinence and retrenchment. . . .

Conservation is something very different from simply leaving oil in the ground or trees in the forests on the theory that by sacrificing lower value uses today we will leave something for the higher value uses of tomorrow when supplies will be scarcer. Using resources today is an essential part of making our economy grow; materials which become embodied in today's capital goods, for example, are put to work and help make tomorrow's production higher. Hoarding resources in the expectation of more important uses later involves a sacrifice that may never be recouped; technological changes and new resource discoveries may alter a situation completely. It may not be wise to refrain from using zinc today if our grandchildren will not know what to do with it tomorrow. But following a course of conservation which, as here suggested, weighs economic factors carefully, is very different from the eat, drink, and be merry philosophy which sees no point in judicious self-restraint and no cause to worry over posterity's welfare.[107]

Conservation, then, does not involve nonuse. Rather, it involves avoidance of economic waste—the recovery of resources whose value exceeds the cost of recovery. It refers to the management of publicly owned resources and the supervision of privately owned resources in the public interest.

State Conservation Measures

For many years, large quantities of natural gas were wasted. As noted earlier, its main function was to drive petroleum to the surface, after which it was vented and burned. A vast surplus of gas existed in the producing fields, but the lack of transportation facilities prevented it from reaching potential consuming markets. Gradually, local uses absorbed much of the surplus. New technology made it possible to return gas to the ground to "repressure" oil pools, thereby increasing the ultimate recovery of low-cost oil as well as conserving gas. But it was not until pipeline technology made long-distance transportation possible that significant markets were developed throughout the country.

State laws to prevent some of the most serious forms of waste were enacted before the turn of the century. An 1878 Pennsylvania statute required that wells be plugged on abandonment, while an 1891 Indiana law prevented the venting or flaring of natural gas. Similar measures were enacted by other gas-producing states during the nineties. Few of the statutes were vigorously enforced. Further, the only law that attempted to deal with the problem of overproduction was one enacted by Oklahoma in 1915, forbidding both physical and economic waste. Then came the large oil and gas discoveries in the 1925 to 1931 period. Chaos soon characterized the industry as production outran market demand and transportation facilities. Producers tried to solve overproduction by voluntary agreements, but the method was unsatisfactory. Producing states

---

[107] President's Materials Policy Commission, *Resources for Freedom* (Washington, D.C.: U.S. Government Printing Office, 1952), Vol. 1, p. 21. Also see S. V. Ciriacy-Wantrup, *Resource Conservation* (Berkeley: University of California Press, 1952), esp. chap. iv.

thereupon enacted stronger laws, entrusting regulatory powers to administrative conservation agencies.[108]

Individual state action, however, has a serious weakness. If one state attempts to limit production, it places its producers at a competitive disadvantage in comparison with producers in other states with no such limitations. As a result, the governors of the major oil- and gas-producing states adopted an Interstate Compact to Conserve Oil and Gas, submitted it for ratification to the legislatures of their states, and then submitted it to Congress for approval. The Compact received Congressional approval in 1935; it has been renewed without amendment ever since. The thirty-three member states (three of which are associate members) agree to enact and continue laws "to conserve oil and gas by the prevention of physical waste thereof, from any cause." The Compact Commission, whose members are the governors of the signatory states, has no power to compel uniform state policies; it can only advise and recommend.

Diversity rather than uniformity is the rule.[109] Present state laws cover such matters as the prevention of physical waste, overproduction, discrimination, and the use of gas for certain purposes. Physical waste in oil-gas fields is to be prevented by such measures as the proper location, spacing, drilling, and operation of wells; establishment of gas–oil ratios; the use of casings; and requirements concerning the capping of wells. The rules regarding spacing may provide for establishment of drilling units for each pool and may permit or require the pooling of interests in a drilling unit. Overproduction is prevented by forbidding production at rates in excess of 25 percent of maximum initial capacity, or by limiting production in excess of transportation and marketing facilities or market demand. State conservation agencies prorate production for each field monthly on the basis of buyers' "nominations" according to sales contracts.[110] A few statutes prohibit discrimination by declaring buyers of gas to be common purchasers and requiring them to take all gas offered or, if unable to take all, to purchase gas on a ratable basis. Finally, some states limit or

---

[108] For example, the Texas Railroad Commission, the Louisiana Commission of Conservation, the California Division of Oil and Gas, the Corporation Commissions of Kansas and Oklahoma, the West Virginia Department of Mines, and the Alabama Oil and Gas Board.

[109] See *A Study of Conservation of Oil and Gas in the United States, 1964* (Oklahoma City: Interstate Oil Compact Commission, 1964). Also see *General Rules and Regulations for the Conservation of Oil and Gas* (Oklahoma City: Interstate Oil Compact Commission, 1969).

[110] Gas prorationing differs significantly from oil prorationing which involves commission control of the amount of oil produced each month. (See Melvin G. de Chazeau and Alfred E. Kahn, *Integration and Competition in the Petroleum Industry* [New Haven: Yale University Press, 1959], esp. chap. vii.) In contrast, gas prorationing does not involve control over the amount of gas produced each month, since state conservation agencies have no jurisdiction over the amount of gas promised by a seller over a contract period.

prohibit the use of gas for certain purposes, such as the manufacture of carbon black.[111]

The state regulatory agencies have systematically enforced these rules. The major wastes have been prevented. Nevertheless, the practice of flaring still exists whenever it does not pay to gather natural gas or to return it to the ground.[112] Flaring may occur in the production of casinghead gas. Approximately one-third of the nation's natural gas supply is produced along with crude oil. In the major oil-producing states, crude oil production is limited under state prorationing laws. Thus, the production of associated gas is likewise limited. When the amount of casinghead gas is small, it may not be economical to build gathering facilities to collect it for sale. Flaring also may occur when a field is not operated as a single unit. Clearly, it is not sensible for a producer to recompress gas at the surface and inject it back into the reservoir only to have it withdrawn by another producer. None of the major producing states, however, requires unitization of a field.

The FPC and Conservation

The Natural Gas Act, as amended, does not mention conservation. But the law provides that in issuing certificates to pipeline companies, the commission "shall have the power to attach to the issuance of the certificate and to the exercise of the rights granted thereunder such reasonable terms and conditions as the public convenience and necessity may require." In determining a rate structure, moreover, the commission must consider the end uses of gas and the availability of competing fuels. The FPC has consistently permitted interested parties concerned with the production or transportation of competing fuels to intervene in certification and rate-making cases. By permitting development of long-distance interstate pipelines to transport gas from the Southwest to northern and eastern markets, high-grade uses have been substituted for low-grade uses near the producing fields.

The commission's consideration of conservation and the end use of gas has been approved by the Supreme Court. In the Hope Natural Gas case, the Court said: "When it comes to cases of abandonment or extension of facilities or services, we may assume that, apart from the express exemptions contained in Section 7, considerations of conservation are material to the issuance of certificates of public convenience and necessity."[113] In a 1961 decision, the Court upheld the commission's right to consider, among other things, both price and proposed use of gas in granting a certificate to build a pipeline.[114] In this

---

111 See Blakeley M. Murphy (ed.), *Conservation of Oil and Gas* (Chicago: American Bar Association, 1949).

112 During 1966, 268 billion cubic feet of natural gas were wasted and lost, compared with 798 billion cubic feet in 1945. American Gas Association, Inc., *1968 Gas Facts*, p. 28.

113 *Federal Power Comm.* v. *Hope Natural Gas Co.*, 320 U.S. 591, 612 (1944).

114 *Federal Power Comm.* v. *Transcontinental Gas Pipe Line Corp.*, 365 U.S. 1 (1961). Increasing concern about air pollution has resulted in a modification of the FPC's

case, the electric utility company serving the New York City area proposed the construction of a pipeline by its own subsidiary to transport gas from producing fields in the Southwest for use as boiler fuel to generate electricity. Direct sales are not subject to the FPC's jurisdiction, but a certificate was required to build the pipeline. The commission held that the price to be paid for the gas was too high and would unbalance the area price level, and that the consumption of natural gas for boiler fuel was an "inferior" use which should be discouraged. The Court agreed.

Many believe, however, that conservation has not received the attention it deserves. Natural gas continues to be consumed in such low-value general uses ("inferior" uses) as a boiler fuel and as a raw material for making carbon black.[115] Diversion from "inferior" to "superior" uses could be accomplished in two ways—by prohibiting low-grade uses of gas or by raising its price. The peak demand for gas occurs during the winter months when it is supplied for residential and commercial space heating. Pipeline and distribution companies, in turn, operate at full capacity. During the summer months, demand declines, and to keep their facilities employed, interruptible sales are made at low rates to industrial users. Low rates are justified by the fact that interruptible sales, which improve the companies' load factors, make some contribution toward fixed costs.[116] Interruptible sales thus help to absorb the cost of building pipelines to high-grade markets and lead to lower rates for peak-period customers. If higher prices were charged, industrial users would tend to turn to substitute fuels, chiefly coal and oil. Moreover, pipeline and distribution companies would find it profitable to develop more summer storage facilities.[117] Gas would be trans-

---

position. In approving the sale of additional gas to Consolidated Edison by Transcontinental in late 1967, for example, the commission said: "Since Transcontinental Gas Pipe Line Corporation is otherwise supported by the record in its proposal to increase its firm sales to Consolidated Edison Company by 55,000 Mcf per day, the effect of this sale on the New York air pollution problem is not controlling. Nevertheless, the serious air pollution problem in New York may be alleviated slightly by the proposal, and to that extent furnishes an additional benefit." *Re Transcontinental Gas Pipe Line Corp.*, 71 PUR 3d 161, 166 (FPC, 1967).

115 "Next to flaring, the most dramatic and apparently wasteful use of natural gas is the making of carbon black. Natural gas is burned off in order to catch carbon black from the smoke. Producers of carbon black stood ready to take the gas near the fields at a steady rate at a time when other customers were lacking. They obtained long-term contracts permitting them to buy gas at very low prices. In view of the fact that there are now demands for natural gas that can afford to pay much higher prices and that there will be even more in the future, there has been some sentiment in favor of prohibiting the burning of gas for carbon black. Some States already prohibit the practice or restrict it to types of gas not suitable for other uses without further processing." President's Materials Policy Commission, *op. cit.*, Vol. III, p. 22.

116 The American Gas Association found that, in 1959, the contribution made to fixed expenses by interruptible gas sales was $392 million. The Independent Natural Gas Association of America found an amount of $394 million in 1960. *Report of the National Fuels and Energy Study Group, op. cit.*, p. 376.

117 At the end of 1967, there were 308 underground gas storage reservoirs operating in the country, with a total capacity of 4.5 trillion cubic feet, located in twenty-five states. Seven states, however, accounted for almost three-quarters of the

ported and stored during the summer season. A larger number of peak-period customers could be served without the necessity of expanding pipeline capacity, thereby minimizing the need of making off-peak interruptible sales. Producers would receive higher profits, but these could be taxed away by the government if above reasonable levels. Such a policy would result in higher prices to consumers, but it would divert natural gas to "superior" uses. Yet, as Wilcox has noted, it would be difficult to so convince the industry's millions of customers (39.7 million at the end of 1967), who have found the past low prices of gas attractive enough to invest in gas-burning equipment.[118] And there are limited geological formations for storing gas.[119]

The Future

The United States faces no immediate shortage of natural gas. Proved recoverable reserves reached 292.9 trillion cubic feet at the end of 1967 (Figure 16-4). During the same year, net production totaled 18.4 trillion cubic feet, while gross additions to reserves were 21.8 trillion cubic feet. In the period 1945-67, gross additions to proved natural gas reserves were equal to 1.6 times net production.[120] And a recent study estimated that total ultimate recoverable natural gas reserves may be in the neighborhood of 2,000 trillion cubic feet, of which some 600 trillion cubic feet have already been found.[121]

---

industry's storage capacity: Pennsylvania, Michigan, Ohio, West Virginia, Illinois, Oklahoma, and California. Most storage facilities are abandoned gas fields into which the gas is injected for withdrawal during winter months. American Gas Association, Inc., *1968 Gas Facts*, p. 71.

[118] Clair Wilcox, *Public Policies Toward Business* (3d ed.; Homewood, Ill.: Richard D. Irwin, Inc., 1966), p. 380.

[119] The American Gas Association, along with others, believes there is no such thing as "inferior" or "superior" use of energy. "Only waste would be inferior. And only release to the atmosphere or flaring would be waste." Further, end-use control might result in protecting traditional fuel markets. Again, in the words of the American Gas Association: "All energy industries would be confronted with a national 'policy' which would equate end-use control with conservation, tinker with the law of supply and demand, label uses willy-nilly as 'inferior' and 'superior,' and treat abundance as if it were scarcity. Free energy competition could never survive in such an atmosphere." *Report of the National Fuels and Energy Study Group, op. cit.*, pp. 377, 381.

[120] See American Gas Association, Inc., *Reserves of Crude Oil, Natural Gas Liquids and Natural Gas in the United States and Canada as of December 31, 1967* (New York, 1968).

[121] T. A. Hendricks, "Resources of Oil, Gas, and Natural-Gas Liquids in the United States and the World," *U.S. Geological Circular 522* (1965). Estimates of natural gas reserves vary widely. See, for example, H. K. Hudson, "Our Future Domestic Natural Gas Supply," 79 *Public Utilities Fortnightly* 29 (January 5, 1967); J. David Mann, Jr., "Sour Notes in 'The Shortage Song'," 79 *ibid.* 15 (June 8, 1967); *Potential Supply of Natural Gas in the United States as of December 31, 1966* (Golden, Colorado: Potential Gas Agency, 1967); and Henry R. Linden, "U.S. Natural Gas Supply and Demand," 81 *Public Utilities Fortnightly* 13 (February 1, 1968).

The industry is developing techniques to produce pipeline quality gas from coal and oil shale on an economical basis. [See 81 *Public Utilities Fortnightly* 46 (February 29, 1968).] And on December 10, 1967, Project Gasbuggy got underway with the underground (4,250 feet below the earth's surface) explosion of a nuclear device in

FIGURE 16–4
Proved Recoverable Reserves and Net Production of Natural Gas
in the United States, 1945–67

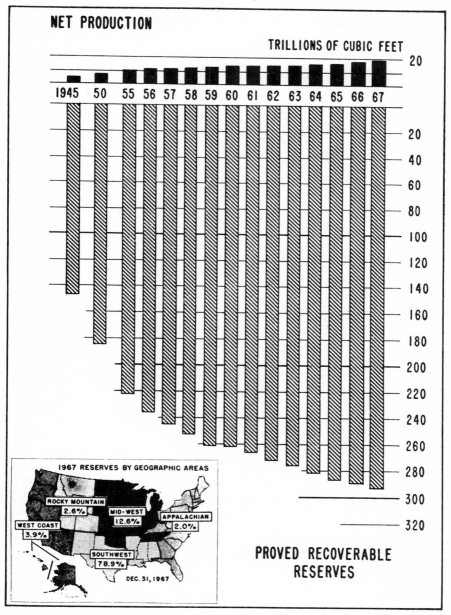

Source: American Gas Association, Inc., *1968 Gas Facts* (New York, 1968), p. 7.

Conservation, however, is still essential. The nation's major sources of power are the fossil fuels—coal, oil, and gas. They also have important nonfuel uses for which substitutes have yet to be found. Further, at some distant period of time,

> . . . more serious problems are likely to arise when natural gas supplies will eventually have shrunk to the point that the general uses in gas producing areas and special uses in all areas are forced to shift to substitute fuels. Costly dislocations may result in the economy of the Southwest, heavy capital costs for conversion will be forced upon nearby and distant customers, and the extensive transportation, distribution, and utilization systems may be rendered useless. The impact could be reduced if it becomes economic to manufacture gas for at least some of these gas customers, presumably from coal, which could then be distributed through portions of existing transmission and distribution lines, though large segments of such lines would probably no longer be used. . . . Meanwhile, in guiding the rapid development of the natural gas industry, it is important for regulatory authorities to bear in mind the ultimate exhaustion of natural gas supplies, with the aim of avoiding costly over-expansion.[122]

CONTROVERSY AND EXPERIMENTATION

The problems that face the producing states and the Federal Power Commission in regulating the natural gas industry are numerous. Solutions, moreover, are complicated by the existence of conflicting economic and political factors, as well as by the need for conservation. There is no question that pipeline and local distribution companies should be regulated; these activities exhibit the traditional economic characteristics associated with regulation. Disputes surround allocation methods, the allowance for incentives, and the proper role of conservation, while the commission annually recommends to Congress that it be given control over direct interstate sales for industrial use, interconnections, security issues of pipeline companies, and stock acquisitions of jurisdictional pipeline firms. Yet, these issues have been overshadowed by the controversy surrounding the regulation of natural gas production.

Many still hold that regulation of the field price of natural gas is unnecessary and perhaps even detrimental to the best interests of the economy. There seems to be little probability, however, that regulation will be abandoned.

---

northwestern New Mexico. (Gasbuggy is a venture of the Atomic Energy Commission, the U.S. Bureau of Mines, and El Paso Natural Gas Company.) The hope is that such nuclear explosions will unlock vast new natural gas reserves (estimated at 300 trillion cubic feet) not currently recoverable by conventional methods. Preliminary reports indicate that the experiment was a success. See Paul Zimmerman, "Project Gasbuggy," *Petroleum Today*, Fall, 1967, pp. 4-8; Herbert G. Lawson, "Peaceful Nuclear Shot," *The Wall Street Journal*, April 22, 1968, p. 34; and *ibid.*, August 9, 1968, p. 24 (for a summary of the preliminary report issued by the participants).

122 President's Materials Policy Commission, *op. cit.*, Vol. III, p. 23.

Thus, the relevant problem is to find an applicable method of rate making for determining the wellhead price of gas. As a lower court expressed it in 1958: "The regulation of the prices at which thousands of 'natural gas companies' may sell to the pipeline companies is a difficult one at best. It is a field which in many respects requires new formulas to test what is just and reasonable."[123]

The FPC has adopted, with approval of the Supreme Court, an area rate concept. Certain guidelines have been set forth. Controversy still exists, however, as to the exact formulae to be applied—the specific details, for example, of the cost computations. In its Permian Basin decision, the Supreme Court itself stated that "area rate regulation of producer prices is avowedly still experimental in its terms and uncertain in its ultimate consequences. . . ."[124] The Court gave the commission wide discretionary powers in developing the area rate methodology, but noted that it "would expect that the Commission will hereafter indicate more precisely the formulae by which it intends to proceed. . . ."[125] And, finally, although much of the groundwork was laid in the Permian Basin proceeding, it seems clear from the Court's opinion that Permian did not answer all the questions—not only as they might pertain to another area, but also for the Permian Basin itself at a later time. For as the Court said: ". . . we must emphasize that we understand the present proceeding to be merely the first of many steps toward a more expeditious and effective system of regulation."[126]

Many issues thus remain to be resolved before the commission's "new formula" can be called a success. Nevertheless, as Priest has observed,

> The future of the natural gas industry, especially in its vital production aspect, has been placed largely in the hands of the FPC. Of course that agency will carefully balance conflicting producer and consumer interests. Of course, it will make every effort to restrict excessive profits. But it must also make sure that the revenues it allows will permit producers (a) to attract capital, including equity capital, and (b) will make possible effective exploration which will appropriately increase natural gas reserves.

> Absent arbitrariness, capriciousness, serious abuse of authority, shocking lack of supporting substantial evidence, the courts almost certainly will not intervene. The commission, therefore, is called upon for as high a quality of regulatory statesmanship as ever has been asked of an American administrative agency.[127]

Natural gas regulation clearly represents a continuing challenge.

[123] *Bel Oil Corp.* v. *Federal Power Comm.*, 255 F. 2d 548, 553 (1958).
[124] *In re Permian Basin Area Rate Cases, op. cit.*, p. 772.
[125] *Ibid.*, p. 800.
[126] *Ibid.*, p. 772, n. 37.
[127] A. J. G. Priest, "Supreme Court Decisions on Gas Rate Cases," 82 *Public Utilities Fortnightly* 29, 34 (October 10, 1968).

| Chapter | COMMUNICATIONS |
| 17 | |

> The words "telegraph" and "telephone" have long ceased to be adequate descriptions of existing telecommunications. In addition to the written and spoken word, today's communications include data, facsimile, and video in systems that can combine part or all of these functions.
>
> — *Walter P. Marshall**

It is reported that Andrew Jackson, for lack of speedy communications, fought the British at New Orleans after peace had been reached in the War of 1812.[1] The incident illustrates a vital point: modern civilization would be unthinkable without rapid communications. Today, as the result of a continuous flow of technological invention and innovation, the world is literally at one's fingertip, and in addition to telephone and telegraph messages, telecommunications includes the transmission of data, facsimile, and video.

The communications industry's leaders continue to be the American Telephone and Telegraph Company and Western Union Telegraph Company. However, competitive forces have added a new dimension to the regulation of an expanding and changing industry. There exists an overlapping zone of service provision in that both A.T.&T. and Western Union have expanded into private line services. As a consequence of the Federal Communications Commission's 1960 decision concerning microwave radio, common carriers have come into increasing competition with private communications systems. And the convergence of communications and computer technologies has raised numerous regulatory and policy questions.

THE COMMUNICATIONS ACT OF 1934

Regulation of the telephone and telegraph companies expanded as their impact on the economy developed and grew. The operations of the telegraph companies, which from the beginning have been interstate in nature, were first regulated at the federal level. In 1866, Congress enacted the Post Roads Act,

---

*Walter P. Marshall, "Western Union: Conquest in Communications," special advertisement supplement, Section 11, *The New York Times*, April 8, 1962, p. 2.
[1] Federal Communications Commission, *Annual Report, 1959*, p. 167.

giving telegraph companies construction rights over the public domain, post roads, and navigable streams and waters, and authorizing the Postmaster General to fix rates annually for government telegrams.[2] In 1887, the Interstate Commerce Commission received Congressional authority to require interconnections among telegraph companies.

The telephone companies, on the other hand, developed and remained for a number of years almost exclusively as local operations. The first regulation, therefore, was by means of municipal franchises covering rates and conditions of service. As their operations expanded beyond municipal boundaries, the various states began exercising jurisdiction over the telephone companies through their existing railroad and public utility commissions. Shortly after the turn of the century, the interstate operations began to assume greater significance, and federal regulation was deemed necessary. Under the Mann-Elkins Act of 1910, broad regulatory powers over interstate and foreign telephone, telegraph, and cable services were delegated to the ICC. The commission was authorized to determine maximum and minimum rates, to establish uniform systems of accounts, and to make valuation studies. Carriers were required to file monthly and annual financial reports.

The ICC, preoccupied with railroad regulatory problems, was also handicapped by the appropriations from Congress which were inadequate to effectively perform its additional responsibilities for the communications common carriers. It did, however, make two significant contributions to the regulatory process: a uniform system of accounts for telephone companies was developed, and valuation studies of communication companies' plants were undertaken. During the period of ICC jurisdiction, formal rate proceedings were at a minimum. Between 1910 and 1934, the commission dealt with telegraph rates in only eight cases, telephone rates in four cases, and cable rates in two cases.[3] In none of these cases were the issues of major importance. In addition, some complaints were filed with the commission and acted on.

From August 1, 1918, to July 31, 1919, the telephone and telegraph companies were taken over and operated by the federal government as a war measure. Under the Transportation Act of 1920, the ICC was directed to prescribe depreciation rates and charges of telephone and telegraph companies. The Willis-Graham Act of 1921 extended the commission's authority to include telephone consolidations and acquisitions of control. In the same year, Congress enacted the Submarine Cable Act, authorizing the Department of State to receive license applications for the landing or operating of ocean cables, while the President was authorized to grant or refuse such licenses.

---

[2] The Post Roads Act was repealed in 1947, thereby ending special domestic telegraph rates for the federal government.

Federal power to regulate interstate and foreign communications rests on both the commerce and postal clauses of the Constitution. See *Pensacola Telegraph Co.* v. *Western Union Telegraph Co.*, 96 U.S. 1 (1877).

[3] James M. Herring and Gerald C. Cross, *Telecommunications* (New York: McGraw-Hill Book Co., Inc., 1936), p. 220.

Early in 1933, an interdepartmental committee was set up by the Secretary of Commerce to study communications regulation. The committee recommended the creation of a single agency to regulate all communications services.[4] In accordance with the committee's recommendation, President Roosevelt sent a special message to Congress on February 26, 1934, urging creation of the Federal Communications Commission. Bills were introduced the following day by Senator Dill and Representative Rayburn. The Senate bill passed the House on June 1, 1934; the conference report was adopted by both houses on June 9; and the Communications Act of 1934 was signed by the President on June 19, 1934. The purpose of the act, as amended in 1937, was to provide for the regulation of interstate and foreign communication by wire and radio,

> ... so as to make available, so far as possible, to all the people of the United States a rapid, efficient, Nation-wide and world-wide wire and radio communication service with adequate facilities at reasonable charges, for the purpose of the national defense, for the purpose of promoting safety of life and property through the use of wire and radio communication, and for the purpose of securing a more effective execution of this policy by centralizing authority with respect to interstate and foreign commerce in wire and radio communication. . . .[5]

With respect to common carriers—telephone, telegraph, and cable—all companies are required to furnish adequate service "upon reasonable request."[6] The commission may order physical connections between carriers, and may establish through routes and charges and determine the division of such charges. All rates, practices, classifications, and regulations must be "just and reasonable"; "unjust or unreasonable" discrimination and "undue or unreasonable preference or advantage" are prohibited. Rates must be filed with the commission and adhered to, and proposed rates may be suspended for a period not to exceed three months to permit an investigation. Common carriers must obtain certificates of public convenience and necessity for the construction, acquisition, or operation of a new line or for the extension of an existing line.[7] The commission may prescribe uniform accounting systems and depreciation charges, and may require records and reports. It was authorized to make valuation studies, and Congress specified that, in making such studies, the

---

[4] *Preliminary Report on Communication Companies* (House Report No. 1273, 73rd Cong., 2d sess.) (Washington, D.C.: U.S. Government Printing Office, 1934), known as the Splawn Report.

[5] The Communications Act of 1934, as amended, 50 Stat. 189, Sec. 1.

[6] With the concurrence of the Secretary of State and the Department of Defense, the commission may authorize a company to land submarine cables in this country to connect with other countries.

[7] There are three exemptions to this requirement: (1) a line within a single state unless the line constitutes part of an interstate line; (2) local, branch, or terminal lines not exceeding 10 miles in length; or (3) any lines acquired by the consolidation of telephone or telegraph companies.

commission "shall be free to adopt any method of valuation which shall be lawful."[8] The FCC was given jurisdiction over consolidations.[9]

The act prohibits interlocking directorates without express commission approval. The FCC, however, was given no control over the security issues of common carriers. The commission was instructed to investigate all transactions between operating companies and affiliated companies, and to report such findings and recommendations, if any, to Congress. The commission also was instructed to inquire into the management of common carriers and to keep itself informed of technical developments and improvements "to the end that the benefits of new inventions and developments may be made available to the people of the United States." Congress, to encourage state and federal cooperation, made provision for establishment of joint boards.

THE TELEGRAPH INDUSTRY

The inventor of the telegraph, Samuel F. B. Morse (a professional portrait painter), began experimentation on an electrical communication system in 1832.[10] By 1838, he had shown that signals could be transmitted by wires and had made public demonstrations. However, it was not until 1843 that Congress passed the Telegraph Act, appropriating $30,000 to construct a commercial telegraph line between Washington and Baltimore. The first public message was sent by Morse on May 24, 1844: "What hath God wrought?" The line proved unprofitable, and after the government refused to buy the invention from Morse and his associates for $100,000 in 1845, the telegraph was developed by private ownership. Funds were raised by Morse and his associates, and the Magnetic Telegraph Company extended its lines to Philadelphia and New York in 1846. Several small telegraph companies, numbering about fifty by 1851, began operations in different sections of the country.[11] Also, in 1851, dispatching of trains by telegraph commenced; indeed, most of the early lines were constructed along the rights-of-way of railroads, and telegraph offices currently are found in railroad stations throughout the country.

[8] The FCC's subsequent decision to use original cost valuations was upheld by the Supreme Court in *American Telephone & Telegraph Co.* v. *United States*, 299 U.S. 232 (1936).

[9] The act prohibits consolidation of a domestic telegraph carrier with an international telegraph carrier; the combination of wire and radio companies is forbidden if the purpose or effect may be "substantially to lessen competition."

[10] For a more complete history of the telegraph industry, upon which this discussion is largely based, see "The Telegraph Industry" in John G. Glover and Rudolph L. Lagai (eds.), *The Development of American Industries* (4th ed.; New York: Simmons-Boardman Publishing Corp., 1959), chap. xxxii. Also see H. H. Goldin, "Government Policy and the Domestic Telegraph Industry," 7 *Journal of Economic History* 53 (1947).

[11] The Morse patent covered the transmission of messages by dots and dashes. Most of the early telegraph companies received licenses under this patent. A few, however, used the House printing telegraph, which transmitted messages by printing in Roman letters. While this system did not prove economical, it was the forerunner of automatic printing telegraphy.

The Western Union Telegraph Company

In 1851, the New York and Mississippi Valley Printing Telegraph Company was incorporated to develop a nationwide telegraph system. At first, the company used the House system of transmission, but the Morse system was in use by 1856. The company constructed a number of lines and acquired others by purchase. In 1856, its name was changed to The Western Union Telegraph Company. Five years later, the company built the first transcontinental telegraph line.

Western Union, in 1866, acquired two significant competitors—the American Telegraph Company and the United States Telegraph Company. In 1881, the Postal Telegraph System entered the field. This company was incorporated as a subsidiary of the Commercial Cable Company, which laid two transatlantic cables in the early 1880's. The development of a successful oceanic cable system requires adequate land line connections to domestic points. Rather than contracting with Western Union for interchange, the company organized the Postal Telegraph Company to build a separate domestic telegraph system. The company was able to operate successfully for many years, but substantial annual deficits followed the stock market crash of 1929. At that time, Postal Telegraph handled about 15 percent of the total domestic telegraph traffic. In 1940, the FCC recommended to Congress that the existing telegraph carriers be consolidated into one or more unified systems. Three years later, Congress amended the Communications Act, and Western Union was permitted to acquire Postal Telegraph, a merger consummated late in 1943.[12]

The merger resulted in Western Union's complete dominance of the public telegraph industry.[13] The company, as of December 31, 1968, had a gross plant investment of $931.1 million and, as of December 31, 1967, had 3,077 telegraph offices and 8,672 telegraph agency stations. Western Union also provides telegraph service between the continental United States and Alaska (both on its own lines and by connection with the Alaska Communications System), Mexico, and Canada, and is the sole agency for land line handling of overseas and ship-shore messages originating or terminating in the continental United States (outside the gateway cities, such as Boston and New York).

Technological Developments

The first telegraph installations consisted of a sending and receiving instrument in each city, connected by iron wire strung on glass bottlenecks fastened to poles as insulators. Only one message at a time could pass in either

---

[12] Western Union was required to divest itself of its international telegraph operations. Divestiture was completed on September 30, 1963, when the facilities were sold to American Securities Corporation.

[13] Five other telegraph companies operate in the United States. Three are Canadian companies, and two—the Colorado and Wyoming Telegraph Company and the Yellowstone Park Company—are small domestic corporations.

direction over this circuit.[14] A good operator could transmit 40 to 50 words per minute. The duplex telegraph, which made possible transmission of two messages simultaneously (one in each direction) over a single wire, was introduced in 1872; the multiplex telegraph, to transmit eight messages simultaneously (four in each direction), was introduced in 1914; and the varioplex telegraph, passing seventy-two messages simultaneously (thirty-six in each direction) was introduced in 1936. Teletypewriter and teleprinter machines came into use around 1925.[15] High-speed switching systems date from 1937; automatic facsimile devices[16] from 1939. Generally, teletypewriters and teleprinters are used between cities where volume is heavy and between business offices and the city telegraph centers, while manual operations continue in areas where message volume is small.

In the late 1950's, Western Union started construction of a transcontinental microwave telegraph network.[17] The network, opened in 1964, represents the most advanced method of telecommunications. It is able to transmit 2,000 telegrams simultaneously in each direction. Further, it is capable of handling all known forms of communications, including voice, data, facsimile, and video, and is relatively immune from interruptions due to storm damage and electrical interference. The microwave system has greatly increased the circuit capacity of Western Union and has added to the range of services being offered by the company.

The Domestic Telegraph Investigation

Despite technological developments, population growth, and increasing business activity, message telegraph volume has been declining for many years. During the period 1945 to 1966, the message telegraph volume fell 70 percent and the number of telegraph offices declined 41 percent, while eleven rate increases resulted in a cumulative increase of 160 percent in the price of message

[14] G. Lloyd Wilson, *Transportation and Communications* (New York: Appleton-Century-Crofts, Inc., 1954), p. 689.

[15] Teletypewriter messages are written by an operator using a keyboard very similar to a typewriter. As the keys are struck, holes are perforated in a narrow, moving paper tape. The tape passes into a transmitter, and the impulses caused by electrical contacts controlled by the holes in the tape flash out over the wire. At the receiving end, the impulses are automatically translated back into characters, printed on tape, and gummed by the operator to message blanks. In contrast, the teleprinter is a printing telegraph sending and receiving machine.

[16] A facsimile machine in a corporate office connects that office with the nearest telegraph center. Subscribers can send and receive telegrams instantly in picture form.

[17] "In essence, microwave systems send signals in the high frequency range, amplify them at intermediate stations, and retransmit them until they reach their destination. Microwaves (which are electromagnetic) are between one and three inches long. Like light waves, they travel in straight lines and do not follow the curvature of the earth. They are focused sharply and aimed from point to point. Less than one watt of power—about the amount needed to light a pocket flashlight bulb—is sufficient to send them on their way between stations on a radio relay route." Herbert H. Goetschius, "Microwave Today and Tomorrow," 43 *Bell Telephone Magazine* 15, 15–16 (Summer, 1964). Microwave relay towers are approximately 30 miles apart.

telegraph between 1945 and 1964. Nevertheless, the message telegraph volume (70.2 million in 1966) indicates that there remains a sizable demand for such service.

In May, 1962, the FCC instituted an investigation of domestic telegraph operations and services. The report of the Telephone and Telegraph Committees (which conducted the inquiry) was issued in December, 1966.[18] The basic question raised was whether the decline in message telegraph service represented the expected response of the price system to a change in consumer wants or whether there were forces distorting the rate relationships between message telegraph and substitute services. If the relative prices confronting consumers adequately reflected the inherent value and cost-of-service characteristics of message telegraph and substitute services, then the decline in the former could be assumed to be the result of consumer choice. If there were forces which distorted these rate relationships, then consumer diversion would have to be explained as a reaction to a series of imperfections in the system of prices. To examine this problem, three areas were considered: (1) the pricing, marketing, and operational practices of the telegraph company; (2) the interrelationships between the Bell System and Western Union; and (3) the limitations or constraints of FCC regulatory policy. With respect to these three areas, the Telephone and Telegraph Committees found:

> Western Union's role in the decline of the message telegraph service is highlighted by its pricing policies. The carrier applied eleven rate increases in the 1945–1964 period to the public message service. The rationalization for this policy of price increases appears to be associated with the need to cover anticipated wage increases, and the need for revenues to support a program of diversification in the Telex and private line telegraph fields. However, as the price of public message telegraph came into proximity with the prices of higher quality alternative communications, users began to divert in an ever-increasing extent, so that subsequent rate increases were not productive of significant additional revenues on a permanent basis. Short-period earnings benefits were achieved by the more recent rate increases because of the ability of the carrier to capitalize on what appears to be a lag in consumer response. [In addition, the carrier resorted to severe cost-cutting and efficiency programs.] But the increased diversion at the higher prices soon erased these benefits and necessitated a repetition of the whole cycle. Over the long run, the consequences of successive price increases in the face of growing consumer price sensitivity, or greater elasticity of demand, could only result in a fall in both message volume and total revenues even at higher unit prices. Western Union never seriously experimented with promotional or incentive prices for message telegraph in an attempt to reverse this trend.

---

[18]*Report of the Telephone and Telegraph Committees in the Domestic Telegraph Investigation*, FCC Docket No. 14650 (December 21, 1966). Also see *Report of the Common Carrier Bureau of the Federal Communications Commission in the Domestic Telegraph Investigation* (Washington, D.C., 1965); and Harry M. Trebing, "The Plight of the Telegraph Service," 15 *MSU Business Topics* 43 (Summer, 1967).

A second factor considered was the relationship between Western Union and the Bell System in domestic communications. The Bell System has occupied a unique position in terms of both Western Union's ability to maintain the public message service and its capacity to diversify in new fields. Bell's impact upon Western Union has been manifest in a number of areas, but principally through (1) the prices or rates set for Bell System services, and (2) the restrictions imposed by Bell on interconnection and the use of facilities leased by Western Union in the provision of its services. Bell's pricing practices have affected Western Union through the rates set for teletypewriter exchange service (TWX), which provided an alternative for certain volume users of the public message service; the rates set for services where direct competition existed between Bell and Western Union (*e.g.*, TWX-Telex and private wire telegraph); and the introduction of volume discounting through TELPAK. AT&T also imposed interconnection and interchange of facilities restrictions on Western Union which served to limit the latter's capacity to compete in the private line voice and alternate voice-record fields.

... The overall relationship among rates for voice and record services is most conspicuously shown in the results of the 1964 7-Way Cost Study, where the earnings of the monopoly voice service, based upon fully allocated investment, were substantially higher than those in the competitive telegraph fields; and where the earnings in the latter fields appear to be below a fair rate of return when related to fully allocated investment and costs. It appears that Bell's prices may have been fixed in the competitive areas without adequate concern as to whether they produced a proper level of earnings, or as to the competitive effect they had upon Western Union.

A third factor considered was the impact of regulatory policy on Western Union's capacity to experiment and promote the public message service. It is clear that Commission policy did not stand as a barrier to the concept of experimentation. On the other hand, we were probably too accommodating in accepting justifications for message telegraph price increases. This is best illustrated by the Commission's allowance of rate increases on the basis of the carrier's claims of anticipated wage-cost pressures which sometimes failed to materialize.[19]

[19]Federal Communications Commission, *Public Notice* (No. 93561, December 22, 1966), pp. 4-6. Several of the Committees' findings are open to dispute. With respect to pricing, the Bell System asserts that a fully allocated investment and cost basis is inappropriate for rate-making purposes. (On the Seven-Way Cost Study, see Chapter 11, pp. 395-96.) Rate-making principles are now being examined by the FCC in Phase 1B of Docket 16258. (See pp. 667-70.) With respect to the alleged restrictions on the use of leased facilities, Trebing has concluded that on the basis of the record developed in the investigation, "it is difficult to argue that the Bell System has employed these restrictions in such a way as to affect the development and promotion of the message telegraph service. Leasing charges are a small element in message telegraph cost, and the Bell System has made circuits readily available. Indeed, there is nothing to suggest that the Bell System makes circuits available in a fashion that discriminates against Western Union in the provision of competitive telegraph services, or that Bell has withheld circuits when Western Union plans to introduce a new record or telegraph offering. Similarly, there is nothing to suggest that the maintenance or quality of circuits leased to Western Union is inferior, or that the restoration of service has been made on a basis that discriminates against Western Union customers." Trebing, *op. cit.*, p. 49.

The report of the Telephone and Telegraph Committees concluded that

. . . the consumers' choice between public message service and alternative communications media was conditioned by a successive series of rate increases needed to support a diversification program into new areas and to off-set Bell's pricing practices in TWX and other competitive services. In such a setting, it is difficult to argue that the resultant price-volume relationships reflect a correct valuation of consumer requirements for the public message service. A different outcome might have been expected had prices been maintained at levels corresponding more closely to value and cost-of-service considerations for public message telegraph and other communications services. This does not necessarily mean that, had prices been permitted to reflect these factors more accurately, the message telegraph service would have retained the position of dominance which it held a half century ago. Nor is it suggested that, even if price had stabilized, message traffic would have enjoyed the same proportional growth as message toll telephone or TWX. But it does indicate that the accelerated decline in volume attributable to the substantial increase in price in the postwar period need not have come to pass. Indeed, in a growing economy, it would not have been improbable to assume that message volume would have stabilized, or possibly demonstrated a slight absolute increase as new usage developed.[20]

Several recommendations were made, the most important being the following. First, an integrated record message service should be created, through the unification of message telegraph, Telex, and the Bell System's TWX in one carrier, namely, Western Union.[21] Second, Western Union should be required to introduce a program of promotional pricing "without delay" and to meet adequate speed and quality-of-service standards so as to maximize usage of each type of message service. Third, certain Bell System–Western Union relationships with respect to facility leasing arrangements, interconnection of services, and minimum prices should be established and/or regulated.[22]

The Diversification of Western Union

In an effort to increase earnings and to meet the growing needs of its customers, Western Union has diversified into other communications services, with emphasis on directly connected customer-to-customer services. The com-

[20] Federal Communications Commission, *Public Notice, op. cit.,* p. 7.

[21] The FCC first suggested that Western Union take over the Bell System's TWX service in 1943, following its hearings on the telegraph company's acquisition of Postal Telegraph. The matter was subsequently explored by the two companies several times, but it was not until early in 1969 that an agreement was reached, under which Western Union will purchase the Bell System's TWX service (subject to approval of the FCC and appropriate state regulatory agencies) for approximately $80 million. *The Wall Street Journal,* January 16, 1969, p. 34.

[22] Federal Communications Commission, *Public Notice, op. cit.,* pp. 9–14.

pany offers a teleprinter exchange (Telex) service [23] and leased wire services (i.e., private line record, voice, alternate voice-data, alternate voice-teleprinter, and alternate facsimile-voice transmission services) in competition with, and with some facilities leased from, the telephone companies.[24] The company's leased wire systems include AUTODIN (automatic digital data network) serving the Department of Defense; ARS (Advanced Record System) designed for the General Services Administration; and nationwide, data-oriented networks for the National Aeronautics and Space Administration, the National Crime Information Center of the Federal Bureau of Investigation, and many commercial and industrial customers. Western Union's transcontinental microwave relay system has resulted in new services, such as Broadband Exchange Service (a service currently under development), which provides instantaneous customer-to-customer voice-band or wider connections that can be used to transmit both voice and nonvoice messages.[25] Also in the experimental stage is a new Hot/Line service; a private point-to-point voice communication service with automatic connections, no dialing, and no minimum time charge. Finally, with the availability of large-capacity, multiple-access computers, the company is offering, or planning to offer, a variety of shared systems and is building an integrated record communication system. One such shared-system service, recently introduced, is called SICOM (Securities Industry Communications), designed for firms in the securities industry.[26]

Western Union's new and expanding services have required the company to undertake the largest construction program in its history. From 1955 through 1961, the company added $138.5 million to its plant; from 1962 through 1968, an additional $455 million was added. The success of this expansion program remains to be seen. However, the company's new services represent a significant

[23] Telex "permits subscribers to dial direct connections with other subscribers, worldwide, for the transmission of messages and data. Telex subscribers can also send Tel(T)ex messages to nonsubscribers by dialing special centers at major cities in the United States and Canada. The centers deliver Tel(T)ex messages as if they were telegrams." Western Union, *Annual Report, 1967*, p. 6.

[24] See T. A. Wise, "Western Union, by Grace of FCC and A.T.&T.," *Fortune*, March, 1959, pp. 114 ff. Western Union's teletypewriter service, Telex, competes with the Bell System's teletypewriter service, TWX; Western Union's leased wire systems with the Bell System's private line services, including TELPAK.

[25] "Broadband Exchange Service makes channels of various bandwidths available at charges based largely on usage. A pushbutton voice instrument is furnished to each subscriber who uses it to call other subscribers, and to select the kind of transmission channel needed for the record transmission device to be used—whether it is a high-speed data transmitter, facsimile machine or other type of business machine. The pushbutton instrument is also used to switch transmission between voice and the particular business machine being used." Western Union, *Annual Report, 1967*, p. 7.

[26] SICOM "interconnects a subscriber's headquarters wire and order rooms, branches and correspondents, the floors of the New York and American Stock Exchanges, and other special points desired. The system ... has been designed and engineered for the fast, efficient and economical transmission and delivery of orders, confirmations, market news reports, administrative messages and other information." *Ibid.*, p. 8.

and growing portion of its annual revenues: in 1968, Western Union's telegram message and money order services accounted for 51 percent of its revenues, its leased systems and related services for 32 percent, and its Telex service for 11 percent (with the remaining 6 percent derived from other services and other income).

THE TELEPHONE INDUSTRY

On March 7, 1876, U.S. Patent No. 174,465, frequently referred to as the world's most valuable patent, was issued to Alexander Graham Bell. Three days later, Bell spoke, and his assistant Thomas A. Watson heard, the first complete sentence ever transmitted by telephone: "Mr. Watson, come here, I want you."

The Domestic Telephone Industry

The domestic telephone industry is dominated by the American Telephone and Telegraph Company. The corporation is both a holding and an operating company. It holds 100 percent of the stock of Western Electric Company, manufacturer and supplier of telephone equipment and installer of central office equipment for A.T.&T. and its associated companies.[27] It owns the Bell Telephone Laboratories jointly with Western Electric. And it owns various amounts of capital stock in twenty-four subsidiary telephone operating companies (Table 17–1). A.T.&T., Western Electric, Bell Labs, and the operating subsidiaries are known collectively as the Bell Telephone System. The parent company, A.T.&T., is divided into two departments—the General Department and Long Lines Department. The General Department provides services to the associated companies, such as basic research and development in telephony (performed by Bell Labs); advice and assistance in engineering, traffic, plant, commercial, accounting, and legal matters; and financial advice and assistance, including assistance in marketing securities and maintenance of a central pool of funds on which the operating companies can draw to meet their day-to-day needs for new capital or for operations. The Long Lines Department provides land line and transoceanic facilities connecting the associated companies into a worldwide system of long distance service.[28]

[27] The Bell System purchases some telephone equipment from independent manufacturers, primarily with Western Electric acting as purchasing agent, but some is bought directly by the associated companies. A small amount of Western Electric equipment is sold to the Graybar Electric Company, which is not affiliated with the Bell System and which, in turn, sells the equipment to other non-Bell System purchasers. There are several independent suppliers of telephone equipment, including Automatic Electric Company and Leich Electric Company (both subsidiaries of General Telephone & Electronics Corporation), Gray Telephone Pay Station Company, Kellogg Switchboard and Supply Company (a subsidiary of International Telephone and Telegraph Company), North Electric Company (a subsidiary of L. M. Ericsson of Sweden), and Stromberg-Carlson Telephone Manufacturing Company (a division of General Dynamics), as well as cable manufacturers such as Anaconda, General Cable, and Whitney Blake.

[28] As a general rule, but with many exceptions, the associated companies supply line facilities for intrastate toll traffic and for interstate traffic involving a distance of 40 miles or under. Long Lines interstate circuits generally involve distances in excess of 40 miles.

TABLE 17-1
Bell System Companies, 1968

Affiliates	Capital Stocks Owned by A.T.&T. Co. (Percent)	Telephones
Principal Telephone Subsidiaries:		
New England Tel. & Tel. Co.	69.5	4,629,415
New York Tel. Co.	100.0	10,817,165
New Jersey Bell Tel. Co.	100.0	4,251,589
Bell Tel. Co. of Pennsylvania	100.0	5,726,742
Diamond State Tel. Co.	100.0	337,180
Chesapeake & Potomac Tel. Co.	100.0	834,043
Chesapeake & Potomac Tel. Co. of Maryland	100.0	2,153,978
Chesapeake & Potomac Tel. Co. of Virginia	100.0	1,724,029
Chesapeake & Potomac Tel. Co. of West Virginia	100.0	622,095
Southern Bell Tel. & Tel. Co.	100.0	5,969,048
South Central Bell Tel. Co.	100.0	5,721,900
Ohio Bell Tel. Co.	100.0	3,733,179
Michigan Bell Tel. Co.	100.0	4,189,643
Indiana Bell Tel. Co., Inc.	100.0	1,442,085
Wisconsin Tel. Co.	100.0	1,591,347
Illinois Bell Tel. Co.	99.3	5,584,892
Northwestern Bell Tel. Co.	100.0	3,557,328
Southwestern Bell Tel. Co.	100.0	9,400,390
Mountain States Tel. & Tel. Co.	86.8	3,659,022
Pacific Northwest Bell Tel. Co.	89.2	2,256,333
Pacific Tel. & Tel. Co.	89.7	9,805,351
Bell Tel. Co. of Nevada[a]		
Total		88,006,754
Subsidiaries Not Consolidated:		
Bell Telephone Laboratories, Inc.	50.0 [b]	
Western Electric Co., Inc.	100.0	
195 Broadway Corp.	100.0	
Other Companies:		
Southern New England Tel. Co.	17.9	1,867,204
Cincinnati & Suburban Bell Tel. Co.	26.7	790,955
Bell Tel. Co. of Canada	2.1	5,450,782
Total		8,108,941

[a] Wholly owned subsidiary of Pacific Tel. & Tel. Co.
[b] Remainder owned by Western Electric Company.
Source: American Telephone and Telegraph Company.

The Bell Telephone System operates nearly 98 percent of all facilities employed in providing long distance telephone communication service in the country. The associated companies provide approximately 84 percent of the facilities used in supplying local telephone service. The Bell System supplies virtually all facilities used in the transmission of radio and television programs, facilities for a significant portion of press news and telephotograph services, and operates a nationwide teletypewriter exchange (TWX) service. It also provides, jointly with foreign telephone administrations, two-way telephone service to almost all other countries of the world. Western Electric accounts for 90 percent of the nation's output of telephonic equipment.

The independent telephone companies, numbering 2,100, supply the remaining local exchange telephone service (Figure 17–1). These companies serve 17.0 million telephones, or 16 percent of the nation's 103.7 million telephones.[29] Whereas the Bell System serves nearly all the big metropolitan centers, most of the independent companies are found in the smaller towns and rural areas. Bell and the independent companies each serve about one-third of the country's geographic area; the remainder consists of unserviceable territory (mountains, lakes, national parks, and so forth). In recent years, the number of independent companies has decreased as a result of purchases and mergers among themselves.[30]

The largest independent telephone company is the General Telephone & Electronics Corporation, a holding company that controlled (at the end of 1967) more than thirty subsidiary operating companies, serving 8.7 million telephones in thirty-four states.[31] General Telephone began as the General Telephone Corporation in 1935—a company that emerged from a bankruptcy proceeding against the Associated Telephone Utilities Company. In 1950, General Telephone acquired a small equipment manufacturer, Leich Electric Company. Five years later, the company acquired Theodore Gary and Company, the second largest independent telephone company, and its subsidiary, the Automatic Electric Company, which was second only to Western Electric as a manufacturer of telephone equipment. In 1959, the company acquired another relatively small manufacturer, Lenkurt Electric Company. In the same year, General Telephone merged with Sylvania Electronics Products, Inc., and changed its name to General Telephone & Electronics Corporation. Thus, the company has extensive telephone manufacturing, as well as research (G.T.&E. Laboratories), facilities. In addition, it is a major manufacturer of electronics systems, electric light bulbs, fluorescent lamps, radio and television receivers, and cameras, and is an important defense contractor. In fact, more than half of General Telephone's annual revenues come from nonutility activities.[32]

American Telephone and Telegraph Company. Bell's experimentation with the telephone was financed by Thomas Sanders and Gardiner G. Hubbard

[29] United States Independent Telephone Association, *Independent Telephone Statistics, 1968 Edition* (Washington, D.C., 1968), Vol. 1, p. 2.

[30] In the early 1930's, there were over 6,400 independent telephone companies, compared with 5,469 companies in 1951, 3,034 companies in 1961, and 2,100 companies at the end of 1967.

[31] The second and third largest independent telephone companies are United Utilities, Inc. (serving 1.6 million telephones in twenty-one states) and Continental Telephone Corporation (serving 1.1 million telephones in forty states), respectively.

[32] In June 1964, the Department of Justice brought suit to enjoin General Telephone's proposed acquisition of four telephone companies, alleging that the acquisition would foreclose competitors of General Telephone from selling equipment to telephone operating companies. (*United States* v. *General Tel. & Electronics Corp.*, Civil Action No. 64-1912 [S.D.N.Y., filed June 19, 1964].) In November 1966, the Justice Department dismissed the suit, saying that since the industry was already vertically

FIGURE 17-1
Independent Telephone Company Exchanges

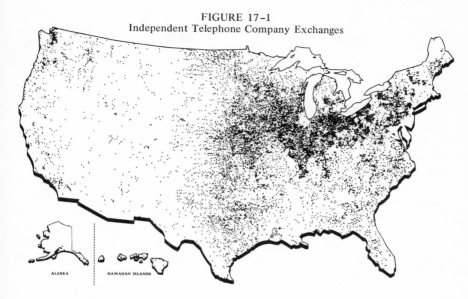

ALASKA   HAWAIIAN ISLANDS

Source: United States Independent Telephone Association, *Independent Telephone Statistics, 1968 Edition* (Washington, D.C., 1968), Vol. 1, p. 10.

who, with the inventor, in 1875 organized a partnership known as the Bell Patent Association. Yet, even after the first successful experiment in 1876, many doubted that the telephone had future significance. Western Union, for instance, in 1876 rejected an opportunity to buy the Bell patent for $100,000. In 1877, the partnership became a Massachusetts voluntary association known as the Bell Telephone Company. Its purpose was to own and control any patents resulting from Bell's experiments. The following year, the association was incorporated in Massachusetts under the name Bell Telephone Company, and in 1879 as the National Bell Telephone Company. In 1880, the Bell interests reorganized to form the American Bell Telephone Company. The company was to manufacture telephones and other equipment, and to construct and operate telephone lines throughout the United States, outside New England.[33]

integrated, "it would be inappropriate to prosecute its suit against a single company at this time." (*The Wall Street Journal*, November 15, 1966, p. 32.) However, following General Telephone's merger with Hawaiian Telephone Company (the fifth largest independent telephone system) and Northern Ohio Telephone Company in 1967, International Telephone & Telegraph Corporation filed a suit on similar grounds. (*International Tel. & Tel. Corp.* v. *General Tel. & Electronics Corp.*, Civil Action No. 2754 [D. Hawaii, filed October 18, 1967]. See *The Wall Street Journal*, October 19, 1967, p. 3.)

[33] Early in 1878, the New England Telephone Company was formed to provide service in that area. The American Bell Telephone Company acquired a portion of the company's stock. The New England Company agreed to lease and not to sell its telephone instruments. The Bell Company, in turn, agreed to cooperate in patent litigation and in establishing connecting lines.

In 1877, Western Union entered into competition, developing telephone exchanges throughout the country under the patents of Elisha Gray and Thomas A. Edison. American Bell filed suit for patent infringement against Western Union in 1878, a suit voluntarily terminated in 1879. Western Union acknowledged the priority of the Bell patents, granted American Bell an exclusive 17-year license to use all its patents, and agreed to pay 20 percent of the cost of any new telephone patents American Bell developed or acquired. American Bell agreed to pay Western Union 20 percent of the rentals or royalties it received for the use of its licenses of telephone instruments, to purchase Western Union's telephone system, and to withdraw from the public message telegraph business.[34]

Throughout this early period, American Bell licensed companies and individuals to operate, and leased telephone instruments to them. "By November, 1879, the parent organization had entered into 185 contracts for the provision of local telephone service; in fact, all of the more productive territory of the country was covered by these license agreements."[35] Five year licenses were common because of the uncertainties of the new ventures. As the industry grew, American Bell granted permanent licenses, taking in return a stock interest in the licensees. The parent company's control was further strengthened by the purchase of additional stock and through consolidations and mergers. In 1881, the American Bell Telephone Company acquired a substantial interest in the Western Electric Manufacturing Company of Chicago and changed its name to the Western Electric Company. Thus, by this date, "a program that envisaged the co-ordination of all phases of the telephone industry was formulated: the supply of local exchange service, the development of long-distance service, and the organization of manufacturing affiliates to supply the necessary equipment were all developed under the control of the parent company."[36]

The American Telephone and Telegraph Company (frequently referred to as the American Company or, popularly, "Mother Bell") was incorporated in February, 1885, as a wholly owned subsidiary of American Bell.[37] Its primary

---

[34] Federal Communications Commission, *Investigation of the Telephone Industry in the United States* (House Doc. 340, 76th Cong., 1st sess.) (Washington, D.C.: U.S. Government Printing Office, 1939), pp. 123–25. "The Vanderbilt interests controlled Western Union at the time and were anxious to forestall the efforts of Jay Gould to acquire the company or achieve a foothold in communications. So when the prospect of a Gould-Bell alliance appeared, Western Union sought a compromise through a patent settlement, even though it possessed patents for the Blake Transmitter which was allegedly superior to anything then available for telephone service. Interestingly, the compromise was not successful in blocking Gould's acquisition of Western Union or in preventing Bell's entry into the telegraph field via private-line telegraph service." Trebing, *op. cit.*, p. 54, n. 8.

[35] Irston R. Barnes, *The Economics of Public Utility Regulation* (New York: F. S. Crofts & Co., 1942), p. 38.

[36] *Ibid.*, p. 39.

[37] A.T.&T. is a New York corporation. Massachusetts law prevented American Bell from holding more than 30 percent of the capital stock of any corporation doing business in the state, paying dividends in its own stock, or selling its stock at less than

purpose was to operate the long distance network connecting the local exchanges of the operating companies. Early in 1900, American Bell transferred all investments in its subsidiaries to the American Company, and the following year the two companies were consolidated, with the American Company becoming the parent holding company. In 1924, Bell Telephone Laboratories, Inc., was established to take over the product development engineering, and a portion of the patent, departments of Western Electric. The parent company's Development and Research Department was transferred to the Labs beginning in 1934.[38]

The growth of the Bell Telephone System has been spectacular (Table 17-2). A.T.&T. is the country's largest corporation, with net telephone plant of $34.8 billion and operating revenues of just over $14 billion. In the post-World War II period, A.T.&T.'s external financing has equaled 10.2 percent of all corporate financing, and its equity financing has been 37.2 percent of that done by all corporations.[39] The company's stockholders, now numbering 3.1 million, have nearly quintupled since 1940. Western Electric is the nation's twelfth largest industrial corporation, with assets of $2.7 billion, revenues of $4 billion, and employees totaling 176,970.[40] Bell Labs, perhaps best known for the

---

the market price as fixed by the Massachusetts Commissioner of Corporations. The company also experienced difficulty in securing permission to increase its capitalization with the growth of its business.

[38] A.T.&T. owned the telephone instruments until December, 1927, when they were sold to the associated companies.

[39] The Bell System's postwar (1946 through 1967) sources of funds compared with those for all corporations are as follows:

	All Corporations		Bell System		Bell System as Percent of All Corporations
	Amount (Millions)	Percent of Total	Amount (Millions)	Percent of Total	
External Financing:					
Stock	$ 33,800	3.0%	$12,569	25.8%	37.2%
Bonds, loans, etc. . . .	194,500	17.5	10,630	21.8	5.5
Total	$ 228,300	20.5%	$23,199	47.6%	10.2%
Internal Financing:					
Retained earnings[a] . .	$ 289,100	26.0%	$ 7,198	14.8%	2.5%
Depreciation	437,600	39.4	18,012	37.0	4.1
Other internal	156,200	14.1	310	0.6	0.2
Total	$ 882,900	79.5%	$25,520	52.4%	2.9%
Total External and Internal	$1,111,200	100.0%	$48,719	100.0%	4.4%

[a] Net income less dividends.
Source: American Telephone and Telegraph Company.

[40] Western Electric has five major subsidiaries: Teletype Corp. (engaged in the manufacture and sale of printing telegraph equipment); Nassau Smelting & Refining Co.

TABLE 17-2
The Bell Telephone System

	1920	1930	1940	1950	1960	1968
Telephones	8,134,000	15,187,000	17,484,000	35,343,440	60,735,073	88,006,754
Average daily conversations:a						
Local	32,489,000	62,550,000	77,706,000	136,394,000	210,360,000	303,535,000
Long distance	636,000	1,484,000	1,597,000	4,388,000	8,733,000	17,827,000
Overseas conversations (total for year)	....	32,821	73,429	1,000,184	3,713,183	15,200,000
Net telephone plant b	$1,082,811	$3,320,277	$3,386,777	$7,275,277	$18,825,273	$34,754,903
Operating revenues b	$ 442,790	$1,077,300	$1,174,322	$3,261,528	$ 7,920,454	$14,100,014
Construction expenditures b	$ 169,000	$ 520,000	$ 290,000	$ 891,000	$ 2,658,381	$ 4,742,144
Operating taxes b	$ 27,452	$ 84,732	$ 184,770	$ 499,452	$ 1,847,702	$ 3,300,010
Employees:						
Telephone companies	228,943	318,119	275,317	532,251	580,405	679,110
Western Electric	39,650	67,763	43,746	73,458	143,352	176,970
Bell Tel. Laboratories	....	5,864	4,638	5,757	12,009	15,938
Total wages b	$ 314,959	$ 680,827	$ 610,815	$2,007,216	$ 4,174,500	$ 6,642,284
A.T.&T. shareowners	139,448	567,694	630,902	985,583	1,911,484	3,142,075

a On basis of present classification (January 1, 1969) between local and long distance.

b Thousands of dollars.

Source: American Telephone and Telegraph Company.

discovery of the transistor and development of Telstar, employs 15,938. It performs the research and development work for the Bell System, amounting to over $300 million annually (including research and development performed within Western Electric, but exclusive of special work done for the federal government).[41]

The Independent Telephone Companies. On issuance of the basic Bell patent in 1876, many competing telephone companies were organized. Between 1877 and 1893, when the original Bell patent expired, American Bell instituted over 600 patent infringement suits. Since many of the defendants went out of business on being sued, only a few of the cases reached the Supreme Court. These cases were combined for purposes of hearings, and on March 19, 1888, the Court, in a 4 to 3 decision, upheld the Bell patents in their entirety.[42]

Consequently, the real growth of the independent telephone companies dates from 1894. Numerous companies were formed in rural areas, although a few entered into direct competition with the Bell System in urban areas. By 1902, out of 1,051 incorporated cities in the United States with a population of more than 4,000, 1,002 were provided with telephone facilities. Independent telephone companies had exclusive service in 137 of these cities, the Bell interests served 414 cities, and the remaining 451 cities were served by both independents and Bell interests.[43] By 1907, the Bell System owned 3.1 million stations, while independent companies owned 3 million.[44]

A.T.&T. acquired a substantial stock interest in Western Union in 1909, an acquisition that was promptly criticized by Postal Telegraph as resulting in discrimination against Postal and in favor of Western Union. The independent companies also charged that the Bell System was refusing satisfactory long distance interconnections. In 1913, in response to a threatened antitrust suit, the so-called Kingsbury Commitment was made whereby A.T.&T. agreed to sell its Western Union stock, agreed to interconnections with those independent telephone companies which met its equipment standards, and promised not to acquire control of competing telephone companies.[45] The Kingsbury Commit-

---

(engaged in the reclamation and sale of nonferrous scrap metals); Manufacturers' Junction Railway Co. (operating an industrial railroad in and about Western's Hawthorne plant, with rail connections with all railroad systems entering Chicago); Western Electric Co. Limited (serving primarily as a patent organization in foreign countries); and Sandia Corp. (operating laboratories for the Atomic Energy Commission). The stock of Bell Laboratories and Bellcom, Inc. (the latter provides technical studies, system planning, analysis and engineering for the National Aeronautics and Space Administration) is owned equally by A.T.&T. and Western Electric.

[41] In addition to its interest in Bell Labs, Western Electric owns a product development and design center in Princeton, New Jersey.

[42] *The Telephone Cases,* 126 U.S. 1 (1888).

[43] Bureau of the Census, "Telephones and Telegraphs, 1902," Bulletin No. 17, as cited in Federal Communications Commission, *Investigation of the Telephone Industry in the United States, op. cit.,* p. 132.

[44] Bureau of the Census, "Special Reports: Telephones, 1907," p. 22.

[45] Letter from N. C. Kingsbury, vice-president of A.T.&T., to the Attorney General of the United States, December 19, 1913. See *Annual Report of A.T.&T.,* 1913, pp.

ment was followed by the Hall Memorandum of 1922, which explained the Bell System's acquisition policy as one opposed to purchases or consolidations with connecting or duplicating companies "except in special cases." The memorandum continued, in part:

> We should consider that such an exception was proved only in cases where it seemed to be demanded either:
> (1) For the convenience of the public as evidenced by the wishes of State authorities or by local public sentiment in or adjoining the territory served; or
> (2) By special reason which made the transaction seem desirable and essential from the point of view of the protection of our own property or the general public service.
>
> * * *
>
> Types of cases which might be expected to come up for consideration under the second general classification would be:
> 1. Companies in which we now have a disproportionately large investment without actual control.
> 2. Cases where connecting company or other telephone property is pressed for sale, and where it seems that the general public service will be improved by its operation as an integral part of our service.[46]

The Hall Memorandum continues to reflect the Bell System's acquisition policy. Generally, since 1922, the Bell System has purchased only distressed companies and has disposed of minority stock interests in independent companies. It has consistently refused to adopt a "balancing purchases agreement" with the independent companies whereby Bell would agree to sell stations to independents in a number equal to the number acquired by Bell,[47] but in several acquisitions it has made offsetting sales to independents. In recent years, mergers among independents to achieve economies of scale, rather than Bell System acquisitions, provide the major explanation for the declining number of independent telephone companies.

The independent companies, moreover, have continued to grow throughout the post-World War II period despite their shrinking number. Population

---

24–26. In 1917, the Kingsbury Commitment was modified whereby A.T.&T. agreed to acquire competing companies only if it gave up an equal number of telephones to an independent company. When, in 1921, the Willis-Graham Act permitted telephone companies to merge or consolidate with competing companies if approved by the state commissions and the ICC, the Kingsbury Commitment was terminated. See letter from the Attorney General of the United States to E. K. Hall, vice-president of A.T.&T., September 19, 1921.

[46] Letter from E. K. Hall, vice-president of A.T.&T., to F. B. MacKinnon, president of the United States Independent Telephone Association, June 14, 1922. A.T.&T. also agreed to give 30 days notice to the USITA before filing with a regulatory commission for approval of such an acquisition.

[47] To adopt such an agreement, the company feels, "would be unbusinesslike, imprudent and absolutely unjustifiable from any point of view. It is too much like drawing a blank check." Letter from E. K. Hall, vice-president of A.T.&T., to F. B. MacKinnon, president of the United States Independent Telephone Association, April 14, 1926.

shifts to smaller communities and diversification of defense and civilian industry have been primarily responsible for this growth. Independent telephones have nearly tripled since 1950. The independents now operate 10,869 exchanges (compared with 6,763 for the Bell System), have invested $8.7 billion in plant, have annual operating revenues of $2.0 billion, and employ 121,410.[48]

The Development of Telephone Communications

In 1877, the first overhead telephone line was erected, from Boston to Somerville, Massachusetts. By 1880, there were 47,900 telephones in the United States. In 1881, telephone service opened between Boston and Providence; in 1884, New York and Boston were connected. Service between New York and Chicago commenced in 1892. Originally, telephones were rented in pairs to individuals for local use, and subscribers had to put up their own lines to connect each other. The switchboard came into existence in Boston in 1877, and the following year New Haven, Connecticut, boasted of the first regular telephone exchange. The dial telephone was invented in 1889 by Almon B. Strowger, a Kansas City undertaker, and the first dial exchange was installed at La Porte, Indiana, in 1895.

Overhead wires soon "blotted out the sky in many cities" and became obstacles to effective firefighting and efficient telephone communications (due to snow and sleet damage). The result was development of overhead and underground cables. The initial long distance underground cables were placed in operation between New York and Newark, New Jersey, in 1902; between New York and Philadelphia in 1906; between Washington and New York in 1912; and between Washington and Boston in 1913. Transcontinental telephone service was inaugurated in 1915 and transcontinental cable service in 1942.

In addition to wire telephone service, radio telephone (wireless telephone) has become of major significance. Radio telephony was first demonstrated in 1915 between Montauk Point on Long Island and Wilmington, Delaware. Transoceanic radio telephony between America and Europe was opened in 1927, between America and South America in 1930. In 1947, an experimental microwave relay system went into operation between New York and Boston; four years later, an improved system was being used to send telephone and telegraph messages and television programs across the country. Today, over half of the communications facilities of A.T.&T.'s Long Lines Department use the microwave medium.

All these developments have resulted from continuous technical pro-

[48]*Independent Telephone Statistics, 1968 Edition, op. cit.*, Vol. 1, pp. 2–3. In 1949, Congress amended the Rural Electrification Act to authorize the agency to make loans to provide, expand, or upgrade rural telephone service. Loans are made at a 2 percent rate of interest for a maximum amortization period of thirty-five years. Eligible borrowers are private telephone companies and cooperatives, but not state or local governmental bodies. Through 1967, REA telephone loans totaled nearly $1.5 billion, providing new or improved service to 2,241,304 subscribers. *Ibid.*, p. 35.

gress.[49] To illustrate: The first commercial coaxial cable (a copper tube about $\frac{3}{8}$ inch in diameter with a single wire suspended inside it), installed between New York and Philadelphia in 1936, could carry 480 simultaneous conversations, compared with the cable being installed between Boston and Miami that will be capable of carrying 32,400 simultaneous telephone conversations.[50] One set of antennas can carry 17,000 simultaneous telephone conversations over the transcontinental microwave relay system. Most domestic telephones are now dial operated for local calls, and direct distance dialing, introduced in 1951, is increasing rapidly (91 percent of the Bell System is equipped for direct distance dialing).

There are indications, moreover, that future developments in the art of telephony will be just as continuous.[51] Push-button dial telephones and picture-phones have been developed and are being introduced to meet future communications needs.[52] Overseas direct dialing started on a test basis in 1967, and should be available to almost all of the world's telephone subscribers during the 1970's. A digital transmission system, which greatly increases capacity and can carry voice, computer data, and pictures at the same time, is gradually being installed.[53] Electronic switching, permitting such new types of services as abbreviated dialing of frequently called numbers and automatic transfer of calls to another number, is also being installed.[54] And research is continuing on a long distance wave-guide—a hollow metallic tube, about two inches in diameter, capable of carrying, simultaneously, hundreds of thousands of long distance telephone conversations along with hundreds of television programs.

The Telephone Investigation of the 1930's

One of the first major actions of the FCC was to initiate an investigation of the telephone industry. This investigation, undertaken at the direction of Congress,[55] was without doubt the most intensive, extensive, and comprehensive

49 See Francis Bello, "The World's Greatest Industrial Laboratory," *Fortune*, November, 1958, pp. 148 ff.

50 See Robert F. Latter, "Modern Coaxial Cable," 43 *Bell Telephone Magazine* 20 (Winter, 1964-65); and "A Cable for Growth," 46 *ibid.* 18 (January-February, 1967).

51 See Statement by Paul A. Gorman in Joint Economic Committee, *New Views on Automation* (86th Cong., 2d sess.) (Washington, D.C.: U.S. Government Printing Office, 1960), pp. 255-67; and Claude M. Blair, "Today's Challenges, Tomorrow's Promise in Communications Technology," 41 *Bell Telephone Magazine* 20 (Summer, 1962).

52 See Eugene Lapé, "Business Experiments with PICTUREPHONE Service," 44 *Bell Telephone Magazine* 54 (Summer, 1965).

53 See "The Code's the Thing," 46 *Bell Telephone Magazine* 20 (July-August, 1967); and *Business Week*, January 13, 1968, pp. 82-84.

54 See Raymond W. Ketchledge, "Electronic Switching," 39 *Bell Telephone Magazine*, 2 (Autumn, 1960); *Business Week*, May 1, 1965, pp. 66-67; Theodore B. Merrill, Jr., "Bell Laboratories' Biggest Job," 44 *Bell Telephone Magazine* 2 (Spring, 1965); and "The Integrated Computer," 47 *ibid.* 8 (May-June, 1968).

55 Public Res. 8, 74th Cong., 49 Stat. 43 (1935).

probe by a regulatory agency of an industry under its jurisdiction. The initial resolution appropriated $750,000 to carry out the mandate of Congress. Two additional appropriations were made in 1936 and 1937, providing a total of $1.5 million for the entire investigation. More than 300 people, primarily lawyers, accountants, and engineers, were engaged in the investigation which lasted over four years. The investigation was carried out in three phases: collection of data from the records and files of A.T.&T. and the associated companies, formal hearings in which evidence was taken and interpreted, and development of the fundamental data and background material relative to basic interstate telephone rate and regulatory problems on which continuing regulation could be built. The basic record of the formal phase of the investigation included 8,441 pages of testimony, 2,140 exhibits, and 77 staff reports.

On June 14, 1939, the commission unanimously adopted its final report.[56] In view of the importance of the investigation, the major findings and summary are quoted at length in the following paragraphs.

Corporate History of the Bell System: . . . The present associated companies of the Bell System, usually covering entire States or groups of States, are the result of many mergers and consolidations in which the parent company of the Bell System consistently followed the policy of increasing its interest in the business of furnishing telephone service. . . . Throughout the history of the Bell System the changing corporate structures have involved a parent company, subsidiaries, and subsidiaries of subsidiaries, but in general the practice of pyramiding securities of the various companies, as practiced by other utilities, has not been indulged in.[57]

Growth of the Bell System: The growth of the Bell System . . . reflects the policy of the management during successive periods. From its early days, until the expiration of the basic patents, the growth was relatively slow. . . . With the expiration of the basic patents and the rise of competition . . . rates were substantially reduced and the market broadened. . . . During the 1920 decade the competitive situation was harmonized to a great extent. The economic developments during this decade further encouraged telephone development. . . .

The general business decline following 1929 inevitably reacted on the telephone business, resulting in a decrease in the number of stations in service . . . together with a great diminution in the extent of the use of toll facilities.[58]

Corporate and Capital Structure of the Bell System: . . . There were in all, at the end of 1934, 273 corporations in which the American Co. either had

[56] Federal Communications Commission, *Investigation of the Telephone Industry in the United States, op. cit.* For a different interpretation of the history of the company during the same period covered by the report, see N. R. Danielian, *A.T.&T.: The Story of Industrial Conquest* (New York: Vanguard Press, 1939). For a more recent critical study of A.T.&T., see Joseph C. Goulden, *Monopoly* (New York: G. P. Putnam's Sons, 1968).

[57] Federal Communications Commission, *Investigation of the Telephone Industry in the United States, op. cit.*, p. 573.

[58] *Ibid.*, p. 574.

direct or indirect ownership of 10 percent or more of the voting securities, or had potential control through various other means. . . . The corporate structure of the Bell System, although involving a large number of operating companies, is simple in comparison with many other enterprises of smaller magnitude; and does not, so far as our investigation discloses, enable it to evade taxation. . . . The relationship of Western Electric Co. to the operating units of the Bell System is such that opportunity is afforded for pyramiding of profits. If Western Electric Co. has made excessive profits on its sales of materials and equipment for the construction of operating telephone plant and if rates for service are adequate to earn a fair return on the cost of such property, a double profit to the holding company will result. . . .[59]

Management and Control of the Bell System: The central management of the Bell System represented by the directors and executive officers of the American Co., and of the predecessor parent companies, has controlled the functions and operations of the system through various means. . . . The separate corporate entity of the associated companies may be said to be merely a legal fiction from the standpoint of the practical direction of every operating function of the entire Bell System. This right of direction is, of course, inherent in the majority stock ownership. . . . Because of this centralized management, effective State regulation cannot be accomplished by reliance entirely on the records of the associated companies, but involves examination of the records of the American Co., Western Electric, and Bell Telephone Laboratories, with respect to which State jurisdiction is limited. Hence effective regulation can be accomplished only by cooperative effort of State commissions and the Federal Communications Commission.[60]

Elimination of Competition: The Bell System has consistently pursued the policy of obtaining control of a Nation-wide unified telephone system. Since its inception the watchword has been "One System, One Policy, Universal Service." In achieving its present dominant position, the Bell System has been successful in the elimination of effective competition. There is today no competition, worthy of the name from the Nation-wide standpoint, with the unified Bell System. . . .

Attempts at this late date to develop a strong, independent telephone system to compete with the Bell System would be futile. Protection of the rate-paying public by means of effective competition is now, and for a number of years has been impossible. Protection of that interest must be accomplished through effective governmental regulation of the telephone industry. . . .[61]

The License-Service Contract: The license-service contract entered into between the parent Bell Co. and the operating companies was an important instrument in the development of the Bell System. The contracts were, in the early days, not only the important source of revenue of the parent company, but were the foundation for control of the operating telephone companies . . . . [T]he importance of the license-service contract today from the

---

[59]*Ibid.,* pp. 575–76.
[60]*Ibid.,* pp. 576–78.
[61]*Ibid.,* pp. 578–79.

standpoint of regulation of telephone rates is the reasonableness of the payments made for services allegedly rendered by the parent company.

. . . The difficulty in determining the appropriate amount to be included in the operating expenses of the associated companies for the services rendered by the American Co. arises because the American Co. performs numerous functions in its capacity as owner of the associated companies, the cost of which should be met by American Co. stockholders and not included in operating expenses of the associated companies. No satisfactory method of segregating and separately accounting for the cost of these various activities has as yet been developed. . . .

The license-service contract covers not only the furnishing of services by the American Co., but also division of revenues on business handled jointly by the long-lines department of the American Co. and the other operating companies of the Bell System. . . . The equitableness of present and past revenue-division practices has never been fully investigated by any regulatory body. . . .[62]

Research: The invention of the telephone itself and the many subsequent advances and improvements in the art of telephony have all been effected through processes of scientific research. . . . The expenditures by the Bell System for research are designed to insure the protection of its investment in the telephone-communications field by keeping abreast or ahead of developments in the art as well as in any potentially competitive fields, and as such they may be considered as properly payable by the stockholders from income rather than as operating expenses of the operating companies. From the standpoint of the telephone subscribers, the research activities of the Bell System have resulted in vastly improved service, and no criticism is intended of the policy adopted of making such expenditures in the interest of improved service. . . . [T]here is at least an attempt to segregate costs of research which bear directly upon telephone service from those which are not so directly related. The so-called telephone activities of the laboratories are the basic source from which many of the nontelephonic products result. The American Co. does not assign any portion of this initial research cost, attributed to telephone activities, to these nontelephonic byproducts and neither does it account for the royalties, or other profits, resulting from these byproducts in determining the revenue requirements from telephone service. This position is inconsistent. . . .[63]

Patents: The Bell System has at all times maintained a controlling patent position as to equipment and instrumentalities necessary for rendering efficient and economical long distance telephone service to the public. . . . By virtue of its policies and practices concerning the acquisition of patents and patent rights, the Bell System has continuously held from year to year a large number of unused patents. Patent suppression is commonly understood to mean ownership and control of patents and the intentional nonuse thereof. With the Bell System the nonuse of patents has resulted in part from acquisitions to protect and maintain as near as possible a complete occupa-

[62]*Ibid.*, pp. 580–81.
[63]*Ibid.*, pp. 581–82.

tion of the telephone field, both as to services to the public and as to the manufacture of equipment therefor.

... The manufacture and sale of patented equipment to the operating companies of the Bell System ... places in the hands of the Western Electric Co. the exclusive right to manufacture and sell all equipment covered by Bell System patents to telephone operating companies. ... This system of manufacture and sale of equipment may be repugnant to the spirit of the antitrust laws of the United States. Such a condition also introduces a problem in the complete and proper regulation of the telephone industry, i.e., it eliminates any possibility of the Bell telephone operating companies securing equipment covered by Bell System patents on a competitive bidding basis. ...

The ownership and control of patents by the American Co. contributes to its ability to control the exploitation of potentially competitive and emerging forms of communications, such as Teletypewriter Exchange Service and two-way public radio telephone service.[64]

Engineering and Standardization: ... The equipment and methods used in the Bell System have been standardized to a remarkable extent with resulting economies in the manufacture of equipment and operation of telephone plant: flexibility in the interchange of equipment and trained personnel between different parts of the System; and a uniformly high quality of service.

... Experts testified that it was their opinion, deduced from records of the American Co., that developments capable of improving the service and increasing its costs have been withheld for considerable periods; that the practice of limiting associated company purchases of apparatus and equipment to those furnished by the Western Electric Co. has prevented the use of improvements in the art developed outside the Bell System for considerable periods after such improvements were available; and that the American Co. has persisted in the installation of certain types of equipment which its studies indicated to be unduly expensive and uneconomical to operate. ...

There is a natural tendency incident to any program of standardization to retard the utilization of technical improvements. On the other hand, the lack of standardization operates to impair uniformity of service when such uniformity is an essential factor in the furnishing of satisfactory service. Such uniformity is an essential of a Nation-wide telephone service. While there may be disadvantages in the application of a rigid program of standardization, which becomes particularly apparent when viewed retrospectively, it is apparent that in the long run the advantages of standardization in the communications field outweigh the disadvantages. The overall results of standardization by the American Co. are such as to justify a continuance of research and standardization.[65]

Western Electric Co. Costs and Prices: ... Western's prices for telephone apparatus and equipment have an appreciable influence on the cost of telephone service. ... If it be assumed that Western's over-all profit has been reasonable and that its manufacturing operations are reasonably efficient, it is

[64] *Ibid.,* pp. 583–84.
[65] *Ibid.,* pp. 584–85.

still necessary that the cost accounting and pricing practices of Western reflect on equitable distribution of costs, plus a reasonable profit, as to each individual item or class of product. Western's costing methods do not provide such a basis. . . .

Comparisons between Western Electric Co.'s and independent manufacturers' prices have been advanced by the associated Bell companies in justification of Western Electric Co. prices advocated by them in rate proceedings. The differences in manufacturing and marketing conditions between Western and the independent manufacturers are such as to make a comparison of their respective prices of little value in testing the reasonableness of Western's prices. . . .

Two methods of regulating or controlling prices of telephone apparatus and equipment appear to warrant consideration. First, the establishment of competition among telephone manufacturers on those items or classes of product which independent telephone manufacturers are able to produce for the use of Bell System companies; and second, regulation of the Western Electric Co., with provision for determination of its valid and reasonable manufacturing costs, including a fair profit, and their effect, in order that proper costs may be available for use in determining reasonable rates.[66]

Depreciation: The depreciation accounting practices of the Bell Telephone System, from its inception to 1913, were variable and erratic. Since 1913, these practices have followed the rules laid down by the Interstate Commerce Commission, and later by the Federal Communications Commission, as interpreted by the American Co. This subject is highly controversial, and the principal difficulties relate not to the mechanics of bookkeeping, but to the determination of the amount to be included annually in operating expenses, and to the relationship of the reserves as accumulated to the accrued depreciation alleged by the companies to exist in the property as of a certain date. . . .

The consolidated depreciation reserve of the Bell System is approximately 30 percent of the book cost of depreciable telephone plant. The system has usually contended in rate cases that its property is depreciated, for rate base purposes, only to the extent of something less than 10 percent. The difference between the amounts obtained by the application of these percentages represents property values which do not exist if its estimates of annual charges for depreciation have been correct; or, if its estimates of annual depreciation have been incorrect, this difference represents an understatement of its profits in the years when this excess was alleged to have accrued . . . .[67]

Toll Activities—Domestic and International: . . . The determination of the reasonableness of toll and exchange rates involves the allocation of property, revenues, and expenses among the several services, interstate toll, intrastate toll, and exchange . . . . The problem of fixing equitable rates for any particular class of service and for any particular community is extremely complicated, and no simplified method of effecting the allocations necessary

[66] *Ibid.*, pp. 586–87.
[67] *Ibid.*, pp. 589–90.

has been developed . . . . A simple and equitable method of allocating property, revenues, and expenses common to two or more of the services rendered by the Bell System (intrastate toll, interstate toll, and exchange) must be developed in order to eliminate costly analyses in connection with individual rate proceedings and to reflect more accurately the profits of the various classes of service in the current operating reports . . . .[68]

Radio Broadcasting: The activities of Bell System companies in the domestic radio-broadcasting field are today limited to the furnishing of the facilities and services necessary for the transmission of broadcast programs over wire lines . . . . At present the Bell System tariffs on file with the Commission prohibit the interconnection of interexchange facilities of other wire carriers with its interexchange–program-transmission network, except where Bell System facilities are not available. This has given rise to certain claims of unjust discrimination . . . .[69]

Noncommunications Activities: Many of the devices covered by patents owned by the Bell System have application outside of the wire- or radio-communication field . . . . The Bell System companies have, in general, endeavored to limit their activities in the noncommunication field to that of licensor . . . . It is the duty of the American Co. to the telephone-using public to exploit fully and completely all the profit opportunities arising from patents or patent rights acquired in the conduct of the telephone business . . . .[70]

Financing of the Bell System: The capital funds required to keep pace with the increasing demand for telephone service were provided principally through the sale of equity securities by the parent company. . . . Prior to 1906 substantially all the long-term-debt issues of the American Co. and its predecessor, American Bell, were sold through competitive bidding. Beginning with 1906, such security issues were sold, without obtaining competitive bids, principally to syndicates of investment bankers. . . . It is not possible from the available evidence, or because of the lack of it, to conclude whether the American Co. and the associated companies have or have not obtained the best prices and the lowest bankers' commissions that the investment market could offer at the time bonds were issued. . . . [T]he investment bankers should be given an opportunity to make competitive bids, and the investment market should be allowed to express itself freely as to the rates of return at which it will supply the telephone business with capital.

The capital structure of the Bell System, with its relatively small proportion of long-term debt and a preponderance of equity financing, reflects a generally conservative financial policy over the years. . . .

It has frequently been asserted by Bell System officials that the policy of paying an annual dividend aggregating $9 on each share of American Telephone & Telegraph Co. common stock is a policy dictated by economic necessity, in the light of the system's large, recurrent, and—until the depression—continuous need for additional financing from sources outside

---

68 *Ibid.,* pp. 591–92.
69 *Ibid.,* p. 592.
70 *Ibid.*

the system itself. Whether this policy has in fact thus been required by economic necessity or is today so required is apparently a matter of judgment upon which opinions may reasonably differ and as to which "proof," in the ordinary sense of that term, is difficult if not impossible to adduce. . . .[71]

The Bell System Pension Plan: In 1913 the Bell System instituted a pension plan designed to take care of the superannuation problem as it affected the Bell System. . . . From 1913 to 1926, inclusive, the plan operated on the pay-as-you-go basis. . . . In 1927 the companies adopted an accrual plan of providing the amounts necessary eventually to pay the pensions called for under its plan. . . . Any accrual and funding basis of providing for pensions results in a lower total charge to operating expenses for pensions actually paid than the pay-as-you-go basis.

Subsequent to 1937 the pension plan of the Bell System has been modified substantially to provide for the elimination of certain undesirable features to which attention was directed by the special-investigation staff.[72]

Public Relations: A history of the Bell System activities in the field of public relations indicates that the system has pursued an active policy of cultivating public good will at considerable expense. There is evidence to indicate that improper influence has been brought to bear upon legislative and regulatory bodies charged with fixing rates for Bell System companies. This practice is clearly against public interest; is condemned; and should not be countenanced by any regulatory body. . . .[73]

Profits of the Bell System: The profitableness of the Bell Telephone System is reflected in the continuous dividends paid by the parent companies since 1880, averaging over 15 percent annually by American Bell Telephone Co. to 1900, and ranging from 7½ to 9 percent annually by the American Co. from 1900 to the present time. . . . The investment of the American Co. and its predecessor, American Bell Telephone Co., in Western Electric Co. has also been very profitable, as indicated by the fact that the cash dividends received from Western from the date of its organization to the end of 1936 have been equivalent to an average annual return of approximately 12 percent on the actual cash invested by them in the capital stock of that company. . . . The conclusion is inescapable that the Bell System has been an exceptionally profitable enterprise since its inception 60 years ago. . . .[74]

As a result of the investigation, the FCC reached major conclusions that have guided its approach to regulating the telephone industry ever since.

The concentration of the Nation's telephone business, and in particular of its interstate telephone business, in the hands of the Bell Telephone System is such that, whereas the problem of regulation is one of large magnitude, it is relatively simplified by reason of this very integration, as contrasted with the railroad, gas, electric-power, maritime, and motor-carrier fields of Federal regulatory effort. The fundamental problem underlying the provision of

[71] *Ibid.*, pp. 593–94.
[72] *Ibid.*, p. 594.
[73] *Ibid.*
[74] *Ibid.*, pp. 595–96.

effective regulation in the interstate telephone field appears to consist largely of developing ways and means, as well as positive and effective machinery, for the continuous acquisition of the basic factual data, and of providing methods for the prompt and adequate digestion and analysis of such facts in such form and manner as to render Commission action thereon readily possible.[75]

* * *

Finally, the telephone investigation conducted by the Federal Communications Commission in response to the mandate expressed in public Resolution No. 8 has served effectively to disclose the nature and magnitude of the telephone industry and of basic telephone-regulatory problems in this country. Through the investigation this Commission has been enabled to bring together for the first time an impressive volume of data in respect to such problems—data both fundamental in import and of permanent value, and which, but for this investigation, would have had to be provided by some other means or agency before effective interstate telephone regulation could be inaugurated. During the course of the investigation, and as a result of the direct efforts of the investigatory staff, telephone-rate reductions now aggregating in excess of $30,000,000 were effected in the interest and for the benefit of the American telephone-using public. In addition, the extent of the problem of future effective interstate telephone rate and service regulation has been thoroughly explored, and the possibilities of cooperation with State regulatory authorities have been canvassed. With the minor exceptions already noted, this Commission is deemed now to be possessed of inclusive statutory authority and, as a direct result of the telephone investigation, to be provided with basic data sufficient to serve as a firm foundation for the inauguration and development of continuous and efficient administrative processes in this highly technical field of governmental effort.[76]

Since 1939, many of the practices questioned in the report have been changed or modified. By 1949, telephone companies had restated their plant accounts on the basis of original cost, reducing by $43 million the net book values on which their rates of return are computed.[77] By 1954, the FCC had completed a program of prescribing depreciation rates for the Bell System, lowering depreciation charges by $29 million annually.[78] Since 1935, there have been over fifty negotiated changes in interstate rates, resulting in an overall net savings to the public (based on 1967 volumes of business) of more than $1.5 billion annually. In addition, as a result of separations changes, there have been equivalent reductions in intrastate revenue requirements totaling more than $350 million annually (based on 1967 volumes of business). Detailed separations procedures have been developed by the National Association of Regulatory

[75] *Ibid.*, p. 596.
[76] *Ibid.*, p. 602.
[77] Federal Communications Commission, *Annual Report, 1949*, p. 104.
[78] Federal Communications Commission, *Annual Report, 1954*, p. 40. Since 1954, the depreciation rates for all Bell System companies have been reviewed every three years and changed as necessary.

Utility Commissioners for separating intra- and interstate plant, expenses, and revenues.[79] A.T.&T.'s license contracts and fees have been investigated and approved.[80] And the FCC has made, or is in the process of completing, lengthy investigations into the costs of, and rates for, private line services offered by both Western Union and the Bell System, and into Bell's tariffs for TELPAK and Wide Area Telephone Service.[81]

Besides all this, the FCC's investigation was of further significance: it formed the basis of—in fact, it made possible—the commission's regulatory procedure known as constant surveillance.[82] Without the data, detailed information, and knowledge about the telephone industry gathered in making the study, the FCC would have been unable to rely so heavily on informal procedures.

The Current Telephone Investigation

On October 27, 1965, the FCC instituted a formal investigation of the rates charged by A.T.&T. and the Bell System companies for interstate and foreign communication services.[83] There appear to be four interrelated problems that formed the basis for the proceeding.[84]

1. The Seven-Way Cost Study. The Seven-Way Cost Study was submitted to the commission by A.T.&T. in connection with the domestic telegraph investigation. The "wide variations" in earnings for different classes of service, as well as the current level of earnings on total interstate operations, "indicate the desirability of a thorough examination by the Commission of

---

[79] See Chapter 6, pp. 157-62.

[80] National Association of Regulatory Utility Commissioners, *Report on Service Charges by the American Telephone and Telegraph Company to the Associated Bell Telephone Companies and Long Lines Department* (New York, 1945). Also see *Consent Decree Program of the Department of Justice* (Hearings before the Antitrust Subcommittee of the Committee on the Judiciary, House, 85th Cong., 2d sess.) (Washington, D.C.: U.S. Government Printing Office, 1958), Part II, Vol. II, pp. 2508-20.

[81] *AT&T and Western Union Private Line Cases,* 34 FCC 217 (1963), 34 FCC 1094 (1963), *aff'd sub nom. Wilson & Co. v. United States,* 335 F. 2d 788 (1964), *cert. denied,* 380 U.S. 951 (1965); *In the Matter of Tariff F.C.C. No. 250, TELPAK Service and Channels,* Docket No. 14251 (December 24, 1964), *aff'd sub nom. American Trucking Ass'ns, Inc. v. Federal Communications Comm.,* 377 F. 2d 121 (1966), *cert. denied,* 386 U.S. 943 (1967); and *In the Matter of Regulations and Charges for Wide Area Telephone Service,* Docket No. 13914 (March 3, 1965). The FCC currently has under consideration TELPAK sharing provisions (Docket No. 17457) of A.T.&T. and Western Union, and rate-making principles for all telephone offerings (Docket No. 16258, Phase 1B).

[82] See Chapter 5, pp. 139-40.

[83] Memorandum Opinion and Order, Docket No. 16258 (FCC 65-959, October 27, 1965). (Hereinafter referred to as the "October 27th Order.") The Bell System's petition for reconsideration was denied by the commission. Memorandum Opinion and Order, Docket No. 16258 (FCC 65-1144, December 22, 1965). In terms of plant investment and revenues, the interstate and foreign services of the Bell System account for approximately 25 percent of its total operations.

[84] See Charles F. Phillips, Jr., "Some Observations on the FCC's Telephone Investigation," 77 *Public Utilities Fortnightly* 23 (February 17, 1966). Also see Ben W. Lewis, "The Great AT&T Investigation," 14 *Challenge* 5 (May–June, 1966).

the interstate rate structure of the Bell System to determine the lawfulness of the rate levels and rate relationships within that structure."[85]

2. Separations Procedures. As noted earlier, separations procedures have been accepted continuously for jurisdictional purposes by all the state commissions and by the FCC on an "interim" basis. They have been modified or revised on several occasions. The investigation "will afford all interested parties an opportunity to present evidence, views, and recommendations concerning these principles and procedures, including the independent segment of the telephone industry which has, in written representations to this Commission, raised certain questions concerning the merits of the recent revision."[86]

3. Rate Base Items. A.T.&T. has long argued that three items—plant under construction, cash working capital, and materials and supplies—should properly be included in the rate base. In the Private Line case, the commission excluded such costs.[87] However, in its reports to the commission, A.T.&T. generally includes these items. "In the investigation which we are hereby instituting, the company will be expected to justify the inclusion of these items, as well as the reasonableness of all other items of rate base, expense, taxes, and reserves upon which it relies in determining its operating results."[88]

4. Western Electric's Prices and Profits. In the Private Line case, the FCC rejected the Bell System's defense of Western Electric's prices and profits on the ground that the evidence presented lacked probative value, but it was unable to reach any conclusions as to what adjustments, if any, were warranted in the claimed revenue requirements of the Bell System. In its October 27th Order, the commission stated that it "will expect the Bell System companies to justify the reasonableness of the prices and profits of Western Electric reflected in their claimed rate base and expenses with due regard to the aforementioned conclusions reached by the Commission in the Private Line case. . . ."[89]

---

[85] October 27th Order, *op. cit.*, p. 2.

[86] *Ibid.* There is a related matter. The state commissions have long expressed concern about the interstate-intrastate rate disparity, frequently arguing that separations procedures place too great a burden on intrastate services. (See Chapter 6, pp. 159–61.) When the FCC announced, in November, 1964, that it had negotiated a $100 million interstate rate reduction with A.T.&T., the California commission (which would have preferred a change in separations procedures that would have reduced intrastate revenue requirements) petitioned the commission for a rehearing. The FCC dismissed the petition, whereupon the California commission filed a court suit challenging the legality of the constant surveillance method of regulation. The FCC was subsequently upheld in the courts. *Public Utilities Comm. of California* v. *United States*, 356 F. 2d 236 (1966), *cert. denied*, 385 U.S. 816 (1966).

[87] *AT&T and Western Union Private Line Cases, op. cit.*

[88] October 27th Order, *op. cit.*, p. 3.

[89] *Ibid.* There were undoubtedly other factors in the FCC's decision to institute a formal telephone investigation, but they are more speculative. It may be that regulators feel the need of periodic full-scale, formal investigations. As former FCC Chairman Henry put it: "In the present circumstances there can be no regulatory order without some reasonably well-defined ground rules—some framework of regulatory principles within which the government's freedom and the company's freedom may be exercised. Such regulatory principles do exist and have always formed the basis for continuing surveil-

The commission subsequently divided the investigation into three parts: Phase 1A—the fair rate of return on A.T.&T.'s interstate and foreign services, the effect of the Bell System's nonuse of accelerated depreciation for income tax purposes on the fair rate of return, the justification for the claimed inclusion of the three rate base items, and separations procedures; Phase 1B—the Bell System's rate structure (i.e., rate-making principles); and Phase 2—the reasonableness of Western Electric's prices and profits and the amounts properly includable as the Bell System's net investment, expenses, and taxes. The commission stated that it would issue an interim order at the conclusion of each part.

On July 5, 1967, the commission issued a unanimous interim decision and order with respect to the four basic Phase 1A issues; on September 13, 1967, it issued another unanimous interim decision and order on reconsideration.[90] In these decisions, the FCC (*a*) held that the Bell System's rate of return on interstate and foreign communication services should be in the range of 7 to 7½ percent; (*b*) stated that the Bell System's nonuse of accelerated depreciation for tax purposes "reduces their risk in comparison with that of entities which do take advantage of accelerated depreciation," but deferred an evaluation of the propriety of the Bell System's nonuse policy until Phase 2; (*c*) included the amount claimed for plant under construction, but excluded the amounts claimed for cash working capital and materials and supplies, thereby ending with a negative working capital allowance (the treatment of which will be considered during Phase 2); and (*d*) was unable to fully resolve the separations issue and, therefore, established a separate proceeding (Docket No. 17975) to further consider such procedures. The Bell System was ordered to reduce its interstate and foreign rates by $120 million—$100 million, effective November 1, 1967, and $20 million, effective August 1, 1968.

---

lance. But they have never been developed by a public hearing as broad-gauged as the one here contemplated. A restatement of these principles, as developed on this record, will better enable the public to judge the reasonableness of its government, and will encourage constructive criticism and scholarly debate. Benefits of this kind will be of lasting importance to all concerned." Memorandum Opinion and Order, Docket No. 16258 (FCC 65-1144), concurring statement of Chairman Henry, p. 3.

[90] *Re American Teleph. & Teleg. Co.*, 70 PUR 3d 129 (FCC, 1967), 71 PUR 3d 273 (FCC, 1967). Phase 1A included three prehearing conferences, seventy-one days of hearings (involving sixty-six witnesses), and two days of oral arguments before the full commission. (The record was certified to the commission for decision without the usual first step of an initial decision by the staff or the hearing examiner—in this case, the Telephone Committee.) The record consisted of 101 exhibits submitted by the Bell System, the commission's staff, and the 103 interveners; five exhibits submitted by "nonparties"; 76 volumes of transcript; and briefs and proposed findings of fact filed by 12 parties—a total of just over 15,000 pages. On the commission's decisions, see Charles F. Phillips, Jr., "Phase 1A of the Telephone Investigation," 80 *Public Utilities Fortnightly* 15 (August 31, 1967) and "The FCC's Phase 1A Interim Order on Reconsideration," 80 *ibid.* 51 (October 12, 1967); Eugene M. Lerner, "The FCC's 7.5 Per Cent Ruling," 80 *ibid.* 40 (October 12, 1967); A. J. G. Priest, "Bell System Interstate and Foreign Rates and Services," 80 *ibid.* 20 (December 21, 1967); and George A. Prendergast, "The FCC Proceedings—Issues and Implications," 82 *ibid.* 17 (September 26, 1968). The separations issue was resolved early in 1969. See Federal Communications Commission, "Report and Order," Docket No. 17975 (FCC 69-65, January 29, 1969).

Phase 1B commenced in the fall of 1967 and is expected to be completed in mid-1969; shortly thereafter Phase 2 will get underway. It seems clear that the current investigation will be one of the most thorough, and also one of the longest, in modern regulatory history.

Western Electric Company

Western Electric is the manufacturing and supply arm of the Bell Telephone System. As described by the FCC:

> Generally, its function is twofold: First, it is the manufacturing branch of the Bell System; and second, it is the purchasing and supply department of the Bell System. In connection with its latter function, Western is also a developer, storekeeper, installer, repairer, salvager, and junker of the Bell System.[91]

Western Electric owns or leases twenty-two manufacturing or related plants and in thirty-five major cities maintains distributing houses from which supplies are furnished to the associated companies. Some of these supplies, such as screws and switchboard equipment, are manufactured by Western Electric; others, such as telephone poles and specially designed telephone trucks, are purchased for resale.[92] The company also installs communication equipment systems (such as central office equipment) for the associated companies, and its distribution centers have facilities for inspecting, repairing, salvaging, and junking telephone equipment.

The Standard Supply Contract. The Standard Supply Contract is an agreement between Western Electric and a Bell operating company which covers all the various functions performed by Western Electric for an associated company. The contract reads, in part:

> The Electric Company will manufacture or purchase materials which the Telephone Company may reasonably require for its business and which it may order from the Electric Company; provided, however, that nothing contained herein obligates the Telephone Company to purchase any materials from the Electric Company.[93]

The contract thus provides that Western Electric will manufacture or purchase materials reasonably required by an associated company, but permits the company (as well as Long Lines Department) to purchase materials from any manufacturer it desires. However, since Western Electric's prices usually are

---

[91] Federal Communications Commission, *Investigation of the Telephone Industry in the United States, op. cit.,* p. 35.

[92] Among Western Electric's purchases in 1966 were 900,000 ball-point pens, 5 million pencils and 9,000 sharpeners, 82 million paper clips, 120,000 typewriter ribbons, 6.5 million erasers, and 36 tons of rubber bands. *The Wall Street Journal,* October 5, 1967, p. 1. In 1967, Western Electric purchased over 150,000 different items from some 45,000 suppliers.

[93] Western Electric Company, *Standard Supply Contract,* June 2, 1930, and supplements, Art. I, Sec. 1.

lower than any other, few outside purchases are made by the associated companies.[94]

Western Electric's Pricing. Western Electric's prices are published on over 100,000 items; prices are also established on thousands of additional items not included in these price lists. The price for an individual product manufactured by the company is built on the "standard shop cost" of the product. The standard shop cost involves a determination of the labor, materials, and manufacturing overhead, assuming a level of output and efficiency.[95] To the standard cost is added (1) current complete cost (e.g., variations from standard shop cost, development expense, merchandising expense, general expense, and federal income taxes) and (2) a margin of profit. The price for an item purchased by the company for resale is similarly established, but the "purchase cost" is the starting point. The amount added to the purchase cost must cover the services performed by Western Electric in purchasing, inspecting, storing, and distributing the item, as well as development expense (where applicable) and federal income taxes, and must afford a return on the investment involved.

The 1956 Consent Decree. On January 14, 1949, the government filed a civil antitrust suit against A.T.&T. and Western Electric, charging that the companies had engaged in a continuing conspiracy to monopolize the manufacture, distribution, and sale of telephones, telephone apparatus, and equipment, in violation of Sections 1 and 2 of the Sherman Antitrust Act.[96] The government asked that: (*a*) Western Electric be separated from A.T.&T. and dissolved into three competing manufacturing companies; (*b*) Western Electric be required to sell its 50 percent stock interest in Bell Labs; (*c*) A.T.&T., Western Electric, and Bell Labs license their patents to all applicants on a nondiscriminatory and reasonable-royalty basis; and (*d*) the Bell operating companies be required to buy all equipment and supplies under competitive bidding.

The heart of the case, therefore, involved the vertical integration of A.T.&T. and Western Electric. The government alleged that the situation created a "closed market" in which the operating companies bought, and Western Electric sold, telephone equipment at noncompetitive prices. As former Attorney General Clark pointed out, "the chief purpose of this action is to restore competition in the manufacture and sale of telephone equipment now produced

---

[94] Typical is the following quotation from a 1966 decision: "In April, 1964, the actual price paid by Bell companies to Western was $10.53 [for the standard telephone handset], and the lowest price for which a similar set could have been purchased elsewhere was $21.63. Other illustrations are found in the record which testify to the fact that significant price differentials, likewise, exist with respect to every comparable item available from other manufacturers supplying the general trade." *Re Southern Bell Teleph. & Teleg. Co.*, 66 PUR 3d 1, 38 (Fla., 1966).

[95] In practice, Western Electric's prices are established for classes of products, rather than for each individual product.

[96] *United States* v. *Western Electric Company, Inc. and American Telephone and Telegraph Company, Inc.*, Civil Action No. 17-49 (D. N.J., filed January 14, 1949). The *Complaint* is reprinted in *Consent Decree Program of the Department of Justice, op. cit.*, Part II, Vol. 1, pp. 1723–95.

and sold almost exclusively by Western Electric at noncompetitive prices."[97]

A.T.&T. and Western Electric denied the charges and requested that the complaint be dismissed.[98] They contended that existing regulatory processes adequately protected the public in furnishing of communications services and in manufacturing of equipment by Western Electric for use in such services. Further, they emphasized that the unification of research and development, manufacturing, and operation in the Bell System was a leading factor in "promoting the efficiency, economy, and dependability of the telephone service." In the defendants' words:

> It makes available to the operating telephone companies equipment of advanced design and high quality at prices substantially lower than would be obtainable in the absence of such unification. It facilitates the standardization of equipment which is essential to efficient operation of an interconnected telephone system. It enables the manufacturing and supply unit to adapt its production and planning to the anticipated needs of the System, stocks of equipment and installation forces for the restoration of service in time of emergency. And it assures that all steps in the development and production of the equipment are planned and carried out with intimate knowledge of the needs of the operating units of the System and with a common incentive to fulfill those needs most effectively. The ultimate beneficiaries of this unification are the users of telephone service, who thereby obtain better service at lower cost.[99]

Seven years later, on January 24, 1956, the suit was settled by a consent decree.[100] A.T.&T. and Western Electric were required to grant licenses to anyone under all existing and future patents. Virtually all patents issued prior to the date of the decree were to be licensed royalty-free; patents issued subsequent to the date of the judgment were to be licensed at reasonable royalties. The defendants were not required, however, to grant any patent license unless the licensee grants to the Bell System licenses it wants for use in its regulated communications business, subject to reasonable royalties.[101] Western Electric was precluded from manufacturing and selling equipment not of a type sold to the telephone operating companies of the Bell System, except for manufacturing equipment or providing services for the government. Western Electric also was required to maintain cost accounting methods consistent with generally accepted

[97] *Ibid.*, p. 1796.

[98] The *Answer* is reprinted in *ibid.*, pp. 1799–1844.

[99] *Ibid.*, p. 1807.

[100] The *Final Judgment* is reprinted in *ibid.*, pp. 1845–63.

[101] An exception to the licensing agreements was made with General Electric Company, Radio Corporation of America, and Westinghouse Electric Corporation. These companies, together with A.T.&T. and Western Electric, had been parties to patent license agreements dated July 1, 1932. The decree did not require licenses to these companies under existing patents to be royalty-free unless they, in turn, granted similar royalty-free licenses to the Bell System.

        On several occasions, A.T.&T.'s licensing agreements have been cited as resulting in the company's control of related industries. See Danielian, *op. cit.*, chaps. v–vii.

accounting principles and to disclose its manufacturing costs. Finally, A.T.&T. and its operating companies were enjoined from engaging in any business other than furnishing common carrier communications services and incidental operations (such as the directory advertising business).[102]

The government has been criticized for signing the consent decree rather than continuing its case for divestiture. Sheahan argues:

> The price of moving Western closer to a regulated public utility status is the sacrificed alternative of choosing instead to secure competition within the telephone equipment industry, and to turn Western toward open competition outside the industry. This alternative was a feasible choice.
>
> Two major steps were required to open up competition. First, Western would have had to be separated from the Bell System, so that equipment choices would no longer be systematically biased in its favor. The second major step is the very gain secured in the settlement: removal of patent restrictions keeping electrical equipment producers out of the telephone field. The change would have had real significance if A.T.&T. no longer had any interest in directing equipment choices to Western. This vast market would have become a real possibility to any aggressive electrical equipment firm. Initially, Western would remain in a very strong position to hold all Bell business. But Federal and the smaller producers already provide important sources of supply to an informed buyer actively seeking the best alternative, and effective purchasing tactics by the Bell companies should have made it possible to open the field quite quickly.[103]

Yet, if there are significant advantages to vertical integration in the telephone industry, the decree would seem appropriate.[104] Moreover, Western Electric's prices, accounting procedures, and profits are under continuous study by the regulatory commissions.

Regulation of Western Electric. The FCC and state commissions lack direct regulatory power over Western Electric. In 1948, the FCC joined with state agencies in a continuing study of the company's prices, costs, and

---

[102] As a result of the decree, Western Electric was required to divest itself of Westrex Corporation (which leased and sold equipment in the motion picture field), the Teletypesetter Corporation (a subsidiary of Teletype Corporation, manufacturing automatic typesetting equipment), and its inventory of train dispatching apparatus and the facilities used in their manufacture, while the Bell System was required to discontinue rendering certain communications services then being provided on a private contract basis.

[103] John Sheahan, "Integration and Exclusion in the Telephone Equipment Industry," 70 *Quarterly Journal of Economics* 249, 267 (1956). Also see Joel B. Dirlam and Alfred E. Kahn, *Fair Competition: The Law and Economics of Antitrust Policy* Ithaca: Cornell University Press, 1954), p. 172; *Report of the Antitrust Subcommittee on the Consent Decree Program of the Department of Justice* (House, 86th Cong., 1st sess.) (Washington, D.C.: U.S. Government Printing Office, 1959), pp. 96–120; and Manley R. Irwin and Robert E. McKee, "Vertical Integration and the Communication Equipment Industry: Alternatives for Public Policy," 53 *Cornell Law Review* 446 (1968), reprinted in 22 *Federal Communications Bar Journal* 131 (1968).

[104] One aspect of the decree which may be of importance in future years concerns the prohibition on A.T.&T. from engaging in, and Western Electric from manufacturing equipment for, private communications business.

profits.[105] As of mid-1968, the average level of prices being charged on sales to the Bell System by Western Electric was 5 percent less than in 1950 (equal to a net reduction of more than $100 million).[106] Western Electric supplies the FCC with quarterly and annual reports containing financial and operating data, which are sent to the state commissions.

Further, as previously discussed, Western Electric's prices and profits are reviewed in rate cases involving A.T.&T. and the associated companies.[107] Western Electric's generally low prices are due to the achievement of economies of scale and to the company's cost reduction program. These, in turn, result from the company's vertical integration with the Bell Telephone System and from its constant effort to achieve cost savings. The downward trend of Western Electric's prices provides concrete evidence of the company's success in this area, as does its relatively low rate of return compared to other major manufacturing companies.[108]

COMPETITION IN THE COMMUNICATIONS INDUSTRY

There is little direct competition among common carriers for residential telephone and telegraph services. Technological advances, however, have introduced important competitive elements into supplying business and government communications needs. Intra-agency rivalry also exists between A.T.&T. and Western Union in the provision of private line and teletypewriter message services.

The "Above 890 Decision": The Impact of Microwave

In 1945, Western Union built the first domestic commercial microwave (radio relay) system to operate between New York City and Philadelphia. Two years later, A.T.&T. opened its initial microwave route between New York and

105 NARUC-FCC Staff Committee on Telephone Regulatory Problems, *Report on Preliminary Survey and Investigation of Western Electric Company, Inc.* (New York, 1948). The study has been updated annually. Two ten-year summaries have been published: NARUC-FCC Staff Committee on Telephone Regulatory Problems, *Report on Operating Results of Western Electric Company, Incorporated, Years 1947 to 1957, Inclusive* (New York, 1958); and NARUC–FCC Staff Subcommittee on Manufacturing and Service Affiliates, *Report on Operating Results of Western Electric Company, Incorporated, Years 1958 to 1967, Inclusive* (New York, 1968).

106 See L. R. Cook, "The Role of the Factory—In the Dollar Transcontinental Telephone Call," 80 *Public Utilities Fortnightly* 26 (October 12, 1967).

107 See Chapter 7, pp. 189–92.

108 A comparison of Western Electric's earnings with those of the 50 largest manufacturing corporations shows that for the period 1925 through 1967, these 50 companies had a margin of profit of 6.0 cents per dollar of sales, as compared with 4.7 cents for Western Electric on its Bell System business, while the return on net investment for these 50 companies was 11.9 percent, compared with Western Electric's earnings of 8.9 percent on its business with Bell System companies. Data supplied by Western Electric Company. For a comprehensive evaluation of Western Electric, see *A Study of Western Electric's Performance* (A Report Prepared by McKinsey & Co., Inc.) (New York: American Telephone & Telegraph Co., 1969).

Boston. Today, microwave networks encompass the nation, transmitting an increasing volume of voice and nonvoice messages.

Until 1959, the FCC licensed private microwave communications systems to government and business units only when they had "special communications needs," such as the lack of common carrier facilities. "This limited approach restricted licensees, other than communications common carriers, to governmental safety organizations such as fire and police and to businesses such as electric utilities, pipeline companies, and railroad companies."[109] Then, on July 30, 1959, the FCC, in its "Above 890 Decision," removed all significant barriers to the installation and operation of private microwave systems by government and business units.[110] Concluded the commission:

> 1. There are now available adequate frequencies above 890 Mc to take care of present and reasonably foreseeable future needs of both the common carriers and private users for point-to-point communications systems, provided that orderly and systematic procedures and proper technical criteria are applied in the issuance of authorizations, and that implementation is consistently achieved with respect to all available and future improvements in the art. There is a demonstrated need for private point-to-point communications systems. Accordingly, the decision looks toward liberalization of the basis for issuance of such authorizations. Availability of common carrier facilities will not be considered as a condition of eligibility for such private users.
>
> 2. There is no basis for generally concluding that the licensing of private communications systems would adversely affect, to any substantial degree, the ability of common carriers to provide service to the general public or adversely affect the users of such common carrier service. Therefore, it is unnecessary to consider whether such licensing is contrary to the public interest.[111]

In short, a finding of special communications needs is no longer a prerequisite to the obtaining of a private communications system license.[112]

The commission's 1959 decision was opposed by the common carriers, including A.T.&T., General Telephone, Western Union, and the U.S. Independent Telephone Association, among others. This group argued that private communications systems would result in higher rates to smaller users, since the overhead of the common carriers would be distributed among a smaller number of customers if large companies were allowed to transmit information by microwave. They contended, further, that since the adequacy of frequency bands is unknown, there is a problem of interference that might affect all types

---

[109] Bernard P. Herber, "The Impact of Microwave on the Telephone Business," 70 *Public Utilities Fortnightly* 214, 215 (1962). Also see Manley R. Irwin, "The Communication Industry and the Policy of Competition," 14 *Buffalo Law Review* 256 (Winter, 1964).

[110] *Allocation of Microwave Frequencies Above 890 Mc.,* 27 FCC 359 (1959).

[111] Federal Communications Commission, Report No. 575, July 30, 1959.

[112] Licenses are issued by the FCC for a maximum of five years before renewal.

of microwave communications. Moreover, the common carriers questioned whether private microwave systems were in the interest of national defense, arguing that a closely controlled system of communications is necessary in time of emergency and suggesting that the common carriers could provide and plan a more efficient national microwave system. Finally, the common carriers maintained that since microwave is a part of the electronics industry—an industry that is competitive—there would be no problem of monopoly (as charged by those favoring private systems) if they were permitted to develop a national system. But the commission, on October 5, 1960, reaffirmed its original order.[113]

Communications and Computers: The Impact of Technology

The electronic computer can provide a wide variety of data processing, computational, and information storage and retrieval services to a large number of users at remote locations.[114] It can also be utilized by communications common carriers as part of their networks as a message switching device. Indeed, the electronic switching system currently being installed by A.T.&T. (and other common carriers) is simply a giant computer. The electronic computer, in short, makes no distinction between communications and calculation: it can switch messages or figure a payroll. Summarizes Strassburg:

> Inasmuch as computers have become standard communications gear, the common carrier networks are no longer confining their service offerings to purely communications service. Taking advantage of the versatility and capacity of their computers, certain carriers are now programming them to provide data processing and information storage and retrieval services in combination with their traditional communications services. At the same time, we find that the nonregulated computer service bureaus, and other entities providing specialized information services over communications channels leased from the carriers, are seeking to furnish their customers with message switching services, an activity which heretofore has been limited to the communications common carrier.[115]

---

[113] *Allocation of Microwave Frequencies Above 890 Mc.,* 29 FCC 825 (1960). Commissioner Craven, in his partial dissent, said: "I fail to understand how the Commission could be so shortsighted as to encourage large businesses to invest huge sums of money for the purpose of using a portion of the spectrum which space communications shortly may need on an unhampered basis." *Ibid.* Herber also has argued that the decision can be challenged in terms of use of the scarce frequency spectrum, as well as in terms of the general use of land, labor, and capital factors of production. Bernard P. Herber, "Telephone Industry Reaction to Microwave Competition," 70 *Public Utilities Fortnightly* 627, 640 (1962).

[114] Users can reach a computer from remote locations via common carrier lines or private microwave lines. Time-sharing services are now being offered, in which a central computer serves many customers over telephone or microwave lines.

[115] Bernard Strassburg, "Communications and Computers: How Shall the Twain Meet?," 82 *Public Utilities Fortnightly* 69 (September 12, 1968). See C. C. Barnett, Jr., and Associates, *The Future of the Computer Utility* (New York: American Management Association, 1967); and Manley R. Irwin, "The Computer Utility: Competition or Regulation?," 76 *Yale Law Journal* 1299 (1967), and "The Computer Utility: A Public Policy Overview," in *Selected Structure and Allocation Problems in the Regulated Industries* (East Lansing: Michigan State Public Utilities Studies, 1969), pp. 1–18.

The convergence of the two technologies thus introduces new competitive forces within the communications and data processing industries.

The Common Carriers' Responses

As a result of the "Above 890 Decision" and of the growing interdependence of communications and computers, private microwave systems have grown in number while computer service bureaus (set up by computer manufacturers) and other data processing and specialized information services (offered by hundreds of nonmanufacturing firms) have been established at a rapid rate.[116] And in October, 1968, A.T.&T. announced the filing of a new tariff under which the telephone network would be opened to a wide variety of customer-provided equipment, including the interconnection of most private systems.[117]

The response of the common carriers has been to offer or propose several new services, primarily intended for customers with heavy (bulk) communications needs. Both the Bell System and Western Union have installed extensive microwave facilities. The Bell System has introduced TELPAK and WATS (Wide Area Telephone Service);[118] Western Union has introduced Telex and numerous leased wire services. In addition, Western Union is in the process of establishing computer centers, not only for its public message and Telex services, but also to provide a variety of data processing, storage and retrieval services as part of its

[116] See Thomas H. Broadus, Jr., and Others, *Microwave Communications* (Boston: Smith & Welsh, Inc., 1961); and Robert McKnight, "Microwave: There's Dramatic Growth Ahead," *Railway Age,* May 23, 1966, pp. 18 ff. As of early 1969, the FCC had not acted on an application from Microwave Communications, Inc., to package communications services between Chicago and St. Louis and to sell them to bulk users.

[117] *The Wall Street Journal,* October 23, 1968, p. 2; and *ibid.,* December 26, 1968, p. 18. For many years (and with certain exceptions), telephone tariffs have prohibited the attachment of devices, other than those supplied by telephone companies themselves, and the interconnection of customer-owned communications systems directly to the telephone network. In 1956, a lower court held that a tariff prohibition of a customer-supplied "foreign attachment" was "an unwarranted interference with the telephone subscriber's right reasonably to use his telephone in ways which are privately beneficial without being publicly detrimental." *Hush-A-Phone Corp.* v. *United States,* 238 F. 2d 266, 269 (1956). Then, in a 1968 decision, the FCC held that A.T.&T.'s existing tariff was "unreasonable, discriminatory, and unlawful" since it prohibited "the use of interconnecting devices which do not adversely affect the telephone system." But the commission said that telephone companies "may submit new tariffs which will protect the telephone system against harmful devices, and may specify technical standards if they wish." *In the Matter of Use of the Carterfone Device in Message Toll Telephone Service,* Docket Nos. 16942 and 17073 (FCC 68-661, June 26, 1968), pp. 6, 9. A.T.&T.'s proposed new tariff is partly in response to these decisions. See William M. Ellinghaus, "Assuring the Quality of Network Service," 82 *Public Utilities Fortnightly* 24 (December 5, 1968).

[118] A.T.&T. reports that it would have offered a service similar to TELPAK in the absence of the "Above 890 Decision," but a company spokesman concedes that the decision "affected the timing and, at least to some extent, the form of the offering." See "Offering Similar to Telpak Would Have Been Made," 28 *Telecommunications Reports* 9 (July 16, 1962).

A.T.&T. also proposed to offer WADS (Wide Area Data Service), but the FCC rejected the initial tariff and ordered the company to cancel its offering. *In the Matter of Regulations and Charges for Developmental Line Switching Service,* Docket No. 14154 (August 5, 1963).

"national information utility" program. The Bell System, which is implementing a program to convert all central offices to electronic switching, has announced that it has no plans to provide a similar information service or to offer data processing services to the public.[119]

Some Regulatory and Policy Issues

The regulatory and policy issues resulting from these developments are as intriguing as they are complex. With respect to the "Above 890 Decision," Herber has stated:

> The manufacturers of private microwave systems are completely unregulated as public utilities and are subject only to the general regulation of antitrust laws—which apply to all businesses, including the utilities. . . . These electronics firms sell microwave systems to "slightly" regulated businesses which purchase and use the systems. The "slight" regulation essentially involves the issuance of a franchise to operate a microwave system and the allocation of a radio-microwave frequency for its operation. The franchise and frequency allocation are attainable "for the asking." Thus, one side of the competitive market—the private systems and their suppliers—faces little or no regulation. However, the other side of the competitive market, the established common carriers such as Bell and Western Union, are closely regulated as public utilities. There is, indeed, a condition of regulatory inequity.[120]

With respect to the increasing difficulty of separating data processing and communications, similar issues arise. Should common carriers be permitted to offer data processing services? Some of the relevant issues in answering this basic question have been raised by Strassburg:

> . . . How, for example, is cost identified, separated, and translated into price when data processing and communications are blended in a single offering utilizing a common plant? If separable, should the communications component be regulated as a common carrier service, whether engaged in by a conventional common carrier or others? If these activities are not separable, will protection of the public interest require regulation of the entire package whether or not offered by common carriers? Or should the answer be to permit free and uncontrolled entry and operation in the market by carrier and noncarriers alike? What are the possibilities of price discrimination? Will not carriers be placed in a position of selling lines to firms with which they compete in service offerings? In short, the burdens and responsibilities imposed upon the commission by such hybrid service offerings are anything but simple. Consider the dilemma that the imperatives of technological progress is presenting the commission. If the logic of technology dictates that a computer can efficiently and economically be programed to furnish data

---

[119] The 1956 consent decree may explain the Bell System's present position regarding computer services, i.e., the decree prevents the Bell System's entrance into other than regulated common carrier offerings.

[120] Herber, "Telephone Industry Reaction . . . ," *op. cit.,* pp. 634-35.

processing and message switching services, would it not be arbitrary policy to prevent maximum exploitation of its potentials by either common carriers or noncommon carriers? Until this threshold question is resolved and rational and realistic policy guidelines are fashioned, both the computer and communications industries may be denied optimum development, with society in general bearing a substantial cost.[121]

There are no easy answers to any of these regulatory and policy questions. If the cost allocation problem could be solved, then a suggestion made by Herber would deserve careful consideration. He recommended that a reappraisal of regulatory philosophy in communications start with a broadly defined communications market, inclusive of both the private systems and the common carriers, within which two submarkets could be identified.

One submarket would be the *residential* segment of communications. Here monopoly power remains great and regulation by means of the public utility concept could be rigorously applied. The second submarket would be in *business-government* communications where the new competition exists. Here the regulation of common carriers could be rigorous, but flexible, in view of the genuine price and nonprice competition existing in this submarket.[122]

Other possible solutions will undoubtedly emerge from the current telephone and computer investigations.

Task Force on Communications Policy

In a Message to Congress in 1967, President Johnson stated that the United States must "review its past activities" in the communications field and "formulate a national communications policy." Toward this end, he announced the appointment of a Task Force (comprised of government officials) to make a comprehensive study of our domestic and international communications posture.[123]

---

[121] Strassburg, *op. cit.*, p. 74. There are many other issues. For example, the emergence of regional and national data banks (storing vast amounts of specialized technical, scientific, educational, and other data) raises the "information privacy" question—how can detailed personal and business data be kept from unauthorized persons or unauthorized use? (See A. R. Miller, "The National Data Center and Personal Privacy," *The Atlantic*, November, 1967, pp. 53–57; and C. R. Sprague and D. N. Ness, "Privacy and a National Data Bank," 60 *Banking* 50 [June, 1968].) All of these issues are now before the FCC: *In the Matter of Regulatory and Policy Problems Presented by the Interdependence of Computer and Communications Services and Facilities*, Docket No. 16979 (initiated in 1966).

[122] Herber, "Telephone Industry Reaction . . . ," *op. cit.*, p. 636.

[123] *Global Communications System,* Message from the President of the United States, August 14, 1967 (House Doc. No. 157, 90th Cong., 1st sess.) (Washington, D.C.: U.S. Government Printing Office, 1967), pp. 2, 8. The President also announced that he had asked the Bureau of the Budget "to make a thorough study of existing governmental organization in the field of communications and to propose needed modifications." *Ibid.*, p. 9.

In examining our international communications posture, the President called on the Task Force to investigate "whether the present division of ownership in our inter-

The Final Report of the Task Force was submitted to President Johnson early in December 1968 and was released by the Nixon Administration (without endorsement) in May 1969.[124] The Task Force viewed the Report "as a compass for policy, not a blueprint" and stated that many of its conclusions were "necessarily tentative." With respect to domestic communications policy, the recommendations of the Task Force fall under three headings, each representing a chapter in the Report.[125]

1. "Domestic Applications of Communication Satellite Technology." Communication satellites "hold sufficient promise for domestic applications in the coming years to warrant a prompt start in that direction," but in view of a number of "unresolved questions" (such as the appropriate use of the electromagnetic spectrum by domestic satellite systems and the issue of general purpose versus specialized systems) it would be "premature to establish full-scale domestic satellite operations at this time or to predict when such a full-scale system would be warranted." Accordingly, the "most prudent course" would be "a modest operational pilot domestic satellite program, with Comsat playing the leading role, as a logical first step."

2. "The Domestic Telecommunications Carrier Industry." "On the basis of existing technology, . . . the basic structural element of domestic tele-communications services—the integrated provision of public message tele-phone service—is satisfactory; and the case for private monopoly regulated by public authority is convincing." However, there should be "more liberalized entry into private line services" by the removal of "unnecessary" telephone company restrictions that limit private interests either in using the telephone network for various types of communications or in establishing their own communications network. (That is, private line systems outside the existing common carrier network should be permitted on a for-hire basis, as well as on a not-for-hire basis.) In turn, the established carriers should be permitted "sufficient flexibility in rates to meet competition" and the FCC should be strengthened "to prevent destructive competition." Computer service companies should be permitted to offer data processing services free of govern-ment regulation. Further studies should be made toward two ends: "opportu-nities for enlarged access to the market for communications equipment" and

---

national communications facilities best serves our needs, as well as which technology can meet new communication requirements in the most effective and efficient manner." The concept of a global system of communications satellites, available to all nations on a nondiscriminatory basis, was affirmed and continuation of the ownership of such a system by an INTELSAT-type consortium (discussed in the next section) was urged. *Ibid.*, pp. 8-9.

124 President's Task Force on Communications Policy, *Final Report* (Washington, D.C.: U.S. Government Printing Office, 1969). All quotations are from this Report. There were dissenting statements by two members of the Task Force and a brief footnote dissent in the international communications chapter by a third member.

125 There were six other chapters in the Report, entitled: "Introduction," "Orga-nization of the United States International Communications Industry," "The Future of INTELSAT," "Satellite Communications and Educational Television in Less Developed Countries," "Future Opportunities for Television," and "The Use and Management of the Electromagnetic Spectrum."

partial consolidation of Western Union's public message service with the Post Office. The jurisdiction of the FCC should be extended to all additions to common carrier plant and equipment and to intercarrier agreements. Finally, the FCC was urged to make "fuller and more sustained use of its power to initiate and conduct long-range studies of the industry" and, thereby, to provide "a desirable catalyst" both in company and in commission policies.

3. "The Roles of the Federal Government in Telecommunications." There should be a new federal government telecommunications "capability" (policy source) in the Executive Branch to coordinate policy now diffused among a "multiplicity of committees," to conduct telecommunications research and development, to allocate the scarce spectrum resource on a rational basis, and to provide policy guidance to the FCC. In addition, the staff of the FCC, as well as the level of the commission's financial support, should be raised.

CABLES AND SATELLITES: A DIGRESSION

While this study is concerned primarily with the domestic operations of the regulated industries, there are two international aspects of communications which deserve brief consideration—submarine cables and satellites. Both these phases of the communications industry, moreover, are in a state of flux. Yet, international communications is a rapidly expanding field. To illustrate: There were 11,000 overseas telephone calls in 1928, compared with 12,300,000 in 1967, the present rate of growth being about 20 percent a year.

Submarine Cables

For many decades, international telecommunications have been made by means of submarine cable and radiophone. The first successful telegraph submarine cable was completed by the Anglo-American Telegraph Company (a British company) between England and the United States in 1866.[126] Since that time, over 3,000 submarine cables have been laid, providing a worldwide telegraph service. There are three major international telegraph carriers: Western Union International, Inc. (formerly the overseas cable division of Western Union, operating 10 transatlantic cables as well as others to South America and the West Indies), International Telephone and Telegraph Corporation (providing telegraph cable service, through four subsidiaries, to Britain, continental Europe, Central and South America, and the West Indies, plus radiotelegraph circuits to these and other points), and RCA Communications, Inc. (a subsidiary of Radio Corporation of America, providing telegraph service to 69 countries, teletype-writer service to 72 countries, and radiophoto service to 46 countries. There are also a number of smaller record carriers, including French Telegraph Cable Company, Press Wireless, Inc., Tropical Radio Telegraph Company, and United

---

[126] For the early history of submarine telegraphy, see Herring and Cross, *op. cit.*, chap. xi.

States-Liberia Radio Corporation, which furnish telegraph services to a limited number of overseas points.[127]

The first overseas commercial telephone service, through the combined use of wire telephony and radio, was opened by A.T.&T. in 1927 between New York and London. Until 1956, international telephone service continued to be provided almost exclusively by A.T.&T. by radiophone. In that year, however, the first transatlantic telephone cable (known as TAT-1) was opened—a cable owned by A.T.&T., Great Britain, and France.[128] The cable marked a significant milestone in communications, since it provided better and more reliable voice communication. Subsequently, four other transatlantic cables were laid: TAT-2 (owned by A.T.&T., France, and Germany) in 1959; CONTAT (owned by the British Commonwealth) in 1961; TAT-3 (owned by A.T.&T. and Great Britain) in 1963; and TAT-4 (owned by A.T.&T., I.T.T., RCA Communications, Inc., Western Union International, Inc., France, and Germany) in 1965.[129] In mid-1964, the first transpacific telephone cable (jointly owned by A.T.&T., Kokusai Denshin Denwa Company, Ltd. of Japan, the Hawaiian Telephone Company, and RCA Communications, Inc.) was opened between the United States—via Hawaii, Midway, Wake, and Guam—and Japan. Submarine telephone cables also provide service to Alaska, Jamaica, Panama, Puerto Rico, Bermuda, Columbia, and the Virgin Islands.[130]

Two policy issues have been raised in recent applications to build submarine cables. The first issue arose in 1963, after A.T.&T. proposed laying TAT-4. The company requested permission from the FCC to offer private line alternate voice and nonvoice service to its customers over the cable, as well as over its existing cables. Mackay Radio and Telegraph Company (a subsidiary of

[127] For a discussion of the operations and problems of the international telegraph carriers, see *Merger of International Telegraph Carriers* (Hearings before the Committee on Interstate and Foreign Commerce, Senate, 86th Cong., 2d sess.) (Washington, D.C.: U.S. Government Printing Office, 1959); Intra-Governmental Committee on International Telecommunications, *Report and Recommendations to Senate and House Commerce Committees* (Washington, D.C., 1966); and President's Task Force on Communications Policy, *Final Report, op. cit.*, chap. ii.

[128] For a more complete discussion, see R. T. Nichols, *Submarine Telephone Cables and International Telecommunications* (Santa Monica: The Rand Corp., 1963).

[129] TAT-4, extending 3,800 nautical miles from Tuckerton, New Jersey, to S. Hilaire, France, is capable of transmitting 138 simultaneous conversations—more than three times as many as TAT-1.

In 1968, the FCC approved a sixth transatlantic cable—TAT-5—to be owned by A.T.&T., I.T.T., RCA Communications, Western Union International, and Italian, Portuguese, and Spanish communications companies. The cable, from Rhode Island to Spain, will have a capacity of 720 circuits and is estimated to cost $90 million. It is expected to be in service in mid-1970.

[130] "In 1957 another type of transmission called 'over-the-horizon' was established for service with Cuba. This medium, which can handle both telephone conversations and television programs, transmits radio signals beyond the curvature of the earth. Unlike microwave systems on land that require intermediate stations every 30 miles or so, the over-the-horizon method can span a distance of some 200 miles in one hop. A similar system linking the U.S. with Nassau in the Bahama Islands was placed in service in 1960." Lowell F. Wingert, "New Tools for Global Communications," 42 *Bell Telephone Magazine*, 2, 6 (Summer, 1963).

American Cable and Radio Corporation which, in turn, is a subsidiary of International Telephone and Telegraph Corporation) filed a competing proposal to lay the fifth transatlantic cable instead of A.T.&T. and opposed A.T.&T.'s request to enter the nonvoice field. In January, 1964, the FCC ruled that the international telegraph carriers could buy channels in A.T.&T.'s transatlantic cables on a perpetual ownership basis, paying a pro rata share for maintenance. Previously, the international carriers were leasing channels—for $102,000 a year per channel—from A.T.&T. Two months later, the commission approved A.T.&T.'s plan for laying the new cable, thereby rejecting Mackay Radio's proposal, but held that all the international carriers except A.T.&T. could offer alternate voice-record service to private customers.[131] The issue demonstrates that just as the dividing line between telephone and telegraph companies has become blurred on the domestic scene, so, too, has advancing technology blurred the distinction on the international front.

The second issue concerns the relationship between cables and satellites. The Communications Satellite Corporation opposed the laying of TAT-5 on the grounds that there would be ample satellite capacity by the time the cable became operational to satisfy communications needs in the Atlantic area, "that the loss of potential satellite traffic to the cable would force satellite per-circuit charges to be higher than would otherwise be necessary, and that the investment in the cable would result in an added burden on the rate payer."[132] A.T.&T. and the other international communications carriers argued that while satellites have an essential role, technological advances have greatly increased the capability of ocean cables and that dependable service requires the use of more than one kind of facility.[133] The FCC, deciding that there will be sufficient traffic to make both cable and satellite systems "economically viable," approved TAT-5, subject to two requirements: first, that rates be reduced by 25 percent and, second, that the cable and satellite circuits be put into use, or filled, at the same proportionate rate.[134]

---

[131] *In the Matter of Transatlantic Telephone Cable No. 4* (P-C-4714-M-1), March 17, 1964. Since 1959, A.T.&T. has been providing over its cables both voice and telegraph data service, under contract, for the Department of Defense. In its decision, the commission also barred expansion of A.T.&T.'s private line services to the government, ruling that if present contracts are terminated, they may not be renewed.

[132] Communications Satellite Corporation, *Annual Report, 1967,* p. 14. Also see *Business Week,* December 16, 1967, pp. 139-40; and *The Wall Street Journal,* February 19, 1968, p. 8. The Communications Satellite Corporation also opposed the laying of a cable between Florida and the Virgin Islands. *The Wall Street Journal,* May 31, 1966, p. 32.

[133] American Telephone and Telegraph Company, *Annual Report, 1967,* p. 8. Bell Telephone Laboratories has designed a unique "sea plow" for use in burying cables beneath the ocean floor, thus protecting them from damage (particularly from fishing vessels). See "Cables under the Sea," 46 *Bell Telephone Magazine* 2 (September-October, 1967).

[134] *The Wall Street Journal,* May 24, 1968, p. 3. On several occasions, it has been recommended that a single international transmission entity, subject to FCC regulation, should be created. See, for example, President's Task Force on Communications Policy, *Final Report, op. cit.,* chap. ii.

Space Communications

The spectacular launching of Telstar I on July 10, 1962, opened a new era in intercontinental communications. Telstar I, owned by A.T.&T., was designed for experimental purposes, but its subsequent success in telephone, television, teletype, facsimile, and data transmission clearly indicated the feasibility of space communications.[135]

Space communications raises a number of interrelated problems, including commercial versus military systems, ownership of an international system, desirability and ownership of a domestic system, and cost of such systems. However, the first problem that had to be faced concerned the question of ownership. President Kennedy, in the summer of 1961, sent a message to Congress urging federal support of a privately owned space communications project.[136] Objections were made to such a privately owned project on the grounds that A.T.&T. would dominate the corporation.[137] But after lengthy debate, Congress authorized establishment of the Communications Satellite Corporation (COMSAT), a privately owned, publicly regulated corporation to develop "as expeditiously as practical, a commercial communications satellite system. . . ."[138] The corporation is subject to FCC regulation and works with the National Aeronautics and Space Administration on research and technical problems and with the State Department in settling international problems which arise. It is also the manager for the International Telecommunications Satellite Consortium (INTELSAT)—an organization of sixty-eight members (countries) which owns the commercial communications satellites.[139]

The act anticipated that ownership of COMSAT would be divided equally

[135] Satellites are of two types—passive and active. The passive merely reflects radio signals from one point to another, while the active picks up signals, amplifies them, and sends them back to earth. Prior to Telstar I, three experimental satellites had been launched: a passive-type balloon satellite named Project Echo and two military communications satellites (Score and Courier I-B), both of the active type.

[136] *New York Times,* July 25, 1961, p. 11.

[137] See *Antitrust Problems of the Space Satellite Communications System* (Hearings before the Subcommittee on Antitrust and Monopoly, Senate, 87th Cong., 2d sess.) (Washington, D.C.: U.S. Government Printing Office, 1962), Parts 1 and 2. Others, who favored private ownership, were concerned with the corporation's rate policies. See Leland L. Johnson, *Communications, Satellites and Telephone Rates: Problems of Government Regulation* (Santa Monica: The Rand Corp., 1961).

[138] The Communications Satellite Act, Public Law 87-624, August 31, 1962. For a discussion of the act, see Senate Report No. 1584 (1962); *The Communications Satellite Act of 1962* (Hearings before the Committee on Foreign Relations, Senate, 87th Cong., 2d sess.) (Washington, D.C.: U.S. Government Printing Office, 1962); Note, "The Communications Satellite Act of 1962," 76 *Harvard Law Review* 388 (1962); and Harvey J. Levin, "Organization and Control of Communications Satellites," 113 *University of Pennsylvania Law Review* 315 (1965).

[139] INTELSAT has been operating under the 1964 Interim Agreement. The agreement provides for definitive arrangements to be negotiated beginning in 1969. (On the initial meetings, see *Business Week,* March 1, 1969, pp. 32–33 and March 22, 1969, p. 46.) The aim of the interim agreement is to develop a single, expanding, global, commercial satellite system open equally to all nations. The Soviet Union has yet to join the consortium.

between the public and communications carriers and specified that the corporation's Board of Directors was to consist of three members appointed by the President with Senate confirmation, six members elected by public stockholders, and six by common carriers holding stock (subject to a provision that no stockholder could elect more than three of the corporation's directors). In its initial offering in 1954, 5 million shares were sold to 130,000 public subscribers, with an additional 5 million shares going to 163 common carriers. However, after subsequent sales to the public of some 1,190,000 shares by common carriers (including 951,250 shares by I.T.T.) reduced the total owned by communications carriers to 38 percent, Congress enacted legislation in 1969 that established a formula whereby the number of directors elected annually by public stockholders and common carriers will be approximately proportional to the total number of shares held by each group.[140]

COMSAT launched INTELSAT I (Early Bird) over the Atlantic Ocean on April 6, 1965—the world's first commercial communications satellite. During 1967, three satellites in the INTELSAT II series (each providing 240 two-way voice circuits) were launched, thereby expanding satellite coverage to more than two thirds of the world.[141] The first successful launch in the INTELSAT III series satellites (providing approximately 1,200 two-way telephone circuits over an expected life of five years) occurred late in 1968. Under construction is a more advanced series of satellites, called INTELSAT IV (having from 3,000 to 10,000 telephone circuits over a seven-year design lifetime), scheduled for launch beginning in 1971.[142] Each satellite in the INTELSAT series has been launched by the National Aeronautics and Space Administration on a cost-reimbursable basis.

The FCC has ruled, at least on an interim basis, that (*a*) all users (except for the government whenever it is in the public interest) must contract with common carriers for satellite services (i.e., COMSAT may not provide direct service) and (*b*) domestic satellite ground stations shall be owned 50 percent by COMSAT and 50 percent by common carriers.[143] But many significant policy issues remain unresolved,[144] including the desirability of a domestic communica-

---

[140]*The Wall Street Journal,* February 28, 1969, p. 3. The four largest common carriers received a total of 4,545,750 shares: A.T.&T., 2,895,750 shares; I.T.T., 1,050,000 shares; General Telephone, 350,000 shares; and RCA Communications, 250,000 shares. I.T.T. reportedly sold most of its shares because it was "in basic disagreement" with COMSAT's policy of attempting to expand its role in international communications. *Ibid.,* December 6, 1968, p. 3.

[141] See "Comsat Keeps Sending Them Up," *Business Week,* October 14, 1967, pp. 186-88.

[142] Communications Satellite Corporation, *Annual Report, 1968,* p. 7. The first launch attempt (in September 1968) in the INTELSAT III series was unsuccessful when the launch vehicle failed, and both it and the satellite were destroyed.

[143] Memorandum Opinion and Statement of Policy, 4 FCC 2d 421 (1966); Second Report and Order, 5 FCC 2d 812 (1966).

[144] See John McDonald, "The Comsat Compromise Starts a Revolution," *Fortune,* October, 1965, pp. 128 ff.; Herman Schwartz, "Comsat, the Carriers, and the Earth Stations: Some Problems with 'Melding Variegated Interests'," 76 *Yale Law Journal* 441 (1967); and Allen E. Throop, "Some Legal Facets of Satellite Communication," 17 *The American University Law Review* 12 (1967).

tions system and, if authorized, its ownership.[145] Regardless of the eventual outcome of these issues, the communications satellite, as President Johnson stated in 1967, "knows no geographic boundary, is dependent on no cable, owes allegiance to no single language or political philosophy. Man now has it within his power to speak directly to his fellow man in all nations."[146]

TECHNOLOGY, COMPETITION, AND THE FUTURE

The communications industry exhibits a pattern of development which is similar to the pattern displayed by other regulated industries: a few startling technological inventions; a period of somewhat chaotic competition, followed by a consolidation movement; and the extension of public regulation to the telephone and telegraph business. And, also like other regulated industries, the rapid pace of technology has introduced important competitive elements into supplying telecommunications services. Both the telephone and telegraph carriers have expanded into supplying private line services; Western Union has established computer centers. But the same technological advances which have tended to blur the traditional distinction between voice and record communication and have made feasible the entry of common carriers into supplying data processing and specialized information services, have likewise made feasible the entry of equipment manufacturers and other firms into supplying communications systems and services.

Significantly, the response of the telephone and telegraph companies to this new competition stands in sharp contrast to that of the railroad industry when it was first faced with intermodal rivalry. As the president of the Illinois Central Railroad has put it: "The railroads lost ground and today are not considered a growing industry because the nature of transportation changed and we did not change with it. We thought of ourselves as railroads first, and only incidentally as transportation companies."[147] In contrast, the telephone and

---

[145] The issues are complex. COMSAT has proposed to put a domestic communication satellite system into operation on a trial basis. The American Broadcasting Company (the television networks pay A.T.&T. some $65 million annually for transmitting their programs by land lines) requested permission to launch a domestic satellite for television broadcast distribution. (The request was rejected as "technically defective" by the FCC.) The Ford Foundation has proposed the establishment of a new nonprofit corporation to distribute television programs via satellite so as to help finance an improved and expanded educational television system. The common carriers have filed proposals for a domestic satellite system to provide all telecommunications service to all users. (The common carriers are opposed to a specialized or "dedicated" system for television distribution on the ground that it violates "the common carrier concept.") See Charles E. Silberman, "The Little Bird that Casts a Big Shadow," *Fortune*, February, 1967, pp. 108 ff.; and President's Task Force on Communications Policy, *Final Report, op. cit.,* chap. v. There is an added complication: satellite to home broadcasting is rapidly becoming technically feasible. See Lawrence Lessing, "Cinderella in the Sky," *Fortune*, October, 1967, pp. 130 ff.

[146] *Global Communications System, op. cit.,* p. 4.

[147] "Rail Problems Can Be Solved by Transportminded Men," 51 *Illinois Central Magazine* 9 (November, 1960).

telegraph common carriers have long considered themselves a part of the broadly defined communications industry, and have reacted to the changing market conditions by offering new services on a competitive basis. Comments one executive:

> The traditional idea of telephone service has been replaced by the much broader concept of total communications. Total communications means getting the right information to the right place at the right time—and by information, we mean voice, data, or video service, carried by wire, cable, microwave, or satellite.[148]

Yet, competition in the provision of communications service has created some difficult regulatory problems, particularly in the area of rate making. In those sectors of the telecommunications business subject to competitive pressures, rates must be competitive if the common carriers are to retain such business in the long run. But how are the competitive and noncompetitive segments to be separated when joint costs are involved, so that unfair advantage and discrimination between the segments are avoided? It is this problem—the mixture of competition and monopoly—that, more than any other, presents regulation with its most significant challenge.

[148] Earle G. Bellamy, quoted in 81 *Public Utilities Fortnightly* 47 (February 29, 1968).

PART IV

An Appraisal—
And a Challenge

Chapter 18

AN APPRAISAL OF

REGULATION

Regulation, like the Constitution under which it functions, is a living thing. It cannot be locked off into any permanent formula. It must change as the economic system in which it operates changes. The good, sound, practical regulation of one decade may not necessarily be the good, sound, practical regulation of another, and the United States Supreme Court has always wisely insisted upon preserving this elasticity.

—Francis X. Welch*

Independent regulatory commissions are a unique American institution. In most other countries of the world, the public utility and transportation industries are owned and operated by governmental agencies. From its very beginning, however, the American economy has been fundamentally a competitive, free-enterprise system. When it became apparent that direct competition between suppliers of utility services was ineffective in securing the public interest, public control was established, but private ownership was maintained. The early forms of control—franchises, charters, courts, and legislatures—proved little more satisfactory than reliance on competition. Consequently, the independent regulatory commission evolved late in the nineteenth century and has been the major form of utility and transport regulation since that time.

Government regulation of private enterprise raises many difficult questions. Even today, after more than three-quarters of a century of experience, the answers to these questions do not command general agreement. Perhaps the most fundamental issue is the balance between government control and private property rights. Some economists and political scientists hold that the provision of utility services is essentially a government operation and emphasize the control function of regulation. Others argue that since the regulated industries have no outstanding differences from other private enterprises, primary reliance should be placed on incentives to attain the social objectives expected from competition. The basic issue has been stated by Brynes to be whether a licensed

---

* Francis X. Welch, "The Effectiveness of Commission Regulation of Public Utility Enterprise," 49 *The Georgetown Law Journal* 639, 672 (1961).

monopoly "should be regulated as an enterprise selling a service, or as a concessionaire providing all there is to be had of it for cost plus a fixed fee. . . . In this view a public utility is created primarily for public purposes and has the status of a trustee; it carries out a function of the state."[1]

Many questions concerning regulatory procedure stem from this basic issue. Some see the necessity for regulation to control every aspect of utility and transport operations, while others feel that regulation should be concerned only with results. Some view regulation as a conflict between the public good and private property rights, requiring a judicial atmosphere and formal proceedings. Others advocate informal administrative methods as ordinarily being the most expeditious means of obtaining the benefits of regulation.

Another major area of disagreement concerns the necessity for, and effectiveness of, regulation. For many years, criticism came mainly from those who held that public regulation was both unnecessary and undesirable.[2] As this type of criticism diminished, new questions have been raised concerning the results of regulation and the possibility of obtaining better results by substituting other forms of regulation for the independent commissions.

It is the purpose of this concluding chapter to review these questions, assuming both that some government regulation of the utility and transportation industries is essential and that government regulation is superior to public ownership. Emphasis is on regulation as a method of control, rather than on the various regulatory problems such as determination of the rate base or the rate of return. The concluding section offers some comments on the future of regulation.

THE REGULATORY PROCESS

The independent regulatory commission combines in the same body legislative, judicial, and executive functions in regulation of an industry. A number of advantages were assumed to accrue to regulatory commissions, including continuity of policy, expertise, impartiality, experimentation, and flexibility in procedures. And independence was designed to gain for commissions the isolation from politics enjoyed by the judiciary. Today, however, all these supposed virtues have been challenged.

✓ *Independence from Political Control*

Independence was thought to isolate the regulatory commissions from undue political pressures, thereby assuring their devotion to the public interest and their impartiality in carrying out their statutory tasks. But commissions, as

---

1 Asher Brynes, "A $500 Million Mistake," *The New Republic,* September 26, 1964, p. 12.

2 See, for example, three articles by Philip Cabot, "Public Utility Rate Regulation," 7 *Harvard Business Review* 257 (1929), 7 *ibid.* 413 (1929), and "Four Fallacious Dogmas of Utility Regulation," 7 *Public Utilities Fortnightly* 719 (1931).

is true with most other branches of government, operate within a political environment.[3] They are dependent on the executive for their members (except in a few states), their budgets must be approved by the executive, their court cases (with a few exceptions) initiated by the attorney general's office, and, in some cases, the executive has statutory control over a commission's internal structure. They get their legal authority and their financial support from the legislative branch, and they are subject to legislative investigation as to personnel and performance. Finally, their authority is subject to judicial interpretation and their decisions to judicial review. The net effect has been to put the regulatory commissions, in Corwin's words, "in the uncomfortable halfway situation of Mahomet's coffin, suspended 'twix Heaven and earth."[4]

Independence, therefore, is difficult to achieve, and even if obtainable, many question its desirability. It is difficult to achieve, because commissions must operate within the existing framework of government and, therefore, must coordinate their activities and policies with other branches of government. It is undesirable, according to some, because independence isolates the commissions from the political support and leadership that is essential for the success of regulation and tends to curtail commission participation in the achievement of national economic objectives.

Outside Pressures. Some observers believe that the regulatory commissions have been subject to improper outside pressures. Schwartz, for example, has argued that the federal commissions have been subjected to pressures from both the executive and legislative branches, thereby resulting in partisan political decisions rather than unprejudiced determinations.[5] Other types of improper pressures were pointed out by Landis:

> Much attention has recently been centered on efforts, unfortunately too frequently successful, to sway the judgment of the members of regulatory agencies by so-called *ex parte* approaches or arguments, usually personalized, made off the record in proceedings that should be decided on the record. The extent of these *ex parte* approaches has only partially been revealed. They come from various sources—the office of the President, members of Congress, and the regulated industries. Some are made in good faith; others to further a personal desire regardless of the public interest. Many of them emanate from lawyers striving to press their clients' cause, indeed, one of the worst phases of this situation is the existence of groups of lawyers, concentrated in Washington itself, who implicitly hold out to clients that they have means of access to various regulatory agencies off the record that are more important than those that can be made on the record. . . .
>
> Instances have also recently been uncovered of actual malfeasance in the sense of bribery among high administrative officials. More serious than these are the subtle but pervasive methods pursued by regulated industries to

---

[3] See Chapter 4, pp. 108–13.

[4] Edwin Corwin, as quoted in Samuel Krislov and Lloyd D. Musolf (eds.), *The Politics of Regulation* (Boston: Houghton Mifflin Co., 1964), p. 93.

[5] Bernard Schwartz, "Crisis in the Commissions," *The Progressive,* August, 1959, p. 13.

influence regulatory agencies by social favors, promises of later employment in the industry itself, and other similar means.[6]

The problem of outside pressures is not unique to the regulatory commissions, nor is it an easy one to solve. Laws exist which make malfeasance a crime. But commissioners and their staffs must keep in constant contact with the industries under their jurisdiction, and the line between proper and improper ex parte contacts is often a fine one to draw. Some have suggested a code of ethics for federal and state employees but, as McFarland has observed, "An alert and devoted public service is the best insurance against improper 'influence' from outsiders. . . . Indeed, it is probably the only way to care for the problem—for such influence takes every variety and quality of forms so that no 'code' could begin to comprehend them."[7] If, then, the ultimate solution to the problem is personnel, it falls on the executive, legislature, and the public, as the case may be, to select or elect people for their competency rather than for their political status. "Good men can make poor laws workable; poor men will wreak havoc with good laws."[8] Higher salaries, particularly at the state level, and longer tenures, perhaps ten years, might be steps in the right direction. But equally important, steps must be taken to insure that the challenge of the job is appealing.

Executive Control or Coordination?   Other observers contend that independence from political control may be undesirable. Bernstein argues:

"Independence" is a device to escape popular politics. It facilitates maximum responsiveness by a commission to the demands and interests of regulated groups. It provides maximum freedom from exposure to popular political forces. It tends to alienate commissions from sources of political strength, especially the president, upon whom regulatory progress may largely depend. Independence acquires a sacred involability because it reduces the effectiveness of regulation and seems to satisfy the Congressional desire to lessen the power and authority of the president.[9]

Separation of Functions.   Some who support this position advocate a drastic change in the nature of regulatory commissions. In general, they believe that the three major functions assigned to commissions—administrative, policy-

---

[6] James M. Landis, *Report on Regulatory Agencies to the President-Elect* (Reprinted as a Committee Print by the Committee on the Judiciary, Senate, 86th Cong., 2d sess.) (Washington, D.C.: U.S. Government Printing Office, 1960), pp. 13–14 (hereinafter referred to as Landis Report). Also see *Independent Regulatory Commissions* (Report of the Special Subcommittee on Legislative Oversight of the Committee on Interstate and Foreign Commerce, House Report No. 2238) (Washington, D.C.: U.S. Government Printing Office, 1961).

[7] Carl McFarland, "Landis' Report: The Voice of One Crying in the Wilderness," 47 *Virginia Law Review* 374, 415 (1961).

[8] Landis Report, *op. cit.,* p. 66. Also see Cornelius J. Peck, "Regulation and Control of Ex Parte Communications with Administrative Agencies," 76 *Harvard Law Review* 233 (1962).

[9] Marver H. Bernstein, *Regulating Business by Independent Commission* (Princeton: Princeton University Press, 1955), p. 101.

making, and adjudication—are incompatible and should be separated. The American Bar Association has long supported the transfer of judicial functions to an administrative court, a position also taken by the President's Committee on Administrative Management in 1937 and by the Hoover Commission in 1955.[10] Two former chairmen of federal agencies, Hector of the Civil Aeronautics Board and Minow of the Federal Communications Commission, have advocated the transfer of all policy-making, planning, and administrative work of the regulatory commissions to an executive agency, with all judicial duties being transferred to an administrative court and all responsibility for investigation and prosecution given to an executive department or agency, such as the Department of Justice.[11] And a former member of the Interstate Commerce Commission has suggested that managerial or administrative duties can best be performed by a single administrator and has urged that those duties be separated from the commission.[12]

Such drastic surgery has not been forthcoming. Jaffe has noted that there is little in our history to suggest "that an executive agency will be much different from an independent agency in periods when public opinion or statutory policy is slack, indeterminate, or lacking in conviction. The odds are that it will respond in much the same way to the climate of opinion."[13] Boyd asks: "How would regulated industries fare if policies of regulation became a campaign issue, as they could under the proposed separation?"[14] Further, policy making and adjudication are so closely related that their separation seems neither desirable nor feasible. In Friendly's words:

> Let me illustrate this from the field of railway rates. If the question is whether a shipment comes within one classification of a tariff or another, that is adjudication clearly enough, with no element of policy making. But a case concerning the fairness or the prejudicial character of rates involves elements of policy, and this even though it arises as a demand for reparations. The policy considerations inherent in such proceedings range from the trivial to the gravest, as in cases relating to the overall rate level or to the

[10] 59 *A.B.A. Rep.* 539-64 (1934); 81 *A.B.A. Rep.* 491-535 (1956); President's Committee on Administrative Management, *Report with Special Studies* (Washington, D.C.: U.S. Government Printing Office, 1937); and U.S. Commission on Organization of the Executive Branch of the Government, *Task Force Report on Services and Procedure* (Washington, D.C.: U.S. Government Printing Office, 1955), pp. 84-88. For a summary, see Robert S. Lorch, "The Federal Administrative Court Idea," 52 *A.B.A. Journal* 635 (1966).

[11] Louis J. Hector, "Problems of the CAB and the Independent Regulatory Commissions," 69 *Yale Law Journal* 931, 960-64 (1960); Letter from Newton N. Minow to the President, May 31, 1963 (mimeographed). Also see Bernard Schwartz, "Administrative Justice and Its Place in the Legal Order," 30 *New York University Law Review* 1398 (1955).

[12] Anthony F. Arpaia, "The Brass Tacks of the ICC Administrative Problem," 65 *Public Utilities Fortnightly* 433, 439-40 (1960).

[13] Louis L. Jaffe, Book Review, "The Independent Agency—A New Scapegoat," 65 *Yale Law Journal* 1068, 1074 (1956).

[14] Alan S. Boyd, "The Scope and Philosophy of Regulatory Commissions," 65 *Public Utilities Fortnightly* 909, 911 (1960).

differentials, or the lack of them, between different ports or between traffic that has or has not moved all the way by rail. To call such cases adjudicative and place their decision in an administrative court would deprive the public of the benefits of the very expertise that is a principal *raison d'être* of the regulatory agency. Moreover, reparations cases and cases involving future rates cannot possibly be divided—often a single case will involve both; yet the fixing of future rates is surely not a "judicial" function.

. . . But even when separation is feasible from a formal standpoint, how can one characterize as adjudication and not policy making a decision whether the service should be operated by an existing airline or by a newly organized enterprise, or the weight to be given to better immediate service to the public as against the benefits thought to be ultimately realizable from fortifying weak carriers against the strong? To analogize decisions on such matters to the ordinary work of the courts is to let words and methods obscure substance.[15]

A less drastic separation of functions *within* the regulatory agencies has been made. After detailed studies of the agencies, a majority of the Attorney General's Committee on Administrative Procedure in 1941 endorsed an internal separation of the prosecution and adjudication functions.[16] Such a separation was subsequently required by the Administrative Procedure Act of 1946.[17] The act established an independent class of hearing examiners, whose appointment, promotion, salary, and tenure are determined by the Civil Service Commission. Further, examiners may not be assigned to other duties, and cases are to be assigned to them in rotation. Woll has noted that the independence of examiners "is an important achievement. The separation of functions must be based upon an independent class of hearing officers; once such independence has been

[15] Henry J. Friendly, "A Look at the Federal Administrative Agencies," 60 *Columbia Law Review* 429, 441-42 (1960). A former chairman of the Securities and Exchange Commission concludes: "To divorce the adjudicatory from the rule making and administrative functions would fragment the regulatory responsibility and deprive both the adjudicators and the rule makers of the valuable feedback between the two regulatory processes." William L. Cary, *Politics and the Regulatory Agencies* (New York: McGraw-Hill Book Co., 1967), pp. 133-34. Also see the testimony of Robert W. Ginnane, *Administrative Process and Ethical Questions* (Hearings before the Special Subcommittee on Legislative Oversight of the Committee on Interstate and Foreign Commerce, House, 85th Cong., 2d sess.) (Washington, D.C.: U.S. Government Printing Office, 1958), pp. 3-7; Carl A. Auerbach, "Should Administrative Agencies Perform Adjudicatory Functions?," *1959 Wisconsin Law Review* 95 and "Some Thoughts on the Hector Memorandum," *1960 Wisconsin Law Review* 183; Earl W. Kintner, "The Current Ordeal of the Administrative Process: In Reply to Mr. Hector," 69 *Yale Law Journal* 965 (1960); William L. Cary, "Why I Oppose the Divorce of the Judicial Function from Federal Regulatory Agencies," 51 *A.B.A. Journal* 33 (1965); and Philip Elman, "A Note on Administrative Adjudication," 74 *Yale Law Journal* 652 (1965).

[16] Attorney General's Committee on Administrative Procedure, *Final Report* (Senate Doc. No. 8, 77th Cong., 1st sess.) (Washington, D.C.: U.S. Government Printing Office, 1941). For a reproduction of the major portions of the Report, see *Administrative Procedure in Government Agencies* (Charlottesville, Va.: The University Press of Virginia, 1968).

[17] 60 Stat. 237 (1946).

destroyed, the prosecuting arm of the agency can easily influence adjudicative decisions." [18]

There is one issue concerning the separation of functions that has caused considerable debate, particularly with respect to the Federal Communications Commission. The procedure long followed by the FCC in rate proceedings "permits the same staff members to investigate, initiate, participate as parties, advocate, inform, and advise the commission ex parte, and then participate in the decision process both as advisers and draftsmen to the commission." [19] In connection with the telephone investigation, former FCC Commissioner Loevinger has argued that the procedure

> . . . is unfair to the telephone company, it is unfair to the public (which is denied effective representation), it is an inefficient and impractical way to conduct an inquiry of this nature, it is contrary to the intent of Congress and to the recommendations of the Administrative Conference of the United States, and it is an unreasonable method of seeking to arrive at an informed, wise, and impartial decision. [20]

And FCC Commissioner Johnson has stated that the procedures,

> . . . while legal and serving Bell as expeditious, have now proved to be unwise in serving the interests of the public, the commission, other participants, and even Bell itself. All have suffered from the role imposed by the commission on the able and dedicated staff of the FCC's common carrier bureau. Neither fish nor fowl, it has been forced to be "non-adversary participant" during the hearings, and "personal staff advisor" during the closed-door sessions thereafter. . . . [21]

Regardless of the legality of the dual role of the FCC's staff, the procedure raises the question of fairness to the parties of record. If such a dual role is essential because of a limited staff, then perhaps the ultimate solution is greater appropriations to enable the commission to separate these functions.

Executive Coordination. Landis, in his 1960 report, rejected a division of functions, urging instead the preservation of the regulatory agencies' integrity and independence. [22] However, he proposed that executive leadership be provided by (1) the creation of a new White House office ("Office for the Oversight

---

[18] Peter Woll, *Administrative Law: The Informal Process* (Berkeley and Los Angeles: University of California Press, 1963), p. 21.

[19] Concurring opinion of Commissioner Loevinger, *Re American Teleph. & Teleg. Co.*, 70 PUR 3d 129, 227 (FCC, 1967).

[20] *Ibid.*

[21] Preliminary concurring statement of Commissioner Johnson, *ibid.*, p. 234. Also see Carl A. Auerbach, "The Controversy over the Role of the FCC's Common Carrier Bureau in Rate Cases" (American Bar Association Annual Report, *Section of Public Utility Law, 1966*), pp. 6–24; Kenneth Culp Davis, "Advocating and Deciding in Rate Cases," *ibid.*, pp. 25–38; and Thomas L. Peterson, "The Hawaii Public Utilities Commission: Separating the Advocative and Advisory Roles of Counsel," 80 *Public Utilities Fortnightly* 73 (September 28, 1967).

[22] Landis Report, *op. cit.,* pp. 82–87.

of Regulatory Agencies") to oversee the regulatory agencies and (2) executive authority to select the chairman of each commission, the chairmen to hold their jobs "at the pleasure of the President."

It is difficult to reconcile these two positions, for agency independence and increased executive control are to some extent incompatible. This problem aside, the most vocal criticism of Landis' proposals has concerned his White House "Overseer." This person, he argued, should not be "a mere Inspector-General," but should be a source of "imaginative and creative activity."[23] The office should watch such matters as regulatory delay and failure to implement statutory policies, and should coordinate policies. Clearly, the chief executive has the duty to see that the agencies are carrying out the laws they were established to administer. Congress has a similar duty, as indicated by the action of the House Committee on Interstate and Foreign Commerce in establishing a permanent Legislative Oversight Subcommittee.[24] If, therefore, the role of the "Overseer" is not to compromise the independence of current agencies and if this could be assured by carefully defining the purposes and limits of the office before it is established, there would be little opposition. But if the "Overseer" were to use his post "as a funnel for regulatory policies originating at the White House," the effect would be to lessen the independence of the commissions.[25] Many believe that independence is still an essential ingredient of the regulatory process.[26]

The Problem of Industry-Mindedness

A regulatory commission must work closely with the industry which it regulates. Some have argued that this industry-agency cooperation results in an inevitable life cycle, thereby describing the evolution of a commission in terms of a biological metaphor.[27] The life of a commission, they say, can be divided into four periods: gestation, youth, maturity, and old age.[28]

The gestation phase includes the period during which legislation is enacted,

[23] *Ibid.*, p. 82.

[24] See 67 *Public Utilities Fortnightly* 461 (1961).

[25] Welch, "The Effectiveness of Commission Regulation . . . ," *op. cit.*, p. 669.

[26] See R. W. Lishman, " 'Independence' in the Independent Regulatory Agencies," 13 *Administrative Law Review* 135 (1960); and Cary, *Politics and the Regulatory Agencies, op. cit.*, pp. 20–23.

[27] ". . . regulatory bodies, like the people who comprise them, have a marked life cycle. In youth they are vigorous, aggressive, evangelistic, and even intolerant. Later they mellow, and in old age—after a matter of ten or fifteen years—they become, with some exceptions, either an arm of the industry they are regulating or senile." John K. Galbraith, *The Great Crash* (Boston: Houghton Mifflin Co., 1955), p. 171.

[28] "The length of each phase varies from one commission to another, and sometimes a whole period seems to be skipped. Some commissions maintain their youthfulness for a fairly long time, while others seem to age rapidly and apparently never pass through a period of optimistic adolescence. Some are adventurous, while others are bound more closely to the pattern established by the oldest commission, the ICC. Such differences add an element of interest and reality to the evolution of commission regulation, but they do not invalidate generalizations about the administrative history of regulation." Bernstein, *Regulating Business by Independent Commission, op. cit.*, p. 74.

providing for a regulatory commission. Since most legislative statutes calling for the regulation of an activity or industry have resulted from a publicly recognized problem, two decades or more may be required to produce such a statute, as illustrated by the political agitation preceding the creation of the ICC in 1887. During this gestation period, so the theory runs, the various contestants seek and oppose government regulation to eliminate the designated evil. As those favoring regulation are concerned more with receiving immediate relief than in developing a long-term philosophy, the net result is a legislative statute that often is lacking in clarity and provides few clear directives to the new commission. Indeed, the proponents of the theory contend that the long period of struggle may well produce a statute that is out of date at the time of its enactment.[29]

Once established, the new commission is apt to be aggressive and to act with vigor. Davis summarizes:

> Characteristically, the great federal regulatory agencies in the early years of their existence have been fired with an inspiration to achieve the goals laid down for them by Congress. During those years the political pressures which have given birth to the agency are still felt, and the agency is acutely aware of its responsibility. Alertness is natural and necessary, for the agency is pioneering; new paths must constantly be broken. The newness of the tasks and the absence of familiar patterns force the agency and its staff to draw constantly upon their own resourcefulness. Young agencies are dominated by the qualities of youth—energy, ambition, imagination.[30]

The youth phase, according to this view, therefore involves a crusading commission. Since the legislative statute resulted from public agitation, the new agency has popular support and attracts a highly qualified staff. The issues are challenging and present ample opportunities for initiative and imagination. The FCC's telephone investigation in the late thirties, to illustrate, provided for many years the groundwork for the commission's regulation of that particular industry.

Gradually, in the cycle theory, a commission matures. Redford describes this phase as follows:

> Later, there comes a period of maturity, when the agency has lost the original political support, when it has found its position among the contending forces in society, and when it has crystallized its own evolved program. It then becomes part of the status quo and thinks in terms of the protection of its own system and its own existence and power against substantial change. Its primary function in government is to operate the mechanisms which have

---

[29] "Because of the rapidity of technological and industrial change and continuing modifications in the economic structure of industry, the regulatory treaty finally hammered out by the House and Senate conferees will be focused on remedying problems that have been acute for many years. The battle to adapt regulatory policy and practices to problems currently emerging in the industrial scene will be fought bitterly during subsequent decades." *Ibid.*, pp. 76–77.

[30] Kenneth C. Davis, *Administrative Law* (St. Paul: West Publishing Co., 1951), p. 164.

been developed in its creative stage and adjust these as circumstances change. This is not to say that it may not still initiate constructive changes, for changes, and even leaps, in administrative program are sometimes made as conditions change, and agencies also may go to the Congress for new directive; but it is too much to expect that, after maturity is reached, government will find all the organization and perspective which it needs in its administrative institutions alone.[31]

During the maturity phase, say the cyclists, both public support and political leadership diminish. The agency tends to become identified with the industry it regulates. Its basic function shifts from one of protecting the public interest to one of protecting the economic health of the industry. "Precedent, rather than prospect, guides the commission. Its goals become routine and accepted."[32]

According to the cycle theory, inertia and a loss of vitality are symptoms of the final phase in a commission's life cycle, old age. The agency no longer enjoys public support or confidence and, cut off from political leadership, it tends to become even more closely allied with the interests of those it regulates. The agency becomes passive and seeks to maintain the status quo in the industry regulated. It tends to become outdated, failing to keep pace with changing technology and economic conditions. To quote Bernstein:

> In the phase of old age the regulatory objectives of a commission are no longer meaningful and appropriate. Not only are there growing doubts about the original objectives laid down vaguely in the enabling statute, but there is even greater doubt about what the objectives ought to be. In their declining days commissions can be described as retrogressive, lethargic, sluggish, and insensitive to their wider political and social setting. They are incapable of securing progressive revision of regulatory policies and fall further and further behind in their work.[33]

Those who support the cycle theory thus hold that a commission is systematically transformed from a vigorous protector of the public interest into an organization captured by the interests being regulated. They contend, further, that in its old age regulation becomes obsolete in that it fails to keep pace with the dynamic changes occurring throughout the economy. The ICC has been the traditional target of the cyclists.[34] Yet, the cycle theory leaves some unanswered questions. If industry-mindedness is a function of a commission's life cycle, why

---

31 Emmette S. Redford, *Administration of National Economic Control* (New York: Macmillan Co., 1952), p. 386. Reprinted by permission of The Macmillan Company.

32 Bernstein, *Regulating Business by Independent Commission, op. cit.*, p. 88.

33 *Ibid.*, pp. 94-95.

34 The pros and cons of the "railroad-mindedness" of the ICC were discussed in a series of articles in the *Yale Law Journal* in 1952 and 1953. See Samuel P. Huntington, "The Marasmus of the ICC," 61 *Yale Law Journal* 467 (1952); Charles S. Morgan, "A Critique of 'The Marasmus of the ICC'," 62 *Yale Law Journal* 171 (1953); C. Dickerman Williams, "Transportation Regulation and the Department of Commerce," 62 *Yale Law Journal* 563 (1953); and "The ICC Re-examined: A Colloquy," 63 *Yale Law Journal* 44 (1953).

is it that many believe the CAB, a relatively young agency, to be as industry-oriented, if not more so, than the older ICC? Further, is not industry-mindedness as closely related to a commission's personnel as to the agency's life cycle? And Jaffe, among others, has argued that agency reliance on the affected interests generally exists from its inception and is administratively rather than industry determined. He explains:

> There are those who say that the ICC is "railroad-minded," as if actions of the ICC favorable to the railroads were a deviation from the expected and relevant norm. The criticisms of the ICC are tendentiously documented and ultimately evasive. There can surely be no question that it was an essential element of the philosophy of the Motor Carrier Act to protect (as the drafters saw the problem) the *regulated* railroad from the *unregulated* motor carrier by subjecting both types of carrier to the same regime of regulation. In the words of a Senate Committee at a somewhat later date (1939), this was not a "railroad philosophy" but a "transportation philosophy." Obviously the implementation of this philosophy as against the previously unregulated motor carrier would favor the railroads. It may be that the ICC is more "railroad-minded" than "motor carrier-minded," but recent criticism has failed to distinguish to what extent it goes beyond the likely consequences of the kind of regulation which presently obtains in this field. The criticism pinning the blame on the ICC, and proposing perhaps this or that reshuffling of administrative power, refuses to face the problems created by regulation as such.[35]

Moreover, the cycle theory implies that effective regulation requires constant conflict between the commissions and the regulated industries. Many commissions, but by no means all, were established amid the glare of publicity attendant on real or alleged abuses by utilities. The immediate objectives of these commissions, of course, were to correct these conditions. Once this short-term goal was attained, commissions could begin to look toward the long-term interest of the consumer. At this stage, the objectives of the commission and the regulated utility begin to merge: the commission's responsibility is to assure so far as possible adequate and increasing supplies of utility services at reasonable rates, while the utility attempts to sell as much of its services as possible at rates that will provide an adequate return. Justice Douglas explained this point in the Hope case in the following words: "The rate-making process under the Act, i.e., the fixing of 'just and reasonable' rates, involves a balancing of the investor and the consumer interest."[36]

Lack of Meaningful Policy Standards

Judge Friendly has argued that a justifiable dissatisfaction with the regulatory process "is the failure to develop standards sufficiently definite to

---

[35] Louis L. Jaffe, "The Effective Limits of the Administrative Process: A Reevaluation," 67 *Harvard Law Review* 1105, 1108-9 (Copyright, ©, 1954 by the Harvard Law Review Association).

[36] *Federal Power Comm. v. Hope Natural Gas Co.,* 320 U.S. 591, 603 (1944).

permit decisions to be fairly predictable and the reasons for them to be understood; this failure can and must be remedied."[37] He continues:

> . . . There have been failures, perhaps excusable, by Congress at the time of initial enactment, failures by the agencies to sharpen the vague contours of the original statute, failures by the legislature to supply more definite standards as growing experience has permitted or even demanded, and failures by the executive to spur the legislature into activity. All these failures have been interdependent: failure by the agency to make clear what it is doing impedes both executive challenge and legislative response. I do not assert that failure has been universal; [there have been] victories as well as defeats. The victories help to show the defeats need not have been suffered.[38]

Intra-Agency Policy Formulation. The regulatory commissions operate under broad standards established by the legislature. There are many examples: "just and reasonable" rates, "undue preference or prejudice," "compensatory," "destructive competition," "public convenience and necessity," and "public interest," to cite but six. These standards, largely resulting from the inability of the legislature to resolve important issues and from the need for flexibility to meet changing conditions in dynamic industries, endow the commissions "with a discretion so wide that they can offer a more or less plausible explanation for any conclusion they choose to reach with respect to many, perhaps the great majority, of the matters coming before them."[39] As Davis has put it: "Because of history or context, vague phrases of this sort may sometimes have considerable meaning. But sometimes they do not. Sometimes telling the agency to do what is in the public interest is the practical equivalent of instructing it: 'Here is the problem. Deal with it.' "[40]

It would be clearly desirable if the legislature could be more specific at the outset. It is difficult to see how an agency can be expected to make policy when the legislature is unable to do so because of conflicting forces. Nevertheless, "fairly broad standards in initial legislative grants to administrative agencies are likely to remain with us, as to some extent, when the statute deals with a novel field, they should."[41] But there is little justification, as Fair has pointed out, for initial statutes that fail to provide a commission with the power to carry out stated policy or that contain inconsistencies in the law.

For example, there is no just basis to criticize the Interstate Commerce

[37] Henry J. Friendly, *The Federal Administrative Agencies: The Need for Better Definition of Standards* (Cambridge: Harvard University Press, 1962), pp. 5-6.

[38] *Ibid.*, p. 6. Also see Harry M. Trebing, "A Critique of the Planning Function in Regulation," 79 *Public Utilities Fortnightly* 21 (March 16, 1967) and "Toward Improved Regulatory Planning," 79 *ibid.* 15 (March 30, 1967).

[39] *Independent Regulatory Commissions* (Staff Report to the Special Subcommittee on Legislative Oversight of the Committee on Interstate and Foreign Commerce, House) (Washington, D.C.: U.S. Government Printing Office, 1960), p. 6.

[40] Kenneth C. Davis, *Administrative Law Treatise* (St. Paul: West Publishing Co., 1958), Vol. I, p. 82.

[41] Friendly, *The Federal Administrative Agencies, op. cit.*, p. 14.

Commission for not carrying out a general plan of consolidation of the railroads, a policy which in the Transportation Act of 1920 was held to be in the public interest, since the Act provided for acquisition of control by stock purchases independent of any consolidation plan and since the Commission was given no power to carry out its plan. Again the Interstate Commerce Act preamble calls for a coordinated and integrated transportation system, yet does not provide for the establishment of through routes between motor carriers and other surface carriers under the Act and actually discourages or restricts acquisition of a carrier by one of another mode of transportation.[42]

Even if it is conceded that the initial standards must be broad, both the legislature and the commissions should define and clarify these standards as experience dictates. However, the statutes which our regulatory agencies seek to enforce are, in the opinion of Rostow,

... usually out of date, often confused, ill-drawn, and needlessly complex. Many of their rules echo forgotten battles, and guard against dangers which no longer exist. They comprise vast codes, understood only by a jealous priesthood which protects these swamps and thickets from all prying eyes. In the main, the agencies follow routines established for the control of local gas companies and street railways. The relevance of the model is not immediately apparent, in dealing with progressive and expanding industries like air transport or trucking.[43]

Consider the ICC's minimum rate power. The power was conferred by Congress in the Transportation Act of 1920, at a time when the railroads enjoyed a virtual monopoly of the nation's transportation system. It has been revised by Congress on two occasions: in 1940, "with language so encompassing as to create as many contradictions as were dissipated," and again in 1958, with "legislation that took with one hand much of what was given to the other."[44] Throughout this period, the commission has failed to define the relevant cost standards or to explain the rationale for its use of a particular one. Fulda thus concludes: "Regrettably one searches in vain for an unambiguous pronouncement of general policy with respect to the various measures of compensativeness. Indeed, the reading of the decisions creates the impression that the Commission selects whichever theory appears best to fit the case at hand."[45] And Williams, after analyzing some 900 railroad cases, concludes:

[42] Marvin L. Fair, "Some Observations on the Theory and Performance of the Independent Regulatory Agencies in Regulating the Public Utility Industries," 27 *I.C.C. Practitioners' Journal* 957, 967 (1960).

[43] Eugene V. Rostow, *Planning for Freedom* (New Haven: Yale University Press, 1959), pp. 311–12.

[44] Friendly, *The Federal Administrative Agencies, op. cit.,* p. 140.

[45] C. H. Fulda, *Competition in the Regulated Industries: Transportation* (Boston: Little, Brown & Co., 1961), p. 370. Also see David Boies, Jr., "Experiment in Mercantilism: Minimum Rate Regulation by the Interstate Commerce Commission," 68 *Columbia Law Review* 599 (1968).

The treatment of the declaration of policy both by the Commission and by the courts, therefore, leaves in doubt the nature of the general objective toward which the Commission should work. In effect the average case is decided without reference to any such objective. In those few instances in which construction of the policy seems almost unavoidable care is taken to skirt the edges; to reach an acceptable decision in the instant case, but one which may not be relied upon as a guide to the decision of future cases.[46]

Or, consider the CAB's domestic air route certification power. Under Section 2 of the Civil Aeronautics Act, the board is directed to consider a number of factors in issuing competitive certificates. In carrying out this directive, however, the board has vascillated and has changed its policy on several occasions.[47] More importantly, it has never spelled out the standards it would apply in situations arising under the Section. Friendly contends:

> . . . It is no answer to take refuge in such cliches as that "no mechanical formula exists whereby statistics can be fed into a machine and an ultimate route decision obtained"—as if anyone had ever contended that it did—and that "the outcome depends upon a balancing and weighting" of many factors such as "diversion, subsidy, cost, need for service, strengthening of weak carrier, competitive balance, [and] adequacy of existing service." The Board ought to have been able to say *something* as to *how* these factors would be weighted—which were more important and which less—and to develop some useful tests of these and other factors through careful economic study. . . .
> The Board's history is a prime example of how an agency's failure to grasp the nettle can make a relatively easy problem hard.[48]

The statutes are also ambiguous concerning current antitrust problems in the regulated industries.[49] A few statutes give antitrust immunity to some or all commission decisions. The Interstate Commerce Act, for example, provides that "any carriers . . . participating in a transaction approved or authorized . . . are relieved from the operation of the antitrust laws. . . ."[50] Generally, however, an

---

[46] Ernest W. Williams, Jr., *The Regulation of Rail-Motor Rate Competition* (New York: Harper & Bros., 1958), pp. 208–9. The Doyle Report argued that "the Commission in its written decisions and its statements to congressional committees provides the best documentation of the thesis that the meaning of minimum rate policy is less certain and its application more confusing than before the addition" of the 1958 amendment. *National Transportation Policy* (Preliminary draft of a Report Prepared for the Committee on Interstate and Foreign Commerce by the Special Study Group on Transportation Policies in the United States, Senate, 87th Cong., 1st sess.) (Washington, D.C.: U.S. Government Printing Office, 1961), p. 405.

[47] See Chapter 12, pp. 413–17.

[48] Friendly, *The Federal Administrative Agencies, op. cit.*, pp. 103–4, 105. Also see Howard C. Westwood, "Choice of the Air Carrier for New Air Transport Routes," Part I: 16 *George Washington Law Review* 1 (1947), Part II: 16 *ibid.* 159 (1948).

[49] See *Report of the Attorney General's National Committee to Study the Antitrust Laws* (Washington, D.C.: U.S. Government Printing Office, 1955), pp. 261–93.

[50] 49 U.S.C. Sec. 5 (11) (1952). Similar relief is granted for rate-making agreements. 49 U.S.C. Sec. 5b (9) (1952). In such circumstances, the Department of Justice may intervene in a case before the commission.

exemption from the antitrust laws is not expressly stated. Thus, in consolidation cases, most regulatory statutes provide that the transaction be "consistent with the public interest."[51] When antitrust exemptions are not specified, conflicts between regulatory standards and antitrust standards may arise.

A recent case is illustrative. Early in 1957, El Paso Natural Gas Company acquired controlling stock interest in the Pacific Northwest Pipeline Corporation. On July 22, 1957, the Department of Justice filed a civil suit against the two companies, charging them with violating Section 7 of the Clayton Act, despite the provision of the Clayton Act which states: "Nothing contained in this section shall apply to transactions duly consummated pursuant to authority given by the . . . Federal Power Commission . . . under any statutory provision vesting such power in such commission. . . ."[52] Subsequently, El Paso applied to the FPC for a certificate of public convenience and necessity authorizing its acquisition, and the court postponed hearings on the antitrust case pending the commission's decision.

On December 23, 1959, the commission granted the certificate, arguing that "we find that any lessening of competition . . . does not prevent our approving the merger because there are other factors which outweigh the elimination of Pacific as a competitor."[53] The state of California appealed the commission's decision, an appeal supported by the Department of Justice. Judge Prettyman upheld the FPC's ruling on March 30, 1961, saying:

> To approve a transaction the Commission must find it to be in the public interest. Clearly, the public interest includes the solution of problems in so important an area of economics and law as the so-called antitrust area. The Commission must consider the public policy, as declared by the Congress, in these respects. . . . We are here dealing with the interweaving of free competition, regulated monopoly, and the public interest. . . . The policy of the antitrust laws is to foster free competition. The policy of regulatory measures such as the Natural Gas Act is public regulation of controlled monopoly, or partial monopoly. . . . A determination that only one regulated utility should operate is not in contravention of the antitrust laws. The antitrust laws and the regulatory laws are not in conflict; they are complementary. Both have as their objective the public interest. . . . The Commission must recognize the policies of the antitrust laws, but it must also recognize its own responsibilities under its own laws.
>
> . . . the Commission weighted one set of factors against the other. It did take into account the policies of the antitrust law and put them in the scale of factors. We think its course of action was its duty, well within its authority, and was a reasonable process. We find no error.[54]

[51] See Federal Communications Act, 47 U.S.C. Sec. 221a, 222(c) (1) (1952); Civil Aeronautics Act, 49 U.S.C. Sec. 488b (1952).

[52] 15 U.S.C. Sec. 18 (1958).

[53] *Re Pacific Northwest Pipeline Corp. and El Paso Natural Gas Co.*, Docket Nos. G-13018 and G-13019, December 23, 1959 (mimeographed), p. 4.

[54] *People* v. *Federal Power Comm.*, 296 F. 2d 348, 353–54 (1961).

The Supreme Court, on appeal, reversed the appellate court, holding that the FPC should have "held its hand" while an antitrust suit was pending in the courts, and ordered the appellate court to vacate the FPC order approving the merger.[55] In November, 1962, the District Court dismissed the antitrust case on the ground that the two companies were not substantial competitors in the California market.[56] But in April, 1964, the Supreme Court reversed the lower court and, in addition, ordered divestiture "without delay."[57] Justice Harlan, who concurred with the majority that the merger was illegal, noted that the case

> ... affords another example of the unsatisfactoriness of the existing bifurcated system of antitrust and other regulation in various fields. ... It would be unrealistic not to recognize that this state of affairs has the effect of placing the Department of Justice in the driver's seat even though Congress has lodged primary regulatory authority elsewhere.
>
> It does seem to me that the time has come when this duplicate and, I venture to say, anachronistic system of dual regulation should be re-examined. ...[58]

Few are likely to disagree with Justice Harlan's plea.[59]

It is not being suggested that regulatory standards can be completely free of ambiguities. Regulation must be flexible enough to adapt to changing economic conditions and technological developments. At the same time, "during three-quarters of a century of regulatory experience in the railroad field and several decades in others, many patterns have recurred frequently enough so that by now it should be possible to articulate bases of administrative determination more specific than we have generally had, even though these cannot be expected to be as immutable as the law of the Medes and Persians."[60] What is needed,

[55] *California* v. *Federal Power Comm.,* 369 U.S. 482 (1962).

[56] The U.S. District Court for Utah made findings of fact and conclusions of law, but issued no written opinion. See *United States* v. *El Paso Natural Gas Co.,* Commerce Clearing House, *1962 Trade Cases,* Par. 70, 571.

[57] *United States* v. *El Paso Natural Gas Co.,* 376 U.S. 651, 662 (1964).

[58] *Ibid.,* pp. 663-64. Because of conflicts over the divestiture decree, the Court's order has yet to be carried out. See *United States* v. *El Paso Natural Gas Co.,* Commerce Clearing House, *1965 Trade Cases,* Par. 71,362, *rev'd sub nom. Cascade Natural Gas Corp.* v. *El Paso Natural Gas Co.,* 386 U.S. 129 (1967).

[59] See Note, "Regulated Industries and the Antitrust Laws: Substantive and Procedural Coordination," 58 *Columbia Law Review* 673 (1958); G. E. Hale and Rosemary D. Hale, "Competition or Control VI: Application of Antitrust Laws to Regulated Industries," 111 *University of Pennsylvania Law Review* 46 (1962), "Mergers in Regulated Industries," 59 *Northwestern University Law Review* 49 (1964), and "Regulation: A Defense to Anti-Merger Litigation?," 54 *Kentucky Law Journal* 683 (1966); John M. Stokes, "A Few Irreverent Comments about Antitrust, Agency Regulation, and Primary Jurisdiction," 33 *George Washington Law Review* 529 (1964); Arthur H. Travers, Jr., "An Examination of the CAB's Merger Policy," 15 *Kansas Law Review* 227 (1967); and Frank W. Frisk, Jr., "Antitrust and Wholesale Power," 26 *Public Power* 24 (October, 1968). For cases dealing with the interaction of antitrust and regulatory standards, see William K. Jones, *Cases and Materials on Regulated Industries* (Brooklyn: The Foundation Press, Inc., 1967), chaps. viii and ix.

[60] Friendly, *The Federal Administrative Agencies, op. cit.,* p. 18.

argues Bernstein, is an appropriate balance between broad and vague policies (which "generally prove to be unsatisfactory guides to decision in adjudicated cases") and policies that are too tight and specific (which "may be applicable only to a relatively few cases").[61]

Policy formulation might also be improved if the decisions and orders of the agencies were written with greater clarity and by the commissioners themselves. Commented Justice Black on a decision of the ICC: "I am compelled to say that the Commission could have informed me just as well if it had written its so-called findings in ancient Sanskrit."[62] And Landis argued: "Opinions of the Interstate Commerce Commission are presently in the poorest category of all administrative agency opinions. Their source is unknown and the practice has grown up of parsimony in discussing the applicable laws in making a determination. Lengthy recitals of the contentions of the various parties are made as a prelude to a succinct conclusion devoid of real rationalization."[63]

The work loads of the commissions, at the federal level and in many of the states, often prevent the commissioners from writing opinions. Consequently, opinion writing is delegated to staff personnel, commonly within an independent Opinion Writing Office. Yet, effective regulation requires that the commissioners take responsibility for all phases of opinions. The Special Subcommittee on Legislative Oversight concluded:

> The subcommittee has been impressed with the need for change in the practices followed by some commissions of letting the commission staff rather than individual commissioners assume responsibility for the preparation of commission decisions and opinions. It is the view of the subcommittee that inconsistencies in commission decisions over the years are traceable to a considerable extent to the failure of following the practice of having the commission, or the majority of the commission, designate individual commissioners to assume responsibility for the preparation of the decisions or opinions of the commission, or the majority of the commission. It is the view of the subcommittee that this practice, which is traditional with the courts and which has been followed by some commissions, should be adopted by all commissions. It is the hope of the subcommittee that this change will produce a sense of personal responsibility of individual commissioners for the decisions and opinions of the commission and will avoid the practice of having commission staffs assume the burden of reconciling inconsistent decisions reached by the commissions.[64]

---

[61] Marver H. Bernstein, "The Regulatory Process: A Framework for Analysis," 26 *Law and Contemporary Problems* 329, 332 (1961).

[62] Dissenting opinion, *Chicago & Eastern Illinois R. Co.* v. *United States*, 375 U.S. 150, 154 (1963).

[63] Landis Report, *op. cit.,* p. 39. As former FCC Chairman Henry said: ". . . many of our hearing records and many of our decisions contain some of the world's greatest collection of useless information." Quoted in *The Wall Street Journal*, January 21, 1966, p. 1.

[64] *Independent Regulatory Commissions* (Report of the Special Subcommittee on Legislative Oversight of the Committee on Interstate and Foreign Commerce, House Report No. 2711) (Washington, D.C.: U.S. Government Printing Office, 1959), p. 41.

Interagency Policy Formulation. The failure to develop meaningful
interagency policy standards has been noted by several observers of the federal
regulatory scene. In the fields of communications, energy, and transportation, a
number of agencies and executive departments share complementary and often
overlapping responsibilities. According to Landis, there is "an almost complete
barrenness" of policy formulation among these various groups. "The few
interagency committees that have been set up have accomplished too little in
conducting their separate approaches to a common problem." [65]

The establishment of the Department of Transportation, bringing most
nonregulatory transport activities of the federal government under one jurisdiction, is a step toward achieving better policy formulation. [66] So, too, is the
creation of the Water Resources Council by the Water Resources Planning Act of
1965. [67] Many believe, however, that further legislation is vitally needed to deal
with the problem. Landis recommended the creation of three coordinating
offices (for communications, energy, and transportation) within the Executive
Office of the President. [68] Some, including Commissioner Tucker of the Interstate Commerce Commission, have urged the uniting of federal transport
regulatory activities by the creation of a National Transportation Commission; a
merger that would result in a stronger regulatory body "more capable of dealing
with transport problems in an equitable and coordinated fashion responsive to
the public demands for transport service rather than modal policy." [69] And
Commissioner Bartley of the Federal Communications Commission has suggested the abolition of that agency, and the establishment of two new
independent agencies (one to regulate broadcasting and the other for common-
carrier regulation) and a new authority for frequency allocations. [70]

The need for greater coordination is clear; the best means of achieving this

[65] Landis Report, *op. cit.,* p. 24.
[66] Prior to the establishment of the Department of Transportation, numerous
proposals had been made to deal with the lack of coordination. See, for example, Report
to the President from the Secretary of Commerce, *Unified and Coordinated Federal
Program for Transportation* (Sawyer Report) (Washington, D.C.: U.S. Government Printing Office, 1949); Commission on the Organization of the Executive Branch of the
Government, *Task Force Report on Regulatory Commissions* (Washington, D.C.: U.S.
Government Printing Office, 1949), Appendix N, chap. iv; *National Transportation
Policy, op. cit.,* pp. 107–15; and D. I. Mackie, "The Necessity for a Federal Department
of Transportation," 8 *Journal of Public Law* 1 (1959).
[67] Public Law 89-80 (1965). See Federal Power Commission, *Annual Report*
(1967), pp. 33–34.
[68] Landis Report, *op. cit.,* pp. 74-81. Cary has argued that the proposal "has
much to be said for it in theory," but seems "unduly optimistic" since it "would
accentuate existing political antagonisms." Cary, *Politics and the Regulatory Agencies, op.
cit.,* p. 34.
[69] William H. Tucker, "Government Organization and Federal Transportation Regulation" (speech before the Board of Directors of the American Trucking Associations,
Chicago, October 19, 1967) (mimeographed).
[70] Robert T. Bartley, "Let's Abolish the F.C.C." (address before the Illinois
Broadcasters Association, Quincy, May 23, 1968) (mimeographed). See *The Wall Street
Journal,* May 24, 1968, p. 12.

goal have yet to be agreed on. At the federal level, and perhaps even at the state level, any means adopted will require a drastic reorganization of the executive branch of the government.

Regulatory Delay

The Achilles heel of the regulatory process is delay.[71] Landis argued:

Inordinate delay characterizes the disposition of adjudicatory proceedings before substantially all of our regulatory agencies. In the Civil Aeronautics Board, for example, the average age of dockets closed by formal proceedings in 1960 was some 32 months. As of June 30, 1959, out of 464 proceedings then pending, 166 had been pending for more than 3 years. . . . In the Federal Power Commission the backlog of pending cases in 1959 was almost four times as great as in 1957. Only last September that Commission announced that it would take 13 years with its present staff to clear up its pending 2,313 producer rate cases pending as of July 1, 1960, and that with the contemplated 6,500 cases that would be filed during that 13 year period it could not become current until 2043 A.D. even if its staff were tripled. Contested proceedings before the Interstate Commerce Commission tend to run from 18 to 36 months, and numerous proceedings before the Federal Communications Commission and the Maritime Board have been pending for more than 3 years. . . . Numerous similar statistics can be gathered from other agencies, including individual instances when even 10 to 14 years have elapsed before a final determination has been made. They all corroborate the fact of interminable delay.[72]

Regulatory delay adversely affects the public welfare in several ways. Delay in the regulatory process may hamper the progress and efficiency of the regulated industries. Delay may prevent consumers from receiving their share of the benefits flowing from progress and efficiency. The first may occur when a rate increase is in order; the second when technological advances indicate a rate decrease. And both occur when the introduction of a new or improved service is postponed.[73] Delay is costly—"costly in terms of the human energies expended by the managements of regulated industries in obtaining approval to do those

[71] Boyd, *op. cit.,* p. 911.

[72] Landis Report, *op. cit.,* pp. 5-6. Also see *Statistical Data Related to Administrative Proceedings Conducted by Federal Agencies—Fiscal 1963* (Committee Print, Committee on the Judiciary, Senate, 88th Cong., 2d sess.) (Washington, D.C.: U.S. Government Printing Office, 1964); *Questionnaire Survey on Delay in Administrative Proceedings* (Committee Print, Prepared for the Committee on the Judiciary by its Subcommittee on Administrative Practice and Procedure, Senate, 89th Cong., 2d sess.) (Washington, D.C.: U.S. Government Printing Office, 1966); and *Evaluation Charts on Delay in Administrative Proceedings* (Committee Print, Prepared for the Committee on the Judiciary by its Subcommittee on Administrative Practice and Procedure, 89th Cong., 2d sess.) (Washington, D.C.: U.S. Government Printing Office, 1966).

[73] See Paul W. MacAvoy and James Sloss, *Regulation of Transport Innovation: The ICC and Unit Coal Trains to the East Coast* (New York: Random House, 1967).

things which must be done; costly in terms of legal fees and the expenses of management personnel engaged in the long-drawn-out proceedings before regulatory agencies."[74] Delay may postpone or even deny justice. Delay causes further delay: When the FPC has a gas pipeline case pending, the affected state commissions are unable to determine proper rates for local distributors. Finally, delay aggravates the problem of ex parte influences.

The causes of regulatory delay are numerous. A major factor is the increasing work load of the commissions. As previously noted, the volume of work has been expanded by new legislation (the Motor Carrier Act of 1935 in the case of the ICC) and by court decisions (the Supreme Court's 1954 Phillips decision in the case of the FPC).[75] Another cause is inadequate budgets. To handle increasing work loads, the commissions must have adequate appropriations and staffs.[76] The lack of clearly defined standards and policies is a third cause of delay. Commissions must interpret broad statutory provisions in regulating a particular industry. Sometimes these statutes are conflicting (regulatory versus promotional duties); other times they are outdated, resulting in overregulation (transportation industry).[77] Poor personnel contributes to the problem. "While regulatory agencies are blessed with a number of highly competent hearing examiners, they are cursed with an equal number of weak ones. The latter compound the problem of regulatory lag through failing their responsibility of determining admissibility of the evidence. This is why some hearings continue ad infinitum."[78] All these are important causes, but they are subordinate to the problem of administrative procedures.

Administrative Procedures. The "judicialization" of proceedings, that is, the tendency to introduce trial-type processes into administrative proceedings, has long been a source of controversy. The Landis Report comments on this as follows:

> Beginning about 1938 concerted efforts were made to deal with these [procedural] problems. At the outset, spurred on by an antagonism to the

74 *Public Regulation of Utility Enterprises* (New York: New York Chamber of Commerce, 1960), p. 21. See Robert W. Gerwig, "Natural Gas Production: A Study of Costs of Regulation," 5 *Journal of Law and Economics* 69 (1962).

75 See Chapter 4, pp. 102-4.

76 Landis Report, *op. cit.,* pp. 6-7. As Commissioner Bartley noted, after explaining the rapidly expanding responsibilities of the FCC: "But the FCC's manpower, as authorized by Congress, instead of keeping pace with the expansion—steadily decreased until 1955, and did not even reach the 1947 level again until 1963. And, in 1967, we had only 71 more employees than in 1947. And many of these were consumed by new management procedures and techniques imposed upon the Commission." Bartley, *op. cit.,* p. 4.

77 "Comprehensive statutory revision should have been effected long ago and should certainly not be postponed any longer. *Every* state system of regulation is outdated. It is too indefinite as to objectives, standards, and procedures. It is not well-suited either for the conservation and promotion of the public interest in the great public services entrusted to private organization, or for clear and consistent protection of the private interests. For the purpose of statutory revision, every state should conduct a comprehensive inquiry as to conditions and needs." John Bauer, *Updating Public Utility Regulation* (Chicago: Public Administration Service, 1966), p. 181.

78 Boyd, *op. cit.,* p. 912.

very powers exercised by the regulatory agencies, the bar as a whole sought to impose the straight-jackets of traditional judicial procedure on the agencies. They were countered by other forces which sought to retain the value of the administrative process but still advocated reforms that would assure fairness in the exercise of powers delegated to the agencies. Some eight years thereafter a compromise between these two opposing views was effected by the enactment of the Administrative Procedure Act of 1946. That Act, however one may evaluate it, is far from a definitive solution of the problems with which it dealt. It has achieved some uniformity of procedure, some assurance of the application of fairer standards, but with its emphasis on 'judicialization' has made for delay in the handling of many matters before these agencies.[79]

The basic problem then is to reconcile the legal and constitutional requirements of due process of law in agency decisions with the demands of promptness and efficiency in achieving statutory duties.[80] Equally important, it is difficult to evaluate the many recommendations for improving administrative procedures, since "the practical and theoretical motivations of reformers differ. Each group seeking change views the administrative process in terms of one aspect of its operation; thus, the official viewpoint of the American Bar Association is based above all on the need to protect the rights of private parties in administrative proceedings, while administrative-minded reformers seek to increase efficiency."[81]

The regulatory commissions have adopted many of the proposals advanced to streamline administrative procedures. Prehearing conferences are used to determine the areas of agreement and of dispute. Previously prepared and published (so-called "canned") testimony often is permitted to limit trial examination. Informal proceedings are increasingly being used in place of formal proceedings. But further remedies would seem desirable. The number of interveners, in many cases, could be limited without any loss to interested parties. "There can be no quarrel with any party presenting his point of view to a regulatory commission, but when the same points of view have been already adequately presented by the public service company or by the staff of the commission, it is a needless waste of time for other groups to plow the same ground a second or third time."[82]

[79] Landis Report, *op. cit.,* p. 16.
[80] *Independent Regulatory Commissions,* Staff Report, *op. cit.,* p. 7.
[81] Woll, *op. cit.,* p. 177.
[82] *Public Regulation of Utility Enterprises, op. cit.,* pp. 23–24. As Welch has observed: "The coal industry and affiliated mining labor interests have almost automatically intervened in every major pipeline certificate case before the FPC for the obvious reason that granting such certificates to build pipelines would mean delivery of gas to markets previously enjoyed by coal or other fuels." Welch, "The Effectiveness of Commission Regulation . . . ," *op. cit.,* p. 663, n. 63. For a discussion of the procedures adopted to expedite the telephone investigation, see Charles F. Phillips, Jr., "Interveners in the Telephone Investigation," 78 *Public Utilities Fortnightly* 26, 34–36 (December 22, 1966). Also see William H. Tucker, "Renovating the Decisional Process in an Independent Regulatory Commission," 35 *I.C.C. Practitioners' Journal* 207 (1968).

Many believe that the key to cutting down procedural delay, at the federal level, is the hearing examiner. Welch argues:

Too often he has been governed by the understandable tendency to let questionable material go into the record so as to give the offering parties the "benefit of the doubt" and make his own position less vulnerable on appeal. This may result in a mass of extraneous material which commissioners and eventually appellate courts are supposed to read. It takes real courage and a good deal of ability to kick irrelevant material out of the record, to cut off counsel mid-flight in the pursuit of testimony obviously not germane, and cutting through the downright "gobbledy-gook" of obscure expert testimony.[83]

Case-by-case adjudication is a slow, costly, and inadequate process for resolving the complex economic issues that characterize the regulation of industry. To be sure, fairness and impartiality must be maintained and informal procedures cannot be used in all instances. But the commissions should be permitted to use informal procedures when applicable. The FCC's policy of primary reliance on continuous surveillance and informal procedures in its regulation of the Bell System is an outstanding example of the benefits that can be derived. Rate reductions made possible by increased efficiency and new equipment have been passed on quickly to subscribers. Innovations in rate making have been made possible and new services introduced.

In an effort to provide for the constant improvement of administrative procedures, the Administrative Conference of the United States was established by Congress in 1964.[84] A permanent, independent government agency, the Administrative Conference has the responsibility of studying and making recommendations for improvement in all federal agency functions which involve "the determination of the rights, privileges, and obligations of private persons through rule making, adjudication, licensing, or investigation." It will make an annual report to the President and to Congress, and will work with the federal departments and agencies in implementing its recommendations.[85]

[83] Welch, "The Effectiveness of Commission Regulation . . . ," *op. cit.*, pp. 665-66. Also see E. Barrett Prettyman, "The President's Conference on Administrative Procedure," 55 *Public Utilities Fortnightly* 61, 67 (1955); *Selected Reports of the Administrative Conference of the United States* (Senate Doc. No. 24) (Washington, D.C.: U.S. Government Printing Office, 1963), esp. pp. 69-114; "ICC Members Blame Some Regulatory Lag on Examiners, Parties, and Budget Limits," *Traffic World*, December 24, 1966, pp. 5-6; and Arthur A. Gladstone, "The Role of the Hearing Examiner," 83 *Public Utilities Fortnightly* 22 (January 16, 1969).

[84] The chairman, appointed by the President with the advice and consent of the Senate for a five-year term, is the only paid full-time member of the conference. At the present time, the conference consists of eighty-two members, a majority being government representatives from federal departments and agencies.

[85] See Jerre S. Williams, "Problems Confronting the Administrative Conference," 82 *Public Utilities Fortnightly* 86 (September 12, 1968).

REGULATION AS A SUBSTITUTE FOR COMPETITION

Criticisms of the regulatory process are numerous and varied. Yet, the shortcomings of regulation cannot be attributed solely to the lack of political control, ex parte influences, industry-mindedness, the failure to develop meaningful policy standards, and undue delay. If all these defects could be remedied, regulation would be more effective, but it would still fall short, in the opinion of some, of the competitive standard.

The Inherent Difficulties

Wilcox has argued that "the difficulties of regulation are largely inherent in the nature of the undertaking itself." In his view:

Taking the place of competition as the method of control, regulation should be expected to yield comparable results. It should not only prevent the regulated industry from charging a monopoly price, impairing the quality of its service, and enjoying a monopoly profit. It should provide an incentive to adopt new methods, to improve quality, to increase efficiency and cut costs, to develop mass markets and expand output by selling at a lower price. It does none of these things.

Regulation, at best, is a pallid substitute for competition. It cannot prescribe quality, force efficiency, or require innovation, because such action would invade the sphere of management. But when it leaves these matters to the discretion of industry, it denies consumers the protection that competition would afford. Regulation cannot set prices below an industry's costs however excessive they may be. Competition does so, and the high-cost company is compelled to discover means whereby its costs can be reduced. Regulation does not enlarge consumption by setting prices at the lowest level consistent with a fair return. Competition has this effect. Regulation fails to encourage performance in the public interest by offering rewards and penalties. Competition offers both.

Regulation is static, backward-looking, preoccupied with the problems of the past. It does nothing to stimulate change, seeking to maintain order on the basis of the old technology. It is slow to adapt to change; new problems appear, but regulatory thinking lags. Competition, by contrast, is dynamic. . . .

Regulation is slower than competition. It must satisfy the requirements of due process: investigate, give notice, hold hearings, study the record, make findings, issue orders, permit appeals. All this takes time and delays action. In some cases, delay may be harmful, as when it permits earnings to rise well above or to fall far below the return required to attract new capital. In other cases, it may be helpful, as when it brakes an inflationary spiral of wages and prices. But here, the merit of regulation lies, not in its efficiency, but in its inefficiency.[86]

Wilcox, however, appears to be comparing some of the alleged short-comings of regulation as it actually exists with the idealistic benefits of the theoretical competitive model. In so doing, he has arrived at a view of regulation which seems too pessimistic, particularly with respect to the nontransport utilities. Put another way, if regulation were as unsuccessful as Wilcox suggests, the gas, electric, and communications utilities could not have contributed so largely to the nation's economic growth. Many of the benefits claimed for competition have been achieved by the utilities under regulation. The growth of the regulated utilities in the postwar period has far exceeded that of the unregulated industries—nearly double the growth rate of the economy as a whole.[87] The productivity of the regulated utilities during the last decade has increased faster than for any other industrial sector.[88] Utility rates have risen far less than prices generally; in many cases they have actually declined. The rate of return earned by utilities has been considerably below that earned by other industries. And, finally, the regulated utilities have accounted for a significant percentage of the nation's capital formation.

One might conclude that regulation has achieved these results directly or, alternatively, that the utilities have achieved these results under the incentives provided by regulation. But regardless of which view one accepts, the fact remains that quality has improved, efficiency has increased, and innovation has been introduced under regulation. Regulation can, and does, "set prices below an industry's costs" when these costs are excessive.[89] Many would argue, and the results would seem to substantiate the point, that regulation has been at least as effective as competition, perhaps more so, in encouraging "consumption by setting prices at the lowest level consistent with a fair return." And, while it is true that formal proceedings in the regulatory process are slow, time-consuming, and expensive, even in the past this type of activity has been only a small portion of the commissions' efforts. With renewed emphasis on informal procedures today, even this small portion is declining. Thus, in the author's opinion, regulation has proven to be a more efficient substitute for competition than many claim, although there remains room for improvement.

[86] Clair Wilcox, *Public Policies Toward Business* (3d ed.; Homewood, Ill.: Richard D. Irwin, Inc., 1966), pp. 476–77. Also see Ben W. Lewis, "Ambivalence in Public Policy toward Regulated Industries," 53 *American Economic Review* 38, 44-45 (1963); and Roger C. Cramton, "The Effectiveness of Economic Regulation: A Legal View," 54 *American Economic Review* 182 (1964).

[87] See Paul W. McCracken, *Economic Progress and the Utility Industry* (Ann Arbor: Bureau of Business Research, The University of Michigan, 1964).

[88] Productivity per unit of input has increased 7 percent annually for gas utilities, 6.5 percent for electric, and 6.3 percent for communications. See Clopper Almon, Jr., *The American Economy to 1975—An Interindustry Forecast* (New York: Harper & Row, Publishers, 1966).

[89] *Market Street Railway* v. *Railroad Comm. of California*, 324 U.S. 548 (1945).

The Role of Competition

Economists who believe that regulation is superior to public ownership, almost unanimously recommend that a greater reliance be placed on competitive forces. The transportation industry is an obvious case in point. Competitive forces have been restrained by restrictions on the entry of new firms. The allocation of both traffic and resources has been distorted by commission policy and public aids. The growth of private and unregulated carriers has been encouraged by regulatory statutes and failure to develop rate structures which meet modern conditions.[90] And, in far too many instances, innovations have been delayed or stifled. As argued in an earlier chapter,[91] it would seem possible and desirable to allow the forces of market competition to allocate traffic to a greater extent than at the present time. For here is a situation, as Barber has pointed out, in which technology over the past forty years or so

> . . . has not only radically changed the character of American transportation but in the process has rendered transport regulation largely anachronistic. Greatly assisted by various forms of government aid, the newer forms of transportation have displaced the once dominant position of the railroads, and have undermined the older regulatory apparatus which rested on the assumption that the ICC was in effective control of the transportation system. It no longer is; competition, albeit limited, has replaced the rail monopoly; and increasing amounts of freight traffic are unregulated. . . .[92]

Few would suggest that competition alone can handle the task. "Interrailroad competition is no more reliable as an economizing instrument than it ever was, but interindustry (rail, water, air, motor transport, and private motor transport) competition is a very lively affair. We cannot and should not ignore it; we should use it (shaping it in the process) and strengthen it."[93]

The task of permitting freer play to competitive forces will not be an easy one. Cramton has noted that "a regulatory scheme is likely to generate interests that make deregulation extremely difficult."[94] Regulators, moreover, tend to

---

[90] Regulation also may have contributed to the overdevelopment of highway trucking transport and the underdevelopment of railroad transport and, in turn, may have exaggerated such problems as those of congestion, noise, smog, transit, and rail passenger service.

[91] See Chapter 14.

[92] Richard J. Barber, "Technological Change in American Transportation: The Role of Government Action," 50 *Virginia Law Review* 824, 884-85 (1964).

[93] Lewis, "Ambivalence in Public Policy toward Regulated Industries," *op. cit.,* p. 51. Also see Walter Adams, "The Role of Competition in the Regulated Industries," 48 *American Economic Review* 527 (1958); James R. Nelson, "The Role of Competition in the Regulated Industries," 11 *The Antitrust Bulletin* 1 (January-April, 1966); and Symposia on "Antitrust and Monopoly Policy in the Communications Industries," 13 *The Antitrust Bulletin* 871 (1968).

[94] Cramton, *op. cit.,* p. 191. Also see Robert A. Nelson, "Interest Conflicts in Transportation," 37 *Journal of Business of the University of Chicago* 167 (1964).

develop a presumption in favor of regulation. Argues Jaffe, with respect to transportation: "In this thinking, competition becomes the equivalent of 'chaos,' of 'waste,' and of 'destruction'; regulation will assure neat, explicable, rationalized ordering of transportation resources, each with its duly appointed role."[95] Stated another way, competitive forces tend to complicate the regulatory process. How, for instance, should a regulatory commission handle such a situation to insure that a regulated company will not use the power at its disposal in the monopoly area of its business to gain an unfair advantage over its rivals in the competitive area? The question is complex, but far too little attention has been devoted to its solution. And as the forces of competition grow stronger, as is now occurring in all of the regulated industries, a solution becomes of even more significance.

Adams and Gray, however, would go further.[96] In those cases when market competition is not feasible, they have recommended development of "institutional" competition. By institutional competition they mean rivalry among different types of utility organization—private, public, and cooperatives. Institutional competition has two important limitations. First, a meaningful yardstick with which to compare the performance of the different forms of organization would have to be developed. Such a yardstick would be extremely difficult to obtain.[97] Second, as Trebing has pointed out, institutional competition would be unable "to accomplish in a positive fashion the ends which it seeks. Under market competition, profits are the stimulus and losses the penalty that eventually drive the inefficient out of business. Institutional competition, on the other hand, possesses at best hazy stimuli and almost completely ineffectual penalties."[98] He concludes:

> Given these limitations, any general attempt to enforce institutional competition is certain to lead to adverse social effects or losses. If the

95 Jaffe, "The Effective Limits of the Administrative Process . . . ," *op. cit.,* pp. 1115–16. Or, as Adams has argued: ". . . Regulation breeds regulation. Competition, even at the margin, is a source of disturbance, annoyance, and embarrassment to the bureaucracy. By providing a yardstick for performance, an outlet for innovation, and a laboratory for experiment, competition subverts the orthodox conformity prescribed by the regulatory establishment. It undermines the static, conservative, and unimaginative scheme of bureaucratic controls, and erodes the artificial values created by protective restrictionism. From the regulator's point of view, therefore, competition must be suppressed wherever it may arise." Walter Adams, "Business Exemptions from the Antitrust Laws: Their Extent and Rationale," in Almarin Phillips (ed.), *Perspectives on Antitrust Policy* (Princeton: Princeton University Press, 1965), p. 283. "Regulation-mindedness," states Wilcox, "is endemic to regulation as such. . . . The regulator's concern is less with the purpose of regulation than with the instrument of regulation itself." Wilcox, *op. cit.,* p. 477.
96 Walter Adams and Horace M. Gray, *Monopoly in America* (New York: Macmillan Co., 1955), chap. iii. Also see Richard Hellman, "Government Competition in the Electric Utility Industry of the United States" (Ph.D. dissertation, Columbia University, 1967).
97 See Chapter 15, p. 581.
98 Harry M. Trebing, "What's Wrong with Commission Regulation?" Part II, 65 *Public Utilities Fortnightly* 738, 747 (1960).

yardstick is based primarily on rates, then service may be allowed to deteriorate in the interests of low prices. Service may also be adversely affected if a particular utility firm falls behind the yardstick standard and, rather than endeavor to improve performance, chooses to recapture its capital through deferred maintenance and replacement. But perhaps the most telling effects of institutional competition will be on the cost of capital, especially for private utilities. The threat of public ownership, whether real or illusory, will give rise to greater feelings of uncertainty among investors, thereby leading to a demand for a greater return on capital devoted to these enterprises. Repercussions, however, would be cumulative and would carry beyond this point, for once the cost of capital increases, the relative yardstick performance of private utilities worsens, thereby triggering a fresh round of anxiety among investors. Ultimately, private utility investment could become less and less profitable as capital costs rise with consequent depressing effects on investment spending and national income.[99]

In summary, while institutional competition seems impracticable, the forces of market competition should be strengthened and used wherever possible. By so doing, the inherent difficulties of regulation can be minimized so that regulation can become a more effective substitute for competition.

Management: Divided Responsibility

Regulation creates another basic problem by dividing the responsibility for management.[100] A company's management, not a regulatory commission, is responsible for the financial success of a firm. Yet, the regulator can and often does interfere with management, and in so doing, he may discourage entrepreneurial initiative and diminish the sense of responsibility.

If the regulator is given a clear mandate to remove a perceived evil, he has an adequate and limited basis for validating his interference with management, and management has a basis for calculating the effects of the interference. But in the absence of a clear mandate, it is not only inevitable, but appropriate that regulation take the form of an accommodation in which industry is the senior partner. This is the essence of "industry-orientation."[101]

Of course, if it could be assumed that most of the regulator's business judgments were superior to those of management, this duplicative effort might result in a net gain. Such an assumption, however, is dubious. As a former member of the CAB has put it: "Members of a regulatory agency must not live in an ivory tower, thinking they know how to operate an air-line better than those actually in the business who know the job firsthand and from the ground

[99] *Ibid.*

[100] See Frederick F. Blachly and Miriam E. Oatman, *Federal Regulatory Action and Control* (Washington, D.C.: The Brookings Institution, 1940), pp. 18–25.

[101] Jaffe, "The Independent Agency: A New Scapegoat," *op. cit.,* p. 1074.

up."[102] But even if commissioners could be assumed to be the better business-men, "there would be offsetting costs." Explains Wilcox:

> Duplication costs money; two managements impose a heavier administrative burden than does one. Negotiation between the managements takes time; decisions are inevitably delayed. Division of authority saps the vitality of an enterprise; diverts energy from the solution of external problems to the prosecution of internal disputes. Managements come to direct their attention more to outsmarting the regulators than to introducing innovations, improving service, and reducing costs.

Regulation dissipates responsibility. The ICC is required, in setting rates, to consider their probable effect upon the volume of traffic. In doing so, it may substitute its own judgment for that of railway managements. And here, if earnings fall, there is no one whom the owners of the roads can hold responsible. The managements are deprived of power; the Commission has power but lacks responsibility. And even if managements are not reversed, decisions are often so delayed that substantial losses are sustained. In cases such as this, management escapes accountability by blaming the regulators. And the regulators are not made accountable by law.[103]

An Obsolete Concept?

Gray, in a well-known article published in 1940,[104] argued that it is fallacious to suppose that the privilege of private monopoly can be harmonized with the public interest by the imposition of regulation. In fact, regulation has failed to limit the power of the very monopolies it has created. The public utility status, he contended, has become "the haven of refuge for all aspiring monopolists who found it too difficult, too costly, or too precarious to secure and maintain monopoly by private action alone," and it has resulted in "institutional decadence." He wrote:

> It [the public utility concept] originated as a system of social restraint designed primarily, or at least ostensibly, to protect consumers from the aggressions of monopolists; it has ended as a device to protect the property, i.e., the capitalized expectancy, of these monopolists from the just demands of society, and to obstruct the development of socially superior institutions. This perversion of the public utility concept from its original purpose was perhaps inevitable under capitalism. Here, as in other areas of our economic and social life, the compelling sanctions of private property and private profit, working within a framework of special privilege, determined the direction and outlook of public policy. Just as in the days of the Empire all roads led to Rome so in a capitalistic society all forms of social control lead

---

102 Chan Gurney, quoted in 73 *Public Utilities Fortnightly* 11 (January 2, 1964).
103 Wilcox, *op. cit.,* p. 478.
104 Horace M. Gray, "The Passing of the Public Utility Concept," 16 *Journal of Land & Public Utility Economics* 8 (1940); reprinted in American Economic Association, *Readings in the Social Control of Industry* (Philadelphia: Blakiston Co., 1949), pp. 280–303.

ultimately to state protection of the dominant interest, i.e., property. The public utility concept has thus merely gone the way of all flesh.[105]

Gray also claimed that the public utility concept has become obsolete, since it is "incapable of securing the social objectives that are essential in the modern economy." Again, to quote from his article:

> ... As previously noted, it was designed to attain limited objectives by negative means. One may read the early public utility statutes in vain to discover any express mandate for the positive promotion of public welfare; the whole tenor of these laws is negative and restrictive; they prohibit certain obvious forms of monopolistic misbehavior but fail to impose definite responsibility for socially desirable action. Thus, public utility companies are under no legal compulsion to conserve natural resources, to utilize capital efficiently, to employ the best known techniques and forms of organization, to treat labor fairly, to extend service to non-profitable areas, to improve public health, to strengthen national defense, to promote technical research, to provide service to indigent persons, to institute rate and service policies that will foster cultural and social values, or to develop related benefits such as navigation, flood control, and irrigation. This being the case, private utility monopolists will have regard for these broad social objectives only when by so doing they can increase or maintain their own profit. Experience has shown that they will not voluntarily strive to attain these ends; moreover, it is clear that public utility regulation, as at present constituted, cannot compel them, against their own interest, to do so.[106]

The attack on the public utility concept by Gray thus involves two elements.[107] In the first place, he argues that regulation has failed to serve as an efficient substitute for competition. Since publication of this article, however, many changes have taken place in the regulatory process. To mention but two: The holding company abuses of the 1920's were corrected under the Public Utility Holding Company Act of 1935 and the Supreme Court's restrictive "fair value" rule of rate making was modified by the Hope decision of 1944. These and other developments have substantially improved the results of regulation in recent years.

In the second place, Gray contends that the limited objectives of a fair profit or of a cost-price philosophy of rate making should be superseded by broad social and national objectives. The phrase "social principles of rate-making" has a variety of meanings, but generally "it refers to any policy of rate control designed to make the supply of utility services responsive to social needs and social costs, and rejecting as even tolerable measures of these needs and

---

[105] *Ibid.,* p. 15.
[106] *Ibid.,* p. 16.
[107] James C. Bonbright, *Principles of Public Utility Rates* (New York: Columbia University Press, 1961), p. 25.

these costs the prices that consumers are able and willing to pay for the services and the money costs that the enterprise must incur in their production."[108] Rate making based upon social principles would be complex. How, for example, are social benefits and social costs to be measured? Similarly, will not the use of the social principles philosophy lead to a distortion between utility rates and other prices, since the others do not reflect social benefits? Business principles, as opposed to social principles, of rate making seem more desirable in the utility and transportation industries.

A CONTINUING CHALLENGE

Private industries in the United States frequently are classified as belonging to either the unregulated sector or the regulated sector. In the unregulated, competition is assumed to prevail; in the regulated, competition is assumed to be limited, at best, and public regulation is undertaken as a substitute. Despite this dichotomy, both competition and regulation have the same basic objectives: the efficient allocation of resources and the protection of consumers against exploitation. It is the means to these ends that are notably different. Competition operates through profit incentives and penalties determined by prices set in the market place. Regulation, however, must set rates itself, thereby determining the profit incentives and penalties.

The lengthy experience of this country with regulation clearly indicates that, like competition, regulation falls short of perfection. Opinions as to the degree of imperfection, however, vary considerably. In the words of Lewis:

> The record of public utility regulation generally since 1907 is neither impressive, nor yet too disheartening. The excessive costs and delays of regulation, its rigidities, and its apparent lack of purpose beyond the settlement of individual controversies, cannot fairly be overlooked. On the other hand, the utilities industries have experienced an enormous physical growth, the increasingly complex problems of regulation have been met by the improvisation of elaborate regulatory machinery, and the period of adjustment has, after all, been short.[109]

According to Bauer:

> Under the conditions that have existed, the wonder is that regulation has worked as well as it has. Although far from satisfactory, it has not been a complete and unmitigated failure. While the commissions have not measured up to high standards, perhaps they have done, in the main, the best they could under all the circumstances. They have carried on their work in an easy going, nonalert way, but they have seldom deliberately flouted the public interest.[110]

108 *Ibid.*, p. 110.
109 Ben W. Lewis, "Public Utilities," in Leverett S. Lyon and Victor Abramson (eds.), *Government and Economic Life* (Washington, D.C.: Brookings Institution, 1940), Vol. II, p. 744.
110 John Bauer, *Transforming Public Utility Regulation* (New York: Harper & Bros., 1950), pp. 137–38.

And in the opinion of Cramton:

> There are inherent limitations on the effectiveness of economic regulation even where public policy is fairly clear and the regulatory task, relatively speaking, is confined and manageable. The simpler case of economic regulation—the determination of maximum rates of a conventional public utility—has not been performed with obvious success. I do not assert that public utility regulation has been a failure. I do maintain, however, that unqualified assertions of its effectiveness would be unwarranted. The lesson of a half-century of experience is that the environment generates enduring problems which limit the potential effectiveness of rate regulation.[111]

Lacking perfection, there is room for improvement. Regulation is, after all, an evolutionary process. In its earlier days, regulation was conceived to be an essentially negative or restrictive force to limit the monopoly power of certain industries and, thereby, to protect utility users from inequitable price discrimination and exorbitant profits. To carry out this task, commissions developed such tools and concepts as establishment of uniform systems of accounts, separations procedures, measures for determining valuation and depreciation, and theoretical principles to use in arriving at a fair rate of return. All these and other regulatory tools were and are essential to effective regulation.

Yet, the great challenge to regulation is to improve its adaptability to a rapidly changing economic environment.[112] Today, regulation must be more than a protector. It cannot attain its objectives merely by protecting consumers from monopoly profits, utility investors from confiscation of their investment, nor utilities from competition. It would be highly desirable if the goals and policies of regulation were more explicit and if the regulatory process could be stripped of its needlessly complex, costly, and often confusing procedures, thus permitting greater flexibility. But above all, regulation needs to adopt dynamic standards to meet the needs of an expanding economy.

The Need for Dynamic Standards

The establishment of dynamic standards will not be easy. A commission must formulate long-range policies or plans and must develop the means to effectuate its policies. Consider the role of profits. Dynamic progress requires

---

[111] Cramton, *op. cit.,* p. 186. Posner, however, has concluded that "public utility regulation is probably not a useful exertion of governmental powers; that its benefits cannot be shown to outweigh its costs; and that even in markets where efficiency dictates monopoly we might do better to allow natural economic forces to determine business conduct and performance subject only to the constraints of antitrust policy." Richard A. Posner, "Natural Monopoly and Its Regulation," 21 *Stanford Law Review* 548, 549 (1969). Also see Adams, "Business Exemptions from the Antitrust Laws . . . ," *op. cit.,* pp. 278–79; Harold Demsetz, "Why Regulate Utilities?" 11 *Journal of Law and Economics* 55 (1968); and Yale Brozen, "Is Government the Source of Monopoly?" 5 *The Intercollegiate Review* 67 (Winter, 1968–69).

[112] See James W. Karber, "Challenge: A Way of Life for the Future," 80 *Public Utilities Fortnightly* 19 (November 9, 1967); George A. Prendergast, "Regulatory Implications of Changing Economic Environment," 80 *ibid.* 37 (November 9, 1967); and Francis X. Welch, "Changing Values in the Regulatory Mix," 80 *ibid.* 61 (November 9, 1967).

technological advance; profits provide the basic incentive for progressiveness. "Cost-plus" regulation, with major emphasis upon limiting profit rates, offers no explicit incentives to a regulated firm. Indeed, as others have observed, regulatory lag may be the most important incentive to efficiency under such a scheme.[113] To encourage efficiency and innovation, therefore, incentive regulatory techniques must be developed.[114] It is not being implied that the rate of return currently being earned by any particular firm is too low. The point is that in determining the proper level of earnings for a regulated company, a commission must not be obsessed with limiting profits; rather, regulation must be a positive system, with consideration given to the role of profits as incentives in addition to the level of earnings needed to attract more capital.[115] The point of reference, moreover, must be long term, for technological progress commonly requires a long time horizon.

Dynamic standards require basic changes in regulatory thinking and in regulatory techniques. With respect to regulatory thinking, more effective economic analysis is needed. Commissioner Johnson, for example, in his "preliminary concurring statement" in Phase 1A of the telephone investigation, listed a series of questions which he thought the commission should direct its attention toward, "other than (or in addition to) the rate-of-return focus dictated by nineteenth century public utility philosophy":

> What are the forces encouraging, or retarding, technological innovation in telephone equipment and service?

113 "Essentially, this is an allegation that imperfections in the regulatory process induce efficiency in production! If true, it intimates that the regulatory process is even more futile than contended by even its most stalwart critics: The argument is that it works well through its imperfections!," Sidney Weintraub, "Rate Making and an Incentive Rate of Return," 81 *Public Utilities Fortnightly* 23, 30 (April 25, 1968).

Baumol has suggested a modification of regulatory lag to provide an explicit incentive to efficiency. Under his proposal, rates would be subject to regulatory reexamination only at periodic intervals, say every three years. During the interim periods, the company would not be allowed to raise its rates ("except under most unusual circumstances"), but it would be permitted to retain all the earnings it makes. Thus, the company would find it profitable to make cost reductions since it could retain "the fruits of its cost-saving efforts." William J. Baumol, "Reasonable Rules for Rate Regulation: Plausible Policies for an Imperfect World," in Almarin Phillips and Oliver E. Williamson (eds.), *Prices: Issues in Theory, Practice, and Public Policy* (Philadelphia: University of Pennsylvania Press, 1967), pp. 114–15.

114 See Weintraub, *op. cit.;* Warren J. Samuels, "Theory of Regulation in Relation to Return," Part I: 80 *Public Utilities Fortnightly* 47 (November 9, 1967), Part II: 80 *ibid.* 34 (November 23, 1967), Part III: 80 *ibid.* 33 (December 7, 1967); and Harold H. Wein, "Fair Rate of Return and Incentives—Some General Considerations," in Harry M. Trebing (ed.), *Performance under Regulation* (East Lansing: Michigan State University Public Utilities Studies, 1968), pp. 39–67.

115 In Butler's words: ". . . I would argue that the goal of regulation is not minimum profits in the regulated industries but rather maximum service to the public at the lowest feasible costs. In many cases, these two requirements may coincide, but I suspect that there may be many other cases where incentives in the form of reasonable rewards through profits could make genuine and lasting contributions to improved service and to reduction in real costs over the longer run." William F. Butler, "The Business Outlook Plus Some Thoughts on Business Regulation," *Telephony*, September 19, 1964, p. 25.

What are the most appropriate rates of change in making new equipment available to the subscriber?

What are the implications for national communications behavior of the ways in which we price telephone service?

What should be the standards by which some rate discrimination (or subsidies) are encouraged and others discouraged?

How should the pricing of telephone service respond as new techniques (satellites, wave guide, lasers) transform an industry of limited capacity into one of excess capacity?

In what ways would more, or less, competition in providing telephone service be useful?

By what procedures and institutional means can the needs and interests of both shareholders and subscribers best be formulated and translated into corporate or national policy? [116]

An attempt to answer these questions would result in a significant shift in traditional regulatory activity and would place greater emphasis upon the economic effects of regulation. In turn, the goal or objective of regulation would become incentive regulation, rather than the traditional, profit limitation goal.[117]

With respect to regulatory techniques, many commissions have attempted to substitute informal procedures for more formal ones. "Periodic and cooperative conferences," argues Welch, "have taken the place of hit-or-miss adversary type proceedings. So, in a sense, you might say that the rate case is really going on all the time."[118] The present methods of continuous regulatory control may contain defects that will have to be ironed out, but in view of the dynamic nature of the economy and of the regulated industries, they are more useful procedures than the older, case-by-case method of more formal proceedings.

The Need for Performance Evaluation

If regulation is to serve as an effective substitute for competition, methods or criteria for evaluating the performance of the regulatory process must be developed. Lewis succinctly summarized the problem several years ago:

Data are available to show the steady increase in the use of electric power, and the general lowering of electric rates—broken down for types of uses, sizes of markets, etc. But these indicate merely what has happened under the exact circumstances that have in fact obtained. There is no universal, objective standard against which the achievements of this industry under regulation may be measured; no way of knowing what the industry might have accomplished if regulatory conditions had been different. Similarly, data are available showing the earnings of the industry, its operations; but with reference to all of these it must still be said that they throw little light either

116 Johnson, *op. cit.,* pp. 233–34.

117 For a more complete analysis, see Lee Loevinger, "Regulation and Competition as Alternatives," 11 *The Antitrust Bulletin* 101 (January–April, 1966).

118 Francis X. Welch, "The Evolution of Utility Regulation," *Telephony*, June 6, 1964, p. 34.

on how much of what has been accomplished has been due to regulation, or what might have been accomplished under regulation of another kind.[119]

In the past, evaluation of regulatory performance has concentrated on procedure. But issues of procedure and organization, while they can either help or hinder the resolution of policy issues, "avoid the important consequences of other types of governmental activities."[120] Further, the effectiveness of the regulatory process cannot be judged by an enumeration of regulatory policies. As Stigler and Friedland have noted, such an enumeration only indicates a desire to regulate, not the effectiveness of regulation. The relevant question, they contend, is whether regulation makes a difference in the behavior of an industry.[121]

Consider, for instance, the argument advanced several years ago by Averch and Johnson that regulation has a tendency to result in overinvestment, or excessive rate base expansion. In their words:

> ... if the rate of return allowed by the regulatory agency is greater than the cost of capital but less than the rate of return that would be enjoyed by the firm were it free to maximize profit without regulatory constraint, then the firm will substitute capital for the other factor of production and operate at an output where cost is not minimized.[122]

Given these assumptions, and on the basis of a careful analysis, they conclude that regulated firms have an incentive to use more capital and that the general level of utility rates will be higher than would be the case if returns were held to cost-of-capital levels.[123]

The Averch-Johnson thesis, which suggests that rate base regulation is deficient, has been the subject of considerable discussion. First, are their assumptions valid? Do regulated firms earn rates of return that are in excess of cost-of-capital levels? Expert opinion differs on this question. Second, to what extent does the model describe the functioning of the utility industry? If, for

[119] Lewis, "Public Utilities," *op. cit.,* p. 744, n. 225. Also see Mark S. Massel, "The Regulatory Process," 26 *Law and Contemporary Problems* 181 (1961); Richard E. Caves, "Direct Regulation and Market Performance in the American Economy," 54 *American Economic Review* 172 (1964); and the articles in Trebing, *Performance under Regulation, op. cit.*

[120] Massel, *op. cit.,* p. 202.

[121] George J. Stigler and Claire Friedland, "What Can Regulators Regulate? The Case of Electricity," 5 *Journal of Law and Economics* 1 (1962).

[122] Harvey Averch and Leland Johnson, "The Firm under Regulatory Constraint," 52 *American Economic Review* 1052, 1053 (1962).

[123] The authors also conclude that regulated firms have an incentive "to operate in some markets even at a loss." *Ibid.,* p. 1063. On the basis of the Averch-Johnson thesis: (*a*) Westfield has argued that utilities are willing to pay increased equipment prices (since this behavior expands the rate base) and (*b*) Klevorick has proposed that "after some point the maximum allowable rate of return on capital would decline with increases in the amount of capital used." See Fred M. Westfield, "Regulation and Conspiracy," 55 *American Economic Review* 424 (1965); and Alvin K. Klevorick, "The Graduated Fair Return: A Regulatory Proposal," 56 *ibid.* 477 (1966). But see Alfred E. Kahn, "The Graduated Fair Return: Comment," 58 *ibid.* 170 (1968).

example, the incentive for rate base expansion is so strong, why have utilities not taken advantage of the opportunity to undertake more rapid investment in underground transmission and distribution facilities, and in air and water pollution control equipment?[124] Could it be that regulatory lag offsets the potential adverse effects of the Averch-Johnson thesis? Third, as Weintraub has noted, the Averch-Johnson analysis, on grounds of efficient resource allocation, "must be correct. . . . But do we want merely to improve resource allocation, or do we intend to advance production techniques? . . . The very incentives to use 'excess' equipment, which Averch and Johnson deplore, may well be forces of some importance in enhancing productivity in the public utility sector and the economy generally. . . . Some allocational inefficiency may be a cost of technological externalities."[125] And, finally, Kahn has argued that the Averch-Johnson effect may have a beneficial aspect in that the incentive to overinvestment may offset the monopolist's tendency to restrict output.[126]

The Averch-Johnson thesis thus raises significant questions concerning the behavior and performance of firms under regulation. Whether one agrees with their findings or not, it is clear that too little is known about how the market performance of an industry is affected by regulation.[127]

The Future

In the future, there must be far more cooperation between the regulator and the regulated if the utility and transportation industries are to reach their maximum potentials. New tools and concepts must be developed, old ones discarded as their usefulness diminishes. "For if regulation ever did become rigid or inflexible it could then become a strait jacket, a stagnation process which would not be in the interests of either the public or the regulated companies."[128] The emphasis, moreover, must be not only on restricting the regulated industries (minimum rates of return, minimum valuation of assets, minimum write-offs for depreciation), but also on promotion. Stated another

---

[124] The Electric Utility Industry Task Force on Environment has estimated that it would cost at least $150 billion to place the nation's overhead electric distribution lines underground (compared with the current electric utility industry investment in overhead lines of about $18 billion). *The Electric Utility Industry and the Environment* (A Report to the Citizens Advisory Committee on Recreation and Natural Beauty by the Electric Utility Industry Task Force on Environment) (New York, 1968), p. 19.

[125] Weintraub, *op. cit.,* pp. 30–31.

[126] Kahn, *op. cit.* On the Averch-Johnson thesis, see William G. Shepherd, "Regulatory Constraints and Public Utility Investment," 42 *Land Economics* 348 (1966); and William R. Hughes, "Comment," in Trebing, *Performance under Regulation, op. cit.,* pp. 73-87.

[127] Two approaches to the problem have been suggested by Caves: (1) a comparison of a regulated industry's performance with "an ideal norm derived from the familiar optimum conditions of economic theory" and (2) a comparison of a regulated industry's performance with the performance of an industry not subject to regulation. (Caves, *op. cit.*, p. 175.) While both approaches involve numerous problems (see Ronald H. Coase, "Discussion," 54 *American Economic Review* 194, 194-96 [1964]), they appear worthy of further research.

[128] Welch, "The Evolution of Utility Regulation," *op. cit.,* p. 34.

way, regulation must never become an end in itself. Both the regulated industries and the commissions must cooperate in developing the required new tools and concepts, and in finding new ways to serve the American public. And, finally, research is needed concerning the development of dynamic standards and the effectiveness of regulation. For these reasons, regulation continues to offer "a challenging opportunity for creative and constructive action."[129]

[129] Walter A. Morton, "Creative Regulation," 39 *Land Economics* 367, 374 (1963).

INDEXES

INDEX OF CASES

INDEX OF NAMES

747

INDEX OF SUBJECTS

A

Abandonment of service, 421
  complete, 421
  partial, 421–22
  railroad discontinuance cases, 422–26
  revocation, suspension, and modification
    of certificates, 426–27
Accelerated depreciation
  commission treatment of, 205–6
  flow through principle, 201–2
  meaning of, 201
  normalization principle, 201–2
Accounting regulation; *see also* Depreciation
  continuing property records, 150–51
  objectives of, 144–46
  retirement unit list, 150
  uniform systems
    balance sheet accounts, 149–51
    comparability, 148
    development of, 146–48
    financial reporting, 148
    income accounts, 151–53
Accrued depreciation; *see* Depreciation
Act to Regulate Commerce (1887)
  emasculation of, 447–49
  provisions, 448–49
  reasons for, 447–48
Actual cost, 218; *see also* Original cost
Actual use principle, in telephone cost
  allocation methods, 158–59
Administrative Conference of the United
  States, 712
Administrative Procedure Act (1946),
  135, 696
Administrative process; *see* Regulatory
  commissions
Advertising expenses, 187–88
Advisory Committee on Energy Supplies
  and Resources, 603–4
"Affected with a public interest"; *see*
  Public interest concept
Agricultural Adjustment Act (1938), 48
Agricultural exemption
  history of, 510 n
  ICC interpretation, 471, 510
  opposition to, 471–72
  reasons for, 510

Agricultural exemption—*Cont.*
  repeal v. extension, 511–12
  significance of, 476–77, 511
  statutory provision, 461–62
Air Commerce Act (1926), 463
Air Line Pilots Association, 530–31
Air Mail Act (1934), 463
Air Quality Act (1967), 567 n
Airline industry
  control of entry, 413–17, 509–10, 704
  labor problems, 530–31
  liability and insurance, 436–37
  market structure, 492–95
  merger policy, 522
  rate of return
    airmail, 277
    freight and passenger service, 276–77
    need for weighted industry rate,
      277–78
    rejection of operating ratio, 275 n
    trunklines, 505
  rates and rate structures
    air freight, 338–40
      deferred air freight service, 340
      "directional" rates, 339–40
    cost considerations, 334–36
    demand considerations, 336
    discrimination, 342–44, 385
    express, 338
    mail, 340–42
      nonpriority mail, 342, 344
      service mail, 341
      subsidy mail, 341–42
    passenger, 336–38
      coach, 336–37
      first class, 336
      promotional, 337–38
  regulation
    declaration of policy, 463–64
    development of, 462–63
    exemptions, 512
    statutory provisions, 464–65
  safety regulation
    air traffic control, 429–31
    investigation of accidents, 432
    role of Federal Aviation Administration, 429
    safety record, 435–36

755

Esch-Cummins Act; *see* Transportation
Act of 1920
Excess capacity, 24 n
and regulation, 26 n
Exchange value, as measure of value, 218,
220 n
Expense ratios, 192–93
Expenses; *see* Operating expenses
Express rates
air express, 338–40
railway express, 325–26

F

Fair Labor Standards Act (1938), 49
Fair rate of return; *see* Rate of return
"Fair value" doctrine, 219–21; *see also*
Reproduction cost
criticisms of, 221, 225–27
legal concept, 219–23
abandonment of, 227–31
measurement, 224–25, 241–43
Farmers' Union, 379 n
Fast Service Shipping Terminals, Inc.,
325 n
Federal Aviation Act (1958), 429, 463
Federal Aviation Administration, 102,
473; *see also* Federal Aviation Agency
air traffic control, 429–31
airport congestion problem, 431
functions of, 429
Federal Aviation Agency, 102
transfer of functions, 463
Federal Aviation Commission, 463
Federal commissions; *see also specific
commissions;* Judicial review; *and*
Regulatory commissions
duties, 104–6
establishment, dates, 102–3
federal-state cooperation, 116–17
financing, 103–5
functions of, 113–14
jurisdiction, 102–3
opposition to, 115–18
organization, 104–5
personnel, 102–4
property valuation, 240–41
uniform systems of accounts, 147
Federal Communications Commission
"Above 890 Decision," 674–76
constant surveillance, 139–40
domestic telegraph investigation, 643–46
jurisdiction, 102–3
private line investigation, 667
property valuation, 240–41
rate regulation, 140
requirements for intervention before,
136 n
statistics, 103

Federal Communications Comm.–*Cont.*
telephone investigations, 658–70
tenure of commissioners, 104
uniform system of accounts, 147
Federal Coordinator of Transportation,
456
reports of, 456 n, 478 n
Federal Highway Administration, 473
safety regulations, motor carriers, 433–
35
Federal Home Loan Bank Board, 102 n
Federal Maritime Board, 102 n, 466 n
Federal Maritime Commission, 102 n, 466
Federal Power Commission
electric power industry regulation
Bureau of Power, 570
development, 565
hydroelectric projects, 565–69
recapture or relicensing, 568
"recreational purposes," 567
types of licenses, 565–66
interstate transmission, 569–70
National Power Survey, 570–72
property valuation, 240–41
reliability recommendations, 573
uniform system of accounts, 147,
149–52
financial reporting, 148
jurisdiction, 102–3, 116–18
natural gas industry
conservation, 632–34
consolidated tax returns, 214–15
jurisdiction, 596–97, 599–604
independent producers, 601–4
integrated producers, 599–601
regulation
certificate power, 597–98, 632
challenge of, 636–37
escalation clauses, 620–21
field price, 604–17
Seaboard formula, 624–25
statistics, 103
tenure of commissioners, 104
Federal Radio Commission, 102
Federal Railroad Administration, 473
Federal Trade Commission, 43, 102 n
report on utility holding companies,
558–60
Federal Water Power Act (1920), 565
Financing regulation
capital structure, 167–72
capitalization, 162–67
reorganization, 173–76
"First" original cost, 218; *see also* Original
cost
Fixed costs; *see* Cost allocation
Flight Engineers International Association,
530

Holding companies—*Cont.*
 electric and gas industries—*Cont.*
  advantages—*Cont.*
   economies, 554–56
   profit motive, 556–58
  definition, 554, 561
  Electric Bond and Share Company, 555
  FTC report on, 558-60
  regulation
   failure of state, 560-61
   federal legislative provisions, 561-63
   under SEC, 563-65
 need for control, 180, 189
  service contracts, 189–91
  write-ups, 144–45, 559-60
 railroad industry, 514–15
 telephone industry
  American Telephone and Telegraph Company, 648–49
  General Telephone & Electronics Corporation, 650
Hoover Commission, 104, 695
Hoover Dam, 546-47

I

Illinois Central Industries, Inc., 515
Illinois Central Railroad, 505 n, 515
Imbedded cost, 284
Imperfect competition; *see* Monopolistic competition; Monopoly; *and* Oligopoly
Income accounts, 151–53
Incremental costs; *see* Marginal costs
Inflation
 compensation for, in rate of return, 291–96
 depreciation allowance, 199–201
 and property valuation, 237, 243–44
Inspector of Gas Meters, 89
Institutional competition, 716–17
Intangibles, 130, 254
 franchise value, 255
 going concern value, 256–57
 good will, 254–55
 leaseholds, 256
 water rights, 255–56
Inter-Agency Committee on Water Resources, 569 n; *see also* Water Resources Council
Interagency ownership, transportation industries
 auxiliary services, 523
 claimed advantages of, 522
 economies of scale, 524
 grandfather clauses, 477–78
 statutory provisions, 477–78, 522–23
 reasons for, 524
Intercoastal Shipping Act (1933), 466, 510 n

Interconnections, electric utilities, 547–50
 major areas served by, 548
 reliability issue, 573–74
Interest during construction as a rate base component, 252–53
International Air Transport Association, 333 n
International Brotherhood of Teamsters, 531
International Telecommunications Satellite Consortium, 684
International Telephone and Telegraph Company, 648 n, 651 n, 681-83
 ownership in COMSAT, 685 n
Interstate Commerce Act; *see* Act to Regulate Commerce; Elkins Act; Hepburn Act; Mann-Elkins Act; Motor Carrier Act; Transportation Act of 1920; Transportation Act of 1940; *and* Transportation Act of 1958
Interstate commerce clause, 46-49
 federal-state conflicts, 115–18
Interstate Commerce Commission
 communications industry
  jurisdiction, 102, 639
  regulation, 639
  uniform system of accounts, 147
 creation of, 88–89
 transportation industries
  depreciation investigation (1926), 152
  financial statements, 148
  jurisdiction, 102–3
  lack of meaningful policy standards, 703–4
  modified procedure, 138
  organization, 105
  property valuation, 240–41
  railroad reorganizations, 173–76
  regulation of rate structures, 368-84
  statistics, 103
  tenure of commissioners, 104
  uniform system of accounts, 147
Interstate Compact to Conserve Oil and Gas, 631
Intracompany transactions, 189–92
Investment cost, 218; *see also* Original cost
Investment tax credit
 meaning of, 206–7
 suspension of, 206 n
 treatment of, 207

J

Joint costs, definition of, 153 n; *see also* Cost allocation
J. P. Morgan and Company, 554
Judicial regulation; *see* Common law
Judicial review, 51–52, 81-82, 111–13